Handbook of Research on Adult Learning and Development

The time is right for this comprehensive, state-of-the-art analysis, integration, and summary of theoretical advances and research findings on adult development and learning—a rapidly growing field reflecting demographic shifts toward an aging population in Western societies. Featuring contributions from prominent scholars across diverse disciplinary fields (education, developmental psychology, public policy, gerontology, neurology, public health, sociology, family studies, and adult education), the volume is organized around six themes:

- Theoretical Perspectives on Adult Development and Learning
- Research Methods in Adult Development
- Research on Adult Development
- Research on Adult Learning
- Aging and Gerontological Research
- Policy Perspectives on Aging

The *Handbook of Research on Adult Learning and Development* is an essential reference for researchers, faculty, and graduate students whose work pertains to adult and lifespan development, adult learning, and adult education, and for practicing psychologists, sociologists, gerontologists, and adult educators.

M Cecil Smith is Professor, Department of Leadership, Educational Psychology and Foundations, Northern Illinois University.

Nancy DeFrates-Densch is an Instructor in the Educational Psychology program, Department of Leadership, Educational Psychology and Foundations, Northern Illinois University.

Handbook of Research on Adult Learning and Development

Edited by

M Cecil Smith

Northern Illinois University

with

Nancy DeFrates-Densch

Northern Illinois University
Assistant Editor

NEW YORK AND LONDON

First published 2009
by Routledge
711 Third Avenue, New York, NY 10017

Simultaneously published in the UK
by Routledge
2 Park Square, Milton Park, Abingdon, Oxon OX14 4RN

Routledge is an imprint of the Taylor & Francis Group, an informa business

Transferred to digital printing 2011

Typeset in Baskerville by EvS Communication Networx, Inc.

Library of Congress Cataloging in Publication Data
Handbook of research on adult learning and development / edited by M Cecil Smith with Nancy DeFrates-Densch.
p. cm.
Includes bibliographical references and index.
1. Adult learning—Research—Handbooks, manuals, etc. 2. Adult education—Research—Handbooks, manuals, etc. I. Smith, M Cecil. II, DeFrates-Densch, Nancy.

ISBN 10: 0-8058-5819-9 (hbk)
ISBN 10: 0-8058-5820-2 (pbk)
ISBN 10: 0-203-88788-3 (ebk)

ISBN 13: 978-0-8058-5819-8 (hbk)
ISBN 13: 978-0-8058-5820-4 (pbk)
ISBN 13: 978-0-203-88788-2 (ebk)

This handbook is dedicated to

Gayle Dubowski
Catalina Garcia
Julianna Gehant
Ryanne Mace
Daniel Parmenter

Contents

Preface

I first became acquainted with the concept of adult development in a graduate course on the topic taught by Professor Art Thomas at the University of Kansas in the early 1980s. I was immediately excited to learn that developmental psychologists were converging on a consensus that developmental processes were lifelong, rather than limited to the first two decades of life. Subsequent coursework in developmental psychology offered by Professor Peter Johnsen at Kansas and by then Professors Nancy W. Denney, Brad Brown, and David Featherman at the University of Wisconsin-Madison in the mid-1980s further solidified my interest in the study of adult development. When I joined the faculty in the educational psychology program at Northern Illinois University in 1988, I was given an opportunity to develop and teach a new graduate course on adult development and aging. Having taught this course approximately every two years since that time has provided me with ample opportunities to immerse myself in the increasingly wide-ranging literature in this remarkable field.

Throughout my career, I have remained deeply interested in connecting the empirical and theoretical work of psychologists—developmental, cognitive, and educational—to that of adult educators. Advances in psychology's understanding of the challenges, changes, and transformations of adult life have much to offer those who teach adult learners or otherwise facilitate adult learning. And, adult education offers a particularly useful window through which to examine developmental change in the adult years. Thus, I have found developmental psychology and adult education to be often complementary disciplines. It is my hope that this handbook reflects and extends these connections.

I wish to express my deep affection and appreciation to those who have supported my work, in large and small ways, during the completion of this volume. My wife, partner, and best friend, Ellin, has been steadfast in her support. Our two boys, Patrick and Kevin, have been endless sources of joy and fascination as they have now reached their young adult years. My former and current graduate students have influenced my thinking about adult development in many significant ways over the course of our conversations. Thanks to Thomas Pourchot, Amy Diaz, Robert "BT" Trierweiler, and Nancy DeFrates-Densch. My educational psychology colleagues at NIU—Lee Shumow, Jennifer Schmidt, David Shernoff, and Stephen Tonks—have provided me with an intellectual environment that is truly stimulating and supportive. Finally, I extend a warm thank you to Naomi Silverman at Routledge who first encouraged me to consider preparing this handbook, and who has nudged it gently through to its completion.

Overview

This handbook is organized into six sections that frame 26 chapters. Part I focuses on contemporary theoretical perspectives that seek to explain the varied dimensions of adult development. Fredda Blanchard-Fields and Antje Stange Kalinauskas (Chapter 1) adopt a life-span developmental lens to describe contemporary theories of adult development that explain observed changes in different domains of functioning. The life-span perspective holds that development is "characterized by multidimensional, multidirectional, and multifunctional processes that involve the constant interplay of gains and losses." The authors summarize recent scientific trends that have influenced theory development, including advances in brain imaging technologies, innovative statistical strategies such as growth modeling that enable more careful examination of intra-individual variability, and increased emphasis on the study of everyday behavior in diverse social contexts. They then examine the role that emotion plays in adult cognitive functioning. Next, the authors describe the interplay of physical health with aging adults' cognitive abilities, highlighting the influence of self-regulatory capacities which affect adults' actions to influence their own development. Finally, Blanchard-Fields and Kalinauskas describe changes in social cognitive skills in adulthood, focusing on the role of individuals' beliefs, values, motivation and goals in their social judgments.

Jennifer Tanner, Jeffrey Jensen Arnett, and Julie Leis describe a relatively recent theoretical advance regarding the early years of adulthood—a period that Arnett has called emerging adulthood (Chapter 2), which comprises the years from 18 to 30. Emerging adulthood is distinct from both adolescence and adulthood proper and is said to be the age of identity explorations, an age of instability, a self-focused period, a time of feeling in-between roles, and an age of great possibilities. Their chapter articulates a three-stage process of *recentering* in which individuals shift their involvements from the dependency of childhood and adolescence to the independence of adulthood. Recentering provides a useful framework for understanding the developmental challenges emerging adults face, according to the authors. Emerging adulthood is a period of plasticity during which the shaping of the adult's life goals is possible and necessary.

In Chapter 3, Carol Hoare argues for a more comprehensive, and less reductionistic, theoretical perspective on adult life span development through an explication of Urie Bronfenbrenner's (2005) bioecological model of human development and Erik Erikson's (1950) biopsychosocial model. Both Bronfenbrenner and Erikson studied the link between individual development and the development of the group and society, and they did so in interdisciplinary fashion. Yet, each was unique in their approaches to understanding the contexts—biological, social, psychological—that shape human development. Hoare notes that these contextual (Bronfenbrenner) and stage (Erikson) models represent only two-thirds of the adult, however, and there remains the need for a larger metamodel that captures not only context and stage, but also the biogenetic (microlevel) factors that contribute to development.

Jan Sinnott describes her Theory of Postformal Thought in Chapter 4. She argues that Postformal Thought is key to adult development, learning, and wisdom. According to Sinnott, the theory draws from extant cognitive developmental theory, native wisdom traditions, and "new" sciences such as quantum physics, chaos theory, and general systems theory. Postformal thinking is necessary to understand the complexities of the modern world, as well as of human emotions and relationships. Postformal Thought is essential to mature adult thinking, according to Sinnott. Postformal Thought is "complex logical thinking that develops in adulthood when we interact with other people whose views about…reality are different from ours." Sinnott argues that teaching adults to think Postformally should be an essential goal both within and outside of educational settings.

Part II focuses on research methods in the study of adult development. There are two chapters. In Chapter 5, Janet Holt describes recent advances in growth modeling providing examples of applications of this analytic approach to understanding development in different areas of adulthood, including personality and cognitive functioning, growth modeling is particularly useful for studying transitions in adult development. Jeff Valentine and Harris Cooper explain the significance of research syntheses and meta-analyses as important tools in the adult development researcher's methodological toolbox (Chapter 6). Meta-analysis involves the statistical analysis of a large collection of results from individual studies such that the sometimes-disparate findings can be integrated. The chapter describes the development of meta-analysis as a legitimate research method in its own right. That is, meta-analysis involves problem formulation, data collection and evaluation, analysis and interpretation, and the reporting of results. After addressing each of these steps in the meta-analysis research process, Valentine and Cooper discuss some potential threats to the validity of meta-analysis findings and ways in which the meta-analyst can avoid such problems. Meta-analytic studies are relatively rare in the field of adult development, suggesting that this method for synthesizing research results is not fully appreciated.

Part III contains nine chapters that describe adult developmental processes within or across different age periods in adulthood (e.g., early adulthood, middle adulthood), as these processes unfold within different social contexts (e.g., marriage and family life, career and work), or within distinct developmental domains (e.g., epistemology, personality, spirituality). Two chapters focus on aspects of personality development in adulthood. Marcia Baxter Magolda, Elisa Abes, and Vasti Torres (Chapter 7) describe adult development during the college years and into the late 20s, with a specific focus on the epistemological development of sexual minority and ethnic young adults. A key task of young adulthood, regardless of sexual orientation or ethnicity, is to construct new meanings for oneself, freed from the meanings that have been uncritically acquired from others (e.g., parents, teachers). Describing the significance of meaning-making in young adulthood and its relationship to learning, they argue that development during this period requires a "fundamental transformation of making meaning from following formulas acquired uncritically...to making meaning by internally choosing one's beliefs, identity, and relationships." Their work is informed by both Kegan's (1994) constructive-developmental and Mezirow's (1990, 2000) transformational learning theories.

Why does personality matter in adulthood? Cory Bolkan, Patricia Meierdiercks, and Karen Hooker suggest (Chapter 8) that personality is important because it is the vehicle by which the innermost aspects of the self are revealed. Personality is the "guiding force" that enables adults to participate in their own development and adaptation across the adult life span. Tracing the history of psychological research on personality, including the extant controversies in the psychology of personality, they note that the field is steadily moving away from the "stability versus change" debate that has characterized personality theorizing and research. Today, conceptions of personality suggest a more nuanced view of change as an individual difference variable that has its own merit. The availability of sophisticated statistical tools such as growth modeling enable assessments of change with increasingly greater precision. Finally, Bolkan et al. describe Hooker and McAdam's (2003) six foci of personality model to account for the processes of stability and change in personality.

In Chapter 9, Ursula Staudinger and Eva-Marie Kessler claim that there are, in fact, two types of personality development: adjustment and maturity. As adults age, they suggest, there is a tendency towards the optimization of adjustment rather than of personality maturity. Personality adjustment refers to how individuals are able to manage changing life opportunities that arise from the various developmental contexts in which they interact. Personality maturation consists of cognitive, emotional, and motivational facets that interact to produce growth. Adjustment and maturity in personality result from different developmental goals. Whereas personality adjustment is normative over the adult life span, the trajectory for personality maturity flattens over adulthood. Personality adjustment is a necessary precondition for personality growth, however, maturity is not possible whenever personality adjustment is in play. Personality maturity appears to be possible only under certain facilitative conditions for most individuals.

Marriage is perhaps the most significant developmental context of adult life, alongside that of the adult's work and career life. Gary Creasey and Patricia Jarvis (Chapter 10) examine the relationship between attachment strivings and marriage, and they articulate the theory and research that seeks to explain successful and unsuccessful martial processes and outcomes. Because attachment functioning is thought to play a significant role in marital functioning, Creasey and Jarvis overview contemporary attachment theory and connect attachment processes with marital functioning, with an eye toward predicting long-term marital success. Securely attached individuals appear to be effective at resolving conflicts with their marital partners, whereas those who have insecure attachments are less skilled at conflict resolution. Also, more secure individuals tend to report greater marital satisfaction and higher marital quality than insecure persons.

Married life places the adult squarely in an extended, and often extensive, network of family relationships through in-law relationships but, principally, within the context of the family that the married couple create through child-bearing and child-rearing. Nadine Marks and Emily Greenfield, drawing upon a life course perspective, bioecological systems theory, and structural interactionism's role-identity theory, examine how family relationships in adult life contribute to one's psychological well-being and feelings of generativity in middle age and beyond (Chapter 11). Marital quality is among the strongest correlates of well-being, according to Marks and Greenfield, and is also associated with greater generativity in adulthood. Parenting, too, plays a role in well-being and generativity; in particular, the quality of one's parenting role influences generativity. Later in midlife, adults often find themselves providing care for their aged parents—a task that can increase one's sense of burden and psychological distress. The evidence presented suggests that family relationships can, and do, influence adult development—both for better and for worse.

A population that has not often been closely studied within the context of adult development consists of sexual minority individuals. Gay, lesbian, and bisexual adults have an array of personal relationships—with lovers and partners, family members, and friends—and these interpersonal connections contribute in myriad ways to their development and well being. Lisa Diamond and Molly Butterworth (Chapter 12) examine these intimate relationships, noting that efforts to understand the sexual-minority life course have contributed to research on adult development in general by highlighting the ways in which diversity and social context influence normative life experiences and trajectories. While societal views about sexual-minority adults' sexual relationships are undergoing change, including legal recognition of same-sex marriages or civil unions in some U.S. states, there is still much stigma and intolerance associated with these relationships. Just as in heterosexual relationships, there is great variability within the sexual-minority population, so drawing simple generalizations about the nature and impacts of sexual minority relationships is unwise and unwarranted. Still, same-sex couples appear to be as satisfied or dissatisfied with their relationships as are heterosexual couples, and for the same reasons. Sexual minority adults appear to be equally capable of parenting as are heterosexual adults, and there is no compelling evidence that children raised in households headed by sexual minority adults suffer for it, in terms of personality or psychological adjustment. Nonetheless, the legal status of same-sex families is often tenuous, which can be stressful for partners, their children, and extended family members.

Gender is both a powerful determinant of one's roles and status and a particular socializing context in itself. Sociologists Phyllis Moen, Erin Kelly, and Rachel Magennis (Chapter 13) analyze the ways in which gender has affected career development for adults (but principally for women) over the past half-century in the United States, acknowledging that adulthood is a fundamentally different experience for women and men owing to biological differences, cultural expectations, and socialization processes. Their chapter describes three related social processes that produce and perpetuate gender differences and disparities in adulthood. These processes are socialization, the allocation of gender roles and responsibilities, and the strategic selections that individual men and women make as they choose to enter or exit particular roles at different times in their lives. Women and men, the authors argue, live different adulthoods because they develop different preferences, and often make different life choices that result from having different expectations and values—a result of gender socialization. There is an increasing degree of variability within and across gender (and age) in adults' life experiences—a trend Moen et al. call converging divergences. Thus, there is—simultaneously—increased similarity for men and women (in, for example, labor force participation), but also increased disparity (in, for example, different expectations regarding paid work or family responsibilities). Coupled with this trend is a lack of normative blueprints that provide guidance regarding gender roles and behaviors. Yet the lack of such scripts or guides also presents opportunities to reimagine and reinvent adult life, regardless of gender.

The development of one's career, and achieving a sense of personal satisfaction through one's work, is a significant challenge for many adults. The workplace provides a context in which adult development can thrive or be impeded. Erik Porfeli and Fred Vondracek (Chapter 14) examine career development in adulthood, noting that the processes of exploring, establishing, and reconsidering one's career may be quite different in the new century, as a number of children today are going to be working in occupations that have not yet been created, while today's workers will be challenged to find new jobs as their occupations become obsolete. Technological advances and globalization of business and industry are two trends having profound effects on career choices and decision-making. Adults today must be willing to engage in ongoing learning to keep pace with these advances and trends. Drawing upon developmental contextualism, developmental systems theory, and the selective-optimization-with-compensation model of life-span adaptation, Porfeli and Vondracek find that adaptive career development involves the expansion, refinement, and integration of various mental processes, biological maturation, and behavior in the pursuit of satisfying careers, an understanding of the world of work, and the means to translate these into a rewarding career.

The final chapter in Section III focuses on the role of religious beliefs and spirituality in adults' lives. Acknowledging that there is a paucity of understanding about religious development in adulthood, Paul Wink (Chapter 15) draws upon life course theory and research to describe life-span changes in adults' religious involvements and church attendance, how the meaning of religiousness changes for adults over time, and changes in spirituality with age. Both religiousness and spirituality are observed to be complex and multifaceted constructs. Yet, religious beliefs and practices show much stability over the life course—highly religious young people tend to remain so in later adulthood; those who are not involved in religion are not likely to change as they age. Today, the numbers of people who identify themselves as spiritual persons, but not religious is increasing—a reflection, perhaps, of changing sociocultural and historical conditions.

Part IV then turns attention to learning in adulthood. The distinction between adult "development" and "learning" is a somewhat arbitrary one, as learning contributes to development and development sets the stage for learning to occur. This close interplay between learning and development will be obvious in many of the chapters contained in this section. Section IV begins with Dennis Thompson's historical overview of research and theorizing in regards to adult learning (Chapter 16), focusing principally upon developments within the past hundred years in the United States. According to Thompson, both developmental psychology and adult education played important roles in the emergence of the study of adult development, with a principal focus on cognitive aging. Psychologists in the early 20th century were eager to know what is gained and what is lost, intellectually, as the adult ages. Early experimental work in cognitive aging was led by Walter Miles and colleagues at Stanford University. The field of adult education was also coming into its own as a discipline by the late 1920s, prompted by individuals such as Eduard Lindeman and, in later years, Malcolm Knowles. Social changes brought about by cataclysmic events such as World War Two also contributed to greater emphasis on adult education. The impacts of the early work in cognitive aging and adult education are still resonant today.

Patricia Alexander, Karen Murphy, and Jonna Kulikowich describe how expertise has been conceptualized, defined, and investigated in Chapter 17. In doing so, the authors review four established programs of psychological research on intellectual abilities and problem solving skills, and they compare these programs on nine evaluative parameters. Contemporary concepts about proficiency view experts as individuals who possess both breadth and depth of knowledge that is highly principled and integrated. Experts are able to "effectively induce or deduce the underlying structure of...problems, and are adept at selecting and applying appropriate problem-solving procedures," drawing upon both their domain knowledge and cognitive strategies effortlessly. Following comparison and analysis of the four models, Alexander et al. make five predictions about the future of theorizing and research on expertise, including the creation of new research design and statistical methodologies that enable more fine-grained (i.e., micro-analytic) investigations of the development of expertise.

Next, in Chapter 18, Cynthia Berg, Michelle Skinner, and Kelly Ko describe an integrative model of everyday problem solving, noting that problem solving in the real world (i.e., outside of the psychology laboratory) is ill-structured, often lacking in a single, correct solution, and taking place in rich interpersonal contexts where others can assist or impede one's problem solving activities. Problem solving often requires adults to not only regulate their cognitive skills and activities, but also their emotions (e.g., distress). The integrative model of problem solving encompasses both well-defined and ill-defined, ill-structured problems as well as the cognitive, emotional, and physiological processes that are involved in everyday problem solving. The model considers how the individual appraises or defines the problem solving situation, their goals for solving the problem, and whether problem solving is to be done independently or in concert with others. Different appraisal processes can produce distinct approaches to solving the problem. Contextual factors, too, will have some bearing on problem solving efforts. In particular, the problem domain and the social context of the problem (e.g., school, work, leisure, health) influence both the determination of one's goals and the strategies used in problem solving. Finally, individual characteristics such as age, gender, and personality variables play important roles in problem solving activities.

Kennon Sheldon (Chapter 19) addresses an important personality development issue in adult learning. That is, how do adults learn to select the best goals for themselves—goals that will be most adaptive, personally expressive, and that promote one's health and happiness? Drawing upon theoretical perspectives from the field of positive psychology, Sheldon examines several motivationally-based theories of positive aging, including Baltes' (2003) selective optimization with compensation model, Heckhausen and Shultz's (1999) model of primary and secondary control, and Carstensen's (1999) socio-emotional selectivity model. All are interpreted in light of Deci and Ryan's self-determination theory (SDT) of human motivation. SDT addresses the nature of optimal, or self-determined, motivation. Self-determined individuals, according to the theory, do what is interesting, personally important, and vitalizing to themselves. Sheldon suggests that, as people age, declines in their cognitive and physical capacities may be counteracted by choosing more self-concordant goals, that is, to take ownership of their personal initiatives. Such actions enable individuals to feel more in control, confident, and competent.

Over the past two decades, Victoria Marsick and her colleagues have studied informal and incidental learning activities both within and outside of the workplace. Informal and incidental learning is defined as learning that occurs outside of formally structured, classroom-based activities within institutions. In Chapter 20, Marsick, Karen Watkins, Mary Wilson Callahan, and Marie Volpe discuss the historical antecedents of informal and incidental learning, and review some key themes and trends in the research on informal and incidental learning. They distinguish between informal learning and incidental learning, noting that while incidental learning occurs by chance, such learning can be beneficial when the adult learner shifts this accidental learning into the informal learning realm where learning is connected to meaningful activities (such as in the workplace). Their chapter also describes their efforts to critically re-examine and reconstruct Marsick and Watkin's (1990) theory, addressing some principal limitations of their theorizing (i.e., a "linear" model that emphasizes cognition over affect and learning in the workplace to the exclusion of other social contexts). The result is a model that grants greater relevance to collective group learning, intellectual reflection, the more intrinsic aspects of learning, and the role of technology in supporting informal and incidental learning.

Literacy is essential to all kinds of learning and to academic, career, and economic success in modern cultures around the world. The abilities to read, write, calculate, and use technologies such as personal computers and other labor-saving gadgets provide tremendous advantages to individuals, enabling them to attain and hold on to jobs, participate in their communities, and advocate for themselves and others. M Cecil Smith describes, in Chapter 21, the characteristics of adult literacy learning and the roles that literacy plays in promoting adult development. Contrasting different theoretical perspectives on literacy and what it means to be literate, the author describes the reciprocal relationship between schooling and literacy, noting that individuals can develop literacy skills outside of school. Because literacy is thought to be essential to productivity in the workplace, nations such as the U.S. have invested considerable resources to assess the literacy proficiencies of their adult populations. Smith reviews three such efforts in the U.S. over the past 25 years, noting that a sizeable portion of the U.S. adult population appears to have less than proficient literacy abilities. Reading, writing, numeracy (math), and technology skills and practices are described, and evidence is provided regarding how literacy influences adults' intellectual, social, and emotional development.

Do civic and community involvement contribute in any meaningful way to adult development? This question is the focus for Susan Jones and Anna Gasiorski in Chapter

22. As the authors note, civic participation, community involvement, and volunteerism provide ways for adults to engage in generative activities that contribute not only to their communities, but also to their personal development and learning. Civic participation, through activities such as voting, public service and volunteerism, are also thought by many to be essential to a healthy democratic society. The Peace Corps is perhaps the most famous government-sponsored institution through which individuals can volunteer their time in service to others, but many people also engage in community service through professional and advocacy organizations, neighborhood groups, and their churches. Educational attainment is strongly associated with individuals' civic participation, with those having more education being more likely to vote and to volunteer on service committees and boards, or work with charitable groups. However, as Jones and Gasiorski note, the relationship between civic participation, service-learning (i.e., public service in exchange for course credit), and adult development is "speculated and presumed [but] not well researched and understood." Thus, the question of whether civic participation is a cause or a consequence of higher moral reasoning abilities, greater compassion and a more well-developed ethical sense, or stronger generative strivings on the part of adults remains unanswered.

Attention deficit/hyperactivity disorders have been well-documented in children and adolescents, and a number of pharmaceutical and behavioral interventions have been developed to assist children and teens who are diagnosed with ADHD. Increasingly, adults with ADHD have come to the attention of psychologists, employers, university instructors, and adult educators. The essential feature of ADHD is, according to Lisa Weyandt (Chapter 23), "a persistent pattern of inattention and/or hyperactivity-impulsivity that is developmentally more frequent and severe than is expected," thus interfering with adult abilities to concentrate—which will ultimately affect their learning. While ADHD is not a learning disability, it often co-occurs with one or more learning disabilities. ADHD is thought to affect about 3%–4% of adults, although estimates vary by age, gender, and the manner is which the disorder is assessed. ADHD has developmental implications for adults, as it is associated with poor social skills, low self-esteem, poor marital adjustment, greater alcohol use, antisocial behavior, and lower educational attainment. Weyandt describes the etiology of ADHD and various treatment approaches, including pharmacotherapy (i.e., stimulant medications, antidepressants) and non-pharmacotherapy methods (i.e., biofeedback, yoga, dietary supplements).

Part V consists of two chapters that present research on various dimensions of aging. First, Ben Mast, Jennifer Zimmerman, and Sarah Rowe describe what neuroscientists understand about age-related changes in the brain, and the implications of these changes for learning in old age (Chapter 24). The authors note that links between age-related changes in the brain and adults' learning activities are not well-established. They draw upon research that examines normal aging of the brain and that which focuses on impaired brain functioning (i.e., dementia), as these two literatures offer significant insights into the links between brain changes and learning late in life. Two broad learning activities are described: formal learning and self-directed learning. The authors review normal cognitive aging in terms of structural brain changes in later life and the common cognitive changes associated with normal aging. They also review some of the extant research on cognitive interventions that are designed to improve elder adults' intellectual functioning. Next, they describe brain changes and the cognitive correlates of these changes in Alzheimer's disease (AD) and preclinical AD syndromes, noting that cognitive training research suggests that some learning remains possible even following the onset of dementia. Baltes and Baltes' (1990) selective optimization with compensation model provides an organizing framework for understanding how older adults can compensate for cognitive declines due to dementia. The authors conclude with an account of how elderly adults might be assisted in achieving successful learning outcomes and to improve some aspects of intellectual functioning in spite of overall declines in their cognitive abilities.

The concept of wisdom—long held to be characteristic of older adults—has captured the attention of philosophers for several millennia and, more recently, has been a focus of much psychological study. In Chapter 25, Monika Ardelt and Steve Jacobs define wisdom, describing the characteristics of wisdom in old age, and the ways in which wisdom may be related to one's sense of personal integrity and life satisfaction. They note that wisdom is best understood as an integration of cognitive, reflective, and affective personality qualities. Ardelt and Jacobs examine the methodological issues that frame the psychological research on wisdom, including the assessment of implicit theories (i.e., folk theories) of wisdom, and the uses of either implicit or explicit theories to measure individuals' wisdom or wisdom-related performance. Next, the authors track the development of wisdom across the life span, concluding that wisdom takes place continuously over the entirety of the life course. Social and personality factors that influence the development of wisdom are described, and the link between wisdom and age is summarized. Ardelt and Jacobs find that researchers generally agree that wisdom is not typical of old age. There is some evidence that those who view negative life situations as opportunities for growth and who successfully overcome life crises are more likely to develop wisdom. However, success in coping with crises and challenges is not equivalent to wisdom. In regard to the connection between wisdom and life satisfaction, wisdom is thought to be important but not necessary to life satisfaction, as other factors and events may contribute as much or more toward one's personal satisfaction in old age.

Part VI concludes the handbook, and its single chapter focuses on policy perspectives in regards to an aging society. Sociologists Judith Treas and Twyla Hill, in Chapter 26, describe recent changes in public policies in response to the changing composition of the aging U.S. population. The authors note that, by the year 2030, 72 million Americans will be age 65 or older and will comprise nearly one in five adults in the U.S. Such profound demographic changes have important implications for national health care policy, affecting public services, Social Security, and Medicare benefits. Educational attainment and adult learning must also be considered when crafting social policy in response to an aging society. While adults today are better educated than their forebears, and are increasingly participating in adult education opportunities, the results from national literacy assessments (as described in Smith's chapter, above) are troubling. High immigration has also contributed to a significant adult population that needs to acquire English literacy skills. The authors describe a shift that is occurring in public policy from one where older adults are viewed as dependent (on government programs such as Social Security to provide financial support) to one where they are encouraged to remain productive, active individuals—and to take responsibility for their own lives. Rescinding the mandatory retirement age is one example of this shift in policy. A consequence of this shift is an implicit demand for older adults to remain healthy, be better informed, literate and knowledgeable, and possess good decision-making abilities so that they can manage their own financial and health care-related affairs. Thus, such policies run the risk of disenfranchising millions of American adults who lack these essential skills and knowledge. Although adults will need to engage in life-long learning (in some cases within formal educational institutions), adult education policies are not yet integrated with public policies related to aging.

Chapter Reviewers

Appreciation is expressed to all of the chapter reviewers for giving their time and expertise.

Pauline Abbott
California State University – Fullerton

Jason C. Allaire
North Carolina State University

Carrie Bassett
The Wisdom Institute, Minneapolis, MN

Alicia Belzer
Rutgers University

Debra L. Berke
Messiah College

Noelle Chesley
University of Wisconsin – Milwaukee

Teresa Cooney
University of Missouri – Columbia

George DuPaul
Lehigh University

Janet Eyler
Vanderbilt University

Judith Glueck
University of Vienna

Derek M. Isaacowitz
Brandeis University

Daniel Keating
University of Michigan

Susanne Lajoie
McGill University

Sylvie Lapierre
University of Quebec

Marylu K. McEwen
University of Maryland

Melvin E. Miller
Norwich University

Mark M. Misic
Northern Illinois University

Allen J. Ottens
Northern Illinois University

Thomas G. Reio, Jr.
Florida Atlantic University

Michaela Riediger
Max Planck Institute for Human
    Development Berlin

Deborah Rohm-Young
University of Maryland

Larry Roper
Oregon State University

Tanja Rothrauff
University of Missouri – Columbia

David A. Shannon
Auburn University

Ilene C. Siegler
Duke University Medical Center

Tawny Smay
Messiah College

John Strucker
Harvard University

Steven Sweet
Ithaca College

Katherine Taylor
St. Mary's College of California

Elizabeth Tisdell
Penn State University – Harrisburg

Marteen Vansteenkiste
Leuven University (Belgium)

Lori Vogelgesang
University of California – Los Angeles

David A. Walker
Northern Illinois University

Lemuel Watson
Northern Illinois University

Jacqueline S. Weinstock
University of Vermont

Kristi Williams
Ohio State University

Part I

Theoretical Perspectives on Adult Development and Learning

Chapter 1

Challenges for the Current Status of Adult Developmental Theories

A New Century of Progress

Fredda Blanchard-Fields and Antje Stange Kalinauskas

In order to understand learning in adulthood, we need to understand developmental changes across the latter half of the lifespan. The purpose of this chapter is to discuss a number of contemporary adult developmental theories that explain changes in different domains of functioning. For instance, strategies for dealing with a novel situation may be different for young and older adults as a function of changes in processing goals. When faced with a new situation, young adults may focus on developing and optimizing new strategies to adapt to the problem situation. Older adults, however, may draw upon an accumulated wealth of strategies in order to regain or maintain a viable solution. Adult development theories can provide us with explanations as to why and how individuals change such processing goals that impact the way they approach the problem.

The general framework for our chapter is a lifespan perspective on development. Baltes and his colleagues (Baltes, 1987, 1997; Baltes, Lindenberger, & Staudinger, 2006) have outlined general theoretical tenets of life-span development characterized by multidirectional, multidimensional, and multifunctional processes that involve the constant interplay of gains and losses within each life period. Applied to a learning situation this means that the learning of a certain skill can involve growth, but this may be at the expense of another skill, therefore implying loss.

By examining contemporary theories through the lens of a lifespan developmental perspective, we hope to illustrate that the core constructs listed above are more fully realized than in earlier thinking. For instance, research focusing on multidirectionality of development has been further enhanced by implementing statistical techniques assessing intraindividual variability. In this case, developmental growth can be distinguished from fluctuations in performance as later described in this chapter. Research focusing on multidimensionality of development has been enhanced with recent attempts to examine developmental linkages in different domains of functioning, such as emotion and cognition or health and cognition.

The lifespan approach takes a functionalist perspective on development. According to this view, the ultimate goal of development is to increase adaptation of the organism to its environment which is achieved through learning. Plasticity and intra-individual variability are key concepts within this perspective because they set the boundaries for the organism's ability to learn and as such adapt to its environment. One of the central questions of adult developmental theory is to understand the boundaries of plasticity. For instance, in the oldest old, the functional reserve capacity of the individual is declining and developmental gains are become increasingly more difficult to achieve. The dynamic of gains and losses, biology and culture need to be investigated within different stages of life to understand the full cycle of adult development.

Another common life-span-related thread that runs through contemporary adult developmental theories discussed in this chapter is that behavior and development are multiply determined. At the simplest level, age is not the best predictor of behavior. Instead, behavior across the lifespan is determined by multiple forces, some of which are age-related (such as biological changes), differing opportunity structures in society, and changes in motivational orientations and emotional functioning. For example, researchers now acknowledge that cognitive change in older adulthood is influenced at multiple levels of analysis including declines in brain volume and density, the positive and negative effects of stereotyping, and deploying attention away from negative stimuli. Furthermore, investigation of these multiple forces on development has become more tractable as new technologies and research methods have evolved, such as brain imagining techniques and extensive multiple-burst micro-longitudinal studies.

This chapter provides an overview of contemporary theories and recent empirical findings of adult development while at the same time outlining future challenges that need to be addressed by these theories. We begin by discussing three factors that influence the development of theories, the availability of new methods of measurement and analysis, the emergence of new phenomena, such as the fourth age, and changes in the science-political agendas that influence the investment of resources into research. Next, several contemporary theories of adult development are described. Whereas we place some theories in their historical context to highlight how they have extended previous thinking in their respective areas, other theories are shown to reflect new and emerging perspectives on adult development and change. We discuss these contemporary theories and provide empirical examples of how they have been tested. Finally, in elucidating each of the newer theories, we suggest how new methods and empirical phenomena can provide challenges for theories of adult development.

Recent Scientific Trends Influencing Theory Development

Psychological theories are advanced when theory-inconsistent findings require the elaboration and refinement of older theories or sometimes the development of completely new theories (Kuhn, 1962). However, there are other factors that influence theoretical development including (1) the development and use of new methods of measurement and analysis that allow the investigation of both recurrent and emerging research questions, (2) the emergence of new phenomena, and (3) science-political agendas that influence the investment of resources into research.

In this section we focus on several noteworthy examples of how these factors have influenced current thinking in human development. First, we focus on neuroimaging as an example of a recent technology that allows the non-invasive investigation of brain functions. Second, we use the sample case of intra-individual variability to illustrate how new methods of data analysis can shape our understanding of developmental processes. Third, we discuss the impact of measures of everyday functioning, such as time-sampling studies that enable us to more closely examine psychological processes as they occur in everyday life. Fourth, we discuss the theoretical implications of the emergence of the fourth age as a likely extended phase of aging for most people. Fifth, we briefly describe how putting aging on the science-political agenda advances the field of adult development.

The Century of the Brain: Observing the Brain Working

The 21st century has been called the century of the brain. Recent technological advances, such as the development of functional magnetic resonance imaging (fMRI) and diffusion tensor imaging (DTI), allow us to study brain structure and functions using non-invasive technologies. Neuronal correlates of behavior can be studied in living individuals. Neuroscientific approaches have been widely applied to research questions that deal with cognitive aging. However, recently researchers have used this technique to investigate processing preferences for emotional compared to neutral information in older adults (Mather, Canli, English et al., 2004). Research in the emerging field of social cognitive neuroscience has shown associations between neural structures and a variety of social cognitive tasks such as person perception, stereotypes, and theory of mind (Amodio & Frith, 2006; Ochsner & Lieberman, 2001). One of the challenges for adult development theories will be to incorporate these models and techniques into their thinking. Finally, the neuroscience approach has taken intervention research to new heights. Now, we cannot only observe change as a result of intervention at the behavioral level but also at the neurological level (Colcombe, Erickson, Raz et al., 2003).

Three approaches to the neuroscience of aging can be distinguished: The neuropsychological, the correlational, and the activation imaging approach (Cabeza, 2004). The majority of work in this area has focused on cognitive aging rather than including the entirety of adulthood. Therefore, we will focus in our discussion on this aspect of adult development. The neuropsychological approach compares the neuropsychological functioning of healthy older adults with adults showing certain pathological patterns. A good example is Parkinson's disease which is accompanied by dopaminergic deficits that affect the frontostriatal system and reduce, for instance, speed of processing. The primary objective of this approach is to identify neural mechanisms that are associated with both normal and pathological decline in cognitive functions. These findings stimulate theoretical development by describing influential factors that warrant theoretical explanation as to how and why these factors may cause cognitive decline as we age.

The correlational approach, on the other hand, tries to link cognitive and cerebral aging. It focuses on the correlation of cognitive behavioral data, such as executive functioning, with neural structural measures, such as white matter deterioration or brain volume. Data from this approach focus on the role of brain structure in explaining cognitive decline (Raz, 2000).

Finally, the activation imaging approach, tries to directly link functional brain data with cognitive behavioral data. This approach allows the in vivo investigation of changes in brain function as they relate to cognitive performance within individuals. For example, studies using this approach found that younger adults' brains show unilateral activation in their brains when they work on cognitive tasks whereas older adults' brains tend to show increased activation in both brain hemispheres (Cabeza, 2002).

Overall, as the sample case of research on cognitive aging demonstrates, theoretical development within the field of adulthood is enriched by neuroscientific methods in several ways. First, theories can be tested using neuropsychological approaches. For instance, the idea of selective allocation of attention can be tested by relating event-related potentials to behavioral data (Wood & Kisley, 2006). Second, changes in performance can be associated with both functional and structural brain variables to explain how the brain influences performance. This is not only applicable to change processes in older adults' brains, but could be also investigated in the maturing brains of adolescents and children. Third, research methods that focus on the architecture and functioning of the brain can help to explain why certain cognitive functions, such as well-practiced tasks, vocabulary, and wisdom can be preserved into old age while other functions, such as processing speed, decline rapidly as people age.

However, neuroscientific methods also have their limits. For instance, documenting activities in different brain regions does not necessarily imply that different psychological processes are involved (i.e., decline in sensory motor functioning, vision and hearing may be similar processes but different regions of the brain). Nevertheless, advances in the field of neuroscience have major impacts on the development of theories of cognitive age because they reveal new findings for which psychological theories have to account and with which they must be consistent.

Statistical Innovations: A New Focus on Intra-individual Change

Past methodological debates have revolved around criticisms of cross-sectional designs comparing young and older persons as adequate tools for studying developmental change. It has been demonstrated that inter-individual differences between young and older adults cannot necessarily be attributed to changes that accompany age. For instance, many human phenomena are non-ergodic. Non-ergodicity refers to the fact that variations between persons (inter-individual variability) and variations within persons (intra-individual variability) are not equivalent (Molenaar, 2004). For example, if we would find that older adults prefer to learn in a face-to-face context, whereas younger adults prefer a computer-based instructional tool, this may reflect generational differences rather than aging-related effects. In this scenario, we would not expect young adults to change their preference as they get older. In other words, the inter-individual difference (i.e., between younger and older adults) would not translate into intra-individual differences.

Furthermore, adult developmental theories are informed by observed behavioral differences between age groups. Thus historically, intra-individual variability has often been considered measurement error or noise (Luszcz, 2004). There are two major problems associated with the cross-sectional approach. First, it is unclear whether behavior measured at a specific point in time is representative of the person's typical behavior. Second, it is questionable whether the differences found between people of different ages are equivalent to the changes that occur within people.

Recently, researchers have turned their attention back to studying the individual as the unit for the observation of developmental change by investigating intra-individual variability. This approach has also been referred to as the person-centered or idiographic approach (Baltes, Reese, & Nesselroade, 1977; Magnusson, 2001; Molenaar, 2004; Nesselroade, 2001, 2004). Again, we will use cognitive aging as an example field in which these ideas have been applied most radically. Here, variability that is due to non-reversible changes, e.g., development due to either learning or cognitive decline, needs to be distinguished from reversible short-term intra-individual variability that reflects fluctuation and reversible changes within individuals, e.g., moods and temporary states (Nesselroade, 2001).

Non-reversible changes are exemplified in developmental changes in cognitive performance over time (see Schaie, 1996). For instance, cross-sectional studies of change often overestimate the amount of change that occurs with age because they reflect inter-individual differences and perhaps cohort effects between age-groups rather than intra-individual change. Also, predictors of cognitive change in old age may differ depending on whether cross-sectional or longitudinal approaches are taken (Sliwinski & Buschke, 1999). Recently new statistical analytical procedures are available to analyze longitudinal data, such as Latent Growth Modeling (LGM) and Multi-Level Models (MLM) (Ghisletta & Lindenberger, 2004; Holt, chapter 5, this volume).

The second form of intra-individual variability is referred to as short-term intra-individual variability. It reflects a person's instability or fluctuation around the individual's mean score. This form of variability has received considerable attention in the psychological literature in the past decade because it has been shown that short-term variability may be an important predictor of different outcomes over and above mean levels of performance (Hultsch, MacDonald, & Dixon, 2002; Li, Aggen, Nesselrode, & Baltes, 2001; Nesselroade & Salthouse, 2004; Ram, Rabbitt, Stollery, & Nesselroade, 2005; Salthouse, Nesselroade, & Berish, 2006). Moreover, measuring any performance using just single assessments becomes questionable as considerable short-term variation and inter-individual differences in short term variation are found even for highly reliable cognitive measures (Salthouse et al., 2006). A life-span perspective is necessary to interpret such variability: Early in the life span, a high amount of intra-individual variability may reflect plasticity and the potential to grow and advance (e.g., Baltes et al., 2006). However, increased intra-individual variability—that is fluctuation—in older adulthood may reflect a decrease in the integrity of the system (Hultsch & MacDonald, 2004; Li & Lindenberger, 1999). As such the intra-individual variability that is associated with temporary states is of high significance to understanding age-related changes that occur across the life span (Hultsch & MacDonald, 2004).

Theories of adult development need to incorporate both mean levels and variability in performance to account for age-associated developmental phenomena. However, it should be noted that there are limitations to the applicability of these designs in some domains of research. For instance, it has to be assumed that repeated exposure to the same material will not influence performance (i.e., practice effects). Basically, studies on intra-individual variability face similar criticisms as within-subjects designs in general (such as longitudinal studies).

Getting Back to "Real Life": Studying Behavior Embedded in Social Context

There is a long history of research in adult development and aging that has embraced the importance of social context by translating behavior from the lab into daily life. Current research trends and methods have enhanced the way we incorporate social context into research designs. Recent advances in the stress and coping as well as the everyday problem solving literature are good examples of this. Both of these areas have utilized interviews and questionnaires to assess retrospective accounts of individuals' actual behavior in handling stress or solving daily hassles and problems. With this approach, we have learned about changes in the way older adults cope with stress, regulate their emotions, and solve problems (Folkman & Lazarus, 1988; Blanchard-Fields, Jahnke, & Camp, 1995). However, these approaches suffer from inherent problems in retrospective accounts that rely on one's memory and one's conceptualization and image of the self.

As opposed to obtaining information retrospectively (e.g., how one handled an emotional situation or assessing perceived stress in life events) a growing trend is to take into consideration the fact that socio-emotional functioning, everyday problem solving, and decision making occur over an extended time frame. Such processes draw upon cognitive, physiological, emotional, and social resources in a time-related fashion. Thus, researchers are now paying particular attention to broadening the assessment of retrospective accounts of successful or unsuccessful outcomes, to solving problems or dealing with stress, to assessing age-related differences in day to day variability in handling ongoing stressful situations or problems. Thus, everyday functioning is related to adaptation to everyday environments by a) examining processes such as problem solving or coping with stress as they naturally occur in daily living and b) relating them to relevant and well-known adaptive outcomes in everyday functioning, both psychological and physiological.

For example, Almeida (2005) examines the measurement of daily stressors in older adults' lives using study designs that allow for the direct examination of how different stressors affect well-being and how personal characteristics influence the daily-stress process. Recent daily assessment methods include responding over the telephone, using personal digital assistants, and Internet reporting. Collecting information about ongoing daily activities circumvents problems with retrospective recall or interviews that can perpetuate memory distortions (Bolger, Davis, & Rafaeli, 2003). Most importantly, Almeida (2005) aptly points out that this methodology assesses within-person processes that chart the day-to-day fluctuations in processes such as stress and well-being, as well as to identify predictors, correlates, and consequences of these fluctuations. In this way, Almeida's research more precisely established the short-term effects of concrete daily experiences.

In sum, a strength of these approaches is that they fully embrace the life-span developmental tenet that behavior is multiply determined. For example, current research not only assesses outcomes of problem solving and coping with stress in terms of psychological well-being, but assesses outcomes at various levels of analysis such as biology in the form of cortisol patterns or allostatic load (Ryff, Singer, & Love, 2004). As indicated above, another strength of these approaches is that it moves beyond a snap-shot of behavior to examining behavior in process across time. There are of course limitations to examining behavior in the natural environment including lack of control over variables, technological limitations in the use of instruments such as PDAs, as well as the degree to which participants comply with procedural instructions. However, in concert with laboratory studies, the future of research in these everyday domains is quite promising.

Emerging Phenomena: Discovering the Fourth Age

Besides the development of new scientific methods, theory development in the field of human development is influenced by the emergence of new phenomena. One example of a relatively new phenomenon is the emergence of the fourth age as a normative condition for most people in our society. The fourth age starts roughly at age 80 or 85 (Baltes, 1997; Laslett, 1991; Neugarten, 1974; Suzman, Willis, & Manton, 1992).

The distinction between the third and fourth age of adulthood is important because most of the positive aspects of aging are found only for the third age. Adults in the third age (aged 65 to 80 years) demonstrate stability in some aspects of intellectual functioning, such as knowledge and expertise (Ackerman, 2000; Baltes & Staudinger, 2000; Schaie, 1996; Singer, Verhaeghen, Ghisletta, Lindenberger, & Baltes, 2003), sustained functional reserve capacity and plasticity (e.g., Baltes & Willis, 1982), desirable levels of social-psychological functioning (Smith & Baltes, 1997), and implementing adaptive goals in daily life (e.g., Riediger, Freund, & Baltes, 2005). The third age is full of positive news.

However, recent empirical evidence has shown that the news for the old-old and oldest-old may not be as promising, i.e., the maintenance of high levels of psychological functioning is more difficult in the fourth age (Gerstorf, Smith, & Baltes, 2006; Smith & Baltes, 1999). Older adults in the fourth age are more likely to be multi-morbid, depressed, and demented (Baltes & Mayer, 1999), show lower levels of cognitive plasticity (Singer, Lindenberger, & Baltes, 2003), as well as decreases in happiness and meaning of life (Smith & Baltes, 1993). The vulnerabilities of very old age provide a challenge for theories of adult development. There may be an increasing need for adult developmental theories to capture the behavioral and psychological dynamics of losses in various domains of life.

Science, Politics, and Social Policy: Furthering the Aging Agenda

Policy makers and researchers alike have noted that the changing population (i.e., the graying of America) focuses us on questions regarding aging at a societal level such as, what effect does an aging workforce have on our economy? To answer this question we need to have a better understanding of the conditions in which the older population functions effectively and under what conditions they are challenged. Thus, for example, the National Institute on Aging has emphasized research that takes into consideration the dynamic interplay between changing biomedical, social, and physical environments. The underlying mission is to establish a knowledge base for maximizing active life and health expectancy with advancing age. Interdisciplinary research is central to establish this kind of knowledge base such as the integration of biology and genetics with behavioral and social sciences. Thus, the newly publicized NIH Roadmap Initiatives sees research teams of the future to be interdisciplinary bringing together biological, behavioral and social sciences to tackle the most pressing health problems. Subsequently, we have seen advances in cognitive neuroscience and aging, genetics, behavior, and aging, and multilevel interactions among psychological, physiological, social, and cultural factors.

For example, the National Institute on Aging has commissioned the National Academy of Sciences to create research agendas for future aging research. Two prominent books have resulted, one focusing on the aging mind (Stern & Carstensen, 2000), the other focusing on social psychology and aging (Carstensen & Hartel, 2006). Each of these research agendas emphasizes an interdisciplinary perspective, which removes the artificial barriers of separate disciplines. This has had far-reaching effects on forging new interdisciplinary research teams with a particular emphasis on the dynamics between a neuroscience approach and other disciplines such as neuro-economics, social neuroscience, and biodemography, among others.

Some Illustrations of Contemporary Theories of Adult Development

In this section we examine a number of areas of adult developmental research that are illustrative of the emerging and new developments in theories of adult development and aging discussed in the first section of the chapter. We focus mainly on areas that have recently benefited from methodological advances and/or have received considerable attention in the literature both in publication proliferation as well as from granting agencies. For each of the following areas, we describe the state of the art, as well as future directions based on the emerging trends.

As indicated above, there are numerous domains covered by adult developmental theories and it is beyond the scope of this chapter to cover them all. We selected theories from a few domains of functioning based on the following criteria: We tried to incorporate "hot topics," areas that receive considerable attention in the literature, such as the relation between cognition and aging and neuroscientific underpinnings of cognitive change. This area is particularly illustrative of how methodological advances have enhanced our understanding of "cognitive aging." Second, we incorporated areas of practical significance, such as the relation between health, cognition, and aging. This exemplifies how the granting agencies putting emphasis on research enhancing the quality of life of older adults has pushed the field forward. Similarly, research on the role of emotion in information processing in older adulthood is also a recent outcome of quality of life issues in older adulthood. Similarly, we describe self-regulation as an area characterized by substantive theoretical elaboration. Finally, we discuss social cognition as a field with a new and growing status in the adult development and aging field. A number of these areas also illustrate how method, empirical findings, and theories work together in enhancing our understanding of adult development.

Emotion and Cognition

As witnessed in various chapters in this book, there is a pervasive and rich history of theory and research examining changes in cognition as we grow older and the extent to which age-related changes in cognition influence the effective functioning of the individual. However, until fairly recently there has been relatively less research on the role emotion plays in cognitive functioning in adulthood and aging. In the past, the focal emotion-related question was whether age differences in performance-inhibiting emotional states (e.g., test anxiety) accounted for age differences in cognitive performance. For example, classic studies by Eisdorfer (1968) argued that age differences in paired associate learning could be an artifact of "overarousal" of older persons in test situations. Historically, for most gerontologists interested in cognitive processes, emotional constructs were really little more than nuisance factors representing possible confounding influences on studies designed to measures age changes in cognition.

This was followed by a line of thinking that treated emotion and affect as a completely separate domain of psychological constructs relevant to aging (Schulz, 1985). This perspective generated a number of emotion-related theoretical questions. For example, researchers questioned whether emotional intensity dampened with increasing age (Diener, Sandvik, & Larsen, 1985; Levenson, Carstensen, Friesen, & Ekman, 1991).

New theoretical trends in research on emotion, cognition, and the aging mind have examined the role of emotions in terms of motivational goals, neurological changes, emotional complexity, and emotion regulation efficacy in cognitive and social cognitive functioning (Blanchard-Fields, 1998; Carstensen, Isaacowitz, & Charles, 1999; Labouvie-Vief, 2003). For example, researchers find that the regulation of emotions improves with age, which has stimulated interest in what accounts for this positive developmental trajectory (Blanchard-Fields et al., 1995; Carstensen, Pasupathi, Mayr, & Nesselroade, 2000; Lawton, Kleban, Rajagopal, & Dean, 1992). The important conclusion coming out of many of these various lines of thinking is that emotion and emotion-related behavior show a positive developmental trajectory in contrast to the well-documented areas of cognitive decline (e.g., in executive processes, working memory).

Most recently, researchers are interested in how this positive developmental trajectory in emotion regulation translates into age-related differences in the way individuals process emotionally-laden information. This interface is reciprocal in that emotion and affect influence cognitive processes (i.e., memory, decision making, social judgments, learning) and cognitions also influence emotions (i.e., mood induction, cognitive appraisal, causal attributions). For example, the emotion-cognitive processing relationship has its roots in cognitive research advocating that when an emotion is experienced, information associated with it is primed and more likely to be recalled (e.g., Bower, 1991; Mandler, 1984; Ortony, Clore, & Collins, 1988). Research in the area of social cognition suggests that when, in a negative mood, individuals may become more critical and search for information to explain their negative feelings (for a review see Forgas, 1995). They tend to engage in more careful and deliberate information processing which leads them to more accurate judgment and decision making. These findings are consistent with the mood-as-input model of affect (Martin, 2001) which proposes that positive moods create a false sense of overconfidence, reducing a participant's willingness to invest additional resources to a task (i.e., increasing more heuristic processing). On the other hand, negative moods create a sense of insecurity within the participant, evoking a state of protective vigilance and a willingness to invest more effort to a task (i.e., a state of more systematic, detail-oriented processing).

It is important to note that the last six years have witnessed a mushrooming of theories and research on the interplay of cognition and emotion from an adult developmental perspective. As evidence, one only has to list current theories on cognition and emotion (e.g., Socioemotional Selectivity Theory and the positivity effect, Dynamic Integration Theory), or peruse the latest handbooks and overview chapters (e.g., Birren & Schaie, 2006; Hoare, 2006), recent trends in grant proposals, scientific presentations, and recent publications such as the special section on cognition and emotion in Psychology and Aging (Blanchard-Fields, 2005). Whereas emotion was once thought of as a confounding variable, it now commands attention in the cognitive aging and neuroscience literature.

Second, there are several areas of theorizing and research that have come to the foreground with respect to the interplay of emotion and cognition. They include the influence of emotion on cognitive processing, and emotion regulation and problem solving. We will briefly review theories and findings in each of these areas.

Is there a positivity effect with aging?   An area that has received much theoretical attention in the extant aging literature is the positivity effect (Carstensen & Mikels, 2005) in which older adults show a processing priority for positive information leading to an accurate recall of positive information. In concert with the positivity effect, a negativity suppression effect (Blanchard-Fields, 2006) results in selective processing to minimize the processing of negative information. Research on both of these selective processing mechanisms has been spearheaded by a social cognitive and emotion-related research approach. The primary question asked is how shifts in goals and motivations change the way older adults process information. However, there is a third approach to selective processing that is most prominent in the social cognitive and neuroscience of aging literature: the negativity effect (Rozin & Royzman, 2001). This reflects a processing priority for negative information leading to an accurate recall of negative information. Given these three theoretical approaches, it is clear that there are a number of ways that individuals selectively process emotional information.

Empirical evidence in light of these theoretical approaches is mixed—reflecting the fact that the current status of research on emotion-cognition interfaces in adulthood and aging represent theories in transition. For example, evidence for older adults focusing more of their attention on positive information is not consistent. Yet, there is more consistent support for the negativity suppression effect, i.e., diverting attention away from negative information. Furthermore, researchers have suggested that an emotional enhancement in memory when processing negative information that is distinctive and salient, i.e., the negativity effect, is similar in both young and older adults or if there are any differences, this effect is diminished with age. Let us illustrate this transition along with recent methodological developments.

Let us briefly examine the evidence for a positivity effect. There are three major findings that suggest that a positivity effect should be prevalent in older adulthood (Carstensen, Mikels, & Mather, 2006). First, there is no evidence for age differences in the functionality of the emotion system. Second, there is evidence for a positive developmental trajectory for improved emotion regulation. Finally, with increasing age, there is an increase in the allocation of resources to emotion and emotion regulation (to enhance their current mood) when processing cognitive tasks. Thus, this motivational shift should have consequences on older adults' cognitive functioning (Carstensen et al., 2006).

The positivity effect is operationalized as age differences in the ratio of positive to negative material in information processing (Carstensen et al., 2006). Researchers find that older adults divert attention away from negative stimuli and in some cases attend more to positive stimuli (Mather & Carstensen, 2003, Experiment 1), i.e., older adults look more at happy faces and look away from angry faces in comparison to young adults. Older adults recalled and recognized more neutral images over negative ones in comparison with young adults and in one experiment they recognized more positive images (Charles, Mather, & Carstensen, 2003, Experiment 1); older adults performed better on a working memory task for positive emotional stimuli in comparison to negative emotional stimuli (Mikels, Larkin, Reuter-Lorenz, & Carstensen, 2005); older adults remembered more positive information during an autobiographical recall task (Kennedy, Mather, & Carstensen, 2004; Levine & Bluck, 1997); and older adults recalled their decisions in a way that was more positive than negative (Mather, Knight, & McCaffrey, 2005).

What happens when research focuses more on a negativity effect? There are studies that, in contrast to the positivity effect, find that older adults spend more time viewing negative stimuli (Charles et al., 2003) and display a negativity effect (Mienaltowski, Corballis, Blanchard-Fields, & Parks, 2006; Thomas & Hasher, 2006; Wood & Kisley, 2006). Grühn, Smith, and Baltes (2005) did not demonstrate a positivity effect in older adults, and instead, found evidence for a reduced negativity effect in older adults when remembering a list of words with negative, positive, and neutral valence. A negativity effect was found in both young and older adults in that they recalled more central elements of a negative scene than neutral peripheral elements. However, with instructions to pay attention to this tendency, only the young adults could overcome this encoding bias, whereas older adults could not overcome the memory trade-off (Kensinger, Piguet, Krendl, & Corkin, 2005).

Despite these mixed findings, we also need to address the important question of how these theoretical approaches inform adaptive functioning in the older adult. From an SST perspective, it is argued that a positivity effect is adaptive for older adults given that they typically have a constrained temporal horizon and thus are motivated to maintain emotionally satisfying experiences (Carstensen et al., 2006). By focusing on the positive to the exclusion of the negative, older adults may be able to create a positive and non-toxic environment that will not strain their limited cognitive as well as physiological resources. Furthermore, it may be the case that this heightened attention to positive emotional information to the exclusion of negative information (negativity suppression effect) may serve as an aid to processing complex material (Carstensen & Mikels, 2005). At a higher level, both of these benefits may operate in service of heightening emotional well-being in older adulthood (Carstensen & Mikels, 2005).

However, this form of processing may also lead to maladaptive effects. For example, it may impede the cognitive processing of important negative information such as information that should be taken into account when making a decision, e.g., the negative side effects of medication or a medical procedure. Along these lines, the counterpoint to the adaptive value of both the positivity and negativity suppression effects is that a negativity effect may be necessary for survival in that it is adaptive to process and attend to pertinent negative material to make adaptive decisions (Rozin & Royzman, 2001). Of course, there are maladaptive outcomes to this effect in that it could lead to overarousal and fragmentation. This could be particularly detrimental to older adults who have lower tolerance for high negative arousal levels (Considine, Magai, & Bonnano, 2002).

In sum, when do emotions help older adults? Simply put, when they create a supportive context for cognitive processing, such as the distinctiveness of emotions, or when it helps older adults process information, such as being able to reduce the number of false memories produced (Kensinger & Corkin, 2004; May, Rahhal, Berry, & Leighton, 2005). It also helps them focus on important information when making decisions (Löckenhoff & Carstensen, 2004; Mikels et al., 2005). When do emotions impede information processing? First, the answer is that emotions that are high in arousal can create interference. For example, situations high in arousal and high in executive control processing demands lead older adults to poor remembrance and processing of information (Kensinger & Corkin, 2004; Mather & Knight, 2005; Wurm, Labouvie-Vief, Aycock, Rebucal, & Koch, 2004). Second, when older adults focus only on positive information their decision making can lead them to overlook important criteria for making a quality decision (Löckenhoff & Carstensen, 2004).

Future research will need to address important theoretical questions that arise from these discrepant findings. For example, can they be integrated into a larger theoretical framework? If emotion regulation and motivation is implicated in the processing of information, we need better outcome measures of the long term consequences in order to truly assess its adaptive value. If older adults are selectively allocating resources toward positive and away from negatively valenced information, we need direct tests of this process. What is the role of arousal? What are the emotion regulation strategies that produce selective attention to emotions? And finally, under what conditions is it important to attend to negative stimuli and when are positivity and negativity suppression effects more adaptive?

Emotion Regulation and Everyday Problem Solving.   As indicated above, research that explicitly examines the extent to which older adults adaptively manage their everyday lives (at least through the third age, 65–80 years of age) reveals positive developmental trajectories in the functioning of older adults. In particular, such positive developmental trends are observed in the strategies and goals older adults use to solve socio-emotional problems and how they regulate emotions in the context of these problems. For example, Blanchard-Fields and colleagues highlight the socio-emotional nature of ill-structured problems, which are unpredictable and continually transforming. Individuals are asked to appraise the causes and demands of the situation and decide between many potentially effective solutions. In these circumstances, older adults are presented with the opportunity to draw on accumulated experience in socio-emotional realms to solve problems effectively. This could involve an immediate proactive plan of action or a combination of regulating one's emotional composure followed by such proactive action. Emotionally laden or interpersonal problems (e.g., the decision to place your mother in a nursing home), along with more instrumental problems (e.g., returning defective merchandise), are presented to participants. They are asked how they would solve the problems or rate the degree to which they would employ particular strategies. Finally, two general categories of strategies: instrumental strategies (e.g., direct action taken to solve the problem) and emotion-regulation strategies (e.g., suppressing feelings, not trying to alter an uncontrollable situation; confronting emotions) were examined.

Findings demonstrate that older adults tend to use a more diverse repertoire of problem-solving and emotion regulation strategies to handle problems that are high in emotional involvement and are interpersonal in nature (Blanchard-Fields, 2007; Blanchard-Fields et al., 1995; Blanchard-Fields, Chen, & Norris, 1997; Blanchard-Fields, Stein, & Watson, 2004). Furthermore, they not only use a variety of strategies, but they use them more effectively than young adults do as indicated by expert panel ratings of the strategies selected (Blanchard-Fields, Mienaltowski, & Seay, 2007). This can lead to a more flexible application of problem solving and emotion regulation strategies to varying contexts. This is especially evident in the way older adults combine the use of emotion-regulation strategies with instrumental strategies in emotionally-charged situations (Blanchard-Fields, 2007; Watson & Blanchard-Fields, 1998). For example, older adults used different strategies depending upon the discrete emotion they felt. When they felt angry, they used proactive strategies such as confronting one's emotions. In contrast, when experiencing sadness they primarily used passive emotion-regulation strategies such as withdrawal. In other words, older adults demonstrate an appreciation of when to be proactive and instrumental, when to passively accept a situation, and when to use a combination of the two. Accordingly, research shows that older adults report that they are better at emotion regulation (Gross, Carstensen, Pasupathi, Tsai, Götestam Skorpen, & Hsu, 1997; Lawton, 2001), report fewer negative emotions in daily life (Carstensen et al., 2000), focus more attention on regulating the emotional aspects of their environment (Carstensen & Mikels, 2005), have the capacity to spontaneously react to negative-emotion-evoking events (Kunzmann & Grühn, 2005), and use more passive emotion regulation coping when a stressful event is appraised as uncontrollable in comparison with young adults (Blanchard-Fields & Irion, 1988).

Whereas findings in this area of research are promising with respect to documenting the adaptive functioning of older adults, they are not without their limitations—in particular the self-report nature of data collection. It will be important for future research to further identify criteria for effective everyday problem solving and emotion regulation by extending outcomes to psychological and physiological well-being. Thus, methodological advances in time sampling techniques will be useful to examine naturally occurring emotional and physiological states that occur in association with day to day problem solving and emotion regulation strategy use. In this way problem solving and emotion regulation can be observed as they occur over time. This approach can examine questions regarding the sequential ordering of strategy use and at what point in the problem solving process are specific strategies effective and non-effective. Finally, what are the mechanisms driving age-related differences in emotion regulation and use of everyday problem solving strategies?

One candidate is affect complexity. Gisela Labouvie-Vief (2003) has examined the construct of cognitive-affective complexity, which involves the balanced integration of emotion and cognition (Labouvie-Vief, 1998; Labouvie-Vief, Hakim-Larson, & Hobart, 1987). Cognitive-emotional complexity involves the ability to integrate emotional and cognitive aspects of self and the environment. At high levels of cognitive-emotional complexity, emotion is seen as jointly reflecting internal states and external contexts. This form of affective complexity demonstrates significant growth until middle adulthood and then shows a decline in later adulthood. It should be noted that this is contrary to research on the positivity effect in that low affect complexity could pose emotion regulation challenges to older adults.

Labouvie-Vief (2003) proposes that older adults who are motivated to maximize positive emotions (i.e., the positivity effect) may be individuals who need to compensate for a decrease in cognitive-affective complexity. Thus, they engage in optimization which is a relatively automatic response to emotions, including passive suppression of negative emotions in favor of positive emotions. Affect differentiation requires more elaborative and cognitive resources in order to differentiate knowledge about one's emotions and confront one's emotions. In support of this, Labouvie-Vief finds that cognitive-affective complexity declines with advancing age, and older adults tend to rely more strongly on optimization strategies than younger age groups.

This theoretical approach is further supported in that older adults who were lower in affect complexity were more likely to use passive emotion regulation strategies (Coats & Blanchard-Fields, 2006). It is suggested that those older adults who are less able to think in complex ways about the role emotions play in the context of everyday situations are the individuals who are more likely to rely on passive strategies. This is consistent with Labouvie-Vief's (2003) theory in that strategies such as avoidance and escape are more commonly endorsed by individuals of low cognitive-emotional complexity. Moreover, the ways that people regulated sadness in everyday problem situations depended upon how likely an individual was to outwardly express sadness. Those older adults who were more expressive when experiencing sadness were also the ones who were more likely to rely on more direct, action-related strategies. The role of affect complexity on problem solving and emotion regulation deserves increasing attention in future research.

Finally, there are other numerous candidates explaining age-related differences in emotion regulation that deserve future investigation including decreases in autonomic and cardiovascular reactivity to emotionally-charged events (Cacioppo, Berntson, Klein, & Poehlmann, 1998; Levenson, Carstensen, Friesen, & Ekman, 1991), motivation to maintain emotional balance related to a reduced future time perspective (Charles & Carstensen, 2007), and the disruptive effects of high arousal level (Wurm et al., 2004).

The Neuro-Scientific Influence on Theories of Cognitive Aging

Cognitive aging is one of the major domains of theories and research in adult development. Classic theories of cognitive aging have been developed based on behavioral data (Salthouse, 1996; Schaie, 1996). In the last years, the availability of neuro-scientific methods has stimulated research that allows us to study cognitive processes—and changes in these processes—in the living brain using non-invasive brain imaging techniques, such as functional magnetic resonance imagery (fMRI) techniques. This opens new opportunities to test models of cognitive aging. Brain research has become increasingly more relevant to cognitive aging research as the focus has shifted from studying pathologies of the brain, such as Alzheimer's or Parkinson's disease, towards investigating normal aging. In addition, neuro-scientific data are more informative for mainstream cognitive aging research because researchers interested in models of cognitive aging become involved in this research and drive advancement in the field by testing established theories using cutting-edge methods. Studies on the structure and function of the brain have therefore become more informative for cognitive aging research as they shift their focus from describing brain activation patterns towards explaining them. Still, because of the relative newness of the available methods the neuroscience of aging is a field that is in need of additional theoretical foundation. The field of cognitive aging is an example of a field that is driven these days by major advances in neuro-imaging techniques that have revealed findings that enhance our understanding of normal and pathological aging and require theoretical explanations (Cabeza, 2004; Hedden & Gabrieli, 2004; Kramer, Fabiani, & Colcombe, 2006).

One of the most influential findings is the greater non-selective activation of brain regions in the aging brain. Older adults' brains tend to show neural activation in regions that are not used by younger adults. Two models that attempt to explain these findings are the HAROLD Model by Cabeza (2002) and the CRUNCH Model developed by Reuter-Lorenz and her colleagues (Reuter-Lorenz, 2002; Reuter-Lorenz & Mikels, 2006). Both models assume that the main reason for greater activation in different brain regions is the need for the recruitment of additional brain regions in order to success-fully execute cognitive functions.

Younger adults show unilateral brain activation when they work on cognitive tasks. In contrast, older adults' brains tend to show increased activation in both brain hemispheres. This finding has led to the development of the HAROLD model, *Hemispheric Asymmetry Reduction in Older Adults* (Cabeza, 2002). The HAROLD model basically describes the empirical finding of reduced lateralization in prefrontal lobe activity in older adults. It also suggests that the function of the reduced lateralization is compensatory, that is additional neural units are being recruited to increase attentional resources, processing speed, or inhibitory control.

According to the *compensation-related utilization of neural circuits hypothesis* (CRUNCH), the aging brain adapts to neurological decline by recruiting additional neural circuits (in comparison to younger adults) to perform tasks adequately (Reuter-Lorenz, 2002; Reuter-Lorenz & Mikels, 2006). Two main mechanisms are suggested that the older brain uses to perform tasks: "More of the same" and "supplementary processes." When task demands are increased, more activation can be found in the same brain region relative to easier tasks. This effect can be found in younger adults as well as in older adults. In older adults neural efficiency declines, therefore, additional neuronal circuits are recruited earlier than in younger adults. "Supplementary processes" are taking place when different brain regions are activated to compensate for lacking processing resources. Reduced lateral-ization is one way of recruiting additional resources. In addition, however, compared to young adults' brains, older adult brains also show over-activation in different brain regions, suggesting that compensation can take different forms in the aging brain.

These findings have stimulated scientific debates on the mechanisms and functional adaptiveness of reduced lateralization. Whereas Cabeza and Reuter-Lorenz and colleagues interpret their findings in the light of a compensational framework, other researchers have challenged this interpretation by suggesting a cortical decline interpretation of the findings (Kramer et al., 2006; Logan, Sanders, Snyder, Morris, & Buckner, 2002). Both with respect to theoretical work and empirical data, the field of neuro-cognition is still in its early stage of development. Therefore definite conclusions about the adaptiveness and functionality of the observed patterns of increased brain activation cannot be drawn.

One of the most significant issues in the theoretical discussion of the implications of neuro-scientific findings is the relationship between brain patterns and behavior. Does the overactivation found in older brains relative to young adults reflect successful compensation or does it reflect greater cognitive deficits? Longitudinal research may be necessary to investigate the time course of neurological decline and additional recruit-ment of resources. Also, studying the effect of cognitive training on lateralization and over-recruitment could provide important insights into the functional meaning of brain activation changes.

Health and Cognition: Healthy Bodies, Healthy Minds

Aging is associated with a variety of declines in both cognitive and physical capacities. Historically, health has been conceptualized mainly as an outcome measure of success-ful development (Rowe & Kahn, 1987) or as a variable used to describe the difference between older and younger samples. In some studies, better than average health is con-sidered to be a necessary condition for participants to be included in studies (Mather & Carstensen, 2003). Recently, this perspective has changed and health is increasingly investigated as a process variable—that can be influenced by life-style variables such as exercise, and that influences other domains of functioning, such as cognitive performance, wisdom, and personality (Aldwin, Spiro, & Park, 2006). In this section, we focus on the relationship between health and cognition that has been investigated most recently using innovative intervention study designs.

The field of health and cognition is another example of a domain of research in which methodological advances led to new findings that require theoretical explanation. In recent years, the dynamic interplay between cognition and health has received increasing attention as studies linking physical exercise to level of mental functioning have reported evidence for a causal relationship between cardio-vascular fitness and cognitive functioning. The main support of a causal relationship between health and cognitive functioning comes from intervention studies demonstrating that exercise training increases cognitive performance (see Colcombe & Kramer, 2003, for a meta-analysis). Evidence for complex relations between physiological and psychological functioning has been discussed before, for example, in research in very old adults demonstrating a strong link between sensory and cognitive performance (Lindenberger, Scherer, & Baltes, 2001).

These findings require additional theoretical work linking body and mind mechanisms. It has been demonstrated that exercise is beneficial. However, the specific mechanisms of physical training need to be theoretically and empirically investigated. For instance, it has been suggested that some forms of exercise, such as aerobic activity training improve executive control functioning (Hall, Smith, & Keele, 2001). Moreover, the specific neurological changes associated with exercise need to be investigated in more detail (Colcombe et al., 2003).

The studies also may have implications for theories on cognitive plasticity. For instance, a certain level of physical plasticity may be required in order to achieve plasticity in cognitive functioning. Moreover, incorporating physical training into cognitive training studies might enhance the transfer of cognitive training. Finally, these studies strongly support the influence of lifestyle on cognitive functioning and therefore have important practical implications.

Self-Regulation and Control in Adult Development

The direction of adult development depends largely on actions an individual takes to shape his or her own development (Lerner & Busch-Rossnagel, 1981). Historically, developmental theories of self-regulation were influenced by general psychological action theoretical approaches (Carver & Scheier, 1999; Gollwitzer & Bargh, 1996; Little, 1989). A life-span perspective on self-regulation led to the development of developmental theories of self-regulation, such as the theory of selective optimization with compensation (Baltes & Baltes, 1990; Freund & Baltes, 2000), the theory of primary and secondary control, and the theory of assimilative and accommodative coping (Brandtstädter & Renner, 1990; Brandtstädter & Greve, 1994). The goal of our chapter is to provide a brief overview of these theoretically refined theories. For a more extensive recent review, see Boerner and Jopp (2007).

These three selected theories identified principles, such as selection, optimization, and compensation or primary and secondary control that are essential to successful development in all phases of life. These models suggest that the relative adaptiveness of engagement and disengagement strategies changes across the life span.

Selective Optimization with Compensation Theory (SOC).   The theory of selective optimization with compensation was proposed by Baltes and Baltes (1990; Freund & Baltes, 2000) as a meta-theory to describe processes that characterize development and facilitate successful aging. Three interrelated processes are distinguished: selection, optimization, and compensation.

Selection describes specialization. In general, specialization characterizes every form of development, from the specialization of embryonic stem cells into different organs, to the physiological fitness of a marathon runner, the structure of a cello player's left and right hands, the development of interests in acquiring knowledge in different fields, or the change in ways of thinking that occurs through life experiences or education. Selection is a necessary condition for development as time, money, and other resources are inherently limited. Once the domains of functioning are selected, the development of these domains can be more or less optimal. The process of *optimization* describes the refinement of means to achieve a desired outcome. Refinement can be achieved through practice or through the use of better means and resources. Finally, *compensation* is a process that is directed towards coping with a loss in means of goal attainment. If previously established means do not lead to the desired outcome, other means may be discovered that can serve the same goal. For instance, a retired CEO may volunteer to advise young entrepreneurs and as such keep his sense of professional efficacy.

The theory of selective optimization with compensation describes processes that can facilitate successful aging. Successful aging in this context involves the attainment of desired outcomes when faced with losses by optimizing the available resources and focusing them on the most important goals. Furthermore, the theory provides a meta-theoretical framework that can be extended in different ways for describing successful development across the lifespan and within different contexts (see B.B. Baltes & Dickson, 2001).

As a meta-model, SOC can be applied to different domains of functioning and levels of analysis. It has been most successfully applied to the domain of goals (Freund & Baltes, 2002). For instance, Li, Lindenberger, Freund, and Baltes (2001) found that older adults prioritized walking over memorizing, suggesting selection of the more important domain of functioning. In addition, when offered external compensatory aids, older adults optimized their walking while younger adults optimized their memorizing. Selective optimization is used to achieve goals. Some goals may change as people age. Ebner, Freund, and Baltes (2006) investigated general goal orientations towards either growth or maintenance/loss-prevention. They found that whereas younger adults focus on growth-related goals, middle-aged and older adults focus on maintenance and loss prevention goals. They argue that the maintenance/loss prevention focus in middle-aged and older adults may be related to the conservation of resources. To support this idea, they found in two experimental studies that when growth-oriented goals were introduced that required more resources than maintenance/loss-prevention goals, both older and young adults chose to focus on maintenance/loss-prevention goals. These findings are consistent with the theoretical ideas of SOC as they show that older adults selectively optimize the domains that are most important to them and that are adaptive.

The Theory of Primary and Secondary Control.   The dynamics between engagement and disengagement processes in successful development were conceptualized in a different way by Heckhausen and Schulz (1995). The theory of control distinguishes two processes: primary and secondary control. Primary control is oriented towards the environment, that is, to achieve changes within the environment to achieve desired outcomes. Secondary control, on the other hand, focuses on the alteration of the self. For example, secondary control can include changing the value of goal attainment and disengaging from a certain goal or attributing failures of goal attainment to external causes.

Heckhausen and Schulz (1995) suggest that primary control is the foremost form of control that is employed because it enables the individual to shape his/her environment to fit particular needs and realize his/her developmental potential. However, secondary control strategies are seen as adaptive when primary control cannot be executed. Because of changing developmental potential of an individual at each segment of the lifespan, different stages in life require different control strategies. Specifically, as aging individuals are becoming increasingly restrained through biological and societal constraints, secondary control becomes an adaptive coping mechanism. Wrosch and Heckhausen (1999) conducted a study in which they investigated the deactivation of partner-relevant goals in late midlife. They found that while young separated adults were actively looking for new partners, people who were in late midlife focused on other social goals, such as the maintenance of friendships. This was interpreted as applying a secondary compensatory control strategy because, in later midlife, the opportunity structures (developmental deadlines) for finding a partner are decreasing.

Assimilative and Accommodative Coping.   The issue of adaptiveness and coping with developmental challenges is also described in Brandtstädter's and colleagues' theory of assimilative and accomodatives modes of coping with critical life events and life transitions: *Assimilation* is adjusting the environment to match one's personal preferences. *Accommodation* is adjusting one's personal goals to constraints of the environment (Brandtstädter & Renner, 1990; Brandtstädter & Greve, 1994). Both processes are seen as adaptive and related to life satisfaction. Assimilative and accommodative tendencies are measured at the dispositional level. Assimilation is reflected in tenacious goal-pursuit, whereas accommodative tendencies are characterized by flexible goal attainment. The balance between gains and losses becomes increasingly negative with old age (Baltes, 1987, 1997). Brandtstädter's model suggests that in order to cope with these developmental changes as people get older there will be a gradual shift from assimilative to accommodative modes of coping.

The three models reported suggest that self-regulation in old age is not characterized by universal disengagement from goals (Cumming & Henry, 1961) but rather by the selection of important domains of functioning. All of these theories describe the dynamic interplay between different strategies to successfully achieve goals. They all suggest that some strategies of goal-achievement may be more adaptive than others and that the specific adaptiveness of strategies changes across the life span as psychological, social, and biological resources change.

The field of self-regulation is an example for a domain of research that is theoretically well substantiated and is in the process of being fine-tuned with innovative studies and new methods, such as time-sampling studies (Riediger et al., 2005), eye-tracking studies (Isaacowitz & Light, 2006), and studies investigating specific behavioral choices instead of general behavioral preferences (Ebner et al., 2006). A challenge for all of these theories is the phenomenon of the fourth age with its prevalent losses in resources, the main question being how very old adults can age successfully.

Social Cognition

In the past sixteen years, there has been considerable growth in theory and research on social cognition and aging (Blanchard-Fields & Hess, 1999; Blanchard-Fields & Horhota, 2006). Instead of something to be controlled, social context has taken its rightful place as an important influence on cognitive functioning as we grow older. Similar to placing information in an emotion-based context, by adopting a social cognitive perspective, researchers in cognitive aging have broadened their understanding of cognitive functioning to include factors such as goals and motivation.

A social cognitive perspective focuses on understanding how people come to learn and make sense of the social world around them including how people think about themselves, others, and the events that occur in everyday life. With respect to aging, this raises questions as to how developmental changes in pragmatic knowledge, social expertise, and values influence social cognitive processes. Even if certain basic cognitive mechanisms decline, older adults may still possess the social knowledge and skills that allow them to function effectively in everyday life. Thus, two theoretical mechanisms that are receiving considerable attention in the social cognition and aging literature are cognitive mechanisms that underlie social cognitive processes and the influence of beliefs, values, and personal dispositions on social cognitive processes.

Cognitive Mechanisms and Social Information Processing. Recent studies on social cognition and aging have investigated whether age-related changes in processing capacity relate to changes in social cognitive processes. Even more importantly, do these age-related processing changes explain age differences in social judgment biases? Recent research draws on theories from social psychology to answer this question (Gilbert & Malone, 1995). When individuals are asked to make an attribution as to the cause of an event such as an interpersonal dilemma, initially they are more likely to attribute the cause to or lay blame on personal characteristics of the target character (i.e., dispositional attributions). Because this type of attribution tends to be more automatic and less cognitively demanding, it typically represents individuals' initial judgment. A second process involves adjusting one's initial blame inference by considering external extenuating circumstances that could have affected the situation. Alternatively, this type of processing requires cognitive effort (Gilbert & Malone, 1995).

There are a number of recent studies suggesting that older adults consistently make dispositional attributions to a greater extent than do young adults (Blanchard-Fields & Beatty, 2005; Chen & Blanchard-Fields, 1997; Follett & Hess, 2002); they rely more on easily accessible heuristics, schemas, and belief systems when forming impressions (Hess, 1999); and they rely more on stereotypes when making source attributions leading to false judgments (Mather, Johnson, & De Leonardis, 1999).

In a number of studies older adults are found to consistently blame characters more (i.e., make dispositional attributions) than young adults do, particularly in relationship dilemmas resulting in a negative outcome (Blanchard-Fields & Beatty, 2005). That older adults are more likely than young adults to make less effortful blame attributions suggests that cognitive mechanisms play a role in social judgments.

Similarly, older adults made higher dispositional ratings than young adults did when given a short time period in which to respond (Chen & Blanchard-Fields, 1997). In contrast, older adults made lower dispositional attribution ratings when they were given more time to think about the situations. Again, this suggests that older adults' dispositional bias is partially due to cognitive limitations that make fast effortful processing difficult. Similar findings were evident with a different social judgment paradigm that used a distracter task instead of limited time (Chen & Blanchard-Fields, 2000). Finally, cognitive mechanisms such as increased rates of false memories also impacted older adults' dispositional attributions (Chen, 2002). Along these lines, Ybarra and Park (2002) found that although reduced cognitive resources did not influence young adults when forming impressions of others, resource limitations did affect older adults' ability to process social information completely.

In sum, evidence suggests that the social judgments of older adults are influenced by cognitive capacity to some extent; older adults tend to rely on easily accessible schematic information more so than young adults. However, processing capacity is not the only possible explanation for these findings. Age-related differences in beliefs, values, motivation, and goals have also been shown to have an impact on social judgments.

Beliefs, Values, and Social Information Processing.   There is growing evidence to suggest that individual differences in attitudes, values, and beliefs may determine the degree to which older adults are susceptible to biased social judgments (Blanchard-Fields & Hertzog, 2000; Hess, 1999). Recall the Chen and Blanchard-Fields (1997) finding that constraints in time pressure increased older adults' use of dispositional attributions, thus implicating a cognitive mechanism. However, in this same study, social beliefs related to the situations were also assessed, and they were the better predictor of when dispositional judgments were made. Social beliefs reflected statements on whether an actor violated a social rule and on how one should behave in a particular relationship situation. Older adults were more likely to generate such beliefs as well as attribute the cause of the negative outcome to dispositional characteristics of that actor. This tendency towards evoked beliefs on the part of older adults in relation to the situational dilemmas accounted for age differences in dispositional biases over and above the influence of cognitive constraints.

Similarly, Klaczynski and Robinson (2000) found older adults accepted evidence that was consistent with their personal positions in a scientific reasoning task and subsequently dismissed evidence that portrayed their beliefs to be inaccurate. Their conclusion was similar to Chen and Blanchard-Fields: Increases in reasoning biases are not occurring due to declines in cognitive ability, but rather to the fact that older adults are more likely than young adults to base their judgments on their own beliefs.

Other researchers have examined motivational goals and dispositional styles that influence social information processing. For example, individuals with a high need for closure (a preference to come to quick and expeditious conclusions) tend to form quick and biased judgments and not consider all the relevant factors (Webster & Kruglanski, 1994). Interestingly, Hess, Waters, and Bolstad (2000) found that need for closure did not influence young and middle-aged adults' social judgments; however, it did predict social judgment biases in older adults. With age-related changes in both cognitive and social resources, it may be the case that motivational factors such as preserving cognitive resources become more important to older adults.

Finally, in a recent study, Blanchard-Fields and Hertzog (2002) examined age differences in blame attributions for characters who behaved traditionally (e.g., a character who insists on marriage before cohabitation) or nontraditionally (e.g., a character who consents to live together before marriage) in interpersonal conflict situations. Individuals who held traditional beliefs about appropriate behavior in interpersonal relationships were more likely to blame individuals whose behavior violated those beliefs. In contrast, individuals who held nontraditional beliefs were more likely to blame traditional characters. Older adults held more traditional beliefs than young adults, and this accounted for older adults' greater tendency to blame nontraditional characters. These studies suggest that generational differences in the content of beliefs and values may contribute to age differences in attributional processing.

Together these findings suggest that older adults are able to apply the rich experience they have accumulated during a lifetime to guide their judgments, especially when it is relevant to their daily life. However, when older adults are in a context in which the task is narrowly defined and the focus is on the ability to produce solutions in a novel context older adults are unable to take advantage of life experiences and perform more poorly.

Evidence for a Cognitive Complexity Mechanism.   Another candidate explanation for age differences in attributional processes is cognitive complexity. From an adult developmental perspective, cognitive complexity is a higher form of reasoning that involves the ability to consider multiple perspectives and causal explanations for behaviors or events (Blanchard-Fields & Norris, 1994; Labouvie-Vief, Chiodo, Goguen, Diehl, & Orwoll, 1995). An individual at higher levels of cognitive complexity should be less prone to making the correspondence bias.

Cognitive complexity in the form of ego level is characterized by the ability to embrace the multifaceted and uncertain nature of people and situations. Individuals with high ego level are more likely to consider both situational and dispositional causes of outcomes in achievement-oriented and interpersonal scenarios (Blanchard-Fields & Norris, 1994). Cognitive complexity in the form of attributional complexity (Fletcher, 1986) (i.e., a preference for complex explanations) also played a role in judgments about actors' attitudes. Young, middle-aged, and older adults watched actors answer questions about social beliefs, such as "Should people have the right to burn flags?" In the choice condition, participants believed the actors could choose how to answer the questions. In the no-choice condition, participants believed the actors were forced to respond a particular way, regardless of their true attitudes. Participants committed the correspondence bias if they rated the actor's true attitude as reflecting their statements, even in the no-choice condition. Individuals with high levels of cognitive complexity were less likely to demonstrate the correspondence bias (Follett & Hess, 2002). Finally, Horhota and Blanchard-Fields (2006) found that young and older adults who were high on attributional complexity did not differ in their attributional processing. However, older adults who were low in attributional complexity committed the correspondence bias more than young adults who were low in attributional complexity did. Again, attributionally complex individuals are more likely to take into account the situational pressure and dispositional factors when making their attributional judgments.

Overall, we find that a simple resource reduction interpretation is inadequate to explain many of the age differences found in social judgments. Instead our review has highlighted the importance of also considering social factors such as cognitive style and values to explain social cognitive functioning.

Age-Related Stereotypes.   Another important mechanism that has taken center stage as an important social factor influencing the nature of cognitive change in older adulthood is age-related stereotyping. Negative stereotypes about aging are pervasive in our society, in particular those that refer to declines in competency. Recent evidence suggests that traditional cognitive aging research may underestimate older adults' cognitive performance due to the debilitating effects of such stereotypes (Andreoletti & Lachman, 2004; Chasteen, Bhattacharyya, Horhota, Tam & Hasher, 2005; Hess, Auman, Colcombe & Levy, 1996; Levy, 1996; Hess, Auman, Colcombe, & Rahhal, 2003). It should be noted that stereotypes are not assumed to fully account for observed declines in cognitive performance, but their activation simply impedes optimal functioning.

Evidence for the negative influence of stereotypes on cognition in older adults suggests that when negative stereotypic traits are activated, memory performance tends to be lower (Hess et al., 2003; Levy, 1996; Rahhal, Hasher, & Colcombe, 2001). This is accomplished by simply framing the task as assessing memory as opposed to a learning task or by telling participants that memory declines with age as opposed to increases with age. More recently, findings reveal that the detrimental effects of negative stereotyping are most prominent with adults who are holding on to more youthful identities (O'Brien &

Hummert, 2006). Furthermore, there is some evidence suggesting a beneficial effect of positive stereotypes on older adults' cognitive performance (Hess et al., 2003; Levy, 1996; Stein, Blanchard-Fields, & Hertzog, 2002). For example, within cultural groups who hold positive views of aging, older adults may show no significant declines in memory performance in comparison to young adults (Levy & Langer, 1994, but see Yoon, Hasher, Feinberg, Rahhal, & Winocur, 2000).

Overall, social cognition and aging research highlights the importance of social factors underlying age-related differences in cognitive functioning. In addition, it suggests that it is important not to limit explanations of cognitive change to cognitive processing mechanisms. The above research suggests that under some conditions motivational goals as well as values and beliefs play a major role in the types of judgments and reasoning observed in older adulthood. It will be important for future research to determine the conditions under which reasoning and judgments reflect cognitive capacity on the part of older adults and the conditions under which such reasoning reflects age differences in social mechanisms, e.g., well-substantiated beliefs or motivational differences or stereotypes.

Challenges for Current Theories of Adult Development

In this chapter we have covered a number of representative theories and empirical findings of adult development that reflect important research innovations and trends in the 21st century. In addition, our review illustrates the ebb and flow of theoretical development. Whereas some theories are well substantiated and are in the process of being more fully elaborated, such as self-regulation theories, other theories are experiencing the growing pains of inconsistent support which should ultimately yield to a more integrated theoretical perspective, i.e., emotion and cognition theories. Furthermore, there are areas of research, such as social cognition and aging that draw upon mainstream psychological theories but need to be elaborated further into lifespan developmental theories. Finally, other fields are in relatively early stages of theoretical development and are in need of additional empirical validation and theoretical refinement, i.e., cognitive neuroscience and, in particular, health.

Recent interest in placing behavior in both in a socio-emotional and biological context has broadened the investigation of adult developmental theories from a unidimensional focus on mechanisms to the consideration of multiple determinants of behavioral change. For example, changes in processing of information are not simply a function of biological decline, but instead are also influenced by social context, motivation, beliefs, emotions, and life experiences. As a result we can observe a proliferation of research examining the nature of the emotion-cognition interface in the aging mind. Motivational shifts towards an increased importance of emotional gratification have been shown to influence older adults' differential allocation of cognitive resources to positive and negative information. Another important determinant of cognitive performance in adulthood is social context, for instance by activating positive and negative stereotypes of aging. Other examples of determinants of behavioral change are life-style interfaces with biology as reflected in the influence of health on cognition.

Our discussion of neuro-scientific methods has demonstrated that cognitive functioning can be understood at new levels. These methods allow us to adequately test conditions under which structural change is associated with decline, compensation, or even improvement in functioning. Rather than using general biological deterioration as the default explanation for cognitive changes, we can now identify specific biological mechanisms reflected in different structures of and activation patterns in the brain. For example, we are now able to differentiate preserved areas of the brain, such as the amygdala, from areas that are more prone to decay, such as specific areas in the prefrontal cortex. These respective areas relate to preserved emotional processing on the one hand, and decline in other more effortful cognitive processes on the other. To summarize, we will revisit the five domains of functioning introduced earlier and discuss challenges they face for the future.

Emotion and Cognition

As indicated earlier, the number of studies examining the interface between emotion and cognition in the aging mind has been rapidly increasing. At this stage, the empirical findings have been somewhat supportive of a shift in motivational goals on the part of older adults. Although the shift towards instantiating emotionally gratifying experience is not challenged, how this shift influences cognitive processing is still to be more fully explained. Future research will need to address important theoretical questions that arise from these discrepant findings. For example, can they be integrated into a larger theoretical framework? As methodologies for time sampling are becoming more accessible and reliable, emotional processing can be more explicitly examined in and generalized to an everyday life-context. Furthermore, the advances in statistical procedure analyzing intraindividual variability and the coupling of psychological constructs will allow for an on-line assessment of the coupling between emotion and cognition. More information is needed on the degree to which emotion processing is resource demanding. Is this a more automatic process for older adults in comparison to young adults or does it strain valuable resources? How is this process reflected in structural and functional changes in the brain?

Neuroscience and Cognition

Advances in neuro-scientific methods have stimulated a vast amount of research in cognition and aging. New findings describing linkages between behavioral and brain data require theoretical explanations. A new challenge for this field is that the same behavior can be related to different neuronal activation patterns. The question remains as to whether they are functionally equivalent, yet represent biologically different mechanisms. In addition, more theoretical and empirical work is needed to investigate whether different changes in the brain may be associated with identical or differential mechanisms. Another challenge is to study changes in the brain longitudinally to investigate causal relationships. For instance, it may well be that certain brain patterns or changes in brain patterns can predict longitudinal behavioral changes. This, in turn, may have implications for pathologies of aging.

There are many open questions for future research to answer. For instance, new methods will allow researchers to combine structural and functional imaging methods. The fourth age is a challenge that all areas of research will have to face in the future. For example, in very old adults there may be limitations in the degree to which the aging brain can compensate through recruitment of alternative areas of the brain. Another challenge for brain research is the issue of variability, both inter-individually and intra-individually. Is aging associated with uniform patterns of changes or are older adults compensating differentially for declines? How variable is the recruitment of additional brain resources within an individual? Is the same brain region consistently recruited for similar and different tasks?

Health and Cognition

The health domain has recently received a lot of attention due to empirical findings linking changes in life-style to changes in cognition. Similar to the domain of neuroscience and cognition, the new empirical findings in this research area require theoretical foundation and explanation. More intervention research is needed to identify causal mechanisms linking health-related life-style and cognition as well as parameters influencing the effectiveness of interventions, such as temporal boundaries. Moreover, the longitudinal effects of training have to be empirically explored and theoretically explained. A unifying theory on health as a process variable still warrants further development. Aldwin, Spiro, and Park (2006) suggest conceptualizing health as a life-long process. They advocate that life-span psychology principles be applied to the study of health, such as multidimensionality including multiple levels of analysis, the need for interdisciplinary approaches, the recognition of the dynamic interaction of gains and losses, and the importance of considering the socio-historical context of health. As a process variable, health needs to be understood as a dynamic and fluctuating state variable rather than as a static trait variable.

Future research in this field is needed to better understand how changes in health are related to changes in other domains of functioning, such as cognition. Because of its fluctuating nature, it will be important to study changes in health, such as illnesses, including recovery, in relation to other domains of functioning. New methods will facilitate the understanding of these phenomena. For instance, measuring biological parameters of stress, such as cortisol, has become increasingly accessible. In addition, time-sampling and longitudinal studies will be necessary to identify specific mechanisms of change.

The findings on health and cognition may also have important implications for studying the fourth age. Plasticity in old age has been found to be limited in testing-the-limits paradigms focusing on cognitive training interventions (Singer et al., 2003). Perhaps, cognitive plasticity could be potentially enhanced through health interventions, such as aerobic exercise training.

Self-Regulation and Control

As outlined earlier, the major theories of self-regulation are theoretically well founded and are at a stage of theoretical refinement. This refinement is mainly aimed at better operationalizing self-regulatory processes as they function inside and outside the laboratory. For instance, Riediger, Li, and Lindenberger (2006) distinguish resource- versus process-based selection. Resource-based selection is applied to situations in which the processing resources are limited because of multiple overlapping tasks consuming the same resources. Process-based selection, on the other hand, refers to selection that is due to a processing conflict between established modes of processing (experientially selected processes) and current actions in new contexts. The preference for habituated processes may impair functioning in new developmental contexts. These more specific predictions can be operationalized and tested empirically and advance our understanding of self-regulation in adulthood and aging. Another open question within the field of self-regulation is the relationships among different models of self-regulation. They all focus on similar questions. At this stage, however, it is still unclear whether differential predictions can be drawn from these models and to what degree they are in accordance or in conflict with each other.

One of the major strengths of this field is the longitudinal investigation of self-regulatory processes in everyday contexts. For instance, Riediger et al. (2005) investigated goal-achievement and goal-coherence in young and older adults using time-sampling methods. They found that older adults selected goals that are more coherent and less conflicting with each other in everyday life.

A challenge for the field of self-regulation research is the fourth age and the increasing vulnerabilities associated with it. For instance, some of the core assumptions of theories of human development, namely, the notion of the individual as a master of his or her own development may be more difficult to find in individuals who are faced with increased losses of control over their environment as well as their own behavior and body.

Social Cognition

Similar to research on emotion and cognition, the major import of the current growth in research placing cognition in a social context is that it has unveiled important areas of reasoning and cognitive functioning that are relatively spared and may even improve in older adulthood. This is illustrated in research assessing the degree to which social cognitive functioning is related to cognitive mechanisms that decline with age as opposed to social cognitive mechanisms that are largely preserved. This research is still in early stages and future research needs to establish the conditions under which older adults' reasoning and decision making is adaptive and the conditions under which older adults fare poorly. Growing trends in social neuroscience have the potential to shed light on preserved processes as is currently being examined in cognitive neuroscience and aging research. Moreover, researchers need to determine the degree to which social cognitive mechanisms such as beliefs, values, and social knowledge account for older adults' preserved performance in everyday life. Finally, given that social psychologists have studied social cognitive phenomenon primarily on college-aged individuals, the influence of developmental theories and developmental research will trigger further advancement in other fields.

The remaining issue in this concluding section is to link the status of adult developmental theories to learning as a lifelong process. First, age-related motivational shifts in goal-orientations and processing preferences have strong implications for designing learning environments for older adults. For example, the fact that older adults have less difficulty processing emotional information while at the same time they focus less on negative information, needs to be taken into consideration when designing learning materials. Similarly, if older adults are more likely to draw upon their rich accumulated experience, care needs to be taken to design materials that are relevant to an older adult's life. Evidence suggests that facilitative social contexts promote optimal functioning on the part of older adults. For instance, creating a social environment that highlights competencies rather than decrements in older adults' functioning may allow older adults to exercise cognitive processes at their full capacity. The revolutionary findings related to health interventions influencing cognition suggest that promoting a healthy lifestyle can facilitate learning. Finally, it should be noted that learning in the service of maintenance is more predominant in older adults, and particularly in the fourth age. Thus, learning is no less important to older adults than it is to young adults as it may enhance the quality of life in the face of a continually rising life expectancy.

References

Ackerman, P. L. (2000). Domain-specific knowledge as the 'dark matter' of adult intelligence: Gf/Gc, personality and interest correlates. *Journals of Gerontology, 55B,* 69–84.

Aldwin, C. M., Spiro, A., Park, C. L. (2006). Health, behavior, and optimal aging: A life span developmental perspective. In J. E. Birren & K. W. Schaie (Eds.), *Handbook of the psychology of aging* (6th ed., pp. 85–104). Amsterdam, Netherlands: Elsevier.

Almeida, D. M. (2005). Resilience and vulnerability to daily stressors assessed via diary methods. *Current Directions in Psychological Science, 14,* 64–68.

Amodio, D. M., & Frith, C. D. (2006). Meeting of minds: The medial frontal cortex and social cognition. *Nature Reviews Neuroscience, 7,* 268–277.

Andreoletti, C., & Lachman, M. E. (2004). Susceptibility and resilience to memory aging stereotypes: Education matters more than age. *Experimental Aging Research, 30,* 129–148.

Baltes, B. B., & Dickson, M. W. (2001). Using life-span models in industrial-organizational psychology: The theory of selective optimization with compensation. *Applied Developmental Science, 5,* 51–62.

Baltes, P. B. (1987). Theoretical propositions of life-span developmental psychology: On the dynamics between growth and decline. *Developmental Psychology, 23,* 611–626.

Baltes, P. B. (1997). On the incomplete architecture of human ontogeny: Selection, optimization, and compensation as foundation of developmental theory. *American Psychologist, 52,* 366–380.

Baltes, P. B., & Baltes, M. M. (1990). Psychological perspectives on successful aging: The model of selective optimization with compensation. In P. B. Baltes & M. M. Baltes (Eds.), *Successful aging: Perspectives from the behavioral sciences* (pp. 1–34). New York: Cambridge University Press.

Baltes, P. B., Lindenberger, U., & Staudinger, U. M. (2006). Life span theory in developmental psychology. In R. M. Lerner & W. Damon (Eds.), *Handbook of child psychology: Vol 1, Theoretical models of human development* (pp. 569–664). Hoboken, NJ: Wiley.

Baltes, P. B., & Mayer, K.U . (1999). *The Berlin Aging Study: Aging from 70 to 100.* New York: Cambridge University Press

Baltes, P. B., Reese, H. W., & Nesselroade, J. R. (1977). *Life-span developmental psychology: Introduction to research methods.* Oxford: Brooks/Cole.

Baltes, P. B., & Staudinger, U. M. (2000). Wisdom: A metaheuristic (pragmatic) to orchestrate mind and virtue toward excellence. *American Psychologist, 55,* 122–136.

Baltes, P. B., & Willis, S. L. (1982). Plasticity and enhancement of intellectual functioning in old age: Penn State's Adult Development and Enrichment Project (ADEPT). In I. M. Craik & S. E. Trehub (Eds.), *Aging and cognitive processes* (pp. 353–389). New York: Plenum Press.

Birren, J. E., & Schaie, K. W. (2006). *Handbook of the psychology of aging.* San Diego: Academic Press.

Blanchard-Fields, F. (1998). The role of emotion in social cognition across the adult life span. In K. W. L. Schaie & M. Powell (Ed.), *Annual review of gerontology and geriatrics* (pp. 238–265). New York: Springer.

Blanchard-Fields, F. (2005). Introduction to the special section on emotion-cognition interactions and the aging mind. *Psychology and Aging, 20,* 539–541.

Blanchard-Fields, F. (2006). *The two faces of processing: Aging and the interface between emotion and cognition.* Paper presented at the Cognitive Aging Conference. Atlanta, GA.

Blanchard-Fields, F. (2007). Everyday problem solving and emotion: An Adult developmental perspective. *Current Directions in Psychological Science, 16,* 26–31.

Blanchard-Fields, F., & Beatty, C. (2005). Age differences in blame attributions: The role of relationship outcome ambiguity and personal identification. *Journals of Gerontology, 60B,* P19–P26.

Blanchard-Fields, F., Chen, Y., & Norris, L. (1997). Everyday problem solving across the adult life span: Influence of domain specificity and cognitive appraisal. *Psychology and Aging, 12,* 684–693.

Blanchard-Fields, F., & Hertzog, C. (2000). Age differences in schematicity. In S. von Hecker, S. Dutke, & G. Sedak (Eds.), *Processes of generative mental representation and psychological adaptation* (pp. 1–24). Dordrecht, The Netherlands: Kluwer.

Blanchard-Fields, F., & Hertzog, C. (2002). *Social schematicity and age differences in attributional biases.* Poster presented at the Cognitive Aging Conference. Atlanta, GA.

Blanchard-Fields, F., & Hess, T. (1999). *Social cognition and aging.* San Diego, CA: Academic Press.

Blanchard-Fields, F., & Horhota, M. (2006). How can the study of aging inform research on social cognition? *Social Cognition, 24,* 207–217.

Blanchard-Fields, F., & Irion, J. C. (1988). The relation between locus of control and coping in two contexts: Age as a moderator variable. *Psychology and Aging, 3,* 197–203.

Blanchard-Fields, F., Jahnke, H. C., & Camp, C. (1995). Age differences in problem-solving style: The role of emotional salience. *Psychology and Aging, 10,* 173–180.

Blanchard-Fields, F., Mienaltowski, A., & Seay, R. B. (2007). Age differences in everyday problem solving effectiveness: Older adults select more effective strategies for interpersonal problems. *Journal of Gerontology: Psychological Sciences, 62B,* P61–64.

Blanchard-Fields, F., & Norris, L. (1994). Causal attributions from adolescence through adulthood: Age differences, ego level, and generalized response style. *Aging, Neuropsychology, and Cognition, 1,* 67–86.

Blanchard-Fields, F., Stein, R., & Watson, T.L. (2004). Age differences in emotion-regulation strategies in handling everyday problems. *Journals of Gerontology, 59B,* P261–P269.

Boerner, K., & Jopp, D. (2007). Improvement/maintenance and reorientation as central features of coping with major life change and loss: Contributions of three life-span theories. *Human Development, 50,* 171–195.

Bolger, N., Davis, A., & Rafaeli, E. (2003). Diary methods: Capturing life as it is lived. *Annual Review of Psychology, 54,* 579–616.

Bower, G. H. (1991). Mood congruity of social judgments. In J. P. Forgas (Ed.), *Emotion and social judgments* (pp. 31–53). Elmsford, NY: Pergamon Press.

Brandtstädter, J., & Greve, W. (1994). The aging self: Stabilizing and protective processes. *Developmental Review, 14*(1), 52–80.

Brandtstädter, J., & Renner, G. (1990). Tenacious goal pursuit and flexible goal adjustment: Explication and age-related analysis of assimilative and accommodative strategies of coping. *Psychology and Aging, 5,* 58–67.

Cabeza, R. (2002). Hemispheric asymmetry reduction in older adults: The HAROLD model. *Psychology and Aging, 17,* 85–100.

Cabeza, R. (2004). Neuroscience frontiers of cognitive aging: Approaches to cognitive neuroscience of aging. In R. A. Dixon, L. Bäckman & L. G. Nilsson (Eds.), *New frontiers in cognitive aging* (pp. 179–196). Oxford, UK: Oxford University Press.

Cacioppo, J. T., Berntson, G. G., Klein, D. J., & Poehlmann, K. M. (1998). Psychophysiology of emotion across the life span. In K.W. Schaie & M. P. Lawton (Eds.), *Annual review of gerontology and geriatrics: Vol 17. Focus on emotion and adult development* (pp. 27–74). New York: Springer.

Carstensen, L. L., & Hartel, C.R. (2006). *When I'm 64.* Washington, DC: National Academies Press.

Carstensen, L. L., Isaacowitz, D. M., & Charles, S. T. (1999). Taking time seriously: A theory of socioemotional selectivity. *American Psychologist, 54,* 165–181.

Carstensen, L. L., & Mikels, J. A. (2005). At the intersection of emotion and cognition: Aging and the positivity effect. *Current Directions in Psychological Science, 14,* 117–121.

Carstensen, L. L., Mikels, J. A., & Mather, M. (2006). Aging and the Intersection of Cognition, Motivation, and Emotion. In J. E. Birren & K. W. Schaie (Eds.), *Handbook of the psychology of aging* (pp. 343–362). San Diego: Academic Press.

Carstensen, L. L., Pasupathi, M., Mayr, U., & Nesselroade, J. R. (2000). Emotional experience in everyday life across the adult life span. *Journal of Personality and Social Psychology, 79,* 644–655.

Carver, C. S., & Scheier, M. F. (1999). Themes and issues in the self-regulation of behavior. In R. S.Wyer (Ed.), *Perspective on behavioral self-regulation* (pp. 1–105). Mahwah, NJ: Erlbaum.

Charles, S. T., & Carstensen, L. L. (2007). Emotion regulation and aging. In J .J. *Gross handbook of emotion regulation* (pp. 307–327). New York: Guilford.

Charles, S. T., Mather, M., & Carstensen, L. L. (2003). Aging and emotional memory: The forget-table nature of negative images for older adults. *Journal of Experimental Psychology: General, 132,* 310–324.

Chasteen, A. L., Bhattacharyya, S., Horhota, M., Tam, R., & Hasher, L. (2005). How feelings of stereotype threat influence older adults' memory performance. *Experimental Aging Research, 31,* 235–260.

Chen, Y. (2002). Unwanted beliefs:Age differences in beliefs of false information. *Aging, Neuropsy-chology, and Cognition, 9,* 217–228.

Chen, Y., & Blanchard-Fields, F. (1997). Age differences in stages of attributional processing. *Psy-chology and Aging, 12,* 694–703.

Chen, Y., & Blanchard-Fields, F. (2000). Unwanted thought: Age differences in the correction of social judgments. *Psychology and Aging, 15,* 475–482.

Coats, A. H., & Blanchard-Fields, F. (2006). *Predictors of emotion regulation strategies in interpersonal problem situations.* Atlanta: Georgia Institute of Technology.

Colcombe, S. J., Erickson, K. I., Raz, N., Webb, A. G., Cohen, N. J., McAuley, E., et al. (2003). Aero-bic fitness reduces brain tissue loss in aging humans. *The Journals of Gerontology, 58,* 176–180.

Colcombe, S. J., & Kramer, A. F. (2003). Fitness effects on the cognitive function of older adults: A meta-analytic study. *Psychological Science, 14,* 125–130.

Consedine, N. S., Magai, C., & Bonnano, G. A. (2002). Moderators of the emotion inhibition-health relationship: A review and research agenda. *Review of General Psychology, 6,* 204–228.

Cumming, E., & Henry, W. E. (1961). *Growing old: The process of disengagement.* New York: Basic Books.

Diener, R., Sandvik, E., & Larsen, R. J. (1985). Age and sex effects for emotional intensity. *Develop-mental Psychology, 21,* 542–546.

Ebner, N. C., Freund, A. M., & Baltes, P. B. (2006). Developmental changes in personal goal orien-tation from young to late adulthood: From striving for gains to maintenance and prevention of losses. *Psychology and Aging, 21,* 664–678.

Eisdorfer, C. (1968). Patterns of federal funding for research in aging. *The Gerontologist, 8,* 3–6.

Fletcher, G. (1986). Attributional complexity: An individual differences measure. *Journal of Person-ality and Social Psychology, 51,* 875–884.

Folkman, S., & Lazarus, R. S. (1988). Coping as a mediator of emotion. *Journal of Personality and Social Psychology, 54,* 466–475.

Follett, K., & Hess, T. (2002). Aging, cognitive complexity, and the fundamental attribution error. *Journals of Gerontology, 57B,* P312–P323.

Forgas, J. P. (1995). Mood and judgment: The affect infusion model (AIM). *Psychological Bulletin, 117,* 39–66.

Freund, A. M., & Baltes, M. M. (2000). The orchestration of selection, optimization and compen-sation: An action-theoretical conceptualization of a theory of developmental regulation. In W. J. Perrig & A. Grob (Eds.), *Control of human behavior, mental processes, and consciousness: Essays in honor of the 60th birthday of August Flammer* (pp. 35–58). Mahwah, NJ: Erlbaum.

Freund, A. M., & Baltes, P. B. (2002). Life-management strategies of selection, optimization and compensation: Measurement by self-report and construct validity. *Journal of Personality and Social Psychology, 82,* 642–662.

Gerstorf, D., Smith, J., & Baltes, P. B. (2006). A systemic-wholistic approach to differential aging: Longitudinal findings from the Berlin Aging Study. *Psychology and Aging, 21,* 645–663.

Ghisletta, P., & Lindenberger, U. (2004). Static and dynamic longitudinal structural analyses of cognitive changes in old age. *Gerontology, 50,* 12–16.

Gilbert, D. T., & Malone, P. S. (1995). The correspondence bias. *Psychological Bulletin, 117,* 21–38.

Gollwitzer, P. M., & Bargh, J. A. (1996). *The psychology of action: Linking cognition and motivation to behavior.* New York: Guilford.

Gross, J. J., Carstensen, L. L., Pasupathi, M., Tsai, J., Götestam Skorpen, C., & Hsu, A. Y. C. (1997). Emotion and aging: Experience, expression, and control. *Psychology and Aging, 12,* 590–599.

Grühn, D., Smith, J., & Baltes, P. B. (2005). No aging bias favoring memory for positive material: Evidence from a heterogeneity-homogeneity list paradigm using emotionally toned words. *Psychology and Aging, 20,* 579–588.

Hall, C. D., Smith, A. L., & Keele, S. W. (2001). The impact of aerobic activity on cognitive function in older adults: A new synthesis based on the concept of executive control. *European Journal of Cognitive Psychology, 13,* 279–300.

Heckhausen, J., & Schulz, R. (1995). A life-span theory of control. *Psychological Review, 102,* 284–304.

Hedden, T., & Gabrieli, J. D. E. (2004). Insights into the ageing mind: A view from cognitive neuroscience. *Nature Reviews Neuroscience, 5,* 87–96.

Hess, T. M. (1999). Cognitive and knowledge-based influences on social representations. In T.M. Hess & F. Blanchard-Fields (Eds.), *Social cognition and aging* (pp. 237–263). San Diego, CA: Academic Press.

Hess, T. M., Auman, C., Colcombe, S. J., & Rahhal, T. A. (2003). The impact of stereotype threat on age differences in memory performance. *Journals of Gerontology, 58B,* P3–P11.

Hess, T. M., Waters, S. J., & Bolstad, C. A. (2000). Motivational and cognitive influences on affective priming in adulthood. *Journals of Gerontology, 55B,* P193–P204.

Hoare, C. (2006). *Handbook of adult development and learning.* New York: Oxford University Press.

Horhota, M., & Blanchard-Fields, F. (2006). Do beliefs and attributional complexity influence age differences in the correspondence bias? *Social Cognition, 24,* 310–337.

Hultsch, D. F., & MacDonald, S. W. S. (2004). Intraindividual variability in performance as a theoretical window onto cognitive aging. In R. A. Dixon, L. Bäckman, & L.G. Nilsson (Eds.), *New frontiers in cognitive aging* (pp. 65–68). Oxford, UK: Oxford University Press.

Hultsch, D. F., MacDonald, S. W. S., & Dixon, R. A. (2002). Variability in reaction time performance of younger and older adults. *Journals of Gerontology, 57B,* 101–115.

Isaacowitz, D. M., & Light, J. C. (2006). The effect of developmental regulation on visual attention: The example of the 'biological clock'. *Cognition & Emotion, 20,* 623–645.

Kennedy, Q., Mather, M., & Carstensen, L. L. (2004). The role of motivation in the age-related positivity effect in autobiographical memory. *Psychological Science, 15,* 208–214.

Kensinger, E. A., & Corkin, S. (2004). The effects of emotional content and aging on false memories. *Cognitive, Affective & Behavioral Neuroscience, 4,* 1–9.

Kensinger, E. A., Piguet, O., Krendl, A. C., & Corkin, S. (2005). Memory for contextual details: Effects of emotion and aging. *Psychology and Aging, 20,* 241–250.

Klaczynski, P. A., & Robinson, B. (2000). Personal theories, intellectual ability, and epistemological beliefs: Adult age differences in everyday reasoning biases. *Psychology and Aging, 15,* 400–416.

Kramer, A. F., Fabiani, M., & Colcombe, S. J. (2006). Contributions of cognitive neuroscience to the understanding of behavior and aging. In J. E. Birren & K. W. Schaire (Eds.), *Handbook of the psychology of aging* (6 ed., pp. 57–83). Amsterdam, Netherlands: Elsevier.

Kuhn, T. S. (1962). *The structure of scientific revolutions.* Chicago: University of Chicago Press.

Kunzmann, U., & Grühn, D. (2005). Age differences in emotional reactivity: The Sample case of sadness. *Psychology and Aging, 20,* 47–59.

Labouvie-Vief, G. (1998). Cognitive-emotional integration in adulthood. In K. W. Schaie & M. P. Lawton (Eds.), *Annual review of gerontology and geriatrics* (Vol. 17, pp. 206–237). New York: Springer.

Labouvie-Vief, G. (2003). Dynamic integration: Affect, cognition, and the self in adulthood. *Current Directions in Psychological Science, 12,* 201–206.

Labouvie-Vief, G., Chiodo, L. M., Goguen, L. A., Diehl, M., & Orwoll, L. (1995). Representations of self across the life span. *Psychology and Aging, 10,* 404–415.

Labouvie-Vief, G., Hakim-Larson, J., & Hobart, C. J. (1987). Age, ego level, and the life-span development of coping and defense processes. *Psychology and Aging, 2,* 286–293.

Laslett, P. (1991). *A fresh map of life: The emergence of the third age.* Cambridge, MA: Harvard University Press.

Lawton, M. P. (2001). *Emotion in later life.* London: Blackwell.

Lawton, M. P., Kleban, M. H., Rajagopal, D., & Dean, J. (1992). Dimensions of affective experience in three age groups. *Psychology and Aging, 7,* 171–184.

Lerner, R. M., & Busch-Rossnagel, N. A. (1981). *Individuals as producers of their development.* New York: Academic Press.

Levenson, R. W., Carstensen, L. L., Friesen, W. V., & Ekman, P. (1991). Emotion, physiology, and expression in old age. *Psychology and Aging, 6,* 28–35.

Levine, L. J., & Bluck, S. (1997). Experienced and remembered emotional intensity in older adults. *Psychology and Aging, 12,* 514–523.

Levy, B. (1996). Improving memory in old age through implicit self-stereotyping. *Journal of Personality and Social Psychology, 71,* 1092–1107.

Levy, B., & Langer, E. (1994). Aging free from negative stereotypes: Successful memory in China among the American deaf. *Journal of Personality and Social Psychology, 66,* 989–997.

Li, K. Z. H., Lindenberger, U., Freund, A. M., & Baltes, P. B. (2001). Walking while memorizing: Age-related differences in compensatory behavior. *Psychological Science, 12,* 230–237.

Li, S., Aggen, S. H., Nesselroade, J. R., & Baltes, P. B. (2001). Short-term fluctuations in elderly people's sensorimotor functioning predict text and spatial memory performance: The MacArthur Successful Aging Studies. *Gerontology, 47,* 100–116.

Li, S., & Lindenberger, U. (1999). Cross-level unification: A computational exploration of the link between deterioration of neurotransmitter systems and dedifferentiation of cognitive abilities in old age. In L. Nilsson & H. J. Markowitsch (Eds.), *Cognitive neuroscience of memory* (pp. 103–146). Ashland, OH: Hogrefe & Huber.

Lindenberger, U., Scherer, H., & Baltes, P. B. (2001). The strong connection between sensory and cognitive performance in old age: Not due to sensory acuity reductions operating during cognitive assessment. *Psychology and Aging, 16,* 196–205.

Little, B. R. (1989). Personal projects analysis: Trivial pursuits, magnificent obsessions, and the search for coherence. In D. M. Buss & N. Cantor (Eds.), *Personality psychology: Recent trends and emerging directions* (pp. 15–31). New York: Springer.

Löckenhoff, C. E., & Carstensen, L. L. (2004). Socioemotional selectivity theory, aging, and health: The increasingly delicate balance between regulating emotions and making tough choices. *Journal of Personality and Social Psychology, 72,* 1395–1424.

Logan, J. M., Sanders, A. L., Snyder, A. Z., Morris, J. C., & Buckner, R. L. (2002). Under-recruitment and nonselective recruitment: Dissociable neural mechanisms associated with aging. *Neuron, 33,* 827–40.

Luszcz, M. A. (2004). What's it all about: Variation and aging. *Gerontology, 50,* 5–6.

Magnusson, D. (2001). The holistic-interactionistic paradigm: Some directions for empirical developmental research. *European Psychologist, 6,* 153–162.

Mandler, G. (1984). *Mind and body.* New York: Norton.

Martin, L. L. (2001). Mood as input: A configural view of mood effects. In L. L. Martin & G. L. Clore (Eds.), *Theories of mood and cognition: A user's guidebook* (pp. 135–157). Mahwah, NJ: Erlbaum.

Mather, M., Canli, T., English, T., Whitfield, S., Wais, P., Ochsner, K., et al. (2004). Amygdala responses to emotionally valenced stimuli in older and younger adults. *Psychological Science, 15,* 259–263.

Mather, M., & Carstensen, L. L. (2003). Aging and attentional biases for emotional faces. *Psychological Science, 14,* 409–415.

Mather, M., Johnson, M. K., & De Leonardis, D. M. (1999). Stereotype reliance in source monitoring: Age differences and neuropsychological test correlates. *Cognitive Neuropsychology, 16,* 437–458.

Mather, M., & Knight, M. (2005). Goal-directed memory: The role of cognitive control in older adults' emotional memory. *Psychology and Aging, 20,* 554–570.

Mather, M., Knight, M., & McCaffrey, M. (2005). The allure of the alignable: Younger and older adults' false memories of choice features. *Journal of Experimental Psychology: General, 134,* 38–51.

May, C. P., Rahhal, T. A., Berry, E. M., & Leighton, E. A. (2005). Aging, source memory, and emotion. *Psychology and Aging, 20,* 571–578.

Mienaltowski, A., Corballis, P. M., Blanchard-Fields, F., & Parks, N. A. (2006). *Electrophysiological studies of age differences in selective attention biases for emotional faces.* Poster presented at the Cognitive Aging Conference. Atlanta, GA.

Mikels, J. A., Larkin, G. R., Reuter-Lorenz, P. A., & Carstensen, L. L. (2005). Divergent trajectories in the aging mind: Changes in working memory for affective versus visual information with age. *Psychology and Aging, 20,* 542–553.

Molenaar, P. C. M. (2004). A manifesto on psychology as idiographic science: Bringing the person back into scientific psychology, this time forever. *Measurement: Interdisciplinary Research and Perspectives, 2,* 201–218.

Nesselroade, J. R. (2001). Intraindividual variability in development within and between individuals. *European Psychologist, 6,* 187–193.

Nesselroade, J. R. (2004). Intraindividual variability and short-term change. *Gerontology, 50,* 44–47.

Nesselroade, J. R., & Salthouse, T. A. (2004). Methodological and theoretical implications of intraindividual variability in perceptual-motor performance. *Journals of Gerontology, 59B,* 49–55.

Neugarten, B. (1974). Age groups in American society and the rise of the young old. *Annals of the Academy of Social and Political Science, 415,* 187–198.

O'Brien, L. T., & Hummert, M. L. (2006). Memory performance of late middle-aged adults: Contrasting self-stereotyping and stereotype threat accounts of assimilation to age stereotypes. *Social Cognition, 24,* 338–358.

Ochsner, K. N., & Lieberman, M. D. (2001). The emergence of social cognitive neuroscience. *American Psychologist, 56,* 717–734.

Ortony, A., Clore, G. L., & Collins, A. (1988). *The cognitive structure of emotions.* New York: Cambridge University Press.

Rahhal, T. A., Hasher, L., & Colcombe, S. J. (2001). Instructional manipulations and age differences in memory: Now you see them, now you don't. *Psychology and Aging, 16,* 697–706.

Ram, N., Rabbitt, P., Stollery, B., & Nesselroade, J. R. (2005). Cognitive performance inconsistency: Intraindividual change and variability. *Psychology and Aging, 20,* 623–633.

Raz, N. (2000). Aging of the brain and its impact on cognitive performance: Integration of structural and functional findings. In F. I. M. Craik & T. A. Salthouse (Eds.), *The handbook of aging and cognition* (pp. 1–90). Mahwah, NJ: Erlbaum.

Reuter-Lorenz, P. A. (2002). New visions of the aging mind and brain. *Trends in Cognitive Sciences, 6,* 394–400.

Reuter-Lorenz, P. A., & Mikels, J. A. (2006). The aging mind and brain: Implications of enduring plasticity for behavioral and cultural change. In P. B. Baltes, P. A. Reuter-Lorenz, & F. Rösler (Eds.), *Lifespan development and the brain: The perspective of biocultural co-constructivism* (pp. 255–276). New York: Cambridge University Press.

Riediger, M., Freund, A. M., & Baltes, P. B. (2005). Managing life through personal goals: Intergoal facilitation and intensity of goal pursuit in younger and older adulthood. *Journals of Gerontology, 60B,* P84–P91.

Riediger, M., Li, S., & Lindenberger, U. (2006). Selection, optimization, and compensation as developmental mechanisms of adaptive resource allocation: Review and preview. In J. E. Birren & K. W. Schaire (Eds.), *Handbook of the psychology of aging* (pp. 289–313). Amsterdam, Netherlands: Elsevier.

Rowe, J. W., & Kahn, R. L. (1987). Human aging: Usual and successful. *Science, 237,* 143–149.

Rozin, P., & Royzman, E. B. (2001). Negativity bias, negativity dominance, and contagion. *Personality and Social Psychology Review, 5,* 296–320.

Ryff, C. D., Singer, B. H., & Love, G. D. (2004). Positive health: Connecting well-being with biology. *Philosophical Transactions of the Royal Society of London, 359,* 1383–1394.

Salthouse, T. A. (1996). The processing-speed theory of adult age differences in cognition. *Psychological Review, 103,* 403–428.

Salthouse, T. A., Nesselroade, J. R., & Berish, D. E. (2006). Short-term variability in cognitive performance and the calibration of longitudinal change. *Journals of Gerontology, 61B,* 144–151.

Schaie, K. W. (1996). Intellectual development in adulthood. In J. E. Birren, K. W. Schaie, R. P. Abeles, M. Gatz, & T. A. Salthouse (Eds.), *Handbook of the psychology of aging* (4 ed., pp. 266–286). San Diego, CA: Academic Press.

Schulz, R. (1985). Emotion and affect. In J. E. Birren & K. W. Schaie (Eds.), *Handbook of the psychology of aging* (pp. 531–543). New York: van Nostrand Reinhold.

Singer, T., Lindenberger, U., & Baltes, P. B. (2003). Plasticity of memory for new learning in very old age: A story of major loss? *Psychology and Aging, 18,* 306–317.

Singer, T., Verhaeghen, P., Ghisletta, P., Lindenberger, U., & Baltes, P. B. (2003). The fate of cognition in very old age: Six-year longitudinal findings in the Berlin Aging Study (BASE). *Psychology and Aging, 18,* 318–331.

Sliwinski, M., & Buschke, H. (1999). Cross-sectional and longitudinal relationships among age, cognition, and processing speed. *Psychology and Aging, 14,* 18–33.

Smith, J., & Baltes, P. B. (1993). Differential psychological aging: Profiles of the old and the very old. *Ageing and Society, 13,* 551–587.

Smith, J., & Baltes, P. B. (1997). Profiles of psychological functioning in the old and oldest old. *Psychology and Aging, 12,* 458–472.

Smith, J., & Baltes, P. B. (1999). Trends and profiles of psychological functioning in very old age. In P. B. Baltes & K. U. Mayer (Eds.), *The Berlin Aging Study: Aging from 70 to 100* (pp. 197–226). New York: Cambridge University Press.

Stein, R., Blanchard-Fields, F., & Hertzog, C. (2002). The effects of age-stereotype priming on the memory performance of older adults. *Experimental Aging Research, 28,* 169–181.

Stern, P., & Carstensen, L. L. (2000). *The aging mind: Opportunities in cognitive aging.* Washington, DC: The National Academies Press.

Suzman, R., Willis, D., & Manton, K. (1992). *The oldest-old.* New York: Oxford University Press.

Thomas, R. C., & Hasher, L. (2006). The influence of emotional valence on age differences in early processing and memory. *Psychology and Aging, 21,* 821–825.

Watson, T. L., & Blanchard-Fields, F. (1998). Thinking with your head and your heart: Age differences in everyday problem-solving strategy preferences. *Aging, Neuropsychology, and Cognition, 5,* 225–240.

Webster, D. M., & Kruglanski, A. W. (1994). Individual differences in need for cognitive closure. *Journal of Personality and Social Psychology, 67,* 1049–1062.

Wood, S., & Kisley, M. A. (2006). The negativity bias is eliminated in older adults: Age-related reduction in event-related brain potentials associated with evaluative categorization. *Psychology and Aging, 21,* 815–820.

Wrosch, C., & Heckhausen, J. (1999). Control processes before and after passing a developmental deadline: Activation and deactivation of intimate relationship goals. *Journal of Personality and Social Psychology, 77,* 415–427.

Wurm, L. H., Labouvie-Vief, G., Aycock, J., Rebucal, K. A., & Koch, H. E. (2004). Performance in auditory and visual emotional stroop tasks: A comparison of older and younger adults. *Psychology and Aging, 19,* 523–535.

Ybarra, O., & Park, D. C. (2002). Disconfirmation of person expectations by older and younger adults: Implications for social vigilance. *Journals of Gerontology, 57B,* P435–P443.

Yoon, C., Hasher, L., Feinberg, F., Rahhal, T. A., & Winocur, G. (2000). Cross-cultural differences in memory: The role of culture-based stereotypes about aging. *Psychology and Aging, 15,* 694–704.

Chapter 2

Emerging Adulthood

Learning and Development During the First Stage of Adulthood

Jennifer L. Tanner, Jeffrey Jensen Arnett, and Julie A. Leis

Inherent in the call for the integration of educational psychology and adult learning (Smith & Reio, 2006) is the need for specific information that speaks to the unique developmental features of discrete adult age periods. Particularly important is the need to recognize the age period between 29 and 30 as a distinct developmental period, emerging adulthood, during which there is great demand for skill and knowledge acquisition as well as maturation as individuals make the transition to adulthood. It is likewise imperative to have appreciation for the diversity of learning experiences that occur during adulthood in general (Smith & Pourchot, 1998) and during emerging adulthood specifically. Given that the post-adolescent years correspond with those spent, by some, in postsecondary education, the college student development literature is often used to frame our understanding of learning, development, and adaptation during this age period. Development and learning during this age period, however, takes place across a variety of contexts, is not limited to those enrolled in college or university, and is distinctly different from development during childhood and adolescence as well as development that occurs in later stages of adulthood.

The distinct experiences of emerging adulthood translate into a need for a unique framework for promoting learning and development during these years. Subjectively, emerging adults experience their roles in the adult world as undetermined because they are in the process of making, but have not yet established themselves in their careers, nor in partnerships, nor families-of-creation. The complexities of adult life that co-exist in adult learners' lives (i.e., balancing one's sense-of-self, work responsibilities, and family demands for time and money) (Smith & Pourchot, 1998) are novel to the emerging adult. Prior to emerging adulthood, learning and development within the role of student is socially mandated, not assumed by choice. At emerging adulthood, learning and development become the responsibility of the individual and prioritization of continued education and maturation requires self-directedness. Given that emerging adults are in the process of determining their goals and directions in life, the connection between education and training is less apparent than for older adults whose learning and education is motivated by the need to obtain, attain, or maintain adult social roles (e.g., careers, families-of-creation).

The fundamental flux of emerging adulthood presents a challenge to programs designed to optimize development and transfer skills and knowledge to emerging adults. Nonetheless, education and development carry a heavy weight during these years. Because emerging adults have yet to enter into adult roles and responsibilities, this is a critical stage for the acquisition of resources. Understanding and incorporating developmental information to meet the unique needs to emerging adults will help optimize learning potential and build a foundation for life-span adult learning.

The goals of this chapter are to provide (1) an overview of contemporary theory framing development between ages 18 and 29, and (2) a review of literature that provides information on the unique features of development during this age period. In the past decade, significant strides have been made to clarify the features of the contemporary transition to adulthood. Arnett (2000, 2004, 2006) reframed the third decade of life as a transitional stage of development, bridging adolescence and adulthood, labeling this age period emerging adulthood to distinguish the age period from adolescence and young adulthood. The subjective experiences of the age period are highlighted through Arnett's work, resulting in a characterization of this developmental stage as the age of instability, of feeling in-between, the self-focused age, the age of identity explorations, of possibilities. From a life-span developmental systems perspective, Tanner (2006) has conceptualized the developmental task of recentering, arguing that this is the key developmental task of emerging adulthood as well as a critical transition in life-span human development. Recentering involves realigning interpersonal relations as well as connections to contexts that facilitate development via dependency (e.g., families, schools) while, at the same time, engaging in temporary and then, finally, permanent commitments and connections to persons and contexts that facilitate development and self-sufficiency via interdependency. The second section of this chapter reviews empirical research highlighting the unique features of this age period, including surveys of literature detailing cognitive development, personality development, ethnic and cultural issues, mental health, physical health, family relationships and support systems, friendships, intimate relationships, media and leisure, education, and career development during the first stage of adulthood.

Theory of Emerging Adulthood: Ages 18–29

The theory of emerging adulthood was proposed by Arnett (2000, 2004, 2006) to identify a new and distinct period of the life course that came to define the experiences of 18- to 29-year-olds in industrialized societies over the past half-century. Prior to the 1950s, few people obtained higher education, and most young men became employed by the end of their teens, if not sooner. In 1950, only 25% of Americans obtained any higher education, and nearly all of them were young men (Arnett & Taber, 1994). Most young women, as well as many young men, remained in their parents' household until they married in their late teens or very early twenties. The median marriage age in the United States as recently as 1960 was just 20.3 for women and 22.8 for men (Arnett, 2000). The entry to parenthood came about a year later, on average. Thus, most young people went directly from adolescence to a settled young adulthood by their early twenties.

Over the past half century, the changes related to the age period from the late teens through the twenties have been dramatic. Participation in higher education has risen steeply, especially among young women. Now over 60% of young persons enter higher education the year after graduating from high school, and among undergraduates in the United States, 57% are women (National Center for Education Statistics, 2005). The median age of first marriage has risen steeply as well, to its current record-high of 26.0 among women and 27.5 among men, with a corresponding rise in the median age of entering parenthood (U.S. Bureau of the Census, 2007). Furthermore, changes in attitudes toward premarital sex have taken place in American society, and the majority of young Americans have sexual intercourse for the first time in their late teens, a decade or more before they enter marriage. About two-thirds cohabit before marriage.

Arnett argues that it no longer makes sense to group 18- to 29-year-olds with "young adults," because—unlike young adults—many emerging adults are not married, do not have children, and have not yet settled into stable full-time work. Nor does it make sense to call them "adolescents," because unlike adolescents they are not going through puberty, they are not in secondary school, and most of them no longer live in their parents' household. Calling them "emerging adults" recognizes that they are distinct in many ways from both adolescents and young adults, and that a new period of the life course has now developed in between these two periods.

So, what is distinctive about emerging adulthood as a period of the life course? Arnett has proposed five features that are prominent in emerging adulthood (Arnett, 2004). Not all emerging adults experience these five features, but these are features that are more prominent during emerging adulthood than during other periods of the life course. According to the theory, emerging adulthood is 1) the age of identity explorations, 2) the age of instability, 3) the self-focused age, 4) the age of feeling in-between, and 5) the age of possibilities.

Identity explorations have been associated in the past with adolescence, because Erikson (1950) proposed in his life-span theory that each period of the life course has a central challenge or crisis, and that adolescents confront an identity crisis. In Erikson's view, adolescents focus on forming an identity, especially with respect to love and work. This may well have been true in the 1940s, when Erikson first formulated his theory. However, today most identity explorations take place in emerging adulthood, according to Arnett. With respect to love, many adolescents experience their first romantic relationships, but it is during emerging adulthood that romantic relationships become more identity focused, as emerging adults ask themselves, "Given what I know about myself, what kind of person would make a good life partner for me?" Similarly, many adolescents have part-time jobs, but it is in emerging adulthood that work becomes more identity-based, as emerging adults seek to find a job that fits well with their sense of what their abilities and interests are.

The identity explorations of emerging adulthood contribute to making it the age of instability because, in the course of their explorations, emerging adults often experience changes in love partners and in educational and occupational paths. They change residences more frequently than in any other part of the life course, for example moving out of their parents' household, living with friends, moving in to cohabit with a partner, moving out again, perhaps moving back home during a transition related to love, education, or work. Although emerging adulthood is largely experienced as positive, and numerous studies have found that median well-being and life satisfaction increase steadily during this age period (e.g., Galambos, Barker, & Krahn, 2006), the instability of the period adds an element of stress and anxiety for many emerging adults.

Emerging adulthood is the self-focused age in the sense that it is the time of life that is the least structured and the least bound by obligations to others. Children and adolescents live with their parents and have to follow the program of daily life laid down by their parents and other adults: living with their parents, going to school, taking part in parent-approved leisure activities. In young adulthood and beyond, obligations to others also structure daily life for most people, in their roles as spouse/partner, parent, and worker. However, emerging adulthood is the time when structure and obligations reach their nadir, and individuals are free to make their own decisions without consulting others and to structure their daily lives as they wish. This does not mean that they are selfish—on the contrary, they tend to be considerably less egocentric than adolescents are—but that they are temporarily relatively free from binding social roles and allowed to live as they wish to a large extent.

Emerging adulthood is the age of feeling in-between adolescence and adulthood. In numerous surveys, in the United States as well as in other industrialized countries, when asked if they have reached adulthood, most emerging adults respond neither yes nor no but "in some ways yes, in some ways no" (Arnett, 2001, 2003; Mayseless & Scharf, 2003; Facio & Micocci, 2003). Their subjective sense of making the transition to adulthood takes place gradually over the course of emerging adulthood. For most, the passage to adulthood is not marked by traditional transition events such as finishing education, marriage, and parenthood, but by more intangible and individualistic criteria, especially these three: accept responsibility for yourself, make independent decisions, and become financially independent. These criteria have been found to rank at the top in a wide range of studies in the United States and other countries, across regions, social classes, ethnic groups, and nationalities.

Finally, emerging adulthood is the age of possibilities in two respects. First, emerging adulthood is a time of high hopes and great expectations. Even if their current lives are stressful and difficult—which is often the case, since many of them are financially strained and are stressfully attempting to balance the demands of education, work, and social relationships—they nevertheless believe almost universally that adulthood will work out well for them in the end. They have high hopes of finding not merely a reliable marriage partner but a "soulmate," and not merely a stable and reasonably well-paying job but a job that is self-fulfilling, an expression of their identity. Second, emerging adulthood is the age of possibilities in the sense that it represents a window of opportunity for people to make dramatic changes in their lives. Children and adolescents are dependent on their parents and cannot leave even if their parents are incompetent or cruel. But emerging adults can leave, and some of them have the freedom to leave a pathogenic family life and make their own decisions which allow them to turn their lives around.

The American college experience and the college environment are well-suited to the developmental features of emerging adulthood. Taking a variety of courses in their first two years of higher education is a form of identity exploration for many emerging adults, as they see what areas resonate most strongly with their own abilities and interests. Explorations in love, too, are facilitated by having so many unattached persons in their age group in the same place. Pursuing a college education is in many ways a self-focused enterprise, because the focus is on building one's own knowledge and credentials, and much of one's time during these years is spent studying and attending classes. The college environment also promotes a sense of feeling in between adolescence and young adulthood, because college students often have more responsibilities than they did as adolescents but fewer than they will in adulthood, especially if they live in a group residential environment such as a dormitory.

Nevertheless, emerging adulthood is not experienced only by college students. Emerging adults who do not pursue higher education also seek satisfying identity-based work, although their explorations may be in different types of jobs rather than different college majors, and they also seek a "soulmate" in marriage. They also experience instability, through frequent job changes in their late teens and early twenties. They are self-focused, as most of them leave their parents' household but wait until at least their late twenties to enter marriage and parenthood. They are as likely as college-attending emerging adults to report the in-between status of feeling adult in some ways but not others (Arnett, 1997). And they have their own dreams, the belief that many doors are still open to them, even though without higher education credentials the attainment of those dreams may be elusive.

Individual Pathways from Adolescence to Young Adulthood

Arnett's theory describes the key population characteristics of the emerging adult age period, pointing to the critical developmental task of gaining self-sufficiency. Subjectively and psychologically, the experience of becoming an adult is a process rather than an event or string of social transitions. Complementing Arnett's characterization of emerging adulthood as a universal stage of development, Tanner (2006) articulated a three-stage process, recentering, that characterizes the individual, developmental process of transitioning from adolescence, through emerging adulthood, into young adulthood.

The developmental process of recentering is formulated utilizing life-span developmental (Baltes, 1997) and life-span developmental systems theories (Lerner, 2002), stressing the relational nature of human development, interactions between individuals and contexts that produce development. Individual pathways of development across emerging adulthood, as with all stages of human development, involve continuities and discontinuities, plasticity, normative and non-normative experiences, and variability in experiences (i.e., individual differences). As individuals move toward greater independence and adult self-sufficiency, as they recenter, development involves both gains and losses.

Recentering is a three-stage process by which individuals shift their primary involvements from the contexts of childhood and adolescence (which promote dependence) to contexts of adulthood (which nourish adult interdependence). Beginning when the individual is embedded in contexts of youth, primarily the family-of-origin (see Figure 2.1a), stage 1 is objectively marked by the legal emancipation of individuals from the responsibility of their parents. Despite a concentration of this occurrence at age 18, a small minority of individuals are emancipated legally as adolescents (e.g., financial emancipation from parents, early graduation from high school), some dissociate from institutional care before age 18 (e.g., runaway youth, those who leave high school before graduation), and a subgroup who reverse the dependent role before age 18 (e.g., those who become parents or take on head-of-household responsibilities). By definition, leaving adolescence and entering emerging adulthood is marked by a weakening of institutional ties. The extent to which resources remain available to the emerging adult (i.e., via families and/or institutions) and opportunities available to the individual represent two sources of individual differences predicting the extent to which an individual experiences emerging adulthood proper.

As adolescents age out of traditional contexts of dependence, they enter emerging adulthood proper, stage 2 (see Figure 2.1b), marked by temporary role commitments that serve the purpose of exploration of adult identities. During this stage, emerging adults progress in identity development by trying out different, albeit temporary commitments, and eliminating those that do not "fit" with their plans and goals. While adolescence is marked by subjective, internalized identity exploration, it is not until emerging adulthood that the active phase of identity exploration begins during which individuals attempt to match their adult senses-of-self with the socially-sanctioned adult roles.

Stage 3 (see Figure 2.1c) of the recentering process occurs when individuals make enduring commitments to relationships and careers, taking on adult roles and responsibilities. These, in turn, serve to sustain adult self-sufficiency. Identity is resolved at the

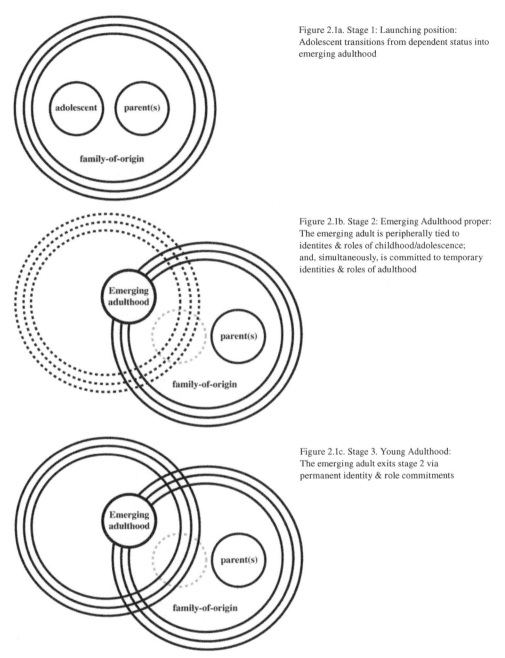

Figure 2.1a. Stage 1: Launching position: Adolescent transitions from dependent status into emerging adulthood

Figure 2.1b. Stage 2: Emerging Adulthood proper: The emerging adult is peripherally tied to identites & roles of childhood/adolescence; and, simultaneously, is committed to temporary identities & roles of adulthood

Figure 2.1c. Stage 3. Young Adulthood: The emerging adult exits stage 2 via permanent identity & role commitments

Figure 2.1 The recentering process.

entry into stage 3 marking the beginning of identity consolidation occurring around such commitments to careers, partners, children, community, and aging parents. Such commitments require stability of responsibility to these roles, to self and to others (Whiting, 1998). After the experimentation of emerging adulthood, and the culling of identity options and roles, the task at hand in young adulthood is the reorganization of self around the roles and responsibilities to which an individual has committed.

The process of recentering is useful for understanding not only normative and non-normative experiences during the first years of adulthood, but it presents a framework for predicting more and less successful adaptation during the transition to adulthood. It is the events and transitions that occur during this age period that are most likely to be considered, by both younger and older adults, the most significant, key marker events that shape their lives (Elnick, Margrett, Fitzgerald, & Labouvie-Vief, 1999; Grob, Krings, & Bangerter, 2001). Despite the fact that adult event transitions (e.g., marriage, parenthood) are rarely considered significant indicators of being an "adult," these events play an important role in the experience of one's life. The extent to which an emerging adult has choice in the process of selecting adult roles and commitments (Rönkä, Oravala, & Pulkkinen, 2003), as well as the extent to which these commitments "fit" an individual, predict successful adaptation (Lerner, 1984).

Facilitated by the availability of both personal and environmental accumulated resources, empirical evidence strongly suggests that conscious exploration and mindful selection of and commitment to adult roles are tied to successful adaptation in emerging adulthood and later stages of adult development. One overarching framework useful for understanding how individuals regulate behavior, development, and adaptation across the life span is the theory of selection, optimization, and compensation (Baltes, 1997). According to this model, emerging adulthood is the critical developmental stage during which individuals select life goals based on available resources and opportunities (Freund & Baltes, 2002; Freund, Li, & Baltes, 1999). Life goals are initiated in adolescence (Lerner, Freund, De Stefanis, & Habermas, 2001) and narrowed, refined, and selected in emerging adulthood (Nurmi, 1993; 1997). The process of articulating and selecting goals, directing one's resources to achieve those goals, and evaluating one's success in meeting identified goals contributes to emerging adult mental health (Nurmi, 1997). For example, Nurmi & Salmelo-Aro (2002) found that depressive symptoms were reduced when emerging adults who had career goals were able to find jobs; among those who had identity goals, depressive symptoms were reduced when they were engaged in contexts that supported identity exploration. In turn, this person-environment fit associated with mental health and personality stability (Roberts, O'Donnell, & Robins, 2004).

The recentering framework provides a lens useful for understanding the developmental challenges of emerging adults engaged in education and training programs during this critical age period. Recentering describes a normative experience in individual development unique to this age period. Understanding individual development from adolescence to young adulthood has implications for determining sources of heterogeneity in adaptation during this developmental period. Variation in ages at which one enters and completes the recentering process, as well as individual differences in functioning during recentering prescribe two specific aspects of the process that lend themselves to assessment of normative vs. non-normative development (Neugarten, 1968). As follows, a comprehensive understanding of the unique developmental characteristics that distinguish this age period from later stages of adulthood is an advantage in work that aims to optimize emerging adult development and learning and to lay the groundwork for continued growth throughout adulthood.

Unique Features of Emerging Adulthood

Cognitive Development

Over the two past decades, developmental science has progressed in its understanding of emerging adulthood as a critical period for the evolution of adult cognitive structures

(Labouvie-Vief, 2006). Coincident with advancements in developmental science, exciting progress in neuroscience has identified significant differences between the adolescent and emerging adult brains (Sowell, Thompson, & Toga, 2004). Evidence of brain reorganization associated with rationale decision-making substantiates the assertion that emerging adulthood is a unique and critical developmental period. Reconceptualizing cognitive development to include age-specific changes of this age period provides a target for programs and policies that aim to facilitate development and adjustment.

The brain's center for reasoning and problem-solving fully develops during the period of emerging adulthood, accomplished by a pruning of gray matter (Giedd et al., 1999). There is an increase in white matter across this same period through the mid-thirties. This combination results in change toward fewer, but faster connections (Gogtay, Giedd, Lusk, Hayashi, Greenstein, Vaituzis et al., 2004). Research comparing brain images (MRI) of first-year college students during their first 6 months of school found changes in several brain regions associated with emotion and motivation, including self-awareness (Bennett & Baird, 2006). The authors concluded that a common change in living associated with the transition to college (e.g., moving over 100 miles away from home) has systematic implications for brain development. Whereas adolescence is the final era of brain plasticity, emerging adulthood corresponds with the final phase of organization of the adult brain—specifically in areas involving the integration of cognition and emotion. In sum, brain processes associated with emotion-regulation and decision making continue to develop through the twenties, identifying a physiological task underlying emerging adult behavior and thinking.

Brain maturation during this age period is reflected in key theories of cognitive development that describe emerging cognitive structures post-adolescence. Perry (1970, 1981), Schaie (1977), and Labouvie-Vief (1980, 1985) have advanced developmental theories indicating that emerging adulthood is a developmental stage during which novel cognitive organizations have the potential to develop in service of the demands of adulthood. For example, Perry (1970, 1981) formulated cognitive growth into nine stages, based on his studies of white, male, Harvard students in the 1950s and 1960s. Perry suggested that typical students entering college (initial transition from adolescence to emerging adulthood) are most likely to cognitively operate "dualistically" (stage 2; i.e., there are right and wrong answers known to authorities) and, those leaving college, typically score between stages 4, "multiplicity" (i.e., there are conflicting solutions; knowledge is opinion) and 5, "relativism and procedural knowledge" (i.e., knowledge is derived from informed opinion; some individuals know more than others on a specific topic).

Making the case that adults change in the ways that they use intellect, Schaie (1977) advanced two stages of adult cognitive development that emerge in response to the demands of adulthood: the achieving and responsibility stages. Following the acquisition stage that reigns during childhood and adolescence, the achieving stage dominates emerging adulthood where previously acquired knowledge is used to establish oneself in the world. In this stage the emerging adult focuses on applying the acquired intellectual skills to real life situations requiring practical problem solving abilities. The individual learns to meet her or his needs within a broader social context than family and school. Of particular importance to this process are the cognitive skills required to monitor one's own behavior.

Labouvie-Vief and colleagues' work traces cognitive growth via changes in self-descriptions that increase across distinct levels monotonically with age (Labouvie-Vief, Chiodo, Goguen, Diehl, & Orwoll, 1995; Labouvie-Vief & Meddler, 2002). At the lowest level, concrete-presystemic, involves descriptions of roles and physical features; while at the highest level, dynamic-intersubjective, "roles and traits are described at a complex psychological level and reflect awareness of underlying, often unconscious motivation and reciprocal interaction" (Labouvie-Vief, 2006, p. 70). Labouvie-Vief argues that emerging adulthood is a distinctly important age period for the emergence and rapid expansion of complex thought structures. Labouvie-Vief's and colleagues' work and findings are consonant with the theory of emerging adulthood and concept of recentering in that the first years of emerging adulthood lack subjective stability, but cognitive and reflective organization increases as individuals transition to adulthood.

Life-span conceptualizations of intellectual development and ways-of-knowing point to the importance of the emerging adult years for acquiring competence. Baltes' review of research on acquisition of wisdom as "an expertise in the conduct and meaning of life" (Baltes & Staudinger, 2000, p. 124) suggests that attaining wisdom-related knowledge and judgment occurs primarily during emerging adulthood, from ages 15 to 25. Across multiple measures of aptitude, there is a decline after maximum levels are achieved in emerging adulthood (i.e., age groups 20–24 and 25–34) in numerical ability, verbal aptitude, clerical perception, finger dexterity, and general intelligence (Avolio & Waldman, 1994). At age 25, there is a point of inflection for cognitive performance where crystallized intelligence (i.e., intelligence as cultural knowledge) stabilizes, but fluid intelligence (i.e., intelligence as basic information processing; Baltes, Staudinger, & Lindenberger, 1999) begins to decline. That is, intelligence as a genetically pre-disposed component of cognitive functioning becomes less salient during emerging adulthood (i.e., mechanics), and knowledge that is culture-relevant and culture-dependent, rich and steeped in experience, becomes more salient (i.e., pragmatics). Through age 25, mechanics and pragmatics are equivalent components of cognition.

In addition to theories of general intelligence, two theories of specific intelligences, practical and emotional intelligences, are particularly salient in considerations of optimizing development in emerging adulthood versus earlier periods of development. As the task of recentering moves to center stage for emerging adults, experimenting with and committing to careers and interpersonal relationships may require a different skill set, or a variety of skills that become necessary when faced with the developmental demands of emerging adulthood. Sternberg and Grigorenko (2002) have defined practical intelligence as "intelligence as it applies in everyday life in adaptation to, shaping of, and selection of environments" (p. 215), and suggest it is complementary to but distinct from crystallized intelligence, as measured by IQ tests. In terms of practical solutions to everyday problems, research indicates that 20 year olds demonstrate less experience with all everyday problems, but provide better solutions than older individuals on average—performing significantly better on some individual items and significantly worse on others (Hershey & Farrell, 1999). Such findings suggest that, in terms of everyday competencies, emerging adults function at similar levels as older adults and that cognitive capacity, as measured by IQ tests, academic achievement, and standardized tests may only partially represent individual differences in capabilities.

Emotional intelligence describes an ability, capacity, or *skill* to perceive, assess, and manage the *emotions* of one's self, of others, and of groups. The Mayer-Salovey model (Mayer & Salovey, 1997) defines emotional intelligence as the capacity to understand emotional information and to reason with emotions, which has been divided into four basic capacities to: (1) accurately perceive emotions, (2) use emotions to facilitate thinking, (3) understand emotional meanings, and (4) manage emotions (see Mayer, Salovey, & Caruso, 2004, for a review). Although there is much controversy concerning the validity of emotional intelligence as a goal of educational practice with children and adolescents (Waterhouse, 2006), the concept of emotional intelligence has been integrated in work on adult learning (MacKeracher, 2004). Academically succesful first-year college students have been demonstrated to have higher levels of emotional intellgence (Parker, Duffy, Wood, Bond, & Hogan, 2005; Parker, Summerfeldt, Hogan, & Majeski, 2004). Considering evidence that more recent cohorts of 18- to 30-year-olds entering the labor market are more likely than past cohorts to value emotional components of their careers and workplace environments (Ng & Burke, 2006; Smola & Sutton, 2002), the salience of emotional intelligence may become a more important determinant of succesful employee-employer match associated with productvity and retention.

Personality Development

Just as cognitive changes are believed to underlie the emergence of abstract thinking and identity exploration characteristic of adolescence, brain maturation associated with increased ability to organize and prioritize can be linked to identity consolidation during emerging adulthood. Once considered a key feature of adolescence proper, Arnett's theory of emerging adulthood (2004) highlights the centrality of achieving identity in emerging adulthood. Cognitive development and maturation of cognitive systems are closely linked to transformations in identity, as well as the actual life experiences that provide opportunities for emerging adults to try out and to choose relevant identities.

Research indicates that the events experienced during emerging adulthood are integrated into individuals' identities and memories more so than those experienced during other age periods (Elnick et al., 1999; Grob et al., 2001; Schuman & Scott, 1989). One explanation for this set of findings is that emerging adulthood is a critical period for the integration of information about one's inner-self as well as one's sociopolitical context. In turn, the shaping of one's identity around salient experiences of the age period has implications for the lens that an individual will use to interpret self-in-society across adulthood.

During emerging adulthood, explorations of multiple roles and relationships gives way to harmonizing one's sense of self. Blos (1962), describing personality development of the postadolescent (between adolescence and adulthood), denoted two stages of identity development, exploration of identity during adolescence and consolidation of identity postadolescence, and noted the following:

> This integration comes about gradually. It usually occurs either preparatory to or coincidentally with occupational choice—provided that circumstances allow the individual any choice at all. The integration goes hand in hand with the activation of social role, with courtship, marriage, and parenthood. The appearance or the manifest role of the young adult—having a job, preparing for a career, being married, or having a child—easily blurs the incompleteness of personality formation. (p. 149)

In sum, adulthood is achieved as a function of consolidation of identity around commitments to careers and families.

Emerging adulthood is a period during which stability of the self is a goal. Empirically, personality traits demonstrate moderate rank-order stability from ages 18 to 26 (Roberts, Caspi, & Moffitt, 2001; Robins, Fraley, Roberts, & Trzesniewski, 2001); however, these years are marked by lower rank-order stability than in adolescence or later adulthood (Roberts, Walton, & Viechtbauer, 2006). Roberts et al. (2006) found that social dominance, conscientiousness, and emotional stability increased and social vitality decreased during this age period compared to changes during later adulthood. Reviewing studies of personality change across the life course, Caspi (1998) concluded that "from late adolescence through early adulthood, most people become less emotionally labile, more responsible, and more cautious" (p. 347). As an exception, Caspi notes that personality change after these years is often associated with specific life events such as the transition to parenthood.

Loevinger's model of ego development (1976) has been used to frame empirical investigations of personality maturation through nine sequential stages, each of which represents a progressively more complex way of perceiving oneself in relation to the world. Ego development is primarily concerned with "impulses and methods for controlling impulses, personal preoccupations and ambitions, interpersonal attitudes and social values" (Blasi, 1998, p. 15). Maturation of ego development increases with age, approximately half a stage per year, but growth slows in emerging adulthood, plateauing at the median stage, self-aware (Cohn, 1998; Westenberg & Gjerde, 1999). The self-aware person sees alternatives, but still in stereotypic categories like age, sex, marital status, and race, rather than in terms of individual differences in traits and needs. Roberts, Caspi, & Moffitt (2001) found that from ages 18 to 26, male and female emerging adults demonstrate increases in self-constraint, moving away from impulsive behavior to greater self-control, demonstrating more reflective, deliberate, and planful behavior. Lasser and Snarey's (1989) interviews with high school students transitioning to college revealed that at the lowest level (pre-conformist) young women report a lack of confidence in their abilities to function independent of their parents, and that at middle stages of ego development (including the self-aware stage), young women are conflicted over their budding independence and ability to maintain attachments with parents. In contrast, at the highest levels of ego development (post-conformist) young women simultaneously express eagerness to gain independence without conflict regarding maintenance of attachment with families-of-origin.

Research on trajectories of ego development across adolescence (ages 14 to 17) indicates that emerging adults (at age 25) who attain or maintain higher levels of ego development report more complex sharing of experiences, more collaborative conflict-resolution strategies, and greater interpersonal understanding; and their young adult peers rate them as less hostile and more flexible (Henninghausen, Hauser, Billings, Shultz, & Allen, 2004). Level of ego development in early emerging adulthood has implications for gains associated with adult self-sufficiency and identity development. For example, Schultz and Selman (1998) found that at age 23, emerging adults with higher levels of ego development have better skills negotiating intimacy and autonomy in close interpersonal relationships compared to those at lower levels (Schultz & Selman, 1998). Similarly, emerging adults classified as higher in ego development at age 21, assessed later at age 52, scored higher in tolerance, achievement via independence, responsibility, and psychological mindedness than those at lower levels of ego development (i.e., self-aware and lower; Helson & Roberts, 1994).

Sense-of-control and mastery over one's environment increases across emerging adulthood (Lewis, Ross, & Mirowsky, 1999). Roberts, Caspi, and Moffitt (2001) also found increases in agentic traits, achievement and social potency which represent pleasure derived from meeting environmental challenges (e.g., establishing a career). Parent education, more than income, is associated with emerging adults' overall sense of control and increases in agency in emerging adulthood (Lewis et al., 1999). Collectively, these studies conclude that increases in mastery result from engagement in roles that, in turn, promote independence—either geographical or financial. Schwartz, Côté, and Arnett

(2005) also found that agency is related to individualization, exploration, and flexible commitment.

Therefore, emerging adulthood is a period of personality development showing plasticity, as demonstrated by empirical studies of change during the age period. The flexibility of personality during emerging adulthood suggests a window of opportunity for shaping personality in the sense that identity remains open and ego development remains amenable. Implications for programs of learning and development during emerging adulthood include the need to consider the process of identity development during these years and understanding the potential for learning experiences to shape individual development beyond this life stage. Moreover, programs designed to encourage learning and development during this age period have the potential to capitalize on this underlying developmental process by using methods that link identity processes with program goals.

Mental Health Problems

A wide-range of mental health problems may interfere with development and learning during emerging adulthood. Serious psychiatric disorder plays a significant role in a large minority of emerging adults' lives. Epidemiologic data indicate that emerging adulthood is a high-risk period for psychiatric disorder. Twelve-month prevalence of psychiatric disorder has been estimated at 25% for 18- 29-year-olds (Robins & Regier, 1991) and 37% for 15- to 24-year-olds (Kessler et al., 1994) in large-scale population studies—higher than in older adult age groups. Lifetime prevalence of any psychiatric disorder has recently been estimated at 52.4% for emerging adults (18–29) and 55.0% for individuals in their thirties and forties, compared to 46.5% for middle-aged (45- to 59-year-olds) and 26.1% for older adults (greater than age 60; Kessler, Berglund, Demler, Jin, & Walters, 2005). In a community sample followed from childhood, lifetime rates of psychiatric disorder increased from ages 21 to 30 (Tanner, Reinherz, Beardslee, Fitzmaurice, Leis, & Berger, 2007). Tracing 12-month prevalence of specific disorders in the same community sample demonstrated decreases in 12-month prevalence of alcohol and drug use disorders, as well as phobias. No significant change in prevalence of major depression or posttraumatic stress disorder was observed.

There is ample evidence to suggest that serious psychopathology affects emerging adults not only via active disorder, but also as a function of past disorder. By age 24, 75% of those who will ever meet criteria for psychiatric disorder will have experienced onset (Kessler et al., 2005), and approximately 75% of emerging adults meeting criteria for a psychiatric disorder have a developmental history (Kim-Cohen, Caspi, Moffitt, Harrington, Milne, & Poulton, 2003; Newman, Moffitt, Caspi, Magdol, Silva, & Stanton, 1996). Psychiatric disorder occurring prior to emerging adulthood has been associated with impaired functioning during these years across a variety of domains (Fergusson & Woodward, 2002; Paradis, Reinherz, Giaconia, & Fitzmaurice, 2006; Reinherz, Giaconia, Carmola Hauf, Wasserman, & Silverman, 1999; Wittchen, Nelson, & Lachner, 1998). Both active and past psychiatric disorder experienced during emerging adulthood is also related to poorer functioning in interpersonal and socioeconomic domains in young adulthood (Tanner et al., 2007).

Classic studies of general mental health of Americans from the mid-1950s through the mid-1970s indicate that the mental health of emerging adults may be significantly different from older adults. Individuals aged 20 and 29 reported higher levels of worries, lower satisfaction with life, were most likely to report having a problem that requires professional help, and reported the highest frequency of being overwhelmed compared to middle-age and older adults. Interestingly, they also reported the highest level of happiness with their current life stage and optimism, or "future morale" (Veroff, Douvan, & Kulka, 1981). Sources of happiness derived from marriage, interpersonal relationships (for men), and jobs were higher among 20–29 year olds compared to older adults. However, sources of unhappiness and worries from marriage and jobs, as well as economic and material issues and personal characteristics were also higher in emerging compared to older adults. These mid-century results foreshadow Arnett's research concluding that the emerging adult years represent an age period of simultaneous excitement and optimism, as well as reactive stress.

Developmental studies that rely on measures of mental health problems other than those used by the medical establishment (i.e., psychiatrists) to assess mental health problems suggest that mental health problems subside, on average, from adolescence to emerging adulthood. Schulenberg and colleagues reported aggregate-level increases in perceived social support, satisfaction with life, self-efficacy, and self-esteem, and significant decreases in loneliness, fatalism, self-derogation, and substance use from ages 18 to 21/22 (Schulenberg, O'Malley, Bachman, & Johnston, 2000). Galambos, Barker, and Krahn (2006) found evidence of intraindividual increase in self-esteem and decrease in anger and depressive symptoms from ages 18 to 25. It has been determined that both incidence (Newman et al., 1996) and 12-month prevalence of psychiatric disorder (Tanner et al., 2007) decrease from 21 to 30. Masten and colleagues found that resilience in the face of childhood and adolescent diversity was maintained in emerging adulthood despite the developmental challenges, and also reported that the age period revealed new cases of resilience (Masten, Burt, Roisman, Obradovic, Long, & Tellegen, 2004; Masten, Obradovic, & Burt, 2006).

Comparing emerging adulthood to later stages of development, on the other hand, indicates that mental health problems are higher in emerging adults than older adults. Mirowsky and Ross (1999) found that rates of depression were higher in the twenties compared to all older age groups, except those in their eighties. Roberts, Caspi, and Moffitt (2001) found a decrease in negative emotionality across the twenties, specifically in regard to feelings of alienation and aggression, but Charles, Reynolds, and Gatz (2001) reported that negative affect is highest in the twenties compared to the later adult years. Prospective studies have also revealed that individuals are less depressed and more mentally healthy at 70 than in early adulthood (Vaillant, 2002). Latent growth models reflecting change in psychological health from ages 14 to 62 indicate stability through age 30 followed by steady increase (Jones & Meredith, 2000).

Grouping individuals based on their mental health problems in adolescence and following them into emerging adulthood indicates that some adolescents afflicted by serious psychopathology are likely to experience persistence into emerging adulthood, but those with low levels of mental health problems are unlikely to experience mental health problems in emerging adulthood. Hofstra and colleagues (Hofstra, van der Ende, & Verhulst, 2001) found that approximately 1 in 5 adolescents (22.3%) with "high" mental health problems remained in the high group 10 years later in emerging adulthood. This finding corresponds with findings from a national epidemiologic study estimating that serious psychopathology is concentrated in a small percentage (22.3%) of the adult U.S. population (Kessler, Chiu, Demler, & Walters, 2005). In contrast, nearly 70% of those "low" in mental health problems in adolescence were classified as low in emerging adulthood (Hofstra, van der Ende, & Verhulst, 2001) and very few reported high problems in emerging adulthood. They found stronger downward compared to upward re-classification. In emerging adulthood, 56.5% of the high group in adolescence had moved into the "moderate" category, and 21.2% were classified in the low group. From the low group, only 27.5% were rated moderate in emerging adulthood and only 3.1% were considered high in mental health problems.

While studies of college students are not necessarily representative of the emerging adult population, they provide some insight into mental health issues of a salient sub-population which may or may not indicate population trends. In recent decades, studies of college student mental health reveal that problems may be increasing, particularly problems tied to developmental issues. Benton, Robertson, Tseng, Newton, and Benton (2003) studied changes in therapist reports of student-client problems across three time periods spanning 13 years (period 1: 1988 to 1992; period 2: 1992 to 1996; period 3: 1996 to 2001). Higher problems in more recent cohorts were found in 13 of 19 problem domains (i.e., developmental, situational, medication use, depression, academic skills, grief, relationships, stress/anxiety, family issues, physical problems, personality disorders, suicidal thoughts, sexual assault). There were no significant changes in manifestations of serious psychopathology: eating disorders, substance abuse, chronic mental health problems, and legal problems. Moreover, the authors report that relationship problems was the most commonly endorsed domain of mental health problems associated with seeking counseling service help, but stress/anxiety emerged as the most commonly reported problem in 1994 and remained the most prevalent through 2001. They concluded with the observation that there is an increase in sub-clinical levels of mental health problems reflecting adjustment difficulties in contrast to increasing serious psychiatric disorder.

Considering that both past and current psychiatric problems undermine educational and occupational adjustment, as well as global functioning in emerging adulthood (Paradis et al., 2006; Tanner et al., 2007), educational and training programs should consider the role that mental health plays in successfully meeting program goals. Integrating mental health resources into programs designed to facilitate development and learning with emerging adults are likely to improve program results.

Physical Health

Compared to mental health problems, rates of serious physical disorders (e.g., cancer, heart disease) are low during emerging adulthood. In 2003, the most recent year for which data are available, only 4% of 18- to 24-year-olds self-reported fair or poor health compared to 6% of 24- to 44-year-olds, 12% of 45- to 54-year-olds, and 19% of 55- to 64-year-olds (National Center for Health Statistics, 2005). Predictors of serious physical illness, however, such as obesity and tobacco use, are frequently—and increasingly—observed among emerging adults. Negative health behaviors practiced during this part of the life span may provide the foundation for health problems in later adulthood (Merluzzi & Nairn, 1999).

In the last decade, as rates of overweight and obesity in Americans have risen, obesity has become one of the most significant health problems for emerging adults, as well as perhaps the greatest predictor of health problems in later adulthood. While emerging adults may have lower rates of overweight and obesity than older adults, approximately three-quarters of emerging adults are overweight or obese (National Center for Health Statistics, 2005), which carries serious implications. For example, being mildly or moderately overweight at ages 20–22 is a significant predictor of obesity by ages 35–37 (McTigue, Garrett, & Popkin, 2002) and being seriously overweight or obese elevates the risk of heart disease, diabetes, high cholesterol, hypertension, and some types of cancer (National Center for Health Statistics, 2005).

The high rates of overweight and obesity seen among emerging adults may be due, in part, to a lack of physical activity. Research has demonstrated a significant decrease in physical activity during the transition from adolescence to young adulthood (Gordon-Larsen, Nelson, & Popkin, 2004), which in turn is independently associated with obesity in young adulthood (Tammelin, Laitinen, & Näyhä, 2004). Furthermore, findings from a population-based, longitudinal cohort study show an inverse relationship between fitness in emerging adulthood and risk factors for cardiovascular disease such as hypertension and diabetes in middle age, even after controlling for body mass index (Carnethon, Gidding, Nehgme, Sidney, Jacobs, & Liu 2003).

Tobacco use is another negative health behavior with serious consequences for emerging adults. Although cigarette smoking is on the decline, approximately one-quarter of American emerging adults still use tobacco. In 2003, approximately 25% of all males and 22% of all females ages 18–24 reported currently smoking cigarettes, contributing to increased risk of heart disease, stroke, lung and other types of cancer, and chronic lung diseases such as emphysema (National Center for Health Statistics, 2005).

Low rates of physical disease during this age period complement the 98% survival likelihood between ages 15 and 34 (Anderson, Kochanek, & Murphy, 1997). However, statistics highlighting health and low rates of mortality and morbidity obscure unique causes of mortality that account for 70% of the deaths in this age group compared to only 8% in the overall population. These are motor vehicle accidents, homicide, HIV infection and suicide, all significantly contributing to the social costs of injury and violence (U.S. Department of Health and Human Services, 2000). Among 26 countries representing Asia, Europe, North America, Latin America, and Oceania, U.S. mortality statistics for each cause of death are outliers across all industrialized nations (Heuveline, 2002). The impulsive and risk-taking behaviors and incomplete brain development of emerging adults have both been implicated as risk factors associated with the high rate of preventable death in this age group.

In general, emerging adulthood is characterized by greater physical health than other stages of the life span. However, emerging adults are not invulnerable to poor health or the precursors of serious physical illness. As more risk factors for common adulthood diseases are discovered, these and behaviors that are often accompanied by negative implications for physical health (i.e., tobacco and alcohol use) will need to be targeted in emerging adults.

Family Relationships

The instability and identity explorations experienced by emerging adults co-occur with changes in family relationships. Most significant is a restructuring of the parent–child relationship. From adolescence to young adulthood, the parent–child relationship evolves from a pattern of child dependence on parents to a relationship between two adults characterized by equality (Aquilino, 2006). This change in the parent–child relationship is recognized by emerging adults as one of the most important markers in becoming an adult (Arnett, 1998).

When and how the restructuring of the parent-child relationship occurs is predicted in a large part by where emerging adults live. Emerging adults leaving home to live independently signals parents that their child is becoming an adult and often leads to reduced conflict and power issues in the relationship (Aquilino, 1997). Aquilino (2006) recently demonstrated that emerging adults living at or close to home have poorer relationships with their parents than emerging adults living farther away (Aquilino, 2006). Closeness with parents may decrease when a grown child leaves home due to reduced time together, geographic distance, and competing demands in emerging adults' lives. Closeness tends to increase again toward the end of emerging of adulthood, as the emerging adult assumes adult roles such as cohabitation, marriage, and labor force entry. Taking on these adult roles is associated with more supportive and less conflicted parent-child relations (Aquilino, 1997, 2006), perhaps because parents are able to see their children in roles that they themselves have been in for an extended period of time.

As emerging adults move out of their parents' home and establish independence from their parents, they may be living apart from their siblings for the first time in their lives, thus altering the sibling relationship as well. In general, research has shown that sibling closeness and interaction decrease in emerging and young adulthood (Cicirelli, 1994). Decreases in proximity and contact are not necessarily associated with decreased relationship quality, however. Research comparing sibling relationships in emerging adulthood with those in adolescence found that emerging adults spend less time and are less involved in joint activities with their siblings than adolescents, but are more involved in emotional exchanges and feel more warmth toward their siblings than adolescents (Scharf, Shulman, & Avigad-Spitz, 2005). In addition, emerging adults have a more mature perspective on their sibling relationships than adolescents. Emerging adults are better able than their adolescent counterparts to understand and respect their siblings' needs, which may play a role in the finding that emerging adults report less intense sibling conflict and rivalry than adolescents (Scharf, Shulman, & Avigad-Spitz, 2005). Furthermore, conflict in emerging adult sibling interactions is not associated with closeness, suggesting that a close sibling relationship in emerging adulthood is not necessarily dependent on the absence of conflict or negative affect in the way that sibling relationships in adolescence often are (Shortt & Gottman, 1997).

Family support during emerging adulthood often comes in the form of material and financial support through residence in the parental household, paying for college, financial subsidies that allow the emerging adult to live independently, or health insurance coverage (Aquilino, 2006). In addition, parents often help support their children as they establish independent households and have their own children (Schoeni & Ross, 2005). A study designed to quantify how much financial assistance and time (e.g., child care, errands, etc.) youth actually receive from their families demonstrated that American emerging adults receive a significant amount of support from their families. Forty-eight percent of 18- to 26-year-olds living independently receive financial help from their parents averaging $2,032 annually (US$, 2001) and 54% of the same demographic receive an average of 488 hours or 12 weeks of full-time, 40 hours per week, support in time per year. Emerging adults living with their parents receive even more assistance. On average, 18- 26-year-olds living at home (college and non-college) receive $4,827 (US$, 2001) in financial help per year (Schoeni & Ross, 2005).

Differences in resources provided by families is one source of heterogeneity predicting pathways to self-sufficiency. Families tend to provide greater resources to emerging adults in their first few years of emerging adulthood compared to the later years. Emerging adults aged 18 to 20 receive, on average, $3,499 a year; those aged 25–26 receive, on average, $2,323 a year (Schoeni & Ross, 2005). Emerging adults from low-income families receive less financial support than those from high-income families, but equal amounts of time from parents. Cross-national and economic trends influence intergenerational transfers (Lee, Lee, & Mason, 2006; Mason, Lee, Tung, Lai, & Miller,

2006). Emerging adults from families with lower socioeconomic status (SES) moved into financial independence earlier, but accelerated more slowly than emerging adults from higher SES families. Female emerging adults from low SES families moved into relationships and parenting more quickly than female emerging adults from higher SES families; males from lower SES families also moved into the parenting role more quickly than their higher SES peers (Cohen et al., 2003). These differences did not disappear when education was considered in the associations. In addition to family income (Avery, Goldscheider, & Speare, 1992), family dynamics such as parental divorce (Aquilino, 2005; Wolfinger, 2003) and high conflict marriages (Amato & Afifi, 2006) influence variation in parental economic support of emerging adult children and home-leaving patterns.

Family relationships, particularly between parents and the emerging adult child, and support received from family members have important implications for successful outcomes in adulthood. The developmental tasks of the emerging adult period present as a challenge to some, making family support during this transition crucial. Research drawing upon a college sample found that both maternal and paternal support predict emerging adult psychological adjustment (Holahan, Valentiner, & Moos, 1994) and support from siblings has been shown to play a role in psychological adjustment as well. High levels of sibling social support are associated with lower levels of loneliness and depression and higher levels of self-esteem and life satisfaction (Milevsky, 2005).

Friendships

Development of intimate relationships and friendships are believed to be an important task of the emerging adult period, particularly because they are considered a resource that help youth master other developmental tasks (Crosnoe, 2000). For example, competence in friendships in emerging adulthood has been shown to be predictive of competence not only in friendships, but also in the areas of work and romantic relationships, in young adulthood (Roisman, Masten, Coatsworth, & Tellegen, 2004). In addition, friendships have significant consequences for emerging adult psychological adjustment and well-being (Bagwell et al., 2005).

Emerging adult friendships appear similar to those of adolescents. Number of friends remains fairly constant during this period and although the amount of time spent with friends is greatest during adolescence, it stays relatively high during emerging adulthood (Hartup & Stevens, 1999). In addition, studies of emerging adult friendships demonstrate that factors characteristic of adolescent friendships such as loyalty, warmth, and sharing of personal experiences remain important (Samter, 2003).

Gender differences present in adolescent friendships also appear to persist into emerging adulthood. Similar to male adolescents, male emerging adults report that time with friends revolves around active pursuits, while female emerging adults report that the majority of their time with friends involves talking (Samter, 2003). Furthermore, emerging adult males report the conversations they have with their same-sex friends center on sports, work, and cars (Caldwell & Peplau, 1982) while emerging adult females are more likely to talk to their friends about themselves, their problems, and their close relationships (Johnson & Aries, 1983). Likewise, research has demonstrated that emerging adult women provide and receive higher levels of support from their friends than men (Fischer, Sollie, Sorell, & Green, 1989). Conversations with close friends in emerging adulthood can be critical in helping to explore and identify a sense of self (Johnson & Aries, 1983).

Friendships may be the most important type of emerging adult relationships. In one of the earliest studies of close relationships across the life span, Shulman (1975), found that when asked to describe the people who composed their personal network, emerging adults (ages 18–30) were significantly more likely not to name any family members (41%) than were young adults (ages 31–44; 34%) and older adults (over age 45; 23%). In addition, emerging adults report that their relationships with their friends are closer, more important, more reciprocal, and characterized by greater positive feelings than their relationships with their siblings (Pulakos, 2001). These findings may be due to the independence emerging adults seek to establish from their families (Pulaskos, 2001).

Indeed, friendships in emerging adulthood are largely predicated on the many transitions that occur during this period of the life span. Role changes associated with career entry appear to be related to a partial withdrawal from friends during emerging adulthood (Fischer, Sollie, Sorell, & Green, 1989). In one study, single emerging adults reported that friends were their most preferred companions or confidants whereas married emerging adults reported that their spouse was the most preferred to fill these roles (Carbery & Buhrmester, 1998). Overall, friendships may reach their peak of functional significance during emerging adulthood, when friends are most likely to fill the role of companion and confidant and are a primary source of social support (Carbery & Buhrmester, 1998).

Considering the salience of friendships during emerging adulthood, it is logical that the quality of emerging adults' relationships with their best friend is related to their adjustment and well-being. Recent research drawing upon an undergraduate sample demonstrated that emerging adults whose friendships are characterized by high levels of conflict and antagonism are more likely to report higher levels of overall symptoms and higher levels of symptoms of hostility and anxiety while emerging adults whose friendships are characterized by greater social support report having higher levels of self-esteem and lower levels of depression symptoms (Bagwell et al., 2005). Similarly, Berry and colleagues (2000) found that ratings of positive and negative affectivity significantly and independently predict the extent to which emerging adults feel close to and are irritated by their friends, respectively, and that emerging adults with high levels of neuroticism have friendships characterized by higher levels of conflict than emerging adults with high levels of agreeableness (Berry, Willingham, & Thayer, 2000).

Intimate Relationships

The transition from adolescence to adulthood is the period of the life span when individuals typically form enduring romantic relationships (Arnett, 2000) and strive to complete intimacy tasks (Erikson, 1982). The small but growing body of research on intimate relationships in emerging adulthood provides evidence that romantic beliefs and behaviors, rates of partnership, and relationship duration and quality differ between emerging adults and adolescents and older adults. While first kisses, first dates, falling in love and sexual intercourse typically occur during adolescence, first serious relationships do not occur until emerging adulthood (Regan, Durvasula, Howell, Ureño, & Rea, 2004). Participants in one longitudinal study were more likely to report having a romantic partner in emerging adulthood (65%) than they were in middle (43%) or late (47%) adolescence, and their emerging adult relationships continued for longer (21.3 months) than their relationships in adolescence (5.1 and 11.8 months for middle and late adolescence, respectively; Seiffge-Krenke, 2003). The frequency of opposite-sex socializing then levels off in young adulthood (Reis, Lin, Bennett, & Nezlek, 1993).

Romantic beliefs and perceptions also vary by stage of the life span. Compared to adolescents, emerging adults are less likely to endorse the romantic belief of idealization (love will be nearly perfect) but do not differ in beliefs of a one and only love partner (there is only one person for each of us) and in love at first sight (Montgomery, 2005). However, emerging adults express higher levels of passionate feelings and intimacy than adolescents (Montgomery, 2005) and perceive their romantic partners as providing more social support in emerging adulthood than in late adolescence (Seiffge-Krenke, 2003). In a study of romantic love across the life course, Montgomery and Sorell (1994) found that unmarried emerging adults' attitudes toward their relationships are more likely to be characterized by possessiveness and dependency and are less likely to be characterized by an altruistic, selfless love than young and middle-aged married adults. In addition, emerging adults report less relationship satisfaction than older adults. Emerging adults' attitudes do not differ from older adults, however, in terms of physical and emotional attraction or the friendship aspects of love.

Predictors of romantic relationships and intimacy in emerging adulthood include both individual characteristics as well as aspects of an individual's family-of-origin. Parenting (Donnellan, Larsen-Rife, & Conger, 2005), family cohesion, mother's marital satisfaction (Feldman, Gowen, & Fisher, 1998), family aversive relationship communication (Andrews, Foster, Capaldi, & Hops, 2000), parent divorce (Shulman, Scharf, Lumer, & Maurer, 2001), and family adaptability (Robinson, 2000) have all been shown to be related to romantic relationships in emerging adulthood. Individual characteristics including self negative-emotionality (Donnellan, Larsen-Rife, & Conger, 2005), antisocial behavior (Andrews, Foster, Capaldi & Hops, 2000), and attachment style (Koski & Shaver, 1997) have also been shown to be associated with emerging adult intimate relationships. In addition, a positive relationship exists between support from one's family and friends and feelings of love, satisfaction, and commitment for both male and female emerging adults (Surra, 1990). Furthermore, social support significantly predicts relationship quality up to a year and a half later, and for females, as support from families and friends increases, relationship stability increases (Sprecher & Felmlee, 1992).

A significant proportion of emerging adult romantic relationships involve cohabitation. In 2003, 15.1% of 20- to 24-year-old males and 20.9% of 20- to 24-year-old females reported living with an unmarried partner (U.S. Census Bureau, 2003). Cohabitation among emerging adults, although receiving increased attention in recent years, is certainly not a new phenomenon. An article published in 1975 reported that cohabitation was the fastest growing life style among 18–24 year olds. Compared with 1960, 50 times as many men and 16 times as many women aged 18–24 reported living with an unmarried partner in 1970 (Lincoln, 1975). An exploratory study of the timing and decision to enter into a cohabitating union showed that emerging adults' decisions to cohabit are based on finances, convenience, their housing situations, because they simply wanted to, and in response to parents/family. Surprisingly, living with a partner as a trial or way to determine compatibility for marriage was the least frequently cited reason for deciding to cohabit (Sassler, 2004). However, cohabitation often leads to marriage. In a cohort born in 1961 in which one-third of the participants experienced cohabitation without marriage by age 23, 50% of the female participants and two-thirds of the male participants who entered into a marital union cohabited prior to doing so (Thornton, 1988).

Based on the 2001 Census, 49% of men and 63% of women who will ever marry, do so by age 29 (Kreider, 2005). Men, on average marry a woman 2 years younger (Martinez, Chandra, Abma, Jones, & Mosher, 2006). Divorce rates for men are estimated at 1% for men between the ages of 20 and 24, and 7.5% between the ages of 25 and 29. For women, respective estimates are higher at 2.6% and 11.9%. For those between the ages of 25 and

29, 15% of the ever-married men and 18.9% of the ever-married women have experienced a divorce (Kreider, 2005).

Sex, fertility, and childbearing play an important role in emerging adults' intimate relationships and partnering. By age 20, 75% of American youth have had premarital sex, by age 30 the figure reaches 90% (Finer, 2007). Despite the commonness of sexual behavior during this age period, there are few studies or reviews of sexual experience and development in emerging adulthood (see, for exception, Lefkowitz & Gillen, 2006). There is some information on sexual identity development among heterosexual (Hoffman, 2004), homosexual, and bisexual (Rosario, Schrimshaw, Hunter, & Braun, 2006) populations that provide a general framework for considering the role of sexuality in emerging adults' lives. However, this topic represents an understudied and underexplored component of emerging adult experience and development.

Rates of pregnancy, abortion, and childbearing provide information concerning the number of emerging adults who experience these events. Approximately 1 in 6 emerging adults experience pregnancy in a given year; women aged 20–24 have the highest pregnancy rate followed by women aged 25–29 (1999; Ventura, Abma, Mosher, & Henshaw, 2003). In 2001, 60% of all pregnancies of 20- to 24-year-old emerging adult women were unintended, 43% among those aged 25 to 29 (Finer & Henshaw, 2006). The unintended pregnancy ratio is highest for women in emerging adulthood, ages 20 to 24, and the unintended pregnancy rate rose between 1994 and 2001 for the 25- to 29-year-old age group (Finer & Henshaw, 2006). Representing 33% of abortions performed between 2000–2001, over one-quarter of a million emerging adult women aged 20 to 24 had an abortion. The second highest percentage by age group was for 25- to 29-year-olds, 23.1% (Jones, Darroch, & Henshaw, 2002; Strauss, Herndon, Chang, Parker, Bowens, & Berg, 2005). In a longitudinal study of adolescent and emerging adult development, Fergusson and colleagues reported that 41% of emerging adult women had become pregnant by age 25 and 14.6% of them reported having an abortion (Fergusson, Horwood, & Ridder, 2006).

Women aged 25 to 29 years had the highest U.S. birth rate of 115.5 per 1,000 births in 2004 (Hamilton, Ventura, Martin, & Sutton, 2005). Of those emerging adults who marry between ages 20 and 22, 82% have a first birth within 4 years; 70% of those who marry at age 23 or older have a first birth within 4 years (Abma, Chandra, Mosher, Peterson, & Piccinio, 1997). Among unmarried mothers, in 2004, childbearing reached a record high of almost 1.5 million births. Over one-half of births to women in their early twenties and nearly 3 in 10 births to women aged 25–29 years were to unmarried women. The birth rate among unmarried women of all ages increased 3%t from 2003 to 2004. In 2004, 35.7% of all births were to unmarried women (Hamilton, Ventura, Martin, & Sutton, 2005).

The relationship between education and learning and partnering and parenting in emerging adulthood is complex. However, attempts to facilitate trajectories of educational attainment, training completions, and successful school-to-work transitions must heed empirical evidence that demonstrates the co-mingling of education, careers, relationships and childbearing during emerging adulthood (Deil-Amen & Turley, 2007; Hynes & Clarkberg, 2005; Teachman & Polonko, 1988).

Media and Leisure

Although the topic of leisure and free-time activity has received the attention of researchers since the 1970s, the majority of work in this area is cross-sectional in design and has focused mainly on children and adolescents or older adults, leaving many questions regarding age differences and changes in leisure activity across the life span unanswered. In general, it appears as if the most significant changes in leisure time occur at major transitional phases in one's life (Raymore, Barber, & Eccles, 2001). Accordingly, in emerging adulthood, a period characterized by multiple transitions, time devoted to leisure use differs from adolescence or later adulthood.

Research examining the role that life transitions play in leisure pattern stability during the transition to adulthood provides support for this claim. Raymore, Barber, and Eccles (2001) demonstrated that for female emerging adults, going to college and or leaving home is associated with stability of leisure patterns while becoming a partner and/or a parent is associated with change in time devoted to leisure. For males, only leaving home is associated with leisure activity in emerging adulthood: this transition is predictive of leisure pattern stability.

Similar findings were demonstrated by Gauthier and Furstenberg (2002) in a study of patterns of time use during the transition to adulthood in nine industrialized countries. The amount of time emerging and young adults (ages 18–34) spend on leisure activities (on average 5.5 hours per day) was impacted by the transition from school to work, from being single to being partnered, and the transition to parenthood. Single, employed emerging and young adults devote less time to leisure activities than their student counterparts (a decrease of 0.6 hours per day), and transitioning from being single to being partnered is associated with a decrease of 0.5 hours per day in time spent on leisure activities for both males and females. The transition to parenthood has the largest effect on leisure: there is a decrease of 0.7 hours per day in time spent on leisure activities among emerging and young adult parents (Gauthier & Furstenberg, 2002).

So, what are emerging adults doing with their leisure time? According to the Bureau of Labor Statistics, in 2005 Americans ages 15–24 spent, per week, 0.54 hours participating in sports and exercise, 1.14 hours socializing and communicating, 2.42 hours watching television, 0.15 hours reading, 0.20 hours relaxing/thinking, 0.64 hours playing games on and using the computer for leisure, and 0.84 hours on other leisure activities, including travel, for a total of 5.55 hours of leisure per week. The only age group who devoted more time to leisure pursuits was Americans ages 65 and older. Although watching TV may be what occupies the majority of leisure time for many emerging adults, a recent Gallup poll (Carroll, 2006) indicates that watching television is not necessarily their preferred activity. When asked to name their favorite way to spend an evening, 41% of 18- to 29-year-olds said their ideal evening involves spending time with family, 14% said watching television, 10% mentioned visiting friends, and 8% reported reading was their favorite way to spend the evening.

It is important that research on leisure activities be expanded upon as emerging adults' leisure behaviors are associated with both psychological (Cassidy, 2005; Haworth & Hill, 1992) and physical health (Gordon-Larsen, Nelson, & Popkin, 2004) and may prove important for adult cognition and learning.

Ethnic and Cultural Issues

Emerging adulthood is culturally bound, existing predominantly "in contemporary industrialized cultures that extend the transition to adulthood until the mid to late twenties" (Arnett, 1998). There appears to be a period between adolescence and adulthood in many cultures, but this stage varies from culture to culture and within minority cultures in America.

Research on emerging adulthood in countries other than America is scarce but demonstrates that the phenomenon does indeed exist in various forms. For example, there is support for emerging adulthood as a distinct developmental period in China, but it is less individualistic than it is in the United States (Nelson, Badger, & Wu, 2004). In a study by Nelson and colleagues, when asked what criteria signified reaching adulthood, Chinese college students most frequently endorsed "accept responsibility for the consequences of your actions," "learn to have good control of your emotions," and "become financially independent from your parents." American emerging adults frequently select the first and last criteria as well (see Figure 2.2). Other responses clearly reflected the collectivistic values and greater importance of obligations toward others characteristic of Chinese culture (Badger, Nelson, & Barry, 2006). Almost all of the students surveyed (89%) endorsed "become capable of supporting parents financially" and "become less self-oriented and develop greater concern for others" (93%) as necessary criteria for attaining adult status (Nelson et al., 2004).

In Argentina, a country that belongs to the Western, Christian, urban, and industrialized cultural group, emerging adulthood exists as a period of the life course for Argentinians in their mid-twenties due to the postponement of marriage and parenthood and continuing education after graduating from high school that are common there (Facio & Micocci, 2003). Argentinians experience emerging adulthood similar to youth in the United States; a longitudinal study of young Argentinians demonstrated that emerging adults experience diverse employment situations and intimate relationships. However, living arrangements are typically more stable than those seen among emerging adults in America. The majority of emerging adults who are not married or cohabiting live with their parents or other relatives; only 12% reported living alone (Facio & Micocci, 2003).

Like emerging adulthood in countries outside of the United States, little is known about this age period among American minority cultures and ethnicities. The extant research suggests that young Americans experience emerging adulthood, regardless of

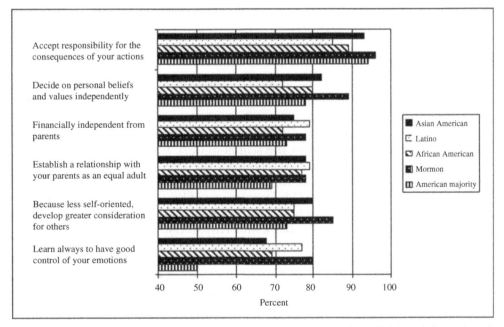

Figure 2.2 Percent indicating that a criterion is necessary for adulthood, by cultural or ethnic group (Arnett, 2003).

culture or ethnicity. However, emerging adults from minority groups, similar to those in other countries, endorse both individualistic and collectivist criteria as necessary requisites for adulthood. For example, results from a study of the transition to adulthood in four American ethnic groups (i.e., Caucasian Americans, African Americans, Latinos, and Asian Americans) indicates that at least 70% of emerging adults across all four groups view the same four criteria (see Figure 2.2) as necessary in order for a person to be considered an adult (Arnett, 2003). In contrast to Caucasian Americans, emerging adults in ethnic minority groups are more likely to favor criteria for adulthood that reflect obligations to others. Emerging adults in all three minority groups endorsed "become less self-oriented, develop a greater consideration for others," as one of the top five criteria associated with transition to adulthood.

Emerging adulthood is also a distinct developmental period in at least some religious minorities in the United States. Youth from the Church of Jesus Christ of Latter-day Saints (the Mormon Church), for example, experience a delay between adolescence and young adulthood, although it is shorter and more structured than emerging adulthood among the American majority (Nelson, 2003). Nelson (2003) has suggested several reasons for this variation. First, the rise in the age of marriage in the United States, a key factor that has contributed to the extended period between adolescence and young adulthood, did not occur among Mormons. Thus the median age of marriage among Mormons is lower than the age of marriage for the U.S. population as a whole, shortening this period of exploration. Second, there are several religious rites of passage that young Mormons experience during the emerging adult years that culminate with adult status in the eyes of the church and community. These rites of passage add structure to the experience of emerging adulthood and emphasize the collectivist perspective of the Mormon Church. Accordingly, the criteria for adulthood most frequently endorsed by young Mormons differ from the criteria of the majority of American emerging adults. Similar to emerging adults in minority ethnic groups in the United States and those in other countries, Mormons endorse both individualistic criteria as well as more collectivist criteria (see Figure 2.2).

Education, Careers, and Financial Independence

The diversity of emerging adult experiences is reflected in the many different pathways they take from formal education, into the world of work, toward financial self-sufficiency. The age at which an individual leaves secondary education, the age at which one enters the labor market, and the pattern of job-holding that follows the exit from formal education each account for variation in the school-to-work transition. In 2000, 86.5% of 18- to 24-year-olds had completed high school. Of the 13% of emerging adults who had not completed high school by age 24 (in 2000), some persisted in their pursuit of a high school diploma into their twenties (U.S. Department of Education, 2001). In more recent years, rates of leaving high school before earning a diploma have decreased; however, race and ethnic differences persist. Black and Hispanic youth are more likely to leave high school before earning a degree (Child Trends, 2007).

Rates of high school completion, graduation with associates and bachelor's degrees, as well as advanced professional degrees have each increased significantly during the past century. Due to increases in more recent years in the number of individuals who have completed both high school and college degrees, the proportion of emerging adults ages 25 to 29 with diplomas is equivalent to the proportion of all adults age 25 and older holding the same degree. Of all adults age 25 and older, in 2005, 85% had at least a high school diploma, 28% had earned a bachelor's degree. In 1985, these numbers, respectively, were 74% and 19% indicating an increase in the percentage of the adult population competing in the labor market with high school and bachelors degrees (Bureau of Labor Statistics, Educational Attainment in the United States, 2005).

Those who do not enroll in 4-year college programs after high school have been labeled the *forgotten half* (W. T. Grant Foundation, 1988), because they represent a vulnerable population, less likely to make transitions to stable, sustaining employment. Economic prospects of this high-risk group declined from the early to the late 1990s (W. T. Grant Foundation, 1998). Of the emerging adult population who leave high school before earning a degree, a significant proportion return to complete a GED, but only some succeed. Of the 53% of high school dropouts accounted for in the National Longitudinal Study of Youth (ages 14 to 22 in 1979; interviewed in 2002), 28% earned a high school (general equivalency) diploma and 14% earned at least some college education. The pathway taken by those who drop-out and go on to earn a GED widens the racial and ethnic gap. By age 35, 6% of whites, 10% of blacks, and 15% of Hispanics or Latinos had not completed high school; and greater than 30% of whites but only 12% of blacks and Hispanics or Latinos had earned college degrees (Yates, 2005).

While those who do not complete college may be more vulnerable on some economic measures, some have argued against the "college-for-all" policy, citing the need to focus broadly on connecting high school graduates to training and careers that match their interests (Rosenbaum, 2002; Rosenbaum & Person, 2003). One established method for connecting non-college-enrolled youth with training and career opportunities is via adult education programs and trainings. Overall, 44% of the U.S. population aged 16 and older participated in adult education 2004–2005; 53% of 16- to 24-year-olds were involved in some form of adult education, higher than any other age group (O'Donnell, 2006). Emerging adults were more likely than older persons to be involved in GED programs and part-time college programs, as well as personal interest courses, and were less likely to be involved in work related trainings (O'Donnell, 2006).

Disparities in educational attainment in emerging adulthood have implications for wages earned across the life span. Lifetime earnings (i.e., synthetic work-life earnings, 1999 US$) for individuals with a high school diploma are estimated at $1.2 million, almost double, $2.1 million for an individual with a bachelor's degree, and $4.4 for an individual with a professional degree (Day & Newburger, 2002). Earning trajectories indicate that for all degree categories except doctoral degrees, annual earnings for 25- to 29-year-olds is under $50,000. By ages 30–34 the earning trajectories of those with bachelor's degrees and higher accelerate past $50,000/year, continuing to increase through the mid-sixties. The earning trajectories of those with associate's degrees and less education do not rise above $50,000/year, representing a relatively flat trajectory (Day & Newburger, 2002). Despite the variation by race, ethnicity, and sex in rates of high school and college completion, earnings differentials between high school and college completers is the same across groups (Perna, 2003).

Higher educational attainment has been linked to establishing career stability and predicts differences in life-span earnings. By age 30, 36.8% of those without a high school diploma had not held an employment relationship for 2 or more years. This was true for only 17.9% of those with a bachelor's degree or higher, despite the former group having a greater number of years of potential employment (calculated from Table 3 of Yates, 2005). The median high school dropout took more than 3 years to start a job that would last a full year, and nearly 11 years before they started a job that would last 3 years. Because less than 50% of the high school dropout sample had yet to hold a job for 5 years at age 35, we cannot determine the median number of years. In comparison, the median high school graduate took 6 years to start a job that would last 3 years and 10 years to start one lasting 5 years. Those with a college degree settled into stable employment much more quickly; within a year and a half they started a job that would last 3 years and it took college graduates less than 4 years to start a job that would last 5 years (Yates, 2005).

Strong associations link first occupation upon entry into the labor market with subsequent earnings and occupational prestige (D'Amico, 1985) and delay of entry into careers has developmental implications for the critical task of gaining financial independence. The challenge of gaining financial stability is not an easy task given that individuals in the emerging adult age group have the lowest earnings, across 19 countries, compared to all other periods of adult labor force involvement (OECD, 1998). Despite, or perhaps given the challenge, career success is associated with adaptation. Gaining status, power, and achieving financial independence through good compensation is associated with decreases in negative emotionality and gains in positive emotionality from 18 to 26 (Roberts, Caspi, & Moffitt, 2003).

Conclusion and Implications

The boundary between childhood and adulthood is not as sharp as it used to be. Emerging adulthood now links the two stages. Development and learning during emerging adulthood shapes and is shaped by the distinctiveness of the developmental period. Because emerging adults are unique in their lack of experience in the adult educational and occupational arenas, traditional education and learning goals including imparting knowledge, providing skills-training, and guiding professional development should be designed differently for this age group to optimize potential for achievement.

There is a naturally occurring window during emerging adulthood to provide opportunities for education and learning because such goals are more common in the twenties period than in later age periods (Nurmi, 1992). Moreover, because life-span goals and patterns of stability are determined, to some extent, during this age period, objectives related to optimizing adult learning and development and priming life-span learners take on special significance. That emerging adulthood can be broadly characterized as an exceptional period of plasticity during which the shaping of life goals in positive ways is possible, rests on specific developmental features that are unique to the age period. Understanding the fundamental characteristics of emerging adult development that make it unique from other periods of the life span has significant implications for work that seeks to facilitate life-span learning. Both normative experiences, as well as sources of interindividual differences may impact and influence pathways of growth and maturation.

The subjective experience of emerging adulthood is critical for tapping into their unique motivations for learning and development. Part of the experience of emerging adulthood is an openness to experience, an eagerness to try new things, and a willingness to learn. Few emerging adults want to obtain a job at 20 that they will have until they are 65. Adulthood is attractive in some ways because it means more stability, but also repellent because emerging adults fear it means stagnation. They expect to continually revise their identities through challenges and new experiences and tend to expect that work will be interesting and fun. They fear that becoming an adult means you no longer grow. One way to avoid this is through continuous learning, perhaps indicated by increasing rates of post-graduate studies after college (U.S. Department of Education, 1999a) and increasingly high rates of enrollment in educational programs among middle-age adults

(U.S. Department of Education, 1999b). Investing in emerging adults through education and facilitating the school-to-work transition for all emerging adults and helping them balance work and family, government can foster an increasingly productive labor force (Fussell, 2002).

Note

Support for this chapter was provided by NIMH Mental Health Services and Systems Training Program Grant 16242-26.

References

Abma, J., Chandra, A., Mosher, W., Peterson, L., & Piccinio, L. (1997). Fertility, family planning, and women's health: New data from the 1995 survey of family growth. National Center for Health Statistics. *Vital Health Statistics, 23*(19).

Amato, P. R., & Afifi, T. D. (2006). Feeling caught between parents: Adult children's relations with parents and subjective well-being. *Journal of Marriage and the Family, 68*(1), 222–235.

Anderson, R. N., Kochanek, K. D., & Murphy, S. (1997). *Report of final mortality statistics, 1995.* Hyattesville, MD: National Center for Health Statistics.

Andrews, J. A., Foster, S. L., Capaldi, D., & Hops, H. (2000). Adolescent and family predictors of physical aggression, communication, and satisfaction in young adult couples: A prospective analysis. *Journal of Consulting and Clinical Psychology, 68*, 195–208.

Aquilino, W. S. (1997). From adolescent to young adult: A prospective study of parent child relations during the transition to adulthood. *Journal of Marriage and the Family, 59*, 670–686.

Aquilino, W. (2005). Impact of family structure on parental attitudes toward the economic support of adult children over the transition to adulthood. *Journal of Family Issues, 26*(2), 143–167.

Aquilino, W. (2006). Family relationships and support systems in emerging adulthood. In J. J. Arnett & J. L. Tanner (Eds.), *Emerging adults in America: Coming of age in the 21st century* (pp.193–217). Washington, DC: American Psychological Association.

Arnett, J. J. (1997). Young people's conceptions of the transition to adulthood. *Youth & Society, 29*, 1–23.

Arnett, J. J. (1998). Learning to stand alone: The contemporary American transition to adulthood in cultural and historical context. *Human Development, 41*, 295–315.

Arnett, J. J. (2000). Emerging adulthood: A theory of development from the late teens through the twenties. *American Psychologist, 55*, 469–480.

Arnett, J. J. (2001). Conceptions of the transition to adulthood: Perspectives from adolescence to midlife. *Journal of Adult Development, 8*, 133–143.

Arnett, J. J. (2003). Conceptions of the transition to adulthood among emerging adults in American ethnic groups. In J. Arnett & N. Galambos (Eds.), *New directions for child and adolescent development: Cultural conceptions of the transition to adulthood* (No. 100, pp. 63–75). San Francisco: Jossey-Bass.

Arnett, J. J. (2004). *Emerging adulthood: The winding road from the late teens through the twenties.* New York: Oxford University Press.

Arnett, J. J. (2006). Emerging adulthood: Understanding the new way of coming of age. In J. J. Arnett & J. L. Tanner (Eds.), *Emerging adults in America: Coming of age in the 21st century* (pp. 3–20). Washington, DC: American Psychological Association Press.

Arnett, J. J., & Taber, S. (1994). Adolescence terminable and interminable: When does adolescence end? *Journal of Youth and Adolescence, 23*, 517–537.

Avery, R., Goldscheider, F., & Speare, A. Jr. (1992). Feathered nest/Gilded cage: Parental income and leaving home in the transition to adulthood. *Demography, 29*(3), 375–388.

Avolio, B. J., & Waldman, D. A. (1994). Variations in cognitive, perceptual, and psychomotor abilities, across the working lifespan: Examining the effects of race, sex, experience, education, and occupational type. *Psychology & Aging, 9*(3), 430–442.

Badger, S., Nelson, L. J., & Barry, C. M. (2006). Perceptions of the transition to adulthood among Chinese and American emerging adults. *International Journal of Behavioral Development, 30*(1), 84–93.

Bagwell, C. L., Bender, S. E., Andreassi, C. L., Kinoshita, T. L., Montarello, S. A., & Muller, J. G. (2005). Friendship quality and perceived relationship changes predict psychosocial adjustment in early adulthood. *Journal of Social and Personal Relationships, 22,* 235–254.

Baltes, P. B. (1997). On the incomplete architecture of human ontogeny. Selection, optimization, and compensation as the foundation of developmental theory. *American Psychologist, 52*(4), 366–380.

Baltes, P. B., & Staudinger, U. M. (2000). Wisdom: A metaheuristic (pragmatic) to orchestrate mind and virtue toward excellence. *American Psychologist, 55,* 122–136.

Baltes, P. B., Staudinger, U. M., & Lindenberger, U. (1999). Lifespan psychology: Theory and application to intellectual functioning. In L. R. Goldberg et al. (Series Eds.), M. R. Rosenzweig & L. W. Porter (Vol. Eds.), *Annual review of psychology, Vol. 50* (pp. 471–507). Palo Alto, CA: Annual Reviews.

Bennett, C. M., & Baird, A. A. (2006). Anatomical changes in the emerging adult brain: A voxel-based morphometry study. *Human Brain Mapping, 27*(9), 766–777.

Benton, S. A., Robertson, J. M., Tseng, W-C., Newton, F. B., & Benton, S. L. (2003). Changes in counseling center client problems across 13 Years. *Professional Psychology: Research and Practice,* 34(1), 66–72.

Berry, D. S., Willingham, J. K., & Thayer, C. A. (2000). Affect and personality as predictors of conflict and closeness in young adults' friendships. *Journal of Research in Personality, 34,* 84–107.

Blasi, A. (1998). Loevinger's theory of ego development and its relationship to the cognitive-developmental approach. In M. P. Westenberg, A. Blasi, & L. D. Cohn (Eds.), *Personality development: Theoretical, empirical, and clinical investigations of Loevinger's conception of ego development* (pp. 13–25). Mahwah, NJ: Erlbaum.

Blos, P. (1962). *On adolescence: A psychodynamic interpretation.* New York: Free Press.

Bureau of Labor Statistics. (2005). *Economic news releases: Time use survey, 2005.* Washington, DC: Author. Retrieved July 20, 2006, from http://www.bls.gov/tus/

Caldwell, M. A., & Peplau, L. A. (1982). Sex differences in same-sex friendship. *Sex Roles, 8,* 721–732.

Carbery, J., & Buhrmester, D. (1998). Friendship and need fulfillment during three phases of young adulthood. *Journal of Social and Personal Relationships, 15,* 393–409.

Carnethon, M. R., Gidding, S. S., Nehgme, R., Sidney, S., Jacobs, D. R., & Liu, L. (2003). Cardiorespiratory fitness in young adulthood and the development of cardiovascular disease risk factors. *Journal of the American medical Association, 290,* 3092–3100.

Carroll, J. (2006). *Family time eclipses TV as favorite way to spend an evening.* Princeton, NJ: Gallup Poll News Service.

Caspi, A. (1998). Personality development across the life course. In W. Damon & N. Eisenberg (Eds.), *Handbook of child psychology, Vol. 3* (5th ed.): *Social, emotional and personality development.* New York: Wiley.

Cassidy, T. (2005). Lesiure, coping and health: The role of social, family, school, and peer relationship factors. *British Journal of Guidance & Counseling, 33*(1), 51–66.

Charles, S. T., Reynolds, C. A., & Gatz, M. (2001). Age-related differences and change in positive and negative affect over 23 years. *Journal of Personality and Social Psychology, 80*(1), 136–151.

Child Trends. (2007). *High school dropout rates.* Retrieved from http://www.childtrendsdatabank.org/indicators/1HighSchoolDropout.cfm

Cicirelli, V. G. (1994). The longest bond: The sibling life cycle. In L. L'Abate (Ed.), *Handbook of developmental family psychology and psychopathology* (pp. 44–59). New York: Wiley.

Cohen, P., Kasen, S., Chen, H., Hartmark, C., & Gordon, K. (2003). Variations in patterns of developmental transitions in the emerging adulthood period. *Developmental Psychology, 39,* 657–669.

Cohn, L. D. (1998). Age trends in personality development: A quantitative review. In P. M. Westenberg, A. Blasi, & L. D. Cohn (Eds.), *Personality development,* 133–143, Mahwah, NJ: Erlbaum.

Crosnoe, R. (2000). Friendships in childhood and adolescence: The life course and new directions. *Social Psychology Quarterly, 63,* 377–391.

D'Amico, R. (1985). The effects of career origins o subsequent socioeconomic attainments. *Work and Occupations, 12*(3), 329–350.

Day, J. C., & Newburger, E. C. (2002). *The big payoff: Educational attainment and synthetic estimates of work-life earnings.* Washington, DC: U.S. Department of Commerce.

Deil-Amen, R., & Turley, R. N. L. (2007). A review of the transition to college literature in sociology. *Teachers College Record, 109*(10), 6–7

Donnellan, M. B., Larsen-Rife, D., & Conger, R. D. (2005). Personality, family history, and competence in early adult romantic relationships. *Journal of Personality and Social Psychology, 88,* 562–576.

Elnick, A. B., Margrett, J. A., Fitzgerald, J. M., & Labouvie-Vief, G. (1999). Benchmark memories in adulthood: Central domains and predictors of their frequency. *Journal of Adult Development, 6,* 45–59.

Erikson, E. H. (1950). *Childhood and society.* New York: Norton.

Erikson, E. H. (1982). *The life cycle completed.* New York: Norton.

Facio, A., & Micocci, F. (2003). Emerging adulthood in Argentina. In J. Arnett & N. Galambos (Eds.), *New directions for child and adolescent development: Cultural conceptions of the transition to adulthood* (No. 100, pp. 21–31). San Francisco: Jossey-Bass.

Feldman, S .S., Gowen, L. K., & Fisher, L. (1998). Family relationships and gender as predictors of romantic intimacy in young adults: A longitudinal study. *Journal of Research on Adolescence, 8,* 263–286.

Fergusson, D. M., & Woodward, L. J. (2002). Mental health, educational, and social role outcomes of adolescents with depression. *Archives of General Psychiatry, 59,* 225–231.

Fergusson, D. M., Horwood, L. J., & Ridder, E. M. (2006). Abortion in young women and subsequent mental health. *Journal of Child Psychology and Psychiatry, 47*(1), 16–24.

Finer, L. B. (2007). Trends in premarital sex in the United States, 1954–2003. *Public Health Reports, 122,* 73–78.

Finer, L., & Henshaw, S. (2006). Estimates of U.S. abortion incidence 2001–2003. New York: Guttmacher Institute.

Fischer, J. L., Sollie, D. L., Sorell, G. T., & Green, S. K. (1989). Marital status and career stage influences on social networks of young adults. *Journal of Marriage and the Family, 51,* 521–534.

Freund, A. M., & Baltes, P. B. (2002). Life-management strategies of selection, optimization, and compensation: Measurement by self-report and construct validity. *Journal of Personality & Social Psychology, 82,* 642–662.

Freund, A. M., Li, K. Z. H., & Baltes, P. B. (1999). Successful development and aging: The role of selection, optimization, and compensation. In J. Brandtstädter & R. M. Lerner (Eds.), *Action and self-development: Theory and research through the lifespan* (pp. 401–434). Thousand Oaks, CA: Sage.

Fussell, E. (2002). The transition to adulthood in aging societies. *The Annals of the American Academy of Political and Social Science, 580,* 16–39.

Galambos, N. L., Barker, E. T., & Krahn, H. J. (2006). Depression, self-esteem, and anger in emerging adulthood: Seven-year trajectories. *Developmental Psychology, 42*(2), 350–365.

Gauthier, A. H., & Furstenberg, F. F. (2002). The transition to adulthood: A time use perspective. *The Annals of the American Academy of Political and Social Sciences, 580,* 153–171.

Giedd, J. N., Blumenthal, J., Jeffries, N. O., Castellanos, F. X., Liu, H., Zijdenbos, A., et al. (1999). Brain development during childhood and adolescence: A longitudinal MRI study. *Nature Neuroscience, 2*(10): 861–863.

Gogtay N., Giedd, J. N., Lusk L., Hayashi, K. M., Greenstein, D., Vaituzis, A. C., Nugent, T. F., Herman, D. H., Clasen, L. S., Toga, A.W ., Rapoport, J. L., & Thompson, P. M. (2004). Dynamic mapping of human cortical development during childhood through early adulthood. *Proceedings of the National Academy of Sciences, 101*(21), 8174–8179.

Gordon-Larsen, P., Nelson, M. C., & Popkin, B. M. (2004). Longitudinal physical activity and sedentary behavior trends: Adolescence to adulthood. *American Journal of Preventive Medicine, 27,* 277–283.

Grob, A., Krings, F., & Bangerter, A. (2001). Life markers in biographical narratives of people from three cohorts: A lifespan perspective in historical context. *Human Development, 44,* 171–190.

Hamilton, B. E., Ventura, S. J., Martin, J. A., & Sutton, P. D. (2005). *Preliminary births for 2004.* Washington, DC: National Center for Health Statistics.

Hartup, W. W., & Stevens, N. (1999). Friendships and adaptation across the lifespan. *Current Directions in Psychological Science, 8,* 76–79.

Haworth, J. T., & Hill, S. (1992). Work, leisure, and psychological well-being in a sample of young adults. *Journal of Community and Applied Psychology, 2,* 147–160.

Helson, R., & Roberts, B. W. (1994). Ego developmental and personality change in adulthood. *Journal of Personality and Social Psychology, 66,* 911–920.

Henninghausen, K. H., Hauser, S. T., Billings, R. L., Schultz, L. H., & Allen, J. P. (2004). Adolescent ego development trajectories and young adult relationship outcomes. *The Journal of Early Adolescence, 24*(1), 29–44.

Hershey, D. A., & Farrell, A. H. (1999). Age differences on a procedurally oriented test of practical problem solving. *Journal of Adult Development, 6*(2), 87–104.

Heuveline, P. (2002). An international comparison of adolescent and young adult mortality. *The Annals of the American Academy of Political and Social Science, 580,* 172–200.

Hoffman, R. M. (2004). Conceptualizing heterosexual identity development: Issues and challenges. *Journal of Counseling and Development, 82*(3), 375–380.

Hofstra, M. B., van der Ende, J., & Verhulst, F. C. (2001). Adolescents' self-reported problems as predictors of psychopathology in adulthood: 10-year follow-up study. *British Journal of Psychiatry, 179,* 203–209.

Holahan, C. J., Valentiner, D. P., & Moos, R. H. (1994). Parental support and psychological adjustment during the transition to young adulthood in a college sample. *Journal of Family Psychology, 8,* 215–223.

Hynes, K., & Clarkberg, M. (2005). Women's employment patterns during early parenthood: A group-based trajectory analysis. Journal *of Marriage and the Family, 67*(1), 222–239.

Johnson, F. L., & Aries, E. J. (1983). Conversational patterns among same-sex pairs of late-adolescent close friends. *Journal of Genetic Psychology, 142,* 225–238.

Jones, C. J., & Meredith, W. (2000). Developmental paths of psychological health from early adolescence to later adulthood. *Psychological Aging, 15*(2), 351–360.

Jones R. K., Darroch, J. E., & Henshaw, S. K. (2002). Patterns in the socioeconomic characteristics of women obtaining abortions in 2000–2001. *Perspectives on Sexual and Reproductive Health, 34*(5), 226–235.

Kessler, R. C., Berglund, P., Demler, O., Jin, R., & Walters, E. (2005). Lifetime prevalence and age-of-onset distributions of DSM-IV disorders in the National Comorbidity Survey Replication. *Archives of General Psychiatry, 62,* 593–602.

Kessler, R. C., Chiu, W. T., Demler, O., & Walters, E. (2005). Prevalence, severity, and comorbidity of 12-month DSM-IV disorders in the National Comorbidity Survey Replication. *Archives of General Psychiatry, 62,* 617–627.

Kessler, R. C., McGonagle, K. A., Zhao, S., Nelson, C. B., Hughes, M., Eshelman, S., Witchen, H. U., & Kendler, K. S. (1994). Lifetime and 12-month prevalence of DSM-III-R psychiatric disorders in the United States. Results frm the National Comorbidity Study. *Archives of General Psychiatry, 51, 8–19.*

Kim-Cohen, J., Caspi, A., Moffitt, T. E., Harrington, H., Milne, B. J., & Poulton, R. (2003). Prior juvenile diagnoses in adults with mental disorder: Developmental follow-back of a prospective-longitudinal cohort. *Archives of General Psychiatry, 60*(7), 709–717.

Koski, L. R., & Shaver, P. R. (1997). Attachment and relationship satisfaction across the lifespan. In R. J. Sternberg & M. Hojjat (Eds.), *Satisfaction in close relationships* (pp. 26–55). New York: Guilford.

Kreider, R. M. (2005). Number, timing, and duration of marriages and divorces: 2001, Table 3. *Current Population Reports* (pp. 70–97). Washington, D C: U.S. Census Bureau. Data for individual race categories: U.S. Census Bureau, Survey of Income and Program Participation (SIPP), 2001 Panel, Wave 2 Topical Module.

Labouvie-Vief, G. (1980). Beyond formal operations: Uses and limits of pure logic in life-span development. *Human Development, 23,* 141–160.

Labouvie-Vief, G. (1985). Logic and self-regulation from youth to maturity: A model. In M. Commons, F. Richards, & C. Armon (Eds.), *Beyond formal operations: Late adolescent and adult cognitive development* (pp. 158–180). New York: Praeger.

Labouvie-Vief, G. (2006). Emerging structures of adult thought. In J. J. Arnett & J. L. Tanner (Eds.), *Emerging adults in America: Coming of age in the 21st century* (pp. 193–217). Washington, DC: American Psychological Association.

Labouvie-Vief, G., Chiodo, L. M., Goguen, L. A., Diehl, M., & Orwoll, L. (1995). Representations of self across the lifespan, *Psychology and Aging, 10,* 404–415.

Labouvie-Vief, G., & Meddler, M. (2002). Affect optimization and affect complexity: Modes and styles of regulation in adulthood. *Psychology and Aging, 10, 404–415.*

Lasser, V., & Snarey, J. (1989). Ego development and perceptions of parent behavior in adolescent girls: A qualitative study of the transition from high school to college. *Journal of Adolescent Research, 4,* 319–355.

Lee, R., Lee, S-H., & Mason, A. (2006). *Charting the economic life cycle.* Working paper no. 12379. Cambridge, MA: National Bureau of Economic Research.

Lefkowitz, E., & Gillen, M. (2006). Sex is just a normal part of life: Sexuality in emerging adulthood. In J. J. Arnett & J. L. Tanner (Eds.), *Emerging adults in America: Coming of age in the 21st century* (pp. 235–255). Washington, DC: American Psychological Association.

Lerner, R. M. (1984). *On the nature of human plasticity.* New York: Cambridge University Press.

Lerner, R. M. (2002). *Concepts and theories of human development.* Mahwah, NJ: Erlbaum.

Lerner, R. M., Freund, A. M., De Stefanis, I., & Habermas, T. (2001). Understanding developmental regulation in adolescence: The use of the selection, optimization, and compensation model. *Human Development, 44*(1), 29–50.

Lincoln, R. (1975). Cohabitation: Fastest growing life style among young adults. *Family Planning Perspectives, 7,* 215.

Loevinger, J. (1976). *Ego development: Conceptions and theories.* San Francisco: Jossey-Bass.

MacKeracher, D. (2004). *Making sense of adult learning.* Toronto: University of Toronto Press.

Martinez, G. M., Chandra, A., Abma, J. C., Jones, J. & Mosher, W. D. (2006). Fertility, contraception, and fatherhood: Data on men and women from cycle 6 (2002) of the National Survey of Family Growth. National Center for Health Statistics. *Vital Health Statistics, 23*(26).

Mason, A., Lee, R., Tung, A-C, Lai, M-S., & Miller, T. (2006). *Population aging and intergenerational transfers: Introducing age into national accounts.* Working paper no. 12770. Cambridge, MA: National Bureau of Economic Research.

Masten, A. S., Burt, K., Roisman, G. I., Obradovic, J., Long, J. D., & Tellegen, A. (2004). Resources and resilience in the transition to adulthood: Continuity and change. *Development and Psychopathology, 16,* 1071–1094.

Masten, A. S., Obradovic, J., & Burt, K. B. (2006). Resilience in emerging adulthood: Developmental perspectives on continuity and transformation. In J. J. Arnett & J. L. Tanner (Eds.), *Emerging adults in America: Coming of age in the 21st century* (pp. 193–217). Washington, DC: American Psychological Association.

Mayer, J. D, & Salovey, P. (1997). What is emotional intelligence? In P. Salovey & D. Sluyter (Eds.), *Emotional development and emotional intelligence: Educational implications* (pp. 3–31). New York: Basic Books.

Mayer, J. D., Salovey, P., & Caruso, D. R. (2004). Emotional intelligence: Theory, findings, and implications. *Psychological Inquiry, 15*(3), 197–215.

Mayseless, O., & Scharf, M. (2003). What does it mean to be an adult? The Israeli experience. *New Directions in Child and Adolescent Development, 100,* 5–20.

McTigue, K. M., Garrett, J. M., & Popkin, B. M. (2002). The natural history of the development of obesity in a cohort of young US adults, 1981–1998, *Annals of Internal Medicine, 136*(12), 857–864.

Merluzzi, T. V., & Nairn, R. C. (1999). Adulthood and aging: Transitions in health and health cognition. In T. L. Whitman, T. V. Merluzzi, & R. D. White (Eds.), *Life-span perspectives on health and illness* (p. 189–206). Mahwah, NJ: Erlbaum.

Milevsky, A. (2005). Compensatory patterns of sibling support in emerging adulthood: Variations in loneliness, self-esteem, depression, and life satisfaction. *Journal of Social and Personal Relationships, 22,* 743–755.

Mirowsky, J., & Ross, C. E. (1999). Economic hardship across the life course. *American Sociological Review, 64*(4), 548–569.

Montgomery, M. J. (2005). Psychosocial intimacy and identity: From early adolescence to emerging adulthood. *Journal of Adolescent Research, 20,* 346–374.

Montgomery, M. J., & Sorell, G. T. (1994). Differences in love attitudes across family life stages. *Family Relations, 46,* 55–61.

National Center for Education Statistics (2005). *The condition of education, 2005.* Washington, DC: U.S. Department of Education. Retrieved from http://www.nces.gov

National Center for Health Statistics. *Health, United States, 2005 with chartbook on trends in the health of Americans.* Hyattsville, Maryland: 2005.

Nelson, L. J., Badger, S., & Wu, B. (2004). The influence of culture in emerging adulthood: Perspectives of Chinese college students. *International Journal of Behavioral Development, 28,* 26–36.

Nelson, L. J. (2003). Rites of passage in emerging adulthood: Perspectives of young Mormons. In J. Arnett & N. Galambos (Eds.), *New directions for child and adolescent development: Cultural conceptions of the transition to adulthood* (No. 100, pp. 33–49). San Francisco: Jossey-Bass.

Neugarten, B. L. (1968). Adult personality: Toward a psychology of the life cycle. In B. L. Neugarten (Ed.), *Middle age and aging.* Chicago: University of Chicago Press.

Newman, D. L., Moffitt, T. E., Caspi, A., Magdol, L., Silva, P., & Stanton, W. R. (1996). Psychiatric disorder in a birth cohort of young adults: Prevalence, comorbidity, clinical significance, and new case incidence from ages 11 to 21. *Journal of Consulting and Clinical Psychology, 64*(3), 552–562.

Ng, E. S. W., & Burke, R. J. (2006). The next generation at work? Business students' views, values and job search strategy: Implications for universities and employees. *Education & Training, 48*(7), 478–492.

Nurmi, J.-E. (1992). Age differences in adult life goals, concerns and their temporal extension: A life course approach. *International Journal of Behavioral Development, 15*(4), 487–508.

Nurmi, J.-E. (1993). Adolescent development in an age-graded context: the role of personal beliefs, goals, and strategies in the tackling of developmental tasks and standards. *International Journal of Behavioral Development, 16,* 169–189.

Nurmi, J.-E. (1997). Self-definition and mental health during adolescence and young adulthood. In J. Schulenberg, J. L. Maggs, & K. Hurrelman (Eds.), *Health risks and developmental transitions during adolescence* (pp. 395–419). New York: Cambridge University Press.

Nurmi, J.-E., & Salmelo-Aro, K. (2002). Goal construction, reconstruction and depressive symptoms in a life-span context: The transition from school to work. *Journal of Personality, 70*(3), 385–420.

O'Donnell, K. (2006). *Adult education participation in 2004–2005.* National Center for Education Statistics. Retrieved from http://nces.ed.gov

OECD. (1998). Work force aging in OECD countries. *OECD Employment Outlook* (pp. 123–150). Paris: OECD Publishing.

Paradis, A. D., Reinherz, H. Z., Giaconia, R. M., & Fitzmaurice, G. (2006). Major depression in the transition to adulthood: The impact of active and past depression on young adult functioning. *The Journal of Nervous and Mental Disease, 194,* 318–323.

Parker, J. D. A., Duffy, J. M., Wood, L. M., Bond, B. J., & Hogan, M. J. (2005). Academic achievement and emotional intelligence: Predicting the successful transition from high school to university. *Journal of the First-Year Experience & Students in Transition, 17*(1), 67–78.

Parker, J. D. A., Summerfeldt, L. J., Hogan, M. J., & Majeski, S. A. (2004). Emotional intelligence and academic success: Examining the transition from high school to university. *Personality and Individual Differences, 36*(1), 163–172.

Perna, L. W. (2003). The private benefits of higher education: An examination of the earnings premium. *Research in Higher Education, 44*(3), 451–472.

Perry, W. G., Jr. (1970). *Forms of intellectual and ethical development in the college years*. New York: Holt, Rinehart, & Winston.

Perry, W. G., Jr. (1981). Cognitive and ethical growth. In A. Chickering (Ed.), *The modern American college* (pp. 76–116). San Francisco: Jossey-Bass.

Pulaskos, J. (2001). Young adult relationships: Siblings and friends. *Journal of Psychology, 123*, 237–244.

Raymore, L. A., Barber, B. L., & Eccles, J. S. (2001). Leaving home, attending college, partnership and parenthood: The role of life transition events in leisure pattern stability from adolescence to young adulthood. *Journal of Youth and Adolescence, 30*, 197–223.

Regan, P. C., Durvasula, R., Howell, L., Ureño, O., & Rea, M. (2004). Gender, ethnicity, and the developmental timing of first sexual and romantic experiences. *Social Behavior and Personality, 32*, 667–676.

Reinherz, H. Z., Giaconia, R. M., Carmola Hauf, A. M., Wasserman, M. S., & Silverman, A. B. (1999). Major depression in the transition to adulthood: Risks and impairments. *Journal of Abnormal Psychology, 108*, 500–510.

Reis, H. T., Lin, Y., Bennett, M. E., & Nezlek, J. B. (1993). Change and consistency in social participation during early adulthood. *Developmental Psychology, 29*, 633–645.

Roberts, B. W., Caspi, A., & Moffitt, T. E. (2001). The kids are alright: growth and stability in personality development from adolescence to adulthood. *Journal of Personality and Social Psychology, 81*(4), 670–683.

Roberts, B. W., Caspi, A., & Moffitt, T. E. (2003). Work experiences and personality development in young adulthood. *Journal of Personality and Social Psychology, 84*(3), 582–593.

Roberts, B. W., O'Donnell, M., & Robins, R. W. (2004). Goal and personality trait development in emerging adulthood. *Journal of Personality and Social Psychology, 87*, 541–550.

Roberts, B., Walton, K. E., & Viechtbauer, W. (2006). Patterns of mean-level change in personality traits across the life course: A meta-analysis of longitudinal studies. *Psychological Bulletin, 132*(1), 1–25.

Robins, L. N., & Regier, D. A. (1991). *Psychiatric disorders in America: The epidemiological catchment area study*. New York: The Free Press.

Robins, R. W., Fraley, R. C., Roberts. B. W., & Trzesniewski, K. H. (2001). A longitudinal study of personality change in young adulthood. *Journal of Personality, 69*(4), 617–640.

Robinson, L. C. (2000). Interpersonal relationship quality in young adulthood: A gender analysis. *Adolescence, 35*, 775–784.

Roisman, G. I., Masten, A. S., Coatsworth, J. D., & Tellegen, A. (2004). Salient and emerging developmental tasks in the transition to adulthood. *Child Development, 75*, 123–133.

Rönkä, A., Oravala, S., & Pulkkinen, L. (2003). Turning points in adults' lives: The effects of gender and the amount of choice. *Journal of Adult Development, 10*(3), 203–215.

Rosario, M., Schrimshaw, E. W., Hunter, J., & Braun, L. (2006). Sexual identity development among gay, lesbian, and bisexual youths: Consistency and change over time. *Journal of Sex Research, 43*(1), 46–58.

Rosenbaum, J. E. (2002). *Beyond empty promises: Policies to improve transitions into college and jobs*. (Contract No. ED99CO0160). Washington D.C.: Office of Vocational and Adult Education, U.S. Department of Education.

Rosenbaum, J. E., & Person, A. E. (2003). Beyond college for all: Policies and practices to improve transitions into college and jobs. *Professional School Counseling, 6*, 252–259.

Samter, W. (2003). Friendship interaction skills across the lifespan. In J. O. Greene & B. R. Burleson (Eds.), *Handbook of communication and social interaction skills* (pp. 637–684). Mahwah, NJ: Erlbaum.

Sassler, S. (2004). The process of entering into cohabitating unions. *Journal of Marriage and Family, 66*, 491–505.

Scharf, M., Shulman, S., & Avigad-Spitz, L. (2005). Sibling relationships in emerging adulthood and in adolescence. *Journal of Adolescent Research, 20*, 64–90.

Schaie, K. W. (1977). Toward a stage theory of adult cognitive development. *International Journal of Aging and Human Development, 8*, 129–138.

Schoeni, R. F., & Ross, K. E. (2005). Material assistance from families during the transition to adulthood. In R. A. Settersten & F. F. Furstenberg (Eds.), *On the frontier of adulthood: Theory, research, and public policy* (pp. 396–416). Chicago: The University of Chicago Press.

Schulenberg, J., O'Malley, P. M., Bachman, J. G., & Johnston, L. D. (2000). "Spread your wings and fly": The course of well-being and substance use during the transition to young adulthood. In L. J. Crockett & R. K. Silbereisen (Eds.), *Negotiating adolescence in times of social change* (pp. 224–255). New York: Cambridge University Press.

Schultz, L. H., & Selman, R. L. (1998). Ego development and interpersonal development in young adulthood: A between-model comparison. In P. M. Westenberg, A. Blasi, & L. D. Cohn (Eds.), *Personality development: Theoretical, empirical, and clinical investigations of Loevinger's conception of ego development* (pp. 181–202). Mahwah, NJ: Erlbaum.

Schuman, H., & Scott, J. (1989). Generations and collective memories. *American Sociological Review, 54*, 359–381.

Schwartz, S. J., Côté, J., & Arnett, J. J. (2005). Identity and agency in *emerging adulthood*: Two developmental routes in the individualization process. *Youth & Society, 37*(2), 201–229.

Seiffge-Krenke, I. (2003). Testing theories of romantic development from adolescence to young adulthood: Evidence of a developmental sequence. *International Journal of Behavioral Development, 27*, 519–531.

Shortt, J. W., & Gottman, J. M. (1997). Closeness in young adult sibling relationships: Affective and physiological processes. *Social Development, 6*, 142–164.

Shulman, N. (1975). Life-cycle variations in patterns of close relationships. *Journal of Marriage and the Family, 37*, 813–821.

Shulman, S., Scharf, M., Lumer, D., & Maurer, O. (2001). Parental divorce and young adult children's romantic relationships: Resolution of the divorce experience. *American Journal of Orthopsychiatry, 71*, 473–478.

Smith, MC., & Pourchot, T. (1998). *What does educational psychology know about adult learning and development?* In MC. Smith & T. Pourchot (Eds.), *Adult learning and development*. Mahwah, NJ: Erlbaum.

Smith, MC., & Reio, T. G. Jr. (2006). Adult development, schooling, and the transition to work. In P. A. Alexander & P. H. Winne (Eds.), *Handbook of educational psychology* (pp. 115–138). Mahwah, NJ: Erlbaum.

Smola, K. W., & Sutton, C. D. (2002). Generational differences: revisiting generational work values for the new millennium. *Journal of Organizational Behavior, 23*(4), 363–382.

Sowell, E. R., Thompson, P. M., & Toga, A.W. (2004). Mapping changes in the human cortex throughout the span of life. *The Neuroscientist, 10*(4), 372–392.

Sprecher, S., & Felmlee, D. (1992). The influence of parents and friends on the quality and stability of romantic relationships: A three-wave longitudinal investigation. *Journal of Marriage and the Family, 54*(4), 888–900.

Sternberg, R. J., & Grigorenko, E. L. (Eds.). (2002). *The general factor of intelligence: How general is it?* Mahwah, NJ: Erlbaum.

Strauss, L. T., Herndon, J., Chang, J., Parker, W. Y., Bowens, S. V., & Berg, C. J. (2005). Abortion surveillance—United States, 2002. *MMWR Surveillance summaries, 54*(SS07), 1–31. Washington, DC: National Center for Chronic Disease Prevention and Health Promotion.

Surra, C. A. (1990). Research and theory on mate selection and premarital relationships in the 1980s. *Journal of Marriage and the Family, 52*, 844–865.

Tammelin, T., Laitinen, J., & Näyhä, S. (2004). Change in the level of physical activity from adolescence into adulthood and obesity at the age of 31 years. *International Journal of Obesity, 28*, 775–782.

Tanner, J. L. (2006). Recentering during emerging adulthood. In J. J. Arnett & J. L. Tanner (Eds.), *Emerging adults in America: Coming of age in the 21st century* (pp.193–217). Washington, DC: American Psychological Association.

Tanner, J. L., Reinherz, H. Z., Beardslee, W. R., Fitzmaurice, G. M., Leis, J. A., & Berger, S. R. (2007). Change in prevalence of psychiatric disorders from 21 to 30 in a community sample. *Journal of Nervous and Mental Disease, 195*(4), 298–306.

Teachman, J. D., & Polonko, K. A. (1988). Marriage, parenthood, and the college enrollment of men and women. *Social Forces,* 67(2), 512–523

Thornton, A. (1988). Cohabitation and marriage in the 1980s. *Demography, 25,* 497–508.

U.S. Bureau of the Census. (2003). *Households and families: 2000.* Washington, DC: U.S. Government Printing Office.

U.S Bureau of the Census. (2007). *Statistical abstracts of the United States.* Washington, DC: U.S. Government Printing Office.

U.S. Department of Education. (1999a). *Digest of education statistics.* Washington, DC: National Center for Education Statistics.

U.S. Department of Education. (1999b). *National household education survey (NHES), adult education interview.* Washington, DC: National Center for Education Statistics.

U.S. Department of Education. (2001). *Dropout rates in the United States: 2000,* NCES 2002-114. Washington, DC: National Center for Education Statistics.

U.S. Department of Health and Human Services. (2000). *Healthy people 2010.* Washington, DC: U. S. Department of Health and Human Services.

Vaillant, G. E. (2002). *Aging well.* New York: Little Brown.

Ventura, S. J., Abma, J. C., Mosher, W. D., & Henshaw, S. (2003). Revised pregnancy rates, 1990–97, and new rates for 1998–1999: United States. *National Vital Statistics Reports, 52*(7). Washington DC: U. S. Department of Health and Human Services.

Veroff, J., Douvan, E., & Kulka, R. A. (1981). *The inner American: A self-portrait from 1957 to 1976.* New York: Basic Books.

Waterhouse, L. (2006). Multiple intelligences, the Mozart effect, and emotional intelligence: A critical review. *Educational Psychologist, 41*(4), 207–225.

Westenberg, P. M., & Gjerde, P. F. (1999). Ego development during the transition from adolescence to young adulthood: A 9-year longitudinal study. *Journal of Research in Personality, 33*(2), 233–252.

Whiting, B .B. (1998). The meaning of independence and responsibility. *Human Development, 41,* 321–322.

William T. Grant Foundation Commission on Work, Family, and Citizenship. (1988). *The forgotten half: Non-college youth in America.* Washington, DC: Author.

William T. Grant Foundation (Halperin, S., Ed.) (1998). *The forgotten half revisited.* Washington, DC: American Youth Policy Forum.

Wittchen, H., Nelson, C. B., & Lachner, G. (1998). Prevalence of mental disorders and psychosocial impairments in adolescence and young adults. *Psychological Medicine, 28,* 109–126.

Wolfinger, N. H. (2003). Parental divorce and offspring marriage: Early or late? *Social Forces, 82*(1), 337–353.

Yates, J. A. (2005). The transition from school to work: Education and work experiences. *Monthly Labor Review, 128*(2), 21–32.

Chapter 3

Models of Adult Development in Bronfenbrenner's Bioecological Theory and Erikson's Biopsychosocial Life Stage Theory

Moving to a More Complete Three-Model View

Carol Hoare

In a discussion that occurred more than 20 years ago, Urie Bronfenbrenner expressed concern about the increasing trend of fragmentation in the field of human development:

> I am reminded in this connection of a well-known fable by the Russian fabulist Krilov, in which a man is speaking of his visit to the zoo and all the creatures that he saw there: 'The tiny flies and beetles, the ladybirds, jewel-like butterflies, and insects with a head no bigger than a pin. What marvels!' 'And did you see the elephant?' asked his friend. 'Oh, do they have one there? I guess I must have missed the elephant.' (Bronfenbrenner, quoted in Bronfenbrenner, Kessel, Kessen, & White, 1986, p. 1219)

Having reviewed theory and research for the prior 100 years, Bronfenbrenner's point was that progress in the discipline of human development throughout the years could be charted by its increasing tendency to look "more and more at less and less" (p. 1219). Grand theories and models had been set aside, the idea of goals or end points toward which development preferentially moves had been abandoned, and tendencies to examine relationships between the broader sociocultural environment and individual development had been jettisoned. Scholars seemed to be "losing their nerve," becoming mere "riders" on a "deconstructionist, postpositivistic, radically relativistic train" (Kessen, in Bronfenbrenner et al., p. 1218).

Now, into the 21st century, partially due to political pressures identified by Bronfenbrenner and colleagues, we study ever narrower and more minute aspects of human qualities to the extent that the entire, highly complex human who advances in developmental space and time seems a mere shadow. This applies to the human attributes we consider in isolation one from another and to the overarching models we use to guide our theory, research, and practice. The end result is a reduction of the entire organism to a partial, lopsided view, a view that varies depending on the lens in use.

Looking to the overarching theoretical models that guide developmental theory and research, we have tended to reduce our models of the complex human "elephant" to either the genetic, biological level (the genome model), the contextual level (the cultural, environmental niche model), or the psychodynamic level (the life stage model). These models vary in view, scope, and level of analysis, but in describing the human each view is only one-third complete. All three models contain data that are necessarily integrated within each person's unique developmental self, one that is historically cumulative and uniquely individual.

In this chapter we take up Krilov's elephant as applied to models of human development. Since a single chapter must be content limited, I consider two of the three models that, given today's knowledge, comprehensively define the adult. These are the contextual and the life stage models. I explore these from the perspectives of Urie Bronfenbrenner's bioecological framework and Erik Erikson's biopsychosocial framework. But first, we explore the reductionistic tendency, one that with respect to examining adults in their lives has a long history of viewing adults as static, non-developmental organisms.

This chapter includes four sections. These are, first, discussion of the tendency in human development to see from within one or another model's lens and the necessity of forging a more comprehensive viewpoint. In this I explore the lessons we might learn from the human tendency to engage in reductionistic, single view thinking. The second section considers contemporary definitions of adult learning and development in their reciprocal associations and their place within models of development. The third section focuses on the contextual and life stage models on the basis of premises established by Bronfenbrenner's bioecological and Erikson's biopsychosocial theories. I note here that both of these theorists focused on the essential role of environmental contexts in shaping, fostering, and thwarting individuals' development, even though Erikson has become known primarily for his life stage concepts. Thus, in this section, considerations of Erikson's thought shifts, first showing his place as a sociocultural contextualist, then elaborating his contextual and stage concepts, and finally focusing on the importance of life stages as essential fuel for current and ongoing development. The concluding section addresses the need to integrate data from all three models of human development—contextual, life stage, and biogenetic—into one metamodel. This is the most comprehensive way forward in our theoretical and research initiatives.

Models as Ways of Seeing in Human Development

As the human cognitive apparatus arranges material in its mental file system, certain content or views predominate while others are moved to the background. The background content then becomes invisible or inconsequential when compared to the predominant view. Examples of this are found in ambiguous figures in which the viewer sees one form (e.g., a vase) as the darkly inked foreground, and other forms (e.g., two persons) when focusing on the pale background. In the psychological realm, in focusing on the contemporary foreground with its influential perspective and data, we frequently fail to consider or discard older views or findings. We often do this not because such perspectives are now incorrect but because the data on which they were based have not been brought up to contemporary times or because such understandings have become so incorporated into our knowledge base that we seem to think we do not need to focus specifically on them. Seeing the persuasive foreground we miss the background, even though both are essential to the complete picture.

In human development today, we focus largely on the more obvious foreground, the *contexts* that shape development. Adult contexts are the personal, highly influential environments (e.g., family milieu, work colleagues and culture, civic commitments and associations), that are nested within the larger macro contexts of life (e.g., the sociocultural, political, ideological environments). Together these contexts form one essential part of our human model, a part that appears discrete and objective, and thus comparatively easy to study. However, if we focus rather differently, we see the background image. This background image represents psychosocial, evolving, life span adults who, while living in various development-shaping prior and current contexts, cannot be extracted from their unique structural, interconnected lives. They are composite humans in the inextricable flow of their complete existence, life-narrative-integrated adults, with their own highly personal, subjective and shifting, content that is difficult to study. This content, expressed through variable contexts, occurs in the stages of adult life; the resolutions of all prior developmental stages exist within each later stage.

Some might claim that the apparently more objective, contextual model represents that which is external to the adult, while the subjective, biopsychosocial life stage model holds content that is internal to the individual. Yet, it has become increasingly clear that the seemingly objective, external context also lives inside and informs our subject, the adult, and his or her sense of the past, present, and future. Thus, for example, a brilliant youth who has the innate talent and interests to become a physician, experiences the ramifications of poverty and lack of acquaintance with professional roles and available resources. As such, access to education leading to a medical degree is denied. The social context, both consciously and unconsciously, is internal to his psyche and sense of possibility. Only 20 to 40 years later, might this person learn of the educational and professional resources that had earlier been available.

We know that development is engineered by genetics in interaction with the environment and a volitional human, by the prenatal and intrauterine environment, by parents or caretakers who have experienced their own developmental positives and negatives, and by resource rich, mediocre, or poor contexts and role models for growth and development in infancy, childhood, and throughout all of the remainder of the life span. Development is also shaped by self-identified and planned futures. Thus as we conceptualize and investigate the adult developmental script, we cannot do other than understand that if we are to appreciate an adult in her or his development, we must understand the forces that have shaped and continue to shape that chronologically mature person, the genetic equipment that was in place from the beginning and which is expressed or dampened over time, the nurturing others and contexts in one unique life, and the way our adult sees the self in the past, present, and future.

Lessons to Learn from Reductionistic Thinking

World Views and Lens-Constricted Models

Sometimes we see things differently because new methods and fresh data undermine prior understandings. Sometimes we look at data differently or are led to see differently because of thinkers who have focused our attention, placing new ways of seeing phenomena on center stage. At other times we see differently because the way we live in the world changes, perhaps suddenly. For example, few U.S. residents see their place in the world today the same as they did prior to the terrorist attacks of September 11, 2001. Adults' thoughts are always related to their perception of history (their own and global history), to the "main currents" of the era, to the experience of one life and period, to the existing "moral climate," and to the "lineage" of thought and discoveries that have occurred up to that point in time (Erikson, 1975, p. 81, 255, 145 respectively). Thus our world view, in our societally nested lives and in the way we see phenomena in our disciplines, is a distorted rendition of reality. We construct reality and in so doing, ours is not an "immaculate perception" (Nietzsche, 1885/1967). Our mind's eye captures and filters for us, and in the final analysis the Talmud is correct: We see things as we are, not as they are (see Taylor, 2006).

In part, humans absorb only a limited portion of reality because the complete, vast, external environment cannot be assimilated by tiny human minds. As Lippmann (1922) said, the mind takes in material from the larger environment and "reconstructs" it on a smaller, simpler scale in order to work with it. Although we must function in the environment as it presents itself to us and as we are able to experience and perceive it, each and every adult brings in a far reduced version of that which is available. We then reorder and remake such personally assimilated reality as a visual, mental construction. This mental reconstruction is made to fit with preferred ideological views and values, with sometimes redrawn understandings of the past, and with projections of visions and a hoped-for future (Erikson, 1977).

The adult tendency to create theories and "schematic" models is evidence of representative, internal "pseudoenvironments" that exemplify thought (Lippmann, 1922, p. 27). The models we use to depict the scientific and social world represent a sometimes sophisticated world view, but this view too is an organization of perceived experience, images, and values. If worldview is indeed a lens through which we appropriate, screen, and understand the environment and our existence in it, this view also exemplifies a "set of interrelated assumptions about the nature of the world" (Overton, 1991, p. 269; see also Koltko-Rivera, 2004; Miller & West, 1993; Pepper, 1942/1970). In our everyday lives and in our discipline-specific models, as Einstein (1945) said, "ideas...(are) as little independent of the nature of our experiences as clothes are of the form of the human body" (p. 2).

Furthermore, the English language leads those who think and speak in its tongue to function in deductive categories, to diminish content downward toward reduction, simplicity, and conceptual dilution. For example, in unabridged English dictionaries, there are more than twice as many words containing the prefix *sub-*, meaning "below," "reduce," or "under," as there are words employing the prefix *super-*, meaning "above" or "of a higher order" (Hoare, 2002, p. 27). English language users are thus led to think as we speak, in subordinate instead of superordinate categories. We abandon expanse and complexity in favor of simplicity and narrowness. Thus, both conceptually and numerically, not only do we diminish the complexity of the external world because of limited minds and experience that help us to "grow" preferential lenses and biases, but thought is further narrowed by the English lexicon.

Stasis and Reductionism in Definitions of Adults: A Brief History

We have come some distance since 184 B.C. when T. Maccius Platus first used the term "adultus" to describe something or someone whose physical form was complete. Having "adulted" meant that one had reached maturity or "ripeness." This ripeness included the peak of seasons, the "sun's full strength," "firmly established states of affairs," and the "distention" or "enlargement" of "fully grown animals, birds, crops, and persons" (Glare, 1982, p. 59). The human adult was amalgamated with all other events, creatures, and planetary occurrences. Physical fullness meant developmental completion. Then, and for nearly all subsequent centuries, the concept of developmental progression in, for example, cognition, identity, insight, intelligence, personality, interpersonal competence, mental maturity, and adaptiveness, were largely absent from concepts about the adult.

In that and many later eras, information about creatures and the world, its topography and other physical characteristics, was the basis for conclusions about the human. Such tendencies evince reasoning by analogy, one of the weakest forms of thinking. In early times, a rudimentary, largely incorrect, knowledge of physics was combined with mythology and magical thinking. These were conveyed through an oral tradition and religious practices. Fears and anxieties inspired much of that tradition, with devils and ill humors warded off by superstition and its various rituals and ministrations.

Even when one considers more recent centuries, static notions about adults continued, then largely inspired by representations of the universe. In the 19th century, for example, the scientific world view held that the planet and humans were central in a non-evolving, static, absolute universe. The predominant world view was Newtonian absolutism. Space was believed immovable and time unalterable. Frames of reference were of one person (or body) relative only to its location and conveyance (e.g., ship or train) alone, not relative to mass or spatial transformation or relative to interaction with other interactive bodies in different frames of reference (Einstein, 1945). Newton's thought was based on notions of Euclidean space and Cartesian coordinates (see Sinnott, 1981), leading to representations of an absolute, uniform, static, and reassuring world. All planets, animals, and particles were believed governed by identical, uniformly applicable, mathematical laws.

Freud's Views About Adults

As the most influential psychologist of the era, Sigmund Freud's voice was prominent. Freud is important to this chapter for he is the progenitor of the idea of psychosexual stages of development, the precursor to Erikson's psychosocial stages. Although Erikson altered Freudian thought substantially, as a student in the Freud School he was informed by Freud's presence, writings, and ways of seeing phenomena.

Writing during the years of 1893 to 1938, owing to his work in neurology and to premises established by the Newtonian-based Hermann Helmholtz school of physiology, Freud held that complex matter, the human included, was reducible to elementary particles and forces. Such forces could be traced back to their geological origins in infancy. Development was not seen as contextually relative, nor did it continue past genital maturity into and through the adult years. Freud depicted the psyche as a Newtonian analogue, a closed, constant system of excitation and discharge, one governed by inertia and Newtonian principles of energy conservation.

Using Newton's very vocabulary, Freud transferred physical principles to the psyche. Freud described "quota" and "quanta" of energy (Freud 1894/1962, p. 60), "mechanical forces" (Freud, 1915/1989b, p. 567), "attraction and repulsion" (Freud, 1940/1969, p. 19), and psychological functions that were specific, localized, quantifiable elements. These elements were "neurones," and neurones were said to retain balance in a state of excitation and discharge (Freud, 1895/1989d, p. 87). Freud's world view expressed the Newtonian "principle of inertia" (Freud, 1895/1989d, p. 88), the "motor force of instincts" (Freud, 1915/1989b, p. 566), "resistance" (Freud, 1940/1965, p. 344), and "discharge" (Freud, 1940/1965, p. 640). As Erikson (1963) said, Freud necessarily saw from within the "thermodynamic" language and views of his day; however, the primacy Freud gave to then-current physical and "histological concepts" led to premises that the adult is a non-developing, static, "neuronic golem" (Erikson, 1975, p. 62). In this Newtonian representation, genital maturity defined adult completion. Freud believed that the adult years were but a barren terrain for development, one in which adults played out their already formed capacities for love and work. Guided by concepts of instincts and neuroses, Freud further claimed that the adult might gain some control over instinctual and neurotic forces, but such control could never be complete.

Furthermore, conceiving of the psychological apparatus as a nearly impermeable, closed system, Freud dissociated the person from important others in the life sphere. Although some Freudians validated the significance of the social world, Sigmund Freud maintained that social groups were completely external to the self and largely of erratic influence. That is, the social "outerworld" surrounded the person but was not internal to the psyche. To Freud, external contexts failed the test of inclusion in individual, analytical depth psychology (see Hoare, 2005). It was inconceivable to Freud that there might be relative spaces in which different persons might know their world and others in that world differently, and in which healthy, positive adult development is not only possible but varies situationally.

As Freud's various case examples show, in patients' relations with other human "objects" he rarely portrayed the context of a social sphere beyond the immediate family, and the family that he occasionally included was the nuclear family of the patient's childhood; the contemporary, postnuclear adult family was largely excluded (e.g., Yankelovich & Barrett, 1970). Intraindividual forces and conflicts governed, and adults were those who were influenced only minimally by others in what we today know of as a shaping, intersubjective, social world.

Freud led thinking along a pathway of stasis and developmental negatives, holding that adulthood was a reenactment of prior life. In this, all one might expect of healthy adults was a comparative absence of the overriding id drives of infancy and of the guilt, fixations, and repressions of childhood. Freud's view was that of a psychological apparatus organized in strata of ever deeper, more primitive layers. One must dig through those layers, searching backward to infantile origins, in order to determine core disturbances (see Erikson, 1958). In fact, although Freud is known to have altered a number of his tenets over time, one of the principal viewpoints he did not change was that of the psyche of origin as a long-buried, archeological artifact.

Freud (1905/1953) saw his work as that of "a conscientious archeologist" who searched through the "mutilated relics of antiquity" (p. 12). Archeological ruins and their unearthing were both the content and the "excavation" technique of psychoanalysis (Freud, 1937/1964, p. 259). He held that "Pompeii," "the tomb of Tut'ankhamum," and repressed material yielded equally "to the work of spades" (p. 260). Expectations for adults were largely expressed in developmental negatives, in terms of what adults should not be and do. By expressing development in terms of absence, most psychologists who came along immediately after Freud failed to examine what adults *are* in their positive development and in their ongoing developmental potentials. A view "backward" to the infancy of personal life, "downward" into the depths of the unconscious, and "inward" to the self, to instincts and pathology, dominated Freud's thought and approach (Erikson, 1987b, p. 598). The world view of Newtonian mechanical forces and pre-Einstein absolutism were among the premises that kept Freud from exploring forward (through developmental life), upward (in consciousness), and outward (toward others). Adulthood was not in focus as a realm in which mental health and normalcy were considered, a period in which development occurs as persons live inter-subjectively with others and in changing environments through time. Far afield were concepts of adults who live in relative social spaces and structures that not only surround, but infuse and govern, great aspects of the psychological system.

By 1920, Freud's ideas of adult developmental stasis informed thought throughout much of the Western hemisphere. Thus, a quarter of the way into the 20th century in the United States little had changed with respect to a product notion of adults. In 1927, the newly begun *Psychological Abstracts* held only five citations using the descriptor *adult*. Those few addressed adult education and the child's views about the adult. One year later, a popular dictionary defined *adult* as one who is "grown up to full age, size and strength: n. a full-grown person, animal or plant" (Devlin, 1928, p. 22). Thus, in mainstream psychoanalysis, in the influential psychological theories of the day, and in everyday thought, the idea of adult developmental progression remained non-existent.

At the time in the United States, with World War I barely resolved and a dramatic influx of immigrants still underway, it was likely thought of as silly to consider what it meant to function as an adult or to change developmentally. It is not that our ancestors had few ideas about what adulthood meant. Everyone *knew* what an adult was: A mature person who behaves according to standards of sound judgment, maturity, able reasoning, and deferral of gratification. Adult attributes were those of "sanity, normality, rationality, continuity, sobriety, responsibility, wisdom, conduct as opposed to mere behavior, the good of the family or group or species as distinct from the desires of the individual" (Stegner, 1978, p. 227; see also Jordan, 1978). Other than in applications to standards of conduct and mature thought, the middle of the 20th century would have to arrive before influential thinkers began to consider the grown person as one who also changed considerably, frequently positively, during the young, middle, older, and aged years of life.

By mid-century, post-Newtonian scientific premises had found their way into psychological thought. Upsetting the conceptual apple cart, the combined discoveries of Copernicus, Darwin, and Einstein had led to realizations that humans are non-central, and, perhaps, even irrelevant, in a relative, evolving universe. Psychologists began to seriously consider the implications to their field of Einstein's discoveries of general and special relativity (respectively, in 1905 and 1926), and, pressed by Darwin's work in evolution, philosophical thought had moved away from belief in a great "chain of being," a hierarchical system in which all creatures are seen as ordered in one, absolute, uniform structure, arranged from lowest to highest (Lovejoy, 1936; see also Lovejoy, 1902, 1930; Wilson, 1980, 1983). Psychological thought began to entertain variable developmental forces and Lewinian fields of forces (Lewin, 1936, 1951).

The *mechanistic*, behavioral world view, with the static, closed, observable, and controllable machine as its metaphor eventually made space for an *organismic* world view of humans. The *organismic view* has as its metaphor the living, breathing organism, one who is seen in many forms, is open to the external world, evolves over time, and organically constructs experience (see Reese & Overton, 1970). The era of psychosocial relativity had begun.

Beginning in the mid-1970s, developmental psychologists began to apply relativistic thought to their work. Among others, Riegel's (e.g., 1975a, b; Wertheimer et al., 1978) work on the dialectics of development, Datan's (1977) applications of dialectical concepts to developmental research, and Gergen's (1977) concepts about change and chance in human development, paved the way (see Sinnott, 1981). Studying Hitler's Germany, the Native American Sioux and Yurok cultures, and the American experience, Erikson's (e.g., 1939, 1942, 1943) concepts about the relativity of cultural understandings, views, and child rearing patterns shaped some of this thought.

Contemporary Definitions: The Developing and Learning Adult

Contemporary concepts now define adult development and learning in new and integrated ways. *Adult development* means:

> systematic, qualitative changes in human abilities and behaviors as a result of interactions between internal and external environments. Interactions and qualitative changes are influenced by genetics, by endogenous and exogenous influences, and by adaptive powers and personal interests. Many abilities are multidimensional.

For example, adult intelligence is comprised of multiple abilities and is intrinsically influenced by personality, motivation, adaptive abilities, and physical and mental health. (Hoare, 2006a, p. 8)

Development means growth and change, those changes that are "orderly, sequential, and lawful" (Endler, Boulter, & Osser, 1976, p. 1). In adulthood, development is bi-directional for there are advances (e.g., introspective ability) and declines (e.g., processing speed). Some declines occur as early as one's late twenties in functions such as psychomotor reflexes (Lu et al., 2004).

With respect to transformations, *qualitative change* means alterations in human functioning and in ways of perceiving and interpreting oneself in the world and in one life narrative. Such changes typically move toward greater expanse and complexity. In this, development is not solely determined quantitatively, for complexity is frequently discounted when human attributes are merely seen in the aggregate. As well, we know that there is great variance among adults. There are significant inter-individual and cohort differences, just as there are differences among adults in genetics, environments, resources, experiences, motivations, and ongoing learning involvement. Inherited tendencies and the sequential contexts of each person's life are equally important. Heated disputes about the comparable weight of nature versus nurture continue on. However, asking whether heredity or environment is more essential to the development of a particular set of attributes is like "asking whether the length or the width is more important in determining the area of a rectangle" (Endler et al., 1976, p. 13). The correct perspective focuses on the key contributions of, and the principal interactions between and among, inherited givens, epigenetics (life stage changes), environmental contexts (both endogenous and exogenous), experiences, intentional choices, and inclinations.

Individuals follow different developmental trajectories in the constancy, development, and deterioration of important attributes and behaviors over time. Each human is a universe of one; thus, as a group, adults necessarily become more heterogeneous over time. Some of adult uniqueness emanates from different roles, experiences, educational backgrounds, family and environmental resources, and motivations. For example, some adults will advance in intellectual acumen, others will deteriorate intellectually, and some will show few or no obvious changes (Ditmann-Kohli & Baltes, 1990; Fillet et al., 2002). Some adults will develop more mature ego defenses during adulthood, while others will fail to develop or regress to immature defenses and coping styles (e.g., Vaillant, 1995, 2000). Some adults will move to the ethical level of principled behavior, while others will remain moral, moralistic, and judgmental. Various life contexts—work, civic, and personal environments—and the important persons in those environments, will catalyze movement in positive or negative directions. Humans are always permeable to their world, to their position in one life narrative, to sociocultural factors, and to key others in their lives. Adult development will vary depending on these factors and because of a unique genetic endowment that interacts with environmental engagement, tasks, opportunities, and interests.

As recent literature (e.g., Hoare, 2006a, b; Smith & Pourchot, 1998) shows, *adult learning* is itself a developmental quality and process. As is true among youth, adult learning is "a change in behavior, a gain in knowledge or skills, and an alteration or re-structuring of prior knowledge; such learning can also mean a positive change in self-understanding or in the development of personal qualities such as coping mechanisms" (Hoare, 2006a, p. 11). Thus, learning is not just an accumulation of information, nor is it merely a change in behavior. Learning includes acquiring or applying information, or changing or re-ordering content in one's cognitive file cabinet. This can mean deleting antiquated content when new knowledge requires this change, as well as subsuming newly acquired information beneath, or super-ordinating it above, prior content. This understanding blurs a prior distinction. Some learning theorists have previously distinguished between knowledge acquisition (learning) and re-structuring knowledge (development) (e.g., Endler et al., 1976). This is an artificial distinction in the absence of studies that show cognitive development during knowledge re-structuring but not during knowledge acquisition. Thus both the acquisition of knowledge and its revision and re-ordering require learning, and cognitive development cannot be separated from such learning.

A number of adult developmental attributes (e.g., intellectual, emotional, insight, self-efficacy) are contingent on learning. And learning during the adult years frequently leads to one or another form of development. As development and learning interact, a scaffolding effect occurs such that learning and development each lead to increments in its essential counterplayer. Both are transformed in the process. Two examples follow.

Living and learning in intricate, complex environments, and learning that goes beyond a person's occupation, predict advances in cognitive development (Pirttila-Backman & Kajanne, 2001). In elders, affluence and interest in cultural and educational activities are associated with cognitive flexibility (Hood & Deopere, 2002; Schaie, 1990, 1993). Cognitive flexibility is also associated with increased learning engagement. In, for example, the prospective, longitudinal Einstein Aging Study, subjects over the age of 75 who engaged in cognitive activities (playing musical instruments or board games, reading) experienced a lower risk for dementia (Verghese et al., 2003).

Insight development has been implicated in additional learning and in the transformation of knowledge into action (e.g., Miller, 2006). "Elaboration" and extended "detailed investigation" (learning) are essential extensions to the developments in awareness that we call *insight* (Pollock, 1981, p. 286). Adults who understand that knowledge is complex, evolving, tenuous, and sometimes contradictory tend to take multiple perspectives, alter their views over time, and avoid early closure in reaching decisions (Pascual-Leone & Irwin, 1998).

Contextual and Life Stage Models

The Contextual Model

In recent decades, psychologists have increasingly moved toward what I have described as the contextual foreground (presented in the first section of this chapter). This foreground is now developmentalists' dominant world view and model. Ongoing dissension persists in the literature with respect to the preeminence that should be attributed to person or environmental attributes; however, the contextual model has eclipsed the life span model (see Cervone, 2004; Cervone, Artistico, & Berry, 2006; Haney, 2002; Mischel, 1990). There are a number of reasons for this dominance in viewpoint, three of which are important to this chapter. These reasons are, first, the way we visually see persons and their related, compelling problems in our world, particularly among youth and elders; second, the movement toward ecologically valid research; and third, our enhanced understanding, recently, about variance in personal outlooks and ways of being in the world, and the way structural social conditions and events shape those perspectives.

Taking these in turn, first, developmental issues are born of what we literally see in the persons around us and what we see from within the vantage point of our social, institutional, problem-oriented structures. In our homes, schools, and communities, we see, literally, children grow and change, becoming more (or less) proficient at language use, mathematical competence, and physical abilities. Among other issues, our recent focus on children and older youth in the elementary and secondary public schooling systems, for example, addresses concerns about declines in student achievement and an alleged deterioration in the competence of public educational systems (e.g., Levine, 2006). Based on such deficit views, anxieties exist about the future ability of the United States to compete in the global economy.

As well, school violence, Internet exploitation of children, and youth substance abuse rivet our attention (see, e.g., Friedman, 2006). Replacing the previous perspective that such problems are preventable, research and practice now tend toward a resilience and compensatory viewpoint relative to children and older youth. That is, experts focus primarily on how we might make up for existing educational deficits, and how, given the tacit belief that social perils and youth disturbances are not fully preventable, we must determine which children are resilient and the circumstances and contexts in which such resilience is expressed (e.g., Haggerty, Sherrod, Garmezy, & Rutter, 1996).

For example, recent data indicate that nearly 50% of high school completers have used one or more drugs illicitly during their secondary school years (Friedman, 2006). In this population, the illicit use of prescription drugs has increased markedly and the use of illicit street drugs continues. Whether obtained through the Internet, from their parents or friends, or on the street, non-medical use of such medications has risen. Sedative use was 7.2% among high school seniors in 2005 (up from 2.89% in 1992); Oxycodone use was 5.5% in 2005, compared with 4.0% in 2002. Interpreting large scale national surveys and follow-up interviews with teens about such drug use, Friedman (2006) found that many such youth used street drugs (e.g., ecstasy, cocaine) for "recreation" and prescription medications for their "practical" needs. "Practical" needs are met with stimulants (to heighten school performance), hypnotics (for sleep), and tranquilizers (for stress reduction). Across the board, experts imply a contemporary impotence in prevention. Substitute agendas include efforts to understand why some youngsters are more resilient in stressful and peer pressure circumstances, why and how some deploy various abnormal coping and adaptation mechanisms (e.g., drug use), and the extent to which professionals can inculcate normal mechanisms in less resilient youth.

Observing, we see visual changes in the elderly as well and, given the growing numbers of aged seniors in our midst, middle-agers, those in various command positions, cannot help but notice the physical deterioration that waits silently to sabotage their lives. In 2005 (the most recent year for which data are available), in the fastest-growing age group, nearly four million Americans were 85 years of age or older, an age group that is projected to number 28 million by 2050 (U.S. Bureau of the Census, 2005). As is true of youth in their early developmental years, changes at the far end of life are so striking that one cannot avoid noticing, paying sustained attention, and posing remedies. Social policy implications (e.g., for Social Security, Medicare) loom large and expensive. That which costs dollars and human resources compels interest, speculation, and remedial approaches.

Adding to our tendency to study those at both ends of life's spectrum is the fact that most studies investigate persons who are readily available in confined settings (e.g., schools, community agencies, college courses, elder care environments). Although there are some stunning exceptions (e.g., Baltes & Mayer, 1999; Roberts & Helson, 1997), time- and context-limited research predominates. Short-term convenience studies are fruitful in a rush-to-publish world and cost far less than longer term cross- or cohort-sequential studies. Such factors have pressed forward the shift to contextual views, to sectioned windows into the lives and problems of people who are contained in various sites.

The second reason for the dominance of the contextual model is that it has become increasingly clear that the laboratory is an artificial milieu in which persons-as-subjects behave artificially, or at least far differently, compared to their performance in the outside, "real" world. For example, an elder adult who in the laboratory fails the test of selecting the correct grocery items based on unit pricing is then observed during actual grocery shopping in the senior residence community. On questioning our senior, the observer learns that the subject has a sophisticated understanding of unit pricing but nonetheless selects the "incorrect" items, doing so because she cannot physically manage to carry the heavier, more cost effective items to her apartment. With such recognitions, a number of investigators have moved in the direction of ecologically valid investigations in which subjects are studied in the actual contexts in which they typically function (see, e.g., Haney, 2002; Neisser & Hyman, 1999).

Third, we have come to realize that "when people live in the world differently," they truly "live in different worlds" (Schweder, 1991, p. 23). Among other factors, recent decades in the United States have been those of rapid fire increases in numbers of "cultural others" and in a growing multiplicity of social, cultural, and racial backgrounds and outlooks (Hoare, 1991). Awareness has also grown that all humans live in a highly permeable, rather small, global environment. Pollutants do not restrict themselves to national boundaries; insulation from nearly immediate information about natural and human-made disasters around the world is almost non-existent in a media-pervasive, information world. Peering down from outer space, satellites have shown us connected world space in stark relief. Our global contextual view is thus need based: An awareness that all share in the potential for destruction has enhanced recognition of our need to understand deeply embedded socio-cultural characteristics, beliefs, differences, and biases. The shared context of one small planet has concentrated our attention. In the United States, this seems to be particularly true since terrorism arrived on home soil.

Understanding how it is that persons live differently in the world also relates to understandings about societal structural differences and access to resources. Belatedly in the United States, we came to understand the relationship between health, including mental health, and socioeconomic status. For example, in the bleak economic conditions of the Great Depression, illness was higher in the 17% of families whose breadwinners were unemployed and in families on relief, in which one in 20 heads of household was disabled. In 1939, the maternal mortality rate for African American women was double that for White women, a ramification of class separation and social deprivation (Hoare, 2002).

Dramatic social events can thwart access to opportunity, intellectual development, and learning, particularly when social class enters the equation. For example, those in the lower socioeconomic, working class, who were forming their identities during World War II and the Great Depression, suffered adverse effects in their learning engagement and emotional functioning. However, among those with adequate personal and emotional resources, social involvement, and middle-class status, the position was reversed. Subsequent learning engagement, identity development, and emotional stability resulted (Caspi & Elder, 1986; Duncan & Agronick, 1995). More recent epic struggles (e.g., the Vietnam War, the Civil Rights movement) have had similar effects, sustaining development for some and undermining it for others (Elder, Rudkin, & Conger, 1994). After the peak years of the Civil Rights era, we became increasingly sensitive to the ways in which structural conditions in society operate to favor some persons in their development and oppress others. We see this in other realms as well. In specific content areas, for example in science and mathematics career options, the person's inclination to transform interests into educational choices and the development of self-efficacy are dramatically affected by barriers and supports in the educational context (Lent, Brown, Brenner, Chopra, Davis, & Talleyrand, 2001).

We know that paid work is inseparable from the society in which that work occurs, and that the deprivation of work opportunities equates with identity deprivation. For example, investigating the influence of increasing individualism in the United States, Roberts and Helson (1997) studied women at four periods over 31 years. They found that increasing individualism, particularly between 1960 and 1985, was associated with enhanced work-based identity development and with increases in self-focus, self-assertion, individuality, and narcissism. Adherence to norms declined. In that longitudinal study, in the years between 1958 and 1989, increases in women's individualism increased and peaked concurrently with trends in the escalation and peak of societal individualism. Work effects were seen in, for example, a growing intolerance for "glass ceilings" and expectations that salaries would be gender neutral (see Moen, Kelly, & Maginnis, chapter 13, this volume). Women's assertiveness also emanated from the feminist movement during those years. The net effect for women, particularly among well-prepared knowledge workers, was that of identity development, personal empowerment, inclusion, and autonomy (Hoare, 2006b). Thus, the social world and changes in that world represent an important set of contexts that both surround and enter each individual's reality.

One Contextual Model, Two Contextual Thinkers

Just as it is uniquely able to adapt to multiple environments, the human species is unique in its ability to design environments that, for better or worse, mold development. In the 20th century, two important thinkers independently studied the shaping roles of large scale and smaller, specific environments. Both worked to help scholars and practitioners understand the ways in which society and everyday contexts shape children and adults, and how positive, development-fostering environments might be designed. These thinkers were Erik Erikson and Urie Bronfenbrenner. Although their disciplines differed, their agendas and their focus on the external milieu that is internal to each person were similar.

Erikson, the psychoanalyst, was born in Frankfurt am Main, Germany, in 1902, and Bronfenbrenner, the developmental psychologist, was born in Moscow in 1917. Their European heritage is important to their work for both theorists conveyed the intellectual breadth of thought that transcended disciplinary boundaries in Europe in the first decades of the 20th century. Immigrants to the United States, both were visionaries who examined the link between individual development and the development of the group and society. Focusing their work sometimes simultaneously on the person and society, some would scorn this tendency as confusing levels of analysis, but neither thinker was deterred by such criticism (Kracke, 1978).

Both the psychoanalyst and the developmental scientist argued for healthy, strong families and supportive communities and institutions, the essence of their generative work. For both, interdisciplinary work was essential to these ends. For Erikson, developmental and societal concerns led to his social criticism and advocacy in support of the needs and rights of all persons. Bronfenbrenner focused more so on social policy, social action, and advocacy for children, concerns that led to his co-founding the national Head Start Program in 1965 (see Wertsch, 2005). He was a participant observer and researcher in the actual settings in which children lived, learned, and played. In such involvement, particularly in originating Head Start, he was indebted to Walter Dearborn who, during his protege's graduate years at Harvard said to him, "Bronfenbrenner, if you wish to understand something, try to change it" (Bronfenbrenner, 1995, p. 606).

Although Bronfenbrenner attended primarily to the needs of children in their development, whereas Erikson's thought considered individuals throughout the entirety of the life span, both held that the extent to which children are focal in a society's concern expresses the extent of the maturational development of that society. Both theorists warned that the late twentieth century harbored dire destructive tendencies. In his last book, Bronfenbrenner (2005) cautioned, "The major social changes taking place recently in modern industrialized societies, especially the United States, may have altered environmental conditions conducive to human development to such a degree that the process of making human beings human is being placed in jeopardy" (p. xxvii). In *his* last publication, Erikson (1985) expressed concern about the potential for species' destruction in a technological, nuclear age. He warned, as he had since 1965, about the necessity for understanding and overcoming the "pseudospecies" (prejudice) mentality, the pan human tendency to see cultural others as so different and inferior that they must be annihilated. He urged all people across the globe to find within and between them the universality of "childhood as a binding all-human phenomenon" before it was too late to do so (p. 217).

In their later years, both Bronfenbrenner and Erikson were particularly concerned about the perils of modern life with its depleted space and time for children to grow and thrive. Today, with more than 5 million stepfamily children, and their higher rates of disciplinary, drop out, and school performance problems, both theorists would likely be even more alarmed. Addressing single-parent families compared to families with two biological parents, Bronfenbrenner (2005) reported that even in single-parent families who live in positive socioeconomic circumstances, children are at risk for "hyperactivity or withdrawal, lack of attentiveness, difficulty in deferring gratification, poor academic achievement, school misbehavior, and frequent absenteeism" (p. 10). The family as a context for development had deteriorated. Citing data from 1996, he found that children (particularly boys) are at a disproportionate risk for a range of connected difficulties, a phenomenon he termed the teenage behavioral syndrome: "Dropping out of school; involvement in socially alienated or destructive peer groups; smoking; drinking; frequent sexual experience; adolescent pregnancy; a cynical attitude toward work; and—in the more extreme cases—drugs, suicide, vandalism, violence, and criminal acts" (p. 10).

In 2006, the U.S. Department of Health and Human Services alerted the country about conditions detrimental to youth and adults. Based on data from 2002, their report shows the relationship among parental educational attainment, teenage sexual activity, child rearing, child support, and poverty. Focusing primarily on males, they found that: men who did not reside with both parents at 14 years of age were more likely to engage in adolescent sexual activity; 50% of men without a high school diploma fathered a child outside marriage, compared with 6% among college degree recipients; 50% of the men who married during their teen years divorced or separated within the subsequent decade, compared with 17% of men marrying at age 26 or older; one-fourth of the 28 million men who have dependent children do not live in the home with those children (Centers for Disease Control, 2006). In terms of monetary and personal resources, including developmental care, parental presence, and positive role modeling and grooming, the environments of single-parent, blended, and re-combined families provide poorer conditions, both for children and the adults in those families.

Even in traditional families, the pace of life and the fact of two working parents have created difficulties. According to the Families and Work Institute, between 1977 and 1997, the number of employees working 50 or more hours per week increased from 24% to 37%, and commuting time also escalated dramatically (Crouter & Bumpus, 2001; Galinsky,

1999). Yet, for some parents there is little choice. In a family of four, with two children under the age of 18, both parents working full time at the federal minimum wage have combined earnings that place their family barely above the U. S. poverty threshold.

Many children have recently expressed discontent, not just about two employed parents and their ever-rising weekly work hours, but about their parents' work-associated stress and its effects of irritability, impatience, and exhaustion when home (Galinsky, 1999). This is on direct lineage with Bronfenbrenner's (1986, 2000, 2005) concerns about the family context as a "chaotic system," one in which "frenetic activity, lack of structure, unpredictability in everyday activities, and high levels of ambient stimulation" are daily experiences (Bronfenbrenner, 2005, p.14).

Bronfenbrenner's Ecological Framework

Although Bronfenbrenner's and Erikson's interests, analyses, and perspectives were similar, they were unique in their approach to the contexts of life that shape development. In this section, I explore Bronfenbrenner's, and in the following section, Erikson's, concepts about important contexts for development.

In his 1942 dissertation, "*Social status, structure, and development in the classroom group,*" we see the beginnings of Bronfenbrenner's studied concern for children in one of their principal contexts. This concern evolved into his research agenda, later expressed as his bioecological model. But it was his childhood experience walking through the woods, swamps, and farmland with his father, a naturalist and a neuropathologist, that led him to see the "functional interdependence between living organisms and their surroundings" (Bronfenbrenner, 1979, p. xii). Bronfenbrenner's thought evolved over time, even past his groundbreaking 1979 volume, *The Ecology of Human Development,* in which he clarified the distinctions, and relationships among, attributes of the micro-, exo-, and macro-systems, and the interactions between those systems and individuals in the systems.

Contexts for development are ecological structures in the life space, topologically nested regions that include inner individual variables (genetic, biological, psychological) and external settings and cultural forces (e.g., economy, political climate). In writing about these variables, Bronfenbrenner (1979) acknowledged his intellectual debt to thinkers such as Lewin, Vygotsky, and Piaget. Based on Lewinian thought, Bronfenbrenner held that interaction exists among forces and regions (Lewin, 1936; Bronfenbrenner, 1977, 1979, 1986). In this, each person possesses a unique phenomenological field, a mental world of personal reality, fantasy, imagination, and unreality (Bronfenbrenner, 1977); this life space perceived is "more important than the actual, the unreal more valid than the real" (p. 202). With Piagetian understandings in hand, Bronfenbrenner understood that reality is relative and gave credibility to the reality in the mind of the knower. Behavior and development are "steered" by interaction between the individual, as that person perceives and constructs reality, and the environment (p. 205). Based on Vygotsky's (e.g., 1978) thought, Bronfenbrenner interpreted the "zone of proximal development" as the family and other close environments. He then moved from that zone to others that fan outward from the person.

Nested Structures.   Concerned about children, their experience and fate in a harried world, Bronfenbrenner directed his research to youth in their various environments of, for example, family constellations, school settings, and child care environments. Figure 3.1 adapts Bronfenbrenner's (1979) framework to the experience of adults. The total environment experienced by the person is a "set of nested structures, each inside the

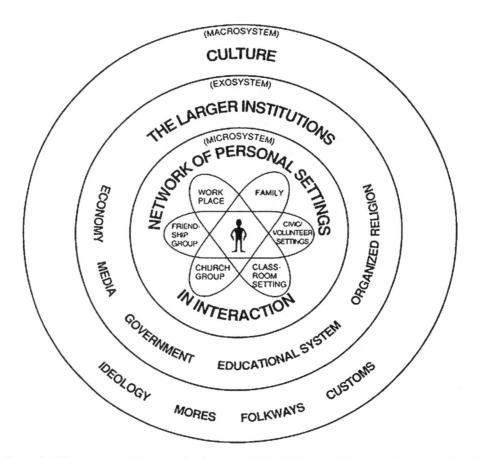

Figure 3.1 The ecology of human development. Adapted from *Children and Families in the Social Environment* (p. 26), by J. Garbarino, 1982, New York: Aldine Publishing Co. With permission.

next, like a set of Russian dolls" (p. 3). The settings that are most proximal to the person exist in the *microsystem*, a network of settings that do not narrowly compartmentalize but interact in the person's psychological life. Among adults, these close-to-the-person contexts (e.g., workplace, family, friendship group, church affiliations, civic settings) include individuals' roles in such settings. Together these are the contexts that most influence ongoing development.

Moving outward, the next tier is the *exosystem* which is comprised of the larger institutions of life in which persons may not necessarily have defined, formal roles, but which nonetheless influence individuals markedly. As expressed in the figure, these are, for example, the economy, government, laws and regulations, organized religion, the educational system, and the media. Their effects are pervasive, if sometimes unconsciously experienced. The ring farthest away from the person is that of the larger culture or society which encapsulates and influences persons. This *macrosystem is* the sociocultural surround, one expressing ideology, views, mores, customs, and, in homogeneous cultures, folkways. Although seemingly less proximal to the person in his or her everyday life, each adult is deeply affected by the content, events, and alterations occurring in that societal context. Bronfenbrenner's *mesosystem* (absent from the figure), is not a delineated structure among the nested tiers, but is that of the person's interactive experience between two or more of the nested settings. Like a bidirectional arrow, the mesosystem reflects the reciprocal influence of the various structures on the person and of the person on the structures. To account for temporal, sociohistorical factors that shape individual development differently, Bronfenbrenner used the term *chronosystem*. For example, egalitarian U.S. educational opportunities and employment possibilities for men and women today are vastly different from the sharply gender-bifurcated possibilities of the 1950s. Different eras and sociopolitical contexts have variable effects on development.

In 2005, Bronfenbrenner defined human development as "the *phenomenon of continuity and change in the biopsychological characteristics of human beings, both as individuals and as groups*" (p. xxviii, italics in the original). He saw this phenomenon as one that traverses the course of life, both within one life and across sequential cohorts throughout history. In that iteration, Bronfenbrenner seemed to give nearly equal weight to the micro-, exo-, and macro-systems, but his writing shows his continued belief that the most proximal zone, the microsystem, exerts the greatest effect on children and families.

In 2005, he wrote about his movement away from considering discrete, nested systems to a perspective of "*interconnected systems*" (p. 1). Presenting nine developmental propositions, the first proposition acknowledges the interaction between heredity and environment and gives credibility to each child's (and adult's) subjective experience. Beginning in childhood, and evolving to later reflect both change and stability, subjective feelings include, for example, "anticipations, forebodings, hopes, doubts, (and) personal beliefs" (p. 5).

There are also objective relationships, some that are proximal, "primary engines," and some that are "remote" (p. 6). These objective attributes are his second and third propositions, some found in his earlier work and others that are based on more recent interpretations. His second proposition is that "over the life course, human development takes place through the processes of progressively more complex reciprocal interaction between an active, evolving biopsychological human organism and the persons, objects, and symbols in its immediate external environment" (p. 6). These interactions are "proximal processes" in which children must experience regular, "enduring" engagement with at least one devoted, attending adult (p. 6). His third proposition is similar to the second, but adds the potential for research in which "process-person-context-time" (PPCT) are examined together (p. 7).

The next two propositions reflect the necessity of each child's experience of strong emotional attachment to an adult and the child's incorporation of resultant positive feelings into his or her own self-system. Each youth needs to actively and regularly experience successively more complicated activities over sustained time with at least one adult who is committed to the child and with whom the child develops a reciprocal attachment (Proposition IV). This is the basis for the child's internalization of parental affection and his or her ability to form interests, engagement, and motivations for exploration (Proposition V).

Proposition VI holds that the ability to successfully master the developmental feats expressed in Propositions IV and V requires that the child have two adults (preferably one of each gender) who are available, loving, and deeply involved with the child. Bronfenbrenner largely referred to the two-parent family, citing data about the disturbed effects shown by children living in many single-parent families, particularly in the absence of a supportive constellation of relatives, neighbors, and concerned others. Nearly as important as its role in nurturing the child is the support such surrogate others provide to the caretaking parent. Bronfenbrenner was concerned about the trend of increased permissiveness, the contemporary family's lack of structure and discipline, showing that many children today are not so much raised and groomed as they are allowed to grow up nearly on their own. In particular, "neglect, abuse, (and) domination" are especially potent predictors of disturbed development and maladaptive behavior among youth (Bonfenbrenner, 2005, p. 12).

Bronfenbrenner (2005) cited evidence in support of each of his first five propositions. However, he held that his final three propositions were tentative, awaiting empirical evidence. In those latter propositions he focused on the influential effects of children on their parents' development. Noting the role reversal that often occurs as parents age and adult children become parents to their parents, he held that when there is little reciprocal attachment during the child's early years, "there may be no attachment at the end" when aging parents need their children's concern, care, and ministrations (p. 13).

Indicating the importance of research designs that link genetics and environmental factors and noting their rarity, in 1986 Bronfenbrenner referenced earlier longitudinal studies by Skeels (Skeels & Dye, 1939; Skeels, Updegraff, Wellman, & Williams, 1938; Skodak & Skeels, 1949), and more contemporary research by Crowe (1974), Hutchings and Mednick (1977), Scarr and Weinberg (1976, 1983), and Schiff (Schiff, Duyme, Dumaret, & Tomkiewicz, 1981, 1982). He also recalculated certain of Bouchard's (e.g., Bouchard & McGue, 1981) data on monozygotic and dizygotic twins, reared together and apart.

For example, Skeels (Skodak & Skeels, 1949) had compared the intellectual development of children raised from their early years in adoptive families with youth reared by their biological parents. Among other findings, advantaged (middle class) home situations and parental engagement resulted in advanced intellectual development among children in adoptive homes. When placed in such circumstances, the mean I.Q. of adoptive children became 20 points higher than that of their biological parents (Skodak & Skeels, 1949). These findings have been replicated among U.S. children (Scarr & Weinberg, 1976) and European youth (Schiff, Duyme, Dumaret, & Tomkiewicz, 1981, 1982).

Recalculating the twin study correlations of Bouchard (e.g., Bouchard & McGue (1981), Bronfenbrenner (1975, 1986) found that although adoptive twins reared apart have different home environments, some share similar community environments. For example, in two samples of 35 and 38 pairs of twins, the mean Binet I.Q. correlation for twins living in the same community and attending the same school was .83 and .87, respectively, while for those reared in different towns it was .67 and .66. When localities were compared on the basis of economics and size, the mean I.Q. correlation of separated adoptive twins residing in similar towns was .86, while for those residing in highly dissimilar communities it was .26.

By the early 1980s, Bronfenbrenner had begun to more closely examine the importance of familial and significant non-familial contexts on adults as well as children. Among others, he cited the work of Mortimer (e.g., Mortimer, Lorence, & Kumka, 1986) and Kohn (e.g., Kohn, 1969; Kohn & Schooler, 1982, 1983). For example, Mortimer found that men who had married in the first decade after college graduation experienced greater career stability, work autonomy, job satisfaction, and higher incomes then those who had remained single. Kohn (1969) showed that men whose jobs demanded subjection to authority required compliance from their children. In contrast, men whose work required autonomy and self-direction expected this of their youngsters. In longitudinal studies addressing work contexts and related job attributes, Kohn and Schooler (1973, 1978, 1982, 1983) found that job conditions requiring self-direction and the use of complex thinking skills were important predictors of intellectual and autonomy development 10 years later. In particular, absence of routinization, job autonomy, and use of complex skills led to increased intellectual flexibility. More recent data support these findings (see Hoare, 2006b, pp. 362–369).

Erikson's Psychodynamic Framework

The Social, Cultural World Inside the Psyche

In human development, Erik Erikson was the first developmental theorist in the United States to capture the contextual and the psychodynamic life stage frameworks as integrated entities. Pre-dating other contextualists, he showed how each person lives in the larger external context of society and culture and in the smaller environments of family, important others, and relationships, themselves reflecting the larger environment. Importantly, Erikson also showed how society and culture are internal to the psyche.

Erikson wrote about the importance of context in two primary ways. The first of these is the broader culture or society, that which infuses and shapes psychosocial attributes. Metaphorically, culture is a "tapestry weaving" (Erikson & Erikson, 1981). Culture embeds and inculcates views, behavior, and developmental grooming through, for example, parent and group imprinting and teaching of children, and among adults, through values, norms, and expectations. Erikson's second use of contexts is that of spheres, those experiential environments that persons' both operate within and envisage.

Society and culture were so important to Erikson's work that late in his life he feared he would appear to have given disproportionate attention to them. But due, perhaps, to the way his identity construct and life stage thought received such inordinate attention, and because he thought in a scanning, inductive manner and wrote diffusely, the contextual aspects of his thought have largely gone by the wayside. In fact, his lifetime of work has largely been diluted to the eight-stage grid of invariant, sequential lifespan development, a fact he abhorred.

As early as 1930 in Vienna, Erikson saw the myriad ways in which the social world both surrounds and lives inside the psyche. Erikson repeatedly addressed the ways different societies, cultural and social groupings, and various external physical attributes such as landscape, topography, and continental attributes, infuse human perceptions. Such external realities are integrated into each person's internal lens, and differences are experienced and expressed as culturally unique ways of being in the world. An ethos of social, cultural rituals and understandings, based on such attributes and on patterns of living, is transmitted to each infant, and this ethos and its norms become more durable as the child develops into an adult, incorporating such knowledge, group habits, customs, mores, and values, along the way. To Erikson, psychological understandings were incomplete to the extent that they failed to incorporate sociocultural attributes and patterns, adaptations to them, and symptoms that show aberrations.

As he began to understand youth in society en route to his later concepts about development in mentally healthy adults, Erikson incorporated three then-new psychoanalytic, developmental perspectives in his thought. The first was Einstein's theory of relativity as it applies to the shaping role of relative familial, group, and sociocultural contexts. The second was knowledge from the border area where psychology meets anthropology. The third was Darwinian evolutionary thought in its forward, adaptational emphasis. These perspectives led him to move beyond Freudian thought. Writing autobiographically in 1975 about his early psychoanalytic training in Vienna Erikson said:

> The question remained, I felt dimly, whether an image of man constructed primarily on the basis of observation in the clinical laboratory might not lack what, in man's

total existence, leads *outward* from self-centeredness to the mutuality of love and communality, *forward* from the enslaving past to the utopian anticipation of new potentialities, and *upward* from the unconscious to the enigma of consciousness. (p. 39, emphasis in original)

With respect to the ways in which culture intersects with universal tendencies of developmental unfolding, infants and children are molded such that cultural differences come about. That is, culture intrudes into ontogenetic development to alter a child's budding, natural inclinations. Through unconscious but systematic "interference" with the child's natural inclinations and impulses, child training and educational intervention lead to the child's regulation in such a way that sociocultural variations in humans are wrought (Erikson, 1939, p. 132). Thus, as adults, humans have been variously calibrated, psychosocially, to a particular cultural, social, or national perspective, its representations and world view. In a nation or culture, inculcated norms, values, and practices endure to the extent that they are useful, psychologically, sociopolitically, economically, and spiritually (Erikson, in Evans, 1967).

Throughout the long human childhood, habituation to and preference for, the familiarity of daily rituals, the repetitive experience of such practices becomes satisfying both in their anticipation and in their ongoing occurrence. In this way, value-honed beliefs, practices, and perspectives are encrypted, and youth are indoctrinated into them. A lens is thus built through which youth see and interpret, producing habits born of a particular view, as well as patterns of blindness. Each young person who has been brought up grows in his or her habituation to a deeply ingrained value system and to its related inner controls. Furthermore, "every conscience," "whether in an individual or a group, has not only specific contents but also its own peculiar logic which safeguards its coherence" (Erikson, 1950, p. 114). Thus, exclusion of inimical foreign values is natural, feels appropriate, and is self-protective.

Learning positives and negatives, what one can and cannot be and do, imprinting positive and negative notions for a variety of values, by adulthood these become the psyche's protective mainstay. That is, cherished ways of being in the world are not abandoned but are built into adult preferences and habits, daily patterns, and biases. Among others, family and group differences in values that express the meaning of *clean, correct, good, industrious, trustworthy,* ways of showing *deference to others, initiative, efficiency, listening* and *speaking,* and a *sense of the Almighty* encode the child's psyche. "Self-idealization" is thus developed, family and cultural traditions are transmitted, and symbols representing group values and mores, some linguistically represented, are preserved (Erikson, 1985, p. 214). Erikson repeatedly described the prolonged human childhood in which children are ritually "speciated" by their experience of a particular family and group. In this, they incorporate and identify with familiar, satisfying routines and views within a unique form of family existence to develop "a distinct sense of corporate identity," one that builds and accumulates to preferences and prejudices of various forms (Erikson, 1977, p. 79). "To have steady values at all," Erikson (1968) wrote, humans "must absolutize them" (p. 241). Absolute values for the self are thus projected as absolute value requirements for others.

Erikson showed how each person is enmeshed in the fabric of family and in the larger culture, society, and nation. For some citizens in certain areas and times, this fabric is integrated and homogeneous, whereas, for others in different places, times, and historical periods, the fabric is loose and heterogeneous. Culture lives inside the person's ideational, linguistic, psychological system and is thus inseparable from the way individuals construe and perceive reality as they move about and pursue their daily lives. Culture is external as well, reverberating in shared ideas, symbols, values, modes of thought, and norms. As such, a person's life in a particular nation enters and fuels the psychological apparatus. Words, ideas, and metaphors, some expressing notions of wide ranging opportunity, freedom, and access, and others expressing notions of restriction, exclusion, and danger, frame thought and the wellspring of security and anxiety that informs its citizens.

Each person's internalization of reality, especially as it represents a group ethos, is powerful. One's fit within the ethos of the group, and the group's fit within the broader society are crucial. *Ethos* is a living code conveying the "interdependence of persons" and the way humans are organized in their relationships with one another (Erikson, 1982, p. 26). It's "inner logic" of shared ideas, values, mores, linguistically expressed symbols, and customs provides a unified way of seeing and interpreting phenomena (p. 36). However strange it might appear to outsiders, each ethos is a nested set of wombs—of family, cultural group, and society—that transport principles of living to infants and children in order to direct, channel, and sublimate behavior. Its modes and values wrap together desires, needs, and traditions to infuse the person's conscious and unconscious. Its consistency, however historically temporary, makes the self and the society of that self seem permanent, even though both are context- and time-limited.

Society nests the person in, for example, ethnicity, religious belonging, family, unique groupings, and distinctive environments. Each person is born into one nuclear family and ethos, only later to live out her or his life traversing variable and changing environmental, temporal, and group-specific contexts. However, conscious and partially unconscious recollections from early life remain ingrained within the psyche.

Unusual for the era, as early as 1939, in his respective writings about the Sioux and Yurok Natives, Germany's World War II era, and the spirit of the U.S. democratic enterprise, Erikson showed the many ways in which the social-political, value driven world exists inside the human mental apparatus. He found "subverbal" ideas to "dominate" and constrict the thought of every nation and cultural group he studied (1942, p. 483). The "Maginot Line" and the "Limes Wall" had suffused the fears and internal divisions of the German people in the 1940s, a citizenry and country that were circled and felt trapped by imposing borders and potential encroachment by others. In technologically advanced societies, geography and space are important as well. In the United States of Erikson's immigration, for example, a land mass protected by vast oceans had created a sense of insular protection, feelings of freedom from the risk of invasion, and isolationist thinking when this was politically expedient. Exploration and expansion, "ranger" imagery, and the equation of a new, separate, independent, nation with a self-made, protean human who can make many things (including the self, over and over) exist in its ideation and its citizens' psychologically grounded sense of self. To our theorist, sensate newness became an "invigorating," "obsessive" replacement for absent national ideas about tradition and permanence (Erikson, 1974, p. 79). The nation's independence, its outgoing nature, and its genial, optimistic attitudes reflected an expansive, open country in which even the exploration of outer space was possible. The American imagination could thus become as vast as its continent and as expansive as its spirit, success, and, sometimes, messianic zeal.

Erikson found that in all such ideas, irrespective of the country, a nation's landscape, its geopolitical existence, and its experience of violation or sense of protection exist in its collective imagery, in anthems and expressions, and in the people's psychologically grounded sense of self. As well, he found a modification of this tendency in all smaller ethnic enclaves, clans, and groups. The society or group's values, norms, freedoms, and fears reside within, and preside, over the individual's psyche.

With respect to the ways in which the unconscious and conscious demonstrate themselves in individual development, Erikson examined how genetically programmed absolutes play out differently. For example, he found cultural differences in trait emphasis, stage length, and the ways in which children's developmental readiness and needs for group incorporation were met. As a psychoanalyst, his focus was on conscious and unconscious expression and subverted needs. Thus, he found, for example, that some cultural, societal groups emphasize oral tendencies, while others emphasize the development of autonomous, aggressive characteristics. Still others, whether for the benefit of the group, the family, or the individual, emphasize the accumulation of wealth. Some societies focus on shaming and shunning as preferred methods of norming, while others inculcate guilt. Such variable emphases are seen in child-rearing, and in training functions and learning systems; they are later manifest in adults who were brought up with such methods. Importantly, the variable anxieties and obsessions of adults that emanate from group- or socioculturally-specific attributes are then mirrored in the anxieties and obsessions of that group's or society's children.

Thus, we must continually attend to the ways in which each culture's and nation's values and ideals are encouraged in its children, and the role of that larger social sphere in emphasizing tendencies that are held dear, while deterring those that are considered onerous. Values, tendencies, and idealized traits learned during childhood persist into, and frequently throughout, the adult years. However, trait causation is not the point:

> We are not saying here that their treatment in babyhood causes a group of adults to have certain traits—as if you turned a few knobs in your child-training system and you fabricated this or that kind of tribal or national character. In fact, we are not discussing traits in the sense of irreversible aspects of character. We are speaking of goals and values and of the energy put at their disposal by child-training systems. (Erikson, 1963, pp. 137–138; emphasis in original)

Unique cultural methods and styles, however internally consistent they are for the group, frequently seemed aberrant, even deviant to outsiders. The stronger a culture, race, or society, and the greater its coherence, the more difficult it is for outsiders to understand it. As though one knows "only the nouns of a foreign language," but not its verbs, adjectives, or clauses, outsiders might only glean some sense of a culture's important meanings and values (Erikson, 1939, p. 145). They will not, however, understand what the traits, habits, routines, and rituals are actually saying, preferring, emphasizing, and omitting, or why this is the case. Important in this are a nation's or culture's concepts of space and time, of past and future. Such notions unify ideas and beliefs, thereby creating some of the greatest differences between one group and another. Each society, Erikson (1975) discovered, adroitly organizes and expresses its unique values and beliefs, and just as "cleverly conceals its irrationalities" (p. 108). Beliefs and irrationalities are the nucleus of rituals, traits, child-rearing methods, ceremonies, and pageantry, all that is found beautiful and endearing, and all that is repugnant.

Although some beliefs are magical, this does not make them any less real or powerful (see Erikson, 1969, pp. 38–39). Outsiders must know that denying the validity of such beliefs does not diminish either their reality or their potency. All humans have their special version of magic and superstitions. These serve as a "collective mastery of the unknown," permitting us to say almost aloud: "I see you! I recognize you!" (Erikson, 1958, p. 60).

Sometimes consciously, but primarily unconsciously, human adults are remarkable in accepting their own forms of logic and illogic, and just as remarkable in countering and resisting the existence and importance of these in nations, societies, cultures, religions, and other important human groupings. For the psyche and in human language, those who are "outside" too readily become "nameless," then "unmeangingful," then "strange," and finallly, "*wrong*" (Erikson, 1966, p. 342).

Although it is beyond the scope of this chapter, Erikson's most powerful identity image is that of the "pseudospecies" inclination, that is, the prejudiced adult (see Hoare, 2002, pp. 41–69). He held that any number of groups act as though they are central in the mind's eye of the divinity who created them. He saw group-based anxieties and prejudices in every culture and group he studied. This, to him, was the basis for judgmental moralism among adults. Showing how easily group-based values and biases turn into prejudice, he examined hostilities between races. Noting animosities between Native and White Americans, for example, he reflected on their blaming tendencies: "The whites *teach* their children to cry,' and 'the Indians *teach* their children to masturbate,' contains a differentiation which creates or rationalizes hate between groups: It implies that foreign customs are based on bad intentions" (Erikson, 1939, p. 131).

Microspheres and Macrospheres.   As did Bronfenbrenner, Erikson conceptualized spaces of involvement. In this, he used the term *sphere,* largely to denote the area in which one functions. Sometimes spheres also meant zones into which ideas and images are visually projected from within the mind's eye.

The earliest developmental sphere is the *autocosm*. This is the infant's first play space, the body of self and of mother, the initial, immediate human "geography" (Erikson, 1963, p. 220). It is one in which the infant first explores the mother with touch, taste, and sight, and later plays within the zone of her or his own infant body. The mother's facial topography is especially important for, to the baby in the first months of life, it is an extension of its own being. In seeing and touching the mysterious protrusions, openings, and flat surfaces of that loved face babies learn all there is to know about their universe at that point in time. Mother *is* universe. Touch, taste, smells, and sounds unite with vision as an organizer of what is seen and experienced to create a fully sensory cosmos. In that first sphere, babies try out behaviors, in effect finding ways to attract and habituate others to their needs.

For children, play configurations are constructed in a *microsphere*. By "configurations," Erikson meant the arrangements that children make with toys and blocks in three-dimensional space and the forms that such constructions take. The term *microsphere* (sometimes *microcosm*) delineates the actual physical space children use to create their toy constructions. This microsphere can be the flat surface of a table or floor on which toys are displayed, a circumscribed area with physical boundaries. The child's use of space and toy forms, and the way toys are symbolically used, paint a picture of that child's ideas, psychological inventions, and conflicts. This micro arena is a suspended reality, a world for imagining, for developing and showing competence, for expressing an "ego ideal," and for refreshing the ego when the big world of people and things is overwhelming. With Huizinga (1950), Erikson saw the microsphere as representing a time-limited, time-out-of-mind space in which the child is free to give reign to the unconscious and to perform his or her own choice of actions. In this temporary habitat, the child tries out fresh identity components, learns and dramatizes what is within and out of bounds, models others, defends against encroachment, and learns how to use toy objects (miniature cars and trucks, toy animals, blocks, tiny wooden dolls) to represent persons, conflicts, and fantasies.

Each micro reality is the young child's work area and escape zone, a safe harbor to which he or she can flee adults' weighty surveillance. In this zone, the child loses the self in creativity and is temporarily free to act out desires unhampered. After his discussions with Piaget in 1955, Erikson saw psychological and cognitive development as one (Erikson, 1987a). Interpreting from the vantage point of the projective medium of child's play, he variously wrote that play serves ego development, aids the child's unmitigated curiosity for learning and for experiencing surprise, serves as a vehicle for deploying the developing cognitive apparatus, permits symbolic improvisations, and permits the child to try on his or her sense of the unique adult roles that each society's rendition of reality presents.

Play is an outlet for imagination and for the release of tensions. Play is serious, a work of the ego. Similar to the time-diffused commitment moratorium of adolescence, the fantasy of play suspends time, permitting a halted arena from which the child can step forward developmentally. In this singular realm, the child takes pleasure in his or her enactments and learns what will be repetitively enjoyable. In the earliest stage a sense of the numenous had been built by the infant's growth in trust colored by mistrust, and in the second stage a sense of the judicious and lawful emanated from rule-learning in the period of autonomy which incorporates shame and doubt. Now a sense of the dramatic develops as a result of time-out-of-mind play initiative, a drama that holds its portion of conscience and guilt.

Expanding upward developmentally and outward spatially, Erikson's term *macrosphere* means the school environment and other large contexts. For the older child, it is the space in which he or she expands the cognitive-psychological equipment by gaining competence in working with things, learning to share, and understanding new freedoms and limits in the larger physical structure and space to which ideas are attached. In the school age proper, the child learns the skills and methods of society. Play is then transformed into concrete work and formal skills, and in this macrosphere of personal industry development, imagination is eventually surrendered to duty.

For adolescents and adults, Erikson's *microsphere* describes ways in which adolescents in their ideological thinking, and adults in their ideational work, project a field of vision as well as the ideas, plans, and models that fit within that field. Adolescent microspheres are projected values and utopian ideas against the prevailing *macrosphere* of the social and political arena that encases the problems of the day. But another uniquely adolescent *macro* environment also exists for such youth. This is the sports field, an engaged zone for competitive action which youth carry along with them into adult life. In those later, larger, adult arenas, youth turn the comparatively benign sportsmanship of their earlier years into political prowess, gaming, and, for some, tactical war maneuvers. All games reflect psychological, social, physical, and cognitive abilities; games also reflect prototypes of power and aggression, both in process and in outcome.

To the adult, *microsphere* is theory and theatre, the eye and visual field projected. Included are the "polis" of the political sphere, as well as the representational drama of theatre, of play acting in the work roles of life, and of entertaining a *microcosm* of ideas. Erikson's take on ideas was that they are each rational adult's mental playing field, the abstract world that cognitively developed adults themselves construct.

An important concept in Erikson's approach to play is vision. The sphere is essential; it is the mind's eye, and a created, projected psychological-visual field. Erikson meant two things by this, first that the infant's vision and, with it, the ability to assimilate impressions, is the earliest organizing element in life, that humans retain early visual pictures from their prelinguistic years, and that such images are transported into later ideas such as worldviews and notions of the Absolute Other, *God* to some. Second, Erikson saw adult visual ideas as the individual's construction of reality, a partial, future-projecting, reality. Individual reality is only partial since humans must reduce the more complex, complete external reality such that their limited human minds can assimilate and handle it. In this, he borrowed Lippmann's (1922) rendition of the way humans reduce the external world, and "reconstruct" it on a smaller, simpler scale in order to work with it.

Stages of Development

One of Erikson's most important contributions was his conception of the human in its developmental, life span completeness at a time when theorists, researchers, and clinicians had begun to study human parts (see Erikson, 1982). His life stage model is an ego developmental theory, one that shows conscious and unconscious forces and attributes in an integrated, cumulative, life narrative. Persons move through sequential stages as they traverse their life cycle. In this, just as society and culture, one's family, and one's school or work environments are contexts, each stage of life is *itself* a context for development.

Each of the eight Eriksonian stages depicts the contextual, ontogenetic origin of a phase-specific crisis and its psychosocial demands and needs, the resolutions of which are recapitulated in all later developmental stages. In this, "a stage is a new configuration of past and future, a new combination of drive and defense, a new set of capacities fit for a new setting of tasks and opportunities, a new and wider radius of significant encounters" (Erikson, 1962, p. 457)

Prior to 1950 when Erikson first presented his life stage theory, psychoanalysts and U.S. developmental psychologists had not seriously entertained the possibility that development continues beyond the period when physical completeness and rational maturity are typically attained. They had not conceptualized ego identity, and had largely failed to consider how it is that the social world infuses the psychosocial human, including the way that world variously offers or withholds developmental opportunities. In showing the nexus between the person and society, in posing an open systems view of development, and in conceptualizing a healthy developmental order and sequence for the entire life span, Erikson's work is a substantial contribution to thought. Furthermore, in his sociocultural agenda, he always searched for ways that society and its institutions might best include and support the developing person, bolstering ego development and its evolution.

Erikson's is a model of opposing polarities that compete with one another in each of the eight stages. For example, in the first stage, the polarity of *trust* vies with its polar opposite *mistrust*. Preferentially, by the end of that stage, the infant will have resolved the conflict in such a way that the health-sponsoring syntonic pole of *trust* will have absorbed the detrimental dystonic pole of *mistrust*. A favorable ratio of both develops, in that both *trust* and *mistrust* emanate, but the most healthy resolution is one in which the balance tips toward trust. That is, the infant knows the dependability of his or her primary caretakers and environment, while harboring a budding sense that one cannot trust every human encounter and situation.

Each set of stage-specific content is termed a *crisis* (e.g., trust/mistrust). *Crisis* means the demands that arise in each specific stage, those with which one is developmentally ready to engage, capable of deploying psychological energy in the encounter. *Polarity* depicts stage opposites. *Versus* conveys the dialectics and tension of the competing, antagonistic forces, *poles*. Using our infant as an example, in trust *versus* mistrust, the best case resolution is one in which the strength of *Hope* emanates from the crisis and its competing polarities. *Hope* expresses the confidence each loved infant has that the world and his or her experience of it holds the promise of safety, security, and ongoing nurturance.

For each stage of life, Erikson thus posed strengths that hold the ego together and, at each stage and cumulatively, illustrate the attributes that show the person's developed capacities. Just as hope, will, purpose, and competence are the principal ego strengths of infancy and childhood, fidelity in ego identity is the strength and competence of adolescence (e.g., Erikson, 1964). In the post-identity development years, ego identity is strengthened through the competencies of love, care, and eventual integration. In all such strengths, the human reaches out to the social world and moves upward in consciousness. Indeed, based on the work of theorists such as Vaillant (1995, 2000), contemporary thought holds that the mature ego defenses of sublimation, suppression, humor, anticipation, and altruism are mechanisms of heightened consciousness; they are developmental progressions from unconscious, less mature defenses such as denial, reaction formation, and projection. And, just as the higher level ego defenses represent movement forward in developmental maturity and upward in consciousness, the more mature defenses are those that are more socially-centered than self-centered, Erikson's (1975) "outward" notion (p. 39).

In his final theoretical book, titling its second section "Ritualization in Everyday Life," Erikson (1977) showed his departure from Freud (1960) who had titled one of his books *The Psychopathology of Everyday Life*. Erikson meant his changed wording to show that one must study and understand normal, healthy, whole humans and their incorporation into society as the basis for all else, mental illness included. Departing from Freud who used the fractured, archeologically examined ill mind, traced back to its origins in infancy, as the frame for portraying neuroses and normalcy, Erikson countered that health, including mental health, cannot be best understood on the basis of mental illness, just as the infantile beginnings of psychological life are not determinative. Persons continue to adapt to life as it unfolds, as the content and the meaning of mastery change with new requirements and abilities. Thus, if early origins are not inviolate, they and related difficulties cannot chart the entire life course. Later nurturance and support, or disintegration and exclusion, can alter any beginning course of events.

Adult Development.   Reading his various publications, notes, and letters, it is clear that just as Einstein worked toward unification theory in physics, Erikson worked to unify the human in its developmental entirety. Early on, he focused on infant and child development and then moved onward in the life trajectory to consider the problem of ego identity. He then turned his attention to adults, considering ongoing ego identity development. This led to framing the meaning of intimacy in young adulthood, and generativity and integration, respectively, in the middle and later years. In this, Erikson used Freud's thoughts as a springboard. Freud is often quoted as having said that being adult means "to love and to work."

In his unpublished notes, Erikson claimed that Freud had also stipulated adulthood's negatives, the developmental traps that each person must confront. To Erikson, these negatives must be countered if one is to move forward, in health and in competence, throughout the rest of life (see Hoare, 2002, 2005). Combining these concepts, intimacy (love) against "isolation" became Erikson's first stage of adulthood proper while generativity (the care of progeny and one's work) against "stagnation" became his second adult stage. He charted the final adult stage as integrity/despair, only to change *integrity* to *integrality* when, as an elder, he understood seniors as those who expend great effort just to keep body and soul together as integral, not necessarily wise and emulated, parcels. Thus, in adulthood proper, in the years of intimacy/isolation, generativity/stagnation, and integrality/despair, identity development is ongoing, presuming that the person's internal and external environments provide the required contexts for such development to occur. And if, as he saw it, identity and integrality are the far distant "I" absorbed eras of adult life, intimacy (through love) and generativity (through care) are the intermediate "we" years, those of engaging deeply, productively, and caringly with others. That is, with ego identity in hand in its early "I" form by late adolescence or early adulthood, identity then becomes "I am who I love" (intimacy/isolation), and "I am who and what I care for" (generativity/stagnation).

In effect, Erikson made explicit an approach and a consciously psychosocial way of thinking about the adult, about humans' collective history, social changes, and the era specific institutions of life. Sometimes subtly and sometimes pointedly, he also planted messages that a developed adult is one who will press the self to think in terms of cultural and historical relativity, to understand that we cannot help but think with the lens and perspective born of one person in a particular time and place, and to advantageously use that which is given in one life and its sequential unfolding. This took us to higher levels of developmental understandings.

Figure 3.2 shows what Erikson meant about the importance of resolving earlier and contemporary stage crises as one approaches and moves through adulthood. It also shows the importance of the adult's own parents or caretakers as nurturers, and the way parental strengths or weaknesses can be passed along from generation to generation. In that figure, an adult moves into the intimacy stage of life. If positive childhood experiences and identifications with mentally healthy, supportive caretakers had been sown, and the ego had developed well in the first four strengths of hope, will, purpose, and competence, if identity is in hand with at least minimal firmness, and if the person's caretakers had themselves developed a favorable ratio of the seven strengths required for the care of that youth, then the individual's adulthood is likely to begin on a secure basis. Care, the ethical basis of the adult's prime years, is the important link between each person's life and prior and future generations. Culture must be supportive as well, for it supports or thwarts each youth in the early stages, as well as in identity formation and ongoing adult identity development. When society is in disarray, when it fails to nurture its young by withholding families and institutions that will ably do so, when it prejudicially closes down opportunities for youth and adults, a firm, positive identity is impossible in the stages that are critical for its development and extension. We have long recognized that in the absence of mentally healthy, nurturant families and other essential environments, ego identity and other maturational forms of development are thwarted to the extent that some persons develop only chronologically.

In his lifetime of work, Erikson made explicit a model of preferential adult development. That is, the adult is one who invests sponsorship, love, and care in the nurturance of others and in the work of the world. In so doing, he committed the naturalistic fallacy of changing an "is" to an "ought," stating in various forums what is required of adults in service to children, to concurrent and later generations of people, and to species survival. He wrote of the various ways in which proximal generations "cogwheel" interdependently one with another, and how they move one another along in their related lives.

The tendency in recent literature is to dispute specific Eriksonian stages, particularly for the adult sequence. Many seem to view Erikson's theory as that which was meant as a timeless system or as the achievement scale he warned against. Yet, he understood from the very beginning of his professional life that truth and facts are not immutable, whereas "a viewpoint or a manner of inquiry" are more inclined to stand the test of time (Coles, p. 162); hence the title of Erikson's (1987b) selected papers as *A Way of Looking at Things*. Speaking of his stage content, Erikson cautioned that it was not a "definitive

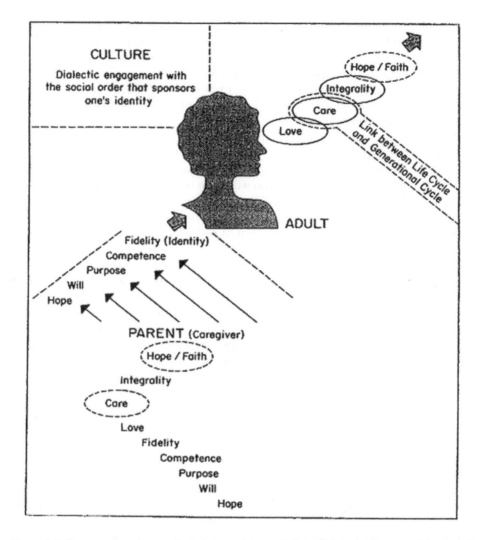

Figure 3.2 Stage progression and vital stage "strengths" in Erikson's Theory of Human Development. From *Erikson on Development in Adulthood: New Insights from the Unpublished Papers* (p. 108), by C. Hoare, 2002, New York: Oxford University Press. Reprinted with permission.

inventory" (Evans, 1967, p. 30). "I only speak," he said, of a "developing capacity to perceive and to abide by values established by a particular living system." In part, the nature of Erikson's stage concepts were, as he knew, tied to the years of its conceptualization.

The temporally ordered, invariant sequence that Erikson conceptualized fit well with what was psychodynamically afoot in mid-20th century, U.S. society, particularly among middle-class, EuroAmericans. Nearly 60 years later, we cannot judge it as invalid for its time and subjects. Instead, we would do well to use his approach in our appraisal of contemporary persons—their developmental trajectory, psychosocial requirements, and concerns—against our changing world, its societies and institutions. We should also retain much of the ground plan he captured, for it remains relevant today.

One can quibble with the adult-specific, invariant order Erikson postulated, of, for example, identity/identity confusion followed by intimacy/isolation. Exceptions to this invariance have been found among some women who seem to have resolved intimacy prior to identity, in sociocentric (largely Eastern) cultures where identity issues are other than those of individualistic achievement, and in those settings in which the mutuality of intimacy is suborned or postponed due to arranged marriages or marriages in which males have multiple mates. Furthermore, in the United States today, any number of 40 year-old mothers of newborns are also grandmothers simultaneously, and the increase in the number and forms of single, blended, and recombined families has added variety, if not a new form of identity/identity confusion.

Thus, there are two ways of considering Erikson's adult stages. The first is to use his approach, but to chart adult developmental stages as they mirror changes in contemporary humans. The second is to understand and apply the meaning of epigenesis and Erikson's ethical stance about the importance of deploying the developmental fuel that is provided in each phase of adult life.

In the first case, understanding that today's adults do not necessarily mirror Erikson's stage invariant order, we can say that the identified unfolding he captured might not strictly apply. For example, identity development might evolve directly into generativity, a caring for one's work and for the people and lives around one. Only then, if at all, might deep intimacy engagement follow. Thus, it depends on how one shuffles the life stage deck of cards. However, it is clear that adults do see themselves, presently and retrospectively, as living in various, sequential rooms of their adult lives. They speak of being, or of having been, young, middle aged, older, and aged, with psychosocial energies, content, and invested meaning-making that changes sequentially through time. For, at its best, adulthood is always a changing landscape in which one partially closes the door to each room of life, and uses the developed investments, capacities, and understandings of each life space as ongoing resources to the developing self. In not entirely closing the doors on any of their prior rooms, adults continue to visualize themselves in, and applying energy to, the key content of those periods of life in order to sustain (or partially undo) prior developmental issues and outcomes. The question then remains as to how current (and future) adults deploy their psychosocial energies, capacities, and variable stage-specific requirements in those critical periods of life. And, how do they use the developed capacities of childhood, adolescence, and their earlier adult stages as resources to themselves in the next life stage?

The second way of considering Erikson's adult developmental stages is to view them as a normative, best case scenario, that is, in terms of what is most developmentally adaptive for adults and children, and for each adult's eventual assessment of the worth of one personal life.

We might ask, as Erikson did, what it is that is given in the ground plan of human design, its unfolding, and developmental readiness. It has long been the case that biological readiness and deterioration factors, as well as facets of mental maturity, define the adult span. For example, mate-seeking characterizes the young adult years (Buss, 1994), and this is often followed by childbearing. Looking only to birth data, the stage of young adulthood, with its intimacy/isolation delineation, remains the most physically appropriate time to bear and begin raising children. Teen pregnancies pose risks for mothers and their infants, and the maternal years after age 35 are risky as well. Thus there are, perhaps, 15 years of young adulthood prime time. After age 35, for example, the risk of bearing a child with a chromosomal disorder (i.e., Down Syndrome) is 1 in 400 at age 35, 1 in 100 at age 40, and 1 in 30 at age 45; these data can be compared with the risk of 1 in 1,250 at age 25 (www.marchofdimes.com). Risks of delivering premature and low birthweight infants also increase substantially after age 35 (Tough et al., 2002), maternal health risks (e.g., diabetes and hypertension) are twice as common in those women (Bianco et al., 1996), and, by age 42, 50% miscarriage rates are reported (Andersen et al., 2000). These data can be combined with knowledge that, in most women sex drive peaks far prior to age 35, and maternal fertility declines in a woman's early thirties. Thus, one might well conclude that the young adult years are indeed the best stage-specific time for bearing children, an outcome of heterosexual intimacy. When one combines biological and morbidity data with our knowledge of psychosocial readiness factors, such information supports the normative best case, if not necessarily contemporary women's variability, of deploying the energies and resources charted by Erikson's intimacy stage.

In the subsequent stage, that of generativity/stagnation, the recognition that one cannot merely produce and discard is explicit in Erikson's concepts. This applies to the care of children who have been born to the adult, to all children in society, and to the care shown in one's work, its products and ideas. Ethically, it is unthinkable to dispose of the next generation, or of other commitments that were born of the engaged work of the adult years. Generative care sows the seeds of adults' later appraisals that their lives had worth and meaning. This is an ethics of adult development as Erikson has been accused, but the alternatives are untenable.

The Need for a Metamodel

Incorporating Context, Life Stages, and Biogenetics

Both Bronfenbrenner's bioecological and Erikson's biopsychosocial frameworks are important representatives of the contextual and life stage models of human development. Returning to the fable that began this chapter, these two models are large scale representations of the complex human. Each model contains substantial data that importantly speak to the principle developmental fuel and environments that frame adults. Two points are important: First, researchers can ill afford to include only one of these models as the exclusive way of framing and examining the human. Second, even when including both the contextual and the stage perspectives, these two models represent only two-thirds of the adult. A larger metamodel must express our thought, one that includes all three views and their intersecting attributes—those of context, stage, and biogenetics—if we are to avoid the reductionistic trap. The challenge to future theorists and researchers in adult development and learning is to incorporate content from within each of these models as we move forward to specify a view of the complete, human adult.

The third model, one not elaborated in this chapter, is that of biogenetics. This is the micro level which, when integrated with contextual and psychodynamic, life stage data, shows the interplay of all three sets of attributes. For example, we recall Bronfenbrenner's (1986) synthesis of findings from, for example, Scarr and Weinberg's (1976, 1983) and Schiff, Duyme, Dumaret, and Tomkiewicz's (1982) studies. When placed in advantageous, middle-class home circumstances, the mean I.Q. of adoptive children became substantially higher than that of their biological parents. Genetic endowment is thus not deterministic, but is altered by family resources and parental engagement. This is in keeping with Erikson's assessment that infantile origins do not necessarily chart the entire life course of adaptations or of aberrations. Among infants, early attachment and engagement are not just primary needs, which of course they are, but there is a complex relationship among genetics, brain plasticity, family environment, parental behavior, cognitive-emotional growth, and the healthy development of an intelligent, social being (see also Cozolino, 2006).

Among adults, recent data show that the adult brain and consequent adult functioning continue to change in important ways. In areas that are critical to development and learning, the adult brain is plastic, forming new neurons, synapses, and capillaries. In particular, neuron growth has been found in the important dentate gyrus of the hippocampus, a location related to learning and memory (Fillit et al., 2002). Such plasticity is reciprocal with learning engagement.

For example, studying London taxi drivers, Maquire and colleagues (2000) found changes in the structure and function of the brain based on learning and experience. London is a large city with an intricate web of roads and streets. For taxi drivers, an intensive two-year period of learning prepares drivers to immediately call forth from memory a visual map of locations, businesses, and routes without the help of road maps. As a result of classroom instruction combined with experience navigating myriad routes, brain neuroimaging showed that drivers' posterior hippocampi, a brain area associated with spatial depictions of the external environment, grew significantly larger than that of control subjects. Subjects with many years of driving experience showed greater hippocampal size than drivers with less experience.

Concluding Premises

The questions we pose and the studies we design are profoundly affected by our view of the world and our models of the human. Just as we have moved beyond the notion of adult stasis, and no longer see the adult in terms of Newton's absolutism or Freud's related mechanics, "neurones," and archeological premises, we must now move beyond seeing from within one or another model alone as we conceptualize adult development. It is important that we understand and incorporate the forces that have shaped and continue to shape the chronologically mature person. In this, perspectives and data are found within the biogenetic, the contextual, and the life stage models, for data from within each of these models are expressed in the adaptive human adult. As was elaborated throughout this chapter, these data necessarily include the nurturing others and important contexts in each unique life, attributes and forces of the broader sociocultural environment, the psychosocial content and resolutions of current and prior life stages, the structural and genetic equipment that was in place from the beginning and which changes its expression dynamically over time, and the way our adult sees the self in the present and into the future. Humans are permeable to their immediate and prior social world, to evolving and interactive biological material, to their position in the connected, always unfolding life span, to national and cultural attributes, and to important others in their personal and work lives. Adult development will vary depending on these facets and on the basis of each adult's ongoing interaction with the environment, with tasks, engagements, motivations, and sense of what the future holds.

Note

I extend my sincere appreciation to my colleague Richard Lanthier and to an anonymous reviewer whose comments helped to refine this chapter.

References

Andersen, A. N., Wohlfahrt, J., Christens, P., Olsen, J., & Melbye, M. (2000). Maternal age and fetal loss: Population based register linkage study. *British Medical Journal, 320*, 1708–1712.

Baltes, P. B., & Mayer, K. U. (Eds.). (1999). *The Berlin aging study*. Cambridge, UK: Cambridge University Press.

Bianco, A., Stone, J., Lynch, L., Lapinski, R., Berkowitz, G., & Berkowitz, R. L. (1996). Pregnancy outcome at age 40 and older. *Obstetrics and Gynecology, 87*(6), 917–922.

Bronfenbrenner, U. (1942). *Social status, structure, and development in the classroom group*. Unpublished doctoral dissertation, University of Michigan.

Bronfenbrenner, U. (1975). Nature with nurture: A reinterpretation of the evidence. In A. Montague (Ed.), *Race and IQ* (pp. 114–144). New York: Oxford University Press.

Bronfenbrenner, U. (1977). Lewinian space and ecological substance. *Journal of Social Issues, 33*(4), 199–212.

Bronfenbrenner, U. (1979). *The ecology of human development*. Cambridge, MA: Harvard University Press.

Bronfenbrenner, U. (1986). Ecology of the family as a context for human development: Research perspectives. *Developmental Psychology, 22*(6), 723–742.

Bronfenbrenner, U. (1995). The bioecological model from a life course perspective: Reflections of a participant observer. In P. Moen, G. H. Elder, Jr., & K. Luscher (Eds.), *Examining lives in context: Perspectives on the ecology of human development* (pp. 599–618). Washington, DC: American Psychological Association.

Bronfenbrenner, U. (2000). Ecological systems theory. In A. E. Kazdin, (Ed.), *Encyclopedia of psychology* (Vol. 3, pp. 129–133). New York: Oxford University Press.

Bronfenbrenner, U. (2005). On the nature of bioecological theory and research. In U. Bronfenbrenner (Ed.), *Making human beings human* (pp. 1–21). Thousand Oaks, CA: Sage.

Bronfenbrenner, U., Kessel, F., Kessen, W., & White, S. (1986). Toward a critical social history of developmental psychology. *American Psychologist, 41*(11), 1218–1230.

Bouchard, T. J., & McGue, M. (1981). Familial studies of intelligence: A review. *Science, 29,* 1055–1059.

Buss, D. M. (1994). *The evolution of desire: Strategies of human mating*. New York: Basic Books.

Caspi, A., & Elder, G. (1986). Life satisfaction in old age: Linking social psychology and history. *Journal of Psychology and Aging, 1,* 18–26.

Cervone, D. (2004). The architecture of personality. *Psychological Review, 111,* 183–204.

Cervone, D., Artistico, D., & Berry, J. M. (2006). Self-efficacy and adult development. In C. Hoare (Ed.), *Handbook of adult development and learning* (pp. 169–195). New York: Oxford University Press.

Coles, R. (1970). *Erik H. Erikson: The growth of his work*. Boston, MA: Little, Brown.

Cozolino, L. (2006). *The neuroscience of human relationships*. New York: W.W. Norton.

Crouter, A. C., & Bumpus, M. E. (2001). Linking parents' work stress to children's and adolescent's psychological adjustment. *Current Directions in Psychological Science, 10* (5), 156–159.

Crowe, R. R. (1974). An adoption study of antisocial personality. *Archives of General Psychiatry, 31,* 785–791.

Datan, N. (1977). After the apple: Post-Newtonian metatheory for jaded psychologists. In N. Datan & H. W. Reese (Eds.), *Lifespan developmental psychology: Dialectical perspectives on experimental research* (pp. 47–58). New York: Academic Press.

Devlin, J. (1928). *New school and office Webster dictionary*. New York: World Syndicate Co., Inc.

Ditmann-Kohli, F., & Baltes, P. B. (1990). Toward a neofunctionalist conception of adult intellectual development: Wisdom as a prototypical case of intellectual growth. In. C. N. Alexander & E. J. Langer (Eds.), *Higher stages of human development* (pp. 54–78). New York: Oxford University Press.

Duncan, L. E., & Agronick, G. S. (1995). The intersection of life stage and social events: Personality and life outcomes. *Journal of Personality and Social Psychology, 69,* 558–568.

Elder, G. H., Jr., Rudkin, L., & Conger, R. D. (1994). Inter-generational continuity and change in rural America. In V. L. Bengston, K. W. Schaie, & L. Burton (Eds.), *Adult intergenerational relations: Effects of societal change* (pp. 30–60). New York: Springer.

Endler, N. S., Boulter, L. R., & Osser, H. (1976). Theories of development. In N. S. Endler, L. R.

Boulter, & H. Osser (Eds.), *Contemporary issues in developmental psychology* (2nd ed., pp. 1–34). New York: Holt, Rinehart & Winston.

Einstein, A. (1945). *The meaning of relativity.* Princeton, NJ: Princeton University Press.

Erikson, E. (1950). *Childhood and society.* New York: W.W. Norton.

Erikson, E. (1958) *Young man Luther.* New York: W.W. Norton.

Erikson, E. (1963). *Childhood and society* (2nd ed.). New York: W.W. Norton.

Erikson, E. (1974). *Dimensions of a new identity.* New York: W.W. Norton.

Erikson, E. (1975). *Life history and the historical moment.* New York: W.W. Norton.

Erikson, E. (1977). *Toys and reasons.* New York: W.W. Norton.

Erikson, E. H. (1939). Observations on Sioux education. *Journal of Psychology, 7,* 101–156.

Erikson, E. H. (1942). Hitler's imagery and German youth. *Psychiatry, 5,* 475–493.

Erikson, E. H. (1943). Observations on the Yurok: Childhood and world image. Monograph. *University of California Publications in American Archeological Ethnology,* 35, 10, iii and 257–302. Berkeley: University of California Press.

Erikson, E. H. (1962). Reality and actuality. *Journal of the American Psychoanalytic Association, 10,* 451–473.

Erikson, E .H. (1964). *Insight and responsibility.* New York: W.W. Norton.

Erikson, E. H. (1966). The ontogeny of ritualization in man. *Philosophical Transactions of the Royal Society of London,* Series B, 251, 772, 337–349.

Erikson, E. H. (1968). *Identity: Youth and crisis.* New York: W.W. Norton.

Erikson, E. H. (1969). *Gandhi's truth.* New York: W.W. Norton.

Erikson, E. H. (1982). *The life cycle completed.* New York: W.W. Norton.

Erikson, E. H. (1985). Pseudospeciation in the nuclear age. *Political Psychology, 6*(2), 213–217.

Erikson, E. H. (1987a). Reprint. The human life cycle. In S. Schlein (Ed.). *A way of looking at things* (pp. 286–292). New York: W.W. Norton. First published in the *International Encyclopedia of the Social Sciences* (New York: Crowell-Collier, 1968)

Erikson, E. H. (1987b). *The papers of Erik and Joan Erikson.* Unpublished manuscripts. Cambridge, MA: The Houghton Library, Harvard University.

Erikson, E., & Erikson, J. (1981). On generativity and identity: From a conversation with Erik and Joan Erikson. *Harvard Educational Review, 51*(2), 249–269.

Evans, R. I. (1967). *Dialogue with Erik Erikson.* New York: Harper & Row.

Fillit, H. M., Butler, R. N., O'Connell, A. W., Albert, M. S., Birren, J. E., Cotman, C. W., et al. (2002). Achieving and maintaining cognitive vitality with aging. *Mayo Clinic Proceedings, 77,* 681–696.

Freud, S. (1953). Fragment of an analysis of a case of hysteria. In J. Strachey (Ed. & Trans.), *The standard edition of the complete psychological works of Sigmund Freud* (Vol. 7, pp. 7–12). London: Hogarth Press. (Original work published 1905)

Freud, S. (1960). *The psychopathology of everyday life.* J. Strachey (Ed. & Trans.), New York: W.W. Norton. (Original work published 1901)

Freud, S. (1962). The neuro-psychoses of defence. In J. Strachey (Ed. & Trans.), *The standard edition of the complete psychological works of Sigmund Freud* (Vol. 3, pp. 43–68). London: Hogarth Press. (Original work published 1894)

Freud, S. (1964). Constructions in analysis. In J. Strachey (Ed. & Trans.), *The standard edition of the complete psychological works of Sigmund Freud* (Vol. 23, pp. 255–269).London: Hogarth Press. (Original work published 1937)

Freud, S. (1965). *The interpretation of dreams.* J. Strachey (Ed. & Trans.), New York: Avon Books. (Original work published 1940)

Freud, S. (1969). *An outline of psychoanalysis.* J. Strachey (Ed. & Trans.). New York: W.W. Norton. (Original work published 1940)

Freud, S. (1989b). Instincts and their vicissitudes. In. P. Gay (Ed.), *The Freud reader* (pp. 562–568). New York: W.W. Norton. (Original work published 1915)

Freud, S. (1989d). Project for a scientific psychology. In P. Gay (Ed.), *The Freud reader* (pp. 86–89). New York: W.W. Norton. (Original work published 1895)

Friedman, R. A. (2006). The changing face of teenage drug abuse – the trend toward prescription drugs. *The New England Journal of Medicine, 354,* 1448–1450.

Galinsky, E. (1999). *Ask the children.* New York: Morrow.

Garbarino, J. (1982). *Children and families in the social environment.* New York: Aldine Publishing.

Gergen, K. (1977). Stability, change, and chance in understanding human development. In N. Datan & H.W. Reese (Eds.), *Lifespan developmental psychology: Dialectical perspectives on experimental research* (pp. 47–58). New York: Academic Press.

Glare, P. G. W. (Ed.). (1982). *Oxford Latin dictionary.* New York: Oxford University Press.

Haggerty, R. J., Sherrod, L. R., Garmezy, N., & Rutter, M. (Eds.). (1996). *Stress, risk, and resilience in children and adolescents: Processes, mechanisms, and interventions.* New York: Cambridge University Press.

Haney, C., (2002). Making law modern: Toward a contextual model of justice. *Psychology, Public Policy, and Law, 8*(1), 3–63.

Hoare, C. (2006a). Growing a discipline at the borders of thought. In C. Hoare (Ed.), *Handbook of adult development and learning* (pp. 3–26). New York: Oxford University Press.

Hoare, C. (2006b). Work as the catalyst of reciprocal adult development and learning: Identity and personality. In C. Hoare (Ed.), *Handbook of adult development and learning* (pp. 344–380). New York: Oxford University Press.

Hoare, C. H. (1991). Psychosocial identity development and cultural others. *Journal of Counseling and Development, 70*(1), 45–53.

Hoare, C. H. (2002). *Erikson on development in adulthood: New insights from the unpublished papers.* New York: Oxford University Press.

Hoare, C. H. (2005). Erikson's general and adult developmental revisions of Freudian thought: "Outward, forward, upward." *Journal of Adult Development, 12*(1), 19–31.

Hood, A. B., & Deopere, D. L. (2002). The relationship of cognitive development to age, when education and intelligence are controlled for. *Journal of Adult Development, 9,* 229–234.

Huizinga, J. (1950). *Homo ludens: A study of the play-element in culture.* Boston: Beacon Press.

Hutchings, B., & Mednick, S. A. (1977). Criminality in adoptees and their adoptive and biological parents: A pilot study. In S. A. Mednick & K. O. Christinesen (Eds.), *Biological bases of criminal behavior* (pp. 127–164). New York: Gardner Press.

Jordan, W. (1978). Searching for adulthood in America. In E.H. Erikson (Ed.), *Adulthood* (pp. 189–199). New York: W.W. Norton.

Kohn, M. L. (1969). *Class and conformity: A study in values.* Homewood, IL: Dorsey.

Kohn, M. L., & Schooler, C. (1973). Occupational experience and psychological functioning: An assessment of reciprocal effects. *American Sociological Review, 38,* 97–118.

Kohn, M. L., & Schooler, C. (1978). The reciprocal effects of substantive complexity of work and intellectual flexibility: A longitudinal assessment. *American Journal of Sociology, 84,* 24–52.

Kohn, M. L., & Schooler, C. (1982). Job conditions and personality: A longitudinal assessment of their reciprocal effects. *American Journal of Sociology, 87,* 1257–1258.

Kohn, M. L., & Schooler, C. (1983). *Work and personality: An inquiry into the impact of social stratification.* New York: Dryden Press.

Koltko-Rivera, M. E. (2004). The psychology of worldviews. *Review of General Psychology, 8*(1), 3–58.

Kracke, W. H. (1978). A psychoanalyst in the field: Erikson's contributions to anthropology. In P. Homans (Ed.), *Childhood and selfhood: Essays on tradition, religion, and modernity in the psychology of Erik H. Erikson* (pp. 147–188). Lewisburg, PA: Bucknell University Press.

Lent, R. W., Brown, S. D., Brenner, B., Chopra, S. B., Davis, T., & Talleyrand, R., et al. (2001). The role of contextual supports and barriers in the choice of math/science educational options: A test of the social cognitive hypotheses. *Journal of Counseling Psychology, 48,* 474–483.

Levine, A. (2006). *Educating school teachers.,* Princeton, NJ: The Education Schools Project.

Lewin, K. (1936). *Principles of topological psychology.* (F. Heider & G. M. Heider, Trans.). New York: McGraw-Hill Book Company.

Lewin, K. (1951). *Field theory in social science.* New York: Harper and Company.

Lippmann, W. (1922). *Public opinion*. New York: Macmillan.

Lovejoy, A. O. (1902). Religion and the time-process. *The American Journal of Theology, 6*(3), 439–472.

Lovejoy, A. O. (1930). *The revolt against dualism*. LaSalle, IL: Open Court.

Lovejoy, A .O. (1936). *The great chain of being*. Cambridge, MA: Harvard University Press.

Lu, T., Pan, Y., Kao, S.-Y., Li, C., Kohane, I., Chan, J., & Yanker, B. A. (2004). Gene regulation and DNA damage in the ageing human brain. *Nature, 429*, 883–891.

Maguire, E. A., Gadian, D. G., Johnsrude, I. S., Good, C. D., Ashburner, J., & Frackowiak, R. S. J., et al. (2000). Navigation-related structural change in the hippocampi of taxi drivers. *Proceedings of the National Academy of Sciences, USA, 97*, 4398–4403.

March of Dimes. (2007). Pregnancy after 35. Retrieved January 17, 2007, from http://www.marchofdimes.com/professionals/681_1155.asp

Miller, M. (2006). Adult development, learning, and insight through psychotherapy: The cultivation of change and transformation. In C. Hoare (Ed.), *Handbook of adult development and learning* (pp. 219–239). New York: Oxford University Press.

Miller, M. E., & West, A. N. (1993). Influences of world view on personality, epistemology, and choice of profession. In J. Demick & P. M. Miller (Eds.), *Development in the workplace* (pp. 3–19). Hillsdale, NJ: Erlbaum.

Mischel, W. (1990). Personality dispositions revisited and revised: A view after three decades. In L. Pervin (Ed.), *Handbook of personality: Theory and research* (pp. 111–134). New York: Guilford.

Mortimer, J. T., Lorence, J., & Kumka, D. (1986). *Work, family, and personality: Transition to adulthood*. Norwood, NJ: Ablex.

Neisser, U., & Hyman, I. (Eds.). (1999). *Memory observed: Remembering in natural contexts*. (2nd ed.). New York: Worth.

Nietzsche, F. W. (1967). *Thus spake Zarathustra* (T. Common, Trans.). New York: Heritage Press. (Original work published 1885)

Overton, W. F. (1991). Historical and contemporary perspectives on developmental theory and research strategies. In R. M. Downs, L. S. Liben, & D. S. Palermo (Eds.), *Visions of aesthetics, the environment and development* (pp. 263–311). Hillsdale, NJ: Erlbaum.

Pascual-Leone, J., & Irwin, R. (1998). Abstraction, the will, the self, and modes of learning in adulthood. In MC. Smith & T. Pourchot (Eds.), *Adult learning and development* (pp. 35–66). Mahwah, NJ: Erlbaum.

Pepper, S. C. (1970). *World hypotheses: A study in evidence*. Berkeley: University of California Press. (Original work published 1942)

Pirttila-Backkman, A. M., & Kajanne, A. (2001). The development of implicit epistemologies during early and middle adulthood. *Journal of Adult Development, 8*, 81–97.

Pollock, G. H. (1981). Reminiscences and insight. *Psychoanalytic Study of the Child, 36*, 279–287.

Reese, H. W., & Overton, W. F. (1970). Models of development and theories of development. In L. R. Goulet & P. B. Balltes (Eds.), *Life-span developmental psychology* (Vol. 1, pp. 115–145). New York: Academic Press.

Riegel, K. F. (1975a). Adult life crisis: A dialectical interpretation of development. In N. Datan & H. Ginsberg (Eds.), *Lifespan developmental psychology: Normative life crisis* (pp. 99–128). New York: Academic Press.

Riegel, K. F. (1975b). Structure and transformation in modern intellectual history. In K. F. Riegel & G. C. Rosenwald (Eds.), *Structure and transformation* (pp. 3–24). New York: Wiley.

Roberts, B. W., & Helson, R. (1997). Changes in culture, changes in personality: The influence of individualism in a longitudinal study of women. *Journal of Personality and Social Psychology, 72*, 641–651.

Scarr, S., & Weinberg, R. A. (1976). IQ test performance of black children adopted by white families. *American Psychologist, 31*, 726–739.

Scarr, S., & Weinberg, R. A. (1983). The Minnesota adoption studies: Genetic differences and malleability. *Child Development, 54*, 260–267.

Schaie, K. W. (1990). Intellectual development in adulthood. In J. E. Birren & K. W. Schaie (Eds.), *Handbook of the psychology of aging* (3rd ed., pp. 291–309). San Diego, CA: Academic Press.

Schaie, K. W. (1993). Age changes in adult intelligence. In D. S. Woodruff & J. E. Birren (Eds.), *Aging: Scientific perspectives and social issues* (2nd ed., pp. 111–124). Monterey, CA: Brooks/Cole.

Schiff, M., Duyme, M., Dumaret, A., & Tomkiewicz, S. (1981). Enfants de travailleurs manuels adoptés par des cadres: Effet d'un changement de categorie sociale sur le cursus scolaire et les notes de QI.P.U.F. (*travaux et Documents,* cahier no. 93, vol. 1). Paris

Schiff, M., Duyme, M., Dumaret, A., & Tomkiewicz, S. (1982). How much *could* we boost scholastic achievement and IQ scores? A direct answer from a French adoption study. *Cognition, 12,* 155–196.

Schweder, R. A. (1991). *Thinking through cultures.* Cambridge, MA: Harvard University Press.

Skeels, H. M., & Dye, H. B. (1939). A study of the effects of differential stimulation on mentally retarded children. *Proceedings and Addresses of the American Association on Mental Deficiency, 44,* 114–136.

Skeels, H. M., Updegraff, R., Wellman, B. L., & Williams, H. M (1938). A study of environment stimulation: An orphanage preschool project. *University of Iowa Studies in Child Welfare, 15*(4).

Skodak, M., & Skeels, H. M. (1949). A final follow-up study of one hundred adopted children. *The Journal of Genetic Psychology, 75,* 85–125

Sinnott, J. D. (1981). The theory of relativity: A metatheory for development? *Human Development, 24,* 293–311.

Smith, MC., & Pourchot, T. (Eds). (1998). *Adult learning and development.* Mahwah, NJ: Erlbaum.

Stegner, W. (1978). The writer and the concept of adulthood. In E. H. Erikson (Ed.), *Adulthood* (pp. 227–236). New York: W.W. Norton.

Taylor, K. (2006). Autonomy and self-directed learning: A developmental journey. In C. Hoare (Ed.), *Handbook of adult development and learning.* (pp. 196–218). New York: Oxford University Press.

Tough, S. C., Newburn-Cook, C., Johnston, D. W., Svenson, L. W., Rose, S., & Belik, J. (2002). Delayed childbearing and its impact on population rate changes in low birth weight, multiple birth, and preterm delivery. *Pediatrics, 109,* 3, 399–403.

U.S. Bureau of the Census. (2005). *United States, 2005 American Community Survey.* (Report S0101). Retrieved January 26, 2007, from U.S. Census Bureau of the Census Reports Online, http://www.census.gov

U.S. Department of Health and Human Services, Centers for Disease Control and Prevention. (2006). *Fertility, contraception, and fatherhood: Data on men and women from Cycle 6 (2002) of the National Survey of Family Growth.* Retrieved September 26, 2006, from National Center for Health Statistics, http://www.cdc.gov/nchs/nsfg.htm

Vaillant, G. E. (1995). *The wisdom of the ego: Sources of resilience in adult life.* Cambridge, MA: Belknap Press.

Vaillant, G. E. (2000). Adaptive mental mechanisms: Their role in a positive psychology. *American Psychologist, 55,* 89–98.

Verghese, J., Lipton, R. B., Katz, M. J., Hall, C. B., Derby, C. A., & Kuslansky, G., et al. (2003). Leisure activities and the risk of dementia in the elderly. *New England Journal of Medicine, 348,* 2508–2516.

Vygotsky, L. S. (1978). *Mind and society: The development of higher psychological processes.* Cambridge, MA: Harvard University Press.

Wertheimer, M., Barclay, A. G., Cook, S. W., Kiesler, C. A., Koch, S., Riegel, K. F., et al. (1978). Psychology and the future. *American Psychologist, 33,* 631–647.

Wertsch, J. V. (2005). Making human beings human: Bioecological perspectives on human development. *British Journal of Developmental Psychology, 23,* 143–151.

Wilson, D. J. (1980). Arthur O. Lovejoy and the moral of the great chain of being. *Journal of the History of Ideas, 41*(2), 249–265.

Wilson, D. J. (1983). Arthur O. Lovejoy. In E. Devine, M. Held, J., Vinson, & G. Walsh (Eds.), *Thinkers of the twentieth century* (pp. 341–342). London: Macmillan.

Yankelovich, D., & Barrett, W. (1970). *Ego and instinct.* New York: Random House.

Chapter 4

Cognitive Development as the Dance of Adaptive Transformation

Neo-Piagetian Perspectives on Adult Cognitive Development

Jan D. Sinnott

Piaget was originally a biologist, and it shows. One of the most important emphases unique to the Piagetian approach to cognitive development and learning is that *adaptation* of the organism is a paramount goal that serves both organism and environment. Sometimes, reading life-span development research and theory, we get the feeling that the human is still the center of the psychological and biological universe. We get the impression that psychological processes just *are*, for their own sakes, without reference to their effectiveness at keeping us alive and thriving. The underpinning of Piagetian and neo-Piagetian theories is the *adaptive nature* of cognitive development.

Piaget, as a biologist, described mechanisms for adaptive cognitive development and processing that allow for gradual good fit between the organism and the environment. The processes rest on the well-known activities of *assimilation* and *accommodation.* In assimilation, already-present knowing schemata take in new information in a way that fits the pattern they already possess. If that pattern proves inadequate to the occasion, accommodation begins to reshape the schemata. The final product is a set of schemata that better fit the environment the person wishes to know.

Similar sorts of mechanisms allow development of more complex levels of cognition that fit the more complex situation of the growing child and adult. When enough discrete elements of information are learned with small modifications in schemata, a rich enough matrix may permit a shift to a new level of complexity of cognition, driven, still, by its potential adaptivity. The more complex cognitive level may be the most adaptive way to process some epistemological tasks; a simpler level may be the most adaptive way to process others. Examples of this will appear later in the chapter. Again, the most important word is *adaptive.*

But what do adults, as opposed to children and adolescents, need to adapt *to*? Here I am talking about adults in general and aging persons in general to simplify our discussion. Here are a few demands that impact upon adults in general and that demand adaptation in epistemology, that is, how we know reality.

The first demand is: with the passage of life time, we need to form close relationships with others (recall Erikson's intimacy, generativity, 1982). For these relationships to work, for some of the time at least, we need to "know" similar realities together. For example, is our marriage healthy or not? Are we good friends? Sometimes we need to arrive at the same judgment of truth or quality along with someone important to us. Are we being treated fairly in our workplace? Is this "quality" work? Is it good for our son to go to war?

The second demand is: we need to keep a consistent sense of self while also personally changing over time. For example, am I a "good" person if I sometimes do "bad" things? How can I reconcile my sense of self as independent and strong with the facts of my personal aging? How can I make an integrated story of my life (recall Erikson's "integrity") with its turns and twists?

The third demand is: if, as many adults do, I give importance to some spiritual meaning or transcendent value for life and death, I need to reconcile my knowing existence as "everyday, finite, and material" with my knowing existence as somehow "larger, spiritual, and transcendent." For example, is death the beginning or the end? Notice that the demand for knowing the "truth" of these realities cannot be met very adaptively simply by picking one pole or the other of the apparent dichotomies. A logic is required that says "yes" to both, that both are "true."

In addition to examining demands to see what adults must adapt to, I might examine the ways of knowing of my many adaptive older relatives, or the ways of knowing of thinkers such as Albert Einstein. When I do this, I also see the need for theorists to develop a description of uniquely adult adaptive cognitive complexity. This would be one that goes beyond the logic of the last stage described by Piaget before his death, that of formal operations (or scientific logical thinking). Albert Einstein's wonderful descriptions of relativity, the knowledge of the Universe delivered by the "new physics," and the wise pronouncements of my relatives all demand an additional epistemology to account for adult knowledge of a non-egocentric but self-referential truth in addition to a scientific truth. A self-referential truth, defined in terms of physics, is that light is both a wave and a particle simultaneously, and the scientist must choose which way to regard it, thereby (partially) creating the "truth" of the situation.

In the next section of this chapter, I will outline my theory, with both its operational and felt connection aspects. In later sections, I will mention some other theories that have some elements of neo-Piagetian approaches. In the important final section, I will address the implications of my theory for two aspects of adult life—couple and family relations and spirituality.

A "Dancing Self" Metaphor for Adult Cognitive Development, Felt Connection, and Transformation of the Self

The metaphor of self-transformation as a dance is important to this chapter. Picture a village circle dance, a traditional folk dance. These folk dances represent the dance of life (or some part of it) in which we all participate. In any circle dance, each of us, in our uniqueness, is important to the dance. Without us, in fact, there would be no dance; traditional village dances are participatory activities, not paid performances.

For the dance to take place, three kinds of relational skills have to be mastered and integrated. The relational skills are analogous to felt connections, discussed below; the integration is analogous to Postformal cognitive operations, also discussed below. First, each of us has to have some balance within the self to move smoothly through the steps of the dance; otherwise we end up stepping on our own feet. Second, each of us has to interact skillfully with other dancers in the circle, or we might crash into each other and fall down. Third, each of us needs to remain connected with the overall purpose of the dance, attuned to the kind of dance this is today, or the circle dance will lose any meaningful pattern. And all these activities must be integrated.

We are each a part of this communal dance activity, but at no time does a self, one of the dancers, disappear. Paradoxically, the more a self learns to be balanced and interwoven and interconnected, the more that single self becomes important to the creation of the dance, perhaps even leading other dancers.

This is an analogy for the dance of transformation of cognitive development and felt connection during adulthood. The most creative accomplishment of any of us in adulthood and old age may be the "living in balance" of this dance (Sinnott, 1994a, 2002c, 2005).

Sinnott's Theory of Adult Cognitive Development: Cognition with Felt Connection

The theory I am about to offer you, the reader, is a complex one with revolutionary implications for the way we conceptualize adult thought development. It is a way to describe how we learn to balance mind, heart, soul, and our relations with others over our lifetimes. It is useful for helping us understand many things, for example, why successful therapists, teachers, and couples *are* successful. Perhaps most important, it is a theory that can open the doors of your world of ideas, generating more and more wonderful questions.

Postformal Thought is the name of my theory, and Postformal Thought appears key to adult development, learning, and wisdom. (When I refer to my own specific theory, Complex Postformal Thought, in this chapter, Postformal will begin with a capital letter.) It is based on an understanding of reality like that which permeates modern sciences. The concepts and skills of Postformal Thought derive from cognitive-developmental theory, native wisdom traditions, "new" sciences such as quantum physics, chaos theory, theories of self-organizing systems, and general systems theory. (For more detail on the new sciences, see the Sinnott references below.) I believe that teaching adults to think Postformally should be an important basic goal whenever we teach adults in the university setting or other contexts.

Postformal thinking operations (or skills) are also models of the thinking skills necessary to understand modern scientific approaches such as quantum physics, general systems theory, chaos theory and theories of self-regulating systems. Postformal thinking skills are needed to allow us to be humanistic, honoring the whole multifaceted person.

To preface the argument I am about to make here, Postformal Thought describes certain cognitive operations. These operations constitute the means for knowing complex realities like those of modern sciences such as quantum physics, as well as those in complex emotions and complex human relations. These operations are similar to the underpinnings of some new views of adult education that seem to work well.

Why do I believe Postformal Thought is so central to mature adult thinking and living? Why do I think Postformal Thought is so important for coping with the challenges of the postmodern era? I think these cognitive skills are so essential because over a period of about 25 years of research I created the theory of complex Postformal Thought precisely as a way to describe several specific phenomena of this positive sort. I had an ambitious agenda. I wanted to cognitively model the step beyond "formal operational (scientific) logic" (developed in adolescence) and describe the thinking of *mature adult* thinkers. I wanted to cognitively model the *wise* thinking possessed by at least some of my mature relatives, friends, and research respondents. I wanted to cognitively model certain logical aspects of the thinking of *great twentieth century scientists* such as Albert Einstein. And I wanted to cognitively model some logical aspects of intense, even intimate, long term *interpersonal interactions that were successful.*

As a university professor, I also saw that I could help students acquire these skills, and that those who had such Postformal skills were more successful in their intellectual and interpersonal pursuits. So, since the whole thrust of this research and scholarship was to capture the thinking and learning related to positive outcomes, I feel confident that the concept of Postformal Thought is related to, and important to, these significant positive outcomes, and even should be taught.

Definition and Description of Postformal Thought

Postformal Complex Thought and the research underlying it are described in my 1998 book, *The Development of Logic in Adulthood: Postformal Thought and Its Applications.* The book outlines the entire Theory of Postformal Thought. Some references that explain this work further are as follows: Cartwright, Galupo & Tyree (in preparation); Galupo, Cartwright & Savage (in preparation); Gavin, Galupo & Cartwright (in preparation); Johnson (1991,1994, 2004); Rogers (1989); Rogers, Sinnott & van Dusen (1991); Sinnott (1981, 1984b, 1989a,b, 1990, 1991a, 1991b, 1993a, 1993c, 1994a, 1994b, 1996, 1997, 1998a,b, 2000, 2002c, 2003b, 2004a, 2004b, 2004c, 2005, 2006a [under review], 2006b); Sinnott & Berlanstein (2006); Sinnott & Cavanaugh (1991); Sinnott & Johnson (1996); Yan (1995); Yan & Arlin (1995). These references also describe the nature of the individual thinking operations that together make up Postformal Thought.

Much of this work was based on the years of research I performed with the support of the National Institute on Aging (NIA) of the National Institutes of Health (NIH), beginning with my postdoctoral training there. I am grateful to the Gerontology Research Center (GRC) there, and the volunteers of the Baltimore Longitudinal Study of Aging (BLSA) and others who were my research respondents.

Postformal Thought is a type of complex logical thinking that develops in adulthood when we interact with other people whose views about some aspect of reality are different from ours. Of course, this kind of interaction is what should occur in educational experiences. From the background of Piagetian theory, Postformal Thought builds upon concrete and formal (scientific) Piagetian thought. It allows a person to deal with everyday logical contradictions by letting that person understand that "reality" and the "meaning" of events are co-created. Both objectivity and a necessary subjectivity are useful in our epistemological understanding of the world. Postformal Thought lets an adult bridge two contradictory "scientifically" logical positions and reach an adaptive synthesis of them through a higher-order logic. The adult then goes on to live the larger reality. So, the larger reality eventually *becomes* "true" with the passage of time. Postformal Thought includes a necessary subjectivity, which means that the knower understands that "truth" is partially a creation of the one who makes those choices.

Postformal Thought uses all the mechanisms identified by cognitive psychology, mechanisms such as memory and attention. It seems to develop later in life, after a certain amount of intellectual and interpersonal experience, according to my earlier research work. For example, only after experiencing intimate relationships, with their shared, mutually constructed logics about the reality of intimate life together, can a person be experienced enough to know that "If I think of you as an untrustworthy partner, then treat you that way, you are likely to truly become an untrustworthy partner."

Here is another example of Postformal Thought. When I begin teaching a college class, the class and I begin to structure the reality or truth of our relationship. We decide on the nature of our relationship, act on our view of it, and mutually continue to create it in the days that follow. These various views, held by class members and by me, form several contradictory logical systems about the reality of our relationship in the class. One student may see me as a surrogate parent and act within the formal logic inherent in that vision, to which I might respond by becoming more and more parental. Another student may logically construct me as a buddy and act within that logical system, to which I might respond by being a buddy also, or by being even more parental to compensate. I might view the class as stimulating or not, and teach in such a way as to make them either. The result, over the time of a semester, will be an organized "truth" about my relationship with this class that is co-created by the class and me.

While Postformal complex thought is *stimulated* by interpersonal interactions among thinkers, once it becomes a thinking tool for a person it may be *applied* to any kind of knowing situation, not just interpersonal ones. I may learn to use the tool of complex Postformal Thought through interactions with my spouse, and go on to use it to think about Newtonian vs. quantum physics. Just as the tool of scientific logic can be used in any context, so the tool of complex Postformal Thought can be used in any context. Of course, decisions need to be made about whether it is an appropriate tool in a given context. Complex Postformal Thought that orders several contradictory logical systems is probably unnecessary for less epistemologically demanding tasks such as rote memorization of an agreed-upon body of material.

Nine thinking operations make up Postformal Thought. Rationale for inclusion of these operations is given in my summary book about the theory (Sinnott, 1998b). The operations include: metatheory shift, problem definition, process/product shift, parameter setting, multiple solutions, pragmatism, multiple causality, multiple methods, and paradox. You can go to the references above to read more about the meaning of each operation term, the ways these operations have been tested, and the research that provides an underpinning for these assertions. I will briefly describe each operation here, giving a simple example of each. Notice that the operations will relate to one another, but will describe different aspects of the complex thinking process. Notice, too, that all the operations relate to problem solving, in the broadest sense.

Metatheory shift is the ability to view reality from more than one overarching logical perspective (e.g., from both an abstract and a practical perspective, or from a phenomenological and an experimental perspective) when thinking about it. For example, do I think of my job as a chance to open my mind to new areas of knowledge, or as collecting a paycheck, or as (of necessity) both?

Problem definition is the realization that there is always more than one way to define a problem, and that one *must* define a problem to solve it, since we all see things like problems through our own unique lenses. For example, I decide as an employee that my "problem" is "how to guess what my supervisor wants," or is "how to serve the public," or is "how to nourish my creativity." Defining the problem in different ways usually leads to different ways to solve it.

Process/product shift is realizing that I can reach a "content-related" solution to a given problem, and/or a solution that gives me a heuristic or a process that solves many such problems. For example, do I learn how to handle the multiple logics of only my colleagues, or do I learn a set of general skills for working with other people in many domains, or both?

Parameter setting is the realization that one must choose aspects of the problem context that must be considered or ignored for this solution. For example, I decide to limit my writing time today to 2 hours. I also ask the question "How am I deciding to approach tasks this way? Is there a better way?" All these decisions and questions set limits for my activity (that is, for my "solution to the problem").

Multiple solutions means that I can generate several solutions, based on several ways to view the problem. For example, I can solve the "problem" of how to be a spiritual person in three ways: join a church, meditate daily on my own, or do good deeds in the world.

Pragmatism in this case means that I am able to evaluate the solutions that I create for this problem, then select that which is "best" by some definition. For example, knowing there are several ways to solve the problem of how to be a spiritual person, I can look at the appropriateness of each. Then I am able, by some criterion, to pick the one that is "best."

Multiple causality is the realization that an event can be the result of several causes. For example, if a friendship fails, I can be aware that it might be due to bad timing (we both have heavy family responsibilities), and lack of common interests, and my inability to think of what my friend might want.

Multiple methods is the realization that there are several ways to get to the same solution of a problem. For example, the solution to my personal problem, dealing with my stubbornness, may be reached by multiple methods. I can accept that I am a stubborn person as well as a kind person, try to modify my stubborn traits, or simply see myself as kind and the other person as unworthy of my attention (e.g., a *polarized position*).

Paradox is realizing that contradictions are inherent in reality, and realizing that the broader view of an event can eliminate contradictions. For example, I see that, paradoxically, starting a family to avoid loneliness may leave me lonelier than before due to my having less time for my friends. In this paradoxical situation, I can only resolve my dilemma by reasoning about it at a more complex level. Perhaps I set a new goal of deciding "What will give the greatest meaning to my existence in the long run, friends or family?" Only I can decide (self-referential thought) to "jump" to a new cognitive level, or not, to address the question and resolve the paradox.

Development of Postformal Thought

The development of Postformal Thought helps explain how adult college students change their thinking styles as they go through the university experience. Younger successful students (e.g., see Perry, 1975) are concrete thinkers who need to know "right" answers. They want to know the "right" personality theory and the "right" major for them to study. They expect an authority to tell them the answer. Professors become the authority figures who provide answers. Then, second, students become relativistic thinkers, shaken by the apparent disappearance of "Truth" ("no right or wrong answers exist," "no way to decide about Truth," "whatever" [translation: "I don't want to even think about this… it is too unimportant or annoying"]). Now they see debates as going on forever, without closure. It doesn't matter which philosophy one professes, which major one takes, it's all the same endless, ongoing debate. Finally, they move on to complex thinking, a type of thinking in which they see that a necessary subjectivity is part of decisions about truth. A passionate commitment to the choice of a "reality" leads to making it "real" in the objective world. That complex thinking appears to be Postformal Thought. At that stage they can say "It's up to me to pick 'the right major,' then make a commitment to it, act as if it is the 'right' choice for me, and see if it works out. It does matter what I pick…not all majors would suit me. But no authority can tell me which will turn out to be 'right.' In fact *no* major will be 'right' unless I commit to it as if some absolute authority told me it is the true major for me!"

This complex kind of thinking skill, once attained in any context, can transfer from context to context. The adult student may have gained insight into the complexity of epistemological truth in the context of major choice, or relationships with peers, or as a politician, and go on to use the skill with family members. People start psychotherapy or challenge themselves with difficult growth activities to achieve just such a transfer to other areas of their lives. However it is gained, the Postformal complex thinker is able to use that set of complex thinking skills in all subject areas and contexts, if he or she chooses to apply it to those contexts.

Two Main Principles

The main characteristics of Postformal cognitive operations (Sinnott, 1998b) are: 1) self-reference (or "necessary subjectivity"); and 2) the ordering of formal operations. Self-reference is a general term for the ideas inherent in the new physics (Wolf, 1981) and alluded to by Hofstadter (1979) using the terms "self-referential games," "jumping out of the system," and "strange loops." The essential notion of self-reference is that we can never be completely free of the built-in limits of our system of knowing, and that *we come to know that this very fact is true.* This means that we somewhat routinely can take into account, in our decisions about truth, the fact that all knowledge has a subjective component and therefore is, of necessity, incomplete. So (we conclude), any logic we use is self-referential logic. Yet we must *act* in spite of being trapped in partial subjectivity. We make a decision about rules of the game (nature of truth), then act based on those rules. Once we come to realize what we are doing, we then can consciously use such self-referential thought.

The second characteristic of Postformal operations is the ordering of Piagetian formal operations (Inhelder & Piaget, 1958). The higher level Postformal system of self referential truth decisions gives order to lower level formal truth and logic systems. One of these logic systems is somewhat subjectively chosen and imposed on data as "true." For example, Perry (1975) describes advanced college students as "deciding" a certain ethical system is "true," while knowing full well that there is no absolute way of deciding the truth of an ethical system.

Looking at another example, relativistic, self-referential organization of several formal operations systems may also be seen. An attorney is trying to decide whether to defend a very young child accused of sexually assaulting another child. There is no conclusive physical evidence and no witnesses were present. Both children are adamant in their stories and both have been known to distort the truth to some degree when they were angry with each other. The attorney must make a commitment to a course of action and follow through on it as if that logical system were true. The attorney knows that, when she acts, that logical system may become true due to her actions, and will then become legal "truth" in court as well as an emotional truth for her and the others involved.

Formal (scientific) logical operations presume logical consistency within a single logical system. Within that single system the implications of the system are absolute. Postformal operations presume somewhat necessarily subjective selection among logically contradictory formal operational systems each of which is internally consistent and absolute.

As is true for other Piagetian thinking operations systems, a knower who is capable of using Postformal Thought skips in and out of that type of thinking. Postformal Thought is not always the best way to process a certain experience; it may be that sensorimotor thought (or some other stage of thought) is most *adaptive* on a given day. Perhaps a thinker with higher order thinking skills is being confronted with a new situation for which he or she has no thinking structures to abstract from and no logical systems to choose among, not even sensorimotor logic.

For example, a grandparent of mine had never learned to drive, although she was a very intelligent woman. When presented with the chance to learn to drive the first thing she did was to read about it, trying to use formal thought. Although she knew, after her reading, about "defensive driving" and other concepts like the logic of the automotive engine, these "higher level" skills did not help much when she first tried to engage the clutch and drive away smoothly. In fact, this particular grandmother was so shocked by her first-time, terrible, actual (physical) driving performance, compared to her excellent book understanding, that she began to panic and let the car roll out of control until it came to a stop against a huge rock. Learning the sensorimotor skill of getting that stick shift car out on the road was "lower level" thinking, but was the most adaptive kind of thinking for that situation. Learning to pick the right level of thought for the occasion may be one thing that people learn is logically possible as they become Postformal.

What characterizes the adaptive power of Postformal Thought? Why is it helpful to an adult? How must an adult structure thinking, over and above the operations of formal-operational adolescents, to be in touch with reality and survive? The question here is not about specific facts that need to be known, but rather about general "higher level" intellectual operations, or processes, that the knower needs to master to make existential sense of life and to make life work in situations which go beyond the demands of lower level thinking.

One key thing competent mature adults seem to need (based on their statements and on observation and task analyses) is to be able to choose one logical model (in other words, one formal operational structure) of the many possible logical models to impose on a given cognitive or emotional reality so that they can make decisions and get on with life. They also need to know that they are making necessarily (partly) subjective decisions about reality when they do this.

Felt Connection and Complex Adult Cognition

What relationship does felt connection—connection among aspects of the self, between self and another, and between self and a Transcendent—have to complex Postformal cognition and learning? Felt connection can be defined as conscious awareness of relatedness to another with an emotional attachment component. Adult cognitive development and the development of complex *felt* connection are motivated by *each other* and ultimately influence each other.

That inter-relationship is described in a new theory (Sinnott, 2005, 2006a,b; Sinnott & Berlanstein, 2006) summarized in Figure 4.1. Let's look at each part of the figure and enlarge upon the complex ideas we find there. Seven aspects of ideas in the figure are outlined below. They are based on research and earlier theoretical work on felt connection. Suggestions for future research can be found in Sinnott and Berlanstein (2006). This aspect of the theory is new and so does not yet enjoy as much empirical support as other aspects of Postformal Theory.

Three Types of Feeling Connected

The first part of Figure 4.1 to notice is that there are three types of feeling connected. These three elements are labeled "connect the sides of the Self," "connect with others," and "connect with the Transcendent." Connecting the sides of the self involves being in touch with and relating to the various aspects of our personalities, including disowned parts like the Shadow (Jung, 1931/1971). How we connect the sides of ourselves (and the *existence* of "sides" of the Self) partly depends on early relationships in the family of origin. Connecting with others involves interactions between or among persons, the conscious or unconscious interpersonal relationship pattern we exhibit today. Connect-

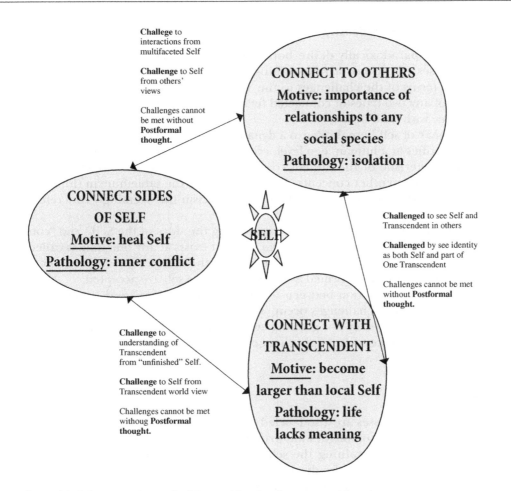

Figure 4.1 Felt connection and adult cognitive development and learning.

ing with the Transcendent involves having an ongoing relationship with something or Someone that is larger than the individual Self, for example, The Great Spirit, the Universe, or God.

Three Dynamic Processes

In the figure each of these three types of feeling connected is united with the other two by lines and arrows going in both directions, indicating that each of the three elements influences and is influenced by the others in a circular fashion. Therefore there are three dynamic processes, the dynamic of which we can discuss and study. The first process is the dynamic interplay between "connecting the sides of the Self" and "connecting with others." The second process is the dynamic interplay between "connecting with others" and "connecting with the Transcendent." The third process is the dynamic interplay between "connecting with the Transcendent" and "connecting the sides of the Self." Interventions and applications, described later, may make use of one or more of these three dynamic processes.

Challenges to the Self's Identity

As humans, we paradoxically desire both continuity and change. The dynamic inter-action processes (those two arrows uniting any two elements in Figure 4.1) also are described in terms of the challenges to the Self, challenges posed by the simultaneous experience of any two types of connected feelings. The two types of connected feelings may not agree with each other.

When I speak of self here, I refer to a dynamic, changing center of events with which a person identifies at a human, ego level, even as it may be constantly transforming. An adaptive characteristic of the human cognitive process is to form concepts and label them as distinct from other concepts. At the same time, the same human thinker might also understand that on the level of physics or mysticism this seemingly concrete thing, the Self, is an illusion.

In the dynamic interaction between "connecting the sides of the Self" and "connect-ing with others" two challenges occur. The self that exists at any one time is called into question by experiencing the reality of others; and the manner in which one perceives and relates to others is transformed as more sides of the self are accepted.

In the dynamic interaction between "connecting with others" and "connecting with the Transcendent," two challenges occur. The manner in which we perceive and relate to others may be changed by our growing awareness of the Transcendent. And our con-nection with the Transcendent might change when challenged by the behavior of others close to us.

Motivation

The three sets of processes are also labeled with a motivation factor in Figure 4.1. That factor suggests *why* a person might want to do the difficult work of rising to the challenge of constructing and maintaining the self when new information emerges during the dynamic interactions. When the dynamic interaction process involves "connecting the sides of the Self" (coupled with some other element), motivation comes from the desire to be more complete or whole, to heal. When the dynamic interaction process involves the element of "connecting with others" (coupled with some other element), motivation comes from our desires to maintain and improve ties with people important to us. When the dynamic interaction process involves "connecting with the Transcendent" (coupled with some other element), motivation comes from the desire to increase our participa-tion in something spiritual, something larger than our local Selves. Motivations can be both practical and existential.

Pathology

There can be a failure to feel connected within any single one of the three types of felt connections mentioned above: within the self; between the self and other persons; and with the Transcendent. These particular failures are labeled *pathology* in Figure 4.1. They have implications for identity and emotional well being.

First, if there are failures in the development of the felt connections within the Self, the person might experience inner conflicts, surprisingly conflicted or self-sabotaging decisions, and a feeling of fragility. The person tends to lose the self upon interacting with others. The person rigidly judges to be "bad" those persons who seem to represent the sides of the self that have not been accepted and integrated. Welwood (1996) dis-cusses this form of projection, especially in the context of relationships.

Failure to establish felt connections with others might lead to different problems. For example, the person might feel isolated or abandoned, as if no one can understand him or her. Intimacy and generativity (Erikson, 1982) might not be possible, then, for that person.

Failure to establish connections with something or Someone larger than the Self, i.e., with some Transcendent meaning for life, may carry yet another set of problems. There may be an existential crisis. The person may be driven by anxiety about death, or may find life tragic and meaningless. For the person, there is nothing that gives a larger platform from which to view current problems or setbacks.

These failures to feel connected, and the resulting difficulties, leave the person with sadness and a yearning to re-weave the web of life, to take part in the dance of life in some more coherent way. But we need those three things mentioned earlier to participate in a healthy way in our modern version of village circle dances. We need to feel mastery of many steps (connection within the Self), to feel connected to other dancers in the circle (interpersonal connection), and to be in connection with the overall pattern the dance represents (connection with the Transpersonal or Transcendent). We need to feel the three types of connection or relationship.

Complex Postformal Thought and Felt Connection

Figure 4.1 also refers to *Postformal Thought* in relation to each challenge. To successfully integrate the types of connections and their sometimes disparate or conflicting ideas, yet preserve a concept of a self that is whole, Postformal complex cognitive operations must be used (Sinnott, 1998b). The conflicting ideas, and the person's high motivation to work out the conflict, provide an occasion for the initial and continuing learning of this complex thinking ability. Possession of this thinking ability provides the means for more easily handling the challenge of conflicting relational structures.

However, a person may suffer from what might be called a *cognitive pathology*. Failure to develop complex Postformal cognitive representations and some integration of the reality of the several types of felt connections, whatever the reason for that failure, leaves the self in a fragmented and conflicted state with few conscious cognitive tools to become whole. The person in such a state may never consciously conceptualize and grasp a way to be able to live with multiple strongly felt connections. Learning is needed. Some examples may clarify this point.

For example, on a cognitive level it may seem impossible to such a person to integrate his or his connections with many other persons of all different types into a unified self that feels whole or connected inside. It will seem like either the whole, integrated self or the deep connections with other persons will have to be sacrificed. The problem is that the person cannot conceive of a way of connecting with others without losing the Self, a very unsatisfactory "borderline" life outcome. Learning the integration can only occur with the learning and use of Postformal Complex Thought.

In a second example of a cognitive failure, the person without complex cognitive representations may be faced with integrating felt connection with others and a felt connection to the Transcendent. The person may conceive of no alternatives but to give up a spiritual search (connection with the Transcendent) in favor of keeping connections with loved ones, or to break connections with the loved ones in order to continue a spiritual search. Again, the person's "solution" leads to a less than satisfactory adult development outcome due to (unnecessary) either/or choices and loss of felt connection of some type. Only a Postformal cognitive representation of self would integrate both aspects of felt connection. Learning can foster this (Sinnott, 1998b).

A final example might add additional light. The person who cannot cognitively represent the complex process of integrating two types of felt connection may have a third type of problem. That person may not be able to conceive of knowing and accepting the multiple sides of the self (some sides of self considered "good," some considered "less than good") *and* feeling (guiltlessly) connected with an angry God figure. A resolution could only occur if one set of felt connections is sacrificed (e.g., surrender of self to the Divine Will or give up religion/spiritual life). Again, the *non*-resolution, based on the inability to conceptualize in Postformal terms at a more complex level, closes off life options for growth and for feeling connected and whole in multiple ways simultaneously.

Learning and Development

Finally, how do learning and development intersect in the model represented in Figure 4.1? We have touched upon these relations above. The Piagetian ideas of assimilation and accommodation are helpful in understanding the intersection of concepts. When the Figure 4.1 indicates that a challenge occurs, the individual receiving new information first tries to assimilate this new information into the cognitive concepts he or she already holds. Those current concepts fit the person's current developmental level. If there *is* a challenge, however, the new information will not fit the old concepts and ways of being in the world. If the individual who is challenged does not ignore that new information but accommodates to it, learning takes place. For a longer discussion of learning and development in adults from this perspective, see Sinnott (1994b; 1998b). At some point, a new developmental level may result from a combination of organic growth and the learning of newly acquired information.

From the preceding discussion we, see how a person *could* come to have a coherent way of thinking about and working with relations that exist in all three areas noted in Figure 4.1: within the self (based upon early experience); interpersonal relations; or relationship with the Transcendent. As a person tries to balance or be *cognitively consistent* about connections in all these areas of relationship, similarity in the existential story of the relationships will be sought because it would make thinking about them easier. If, for example, parts of myself cannot be trusted, *and* other people cannot be trusted, *and* God cannot be trusted, my thinking about life is simplified in one coherent pattern of distrust.

Related Perspectives on Adult Cognitive Development and Learning

Several authors have discussed adult cognitive development in earlier work that predates this handbook. With apologies for necessarily incomplete listings of authors, I will describe the general direction this work took. The several authors can be organized into two general groups.

Beginning in the late 1970s and early 1980s, thinkers in the first group were attempting to "go beyond Piagetian formal operations" to see what the next stage might be. (Piaget himself was beginning to be interested in similar questions when he died in old age.) They often presented lectures at the periodic Harvard University Conferences on Postformal Thought, later the Adult Development Conferences. Those lectures are summarized in the following edited books: Commons, Armon, Kohlberg, Richards, Grotzer, and Sinnott (1990); Commons, Richards & Armon (1984); Commons, Sinnott, Richards, and Armon (1989); and, Sinnott (1994b). (Also see the Sinnott references listed earlier in this chapter.) Many of these presenters did not test their ideas with research, nor did more than one or two studies.

One example of thinking among those in the first group are the ideas of Arlin (1975, 1984). Her presentation and research described how adult cognitive development may achieve a new stage making us specialists in "problem finding," identifying the latent problem in a complex situation. Another example is Koplowitz (1984) who saw cognitive development during adulthood as leading to "unitary thought." Unitary thought accepts that all things are causally connected, that there is essential underlying unity in variables, and that boundaries and "permanent objects" are constructed, not given.

In the second group are authors coming mainly from adult education traditions. Rather than developing entire theories of adult cognitive development, these writers usually were interested in examining how adults might learn or teach, *if* they have cognitive strengths, weaknesses and goals different from younger persons. These writers include: Baltes & Baltes (1990); Kegan (1982); Kramer & Bacelar (1994); Labouvie-Vief & Hakim-Larson (1989); Lee (1991, 1994); Meacham & Boyd (1994); Mezirow & Associates (2000); and Sternberg & Berg (1992). Some in this group can also be found in the first group.

One example of the thinking of individuals in the second group is the work of Sternberg and Berg (1992). They describe learning in adulthood as directed toward practical problem solving and the mastery of tacit knowledge. Tacit knowledge is defined as the semi-automatic knowledge of how things work in the real world, e.g., how office politics operates. A second example from group two is Mezirow (2000). In his writing the adult is described as learning to shift cognitive contexts and currently existing frames of reference. Meaning is therefore transformed in many ways. This creates cognitive change. In Kegan's (1982) "evolving self" view, self-construction is the most important task of adult cognitive development. Adults learn both information and transformation. This epistemological transformation is a lifelong cognitive development process during which adults grow a self-authoring mind and a self-transforming mind.

These very brief mentions of some of the other approaches somewhat related to the main theme of this chapter are offered to the reader to allow for further exploration given the history and the breadth of the field. To date, the most developed theory of adult cognitive development with a neo-Piagetian "flavor" is that of Sinnott, with its research and extensive applications.

The remainder of this chapter will be focused on applications of Sinnott's theory to adult life tasks. These tasks overall include creating an identity, maintaining intimate and family relationships, dealing with the workplace, achieving generativity, achieving integrity, avoiding psychopathology, continuing one's education, creating a structure for the university suitable to adult learning, and developing an appropriate spirituality.

Applications of the Theory of Postformal Adult Cognitive Development

In this final section of the chapter, we explore just a few of the adult-life applications that make the ideas of Postformal Thought, with its association to felt connection, so useful for the study of adult development. It is worth re-emphasizing that cognitive development cannot be separated from its intersection with the complex web of felt connections that adults value. Postformal cognition and felt connection go hand in hand. For a reminder, look again at Figure 4.1 and at the earlier description of the development of this complex thought.

Let's look first at the effects of developing complex thought on couple and family relations. Second, let's very briefly look at the relation between adult cognitive development and spirituality in adulthood.

Couple and Family Relations

Intimate relationships are intense and important interactions, by definition. Emotions weave through each interaction and often contribute too much heat to any light which cognition may shed. Framing actions of family members has implications for daily encounters and decisions, far more so than anything that might happen in other settings with comparative strangers. For a couple or a family that remains together for a longer period of time, the entire enterprise is colored by the history of past cognition, felt connection, emotion, and action.

Styles of dealing with this intensity are defined by the emotional defense patterns, the felt connections, the shared cultural reality, the history, and the cognitive development of each person in the relationship. The presence or absence of Postformal thinking can skew individuals' defense styles and their responses to shared cultural reality and the history of that couple or family. Similarly, the emotionally based defense mechanisms, the shared culture, and the relationship history can distort the development or use of Postformal thought by individuals or intimate groups at later points in their history. Further, these patterns are taking shape within the psychodynamics of each individual, within the individual's ongoing dialogue between the ideal and real self-in-relationship, between members of the couple, in the couple as a unique living system in its own right, between the family system and society, *and* in the family as a living system. Notice that even the relationship itself begins to take on a life of its own, going on with a history somewhat separate from the histories of the individuals within it. It is as if additional layers of complexity were overlaid on "triangular" theories of intimate relations such as Sternberg (1986) or Marks (1986), and on relational "stage" theories like Campbell (1980) such that each triangle of relationship features or each stage becomes *four* dimensional and transforms over time!

Researchers and therapists who discuss processes in couples and families usually tend to focus on only one or two of those several elements of the volatile intimacy mix, and then shape questions or therapeutic processes around that element. Sometimes the nature of the problem demands this reductionism; sometimes the therapist's skills are stronger in that area; sometimes there is simply not enough time. Ironically, when I focus on the element of Postformal thought in this chapter, I employ a similar narrowing of vision since I am looking most of all at a cognitive logical process and a felt connection process rather than at some other sort of process. My plan, though, is to bring the discussion around full circle to show the interplay of *all* the forces as they are affected by and as they affect Postformal thought.

In this part of the chapter, we will begin our discussion by examining the interplay and mutual causality of each of the main felt connection relational elements (i.e., defense patterns, cultural reality, and relationship history) and Postformal thought development. How might Postformal thinking help couples and families stay together happily? How might their relational life stimulate the development of Postformal thought? We will examine how these connections relate to marital and family harmony and distress. Then, we will summarize a sample of some research on the felt connection element of couple relations, a project initiated by Rogers (1989; Rogers, Sinnott & Van Dusen, 1991), in which Postformal thought is taken into account as a factor.

Postformal Thought and Other Elements in Intimate Behavior

The adaptive value of Postformal thought is that it can help bridge logical realities so that partners in a relationship can re-order logically conflicting realities in more complex ways. This skill can let the knower(s) handle more information, live in a state of multiple realities even if those realities logically conflict, and become committed enough to a chosen reality to go forward and act, thereby reifying the chosen (potential) reality.

In an intimate relationship, individuals attempt to join together to have one life, to some degree. As the Apache wedding blessing says, "Now there is one life before you ... (so)...enter into the time of your togetherness." For a couple, three "individuals" begin to exist: partner #1, partner #2, and their relationship that begins to take on a life of its own. For a family, of course, there are even more "individuals" present, as pioneering family therapist Virginia Satir (1967) noted when she worked with not only the real humans in her office but also with the remembered aspects of other absent relatives with whom the real humans psychologically have felt connections. To have that one life together, to whatever extent they wish to have it together, the logics of the individuals must be bridged effectively. Those logics might be *about* any number of things, some of which may not sound especially "logical" (in the narrow sense of the word we are accustomed to), including concepts, roles, perceptions, physical presence, emotions, and shared history.

Effects of Individual's Cognitive Postformal Skills on Intimate Relationships

In some cases, the individual has access to a cognitive bridge across realities, but not a Postformal one. After all, realities *are* bridged, though poorly, if one person in a relationship dominates another and that one's reality becomes the other's, too. But this domination does not require a synthesis of logics since one logic is simply discarded.

There is a variation on this theme. Two members of an intimate union, because of religious beliefs or personal emotional needs, also may drop their own logics to give preference to that of the new "individual," "the relationship," letting its role-related reality dominate both of their own individual ones. This, too, is not a Postformal synthesis but a capitulation.

A converse scenario might find the logic of that third individual, "the relationship," dominated and discarded by one or both partners' logics. In all these cases one "individual" has lost part of the "self," most likely in order to maintain the relationship.

Members of the intimate partnership may find this winner/loser solution to conflicts large and small to be the best fit for them; they may not be capable of any higher-level solution, may not be motivated to find it, or may not be emotionally ready for one. Postformal thought is not involved in this sort of resolution. Perhaps this less skilled behavior is so incorporated into their shared history that it would be a challenge to their relational identity for them to have a relationship without it. But it is not Postformal thinking, and it is less adaptive overall than Postformal thinking would be.

Predictable Couple Problems When One Logic Dominates (Non-Postformal)

When one logic dominates the other a chance for growth is lost. There also are emotional overtones that begin to color the relationship processes and relationship history. The partner or family member whose logic was dominated usually exacts a price, whether consciously or unconsciously, expecting a payback to allow the balance of power to return to the relationship. And less information can be taken in, integrated, and acted upon by an individual using one simpler logic (e.g., in Piagetian terms, concrete operational logic), as opposed to two logics or as opposed to a more complex single one such as Postformal logic.

There are several predictable outcomes that are less than optimal when one logic dominates another. Lack of movement forward toward Postformal thought slows the individual's growth. Having a single dominant logic begins or continues a story in the relationship history that is a story about winners and losers and simplistic cognitions about complex life events. It slows the individuals' movement toward understanding and learning how to work with the shared cultural reality. It does prevent any challenge to whatever emotional defenses the individuals may have used in the past, but keeps the peace at a cost.

A special case occurs if the intimate group is a family with minor children, none of whose members happen to use Postformal thought. The predictable difficulties mentioned in the last section are multiplied in a situation with more individuals. It is harder for children to gradually learn a more skilled cognitive approach where there are no daily role models. It is harder for the children to grow up, create their own personal view of the world, and leave that family when power struggles centering on control of the family reality have been going on for so long in their own family history.

Benefits of Using a Complex Postformal Logic

Alternatively, the bridge across realities may be a Postformal one. The incompatible several logical realities of the relationship then might be orchestrated more easily and orchestrated at a higher cognitive level to permit a more complex logic of the relationship to emerge. Postformal thinkers can adapt to the challenges of intimate relationships better than those without Postformal thought because no one's logic needs to be discarded for the relationship to go on. For the Postformal couple, power and control are not the same level of threat looming on the relational horizon as they are for the individuals without Postformal thought who must worry about cognitive survival of individuality in their relationships. Shared history for the Postformal intimates reflects the synthesis of cognitive lives rather than alternating dominance of one reality/life over another. Each logical difference or disagreement ends up being another piece of evidence that the relationship remains a win-win situation for individuals within it. This enhances the relationship's value and tends to stabilize it even further.

In the situation where one individual in the relationship is the *only* Postformal one, we see a different opportunity and challenge. Several resolutions are possible each time an interpersonal logical conflict occurs. Perhaps the less cognitively skilled individual(s) will use this chance to grow cognitively, with predictable benefits. From my point of view, this is the best outcome and one of the desirable features of having intense intimate relationships and felt connections.

Alternatively, perhaps the increasingly aggravated Postformal individual will let emotions overtake him or her and will temporarily resolve the situation by regressing cognitively and acting out against or withdrawing from others in the situation. This will lead to the previously mentioned predictable problems for couples using lower level logics.

Perhaps the more cognitively skilled individual will decide to wait and hope that the other(s) will come around to a more skilled view of the situation, in time. This tactic is easier for that *Postformal* person to tolerate since the Postformal individual sees the bigger picture and does not have to take the power struggle quite as seriously as other members of the intimate group. But predictable conflicts will still occur and growth may be stalled.

A special situation occurs when this intimate group is a family with minor children. The Postformal parent has reason to believe that the children will develop further and possibly become Postformal thinkers themselves. The Postformal parent might consciously try to encourage the cognitive development of those children in the direction that the Postformal parent has mastered. The mismatch in cognitive levels will not be a cause for frustration, in this case, but rather for challenge and hope for the future development of the children.

The Other Side of the Coin: Effects of Intimate Relationship Factors Influencing Postformal Thought Development

The factors in ongoing intimate relationships that we have been discussing—mainly felt connection, emotional defense mechanisms, shared relationship history, and shared cultural reality—potentially can influence the development and use of Postformal thought, not just be influenced by it. For example, if an individual is emotionally damaged and is responding to all situations out of need, that person is less likely to take a risk in a relational situation and let go of his or her own cognitive verities long enough to be willing to bridge to someone else's realities. Even the Postformal thinker would not be likely to use that level of logical thought in such an interpersonal contest in which he or she is emotionally needy or "one down." Just as negative emotions often dampen the higher-level creative spirit, emotional damage means the individual tries to regain safety before meeting the higher level needs of the relationship (other than those in which s/he is the nurtured one). Children in a relationship where the parents are damaged emotionally, or children who themselves are emotionally damaged, will find it harder to learn Postformal responses to family dynamics. Such families function at the lower levels of unproductive patterns on the Beavers Scale, for example (Beavers & Hampson, 1990), described so well by Scarf (1995) in her book on the intimate worlds of families. The life-and-death emotional struggles that occupy such families prevent those children from having the emotional space or energy to bridge realities.

Shared relationship history also is a strong force influencing Postformal thinking. The habits of relating and felt connection that individuals have developed in earlier years tend to perpetuate themselves over the lifetime. If those habits do not include Postformal cognitive processes for relating at the time that a given relationship begins, and if many years are spent bridging the related individuals' realities in a *non*-Postformal way, than it will be increasingly difficult for anyone (child or adult) in the relationship to move on to a Postformal way of relating, violating earlier habit.

An exception to this is the family situation in which parents may be Postformal but young children are not. Postformal parents may find this cognitive discrepancy easier to bear than less cognitively skilled parents, but still will be influenced by living in relationships in which they are always using a logical level that is beneath their own. One's tendency to permanently distort perceptions about an intimate's logical skills, based on the cognitive skills they have shown during the history of our relationship with them, is very strong. We see just how strong when we see parents relating to their adult children as if those adults are *still* very young children. Parents must make significant efforts to overcome history, or at least reconsider whether historical patterns need to be revised before using them to predict today's behavior. Intimates influenced by their history face an equally daunting task if they want to relate on a new (to them), more skilled, logical level.

Shared cultural reality (or social forces and roles) also influences the ways that Postformal thinking can be used in intimate relationships. This is a domain where social roles often interfere with the choice of possible processes of relating and possible concepts of relationships. The shared reality of the social roles "appropriate" for various intimate relationships must be a "lowest common denominator" reality that the vast majority in a society can achieve, or pretend to achieve. The shared social role reality for couples' relations and family relations is often structured enough and at a low enough skill level that no bridging of conflicting logical realities is necessary at all. All that is necessary is to act out the appropriate roles in a convincing way and to make the socially appropriate comments about feelings connected to those roles. Tradition does save cognitive energy!

(Notice that this is the first time in this discussion that we need to consider whether a couple or family is heterosexual or homosexual, legally married or not, childless or not, a May/December union, divorced or previously married, with or without stepchildren or other relatives. Other than here in this paragraph, the processes discussed in this chapter apply to all of these differing roles and family configurations. Only the shared social cognition element discriminates among the various family configurations. Persons in all the various family configurations *can* use the same cognitive relational processes and can experience the same styles of relating and felt connection.)

A conflict may occur when the views of any knower (e.g., "the couple") about the reality of their relationship come into conflict with the views of society about their intimate relationship. This conflict might be the stimulus for the growth of a Postformal way of seeing their relationship and seeing the world. For example, it has not been many years since the existence of a childless marriage was considered an ongoing tragedy for everyone and, if intentional, a sign of problems in one's personality and maturity level. Imagine a couple who feel very happy in their relationship, even secretly happy to have evaded the encumbrance of children, coming face to face with this tragic and pathologized view of their "selfish" childless life together and their part in the "problem." Knowing that such a view does not square with their personal knowledge may be the impetus for them to realize Postformal elements of knowing, perhaps for the first time. The motivation in this case is social.

When the reality of one person in the relationship clashes with another's view, the intensity of the bond is what motivates them to seek a resolution. This is a push toward development of Postformal thought, or perfection of it, since lower level logics will leave the conflict unresolved. Since framing such a situation Postformally can help keep blame and anger at bay, Postformal skills are often welcome conflict resolution devices.

The recent past has been a time of social change, especially in regard to the forms of intimate relations. While there are inherently limited possibilities for intimate relationship behavior in the human behavioral repertoire, some of those possibilities are more fashionable than others at a given time. Living at a time of social change means that the individual and even the relationship is challenged to cross logical realities about itself without losing itself, all the while under shifting shared social reality pressures. Access to Postformal thought makes it easier for the social change shift to occur while an identity is maintained by a person or a relationship.

Postformal Thought, Distress, and Healing in Intimate Relationships

You may have gathered from the discussion above that acknowledging the role of Postformal thought in intimate ongoing relationships might lead to some new ways of conceptualizing couple and family distress and some new approaches to healing distressed relationships. Postformal thought may be an additional tool for keeping relationships from running into serious trouble when the inevitable difficult times occur. But Postformal Thought may be the source of discord, too.

Looking at the bad news first, attaining this more complex cognitive level might lead to trouble and discord in a relationship. Imagine the case of a couple, neither of whom was Postformal when they first became a couple. Time and the events of life passed, and one (but only one) member of the couple developed the ability to think Postformally. This led to their each seeing the world and their life together from very different vantage points on many occasions, living different cognitive lives within the boundaries of their life together. For a couple that desires a deep level of closeness, this becomes a challenging situation; they no longer "speak the same language." Of course, differences of opinion, differences in ways of seeing the reality of the world, happen for every couple, to some degree, at one time or another in their relationship, and their task as a couple is to grow through the difficulty and build a stronger union. However, in the case of a difference in the ability to understand at a Postformal level, the couple has begun a time of profound and far-reaching differences in world views. The very nature of their usual realities is different much of the time; one sees it as concrete and existing "out there," while the other sees it as co-constructed and co-created through commitment to its reality. Even more challenging, one of the partners (the Postformal one) can visit the reality of the other (the non-Postformal one), but the other cannot yet visit back. So when one develops cognitively but the other does not, discord in world views may provide a challenge.

A second piece of potential bad news related to Postformal thought and relationships is the type of pathology that may intrude when any unskilled behavior becomes unskilled in a much more complex, Postformal way. For example, if a couple is temporarily waging a power struggle with one another, they have access to a *far broader* range of strategies to do so if they are Postformal, since weapons like sarcastic remarks can be used at several cognitive levels of the argument.

In spite of these negative possibilities, it has been my impression that the positive features which Postformal thought might bring to a relationship difficulty far outweigh the negative ones. In a time of conflict members of a couple have to handle emotions and felt connections and deal with their individual unskilled behaviors. If they can do so looking from an over-arching logical vantage point that gives them "the big picture," it is easier for them to gain perspective on their individual problems and avoid blaming each other. They can weather the changes in the developing relationship better than the members of the non-Postformal couple who see the world in polarized terms. Let's look at one practical area of life in intimate relations where Postformal thought may make a difference: the roles related to gender (sex roles, sex role stereotypes) and behavior related to those masculine/feminine roles. I have written about this topic rather extensively, and have included it in my research efforts, because gender roles and the co-creation of social roles have been a central aspect of historically recent social changes in the United States (Cavanaugh, Kramer, Sinnott, Camp, & Markley, 1985; Sinnott, 1977, 1982, 1984a, 1986; 1987, 1993b; Sinnott, Block, Grambs, Gaddy, & Davidson, 1980; Sinnott & Shifren, 2002; Windle & Sinnott, 1985).

"Gender role" is a different concept than sexual identity, sexuality, or masculine/feminine behavior. Gender roles may at various times be ambiguous, polarized into opposites, synthesized into androgenous larger versions, reversed, or transcended entirely. The general age-related progression of gender role development is from polarizing masculine/feminine roles to transcending roles entirely in favor of giving energy to other parts of identity. Gender related roles enter discussions of intimate relations because couples tend to divide the work of living together, and gender has often been used by society to define roles. Couples enter relationships, even homosexual ones, with ideas of what is proper socially dictated masculine and feminine behavior. Sometimes identity is being challenged when there is conflict over role related behavior, making an apparently simple negotiation over something concrete like housework into a complex, full-blown struggle over identity and worth. If a couple is struggling about gender role related behavior, Postformal thought makes it easier to sort things out. A Postformal partner can readily understand that, if he or she gets beyond emotional or habitual reactions, the roles can be validly co-constructed by them in any number of ways, as logical systems to which they commit themselves and weave into their lives. That partner can also understand that a gender role and its related behavior is only a minor part of his or her constantly transforming identity and is a poor index of personal worth. For the Postformal partners, the negotiation then moves back to the domain of "what job do I *want?*" rather than remaining in the domain of identity and worth: "I'm a terrible person if you make more money (less money) than I do, and my *identity* is in danger."

In terms of doing therapy with a Postformal couple or with the members of a couple, at least one of whom is Postformal, their level of cognition can be a real asset or a real drawback. The couple that understands that they are co-creators of the reality of their relationship, to some degree, finds it easier to open to possibilities and to change, in spite of history. They already feel that power and choice are partly in their hands, and that taking action is part of creating something new. They know that partners seldom have absolute characteristics that are unmodifiable. Given the motivation to reduce pain and create a better shared relationship, progress is made with comparative ease. If the motivation is to obstruct change, though, the Postformal client can create more ways to avoid real consideration of issues than other clients can, all things being equal. Defenses can be more sophisticated.

One Study of Couple Relations and Postformal Thought

If the availability of Postformal thought is related to the quality of intimate relations, we should be able to see an empirical connection between those two variables. Rogers (1992; Rogers, Sinnott, & Van Dusen, 1991) set out to investigate the joint cognition of two persons trying to solve their Postformal problems together. These two persons might be longer-term married adults or strangers in a dyad, which might influence their cognition. Rogers also wanted to examine marital adjustment and social behaviors evident during problem solving. She expected that well adjusted married dyads would demonstrate more Postformal problem solving and more socially facilitative behaviors than the poorly adjusted married dyads.

Forty heterosexual couples between the ages of 35 and 50 were recruited. They were mainly Caucasian, married for an average of 15 years, 75% for the first time, 25% having had a long term previous marriage. Forty-one percent had a bachelors, masters, and/or Ph.D. degrees. After individuals were prescreened for intelligence they were tested for marital adjustment using Spanier's (1976) Dyadic Adjustment Scale, a widely used self report instrument, which tests for, among other things, dyadic cohesion, consensus, and satisfaction. The individuals were randomly assigned to work in one of the following contexts: well-adjusted couple, working as a couple; poorly adjusted couple, working as a couple; well-adjusted-couple individuals, working with someone not their spouse; and poorly-adjusted-couple individuals working with someone not their spouse. Then each "couple" (real or artificial) was videotaped solving the Postformal logical problems. Tapes were scored according to the coding schemes of Pruitt and Rubin (1986) and Sillars (1986) to obtain counts of the social behavior factors of avoidance, competition/contention, accommodation/yielding, and cooperation/collaboration.

While marital adjustment or dyadic context scores did not relate to using formal logical operations, these variables were related to using Postformal operations. Eighty percent of the maritally well adjusted dyads, both real couples and well adjusted members of couples paired with well adjusted strangers, gave evidence of significantly more Postformal thinking operations than the poorly adjusted did. This was especially true for responses to the problems with an interpersonal element. Analyzing facilitative social behaviors from the videotape, Rogers once again found that the ability to use formal operations did not relate to the social behaviors while use of Postformal operations did. For example, dyads without Postformal thought demonstrated more contentious and competitive behaviors while problem solving.

Rogers' results support the theory described earlier in this chapter. Postformal thinking and adjustment in intimate relationships were positively related. Some generalized ability seemed to be present which operated whether or not the spouses were working with each other or with strangers of equal cognitive developmental status. It may have operated by means of facilitating positive types of social behaviors and interactions, as evidenced by the fact that Postformal thinkers produced more cooperative and fewer avoidant behaviors. Postformal thinkers seemed to explore and create to a greater degree, tolerate others' ways of seeing reality, and ultimately be able to commit to one solution. When working with strangers, they also took more pains to communicate "where they were coming from" in their views of a problem's many potential realities. Rogers' work suggests that Postformal thinking is useful in intimate relationships. In the next section we very briefly explore cognitive development of a Postformal type and issues of spirituality.

Cognitive Development and Spirituality

In this section, we will discuss four related ideas. First, we propose that spirituality (as opposed to religiosity) makes use of the type of complex cognition which we have described earlier, a type known as Postformal thought. Second, we examine how we might perform psychological research on spiritual development using the theory of Postformal thought. Third, we examine the overlap between the new physics, Eastern spirituality, and Postformal thinking. Finally we propose that being able to think Postformally facilitates the individual's being able to live in balance—integrating mind, felt connections, emotions, body, and spirit into the dance of living.

Does spirituality grow with the aid of postformal thought? Religiosity and spirituality are two surprisingly separate things. To be religious is to observe the dictates and customs of a particular "church." To be spiritual, or to be a mystic, demands that we look with the eyes of a lover both on the world around us and on our fellow beings. Spirituality demands that we consciously shift realities and "know" the lovable quality of what we see at several levels, in order to love at least one aspect of it. Religiousness is different from spirituality; we can be religious using concrete or formal thought without making the Postformal cognitive shifts that spirituality demands. I can observe the dictum to give alms because my church says to do so without ever taking the spiritual leap of loving, identifying with, and empathizing with the dirty panhandler annoying me today. With maturity adults often become more religious and more spiritual. Adulthood encourages the awareness of death, and that awareness helps motivate both our obedience to religious customs and rules and our cognitive wrestling with the spiritual and mystical aspects of "de-identifying" with our mortal bodies.

Spirituality and spiritual knowing are important to humans, at least based on what they say and do in all cultures. Both are just beginning to get attention in life-span studies, especially life-span studies of cognition (APA Committee on Aging, 2005; Sinnott, 1993c, 1994a, 2000, 2001, 2002a, 2002b, 2003a, 2006a [under review], 2006b). Yet we are thinking beings who do conceptualize the spiritual and the transcendent, who think about and yearn for unitative states of being united with God or Universal Consciousness. When we think about spiritual things, we want our thoughts to make sense, to us and to others around us, as potentially *shared* cognition.

Several authors have addressed some aspect of the spirituality/cognition interface and its complexity over the course of the life span. Jung (1943, 1964) discussed the idea that spirituality is the product of a life-span maturational process. As Wink and Dillon (2002) explained, when middle aged and older adults experience the ambiguity and relativity of human life, they learn to go beyond linear logical modes of understanding reality. They use more evolved ways of conceptualizing the world, incorporating paradox, feelings and context into logic when making spiritual judgments (Wink & Dillon, 2002).

Labouvie-Vief, DeVoe, and Bulka (1989) also described a positive age-related ability to integrate cognitive and emotional perspectives leading to a greater comfort with metaphor and subjectivity, an ability not unlike Postformal Thought. Emmons (1999) discussed the notion of spiritual intelligence that enhances the adaptivity of an individual.

Wink and Dillon (2002) tested the correlation between spirituality among individuals in their 60s and 70s and cognitive commitment on the CAQ (the California Q-set, a 100-item ipsative measure of personality) (Block, 1978). They found that, for women, cognitive commitment scored from interview material decades earlier was correlated with spirituality in their 60s and 70s.

Cartwright (2001) addressed cognitive development and spirituality and reviewed recent research and theory with the goal of making connections between these domains. She discussed features of individuals' conceptions of their relationships to an External Power. She noted that some theorists have suggested parallels between children's understanding of religious or spiritual concepts and Piaget's stages of cognitive development (e.g., Elkind, 1997; Fleck, Ballard, & Reilly, 1975).

Spirituality has also been connected with the Felt Connection aspect of the Postformal Theory. Both Conn (1993) and Fowler (1981) hold that many relationships—between self, others, and a transcendent power—are important to spirituality. Kramer (2002), in her psychobiographical analysis of the suicidal decision of Clara, examined Clara's several types of relationships including her spiritual relationship with the transcendent. Kramer especially focused on the construction of the self within all these sometimes conflicting relationships. These analyses suggest that the Felt Connection portion of the Postformal Theory, described above, is also related to the development of mature spirituality.

But it may be time at this point in the history of our profession to try to make this illusive integration between psychological science and spirituality. We see all around us, for example in the integration of new physics with Eastern spirituality, that the old ways of describing reality are being reformulated and expanded because they are too limited to describe the current changes we see. Now we study the evolution of consciousness, but such a concept as consciousness was not even acknowledged in the psychology of the 1960s.

The question of the nature of the logical operations connected to knowing the spiritual eventually arises. How can we even *think* about the ideas of spirituality which violate the scientific logic of our formal operational minds? How can we make any kind of cognitive sense of the multiple realities of the new physics and quantum theory, much less of spirituality and mysticism? Spiritual ideas seem opposed to logic of any kind.

The purpose of this section is to suggest a way to make some integration between our psychological science and our spiritual experiences by seeing them both as knowable in Postformal operational terms. As psychologists and scientists we may find it useful to understand the cognitive processes involved in complex, transcendent, spiritual knowing, as well as how such thinking becomes part of the skills and processes and experience of the normal, non-pathological, developing human. The concepts of Postformal thought can help us do this. We also need to explore how ideas of transcendence, multiple realities, and "higher" meaning in life might be modeled in our cognitive language. We can apply the model of Postformal thought. Postformal thought can help us understand how we can know these experiences from a cognitive point of view, and can help us generate testable, even experimental, hypotheses about this knowing. The part of the theory focused on *felt connection with the transcendent* would be very important to this exploration.

From our own experience and from descriptions by others, we know that individuals do this multiple-reality knowing in many contexts. Analyses of thinking that are done in terms of Postformal thought specifically address the question of how two logically disparate frames for reality can coexist in a coordinated way in the human mind. How can the transcendent thinker see life as both "real" and "maya" (illusion) and still function? Postformal thinking may help explain how humans can function on a day-to-day, practical level while experiencing the conflicting basic logical frameworks that underlie spiritual knowing. Could Postformal thought be among the logical processes that allow this transcending of multiple realities and even of "self" and this achievement of a unitative spiritual state?

We also see characters in classics of fiction display multiple-reality knowing as part of their spiritual experiences. For example, Jean Valjean, in *Les Miserables* (Hugo, 1938), asks who he *is*, convict, spiritually condemned man, pillar of the community, or one whose life has been purchased by God for a special role in doing good works. When he asks these questions he must develop to a point where his "self" can bridge across those smaller selves within each of those contradictory logics to arrive at a larger self that is part of the spiritual, unitative self. This sounds like an activity of Postformal thought, being refined by felt connection.

Madeline L'Engle, in her classic "children's" book *The Wind in the Door* (1974), shows us a heroine who must shift her views of who and what she and others are (on the level of spirit) to prevent the physical death of her brother. In doing so, she transforms the logic of self, life, and death from a concrete one to a transcendent one in which the unlovable (on the everyday level) is also lovable (in the sense of agape, on the spiritual level). The demand to do so, motivated by felt connection, helps her develop Postformal thought.

Points of Interface.   There are four potential points of interface between the two domains of Postformal cognitive development and spirituality, points from which it would be easy to start our studies. See Figure 4.1 again; there could be many more. These four are: the *form* of this logic; the *developmental process* to attain this thought; the connection between this sort of thought, its underlying logic, and *felt connection*, emotion, and will; and the multi-person, *cooperative cognition* element.

With respect to the *form* of this logic, the scientist can examine the information processing and the cognitive style of any thinker, including the thinker in a unitative state. The scientist can elaborate on the logical processes being used by that thinker (as Piaget elaborated on the processes of infants and scientists) whether that thinker is Blake or an adolescent, St. Teresa or an Alzheimer disease patient, Buckminster Fuller or an unknown gifted musician. Cognitive developmental psychologists can examine the memory, problem solving, and the logic of the healthy, spiritually questing person. Tart (1983) explored the cognitive processes of those in many states of consciousness; we can explore the logic of mystics and spiritually questing persons in many settings.

The developmental process by which a person arrives at multi-reality logic skills is also ripe for study. Wilber (1995) offers a complex developmental model that could inspire years of study. Pearce (1973) has described developmental stages in which the first pass through the stage leads to *intra*-psychic growth while the second pass through the same stages leads to transpersonal psychological growth. That second pass through the stages is expected, Pearce says, in the middle and later years of adult life. But not every adult achieves this growth. What makes the difference?

A third way to approach the cognitive study of spiritual development is to tap the methods that incorporate felt connection, emotion, and will (or intention) into cognition. Since spiritual experience is often felt to be an emotional knowing and connection that does demand the use of intention and will, being able to incorporate such elements into studies is important. Emotional reactions might be one way to enlarge problem space to permit an enlarged world view such as Postformal or spiritual thought to develop.

A fourth set of studies may be equally difficult, but also possible. Studies of *cooperative cognition* are fairly rare in standard cognitive experimental settings where variables can be controlled in ways that are not practical in real life organizational or educational settings. Studying multi-person cognition would help us understand spirituality in two ways. First, we could understand how the shared belief system challenges or facilitates cognitive growth. Second, unitative states are, in certain ways, shared cognitive states. So, these four areas (process, development, emotion and will, multi-person cognition) offer a promise of research utility in our study of the cognitive aspects of spirituality.

A Necessary Skill.   We propose that Postformal thought is a necessary cognitive skill for deep, mature, thoughtful spiritual development and that it can be found in the thinking of spiritually wise individuals, saints, and mystics. We propose that it is the form logic takes in these mature thinkers and that it develops through the thinkers' relationships with others, God, and the universe. It includes the union of mind and emotion as well as a modified and expanded concept of self.

Postformal thought could allow the mature spiritual thinker to know that he or she is operating by two or more mutually contradictory but simultaneous logics while that thinker is experiencing higher awareness. Postformal thought could leave him or her comfortable with that knowing and with the behavior that flows from that knowing. The spiritual seeker who (as the saying goes) experiences all persons as Buddha, all places as Nirvana, and all sounds as Mantra is either totally out of touch with ordinary reality (without a reality to replace it), or much more able to orchestrate the multiple ordinary and non-ordinary states of consciousness described by Tart (1983) by virtue of improved cognitive abilities. What if the built-in human possibilities include a cognitive possibility of transcending the prison of our own cognition to enjoy a god's eye view of it?

The spiritual yearnings that accompany generativity and integrity for many persons often demonstrate thinking processes similar to Postformal thought, as do the comments of the wise ones, mystics, and saints of all spiritual traditions (Smith, 1991). Underhill (1961) may have said it best, writing that the mystic lives in a world unknown to most others where he or she sees through the veil of imperfection to view creation with God's eyes. The mystic is lifted out of the self to a higher self in order to see everything and everyone as lovable. There is a sense of choice about whether one spend a certain hour or day in a place of limited (ordinary) understanding or in a place of the larger understanding. The shaman walks in the upper and lower worlds, as animal spirit and human spirit simultaneously. Don Genero (Castaneda, 1971) can choose to see in a unitative way, with the eyes of the sorcerer, or see in the more ordinary way; he can violate physical laws or obey them. Spiritual seekers who are mystics say that they share in all of being while being one part of it. To sustain and understand these experiences takes the ability to coordinate multiple contradictory formal logical systems and to be able self-referentially to choose one to commit to at a given moment.

Some Testable Hypotheses and Some Difficulties in Studying These Relations

Next, I briefly describe four sample hypotheses with which we could test some relations between Postformal cognition and higher level spiritual development.

Hypothesis 1.   Individuals who report a unitative state of consciousness show Postformal operations; those not reporting unitative states may or may not show Postformal operations.

One might sample meditators, university students, the public at large, religious leaders, older adults labeled "wise," or master transpersonal therapists (among others) to find individuals reporting experiences of unitative states. Some of these groups would be expected to report them more frequently than others would. They would be tested for Postformal thought and for felt connections with the transcendent which are balanced in a Postformal way with other types of felt connections.

Conversely, one might hypothesize that Postformal thinkers are more likely to have unitative states of consciousness than non-Postformal thinkers. This direction of causality (that the cognitive state causes the unitative state to be conscious and reportable) better reflects the direction in which events probably occur. (However, it would probably be more fun for the researcher to use the hypothesis variation stated first. Using that one permits conversations with groups of individuals expressly chosen for their interesting spiritual experiences.)

Hypothesis 2.   Those reporting unitative states have highly efficient styles of processing large amounts of conflicting information and would function better in the face of that overload than those not reporting unitative states. We hypothesize that relation because of the underlying Postformal thought components that organize disparate realities more effectively.

Hypothesis 3.   Middle aged and older persons, whose life tasks involve developing generativity and integrity, are more likely to describe spiritual searches that link them with others and that operate to give a unity and meaning to their lives than are younger persons. They are even more likely to do so if they demonstrate use of Postformal operations. The rationale for this hypothesis is that underlying Postformal cognitive skills provide a similar form to personality development and to spiritual development, both of which serve the good or adaptation of the person.

Hypothesis 4.   Choice of the experience of life events, workshops involving self development, or psychotherapy where one challenges the meaning of one's life and the grounds of the self are likely to let a person make a transition to both Postformal thought and spiritual development. The rationale for this hypothesis is that a challenge of serious magnitude is needed to motivate reorganizing complex cognitive structures with the concomitant ability to articulate the aspects of deeper spiritual development.

Below are listed several difficult aspects of all the studies just proposed above.

1. It is difficult to reach agreement on what constitutes spiritual development, unitative experiences, and other aspects of advanced spirituality. Concrete polarized language is a significant problem. Operational definitions need to be crafted carefully.
2. If we are researching an "advanced" cognitive or spiritual state, relatively few persons will have experienced it. We will need large samples to find enough target respondents. Few will read the reports we generate about the phenomenon with enough understanding and interest. Few will want to review proposals or journal articles favorably, or generally support the effort.
3. Cognition, spirituality, and science have traditionally been split apart. Trying to find the bridges among them frightens both the complex thinkers who fear reductionism and the orthodox thinkers who fear bad science.
4. Some argue that we should not even try to scientifically study these subjects because such studies are really attempts to advocate a particular religion or some single value system, not about science.

However, these objections and difficulties can be answered. Spirituality and spiritual yearnings cross cultures and religions and can be seen in some form in all human groups. Nothing at all is value free; science in its traditional form has its own values and hidden or overt basic paradigms. Also, *all* behavior should be open to scientific investigation, if science is the powerful tool we believe it is. Using several tools can give us measures of a phenomenon from several additional perspectives. There is general agreement between both traditional and nontraditional scientists that study of only selected facets of a phenomenon by either group is always expected to yield limited information, whether in the field of spirituality or particle physics. So, it appears that none of the difficulties mentioned above is sufficient to keep us from conducting some innovative and "clean" (from a traditional scientific perspective) research on cognitive aspects of spiritual development. What is left to prevent us from approaching the study of this phenomenon?

New Physics, Eastern Spirituality, and Postformal Thought

It has been more than 30 years since Western culture, as a whole, rediscovered Eastern spiritual systems and mediated that understanding through selected concepts of the new physics. These phenomena have, in turn, been linked culturally with an emerging sense of global community. We have seen what could be described as a "sudden" interest in new ways of conceptualizing all levels of realities and relationships-over-time in physical, psychological, and spiritual realms. The "new" paradigms, of course, are really one of the several basic philosophical stances vis-à-vis reality, recycled throughout human history, each time dressed in the current fashion and the necessary accessories appropriate to the historical context in which they emerge. Within psychology, this "new" paradigm found varieties of expression in the sub-fields of: cognitive psychology (especially study of consciousness and intention); chaotic, evolving, and general systems models of behavior; humanist psychology; existential psychology; transpersonal psychology; and the psychology of mind/body interactions.

The key point relevant to this chapter is that the new physics, Eastern, transpersonal and other rediscovered spiritual traditions, and other emerging "new" paradigms all include a view of logical known reality that is like that described in the Theory of Postformal Thought. Postformal Thought can help us study how the human mind "knows" the "unknowable" (Sinnott, 1994a). We are not arguing the reductionist position that any of these new paradigms are "only" Postformal thought in disguise. Rather, we argue that the epistemology is similar for each. In other words, it seems possible that the intellectual operations by which the human mind knows reality in all these fields are similar ones. Physics and the reality of the spiritual realm both seem to reflect the self-referential awareness of truth possessed by the individual with access to Postformal thought. The co-constructed truth to which we make a passionate commitment of our lives, which we come to and leave as we shift our realities, may be spoken of in different words by Schroedinger or by a mystic, but the final epistemological result is the same. Each field seems to express a different side of the same Postformal reality in its own epistemology.

Living in Balance: Mind, Felt Connection, Emotions, and Body, with Spirit

I propose that access to Postformal thought permits the individual to balance, to orchestrate the physical and mental elements of the self not only with each other but also with the element of spirituality. For example, the body self may be very interested in having sex with an attractive person it met this summer. The emotional self may feel felt connection and love toward a long-term partner and guilt (in a complicated historical scenario involving relations with our parents) about even being aware of this attraction, much less acting on it. Meanwhile the intellectual self may be thinking through the meaning of this attraction, and how much it should say about it to its partner (to be honest about trouble in our relationship yet avoid bad feelings hurting the long-term relationship). The spiritual self, in this example, has a strong felt connection with God. The spiritual self may have an intuitive sense that the encounter is needed to learn something, somehow, about the nature of universal love (what? how?) by means of interaction with this person. Finally, the lack of felt connection between the part of my personality that is stimulation-seeking and the part that is an introvert creates conflict within.

In this example, each aspect of the self may offer a different vote about the behavior that should occur here, and some of the behavioral votes may contradict each other. In fact, the human condition is as interesting as it is because these balancing dilemmas are so frequent. Yet *some* behavior must be chosen actively or passively by the human who wishes to survive and thrive. Denial of any aspect of our complex human agendas, refusing to honor that aspect's needs, leads to trouble down the road in the form of mental or physical or emotional or spiritual illness. It is only when we can work out a balance among the needs of aspects of the self that we can make choices that maximize our ability to fulfill the needs of all aspects of the self.

Using our spiritual challenges and spiritual awareness with a logic that overarches the several often-contradictory logical system demands can hardly be expected to occur if the Postformal cognitive system has not yet developed. While the body and mind and emotional systems can to some degree "run on automatic" or instinct, spirit cannot be added to a coordinated conscious and mature balance honoring all of these without the operations of Postformal thinking. Postformal thought would seem to provide the conscious balance-forging tools to make it possible to creatively reach this sophisticated, transpersonal balance for ourselves, or to reach it through awakening in an intimate relationship with a partner.

Conclusion

I have explored some neo-Piagetian approaches to adult complex cognitive development, with an emphasis on Sinnott's theory of Postformal Thought. As seen in this chapter and in Figure 4.1, Postformal Thought is deeply integrated with our three major felt connections, first the connection among all elements of our personalities, second the connection with each other, and third the connection with the Transcendent. Finally, I explored two of the many applications of the Theory, with many more available in Sinnott's (1998) book and in other sources cited in this chapter. This overall approach suggests answers to many mysteries of adult cognitive development as well as to many of the challenges adults face. Research is ongoing to examine the relations between several additional variables and Postformal Thought.

This chapter offers a theoretical advance for the field since it integrates objective logic and subjective aspects of adult developmental experience. It also integrates key intra-personal and inter-personal aspects of adult human experience including the understanding of self, of others, and of the transcendent. It presents new theories that have the potential to offer explanations for a wide range of adult experience and developmental phenomena. Testable hypotheses are offered.

Cognitive development, as discussed here, can describe a dance of adaptive adult transformation. We are challenged to learn our own steps (i.e., to know ourselves), to learn to dance with others (i.e., to thrive in an interpersonal milieu), and to find meaning in the dance (i.e., to address existential questions and find meaning in our lives). If we can think about these parts of the dance in more effective and adaptive ways, using Postformal Thought, the challenges of life-long adaptation will be easier to meet.

References

American Psychological Association Committee on Aging (J. D. Sinnott, member). (2005). *Life plan for the life span*. Washington, DC: Author.

Arlin, P. (1975). Cognitive development in adulthood. A fifth stage? *Developmental Psychology, 11*, 602–606.

Arlin, P. (1984). Adolescent and adult thought: A structural interpretation. In M. Commons, F. Richards, & C. Armon (Eds.), *Beyond formal operations*, (pp. 258–271). New York: Praeger.

Baltes, P. B., & Baltes, M. M. (1990). *Successful aging: Perspectives from the behavioral sciences*. New York: Cambridge University Press.

Beavers, W., & Hampson, R. (1990). *Successful families: Assessment and intervention*. New York: Norton.

Block, J. (1978). *The Q-sort method in personality assessment and psychiatric research*. Palo Alto, CA: Consulting Psychologists Press.

Campbell, S. (1980). *The couple's journey: Intimacy as a path to wholeness*. San Luis Obispo, CA: Impact.

Cartwright, K. B. (2001). Cognitive developmental theory and spiritual development. *Journal of Adult Development, 8*, 213–220.

Cartwright, K. B., Galupo, M. P., & Tyree, S. D. (in preparation). *Reliability and validity of the Complex Postformal Thought Questionnaire*.

Castenada, C. (1971). *A separate reality*. New York: Washington Square Press.

Cavanaugh, J. C., Kramer, D., Sinnott, J. D., Camp, C., & Markley R. P. (1985). On missing links and such Interfaces between cognitive research and everyday problem solving. *Human Development, 28*, 146–168.

Commons, M., Armon, C., Kohlberg, L., Richards, F., Grotzer, T., & Sinnott, J. D. (Eds.), (1990). *Adult development: Models and methods in the study of adolescent and adult thought*. New York: Praeger.

Commons, M., Richards, F., & Armon, C. (Eds.). (1984).*Beyond formal operations: Late adolescent and adult cognitive development.* New York: Praeger.

Commons, M., Sinnott, J. D., Richards, R., & Armon, C. (Eds.). (1989). *Adult development II: Comparisons and applications of adolescent and adult development models.* New York: Praeger.

Conn, J. W. (1993). Spirituality and personal maturity. In R. J. Wicks, R. D. Parsons, & D. Capps (Eds.), *Clinical handbook of pastoral counseling, Volume 1, Expanded edition* (pp. 37–57). Mahwah, NJ: Paulist Press.

Elkind, D. (1997). The origins of religion in the child. In B. Spilka & D. N. McIntosh (Ed.), *The psychology of religion* (pp. 97–104). Boulder, CO: Westview Press.

Emmons, R. A. (1999). *The psychology of ultimate concerns.* New York: Guilford Press.

Erikson, E. (1982). *The lifecycle completed.* New York: Norton.

Fleck, J. R., Ballard, S. N., & Reilly, J. W. (1975). The development of religious maturity: A three stage model. *Journal of Psychology and Theology, 3,* 156–163.

Fowler, J. W. (1981). *Stages of faith: The psychology of human development and the quest for meaning.* New York: Harper Collins.

Galupo, M. P., Cartwright, K. B., & Savage, L. S. (in preparation). *Cross-social category friendships as a context for postformal cognitive development.*

Gavin, J. L., Galupo, M. P., & Cartwright, K. B. (in preparation). *The role of postformal cognitive development in death acceptance.*

Hofstadter, D. R. (1979). *Godel, Escher, and Bach: An eternal golden braid.* New York: Basic Books.

Hugo, V. (1938). *Les miserables* (Lascelles Wraxall, Trans.). New York: Heritage Press.

Inhelder, B., & Piaget,J. (1958). *The growth of logical thinking from childhood to adolescence.* New York: Basic Books.

Johnson, L. (1991). Bridging paradigms: The role of a change agent in an international technical transfer project. In J. Sinnott & J. Cavanaugh (Eds.), *Bridging paradigms: Positive development in adulthood and cognitive aging* (pp. 59–72). New York: Praeger.

Johnson, L. (1994). Nonformal adult learning in international development projects. In J. D. Sinnott (Ed.), *Interdisciplinary handbook of adult lifespan learning* (pp. 203–217). Westport, CT: Greenwood Press.

Jung, C. (1931/1971). The stages of life. In J. Campbell (Ed.), *The portable Jung.* New York: Viking.

Jung, C. G. (1943). *On the psychology of the unconscious.* In H. Read, M. Fordham, & G. Adler (Eds.), *Jung, collected works, Volume 7.* Princeton, N.J.: Princeton University Press.

Jung, C. G. (1964). *Man and his symbols.* New York: Laurel.

Kegan, R. (1982). *The evolving self.* Cambridge, MA: Harvard University Press.

Koplowitz, H. (1984). A projection beyond Piaget's formal operations stage: A general systems stage and a unitary stage. In M. Commons, F. Richards, & C. Armon (Eds.), *Beyond formal operations* (pp. 272–296). New York: Praeger.

Kramer, D. A. (2002). A psychological analysis of faith, hope and despair in suicide. *Journal of Adult Development, 9,* 117–126.

Kramer, D. A., & Bacelar, W. T. (1994). The educated adult in today's world: Wisdom and the mature learner. In J. D. Sinnott (Ed.), *Interdisciplinary handbook of adult lifespan learning* (pp.31–50). Westport, CT: Greenwood.

Labouvie-Vief, G., DeVoe, M., & Bulka, D. (1989). Speaking about feelings: Conceptions of emotion across the lifespan. *Psychology and Aging, 3,* 425–437.

Labouvie-Vief, G., & Hakim-Larson,J. (1989). Developmental shifts in adult thought. In S. Hunter & S. Sundel (Eds.).*Midlife myths.* Newbury Park, CA: Sage.

Lee, D. (1991). Relativistic operations: A framework for conceptualizing teachers' everyday problem solving. In J. Sinnott & J. Cavanaugh (Eds.), *Bridging paradigms: Positive development in adulthood and cognitive aging* (pp. 59–72). New York: Praeger.

Lee, D. M. (1994).Models of collaboration and adult reasoning. In J. D. Sinnott (Ed.), *Interdisciplinary handbook of adult lifespan learning* (pp.51–60). Westport, CT: Greenwood.

L'Engle, M. (1974). *A wind in the door.* New York: Dell.

Marks, S. (1986). *Three corners: Exploring marriage and the self.* Lexington, MA: D.C. Heath.

Meacham, J. A., & Boyd, C. (1994). Expanding the circle of caring: From local to global. In J. D. Sinnott (Ed.), *Interdisciplinary handbook of adult lifespan learning* (pp. 61–73). Westport, CT: Greenwood.

Mezirow, J., & Associates (2000). *Learning as transformation.* San Francisco: Jossey-Bass.

Pearce, J. (1973). *The crack in the cosmic egg.* New York: Pocket Books.

Perry, W. G. (1975). *Forms of ethical and intellectual development in the college years.* New York: Holt, Rinehart & Winston.

Pruitt, D., & Rubin, J. (1986). *Social conflict.* New York: Random House.

Rogers, D. R. B. (1989). *The effect of dyad interaction and marital adjustment on cognitive performance in everyday logical problem solving.* Unpublished doctoral dissertation, Utah State University, Logan, UT.

Rogers, D. R., Sinnott, J. D., & van Dusen, L. (1991). *Marital adjustment and social cognitive performance in everyday logical problem solving.* Paper presented at Sixth Adult Development Conference, Boston.

Satir, V. (Ed.) (1967). *Conjoint family therapy.* Palo Alto, CA: Science and Behavior Books.

Scarf, M. (1995). *Intimate worlds: Life inside the family.* New York: Random House.

Sillars, A. (1986). *Manual for coding interpersonal conflict.* Unpublished manuscript, University of Montana, Department of Interpersonal Communications.

Sinnott, J. D. (1977). Sex-role inconstancy, biology, and successful aging: A dialectical model. *Gerontologist, 17,* 459–463.

Sinnott, J. D. (1981). The theory of relativity: A metatheory for development? *Human Development, 24,* 293–311.

Sinnott, J. D. (1982). Correlates of sex roles in older adults. *Journal of Gerontology, 37,* 587–594.

Sinnott, J. D. (1984a). Older men, older women: Are their perceived sex roles similar? *Sex Roles, 10,* 847–856.

Sinnott, J. D. (1984b). Postformal reasoning: The relativistic stage. In M. Commons, F. Richards, & C. Armon (Eds.), *Beyond formal operations* (pp. 298–325). New York: Praeger.

Sinnott, J. D. (1986). *Sex roles and aging: Theory and research from a systems perspective.* New York: S. Karger.

Sinnott, J. D. (1987). Sex roles in adulthood and old age. In D. B. Carter (Ed.), *Current conceptions of sex roles and sex typing* (pp. 155–180). New York: Praeger.

Sinnott, J. D. (1989a). General systems theory. In L. Poon, D. Rubin, & B. Wilson (Eds.), *Everyday cognition in adulthood and old age* (pp.59–70). New Rochelle, NY: Cambridge University Press.

Sinnott, J. D. (1989b). Lifespan relativistic postformal thought. In M. Commons, J. Sinnott, F. Richards, & C. Armon (Eds.), *Beyond formal operations I* (pp. 239–278). New York: Praeger.

Sinnott, J. D. (1990). *Yes, it's worth the trouble! Unique contributions from everyday cognition studies.* Paper presented at the Twelfth West Virginia University Conference on Lifespan Developmental Psychology: Mechanisms of Everyday Cognition, Morgantown, WV.

Sinnott, J. D. (1991a). Limits to problem solving: Emotion, intention, goal clarity, health, and other factors in Postformal thought. In J. D. Sinnott & J. Cavanaugh (Eds.), *Bridging paradigms: Positive development in adulthood and cognitive aging.* New York: Praeger.

Sinnott, J. D. (1991b). What do we do to help John? A case study of everyday problem solving in a family making decisions about an acutely psychotic member. In J D. Sinnott & J. Cavanaugh (Eds.), *Bridging paradigms: Positive development in adulthood and cognitive aging* (pp. 203–220). New York: Praeger.

Sinnott, J. D. (1993a). Teaching in a chaotic new physics world: Teaching as a dialogue with reality. In P. Kahaney, J. Janangelo, & L. Perry (Eds.), *Theoretical and critical perspectives on teacher change* (pp.91–108). Norwood, NJ: Ablex.

Sinnott, J. D. (1993b). Sex roles. In V. S. Ramachandran (Ed.), *Encyclopedia of human behavior, Vol. 4* (pp. 151–158). New York: Academic.

Sinnott, J. D. (1993c). Use of complex thought and resolving intragroup conflicts: A means to conscious adult development in the workplace. In J. Demick & P. M. Miller (Eds.), *Development in the workplace* (pp. 155–175). Hillsdale, NJ: Erlbaum.

Sinnott, J. D. (1994a). Development and yearning: Cognitive aspects of spiritual development. *Journal of Adult Development, 1,* 91–99.

Sinnott, J. D. (1994b). *Interdisciplinary handbook of adult life span learning.* Westport, CT: Greenwood.

Sinnott, J. D. (1996). The development of complex reasoning: Postformal thought. In F. Blanchard-Fields & T. Hess (Eds.), *Perspectives on cognitive change in adulthood and aging.* New York: McGraw-Hill.

Sinnott, J. D. (1997). Brief report: Complex postformal thought in skilled research administrators. *Journal of Adult Development, 4*(1), 45–53.

Sinnott, J. D. (1998a). Creativity and postformal thought. In C. Adams-Price (Ed.), *Creativity and aging: Theoretical and empirical approaches.* New York: Springer.

Sinnott, J. D. (1998b). The development of logic in adulthood: Postformal Thought and its applications. In J. Demick (Ed.), *Plenum series on adult development.* New York: Plenum.

Sinnott, J. D. (2000). Cognitive aspects of unitative states: Spiritual self-realization, intimacy, and knowing the unknowable. In M. E. Miller & A. N. West (Eds.), *Spirituality, ethics, and relationship in adulthood: Clinical and theoretical explorations* (pp.177–198). Madison, CT: Psychosocial Press.

Sinnott, J. D. (Special issues editor) (3 Issues: 2001, 2002a, 2002b). Special issues: Spirituality and adult development. *Journal of Adult Development, 8*(4), *9*(1, 2).

Sinnott, J. D. (2002c). Postformal Thought and adult development: Living in balance. In J. Demick & C. Andreoletti (Eds.), *Adult development* (pp. 221–238). New York: Plenum.

Sinnott, J. D. (2003a). *Spirituality, development and healing: Lessons from several cultures.* Paper presented at Loyola College Midwinter Conference on Religion and Spirituality, Columbia, MD.

Sinnott, J. D. (2003b). Teaching as nourishment for complex thought. In N. L. Diekelmann (Ed.), *Teaching the practitioners of care: New pedagogies for the health professions* (pp. 232–271). Interpretive studies in healthcare and the human services Series. Madison, WI: University of Wisconsin Press.

Sinnott, J. D. (2004a, March). *Feeling connected, spirituality, and adult development: A new theory of their interrelationships.* Invited paper presented at the Annual Conference on Research and Spirituality, Loyola College, Columbia, MD.

Sinnott, J. D. (2004b). *Learning as a humanistic dialogue with reality. New theories that help us teach the whole person: Context of learning and complex thought: Implications for modern life.* Invited monograph, University of Stockholm, Sweden.

Sinnott, J. D. (2004c). *Learning as a humanistic dialogue with reality; New theories that help us teach the whole person: Complex Postformal Thought and its relation to adult learning, life span development, and the new sciences.* Invited monograph, University of Stockholm, Sweden.

Sinnott, J. D. (2005). The dance of the transforming self: Both feelings of connection and complex thought are needed for learning. In M. A. Wolf (Ed.), *Adulthood: New terrain* (pp.27–37). San Francisco, CA: Jossey-Bass.

Sinnott, J. D. (2006, under review a). Coherent themes: Individuals' relationships with God, their early childhood experiences, their bonds with significant others, and their relational delusions during psychotic episodes all have similar holistic, existential and relational themes. *Journal of Adult Development.*

Sinnott, J. D. (2006b). Spirituality as "feeling connected with the transcendent": Outline of a transpersonal psychology of adult development of self. *Religion, Spirituality, and the Scientific Study of Religion 16,* 287–308.

Sinnott, J. D., & Berlanstein, D. (2006). The importance of feeling whole: Learning to "feel connected," community, and adult development. In C. H.Hoare (Ed.), *Oxford handbook of adult development and learning* (pp. 381–406). New York: Oxford University Press.

Sinnott, J. D., Block, M., Grambs, J., Gaddy, C., & Davidson, J. (1980). *Sex roles in mature adults: Antecedents and correlates.* College Park, MD: Center on Aging, University of Maryland.

Sinnott, J. D., & Cavanaugh, J. (Eds.) (1991). *Bridging paradigms: Positive development in adulthood and cognitive aging.* New York: Praeger.

Sinnott, J. D., & Johnson, L. (1996). *Reinventing the university: A radical proposal for a problem focused university.* Norwood, NJ: Ablex.

Sinnott, J. D., & Shifren, K. (2002). Gender and aging: Transforming and transcending gender roles. In J. Birren & K. W. Schaie (Eds.), *Handbook of the psychology of aging* (5th ed., pp. 454–476). San Diego, CA: Academic Press.

Smith, H. (1991). *The world's religions*. San Francisco: Harper.

Spanier, G.B. (1976). Measuring dyadic adjustment: New scale for assessing the quality of marriage and similar dyads. *Journal of Marriage and the Family, 38,* 15–28.

Sternberg, R. J. (1986). A triangular theory of love. *Psychological Review, 93,* 119–135.

Sternberg, R. J., & Berg, C. A. (1992). *Intellectual development*. New York: Cambridge University Press.

Tart, C. (1983). *States of consciousness*. El Cerrito, CA: Psychological Processes.

Underhill, E. (1961). *Mysticism*. New York: Dutton.

Welwood, J. (1996). *Love and awakening*. New York: Harper Collins.

Wilber, K. (1995). *Sex, ecology, spirituality: The spirit of evolution*. Boston: Shambala.

Windle, M., & Sinnott, J. D. (1985). A psychometric study of the Bem Sex Role Inventory with an older adult sample. *Journal of Gerontology, 40,* 336–343.

Wink, P., & Dillon, M. (2002). Spiritual development across the adult life span: Findings from a longitudinal study. *Journal of Adult Development, 9,* 79–94.

Wolf, F. A. (1981). *Taking the quantum leap*. New York: Harper and Row.

Yan, B. (1995). *Nonabsolute/relativistic thinking (N/R): A possible unifying communality underlying models of Postformal reasoning*. Unpublished doctoral dissertation, University of British Columbia, Vancouver.

Yan, B., & Arlin, P. K. (1995). Nonabsolute/relativistic thinking: A common factor unifying models of Postformal reasoning? *Journal of Adult Development, 2,* 223–240.

Part II

Research Methods in Adult Development

Chapter 5

Analyzing Change in Adulthood with Multilevel Growth Models

Selected Measurement, Design, and Analysis Issues

Janet K. Holt

Current perspectives acknowledge that adult development is a lifelong process. Life-span development involves both gains and losses in skills and abilities. Life-span development is multidimensional, multidirectional, and multicausal, and is embedded in historical, cultural, and social contexts. As such, the study of developmental processes across the life span involves multidisciplinary approaches. Knowledge of these characteristics is, therefore, critical for informing the selection of methodology to study development processes in adulthood. The life-span perspective implies that developmental studies measuring change over time are preferred to non-developmental studies because the former are better able to uncover patterns of change (i.e., growth or decline) over time. The characteristics of life-span processes also imply that the methodology used to assess developmental changes should facilitate the modeling of a complex system of development. Methodology should be sensitive to maturational patterns, the effects of life events, and allow for the incorporation of an array of contextual variables to best describe the rich influences of historical, cultural, and social contexts on individuals.

Developmental Research Designs

Various methods have been employed for developmental studies such as cross-sectional studies in which different age groups are compared at a particular point in time. For instance, a research study might be conducted to survey individuals of different ages about their liberal-conservative attitudes and thereby determine how different aged individuals align on a liberal-conservative scale. Such a design can be useful for obtaining a snapshot of age-related views in regards to a specific issue. However, only weak inferences regarding developmental trends can be made from cross-sectional studies because of the confounding of age, cohort (i.e., birth year), and time of measurement effects. In this example, an investigator cannot infer if a person's liberal-conservative views are likely to change over time due to age-related trends or if any age-related differences in attitudes of liberal-conservative views are due to the normative views of the generation of individuals living in that time period.

An alternate developmental research design is the time-lag design, in which different groups of same-aged individuals are compared at different time periods. For instance, a comparison of literacy rates of 25 year olds from the National Adult Literacy Study of 1992 (U.S. Department of Education, 1993) and the National Assessment of Adult Literacy of 2003 (U.S. Department of Education, 2005) is a time-lag design. Same aged individuals could be compared 11 years apart to determine if literacy rates have changed over the decade. Although age is held constant in this design, cohort and time of measurement vary. This design is useful for showing trends that have changed across different time periods, although it is still difficult to discern if any observed changes are due to birth cohort (e.g., the normative literacy rates of a particular generation of individuals) or if the changes are due to the time of data collection (e.g., particular emphases on literacy in 1992 and 2003). Moreover, this design does not allow the investigator to determine any age-related changes that might occur.

A preferred design for showing age-related changes is the longitudinal design in which data are collected on the same individuals over different time points. In this case, time of measurement is set at fixed time points and the cohort is held constant, but age varies. An example would be the study of career aspirations of individuals from the 1988–2000 National Educational Longitudinal Study (NELS, p. 88) across the 12 years of the survey. Individuals who were in eighth grade in 1988 would have typically been eight years out of high school in 2000. A difficulty with this design is that it does not allow the investigator to make inferences to other cohorts (e.g., would individuals' career aspirations have the same pattern if the study began in 1970, or in 2000?) or other times of measurement (e.g., would individuals' career aspirations have been different if the sample was selected in 2008?). Two other pragmatic concerns with the longitudinal design are the investiture of both time and money to conduct a study over a lengthy time period, as well as problems with attrition of participants in long-term studies of the same individuals. Difficulties tracking individuals over time as well as maintaining participants' long-term interest in the study often results in increased attrition as the study progresses. Large-scale longitudinal surveys often employ sophisticated techniques for freshening the sample with like individuals to compensate for attrition, although this is less common in small-scale studies conducted by individual researchers. Although imperfect, the longitudinal design is a solid design for inferring change over time as long as the results are not generalized beyond the cohort and times of measurement studied.

There are also designs that can control for the confounding of age, time of measurement, and cohort in longitudinal studies. An example is the cohort-sequential design (Schaie, 1965, 1986). Using this method, the period of study can be accelerated by using more than a single cohort of individuals. For example, a study of middle-aged individuals from 40 to 50 years old could be conducted on two cohorts, one at age 40, at the onset of the study, and another at age 44, at the onset of the study. If measurements on each cohort are made yearly for six years, data collection would be accelerated from 10 years to six years. A comparison of the overlapping growth trajectories between the two cohorts during the period from 44 to 46 years of age will determine if there is a possible cohort effect. A cohort effect should be suspected if the growth trajectories are different between the two groups in these overlapping years, although, the period effect could not be ruled out as a possible explanation for any differences between the two groups. In contrast, if the trajectories are the same in the overlapping years between the two cohorts, this would be a strong indication that there was no cohort effect. Other modifications of this design can be made to further untangle age and time of measurement effects (Singer & Willett, 1996).

Measurement of Outcomes for Growth Modeling

Reliability and validity, the cornerstones of sound measurement, are essential to assess in longitudinal studies to ensure that outcome measures are stable over time and are measuring the intended constructs. Standard methods, such as coefficient alpha or Kuder-Richardson 20 or 21, can be used to assess internal consistency reliability. Other means of assessing reliability that may be appropriate are alternate forms reliability—if more than one form was used for measurement—or inter-rater reliability if multiple raters were used (Allen & Yen, 1979; Nunnally, 1978).

However, the determination of temporal stability is particularly relevant to ensure that scores on the measures are stable over the time period under study. If the outcome measure has low temporal stability, then any change that occurs cannot be attributed to developmental change but only to changes in the measurement process. Because the goal of most developmental studies is to discern relatively stable trends that exist over time, this goal will be completely negated if the measurements are not stable over time due to measurement unreliability. Therefore, it is critical to assess temporal stability in developmental studies. Typically, this is done via test-retest reliability by measuring the outcome on the same group of individuals at two time points and correlating their scores. The time lag between the two measurement points should be long enough to ensure that respondents do not remember the items from the previous assessment and short enough to ensure that no significant learning has occurred. For more details on test-retest reliability the reader is referred to the Standards for Educational and Psychological Measurement (American Educational Research Association, 1999).

In addition to ensuring precision in measurement via measures of reliability, the validity of the scores indicates how well the measure is assessing the intended construct or content. Several forms of validity are well known: content validity to ensure the content coverage of the assessment is complete and aligns with educational objectives; criterion-related validity to determine a) that the measure has concurrent validity with other established measures, and b) predictive validity of hypothesized outcomes; and construct validity, to ensure that the measure is assessing the intended construct that is was designed to assess. For further information regarding any of these types of validity see the Educational and Psychological Standards (American Educational Research Association, 1999).

In longitudinal studies in which the outcome is assessed at various time points, another aspect of validity that is critical is whether the construct, as measured, remains constant over time. Variance in the construct can occur because of testing or instrumentation threats (Campbell & Stanley, 1963; Cook & Campbell, 1979), but can also occur when there are interactions of development with the assessment tool (Baltes, Reese, & Nesselroade, 1988; Hartmann, 2006). This specific form of measurement nonequivalence, developmental nonequivalence, can be problematic in long-term studies or in studies in which the outcome is undergoing rapid change, such as during critical transition periods. For example, if the number of visits to the doctor is used as a measure of health and this outcome is measured across several years, the reasons why individuals are going to the doctor may change during the course of the study. Perhaps younger individuals with good health insurance coverage visit the doctor for preventative medicine and minor procedures that are not related to critical health issues, while older individuals with more limited health insurance coverage visit the doctor only for critical medical health issues. In this case, the meaning of the number of visits to the doctor (as a proxy for health) changes across time and does not have measurement equivalence over time. As a result, a growth model of changes in health might not seem to be changing dramatically over time—as true changes in health would indicate. In this case, the meaning of the measuring instrument changes from behavior related to preventative and/or minor health issues to behavior related to major health issues. Measurement invariance is often assessed with multiple-groups confirmatory factor analysis (CFA) to determine if the relationship of the construct to its indicator variables remains constant across time.

Measurement concerns in longitudinal studies involve several factors including careful consideration of reliability, particularly temporal stability, and validity, especially measurement equivalence over time. Thus, the data analysis methods discussed in this chapter assume that the outcomes being assessed have solid evidence of validity and reliability in ways that ensure that outcomes are precise, stable, and meaningful over time.

Comparison of Analytic Methods for Modeling Change

Repeated measures analysis has been the traditional approach to analyzing data collected over time. However, both univariate and multivariate repeated measures are best suited for analyzing data from experimental designs in which time points are equally spaced, the data collection schedule is time structured (i.e., the same for every individual) and balanced (i.e., the same number of time points are collected for every individual). Yet, in non-experimental situations, this is rarely the case. Additionally, traditional repeated measures analyses assume that all individuals have a common trend line and do not account for situations in which individuals have randomly varying trend lines. Moreover, by default, these traditional longitudinal analyses discard participants without complete data for all time points using listwise deletion. This often results in a much-reduced data set that does not accurately represent the originally sampled population. In traditional univariate or multivariate repeated measures analyses, it is assumed that any missing data are missing completely at random (MCAR; Little & Rubin, 1987, 1989). This assumption is fairly restrictive because the value on the missing variable, if it were observed, is assumed to be missing completely at random and to be independent of all other variables in the analysis. However, the attrition of participants in longitudinal studies could, perhaps, be related to variables under study and we cannot typically assume that the values on missing variables are MCAR. It is clear that repeated measures would not be adequate in the vast majority of longitudinal studies that are non-experimental in nature and are occurring in the context of adulthood in which the complexity of family, work, and social activities influence the data collection schedule.

In contrast, in multilevel modeling, the data are a series of observations nested within the individual. Therefore, the structure of the data can be person-specific and much more flexible. This approach allows for data that are collected at unequally-spaced waves of data collection that have varying schedules and numbers of observations across different individuals. In multilevel modeling, data at level 1 are assumed to be missing at random (MAR; Little & Rubin, 1987, 1989), a less restrictive assumption than MCAR. Data that are MAR are assumed to be unrelated to the value on the missing variable, similarly to MCAR, however, under MAR the missing value may be related to other variables in the analysis. This is a much more tenable assumption when there is attrition in panel data in which the missingness may be related to other known variables. As long as those variables are measured and included in the analysis, then we can assume that the data meet the MAR assumption.

Estimating person-specific growth trajectories is another advantage of multilevel growth modeling because the variability among the trajectories of different individuals can be estimated and modeled with person- or organization-level covariates. This reconceptualization of repeated measures analyses to multilevel growth modeling (MLGM) results in a flexible modeling approach that more aptly captures individual differences and the inherent complexity in developmental change.

Modeling Individual Differences in Growth Trajectories

In 1979, Baltes and Nesselroade put forth several tenets of sound longitudinal design for developmental research. Hoeksma and Koomen (1992) later demonstrated how multi-level modeling can be used to meet all of these tenets of longitudinal research. The key feature of multilevel growth modeling that is a strength for developmental research is the ability to model intra-individual change while concomitantly modeling inter-individual growth patterns. Intra-individual change, or an individual's variation around his/ her trend line, is captured in the level-1 equation of multilevel growth models and the inter-individual differences in growth patterns are encapsulated in the level-2 equations of individual differences. In other words, in MLGM one does not need to assume that the normative growth pattern holds for all individuals. As noted by Mroczek and Spiro (2003), the notion that individuals vary in their developmental pathways is a basic tenet of life-span developmental theory. Likewise, the models discussed in this chapter allow the estimation of random variability in growth parameters, as well as the possibility of modeling the variability in growth patterns with a set of relevant predictors. So, the match between MLGM and life-span development seems a natural one that allows researchers to model the complexity of growth and decline that occur with development and age and to explain this variability with covariates that capture history and age-graded effects, as well as interventions and natural interactions with the environment.

The analytic methods described in this chapter focus on recent advances in multi-level growth modeling (Raudenbush & Bryk, 2002; Singer & Willett, 2003), however, the development of these methods originate from Rogosa and Willett (Rogosa, 1988; Rogosa, Brandt, & Zimowski, 1982; Rogosa & Willett, 1985; Willett, 1988). These models of individual differences in growth trajectories are especially pertinent for longitudinal studies and can be used to: track developmental trends over time, take into account con-textual factors that situate the study, and, estimate the amount of individual variability in growth patterns. Multilevel growth modeling methods are part of a broader class of random coefficients models that includes latent growth curve modeling. Both methods can be used to model intra-individual and inter-individual variability in growth and the same growth parameters can be estimated from both types of models (see Holt, 2008, for a comparison of these methods). The focus of the remainder of the chapter is on selected multilevel growth modeling methods that are pertinent to adult development. Additionally, analytic methods that allow one to model varied patterns of change, such as linear, curvilinear, and discontinuous growth models, while still accounting for contextual factors and moderating effects, are introduced.

Linear and Quadratic Growth Models

In MLGM each individual's growth curve is estimated in a level-1 model and the differences among growth curves of different individuals are modeled at level 2. Because each individual has a separately estimated growth model, the number and spacing of observations can vary across individuals, however, one more wave of data is needed than the number of growth parameters to be estimated. Increasing the number of waves of data collection has many advantages in growth modeling. Foremost, having a sufficient number of waves of data allows the study of not only whether change occurred, but also the shape of the growth trajectory. Second, as illustrated by Willett, Singer, and Martin (1998), the precision of estimates of individual growth trajectories can be dramatically affected by adding more waves of data collection. In this section, linear and quadratic multilevel growth models are discussed, as well as variants of these models that are useful for modeling change in adult development.

Linear Growth Model

A typical linear growth model has two level-1 growth parameters, the intercept and linear slope (see Equation 1). The outcome, y, is measured for $i = 1, \ldots, n$ subjects

$$y_{ti} = \pi_{oi} + \pi_{li} \, (\text{time})_{ti} + e_{ti} \tag{1}$$

across $t = 1, \ldots, T$ time points or waves. The growth parameters, π_{oi} and π_{li}, represent the intercept and slope, respectively, for person i and e_{ti} is the within-person residual not accounted for by the specified growth parameters. The intercept is the outcome when time equals 0 and the slope is the linear rate of change in the outcome across the time period studied. The within-person residual is the deviation of the outcome at time t for person i from their predicted trajectory. This level-1 residual will be larger when there is less precision in estimating the individual's growth curve. Three waves of data are required to estimate a linear model in MLGM, however, as mentioned previously, additional waves will increase the precision of the estimated level-1 growth trajectories. Equation 1 closely resembles a linear regression equation regressing y on *time*, except that the subscript i indicates that the equation is person-specific; that is, a separate growth trajectory is estimated for each person. In level 2, a separate equation is constructed to model each level-1 growth parameter across the individuals (see Equation 2). Equations 1 and 2 combined represent the unconditional linear growth model with random slopes and intercepts. Both the

$$\begin{aligned} \pi_{0i} &= \beta_{00} + r_{0i} \\ \pi_{li} &= \beta_{10} + r_{li} \end{aligned} \tag{2}$$

individual's intercept and slope are estimated from a fixed effect, β, and a random component, r. The fixed effects in this level-2 model, β_{00} and β_{10}, represent the intercept and the average rate of change, respectively, estimated across all persons. Whereas, the random, effects, r_{0i} and r_{li}, represent the individual's deviation from the mean intercept and slope, respectively, and together comprise the level-2 residuals. Figure 5.1 illustrates the variability in linear growth trajectories with varied intercepts, π_{0i}, and linear slopes, π_{li}, for different individuals. This type of growth pattern would be captured with multilevel modeling but not by a traditional regression model because of the allowance for random variability of individual growth curves in MLGM.

Variances/Covariances of the Linear Model. The variance of the residuals from both the level-1 and level-2 growth models is also estimated with MLGM. The variance of the level-1 residuals, VAR $(e_{ti}) = \sigma^2$, indicates the amount of variability of the observations around the linear trend line, whereas at level 2 VAR$(r0i) = \tau_{00}$ is the variability in the intercept and VAR$(r_{li}) = \tau_{11}$ is the variability in the linear trend among individuals. The covariance term, τ_{01} or τ_{10}, describes the covariation between the intercept and the linear rate of growth across individuals. The variance/covariance matrix that contains these elements is designated T, in which the diagonal elements are the variances and the off diagonal elements are the covariance (see Equation 3).

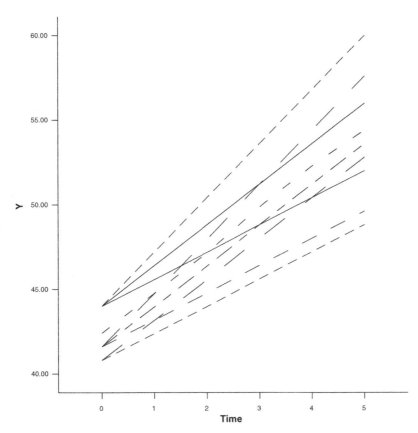

Figure 5.1 Random variation in linear growth.

$$T = \begin{bmatrix} \tau_{00} & \tau_{01} \\ \tau_{10} & \tau_{11} \end{bmatrix}$$

(3)

Covariates.   Covariates can be integrated into the model at levels 1 and/or 2 to account for some of the residual error variability. Predictors that are measured over time at the same intervals as the dependent measure can be incorporated into the level-1 model as *time-varying* covariates. These predictors are useful for accounting for some of the variability in the observations around the trend line, such as the covariate, a_{ti}, in Equation 4. In contrast, *time-invariant* covariates can be used at level two to account for variation in growth parameters across individuals. Time invariant covariates can be used to model variation in the intercept or in the linear rate of change or both. It is important to note that in MLGM the file containing the level-2 data must be complete and not include any missing data. For more information regarding the structure of the data files, see Holt (2008). In Equation 4, the time-invariant covariate, X_i, is accounting for variability in the intercept, π_{0i} and in the linear rate of change, π_{1i}. The level-2 coefficient, β_{11}, estimates the cross-level interaction between this covariate and the linear growth parameter, π_{1i}, at level 1. This would constitute a moderator effect in a 2-level growth model and, importantly for developmental research, this allows researchers to study effects that would explain the inter-individual variability in age-related trends.

$$Y_{ti} = \pi_{0i} + \pi_{1i}\,(time) + \pi_{2i}a_{ti} + e_{ti}$$
$$\pi_{0i} = \beta_{00} + \beta_{01}X_i + r_{0i}$$
$$\pi_{1i} = \beta_{10} + \beta_{11}X_i + r_{1i}$$
$$\pi_{2i} = \beta_{20} + \beta_{21}X_i + r_{2i}$$

$$(4)$$

Recentering Time.   In MLGM the variable indicating the passage of time (e.g., year, grade, age) is often recoded such that zero is a meaningful point of reference. Biesanz, Deeb-Sossa, Papakakis, Bollen, and Curran (2004) suggest that the coding of time in multi-level modeling should facilitate interpretability and should focus on the main period of interest in the study. For instance, in a study of early adult development in persons aged 21 to 29, age could be recentered such that at age 21 age is coded zero (i.e. $age_{ti} - 21$) or, likewise, age could be recoded such that age 29 is coded zero (i.e. $age_{ij} - 29$). In the former situation, the intercept in Equation 1, π_{0i}, would be interpreted as the outcome for person i at initial status, whereas in the latter situation it would be interpreted as the outcome for person i at final status. Because these intercepts become outcomes at level 2 and their variance is modeled with covariates, it is important to have an interpretable measurement point for the intercept that is of interest in the study. Other options for recentering time include the midpoint, in this example, age = 25, in order to interpret the intercept at the midpoint in the study.

Assumptions.   Assumptions are made regarding both the random components of the level one and level two models, as well as specification assumptions about the relationship of the variables to the random components. For a detailed explanation of assumptions, see Raudenbush and Bryk (2002, pp. 255–256). One important assumption is that both level one and level two residuals are assumed to be independently and normally distributed. Nonnormality introduced at level one must be taken into consideration, as it will bias the standard errors at both levels one and two. Examination of the residuals with normal probability plots is an accepted procedure for determining if this assumption is met. Separate normal probability plots need to be constructed for each level of residuals (e.g., e_{it}, r_{0i}, r_{1i}). A complication in this process is that the residual distributions will change across the different models in the model-building process. Hox (2002) recommends checking the residuals in the intercept only model to determine if data transformation or outlier deletion needs to occur before adding covariates. Holt and Collins (2001) discuss a method for detecting outliers in growth models by identifying unusually steep or flat growth trajectories.

Multilevel Mediational Models.   The classic mediational model advanced by Baron and Kenny (1986) can be applied to multilevel models as well; however, this model can take on various forms when extending to the multilevel framework. With a basic 2-level multilevel model, the mediational effects can operate within level 1 or across levels 1 and 2. The outcome that is affected by the mediator will always be at the lowest level and the mediation chain can proceed from a higher to a lower level but never the reverse (Krull & MacKinnon, 2001). Three types of mediational models can occur in a basic 2-level multilevel model (Krull & MacKinnon, 2001). The 1 – 1 – 1 mediation model operates entirely at level 1, which includes both the mediator and the variable of interest. An example is the effect of being a first born child on one's adult leadership ability if the effect of being a first born is mediated by parenting practices, all assessed at the individual level. In the 2 – 1 – 1 mediation model, the initial variable of interest is at level 2 and the mediator is at level 1. An example of this type of mediational model is the effect of childhood neighborhood poverty level on one's adult leadership ability, mediated through parenting practices. In this case, the initial variable, childhood neighborhood poverty level, is at level 2 and the mediator (i.e., parenting practices) and outcome are measured at level 1. Finally, in the third type of mediational model, 2 – 2 – 1, both the initial variable of interest and the mediator are assessed at level 2. For example, the effect of childhood neighborhood poverty level of on one's adult leadership ability, as mediated through citizenship participation (e.g., volunteering) fits this type of model because both citizenship participation and neighborhood poverty level are measured at level 2 (e.g., neighborhood) and the outcome is at the individual level. The difference in the coefficient for the initial variable between a model without the mediator and one with the mediator constitutes the mediated effect. The method for estimating the variance of the mediated effect as the product of random effects (Sobel, 1982) is extended to the multilevel context (Krull & MacKinnon, 1999; MacKinnon, Warsi, & Dwyer, 1995), such that a significance test of the mediated effect can be obtained. For further information on the mediation model in the multilevel context, see Krull and MacKinnon (1999, 2001) and MacKinnon, Lockwood, Hoffman, West, and Sheets (2002).

Application of Multilevel Linear Growth Modeling.   To illustrate MLGM in an adult development context, assume that a series of memory tasks were administered six times in adulthood approximately two years apart to a sample of 50 adults between the ages of 45 and 55. Therefore, the duration in months between observations was 10 years (120 months) with measurements approximately every 24 months. However, it is conceivable that not every individual was measured at exactly 24-month intervals due to work schedules, travel plans, illnesses and other reasons. Hence, the measurements were taken as close to 24-month intervals as possible and time of measurement was recorded. If we assume that the series of tasks can be compiled into a composite score with adequate reliability and validity for this sample, we might use the MLGM to study cognitive changes in memory in middle-aged individuals. In this case the outcome, Y_{ti} is the score on the composite memory measure and $time_{ti}$ is the recorded measurement point at time t for person i. If we center time at age 45, then the intercept, β_{00}, is the average memory at age 45 and β_{10} is the linear rate of change in memory from age 45 to 55. Additionally, τ_{00} is the inter-person variability in memory at age 45 and τ_{11} is the inter-person variability of the linear rate of change in memory between 45 and 55 years of age. If we take this analysis one step further, we can decide on variables that are important correlates of this variability and incorporate them into the multilevel growth model. For instance, overall health, activity level, and work status might be some of the variables that are important to incorporate into the model as time-varying covariates. These variables would then be added to the level-1 model (i.e., a_{ti}) and would account for the intra-individual variance in the scores, σ^2, or the deviations of the observations from the linear growth trajectory. Additionally, demographic attributes such as gender and race might be important time-invariant covariates to model differences in growth parameters. These variables can be incorporated into the level-2 model (e.g., X_j) to account for some of the inter-individual variance in memory at age 45 (i.e., at the centering point), τ_{00}, and in the linear slope, τ_{11}. Using MLGM allows for some flexibility in the data collection schedule and the resulting model would be a rich model of memory changes during middle adulthood that correlates changes in health, activity level and work status with memory and models how these relationships vary by gender or race.

Quadratic or Higher-Order Growth

Sometimes change is not expected to be a linear trend; it could be exponential, quadratic, or a higher-order polynomial. The linear trend may become flatter over time, indicating a deceleration of the linear growth rate; alternately, the linear trend may increase or become steeper over time, indicating an acceleration of the linear trend. Either of these situations can be modeled with a quadratic growth model. The quadratic component of a MLGM is fitted to the data simply by squaring the time variable and adding it to the level-1 model (see Equation 5). The coefficient for the squared term at level 1, π_{2i}, is the change in the linear growth rate with the passage of time. In other words, it indicates the amount of curvature in the growth trajectory. In a quadratic growth model, the linear growth rate changes over time and is not constant as in the linear growth model. Therefore, the meaning of the linear term, π_{1i}, is different from a strictly linear model because there is not simply one linear rate of growth; the linear rate of growth in a quadratic model indicates the linear rate of change *at the centering point*. This is equivalent to the slope of the line tangent to the growth curve or when time equals the centering point. Note that time and time squared are highly correlated in their original metric, however, if each score is recentered at the midpoint and then squared, the correlation between the two scores is much reduced from the uncentered pair. Hence, centering at the midpoint substantially reduces some of the collinearity between the two level-1 predictors. Because the level-1 model now includes three growth parameters, the minimum number of waves of data needed to estimate this model increases to four.

$$y_{ti} = \pi_{0i} + \pi_{1i}(time)_{ti} + \pi_{2i}(time)_{ti}^2 + e_{ti}$$
$$\pi_{0i} = \beta_{00} + r_{0i}$$
$$\pi_{1i} = \beta_{10} + r_{1i}$$
$$\pi_{2i} = \beta_{20} + r_{2i} \tag{5}$$

In equation 5, we can see that the linear and quadratic level-1 growth parameters, as well as the intercept, become outcomes at level two. The fixed effects, β_{00}, β_{10}, and β_{20}, in Equation 5 estimate the population growth parameters: the intercept at the centering point, linear slope at centering point, and quadratic slope across time, respectively, for all individuals. Additionally, the deviations of the individuals from the estimated population parameters are captured in the residuals, u_{0i}, u_{1i}, and u_{2i}. There are four combinations of direction of linear and quadratic growth parameters that can occur. A positive linear parameter and positive quadratic parameter indicate that there is growth at the centering point and that this growth accelerates over time (see Figure 5.2a).

If the linear trend is positive and the quadratic trend is negative, this indicates that there is growth at the centering point, but this growth decelerates over time (see Figure 5.2b). In contrast, if the linear trend is negative and the quadratic trend is positive, then linear change is declining at the centering point and this trend is decelerating over time (see Figure 5.2c). Whereas if the linear trend is negative and the quadratic trend is also negative, the linear change at the centering point is declining and there is an acceleration in this decline over time (see Figure 5.2d).

Figure 5.3 depicts the predicted individual growth trajectories with a quadratic trend similar to the pattern in Figure 5.2b (i.e., positive linear trend and negative quadratic trend). The growth pattern in Figure 5.3 indicates that there is variation among individuals in their predicted trajectories and it is this variation that is estimated in the quadratic MLGM and can be explained by incorporating covariates in the level-2 equation for π_{2i}.

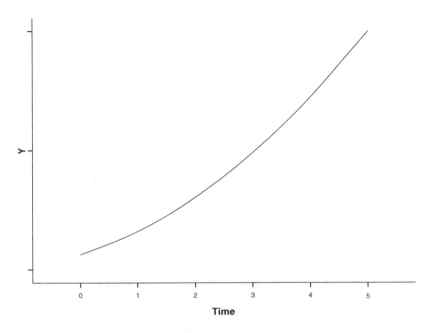

Figure 5.2a Linear and quadratic growth patterns. Positive linear and positive quadratic trend.

Variance/Covariances of the Quadratic Model.   The variance of the level-1 residuals, VAR (e_{ti}) = σ^2, still indicates the amount of variability of the observations around the trend line, although, in this model, the trend line is curvilinear. At level 2, VAR(r_{0i}) = τ_{00} is the variability in the intercept and VAR(r_{1i}) = τ_{11} is the variability in the linear trend, both at the centering point. An additional variance term is estimated, VAR(r_{2i}) = τ_{22}, which is

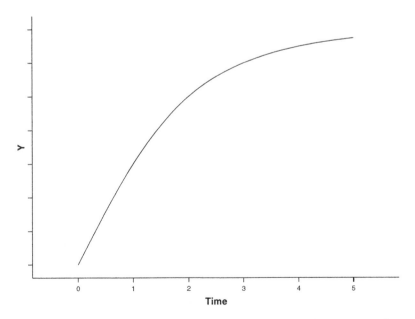

Figure 5.2b Linear and quadratic growth patterns. Positive linear and negative quadratic trend.

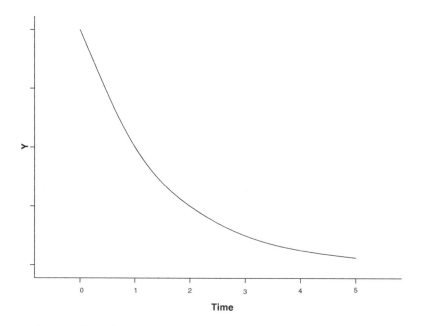

Figure 5.2c Linear and quadratic growth patterns. Negative linear and positive quadratic trend.

the variability in the quadratic curvature among individuals. The covariance term, τ_{01} or τ_{10}, describes the covariation between the intercept and the linear rate of growth, both at the centering point, across individuals. Two additional covariances are estimated in the quadratic model: τ_{02} or τ_{20}, which is the covariance of the intercept at the centering point and the quadratic curvature and τ_{12} or τ_{21}, which estimates the covariance between

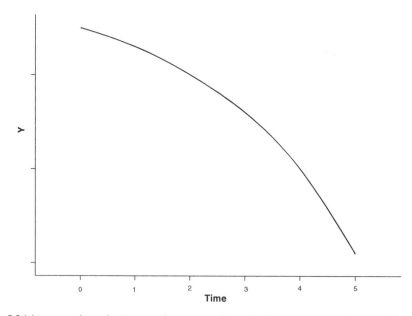

Figure 5.2d Linear and quadratic growth patterns. Negative linear and negative quadratic trend.

the linear slope at the centering point and the quadratic curvature. The variance/covariance matrix for the quadratic model with random slopes and intercepts is given in Equation 6.

$$T = \begin{bmatrix} \tau_{00} & \tau_{01} & \tau_{02} \\ \tau_{10} & \tau_{11} & \tau_{12} \\ \tau_{20} & \tau_{21} & \tau_{22} \end{bmatrix}$$ (6)

Covariates.   Predictors of change can be incorporated into the quadratic growth model similar to the linear model. Although, in the quadratic growth model there are two outcomes that directly measure change, the linear growth rate at the centering point, π_{1i}, and the deceleration or acceleration in growth over time, π_{2i}. Consequently, time-invariant covariates can be used to predict either or both of these outcomes. If the goal is to predict overall acceleration or deceleration across the study period, then the covariates can be entered into the level-2 model predicting π_{2i}. Or, if the goal of the study is to predict changes in all three level-1 growth parameters, π_{0i}, π_{1i}, and π_{2i}, the covariates can be added to all three of the level-2 equations.

Higher-Order Models.   In some cases we might expect two continuous phases of growth, depending on the outcome and the duration of study. For instance, this might involve an early acceleration in growth followed by a decline. With these types of growth patterns,

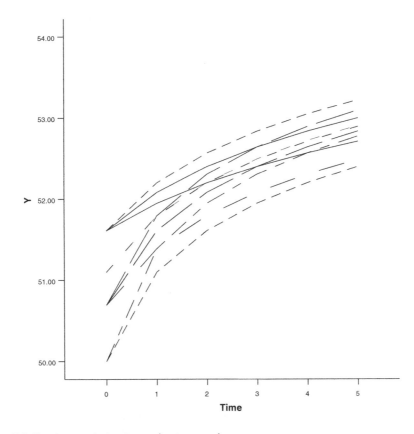

Figure 5.3 Random variation in quadratic growth.

the researcher can estimate any change in acceleration or deceleration that occurs when undergoing a transition from one phase to another by including a cubic term in the level-1 model. Other higher-order models can be constructed as well. As noted before, the number of waves needed for polynomial models is the number of parameters being estimated plus one; therefore, five waves are needed for the cubic model because four growth parameters are being estimated (i.e., intercept, linear term, quadratic term, and cubic term). Also note that only the highest-order polynomial in the model is interpreted across time (e.g., cubic term in cubic model) and the other terms are interpreted at the centering point (e.g., intercept, linear term, and quadratic term in cubic model).

Effect Sizes and Power in Multilevel Models.   Calculating power in multilevel designs is generally complex, especially when there are random slopes. If only the intercepts vary randomly, then the power of a treatment effect can be determined using Cohen's (1992) recommended power procedures and adjusting the sample size for the design effect (Hox, 2002). However, if random slopes are also modeled, then the *a priori* power calculations must take into account the variation across sites in the treatment effect and the intraclass correlation (Hox, 2002). General procedures for assessing power in a multilevel design are discussed by Hox and the specific case of power in the multi-site experimental design is discussed by Raudenbush and Liu (2000).

Raudenbush and Liu (2001) have simplified the power analysis procedure for assessing treatment effects in growth models by using an orthogonal polynomial model. If the goal is to assess differences in treatment effects in linear or quadratic growth parameters, then the standardized effect size on polynomial, p, is defined as:

$$\delta_p = \beta_p / \sqrt{\tau_{pp}} \tag{7}$$

(Raudenbush & Liu, 2001). If the difference of the linear trend across treatment groups is the desired effect, then β_{11} from Equation 4 and τ_{11} are substituted into Equation 7; however, if the effect of treatment on the quadratic polynomial is of interest, then β_{21} from a quadratic model with a treatment variable and τ_{22} is substituted. Power for this effect depends on the noncentrality parameter, $\lambda = n\delta^2\alpha_p/4$, where n is sample size and α_p is the person-specific reliability coefficient (Raudenbush & Liu, 2001). The reliability coefficient in turn depends on the study duration, the frequency of observations, and the within-person and between-person variance components. Raudenbush and Liu (2001) describe a simplified six-step process for determining power by estimating each of these components. Further, they supply SAS code for carrying out these power calculations in polynomial models.

Growth Modeling and Developmental Processes

Growth modeling particularly lends itself to the study of adult development because we can estimate an overall population trend of decline or growth in a relevant outcome, but perhaps more importantly, estimate the variability in the inter-individual growth patterns and model this variability in the growth parameters. Hence, we do not need to assume that everyone changes at the same rate or even in the same way. Also, the multilevel nature of the model allows the researcher to form rich contextual models that take into account a wide array of covariates that may be measured across time, at the individual level, or even at the neighborhood, school, or organizational level.

Imagine that the goal of a study is to model change in literacy as adults age. An appropriate growth model might be a quadratic model similar to Figure 5.2b that can account for deceleration in the growth rate as individuals age. Suppose individuals are sampled yearly between ages 40 and 60. If we choose age 50 as a centering point, then the intercept, π_{0i}, describes the literacy level for individual i at age 50 and the linear growth rate, π_{1i}, describes the individual's linear rate of growth in literacy at age 50. Moreover, π_{2i} describes the decline in literacy for individual i that occurs over the course of the study, from age 40 to 60. If we allow the coefficients to randomly vary at level 2 by incorporating error terms into the level-2 models, everyone does not need to have the same predicted literacy level at age 50, nor do they need to have similar predicted trajectories of decline.

If we expect there to be a rich array of contextual variables, such as family income level, employment status, number of books in the home, health status, and education level that might account for some of this variability in levels and trajectories of literacy, these can be taken into account. These contextual variables are examples of individual-level variables and can be added either as time-varying covariates in level 1, if they changed over time (e.g., health status, employment status), or as time-invariant covariates in level 2, if they remained fairly constant over the course of the study (e.g., family income level, number of books in the home, education level). By adding these contextual variables to the model, we can also determine if there is still significant decline and significant variance in growth parameters after taking these variables into account. If, after adding the contextual variables to the model, there is not significant variance in the growth parameters, then we can conclude that the contextual model is fairly complete in accounting for sources of variation in the decline of literacy with age.

Although I have captured some of the more common linear and quadratic models that are used in multilevel modeling, this is not an exhaustive account. The flexibility of multilevel growth modeling makes it feasible to adapt the model to the questions of the research study. For example, the structure of time and time-varying covariates do not need to be equivalent for every individual. As long as missing observations are MAR, different individuals could have had data collected at different times and unequal intervals of time between data collection points. Also, both the random and the structural component of the model can vary. For instance, not every study will have both time-varying and time-invariant covariates, or some models may have some fixed growth parameters that do not vary randomly from the prototypical growth curve. Further, the researcher can use the time-invariant covariates in one level-2 equation but not another if it makes theoretical sense to do so.

Another dimension in which the model can be expanded is by adding a third organizational level in which the effects of neighborhood, school, or organization variables on the growth parameters are investigated. If there are a large number of organizations sampled and the researchers posit that the unique effect of the organization was randomly distributed, then the organization can be used as a third level in the multilevel model. This would be possible if the sampling design was such that organizations were first randomly selected and then individuals within the organizations were randomly selected for the longitudinal study. Variables associated with characteristics of the organization can then be used as predictors at this level. For further discussion on this type of model see Raudenbush and Bryk (2002, pp. 237–245).

Applications of Growth Modeling to Adult Development

Intraindividual Change in Personality Traits.   In a study of intraindividual change in personality traits in men from the Normative Aging Study, Mroczek and Spiro (2003) illustrate an application of linear and quadratic growth modeling to adult development in a cohort sequential design. In a 12-year period, 1,663 men were measured up to five times on two personality characteristics: extraversion and neuroticism. The participants were categorized into three birth cohorts: those born between 1) 1897 and 1919, 2) 1920 and 1929, and 3) 1920 and 1945. Additionally, data on health status, memory complaints, and selected life events were used as predictors of growth and decline in extraversion and neuroticism.

Extraversion was best described by a linear model, although there was not a significant fixed effect for the linear trend, β_{10}; in other words, the overall change across time in extroversion was not significantly different from 0 (Mroczek & Spiro, 2003). However, there was significant random variation in the linear trend, τ_{11}, indicating that at least some of the individual linear growth trajectories, π_{1i}, were different from 0. Therefore, covariates were used to explain this variation in the growth trend. Most notably, the authors found that birth cohort, when entered as a level-2 predictor, X_i, accounted for significant variation in the level of extraversion at the centering point (age 63) and in the linear rate of extroversion across time. When plotting out the actual slopes for the three birth cohorts, extraversion increased over time for the first two cohorts and decreased over time for the older cohort. The authors were able to determine that the difference in trends was due—at least in part—to birth cohort because there were different trends for the different cohorts, even when studying the same age range. Therefore, they could be reasonably certain that birth cohort effects were not due to age differences. The middle cohort, for instance, had an upward trend in extraversion between ages 70 and 75, whereas the older cohort had a decline in extraversion in this same age range. Memory complaints explained some of the differences in extraversion at age 63, but none of the other predictors accounted for significant variance in the linear rates of growth.

Mroczek and Spiro (2003) found a different pattern in the growth trajectory of neuroticism over time—both the linear and the quadratic fixed effects, β_{10} and β_{20}, respectively, were significantly different from 0. The overall trajectory line was a declining trend that decelerated over time (see Figure 5.2c). Additionally, the random effects for the intercept and linear slope at age 63 were significant, but there was not significant variability in the deceleration parameter. This indicates that there is random variation in the individual levels of neuroticism at age 63, π_{0i}, and in the instantaneous linear slope at age 63, π_{1i}, but the quadratic trend, π_{2i}, is fairly consistent across individuals. Birth cohort was added as a level-2 predictor, X_i of the level of neuroticism at age 63, the linear rate of decline of neuroticism at age 63, and the deceleration of the decline across the years. The coefficients for X_i: β_{01}, β_{11}, and β_{21}, test the interaction or the moderating effect of birth cohort on the growth trajectory of neuroticism. Birth cohort was not related to the deceleration of the decline across the years but was related to level and linear slope of neuroticism at age 63. Specifically, the younger cohort experienced a lower level and steeper decline in neuroticism at age 63 than the older cohort. Personality variables entered at level-2 also proved to be important predictors of the decline in neuroticism among men. Memory complaints were associated with a higher level of neuroticism, whereas death of a spouse and marriage/remarriage were associated with a steeper decline. Death of a spouse was also associated with a higher level of neuroticism at age 63, however. Via growth modeling methods, the authors were able to test for inter-individual differences in the growth and decline of personality development as predicted by life-span developmental theory and demonstrate the correlation of these growth patterns with cohort effects, as well as life events.

Genetic and Environmental Influences on Cognitive Functioning.   In a study of the relationship of declining cognitive functioning with aging and the genetic and environmental influences of this decline, Reynolds, Finkel, McArdle, Gatz, Berg, and Pedersen (2005) used latent growth curve modeling (LGM; McArdle & Nesselroade, 2003). Growth trajectories of four measures of cognitive functioning: a) crystallized, b) fluid, c) memory, and d) perceptual speed abilities, were constructed for 798 nondemented twins at least 50 years of age to determine a) the amount of variance in growth attributable to genetic or environmental factors and b) whether different factors were related to level of cognitive functioning as opposed to rate of change in cognitive performance. They fitted a quadratic growth model centered at age 65 in order for the intercept and linear growth to be at an interpretable time point, as they defined old age as those 65 and older. By accounting for whether the twins were reared apart or together and whether they were monozygotic or dizygotic twins, they were able to apply biometrical analyses to determine heritability coefficients and the relative importance of genetic versus environmental influences on the three growth parameters, β_{00}, β_{10}, and β_{20}, the level of cognitive functioning at age 65, the linear slope in cognitive functioning at age 65, and the curvature in the trend from age 50 to 80, respectively. They found that the hertitabilities were strongest for level of cognitive functioning at age 65 and were weakest for the linear slope of cognitive functioning at age 65. They concluded that environmental variances increase steadily after age 65 and that the forces responsible for cognitive change are more environmental in nature than are the forces that are responsible for changes in the level of cognitive functioning. They also determined that non-shared environmental influences became more important after age 65 (Reynolds et al.).

Changes in Inter-Individual Variability in Cognitive Performance with Age.   Latent growth modeling was also used in a study that investigated age-related changes in cognitive performance in a) episodic recall, b) semantic knowledge, c) semantic fluency, and d) visuospatial ability in adults aged 35–80 years (de Frias, Lövdén, Lindenberger, & Nilsson, 2007). A cohort-sequential design was used in which cohorts were formed with groups that spanned five years in age. Participants' performance was assessed over a 10-year period with three waves of observations. The investigators fitted a curvilinear growth model with an intercept and slope factor and centered at the first time point or initial status for each age cohort. They used a technique in LGM, latent basis modeling, that allows the shape of the curve to be estimated rather than pre-specified. (For further explanation of latent basis modeling, see Holt, 2008.) By investigating the within-cohort variances in the intercept and slope, as well as the between-cohort variances and covariances, the authors were able to explain the magnitude and structure of change in cognitive performance across cohorts. Key findings from this study were the following: Correlations among measures of cognitive performance increased with age but not before old age (over 65 years). Also, inter-individual variability of the slope could only be detected in old age. The authors claim that the results support the dedifferentiation hypothesis, i.e., development of intellectual abilities in old age is increasingly controlled by a collection of sources because different cognitive abilities appeared to function as a system in old age but not before (de Frias et al. et al., 2007).

In all of these research examples, the investigators were able to make relatively strong conclusions regarding age-related trends because of a) the design of the study (i.e., two studies used cohort sequential designs) and b) the growth modeling method that took into account both variation around the growth trajectories and variation among individuals in the growth trajectories. These types of analyses would not have been possible with traditional repeated measures methods—it is only with random coefficient methods that the variability among individuals in the growth patterns are estimated and modeled.

Modeling Growth Across Adult Transitions

Developmental milestones serve as somewhat arbitrary markers on development. In infancy, this might include transition from crawling to walking, or the acquisition of language in toddlerhood. Attaining puberty is considered a developmental milestone in early adolescence. Developmental milestones in adult life tend to have a social component, such as entry into the workplace, marriage, or retirement. Many milestones tend to occur at similar times and therefore, the effect they have on the growth trajectory can be expected to occur at the same time for all individuals. Adults are, however, less likely to achieve developmental milestones or to make critical life transitions at the same age. Adults' transitions often depend upon their family, work, military, educational, and other personal life experiences. For instance, getting married or divorced, changing jobs or work status, experiencing the onset of a major illness, or transitioning from military to civilian life are transitions that occur at different ages for different adults. These transitions often produce a cascade of events that compound their impact the person's physical and emotional well being. For instance, developing a serious illness may cause the adult worker to lose her job, and consequently, her health insurance. So, the effects of the illness might have dramatic effects not only on physical, but psychological—and economic—well being. These two characteristics of adult transitions (e.g., different persons experience the same transition at different ages, and the compounding nature of the transition's impact) have important implications for choosing an appropriate statistical model. The model must be flexible enough to allow for variability in the timing of the transition across persons and must be able to detect changes that might occur abruptly and dramatically. The linear and quadratic growth models allow for random variation among growth trajectories of different persons. However, this type of model will not aptly capture abrupt change that might result when an individual experiences a critical life transition. Multiphase models that specifically model multiple distinct phases can capture this type of change.

Multiphase Models

In applications in which all individuals are expected to cross a transition at a particular time or when a specific time period is of interest, a piecewise linear model can be used. Here, the ages or times associated with each phase are identified and coded to depict the expected linear growth rate in each phase (Finkel, Reynolds, McArdle, Gatz, & Pedersen, 2003; Holt, 2008; Raudenbush & Bryk, 2002). To adequately model this type of transition, the variable that encodes the transition is incorporated into a random coefficients model, such as a MLGM.

Piecewise Linear Growth.   When developmental transitions occur at common points in time, the piecewise model can be used to effectively model this change. Figure 5.4a illustrates the type of change that can be captured by a piecewise linear growth model. As illustrated, the phase change occurs at the same time for all individuals in which the rate of decline increases after time = 2. Variations of this model include a two-rate model,

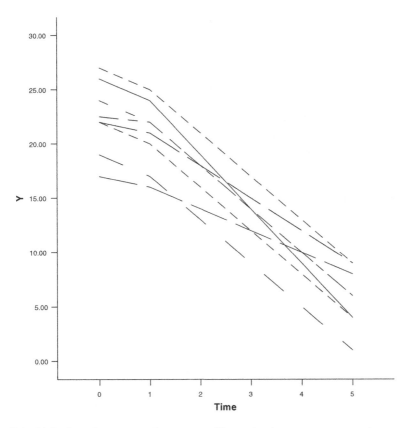

Figure 5.4a Multiphase linear growth patterns. Change in slope at a common time.

an increment/decrement model, and alternate models for discontinuities in growth rates (Raudenbush & Bryk, 2002, pp. 178–179; Singer & Willett, 2003, pp. 207–208). The essence of this growth model is to estimate linear growth for each distinct phase with a separate parameter in the level-1 model. However, this is restricted to the case in which all persons are expected to shift phases (transitions) simultaneously in order for the time frame for each phase to be specified in the model.

The piecewise linear model was used by Bartholow, Sher, and Krull (2003) in a study of heavy drinking during emerging adulthood (approximately ages 18 to 25) and early adulthood (young adulthood later than 25 years old). Heavy drinking was expected to dramatically change after the college years; specifically, the authors predicted that the linear rate of change in heavy drinking would decrease after the college years. Consequently, the transition point in this study was identified for all individuals as four years after high school. Two separate linear rates of growth were estimated by applying a piecewise linear model in which the first parameter modeled the rate of linear change of heavy drinking in emerging adulthood (i.e., the college years) and the second phase modeled the rate of linear change in this outcome in young adulthood (i.e., post-college to eight years after college). The authors denoted this as the continuous model. They also tested a discontinuous model in which a third parameter was added to the level-1 model to estimate the change in the level of the heavy drinking (i.e., change in elevation) that would occur with an abrupt shift in environment when transitioning from the college years to the post-college years (i.e., year 4 to year 7). The continuous model showed an increase in heavy drinking during the college years followed by a decline in the post-college years. Further, the level of heavy drinking in year one and the rate of increase in heavy drinking in the college years varied randomly. A comparison of the continuous and discontinuous models indicated that most of the variance in the rate of decline in the post-college years occurred between years 4 and 7 and when this was accounted for by an additional parameter modeling the abrupt change between college and post-college years, the discontinuous model was a better fit to the data. Both time-varying (i.e., peer norms about alcohol use) and time-invariant covariates (i.e., temperament, gender, Greek organization participation) were used to model changes in growth rates, as well as changes in elevation. The interaction of gender and Greek involvement affected the coefficient for the elevation change. College men in the Greek system experienced the sharpest drop in heavy drinking between year 4 and year 7. However, when the time-varying covariate, peer norms, was added to the model, the Greek effect was attenuated for males and eliminated for females. The piecewise linear growth model was appropriate for this study because the time frames for each phase (i.e., first four years out of high school and post-college to year 11) could be specified in advance and the time of transition was common to all participants.

Individually Varying Discontinuities.   In much developmental research, individuals may transition from one developmental phase to another at different points and the time of transition cannot always be identified in advance. Consequently, the piecewise linear model cannot be applied and alternate analysis methods are needed that are more flexible to allow individual variation in the time of transition. As illustrated in Figure 5.4b, individuals may undergo an abrupt shift or change in the outcome between phases and this may not necessarily occur at the same time for everyone. In this illustration, the phase shift occurs sometime between time = 1 and time = 4 and is characterized by a drop in the outcome value. To model discontinuous individual change, a variable that encodes movement from one phase to another is included as a time-varying predictor in the MLGM. Typically, this is a binary indicator with 0 indicating that the shift across the transition period has not occurred and 1 indicating that the shift has occurred. The change in elevation of the outcome is estimated by the coefficient for this binary predictor. For example, in a study of independent living among elderly (ages 65 and older), a general decline in independent living might be expected during this age range. However, if a critical event occurred that precipitated this decline more rapidly, such as the loss of the person's driver's license, then an abrupt shift in independent living might be predicted to occur.

Equation 8 is a discontinuous model of change that allows for the transition point to vary randomly. In this case, it models this shift in IL_{ti}, independent living for

$$IL_{ti} = \pi_{0i} + \pi_{1i} (age - age_{70})_{ti} + \pi_{2i} DLL_{ti} + e_{ti}$$
$$\pi_{0i} = \beta_{00} + r_{0i}$$
$$\pi_{1i} = \beta_{10} + r_{1i}$$
$$\pi_{2i} = \beta_{20} + r_{2i} \tag{8}$$

individual i at time t as a function of age, measured in years and centered at age 70, and DLL_{ti}, driver's license loss for individual i at time t, such that if the individual has a valid driver's license, the variable assumes a value of 0 and when the individual loses his/her license then the variable increments to a value of 1. If we assume that measurements are taken every year for 20 years from age 65 to age 85, and driver's license loss is measured

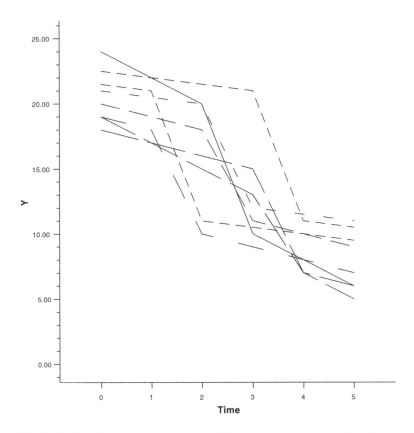

Figure 5.4b Multiphase linear growth patterns. Change in elevation at varied times.

every year, then (hypothetically) a person can hold a license one year, lose it the next, and reacquire it the third year. However, the typical pattern is that one has the driver's license until the year that they fail the test or choose not to take the test due to disability, health, or other problems, and then do not reacquire the license. So, we would expect the values for DLL over time for a person to be a string of 0s until the loss and then it will be a 1 for every subsequent year. In this case, π_{1i} is the presumptive linear rate of decline in independence that would normally occur for persons between the ages of 65 and 85 who have a driver's license and π_{2i} is be the change in average independence that would occur when DLL changes from a 0 to a 1 or when the person loses his or her license. And, the corresponding population average values for the linear rate of decline in independence for those with a license and the change in independence resulting from driver's license loss is β_{10} and β_{20}, respectively. By incorporating the time-varying variable, DLL_{ti}, one is able to estimate the change in independent living from a driving to a non-driving phase, no matter the age at which the driver's license loss occurred.

Suppose the loss of a driver's license is precipitated by a health condition and then the combination of the health condition with the loss of the license leads to a dramatic decline in independence. This model might then be insufficient to also capture the abrupt change in the rate of decline of independent living. In this case, an interaction shift model better represents this change (see Equation 9). If a person's rate of decline abruptly accelerates with the driver's license loss, π_{3i}

$$IL_{ti} = \pi_{0i} + \pi_{1i}(age-age_{70})_{ti} + \pi_{2i}DLL_{ti} + \pi_{3i}[(age-age_{70}) \times DLL]_{ti} + e_{ti}$$
$$\pi_{0i} = \beta_{00} + r_{0i}$$
$$\pi_{1i} = \beta_{10} + r_{1i}$$
$$\pi_{2i} = \beta_{20} = r_{2i}$$
$$\pi_{3i} = \beta_{30} + r_{3i} \qquad\qquad (9)$$

will capture the magnitude of this increment in decline for person i. In other words, π_{2i} estimates the shift in elevation of independent living for person i and π_{3i} indicates the change in the linear rate of change of independent living for person i as he or she transitions from driving to non-driving status. The population average increment to the decline is estimated by β_{30}. This type of phase change is illustrated in Figure 5.4c. Like Figure 5.4b, there is an abrupt decline in the value of the outcome sometime between time = 1 and time = 4. However, the drop in elevation is also accompanied by a change in slope which, in this example, is an increased rate of decline.

By incorporating other covariates to the model we can account for some of the variability in the patterns of change. In this example, one can model how changes in the person's environment might attenuate the effect of the driver's license loss. For instance, we could investigate the mitigating effect of having a strong social support network on this loss of independence by incorporating measures of social support (SS) into the level-2 equations (see Equation 10). The effect of social support for 70 year olds with a driver's license is estimated by

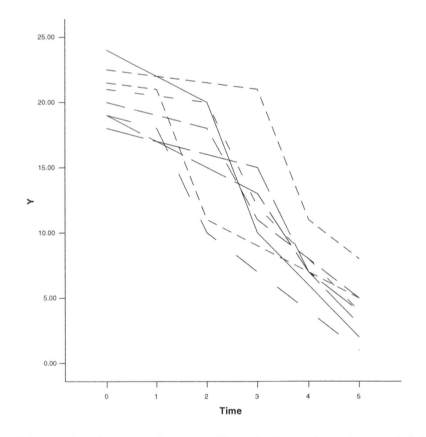

Figure 5.4c Multiphase linear growth patterns. Change in slope and elevation at varied times.

$$IL_{ti} = \pi_{0i} + \pi_{1i}(age-age_{70})_{ti} + \pi_{2i}DLL_{ti} + \pi_{3i}[(age-age_{70}) \times DLL]_{ti} + e_{ti}$$
$$\pi_{0i} = \beta_{00} + \beta_{01}SS_i + r_{0i}$$
$$\pi_{1i} = \beta_{10} + \beta_{11}SS_i + r_{1i}$$
$$\pi_{2i} = \beta_{20} + \beta_{21}SS_i + r_{2i}$$
$$\pi_{3i} = \beta_{30} + \beta_{31}SS_i + r_{3i} \tag{10}$$

β_{01} and the effect on the decline in independent living is estimated by $\beta_{11.}$ The mitigating effect of social support on the drop in decline in independent living for those who lose their driver's license is indicated by β_{21} and the mitigating effect of social support on the change in the rate of decline in independent living is indicated by β_{31}.

Conclusion

The advantages of using MLGM to model the shifts that occur as adults cross critical transitions in their life, are the ability to a) allow the transition point to vary across individuals, b) formulate individualized models of change, and c) model the variability in the growth trajectories as a function of a rich array of contextual variables. Although linear and quadratic models are often constructed to model age-related changes over time, the menu of growth modeling choices includes a wide variety of methods to suit different developmental patterns and take into account gradual as well as abrupt changes that can occur over time. Consequently, this allows the investigator to construct statistical models that capture the varied types of changes that occur in adults' lives and mirror the complexities that affect the growth or decline of a wide array of adult characteristics and abilities.

References

Allen, M .J., & Yen, W. M. (1979). *Introduction to measurement theory.* Long Grove, IL: Waveland.

American Educational Research Association, American Psychological Association, and the National Council on Measurement in Education. (1999). *Standards for educational and psychological testing.* Washington DC: Author.

Baltes, P. B., & Nesselroade, J. R. (1979). History and rationale of longitudinal research. In J. R. Nesselroade & P. B. Baltes (Eds.), *Longitudinal research in the study of behavior and development* (pp. 1–39). New York: Academic Press.

Baltes, P. B., Reese, H. W., & Nesselroade, J. R. (1988). *Life-span developmental psychology: Introduction to research methods.* Monterey, CA: Brooks/Cole.

Baron, R. M., & Kenny, D. A. (1986). The moderator-mediator variable distinction in social psychological research: Conceptual, strategic, and statistical considerations. *Journal of Personality and Social Psychology, 51,* 1173–1182.

Bartholow, B. D., Sher, K. J., & Krull, J. L. (2003). Changes in heavy drinking over the third decade of life as a function of collegiate fraternity and sorority involvement: A prospective, multilevel analysis. *Health Psychology, 22,* 616–626.

Biesanz, J. C., Deeb-Sossa, N., Papakakis, A. A., Bollen, K. A., & Curran, P. J. (2004). The role of coding time in estimating and interpreting growth curve models. *Psychological Methods, 9*(1), 30–52.

Campbell, D. T., & Stanley, J. C. (1963). *Experimental and quasi-experimental designs for research.* Chicago, IL: Rand McNally.

Cohen, J. (1992). A power primer. *Psychological Methods, 112,* 155–159.

Cook, T. D., & Campbell, D. T. (1979). *Quasi-experimentation: Design and analysis issues for field settings.* Boston, MA: Houghton Mifflin.

de Frias, C. M., Lövdén, M., Lindenberger, U., & Nilsson, L. G. (2007). Revisiting the dedifferentiation hypothesis with longitudinal multi-cohort data. *Intelligence, 35,* 381– 92.

Finkel, D., Reynolds, C .A., McArdle, J .J., Gatz, M., & Pedersen, N .L. (2003). Latent growth curve analyses of accelerating decline in cognitive abilities in late adulthood. *Developmental Psychology, 39,* 535–550.

Hartmann, D. P. (2006). Assessing growth in longitudinal investigations: Selected measurement and design issues. In D. M. Teti (Ed.), *Handbook of research methods in developmental science* (pp. 319–339). Malden, MA: Blackwell.

Hoeksma, J. B., & Koomen, H. M. (1992). Multilevel models in developmental psychological research: Rationales and applications. *Early Development and Parenting, 1,* 157–167.

Holt, J. K. (2008). Modeling growth using multilevel and alternative approaches (pp. 111–159). In A. A. O'Connell & D. B. McCoach (Eds.) *Multilevel analysis of educational data* (Volume 3). Quantitative Methods in Education and the Behavioral Sciences: Issues, Research and Teaching Series. Charlotte, NC: Information Age.

Holt, J. K., & Collins, V. L. (2001). Dynamic accountability systems: Multilevel modeling of educational growth. *Multiple Linear Regression Viewpoints, 27,* 46–52.

Hox, J. (2002). *Multilevel analysis: Techniques and applications.* Mahwah, NJ: Erlbaum.

Krull, J. L., & MacKinnon, D. P. (1999). Multilevel mediation modeling in group-based intervention studies. *Evaluation Review, 23,* 418–444.

Krull, J. L., & MacKinnon, D. P. (2001). Multilevel modeling of individual and group level mediated effects. *Multivariate Behavioral Research, 36,* 249–277.

Little, R. J., & Rubin, D. B. (1987). *Statistical analysis with missing data.* New York: Wiley.

Little, R. J., & Rubin, D. B. (1989). The treatment of missing data in multivariate analysis. *Sociological Methods & Research, 18,* 292–326.

MacKinnon, D. P., Lockwood, C. M., Hoffman, J. M., West, S. G., & Sheets, V. (2002). A comparison of methods to test mediation and other intervening variable effects. *Psychological Methods, 7,* 83–104.

MacKinnon, D. P., Warsi, G., & Dwyer, J. H. (1995). A simulation study of mediated effect measures. *Multivariate Behavioral Research, 30,* 41–62.

McArdle, J. J., & Nesselroade, J. R. (2003). Growth curve analysis in contemporary psychological research. In J. A. Schinka & W. F. Velicer (Eds.), *Handbook of psychology: Vol. 2. Research methods in psychology* (pp. 447–480). New York: Wiley.

Mroczek, D. K., & Spiro, A. (2003). Modeling intraindividual change in personality traits: Findings from the Normative Aging Study. *Journal of Gerontology, 58B,* 153–165.

Nunnally, J. C. (1978). *Psychometric theory* (2nd ed.) New York: McGraw-Hill.

Raudenbush, S. W., & Bryk, A. S. (2002). *Hierarchical linear models: Applications and data analysis methods* (2nd ed.). Newbury Park, CA: Sage.

Raudenbush, S. W., & Liu, X. (2000). Statistical power and optimal design for multisite randomized trials. *Psychological Methods, 5,* 199–213.

Raudenbush, S. W., & Liu, X. (2001). Effects of study duration, frequency of observation, and sample size on power in studies of group differences of polynomial change. *Psychological Methods, 6,* 387–401.

Reynolds, C. A., Finkel, D., McArdle, J. J., Gatz, M., Berg, S., & Pedersen, N. L. (2005). Quantitative genetic analysis of latent growth curve models of cognitive abilities in adulthood. *Developmental Psychology, 41,* 3–16.

Rogosa, D. R. (1988). Myths about longitudinal research. In K. W. Schaie, R. T. Campbell, W. M. Meredith, & S. C. Rawlings (Eds.), *Methodological issues in aging research* (pp. 171–209). New York: Springer.

Rogosa, D. R., Brandt, D., & Zimowski, M. (1982). A growth curve approach to the measurement of change. *Psychological Bulletin, 92,* 726–748.

Rogosa, D. R., & Willett, J. B. (1985). Understanding correlates of change by modeling individual differences in growth. *Psychometrika, 50,* 203–228.

Schaie, K. W. (1965). A general model for the study of developmental problems. *Psychological Bulletin, 64*, 91–107.

Schaie, K. W. (1986). Beyond calendar definitions of age, time, and cohort: The general developmental model revisited. *Developmental Review, 6*, 252–277.

Singer, J. D., & Willett, J. B. (1996). Methodological issues in the design of longitudinal research: Principles and recommendations for a quantitative study of teachers' careers. *Educational Evaluation and Policy Analysis, 18*, 155–195.

Singer, J. D., & Willett, J. B. (2003). *Applied longitudinal data analysis: Modeling change and event occurrence.* New York: Oxford University Press.

Sobel, M. E. (1982). Asymptotic confidence intervals for indirect effects in structural equation models. In S. Leinhardt (Ed.), *Sociological methodology 1982* (pp. 290–312). Washington, DC: American Sociological Association.

U.S. Department of Education (1993). *National Adult Literacy Survey.* Washington, DC: National Center for Education Statistics.

U.S. Department of Education (2005). *National Assessment of Adult Literacy.* Washington, DC: National Center for Education Statistics.

Willett, J. B. (1988). Questions and answers in the measurement of change. In E. Z. Rothkopf (Ed.). *Review of Research in Education, 1988–1989* (pp. 345–422). Washington, DC: American Educational Research Association.

Willett, J. B., Singer, J. D., & Martin, N. C. (1998). The design and analysis of longitudinal studies of development and psychopathology in context: Statistical models and methodological recommendations. *Development and Psychopathology, 10*, 395–426.

Chapter 6

Research Synthesis and Meta-Analysis

Jeffrey C. Valentine and Harris Cooper

Imagine that you are the head of a large non-profit foundation that has, as its mission, the goal of improving adult literacy. The foundation's board of directors is particularly interested in developing a new intervention specifically targeted at adults who are not functionally literate. What might such an intervention look like? To find this out, you ask your crack staff of researchers to search the literature for "best practices" in adult literacy programs. If your staff is thorough, it is likely that they will find multiple studies that claim to have implemented and/or tested best practices, and it is likely to be the case that the studies seem to reach different conclusions about which practices are most effective. How should you proceed?

This chapter addresses some of the possibilities for making sense out of a body of research evidence. Progress in any scientific field depends on the accumulation of knowledge, and the accumulation of knowledge depends greatly on the methods used to integrate individual studies into a coherent whole. You will see in this chapter that we are predisposed to a particular type of review, specifically one that is conducted with a similar degree of transparency and rigor as the best scientific studies. In the past, reviewing the literature on best practices in adult literacy would usually have involved a narrative review, in which a scholar would gather some studies that were relevant, read them, then pronounce on what those studies have to say. Typically, little attention has been paid to whether the studies could claim to be representative of the studies that had been conducted, and almost nothing was said about the standards of proof that were employed during the review. Further, results were often presented in impressionistic terms, with little insight provided about the magnitude of some relation (e.g., in the context of an adult literacy intervention, *how much* of an effect the intervention had on participants). Increasingly, however, scholars recognized that literature reviews did not meet the standards of rigor and transparency required in primary research.

At the same time, the amount of available research in the social and medical sciences increased dramatically. A savvy and conscientious scholar might be able to reasonably synthesize the results of a few studies. But what were Bob Rosenthal and Don Rubin (Rosenthal & Rubin, 1978), to do when, in the course of looking for studies that investigated expectancy effects, they found 345 studies? Or Jack Hunter and Frank Schmidt (Hunter & Schmidt, 1979, when they found over 900 estimates of the differential validity of employments tests by race? According to Glass (1976), when faced with this situation reviewers would likely "carp on the design or analysis deficiencies of all but a few studies—those remaining frequently being one's own work or that of one's students or friends—and then advance the one or two 'acceptable' studies as the truth of the matter" (p. 6).

In contrast to the narrative review, a systematic research synthesis (or simply, a systematic review) employs a collection of methodological and statistical techniques designed to improve upon the integration of empirical studies. Systematic research syntheses employ literature searching strategies that are meant to minimize differences between retrieved studies and studies that could not be located. Decisions about whether to include or exclude studies based on methodological quality or other criteria are made explicit prior to their application and are applied even-handedly. The extraction of information from research reports is carried out using coding rules similar to those developed for the scientific analysis of document content. Meta-analysis, or the statistical integration of the results of studies, is conducted using open standards of proof, and is approached with the same structure and rigor as is data analysis in primary studies.

From the outset, it is important to recognize that these procedures, including meta-analysis, are not a complete solution to the problems faced by research synthesists. Indeed, meta-analysis is unsuited to addressing certain kinds of questions. For example, theoretical analyses, taxonomic studies, and qualitative research cannot be analyzed using meta-analytic techniques. A scholar interested in tracing the historical development of the concept of literacy would not find meta-analysis a useful tool. In addition, a basic premise behind the use of statistics in research synthesis is that a research body of conceptually relevant studies exists. If this assumption is not met, a quantitative research synthesis cannot be done. And more generally, as Wachter and Straf (1990) point out, meta-analysis is no substitute for wisdom. A statistical method cannot generate theories or hypotheses that do not already exist, nor can it tell us what topics are important to study. Even less ambitiously, a statistical method cannot point out to its user what variables should be examined as moderators of relationships. These can only be accomplished through the thoughtful application of the human intellect.

In this chapter, we describe the ways in which systematic research synthesis can be an improvement over traditional narrative reviews. Also, we will describe briefly the processes by which a systematic review is carried out. We do not aim to cover all the details of how to conduct a systematic review. For such coverage, we can recommend texts by Cooper (1998), Cooper and Hedges (1994), and Lipsey and Wilson (2001). To help illustrate certain concepts and practices, we will refer to a systematic review by Torgerson, Porthouse, and Brooks (2005), as it is representative of the kind of reviews that can be done in the area of adult literacy.

A Brief History of Research Synthesis and Meta-Analysis

A century ago, Karl Pearson conducted what is believed to be one the first statistical syntheses of results of independent research (Pearson, 1904). Pearson gathered data from eleven studies of the effect of a vaccine against typhoid and for each study he calculated a new statistic called the correlation coefficient. He averaged the correlations and concluded that other vaccines were more effective. Three decades later, Ronald Fisher presented a technique for combining the probability values that came from statistically independent tests of the same hypothesis (Fisher, 1932). Early work on quantitative procedures for integrating results of independent studies was ignored for many years. However, the twin problems of (a) the lack of rigor in traditional literature reviews and (b) the dramatic increase in the numbers of studies available for review led to a revival of sorts.

Glass (1976) coined the term meta-analysis to stand for "the statistical analysis of a large collection of analysis results from individual studies for purposes of integrating the findings" (p. 3). Shortly thereafter, Cooper (1979) and Cooper and Rosenthal (1980) made the empirical case for meta-analysis by showing that narrative review procedures led to inaccurate or imprecise characterizations of the cumulative research results. Glass, McGaw, and Smith (1981) then proposed that meta-analysis be viewed as a new application of analysis of variance and multiple regression procedures, with the outcomes of studies, in the form of effect sizes, treated as the criterion variable and the features of studies as the predictor variables. Hunter, Schmidt, and Jackson (1982) introduced an alternative meta-analytic model that (a) compared the observed variation in study outcomes to that expected by sampling error and (b) corrected the mean and variance of observed effect sizes for known sources of bias (e.g., measurement error, restrictions in sampled ranges). Rosenthal (1984) presented a compendium of meta-analytic methods including combining significance levels, effect size estimation, and the search for moderators of study results. Importantly, Rosenthal's procedures for testing moderators of effect sizes were not based on traditional inferential statistics, but on a new set of techniques involving assumptions tailored specifically for the analysis of study outcomes.

Simultaneous with the development of meta-analysis procedures, several attempts were undertaken to examine and place research synthesis in the context of a scientific process. In 1971, Feldman published an article entitled "Using the work of others: Some observations on reviewing and integrating" in which he wrote, "Systematically reviewing and integrating ... the literature of a field may be considered a type of research in its own right—one using a characteristic set of research techniques and methods" (Feldman, 1971, p. 86). In the same year, Light and Smith (1971) presented a "cluster approach" to research synthesis that was meant to redress some of the deficiencies in the existing strategies. They argued that, if treated properly, the variation in outcomes among related studies could be a valuable source of information, rather than a source of consternation as it appeared to be when treated with traditional reviewing methods.

Two papers that appeared in the *Review of Educational Research* in the early 1980s brought the meta-analytic and review-as-research perspectives together. First, Jackson (1980) proposed six reviewing tasks "analogous to those performed during primary research" (p. 441). His paper employed a sample of 36 review articles from prestigious social science periodicals to examine the methods used in syntheses of empirical research. His conclusion was that "relatively little thought has been given to the methods for doing integrative reviews" (p. 459).

Cooper (1982) drew the analogy between research synthesis and primary research to its logical conclusion. He presented a five stage model of the review that viewed research synthesis as a data gathering exercise and, as such, applied to it criteria similar to those employed to judge primary research. Cooper argued that, similar to primary research, a research review involves problem formulation, data collection (the literature search), data evaluation, data analysis and interpretation (the meta-analysis), and public presentation. For each stage, Cooper codified the research question, its primary function in the review, and the procedural differences that might cause variation in the conclusions of different reviews. In addition, Cooper applied the notion of threats-to-inferential-validity—introduced by Campbell and Stanley (1966; also see Cook & Campbell, 1979) for evaluating the utility of primary research designs—to research synthesis. He identified numerous threats to validity associated with reviewing procedures that might undermine the trustworthiness of a research synthesis' findings.

Light and Pillemer (1984) offered a text that emphasized the use of research synthesis to inform social policy. Their approach highlighted the importance of meshing quantitative procedures and narrative descriptions in the interpretation and communication of synthesis results. Hedges and Olkin's (1985) text, titled *Statistical Procedures for Meta-*

Analysis, covered a wide array of meta-analytic procedures and established the procedures' legitimacy by presenting rigorous statistical proofs.

During and after the years that the works mentioned above were appearing, the use of meta-analysis spread from psychology and education through many disciplines, especially social policy analysis (Light, 1983) and the medical sciences (see *Statistics in Medicine,* 1987, Vol. 6, No. 3). These developments led Greenberg and Folger (1988) to state that "if the current interest in meta-analysis is any indication, then meta-analysis is here to stay" (p. 191).

Since the mid-1980s, several full-text treatments have appeared on meta-analysis. Some of these treat the topic generally (e.g., Cooper, 1998; Hunter & Schmidt, 1990; Lipsey & Wilson, 2001), some treat it from the perspective of particular research design conceptualizations (e.g., Eddy, Hasselblad, & Shachter, 1992), some are tied to particular software packages (e.g., Johnson, 1989), and some look at potential future developments in research synthesis (e.g., Wachter & Straf, 1990, Cook et al., 1992). In 1994, the first edition of *Handbook of Research Synthesis* was published (Cooper & Hedges, 1994). This book included 32 chapters contributed by specialists in information science, computer software, and statistics, as well as experts in the use of research synthesis for psychology, medicine, education, and public policy.

Components of Research Synthesis

As we discussed earlier, systematic research syntheses are conducted much like primary research (Cooper, 1998). A problem is formulated, data are collected, evaluated, analyzed, and interpreted, and results are presented to the public. In a sense, research synthesis may be thought of as a form of survey research, in which studies (as opposed to people) are the population of interest (Lipsey & Wilson, 2001). The "response" offered by the research report is called an effect size and the "demographics" related to the response are the characteristics of the study (its design, implementation characteristics, and sample). An effect size is a measure of the magnitude of the relationship in question. For example, a study investigating the relationship between literacy and socio-economic status (SES) might result in a correlation coefficient between these two variables; this correlation is the effect size. However, before the effect size is calculated, the researcher has made numerous decisions that unfold in systematic order. We will now discuss each stage of research synthesis.

Problem Formulation

In its most basic form, problem formulation involves identifying at least two relevant variables, specifying the anticipated relation between them, and providing a rationale for relating the variables to one another. So for example, my variables of interest might be adult literacy and SES. One might suspect that these are positively related (i.e., as wealth increases so does literacy), with two complementary reasons being (a) that having low literacy reduces one's value in the workforce and (b) being poor often involves a restriction in access to activities and materials that would enhance literacy.

While the problems addressed by primary researchers are limited only by their imaginations and funding levels, research synthesists have no choice but to study topics that have already appeared in the empirical literature. In fact, a topic may not be suitable for review unless a substantial number of studies have taken it as a problem. This does not mean, however, that research synthesis is not a creative enterprise. Instead, the creativity enters when the synthesist must make sense of many related but not identical studies. More often than not, the cumulative results of studies are many times more complex than the result of any single study.

The most important issues that arise in defining the problem for research syntheses are (a) how broadly to define the conceptual variables of interest and (b) how to handle multiple operational definitions of the same conceptual variables. Although no two participants in any single study will be treated exactly alike, this variability within studies is small compared to the variability produced by differences in operationalizations across studies.

Torgerson et al. (2005) were interested in interventions designed to increase the literacy and/or numeracy of adults. This is a broad research question made necessary by the relative lack of research in this area. As such, their research problem formulates a very general question: For adults, is there a relationship between receiving an intervention designed to enhance literacy or numeracy and outcomes in those areas, relative to individuals who do not receive such an intervention?

Optimally, a research synthesist will specify in advance the conceptual definitions of a variable covered by the review and will then assess the fit between this definition and the operations employed in any given study. In practice, it is often necessary for the synthesist to retain some flexibility in judging the relevance of a given operation of the dependent variable. Variables can be operationalized in a surprising number of ways, and it is rare to have perfect knowledge of this diversity before undertaking a search of the literature. Thus, more so than is true in primary research, problem formulation in research synthesis is an iterative process. The synthesist begins with a defined concept and known operational realizations but these two ideated sets are refined as the subsequent stages of the review proceed. In the case of Torgerson et al. (2005), the research question is so broad that this activity was not necessary, but generally synthesists will have to wrestle with this problem.

The Literature Search

For the research synthesist, the data collection stage involves gathering studies and making judgments about their relevance to the question at hand. Too often, scholars conducting a narrative research review rely on a convenience sample of studies on which to base their conclusions. For example, the reviewer might only include studies published in a few selected journals plus those that have come to their attention through informal means. Thus, the studies reviewed are neither exhaustive nor representative of all studies that have been conducted on the topic of interest.

Systematic research synthesists are advised to operate with the goal of obtaining all relevant research (Cooper, 1998; Lipsey & Wilson, 2001), regardless of whether or where it was published. Of course, whether this goal is ever obtained is unknowable. Indeed, we can be reasonably certain that the goal is often unobtainable. Setting the goal, however, does lead to the use of comprehensive searching strategies that are meant to reduce biases in the results of obtained literature. Here, bias is defined as systematic differences in the outcomes of studies that do and do not come to the attention of the synthesist.

One important question faced by research synthesists involves whether to include unpublished research. Two reasons are frequently given for excluding unpublished research reports. The first is that the research base has the potential for becoming too large and unwieldy for a narrative review. Meta-analysts solve this problem by using computers to help store, sort, and analyze study results.

The second reason given is that unpublished research is often of lesser quality than published research. We would argue that this is too simple a conclusion. For example, researchers may not publish their results because publication is not their objective and if so this decision is independent of the quality of their work (see Cooper, DeNeve, & Charlton, 1997). Conversely, most researchers would agree that some low quality research does get published. Suffice it to say that the quality of research, published and not, is distributed along overlapping continua.

Moreover, research is often turned down for publication for reasons other than quality (Greenwald, 1975). In particular, research papers failing to achieve standard levels of statistical significance are frequently left in researcher's "file drawers," a problem known as publication bias. The concern here is that studies revealing smaller effect sizes will be systematically censured from the published literature and therefore estimates of effect in the published literature may make relationships appear stronger than if all estimates were available to the synthesist. For this reason, it is now accepted practice that rigorous research syntheses will include both published and unpublished research.

Torgerson et al. (2005) employed two main strategies to find relevant literature. They conducted keyword searches of several databases (including a specialty database that houses unpublished research), and also examined the reference sections of research reviews that were identified in their search for additional studies. Reviewers might also try contacting leading researchers, relevant professional organizations, and agencies known to fund work in the area of the research question.

Data Collection and Evaluation

In a typical research synthesis, trained personnel use standardized coding procedures to extract the desired information from research reports. The process is analogous to collecting data on a survey questionnaire or, more directly, to the content analysis of documents (Weber, 1990). The coding sheet contains information about the background characteristics of the reports (e.g., author, year of publication) as well as the specifics of the study, such as sample size and composition, research methodology, and study results. While some collected information will be the same regardless of the topic under consideration (for example, all reviewers will collect information on sample sizes), other coded study characteristics will be unique to the substantive topic of interest. Lipsey (1994) discusses how synthesists can go about identifying study features that might influence study outcomes.

Stock (1994) presented a detailed discussion of how to assemble a coding guide for a research synthesis. A good coding guide will facilitate complete, unambiguous, and reliable extraction of all relevant data in a research report. Among the issues Stock addressed, none is more important than the reliability of data extraction.

Reliability of Data Extraction. Traditional narrative reviewers give very little (if any) attention to the reliability of their descriptions of studies. On the other hand, systematic research reviewers pay special attention to errors that occur when extracting data from a research report. There are several sources of error in research reviews. One source of error occurs when primary researchers do not report or poorly report data that are of interest to the research synthesist. This occurs, for example, when researchers performing research on adult literacy neglect to describe how samples were obtained. To counter this problem, the synthesist may choose to contact the study authors directly for assistance. DuBois, Holloway, Valentine, and Cooper (2002) utilized this approach in a meta-analysis of the effectiveness of youth mentoring programs and had moderate success. When a research report contained missing or incomplete data, these authors attempted to contact the primary author through electronic mail. Success in both contacting study authors and retrieving data were dependent on the amount of time that had passed since original publication of the research report; we had very little success with reports that were more than 10 years old, but were able to retrieve some information from newer reports. While labor intensive, this approach added data to the synthesis that would have been otherwise unavailable, increasing the representativeness of the data set. One can only hope that the current trend of decreasing costs for electronic storage will increase the probability that study authors will be willing and able to accommodate these requests in the future.

Research reviewers are not immune to making mistakes themselves. To assess the extent to which study information has been reliably extracted from research reports, most research synthesis texts suggest performing some sort of reliability assessment. This involves employing procedures akin to those used in assessing interjudge reliability in other research domains (e.g., Lipsey & Wilson, 2001; Orwin, 1994). At a minimum, a reliability assessment will involve at least two (and possibly more) coders working independently. If a substantial number of studies have met inclusion criteria, the reliability assessment could be conducted by having one of the researchers code a randomly sampled subset of studies. With a smaller number of studies, best practice is to have researchers independently code all studies. Disagreements then may be resolved in conference and/or by a third reader. This procedure raises the effective reliability of codes to very high levels, and is the approach adopted by Torgerson et al. (2005).

Empirical results suggest that different types of information about research are extracted from reports with different levels of reliability. For example, Stock, Okun, Haring, Miller, Kinney, and Ceurvorst (1982) found that, among 27 types of information extracted from research reports describing studies of the predictors of life satisfaction, the mean reliability coefficient (uncorrected for chance), was $r = .88$. Eighteen of the 27 characteristics had a reliability coefficient greater than or equal to .90, and an additional six characteristics had a reliability coefficient of $.80 \leq r \leq .90$. Two characteristics had reliabilities below .60, suggesting that they could not be reliably coded by the readers. One of these codes was "quality of study."

Judging Research Quality.   It is a truism that a research synthesis is only as good as the studies that go into it. While multiple operationism can overcome some deficiencies in research design (see Cook & Campbell, 1979), if only low quality studies have been conducted on the topic of interest, one cannot expect a synthesis to yield interpretable findings. Of course, this holds true whether traditional narrative review procedures or meta-analysis are employed.

In some instances, research synthesists are interested in a variable that requires a high degree of inference on the part of the coders. Among these, the most frequent high inference codes occur because the synthesists wish to determine whether "study quality" moderates the estimated magnitude of the relationships in question. For example, do "high quality" studies reveal larger or smaller effects of an adult literacy intervention than "low quality" studies? Assessing whether a study is "good" or "bad" requires a complex judgment on the part of the coder, and the level of inference required may introduce error in the research review. As suggested by Stock et al. (1982), arriving at a dichotomous decision about study quality (good vs. bad) or even reducing study quality to a single continuous dimension can be difficult.

This is not to suggest that all high inference codes are unreliable. For example, Miller, Lee, and Carlson (1991) had judges read a description of an experimental manipulation. Judges made inferences about the affective, cognitive, and behavioral responses of study participants. Results suggested that judges effectively inferred participant affective responses, but did not reliably infer participant behavior or attitude change.

Research reviewers often employ quality scales designed to help them quantify the quality of a study's design and implementation. However, these scales unfortunately have little to recommend them. They generally lack sufficient operational specificity and they are based on criteria that lack empirical support. In a demonstration of these problems Jüni, Witschi, Bloch, and Egger (1999) applied 25 different quality scales to 17 studies reporting on trials comparing the effects of low-molecular weight heparin (LMWH) to standard heparin on the risk of developing blood clots after surgery. After applying the 25 quality scales to the 17 trials, the authors then performed 25 different meta-analyses examining, in each case, the relationship between study quality and the effect of LMHW (relative to standard heparin). Then, the authors examined the conclusions of the meta-analyses separately for "high" and "low" quality trials. For six of the quality scales, the "high quality" studies suggested no difference between LMWH and standard heparin, while the "low quality" studies suggested a significant positive effect for LMWH. For seven other quality scales, this pattern was reversed. That is, the "high quality" studies suggested a positive effect for LMWH, while the "low quality" studies suggested no difference between the two conditions. The remaining 12 quality scales resulted in conclusions that did not differ between "high" and "low" quality trials. Thus, Jüni et al. (1999) suggested that the clinical conclusion about the efficacy of the two types of heparin depended on the quality scale used.

The dependence between the outcomes of the synthesis and the quality scale used reveals a critical problem with the scales. A team of scholars could have chosen Quality Scale A, used it to exclude low quality studies, and then concluded that LMWH is effective. Starting with the same research question, another team of scholars could have chosen Quality Scale B, used it to exclude low quality studies, then concluded that LMWH is no more effective than standard heparin. As such, the scales appear to have been at best useless and at worst misleading (Berlin & Rennie, 1999).

Examination of the quality scales used makes it easy to see why this result occurred. The 25 quality scales often focused on different dimensions, and analyzed a differing number of dimensions (ranging from 3 to 34), including dimensions that are unrelated to validity in the traditional sense (e.g., whether or not an institutional review board approved the study). Even when the same dimension was analyzed, the weights assigned to the dimension varied. For example, one scale allocated 4% of total points on their scale to the presence of randomization, and 12% of the points to whether or not the outcome assessor was unaware of the condition the participants were in (called masking). Another scale very nearly reversed the relative importance of these two dimensions, allocating 14% of the total points to randomization and 5% to masking. Simply stated, there is no empirical justification for these weighting schemes, and the result in the absence of that justification is a hopelessly confused set of arbitrary weights.

Further, the scales reviewed by Jüni et al. (1999) share a reliance on single scores to represent a study's quality. Especially when scales focus on more than one aspect of validity, the single score approach results in a score that is summed from very different aspects of study design and implementation, many of which are not necessarily related to one another. For example, there is no necessary relation between the validity of outcome measures and the mechanism used to allocate participants to groups. When scales combine disparate elements of study design into a single score, it is likely that important considerations of design are being obscured. For example, a study with strong internal validity but weak external validity can get a score identical to a study with weak internal validity and strong external validity. If the quality of these studies is expressed as a single number, how would one know the difference between these studies with such very different characteristics?

As such, we think the best strategy for addressing study quality in a research synthesis is for the reviewers to think deeply about the features of study design, implementation, and analysis that are likely to affect study results in their area and to carefully code studies on these dimensions. The reviewers can then explore the relation between these characteristics and study outcomes. Further, if the reviewers have a strong basis for believing that a characteristic biases a collection of studies, then studies with that characteristic could be excluded from the review (but note that, as much as possible, decisions like these should be made before data collection begins).

Torgerson et al. (2005) employed quality criteria in this manner, using items that were suggested by the CONSORT statement (Moher, Schulz, & Altman, 2001). The CONSORT statement addresses aspects of study design and implementation that ought to be reported in a study write up. Torgerson et al. then described where each of the included studies fell on each quality dimension.

The Statistical Analysis and Interpretation of Combined Study Results

In this section we discuss statistical methods that help reviewers summarize research results. Meta-analyses generally lead to more precise and reliable conclusions about a research base than does the narrative integration of research. An empirical example demonstrates this point. Cooper and Rosenthal (1980) randomly assigned 41 faculty and graduate students in a psychology department to read seven articles addressing the question of sex differences in task persistence. All participants read the same seven articles chosen to suggest that women have greater task persistence than men. Some participants were assigned to a meta-analysis condition, in which they were given detailed instructions about how to combine the study's significance levels and to obtain an overall estimate of the effect size for the seven studies. Participants assigned to the narrative review condition were simply told to use whatever procedures they typically would use to assess the literature.

After the participants completed their reviews, they were asked whether the articles they read supported the conclusion that women exhibit greater task persistence than men. Participants could respond "definitely yes," "probably yes," "can't tell," "probably no," or "definitely no." Among the narrative reviewers 73% found definitely or probably no support for the hypothesis compared with only 32% of participants using the meta-analytic technique. In fact, the combined probability that the null hypothesis was true was $p < .005$, indicating over twice as many inferential errors by the narrative than the quantitative reviewers. This study suggests that meta-analysis can be a superior data integration strategy.

As we mentioned in the introduction, traditional narrative reviewers are unable to generate effect sizes for the hypotheses they test, and do not employ strategies for weighting individual studies proportional to their size or quality. Rather, most narrative reviewers use, explicitly or not, a vote-count of studies. Often, this procedure leads to inferential errors.

The Vote-Count. Typically, when conducting a vote count, the reviewer assigns research reports to one of three categories: either the relation between the two variables is significantly positive, significantly negative, or the null hypothesis cannot be rejected (Bushman, 1994). The number of reports in each category is counted, and a decision rule is applied to the count to determine what the research base suggests about the relation. The category with the largest number of votes wins.

The vote count is intuitively appealing. However, it has few defenders as a final data analysis strategy. Hedges and Olkin (1985) have demonstrated that in many instances in the social sciences, vote counts have power characteristics that are inversely related to the number of studies contained in the review. That is, counterintuitively, when a real but moderate effect exists in a population of studies that are carried out with less-than-ideal statistical power characteristics, the *more* studies that a review covers, the *less* likely it is that a vote count will reject the null hypothesis. In addition, the vote counting strategy does not differentially weight studies based on sample size. This is a problem because a study with 100 participants and a study with 1,000 participants are given equal weight, even though the larger study provides the more precise and reliable estimate of the effect. Further, the effect size of the studies reviewed is not considered. A study showing small negative effects is given the same weight as a study showing large positive ones. For these reasons, vote counting is not considered a credible analytic strategy for drawing inferences (Cooper & Dorr, 1995).

Effect Size Metrics. As an alternative to vote counting procedures, meta-analysts will (a) calculate an effect size for the outcomes of hypothesis tests in every study, (b) average these effect sizes across hypothesis tests to estimate general magnitudes of effect, and (c) compare effect sizes to discover if variations in outcomes exist and, if so, what features of comparisons might account for them.

Cohen (1988) defined an effect size as "the degree to which the phenomenon is present in the population, or the degree to which the null hypothesis is false" (pp. 9–10). For the meta-analyst, estimates of effect size are the most crucial output of studies. Because the reporting of effect sizes in primary research is not yet universal, a meta-analyst often must estimate or calculate the effect size from other statistics present in a research report (see Rosenthal, 1984, for many of these approaches). Often, they also must adjust an effect size estimate to remove certain sampling biases.

Two effect size metrics are most applicable to research on adult literacy. The first, known as the standardized mean difference (or *d*-index, Cohen's *d*, or simply as *d*) by is a scale-free measure of the separation between two group means (Cohen, 1988). Calculating the basic standardized mean difference for any comparison involves dividing the difference between the two group means by their average (or pooled) standard deviation. This calculation results in a measure of the difference between the two group means expressed in terms of their common standard deviation. For example, a standardized mean difference of .25 indicates that one-quarter standard deviation separates the two means.

Because the interpretation of the standardized mean difference effect size is not intuitively transparent in many contexts, Cohen (1988) presented a measure associated with it called U_3. U_3 describes the percentage of the sample with the lower mean that was exceeded by the average (or 50th percentile) score in the higher-meaned group. When $d = 0$, $U_3 = 50\%$, suggesting that half of the scores in the lower-meaned group were exceeded by the mean of the higher-scoring group. Of course, this suggests no difference between the groups. When $d = .50$, or when the higher-scoring group mean is one-half standard deviation above the lower-scoring group mean, $U_3 = 69\%$. This suggests that 69% of the scores in the higher-meaned group exceed the average score in the lower-meaned group.

A related way to think about the interpretation of the standardized mean difference effect size is that it represents the probability that a randomly selected member of the treatment group will outscore a randomly selected member of the comparison group. For example, assume that a meta-analysis of adult literacy programs found that the average effect size was $d = +.50$, with the positive sign in front of the d-index, indicating that the participants in the intervention outscored the participants in the comparison condition. The $d = +.50$ can be interpreted as a 69% chance that a randomly-chosen participant receiving the literacy intervention would outscore a randomly-chosen comparison group member. If the studies in this review were all randomized experiments, we would have a strong basis for believing that, if the intervention were not effective at all, a randomly-drawn intervention group member would have a 50% chance of outperforming a randomly-drawn comparison group member.

The second effect size metric well-suited to research in adult literacy is the r-index, or correlation coefficient. The correlation coefficient is familiar to most researchers and students. However, interpretations of the correlation coefficient that rely on the proportion of variance explained (i.e., r^2), are frequently misinterpreted even by experienced researchers (cf, Abelson, 1985; Rosenthal & Rubin, 1982). The physicians' aspirin study (Steering Committee of the Physicians' Health Study Research Group, 1988) provides a particularly compelling example. Over a 5-year period, approximately 22,000 physicians with a history of heart attack took either 325 mg. of aspirin every other day or they took a placebo. The data showed that 1.7% of the placebo group and .09% of the aspirin group had a second heart attack during the course of the study. The correlation associated with these data was $r = .03$, and $r^2 = .0009$, a seemingly trivial relationship. However, this effect means that taking an aspirin every other day was associated with a significant reduction in the risk of having a second heart attack. In fact, risk of a second heart attack was reduced by more than one-third (Rosenthal & Rosnow, 1991). Olkin (1992), citing Chalmers (n.d.) suggests that had research synthesis techniques been applied to the efficacy of aspirin in reducing the risk of a second heart attack, sufficient evidence demonstrating the clinical benefits of aspirin existed as early as 1976, with an estimated savings of 10,000 to 20,000 lives over the next decade.

Typically, the correlation coefficient is used to express the relationship between two continuous variables, such as continuous measures of literacy and earnings per year. On the other hand, the d-index is used to relate one dichotomous variable to a continuous variable, such as comparing groups of qualitatively different participants (e.g., males and females, Whites and African Americans), on a continuous measure, such as literacy. The choice of metric is determined by which fits best with the characteristics of the variables under consideration.

Identifying Independent Samples.   A statistical problem arises when a single study contains multiple effect size estimates taken on the same sample of participants. There are several approaches meta-analysts use to handle such dependent effect sizes. Some treat each effect size as independent, regardless of the number that comes from the same sample of people. They assume that the effect of violating the independence assumption is not substantial. Other meta-analysts use the study as the unit of analysis. They calculate the mean effect size or take the median result and use this value to represent the study.

Sophisticated statistical models also have been suggested as a solution to the problem of dependent effect size estimates (Gleser & Olkin, 1994; Raudenbush, Becker, & Kalaian, 1988), but due to their complexity they are yet rarely found in practice.

Examining Effect Size Distributions.   Inspecting the effect size distribution is an important part of a complete meta-analysis. This information often includes stem-and-leaf displays and/or funnel plots (Greenhouse & Iyengar, 1994) that help convey information about the magnitude and variation in effect sizes, as well as help assess whether publication bias might exist in the sample of comparison outcomes (see below for a discussion of publication bias).

The distribution of effects will also be examined to determine whether it contains statistical outliers (Barnett & Lewis, 1978). As with data based on primary research, if outliers are present meta-analysts then must decide how to treat them. Some synthesists remove them from the data set entirely while others will modify the outlying values so as to make them conform more closely to the general distribution of results. For either option, the meta-analysts wish both to make the distribution of effects more normal and to mitigate the effect of a few extreme values on measures of central tendency and dispersion, and on subsequent moderator analyses. Whichever option is chosen, it is important to inform the readers so they may make their own judgments about the adequacy of the strategy.

Averaging Effect Sizes and Measuring Their Dispersion.   The most pivotal outcomes of a meta-analysis are the average effect sizes and measures of dispersion that accompany them. Weighted procedures are typically used to calculate average effect sizes across comparisons. In this procedure, each independent effect size is first multiplied by the inverse of its variance and the sum of these products is then divided by the sum of the inverses.

The weighting procedure is generally preferred to not weighting because it gives greater weight to effect sizes based on larger samples. Also, as noted above, confidence intervals are calculated for weighted average effects. Many texts, including Hedges and Olkin (1985), Shadish and Haddock (1994), and Lipsey and Wilson (2001) provide procedures for calculating the appropriate weights and confidence intervals.

In addition to the confidence interval as a measure of dispersion, research synthesists usually carry out a highly informative procedure called a "homogeneity analysis." A homogeneity analysis compares the amount of variance in an observed set of effect sizes with the amount of variance that would be expected by sampling error alone. If there is greater variation in effects than would be expected by chance, then the meta-analyst begins the process of examining moderators of hypothesis test outcomes. (Note also that the meta-analyst may search for moderators in the absence of a statistically significant homogeneity analysis if there are good theoretical reasons for doing so.)

Artifactual Influences of the Size of Observed Effects.   There are numerous factors that influence the magnitude of an observed relation between two variables other than the "true" relationship. In particular, meta-analysts must pay attention to factors that might attenuate the magnitude of the effect size. For example, both (a) unreliability in the scores used to measure the dependent variable and (b) artificially dichotomizing continuous scores on the dependent variable into groups (that is, turning a continuous measure of SES into middle and low wealth groups) will lead to smaller observed effect sizes than the "actual" effect in the population. The synthesist must decide how this attenuation should be treated. One approach is to estimate the degree to which the effect size has been attenuated due to these and other related issues. Procedures for carrying this out are described in Hunter and Schmidt (1990).

A final influence on effect sizes is the number of factors employed in a research design. If the research design includes more factors than the reviewer is interested in, the reviewer is faced with the choice of either using a standard deviation reduced by the inclusion of additional factors (inflating the estimate of the effect size), or attempting to retrieve the standard deviation that would have been obtained if all extraneous factors had been ignored. Whenever possible, this latter strategy should be employed. In practice, however, it is often difficult to retrieve this estimate. In such cases, we recommend examining whether or not the number of factors involved in the studies is correlated with effect size.

Fixed and Random Effects Models of Error.   Another aspect of conducting a meta-analysis that recently has received considerable attention involves the decision about whether a fixed-effects or random-effects model of error influences the generation of study outcomes. In a fixed-effect analysis, each effect size's variance is assumed to reflect only sampling error (i.e., error solely due to participant differences) and thus can be taken into account through the procedures described previously for weighting effect sizes by sample size. When a random-effect analysis is carried out, a study-level variance component is assumed to be present as an additional source of random influence. Hedges and Vevea (1998) state that fixed-effect models of error are most appropriate when the goal of the research is "to make inferences only about the effect size parameters in the set of studies that are observed (or a set of studies identical to the observed studies except for uncertainty associated with the sampling of subjects)" (p. 3). A further statistical consideration is that in the search for moderators, fixed-effect models may seriously underestimate, and random-effects models seriously overestimate, error variance when their assumptions are violated (Overton, 1998). In view of these competing sets of concerns, one approach is to consider applying both models in all primary study analyses (e.g., Cooper et al., 2000). Specifically, all analyses could be conducted twice, once employing fixed-effect assumptions and once using random-effect assumptions. Differences in results based on which set of assumptions is used can be incorporated into the interpretation and discussion of findings.

Moderator Analysis.   The search for why the outcomes of hypothesis tests differ is the most interesting and informative part of conducting a meta-analysis. Because effect sizes are sample statistics, they will vary somewhat even if they all estimate the same underlying population value. Homogeneity analysis allows the meta-analyst to test whether sampling error alone accounted for this variation or whether features of studies, samples, treatment designs, or outcome measures also play a role. The synthesist calculates average effect sizes for subsets of studies, comparing the average effect sizes for different methods, types of programs, outcome measures, and participants and compares these to determine if they provide insight into what influences the strength and/or direction of the relationship. In fact, the synthesist can ask questions about variables that moderate outcomes even if no individual study has included the moderator variable. For example, a meta-analyst can ask whether the effects of a literacy intervention differ for low vs. middle SES individuals, even if no single study ever included both of these groups. The results of such a comparison of average effect sizes can suggest whether this student characteristic would be important to look at in future research and/or as a guide to policy.

After calculating the average effect sizes for different subgroups of comparisons, the meta-analyst statistically tests whether the group factor is reliably associated with different magnitudes of effect. Three statistical procedures for examining variation in effect sizes have appeared in the literature. The first approach applies statistical procedures typically used on primary research data, like ANOVA or multiple regression. The effect sizes serve as the dependent variable and comparison features serve as independent or predictor variables. This approach has been criticized based on the questionable tenability of the underlying assumptions (see Hedges & Olkin, 1985). Most notably, traditional inferential statistics assume that the error in measurement is relatively homogeneous across data points (the assumption of homoscedacity). This assumption is often violated in meta-analytic data sets.

The second approach compares the variation in obtained effect sizes with the variation expected due to sampling error (Hunter & Schmidt, 1990). This approach involves calculating not only the observed variance in effects but also the expected variance, given that all observed effects are estimating the same population value. A formal statistical test of the difference between these two values is typically not carried out. Rather, the meta-analyst adopts a critical value for the ratio of observed-to-expected variance to use as a means for rejecting the null hypothesis. The meta-analyst might also adjust effect sizes to account for methodological artifacts such as sampling error, range restrictions, or unreliability of measurements.

The third approach involves the homogeneity statistic described above. Analogous to ANOVA, comparisons are grouped by features and the average effect sizes for these groups are tested to determine if the averages are drawn from the same population. If this hypothesis is rejected, the grouping variable remains a plausible potential moderator of effect.

Sensitivity Analysis.   An additional step in meta-analysis which is gaining popularity is the performance of sensitivity analyses. A sensitivity analysis is used to determine if and how the conclusions of an analysis might differ if it was conducted using different statistical procedures or assumptions. There are numerous points at which a meta-analyst might decide a sensitivity analysis is appropriate. For example, there might be a set of comparisons that fall at the edge of the conceptual definition of what constitutes an acceptably valid measure of SES. The effects of SES might be tested with and without the inclusion of these comparisons. Or, some evaluations of the relation between SES and literacy have missing data. These comparisons might be omitted from one analysis and included in another analysis that makes conservative assumptions about what those values might be.

In sum then, meta-analysts have a wide array of techniques at their disposal. Some of these techniques have been developed specifically for analysis of meta-analytic data sets and others have been adopted from other research methodologies. The specific techniques used in any meta-analysis will differ somewhat depending on the characteristics of the data set and the questions asked by the research synthesist.

Assessment of the Potential for Publication Bias.   As defined earlier, publication bias refers to the well-documented tendency for studies lacking statistically significant effects to go unpublished. All else being equal, studies with "less" statistical significance have smaller intervention effects. Given that these studies are less likely to be published, the risk is that a review might present an overly optimistic (i.e., biased) picture of the evidence. As such, it is increasingly common for reviewers to assess the likelihood that publication bias has affected their results. Rothstein, Sutton, and Borenstein (2005) present a comprehensive overview of the problem of publication bias as well as its assessment. One relatively common technique involves a trim and fill analysis (Duval & Tweedie, 2000). This analysis is based on the assumption that the effects in the observed studies (i.e., the studies included in the review) are drawn from a normally distributed population of effects. With this assumption in mind, the trim and fill analysis essentially examines the distribution of observed effects and "fills" in any effects that appear to be missing. The analysis will generate a new distribution of effects that conforms to the assumption of a normal distribution, and also provides a new estimated effect size that can be compared to the effect size estimated from the observed studies. If the conclusion about the effects of the intervention is similar in both analyses, it lends greater weight to the confidence that can be placed in the conclusion. If the trim and fill analysis suggests that publication bias might be playing a role, caution is warranted.

Unfortunately, the trim and fill analysis is not a perfect solution to the problem of publication bias. The analysis exploits a frequent negative correlation between effect size and study size (ideally, these would be independent). However, there may be good reasons for, say, larger studies to yield smaller effect sizes. For example, interventions may be more difficult to implement as the number of participants increases. If implementation quality is positively related to study outcomes (i.e., better implementation = better outcomes), then this might show up as a negative correlation between study size and study outcomes (i.e., larger studies have smaller effects because they are more difficult to implement with good fidelity). As such, in this case a trim and fill analysis might mistake a problem with implementation fidelity as a problem with publication bias. Despite this limitation, techniques to help assess the plausibility of publication bias should be routinely undertaken in research syntheses. Torgerson et al. (2005) did not carry out a trim and fill analysis, but did produce graphics called funnel plots. These are plots of effects sizes (on the x-axis) and their standard errors (on the y-axis). Just like with the trim and fill analysis, the distribution of effect sizes is analyzed for gaps (the difference is that the analysis is done visually instead of statistically). A good source for issues related to publication bias (including a more complete treatment of funnel plots and the trim and fill procedure) is Rothstein, Sutton, & Borenstein (2005).

When Should a Meta-Analysis Not Be Done?   Recall that Torgerson et al. (2005) developed a very broad question for their research synthesis. They did this because they anticipated that they would find relatively few studies; their intuitions were correct. In all, they identified only 18 studies of an experimental or quasi-experimental nature, and only 9 of these presented data. Given that these 9 studies included interventions designed to affect literacy, numeracy, or both, they reasonably felt that combining these studied was not appropriate. Instead, these reviewers presented tables that detailed for readers important characteristics of studies, such as design, sample size and characteristics, intervention characteristics, and outcome measures. They also provide paragraph descriptions of each study that met inclusion criteria. They conclude by stating:

> It is of concern that the few trials that have been undertaken tend to be of low methodological quality ... substantial heterogeneity between the included studies ... makes it difficult to draw either quantitative or qualitative conclusions about which particular forms of intervention are effective. (p. 99)

We agree with this general approach. Ideally, the conditions under which synthesists will meta-analytically combine data will be operationalized before the data have been collected.

Public Presentation

Research is not complete until results are shared with the scientific community (American Psychological Association, 2001). We have already touched on some of the issues related to public presentation in previous sections. For example, the research synthesist must take care to interpret and report effect sizes in such a manner as to be understandable to the intended audience. Two other potential sources of invalidity are relevant to the public presentation stage. First, leaving out evidence regarding possible moderating influences on main effects can jeopardize the trustworthiness of the conclusions presented by the research synthesist. Second, the research synthesist should ensure that the synthesis techniques employed are transparent to the reader. That is, the synthesist should provide enough information so that readers can critically assess the methods, strengths, and weaknesses of the research synthesis. Halvorsen (1994) and Light, Singer, and Willett (1994) present numerous suggestions regarding effective public presentation techniques.

Other Threats to Validity in Conducting Research Synthesis

As we suggest above, using rigorous and systematic rules for synthesizing a literature does not ensure that the resulting inferences will be infallible. Cooper (1982) pointed to several threats to the validity of research synthesis conclusions. For example, during problem formulation threats to the validity of a synthesis could occur if the synthesist did not pay proper attention to conceptual distinctions in definitions and hypotheses that were viewed as important by others in the field. The validity of a literature search could be compromised by the use of a few selective sources of research reports or by publication bias. The validity of data evaluation can be threatened if information from research reports is missing, or if the individuals extracting information from documents are poorly trained.

Many more threats to the validity of a research synthesis can be identified (Matt & Cook, 1994). We will elaborate on two here. One obvious threat to the validity of meta-analytic conclusions involves the rules of inference employed by a synthesist. The possibility always exists that the meta-analyst has used an invalid rule for inferring a characteristic of the target population. This occurs because the target population does not conform to the assumptions underlying the analysis techniques. Of course, this is not a shortcoming unique to the use of quantitative integration techniques. In non-quantitative syntheses, rules of inference also must be used but it is difficult to gauge their appropriateness because they are not very often made explicit. For meta-analyses, the suppositions of statistical tests are generally known and some statistical biases in reviews can be removed.

Another threat to validity is that the meta-analyst might capitalize on or suffer because of the probabilitistic nature of statistical findings. First, as in primary research, the meta-analyst might conduct many statistical tests without adjusting for "synthesis-wise" error rates. Second, because of gaps in the literature, a meta-analyst might discover so few tests of a particular hypothesis that the statistical power of the meta-analysis is low. Unlike a primary researcher, the meta-analyst cannot sample more participants (or in this case, generate more studies) so as to increase the sensitivity of tests. It is possible, however, to expand the search for relevant research.

The Contribution of Systematic Research Reviews

Systematic research reviewing is not a perfect solution to the problems faced by social and behavioral scientists. But still, it can make important—indeed essential—contributions to the scientific enterprise. The use of proper procedures for the synthesis of multiple studies does more then simply ameliorates the problems associated with the traditional narrative review. Systematic research synthesis transforms the difficulties into strengths. Variation in the context, design, and sampling characteristics of individual studies are sources of consternation when studies are examined individually, serially, and narratively. When multiple studies, each limited in their representation of context, design, and sample, are treated as data points in a second round of scientific investigation they contribute jointly to confident, general, and properly contextualized conclusions about relationships and hypotheses.

Because of the potential value of systematic research reviews in the policy domain, both the producers and consumers of reviews now agree they must think about what distinguishes good from bad reviews. Further, they agree that without high-quality reviews, both theoreticians and practitioners will question the value of research for assisting the development of effective explanations for behavior and behavioral interventions.

References

Abelson, R. P. (1985). A variance explanation paradox: When a little is a lot. *Psychological Bulletin, 97*, 129–133.

American Psychological Association (2001). *Publication manual of the American Psychological Association* (5th ed.). New York: Author.

Barnett, V., & Lewis, T. (1978). *Outliers in statistical data.* Chicester, England: Wiley.

Berlin, J. A., & Rennie, D. (1999). Measuring the quality of trials. *Journal of the American Medical Association, 282*, 1083–1085.

Bushman, B. J. (1994). Vote-counting procedures in meta-analysis. In H. Cooper & L. V. Hedges (Eds.), *Handbook of research synthesis* (pp. 193–213). New York: Russell Sage.

Campbell, D. T., & Stanley, J. C. (1966). *Experimental and quasi-experimental designs for research.* Chicago: Rand McNally.

Cohen, J. (1988). *Statistical power analysis in the behavioral sciences.* Hillsdale, NJ: Erlbaum.

Cook, T. D., & Campbell, D. T. (1979). *Quasi-experimentation: Design and analysis issues for field settings.* Chicago: Rand McNally.

Cook, T. D., Cooper, H. M., Cordray, D. S., Hartmann, H., Hedges, L. V., Light, R. J., Louis, T., & Mosteller, F. (1992). *Meta-analysis for explanation: A casebook.* New York: Russell Sage.

Cooper, H. M. (1979). Statistically combining independent studies: A meta-analysis of sex differences in conformity research. *Journal of Personality and Social Psychology, 37*, 131–146.

Cooper, H. M. (1982). Scientific guidelines for conducting integrative research reviews. *Review of Educational Research, 52*, 291–302.

Cooper, H. M. (1998). *Synthesizing research: A guide for literature reviews* (3rd ed.). Thousand Oaks, CA: Sage.

Cooper, H., Charlton, K., Valentine, J. V., & Muhlenbruck, L. (2000). Making the most of summer school: A meta-analytic and narrative review. *Monographs on Child Development, 65*(1). Malden, MA: Blackwell Press.

Cooper, H., DeNeve, K., & Charlton, K. (1997). Finding the missing science: The fate of studies submitted for review by a human subjects committee. *Psychological Methods, 2*, 447–452.

Cooper, H., & Dorr, N. (1995). Race comparisons on need for achievement: A meta-analytic alternative to Graham's narrative review. *Review of Educational Research, 65,* 483.

Cooper, H., & Hedges, L. V. (1994). *Handbook of research synthesis.* New York: Russell Sage.

Cooper, H. M., & Rosenthal, R. (1980). Statistical versus traditional procedures for summarizing research findings. *Psychological Bulletin, 87,* 442–449.

DuBois, D. L., Holloway, B. E., Valentine, J. C., & Cooper, H. (2002). Effectiveness of meta-analytic programs for youth: A meta-analytic review. *American Journal of Community Psychology, 30,* 157–197.

Duval S. J., & Tweedie R. L. (2000). A non-parametric "trim and fill" method of accounting for publication bias in meta-analysis. *Journal of the American Statistical Association, 95,* 89–98.

Eddy, D. M., Hasselblad, V., & Schachter, R. (1992). *Meta-analysis by the confidence profile method.* Boston, MA: Academic Press.

Feldman, K. A. (1971). Using the work of others: Some observations on reviewing and integrating. *Sociology of Education, 4,* 86–102.

Fisher, R. A. (1932). *Statistical methods for research workers.* London: Oliver & Boyd.

Glass, G. V. (1976). Primary, secondary, and meta-analysis of research. *Educational Researcher, 5,* 3–8.

Glass, G. V., McGaw, B., & Smith, M. L. (1981). *Meta-analysis in social research.* Beverly Hills, CA: Sage.

Glass, G. V., & Smith, M. L. (1979). Meta-analysis of research on class size and achievement. *Educational Evaluation and Policy Analysis, 1,* 2–16.

Gleser, L. J., & Olkin, I. (1994). Stochastically dependent effect sizes. In H. Cooper & L. V. Hedges (Eds.). *Handbook of research synthesis.* New York: Russell Sage.

Greenberg, J., & Folger, R. (1988). *Controversial issues in social research methods.* New York: Springer-Verlag.

Greenhouse, J. B. & Iyengar, S. (1994). Sensitivity analysis and diagnostics. In H. Cooper & L. V. Hedges (Eds.), *Handbook of research synthesis* (pp. 383–398). New York: Russell Sage.

Greenwald, A. (1975). Consequences of prejudice against the null hypothesis. *Psychological Bulletin, 82,* 1–20.

Halvorsen, K. T. (1994). The reporting format. In H. Cooper & L. V. Hedges (Eds.), *Handbook of research synthesis* (pp. 425–438). New York: Russell Sage.

Hedges, L. V., & Olkin, I. (1985). *Statistical methods for meta-analysis.* Orlando, FL: Academic Press.

Hedges, L. V., & Vevea, J. L. (1998). Fixed and random effects models in meta-analysis. *Psychological Methods, 3,* 486–504.

Hunter, J. E., & Schmidt, F. L. (1990). *Methods of meta-analysis: Correcting error and bias in research findings.* Beverly Hills, CA: Sage.

Hunter, J. E., Schmidt, F. L., & Hunter, R. (1979). Differential validity of employment tests by race: A comprehensive review and analysis. *Psychological Bulletin, 86,* 721–735.

Hunter, J. E., Schmidt, F. L., & Jackson, G. B. (1982). *Meta-analysis: Cumulating research findings across studies.* Beverly Hills, CA: Sage.

Jackson, G. B. (1980). Methods for integrative reviews. *Review of Educational Research, 50,* 438–460.

Johnson, B. (1989). *DSTAT: Software for the meta-analytic review of research literatures.* Hillsdale, NJ. Erlbaum.

Jüni, P., Witschi, A., Bloch, R., & Egger, M. (1999). The hazards of scoring the quality of clinical trials for meta-analysis. *Journal of the American Medical Association, 282,* 1054–1060.

Light, R. J. (Ed.) (1983). *Evaluation studies review annual* (Vol. 8). Beverly Hills, CA: Russell Sage.

Light, R. J., & Pillemer, D. B. (1984). *Summing up: The science of research reviewing.* Cambridge, MA: Harvard University Press.

Light, R. J., Singer, J. D., & Willett, J. B. (1994). The visual presentation and interpretation of meta-analyses. In H. Cooper & L. V. Hedges (Eds.), *Handbook of research synthesis* (pp. 439–453). New York: Russell Sage.

Light, R .J., & Smith, P. V. (1971). Accumulating evidence: Procedures for resolving contradictions among research studies. *Harvard Educational Review, 41,* 429–471.

Lipsey, M. W. (1994). Identifying potentially interesting variables and analysis opportunities. In H. Cooper & L. V. Hedges (Eds.), *The handbook of research synthesis* (pp. 111–123). New York: Russell Sage.

Lipsey, M. W., & Wilson, D. B. (2001). *Practical meta-analysis.* Thousand Oaks, CA: Sage.

Matt, G. E. & Cook, T. D. (1994). Threats to the validity of research syntheses. In H. Cooper & L. V. Hedges (Eds.), *Handbook of research synthesis* (pp. 503–520). New York: Russell Sage.

Miller, N., Lee, J., & Carlson, M. (1991). The validity of inferential judgments when used in theory-testing meta-analysis. *Personality and Social Psychology Bulletin, 17,* 335–343.

Moher, D., Schulz, K. F., & Altman, D. G. for the CONSORT Group (2001). The CONSORT Statement: Revised recommendations for improving the records of parallel-group randomised trials. *The Lancet, 357,* 1191–1194.

Olkin, I. (1992, July/August). Reconcilable differences: Gleaning insight from conflicting scientific studies. *The Sciences,* 30–36.

Orwin, R. G. (1994). Evaluating coding decisions. In H. Cooper & L. V. Hedges (Eds.), *Handbook of research synthesis* (pp. 139–162). New York: Russell Sage.

Overton, R. C. (1998). A comparison of fixed-effects and mixed (random-effects) models for meta-analysis tests of moderator variable effects. *Psychological Methods, 3,* 354–379

Pearson, K. (1904). Report on certain enteric fever inoculation statistics. *British Medical Journal, 3,* 1243–1246.

Raudenbush, S. W., Becker, B. J., & Kalaian, H. (1988). Modeling multivariate effect sizes. *Psychological Bulletin, 103,* 111–120.

Rosenthal, R. (1984). *Meta-analytic procedures for social research.* Beverly Hills, CA: Sage.

Rosenthal, R., & Rosnow, R. L. (1991). *Essentials of behavioral research: Methods and data analysis* (2nd ed.). New York: McGraw Hill.

Rosenthal, R., & Rubin, D. (1978). Interpersonal expectancy effects: The first 345 studies. *Behavioral and Brain Sciences, 3,* 377–415.

Rosenthal, R., & Rubin, D. (1982). Comparing effect sizes of independent studies. *Psychological Bulletin, 92,* 500–504.

Rothstein, H. R., Sutton, A. J., & Borenstein, M. (Eds.) (2005). *Publication bias in meta-analysis: Prevention, assessment, and adjustments.* Chichester, England: Wiley.

SAS Institute. (1992). *SAS user's guide: Statistics* (Version 6). Cary, NC: Author.

Shadish, W. R., & Haddock, C. K. (1994). Combining estimates of effect size. In H. Cooper & L. V. Hedges (Eds.). *Handbook of research synthesis* (pp. 261–282). New York: Russell Sage.

Steering Committee of the Physicians' Health Study Research Group (1988). Preliminary report: Findings from the aspirin component of the ongoing physicians' health study. *New England Journal of Medicine, 318,* 262–264.

Stock, W. A. (1994). Systematic coding for research synthesis. In H. Cooper & L. V. Hedges (Eds.), *Handbook of research synthesis* (pp. 125–138). New York: Russell Sage.

Stock, W. A., Okun, M. A., Haring, M. J., Miller, W., Kinney, C., & Ceurvorst, R. W. (1982). Rigor in data synthesis: A case study of reliability in meta-analysis. *Educational Researcher, 11*(6), 10–14, 20.

Torgerson, C., Porthouse, J., & Brooks, G. (2005). A systematic review of controlled trials evaluating interventions in adult literacy and numeracy. *Journal of Research in Reading, 28,* 87–107.

Wachter, K. W., & Straf, M. L. (Eds.). (1990). *The future of meta-analysis.* New York: Russell Sage.

Weber, R. P. (1990). *Basic content analysis* (2nd ed.). Thousand Oaks, CA: Sage.

Part III

Research on Adult Development

Epistemological, Intrapersonal, and Interpersonal Development in the College Years and Young Adulthood

Marcia Baxter Magolda, Elisa Abes, and Vasti Torres

One of the hallmarks of young adulthood is shifting from a life guided by adult authorities to guiding one's adult life. On the surface, this task appears to be one of gaining employment, living independently and entering into adult relationships. However, as Robert Kegan (1994) persuasively articulated, there are mental demands of adult life underlying these tangible tasks. Whether at work, school, or home, Kegan argued that adults are expected to be self-initiating, guided by their own visions, responsible for their experience, and able to bring these capacities into interdependent relations with diverse others (pp. 302–303). Taking responsibility for one's life is a complex and challenging experience that involves, among other things, realizing your role in composing reality, making meaning for yourself instead of accepting meaning others make for you, sorting out who you are (e.g., complex social identities), what you believe, and how you want to relate to others. Jordana, a 19-year-old Latina college sophomore, described a crucial aspect of this shift:

> Normal makes me angry a little bit. Because it's what I've been trying to reach, and I couldn't reach it, you know? And it was a liberation when I realized, there is no normal! And then you come to realize everybody doesn't know that! Evidently I know it, but not everybody knows it, and now I have to go and convince the world that there is no normal, and that's really difficult. Especially when they think they're normal or something. (Abes & Jones, 2004, p. 622)

Although Jordana shares this perspective in the course of exploring her lesbian identity, she could be speaking for the multitude of young adults who struggle with the discovery that what they've been taught is "normal" is not the only perspective (or truth) from which to approach adult life. Whether it is racial, ethnic, gender, class or sexual orientation stereotypes, religious or secular values, or career expectations, young adults discover that adults around them composed these "normals" and they can recompose them to define themselves. Like Jordana, they experience the tension between liberation from external forces, the pressure of responsibility to define a new normal for themselves, and the nagging desire to be "normal."

What role does—or should—the college experience play in this shift? Some regard college as acquiring skills and information for the tangible tasks of adulthood, primarily gainful employment. As Kegan (1994) and other developmental scholars illustrate, success in adult life requires developing complex ways of making meaning that enable one to meet the mental demands of modern life. The shift from an externally guided life to guiding one's life requires a fundamental transformation of making meaning from following formulas acquired uncritically from external authorities to making meaning by internally choosing one's beliefs, identity and relationships (Baxter Magolda, 2001,

2004b; Kegan, 1994). This chapter is about this developmental transformation in meaning-making and its relationship to learning.

Learning and Developmental Frameworks

We use as starting points Kegan's (1982, 1994, 2000) constructive-developmental psychological line of thought and Mezirow's (2000) transformational learning educational line of thought. Mezirow described transformational learning as:

> the process by which we transform our taken-for-granted frames of reference (meaning perspectives, habits of mind, mind-sets) to make them more inclusive, discriminating, open, emotionally capable of change, and reflective so that they may generate beliefs and opinions that will prove more true or justified to guide action. (2000, pp. 7–8)

Mezirow (2000) emphasized that transformational learning focuses on "how we learn to negotiate and act on our own purposes, values, feelings, and meanings rather than those we have uncritically assimilated from others" (p. 8). Transformational learning requires fundamental shifts in meaning-making that Kegan (1994) describes as "growth of the mind" (p. 34). The constructive-developmental perspective hinges on the notions that humans construct and organize reality and that our constructions "evolve through eras according to regular principles of stability and change" (Kegan, 1982, p. 8). At any given point in time, our meaning-making structures are a combination of elements over which we have control (what Kegan calls *object*) and elements that have control over us (what Kegan calls *subject*). Object is "distinct enough from us that we can do something with it" (Kegan, 1994, p. 32); subject "refers to those elements of our knowing or organizing that we are identified with, tied to, fused with, or embedded in. We *have* object; we *are* subject (1994, p. 32, italics in original). Growth of the mind comes from "liberating ourselves from that in which we were embedded, making what was subject into object so that we can 'have it' rather than 'be had' by it" (1994, p. 34). A key task of young adulthood, and of learning in college, is to liberate oneself from meanings uncritically assimilated from others to construct new meanings for oneself. This sounds like exactly the kind of expectation college faculty and administrators have of college students.

Transformational learning supports informational learning because "*what* individuals learn and claim to know is grounded in *how* they construct their knowledge" (King & Baxter Magolda, 1996, p. 165, italics added). Consider this example. A zoology professor advanced this goal for his students: "I want them to understand how information is gained. I want them to appreciate what facts really mean. Tentative facts. That's what all of science is. Subject to change and revision" (Baxter Magolda, 1999, p. 3). Ann, a college senior in this course, reacted at the end of the term with this comment: "He was trying to give examples to show what happened. But if he had … just said the point, I would believe him because he is the teacher. I don't need the proof. It's not like I'm going to argue with him about it" (Baxter Magolda, 1999, p. 3). *How* Ann constructed knowledge (i.e., knowledge is certain, the teacher as authority has this knowledge, students accept it) mediated *what* she learned in the course. She attempted to memorize the facts rather than gain an understanding of how they were constructed and how they might be reconstructed as new scientific evidence comes to light.

Ann's story demonstrates the link between learning and development; however, it also demonstrates the integrated approach we take to development in this chapter. Part of

Ann's approach to learning in zoology was based on her assumptions about the nature of knowledge, or the epistemological dimension of development. An equally important influence was how she perceived herself as a learner, or the intrapersonal dimension of development, and how she perceived her relationship with her instructor, or the interpersonal dimension of development. She perceived herself as a passive recipient of knowledge rather than as a constructor of knowledge, thus she did not need the proof in order to believe the professor. She could not conceive of arguing with him because her role was to receive the knowledge he already possessed. The way young (and older) adults construct knowledge, their identities, and their relationships with others combine to form the ways they organize their experience (Baxter Magolda, 2001; Kegan, 1994).

Today's College Students

Today's college students enroll in higher education at various stages of life, come from various social contexts, and engage the college experience for diverse purposes. Much of the college student development literature focuses on traditional-aged students who attend college between the ages of 18 and 24. Developmental literature on adults from their twenties to mid-life, often constructed outside the context of college, informs our understanding of the development of those who enter college at later ages. These two lines of research are often separate; we use both to augment contemporary longitudinal studies of college student and young adult development to paint a comprehensive picture of the possibilities of development in college.

We also intentionally focus our exploration of adult development on diverse populations to portray the complexity of development mediated by social context. We include in our discussion both women and men, people of color and Whites, people from varied social classes, and people with varied sexual orientations. Doing so enables us to explore crucial social mediators of development such as oppression, stereotyping, and privilege (Pizzolato, 2003; Steele & Aronson, 1995; Torres, 2003a; Torres & Hernandez, 2007; Torres, Howard-Hamilton & Cooper, 2003).

Organization of the Chapter

We begin by articulating the elements and nature of an integrated view of adult development based on contemporary research. We outline the epistemological, intrapersonal, and interpersonal dimensions of development and highlight how they interweave throughout various ways of making meaning. We introduce the role of individual and contextual factors in mediating how adults make meaning. Rather than summarizing multiple theories of this kind of development, we place the person in the foreground of our integrated exploration of development in college. To illustrate this integrated view of development, we use longitudinal data from all three authors' research to offer a portrait of adults who are externally defined, of adults struggling with the transition from external to internal definition, and of adults who are internally defined. In each of these segments, we incorporate research that informs various dimensions of these portraits and that demonstrates the effect of social context on these portraits. We organize the chapter this way to offer an integrated view of development rather than a compendium of theoretical perspectives, many of which focus on only one dimension. We intentionally begin with the particular—dynamics of gender, race, ethnicity, social class, and sexual orientation—to emphasize the dynamic and varied nature of developmental possibilities. We incorporate seminal theoretical perspectives and their important contributions to understanding development, yet simultaneously foreground the particulars that help us understand today's diverse college students.

Next, we explore research linking development and learning. We then devote considerable attention to how higher education can promote the transformative learning and ways of making meaning needed by young adults to succeed in adult life. We review contemporary models of practice that emerge from the integrated view of development we advance in sufficient detail for readers to analyze and alter their educational practice to promote learning and development. We raise practical issues inherent in enabling the fundamental shift in meaning-making toward self-authorship. Finally, we introduce research that challenges this developmental trajectory, using this research in juxtaposition to the integrated view to identify future research questions.

Integrated View of Development

> One thing that is very apparent to me—I spent the entire decade of my 20s getting in touch with who I was and what is important to me.—Kurt (Baxter Magolda, 2004b, p. 24)

Kurt, a participant in Baxter Magolda's (2001) longitudinal study of young adult development, articulated the driving questions he and his peers grappled with during their twenties. Dealing with the "who am I?" question meant figuring out one's identity in all of its multiple dimensions. More importantly, it meant figuring it out for oneself rather than accepting external definitions of who one *should* be. Kurt noted, "You have to learn that it does come from inside. For a while you think others can make decisions; you learn in the end that it comes down to you" (Baxter Magolda, 2001, p. 127). Kurt's "what is important to me" encompasses two closely related questions: "how do I know?" and "what relationships do I want?" Young adults grow up learning what external authorities know. At some point, usually during college, they realize that knowledge claims come from inside as well. Thus, figuring out the basis for one's beliefs and values is another major task of young adulthood. A closely related task is ascertaining how to relate to others in the world based on these beliefs, values and identities. Kurt's commentary highlights the three major dimensions of adult development that lurk underneath most societal expectations of young adults. Society expects that young adults become effective citizens who make mature decisions for themselves and others, have a solid sense of who they are, and engage in mature relationships require maturity on the epistemological, intrapersonal, and interpersonal dimensions of development.

The Epistemological Dimension: How Do I Know?[1]

How people use assumptions about the nature, limits, and certainty of knowledge to make knowledge claims is the *epistemological* dimension of development. Mature decision-making requires viewing knowledge as contextual, or constructed using relevant evidence in a particular context. A contextual view of knowledge recognizes that multiple perspectives exist depending on how people structure knowledge claims. This makes shifting perspectives and using multiple cultural frames possible. It further requires the capacity to participate in constructing, evaluating, and interpreting judgments in light of available evidence and frames of reference. Contextual knowers construct knowledge claims internally, critically analyzing external perspectives rather than adopting them uncritically. Increasing maturity in knowledge construction yields an internal belief system that guides thinking and behavior, yet is open to reconstruction given relevant evidence. Mature decision-making and problem-solving depend on these epistemological capacities. This dimension is central to achieving cognitive maturity as well as a necessary ingredient for achieving a solid sense of self and mature relationships.

Intrapersonal Dimension: Who Am I?[2]

How people view themselves and construct their identities is the *intrapersonal* dimension of development. An integrated identity requires the ability to reflect on, explore and choose enduring values. It requires coordinating various characteristics (including social identities of race, ethnicity, sexual orientation, gender, and social class) to form a coherent identity that gains stability over time yet is open to growth. To be coherent and enduring, this integrated identity must be internally constructed rather than adopted to seek external approval. An integrated identity serves as a foundation for interpreting experience and conducting oneself in the world. Understanding one's particular history, confidence, the capacity for autonomy and connection, and integrity all depend on these intrapersonal capacities. These intrapersonal developmental capacities are central to achieving an integrated identity as well as necessary for mature decision-making and mature relationships. For example, constructing an internal belief system and using it in decision-making (i.e., cognitive maturity) requires an internal identity that is not overly dependent on the views of others. Similarly, choosing one's values and identity characteristics (i.e., integrated identity) requires contextual knowing in which one takes responsibility for constructing knowledge.

Interpersonal Dimension: How Do I Relate to Others?[3]

How people view themselves in relation to others and how they construct relationships is the *interpersonal* dimension of development. Mature relationships are characterized by respect for both self and others' particular identities as well as by collaboration to negotiate and integrate multiple perspectives and needs. The capacity for interdependence is the foundation of mature relationships. Interdependence requires openness to other perspectives without being consumed by them. An integrated identity makes this interdependence possible by prioritizing self-approval as a criterion with which to judge others' perspectives. This is not a return to egocentricity but rather a turning away from self-sacrifice to please others (illustrated in Kurt's narrative later in the chapter). Kegan (1994) describes this as having relationships rather than being had by them. From this vantage point, it is no longer threatening to see differences (e.g., cultural, political, geographical) or to acknowledge that people hold multiple perspectives; this capacity enables the individual to become interculturally mature (Kegan, 1994; King & Baxter Magolda, 2005; King & Shuford, 1996). Mutuality (Jordan, 1997, 2004) is possible due to the capacity to explore others' perspectives as well as one's own. These interpersonal capacities are central to mature relationships as well as to having a solid sense of self and mature decision-making. For example, constructing an internal belief system (i.e., cognitive maturity) and achieving an integrated identity both require avoiding being consumed by others' perspectives. Similarly, authentic engagement in interdependent relationships requires an integrated identity. It also requires the acceptance of multiple perspectives and the internal belief system possible with cognitive maturity.

Journey Toward Self-Authorship

Reliance on external authority for one's beliefs, identity and relations with others is typical in the late teens and early twenties (Baxter Magolda, 2001; Kegan, 1994; King & Kitchener, 1994; Parks, 2000). Baxter Magolda (2001) captured this notion with the phrase, *following external formulas*. The epistemological dimension of this reliance is characterized by viewing knowledge as certain or partially certain and held by authorities. The lack of an internal basis for evaluating knowledge claims, or even the lack of awareness that an internal basis is important, results in externally defined beliefs. This can result in viewing different cultural practices as wrong or accepting negative stereotypes about social identities (Abes & Jones, 2004; King & Baxter Magolda, 2005; Torres & Baxter Magolda, 2004). In the intrapersonal realm, there is a similar lack of awareness of one's own values and social identity. The lack of coordination of multiple components of identity (e.g., race, ethnicity, sexual orientation, social class, gender) and a high need for others' approval yield an externally defined identity susceptible to changing external pressures and stereotypes. Difference is often viewed as a threat to identity from this perspective. This susceptibility plays out in the interpersonal dimension as dependent relations with similar others are the source of identity and needed affirmation. Participation in relationships is framed as acquiring others' approval.

Shifts in all three dimensions emerge when young adults encounter difficulty following external formulas. The increasing awareness of one's role in composing reality leads young adults into a *crossroads* where tension between external authority and the growing internal voice abounds (Baxter Magolda, 2001). The epistemological dimension is marked by an evolving awareness and acceptance of uncertainty and multiple perspectives. An accompanying shift from accepting authority's knowledge claims to personal processes for adopting knowledge claims raises the specter of "how I know." Young adults at this crossroads recognize the need to take responsibility for choosing their own beliefs. A similar set of realizations occurs in the intrapersonal dimension as awareness of one's own values and sense of identity, distinct from external others' perceptions, evolves. The resulting tension between emerging internal values and external pressures prompts self-exploration and recognition of the need to take responsibility for crafting one's own identity internally. This often entails exploring various aspects of social identities as well as immersion in those "cultures" (Abes & Jones, 2004; Helms, 1995; Torres & Baxter Magolda, 2004; Torres & Hernandez, 2007). Young adults realize the need to bring this newly crafted identity into relationships. A growing awareness of the limitations of dependent relationships leads to a struggle to reconstruct or extract oneself from these relationships. An increased willingness to interact with diverse others and refraining from judgment emerges as affirmation needs recede (King & Baxter Magolda, 2005).

Self-authorship reflects maturity on all three developmental dimensions. Baxter Magolda's longitudinal participants who achieved self-authorship acknowledged the uncertainty of knowledge and crafted their own internal belief systems. They engaged in intense self-reflection to explore and choose their internal values and identity. This sometimes involved renegotiating relationships to balance their internal beliefs and identity with those of others in a mutual fashion. Kegan (1994) described self-authorship as fourth order, a way of making meaning in which values, beliefs, convictions, generalizations, ideals, abstractions, interpersonal loyalty and intrapersonal states of mind emerge from being co-constructed with others external to the self. He wrote that fourth order meaning-making:

takes all of these as objects or elements of its system, rather than the system itself; it does not identify with them but views them as parts of a new whole. This new whole is an ideology, an internal identity, a *self-authorship* that can coordinate, integrate, act upon, or invent values, beliefs, convictions, generalizations, ideals, abstractions, interpersonal loyalties, and intrapersonal states. It is no longer *authored by* them, it *authors them* and thereby achieves a personal authority. (1994, p. 185, italics in original)

As Kurt noted, emerging from co-construction to achieve self-authorship took most of his twenties. Parks (2000), writing about faith development in young adulthood, asserted that between the ages of 17 and 30 a distinctive mode of making meaning emerges that "includes: (1) becoming critically aware of one's own composing of reality, (2) self-consciously participating in an ongoing dialogue toward truth, and (3) cultivating a capacity to respond—to act—in ways that are satisfying and just" (p. 6). Parks noted that this mode of meaning-making emerges as young adults struggle with questions about forms of knowing (i.e., epistemological dimensions), forms of dependence (i.e., intrapersonal dimension), and forms of community (i.e., interpersonal dimension).

Individual and Contextual Dynamics

Although researchers report observing this overarching trajectory toward self-authorship in multiple young adult populations, the pace at which it occurs and the particulars of the journey vary across contexts. Part of the complexity of this multi-dimensional transformation is the dynamic blend of individual and environmental factors that mediate it. Kegan (1982) noted that we make meaning in the space between our experiences and our reactions to them—"the place where the event is privately composed, made sense of, the place where it actually *becomes* an event for that person" (p. 2, italics in original). The meaning we make of our experiences, and how we make that meaning (through our epistemological, intrapersonal and interpersonal capacities) determines the salience of experiences in our development. Thus environmental factors—everything from our immediate contexts to larger societal contexts—play a part in our developmental journeys to the extent and the way in which we make meaning of them. For example, Zaytoun (2003) explored how social contexts might shape conceptualizations of self, knowing, and relationships. She argued, "When social identity is considered in self-concept construction, broader possibilities emerge for thinking about self and interconnectedness. The self is intricately imbedded in relationships not only to other people, but to aspects of the world that include social groups, communities, and inanimate and spiritual entities that are deemed important to the individual according to social influence and identity categories within which they relate" (p. 86). Similarly, Goldberger (1996) illuminates how familial, community, cultural and political contexts mediate orientation to authority, a component of ways of knowing. Helms (1995) describes racial identity development as occurring "by way of the evolution or differentiation of successive racial identity statuses, where *statuses* are defined as the dynamic cognitive, emotional, and behavioral processes that govern a person's interpretation of racial information in his or her interpersonal environment" (p. 184, italics in original). Among the environmental factors that interact with the pace and particulars of development are societal structures such as heterosexism, ethnocentrism, classism, and racism, and the resulting binary relationships associated with privilege and oppression.

Empirical studies illuminate some of these possibilities. Abes and Jones (2004) demonstrated that lesbian college students' meaning-making structures filtered contextual influences such as family background, peer culture, stereotypes and norms, many of which were grounded in heterosexist assumptions. They wrote, "As meaning-making grew more complex, the participants grew more capable of filtering contextual influences, and thus were increasingly able to decide for themselves how context shaped their identity" (p. 619). Torres' (2003a) longitudinal study of Latino/a young adults revealed that those who grew up in environments with greater diversity and acculturated parents developed their ethnic identity and openness to multiple cultures more easily than those who grew up in majority White culture. Those who perceived themselves as privileged did not believe negative stereotypes applied to them but applied the stereotypes to others; those who perceived less privilege were open to others and more likely to have experienced and to be aware of racism.

Pizzolato (2003) reported how the experiences of high-risk college students prompt movement toward self-authorship prior to college. Attending college was often in conflict with what their peers and communities expected of them, and their peers' negative behavior often served as the dissonance that prompted high-risk students to internally define attending college as a goal. Their self-authorship, however, wavered early in college as others' doubts about their capability and marginalization of their identities pushed them to behave in ways to gain acceptance rather than in ways consistent with their internal goals. Personal characteristics and coping strategies influenced the ways these students made sense of these challenges and their ability to return to self-authorship. These examples, which we will pursue in more depth in the discussion that follows, underscore the importance of taking an integrated, multidimensional approach to young adult development that acknowledges the dynamic interaction between personal and contextual factors.

Journeys from External to Internal Authorship

We use narratives from our three longitudinal studies to explore what an integrated view of adult development looks like across the trajectory from external to internal definition. Abes' 2-year longitudinal study (2003, in press; Abes & Jones, 2004) explores lesbian identity development and relationships among multiple social identities such as race, ethnicity, sexual orientation, and faith. Baxter Magolda's 22-year longitudinal study (1992, 2001) of young adults from age 18 to 40 explores the evolution of epistemological, intrapersonal and interpersonal development toward self-authorship. Torres' 4-year longitudinal study (2003a, 2004; Torres & Hernandez, 2007) of Latino/a student development explores the multiple dynamics of cultural choices made during college. Narratives from these three studies illustrate both overarching patterns of adult development and particulars that vary due to individual and contextual factors. Although we sketch three broad phases of development—external formulas, crossroads, and self-authorship—as an overarching pattern evident in each study, the narratives illustrate individual variation within this pattern. We incorporate the developmental literature, as well as literature related to race and class, in the discussion of these narratives to demonstrate how literature that addresses separate dimensions of development can be linked to form an integrated view.

Following External Formulas

Young adult college students often make their way in the world following formulas obtained from external sources (Baxter Magolda, 2001). They take what they are told as *Truth* or "normal," and this foundation guides their beliefs, values, identity and relationships with others. This interconnectivity among the three dimensions sustains their reliance on external formulas to succeed in college and adult life. Although we bring each dimension to the foreground for exploration and highlight it with participant quotations, the participants' comments routinely blend beliefs, identity and relationships. Movement from these external formulas emerges only when sufficient dissonance occurs in at least one of the dimensions to spark development.

Adopting External Truths.   Martin, a participant in Torres' longitudinal study, offers a perspective on his Latino culture and Anglo culture that exemplifies external formulas:

> My cousin, she got married to someone who is an Anglo, but he doesn't even look like an Anglo. He's like a Mexican. He is always partying and making jokes and everything. And when they got married, I was expecting his family to be serious. So I was like, all the family was dancing, and I was like okay. (Torres & Hernandez, 2007, p. 567)

Martin's source of information on Anglo culture, and thus his assumptions that Anglos were serious, was television. He followed this external formula to determine how Anglos should be, because he did not have the epistemological capacity to evaluate the validity of the external authority. He used the experience living in an area of the United States where Latinos compose the majority as the source of his perspective of what was normal. Without the ability to evaluate these external formulas, Martin accepted them as knowledge. Nora, another participant in the same study, also saw the differences between cultures as externally defined. She saw Mexicans as being stricter and Americans as being liberal. She had limited experiences with Anglos because she attended a private Mexican high school; her parents had explained this external formula and she accepted it as truth (Torres, 2005).

These dichotomous views of the world, based on the belief that knowledge is certain, are characteristic of college students relying directly on external authority for the truth. Perry (1970) called this dualistic thinking, reflecting the notion that since knowledge is certain perspectives are sorted into two categories: right and wrong. Similarly, Baxter Magolda's (1992) absolute knowers believed that knowledge was certain and possessed by authorities. Belenky, Clinchy, Goldberger, and Tarule (1986) observed this way of making meaning in their received knowers who focused on taking in knowledge from authorities. King and Kitchener's (1994) pre-reflective thinkers also relied on authorities for certain knowledge and relied on direct observations to ascertain what to believe if knowledge was temporarily uncertain. Parks (2000) noted this authority-bound way of knowing in faith development. Belenky et al. identified an even more profound absence of voice—silence—in their "youngest and the most socially, economically, and educationally deprived" participants (p. 24). This lack of voice also emerged in a project that brought together isolated, poor, rural mothers (Belenky, Bond, & Weinstock, 1997), indicating that social class can play a mediating role in epistemological development.

As students encounter dissonance, they become aware of uncertainty in various areas of knowledge and multiple perspectives. However, they have not yet developed the epistemological capacity to evaluate evidence and make decisions about what to believe, so they continue to rely on external formulas. One typical context in which this occurs is career decisions. Kurt describes the external formulas that guided his career choices:

> I've been wanting to be an attorney. That's been something that's driven me ever since sixth grade. I was steered away from that for a while. People were saying, "Kurt,

there are too many attorneys. Go be something else. Be a businessman." And I'm like, "Okay." So I did that, and then I took a couple of years in the business school, and I'm like, "No, I don't want to do this. I want to be an attorney." The fact that I still think I want to be an attorney motivated me to go after this position, because they're going to be paying for my law school. I was like, "Kurt, as long as the opportunity presents itself, you can't let those kinds of things pass you by and not take advantage of them." Another priority I had for this position was, I guess it was just because it's the right thing for me to do right now. (Baxter Magolda, 2004b, p. 26)

Kurt listened to authorities earlier to pursue business. When he realized he did not like business, he sought an opportunity that would help him become an attorney. He saw this position as helping him know whether he wanted to be an attorney and providing the financial ability to pursue it. He discovered that he could no longer rely on authority for right answers, so he sought out a process that would help him arrive at the right answer. Although he is not accepting authority without question, his approach still reflects following an external formula toward career success. Kurt's focus on a process is consistent with Perry's (1970) description of early multiplicity when students realize that some knowledge is not known at present even to authorities and they need a new way to resolve questions. Baxter Magolda (1992) labeled this way of making meaning transitional knowing, describing it as a shift from acquiring knowledge from authorities to attempting to understanding it. King and Kitchener (1994) portray a similar way of making meaning in the latter stage of pre-reflective thinking in which some knowledge is temporarily uncertain. Students using these ways of making meaning rely on authorities to guide them through these uncertain arenas. Belenky et al.'s (1986) subjective knowing is a version of this same meaning-making, but women in their study tended to rely on experience at this juncture rather than authorities.

Despite similarity in following external formulas for what to believe, women and men often exhibit varying styles in how they follow these formulas. Belenky et al. (1986) first described a connected version of epistemological development that emerged from their participants' tendency to try to believe what they heard first, or to connect to what they were trying to know, prior to trying to doubt it. This contrasted with Perry's (1970) description of an agentic style of knowing in which students stood apart from what they were trying to know. Baxter Magolda's (1992) participants' use of both connected and separate styles of knowing revealed that the styles reflected equally complex ways of knowing and that while gender-related, the styles were not gender exclusive. Day Shaw (2001) observed these same connected and separate styles in the external ways of knowing Black and Latino students in her study expressed.

Adopting Externally Defined Identities.   Relying on external authorities for what to believe translates to using external formulas to define one's identity. In the case of students from some non-majority groups, they also use them to decide what identity labels to adopt. For example, Bob explained that his parents tell him he is, "Hispanic because I was born in the United States, and Mexican … because everyone in my family is Mexican" (Torres, 2004, p. 462). When asked what the label meant to him, he responded with an explanation that focused on geographic meaning instead of internal meaning (Torres, 2004). This relatively superficial geographic meaning illustrates that Bob has yet to construct his own ethnic identity. For Latino/a students and other diverse ethnic populations, their initial identity label can come from their parents whose authority they accept (Torres, 2004).

Similarly, many White students adopt external definitions of identity and values from their families of origin. Helms' (1995) model of White racial identity ego statuses explains that Whites in the contact status are "satisfied with the racial status quo and oblivious to racism and one's participation in it" (p. 185). Identity development theorists refer to unexamined identities as foreclosed (Josselson, 1987; Marcia, 1966, 2002; Phinney, 1990) because the commitment to an identity is made without exploration of possibilities or internal construction of values. Phinney (1993) described acceptance of external meanings without evaluation or exploration as unexamined ethnic identity. Similarly, Helms (1995) described external self-definition as a characteristic of her conformity (pre-encounter) racial identity status for people of color. Ossana, Helms, and Leonard (1992) described the pre-encounter stage of their womanist identity model as conformity to societal gender roles. Day Shaw (2001) noted that some of the college students in her study who used absolute and transitional knowing reflected characteristics of the pre-encounter status in their expectations of same-race faculty.

Unlike Bob, some students use an identity label to express themselves. Billie, one of Abes' longitudinal participants, came out as a lesbian to her friends and family while in college. While she found this process liberating, she accepted an external construction of the meaning of the label lesbian.

> I myself have no problem with labels... I think it's like trying to figure yourself out... It's just a part of it what I don't really have to worry about, because I don't have to think about it. It took me a while to find my place. So I'm comfortable in that place for now. I don't want to be changing it... I have a place in the world. (Abes & Jones, 2004, p. 620)

In Billie's case, she found the label "lesbian" as a way to express her sexual orientation identity and find a place in the world. However, Billie did not question any of the social norms in constructing this identity. Accepting an external definition of lesbian "settled" Billie's identity so that she no longer had to worry about it. However, it clearly was not an integrated identity that would have freed her from fear of others' judgments. She reported that in her interpersonal life she preferred to conform to others' expectations so that attention would not be drawn to her:

> When you go out of your comfort zone, and you find yourself with all these people that don't know you and the kind of person you are and are going to judge you by the things you do... I like to be inconspicuous. (Abes, 2004, p. 620)

At this point, Billie had not established what D'Augelli (1994) would call an internalized personal identity status.

Reliance on external influences for the meaning of one's sexual orientation encompasses several stages of Cass's (1984) theory of homosexual identity development. Cass, one of the early theorists on sexual orientation identity development, describes development from awareness of one's sexual orientation to integration of the identity into one's self concept. External influences facilitate development from a negative to positive association with one's gay identity. Reliance on external influences also encompass multiple stages in McCarn and Fassinger's (1996) theory of lesbian identity development, which describes simultaneous processes of an increasing commitment to and internalization of individual sexual identity and group membership identity.

Externally Defined Relationships.   Reliance on others for one's beliefs and identity yields using external formulas to construct relationships. As noted earlier, Billie hesitated to go against others' expectations. She wore a skirt to an athletic banquet despite preferring to wear men's clothes because she did not want to stand out as the lesbian among her team. Avoiding difference is characteristic of relationships at this juncture. Lauren, a participant in Baxter Magolda's study, articulated that difference interferes with being good friends:

> I lived with my best friend last year, and that might have been a mistake because we fought over trivial matters. But it turned into bigger things. This year, we live in the same house, but on different floors. We haven't had a fight yet. It's important to learn that they're your friends; however, you can't eat, breathe, and live twenty-four hours a day with them. (Baxter Magolda, 1992, pp. 313–314)

Lauren and her best friend were able to maintain a good relationship as long as they did not have to face their differences.

Similarly, KT, a participant in Abes' study (2003), kept her interest in religion secret from her friends to maintain their friendship. She explained:

> None of my friends go to Church ... Knowing that I want to go to Church and find a Church, I really keep that a secret because everything that they say about religion is bad. They'll bring up something the protestors will say at Pride or something like that. And how, you know, well God says it's bad, why do you want to go to Church?... But I keep it a secret. I'm in the closet about religion. I haven't met any of my close friends that want to go to Church. So I don't really like to talk about religion period. I just keep it a secret.... But I believe in religion, I believe in a higher power. (p. 111)

Because her lesbian friends do not support going to church, KT avoids sharing this important aspect of herself to avoid controversy and maintain relationships.

For many Latinas, cultural gender expectations limit their ability to experience new settings and encounters. Maria described the tension she had with her parents letting her attend university functions outside of the classroom setting:

> They are so strict. I have to sometimes go to meetings and projects and they are like—"Well no." And I am like, "Well this is different. It is not high school, it is not grammar school. It is college, I need to go out." (Torres, 2004, p. 464)

Maria had negative support to venture past the safety of her home environment. This made it difficult for her to develop interpersonal relationships that allowed her to experiment and explore her own sense of self. Marcia (2002) asserted that young adults in foreclosed identity status were likely to accept relationships that are within a narrowly unexplored identity status. Without the freedom to have new experiences, these individuals maintain an externally defined identity and interpersonal relationships that support this unexplored sense of self.

Maria's experience highlights the complications of both ethnic and gender dynamics in coping with others' expectations in relationships. Torres (2004) and Day Shaw (2001) demonstrate the strong influence of family expectations in Latino/a and Black students' development, revealing that students stay in connection with their parents by reshaping relationships as they develop personally. Family expectations played a strong role in Baxter Magolda's (1992) White students' lives as well; however, gender-related socialization mediated this influence. The majority of the men in her study experienced socialization toward agency (Bakan, 1966) or the expectation that they would separate from authorities (including family) and become autonomous individuals. The majority of the women in the study experienced socialization toward communion (Bakan, 1966) or the expectation that they would connect with and function collaboratively with others. Surrey (1991), reporting on the work of numerous scholars of women's development, described the latter as "self-in-relation," noting that for women, "the primary experience of self is relational, that is, the self is organized and developed in the context of important relationships" (p. 52). This contrast of agency and communion is also reflected in moral reasoning via external formulas. Kohlberg's (1984) conventional reasoning reflects agency in its focus on goodness as doing what is expected given roles one occupies whereas Gilligan's (1982) conventional reasoning reflects communion in its focus on goodness as caring for others. Chickering and Reisser (1993) noted the importance of relationships in identity formation by linking the vectors developing mature interpersonal relationships and establishing identity.

External Formulas for Beliefs, Identity, Relationships.   Following external formulas in one dimension influences other dimensions and one's overall meaning-making capacity. Uncritical acceptance of knowledge from external sources is accompanied by a lack of awareness of one's values because there is no awareness that multiple possibilities for what to believe or value exist. This lack of awareness of one's values is reflected in adopting external definitions of identity, which make negotiating relationships with others whose expectations differ across contexts difficult. This is particularly challenging for those who use Kegan's third order meaning-making in which they internalize others views to the point that theirs are overshadowed. Without sufficient dissonance about what is normal, these adults continued to follow their externally derived formulas. When following external formulas no longer resulted in satisfaction or success, they needed support to explore alternative messages to help them develop into the crossroads and a more internally defined sense of self.

Development at the Crossroads

When sufficient dissonance sparks development beyond exclusive reliance on external meaning-making, adults move into the crossroads of their developmental journey toward self-authorship. Kegan (1994) described development through the crossroads as one of the most significant and difficult transitions of adult life. In the crossroads, adults grow aware of the shortcomings of external formulas for what they believe and value, how they relate to others, and how they understand their identity; as part of that process, they begin to develop internal ways of making meaning. Those recently entering a crossroads gradually rely less on external formulas; as their internal voice develops and takes hold, active questioning of external formulas gives way to growing reliance on internal meaning-making. As the narratives that follow demonstrate, the tension between external and internal sources simultaneously occurs in defining beliefs, identity and relationships.

Struggling to Internally Define Beliefs.   Carmen, a participant in Abes' longitudinal study, illustrates meaning-making in the crossroads. Self-identified as either bisexual or lesbian, Carmen's quest for self-understanding regarding her sexual orientation identity is infused with musings reflecting her simultaneous feelings of normalcy and abnormality. Carmen's struggle is laced with conflicts and tensions between her growing internal beliefs and her perceptions of society's norms and expectations. Pondering "whether I was with a guy and chose to be normal, or whether I was with a girl and chose to be abnormal" acted as a refrain throughout her story. Framing her sexual orientation identity in terms of this decision is a reflection of Carmen wanting to fit in with society's perspective on normal, at the same time that she tentatively believes she can define her own norms. Carmen explained:

> I really do think I'm normal, but I recognize that other people don't think that I'm normal, and I want them to think that I'm normal. I don't want to be a big weirdo.
>
> ... I *do* think I'm normal, but in certain ways, I recognize that I'm not normal as far as statistical or the average person is. That makes me abnormal. But I think I'm more normal ... it's not at all [important to be normal]. Like, not at all. I really just want to be myself. And as long as I'm happy, I don't really care about what others think. (Abes, 2003, pp. 100–102)

Positive messages from friends who did not identify as heterosexual and healthy intimate relationships provided Carmen with sufficient dissonance to begin perceiving the shortcomings of relying on external formulas for the meaning of a "normal" sexual orientation identity. Still, her internally defined understanding of normal was tentative as she had not yet committed to an internal belief system, suggesting her epistemological meaning-making was at a crossroads.

Similarly, Torres' (2004) participants encountered dissonance with relying on external stereotypes to define themselves. Perceiving themselves as not fitting into the majority culture prompted them to redefine how racist stereotypes would influence how they saw themselves. For example, Angelica's academic coursework prompted her to question how stereotypes of Latinos influenced her. Prior to starting college, Angelica asked her mother to not answer the phone in case her new college roommate called. She felt her mother's Spanish accent would create an image about Mexicans and she did not want to address this potential negative imagine. In her third year of college she reflected back on this story and how her behavior influenced others.

> I didn't think about the impact of me saying that to my mother, but my mom kind of understood at the time. Nor did I understand the impact of what I was saying in general... I remember my mother did answer the phone when they did call, and she apologized to me. (Torres & Baxter Magolda, 2004, p. 342)

At this point, Angelica was willing to question the stereotypes she believed about Mexican Americans and how those stereotypes might impact others. Earlier in her college years she had accepted externally defined stereotypes as true, though they did not pertain to her. She is no longer willing to accept this external definition of how Latinos are stereotyped and entered a crossroads to examine her beliefs more closely and to behave differently.

One of the hallmarks of the epistemological dimension of the crossroads is a growing awareness and acceptance of uncertainty and multiple perspectives. Career decision-making is a context in which growing awareness and acceptance of uncertainty and multiple perspectives are often evident. In contrast to Kurt, who made meaning of his career decisions using external formulas, Al, another participant in Baxter Magolda's longitudinal study, demonstrates meaning-making at the crossroads. Al began to recognize his need to take responsibility for his own beliefs about the meaning of success as he grew dissatisfied with his career path. Al was coming to understand that there was not one right career for him. Whereas immediately after graduation he relied on external formulas for success, such as financial rewards and marketability, he started to realize within his first couple years on the job that his own internally defined measure of success—happiness—was also an important consideration. Al explained:

> After you've worked a year or so, you start to realize you're going to be working the rest of your life. I mean, you realize you're going to have to get a job, but you really don't feel what it's all about until you get out there and do it. After a year, I learned a lot with the company I worked for. And I didn't dislike it. I just figured I'm gong to work until I'm 65 anyway, I ought to do what I've always thought I wanted to do. And if I'm ever going to do it, I need to get started. Even that freshman year in college, I thought would want to be a doctor. But what was holding me back was (a) I wasn't sure I wanted to spend that much time getting there, and (b) I have never been a real science fan. Now I'm looking at the end of the road rather than what it takes to get there. I think the bottom line is, "are you going to be happy in what you're doing?" The biggest thing is what am I really doing? In my job, I never really felt like it was the kind of help I wanted to give to people. (Baxter Magolda, 2001, p. 101)

Starting to realize there were multiple perspectives on the meaning of career success and that he could determine his own beliefs for what makes him happy in work, but not yet committed to this course of action, Al illustrates epistemological crossroads. Al's recognition that he could determine his own beliefs represents a shift to independent knowing (Baxter Magolda, 1992) in which uncertainty becomes the norm and students realize that they can craft their own perspectives. However, as Perry (1970) pointed out, this early relativism is a way of making meaning in which learners have no criteria for distinguishing one opinion from another. King and Kitchener (1994), calling this meaning-making quasi-reflective, report that their participants initially took an idiosyncratic approach to knowledge claims and later used rules of inquiry in a particular context to sort out what to believe. Belenky et al. (1986) reported that women in their study used procedural knowing (perhaps a version of rules of inquiry) to compare and contrast interpretations. Some used separate procedures, doubting alternative interpretations and taking detached stance toward arguments; others used connected procedures, trying first to believe alternative interpretations and taking an attached stance toward arguments (Clinchy, 2002).

Struggling to Internally Define Identity.   The struggle between external and internal sources of what to believe plays out in young adults' perceptions of their identities The longitudinal studies of both Abes (2003) and Torres (2004) demonstrate a few possibilities for how young adults perceive their marginalized social identities when making meaning at the crossroads. In Torres' study of Latino/a identity, the crossroads were apparent through participants' growing awareness of the influence of negative stereotypes and the extent to which they internalized these stereotypes. For instance, Nora, a Mexican American woman who transferred to a predominantly White institution during her third year of college entered the crossroads in how she made meaning of her ethnicity by having to create her own symbols about how to see herself in a context that sees being Latino as negative. After transferring, she became more proud of her ethnicity as she became aware of and worked through other people's negative stereotypes of Latinos. Nora explained:

> The fact that I am a minority … and people have told me, friends of mine, that there are still people that don't like Mexicans or any other culture. I guess they think Mexicans are all the same, they always describe them as short, lazy, you know? Like I said, there are still people that don't like the way we are. (Torres & Hernandez, 2007, p. 565)

Interacting with a racially and ethnically diverse group of peers also was an impetus for her transition into the crossroads as she came to understand different stereotypes associated with their identities, allowing her to reflect on the meaning of being Latina.

Nora's experience resonates with Helms' (1995) description of the dissonance (encounter) racial identity ego status experienced by people of color. Encountering dissonance with previously held definitions prompts exploration and reconsideration of those ideas in the immersion/emersion status. Similarly, ethnic identity search/moratorium is characterized by exploration and translation of cultural beliefs into behavior. This exploration can also create dissonance about how previous beliefs were created and the role the majority culture plays in marginalizing non-majority cultures (Phinney, 1993). Whites can also experience dissonance at the disintegration status when they struggle to face their privilege in the search for their own understanding of racism in the immersion/emersion status (Helms, 1995).

Similarly, in Abes' study (2003) one aspect of the crossroads was the clashing of the internalization of other people's negative perceptions of same-sex relationships and a growing internal voice that perceived these relationships in a positive light. For instance, Gia, a fourth-year student, who was dating a woman whose family disapproved of their relationship lamented:

> I'm having to deal with my girlfriend's family and they're not very happy about me…. So, I've been thinking a lot more about people and how against gay people they really are…. It makes me angry, and it makes me also I think, somewhere inside, I want to hide it. Even though I know hiding isn't right. It's starting to have that kind of effect on me, and it's bothersome. And that's what makes me angry. It's like why are these two people, who are ignorant, going to get me to think badly about myself or my relationship…. And it's so funny because I know what I know about the gay community, my life, how I feel about me. I'm very secure about myself. And then have these two people who are challenging that, and I'm allowing that. So it really frustrates me … That's where the anger comes in. Because inside I'm like, why should I want to melt into the mainstream, just because these two people don't like it…. Their homophobia is like starting to seep into me…. Why should I let their ideas like start seeping into me…. It's like this really complex problem right now.

Although Gia was very much aware of the influence of other people on the meaning she made of her sexual orientation identity, she was not able to resolve this tension in a manner consistent with the sense of self to which she aspired.

Tensions between external formulas and their growing internal voices are also apparent in how young adults construct relationships among their multiple social identities. For instance, Carmen, for whom her Puerto Rican culture is very important, was aware that her family does not approve of her sexual orientation, which she attributes to their

Puerto Rican culture. Although she typically is very concerned about what other people think about her (despite her assertion earlier to the contrary), Carmen neither thinks less of herself nor is uncomfortable with her sexual orientation as result of her family's attitude. Instead, with some disappointment, she has accepted that they are entitled to their opinion and is honest with her family about her identity. Yet, at the same time that she is trying to think for herself, Carmen has resigned herself to believing that she cannot be completely honest about whom she is when she is with her Puerto Rican family, and for the time being, explains that she is satisfied with this arrangement:

> When I'm around a bunch of Puerto Ricans, I'm not going to be like, yeah I'm gay. ... If we're getting together, if the focus is more towards being about my culture or doing something with that aspect of my life ... then I guess the two are separate there.... Eventually I hope like when my kids' kids are alive it's not such a big issue. And I don't see it happening ... Not that I don't think I can make a difference with a few of my relatives opinions or anything but ...I don't see why the two really need to come together. (Abes, Jones, & McEwen., 2007, p. 10)

While she stated that the two don't have to come together, it is hard for her to understand why they cannot. Like Gia, Carmen is aware of the tension, but does not yet have the intrapersonal maturity to resolve the tension to construct an internally defined self. Both women's stories reflect the intertwining of epistemological, intrapersonal and interpersonal meaning-making.

Struggling to Internally Define Relationships.   The inner conflict between reliance on external formulas and developing internal voices for defining beliefs and identity also plays out in the interpersonal domain. One of the ways in which interpersonal crossroads are apparent is through developing a sense of and need for agency in relationships, while realizing the shortcomings of maintaining relationships only by meeting the expectations of other people. For instance, as Kurt from Baxter Magolda's longitudinal study became increasingly aware of and dissatisfied with his dependence on others to make him happy, he started to realize that he was not content following the formula for career success set forth for him as a legal assistant. Kurt explained:

> I'm the kind of person who is motivated by being wanted, I think. I've gone to a couple of workshops and, either fortunately or unfortunately, I'm the kind of person who gets my self worth on whether or not other people accept me for what I do or other people appreciate what I'm doing.... I'm coming from a position where I get my worth and my value from other people, which is, I think, wrong for me to do. But that's where I am right now. I feel like whether or not I choose to be happy is dependent on me and only me. If I say, "you made me mad," or the converse, "you made me happy," then I'm giving all of the power that I have to you. The power of choice is mine; I have a choice of how I want to perceive each and every situation in my life.... Obviously I'm not to that point yet because I choose to make myself happy and myself sad on what other people are thinking. But I think I'd like to someday get to a point where I can say, "okay, that's your perception. I am not dependent on you for my happiness or my sadness." (Baxter Magolda, 2001, pp. 98–99)

Kurt's internal struggles between his growing self-awareness of his dependence on others and his inability to act on this newfound awareness illustrate interpersonal crossroads.

He is able to identify shortcomings of his third order constructions and dependence on others; he can verbalize that the power of choice is his, but he is not yet able to stand apart from these relationships to take up that power.

For many Latino/a young adults managing family expectations is part of the process for entering into a crossroads. The expectation that family is central can place external pressures on Latino/a young adults. For many students this crossroads has both interpersonal and intrapersonal developmental implications. Interpersonally they must decide on the kinds of friends they want, while also managing the cultural expectations that come with familialism. Angelica's struggle focused on being half Anglo and half Latina. She described her process like this:

> I'm a lot more critical of my father's role in my life and what he represents. Since my freshman year, I think my mother and I have gone from mother-daughter relationship to the friend-friend relationship.... A lot more connection in our relationship,... we discuss a lot how I was socialized, how I was raised, how I viewed things then. But I think even now, if were to discuss a lot more my relationship with my mother it would be a lot more—it would have a little more content because I know her more as a person, and how she sees this. (Torres & Baxter Magolda, 2004, p. 341)

In Angelica's case, she maintains her connection to her mother, but reformulated the relationship in order to express her own thoughts. This crossroads allowed her to continue being close to her mother while also experiencing her own meaning independent of her parents' opinions. This reformulated relationship allowed her to maintain her cultural congruence with family, but also be able to disagree with some parental expectations. She is approaching a mutual relationship in which she can authentically express herself without sacrificing her own needs or those of her family.

Leah, a participant in Abes' study, was aware that she was losing her sense of identity as a result of a relationship, including her comfort with her sexual orientation identity, the value she places on being part of a GLBT community, and her perception of normalcy with regard to sexual orientation identity. Although aware of the negative impact the relationship had on her sense of self, she was not prepared to change the dynamic of the relationship such that she maintained greater agency. Leah elaborated:

> I was dating someone who was out ... and at that point we were kind of in a similar place, we were both very involved with the GLBT [gay, lesbian, bisexual, transgender] community, both kind of more activism and involvement and also more socially.... But the person I'm dating now ... she isn't even out.... So I shifted from this out and involved and just really a part of a GLBT community to this, I feel almost like I'm in the closet a little bit. We're very much private about our lives, about our relationship. We don't do that many gay things ... I miss it a lot.... I feel like I've almost regressed a little bit back into the closet and a little bit back into this thought of "can I have a normal life?" I mean, given that; and so partially because I define a lot of these things so much by who I'm with, and I'm with someone now who's closeted and I can't right now see this point in our lives that you know that we'll both be out and we'll both be comfortable with it ... I don't foresee that as much. I just don't see that with her because I don't see that comfort with her. So I'm beginning to question it in me, too.... I guess my model of normal might even just be the way a heterosexual would do it. Which I hate to say, but maybe that's what I think right now. (Abes, 2003)

Leah's own concept of her sexual identity falters in maintaining this relationship, reflecting that her earlier sense of herself was constructed in a relationship and community more open about sexual orientation. When she shifted to this relationship with a closeted partner, she began to question herself.

Struggling to Internally Define Beliefs, Identity, and Relationships.   As each of these participant excerpts demonstrates, the three domains of development are interdependent. For instance, while Leah's excerpt brings to the forefront crossroads in her interpersonal development, it also demonstrates the influence the relationship with her girlfriend is having on the meaning she makes of her sexual orientation identity. Likewise, her realization that she might be defining "normal" through the dominant heterosexual paradigm speaks to the epistemological domain as she questions the meaning of "normal" (as did Carmen), raising the question of how she resolves inconsistencies among multiple perspectives, including inconsistencies among her own perspectives. Unlike Carmen, who appears to be at early phase within the crossroads of her development, Leah and Angelica appear to be at a more mature place within their crossroads, approaching an integrated self-authored identity. Through Leah's complex analysis of the nature of her relationship with her girlfriend and Angelica's reformulated relationship with her mother, they both appear to be closer epistemologically to making meaning through an internal belief system. They will not be able to wholly do so however until they move through the crossroads of their interpersonal development.

Self-Authorship

Leaving the crossroads and allowing one's internal voice to move to the foreground to mediate external influence yields self-authorship. The shift of internal voice to the foreground takes place in all three developmental dimensions. Dawn, one of Baxter Magolda's longitudinal participants, articulates this multi-dimensional shift in her late twenties:

> The more you discover about yourself, the more you can become secure with it. And that obviously leads to greater self-confidence because you become comfortable with who you really are. My confidence level is so much better than it ever has been. I'm more willing to express my ideas and take chances expressing my ideas. "Who cares what people think?" sort of thing. When you're not as self-confident, you're afraid that people are going to laugh at what you think or you're afraid that they're going to think you're stupid—it's all those petty, little things that inhibit us. Whereas when you're confident, you are more willing to say, "This is my opinion; this is why I hold this opinion. You may agree with it or not, but this is what—with my mind I have formulated this opinion and that's how I think and feel." And I think self-awareness too, because you realize that it doesn't really matter if other people agree with you or not. You can think and formulate ideas for yourself and ultimately that's what's important. You have a mind and you can use it. That's probably the most important thing, regardless of the content of what your thoughts and opinions are. I suppose it's very idealistic to think that everybody can see that. It's the fact that you can form an opinion that's more important than the opinion itself. (Baxter Magolda, 2001, pp. 152–153)

Dawn conveyed that self-discovery led to self-confidence and comfort with her identity. This internally-defined identity allowed her to express her ideas without fearing others' reactions. She exhibited the capacity to engage in relationships with others whose perspectives differ from hers without feeling threatened. These insights led her to the notion that she could think and formulate ideas for herself to craft her own belief system. She realized that the process of deciding what to believe and value is more important than the content of what one believes and values.

Internally Defining a Belief System and Identity.   Formulating ideas for oneself reflects mature forms of epistemological development. As external authority shifts to external influence, the recognition that knowledge is uncertain and relative to particular contexts emerges. As the internal voice comes forward, one recognizes the need (and responsibility) to judge evidence in context to decide what to believe. Theorists describe this mature epistemology as relativism (Perry, 1970), constructed knowing (Belenky et al., 1986; Clinchy, 2002), contextual knowing (Baxter Magolda, 1992, 2001, 2004a), reflective judgment (King & Kitchener, 1994, 2002, 2004), and the coordination of abstract systems (Fischer, 1980; Kitchener & Fischer, 1990). The hallmark of self-authorship in this dimension is weighing multiple perspectives based on criteria relevant to the context to craft one's own belief system. What is normal or true now becomes internally constructed.

For many college students, crafting their own belief system involves choosing cultural values, religious beliefs, and making sense of marginalization they experience due to their gender, race, ethnicity, sexual orientation, or social class. Thus the intrapersonal dimension, or how one constructs one's identity, is intricately tied to the epistemological dimension. Dawn's earlier notion about formulating opinions with her own mind translated to how she made sense of her sexual orientation. She reported:

> That has contributed a great deal to how I see things and how I think. Getting to where I am now, the confidence thing; you know you have the inner strength to stand apart from the mainstream. I don't have to be a duck in a row, following what everyone else is doing. Whether it has to do with being gay or not. The best way I can explain it is learning to walk. You get stronger and finally run. It is a release, where you are willing to let go of clutter that people throw at you. (Baxter Magolda, 2001, p. 183)

Dawn illustrates that crafting one's own beliefs, particularly when they require standing apart from the mainstream, requires not only the ability to weigh evidence but inner strength to stand on one's convictions.

Jacky, a college junior in Abes' longitudinal study, used discriminatory experiences as a stimulus for "researching various political and identity-based issues, reading in-depth about all sides of an issue and then reaching her own conclusions after a logical analysis of multiple perspectives" (Abes et al., 2007, p. 11). Struggling financially due to lack of domestic partnership benefits, she offered:

> It doesn't make me feel sorry that I'm gay or anything like that, but it makes me wish I could be more able to change the system… I'm Black, gay, and female, and leftist … and I'm not a Christian.… It makes me follow politics that much more.… It helped me shape my opinions and my politics and my point of view. (Abes et al., 2007, pp. 11–12)

Experiencing discrimination on a number of fronts prompted Jacky to explore and self-author her point of view and her identity. The way in which Jacky makes meaning of her sexual orientation identity resonates in some respects with McCarn and Fassinger's (1996) description of the internalization/synthesis stage of lesbian identity development. In that stage, individuals internalize their sexual orientation, both individually and as a member of an oppressed group, as one aspect of their overall self-concept.

Goldberger's (1996) cultural interviews illustrated that people of color, immigrants, and members of the working class often develop contextual knowing by virtue of their marginality because they experience firsthand the situational and power-related nature of ways of knowing. Similarly, Pizzolato (2003) found that high-risk students' encounters with provocative experiences such as those Jacky described often prompted the disequilibrium needed to get them to revise their goals and conceptions of themselves. Students with low privilege lacked external formulas for succeeding in college and tended to develop self-authorship earlier than those with high privilege. Clarity about their goals from being self-authored also helped them address marginalization when they attended college. Although Pizzolato (2004) found that high-risk students' self-authorship was shaken initially by discriminatory experiences, those who were clear about their goals and used effective coping skills were able to solidify their self-authored vision of themselves. Helsing, Broderick, and Hammerman (2001) also speak to this resiliency on the part of self-authored English as a second language students:

> Self-authoring students seem better able to evaluate and critique the messages they receive about race, class, linguistic, and cultural differences. As they move away from Socializing ways of understanding, they develop the ability to reflect on the standards and values of their cultural surround, reviewing them according to their own internal standards and values. Thus, even if the culture messages imply their inferiority, they are able to reject these messages and disregard negative feedback that contradicts their own values and standards. (p. 179)

Creating one's own internal standards makes one less susceptible to external standards. Using internal standards for self-definition is also characteristic of Helms' (1995) internalization status, in which people of color internally define racial attributes and have the capacity to respond objectively to members of the dominant group, and her autonomy status, in which Whites gain the capacity to relinquish the privileges of racism.

Similarly, self-authored students are able to internalize choices between cultures to create their own principles. In her final year of college, Jackie, a participant in Torres' (2003a) study, considered the cultural expectations to be near family as one criterion among many. Describing her decision-making process, she offered:

> I think they just happen. I think about where it would be best. I mean if different options come up, I consider them and I say okay, if I do take this path, you know, what is it going to offer me? And how am I going to better my career and myself as a person? (Torres & Hernandez, 2007, p. 563)

Her internalized sense of self was evident in the process she used to tell her mother about her choices after college. She said, "it takes a lot of explaining …, but I think she [mother] knows that I haven't really messed up on my way here, so chances are that I am making the right choices" (fourth year interview). The act of explaining her choices from an internalized position helped Jackie feel like she could be independent while also respecting the cultural expectations of her family.

As is evident from these examples, self-authoring one's belief system and identity are arduous processes. Dawn, who articulated a self-authored perspective in her late twenties, reports how the process is still salient in her life at age 33:

> There is so much processing going on, what I do on a daily basis, trying to fit all the pieces of the puzzle together. I think I'm definitely at a point where I am really defining a lot about my life. Not that it is discovering new things ... but bringing everything that I've ever thought and believed into a much clearer focus for myself.... The whole thought process of just taking stock of where you are in your life. It's like putting your life through a sieve, getting the big awkward chunks out of your life, getting the nice finely sifted residue—it is kind of sorting it all out. What is the essence of you and what isn't? What is important to the essence of you and what isn't? (Baxter Magolda, 2004b, pp. 18–19)

Self-authored adults continue this sifting to refine the essence of their identities. Josselson (1987; 1996) chose the words identity achievers and pathmakers for her participants who explored multiple possible selves and committed to a self-authored version of their identity. She noted that these women did not abandon their prior selves but rather "sifted through what they had been, thinking about each piece, deciding to keep most of what was already there, modifying or adding new pieces" (1996, p. 75). Ossana et al.'s (1992) internalization stage involved women incorporating a positive definition of womanhood into their identity, taking into account but not controlled by the views of other women regarding the role of women. Baxter Magolda's (2001) participants demonstrated that this sifting process required both agentic and communion styles.

Torres' longitudinal participants who became self-authored had engaged in this sifting process in defining their own internal cultural identity. For Vanessa, part of her sifting was deciding how to teach her children about her culture and deciphering what was her responsibility and what was up to them. As a non-traditional age college student, she was self-conscious about her abilities in both English and Spanish languages. By her fourth year of college, she had selected Spanish as a minor in order to improve her language skills. In addition, her children began asking why they don't speak Spanish well and attempted to blame her for not speaking the language. Vanessa responded to them with an inner sense of her identity that is not dependent on what others think. She told them, "I spoke to you [in Spanish]; your grandfather and grandma spoke to you. Why didn't you pick it up?" (Torres & Hernandez, 2007, p. 566).

Self-authoring one's identity involves not only crafting particular social identities but also forming an internal identity that incorporates all the possible social identities one possesses. Beth, a college junior in Abes' study, explained how she was gradually perceiving the concept of identity fluidity, which she learned about through the study of queer theory, as relevant to not only her sexual orientation and gender but also her religion, and to a lesser extent race. In the course of this explanation, she shared how she perceived an integrated relationship among her multiple social identities:

> I'm seeing so many things as not so defined ... my religious identity for example, which has always been very primary to me, is still very important to me, but it also is a lot less defined, exists along a continuum and less in a specific label. There are issues with that I'm still working out with myself ... if I don't believe in God and don't want to have a traditional Jewish marriage, can I still identify as culturally Jewish, what does that mean ... how does that intersect with queer identity ... But I don't see my Jewish identity as my prime role in my life. I don't see being queer as the prime role

in my life. I don't see being White or middle class or a student or maybe somebody who wants to be an academic someday as the one thing that must define me. I am this collection of things…. some of which are label-able, some of which are stories or experiences or the exact combination that only exists within me, or how I interpret them. I know, I'm been kind of going through an anti; not anti-labels phase, because obviously labels are important to communicate, but … I don't feel comfortable as defining myself as a list of identities, I just seeing myself as a combination of those and a lot of other things that I don't label…. I recognize that there are aspects of my identity that if taken out of the whole picture are defined as or are definable, mostly as sexuality, or religion or career goal, or family or whatever. So in that way I do recognize that they are definable by separate terms but I also don't think that the way I think about any one of them would be the same if I didn't have all those other things. The way I think about my relationship with my family for example, might be this is how I relate to my mother, this is how I relate to my sister, this is how I relate to my stepfather and my outside family and everything else. That said, that relationship with them would be entirely different if it weren't influenced by that—all those other things, you know, sexuality, religion, etc.

Beth's complex understanding of identity fluidity shaped the way she internally integrated various aspects of her identity. Abes et al.'s (2007) reconceptualization of the Model of Multiple Dimensions of Identity (Abes, Jones, & McEwen, 2007) suggests that one's meaning-making capacity acts as a filter through which one reshapes contextual influences on social identities. Beth's ability to construct her social identities as a complex system stems from her ability to internally choose her values. Her way of constructing knowledge about identity and how her particular identities interrelate affects her identity development as well as her relationships with others. These attributes resonate with Helms' description of the integrative awareness status in which people of color have the "capacity to value one's own collective identities as well as empathize and collaborate with members of other oppressed groups" (1995, p. 185).

Internally Defining Relationships.   As Beth's comments illustrate, how one views oneself is closely related to how one views relationships. Dawn spoke to this intersection of identity and relationships:

> You take in information and see how it feels given your accumulation of life experiences to that point. If it feels right you keep it; if it doesn't, you let it go…. I think a lot of it also has to relate to the self, how you view yourself. If you respect yourself, if you have confidence in your ability, that changes your whole perspective. If you respect yourself, it is pretty much a given that you will respect others. Treating others with compassion and understanding can only happen when you've achieved a certain level of that yourself. Just thinking about the energy of the world and how we treat each other and how—that is a big defining thing for me right now. Stepping into that realm of not judging people, treating them with compassion, acting in my life without judging and with compassion. (Baxter Magolda, 2004b, p. 20)

Dawn conveyed that her internal identity and subsequent respect for herself allowed her to respect others and refrain from judging them. This ability to explore one's own and others' perspectives enables what Jordan (1997) calls mutuality. In a relationship characterized by mutuality each party is able to "represent her or his own experience in a relationship, to act in a way that is congruent with an 'inner truth' and with the context, and to respond to and encourage authenticity in the other person" (p. 31). This capacity to be authentic enhances intercultural relationships because it enables taking others' cultural perspective and the ability to act from another frame of reference, both characteristics of Bennett's (1993) complex stages of ethnorelative perspectives. In his stage of integration, individuals integrate disparate aspects of their identities as they move between cultural perspectives.

Internally Generated Beliefs, Identity and Relationships.   As these narratives reveal, separating epistemological, intrapersonal, and interpersonal dimensions is difficult. Self-authoring one's view of the world requires reflection on what one believes and values, which contributes to the establishment of an internal identity. Similarly, constructing a self-authored identity requires this reflection, which in turn heightens the ability to construct knowledge internally. A self-authored internal identity frees adults from the constant need for affirmation from others, enabling them to function authentically in relationships. The security of an internal, integrated identity prompts interest in exploring multiple frames of reference which leads to mutual relations with diverse others. Contextual influences and social environments are mediated by self-authored internal belief systems, leaving a person less susceptible to negative external influences. This shift begins as one becomes the author of one's life and becomes increasingly solid as internal belief systems and identities become one's internal foundation (Baxter Magolda, 2001). Parks (2000) similarly portrays this in the realm of faith development as a tested commitment in which "one is willing to make one's peace and to affirm one's place in the scheme of things (though not uncritically)" (p. 69). This tested commitment is accompanied by a confident inner-dependence (the intrapersonal dimension) similar to Kegan's (1994) fourth order self-authorship. Solidifying one's internal foundation is similar to Parks' convictional commitment and interdependence, both captured in Kegan's fifth order meaning-making where interdependence between self and other is the hallmark. This interdependence stems from individuals viewing themselves as a partial construction of all they can be and viewing relationships as a "context for a sharing and an interacting in which both are helped to experience their 'multipleness,' in which the *many* forms or systems that *each self* is are helped to emerge" (1994, p. 313, italics in original).

Intersections of Development and Learning

These extensive narratives from our three longitudinal projects support long-standing propositions about the intersections of development and learning. Narratives we used to highlight the epistemological dimension reveal that, "what individuals learn and claim to know is grounded in how they construct their knowledge" (King & Baxter Magolda, 1996, p. 165). Those constructing knowledge via external formulas accepted truths from authorities, those constructing knowledge via the crossroads struggled to understand what to learn and how to construct knowledge, and those achieving self-authorship were able to assess evidence in context to decide what to believe. Thus, the experiences of these participants demonstrate the intersection of Kegan's (1982, 1994, 2000) psychological constructive-developmental line of thought with Mezirow's (1990; 2000) educational transformational learning line of thought. Mezirow (2000) writes, "Formulating more dependable beliefs about our experience, assessing their contexts, seeking informed agreement on their meaning and justification, and making decisions on the resulting insights are central to the adult learning process" (p. 4). Kegan (1994) points out that this learning process requires transformations of the way we make meaning away from authority dependence to self-authorship. Most college mission statements and national higher education reports call for cognitive maturity as a learning outcome. Baxter Magolda (2004b) articulated the epistemological developmental foundation of this outcome as "viewing knowledge as contextual and developing an internal belief system via constructing, evaluating, and interpreting judgments in light of available frames of reference" (p. 8). Constructing knowledge from external formulas or the crossroads is insufficient to meet this learning outcome and insufficient for learning in adult life (Baxter Magolda, 2004b; Kegan, 1994; Mezirow, 2000). Constructing knowledge via authority-dependence also contributes to accepting negative stereotypes about one's racial, ethnic, gender, sexual orientation, or social class identity (Abes & Jones, 2004; King & Baxter Magolda, 2005; Ortiz, 2004; Torres & Baxter Magolda, 2004; Torres & Hernandez, 2007) that inhibit cognitive maturity.

The intersections of epistemological and intrapersonal development in the narratives reflect King and Baxter Magolda's (1996) proposition that "how individuals construct knowledge and use their knowledge is closely tied to their sense of self" (p. 166). Our longitudinal participants, whose identities were externally defined, did not see themselves as capable of constructing knowledge and thus accepted knowledge uncritically. They were unable to reconstruct negative stereotypes about their social identities or reconstruct limited perspectives of race, ethnicity, gender, class, or sexual orientation until their internal voices came to the foreground near the end of the crossroads. Cognitive maturity is a necessary but insufficient condition for a complex, integrated identity. College learning outcomes such as students understanding their own history, functioning autonomously yet in connection with others, and integrity all require an intrapersonal developmental foundation. This foundation is the ability to "choose [one's] own values and identity in crafting an internally generated sense of self that regulates interpretation of experience and choices" (Baxter Magolda, 2004b, p. 8). This intrapersonal foundation underlies transformational learning's "crucial mode of meaning making: becoming critically aware of one's own tacit assumptions and expectations and those of others and assessing their relevance for making an interpretation" (Mezirow, 2000, p. 4).

The narratives also illustrate that how one constructs and uses knowledge is intricately tied to relationships. Managing others' assumptions and expectations effectively requires complex ways of knowing, an internally generated identity, and the ability to form mature relationships with others in which one's own views are not subsumed by others' views. We expect these mature relationships of college students and graduates so that they are able to interact effectively with diverse others. Mature relationships require an interpersonal developmental foundation characterized by a "capacity to engage in authentic, interdependent relationships with diverse others in which self is not overshadowed by the need for others' approval" (Baxter Magolda, 2004b, p. 8). Until our participants' internal voices came to the forefront near the end of the crossroads, others' approval inhibited their learning.

Brookfield (2005) identified a series of adult learning tasks that resonate with transformational learning and constructive-developmental meaning-making. He argued that creating a just society requires:

Learning to recognize and challenge ideology that attempts to portray the exploitation of the many by the few as a natural state of affairs, learning to uncover and counter hegemony, learning to unmask power, learning to overcome alienation and thereby accept freedom, learning to pursue liberation, learning to reclaim reason, and learning to practice democracy. (p. 39)

These learning tasks all require self-authorship. Thus guiding students in the journey toward self-authorship should be a central component of promoting learning in college.

Promoting Adult Development and Learning in College

The integrated view of development and the intersection of development with learning illustrates that bringing all three developmental dimensions into the learning process is crucial for transformational learning and achieving self-authorship. Feminist (e.g., Hooks, 1994; Maher & Tetrault, 1994; Noddings, 1984; Ropers-Huilman, 1998), liberatory (e.g., Freire, 1988; Shor, 1992), constructivist (e.g., Twomey-Fosnot, 1996), narrative (e.g., Brooks, 2000; Hopkins, 1994), and culturally relevant (Ladson-Billings, 1998) pedagogy have all succeeded in bringing various dimensions into teaching and learning and welcoming learners as partners. However, only constructivist-developmental pedagogy (e.g., Baxter Magolda, 1999; Belenky et al., 1986; Kegan, 2000; King & Kitchener, 1994; Perry, 1988) explicitly links college students' developmental journey to the learning process. To help educators envision explicitly incorporating diverse students' development into learning, we explore a constructive-developmental model, The Learning Partnerships Model, which emerged from Baxter Magolda's 20-year longitudinal study of young adult learning. This model resonates with previous constructive-developmental pedagogical models.

The Learning Partnerships Model.   The wide array of individual and contextual factors mediating the overarching journey toward self-authorship pose major challenges for educators trying to link learning to students' development. The Learning Partnerships Model (LPM; Baxter Magolda, 2004a) offers one way to link learning to the diverse experiences of today's students. Although the tenets of the model emerged from a longitudinal study with one group of young adults, the model has been used successfully in diverse curricular, cocurricular, faculty development, and student affairs organization settings (Baxter Magolda & King, 2004). Because the model hinges on mutual partnerships with students, it offers educators a means through which to invite students' individual development into learning.

The LPM helps learners shift from authority dependence to self-authorship by challenging them to see the complexity of and their role in composing reality and supporting them in coordinating their beliefs, values, and interpersonal loyalties. The model balances guidance with empowerment. Learning partnerships challenge authority dependence via *three core assumptions* about learning: knowledge is complex and socially constructed, one's identity plays a central role in crafting knowledge claims, and knowledge is mutually constructed via the sharing of expertise and authority. Portraying knowledge as a complex result of experts negotiating what to believe gives learners access to the process of learning and deciding what to believe. Assuming that one's identity plays a central role in this process opens the door for learners to see their role in knowledge construction. Assuming knowledge is mutually constructed emphasizes the shared responsibility to engage multiple perspectives to decide what to believe. All three assumptions emphasize autonomy through personal responsibility for learning and molding beliefs. They simultaneously emphasize connection through the necessity to connect to one's own and others' perspectives.

Learning partnerships support self-authorship via *three principles*: validating learners' capacity as knowledge constructors, situating learning in learner's experience, and defining learning as mutually constructing meaning. Validating learners' capacity to learn and construct knowledge is necessary for them to see themselves as creators of their beliefs. Situating learning in their experience instead of the experience of authority gives them a context from which to bring their identity to learning. Defining learning as a mutual process of exchanging perspectives to arrive at knowledge claims supports their participation in the social construction of knowledge.

The three principles model autonomy through encouraging learners to bring their experience and construct their own perspectives. The principles model connection through encouraging learners to connect to their own and others' experience and ideas. The blend of challenge and support in the LPM provides guidance and empowerment simultaneously, modeling the blend of connection and autonomy inherent in the nature of self-authorship. Because learning partnerships are mutually crafted to incorporate learners' perspectives, learners' epistemological, intrapersonal and interpersonal development drives the partnership. Partnerships with learners who follow external formulas require high support to cope with the challenges. Partnerships evolve as students move through the journey toward self-authorship. Rather than having to know students' development in advance, educators learn about students' development in the practice of partnering with them in the learning process.

Educators have used the LPM effectively in a variety of contexts. Use of the LPM in Casa de la Solidaridad, a one-semester length cultural exchange program in El Salvador, aims to challenge students' perceptions about global justice and human liberation and self-author their values (Yonkers-Talz, 2004). Yonkers-Talz designed the Casa to reflect the components of the LPM. Challenge is inherent in a cultural immersion program such as the Casa. A praxis course to integrate learning from students' field placements in the community emphasizes knowledge as complex and socially constructed. Sustained individual and community reflection in the living-learning community keep self central to knowledge construction. The living-learning community and pedagogy of the Casa model sharing authority and expertise. Mutual relationships within the Casa community and with the Salvadorians define learning as a mutual process. The six courses students take while at the Casa integrate the subject matter with their field placements. Staff support, community living, and the pedagogy of the Casa validate students' capacity to know. Yonkers-Talz (2004) shares powerful stories from Casa participants that show how their views of the world, themselves, and their role in the world became more complex via this experience.

The LPM guides the Urban Leadership Internship Program at Miami University. This program challenges students to clarify their vocation and identity through a 10-week summer internship involving work, service and urban exploration. Egart and Healy (2004) implemented the six LPM components in the structure of the program. The interns' role and responsibilities in their urban placement and community convey that knowledge is complex and socially constructed. The interns need to negotiate their new environment and identity, making self central to knowledge construction. The interns work mutually with their peers to share authority and expertise. Collaboration among co-workers, roommates, supervisors and the program coordinators supports students in defining learning as a mutual process. Learning is automatically situated in the interns' experience in their jobs and community service in the urban setting. Group work and reflective writing offer validation for their capacity as knowers. Egart and Healy reported that "students had an integrated view of themselves and the world that was larger and more complex than they had had before the internship began. This shift in perspective encompassed a new view of self in relation to others, to knowledge, and, inwardly, toward self" (2004, p. 144).

Hornak and Ortiz (2004) used the LPM in conjunction with Ortiz and Rhoads' (2000) Multicultural Educational Framework (MEF) to promote a multicultural outlook in a community college business course. The concept of developing a multicultural outlook emphasized knowledge as complex and socially constructed. The MEF focuses on the role of self in understanding race and privilege, making self central to knowledge construction. The class reconstructed race and privilege collaboratively, modeling sharing authority and expertise. Group processing of reflections, observations and experiential activities emphasized the mutual nature of learning. Cultural observations and immersions situated learning in students' experience and reflections on their own and others' cultures validated their capacity to know. Students in the course made progress on revisioning their own pasts, learning about other cultures, and beginning to understand how culture is created. They struggled with owning White privilege, lack of exposure to diverse others, and seeing how a multicultural perspective was applicable to their lives. Hornak and Ortiz concluded that "if diversity educators incorporate the assumptions and principles of the Learning Partnerships Model in their multicultural educational efforts, students would be more likely to see themselves as intimately involved in culture as it is perpetuated and culture as it is changed" (pp. 121–122).

The LPM guided the implementation of a four-year writing curriculum (Haynes, 2004), the nature of a higher education masters curriculum (Rogers, Magolda, Baxter Magolda, & Knight-Abowitz, 2004), the Community Standards Model for residential living (Piper & Buckley, 2004), an academic advising retention program (Pizzolato & Ozaki, 2007), and an interdisciplinary general education program (Bekken & Marie, 2007). It played a central role in faculty development (Wildman, 2004) and reorganizing a student affairs division (Mills & Strong, 2004). Designing learning partnerships involves analyzing the learning goals of a particular context to determine the developmental demands they place on learners. Assessing the degree to which these vary from the developmental capacities learners currently possess helps educators design ways to construct the six components of the LPM in ways that challenge and support learners appropriately. A step-by-step design process (King & Baxter Magolda, 2004) aids educators in conceptualizing learning partnerships.

Counteracting Messages that Oppress Development.   As we have noted earlier, negative external messages sometimes provide dissonance that promotes development (Abes, 2004; Pizzolato, 2005). Yet for students from underrepresented groups, negative external messages can also be damaging to their epistemological, intrapersonal and interpersonal development. Steele and Aronson (1995) refer to the effects of this negative stereotyping as stereotype threat. This phenomenon occurs when individuals believe negative stereotypes associated with their social identity group to the point that these negative images influence how they see themselves and their interactions with others. Sagi, a participant in Torres' (2003) longitudinal study, is an example of a young adult who believed that people who spoke English with an accent were less intelligent and less prepared than native speakers. Instructors and students' behaviors reinforced this externally defined sense of self. Because Sagi had an externally defined intrapersonal sense of herself, she took these behaviors as confirmation that she was less intelligent (Torres & Baxter Magolda, 2004).

Part of constructing a learning partnership with students in this situation involves introducing alternative messages to change the negative external messages to positive internal messages. For Sagi, Torres served as an external messenger with a different view of accents. Torres is a native Spanish speaker and was able to give Sagi examples of successful Latinos in the United States who had strong Spanish accents. Entertaining an alternative interpretation for others' behaviors, Sagi began to see her accent as a sign that she speaks another language and therefore has some advantage over someone who speaks only one language (Torres & Baxter Magolda, 2004). Alternate messages can also be provided at a program or institutional level by acknowledging and confronting racist behavior, structuring programs that contest dominant ideology and promote social justice, and seeking out students' experiential knowledge (Villalpondo, 2004).

Mentors and Learning Partnerships.   Mentoring has been a mainstay of research on helping college students to develop. Chickering and Reisser (1993) highlighted the important role of faculty relationships to multiple vectors of students' identity development. Daloz (1986, 1999) painted an in-depth picture of how mentors can accompany adult learners throughout the developmental journey toward self-authorship. Parks (2000) extends the idea of mentoring to the community level, describing mentoring environments as providing "a network of belonging, big-enough questions, encounters with otherness, important habits of mind, worthy dreams, access to key images, concepts (content), and practices that mediate these gifts of a mentoring community" (p. 135).

Because of the potentially negative messages young adults from non-majority cultures receive, it is critical that mentors help them create alternative cognitive maps that are inclusive of their own values and beliefs. Mentors can assist young adults to develop internal messages for success by teaching them how to create a cognitive map that includes positive symbols, self-reflection, self-regulations, and forethought and promotes internalized values that can help them maneuver the outside world in order to meet their goals (Torres, 2006). Fries-Britt (2000) articulated how positive interactions with faculty helped high-achieving Black students acknowledge their intellectual ability. Similarly, Abes and Jones (2004) found that positive interactions with lesbian faculty and staff allowed several of the participants to realize for the first time that lesbians could be successful, professional women, debunking previously held stereotypes. Torres noted that the success of many academic support programs for underrepresented students is often based on the coordinated mentoring participants receive. This coordination builds bridges between academic and personal support services. At one Hispanic-serving institution, at-risk students who participated in the culturally sensitive academic support program "had a 4% higher one-year persistence rate than the general freshman cohort" (Torres, 2003b, p. 344). The learning partnerships described by Baxter Magolda's longitudinal participants and participants in programs using the LPM all reinforce the notion that learning partnerships engage students with mentors who provide good company for their developmental journeys.

Challenges in Learning Partnerships.   It should be evident by now that the developmental journey we describe here is not a clean, linear path to increasingly sophisticated skills. It is, instead, a messy process of steps forward, back and sideways to sort through the conflicts inherent in crafting one's own beliefs and identity in the process of redesigning one's relationships with significant others and to the world at large. Arriving at the complex phases of the journey requires struggling through the transformations. Although evidence supports the necessity of giving students responsibility to enable transformations, doing so is uncomfortable when they have yet to develop ways of taking up this responsibility wisely. Educators worry that giving students more responsibility in learning interactions may result in decreased learning or that progress toward learning outcomes will be unclear. Educators worry that giving students more responsibility for everyday decision-making may result in poor decisions regarding well-being, relationships, and civility among diverse peers. These risks are highest in the space between following external formulas and self-authorship—that space in which students are exploring to decide what to believe.

These risks are not lost on parents who are more involved in their students' lives than in earlier generations (Coburn & Treeger, 2003). These parents have devoted considerable energy to providing the best experiences to help their children succeed. They often regard the college experience as one more part of the process to propel their children to success in adult life. They are not accustomed to failure or mishaps along the journey. This concern for success, various cultural mores, and concern about the values their children may adopt sometimes lead parents to challenge allowing increased autonomy for their children. Parents may also struggle with institutions' approaches to engaging their students in exploring White privilege, racism, heterosexism, and classism. Establishing partnerships with parents, with whom the university shares a common goal—preparing college students for meaningful adult lives—is an essential new challenge in higher education practice (Coburn & Treeger, 2003).

Educators' perspectives sometime conflict with partnerships that promote self-authorship. Most educators are socialized to pass their expert knowledge on to novice learners in an organized and efficient way. Working collaboratively with learners to help them struggle with a concept takes longer than telling them the concept. Collaborating with students to influence student behavior is more challenging than managing systems to control student behavior. Educators' assumptions about authority, learning, and students capacities for self-authorship mediate their ability to implement contemporary (and in some cases long standing) research demonstrating that students do not learn responsibility and self-authorship unless they have a chance to practice it. The Learning Partnerships Model does not advocate total student autonomy. It does, however, advocate willingness to balance guidance with empowerment to help students shift from external to reasoned internal authority.

Future Research and Challenges

Many questions remain regarding whether development follows a consistent trajectory and the degree to which these trajectories are linear versus fluid. Renn (2003, 2004) argues that racial identity models fail to capture the complexity of mixed race college students. Renn's (2004) cross-sectional study identified five identity patterns: monoracial identity, multiple monoracial identities that shift according to the situation, multiracial identity, extraracial identity (opting out of identifying by racial categories), and situational identity that varies by context. Renn uses an ecology model to explore the dynamics of development within these patterns, including how individual characteristics and multiple ecological contexts intersect, rather than exploring how identities evolve over time. Future research might explore whether the complexity of students' meaning-making capacity is one of the individual characteristics that contributes to their approach to handling conflicting contexts and imposing societal structures within this ecology model.

Kodama, McEwen, Liang, and Lee (2002) focused on the multiple contexts in which Asian American students develop their identity for the purpose of reconceptualizing Chickering and Reisser's (1993) psychosocial development theory. They explained that

Asian American students develop their identity in the context of traditional family values and cultural norms, as well as the "mores of the dominant culture," (p. 46) in particular racism. Kodama et al. altered the order and emphasis placed on particular vectors, and used terms identifying vectors to describe the general content areas for development rather than specific tasks. Identity and purpose are central to the model and develop within the context of racism and traditional cultural and family values. "Increased awareness of the relationship of self to the two domains [contexts] promotes the development of identity and purpose, which in turn influences change and growth among the five developmental tasks" (p. 49), including emotions, competency, interdependence, relationships, and integrity. Future research might consider how meaning-making complexity interfaces with the students' ability to understand and own their relationship with traditional norms and values of their culture and racism.

A few recent studies have considered relationships among multiple socially constructed identities, such as race and gender in relation to ego (Miville, Darlington, Whitlock, & Mulligan, 2005), race and faith (Stewart, 2002), and race and religious orientation (Sanchez & Carter, 2005). Challenging a linear trajectory, Love, Bock, Jannarone, and Richardson (2005) explored how college students experience interactions between their spiritual identity and sexual orientation identity. They described students as "reconciled" when these aspects of their identity "were two mutually interacting aspects of an integrated self or identity" (p. 199), but cautioned that the process of reconciliation is non-linear because students occasionally experienced dissonance between their spirituality and sexuality. Additional research exploring the role of meaning-making capacity as an avenue for understanding how students negotiate the changing contexts and meanings associated with the fluid development of their multiple identities would add to our understanding of student development. Moving in this direction, Abes, Jones, and McEwen (2007) recently reconceptualized the Model of Multiple Dimensions of Identity (Jones & McEwen, 2000), a conceptual model portraying relationships between environmental contexts and the relative salience of college students' socially constructed identities. Still, Abes and Kasch (2007) challenged whether the reconceptualized model goes far enough in portraying identity fluidity. They used queer theory to question whether the developmental trajectory toward increased meaning-making capacity is based on a heteronormative depiction of development that does not account for the fusion of multiple identities that are constantly in motion.

Other recent research specifically describes a developmental trajectory in the intrapersonal domain. Using language that resonated with an external to internal trajectory, Stevens's (2004) offered a model of gay identity development within the college environment that depends on a growing sense of empowerment, or "an inner strength that weathers more and various environmental situations" (p. 198). Stevens explained that empowerment "moved from an environmentally influenced or situational understanding given particular environmental conditions to a more internally based understanding where the participant had a self-awareness about the skills and knowledge he had to control a situation regarding his own needs and those of the gay community, in general, regardless of the environmental conditions" (p. 198). It would be fruitful to explore whether this growing sense of empowerment that fosters an internally based understanding of self might depend also on growing cognitive and interpersonal complexity.

There is a need for additional research focusing on the development of diverse college students. College students did not comprise significant portions of the samples for much of the developmental literature on socially constructed identities. For instance, much of our understanding of Black identity development is grounded in Cross (1995) and White identity in Helms (1995). Pope (1998; 2000) linked these racial identity concepts to college students' psychosocial development as described by Chickering and Reisser (1993). Additional research focusing on the nature of developmental processes for diverse college students is needed. Much of the literature on relational development is based on women; studying the relational development of both genders is important. The major longitudinal studies of students' intellectual development are based on predominantly White samples; similar research needs to be conducted with diverse groups (Moore, 2002). Although there is a strong literature on racial climate on campus, students' development is often not a key focus of that research.

Higher Education's Responsibility

In the face of a complex, diverse, and global society fraught with ideological, economic, and cultural conflict higher education must do more to help college graduates develop capacities to function effectively in adult life (Meszaros, 2007). Enabling the journey toward self-authorship and mature interdependence not only enhances students' ability to meet college learning goals (e.g., critical thinking, effective problem-solving in their disciplines, intercultural maturity, wise decision-making) but also prepares young adults for the challenges of work, community relations, and personal life. We possess knowledge about how to enable this developmental transformation. Now it is our responsibility to partner with students to implement it.

Notes

1. Adapted from M. B. Baxter Magolda (2004). Self-authorship as the common goal of 21st century education. In M. B. Baxter Magolda & P. M. King (Eds.), *Learning partnerships: Theory and models of practice to educate for self-authorship* (pp. 1–35). Sterling, VA: Stylus.
2. Adapted from M. B. Baxter Magolda (2004). Self-authorship as the common goal of 21st century education. In M. B. Baxter Magolda & P. M. King (Eds.), *Learning partnerships: Theory and models of practice to educate for self-authorship* (pp. 1–35). Sterling, VA: Stylus.
3. Adapted from M. B. Baxter Magolda (2004). Self-authorship as the common goal of 21st century education. In M. B. Baxter Magolda & P. M. King (Eds.), *Learning partnerships: Theory and models of practice to educate for self-authorship* (pp. 1–35). Sterling, VA: Stylus.

References

Abes, E. S. (2003). *The dynamics of lesbian college students' multiple dimensions of identity*. Unpublished dissertation, The Ohio State University, Columbus.

Abes, E. S. (2007). Applying queer theory in practice with college students: Transformation of a researcher's and a participant's perspectives on identity. *Journal of LGBT Youth, 5*, 55–75.

Abes, E. S., & Jones, S. R. (2004). Meaning-making capacity and the dynamics of lesbian college students' multiple dimensions of identity. *Journal of College Student Development, 45*(6), 612–632.

Abes, E. S., Jones, S. R., & McEwen, M. K. (2007). Reconceptualizing the Model of Multiple Dimensions of Identity: The role of meaning-making capacity in the construction of multiple identities. *Journal of College Student Development, 48*(1), 1–22.

Abes, E. S., & Kasch, D. (2007). Using Queer Theory to explore lesbian college students' multiple dimensions of identity. *Journal of College Student Development, 48*(6), 1–18.

Bakan, D. (1966). *The duality of human existence: An essay on psychology and religion*. Chicago: Rand McNally.

Baxter Magolda, M. B. (1992). *Knowing and reasoning in college: Gender-related patterns in students' intellectual development*. San Francisco: Jossey-Bass.

Baxter Magolda, M. B. (1999). *Creating contexts for learning and self-authorship: constructive-developmental pedagogy.* Nashville, TN: Vanderbilt University Press.

Baxter Magolda, M. B. (2001). *Making their own way: Narratives for transforming higher education to promote self-development.* Sterling, VA: Stylus.

Baxter Magolda, M. B. (2004a). Learning Partnerships Model: A framework for promoting self-authorship. In M. B. Baxter Magolda & P. M. King (Eds.), *Learning partnerships: Theory and models of practice to educate for self-authorship* (pp. 37–62). Sterling, VA: Stylus.

Baxter Magolda, M. B. (2004b). Self-authorship as the common goal of 21st century education. In M. B. Baxter Magolda & P. M. King (Eds.), *Learning partnerships: Theory and models of practice to educate for self-authorship* (pp. 1–35). Sterling, VA: Stylus.

Baxter Magolda, M. B., & King, P. M. (Eds.). (2004). *Learning partnerships: Theory & models of practice to educate for self-authorship.* Sterling, VA: Stylus.

Bekken, B. M., & Marie, J. (2007). Making self-authorship a goal of core curricula: The Earth Sustainability Pilot Project. In P. S. Meszaros (Ed.), *Self-authorship: Advancing students' intellectual growth. New Directions for Teaching and Learning* (Vol. 109, pp. 53–67). San Francisco: Jossey-Bass.

Belenky, M., Bond, L. A., & Weinstock, J. S. (1997). *A tradition that has no name: Nurturing the development of people, families, and communities.* New York: Basic Books.

Belenky, M., Clinchy, B. M., Goldberger, N., & Tarule, J. (1986). *Women's ways of knowing: The development of self, voice, and mind.* New York: Basic Books.

Bennett, M. (1993). Towards ethnorelativism: A developmental model of intercultural sensitivity. In M. Paige (Ed.), *Education for the intercultural experience* (pp. 21–71). Yarmouth, ME: Intercultural Press.

Brookfield, S. D. (2005). *The power of critical theory: Liberating adult learning and teaching.* San Francisco: Jossey-Bass.

Brooks, A. K. (2000). Transformation. In E. Hayes & D. D. Flannery (Eds.), *Women as learners* (pp. 139–153). San Francisco: Jossey-Bass.

Cass, V. C. (1984). Homosexual identity formation: Testing a theoretical model. *Journal of Sex Research, 20,* 143-167.

Chickering, A. W., & Reisser, L. (1993). *Education and identity* (2nd ed.). San Francisco: Jossey-Bass.

Clinchy, B. M. (2002). Revisiting *Women's Ways of Knowing.* In B. K. Hofer & P. R. Pintrich (Eds.), *Personal epistemology: The psychology of beliefs about knowledge and knowing* (pp. 63–87). Mahway, NJ: Erlbaum.

Coburn, K. L., & Treeger, M. L. (2003). *Letting go: A parent's guide to understanding the college years.* New York: HarperCollins.

Cross, W. E., Jr. (1995). The psychology of Nigrescence: Revising the Cross model. In J. G. Ponterotto, J. M. Casas, L. A. Suzuki, & C. M. Alexander (Eds.), *Handbook of multicultural counseling* (pp. 181–198). Thousand Oaks, CA: Sage.

Daloz, L. A. (1986). *Effective teaching and mentoring: Realizing the transformational power of adult learning experiences.* San Francisco: Jossey-Bass.

Daloz, L. A. (1999). *Mentor: Guiding the journey of adult learners.* San Francisco: Jossey-Bass.

D'Augelli, A. R. (1994). Identity development and sexual orientation: Toward a model of lesbian, gay, and bisexual development. In E. J. Trickett, R. J. Watts, & D. Birman (Eds.), *Human diversity: Perspectives on people in context* (pp. 312–333). San Francisco: Jossey-Bass.

Day Shaw, J. (2001). *An application of Baxter Magolda's epistemological reflection model to Black and Latino students.* Unpublished dissertation, Florida State University, Tallahassee.

Egart, K., & Healy, M. (2004). An urban leadership internship program: Implementing learning partnerships "unplugged' from campus structures. In M. B. Baxter Magolda & P. M. King (Eds.), *Learning partnerships: Theory and models of practice to educate for self-authorship* (pp. 125–149). Sterling, VA: Stylus.

Fischer, K. W. (1980). A theory of cognitive development: The control and construction of hierarchies of skills. *Psychological Review, 87*(6), 477–531.

Freire, P. (1988/1970). *Pedagogy of the oppressed.* New York: Continuum.

Fries-Britt, S. (2000). Identity development of high-ability Black collegians. In M. B. Baxter Magolda (Ed.), *Teaching to promote intellectual and personal maturity: Incorporating students' worldviews and identities into the learning process. New directions for teaching and learning* (Vol. No. 82, pp. 55–65). San Francisco: Jossey-Bass.

Gilligan, C. (1982). *In a different voice.* Cambridge, MA: Harvard University Press.

Goldberger, N. R. (1996). Cultural imperatives and diversity in ways of knowing. In N. R. Goldberger, J. M. Tarule, B. M. Clinchy & M. F. Belenky (Eds.), *Knowledge, difference, and power: Essays inspired by Women's Ways of Knowing* (pp. 335–371). New York: Basic Books.

Haynes, C. (2004). Promoting self-authorship through an interdisciplinary writing curriculum. In M. B. Baxter Magolda & P. M. King (Eds.), *Learning partnerships: Theory and models of practice to educate for self-authorship* (pp. 63–90). Sterling, VA: Stylus.

Helms, J. E. (1995). An update of Helms's white and people of color racial identity models. In J. G. Ponterotto, J. M. Casas, L. A. Suzuki, & C. M. Alexander (Eds.), *Handbook of multicultural counseling* (pp. 181–198). Thousand Oaks, CA: Sage.

Helsing, D., Broderick, M., & Hammerman, J. (2001). A developmental view of ESOL students' identity transitions in an urban community college. In R. Kegan (Ed.), *Toward a new pluralism in ABE/EDOL classrooms: Teaching to multiple "cultures of mind"* (Vol. 19, pp. 77–228). Cambridge, MA: National Center for the Study of Adult Learning and Literacy, Harvard Graduate School of Education.

Hooks, B. (1994). *Teaching to transgress: Education as the practice of freedom.* New York: Routledge.

Hopkins, R. L. (1994). *Narrative schooling: Experiential learning and the transformation of American education.* New York: Teachers College Press.

Hornak, A., & Ortiz, A. M. (2004). Creating a context to promote diversity education and self-authorship among community college students. In M. B.axter Magolda & P. M. King (Eds.), *Learning partnerships: Theory and models of practice to educate for self-authorship* (pp. 91–123). Sterling, VA: Stylus.

Jones, S. R., & McEwen, M. K. (2000). A conceptual model of multiple dimensions of identity. *Journal of College Student Development, 41*(4), 405–413.

Jordan, J. V. (Ed.). (1997). *Women's growth in diversity: More writings from the Stone Center.* New York: Guilford.

Jordan, J. V. (2004). Toward competence and connection. In J. V. Jordan, M. Walker, & L. M. Hartling (Eds.), *The complexity of connection: Writings from the Stone Center's Jean Baker Miller training institute* (pp. 11–27). New York: Guilford.

Josselson, R. (1987). *Finding herself: Pathways to identity development in women.* San Francisco: Jossey-Bass.

Josselson, R. (1996). *Revising herself: The story of women's identity from college to midlife.* New York: Oxford University Press.

Kegan, R. (1982). *The evolving self: Problem and process in human development.* Cambridge, MA: Harvard University Press.

Kegan, R. (1994). *In over our heads: The mental demands of modern life.* Cambridge, MA: Harvard University Press.

Kegan, R. (2000). What "form" transforms? A constructive-developmental approach to transformative learning. In J. Mezirow (Ed.), *Learning as transformation: Critical perspectives on a theory in progress* (pp. 35–69). San Francisco: Jossey-Bass.

King, P., & Baxter Magolda, M. (1996). A developmental perspective on learning. *Journal of College Student Development, 37*(2), 163–173.

King, P. M., & Baxter Magolda, M. B. (2004). Creating learning partnerships in higher education: Modeling the shape, shaping the model. In M. B. Baxter Magolda & P. M. King (Eds.), *Learning partnerships: Theory and models of practice to educate for self-authorship* (pp. 303–332). Sterling, VA: Stylus.

King, P. M., & Baxter Magolda, M. B. (2005). A developmental model of intercultural maturity. *Journal of College Student Development, 46*(6), 571–592.

King, P. M., & Kitchener, K. S. (1994). *Developing reflective judgment: Understanding and promoting intellectual growth and critical thinking in adolescents and adults.* San Francisco: Jossey-Bass.

King, P. M., & Kitchener, K. S. (2002). The reflective judgment model: Twenty years of research on epistemic cognition. In B. K. Hofer & P. R. Pintrich (Eds.), *Personal epistemology: The psychology of beliefs about knowledge and knowing* (pp. 37–61). Mahwah: NJ: Erlbaum.

King, P. M., & Kitchener, K. S. (2004). Reflective judgment: Theory and research on the development of epistemic assumptions through adulthood. *Educational Psychologist, 39*(1), 5–18.

King, P. M., & Shuford, B. A. (1996). A multicultural view is a more cognitively complex view cognitive development and multicultural education. *The American Behavioral Scientist, 40*(2), 153–164.

Kitchener, K. S., & Fischer, K. W. (1990). A skill approach to the development of reflective thinking. In D. Kuhn (Ed.), *Contributions to human development: Developmental perspectives on teaching and learning* (Vol. 21, pp. 48–62). Basel, Switzerland: Karger.

Kodama, C. M. McEwen. M. K., Liang, C. T. H., & Lee, S. (2002). An Asian American perspective on psychosocial student development theory (pp. 45–59). In M. K. McEwen, C. M. Kodama, A. N. Alvarez, S. Lee, & C.T.H. Lian (Eds.), *Working with Asian American college students. New Directions for Student Services*, No. 97, San Francisco: Jossey-Bass.

Kohlberg, L. (1984). *Essays on moral development. Volume 1.* The philosophy of moral development. New York: Harper & Row.

Ladson-Billings, G. (1998). Who will survive America? Pedagogy as cultural preservation. In D. Carlson & M. W. Apple (Eds.), *Power, knowledge, pedagogy: The meaning of democratic education in unsettling times* (pp. 289–304). Boulder, CO: Westview Press.

Love, P. G., Bock, M., Jannarone, A., & Richardson, P. (2005). Identity interaction: Exploring the spiritual experiences of lesbian and gay college students. *Journal of College Student Development, 46*, 193–209.

Maher, F. A., & Tetrault, M. K. T. (1994). *The feminist classroom: An inside look at how professors and students are transforming higher education for a diverse society.* New York: Basic Books.

Marcia, J. E. (1966). Development and validation of ego-identity status. *Journal of Personality and Social Psychology, 3,* 551–558.

Marcia, J. E. (2002). Identity and psychosocial development in adulthood. *Identity: An International Journal of Theory and Research, 2*(1), 7–28.

McCarn, S. R., & Fassinger, R. E. (1996). Revisioning sexual minority identity formation: A new model of lesbian identity and its implications for counseling and research. *The Counseling Psychologist, 24,* 508–534.

Meszaros, P. S. (Ed.). (2007). *Self-authorship: Advancing students' intellectual Growth. New directions for teaching and learning* (Vol. 109). San Francisco: Jossey-Bass.

Mezirow, J. (Ed.). (1990). *Fostering critical reflection in adulthood: A guide to transformative and emancipatory learning.* San Francisco: Jossey-Bass.

Mezirow, J. (Ed.). (2000). *Learning as transformation: Critical perspectives on a theory in progress.* San Francisco: Jossey-Bass.

Mills, R., & Strong, K. L. (2004). Organizing for learning in a division of student affairs. In M. B. Baxter Magolda & P. M. King (Eds.), *Learning partnerships: Theory and models of practice to educator for self-authorship* (pp. 269–302). Sterling, VA: Stylus.

Miville, M. L., Darlington, P., Whitlock, B., & Mulligan, T. (2005). Integrating identities: The relationships of racial, gender, and ego identities among White college students. *Journal of College Student Development, 46,* 157–175.

Moore, W. S. (2002). Understanding learning in a postmodern world: Reconsidering the Perry scheme of intellectual and ethical development. In B. K. Hofer & P. R. Pintrich (Eds.), *Personal epistemology: The psychology of beliefs about knowledge and knowing* (pp. 17–36). Mahwah, NJ: Erlbaum.

Noddings, N. (1984). *Caring: A feminine approach to ethics & moral education.* Berkeley: University of California Press.

Ortiz, A. M. (2004). Promoting the success of Latino students: A call to action. In A. M. Ortiz (Ed.) *Addressing the unique needs of Latino American students. New Directions for Student Services* (No. 105). San Francisco: Jossey Bass.

Ortiz, A. M., & Rhoads, R. A. (2000). Deconstructing whiteness as part of a multicultural educational framework: From theory to practice. *Journal of College Student Development, 41*(1), 81–93.

Ossana, S. M., Helms, J. E., & Leonard, M. M. (1992). Do "womanist" identity attitudes influence college women's self-esteem and perceptions of environmental bias? *Journal of Counseling and Development, 70*, 402–408.

Parks, S. D. (2000). *Big questions, worthy dreams: Mentoring young adults in their search for meaning, purpose, and faith*. San Francisco: Jossey-Bass.

Perry, W. G. (1970). Forms of intellectual and ethical development in the college years: A scheme. Troy, MO: Holt, Rinehart, & Winston.

Perry, W. G. (1988). Different worlds in the same classroom. In P. Ramsden (Ed.), *Improving learning: New perspectives*. East Brunswick, NJ: Nichols.

Phinney, J. S. (1990). Ethnic identity in adolescents and adults: Review of research. *Psychological Bulletin, 108*, 499–514.

Phinney, J. (1993). A three-stage model of ethnic identity development. In M. Bernal & G. Knight (Eds.), *Ethnic identity: Formation and transmission among Hispanics and other minorities* (pp. 61–79). Albany: State University of New York Press.

Piper, T. D., & Buckley, J. A. (2004). Community standards model: Developing learning partnerships in campus housing. In M. B. Baxter Magolda & P. M. King (Eds.), *Learning partnerships: Theory and models of practice to educate for self-authorship* (pp. 185–212). Sterling, VA: Stylus.

Pizzolato, J. E. (2003). Developing self-authorship: Exploring the experiences of high-risk college students. *Journal of College Student Development, 44*(6), 797–812.

Pizzolato, J. E. (2004). Coping with conflict: Self-authorship, coping, and adaptation to college in first-year, high-risk students. *Journal of College Student Development, 45*(4), 425–442.

Pizzolato, J. E. (2005). Creating crossroads for self-authorship: Investigating the provocative moment. *Journal of College Student Development, 46*(6), 624–641.

Pizzolato, J. E., & Ozaki, C. C. (2007). Moving toward self-authorship: Investigating outcomes of learning partnerships. *Journal of College Student Development, 48*(2), 196–214.

Pope, R. L. (1998). The relationship between psychosocial development and racial identity of Black college students. *The Journal of College Student Development, 39*, 273–282.

Pope, R. L. (2000). The development between psychosocial development and racial identity of college students of color. *The Journal of College Student Development, 41*, 304–314.

Renn, K. (2003). Understanding the identities of mixed-race college students through a developmental ecology lens. *Journal of College Student Development, 44*(3), 383–403.

Renn, K. A. (2004). *Mixed race students in college: The ecology of race, identity, and community on campus*. Albany: State University of New York Press.

Rogers, J. L., Magolda, P. M., Baxter Magolda, M. B., & Knight-Abowitz, K. (2004). A community of scholars: Enacting the Learning Partnerships Model in graduate education. In M. B. Baxter Magolda & P. M. King (Eds.), *Learning partnerships: Theory and models of practice to educate for self-authorship* (pp. 213–244). Sterling, VA: Stylus.

Ropers-Huilman, B. (1998). *Feminist teaching in theory & practice: Situating power & knowledge in poststructural classrooms*. New York: Teachers College Press.

Sanchez, D., & Carter, R. T. (2005). Exploring the relationship between racial identity and religious orientation among African American college students. *Journal of College Student Development, 46*(3), 280–295.

Shor, I. (1992). *Empowering education: Critical teaching for social change*. Chicago: University of Chicago Press.

Steele, C. M., & Aronson, J. (1995). Stereotype threat and the intellectual test performance of African Americans. *Journal of Personality and Social Psychology, 69*(5), 797–811.

Stevens, R. A. (2004). Understanding gay identity development within the college environment. *Journal of College Student Development, 45*(2), 185–206.

Stewart, D. L. (2002). The role of faith in the development of an integrated identity: A qualitative study of a Black students at a White college. *Journal of College Student Development, 43,* 579–596.

Surrey, J. L. (1991). The "Self-in-relation": A theory of women's development. In J. V. Jordan, A. G. Kaplan, J. B. Miller, I. P. Stiver, & J. L. Surrey (Eds.), *Women's growth in connection: Writings from the Stone Center* (pp. 51–66). New York: Guilford.

Torres, V. (2003a). Factors influencing ethnic identity development of Latino college students in the first two years of college. *Journal of College Student Development, 44*(4), 532–547.

Torres, V. (2003b). Student diversity and academic services: Balancing the needs of all students. In G. L. Kramer (Ed.), *Student academic services: An integrated approach* (pp. 333–351). San Francisco: Jossey-Bass.

Torres, V. (2004). Familial influences on the identity development of Latino first year students. *Journal of College Student Development, 45*(4), 457–469.

Torres, V. (2005, October). *Considering the ethnic identity of Latino college students within holistic development.* Keynote speaker for Drive-in Conference. Virginia Tech, Blacksburg, VA.

Torres, V. (2006). A mixed method study testing data-model fit of a retention model for Latino students at urban universities. *Journal of College Student Development, 47*(3), 299–318.

Torres, V., & Baxter Magolda, M. B. (2004). Reconstructing Latino identity: The influence of cognitive development on the ethnic identity process of Latino students. *Journal of College Student Development, 45*(3), 333–347.

Torres, V., & Hernandez, E. (2007). The influence of ethnic identity on self-authorship: A longitudinal study of Latino/a college students. *Journal of College Student Development, 48*(5), 558–573.

Torres, V., Howard-Hamilton, M. F., & Cooper, D. L. (2003). *Identity development of diverse populations.* (ASHE-ERIC Higher Education Report, Vol. 29, No 6). San Francisco: Jossey-Bass.

Twomey-Fosnot, C. (Ed.). (1996). *Constructivism: theory, perspectives, and practice.* New York: Teachers College Press.

Villalpando, O. (2004). Practical considerations of critical race theory and Latino critical theory for Latino college students. In A. M. Ortiz (Ed.), *Addressing the unique needs of Latino American students. New Directions for Student Services* (no. 105, pp. 41–50). San Francisco: Jossey-Bass.

Wildman, T. M. (2004). The Learning Partnerships Model: Framing faculty and institutional development. In M. B. Baxter Magolda & P. M. King (Eds.), *Learning partnerships: Theory and models of practice to educate for self-authorship* (pp. 245–268). Sterling, VA: Stylus.

Yonkers-Talz, K. (2004). A learning partnership: U. S. college students and the poor in El Salvador. In M.B. Baxter Magolda & P.M. King (Eds.), *Learning partnerships: Theory and models to educate for self-authorship* (pp. 151–184). Sterling, VA: Stylus.

Zaytoun, K. (2003). *Theorizing at the borders: A feminist, interdisciplinary exploration of the development of adult consciousness.* Doctoral Dissertation, Miami University, Oxford, Ohio.

Chapter 8

Addressing Stability and Change in the Six-Foci Model of Personality

Personality Development in Midlife and Beyond

Cory R. Bolkan, Patricia Meierdiercks, and Karen Hooker

The idea that personality is vital to understanding human behavior captured the attention of life-span researchers during the last half of the twentieth century. During this time, some researchers focused attention on relatively stable aspects of the broad construct of personality while others focused on those that were not. The complexity of determining continuity, change, and development within and between individuals has led to a myriad of studies and a multitude of findings. In this chapter, we provide an overview of personality research by relying on a comprehensive framework called the *six-foci model* of personality (Hooker & McAdams, 2003). We will highlight key linkages between personality and quality of life outcomes while also emphasizing the potential for personality growth during the second half of life.

We begin by drawing attention to why personality matters. We then provide a historical overview of the study of personality, synthesizing key empirical findings and addressing controversies and problems in personality development throughout the middle and later years. A discussion of current research follows, and we focus throughout on important questions as to how and why certain aspects of personality change or remain the same, how personality serves as both a risk and protective factor, how it influences the aging process, and how it influences the capacity to flourish during the second half of life.

Why Personality Matters

Personality matters because it is the vehicle through which we reveal our innermost selves. Inextricably intertwined with self, personality produces uniquely patterned ways of being human in the natural world. Fused, yet conceptually distinct (Allport, 1937, 1955; Hooker, 1999; Markus, 1983), personality and self shape who we are, how we become, what we do, where we are going, and help to explain why some people flourish and others do not. As unique individuals, we have idiosyncratic ways of interpreting, engaging with, and responding to different opportunities and constraints. As a result, heterogeneity increases within and between individuals over time. Consequently, heterogeneity in personality, health, cognition, and abilities tends to peak during the later adult years. Identifying the personality structures and processes that contribute to increasing heterogeneity can provide researchers with insight into linkages between personality and important life outcomes such as the link found between neuroticism and mortality, which we will discuss later in the chapter. This notion also highlights how personality acts as a guiding force that allows us to participate in our own development and adaptation across the life span (Bandura, 2001; Brandtstädter & Lerner, 1999; Ford, 1987).

Personality and self also contribute to our sense of well-being. Recent evidence suggests that individuals who lack a coherent sense of self amass cumulative negative effects across the life span and these effects have great impact on adults during their later years

(Diehl, Hastings, & Stanton, 2001). McAdams (2006), for example, found that adults with a weak sense of self-coherence were vulnerable to low self-esteem and depression. More positively, a coherent sense of self precludes the need for reinventing ourselves with each new day, contributing to the predictability of thoughts, feelings, and behaviors across contexts and situations. As a result, having a coherent sense of self facilitates our interface with the world and frees personal energy for more meaningful endeavors.

Personality is commonly used to illustrate the individual and distinct characteristics that differentiate one person from another. For example, knowledge about seemingly stable dispositions (e.g., responsible, outgoing, introverted, gregarious) people display can help us to relate and interact with others. It enhances our understanding of who they are and helps us to predict their behavior. Although this global, established knowledge of personality disposition is clearly useful in knowing another person, it is evident that it cannot possibly fully explain and describe the complexities of one's true self. For instance, because one is introverted at the office meeting, does not necessarily indicate this same person will be introverted at the office picnic. Humans are multi-faceted, influenced by time and context, and capable of personality change. This opportunity for change is particularly exciting because it means that we are capable of continued growth in this domain well into later life.

Two distinct lines of personality research (trait research and social-cognitive research) have emerged to help scientists gain a better understanding of personality structures and processes. We will briefly discuss both of these lines of research in the subsequent section; however, it is at the confluence of these two distinct paths that we hope to find who we are and what can be expected of our aging self. The convergence of both trait and social cognitive lines of personality research will be reflected in our discussion of the *six foci model* of personality.

How the Science of Personality Came to Be

The study of personality development began with Freud's theoretical work on psycho-sexual development (for a general overview of Freudian theory, see Westen, 1990). Today, the field of personality psychology embodies a vast complex of theoretical frameworks, research methods, topics, and issues. Dispositional traits, identity and self-processes, coping strategies, emotions, and affect regulation are just a few of the topics subsumed under this research umbrella. Traits have received a great deal of attention, leading some to assume traits define personality (Allport, 1955; McAdams, 1995). The widespread acceptance and prevalent use of the "five-factor" and "Big Five" models of personality (Goldberg, 1993; McCrae & Costa, 1994) played a key role in shaping this definition. Many critics, however, argued for a definition of personality that emphasized its dynamic, organized, internal, psychophysical properties, one not dominated by fixed and stable properties.

Traits versus Whole Persons

Trait research has advanced our understanding of personality development. Nevertheless, theorizing about *whole* persons becomes problematic using this line of research. Humans are more than the embodiment of dispositional traits. Cantor (1990), for example, strongly opposed the idea that people simply "have" personalities and noted that what they "do" was often overlooked. What people try to do within their own unique contexts and situations influences the person they are and want to become. Personality researchers need to account for the ways in which personal characteristics and active processes shape a person's world, and how, in turn, these interactions influence social cognitions and the personal meanings people construct (Markus, 2004). Idiographic research, describing individual differences rather than generalizing across populations, will play an important role in advancing current theories of adult personality development. Furthermore, by moving even more toward an *idiothetic* approach (Lamiell, 1981), combining idiographic (i.e., individual trajectories) with nomothetic (i.e., generalize across persons) methodological techniques (Nesselrode, 1990), scientists can provide a more accurate accounting of these interactions and outcomes.

Need for an Integrative Framework

Friction emerged in the field because of incongruities in the domains studied, frameworks applied, and methodologies used. These incongruities sparked years of debate as to whether personality was consistent or capable of change. Today, researchers have moved toward a more integrative perspective of personality, one that accounts for and clearly describes the whole person. Current personality researchers need integrative definitions and frameworks that allow for a full and rich accounting of individuals as unique whole persons. McAdams and Pals (2006) proposed five principles (referred to as the "New Big Five") to facilitate this integration. These principles include accounting for the dynamics that take place between (a) an individual's unique patterning of dispositional traits, (b) the characteristic ways in which individuals adapt to the world, (c) the themes individuals use in life narratives, (d) the evolutionary demands placed on the human species, and (e) the culture in which these demands are embedded. In addition, Hooker and McAdams (2003) developed the integrative *six-foci model* of personality; the emergence of this model (Hooker & McAdams, 2003), in addition to the "New Big Five" principles (McAdams & Pals, 2006), hold promise for nudging the conversation toward an amicable resolution.

Theories of Adult Personality Development

We have learned much about how structural and contextual factors (e.g., socioeconomic status) influence human adaptation. We know less, however, about how dynamic transactions between individuals, person-related variables, and different types of supporting or constraining environments shape human development. Knowing an individual's personality type and the ways in which she or he responds to specific contexts and social situations provides important information about health-related behaviors across the life span (e.g., social support, coping strategies, exercise, and nutrition). This information becomes especially important to later life development when the cumulative effects of these transactions become most pronounced.

Originators of Seminal Ideas

William James (1890), the founder of American psychology, stated "personality is set like plaster by age 30" (p. 126), which implied that personality did not develop beyond early adulthood. Many preeminent scholars, such as Jung (1933), Erikson (1959), and Labouvie-Vief (1982), disagreed with this line of thinking and developed theoretical frameworks for understanding personality development throughout adulthood. Jung (1933), for example, emphasized self-preoccupation and self-discovery as age-graded developmental tasks extending beyond childhood. Erikson (1959) developed an eight-stage model of psychosocial development linking development to age-related tasks and psychosocial crises; he was the first to propose a model of development that spanned from infancy to old age. He also coined the term *generativity*, or one's concern of establishing and guiding the next generation, which emerges in middle to later adulthood. We will discuss this concept in detail later in the chapter. Finally, Labouvie-Vief (1982) extended Piagetian theory into the adult years. More specifically, she refuted the notion that abstract skills first emerged in adolescence and were indicative of cognitive maturation. Instead, she has argued that adults continue to build on these skills to develop further rational thought well into adulthood.

The work of these early scholars provided a catalyst for the continued empirical study of personality development beyond childhood. Bernice Neugarten, another pioneer of gerontological research, also challenged researchers to reconsider traditional views of aging. She, along with University of Chicago colleagues such as Robert Havighurst, launched the Kansas City Studies of Adult Life, in which they explored age norms and constraints. She drew attention to the variability of life patterns, expectations, timing, and timetables by introducing concepts such as "social clocks" and noted that chronological age can be a poor indicator of biological, psychological or social age (Neugarten, 1996; Neugarten & Hagestad, 1976). The collected work of Neugarten (1968, 1979, 1996) highlights a contextual and sociocultural perspective in which both social roles and the sequencing of life events influence normative adult development into later life. Neugarten urged researchers in the field to challenge commonly held beliefs about adult development and how people age. Today, most life-span researchers of personality take for granted the once controversial notion that personality development extends beyond childhood. This new image of adults and the aging process opened doors to new lines of inquiry (see Caspi, 2000; Caspi, Bem & Elder, 1989; Light, Grigsby, & Bligh, 1996; Roberts, Caspi, & Moffitt, 2001, 2003; Scarr & McCartney, 1983).

Problems and Controversial Issues

Personality has always been an elusive concept, which explains the inconsistencies in its various conceptualizations. These inconsistencies make interpreting research findings both challenging and confusing. Psychodynamic theorists, for example, explain behavior primarily in relation to personality structures formed early in childhood whereas behavioral theorists do so primarily in terms of an individual's cumulative experience. These different worldviews fueled an historic debate in the field of personality, providing the impetus for many contemporary personality researchers to move toward a more assimilated and balanced perspective. Personality research has currently moved toward integration, ever mindful of the contrasting sentiments that once disunited the field. In this section, we draw attention to some of the key debates.

Nature versus Nurture.   Researchers in the 1970s, concerned about the limitations of the research approaches then in use, argued that environmental factors shaped personality and accounted for human behavior (e.g., Mischel, 1968, Fiske, 1974). Their critiques accentuated the differences between research programs, diminishing interest in personality as a science (West, 2003). Since then, major contributions to personality and psychological research have reinvigorated the field. Empirical evidence from dispositional trait research indicated that general consistencies in individual personality differences did exist, were stable, and could predict life outcomes (Hogan, Johnson, & Briggs, 1997;

Matthews, Deary, & Whiteman, 2003). Furthermore, evidence in support of the relative importance of genetic factors for certain traits emerged among older twins in the Swedish Adoption/Twin Study of Aging (Pedersen, Plomin, McClearn, & Friberg, 1988). Today, the study of dispositional traits continues to play a vital role in psychological research, becoming one of the most visible contributions of the personality psychology field.

The "Big Five" traits framework (i.e., openness to experience, conscientiousness, extraversion, agreeableness, and neuroticism—OCEAN) provides clarity and has thus been well received. Moreover, empirical evidence supports the universality and stability of these factor-analytically-derived global traits across all periods of the adult life span. Cross-cultural studies using the trait framework have corroborated these findings (McCrae & Terracciano, 2005). Even so, many researchers argue that personality psychology should offer more to the discipline of psychology. They specifically call for a more comprehensive framework that can provide in addition to clarity, the means for understanding the *whole* person throughout the life span (Hooker & McAdams, 2003; McAdams & Pals, 2006).

In response to an increasing awareness of this problem, the study of personality has moved toward adopting a general life span developmental approach (Baltes & Baltes, 1990). Life-span developmental theorists examine both consistency and change in personality (or growth and decline) recognizing that processes of adaptation throughout one's life span can result in wide variability in human development as individuals age. We will further highlight the complexity of ascertaining personality stability and change as we segue into methodological issues.

Theories, Methodologies, and Measures

Theoretical perspectives and methodological approaches influence what and how stability and change are measured. Incongruent theoretical perspectives and methodological approaches drove the schism that divided the field. Cumulative evidence indicated that personality traits were consistent over time when based on the stability of correlation coefficients (McCrae & Costa, 1999; Roberts & DelVecchio, 2000), yet critics argued that normative stability in personality traits should not be interpreted as a lack of individual change (Nesselroade, 1990). Semantic problems also muddled the discourse. Roberts, Walton, and Viechtbauer (2006), for example, found that key terms such as "stability" and "change" were used broadly despite being derived from different indices of continuity and change that were largely independent of each other (Block, 1981; Mortimer, Finch, & Kumka, 1982).

The field is moving away from the "stability versus change" debate and toward a more nuanced conception of change as an individual difference variable with its own distinct merit (Mroczek, Spiro, & Griffin, 2006). Longitudinal personality studies have often used rank-ordering as a means of measuring personality consistency despite the limited information this approach can provide. Rank-ordering can only provide information about an individual's placement within a group when ranked on a specific outcome that is measured over time. Although many important personality studies have relied on this method (see Roberts & DelVecchio, 2000; see Roberts, Walton, & Viechtbauer, 2006), rank ordering is limited in what it can reveal about individual stability and change. An individual can maintain rank order consistency within a group, for example, despite experiencing significant individual changes not captured by the resulting correlation coefficients. Widespread reliance on repeated-measures means in longitudinal studies has likely led some researchers to make stronger statements about personality stability than would have been warranted had they used a more progressive analytic technique.

Complex statistical models today, such as latent growth curve modeling or structural equation modeling, are more sophisticated than ever before, capable of measuring change with greater precision. These recent innovations keenly position researchers to advance knowledge of individual differences in personality change (McArdle, 1991; Nesselroade & Featherman, 1991; Nesselroade & Ram, 2004). Longitudinal studies are now capable of demonstrating that personality consistency and change, although conceptually and empirically independent of one another, do simultaneously exist (Roberts et al, 2006; Roberts, Helson, Klohnen, 2002). Incorporating these disparate synchronies into a single integrative framework has proved a challenge for the field.

An Integrative Framework

With the intent of accounting for both stability and change, Hooker and McAdams (2003) designed the *six-foci of personality* model of personality development. This model integrates personality processes and structures within a levels-of-analysis framework. It incorporates well-known trait and social-cognitive approaches, allowing for simultaneous examination of stability and change as well as structures and processes. Founded on Developmental Systems Theory (Ford & Lerner, 1992), this model emphasizes the plasticity, multidirectionality, and organizing properties of persons, which parallels life-span developmental psychology (Baltes, Lindenberger, & Staudinger, 1998). Consequently, the full complexity of personality as experienced by unique individuals is taken into consideration, which helps to explain how dynamic transactions between individual personalities and contexts continuously shape the contours of individual lives (e.g., see Mroczek & Spiro, 2003).

The Six Foci of Personality

Structures, Processes, and Levels of Analysis

The six foci represent an essential element of either a *structure* (i.e., trait, personal action construct, or life story) or a *process* (i.e., psychological states, self-regulation, or self-narration) in linked pairs that parallel one another on separate analytical planes. Structures are rooted in trait approaches whereas processes derive from the social-cognitive approaches.

These three paralleling structure-process pairs characterize each of the three levels of analysis. The levels represent the idea that *all* people fall on a continuum of a relatively universal set of traits (Level I); that particular goals and developmental tasks are relevant to *some*, but not all people (Level II); and that life stories are *unique* to each person (Level III) (Hooker & McAdams, 2003). This model reflects the current direction in the personality field by demonstrating that both idiographic and nomothetic approaches can be integrated into one personality framework (Hooker & McAdams, 2003). We organize our discussion of the model and of contemporary personality research along these three analytical planes.

Level One: Traits and States

Dispositional traits, a structure construct, accounts for broad consistencies in behavior across time and situations (e.g., agreeableness, neuroticism). States, a process construct, include the intraindividual processes that bring about dynamic change (e.g., emotions, mood). Fleeson's (2001) research integrates both structure and process along the line of reasoning that if states represent a person's everchanging and on-going thoughts, feelings, and behaviors, then traits might be the most common type of state experienced across time and situations. Global traits reveal valuable information about a person and can be useful for understanding certain human behaviors, critics contend, however, that traits provide only general labels (McAdams, 1995; McAdams & Pals, 2006).

Traits.   Costa and McCrae's (1980) five-factor model (FFM) of personality has been well received in the gerontological literature because of its clarity and extensive research on the universality and stability of global traits across the life span. As noted earlier, within the field of psychology, personality traits have arguably been one of the most recognizable contributions of the personality field (McAdams & Pals, 2006). Trait theorists maintain that the FFM traits remain virtually unchanged throughout the life span because of the stability of the biological origins from which they derive. Most personality scientists agree that stable global traits exert important influences on a person's sense of identity, but discussions become more contentious when topics turn to central issues such as whether traits comprise the core of personality or whether experiences (e.g., culture, social roles, and relationships) make substantial contributions to personality development.

Numerous studies (cf. McCrae & Costa, 1990) have revealed moderate to high levels of stability on the "Big Five" traits across periods spanning up to 30 years. Nevertheless, psychologists are beginning to question their assumptions about the stability of traits. Meta-analyses of personality trait research have revealed the simultaneous coexistence of both stability and change in traits (Roberts et al., 2006). These findings align with the tenets of life span developmental theory in that development occurs within biopsychosocial changes elicited by any combination of normative age-graded, history-graded, or non-normative life events.

Age-graded experiences such as starting a family or launching a career have been linked to mean level differences in "Big Five" traits when comparing younger and older adults. Roberts, O'Donnell, and Robins (2004), for example, found higher levels of trait conscientiousness and agreeableness expressed when individuals engaged in work or marriage-related goals compared to times when these goals were not pursued. These shifts in the expression of personality traits coincided with the respondents' specific goal pursuits. Similarly, Martin and Mroczek (2004) found lower levels of trait extroversion and agreeableness expressed during midlife when family and work overload were present compared to times when they were not. Negative affect, often correlated with trait neuroticism, showed a decreasing trend across midlife in another study in which positive affect showed the opposite trend (Mroczek & Kolarz, 1998). These findings draw attention to ways in which goals and life circumstances can influence the level of personality trait expressed, especially during midlife and beyond.

In general, neuroticism, extraversion and openness to experience tend to decrease with age (McCrae & Costa, 2003) whereas agreeableness and conscientiousness tend to increase throughout adulthood (McCrae & Costa, 2003; Mroczek & Spiro, 2003). Mroczek and Spiro (2003) also found a tendency toward increased emotional stability and social dominance that continued into old age. These studies, as well as studies on centenarians, indicate that traits are malleable even among the oldest old (Adkins, Martin, & Poon, 1996).

Roberts and DelVecchio (2000) report that trait stability appears to peak in middle age, when most individuals have been able to assimilate more experiences into their identities and have achieved the ability to choose environments that fit well with their identities. This finding is also reflective of research regarding adults' ability to self-regulate; with age, individuals are more adept at emotion regulation and adjusting to life tasks. We will further address self-regulatory processes in a later section.

Helson, Jones, and Kwan (2002) proposed viewing personality as consistent yet adaptive to changing biological and environmental context. The five-factor model has limitations in predicting specific behaviors, especially with respect to describing an individual's contextualized life (McAdams, 1992). Models that focus exclusively on the first level of analysis create what McAdams (1992) termed a "psychology of the stranger," a psychology based only on what we need to know about a person when we know nothing about them at all. The "Big Five" model of personality is in prominent use today, despite falling short on the task of limning whole persons.

States. Moods, fatigue, hunger, and anxiety are a few of the constructs typically studied within this domain. States are transient processes involving short-term change. Because of the transitory nature of states, research methods must account for state's inherent lability. Researchers studying traits expect stability with minimal change (Nesselroade, 1987; Nesselroade & Featherman, 1991) in contrast to those studying affective states who expect them to display considerable change. Analyses of states require intensive, repeated measurements capable of capturing intraindividual variability. Inherent methodological challenges may explain the relative dearth of empirical literature on personality states juxtaposed to volumes on traits.

Despite methodological challenges, researchers studying moment-to-moment changes within individuals contend that this research provides valuable information. For example, a construct typically thought to be stable (i.e., temperament, traits), may reveal ordered patterns of change when using methodological approaches designed for its capture (Fleeson, 2001; Nesselroade, 1990). Fleeson (2001), for example, empirically demonstrated that, despite wide inter-individual variability, individuals report a full spectrum of behaviors for different traits when measured over a period of several weeks. His studies revealed that some individuals felt extroverted one day, but less so the next. Similarly, between-individual differences in levels of traits correlated with the daily frequencies of actions consistent with that trait (Fleeson, Malanos, & Achille, 2002). These studies demonstrate that research on states hold promise for capturing intraindividual personality processes, but also demonstrate the need for studies that track variability over long periods.

Level Two: Personal Action Constructs and Self-Regulatory Processes

Personal action constructs (PACs) represent an individual's goals, developmental tasks, and personal motivations (Little, 1983) contextualized within time, place, and social roles. *Self-regulatory processes* represent the parallel process construct situated on this second analytical plane. These processes (e.g., self-efficacy, outcome expectancy) relate to specific domains such as work or family (Bandura, 1997, Lachman, 2004) and serve as the means by which people actively direct their own lives (Carver & Scheier, 1998). Together, PACs and self-regulatory processes shed light on individual goals, strivings, and possible selves (Markus & Nurius, 1986). To know a person well entails more than knowing a personality quotient; it means reconciling the difference between what a person sees as important—wants, goals, plans, and strivings—and the contexts and situations that life provides (McAdams, 1992). PACs strongly affect the course of events and provide a candid portraiture of adult personality.

Personal Action Constructs.   PACs represent the motivational aspects of human behavior embedded within time, place, and social role. PACs, defined as goal constructs, reflect certain states people seek to obtain, maintain, or avoid (Emmons, 1996). They exemplify what people want during particular times in specific domains; they are the strategies, plans, and defenses people use to secure longings and avoid detestations.

Individuals achieve outcomes via cognitive-behavioral strategies (e.g., self-regulatory processes), but only to the extent that contextual factors (e.g., person-environment interactions) tolerate such goals. Many researchers conceptualize motivation in terms of PACs or personal goals but differ in the terms used in their operationalization. Little's (1983) *personal projects*, Emmons' (1986) *personal strivings*, Markus's (1983) *possible selves* and Cantor's (1990) *life tasks* are just a few of the constructs currently serving as representatives of PACs. Each construct measures motivation from a slightly different perspective (i.e., level of abstraction or temporal frame), yet there are commonalities among them (Nurmi & Salmela-Aro, 2002). Each emphasizes individual motivations and directions of behavior (Allport, 1961; Emmons, 1986). These constructs remain malleable across the life span, existing within an organized hierarchical system of motivational structures (Emmons, 1986) and adapting in response to person-environment interactions. Researchers can capture the dynamic transactions that occur between cognitions, emotions and environments through PACs (see Mischel & Shoda, 1998).

Possible selves may prove to be one of the most promising new areas of inquiry in relation to PACs. They represent *hoped-for selves* (i.e., what people are trying to become) and *feared selves* (i.e., what people are afraid of becoming). These highly personalized images of a person provide insight into the incentives directing individuals toward goals they should pursue, avoid, or abandon. Possible selves tend to remain stable long enough to be measured with scales that are psychometrically sound (Hooker, 1999; Ryff, 1991), yet change in response to efforts at personal growth (Cross & Markus, 1991; Frazier et al., 2000; Hooker, 1992). Younger adults, for example, often envision a greater number of possible selves related to career, whereas older adults tend to envision greater numbers related to health (Cross & Markus, 1991). Possible selves change in correspondence with normative developmental tasks (Hooker, 1999) and in concert with the functions of Baltes and Baltes' (1990) selection, optimization, and compensation (SOC) theory. As such, possible selves may play a key role in successful adult development.

Self-Regulatory Processes.   Self-regulatory processes such as self-efficacy and sense of control (a construct associated with self-efficacy) have been studied extensively over the decades. Researchers in the field of adult development and aging have been particularly interested in sense of control (Langer & Rodin, 1976; Schulz, 1976) in relation to specific developmental domains and outcomes (Lachman, 1986; Lachman & Weaver, 1998). This line of research has produced numerous studies demonstrating a link between rates of mortality in institutionalized older adults and sense of personal control (Langer & Rodin, 1976; Eizenman, Nesselroade, Featherman, & Rowe, 1997). Feeling a sense of mastery has also been linked to the effectiveness of stress reduction strategies used by adults facing a complexity of midlife challenges (Lachman & Bertrand, 2001).

The most consistent finding regarding age differences in self-regulation pertains to studies on resilience. People maintain and regain levels of subjective well-being and adjust to life tasks more effectively as they age (Staudinger & Kunzmann, 2005). Self-evaluation, emotion regulation, and goal setting are among the most potent of these self-regulatory processes (Staudinger & Kunzmann, 2005). Heckhausen's (2001) research, for example, draws attention to the way middle-aged adults use compensatory strategies and adaptive behaviors to maintain resilience in the face of age-related loss. Despite the increased likelihood of encountered instead of elicited experiences in old age, most older-aged adults maintain their sense of control and personal agency (Staudinger & Kunzmann, 2005).

The SOC model (Baltes & Baltes, 1990; Baltes & Carstensen, 1999; Freund & Baltes, 2000) explains the maintenance of self-regulation across the life span in terms of three processes—selection, optimization, and compensation—regarded by life-span researchers as the universal principles of developmental regulation. These universal adaptive processes include selecting goals or outcomes, optimizing the means to achieve these goals or outcomes, and compensating for loss so that successful outcomes can still be achieved (Baltes & Baltes, 1990). This model provides a general framework for understanding adaptive processes across the life span as well as across multiple domains. Baltes and Carstensen (1999), for example, applied the SOC model to the goal processes older adults use in their social relationships. They found that many older adults select goals related to maintaining family relationships, optimize these goals by investing more time in family relationships (compared to other types of relationships), and compensate for the loss of friendships and other relationships by maximizing salience of family ties.

Time abrogates from each of us resources once taken for granted. As such, aging brings with it the challenge of balancing potential resource gains (e.g., practical knowledge, material belongings) with those involving losses (i.e., physical decline). The strategic selection and pursuit of goals that maximize gains and minimize losses helps to enhance our ability to adapt as we age (Baltes & Baltes, 1990; Riediger, Freund, & Baltes, 2005). Research on personal action constructs and the processes of self-regulation not only provide insight into adult personality development, but also play a key role in optimal aging.

Level Three: Life Story and Self-Narration Processes

Life stories are the internalized structures reflective of an individual's contextualized life; it is here that the narrative unfolds in kinship with experience and self-understanding. People create life stories by reconstructing the past and anticipating the future and in so doing, engender a sense of meaning, unity, and purpose in their lives. True to narrative form, these internalized stories give license to plots, characters, images, themes, and scenes, with each act of revision a window into self-understanding. Narrating the life story to others through remembering, reminiscing, or storytelling entails inducing certain social cognitive processes. Human individuality and the uniqueness of each individual will most likely to be revealed within this third level of the six-foci model.

Life Story.   Life stories continually evolve as new themes within relationships emerge and interweave with changing plots and life settings. Consequently, identity and creation of self elicit empirical attention throughout the adulthood years (e.g., Labouvie-Vief et al., 1995; Whitbourne & Connolly, 1999). The life-narrative approach is an emergent field of study in the science of personality development. We can learn much about personality by discovering how and why individuals select and reconstruct experiences to align with present goals and perceptions as viewed through the lens of an uncertain but anticipated future. When woven together these richly textured threads create a unified and coherent structure, what McAdam's (1995, 2006) christened the revitalizing life myth. These life myths facilitate the integration of life experiences into a coherent identity structure.

The life-narrative approach uses life stories to peer into personality and surmise the structures and processes that inhere in its core. The main characters in life stories represent idealizations of the self. Integrating these various aspects of self becomes a major challenge during middle and later adulthood when attention often turns toward creating a satisfying ending. When well crafted, endings provide the means through which self can leave a legacy and foster new beginnings. Life stories in middle and older adults have a clear quality of "giving birth to" a new generation, a notion essentially identical to generativity (Erikson, 1959; McAdams, 1995). Generativity marks the attempt to create an appealing story "ending," one that fosters new beginnings in generations to come. People derive personal meaning from being generative by constructing a life story or narrative that helps them create a particular identity (Whitbourne, 1999). The changing personality identity, as reflected in the conveyance of emotions in the narrative of a person's life story (e.g., from tragedy to resilience), is paramount to understanding the person. Life stories provide the means by which people prove to themselves and others that they have either changed or remained the same, identifying specific events to support their claims.

Whitbourne (1987), a pioneer in identity research, believes people construct their own ideas about how their lives should proceed. Her research on identity assimilation (i.e., using existing identity) and accommodation (i.e., adjusting existing identity) found that identity assimilation was used prominently among older adults but also that identity accommodation was more prominent among adults in their earlier years (Sneed & Whitbourne, 2003). Moreover, identity assimilation helped older adults minimize negativity, which also tended to be associated with maintaining and enhancing positive self-regard. In contrast, identity accommodation in older adults was associated with poor psychological health. The ability to integrate age-related changes into one's identity and maintain a positive view of self is crucial to aging successfully (Holahan, 2003; Sneed & Whitbourne, 2003). This emergent field of identity development relies on life narratives, the internalized and evolving story that integrates past, present, and future into a coherent and vitalizing myth (McAdams, 1995, 2001). Self-narrative processes guide the telling of these stories.

Self-Narration Processes.   Remembering, reminiscing, and storytelling evolve within the social contexts of people's everyday lives (Bronfenbrenner, 1977, 1979), attesting to self's co-constructed nature. In essence, the audience either affirms or refutes who we think we are by their reactions to us during social interactions. These dynamic transactions subsequently influence the way the narrative evolves and how identities of both narrator and audience become co-constructed. Reciprocal interactions between autobiographical memories (i.e., long term memories) and self also influence the narrative process.

Current evidence suggests that differences exist between younger and older adults in relation to autobiographical memories. Older adults, for example, may be more likely to preserve self-relevant and emotionally intense memories than younger adults (Dijkstra & Kaup, 2005). Moreover, what a person remembers and tells about their personal history may change to align with current realities such as audience or current situational environment (Wilson & Ross, 2003). Autobiographical memories promote self-continuity, which can be important to goal-striving, self-knowledge, and well-being.

Contextual factors play a role in influencing a person's ability to secure an audience to listen to one's life story. Because memory is constructive, the narration of a person's life history evolves through a dynamic process of interaction with social partners. Consequently, developmental level, audience, or social context may change the ways in which individuals tell their stories (Adams, Smith, Pasupathi & Vitolo, 2002; Bartlett, 1932; Fiese, Hooker, Kotary, Schwagler, & Rimmer, 1995; Pasupathi, 2001).

In summary, despite the complexity of the *six-foci model*, the advantages of relying on such a comprehensive model of personality development cannot be ignored. This model captures the simultaneous development of both stability and change as they operate in tandem to create a coherent sense of an embodied self that we can then present to world. This model also accounts for both perspectives of stability and change, providing a foundation for the development of a common language, which in turn will strengthen the science of adult personality (Hooker & McAdams, 2003).

The Importance of Personality

Gerontologists have identified health-related behaviors, such as maintenance of proper nutrition and daily exercise, as key determinants in one's ability to age optimally. Although demographic variables (e.g., education, socioeconomic status, or gender) may serve as key risk or protective factors in predicting certain health-related behaviors, the individual person within whom these factors reside is also a critical antecedent to successful aging. For example, the type of person one is (e.g., reliability, warmth) and what an individual is attempting to accomplish (i.e., personal goals) will likely influence most behavioral outcomes such as social support, coping strategies, stress, or exercise (Hooker & McAdams, 2003). Consequently, increased understanding of how personality interacts with behavior will enable us to predict health outcomes with improved accuracy. This notion links us back to the beginning of this chapter in which we proposed why personality matters. As we begin to conclude this chapter, we will continue to underscore the importance of personality, by focusing on how it affects health, well-being, and behavior.

Health.   The idea that personality is strongly linked to health and longevity is long-standing (for reviews see Aldwin, Levenson, & Gilmer, 2004; Contrada, Cather, & O'Leary, 1999; Smith & Gallo, 2001). This line of empirical inquiry highlights the importance of having an understanding of the intersection between disease processes, personality, and aging (Siegler, 1989). The research in this area is broad and remains an important topic in personality psychology, health psychology, and behavioral medicine disciplines. Although it is beyond the scope of this chapter to include a review of all personality, health, and aging research, we will provide some evidence of the magnitude of these associations.

Early studies on personality and health previously relied on subjective measures, which made the interpretation of this association difficult (Costa & McCrae, 1987). Current studies, however, that focus on definitive methodological approaches, include prospective designs, and well-validated measures of both personality and health outcomes, provide a more objective assessment of identifying the influence personality can have on health (Smith & Spiro, 2002; Wilson et al., 2004). Researchers have examined this relationship in numerous studies, primarily relying on personality traits as predictors.

Previous research has established both neuroticism and conscientiousness as predictors of longevity, disease progression, and mortality (Bogg & Roberts, 2004; Wilson et al., 2004, 2005). Even after controlling for the confounding effects of socioeconomic status and lifestyle factors, older individuals who were more neurotic almost doubled their risk of death (Wilson et al., 2004, 2005). Additionally, the more stable the pattern of neuroticism or increasing neuroticism over time, the greater the likelihood of compromised health in later life (Mroczek & Spiro, 2007; Wilson et al., 2004). High levels of conscientiousness, on the other hand, were strong predictors associated with survival and inversely related to all risky health-related behaviors (Bogg & Roberts, 2004; Weiss & Costa, 2004). More specifically, older adults with high conscientiousness scores cut their risk of death by half (Wilson et al., 2004).

Although neuroticism is associated with poorer health outcomes, we should not discount the potential beneficial effects of such a common personality trait. For example, high trait anxiety (similar to neuroticism) was associated with an increased risk of non-accidental death in later life, despite its association with a decreased risk of accidents and accidental death in early adulthood (Lee, Wadsworth, & Hotopf, 2005). Theoretically, neuroticism is indicative of increased sensitivity and fear of potentially dangerous situations, thereby reducing the risk of accidental death early in life. Finally, the direction of change in neuroticism, particularly if it continues to increase over time, may be more important in predicting mortality than simply possessing this particular trait (Mroczek & Spiro, 2007).

Personality traits are also strong antecedents to additional health outcomes such as cardiovascular disease. For example, hostility assessed during late adolescence was associated with increased likelihood of smoking, excessive alcohol intake, and higher depression up to 30 years later (Siegler et al. 2003). Interest in this area grew from research on Type A and Type B personalities in which hostile Type A behavior patterns were linked to coronary disease (see Friedman & Rosenman, 1974) and research into this phenomenon continues to flourish (see Smith & Spiro, 2002). Finally, there is additional evidence that personality traits may also be associated with specific chronic conditions and other lifestyle choices such as tobacco use (Munafo & Black, 2007).

Although these findings indicate that personality traits have a stable and cumulative effect on both health and longevity, disentangling a direct causal pathway between personality and health can be challenging. Research that includes nonlinear effects of personality traits as well as the within-person variability (rather than focusing on average effects) is necessary to clarify these relationships. Because the majority of empirical results exploring the relationship between personality and health have relied primarily on trait measures of personality, we encourage readers to also consider the role that personality processes (e.g., attitudes, beliefs, goals) likely play in important health outcomes. For example, mastery and sense of coherence are associated with lower rates of mortality from all causes, even after adjusting for chronic physical disease (Surtees et al, 2006).

Well-Being.   The importance of personality processes and health is evident in psychological well-being outcomes. The fact that unique people faced with diverse life circumstances claim to experience similar levels of well-being, highlights the complexity of analyzing individual well-being. Markus, Ryff, Curhan, and Palmersheim (2004) suggest that well-being is intimately tied to people's understanding of themselves, their actions, and their places in the world. Additionally, their perception of the world is determined by the opportunities and constraints associated with their individual lives. Well-being reflects and requires the sense that one fits in, belongs, or is a member in good standing in some set of communities, so any measurement of well-being may also require an assessment of these contexts. Most midlife Americans believe that social relations and health are necessary aspects of a good middle and future life (Markus, Ryff, Curhan, & Palmersheim, 2004). Two other concepts they reported as central to well-being included developing aspects of the self (e.g., loving the self, pursuing goals, experiencing autonomy) and enjoying life as it progresses (Markus, Ryff, Curhan, & Palmersheim, 2004).

Multiple studies have demonstrated that there is a minimal decrease in life satisfaction and subjective well-being in old age (Diener & Suh, 1998; Kunzmann, Little, & Smith, 2000). Because the likelihood of experiencing a chronic condition or decline in physical functioning increases with age, the stability of subjective well-being is an interesting phenomenon. This finding highlights the role of developing aspects of the self, self-regulation and resilience to achieving successful aging. Having a sense of coherence, or an integrated self, is an important element to well-being in older adults (Schneider, Driesch, Kruse, Nehen, & Heuft, 2006) and may offset age-related losses.

Ryff (1989, 1991) has been a pioneer in research on well-being in adulthood. Her work has resulted in the identification of six dimensions of psychological well-being for adults: self-acceptance, positive relations with others, autonomy, environmental mastery, purpose in life, and personal growth. Distinctive personality traits have been associated with each aspect of well-being; for example, self-acceptance, environmental mastery, and purpose in life were linked with neuroticism, extraversion, and conscientiousness (Schmutte & Ryff, 1997). Other personality traits (i.e., optimism, extraversion) are strong predictors of most components of well-being (Diener & Lucas, 1999; McGregor & Little, 1998; Wilson et al., 2005). In fact, positive affect has predicted survival up to six decades later in life (Danner, Snowdon, & Friesen., 2001).

The effects of personality disorders may also be useful in demonstrating how crucial a well-functioning personality is for mental health and well-being (Widiger, Verheul, & Wim vanden Brink, 1999). It has been argued that mental health symptoms are an extreme manifestation of normal personality traits (Claridge & Davis, 2003). When personality traits become maladaptive and inflexible, it can result in significant functional impairment and subjective distress. In this scenario, one may need clinical intervention to alleviate this distress. This highlights the value of a malleable versus rigid personality to achieve mental health.

Some research suggests a general continuity of personality characteristics across the life span, with some decline in impulsivity (Molinari & Krunik, 1999) and potential decline in personality disorders in adulthood compared to adolescence (Johnson et al., 2000). This is reflective of the general trends for better emotion and self-regulation with age. Similar to research on physical health outcomes, however, the association between psychological wellness and personality is strong, but also quite complex.

Counseling and Adult Learning

Personality can play an important role in counseling and adult learning domains. Individuals' future goals (such as their possible selves) are one specific aspect of personality that demonstrate potential for positive effects on both counseling and adult learning. As described previously in the chapter, possible selves are a potentially useful motivational tool for affecting change in individuals. A valuable feature of the possible selves construct is the way it links motivational, cognitive, and emotional self-systems. When an individual's goals for the future are represented as possible selves, one may be more motivated to work toward this goal (Markus & Nurius, 1986). In addition, one's ability to select and pursue goals is closely tied to emotions, which in turn can guide individual daily action (Hooker, 1999).

Researchers have already begun integrating the use of possible selves into such fields as occupational counseling, school achievement, adult learning, and substance abuse counseling with some preliminary success (Martz, 2001; Oyserman, Terry, & Bybee, 2002; Packard & Nguyen, 2003). The need for ongoing, future research regarding this construct and its usefulness in improving the quality of human lives is still necessary. Counselors and therapists, for example, might obtain more insight into their clients' distress by eliciting their possible selves and self-regulatory processes (Dunkel, Kelts, & Coon, 2006). Additionally, they might be able to better motivate clients to adhere to treatment plans if they had a clearer understanding of their clients' volitional processes. Future studies designed to explore the practicality and usefulness of integrating this construct into counseling and clinical domains are needed (Allen, Woolfolk, Gara, & Apter, 1996).

Other lines of research are exploring how possible selves may be useful in adult learning (Cox, 2006; Fletcher, 2007). Because the attainment of possible selves occurs in a social context, Fletcher (2007) asserts that mentoring relationships are one means of helping individuals reach their goals. Mentors can help adult learners create a more detailed and well-defined possible self to motivate individuals toward more purposeful and intentional behavior. Possible selves are particularly useful in this domain because they enable people to see and articulate a vision of who they are, who they want to become, as well as how, and what they want to learn.

Summary and Future Directions

As emphasized throughout this chapter, personality matters. It is a crucial human element and can provide insight into human behavior. Additionally, personality is a multifaceted construct. It encompasses an individual's unique enduring traits, ephemeral states, goal processes, self-regulation, integrative life stories, and self-narration processes. Each of these features is represented in the six-foci approach to understanding personality, which provides a useful model for addressing the complexity of personality science. Because the discipline of personality is so expansive, we were unable to address all areas of the field, however, we provided ample evidence that each element of personality plays a vital role in optimal aging and that both personality stability and change are universal aspects of personality.

The field of personality and adult development is flourishing and we anticipate that it will continue to thrive, in part because it shows promise as an area in which adults have the potential for growth well into later life. Through midlife and beyond, adults are capable of striving for and experiencing gains in integrity, self-transcendence, and wisdom, as well as creating and attaining personal goals to promote optimal aging across the life span. Personality variables are a driving force behind these gains. Studying personality with a triangulated approach and from a life span developmental perspective will allow us to continue to answer interesting questions about how we change, learn, develop, or even remain the same over time.

References

Adams, C., Smith, M. C., Pasupathi, M., & Vitolo, L. (2002). Social context effects on story recall in older and younger women: Does the listener make a difference? *Journal of Gerontology: Psychological Sciences, 57*B, 28–40.

Adkins, G., Martin, P., & Poon, L. W. (1996). Personality traits and states as predictors of subjective well-being in centenarians, octogenarians, and sexagenarians. *Psychology and Aging, 11*, 408–416.

Aldwin, C. M., Levenson, M., & Gilmer, D F. (2004). *Health, illness, and optimal aging.* Thousand Oaks, CA: Sage.

Allen, L. A., Woolfolk, R. L., Gara, M. A., & Apter, J. T. (1996). Possible selves in major depression. *Journal of Nervous & Mental Disease, 184*(12), 739–745.

Allport, F. H. (1937). Teleonomic description in the study of personality. *Character and Personality, 5,* 202–214.

Allport, G. W. (1955). *Becoming: Basic considerations for psychology of personality.* New Haven, CT: Yale University Press.

Allport, G. W. (1961). *Pattern and growth in personality.* New York: Holt, Rinehart and Winston.

Baltes, M. M., & Carstensen, L. L. (1999). Social psychological theories and their applications to aging: From individual to collective. In V. Bengtson & K.W. Schaie (Eds.), *Handbook of theories of aging* (pp. 209–226). New York: Springer.

Baltes, P. B., & Baltes, M. M. (1990). Psychological perspectives on successful aging: The model of selective optimization with compensation. In P. B. Baltes & M. M. Baltes (Eds.), *Successful aging: Perspectives from the behavioral sciences* (pp. 1–34). New York: Cambridge University Press.

Baltes, P. B., Lindenberger, U., & Staudinger, U. M. (1998). Life-span theory in developmental psychology. In R. M. Lerner (Ed.), *Handbook of child psychology, Vol. 1: Theoretical models of human development* (5th ed., pp. 1029–1143). New York: Wiley.

Bandura, A. (1997). *Self-efficacy: The exercise of control.* New York: Freeman.

Bandura, A. (2001). Social cognitive theory: An agentic perspective. *Annual Review of Psychology, 52,* 1–26.

Bartlett, F. (1932). *Remembering: A study in experimental and social psychology.* New York: Cambridge University Press.

Block, J. (1981). Some enduring and consequential structures of personality. In A. I. Rabin (Ed.), *Further explorations in personality* (pp. 27–43). New York: Wiley.

Bogg, T., & Roberts, B. W. (2004). Conscientiousness and health-related behaviors: A meta-analysis of the leading behavioral contributors to mortality. *Psychological Bulletin, 130*(6), 887–919.

Brandtstädter, J., & Lerner, R. M. (Eds.). (1999). *Action and self-development: Theory and research through the life span.* Thousand Oaks, CA: Sage.

Bronfenbrenner, U. (1977). Toward an experimental ecology of human development. *American Psychologist, 32,* 513–530.

Bronfenbrenner, U. (1979). *The ecology of human development.* Cambridge, MA: Harvard University Press.

Cantor, N. (1990). From thought to behavior: "Having" and "doing" in the study of personality and cognition. *American Psychologist, 45,* 735–750.

Carver, C. S., & Scheier, M. F. (1998). *On the self-regulation of behavior.* New York: Cambridge University Press.

Caspi, A. (2000). The child is father of the man: Personality continuities from childhood to adulthood. *Journal of Personality and Social Psychology, 78,* 158–172.

Caspi, A., Bem, D. J., & Elder, G. H., Jr. (1989). Continuities and consequences of interactional styles across the life course. *Journal of Personality, 57,* 375–406.

Claridge, G., & Davis, C. (2003). *Personality and psychological disorders.* New York: Oxford University Press.

Contrada, R. J., Cather, C., & O'Leary, A. (1999). Personality and health: Dispositions and processes in disease susceptibility and adaptation to illness. In L.A. Pervin & O.P. John (Eds.), *Handbook of personality* (2nd ed., pp. 576–604). New York: Guildford.

Costa, P. T., & McCrae, R. R. (1987). Neuroticism, somatic complaints, and disease: Is the bark worse than the bite? *Journal of Personality, 55,* 299–316.

Costa, P. T., Jr., & McCrae, R. R. (1980). Still stable after all these years: Personality as a key to some issues in adulthood and old age. In P. B. Baltes & O. G. Brim, Jr. (Eds.), *Life-span development and behavior* (Vol. 3, pp. 65–102). New York: Academic.

Cox, E. (2006). An adult learning approach to coaching. In D. Stober & A. Grant, (Eds.), *Evidence based coaching handbook* (pp. 207). New York: Wiley.

Cross, S., & Markus, H. (1991). Possible selves across the lifespan. *Human Development, 34,* 230–255.

Danner D., Snowdon, D. A., & Friesen, W. V. (2001). Positive emotions in early life and longevity; findings from the Nun Study. *Journal of Personality and Social Psychology, 80*(5), 804–813.

Diehl, M., Hastings, C. T., & Stanton, M. (2001). Self-concept differentiation across the adult life span. *Psychology and Aging, 16*(4), 643–654.

Diener, E., & Suh, M. E. (1998). Subjective well-being and age: An international analysis. In K. W. Schaie & M. P. Lawton (Eds.), *Annual review of gerontology and geriatrics* (Vol. 17, pp. 304–324). New York: Springer.

Diener, E., & Lucas, R. (1999). Personality, and subjective well-being. In D.Kahneman, E. Diener, & N. Schwarz (Eds.), *Well-being: The foundations of hedonic psychology* (pp. 213–229). New York: Russell Sage.

Dijkstra, K., & Kaup, B. (2005). Mechanisms of autobiographical memory retrieval in younger and older adults. *Memory & Cognition, 33*(5), 811–820.

Dunkel, C., Kelts, D., & Coon, T. (2006). Possible selves as mechanisms of change in therapy. In C. Dunkel & J. Kerpelman (Eds.), *Possible selves: Theory, research, and application.* New York: Nova Science.

Eizenman, D. R., Nesselroade, J. R., Featherman, D. L., & Rowe, J. W. (1997). Intraindividual variability in perceived control in an older sample: The MacArthur successful aging studies. *Psychology & Aging, 12,* 489–502.

Emmons, R. A. (1986). Personal strivings: An approach to personality and subjective well-being. *Journal of Personality and Social Psychology, 51,* 1058–1068.

Emmons, R. A. (1996). Striving and feeling: Personal goals and subjective well-being. In J. Bargh & P. Gollwitzer (Eds.), *The psychology of action: Linking motivation and cognition to behavior* (pp. 314–337). New York: Guilford.

Erikson, E. H. (1959). *Identity and the life cycle.* New York: International Universities Press.

Fiese, B., Hooker, K., Kotary, L., Schwagler, J., & Rimmer, M. (1995). Family stories: Gender differences in the early stages of parenthood. *Journal of Marriage and the Family, 57,* 763–770.

Fiske, D. W. (1974). The limits for the conventional science of personality. *Journal of Personality, 42*(1), 1–11.

Fleeson, W. (2001). Toward a structure- and process-integrated view of personality: traits as density distribution of states. *Journal of Personality & Social Psychology, 80*(6), 1011–1027.

Fleeson, W., Malanos, A. B., & Achille, N. M. (2002). An intraindividual process approach to the relationship between extraversion and positive affect: is acting extraverted as "good" as being extraverted? *Journal of Personality & Social Psychology, 83*(6), 1409–1422.

Fletcher, S. (2007). Mentoring adult learners: Realising possible selves. *New Directions in Adult Learning.* San Francisco: Jossey-Bass

Ford, D. H. (1987). *Humans as self-constructing living systems: A developmental perspective on behavior and personality.* Hillsdale, NJ: Erlbaum.

Ford, D. H., & Lerner, R. M. (1992). *Developmental systems theory: An integrative approach.* Newbury Park, CA: Sage.

Frazier, L. D., Hooker, K., Johnson, P. M., & Kaus, C. R. (2000). Continuity and change in possible selves in later life: A 5-year longitudinal study. *Basic and Applied Social Psychology, 22,* 235–241.

Freund, A. M., & Baltes, P. B. (2000). The orchestration of selection, optimization,and compensation: An action-theoretical conceptualization of a theory of developmental regulation. In W. J. Perrig, & A. Grob (Eds.), *Control of human behavior, mental processes, and consciousness: Essays in honor of the 60th birthday of August Flammer* (pp. 35–58). Mahwah, NJ: Erlbaum.

Friedman, M., & Rosenman, R. H. (1974). *Type A behavior and your heart.* New York: Knopf.

Goldberg, L. (1993). The structure of phenotypic personality traits. *American Psychologist, 48,* 26–34.

Heckhausen, J. (2001). Adaptation and resilience in midlife. In M. E. Lachman (Ed.), *Handbook of midlife development* (pp. 345–394). New York: Wiley

Helson, R., Jones, C. J., & Kwan, V. S. Y. (2002). Personality change over 40 years of adulthood: HLM analyses of two longitudinal samples. *Journal of Personality and Social Psychology, 83,* 752–766.

Hogan, R., Johnson, J., & Briggs, S. (Eds.). (1997). *Handbook of personality psychology.* San Diego, CA: Academic.

Holahan, C. K. (2003). Stability and change in positive self-appraisal from midlife to later aging. *International Journal of Aging and Human Development, 56,* 247–267.

Hooker, K. (1992). Possible selves and perceived health in older adults and college students. *Journal of Gerontology: Psychological Sciences, 47,* 85–95.

Hooker, K. (1999). Possible selves in adulthood: Incorporating teleonomic relevance into studies of the self. In T. M. Hess & F. Blanchard-Fields (Eds.), *Social cognition and aging* (pp. 97–122). New York: Academic.

Hooker, K., & McAdams, D. P. (2003). Personality reconsidered: A new agenda for aging research. *Journal of Gerontology: Psychological Sciences, 58,* 296–304.

James, W. (1890). *The principles of psychology.* New York: Dover.

Johnson, J. G., Cohen, P., Kasen, S., Skodol, A. E., Hamagami, F., & Brook, J. S. (2000). Age related change in personality disorder trait levels between adolescence and adulthood: A community-based longitudinal investigation. *Acta Psychiatrica Scandinavica, 102*(4), 265–275.

Jung, C. G. (1933). *Modern man in search of a soul.* New York: Harcourt.

Kunzmann U., Little T. D., & Smith, J. (2000). Is age-related stability of subjective well-being a paradox? Cross-sectional and longitudinal evidence from the Berlin Aging Study. *Psychology & Aging, 15,* 511–526

Labouvie-Vief, G. (1982). Growth and aging in life span perspective. *Human Development, 25,* 65–88.

Labouvie-Vief, G., Chiodo, L. M., Goguen, L. A., Diehl, M., & Orwoll, L. (1995). Representations of self across the life span. *Psychology & Aging, 10,* 404–415.

Lachman, M. E. (1986). Locus of control in aging research: A case for multidimensional and domain-specific assessment. *Psychology & Aging, 1*(1), 34–40.

Lachman, M. E. (2004). Development in midlife. *Annual Review of Psychology, 55,* 305–331.

Lachman, M. E., & Bertrand, R. M. (2001) Personality and the self in midlife. In M. E. Lachman (Ed.), *Handbook of midlife development.* New York: Wiley.

Lachman, M. E., & Weaver, S. (1998). Sociodemographic cariations in the sense of control by domain: Findings from the MacArthur Studies of Midlife. *Psychology and Aging, 13,* 553–562.

Lamiell, J. T. (1981). Toward an idiothetic psychology of personality. *American Psychologist, 36,* 276–289.

Langer, E., & Rodin, J. (1976). The effects of choice and enhanced personal responsibility for the aged: A field experiment in an institutional setting. *Journal of Personality and Social Psychology, 61,* 191–198.

Lee, W. E., Wadsworth, M. J., & Hotopf, M. (2005). The protective role of trait anxiety: A longitudinal cohort study. *Psychological Medicine,* 1–7.

Light, J. M., Grigsby, J. S., & Bligh, M. C. (1996). Aging and heterogeneity: Genetics, social structure, and personality. *The Gerontologist, 36*(2), 165–198.

Little, B. R. (1983). Personal projects: A rationale and method for investigation. *Environment and Behavior, 15,* 273–309.

Markus, H. R. (1983). Self-knowledge: An expanded view. *Journal of Personality, 51, 3,* 543–565.

Markus, H. R. (2004). Culture and personality: Brief for an arranged marriage. *Journal of Research in Personality, 38,* 75–83.

Markus, H., & Nurius, P. (1986). Possible selves. *American Psychologist, 41,* 954–969.

Markus, H. R., Ryff, C. D., Curhan, K. B., & Palmersheim, K. A. (2004). In their own words: Well-being at midlife among high school and college educated adults. In O. G. Brim, C. D. Ryff, & R. C. Kessler (Eds.), *How healthy are we? A national study of well-being at midlife* (pp.273–319). Chicago: University of Chicago Press.

Martin, M., & Mroczek, D. K. (2004). Are personality traits across the lifespan sensitive to environmental demands? *Journal of Adult Development,* 1–27.

Martz, E. (2001). Expressing counselor empathy through the use of possible selves. *Journal of Employment Counseling, 38,* 128–133.

Matthews, G., Deary, I. J., & Whiteman, M. C. (2003). *Personality traits*. New York: Cambridge University Press.

McAdams, D. P. (1992). The five factor model in personality: A critical appraisal. *Journal of Personality, 60,* 329–361.

McAdams, D. P. (1995). What do we know when we know a person? *Journal of Personality, 63,* 365–396.

McAdams, D. P. (2001). The psychology of life stories. *Review of General Psychology, 5,* 100–122.

McAdams, D. P. (2006). *The redemptive self: Stories Americans live by.* New York: Oxford University Press.

McAdams, D. P., & Pals, J. (2006). A new big five: Fundamental principles for an integrative science of personality. *American Psychologist, 61*(3), 204–217.

McArdle, J. J. (1991). Structural models of development theory in psychology. *Annals of Theoretical Psychology, 7,* 139–159

McCrae R. R., Costa P. T., Jr.(1990) *Personality in adulthood.* New York: Guilford.

McCrae, R. R., & Costa, P. T. (1994). The stability of personality: Observation and evaluation. *Current Directions in Psychological Science, 3,* 173–175.

McCrae, R. R., & Costa, P. T. (1999). A five-factor theory of personality. In L. A. Pervin & O. P. John (Eds.), *Handbook of personality: Theory and research* (2nd ed., 139–153). New York: Guilford.

McCrae, R. R., & Costa, P. T. (2003). *Personality in adulthood: A five-factor theory perspective* (2nd ed.). New York: Guilford.

McCrae, R. R., & Terracciano, A. (2005). Universal features of personality traits from the observer's perspective: Data from 50 cultures. *Journal of Personality & Social Psychology, 88*(3), 547–561.

McGregor, I., & Little, B. R. (1998). Personal projects, happiness and meaning: On doing well and being yourself. *Journal of Personality and Social Psychology, 74,* 494–512.

Mischel, W. (1968). *Personality and assessment.* New York: Wiley.

Mischel, W., & Shoda, Y. (1998). Reconciling processing dynamics and personality dispositions. *Annual Review of Psychology, 49,* 229–258.

Molinari, V., & Krunik, M.E. (1999). Age-related personality differences in inpatients with personality disorder: A cross-sectional study. *Journal of Clinical Gerontology 5*(3), 191–202.

Mortimer, J. T., Finch, M. D., & Kumka, D. (1982). Persistence and change in development: The multidimensional self-concept. In P. B. Baltes & O. G. Brim (Eds.), *Life span development and behavior* (pp. 216–313). New York: Academic.

Mroczek, D. K., & Kolarz, C. M. (1998). The effect of age on positive and negative affect: A developmental perspective on happiness. *Journal of Personality and Social Psychology, 75,* 1333–1349.

Mroczek, D. K., & Spiro, A., III. (2003). Modeling intraindividual change in personality traits: Findings from the normative aging study. *Journal of Gerontology: Psychological Sciences, 58B*(3), P153–P165.

Mroczek, D. K., & Spiro, A. (2007). Personality change influences mortality in older men. *Psychological Science, 18* (5), 371–376.

Mroczek, D. K., Spiro, A., & Griffin, P. (2006). Personality and aging. In J. E. Birren & K. W. Schaie (Eds.), *Handbook of the psychology of aging* (6th ed., pp. 263–377). San Diego, CA: Elsevier.

Munafo, M. R., & Black, S. (2007). Personality and smoking status: A longitudinal analysis. *Nicotine & Tobacco Research, 9*(3), 397–404.

Nesselroade, J. R. (1987). Some implications of the trait-state distinction for the study of development over the life span: The case of personality. In P. B. Baltes, D. L. Featherman, & R. M. Lerner (Eds.), *Life-span development and behavior* (Vol. 8, pp. 163–189). Hillsdale, NJ: Erlbaum.

Nesselroade, J. R. (1990). Adult personality development: Issues in assessing constancy and change. In A. Rabin, R. A. Zucker, R. A. Emmons, & S. Frank (Eds.), *Studying persons and lives* (pp. 41–85). New York: Springer.

Nesselroade, J. R., & Featherman, D. L. (1991). Intraindividual variability in older adults depression scores: Some implications for developmental theory and longitudinal research. In D. Magnusson, R. L. Bergman, G. Rudinger, & B. Torestad (Eds.), *Problems and methods in longitudinal research: Stability and change* (pp. 47–66). Cambridge, MA: Cambridge University Press.

Nesselroade, J. R., & Ram, N. (2004). Studying intraindividual variability: What we have learned that will help us understand lives in context. *Research in Human Development 1*(1 & 2), 9–29.

Neugarten, B. L. (1968). Adult personality. In B. L. Neugarten (Ed.), *Middle age and aging* (pp. 137–147). Chicago: University of Chicago Press.

Neugarten, B. L. (1979). Time, age, and the life cycle. *American Journal of Psychiatry, 136*(7), 887–894.

Neugarten, B. L. (1996). *The meanings of age: Selected papers of Bernice Neurgarten*. Chicago: University of Chicago Press.

Neugarten, B. L., & Hagestad, G. O. (1976). Age and the life course. In R. Binstock & E. Shanas (Eds.), *Handbook of aging and the social sciences* (pp. 35–55). New York: Van Nostrand Reinhold.

Nurmi, J., & Salmela-Aro, K. (2002). Goal construction, reconstruction and depressive symptoms in a life-span context: The transition from school to work. *Journal of Personality, 70*(3), 385–420.

Oyserman, D., Terry, K., & Bybee, D. (2002). A possible selves intervention to enhance school involvement. *Journal of Adolescence, 24*, 313–326.

Packard, B. W., & Nguyen, D. (2003). Science career-related possible selves of adolescent girls: A longitudinal study. *Journal of Career Development, 29*(4), 251–263.

Pasupathi, M. (2001). The social construction of the personal past and its implications for adult development. *Psychological Bulletin, 127*(5), 651–672.

Pedersen, N. L., Plomin, R., McClearn, G. E., & Friberg, L. (1988). Neuroticism, extraversion, and related traits in adult twins reared apart and reared together. *Journal of Personality and Social Psychology, 55*(6), 950 – 957.

Riediger, M., Freund, A. M., & Baltes, P. B. (2005). Managing life through personal goals: Inter-goal facilitation and intensity of goal pursuit in younger and older adulthood. *Journal of Gerontology: Psychological Sciences, 60*B, 84–91.

Roberts, B., O'Donnell, W., & Robins, R. W. (2004). Goal and personality development. *Journal of Personality and Social Psychology, 87*, 541–550.

Roberts, B. W., & DelVecchio, W. F. (2000). The rank-order consistency of personality from childhood to old age: A quantitative review of longitudinal studies. *Psychological Bulletin, 126*, 3–25.

Roberts, B. W., Caspi, A., & Moffitt, T. (2001). The kids are alright: Growth and stability in personality development from adolescence to adulthood. *Journal of Personality and Social Psychology, 81*, 670–683.

Roberts, B. W., Caspi, A., & Moffitt, T. E. (2003). Work experiences and personality development in young adulthood. *Journal of Personality and Social Psychology, 84*, 582–593.

Roberts, B. W., Helson, R., & Klohnen, E. C. (2002). Personality development and growth in women across 30 years: Three perspectives. *Journal of Personality, 70*, 79–102.

Roberts, B. W., Walton, K. & Viechtbauer, W. (2006). Patterns of mean-level change in personality traits across the life course: A meta-analysis of longitudinal studies. *Psychological Bulletin, 132*, 1–25.

Ryff, C. D. (1989). Happiness is everything, or is it? Explorations on the meaning of psychological well-being. *Journal of Personality and Social Psychology, 57*, 1069–1081.

Ryff, C. D. (1991). Possible selves in adulthood and old age: A tale of shifting horizons. *Psychology & Aging, 7*, 507–517.

Scarr, S., & McCartney, K. (1983). How people make their own environments: A theory of genotype greater than environment effects. *Child Development, 54*(2), 424–35

Schmutte, P. S., & Ryff, C. D. (1997). Personality and well-being: Reexamining methods and meanings. *Journal of Personality and Social Psychology, 73*(3), 549–559.

Schneider, G., Driesch, G., Kruse, A., Nehen, H., & Heuft, G. (2006). Old and ill and still feeling well? Determinants of subjective well-being in >60 year olds: The role of the sense of coherence. *American Journal of Geriatric Psychiatry, 14*(10), 850–859.

Schulz, R. (1976). Effects of control and predictability on the physical and psychological well-being of the institutionalized aged. *Journal of Personality and Social Psychology, 33*, 563–573.

Siegler, I. C., Costa, P. T., Brummett, B. H., Helms, M. J., Barefoot, J. C., Williams, R. B., et al. (2003). Patterns of change in hostility from college to midlife in the UNC Alumni Heart Study predict high-risk status. *Psychosomatic Medicine, 65,* 738–745.

Siegler, R. S. (1989). Mechanisms of cognitive development. *Annual Review of Psychology, 40,* 353–379.

Smith, T. W., & Gallo, L. C. (2001). Personality traits as risk factors for physical illness. In A. Baum, T. Revenson, & J. E. Singer (Eds.), *Handbook of health psychology* (pp. 139–172). Hillsdale, NJ: Erlbaum.

Smith, T. W., & Spiro, A., III. (2002). Personality, health, and aging: Prolegomenon for the next generation. *Journal of Research in Personality, 36,* 363–394.

Sneed, J. R., & Whitbourne, S. K. (2003). Identity processing and self-consciousness in middle and later adulthood. *Journal of Gerontology: Psychological Sciences and Social Sciences, 58,* 313–319.

Staudinger, U., & Kunzmann, U. (2005). Positive adult personality development: Adjustment and/or growth? *European Psychologist, 10*(4), 320–329.

Surtees, P., Wainwright, N., Luben, R., Khaw, K., & Day, N. (2006). Mastery, sense of coherence, and mortality: Evidence of independent associations from the EPIC-Norfolk prospective cohort study. *Health Psychology, 25*(1), 102–110.

Weiss, A., & Costa, P. (2004). Domain and facet personality predictors of all-cause mortality among Medicare patients aged 65–100. *Psychosomatic Medicine, 67,* 724–733.

West, S. G. (2003). Towards finding the person in the data of personality. *Journal of Personality, 71*(3), 299–318.

Westen, D. (1990). Psychoanalytic approaches to personality. In L. A. Pervin (Ed.), *Handbook of personality: Theory and research* (pp. 21–65). New York: Guilford.

Whitbourne, S. K. (1987). Personality development in adulthood and old age: Relationships among identity style, health, and well-being. *Annual Review of Gerontology and Geriatrics, 7,* 189–216.

Whitbourne, S. K. (1999). Identity and adaptation to the aging process. In C. Ryff & V. Marshall (Eds.), *The self and society in aging processes* (pp.122–149). New York: Springer.

Whitbourne, S. K., & Connolly, L. A. (1999). The developing self in midlife. In S. B. Willis & J. Reid (Eds.), *Life in the middle: Psychological and social development in middle age* (pp. 25–45). San Diego, CA: Academic.

Widiger, T. A., Verheul, R., & vanden Brink, W. (1999). Personality and psychopathology. In L. A. Pervin & O. P. John (Eds.) *Handbook of personality: Theory and research.* New York: Guilford.

Wilson, A. E. & Ross, M. (2003). The identity function of autobiographical memory: Time is on our side. *Memory, 11*(2), 137–149.

Wilson, R. S., Krueger, K. R., Gu, L., Bienias, J. L., Mendes De Leon, C. F., & Evans, D. A. (2005). Neuroticism, extraversion, and mortality in a defined population of older persons. *Psychosomatic Medicine, 67,* 841–845.

Wilson, R. S., Mendes de Leon, C. F., Bienas, J. L., Evans, D. A., & Bennett, D. A. (2004). Personality and mortality in old age. *Journal of Gerontology: Psychological Sciences, 59*B, 110–116.

Chapter 9

Adjustment and Growth

Two Trajectories of Positive Personality Development across Adulthood

Ursula M. Staudinger and Eva-Marie Kessler

Theories of personality development typically describe changes in personality functioning during adulthood as "maturation" or "growth." In a similar fashion, adult developmentalists have interpreted recent empirical findings on age-related changes in personality measures as being indicative of maturation across adulthood. We would like to suggest that not necessarily can any personality change occurring during adulthood and old age be interpreted as maturation, even though personality maturity is probably one of the few positive facets of the aging stereotype. It is part of lay wisdom that if there is anything positive about aging it is that we gain in experience and become more mature and dignified or even wise as we grow older (Heckhausen, Dixon, & Baltes, 1989). However, one of us has recently argued that the observed pattern of personality development across adulthood suggests that there are not one, but rather two types of positive personality development, that is, adjustment and growth (Staudinger, Doerner, & Mickler, 2005; Staudinger & Kunzmann, 2005). In this chapter, in contrast to some of the extant literature and lay theory, we will argue that as we age, on average, we tend towards optimizing adjustment rather than personality growth.

In the first section of this chapter, we will introduce our notions of adjustment and growth by outlining definitions and empirical markers for these two types of positive personality development during adulthood. In the second section, we will discuss and summarize empirical findings on age trajectories of personality development and thereby provide empirical support for these two kinds of developmental trajectories.

Two Types of Positive Adult Personality Development

Defining Personality Adjustment

Personality adjustment, according to our definition, refers to how well an individual is able to manage changing opportunities and constraints that arise from history-graded, age-graded, and idiosyncratic developmental contexts.

The criteria according to which the quality of adjustment is assessed can either be subjective or objective in nature. The prototypical subjective criterion of adjustment is how good one feels about the self (in a world of others). Bauer and McAdams (2004) have recently labelled this facet of positive development "socio-emotional well-being." The classical objective criterion of adjustment is the degree to which an individual, according to societal norms, is successful in negotiating and mastering societal and biological demands, as well as their interaction. Helson and Wink (1987) have described the latter kind of positive development as functioning effectively within society or as social maturity. Freud's theory of personality development is a prototypical example of an ontogenetic theory of adjustment (Freud, 1953).

For any human being, adjustment is an obligatory task throughout the life course (for the distinction between obligatory and optional tasks see also Schindler & Staudinger, in press). In its extreme form, adjustment can be a question of survival. With increasing age, however, adjustment becomes more challenging due to increasing constraints in and decreasing opportunities for replenishment of societal and material as well as biological resources (Staudinger, Marsiske, & Baltes, 1995). At the same time, fortunately, there is a normative increase (or at least maintenance) of personal resources that support the capacity for adjustment, such as professional skills, increasing competence in everyday problem-solving, adjustment-related self-regulation, and social support. Furthermore, the age-related increase in the awareness of life's finitude seems to be a strong and successful motivator for adjustment—at least in the sense of socio-emotional well-being (Charles & Carstensen, 1999).

The survival and success of any human community is dependent on a high "incidence rate" of successful adjustment. Societies usually cannot and do not leave adjustment processes to chance but take precautions to optimize them (e.g., schooling system, educational and developmental tasks (Staudinger & Kunzmann, 2005). Such measures, usually subsumed under the heading "socialization," need to take care, however, that they do not lose sight of the synchronization of the subjective and objective side of adjustment. These two facets of personality adjustment not necessarily coincide at any given point in time. However, a society is well advised to take precaution that in the long run mastering rules and expectations (at least to a certain degree; objective adjustment) is not conflicting with individual members if this society leading a happy life (subjective adjustment) and vice versa. If this calibration process gets out of balance for many individuals it may result in political unrest, if it is the case for only some individuals it may result in emigration or psychopathology.

Defining Personality Growth/Maturity

We define personality maturity in terms of three facets, including a cognitive, emotional and motivational facets that entail: (i) deep and broad insight into self, others and the world, (ii) complex emotion-regulation (in the sense of tolerance of ambiguity), and (iii) a motivational orientation that is transcending self-interest and is investing in the well-being of others and the world. Note that all three facets need to come together in order for personality maturity to emerge.

Again, there is a subjective as well as an objective side to personality maturity. The subjective facet of personality maturity is indexed by the degree to which an individual experiences and strives for personal growth as well as feels love and a need to care of others. Ryff's (1989) dimensions of personal growth and purpose in life prototypically describe the subjective facet of personality maturity. The objective facet of personality maturity is indexed by the degree to which an individual is able to approximate the ideal of personality development of wisdom as it has been described through historical times and across different cultures (Baltes & Staudinger, 2000). Ideal endpoints of human development have also been described in a number of developmental theories, for example, Erikson (1959), Kohlberg (1963), Labouvie-Vief (1982) or Loevinger (1976); for a review see Baltes, Lindenberger & Staudinger (1998). Mostly, these models work with a Piagetian notion of development assuming that it is the dialectic between assimilation and accommodation that promotes growth. In other words, our expectations need to continuously be challenged by new experiences and we need to *emancipate* ourselves in thinking and feeling and *transcend* the structures within which we have been socialized (e.g., Chandler

& Holliday, 1990). Thus, in contrast to adjustment, the gist of growth is not the mastery of given structures and procedures but their transcendence.

We submit that personality growth is not an obligatory, but rather an optional task for the individual throughout the life course. And in fact, the support that modern industrialized societies invest in this kind of positive development is usually far less than the support for personality adjustment. In the same vein, deviations of one' own subjective perception from culturally ideal standards of personality growth are quite rarely punished. This lack of facilitating societal mechanisms most likely contributes to the fact that the capacities for personality growth are less easily acquired than strategies for adjustment and that age-related increases in personality maturity are a rather rare event (e.g., Staudinger, 1999a).

It will be interesting to observe how modern industrialized societies will behave as they try to adapt to the massive increase in average life expectancy, increasing uncertainty due to fast changes as well as to increased cultural diversity in lifestyles due to migration and globalization. We argue that the innovativeness of a society, and therefore its long-term success and survival, is dependent on a certain percentage of individuals that does not only master and negotiate given rules, norms and expectations, but transcends given societal circumstances. Times of thorough historical change may require more societal investment in personality growth than usually is the case.

The two tracks of personality development, adjustment and growth, do not operate independently from each other. Primarily authors with a background in (positive) mental health have viewed adjustment as one important component of maturity (Allport, 1961; Freud, 1923/1961; Ryff, 1989; Sullivan, 1972). However, there is also another tradition that views adjustment as unrelated (Bauer & McAdams, 2004; Helson & Wink, 1987; Loevinger, 1976) or even negatively related with maturity (e.g., Mead, 1934). Fromm (1941) considered adjustment even as the most universal form of neurosis. In order to understand the rather complicated causal connection between these two trajectories of positive personality development, lifespan psychologists, as a first step, need to agree upon indicators of personality adjustment and maturity and then collect evidence on how those indicators change across time and how they are interrelate across time.

So far, we have presented theoretical evidence that the two trajectories of adult personality development result from different developmental goals, are embedded in different facilitative structures, and demonstrate different incidence rates. In the following, we will consult empirical evidence on age-related changes in different indicators of adjustment and maturity.

Indicators and Facets of Personality Adjustment and Maturity

A number of different indicators/facets of personality adjustment and maturity can be identified in the literature. We have selected some structural and some process-related personality concepts to exemplify our notions of personality adjustment and maturity: the Big Five, psychological well-being, self-concept, self-concept maturity, personal wisdom, and ego development on the structural side, and values, coping strategies, systemic regulatory processes (SOC), and emotion regulation on the process side (Funder, 2001; Staudinger & Pasupathi, 2000).

Many efforts to understand and identify indicators of personality development have focused on structural characteristics. However, structural approaches typically do not consider the underlying processes or dynamics, nor do they focus on the interplay between dispositions and particular situations (Mischel & Shoda, 1999). Most likely, several important processes are involved in any given disposition. Understanding such processes is essential first to understanding how people will encode and respond to different situations that have implications for personality adjustment and growth, and second to developing interventions that promote positive development (Mischel & Mendoza-Denton, 2003). The following section is therefore divided into two parts, the first deals with structural and the second with process-related markers of adjustment or maturity.

For each of the concepts, Table 9.1 and Table 9.2 depict markers of personality adjustment and/or maturity. Note that some of the indicators were originally conceptionalized by researchers in order to describe positive functioning (adjustment and/or maturity), whereas others were not. In the latter case, we assigned them to either the adjustment or the growth trajectory based on the conceptualization of adjustment and growth introduced above.

Three further issues deserve consideration before we review the empirical evidence: (1) intentionality or automaticity; (2) correlates, antecedents, and consequences of adjustment and maturity; and (3) components or integrate whole. First, the issue arises whether the development of indicators of personality adjustment and maturity is conscious and intentional or whether it also encompasses automatic or intuitive processes. Even though reflexivity is one of the major discriminating features of the human species, it may not necessarily be the case that all positive features are conscious and linked to intentional action or reaction (Aspinwall & Staudinger, 2003). Rather, it is possible that human evolution, as well as ontogenesis, has produced "growth" as well as adjustment patterns of perception, action and reaction on an automatic and unintentional level (Berridge, 1999). Furthermore, we know from research on the acquisition of expertise that originally deliberative and intentional behavior across time becomes automatic and effortless. Thus, we proceed from the assumption that indicators of adjustment and

Table 9.1 Summary of Structural Indicators/Facets of Personality Adjustment and Growth

Personality Concepts	Indicators/Facets of Adjustment	Indicators/Facets of Growth/Maturity
Big Five	Emotional stability, agreeableness, conscientiousness (social)	Openness to experience, (social vitality)
Psychological Well-Being	Environmental mastery, self-acceptance	Personal growth, purpose in life
Self-Concept	Medium level of complexity of self-conceptions, associated with high level of self-concept integration	Medium complexity, high integration in content and valence, self-enhancing values, high self-esteem
Self-Concept Maturity	Medium level of complexity of self-conceptions, associated with high level of self-concept integration	High complexity, medium integration in content and valence, self-transcendent values, moderate self-esteem
Personal Wisdom	Medium ratings on the two criteria of self-insight and heuristics for growth, low ratings on interrelating the self, self-relativism, tolerance of ambiguity	High ratings on all five criteria: rich self-insight, heuristics for growth and self-regulation, interrelating the self, self-relativism, tolerance of ambiguity
Ego Development	Stage 3 (Conformist), Stage 4 (Self-aware), Stage 5 (Conscientious)	Stage 7 (Individualistic), Stage 8 (Autonomous)

maturity and their development can be conscious and intentional as well as automatic in nature. Second, indicators can differ in as much as they represent either direct operationalizations of adjustment or maturity or an antecedent or a consequence of personality adjustment or maturity. And finally, in a related vein, indicators differ in as much as they either contribute one facet to personality adjustment or maturity or represent adjustment or maturity as such.

Age Trajectories of Structural Markers of Personality Adjustment and Maturity

The Big Five

Relating our distinction between personality adjustment and maturity to the Big Five personality model developed and advocated by Costa and McCrae (1980), it is the absence of neuroticism, and the presence of agreeableness and conscientiousness that is associated with personality adjustment. The presence of openness to experience, in contrast, is related with personality growth. Extraversion is a quite complex characteristic that has been suggested to be composed of two facets, social assurance and social vitality (Helson, Kwan, John, & Jones 2002; Roberts, Robins, Caspi, & Trzesniewski, 2003). Social assurance (e.g., dominance, norm adherence, independence) increases with age and fits well with our notion of personality adjustment, whereas social vitality (e.g., sociability, empathy, social presence) seems to be one antecedent for personality growth and shows age-related decreases.

Empirical evidence suggests that during adulthood (the lack of) neuroticism is a good predictor of adjustment. Across studies, neuroticism shows strong links with negative affect (Costa & McCrae, 1980; Diener & Fujita, 1995; Watson & Clark, 1992). Neuroticism has often been viewed as the dispositional underpinning of negative affect and even has been used as a negative indicator of mental health. Furthermore, agreeableness and conscientiousness are moderately strong predictors of adjustment. Agreeableness and conscientiousness seem to be associated with subjective well-being instrumentally by engendering conditions and behaviors that facilitate or maintain subjective well-being. In fact, agreeableness and conscientiousness have been shown to predict subjective well-being over and above neuroticism (McCrae & Costa, 1991).

In contrast, openness to new experiences is discussed as the most central concomitant of personality maturity (Compton, 2001; Schmutte & Ryff, 1997; Staudinger, Lopez, & Baltes, 1997). In this vein, openness to experience shows strong associations with "purpose in life" and "personality growth," as defined below (Schmutte & Ryff, 1997). In a similar fashion, openness is positively correlated with ego development (Einstein & Lanning, 1998; McCrae & Costa, 1980), emotional complexity (Kang & Shaver, 2004), maturity of coping strategies (Costa, Zonderman, & McCrae, 1991), general and personal wisdom (Staudinger et al., 2005), and various other constructs related to personality growth (McCrae & Costa, 1997). At the same time, openness to new experience is not significantly correlated with indicators of adjustment such as subjective well-being. The reason may be that new experiences often imply challenges to adjustment that are not always mastered.

Taking into account cross-sectional and longitudinal evidence, the empirical consensus regarding stability and change of the five "basic" personality traits can be described as follows: Neuroticism decreases across adulthood (Mroczek & Spiro, 2005; Roberts, Walton, & Viechtbauer, 2006) and may show some increase again very late in life (Small, Hertzog, Hultsch, & Dixon, 2003); agreeableness and conscientiousness increase during adulthood (Helson & Kwan, 2000; Srivastava, John, Gosling, & Potter, 2003); and, openness to new experiences declines in later adulthood (Roberts et al., 2006). In an interesting cross-sectional study comparing samples between age 14 and 83 years from Korea, Portugal, Italy, Germany, Czech Republic, and Turkey, McCrae and colleagues (McCrae et al., 2000) found a highly similar pattern of mean-level age differences in these different cultures.

We suggest that this pattern of mean-level changes across adulthood and into old age, that is, the decrease in neuroticism combined with increases in agreeableness and conscientiousness can be interpreted as evidence for a normative increase in personality adjustment across the life span. The decline in openness that is observed in later adulthood according to our approach reflects the fact that personality maturity does not show normative increase but rather stability and later even decline.

Psychological Well-Being

Another theoretical framework that informs us of our two types of personality development across adulthood is the conception of "psychological well-being," as defined by Carol Ryff (Ryff, 1989; Ryff & Keyes, 1995). She developed a measure of psychological well-being based on models of personality development. This measure encompasses the following dimensions: *environmental mastery* (choosing or creating environments suitable to one's psychic conditions), *self-acceptance* (holding positive attitudes toward oneself), *autonomy* (having an internal locus of evaluation), *positive social relations* (ability to form warm, trusting interpersonal relations), *personal growth* (continuing to develop one's potential, to grow and expand as a person), and *purpose in life* (beliefs that convey the feeling there is purpose in and meaning to life).

In factor analyses, the dimensions of environmental mastery and self-acceptance load on the same factor conjointly with indicators of adjustment such as life satisfaction and positive/negative affect (Compton, 2001; Keyes et al., 2002; Mickler & Staudinger, 2007). The behaviors and attitudes subsumed under "personal growth" and "purpose in life" do not primarily serve adjustment-related goals but help to grow and transcend given structures. Indeed, personal growth and purpose in life show close relations with indicators of personality maturity such as personal wisdom and self-concept maturity (Doerner & Staudinger, 2007; Mickler & Staudinger, 2007). Autonomy and positive relations seem to be of relevance for both personality growth and adjustment. The ability for having intimate relationships and to evaluate oneself by personal standards are clearly a characteristic of a mature personality (Allport, 1961; Heath & Heath, 1991; Maslow, 1994), but, at the same time, represent important prerequisites for adjustment.

And, again, environmental mastery and self-acceptance follow a different age trajectory than personal growth and purpose in life during adulthood and old age. Replicating the trends of prior findings, in a large representative sample (N = 1108) purpose in life and personal growth showed negative age differences (with scores of the oldest respondents significantly lower than those of the two younger age groups; Ryff & Keyes, 1995). In contrast, the other two facets—environmental mastery and self-acceptance—showed positive age differences. These positive age differences again can be described as highly functional for mastering developmental tasks.

In sum, we suggest that the pattern of mean-level changes in environmental mastery and self-acceptance is indicative of normative (in the sense of statistical average) age-related increases in personality adjustment. Simultaneously, the developmental pattern in personal growth and purpose in life seems indicative of a decrease in personality maturity. Again, as before in the case of the Big Five, we find a distinctive developmental pattern for indicators of personality adjustment as compared to those of growth.

Self-Concept and Self-Concept Maturity

Both in the literature on personality adjustment and on growth, there is a long tradition to investigate the structure of the self-concept as an indicator of positive personality functioning. The structure of the self-concept is often investigated in terms of (1) its *complexity* and (2) its *integration* (Campbell, Assanand, & Di Paula, 2003). There are certain conceptual differences in what is meant by complexity.

Complexity has been defined as the number of factors, perspectives and roles involved in one's thoughts and actions (Allport, 1961), the interlocking of multiple psychological functions (such as emotion, cognition, and motivation; e.g., Labouvie-Vief, 1982), and the level of abstraction and reasoning underlying one's motives (Loevinger, 1976; Maslow, 1994). Complexity as used here refers to the number of perspectives an individual adopts with regard to himself or herself, as indicated by the number of non-redundant self-aspects or content categories of the self-definition (Linville, 1987). *Integration* often is defined as the similarity of self-aspects, as indicated by the correlation of trait ratings across different domains of the self-concept (Donahue, Robins, Roberts, & John, 1993). High similarity between self-aspects indicates high self-concept integration (Diehl, Hastings, & Stanton, 2001).

Research has shown that it is important to consider *complexity* and integration conjointly when investigating personality adjustment. A moderately complex, but highly integrated self-concept has been demonstrated to be associated with adjustment as previously defined (for a review, see Doerner, 2007). In a recent study on self-concept maturity, however, we found that it was high complexity combined with only a moderate degree of integration that was indicative of personality maturity (Doerner & Staudinger, 2007).

Unfortunately, different investigators have used different measures to assess the structure of the self-concept. Little is known about the validity of those instruments, and, thus, the results are often difficult to compare. Some authors use open self-descriptions (Freund & Smith, 1999; Labouvie-Vief, Chiodo, Goguen, Diehl, & Orwoll, 1995), whereas others use prefixed lists (Fitts, 1977; Gough & Bradley, 1996). Therefore, despite a huge amount of literature on the structure of the self-concept, its association with indicators of positive development has not been fully understood yet. It is much better understood, however, in terms of adjustment than in terms of growth.

Number of Self-Aspects, Self-Concept Complexity: Age Differences, Adjustment and Growth. The few studies that have investigated the number of self-aspects separately from their integration have mostly demonstrated the "stress-buffering" effect that an accrual of roles has on mental health, particularly in old age (Coleman, Antonucci, & Adelmann, 1987; Dietz, 1996; Helson, Elliot, & Leigh, 1990; Thoits, 1986; Vandewater, Ostrove, & Stewart, 1997). Studies that examine the effect of number of self-aspects on psycho-social adjustment come to the same conclusion (Koch & Shepperd, 2004; Rafaeli-Mor & Steinberg, 2002; Solomon & Haaga, 2003). However, a very large number of self-aspects can also be indicative of role strain or identity uncertainty (Block, 1961). Furthermore, a high number of self-aspects frequently goes along with an intense engagement in self-reflection, which in turn is more likely to induce negative affect, self-doubts, and uncertainty (Brown & Dutton, 1995; Silvia & Gendolla, 2001; Wicklund & Eckert, 1992; Wilson & Dunn, 2004).

Therefore, there is empirical reason to assume that it is indeed a medium number of self-domains that is optimal with regard to adjustment (Doerner & Staudinger, 2007).

Across different approaches, self-concept complexity has been considered as an important facet of personality maturity (Allport, 1961; Maslow, 1994; Loevinger, 1976; Heath, 1968; Labouvie-Vief, 1982). The very few empirical studies on the association of self-complexity and personality maturity support this assumption. Labouvie-Vief, Chiodo, Goguen, Diehl, and Orwoll (1995) used open self-descriptions as a measure of self-complexity and found a significantly positive relation between this measure and ego development. In a study by Hauser, Jacobson, Noam, and Powers (1983), complexity of the self-concept was defined as complexity vs. simplicity in rating patterns across a number of self-descriptive attributes (e.g., patient, hostile) and a number of relevant contexts (e.g., now; in the eyes of my friend). This measure of self-complexity was significantly related to ego development in an adolescent sample. Furthermore, two studies by Evans (Evans, 1994; Evans, Brody, & Noam, 2001) yielded a significant association between self-concept complexity and the maturity of psychological defenses and ego development, respectively. In this study, self-concept complexity was assessed as the similarity between reactions to various self-relevant scenarios. However, different authors (Assagioli, 1978/1989; Block, 1961; Erikson, 1968; James, 1890/1948; Rogers, 1961) have argued that a high level of self-complexity comes always at the risk of losing consistency and a sense of self. Therefore, the cognitive dimension of personality growth has to be characterized by a high degree of self-concept differentiation as well as a medium degree of self-concept integration—that is, a proper balance between role rigidity and role confusion (Block, 1961; Doerner & Staudinger, 2007).

In contrast to widely held theoretical assumptions about age trajectories in self-concept complexity, but in line with the present distinction between personality adjustment and maturity, the empirical evidence neither illustrates an increase (as suggested by Markus & Herzog, 1991; Neugarten. 1968; Perlmutter, 1988) nor a decrease (as suggested by disengagement theory, i.e., Cummings & Henry, 1961) in the number of self-aspects across the life span. Instead, the number of self-aspects seems to remain relatively stable throughout adulthood, although empirical evidence is scarce. For example, in a cross-sectional study conducted by Mueller, Wonderlich, and Dugan (1986), college students and older adults were asked to select self-descriptive attributes from a large set of descriptors. No age differences were found in number of selected attributes. Doerner and Staudinger (2007) recently yielded a similar result. Using an adapted version of the Linville self-complexity measure (Linville, 1985), they found no difference in number of self-aspects between younger and older adults (20–40 years vs. 60–80 years old).[1] It seems that the structure of the self-definition is not very sensitive towards age-graded changes in life circumstances.

Self-Concept Integration: Age Differences, Adjustment, and Growth.   In terms of the relationship between self-concept integration and adjustment, on theoretical grounds, a case has been made for a quadratic relationship—such that a medium degree of self-concept integration would be associated with the highest level of adjustment (Block, 1961). However, empirical evidence, despite some inconsistent findings (Gramzow et al., 2004), all in all confirms a linear association between self-concept integration on psychological health and well-being (Campbell et al., 2003; Diehl et al., 2001; Lutz & Ross, 2003). Even though high integration is associated with adjustment throughout adulthood, first results indicate that this effect is significantly more pronounced in older adults (Diehl et al., 2001).

In terms of age trajectories in self-concept integration, it is widely assumed that it is around the onset of adulthood that the conflicts of adolescence raised by opposing self-aspects tend to alleviate, and the self-structure becomes more and more integrated across adulthood (Arnett, 2000; Moneta, Schneider, & Csikszentmihalyi, 2001). Most theories and evidence covering adulthood expect this trend to continue linearly over the rest of the life span (Markus & Herzog, 1991; Neugarten, Havighurst, & Tobin, 1961; Whitbourne & Connolly, 1999). When it comes to empirical research, in one of the few studies on this topic, cross-sectional data indicate an inverted-u-shaped relationship between self-concept integration and chronological age for the age range from 20 to 88 years, with the peak (i.e., the highest degree of self-concept integration) being located in middle adulthood (Diehl et al., 2001). In contrast, Doerner and Staudinger (2007) found that the degree of integration of self-aspects is higher for older adults (60–80 years) than for younger adults (20–40 years). The latter result at least indirectly corresponds to the increase in identity certainty across adulthood (Cramer, 2004; Sheldon & Kasser, 2001; Stewart & Ostrove, 1998).

In sum, we demonstrated that the self-concept is a domain of psychological functioning that is highly relevant to our notions of personality adjustment and maturity. However, the association with indicators of adjustment and maturity has not yet been fully understood. Furthermore, empirical evidence on age trajectories, particularly with regard to self-concept integration, is equivocal (partly due to variation in measurement). Therefore, the presently available results only provide first evidence with regard to our distinction between personality adjustment and personality maturity: The finding that self-concept complexity remains stable throughout adulthood supports our assumption that personality growth may not increase normatively in old age. And at the same time, the result that self-integration seems to increase with age supports our tenet that personality adjustment increases normatively during adulthood and old age.

Self-Concept Maturity: Definition and Age Trends.   Most of the available self-concept research has concentrated on the stress-buffering effect of self-concept structure (see also Baltes, Staudinger, & Lindenberger, 1996). Only recently, a measure of personality maturity based on the self-concept literature has been developed (Doerner & Staudinger, 2007). Besides considering the facets of self-complexity and self-integration jointly, it is necessary to introduce an emotional as well as a motivational facet to arrive at an indicator of personality maturity. Thus, the recently developed measure of self-concept maturity combines five self-concept facets. These facets are complexity of self-concept content, self-concept integration, balance of self-related affect, self-esteem, and value orientation. Each of the five facets has to show a specific value and all five have to be considered jointly in order to assess personality maturity: High complexity, medium integration, a balanced experience of positive as well as negative self-related emotions, self-transcending values and a medium level of self-esteem were defined to index personality maturity. In contrast, using the same self-concept facets, personality adjustment was indexed by the joint occurrence of medium complexity, high integration, more positive than negative self-related emotions, self-enhancing values and high self-esteem. As expected, self-concept maturity did not show age differences whereas self-concept adjustment demonstrated positive age differences (Doerner & Staudinger, 2007).

Personal Wisdom

Recently, Mickler and Staudinger (in press) conceptualized personal wisdom as a person's deep insight and judgment into his or her own life and personality. Based on the wisdom literature as well as the literature on personality maturity (Allport, 1961; Bühler, 1968; Erikson, 1950; Freud, 1917/1993; Jung, 1933; Labouvie-Vief, 1982; Maslow, 1994; Rogers, 1961), five criteria of personal wisdom were defined. There are two *basic* criteria: deep, broad and balanced self-knowledge, and heuristics or strategies of growth and self-regulation. These are considered to be necessary but not sufficient to define personal wisdom. There are three *meta*-criteria: interrelating the self, self-relativism, and tolerance of ambiguity. These are more specific, require more complex judgmental processes and are more difficult to acquire. Based on an adapted version of the Berlin (general) wisdom paradigm (Baltes, Smith, & Staudinger, 1992), personal wisdom is measured by first using a thinking-aloud task and, subsequently, a rating procedure is applied to these response protocols (Mickler & Staudinger, 2007).

The first basic criterion of personal wisdom is rich *self-knowledge*, that is, deep insight into oneself. A self-wise person should be aware of his or her own competencies, emotions and goals and have a sense of meaning in life. The second basic criterion requires of a self-wise person to have available *heuristics* for growth and self-regulation (e.g., how to express and regulate emotions or how to develop and maintain deep social relations). Humor is an example of an important heuristic that helps one to cope with various difficult and challenging situations. *Interrelating the self*, the third criterion, refers to the ability to reflect on and have insight in the possible causes of one's behavior and/or feelings. Such causes can be age-related or situational or linked to personal characteristics. Interrelating the self also implies that there is an awareness of one's own dependency on others. The fourth criterion is called *self-relativism*. People high on self-relativism are able to evaluate themselves as well as others with a distanced view. They critically appraise their own behavior but at the same time display a basic acceptance of themselves. They also show tolerance for others' values and lifestyles—as long as they are not damaging to self or others. Finally, *tolerance of ambiguity* involves the ability to recognize and manage the uncertainties in one's own life and one's own development. It is reflected in the awareness that life is full of uncontrollable and unpredictable events, including death and illness. At the same time, tolerance for ambiguity includes the availability of strategies to manage this uncertainty through openness to experience, basic trust, and the development of flexible solutions.

In a first study, this performance measure of personal wisdom was positively correlated with other performance measures of personality maturity such as Loevinger's (1970) ego development, the measure of self-concept maturity, just presented, but also with self-report measures of personality growth, such as Ryff's personal growth and purpose in life (Mickler & Staudinger, in press). Furthermore, the measure was uncorrelated with indicators of adjustment, such as life satisfaction, and negative or positive emotions. Openness to experience emerged as an important predictor of personal wisdom. Furthermore, psychological mindedness, a construct measuring interest in thoughts and feelings of other people (Gough, 1957), was significantly correlated with personal wisdom.

When it comes to age trajectories, we have recently provided first evidence that, whereas general wisdom remains stable over the adult years and does not show normative increases (Baltes & Staudinger, 2000), age differences in personal wisdom seem to be less favorable. Overall, older adults scored lower on personal wisdom. When analyzing the data separately for the meta-criteria and the basic criteria, older adults performed lower than the young adults with regard to the meta-criteria, but older adults showed a tendency to perform better than younger adults on the two basic criteria.

Overall, personal wisdom as one indicator of personality maturity shows stability or even slight decline with age and thus supports the assumed trajectory of personality maturity during adulthood. Clearly, however, personal wisdom cannot be considered independent of adjustment. Rather, it is most likely that there is a threshold relationship between adjustment and wisdom. In that vein, it is interesting to note that five personal-wisdom criteria show differential associations with age as well as adjustment. The basic criteria show relationships with adjustment and at the same time demonstrate slight age-related increase. The three meta criteria showed no relationship with indicators of adjustment and demonstrate slightly negative age trends.

Ego Development

One concept that has gained much prominence as an indicator of personality growth is ego development, as defined by Jane Loevinger (Loevinger, 1976, 1998). She attempted to capture character development in a stage-model following the Piagetian model of cognitive development, but with a focus on character rather than cognitive changes. Loevinger conceived the stages of ego development as a successive progression toward psychological maturity, developing along the four dimensions of impulse control, interpersonal style, conscious preoccupations, and cognitive styles (Blasi, 1998; Manners & Durkin, 2001). The model comprises eight stages (impulsive, self-protective, conformist, self-aware, conscientious, individualistic, autonomous, integrated) that are characterized by increasingly mature versions of the four dimensions mentioned earlier. The eighth stage, the integrated stage, is rarely observed in random samples (Loevinger, 1998).

Loevinger (1976) proposed that there is stability in ego development across adulthood and into old age. Accordingly, after adolescence individuals sufficiently know about the human condition and contextual demands are less prone to challenge personality functioning any longer. Furthermore, Loevinger argued that most people proactively select their environments according to their own ego level, thereby inhibiting personality growth. And, indeed, empirical results show no age differences in ego level between 25 and 80 years (Cohn, 1998; McCrae & Costa, 1980). Most adults are categorized to be in the third to fifth stage, that is, the conformist, self-aware, and conscientious stage, with the self-aware stage being the modal stage in late adolescence and adult life (Loevinger, 1997). Overall, these results support our proposal that aging and old age may not automatically bring personality growth.

Within the conceptual framework of ego development, the autonomous and the integrated stages tap into our notion of personality growth. Accordingly, people at these stages are able to cope with conflict and have an interdependent interpersonal mode; they are preoccupied by self-fulfillment and are aware of the multifaceted complexity of situations and life choices. Whereas ego levels below the third stage (i.e., conformist) are maladaptive for mastering the challenges of life, the third to fifth stages can be interpreted as indicators of what we have called personality adjustment.

In a recent study, positive correlations between ego level and psychometric indicators of personal growth such as personal wisdom were obtained (Staudinger et al., 2005). Furthermore, evidence from the Mills Study (Helson & Roberts, 1994) demonstrated that ego level was related to the "appreciation of the other's individuality," and the individuality of the integration and conscious development of a personal philosophy of life (Helson & Roberts, 1994), as assessed by the revised California Psychological Inventory (Gough, 1964). Thus, it seems more than meaningful to consider ego level as one operationalization of personality maturity.

Table 9.2 Summary of Process-Related Indicators/Facets of Adjustment and Personality Growth

Personality Concepts	Facets of Adjustment	Facets of Growth/Maturity
Self-regulation: Coping	Large repertoire of coping styles and compensatory strategies, coping styles applied as flexibly as possible depending on situational opportunities and constraints	Large repertoire of coping styles and compensatory strategies, at least medium amount of persistence in goal pursuit and accurate perception of reality
Systemic Regulatory Processes	Selective optimization with compensation (adjustment algorithm)	Selective optimization with compensation (growth algorithm)
Motivation: Values and Personal Strivings	Self-enhancing values (e.g. ego-centeredness, achievement, stimulation, conformity)	Self-transcendent values (universalism and benevolence), generativity
Emotion Regulation	Positive affect balance, high degree of life satisfaction	Affect complexity

Process-Related Markers of Personality Adjustment and Growth

Table 9.2 lists the process-related constructs that are considered in the following and shows how they contribute to our distinction between personality adjustment and personality maturity.

Coping Strategies

The long research tradition in the investigation of coping strategies (e.g., emotion-focused vs. problem-focused coping) also provides support for the usefulness of our distinction between personality adjustment and growth. Coping strategies represent important sources that contribute both to adjustment and growth. In general, we argue that whether a coping strategy should be labeled adjustment- or growth-related is not primarily due to the type of strategy, such as an agentic strategy (i.e., assimilative, primary control, or problem-focused coping) or a yielding strategy (i.e., accommodative, secondary control, or emotion-focused coping). Rather, the distinction between adjustment and growth is indexed by the algorithm according to which either agentic or yielding strategies are employed. Contemporary models of coping have focused on how coping mechanisms contribute to successful development in the sense of adjustment. Overall, these models have suggested that successful development is associated with access to, and flexible selection from, a repertoire of coping styles and compensatory strategies (Baltes et al., 1998). This implies that a person who copes successfully is highly flexible in applying both agentic and yielding strategies (Brandtstädter & Greve, 1992; Heckhausen & Schulz, 1995). For example, rather than any particular form of coping, better mental health (i.e., one indicator of adjustment) is related to a greater repertoire of coping responses (Forster & Gallagher, 1986). Further, it seems that it is not only the variety of available coping styles that is adaptive but rather it is a specific selection of responses. For example, older individuals who reported selective flexibility in coping (endorsing some coping styles very strongly and others not at all) also demonstrated high levels of subjective well-being (Staudinger & Fleeson, 1996). To the best of our knowledge, flexibility in applying agentic and yielding strategies has not been empirically tested with regard to their predictive value in personality growth/maturity.

Yielding strategies have consistently been found to increase with age (Brandtstädter & Renner, 1990; Wrosch, Heckhausen, & Lachman, 2000). That is, in comparison to younger adults, older adults demonstrate an accommodative coping style in the face of adversity or failure. In this vein, it was demonstrated that people become increasingly better at adjusting to losses and negative events with age—for example, by disengaging from blocked goals (Wrosch, Scheier, Carver, & Schulz, 2003), re-scaling personal expectations to the given situation (Rothermund & Brandtstädter, 2003), or letting go of self-images that do not fit the actual self anymore (Greve & Wentura, 2003; Freund & Smith, 1999). Such actions can also be interpreted as pragmatic responses to declines in the mechanics of life (Schindler & Staudinger, 2005). All in all, empirical evidence suggests that differences in the endorsement of coping mechanisms are more a function of the type of stressful event than of age per se (McCrae, 1989).

In contrast to yielding strategies, findings with respect to the development of agentic and assimilative strategies are not completely consistent. With a few exceptions (e.g., Brandtstädter & Renner, 1990) most authors speak, for instance, of stable or even increasing primary control across adulthood (Staudinger, Freund, Linden, & Maas, 1996; Wrosch et al., 2000), including investment of resources such as effort, time, and skills to achieve a chosen goal. Furthermore, older adults seem to be more flexible in adapting their coping response to the characteristics of the situation than do younger adults (Aldwin, 1991). Conversely, younger adults are more likely to adhere to their established goals, even if these goals are no longer obtainable (Brandtstädter & Renner, 1990). Of course, this capacity for adaptation may find its limits in extreme situations, such as the challenges of advanced very old age (Baltes & Smith, 2003).

In contrast to stereotypical views of the elderly as rigid, the evidence for coping behavior points to an increase in adjustment to life's demands across adulthood. Yielding strategies and flexibility in coping strategies strongly contribute to adjustment in the face of physical vulnerability well into old age. By adjusting their coping behaviors to the controllability of specific health and social stresses, older adults can maintain both their psychological and physical health.

When it comes to pursuing the goal of personality growth rather than that of optimal adjustment, however, at least some of the yielding strategies mentioned above counteract rather than support personality growth. According to several personality theorists (Allport, 1961; Haan, 1977; Maslow, 1994), the mature personality is characterized by efforts to both see one's self and one's environment realistically and to continuously, and tenaciously pursue one's goals. According to this portrayal of the mature personality, reinterpreting a failure one-sidedly in a positive manner indicates that the person is not able to accept negative events and unpleasant truths about oneself. Coping in the sense of striving for personality growth, therefore, entails—apart from seeing the opportunities in a failure—also analyzing the mistakes, weaknesses, and circumstances that have contributed to the failure. Thus, coping behavior that takes note of failures and tries to learn from them without becoming depressed contributes to personality growth. Not necessarily does this kind of coping—on the short run—contribute to subjective well-being (i.e., personality adjustment).

In the light of these considerations, distinguishing two types of personality development—that is, personality adjustment and growth—adds a new argument to the long-standing controversy of whether regressive coping strategies or mature mechanisms increase with age. Pfeiffer (1977) suggested that, with increasing age, regressive tendencies increase. In contrast, Vaillant (1977), in line with developmental and lay theories of personality, reported an age-related increase in "mature" coping mechanisms. It seems that differentiating between personality adjustment and personality growth might solve some of the inconsistencies in this debate. In the face of difficulties, yielding strategies contribute to the maintenance or recovery of our subjective well-being and thereby index personality adjustment. Thus, the age-related increase in yielding strategies is another piece of evidence that shows that, as we age, we display a higher level of adjustment.

Systemic Regulatory Processes

In the following, we discuss an even more general self-regulating mechanism which, according to lifespan psychology, is assumed to be the most effective in promoting positive (personality) development. This mechanism is *selective optimization with compensation* (SOC; Baltes & Baltes, 1990). It is argued that the coordinated use of strategies such as selection, optimization, and compensation can (a) increase one's resources in the sense of developmental enhancement, (b) help maintain functioning in the face of life's challenges, and (c) help regulate impending losses in resources. Applying our distinction between personality adjustment and maturity, it is again not the three strategies per se that are prone to support personality adjustment or growth. Rather, it is the algorithm according to which the three processes are applied and the goals which are pursued when using the three mechanisms. A thought experiment may be helpful to clarify what we mean by algorithm: Selective goal investment right after difficulties in goal attainment have occurred may contribute to maintaining well-being and, thereby, further personality adjustment. At the same time, opportunities to push ahead personal limits may be missed, and thereby limit the potential to facilitate personality growth.

The following definitions of the SOC components are taken from Freund and Baltes (1999). The primary focus of selection is to give direction to behavior, that is, to shape the development and allocation of resources in a non-random manner, especially because resources are limited to begin with. Elective selection of goals (ES) occurs when goal selection is guided primarily by preference or social norms, and not imposed by a loss in resources across time. For instance, consider when a student decides to study biology rather than chemistry. Loss-based selection (LS) occurs when the individual is pressured to change his or her goals (or goal hierarchy) by the loss of some internal (e.g., physical strength) or external resource (e.g., money). For instance, deciding against the usual vacation plans due to financial constraints, or deciding to discontinue an activity in a sports club because of health constraints. Optimization (O) refers to the acquisition, refinement, and use of means to achieve goals. General categories of optimization include persistence, practice, learning of new skills, modeling of successful others, as well as the scheduling of time and energy. Compensation (C) concern the acquisition and use of alternative means to maintain a given desired level of functioning in the face of actual or anticipated decreases in resources.

Initial self-report and observational studies lend support to the assumption that individuals show higher levels of personality adjustment, both short-term and long-term, when they engage in selection, optimization, and compensation (Baltes et al., 2006). One example is the management of the family-career interface. Both cross-sectionally and longitudinally, partners who reported higher use of SOC-related behaviors obtained higher levels of well-being (Baltes & Heydens-Gahir, 2003; Wiese, Freund, & Baltes, 2002). Similar findings were obtained with regard to the challenges faced by college students (Wiese & Schmitz, 2002). As another example, older people suffering from osteoarthritis successfully managed their illness by use of behaviors that are consistent with selection, optimization, and compensation (Gignac, Cott, & Badley, 2002). Again, as in the case of coping strategies, there is no evidence that points to the relationship between SOC and measures of personality growth.

Across adulthood and into old age, cross-sectional data have demonstrated age-related increases of optimization and compensation from young to middle adulthood and a decrease in later adulthood (Freund & Baltes, 2002). The authors interpret this finding as a sign that the use of SOC strategies itself is effortful and that, due to age-related losses in resources, older adults might be constrained in the employment of these strategies. However, it may also be the case that, due to increased selectivity, less and less compensation is actually necessary (Freund & Baltes, 1998; Freund & Baltes, 2002). At the same time, despite such declines in the frequency of self-reported optimization and compensation, the elderly do continue to use these strategies, and if they do so, they display higher levels of well-being (Baltes & Lang, 1997; Freund & Baltes, 1998). There were no age differences in loss-based selection. There was an increase in the endorsement of elective selection from young to middle and from middle to later adulthood. According to Freund & Baltes (2002), this result points to the fact that young adults experience a high need to explore the different pathways of life. By middle and especially later adulthood, however, pathways of life are more or less set and subsequently pursued (Baltes & Baltes, 1990).

This pattern of results bears some relevance with regard to our tenet that personality growth does not occur normatively with age. The normatively observed pattern of SOC employment (i.e., increased selection, decreased compensation and optimization) supports personality adjustment. In order for personality growth to emerge, the SOC strategies need to be orchestrated differently and in terms of a different goal, that is, the promotion of personality growth rather than the maintenance or recovery of subjective well-being (Staudinger, 1999). In the same vein, the normatively observed goal selection taking place in adulthood later on constrains the possible range of new and challenging experiences (a necessary ingredient of continued growth). Thus, a lot of selection during adulthood and old age will most likely constrain personality growth. Besides the pattern of SOC employment, however, it is also crucial to consider which overarching goal is pursued by using the three strategies. Is the overarching goal to maintain and/or regain well-being (personality adjustment), or is the goal to advance one's insight and understanding of the self and the world (personality maturity)?

Values and Personal Strivings

Indicators of personality adjustment and growth can also be found in the area of motivational functioning—in particular when it comes to values and personal strivings. Values, defined as cognitive representations of desirable, abstract goals that motivate actions (Rokeach, 1973; Schwartz, 1992), as well as the degree to which they are realized by an individual, have been described as important antecedents of adjustment (Sagiv & Schwartz, 2000). Furthermore, specific types of values have been described by almost all personality theorists as part and parcel of personality maturity. Examples include Rogers' (1961) notion of organismically based values, Fromm's (1947) concept of "being" value orientation, and Kasser and Ryan's (1996) notion of intrinsic values. The values we pursue determine the social goals and the means that are ethically appropriate to achieve these goals (Achenbaum & Orwoll, 1991; Allport, 1961; Orwoll & Perlmutter, 1990). Therefore, values may or may not direct complex and integrated cognition in a mature direction. As Noam (1998) pointed out, even though persons might "be capable of developing complex understanding of themselves and others," they can "use their insights in the service of self-alienation, self-hate, and contempt for others" (p. 289).

According to Schwartz (1992), values can be distinguished according to whether they are self-transcending or self-enhancing. Self-enhancement reflects a self-serving and self-gratifying attitude, as indicated by hedonism, achievement and power. Self-transcending values reflect both universalism (i.e., preference for social justice and tolerance, and appreciation of beauty and nature) and benevolence (i.e., preference for the welfare of others with whom one has personal contact). In the following, we argue that self-enhancing values are concomitant of adjustment, whereas self-transcendent values are a pivotal marker for personality growth.

A study examining the associations between value priorities and well-being found that those with high levels of affective well-being are more likely to adhere to values related to achievement, self-direction, stimulation, tradition, conformity and security (Sagiv & Schwartz, 2000). Furthermore, studies contrasting happy with unhappy people have shown that one of the main differences is their hedonic orientation. People who are happy frequently name it as a conscious goal to enjoy their lives, seek positive experiences, and look for stimulation and sensual pleasure (Diener & Fujita, 1995; Lyubomirsky, 2001; Sheldon, Ryan, Deci, & Kasser, 2004). At the time, it was found that a focus on financial success, physical appearance, and social recognition was correlated with lower levels of well-being. However, aspirations concerning physical health, the community, and self-acceptance were positively related with well-being (Chan & Joseph, 2000; Schmuck, Kasser, & Ryan, 2000; Sheldon & Kasser, 2001; Sheldon et al., 2004). Thus, it seems that both self-enhancing and ego-centered goals as well as goals pursuing sustainable and self-transcending issues, such as health and social relations (instead of elusive values like money and beauty), are associated with higher levels of subjective well-being. This pattern of results reflects the fact that adjustment and growth are not independent but related.

Furthermore, there is consensus in theories of personality growth, such as in Maslow, Allport, Erikson, or Heath that it is a motivational orientation towards self-transcendence and generativity or—in Heaths' (1968) words— "allocentrism" that characterizes personality maturity (see also Doerner, 2006). Empirical evidence for this notion comes from studies on personal as well as general wisdom. Kunzmann and Baltes (2003) demonstrated that general wisdom-related performance is positively associated with other-related values (i.e., values relating to the well-being of friends, societal engagement) and such self-related values that are oriented toward self-actualization and insight into life in general. Simultaneously, general wisdom was uncorrelated to values revolving around a pleasurable life. Furthermore, using Schwartz's value scale (1992), Mickler and Staudinger (in press) found that personal wisdom was positively correlated with universalistic and benevolent values; simultaneously, personal wisdom was uncorrelated to adaptive motives such as power, achievement and hedonism.

There is a rich research tradition concerning the development of self-enhancing versus self-transcending values across the life span. However, there is not very much evidence on age differences in values that tap our differentiation between self-enhancing versus self-transcending values. Age-related differences in values have been primarily demonstrated, on the one hand, in terms of value stability and increasing conservatism and, on the other hand, in terms of changes in the relative importance of instrumental as compared to teleological values (Glenn, 1980; Pennebaker & Stone, 2003; Ryff & Baltes, 1976). In a recent study using the Schwartz value scale, it was demonstrated that older participants (aged 60–80 years) reported a higher degree of self-transcending values as compared to young participants (aged 20–40 years) (Doerner & Staudinger, 2007). As predicted, on the benevolence as well as the universalism scale, older participants exhibited a higher mean score than young participants. This finding is in line with the results reported by Kunzmann and Baltes (2003). In this study, it was also shown that hedonistic values showed negative age differences. Such findings are somewhat at odds with the result that universalism is strongly associated with openness (at least in young adults; Roccas, Sagiv, Schwartz, & Knafo, 2002), and openness, as we know, decreases with age. However, this seeming contradiction may be related to differences in the age ranges under consideration or with the kind of universal value under consideration.

These first empirical results suggest that older people in general might adhere more strongly to values that represent self-transcendence as compared to younger people. According to our definition of personality growth, this result suggests that the motivational facet of personality growth, that is, self-transcendence, might show a normative increase in old age. Age trends in self-transcending values parallel findings on generative strivings (McAdams, de St. Aubin, & Logan, 1993; Midlarsky & Kahana, 1994; Sheldon & Kasser, 2001). However, since value orientations are highly susceptible to cultural influences, the effect possibly is not only driven by age, but also by cohort membership. As a consequence, it seems important to replicate these results in a longitudinal design or with regard to different cohorts (Bauer & McAdams, 2004; Sheldon, 2005).

Emotion Regulation

Dimensions of subjective well-being—positive affect, negative affect, and life satisfaction—are traditionally used as the central indices of adjustment in psychological research. In such research, life satisfaction is often equated with adjustment (Diener & Suh, 1998). And, indeed, there is considerable empirical evidence that positive affect plays an extremely important role in adaptation. Isen (1999; Isen, Daubman, & Nowicki, 1987) suggested that moderate positive affect promotes problem solving as well as perseverance and success in decision making. Across the life span, positive affect is described as fostering the integration of experience and promotes "growth" as well as the restoration of social, cognitive and physical resources (Fredrickson, 2000, 2001). Negative affect, even though it promotes realistic, analytic thinking, exhausts energy and debilitates adaptive coping with uncontrollable events (e.g., Cole, Michel, & Teti, 1994). Negative affect is also often regarded as an indicator of neuroticism and (lack of) mental health. Thus, negative emotions may be described as constraining personality adjustment.

Emotion Regulation and Personality Adjustment.   When it comes to affective developmental across the adult life span, the ability to maintain high levels of subjective well-being (i.e., maintaining or achieving adjustment)—despite multiple losses at least into "young" old age—is a core finding indicative of the resilience of the aging self (Staudinger et al., 1995). With a few exceptions, findings unequivocally suggest a higher level of overall negative affect in young adults as compared to successive age groups. The negative age trend levels off in early old age (Carstensen, Pasupathi, Mayr, & Nesselroade, 2000; Gross, Carstensen, Tsai, Skorpen, & Hsu, 1997; Mroczek & Kolarz, 1998). Findings on the development of positive affect, however, have been rather mixed. Previous studies have found either decline, stability, or even increase in overall positive affect. Recently, we have argued that these inconsistencies can be partially resolved by differentiating between high and low arousal states of positive affect. In line with this assumption, we found that older participants showed a higher level of positive, low arousal affect (e.g., serene). Simultaneously, older participants did not significantly differ from the two younger age groups in positive, high arousal affect (e.g., excited) (Kessler & Staudinger, 2007). However, it also seems that, in very old age, the potential of adjustment decreases due to the tremendous increase in losses and negative events. In this vein, in a sample of participants between the ages of 74 and 103 years, Smith and Baltes (1997) found increasingly negative affective states with age. Furthermore, a longitudinal study over a period of 22 years indicated that life satisfaction peaked at 65 and declined in the seventh decade (Mroczek & Spiro, 2005). Overall, this developmental pattern of emotions is indicative of an increase in personality adjustment from earlier phases of adulthood to "young" old age and a decline in very old age.

Recently, it has been speculated about the regulatory processes that underlie the high levels of positive emotions in old age. One line of research has argued that affect regulation may improve as people age due to learning and practice (Lawton, 1996). In other words, through years of practice we learn to regulate our affective responses and thus, in old age, we report to be better able to deal with and to control emotions than younger people. And indeed, older people report a "higher" ability to control their emotions and to maintain a neutral emotional state (Gross, Carstensen, Pasupathi et al., 1997; Lawton, Kleban, & Dean, 1993). Others have argued that older individuals might be better able to cope in anticipation of emotion-laden situations (Gross, 1998; Gross, Carstensen, Tsai et al., 1997; Magai, 2001) due to an increase in the richness and effectiveness of available emotion schemas. Recently, we have shown that there is an age-related advantage in the regulation of affect which in turns shows a strong association with age-related differences in affective patterns. Specifically, the efficiency of affect regulation in the face of difficulties and/or threatening situations emerged as a central mediator in the age-affect relationship (Kessler & Staudinger, 2007).

In the same context, Socioemotional Selectivity Theory argues that high levels of emotional well-being in old age are not primarily a result of regulatory practice, but rather a result of perceived time left in life (Carstensen, 1991; Carstensen, Isaacowitz, & Charles, 1999). In fact, these two explanations of age-related affective differences (i.e., practice vs. time perspective) may complement each other rather than be mutually exclusive. As people move through adulthood, due to the social-cognitive construal of time, they shift their motivational orientation away from information search towards emotion regulation. Accordingly, as people age, they gear their lives, especially their social lives, toward maximizing positive and minimizing negative affect. In contrast, young people see the future as being largely open. Therefore, they are more focused on the acquisition of new knowledge. In support of this assumption, studies on attention and memory for positive/negative stimuli have found three things. First, during initial attention, older adults seem to avoid negative information (Mather & Carstensen, 2003), unless this information is threatening or extremely aversive (Mather & Knight, 2006). Second, older adults remember a lower proportion of negative stimuli than younger adults do (Charles, Mather, & Carstensen, 2003). Third, there is a positivity effects in older adults' autobiographical memories (e.g., Kennedy, Mather, & Carstensen, 2004). This so-called positivity bias in attention and memory was consequently cited as the regulatory mechanisms underlying emotional adjustment.

Emotion Regulation and Personality Growth.   Applying our notion of personality growth to markers of emotional functioning, affective complexity (defined as a high degree of affective differentiation and the co-existence of positive and negative emotions) can be regarded as an indicator of personality growth. Growth theorists have described affective complexity as a central prerequisite of the capacity to view the self in an open and tolerant fashion (e.g., Loevinger, 1976). The few studies that so far have investigated developmental trajectories in affective complexity used two different approaches, one building on the covariation of self-reported positive and negative emotions (e.g., Carstensen et al., 2000; Larsen & Cutler, 1996; Ong & Bergeman, 2004), the other building on the complexity of adults' self-statements in self-narratives (Labouvie-Vief, DeVoe, & Bulka, 1989).

Within the first approach, affective complexity is based on the self-reported frequency of emotions using an event-sampling method. Affective complexity is defined by (1) the number of dimensions characterizing a person's intraindividual emotional experience, and by (2) the average intraindividual correlation between positive and negative affect within a (short) sample period of time. A higher number of dimensions is interpreted as a high degree of differentiation between different kinds of discrete emotions. A high intraindividual correlation between positive and negative affect on the same occasion is interpreted as a high degree of "poignancy." In a recent study by Carstensen et al. (2000), it was found that affective complexity increases with age. More dimensions were required to reflect the structure of older as compared to younger participants´ emotions. Furthermore, although the average correlation between positive and negative affect within a sampled moment was negative at all ages, the negative correlation was increasingly smaller at older ages. Interpreting these results as indicative of higher levels of complexity, however, might be problematic as the results do not provide information on the temporal order of positive and negative emotions. Specifically, these results do not necessarily indicate that an individual *concurrently* experiences different and even opposing emotions. This, however, is the central aspect to the common understanding of affective complexity. Rather, it could also be that there is a dynamic interplay between positive and negative emotions with older people using positive emotions more often to "undo" negative emotions. Supportive of this interpretation is the finding that, in the same study as well as in another study by Ong and Bergeman (2004), affective complexity was negatively associated with negative affect, neuroticism and daily stress. These empirical results suggest that the affective complexity measure, as used by this line of research, might be an indicator of personality adjustment (rather than maturity) which seems to increase as people age.

A second line of research on affective complexity might more directly tap our notion of personality growth and that of other growth theorists: Labouvie-Vief builds on the conceptual complexity, openness and multivalence of adults' self-representations. She found that in self-descriptions, older people have representations of the self that are characterized, among others, by a low degree of blendings of emotions and high levels of repression (Labouvie-Vief et al., 1995; Labouvie-Vief & Medler, 2002). These results suggest that emotion-regulation resources in older people seem to be oriented less towards personality growth and more towards to optimizing well-being, that is, personality adjustment.

Conclusion

In contrast to the assumption that "personality is set like plaster" (Costa & McCrae, 1994), the present chapter has first of all provided ample evidence for one of the central assumptions of lifespan psychology, namely, that there is dynamic and continued personality change throughout the adult life span (Baltes, Reese, & Lipsitt, 1980; Erikson, 1963). The chapter has also demonstrated that personality development as much as cognitive development is a multidimensional phenomenon. Overall, we have shown that it is theoretically as well as empirically useful to integrate such changes under the heading of two types of personality change across adulthood, that is, personality adjustment and personality maturity (Staudinger, 2005; Staudinger & Kunzmann, 2005).

Our integrative overview of empirical results on personality-related measures indicates that there appear to be normative gains in personality adjustment and a flattening of the personality-growth trajectory during adulthood. At the same time, the age-related increase in self-transcendent values and generative strivings might be regarded as preliminary evidence that the normative stability in personality growth is primarily due to the cognitive and the emotional facets of personality growth rather than the motivational facet.

Clearly, personality adjustment and maturity are not independent. Rather, a certain level of personality adjustment is a necessary precondition for the pursuit of personality growth. However, we argue that when it comes to optimizing personality adjustment the possibility of also making progress on the growth trajectory is excluded. More systematic and longitudinal research is needed in order to buttress such theoretical considerations about the ontogenetic orchestration of personality adjustment and growth.

From what we have argued so far, it might appear as if the observed stability in personality maturity is a "natural law" and thereby fixed. Rather, we would like to argue that gains in personality maturity are possible, but that it takes a very special constellation of personal and contextual factors. When it comes to personal factors, a certain level of trait-related openness to new experience and internal control is necessary to achieve more complex forms of personality maturity—as expressed in personal wisdom. Simultaneously, continued access to environmental contexts that allow for and ask for unexpected and challenging experience is necessary. Muehlig-Versen and Staudinger (2007) recently found, in a quasi-experimental longitudinal study, that older people who participated in a special volunteering program that included a specific volunteering training and who reported above median internal control beliefs, showed higher levels of personal growth and openness compared to baseline assessment three months earlier and to a control group of volunteers who had not participated in the training. For personal growth, this increase remained stable one year later; for openness, the increase continued one year later.

However, even though under such facilitative conditions it seems that personality growth is possible in old age, the perception of life's finitude may constitute a built-in constraint to personality growth. It has been suggested that one important way to overcome this "natural" barrier to personality growth is to pass on life experience to members of the young generation and thereby experience something like "symbolic immortality" (Kotre, 1984). We have recently conducted an experimental study that provided some support for this assumption. We found that intergenerational settings that were supportive of the generativity theme increased affective complexity (i.e., personality maturity) in older adults (Kessler & Staudinger, 2007).

In the future, it will be necessary to explore the (ontogenetic) relationship between these two forms of positive development in more detail to better understand the relationship between successfully adjusting to the given cultural (and biological) context and growing beyond.

References

Achenbaum, W., & Orwoll, L. (1991). Becoming wise: A psycho-gerontological interpretation of the Book of Job. *International Journal of Aging & Human Development, 32*(1), 21–39.

Aldwin, C. M. (1991). Does age affect the stress and coping process? Implications of age differences in perceived control. *Journal of Gerontology, 46*, 174–180.

Allport, G. W. (1961). *Pattern and growth in personality.* New York: Holt, Rinehart and Winston.

Arnett, J. J. (2000). Emerging adulthood: A theory of development from the late teens through the twenties. *American Psychologist, 55*, 469–480.

Aspinwall, L. G., & Staudinger, U. M. (2003). A psychology of human strengths: Some central issues of an emerging field. In L. G. Aspinwall & U. M. Staudinger (Eds.), *A psychology of human strengths. Fundamental questions and future directions for a positive psychology* (pp. 9–22). Washington, DC: American Psychological Association.

Assagioli, R. (1989). Self-realization and psychological disturbance. In S. Grof & C. Grof (Eds.), *Spiritual emergency: When personal transformation becomes a crisis* (pp. 29–49). Los Angeles: Jeremy P. Tarcher, Inc. (Original work published 1978)

Baltes, B. B., & Heydens-Gahir, H. A. (2003). Reduction of work-family conflict through the use of selection, optimization, and compensation behaviors. *Journal of Applied Psychology, 88*, 1005–1018.

Baltes, M. M., & Lang, F. R. (1997). Everyday functioning and successful aging: The impact of resources. *Psychology and Aging, 12*, 433–443.

Baltes, P. B., & Baltes, M. M. (1990). Psychological perspectives on successful aging: The model of selective optimization with compensation. In P. B. Baltes & M. M. Baltes (Eds.), *Successful aging: Perspectives from the behavioral sciences* (pp. 1–34). Cambridge, UK: Cambridge University Press.

Baltes, P. B., & Freund, A. M. (2003). Human strengths as the orchestration of wisdom and selective optimization with compensation. In L. G. Aspinwall & U. M. Staudinger (Eds.), *A psychology of human strengths: Fundamental questions and future directions for a positive psychology* (pp. 23–35). Washington, DC: American Psychological Association.

Baltes, P. B., Lindenberger, U., & Staudinger, U. M. (1998). Life-span theory in developmental psychology. In R. M. Lerner (Ed.), *Handbook of child psychology: Vol. 1. Theoretical models of human development* (5th ed., pp. 1029–1143). New York: Wiley.

Baltes, P. B., Lindenberger, U., & Staudinger, U. M. (2006). Life-span theory in developmental psychology. In R. M. Lerner (Ed.), *Handbook of child psychology: Vol. 1. Theoretical models of human development* (6th ed.). New York: Wiley.

Baltes, P. B., Reese, H. W., & Lipsitt, L. P. (1980). Life-span developmental psychology. *Annual Review of Psychology, 31*, 65–110.

Baltes, P. B., & Smith, J. (2003). New frontiers in the future of aging: From successful aging of the young old to the dilemmas of the fourth age. *Gerontology & Geriatrics Education, 49*, 123–135.

Baltes, P. B., & Staudinger, U. M. (2000). Wisdom. A metaheuristic (pragmatic) to orchestrate mind and virtue toward excellence. *American Psychologist, 55*(1), 122–136.

Bauer, J. J., & McAdams, D. P. (2004). Growth goals, maturity, and well-being. *Developmental Psychology, 40*, 14–127.

Berridge, K. C. (1999). Pleasure, pain, desire, and dread: Hidden core processes of emotion. In D. Kahneman, E. Diener, & N. Schwarz (Eds.), *Well-being: The foundations of hedonic psychology* (pp. 525–557). New York: Russell Sage.

Blasi, A. (1998). Loevinger's theory of ego development and its relationship to the cognitive-developmental approach. In P. M. Westenberg, A. Blasi, & L. D. Cohn (Eds.), *Personality development: theoretical, empirical, and clinical investigations of Loevinger's conception of ego development* (pp. 133–143). Mahwah, NJ: Erlbaum.

Block, J. (1961). Ego identity, role variability, and adjustment. *Journal of Consulting Psychology, 25*, 392–397.

Brandtstädter, J., & Greve, W. (1992). Das Selbst im Alter: Adaptive und protektive Mechanismen. *Zeitschrift für Entwicklungspsychologie und Pädagogische Psychologie, 24*(4), 269–297.

Brandtstädter, J., & Greve, W. (1994). The aging self: Stabilizing and protective processes. *Developmental Review, 14*, 52–80.

Brandtstädter, J., & Renner, G. (1990). Tenacious goal pursuit and flexible goal adjustment: Explication and age-related analysis of assimilative and accomodative strategies of coping. *Psychology and Aging, 5*(1), 58–67.

Brown, J. D., & Dutton, K. A. (1995). Truth and consequences: The costs and benefits of accurate self-knowledge. *Personality & Social Psychology Bulletin, 21,* 1288–1296.

Bühler, C. (1968). The general structure of the human life cycle. In C. Bühler & F. Massarik (Eds.), *The course of human life: A study of goals in the humanistic perspective* (pp. 12–26). New York: Springer.

Campbell, J. D., Assanand, S., & Di Paula, A. (2003). The structure of the self-concept and its relation to psychological adjustment. *Journal of Personality, 71,* 115–140.

Carstensen, L. L. (1991). Selectivity theory: Social activity in life-span context. In K. W. Schaie (Ed.), *Annual review of gerontology and geriatrics* (pp. 195–217). New York: Springer.

Carstensen, L. L., Isaacowitz, D. M., & Charles, S. T. (1999). Taking time seriously: A theory of socioemotional selectivity. *American Psychologist, 54*(3), 165–181.

Carstensen, L. L., Pasupathi, M., Mayr, U., & Nesselroade, J. R. (2000). Emotional experience in everyday life across the adult life span. *Journal of Personality and Social Psychology, 79*(4), 644–655.

Chan, R., & Joseph, S. (2000). Dimensions of personality, domains of aspiration, and subjective well-being. *Personality & Individual Differences, 28,* 347–354.

Chandler, M. J., & Holliday, S. (1990). Wisdom in a postapocalyptic age. In R. J. Sternberg (Ed.), *Wisdom: Its nature, origins, and development* (pp. 121–141). New York: Cambridge University Press.

Charles, S. T., Mather, M., & Carstensen, L. L. (2003). Aging and emotional memory: The forgettable nature of negative images for older adults. *Journal of Experimental Psychology, 132*(2), 310–324.

Cohn, L. D. (1998). Age trends in personality development: A quantitative review. In P. M. Westenberg, A. Blasi, & L. D. Cohn (Eds.), *Personality development: Theoretical, empiricial, and clinical investigations of Loevinger's conception of ego development* (pp. 133–145). Mahwah, NJ: Erlbaum.

Cole, P. M., Michel, M. K., & Teti, L. O. D. (1994). The development of emotion regulation and dysregulation: A clinical perspective. *Monographs of the Society for Research in Child Development, 59*(2-3), 73–100, 250–283.

Coleman, L. M., Antonucci, T. C., & Adelmann, P. K. (1987). Role involvement, gender, and well-being. In F. J. Crosby (Ed.), *Spouse, parent, worker: On gender and multiple roles* (pp. 138–153). New Haven, CT: Yale University Press.

Compton, W. C. (2001). Toward a tripartite structure of mental health: Subjective well-being, personal growth, and religiosity. *The Journal of Psychology, 135,* 486–500.

Costa, P. T., & McCrae, R. R. (1980). Still stable after all these years: Personality as a key to some issues in adulthood and old age. In P. B. Baltes & O. G. Brim (Eds.), *Life-span development and behavior* (Vol. 3, pp. 66–102). New York: Academic Press.

Costa, P. T., & McCrae, R. R. (1994). Set like plaster? Evidence for the stability of adult personality. In T. F. Heatherton & J. L. Weinberger (Eds.), *Can personality change?* (pp. 21–40). Washington, DC: American Psychological Assocation.

Costa, P. T., & McCrae, R. R. (1998). Trait theories of personality. In D. F. Barone, M. Hersen, & V. B. Van Hasselt (Eds.), *Advanced Personality* (pp. 103–121). New York: Plenum.

Costa, P. T., Zonderman, A. B., & McCrae, R. R. (1991). Personality, defense, coping, and adaptation in oder adulthood. In E. M. Cummings, A. L. Greene, & K. H. Karraker (Eds.), *Life-span developmental psychology: Perspectives on stress and coping* (pp. 277–293). Hillsdale, NJ: Erlbaum.

Cramer, P. (2004). Identity change in adulthood: The contribution of defense mechanisms and life experiences. *Journal of Research in Personality, 38,* 280–316.

Cummings, E. M., & Henry, W. E. (1961). *Growing old: The process of disengagement.* New York: Basic Books.

Diehl, M., Hastings, C. T., & Stanton, J. M. (2001). Self-concept differentiation across the adult life span. *Psychology and Aging, 16,* 643–654.

Diener, E., & Fujita, F. (1995). Resources, personal strivings, and subjective well-being: A nomothetic and idiographic approach. *Journal of Personality and Social Psychology, 68*(5), 926–935.

Diener, E., & Suh, E. M. (1998). Subjective well-being and age: An international analysis. In K. W.

Schaie & M. P. Lawton (Eds.), *Annual Review of Gerontology and Geriatrics* (Vol. 8, pp. 304–324). New York: Springer.

Dietz, B. E. (1996). The relationship of aging to self-esteem: The relative effects of maturation and role accumulation. *International Journal of Aging & Human Development, 43,* 249–266.

Doerner, J., & Staudinger, U. M. (2007). Self-concept Maturity—A new measure of personality growth: Validation, age effects, and first processual explorations. Manuscript in preparation.

Donahue, E. M., Robins, R. W., Roberts, B. W., & John, O. P. (1993). The divided self: Concurrent and longitudinal effects of psychological adjustment and social roles on self-concept differentiation. *Journal of Personality & Social Psychology, 64,* 834–846.

Einstein, D., & Lanning, K. (1998). Shame, guilt, ego development, and the five-factor model of personality. *Journal of Personality, 66,* 556–582.

Erikson, E. H. (1950). *Childhood and society.* New York: Norton.

Erikson, E. H. (1959). *Identity and the life cycle. Psychological issues monograph 1.* New York: International University Press.

Erikson, E. H. (1963). *Childhood and society* (2nd ed.). New York: Norton.

Erikson, E. H. (1968). *Identity. Youth and crisis.* New York: Norton.

Evans, D. W. (1994). Self-complexity and its relation to development, symptomatology and self-perception during adolescence. *Child Psychiatry and Human Development, 24,* 173–182.

Evans, D. W., Brody, L., & Noam, G. G. (2001). Ego development, self-perception, and self-complexity in adolescence: A study of female psychiatric inpatients. *American Journal of Orthopsychiatry, 71,* 79–86.

Fitts, W. H. (1977). Tennessee Self-Concept Scale—"English". In R. S. Andrulis (Ed.), *Adult assessment: A source book of tests and measures of human behavior.* Springfield, IL: Charles C. Thomas.

Forster, J. M., & Gallagher, D. (1986). An exploratory study comparing depressed and nondepressed elders coping strategies. *Journal of Gerontology, 41,* 91–93.

Fredrickson, B. L. (2000). Cultivating positive emotions to optimize health and well-being. *Prevention and Treatment, 3.*

Fredrickson, B. L. (2001). The role of positive emotions in positive psychology: The broaden-and-build theory of positive emotions. *American Psychologist, 56*(3), 218–226.

Freud, S. (1993). *Vorlesungen zur Einführung in die Psychoanalyse.* Frankfurt: Fischer. (Original work published 1917)

Freund, A. M., & Baltes, P. B. (1999). Selection, optimization, and compensation as strategies of life management: Correlations with subjective indicators of successful aging. *Psychology and Aging, 13*(4), 531–543.

Freund, A. M., & Baltes, P. B. (2002). Life-management strategies of selection, optimization, and compensation: Measurement by self-report and construct validity. *Journal of Personality and Social Psychology, 82*(4), 642–662.

Freund, A. M., & Smith, J. (1999). Content and function of the self-definition in old and very old age. *Journals of Gerontology: Series B: Psychological Sciences and Social Sciences, 54B*(1), P55–P67.

Fromm, E. (1947). *Man for himself.* New York: Rinehart.

Funder, D. C. (2001). Personality. *Annual Review of Psychology, 52,* 197–221.

Gignac, M. A. M., Cott, C., & Badley, E. M. (2002). Adaptation to disability: Applying selective optimization with compensation to the behaviors of older adults with osteoarthritis. *Psychology and Aging, 17,* 520–524.

Glenn, N. D. (1980). Values, attittudes, and beliefs. In O. G. Brim & J. Kagan (Eds.), *Constancy and change in human development* (pp. 596–640). London: Harvard University Press.

Gough, H. G. (1957). *Manual for the California Psychological Inventory.* Palo Alto, CA: Consulting Psychologists Press.

Gough, H. G. (1964). *The California Psychological Inventory.* Palo Alto, CA: Consulting Psychologists Press.

Gough, H. G., & Bradley, P. (1996). *Manual for the California Personality Inventory Manual* (3rd ed.). Palo Alto, CA: Consulting psychology press.

Gramzow, R. H., Sedikides, C., Panter, A. T., Sathy, V., Harris, J., & Insko, C. A. (2004). Patterns of self-regulation and the Big Five. *European Journal of Personality, 18,* 367–385.

Greve, W., & Wentura, D. (2003). Immunizing the self: Self-concept stabilization through reality-adaptive self-definitions. *Personality and Social Psychology Bulletin, 29*(1), 39–50.

Gross, J. J. (1998). Antecedent- and response-focused emotion regulation: Divergent consequences for experience, expression, and physiology. *Journal of Personality and Social Psychology, 74*(1), 224–237.

Gross, J. J., Carstensen, L. L., Pasupathi, M., Tsai, J., Gotestam Skorpen, C., & Hsu, A. Y. (1997). Emotion and aging: Experience, expression, and control. *Psychology and Aging, 12*(4), 590–599.

Gross, J. J., Carstensen, L. L., Tsai, J., Skorpen, C. G., & Hsu, A. Y. C. (1997). Emotion and aging: Experience, expression, and control. *Psychology and Aging, 12*(4), 590–599.

Haan, N. (1977). *Coping and defending: Processes of self-environment organization.* New York: Academic Press.

Hauser, S. T., Jacobson, A. M., Noam, G., & Powers, S. (1983). Ego development and self-image complexity in early adolescence. Longitudinal studies of psychiatric and diabetic patients. *Archives of General Psychiatry, 40*, 325–332.

Heath, D. H. (1968). *Growing up in college.* San Francisco: Jossey-Bass.

Heath, D. H., & Heath, H. E. (1991). *Fulfilling lives: Paths to maturity and success.* San Francisco: Jossey-Bass/Pfeiffer.

Heckhausen, J., & Schulz, R. (1995). A life-span theory of control. *Psychological Review, 102*(2), 284–304.

Helson, R., Elliot, T., & Leigh, J. (1990). Number and quality of roles: A longitudinal personality view. *Psychology of Women Quarterly, 14*, 83–101.

Helson, R., & Kwan, V. S. Y. (2000). Personality development in adulthood: The broad picture and processes in one longitudinal sample. In S. Hampson (Ed.), *Advances in personality psychology* (Vol. 1, pp. 77–106). London: Routledge.

Helson, R., Kwan, V. S. Y., John, O. P., & Jones, C. (2002). The growing evidence for personality change in adulthood: Findings from research with personality inventories. *Journal of Research in Personality, 36*, 287–306.

Helson, R., & Roberts, B. W. (1994). Ego development and personality change in adulthood. *Journal of Personality & Social Psychology, 66*(5), 911–920.

Isen, A. M. (1999). Positive affect. In T. Dalgleish & M. Power (Eds.), *The handbook of cognition and emotion.* (pp. 521–539). New York: Wiley.

Isen, A. M., Daubman, K. A., & Nowicki, G. P. (1987). Positive affect facilitates creative problem solving. *Journal of Personality and Social Psychology, 52*(6), 1122–1131.

James, W. (1948). *Psychology: Briefer Course.* New York: Henry Holt & Company. (Original work published 1890)

Jung, C. (1933). *Modern man in search of a soul.* New York: Hartcourt, Brace and World.

Kang, S.-M., & Shaver, P. R. (2004). Individual Differences in Emotional Complexity: Their Psychological Implications. *Journal of Personality, 72*, 687–726.

Kasser, T., & Ryan, R. M. (1996). Further examining the American dream: Differential correlates of intrinsic and extrinsic goals. *Personality and Social Psychology Bulletin, 22*, 280–287.

Kennedy, Q., Mather, M., & Carstensen, L. L. (2004). The role of motivation in the age-related positivity effect in autobiographical memory. *Psychological Science, 15*(3), 208–214.

Kessler, E.-M., & Staudinger, U. M. (2007). Intergenerational potential: Effects of social interaction between older adults and adolescents. *Psychology and Aging, 22*(4), 690–704.

Keyes, C. L. M., Shmotkin, D., & Ryff, C. D. (2002). Optimizing well-being: The empirical encounter of two traditions. *Journal of Personality and Social Psychology, 82*, 1007–1022.

Koch, E. J., & Shepperd, J. A. (2004). Is Self-Complexity Linked to Better Coping? A Review of the Literature. *Journal of Personality, 72*, 727–760.

Kotre, J. (1984). *Outliving the self: Generativity and the interpretation of lives.* Baltimore, MD: John Hopkins University Press.

Kunzmann, U., & Baltes, P. B. (2003). Wisdom-related knowledge: Affective, motivational, and interpersonal correlates. *Personality & Social Psychology Bulletin, 29*, 1104–1119.

Labouvie-Vief, G. (1982). Dynamic development and mature autonomy: A theoretical prologue. *Human Development, 25*, 161–191.

Labouvie-Vief, G., Chiodo, L. M., Goguen, L. A., Diehl, M., & Orwoll, L. (1995). Representations of self across the life span. *Psychology and Aging, 10*(3), 404–415.

Labouvie-Vief, G., DeVoe, M., & Bulka, D. (1989). Speaking about feelings: Conceptions of emotion across the life span. *Psychology and Aging, 4,* 425–437.

Labouvie-Vief, G., & Diehl, M. (2000). Cognitive complexity and cognitive-affective integration: Related or separate domains of adult development? *Psychology and Aging, 15*(3), 490–504.

Labouvie-Vief, G., & Medler, M. (2002). Affect optimization and affect complexity: Modes and styles of regulation in adulthood. *Psychology and Aging, 17*(4), 571–588.

Larsen, R. J., & Cutler, S. E. (1996). The complexity of individual emotional lives: A within-subject analysis of affect structure. *Journal of Social and Clinical Psychology, 15,* 206–230.

Lawton, M. P. (1996). Quality of life and affect in later life. In C. Magai & S. H. McFadden (Eds.), *Handbook of emotion, adult development and aging* (pp. 327–348). San Diego,CA: Academic Press.

Lawton, M. P., Kleban, M. H., & Dean, J. (1993). Affect and age: Cross-sectional comparisons of structure and prevalence. *Psychology and Aging, 8*(2), 165–175.

Linville, P. W. (1985). Self-complexity and affective extremity: Don't put all of your eggs in one cognitive basket. *Social Cognition, 3,* 94–120.

Linville, P. W. (1987). Self-complexity as a cognitive buffer against stress-related depression and illness. *Journal of Personality & Social Psychology, 52,* 663–676.

Loveinger, J. (1970). *Measuring ego development.* San Francisco: Jossey-Bass.

Loevinger, J. (1976). *Ego development: Conception and theory.* San Francisco: Jossey-Bass.

Loevinger, J. (1997). Stages of personality development. In R. Hogan, J. Johnson & S. Briggs (Eds.), *Handbook of personality psychology.* San Diego, CA: Academic Press.

Loevinger, J. (1998). Completing a life sentence. In P. M. Westenberg, A. Blasi & L. D. Cohn (Eds.), *Personality development: Theoretical, empirical, and clinical investigations of Loevinger's conception of ego development.* Mahwah, NJ: Erlbaums.

Loevinger, J., & Wessler, R. (1978). *Measuring ego development I: Construction and use of a sentence completion task.* Mahwah, NJ: Erlbaum.

Lutz, C. J., & Ross, S. R. (2003). Elaboration versus fragmentation: distinguishing between self-complexity and self-concept differentiation. *Journal of Social & Clinical Psychology, 22,* 537–559.

Lyubomirsky, S. (2001). Why are some people happier than others? *American Psychologist, 56,* 239–249.

Magai, C. (2001). Emotions over the life span. In J. E. Birren & K. W. Shaie (Eds.), *Handbook of the psychology of aging* (pp. 399–426). San Diego, CA: Academic Press.

Manners, J., & Durkin, K. (2001). A critical review of the validity of ego development theory and its measurement. *Journal of Personality Assessment, 77,* 541–567.

Markus, H. R., & Herzog, A. R. (1991). The role of the self-concept in aging. In K. W. Schaie & M. P. Lawton (Eds.), *Annual Review of Gerontology and Geriatrics* (Vol. 11, pp. 110–143). New York: Springer.

Maslow, A. H. (1994). *Motivation und Persönlichkeit.* Hamburg: Rowohlt.

Mather, M., & Carstensen, L.L. (2003). Aging and attentional biases for emotional faces. *Psychological Science, 14*(5), 409–415.

Mather, M., & Knight, M. R. (2006). Angry faces get noticed quickly: Threat detection is not impaired among older adults. *Journals of Gerontology: Series B: Psychological Sciences and Social Sciences, 61B*(1), P54–P57.

McAdams, D. P., de St. Aubin, E., & Logan, R. L. (1993). Generativity among young, midlife, and older adults. *Psychology and Aging, 8*(2), 221–230.

McCrae, R. R. (1989). Age differences and changes in the use of coping mechanisms. *Journal of Gerontology, 44,* 919–928.

McCrae, R. R., & Costa, P. T. (1980). Openness to experience and ego level in Loevinger's Sentence Completion Test: Dispositional contributions to developmental models of personality. *Journal of Personality and Social Psychology, 39*(6), 1179–1190.

McCrae, R. R., & Costa, P. T. (1991). Adding Liebe und Arbeit: The full five-factor model and well-being. *Personality & Social Psychology Bulletin, 17,* 227–232.

McCrae, R. R., & Costa, P. T. (1997). Conceptions and correlates of openness to experience. In

R. Hogan, F. Johnson, & S. Briggs (Eds.), *Handbook of personality psychology* (pp. 825–847). San Diego, CA: Academic Press.

McCrae, R. R., Costa, P. T., Ostendorf, F., Angleitner, A., Hrebickova, M., Avia, M. D., et al. (2000). Nature over nurture: Temperament, personality, and life span development. *Journal of Personality and Social Psychology, 78*(1), 173–186.

Mickler, C., & Staudinger, U. M. (in press). Personal wisdom: Measurement, validation and age differences. *Psychology and Aging.*

Midlarsky, E., & Kahana, E. (1994). *Altruism in later life.* Thousand Oaks, CA: Sage.

Mischel, W., & Mendoza-Denton, R. (2003). Harnessing willpower and socio-emotional intelligence to enhance human agency and potential. In L. G. Aspinwall & U. M. Staudinger (Eds.), *A psychology of human strengths: Fundamental questions and future directions for a positive psychology* (pp. 245–256). Washington, DC: American Psychological Association.

Mischel, W., & Shoda, Y. (1999). The cognitive-affective personality system. Integrating dispositions and processing dynamics within a unified theory of personality. In L. A. Pervin & O. P. John (Eds.), *Handbook of personality: Theory and research* (pp. 197–218). New York: Guilford.

Moneta, G. B., Schneider, B., & Csikszentmihalyi, M. (2001). A longitudinal study of the self-concept and experiental components of self-worth and affect across adolescence. *Applied Developmental Science, 5*, 125–142.

Mroczek, D. K., & Kolarz, C. M. (1998). The effect of age on positive and negative affect: A developmental perspective on happiness. *Journal of Personality and Social Psychology, 75*(5), 1333–1349.

Mroczek, D. K., & Spiro, A. I. (2005). Change in life satisfaction during adulthood: Findings from the Veterans Affairs Normative Aging Study. *Journal of Personality and Social Psychology, 88*(1), 189–202.

Mueller, J. H., Wonderlich, S., & Dugan, K. (1986). Self-referent processing of age-specific material. *Psychology and Aging, 1*, 293–299.

Mühlig-Versen, A., & Staudinger, U. M. (2007). Personality change in later adulthood: The role of learning and activism. Manuscript in preparation.

Neugarten, B. L. (1968). The awareness of middle age. In B. L. Neugarten (Ed.), *Middle age and aging* (pp. 88–92). Chicago: University of Chicago Press.

Neugarten, B. L., Havighurst, R. J., & Tobin, S.S . (1961). The measurement of life satisfaction. *Journal of Gerontology, 16*, 134–143.

Noam, G. (1998). Solving the ego development — mental health riddle. In P. M. Westenberg, A. Blasi, & L. D. Cohn (Eds.), *Personality development: Theoretical, empirical, and clinical investigations of Loevinger's conception of ego development* (pp. 271–295). Mahwah, NJ: Erlbaum.

Ong, A. D., & Bergeman, C. S. (2004). The complexity of emotions in later life. *Journal of Gerontology: Psychological Sciences, 59*(3), 117–122.

Orwoll, L., & Perlmutter, M. (1990). The study of wise persons: Integrating a personality perspective. In R. J. Sternberg (Ed.), *Wisdom: Its nature, origins, and development* (pp. 160–177). New York: Cambridge University Press.

Pennebaker, J. W., & Stone, L. D. (2003). Words of wisdom: Language use over the life span. *Journal of Personality and Social Psychology, 85*(2), 291–301.

Perlmutter, M. (1988). Cognitive potential throughout life. In J. E. Birren & V. L. Bengtson (Eds.), *Emergent theories of aging* (pp. 247–268). New York: Springer.

Pfeiffer, E. (1977). Psychopathology and social pathology. In J. E. Birren & K. W. Schaie (Eds.), *Handbook of the psychology of aging* (pp. 650–671). New York: Van Nostrand Reinhold.

Rafaeli-Mor, E., & Steinberg, J. (2002). Self-complexity and well-being: A review and research synthesis. *Personality and Social Psychology Review, 6*, 31–58.

Roberts, B. W., Robins, R. W., Caspi, A., & Trzesniewski, K. H. (2003). Personality trait development in adulthood. In J. L. Mortimer & M. Shanahan (Eds.), *Handbook of the life course* (pp. 579–598). New York: Plenum Press.

Roberts, B. W., Walton, K. E., & Viechtbauer, W. (2006). Patterns of mean-level change in personality traits across the life course: A meta-analysis of longitudinal studies. *Psychological Bulletin, 132*(1), 1–25.

Roccas, S., Sagiv, L., Schwartz, S. H., & Knafo, A. (2002). The big five personality factors and personal values. *Journal of Personality & Social Psychology, 28*, 789–801.

Rogers, C. R. (1961). *On becoming a person.* Boston: Houghton Mifflin.

Rokeach, M. (1973). *The nature of human values.* New York: Free Press.

Rothermund, K., & Brandtstädter, J. (2003). Depression in later life: Cross-sequential patterns and possible determinants. *Psychology and Aging, 18*, 80–90.

Ryff, C. D. (1989). Happiness is everything, or is it? Explorations on the meaning of psychological well-being. *Journal of Personality and Social Psychology, 57*(6), 1069–1081.

Ryff, C. D., & Baltes, P. B. (1976). Value transitions and adult development in women: The instrumentality-terminality hypothesis. *Developmental Psychology, 12*, 567–568.

Ryff, C. D., & Keyes, C. L. M. (1995). The structure of psychological well-being revisited. *Journal of Personality & Social Psychology, 69*, 719–727.

Sagiv, L., & Schwartz, S.H. (2000). Value priorities and subjective well-being: direct relations and congruity effects. *European Journal of Social Psychology, 30*, 177–198.

Schindler, I., & Staudinger, U. M. (2005). Lifespan perspectives on self and personality: The dynamics between the mechanics and pragmatics. In W. Greve, K. Rothermund, & D. Wentura (Eds.), *The adaptive self: Personal continuity and intentional self-development* (pp. 3–30). Göttingen: Hogrefe/Huber.

Schmuck, P., Kasser, T., & Ryan, R.M . (2000). Intrinsic and extrinsic goals: Their structure and relationship to well-being in German and U.S. college students. *Social Indicators Research, 50*, 225–241.

Schmutte, P. S., & Ryff, C. D. (1997). Personality and well-being: Reexamining methods and meanings. *Journal of Personality and Social Psychology, 73*(3), 549–559.

Schwartz, S. H. (1992). Universals in the content and structure of values: Theoretical advances and empirical tests in 20 countries. In M. P. Zanna (Ed.), *Advances in experimental social psychology* (Vol. 25, pp. 1–65). San Diego, CA: Academic Press.

Sheldon, K. M. (2005). Positive value change during college: Normative trends and individual differences. *Journal of Research in Personality, 39*, 209–223.

Sheldon, K. M., & Kasser, T. (2001). Getting older, getting better? Personal strivings and personality development across the life-course. *Developmental Psychology, 37*, 491–501.

Sheldon, K. M., Ryan, R. M., Deci, E. L., & Kasser, T. (2004). The independent effects of goal contents and motives on well-being: It's both what you pursue and why you pursue it. *Personality & Social Psychology Bulletin, 30*, 475–486.

Silvia, P. J., & Gendolla, G. H. E. (2001). On introspection and self-perception: Does self-focused attention enable accurate self-knowledge? *Review of General Psychology, 5*, 241–269.

Small, B. J., Hertzog, C., Hultsch, D. F., & Dixon, R. A. (2003). Stability and change in adult personality over 6 years: Findings from the Victoria Longitudinal Study. *Journals of Gerontology: Series B: Psychological Sciences and Social Sciences, 58B*(3), P166–P176.

Smith, J., & Baltes, P. B. (1997). Wisdom-related knowledge: Age/cohort differences in responses to life planning problems. *Developmental Psychology, 26*, 494–505.

Solomon, A., & Haaga, A. F. (2003). Reconsideration of self-complexity as a buffer against depression. *Cognitive therapy and research, 27*, 579–591.

Srivastava, S., John, O. P., Gosling, S. D., & Potter, J. (2003). Development of personality in early and middle adulthood: Set like plaster or persistent change? *Journal of Personality and Social Psychology, 84*(5), 1041–1053.

Staudinger, U. M. (1999). Social cognition and a psychological approach to an art of life. In F. Blanchard-Fields & T. Hess (Eds.), *Social cognition, adult development and aging* (pp. 343–375). New York: Academic Press.

Staudinger, U. M. (2005). Personality and aging. In M. Johnson, V. L. Bengtson, P. G. Coleman, & T. Kirkwood (Eds.), *Cambridge handbook of age and ageing* (pp. 237–244). Cambridge, England: Cambridge University Press.

Staudinger, U. M., Doerner, J., & Mickler, C. (2005). Wisdom and Personality. In R. Sternberg & J. Jordan (Eds.), *Handbook of Wisdom* (pp. 191–219) New York: Cambridge University Press.

Staudinger, U. M., & Fleeson, W. (1996). Self and personality in old and very old age: A sample case of resilience? *Development and Psychopathology, 8,* 867–885.

Staudinger, U. M., Freund, A. M., Linden, M., & Maas, I. (1996). Selbst, persönlichkeit und lebensgestaltung im alter: Psychologische widerstandsfähigkeit und vulnerabilität. In K.U. Mayer & P.B. Baltes (Eds.), *Die Berliner Altersstudie* (pp. 321–351). Berlin: Akademie Verlag.

Staudinger, U. M., & Kunzmann, U. (2005). Positive adult personality development: Adjustment and/or growth? *European Psychologist, 10*(4), 320–329.

Staudinger, U. M., Lopez, D. F., & Baltes, P. B. (1997). The psychometric location of wisdom-related performance: Intelligence, personality, and more? *Personality and Social Psychology Bulletin, 25*(11), 1200–1214.

Staudinger, U. M., Marsiske, M., & Baltes, P. B. (1995). Resilience and reserve capacity in later adulthood: Potential and limits of development across the life span. In D. Cicchetti & D. J. Cohen (Eds.), *Developmental psychopathology* (Vol. 2. *Risk, disorder, and adaptation,* pp. 801–947). New York: Wiley.

Staudinger, U. M., & Pasupathi, M. (2000). Life-span perspectives on self, personality, and social cognition. In T. A. Salthouse & F. I. M. Craik (Eds.), *The handbook of aging and cognition* (2nd ed., pp. 633–688). Mahwah, NJ: Erlbaum.

Stewart, A. J., & Ostrove, J. M. (1998). Women's personality in middle age. Gender, history, and midcourse corrections. *American Psychologist, 53,* 1185–1194.

Thoits, P. A. (1986). Multiple identities: Examining gender and marital status differences in distress. *American Sociological Review, 51,* 259–271.

Vaillant, G. E. (1977). *Adaptation to life.* Boston: Little Brown.

Vandewater, E. A., Ostrove, J. M., & Stewart, A. J. (1997). Predicting women's well-being in midlife: The importance of personality development and social role involvements. *Journal of Personality and Social Psychology, 72,* 1147–1160.

Watson, D., & Clark, L. A. (1992). On traits and temperament: General and specific factors of emotional experience and their relation to the Five-factor Model. *Journal of Personality, 60,* 441–476.

Whitbourne, S. K., & Connolly, L. A. (1999). The developing self in midlife. In S. L. Willis & J. D. Reid (Eds.), *Life in the middle. Psychological and social development in middle age* (pp. 25–45). San Diego, CA: Academic Press.

Wicklund, R. A., & Eckert, M. (1992). *The self-knower: A hero under control.* New York: Plenum Press.

Wiese, B. S., Freund, A. M., & Baltes, P.B. (2002). Subjective career successand emotional well-being: Longitudinal predictive power of selection, optimization and compensation. *Journal of Vocational Behavior, 60,* 321–335.

Wiese, B. S., & Schmitz, B. (2002). Studienbezogenes handeln im kontext eines entwicklungspsychologischen meta-modells. *Zeitschrift für Entwicklungspsychologie und Pädagogische Psychologie, 34,* 80–94.

Wilson, T. D., & Dunn, E. W. (2004). Self-knowledge: Its limits, value and potential for improvement. *Annual Review of Psychology, 55,* 493–518.

Wrosch, C., Heckhausen, J., & Lachman, M. E. (2000). Primary and secondary control strategies for managing health and financial stress across adulthood. *Psychology and Aging, 15*(3), 387–399.

Wrosch, C., Scheier, M. F., Carver, C. S., & Schulz, R. (2003). The importance of goal disengagement in adaptive self-regulation: When giving up is beneficial. *Self and Identity, 2,* 1–20.

Chapter 10

Attachment and Marriage

Gary Creasey and Patricia Jarvis

An objective of this chapter is to articulate theory and research that may help us better understand successful marital processes and outcomes. Quite understandably, there are many theories that attempt to explain long-term marital stability, and there are numerous comprehensive analyses concerning conceptual, methodological and theoretical issues related to this field (Karney & Bradbury, 1995; Gottman & Notarius, 2002). Such another analysis is not the objective of the present review, rather, in this chapter; the role of adult attachment functioning in predicting important marital outcomes will be specified. This particular approach is not entirely novel, in that there is both existing theory (Karney & Bradbury, 1995) and research (e.g., Treboux, Crowell, & Waters, 2004) that have attempted to better establish such links. On the other hand, we suggest herein that such theory and research have not been well integrated, and links between attachment functioning and relationship success primarily are limited to studies involving college student dating couples. Although such research has paved some important groundwork in this area, it is unreasonable to predict that research findings from one very select population automatically generalize to another.

A chapter on attachment relationships within the context of marriage is an important topic for a handbook devoted to adulthood and adult development. Marriage is a significant behavioral context in which the majority of adults are situated at some time in their lives. Therefore, marriage provides an important setting for adult development to unfold. This chapter is organized into several sections. First, conceptual, theoretical and methodological advancements pertaining to the study of marital functioning are articulated. Next, basic research findings regarding marriage are presented, as well as the applicability of these results to popular theories of long-term marital success. Because attachment functioning may play a major role in explaining marital functioning, contemporary attachment theory is overviewed, as well as major methodological issues that face researchers that use this approach. Next, studies that have connected attachment processes with marital functioning are specified. The chapter concludes with a critique of this existing research, as well as a discussion regarding how attachment theory and methods can be better integrated into marital research.

Our chief focus on marital couples obviously ignores other important populations, namely same-sexed couples in long-term, committed, romantic relationships. This omission is a limitation of the review; however, there is another chapter devoted to same-sex relationships in this current volume (i.e., chapter 12). Further, there are heterosexual couples involved in lengthy and exclusive relationships that do not marry. The omission of this couple, however, pertains more to a lack of systematic research than anything else, in that, very few studies have been conducted with these dyads, and virtually none have focused on attachment issues. Finally, little is known about how adult attachment functioning influences committed relationships in other cultures. All of these populations need more study to determine if the associations between attachment processes and marital success identified in the current review could be applied to other groups of adults in committed romantic relationships. Such studies may reveal that involvement in a high quality, secure romantic relationship over time may be more important for health and development than whether or not one is married in the legal sense.

Marriage and Divorce in the United States

Marriage is an important normative event for most adults in the United States, albeit not all people marry. In 2004, about 72% of the adult population in the United States had experienced one marital relationship, although, about 31% of men and 25% of women over 15 had never married (United States Census Bureau, 2004). Whereas most people marry, many adults today are postponing this important, legally recognized commitment. For example, between 2000 and 2003 the median age for first marriages was 27 and 25 years of age for men and women, respectively (Johnson & Dye, 2005). According to the aforementioned report, these averages are influenced by geographic region in that the median age for first marriages are higher in the Northeast and West, and lower in the Midwest and South. These regional statistics are influenced by many factors; however, it is estimated that rural adults marry at younger ages than people living in urban areas. Thus, this consideration could explain these geographic regional differences.

While marriage remains an institution in the United States, it is apparent when reviewing empirical research regarding this context, as well as a more causal review of mass media coverage of this topic, that more attention focuses on problematic/failed marriages than healthy relationships. The suspected instability of many marriages, experts claim, is supported by the "divorce rate," a figure that ranges from 50% to a jarring 75% (Martin & Bumpass, 1989)—depending on one's source. Perhaps to support these claims, in 2003 there were about 7.5 marriages per 1,000 adults and 3.8 divorces (National Center for Health Statistics, 2003). Further, when reviewing the number of marriages and divorces that occurred between January and August, 2005, most states report divorce rates of over 50% (National Vital Statistics Reports, 2006). These statistics appear alarming because an additional (and difficult to document) percentage of marriages remain in "permanent separation" limbo.

On the other hand, most marriage and family experts acknowledge that some of these pessimistic statistics are misleading. For example, simply comparing the number of new certified marriages to finalized divorces—whether at the national, state, or county/city level—is problematic because these data are drawn from very different populations of adults. Consider that the former pool is drawn from a more limited sample of adults (largely adults in their 20s), whereas the latter sample is drawn from a much larger population of married adults.

A more representative statistic, and one not widely cited in empirical studies or the media, concerns the percentage of marital couples that *actually become* divorced. According to U.S. Census statistics, the percentage of white, non-Hispanic adults in first time marriages that eventually divorce is about 30% (Bramlett & Mosher, 2001), a percentage that is lower now than 30 years ago (Kreider, 2001). It is also interesting that large-scale, longitudinal studies of community-residing adults rarely yield divorce rates over 25 to 30%. About the only consistent statistic on divorce concerns timing; most studies suggest divorce is most likely to occur in first-time marriages during the first 10 years of the relationship (Bramlett & Mosher, 2001).

Although the percentages of adults that eventually become divorced may be lower than normally expected, marital dissolution and severe marital distress are pressing problems. While there are clearly cases when marital dissolution appears justified (e.g., an abusive relationship), the potential financial, emotional, psychological, and interpersonal risks of divorce are well known. In addition, ongoing marital discord presents potential health problems to husbands and wives, as well as for children residing in the household (Whisman & Bruce, 1999). Thus, when examining variables that predict marital success, it is prudent to identify constructs that influence both marital stability and satisfaction.

What Predicts Marital Quality and Stability?

Although some adults in distressed marriages may escape the potential physical and health outcomes commonly associated with such relationships, it is also true that poor marital quality (i.e., marital satisfaction) is an obvious predictor of marital stability. That is, consideration of divorce or separation, or marital dissolution is frequently preceded by chronic marital distress. Of course, most married adults occasionally feel dissatisfied in their relationship; thus, predicting marital stability with some degree of certainty requires a multivariate assessment of the marriage beyond an evaluation of marital satisfaction.

Marital quality is a benchmark variable that refers to the adult's overall evaluation of marital health. It is often used as an index of marital distress or satisfaction. In terms of assessment, two of the most commonly used measures are the 15-item Marital Adjustment Test (MAT; Locke & Wallace, 1959) and the 32-item Dyadic Adjustment Scale (DAS; Spanier, 1976). The DAS was developed from the shorter MAT and taps agreement about standard marital issues (e.g., finances, sex, careers), and how frequently the couple does things together (e.g., household projects; recreation). Yet, there are concerns with this widely used assessment. Items on marital quality measures, such as the DAS, sometimes are similar to items on other measures of marital functioning (Fincham, 1998). There are multiple DAS items that inquire about specific types of conflict in the relationship; thus, it would not be surprising to obtain a significant correlation between the DAS and a conflict tactics measure because of item redundancy. Further, polling adults about how often they do things together (e.g., laughing, kissing) or how much they agree on issues (e.g., family matters)—standard DAS items—does not provide a measure of the adult's evaluation of the marriage. Thus, marital quality may be best assessed using shorter, more direct measures of marital satisfaction (Fincham, 1998). For instance, the Kansas Marital Satisfaction Scale (Schumm et al., 1986) contains three short items that specifically inquire about marital satisfaction, such as "How satisfied are you with your marriage"?

How is marital quality, as a variable, used in research? Because chronic marital distress almost always precedes marital dissolution, marital satisfaction is often treated as an outcome, rather than independent variable for research purposes. That is, there is a process to separation and divorce; most couples who ultimately divorce do so via a lengthy period of marital dissatisfaction, followed by serious consideration of divorce, to actual separation and divorce (Gottman & Levenson, 1992). Thus, the successful *prediction* of which couples will become highly (and consistently) dissatisfied or satisfied over the course of their marriage constitutes an important research agenda.

Thus, what variables can reliably predict marital quality? Perhaps the starting place is to adopt a demographic approach—a tact that is frequently used by scholars who possess large, epidemiological data sets involving marital couples. When embracing such a perspective, it has been documented that adults who marry young, are unemployed, of low education, or possess a divorce history are more prone to marital distress and divorce (Heaton, Albrecht, & Martin., 1985; Morgan & Rindfuss, 1985; Kurdek, 1993). However, while all of these variables hold some predictive power in forecasting marital distress and stability, they are relatively immune to change or intervention.

Why is there a connection between such demographic variables and marital distress? Quite possibly, there are additional variables that explain such an association. For example, according to the *stress/crisis perspective* (Karney & Bradbury, 1995), an accumulation of chronic life stressors can lower marital satisfaction more quickly among couples in certain demographic groups than dyads that have considerable resources (i.e., education, maturity, finances). That is, although chronic life stress and major life events (e.g., sudden financial hardship) are tied to marital quality in many couples (e.g., Bolger, DeLongis, Kessler, & Wethington, 1989), it is probable that young couples and/or couples with less economic means may be especially challenged in such circumstances.

Marital duration and age have been identified as variables that are diagnostic of marital quality. That is, most divorces occur within the first 10 years of marriage, and it has been widely held that marital satisfaction shows a curvilinear path over the course of the marriage. Although most of our knowledge about this subject has been gleaned from cross-sectional studies, marital satisfaction starts initially high during the newlywed period, appears to drop somewhat after childbirth, declines further as offspring negotiate adolescence, and then increases when children begin to leave the household (Doherty & Jacobson, 1982; Orbach, House, Mero, & Webster, 1996).

The finding that older couples (e.g., 60–70 years of age) report less conflict and display better conflict management skills compared to younger couples (Levenson, Carstensen, & Gottman, 1993) has been taken as support for another major perspective of long-term relationship development known as *socioemotional selectivity theory*. This approach assumes that there is an increasingly important need for supportive, close affiliations during later adulthood. Because of this need, older adults begin narrowing their social networks to achieve more emotional closeness within their most important relationships (Carstensen, 1991). Thus, the finding that older adults report more closeness in their marriages, fewer conflicts, and higher marital satisfaction has been taken as support for this approach (Levenson et al., 1993).

However, there have been recent concerns raised about the interpretation of these study results (Glenn, 1998; Hatch & Bulcroft, 2004). Most of the studies that support socioemotional selectivity theory have utilized cross-sectional designs. It is possible that the older couples *appear* to resolve conflict better because their peers or contemporaries who could not do so became divorced. This finding would suggest that the differences between younger (some of which will become divorced) and older couples could be due to non-equivalent sampling.

Further, in such cross-sectional studies, it is difficult to ascertain whether age, marital duration, or generational differences between the age groups are influencing the data. For example, during the Great Depression family members were routinely separated due to economic hardship and unemployment. Perhaps just remaining together as a couple was enough to serve as a model for a successful marriage, and these demanding times mandated conflict avoidance or quick marital conflict resolution. If any of these ideas are correct, then it is possible that the older marital couples of today have always had satisfying marriages (according to their definition) and had fewer conflicts than today's more confrontational younger couples. Indeed, studies incorporating sequential designs have documented that marital quality may be better predicted by cohort differences than age effects (Glenn, 1998). Thus, while socioemotional selectivity theory appears to be a plausible theory regarding the evolution of general close relationships during adulthood, whether marital relationships, in particular, become closer and less conflict-ridden with age is debatable in light of these recent methodological challenges.

The association of broad demographic variables—such as age, education, or financial status—with marital quality and stability is a necessary first step in understanding risk and protective factors that might influence the marital process. Further, these may be the only data a researcher has at their disposal when using archival data sets involving large, community-residing marital samples. However, concluding that demographic variable "X" is associated with marital stability is like ascertaining that it usually rains when the barometer falls. It is difficult to conduct interventions at this level, much as it is difficult to change a weather pattern. Further, ascertaining that age or social class is correlated with marital success tells us little about the mechanisms responsible for the development or deterioration of a marriage.

Thus, to better clarify predictions, experts that conduct intervention work with marital couples often assess intrapersonal and interpersonal variables that may contribute to marital quality. Intrapersonal variables reside within the individual person and interpersonal variables reside at the level of the couple. These variables are attractive for study because they can be defined, measured, evaluated, and may be amenable to intervention efforts (Baucom & Epstein, 1990).

Intrapersonal Variables

Intrapersonal variables can either be proximal or distal (Karney & Bradbury, 1995). In terms of proximal variables, the aforementioned stress/crisis perspective of marital functioning stipulates that high levels of current, personal stress may produce more marital strain—a finding that has been well replicated (Bolger et al., 1989). Further, there may be other proximal variables that mediate or moderate associations between problematic temporal variables and marital functioning. For example, the way an adult copes with occupational stress may mediate associations between such stress and marital quality, or a large social support network may moderate such associations. Thus, the relationship between any given proximal intrapersonal variable (e.g., stress) and marital quality, could theoretically be mediated (e.g., personal coping styles), or moderated (e.g., social support networks) by other temporal variables.

There are also distal, intrapersonal variables that adults bring with them into new relationships (Karney & Bradbury, 1995); adults have differential past experiences that may have import in a new marriage. There is some evidence that adults who witnessed severe inter-parent discord or whose parents divorced may have more difficulties negotiating marital relationships compared to adults who have not experienced such events (Wallerstein & Lewis, 2004). Of course, linking distal developmental history variables, such as child maltreatment or parental divorce, to present marital functioning is somewhat akin to associating demographic variables to the marital process. One, it is difficult to change or conduct interventions with such information, and two, it is difficult to ascertain the mechanisms that link the variables.

To illustrate, serious inter-parent conflict experiences, or even a parental divorce may be co-morbid with other childhood variables, such as child maltreatment or peer victimization (Cummings & Davies, 1994). Such co-morbidity makes it notoriously difficult to isolate any specific developmental history variable that might be influencing a current close relationship. Simple links between such variables and marital functioning are further mitigated by longitudinal findings that suggest many adults who have experienced adverse pasts (e.g., serious domestic conflict) are in satisfying marriages (Werner & Smith, 2001). It appears these adults have overcome previous risks and are functioning well in their relationships.

Another variable that couples bring with them into new marriages, and one that can be more reliably assessed than the adult's recall of childhood/adolescent relationship experiences, is personality functioning. This intuitively seems like an interesting area of study because personality traits, such as extroversion, agreeableness and openness to experience have been associated with life goals, interests, and needs. A couple who shares similar interests and goals would then be predicted to score high on compatibility, a premise that supports another theory concerning the prediction of successful marital processes—the *similarity hypothesis* (e.g., Bentler & Newcomb, 1978). That is, it is assumed that new couples who share similar interests, activities, and values will experience more satisfying marriages than couples who are more dissimilar. However, while a compelling hypothesis, the notion that compatibility singularly predicts marital success is one that has only received weak support (Kurdek, 1993; Watson et al., 2004).

Of course, personality characteristics could influence other components of marriage that may play a more central role in predicting marital satisfaction and stability, such as marital behavior or relationship cognitions (e.g., partner attributions). It is in this arena that research has been most promising; in particular, neuroticism—a personality disposition marked by high negative mood—is positively correlated with marital distress and instability (Kelly & Conley, 1987; Kurdek, 1993). Further, the relationship between a more distal variable, such as personality, and marital quality, can also be mediated or moderated by other variables. For example, adults who report high levels of general negative affect often possess problematic relationship cognitions, such as unrealistic expectancies regarding their partner or distorted attributions, such as, "She works long hours because she is interested in her co-worker" (Karney, Bradbury, Fincham, & Sullivan, 1994). Further, more neurotic adults who possess high levels of negative affect display more problematic marital behaviors. Pasch, Bradbury, and Davila (1997) noted that spouses who report more generalized negative affect were less receptive to supportive behaviors exhibited by their partners as they disclosed personal problems.

A related topic is that the personality structure of one adult may not mesh well with the partner. For example, a highly anxious person may not experience major marital problems if their spouse is less aroused or reactive to stress. However, this premise underscores a central problem with marital research in that many researchers often gather comprehensive data on one partner without garnering a similar assessment on the other partner. The fact of the matter is that there are two partners; thus, the contribution of each partner's developmental history and personal functioning must be considered when making predictions. Further, most studies linking personality and marital functioning are cross-sectional; there may be times personality dispositions are less tied to marital quality. In a longitudinal study, Karney and Bradbury (1995) noted that newly-wed assessments of neuroticism were correlated with initial marital satisfaction, but was not predictive of changes in marital satisfaction over time. This finding suggests that personality plays an early role in marital satisfaction, but by itself is not a central cause of later marital instability.

Although links between personality functioning and marital behavior are well established, it is also known that problematic personality dispositions are difficult to "cure" and are at best managed (Butz & Austin, 1993). Thus, personality is somewhat akin to developmental history—we can assess it, but may not be able to treat it. However, there are other intrapersonal variables that have received attention, such as marital cognitions. This construct concerns the couple's broad-based beliefs about marriage. Perhaps the earliest work in this area was assumed under *social exchange theories*, or the perspective that marriages begin, develop, and stay stable due to the perceived advantages and disadvantages of being married to the present partner, perceived barriers to relationship termination, and the attractiveness of alternatives to the present relationship (Levinger, 1976). According to this perspective, a relationship will end when the partner perceives little benefit to the present relationship, views few barriers or liabilities to ending the relationship, and attractiveness to alternatives to the present relationship are high (Karney & Bradbury, 1995). However, while people considering divorce probably make such appraisals, it does not explain how or why adults come to think this way (Karney & Bradury, 1995). Additionally—and the following statement does not assume social exchange theory is necessarily a bad theory of marriage—it is somewhat hard to imagine how such broad marital cognitions would be amenable to intervention or change.

A more recent approach concerns the assessment of more specific attitudes, expectancies, standards, and attributions adults possess regarding their partner. Studies have documented that women report more marital satisfaction when they perceive their spouses to be supportive and emotionally close (Mills, Grasmick, Morgan, & Wend, 1992). This finding has been documented for couples during the early (Julien & Markman, 1991) and later years of marriage (Acitelli & Antonucci, 1994). Further, marital partners who possess negative attitudes, expectancies and attributions regarding their partner report more marital distress and display more problematic marital behavior than their counterparts who do not hold such expectancies (Baucom & Epstein, 1990; Bradbury & Fincham, 1992; Fincham & Bradbury, 1987). Although much of this research is cross-sectional, there are longitudinal studies that have documented that problematic relationship cognitions are diagnostic of marital distress and dissolution over time (Carrère, Buehlman, Gottman, Coan, & Ruckstuhl, 2000). New researchers that desire to study marital relationship cognitions will note that this field is very large, and one should be sensitive to the fact that relationship standards, beliefs, expectancies, attitudes, and attributions all represent different constructs and are assessed with different instruments (Fincham, 1998).

The links between relationship cognitions and marital quality—as assessed via marital satisfaction—are so strong, it has been questioned whether or not these cognitions are just an artifact of such quality. That is, people in distressed marriages may develop distressed cognitions over time, rather than the other way around. This bias, known as the *sentiment override hypothesis* assumes that adults in highly distressed marriages possess a generalized negative sentiment regarding their partner that contaminates the way they complete self-report measures regarding their partner (Weiss & Heyman, 1990). For example, the adult may rate their partner as "always cruel" when, in fact, a casual observer would perceive the partner in a different light. Because it is important to establish that any relationship cognition measure assesses something distinct from marital quality, it has become a matter of practice to control for marital satisfaction when linking marital cognitions to reports of marital behavior.

To sum, there are numerous intrapersonal variables that can influence marital quality and stability. Marital partners bring certain vulnerabilities and strengths into relationships, and there are ongoing temporal variables, such as occupational stress, that adults "bring home" with them that may alter the course of a marital relationship for better or worse. Of course, while it is understandable that such intrapersonal variables are important for empirical scrutiny, it is also true that marital quality and behavior is shaped by the way the couple "partners" or interacts on a daily basis. The study of such interpersonal variables will be specified next.

Interpersonal Variables

There exist different theories that account for how interpersonal variables may influence marital quality and stability. These theories are largely behavioral, and assume that certain patterns of marital behavior forecast subsequent satisfaction and stability. For example, "Well, we just do not communicate anymore," seems to be the mantra of the typical distressed couple. Good communications skills are more highly correlated with marital satisfaction than any other type of marital behavior (e.g., frequency of sex, time spent together, shared activities) (Jacobson, Waldron, & Moore, 1980), and the primary presenting problem of couples in marital therapy (Smith, Vivian, & O'Leary, 1990). The predictive power of communication has also been studied in a number of longitudinal studies. For example, communication abilities in the early parts of marriage (e.g., premarital, newlywed) are diagnostic of changes in marital quality during the earliest months as well as later years of a marriage (Gottman & Krokoff, 1989; Markman, 1981).

Although some of the earliest work in this area focused on the effectiveness of couple problem-solving skills and conflict resolution, the long-term ramifications of such behavior are only more recently understood. For example, while at one time marital therapists may have encouraged couples to resolve their differences at all costs, one might wonder how this feat could be accomplished if the matter were *irresolvable*. Further, it is true that highly satisfied couples in long-term marriages often argue about the same subjects—suggesting that some couples, even happily married ones, have never resolved certain issues in their relationship (Gottman, 1994). Thus, there must be something else about the content of communication that is diagnostic of marital success.

A major agenda for research and practice during the last two decades has been to focus more thoroughly on the emotional content of couple communication. This "affective behavior" is diagnostic of relationship success across many close relationships (e.g., marital; long-term dating, same-sexed romantic relationships, dyadic friendships) (Arellano & Markman, 1995; Creasey, Kershaw, & Boston, 1999), predicts stability in relationships across different ethnic/racial groups (Oggins, Veroff, & Leber, 1993), and is an important component for relationship quality across most cultures (Gottman & Levenson, 1986).

Two major approaches that have been developed to study the emotional content of communication consist of social support and conflict management paradigms. A standard social support paradigm, developed by Bradbury and colleagues, consists of asking one member of the couple to divulge a personal problem, while the second plays the role of the empathic listener. After this observation (10–15 minutes), the couple switches roles and their behaviors are subsequently coded. For example, when using Bradbury's Social Support Interaction Coding System (Bradbury & Pasch, 1994), the rater considers the behavior of the "helper" (e.g., positive instrumental or emotional support), as well as the "helpee" (e.g., clear communication of the problem).

In the conflict management paradigm, the couple must discuss sources of relationship contention. There are different methods that can be used to assess the couple's conflict management skills; however, one popular method consists of asking the couple to resolve a minor relationship conflict, followed by a major one (Creasey, 2002; Simpson, Rholes, & Phillips, 1996). One of the most effective methods to capture the emotional content of the conflict management behavior is the Specific Affect Coding System (Gottman,

1996). When using this system, the coder uses voice tone and content, body posture, eye movements, and so on to evaluate both positive (e.g., validation, affection, interest) and negative (e.g., contempt, defensiveness, belligerence) conflict management skills.

The results of marital behavior collected in both social support and conflict management paradigms have led to some very compelling results that have implications for both research and practice. For example, while it has been widely documented that men and women report very different levels of emotional support in their marriage, there have not been consistent gender differences in the use of positive social support strategies during actual couple observations (Pasch et al., 1997). Further, the behavior exhibited in such paradigms is more diagnostic of future marital satisfaction and stability (Pasch & Bradbury, 1998) than data collected via self-report methods.

The outcomes for couples observed in conflict paradigms are also compelling. A high amount of negativity in conflict observations, as well as a high imbalance of positive and negative behaviors (e.g., many more negative than positive behaviors), forecasts future declines in marital satisfaction (Gottman, 1993; Pasch & Bradbury, 1998; Smith et al., 1990). High marital distress is correlated with more negative conflict management behaviors (i.e., high levels of negative affect during conflict) at all stages of marriage (Carstensen, Gottman, & Levenson, 1995). However, unlike behavior witnessed in social support paradigms, there are somewhat clear gender differences pertaining to conflict management styles. At all ages, women are more confrontational and display more negative affect (e.g., anger; sadness), whereas men are more often defensive and tend to escape or avoid conflict (Carstensen et al., 1995; Gottman & Krokoff, 1989). High amounts of certain negative behaviors, such as mutual contempt and belligerence, or high levels of wife criticism and husband defensiveness, are predictive of later divorce (Gottman, 1993, 1994). Thus, the data gleaned from a conflict management paradigm possess important predictive validity.

One might ask, "Should I use a social support or conflict management paradigm?" Although choice of methods is always dependent on the original research questions, we recommend the use of both assessments. Whereas behaviors captured in both paradigms are diagnostic of marital success (Heyman, 2001; Pasch & Bradbury, 1998), the positive and negative behaviors observed in these methods do not always correspond or overlap. That is, a spouse that is unsupportive to their partner's personal problems does not always have problems resolving conflict. Further, in terms of predicting marital success, although there is some shared variance concerning behaviors derived from these paradigms, there is unique predictive variance accounted for as well via each assessment (Pasch & Bradbury, 1998).

In summary, the reader is probably considering at this juncture that there are a wide assortment of demographic, intrapersonal, and interpersonal variables that could be used to study the ontogeny of marital quality and success over time. One lesson that has been learned from decades of marital research is that there are innumerable variables that influence the thinking and behavior of both members of the couple, including each other's thinking and behavior. For example, there are probably some adults who are experts at conflict management and routinely engage in behaviors that diminish a negative tide of problems as they emerge during a conflict discussion. However, it is difficult to firmly conclude that such phenomena occur because of the way marital studies are frequently designed and the couple data analyzed. Many marital and dating relationship studies rely on the perceptions of a single partner, and do not record the thinking or behavior of both partners.

Further, there are studies that do include observations of both members of the couple, but the researchers analyze their data at the level of the individual, rather than the couple. For example, consider a researcher that is interested in associating occupational distress with marital behavior. It is quite popular, in such a study, to correlate the husband's distress with his behavior, and then associate the wife's distress with her behavior. However, the marital landscape is richer and more complicated than this particular analysis reveals. It is possible that the behavior of any one given marital partner is influenced not only by his or her distress, but the distress and behavior of the partner as well. An additional consideration is that this finding might be stronger for husbands than wives (or vice versa). Perhaps the difficulty facing researchers is that analyzing marital data at the level of the couple is somewhat complex, and requires one to consider husband and wife data *over* the course of the interaction (i.e., marked by time). Further, there are specific data entry and analytic considerations for evaluating such interactions. Interested readers regarding this issue may wish to consult particularly accessible sources by Kashy and Kenny (Kashy & Kenny, 2000; Kenny, Kashy, & Cook, in press).

Predicting Long-Term Marital Success: An Integrative Approach

Thus, there are a number of important variables that forecast marital success. A watershed event for marital researchers consisted of a now classic publication by Karney and Bradbury (1995) that delineates a vulnerability-stress-adaptation perspective regarding the marital process. In this model, *marital quality* is assumed to be a dependent variable, and is best predicted by marital adaptive processes, such as relationship cognitions (e.g., marital attributions) and behavior (e.g., socially supportive behavior; conflict management techniques). Further, it is correctly assumed that there are various enduring vulnerabilities, such as personality or developmental history variables that impinge on marital cognitions and behavior. However, more temporal stressful events and the aforementioned adaptive processes mediate the connections between such vulnerabilities and marital quality. Thus, a person possessing high levels of general negative affect may create more stress in their lives, which in turn, influences the way they think about their partner, or behave towards them. It is clear from reviewing this conceptual model that these marital experts have developed an important, testable framework for better understanding the marital process.

One of the central vulnerabilities alluded to in Karney and Bradbury's (1995) framework concerns the role of adult attachment functioning. In their theoretical framework, adult attachment is assumed to play the role of an enduring vulnerability that has a possible direct function in predicting both marital cognitions and behavior that, in turn, forecasts marital quality and stability. However, these theorists also assume that the strongest link between attachment and marital quality is indirect, and that, secure and insecure people may encounter different stressors or possess different stress appraisals that in turn affect marital quality. This idea is akin to a mediation model; it is theoretically assumed that Variable A (attachment functioning) causes Variable B (stress appraisal; poor coping), which in turn predicts an outcome, Variable C (adaptive processes). Given the central role of stress in mainstream attachment theories, this mediational model is well theorized, yet, attachment theory provides a framework for offering additional hypotheses. For example, the attachment system is presumed to activate during times of major stress, thus it is quite possible that the effects of stress (e.g., major financial problems) will adversely affect marital relationships in cases when one or both partners are insecure.

Indeed, in subsequent updates to the Karney and Bradbury model, it has been acknowledged that the outlined variables potentially can have reciprocal pathways

(Davila, Karney, & Bradbury, 1999). Thus, a highly satisfying marriage could buffer the impact of stressful events, or even influence attachment functioning. For example, it is possible that high marital satisfaction may alter the way the adult thinks about his or her own attachment functioning (cf., Bowlby, 1988).

Of course, there has been a substantial amount of attachment research involving marital couples pursued since 1995. There have also been important theoretical advances on this subject since the Karney and Bradbury (1995) publication. In the initial review, these authors relied heavily on Hazan and Shaver's interpretation of attachment theory that, at the time, suggested that an adult's ideology of close relationships is based on models of close relationships developed during infancy and childhood (Hazan & Shaver, 1987, 1994). Thus, a secure child should grow up to be a secure adult and to function well in all close relationships. Such a straightforward explanation of the role of adult attachment in predicting marital success is probably too simplistic, and even Karney and Bradbury voiced concerns that the relationship between adult attachment security and successful marital functioning may be moderated by other variables, such as the marital partner's attachment functioning. Another issue, and one not voiced in Karney and Bradbury's (1995) work, pertains to growing concerns regarding certain measurement techniques in the field of adult attachment (Waters, Crowell, Elliott, Corcoran, & Treboux, 2002).

In terms of the sections to follow, we overview some of these advancements, as well as lingering concerns in this exciting area of research. Thus, we begin with a survey of attachment theory and its theoretical role in predicting success in close relationships during adulthood. Next, methodological approaches regarding the assessment of adult attachment will be overviewed. After this discussion, marital studies that have involved attachment as a primary variable will be overviewed. Finally, alternative ways to consider the role of attachment functioning in marriage are presented, as well as suggestions for future research.

Contemporary Attachment Theory

The theoretical basis for most studies involving marital couples has been paved via Bowlby's ethological attachment theory. For many years, much of the empirical research involving his approach concentrated on infants. Bowlby (1969/1982) posited that close attachment relationships between infants and caregivers were necessary from a survival standpoint. In the spirit of ethological theory, Bowlby (1969/1982) asserted that attachment bonds should be witnessed across all cultures around the world. Ainsworth (1967) provided support for this premise by documenting that classic signs of infant-caregiver attachment (e.g., proximity seeking; stranger distress) can indeed be witnessed in other culture. However, while Ainsworth's work suggested that almost all infants become attached to caregivers, the caregiving environment has been theorized to produce differences in the *quality* of this attachment. To better capture this diversity, Ainsworth and colleagues developed the Strange Situation procedure (Ainsworth, Blehar, Walters, & Wall, 1978) in which infants are separated from, and reunited with their primary caregiver, as well as a "stranger" over the course of brief observational segments.

To assess quality of attachment, Ainsworth developed a classification system that identified three organized patterns of attachment. *Secure* infants actively explore their environment when not distressed; yet seek comfort and proximity from caregivers when upset, and a caregiver can readily comfort these babies. *Avoidant* infants distance themselves from caregivers and rely on themselves (or focus on the environment) for comfort. *Ambivalent* or *resistant* infants have difficulty with exploration, often angrily seek contact with caregivers during times of duress, and yet cannot be comforted. The latter two classifications are signs of attachment insecurity. Attachment security is considered the modal attachment classification, and most closely linked with healthy development.

Infant attachment classifications modestly predict important outcomes during childhood and adolescence, such as social competence in the peer group, the ability to cope with stress, psychological health, and school adjustment (Thompson, 1999). There are a number of methodological and theoretical advancements in the field of adult attachment that allow for more systematic testing of Bowlby's original theoretical perspective. Bowlby's theory regarding the development of generalized attachment representations was advanced by the development of the Adult Attachment Interview (AAI; George, Kaplan, & Main, 1996). This 20-item interview was designed to assess one's state of mind regarding attachment to principal caregivers during childhood and adolescence, and is used to measure "the security of attachment in its generality rather in relation to any particular present or past relationship" (Main, Kaplan, & Cassidy, 1985, p. 78).

The AAI assesses cognitive processing of attachment relevant information in response to past, current, and future attachment experiences. Like the infant Strange Situation, the AAI coding scheme yields three organized attachment classifications (i.e., secure, dismissive, and preoccupied), but these evaluations are based primarily on the person's state of mind regarding attachment. After these classifications are derived, interviews can be classified as *unresolved/disorganized* with respect to past abuse or loss. It is important to note that reports of significant childhood maltreatment, as an example, do not automatically lead to an unresolved attachment classification.

Most adults do not find themselves squarely centered within these attachment categories. For instance, a secure adult may show some dismissing or preoccupied tendencies. Although the AAI classification allows coders to further subcategorize adults to capture such trends, this strategy is rarely undertaken because only a few participants in any given study may be represented within any subcategory. Partly in response to this issue, Kobak (1993) developed the 100-item Adult Attachment Interview Q-sort. When using this method, trained raters sort the items, printed onto cards, into a pre-determined distribution. Although this method has not been widely used by marital researchers, the approach possesses good psychometric properties and scores garnered from this instrument are associated with the traditional attachment categories in predictable ways (Allen, McElhaney, Kuperminc, & Jodl, 2004; Kobak, Cole, Ferenz-Gilles, Fleming, & Gamble, 1993).

The development of the AAI represented a major advancement in the field of adult attachment and lends the researcher an important method to assess adult generalized attachment representations. Further, in relation to marital research, Bowlby's theory regarding generalized attachment representations, and the adult attachment classifications derived from the AAI that are thought to reflect these mental models, have important implications for considering the role of developmental history in predicting marital functioning. That is, a thorny issue for marital researchers has been the obvious methodological limitations inherent in assessing the adult's recall of past childhood events (such as the intensity or frequency of parental discord) that may have a bearing on present marital thinking or behavior. Experts that embrace attachment theory, in terms of Bowlby's tradition, would argue that obtaining a catalog of all of these possible events—whether real or imagined may be less rewarding than an accurate assessment of generalized attachment representations (cf. Hesse, 1999). That is, what has the most important impact on adult relationship functioning is not whether something good or bad happened during childhood. Rather, it is the state of mind regarding the recollection of past events that has the most important bearing on current mental and interpersonal health.

Because the AAI requires considerable training to master, there are a number of self-report questionnaires that assess general attachment security, such as the Attachment History Questionnaire (Pottharst, 1990), Inventory of Parent and Peer Attachment (Armsden & Greenberg, 1987), and Reciprocal and Avoidant Attachment Questionnaires for Adults (West & Sheldon, 1988), and a self-administered q-sort procedure, the Adult Attachment Q-sort (AAQS; Creasey, 2005).

Generalized attachment representations have been proposed to exert influence in very close relationships, and play a major role in the development of parenting, marital or long-term, committed romantic relationships, and adult child-parent caregiving relationships (Waters, Corcoran, & Anafarta, 2005). Although a case can be made that these representations influence all of these relationships similarly, the dynamics and needs in the relationships are different. Thus, whereas generalized representations are assumed to have a global influence on adult thinking, emotions, and behavior in very close relationships, adults may tailor their representations to adjust for the different relationship dynamics and demands across different attachment affiliations. For example, while infants are highly dependent on their parents, the encouragement of such one-sided dependence is unhealthy in adult relationships. Thus, although parent-infant and adult-romantic partners qualify as attachment figures, the perceptions of closeness, dependability, anxiety, trust, and commitment in these affiliations are dependent on the nature and maturity of the relationship (Hazan & Shaver, 1987; Collins & Read, 1990).

In this regard, it is predicted that adults possess generalized representations, but eventually acquire relationship-specific representations as well (Creasey & Ladd, 2005; Furman & Simon, 2006; Roisman, Collins, Sroufe, & Egeland, 2005; Treboux et al., 2004). Paramount to this present chapter is the development of relationship specific expectancies of self and partners in romantic relationships. Hazan and Shaver (1987) proposed that romantic love could be conceptualized as an attachment process, speculating that that the "attachment styles" of romantic couples were similar to what was originally observed by Ainsworth in her work with infants. These researchers constructed an attachment style measure in which respondents endorsed brief paragraphs depicting different patterns of attachment analogous to Ainsworth's three organized attachment strategies. A secure adult trusts and feels emotionally close to others, experiences low relationship anxiety, and is comfortable depending on partners (and vice versa). An avoidant adult is uncomfortable with emotional closeness, reports low relationship anxiety, yet, feels uncomfortable depending on partners. Finally, an anxious or ambivalent adult reports high relationship anxiety, expresses concerns over partner availability, and has little trust in relationships.

Hazan and Shaver's perspective on adult attachment has been extended on theoretical and methodological grounds. If working models of romantic relationships reflect both thinking about the viability of oneself as an attachment figure, as well as thinking about the worthiness of the romantic partner as attachment figure, then one could view themselves positively and/or negatively on these two self-other dimensions. Thus, according to Bartholomew and colleagues (Bartholomew, 1990; Bartholomew & Horowitz, 1991), on conceptual grounds, there should be four adult attachment prototypes, represented by attachment *security* (positive self, positive other), *avoidance* (positive self, negative other), *preoccupation* (negative self, positive other) and *fearfulness* (negative self, negative other). To capture thinking across self-other dimensions, Bartholomew developed a series rating scales to assess attachment styles in close adult relationships (Griffin & Bartholomew, 1994) in which the adult considers to what degree they are secure, avoidant, preoccupied, or fearful.

Other attachment questionnaires also yield continuous ratings of attachment security based on these self-other dimensions that tap feelings of closeness, dependability, and anxiety in close emotional relationships. However, respondents are provided different directions on how to complete these measures across studies. For example, respondents may be asked to consider how they generally view close relationships or be specifically instructed to think about romantic relationships. In the former case, the researcher is intent on assessing a more generalized way of thinking about attachment, as opposed to the adult's thinking about a specific relationship. Thus, it is possible that many of the aforementioned survey methods can be used to assess generalized attachment or more specific representations. However, we noted in our review of attachment-based studies using the aforementioned questionnaires that it was sometimes difficult to discern whether the research participants were instructed to think about their relationships with romantic partners, or if they were asked to consider their thinking in all adult close relationships.

Although considerable controversy remains whether adult attachment functioning is best captured via categories/prototypes or dimensions, a recent review of studies involving five popular attachment measures revealed that self-reported attachment security was consistently related to more romantic relationship satisfaction when using either approach (Stein et al., 2002). However, a number of experts believe that, on statistical grounds, it is best to use a dimensional method (Fraley & Waller, 1998). This is a prudent idea because most adults classify themselves as secure on attachment questionnaires and usually only a handful classify themselves as wholly preoccupied or fearful (Kobak & Hazan, 1991). Further, aside from preserving statistical power, it has been noted in adult attachment studies using narrative methods (such as the AAI) that many secure people, for instance, show some preoccupied or dismissing tendencies. A dimensional approach thus allows the researcher to study attachment processes in a continuous manner to capture such tendencies. When doing so, large-scale, factor analytic studies of popular attachment questionnaires have revealed that the underlying structure of such attachment measures can be reduced to two major higher-order continuous scales: Secure—Avoidance; Secure—Anxiety (Brennan, Clark, & Shaver, 1998; Fairchild & Finney, 2006). In most recent studies of adult attachment using questionnaire methods, researchers have used these two scales to assess attachment functioning. Whereas most attachment measures that assess romantic relationship representations are questionnaires, there are narrative or interview schedules that assess these relationship specific attachment representations (e.g., Current Relationship Interview, Crowell & Owens, 1996).

Thus, there exists a vast, somewhat conflicting literature on adult attachment that can be somewhat confusing to a new researcher. There are two major constructs—generalized and relationship specific attachment representations—that can be assessed by narrative/interview methods, questionnaires, and even q-sort procedures, such as the Marital Q-set (Kobak & Hazan, 1991) and the Romantic Partner Attachment Q-sort (Creasey, 2006). However, on conceptual and methodological grounds, it is hotly debated whether self-report questionnaires represent a valid approach to assess these mental models. It is assumed that attachment representations reside partly outside conscious awareness, which means, that some adults may perceive themselves to be secure, when in fact they are not classified that way when using narrative methods.

This concern becomes more of an issue when one considers that security scores gleaned from questionnaires often do not parallel attachment classifications garnered from interview schedules (Crowell, Fraley, & Shaver, 1999; Holtzworth-Munroe, Stuart, & Hutchinson, 1997; Simpson, Rholes, Orina, & Grich, 2002). Further, while attachment classifications yielded from interview protocols are often quite stable over time (Treboux et al., 2004)—suggesting a formation of a stable, internalized working model of attachment—attachment data garnered from attachment questionnaires has displayed less success. Although security scores garnered from questionnaires display short-term stability (e.g., 3-weeks) (Sibley, Fischer, & Liu, 2005), they are often unstable over longer periods of time (Baldwin & Fehr, 1995; Fuller & Fincham, 1995). It has been suggested in this regard that these assessments may more likely tap current relationship feelings, as opposed to a deeply stored, internal working model of attachment (Waters et al., 2002).

Psychometric work on attachment instruments, is not often extensive, and is limited to the work of the researchers who developed the instruments. Thus, it is prudent to recommend that marital researchers interested in the impact of attachment functioning on marital health consider collecting additional data on general mood, personality, and social desirability—which would yield more complete, if no less complex, assessments of adult attachment.

Attachment and Marriage: Theoretical Associations

When considering some of the recent trends in adult attachment theory and research, it could be argued that central elements of Karney and Bradbury's (1995) theoretical framework of the marital process can be retained; however, other ideas can be added. In terms of the original framework, it is sensible to predict that attachment functioning has an important role in explaining the development of adaptive processes (e.g., conflict management skills) in a marital relationship. Further, it can be speculated that generalized attachment relationships play a more important task in the courtship period of a romantic relationship, and the early years of marriage, than in the later years. That is, this thinking represents a potential asset or liability that adults bring into very close relationships. Indeed, given the relationship standards of secure people, it would seem prudent to theorize that secure adults are more likely to find themselves in long-term relationships with similar-minded, secure adults (Mikulincer, Florian, Cowan, & Cowan, 2002). However, the notion that secure or insecure adults choose marital partners who are similar to themselves on attachment concerns is controversial and is explored further in this review.

Generalized attachment representations should also shape the attitudes, expectancies, and attributions we make about romantic partners (e.g., Collins, 1996). Secure adults should function as good support figures (or a secure base) for their partner and would more effectively resolve conflict than insecure adults. Thus, one can justify that generalized attachment representations forecast the development of adaptive processes (e.g., conflict management behavior) in a marital relationship (at least in the early years of the marriage), and that, such adaptive processes will mediate associations between these representations and marital quality.

Of course, with time, adults also develop specific attachment representations about romantic partners. Thus, a theoretical issue concerns the role of generalized and specific attachment representations in the marital process and how marital behavior and quality is influenced when these models are compatible or incompatible. Although making predictions about marital success seems straightforward—for example, possessing insecure generalized and partner representations should spell doom for any close relationship—the extant research produces a more complex picture of this process.

Another consideration is that the relative influence of other potential variables that might affect marital quality can be weakened or strengthened by attachment functioning. For example, adults with mental health problems or certain personality difficulties (e.g., neuroticism) may be very difficult to cope with if they also possess insecure attachment representations. On the other hand, as an example, a depressed or highly impulsive adult who possesses a secure attachment representation may be able to negotiate marital interactions as well as an adult without such difficulties. Thus, the relationship between enduring vulnerabilities residing in the individual and marital quality and behavior could very well be moderated by attachment functioning.

Although some may consider attachment functioning to be more or less a trait, attachment representations probably do not influence adaptive behavior/thinking in relationships and subsequent marital success in such a straightforward manner. For example, stress plays a central role in attachment theory, and also has a place in theoretical frameworks of marital functioning (Karney & Bradbury, 1995). Because stress is assumed to activate the attachment system, it is plausible to theorize that attachment functioning is most relevant when adults are facing major life events (e.g., becoming a parent) or chronic daily distress. Major stressors also may spark considerable discussion and conflict in couples, and/or one partner may need considerable support from the other. Thus, the relative influence of attachment functioning on marital behavior and stability may be somewhat dependent on ongoing stressors and demands in the adults' lives. In other words, there may be times in the life course of the marriage when attachment functioning does *not* play a role in shaping the daily thinking, emotions, and behavior of couples.

Another consideration is that working models of relationships, while theorized to be resistant to change, are open to revision (Bowlby, 1969/1982). It is possible that vulnerabilities within the adult, or the environment, can overwhelm the attachment functioning of even a secure person. For example, an adult with a history of depression that is otherwise secure may find themselves becoming more insecure if their lives are highly demanding or they encounter some major life event that is attachment relevant, such as their partner taking a job that requires considerable travel. Thus, there could be characteristics within the individual (e.g., personality, mental health functioning) that encourage changes in attachment functioning that, in turn, impinge on the marital relationship (Davila et al., 1999).

There can also be other attachment-relevant, major life events that have implications for attachment change, such as marriage itself. In fact, Bowlby (1969/1982) theorized that becoming married has important implications for potential modification of relationship representations. For example, because the honeymoon period is marked by high marital satisfaction, perhaps adults develop more secure representations of their partners. Such a finding could suggest that attachment representations might change as a result of the marital behavior of the partner (Davila et al., 1999). A partner who is unfaithful may cause an otherwise trusting, secure partner to become insecure regarding the relationship. Thus, while we assume that attachment functioning has a strong role in predicting marital behavior and quality, it can be theorized that the relationship between these variables is reciprocal as well.

Attachment and Marriage: A Review of the Research

In this section, research that has associated attachment processes with marital functioning are considered. In the first segment, we examine the phenomena of associative mating, exploring the possibility that adults with certain attachment stances marry partners having similar models. Next, because attachment functioning is theorized to influence adaptive processes in a marriage, such as conflict management skills, research that has associated adult attachment with such behavior will be specified. Because marital quality influences long-term marital stability, we next examine research that has correlated attachment functioning with marital satisfaction. Finally, we turn to research that has identified variables that might alter attachment representations over time.

Associative Mating

Do either secure or insecure people tend to marry partners with similar generalized attachment stances? Answering this query depends on the way generalized attachment representations are assessed. When adults are asked to categorize themselves as secure or insecure on self-report attachment questionnaires, there is high concordance for associative mating. Adults who consider themselves generally secure are often married to secure partners (Senchak & Leonard, 1992). What factors might account for such a finding? One possibility is that secure adults are overly "choosey" during the mate selection process, and negotiate a series of dating relationships before settling down into a more committed relationship that is compatible with their working model of what defines a successful, long-term relationship. Thus, because generally secure adults display highly supportive behavior in close relationships, we would expect that their secure partner is exhibiting the types of positive behaviors and emotions during the courtship period that serve as a reinforcing signal for a secure attachment representation. Of course, because there are few studies that have tracked adults through the courtship process, most of these ideas are at best speculative.

On the other hand, the finding that generally secure adults marry secure partners may be overly amplified by the fact that very high percentages (75% or more) of people categorize themselves as "secure" on attachment style questionnaires (Kobak & Hazan, 1991; Volling, Notaro, & Larsen, 1998). Thus, it is not surprising that high associative mating is particularly confined to adults who report that they are secure people, and in marital couples, there does not seem to be consistent pairing of any particular insecure attachment style. For example, more avoidant adults do not seem to pair with other avoidant adults. Further, the fact that secure adults do sometimes marry insecure partners is also a curiosity; however, this finding could be due to the fact that most adults, whether they are secure or insecure, often prefer secure people as potential romantic partners (Latty-Mann & Davis, 1996). If most people, regardless of attachment security, admire the relationship qualities of secure people, then there are only so many secure adults available for long-term romantic relationships. Thus, according to some attachment experts, the associative mating of secure adults has much to do with the availability of secure partners, and secure people are the one's most likely to "attract and keep them" (Kirkpatrick, 1998, p. 376).

However, it is interesting that when generalized attachment representations are assessed using narrative methods, such as the Adult Attachment Interview (AAI), there appear to be lower levels of associative mating and no predictable "partnering" of people with various insecure styles (e.g., dismissing/avoidant male; anxious/preoccupied

286 Gary Creasey and Patricia Jarvis

women) (Crowell, Treboux, & Waters, 2002; Dickstein, Seifer, St. Andre, & Schiller, 2001; Paley, Cox, Burchinal, & Payne., 1999). If there is a trend, secure people are more likely married to secure partners; however, this finding is less strong than what has been documented when attachment is assessed via self-report questionnaires. These somewhat divergent findings could be due to certain nuances of narrative and questionnaire-based attachment measures that assess generalized attachment representations. Because self-report attachment questionnaires have been charged to be stronger measures of personality than attachment functioning (Waters et al., 2002), it could be that the associative mating between secure-secure adults is more due to compatibility of personality dispositions than attachment stances. This idea can be somewhat supported by critiquing popular items on self-report attachment questionnaires, such as, "*I find it easy to depend on others*," or "*I find it difficult to get emotionally close to others*." Because attachment figures, per se, are not specifically mentioned as relationship targets, it is possible that personality traits such as neuroticism or general agreeableness influence the adult's responses on these surveys more than general attachment functioning. If this concern is true, then it would not be surprising to find a convergence of attachment styles in marital couples because the measures may be assessing personality compatibility as opposed to a stable, internalized attachment representation.

Although it is debatable whether generalized attachment representations play a strong role in eventual mate selection, it does appear that these general representations forecast how the adult views their partner as an important attachment figure. For example, generalized attachment representations predict the ontogeny of partner-specific representations Crowell, Treboux, & Waters, 2002; Treboux et al., 2004). That is, a generally secure adult tends to hold a secure representation regarding their partner.

Attachment and Adaptive Processes

Because of the close ties of adaptive processes to marital quality and stability, it comes as no surprise that many studies have linked attachment functioning to important marital behaviors, such as conflict management tactics. It is compelling that the marital behaviors most frequently targeted for study—namely conflict management behaviors and the ability to function as an important source of support for a partner—are also "emotionally laden" behaviors. Because adult attachment pertains to a close emotional relationship, the relevance of attachment functioning to such adaptive processes in marriage would seem self-evident. Further, in cases where couples are encouraged to openly resolve conflict, or function as support figures to one another, the researcher is providing a potential context for activation of the attachment system (cf. Simpson et al., 1996). Thus, these particular marital interactions can be viewed as especially salient outcome variables for study in attachment-based research.

Conflict Management Skills. Most of the attachment research involving marital behavior has focused on associating attachment security with the ability to manage conflict with the partner. Theoretically, if a generalized attachment representation is a broad knowledge or resource base regarding emotional relationships (Treboux et al., 2004), generally secure adults should have a good working knowledge of how to regulate negative affect and relate to others (Kobak & Sceery, 1988; Powers, Pietromoaco, Gunlicks, & Sayer, 2006) and would more smoothly negotiate marital conflict than insecure adults. This premise has been supported when adults, themselves, are the informants of such conflict behavior. For example, a secure generalized attachment representation, whether measured via narrative (Crowell, Treboux, & Gao, et al., 2002) or questionnaire (Senchak & Leonard, 1992) methods, is tied to fewer self-reported conflict management problems in marital relationships.

Further, in studies involving direct observations of couple conflict management, most research has documented that attachment security has a role in predicting the use of more positive conflict tactics (Cohn, Silver, Cowan, Cowan, & Pearson, 1992). Adults with secure generalized attachment representations, as assessed by the Adult Attachment Interview, resolve conflict better than adults classified as dismissing or preoccupied. Further, preoccupied adults appear to resolve conflict somewhat more effectively than dismissing people (Babcock, Jacobson, Gottman, & Yerrington., 2000; Paley et al., 1999)—a finding that somewhat parallels the results of studies involving dating couples that have used similar methods (e.g., Creasey, 2002). This finding is curious, because it is well known that preoccupied adults lace attachment interviews (as well as therapy sessions) with angry discourse, and are often highly blaming of others for their relationship problems. One would think that their conflict interactions with marital partners would be equally chaotic; however, this does not appear to be the case. It has been speculated that more preoccupied or anxious adults, partly due to their lack of interpersonal relationship confidence or potential fears of abandonment may be somewhat inhibited during conflict negotiation (Creasey & Ladd, 2004; Feeney, 1998). However, after the interaction, they may obsessively ruminate over the encounter or bitterly complain to others about the behavior of their partner at a later date (Slade, 1999).

Although more secure adults seem to "argue better" than insecure people, it is less well known if generally secure, dismissing, or preoccupied adults possess any particular "style" of conflict negotiation. This is an important agenda for study, because certain conflict management profiles, such as angry, critical, attacking behaviors, or conflict withdrawal are tied to eventual relationship dissolution (Gottman, 1994). In terms of the latter, gradual disengagement from conflict by men is viewed as a major precursor to the divorce process, and we are encouraged by studies that have documented that secure men are generally more involved in marital interactions than their insecure counterparts (Cohn et al., 1992). However, it may be difficult to predict a certain "style" of conflict for any given secure, dismissing, or preoccupied adult because their thinking and behavior during the interaction is influenced by the attachment stance and behavior of their partner. This is an area that needs more investigation.

Researchers rarely focus on the conflict behavior of adults classified as unresolved due to loss or trauma (i.e., when using the Adult Attachment Interview) or who classify themselves as fearful on attachment style questionnaires. This might be an important research area, because it has been noted that unresolved adults in committed dating relationships show differential conflict management behavior in comparison to dismissing or preoccupied adults, such as overly controlling behavior (Creasey, 2002). Further, there is evidence to suggest that unresolved or fearful marital partners are more verbally and physically aggressive than secure, dismissing, or preoccupied adults (Crowell, Treboux, & Gao, et al., 2002; Dutton, Saunders, Starzomski, & Bartholomew, 1994; Holtzworth-Munroe et al., 1997).

Although it is understandable that generalized attachment representations may have some role in forecasting conflict management behavior, we also gradually develop partner-specific attachment representations. Like the findings associating generalized attachment representations and conflict behavior, it has been documented that secure representations regarding marital partners are positively associated with more positive behavior, and more insecure representations are related to the use of more problematic behavior, such as hostile, verbal aggression (Treboux et al., 2004; Alexandrov, Cowan, & Cowan, 2005).

Similar to the research results regarding generalized attachment representations, adults who possess secure, dismissing, or preoccupied attachment stances regarding their marital partner do not seem to show any particular "style" of conflict behaviors in research to date. This finding could be due to the idea that adult conflict management behavior is heavily dependent on the attachment functioning and conflict management skills of the partner. For example, a dismissing adult may not be overly defensive when engaged in conflict with a secure partner. Further, another theory—and one that will be examined more thoroughly in a later section—is that the major predictor of marital behavior concerns the compatibility of our generalized attachment representation and our representation of our partner. For example, what type of conflict management behavior is observed when an adult possesses a secure generalized attachment representation, yet holds an insecure representation regarding his or her marital partner?

Supportive Behavior.   Like conflict management abilities, the aptitude to provide and receive emotional support from marital partners is an important predictor of marital success. Similar to the findings regarding associations between attachment and conflict behaviors, adults who rate themselves as generally secure via surveys report high levels of supportive interchanges in their marriages (Cobb, Davila, & Bradbury, 2001). On the other hand, it is difficult to interpret such findings when data are from a single informant.

When analyzing supportive behavior at the observational level, adults who possess secure generalized (Crowell, Treboux, & Gao, et al., 2002b), or secure partner-specific (Kobak & Hazan, 1991; Treboux et al., 2004) attachment representations possess the ability to both effectively provide and receive social support in response to personally distressing issues. These findings have been replicated in younger and older couples, when using both narrative and q-sort methods (e.g., Marital Attachment Q-sort) (Kobak & Hazan, 1991). Further, Crowell and colleagues have noted that highly skilled adults are not only secure people, but also these skills seems to develop further over the course of the marriage in these secure adults (Crowell, Treboux, & Waters., 2002; Treboux et al., 2004).

Such highly skilled adults are assumed to have developed "secure base" behavior, and are thus able to show better interest in their partner's concerns, can more optimally recognize and interpret their partner's distress, and can more effectively respond to such distress over the life course of a marriage. Because these behaviors are highly indicative of an attachment relationship (e.g., Ainsworth, 1989), these researchers could be given credit for successfully specifying the evolution of such a relationship, which provides support for the idea that marital partners are true attachment figures. Perhaps this is the reason that researchers have had mixed success in drawing connections between attachment functioning (whether assessed via narrative or questionnaire methods) and supportive behavior in dating samples (e.g., Simpson et al., 2002). These mixed findings could be due to the fact that many dating couples have not yet formed a true attachment alliance, that is, the ability to effectively provide and receive support during personal distress are hallmark behaviors associated with true attachment relationships (Cassidy, 1999).

It should be noted that there is one study in which relations between attachment and supportive behavior in marital couples were specified using multiple measures of attachment. In a longitudinal study of married couples over a six-year period, Treboux and colleagues (2004) assessed generalized attachment representations using the Adult

Attachment Interview, and partner specific attachment representations using both the Current Relationship Interview and the Experiences in Close Relationships Scale (Brennan et al., 1998). In this study, relatively strong connections were noted between the interview-based assessments and the presence of supportive behavior in marital couples; yet, self-reported partner security was not significantly related to these behavioral observations. This was curious, in that the questionnaire used to assess partner attachment security contained questions pertaining to partner support and dependence. Thus, one's perception of a secure attachment, as assessed via self-report questionnaires, may not always mesh well with observations of supportive behavior in the relationship.

To summarize, attachment functioning plays a role in forecasting the development of important marital behavior. Secure people are effective at resolving conflicts and are able to competently provide and receive social support, whereas more insecure people are less skilled at these abilities. However, although there are a growing number of studies that have linked attachment processes to observed marital behavior, in some cases, we have only scratched the surface. It is still somewhat unclear how the attachment representations of both partners "work together" to produce a coherent and predicable set of marital behaviors. Also, it is very rare for researchers to study the marital behavior of couples sequentially over time. That is, we need to better pinpoint the actions of couples that *lead to* more or less supportive behavior over the course of an interaction.

Further, we proposed that attachment functioning can potentially moderate associations between intrapersonal, contextual, interpersonal variables and marital behavior. It is somewhat rare to locate studies that take these factors into consideration, and again, there may be times during the lifecycle of a marriage when connections between attachment functioning and marital behavior are stronger. For example, Paley and colleagues (2005) noted that marital and family interactions over the course of pregnancy are considerably worse when one (particularly new fathers) or both partners possess attachment insecurity. Thus, it is evident that more research is needed in this area in light of the aforementioned concerns.

Attachment and Marital Quality

Because marital quality (i.e., satisfaction or distress) is such a benchmark variable for marital researchers, it is not surprising that there are studies that have linked attachment functioning with this construct. The association between attachment and marital quality, not surprising, is a controversial issue, and is often dependent on the manner in which attachment is assessed. For example, generalized and partner-specific attachment representations assessed via attachment questionnaires are almost always associated with marital quality in predictable ways. That is, adults who perceive themselves to be generally secure or possess secure partner representations often report much higher marital satisfaction than adults who report themselves as insecure (Davila, Bradbury, & Finchman., 1998; Davila & Bradbury, 2001; Feeney, 1994, 1999; Hollist & Miller, 2005; Lussier, Sabourin, & Chantal., 1997; Mayseless, Sharabany, & Sagi, 1997; Treboux et al., 2004). In fact, and consistent with attachment theory, secure attachment representations have been shown to buffer couples from serious marital dissatisfaction during potential times of duress, such as when couples are faced with major family illnesses (Berant, Mikulincer, & Florian, 2003), when negotiating marital stressors (e.g., infertility) (Mikulincer, Horesh, Levy-Shiff, Manovich, & Shalev, 1998), and during the transition to parenthood (Curran, Hazen, Jacobvitz, & Feldman, 2005; Simpson, Rholes, Campbell, Tran, & Wilson., 2003).

In fact, sometimes the association between self-reported attachment and marital quality is *extremely* robust. Treboux and colleagues (2004) noted that self-reported, partner-specific attachment anxiety or avoidance highly predicted less marital satisfaction, as assessed by the Dyadic Adjustment Scale (Spanier, 1976) (respective correlations –.52 and –.61). Indeed, while some have charged that attachment questionnaires may be proxy measures of general personality (Waters et al., 2002) and/or subject to self-presentational biases, another interpretation is that they might be redundant assessments of marital satisfaction. That is, adults who are currently satisfied with their marriages may report that they are comfortable depending on their partner, feel emotionally close to him or her, and perceive little relationship anxiety. Thus, it could be that these surveys are tapping current feelings toward a partner; akin to supporting the sentiment override hypothesis reported earlier in this chapter. The concern arises that the measures may not be tapping any type of stable, internalized model regarding attachment (cf. Treboux et al., 2004).

The association between attachment functioning and marital satisfaction is less straightforward when considering studies that assess attachment processes using interview-based measures. While some have linked secure generalized attachment representations with higher marital quality (Das Eiden, Teti, & Corns, 1995), other research has established less strong associations (Cohn et al., 1992; Paley et al., 1999). Further, it is somewhat surprising that attachment classifications derived from interviews designed to assess relationship specific, attachment representations with marital partners are only modestly correlated with marital satisfaction (Treboux et al., 2004). This is a surprising finding, because classifications derived from attachment interviews are generally well correlated with objective assessments of marital behavior, such as conflict management behavior. However, it is also possible that the attachment constructs assessed via interviews are not temporary feelings the adult currently possesses regarding their partner. Rather, if these interviews were truly assessing internalized representations, then it would be expected that assessments such as the Adult Attachment Interview or the Current Relationship Interview might be more diagnostic of marital stability than any contemporaneous assessment of marital satisfaction. This particular premise has been borne out, in that attachment security in the early years of marriage is diagnostic of marital stability and dissolution (Treboux et al., 2004).

In sum, most studies document modest associations between attachment representations assessed via narrative methods and self-reported marital quality. This is not that surprising as a deeply internalized attachment presentation of a romantic partner may not always coincide with the way one currently feels about that partner. Further, the associations between attachment processes and marital satisfaction are purported to be more indirect than direct. Kobak and Hazan (1991) determined that the most highly skilled couples were ones who had partners with secure attachment representations. Indeed, there do exist some studies in which, both generalized attachment and partner-specific representations are assessed concurrently to forecast marital functioning. We next turn to some of this exciting work.

Compatibility of Attachment Representations

A recent research avenue concerns the compatibility of attachment security, or the joint role of husband and wife attachment representations in predicting marital functioning. Because attachment functioning does not strongly predict associative mating (Paley et al., 1999; Dickstein et al., 2001), it is possible that one marital partner may possess a secure generalized attachment representation whereas the other may be insecure. Further, while secure generalized attachment representations are related to the development of a secure partner representation, this is not always the case (Crowell et al., 1999; Simpson et al., 2002). Thus, it is possible that one could possess a secure generalized attachment representation, yet, possess considerable insecurity regarding the partner.

In terms of generalized attachment representations, like research with dating couples (Creasey, 2002; Kirkpatrick & Davis, 1994), there is evidence that husband-wife attachment compatibility has an effect on marital satisfaction and behavior. Not surprisingly, marital health appears better when both partners are secure, and less optimal when both are insecure (e.g., Volling et al., 1998); however, this finding is stronger in studies that include self-report measures of attachment rather than narrative methods (e.g., Paley et al., 1999). In any case, regardless of the instrumentation choice, associations between joint generalized attachment representations and marital health/behavior in most studies are consistent, but also of modest strength.

Regarding the compatibility of partner-specific representations, most research suggests that marital behavior and satisfaction are higher when both partners' hold secure attachment stances of one another (Alexandrov et al., 2005; Dickstein et al., 2001; Kobak & Hazan, 1991). However, more recent research has examined the compelling idea that marital quality and health may be best determined by an assessment of *both* generalized and partner-specific attachment representations. Because these models are not always compatible (Dickstein, Seifer, Albus, & Magee, 2004), it is possible, for example, that an adult could possess an insecure generalized attachment representation and a secure partner attachment representation. Unfortunately, the exploration of this idea is somewhat underdeveloped because of the paucity of studies that have involved assessments of both types of attachment representations. Further, a coherent set of results or findings does not seem to be apparent when these representations are assessed using different methods (e.g., parent representation: questionnaire; generalized representation: interview) (Treboux et al., 2004; Simpson et al., 2002). However, Crowell and colleagues (Crowell, Treboux, & Waters 2002; Treboux et al., 2004) examined the impact of generalized and partner-specific representations over a six-year period, from the engagement period through the early years of marriage, using the AAI and the CRI.

The results of the aforementioned investigations support the premise that couples that contain an adult who possesses secure generalized- and secure partner-specific representations (or secure/secure) have better marital outcomes than adults who possess alternative models of relationships. Individuals who possess such secure/secure representations report positive appraisals regarding their partners and marriage, report low levels of relationship conflict, and function as effective support figures to their partner when they report contemporaneous stressors in their lives (Crowell, Treboux, & Gao, et al., 2002). The ability to serve as a support figure to a spouse in the face of stressful events is a benchmark criteria for a competent attachment figure.

Further, the suggestion that an insecure generalized attachment representation and an insecure partner representation (or insecure/insecure) spells marital doom would be challenged by this research. Insecure/insecure adults display low rates of socially supportive behavior and more relationship conflict; however, they do not report high amounts of marital dissatisfaction. As suggested by Treboux and colleagues (2004), perhaps these adults are comfortable with having their attachment representations confirmed and have become used to relationship adversity. These results confirm what has been demonstrated in the dating literature; couples possessing considerable attachment insecurity show high rates of relationship problems, but are more likely to remain together than couples containing a secure and insecure partner (Creasey, Ladd, Dansfield, Giaudrone, & Johnson, 2005).

Indeed, couples are more likely to divorce if one member of the couple displays a secure representation, but has an insecure representation of their marital partner (or *secure/insecure*) (Crowell, Treboux, & Waters 2002). Further, secure/insecure individuals report the most relationship distress and exhibit some of the worst relationship behavior when they report major stress in their lives (Treboux et al., 2004). Quite understandably, this incompatibility in attachment representations is problematic because the partner's behavior, which is viewed as the chief force behind the development of partner representations (Davila et al., 1999), is inconsistent with the way the adult generally has come to think about attachment relationships. Although this is not something the secure/insecure adults may routinely think about, perhaps this idea becomes more apparent when an adult needs the support of a partner during times of stress and does not receive it.

Another intriguing finding concerns adults who possess an insecure generalized attachment representation, yet, have come to develop a secure representation of the partner (i.e., insecure/secure). Treboux and colleagues (2004) have noted that insecure/secure individuals report more relationship problems with spouses than adults that possess secure/secure attachment representations, but possess positive feelings towards their spouses and report low levels of conflict when they are experiencing low levels of stress. This finding has been partially replicated by others (e.g., Alexandrov et al., 2005), suggesting that a secure partner representation may serve as a buffer in preventing negative conflict escalation and preserving relationship harmony.

In summary, adults develop multiple mental models of relationships. A generalized representation is based on years of experience with principal attachment figures, whereas a relationship-specific representation is based on experiences with one person. While these models can be compatible, incompatibility is not necessarily a negative thing, at least in cases when the adult possesses an insecure generalized attachment representation, yet, possesses a secure representation of their partner. What is intriguing about this finding is that this generally insecure adult may have developed a secure representation of their partner, even in cases where that partner themselves is not necessarily secure (Crowell, Treboux, & Waters 2002).

What remains unclear is how mental models of partners evolve and synthesize, and if they are as resistant to change as more generalized attachment representations. In addition, while it is widely theorized that attachment representations "wag the tail," at least in terms of forecasting marital thinking/behavior, it is just as probable that this process can work in reverse order. Thus, although attachment representations are resistant to change, they are open to revision. In the next section, we will delineate variables that are thought to possibly alter attachment stances over time.

Changes in Attachment Functioning

Although attachment functioning is theorized to remain stable, there might be intrapersonal, interpersonal, and contextual factors that spur revision of attachment representations (Allen et al., 2004). Further, these factors probably do not function in a vacuum and can work in concert together. As an example, intrapersonal factors are analogous to enduring vulnerabilities, and the one most heavily discussed by Bowlby (1980) was depression. Certainly, depression can be viewed as an outcome of insecure attachment functioning because the individual potentially has received the message that they are unloved (Bretherton, 1985). However, not all depressed adults are insecure, but such adults are potentially vulnerable to become insecure if they experience marital difficulties (an interpersonal factor), or major life stress (a contextual factor). In such cases, depressive symptoms could hypothetically worsen, and overwhelm the attachment system, which could lead to more insecurity over time (Bowlby, 1980). These are compelling ideas, but equally interesting would be the delineation of variables that lead to more security in adults over time. Unfortunately, this is an area that is more uncharted because such research requires an ambitious longitudinal design and the use of such designs are relatively lacking in most attachment-romantic relationship research.

However, there are scattered studies that have examined how certain intrapersonal variables—such as educational background, mental health history, and personality—may influence attachment functioning over time in marital couples (Crowell, Treboux, & Waters 2002; Davila et al., 1999). For example, highly educated people are more likely to develop secure partner representations, and individuals with poor mental health or certain personality dispositions (e.g., neuroticism) are more likely to shift from secure to insecure attachment stances (Davila et al., 1999). The role of personality, mental health, and educational status have been linked to attachment change processes in other populations, such as adolescents (Allen et al., 2004), and could serve either as risk or protective factors. As alluded to earlier, as an example, an individual with mental health problems could conceivably possess a secure attachment stance, yet, become more insecure over time if they lack a good social support network or encounter a major change in their attachment context (e.g., a spouse whose job requires considerable travel). One might expect that these individuals are more likely "wavering secures" and that major life changes may make them prone to develop more attachment insecurity than an adult without such vulnerabilities (Treboux et al., 2004).

Bowlby (1988) also proposed that marriage, in itself, might cause shifts in attachment representations over time. Some of the seminal work in this area has examined if positive marital functioning (an interpersonal variable) can have a constructive influence on the attachment system. Some researchers have examined if the development of a secure partner representation, in the face of positive marital behavior and high levels of marital quality, can potentially alter deep-rooted generalized attachment representations. For example, several studies have documented that attachment representations become more stable and secure during the honeymoon or newlywed period (e.g., Davila et al., 1999). In one study, Crowell, Treboux, and Waters (2002) noted that the presence of supportive marital behavior and a secure partner representation forecasted changes in generalized attachment representations, that is, from an insecure to secure stance. It is interesting to note that while most adults did not show major changes in generalized attachment representations, these were the major conditions that most likely provoked a change from a generally insecure to secure stance. Thus, there is the distinct possibility that secure partner representations, quite predictably, evolve from highly supportive marital behavior, where the partner repeatedly shows evidence that they are an important and effective attachment figure in the adult's life. This behavior, and the evolution of such thinking, wholly contradicts a deeply ingrained generalized attachment representation. What is somewhat surprising about such a finding is that the aforementioned researchers observed these changes over 2- to 6-year time intervals, a relatively short time frame when one considers the lifespan of a successful, long-term marriage.

It has also been suggested that chronic stress or major life stressors may also play a role in altering attachment representations. Because it is well known that stress can impinge on marital behavior, such conditions could alter attachment representations. For example, Crowell, Treboux, and Waters (2002) noted more instability in attachment functioning over time when the couple encountered more negative life events. These researchers documented that the increases in these life events, such as serious financial problems, were more likely to lead to marital conflict, which in turn, predicted increases in insecurity. This finding has been replicated in other populations (e.g., adolescents) (Allen et al., 2004), and again presumably is due to a renegotiation of attachment representations in the face of the increased relationship conflict.

It should be pointed out again that longitudinal studies involving marital couples suggest that attachment representations are usually stable over time, which supports Bowlby's (1988) contention that internal working models are resistant to change. However, this work suggests that attachment representations are open to revision, in the face of personal, interpersonal, and contextual variables. The finding that these representations can change also supports the idea that there is not a clear direction of effect when it comes to the assessment of marital variables, such as attachment and marital quality, and that their association is indeed bi-directional over time and should be studied using time sensitive research designs.

Conclusions

Perhaps one of the most important contributions to the marital literature concerns the recent integration of adult attachment in major theoretical frameworks outlining variables that forecast marital quality and stability. It has long been held that the attachment system represents an important organizational construct for making predictions about success in close relationships during childhood, adolescence, and adulthood (Sroufe, 2005). Indeed, much of the marital research has taken this stance, and a majority of studies have documented that more secure adults display better marital behavior and achieve higher marital quality than more insecure adults.

Perhaps the most predominate finding we uncovered was that adults with secure attachment representations who are married to more secure partners display the most optimal marital functioning, a finding that is consistent with attachment theory, and not wholly unsurprising. Secure adults are highly valued by other secure and insecure adults, as more viable marital partners (Kirkpatrick, 1998) and they "show why" during conflict interactions, or during times when they are needed (Crowell, Treboux, & Gao, et al., 2002). Further, many studies have demonstrated that secure adults are more psychologically healthy and emotionally mature than insecure adults (Dozier, Stovall, & Albus, 1999), are more forgiving (Kachadourian, Fincham, & Davila, 2004), and are more sensitive parents (Hesse, 1999). Further, the finding that attachment security is the predominate attachment stance across cultures, and that most secure adults are married to secure partners, may be one reason that the majority of marriages do not experience health-threatening marital dissatisfaction or failure.

While it is not surprising that secure adults married to secure partners have more successful marriages, what is missing are studies that show more clear outcomes for adults who display other types of attachment pairings. In addition, we are not sure what to make of studies that conclude that more insecure adults manage conflict "worse" than secure adults, as well as research that documents that they are "less supportive" partners. It would seem that we could predict, using attachment theory, unique patterns of interaction concerning adults that are more dismissing/avoidant, anxious/ preoccupied, or unresolved/fearful. However, this is a daunting task because attachment security is the most predominate attachment stance across cultures (van IJzendoorn & Sagi, 1999); thus, there are fewer numbers of insecure people available in any given study.

Thus, while we know that the marital behavior and quality of couples is best when both adults are secure, much less is known about unique modes of interaction among couples with alternative representations at the dyadic level (e.g., dismissing husband/ preoccupied wife; unresolved husband/secure wife). Again, this is an important agenda, because there are small scale studies suggesting that the adult attachment pairing most commonly witnessed in marital treatment settings is the highly engaged, preoccupied wife accompanied by a reluctant, dismissing husband (Byng-Hall, 1999). Unfortunately, it is difficult to interpret the meaning of this finding. Is this the type of couple most likely headed to marital disharmony, or is this the type of couple that is most likely to self-refer themselves to treatment? The answers to such questions are critical on a number of fronts. For example, it is well known that one type of marital couple that frequently experiences a divorce is the "demand-withdrawal" couple, marked by a highly critical, engaged wife and a stonewalling, inattentive, non-engaged husband (Heavey, Christensen, & Malamuth, 1995). Is the aforementioned attachment configuration predictive of such interactive behavior? This is an important issue, because this connection between these attachment stances and this profile of interactive behavior has been somewhat supported in dating couples (Feeney, 1994; Kirkpatrick & Davis, 1994). Further, other couples who show a risk for divorce are dyads marked by a highly controlling spouse and a nervous, tentative partner, as well as couples who display bitter, contemptuous, mutual hostility (e.g., Gottman, 1994).

The field has been somewhat handicapped because attachment methods that require a classification scoring system frequently yield low numbers of adults who are "purely" preoccupied or unresolved. This problem, to some degree, could be addressed via methodological advancements in this field. For example, many of the recently developed attachment questionnaires, such as the Experiences in Close Relationship Scale-Revised (Fraley, Waller, & Brennan, 2000), allow researchers to assess general attachment security, anxiety, and avoidance in a more continuous manner. This type of assessment strategy makes theoretical sense in that secure people often report varying degrees of insecurity, and the same is true for more insecure adults. While some experts are critical of attachment questionnaires (Waters et al., 2002), there do exist alternative ways to continuously score narrative methods that assess generalized attachment representations (Adult Attachment Interview Q-sort; Kobak, 1993) and there are q-sort methods (Marital Attachment Q-sort; Kobak & Hazan, 1991; Romantic Partner Q-sort; Creasey, 2006) available to assess partner attachment security, avoidance, and anxiety in a continuous manner.

The aforementioned concern suggests a high need for more research in this area, but overall, it appears from the available research that secure attachment functioning is a valuable resource for marital couples. Further, because attachment is viewed as an organizational construct, it has been widely proposed that attachment functioning at any age could serve as a major buffer from past and present adverse events. As articulated recently by Sroufe (2005), "Secure people are just simply robust." However, another lesson we learned from this review was that attachment security, in adults, does not seem to have a unilateral, main effect influence on interactive behavior in marital relationships. Attachment security can thus serve as both a mediator and moderator variable in theoretical frameworks of the marital process.

The idea that attachment functioning may play a role in moderating associations between personal/contextual risk factors and marital functioning is an exciting one because certain variables, such as general personality functioning or serious financial hardship cannot really be "cured." On the other hand, the idea that attachment functioning plays more of a moderating than a mediating role is not widely articulated in current theories of the marital process (e.g., Karney & Bradbury, 1995). We think this is a mistake because, in many ways, attachment functioning is quite stable over time, and resistant to major changes. This finding serves as verification that attachment functioning may not, in many instances, serve well as a mediating variable.

Of course, Bowlby (1988) argued that if the conditions are right, then attachment functioning can change over time, and in such cases, this construct therefore becomes more of a mediator than moderator variable. As alluded to before, highly stressful situations or personal vulnerabilities, such as depression, may potentially overwhelm the attachment system and result in more insecurity over time (Allen et al., 2004; Bowlby, 1980), which then leads to more marital distress. In fact, it is likely that these two constructs—namely, stress and depression—are not always independent of one another. As suggested above, it is probable that at most times, attachment moderates associations between depression and marital health, thus, serving a protective or buffering role. However, perhaps the "dam breaks" when the adult becomes highly stressed, resulting in increased insecurity and eventual marital problems. In this case, attachment is *mediating* the association between enduring vulnerabilities and marital health, and is not playing any moderating role. Therefore, the exact role of attachment functioning, in terms of serving as a mediating or moderating influence in terms of predicting marital functioning, may change with life circumstances or even maturity itself.

Thus, it is suggested that attachment functioning can change over time, and quite possibly develops for the better in many marital couples. However, there is little research that has traced the ontogeny of attachment processes over the course of a marriage (see studies by Crowell, Treboux, & Waters, 2002; Davila et al., 1999; Simpson et al., 2002; Treboux et al., 2004, for notable exceptions), and the extant work tends to involve the longitudinal study of newlywed or engaged couples over brief time periods. The evolution of attachment functioning throughout the marital life cycle would seem to be an important area of study. In fact, we are reminded of the comment that older adults frequently make to young teen couples that are contemplating marriage, "Marriage lasts a long time....the way you think about him/her may be different twenty years from now."

Indeed, it is probable that the way we think about attachment issues, and our marital partner as an attachment figure, may change with cognitive development and changing life circumstances across adulthood. Whether or not attachment becomes more or less a salient issue over time is debatable, for example, if the prime evolutionary significance of adult attachment is mating, reproduction, and parental investment (Kirkpatrick, 1998). One could then argue that marital relationships become less salient from an attachment standpoint as children mature and leave home. On the other hand, some theorists posit that close emotional relationships become more salient as we age (Carstensen, 1991), particularly as we negotiate emerging attachment concerns during later adulthood (e.g., grandparenthood). Of course, supporting either hypothesis is difficult because there is a serious lack of longitudinal work in this area.

Another issue we addressed in this chapter concerned the possibility that adults possess multiple attachment representations. From a conceptual standpoint, this is one of the most important advancements in this field; for example, adults possess both generalized and partner-specific attachment representations (Treboux et al., 2004). While this idea makes sense, it is quite rare for researchers to assess these multiple representations concurrently in *both* partners, despite emerging evidence that suggests marital behavior/quality is best predicted by an assessment of the compatibility or incompatibility of generalized-partner attachment representations. On a related point, the set of intrapersonal, interpersonal, and contextual variables that best forecast the development of partner-specific representations remains to be identified.

In terms of methodological issues addressed in review, perhaps one of the most pressing concerns pertains to choice of measurement techniques to assess both marital functioning and adult attachment. The good news is that there are some very strong assessment techniques used to assess marital behavior, cognitions, and quality. Further, marital stability can be readily ascertained via targeted queries (e.g., still married, divorced, separated). A difficulty is that divergent results are produced in studies that measure attachment functioning using narrative and questionnaire methods. The long-held viewpoint was that the assessments were targeting different types of representations using different methods (Crowell et al., 1999). For example, for many years, generalized attachment representations—that are presumed to reflect a lengthy history of relationship experiences with principal caregivers—were assessed via narrative methods. In contrast, more partner-specific representations were assessed via questionnaire methods.

However, more recent research, in which the same attachment representation has been simultaneously assessed using different methods (e.g., narrative and questionnaire) has suggested that narrative-based attachment data is more strongly tied to observations of marital behavior, whereas questionnaire-based data is more highly related to perceptions of marital functioning (Waters et al., 2002). The concern that is raised here is that attachment questionnaires that inquire about feelings towards romantic partners (e.g. "I tend to be mistrusting of romantic partners") may not be assessing a stable, internal working model of attachment, but rather, one's current marital satisfaction. In a worst-case scenario, it could be argued that these surveys are not functioning as attachment measures, but rather, proxy measures of marital satisfaction (Treboux et al., 2004). There is some evidence to support this argument; attachment functioning assessed via narrative methods is more stable than if measured using questionnaires (Crowell, Treboux, & Waters, 2002), and the attachment styles assessed via questionnaires sometimes show overly robust associations with marital satisfaction. Thus, there may be some pressure on attachment researchers that use such assessments to demonstrate that their instruments are assessing something distinct from marital satisfaction.

On the other hand, let us not assume that intensive, narrative methods that purportedly assess attachment representations are immune from concerns either. These interview techniques largely require intensive training to administer and score. Further, the psychometric properties of the interview methods described in this chapter have been largely determined in the labs of the developers of these instruments. In addition, while interview methods, are thought to tap the conscious and unconscious elements of attachment representations, there has not been intensive research to support the idea that this method assesses information stored at the unconscious level (Shaver & Mikulincer, 2002).

In closing, there is a high need for more industrious research that links attachment processes to marital health and success. This work is exciting on both a theoretical and practical level. Although attachment representations are somewhat resistant to change, it is widely believed that they can be altered, unlike personality, and thus represent a prime intervention target for marital therapists. Indeed, it is somewhat curious that connections have not been better drawn between more specific marital relationship cognitions and generalized/partner attachment representations. That is, within a cognitive-behavioral framework of marital therapy, it is assumed that problematic marital behavior is largely based on faulty or distorted attitudes, expectancies, attributions and standards for both marital partners as well as the concept of a marital relationship, in itself. Thus, a chief goal of treatment is to alter these marital cognitions, in the hope that healthy changes in thinking may modify problematic marital behavior (Baucom & Epstein, 1990). In particular, certain insecure attachment stances may predict unique types of expectancies, standards, and attributions adults may hold for marital partners. A final research agenda may be to conduct more research connecting different adult attachment classifications or styles with specific types of marital cognitions. Documenting unique profiles of thinking in these adults may have implications for more individualized marital therapy (Byng-Hall, 1999), in that, the approach to changing one's thinking about the marital relationship may be dependent on the adult's attachment stance, as well as their partner's.

References

Acitelli, L., & Antonucci, T. (1994). Gender differences in the link between marital support and satisfaction in older couples. *Journal of Personality and Social Psychology, 67,* 688–698.

Ainsworth, M. (1967). *Infancy in Uganda: Infant care and the growth of attachment.* Baltimore: John Hopkins University Press.

Ainsworth, M. (1989). Attachments beyond infancy. *American Psychologist, 44,* 709–716.

Ainsworth, M., Blehar, M., Walters, E., & Wall, S. (1978). *Patterns of attachment: A psychological study of the strange situation.* Hillsdale, NJ: Erlbaum.

Alexandrov, E., Cowan, P., & Cowan, C. (2005). Couple attachment and quality of marital relationships: Method and concept in the validation of the new couple attachment interview and coding system. *Attachment and Human Development, 7,* 123–152.

Allen, J., McElhaney, K., Kuperminc, G., & Jodl, K. (2004). Stability and change in attachment security across adolescence. *Child Development, 75,* 1792–1805.

Arellano, C., & Markman, H. (1995). The managing affect and differences scale (MADS): A self-report measure assessing conflict management in couples. *Journal of Family Psychology, 9,* 319–334.

Armsden, G. C., & Greenberg, M. T. (1987). The inventory of parent and peer attachment: Individual differences and their relationship to psychological well-being in adolescence. *Journal of Youth & Adolescence, 16*(5), 427–454.

Babcock, J., Jacobson, N., Gottman, J., & Yerrington, T. (2000). Attachment, emotional regulation, and the function of marital violence: Differences between secure, preoccupied, dismissing violent and nonviolent husbands. *Journal of Family Violence, 15,* 391–409.

Baldwin, M., & Fehr, B. (1995). On the instability of attachment: A construct validation of two self-report measures. *Personal Relationships, 2,* 247–261.

Bartholomew, K. (1990). Avoidance of intimacy: An attachment perspective. *Journal of Social and Personal Relationships, 7,* 147–178.

Bartholomew, K., & Horowitz, L. (1991). Attachment styles among young adults: A test of a four-category model. *Journal of Personality and Social Psychology, 61,* 226–244.

Baucom, D., & Epstein, N. (1990). *Cognitive-behavioral marital therapy.* New York: Brunner/Mazel.

Bentler, P., & Newcomb, M. (1978). Longitudinal study of marital success and failure. *Journal of Consulting and Clinical Psychology, 46,* 1053–1070.

Berant, E., Mikulincer, M., & Florian, V. (2003). Marital satisfaction among mothers of infant with congenital heart disease: The contribution of illness severity, attachment style, and the coping process. *Anxiety, Stress, and Coping, 16,* 397–415.

Bolger, N., DeLongis, A., Kessler, R., & Wethington, E. (1989). The contagion of stress across multiple roles. *Journal of Marriage and the Family, 51,* 175–183.

Bowlby, J. (1980). *Attachment and loss: Vol. 3: Loss: Sadness and depression.* New York: Basic.

Bowlby, J. (1982). *Attachment and loss: Vol. 1: Attachment* (2nd ed.). New York: Basic. (Original work published 1969)

Bowlby, J. (1988). *A secure base: Clinical applications of attachment theory.* London: Routledge.

Bradbury, T., & Fincham, F. (1992). Attributions and behavior in marital interaction. *Journal of Personality and Social Psychology, 63,* 613–628.

Bradbury, T., & Pasch, L. (1994). *Social Support Interaction Coding System.* Psychology Department, University of California, Los Angeles.

Bramlett, M., & Mosher, W. (2001). *First marriage dissolution, divorce, and remarriage: United States. Advance Data, # 23.* Centers for Disease Control, Atlanta, GA.

Brennan, K., Clark, C., & Shaver, P. (1998). Self-report measurement of adult attachment: An integrative overview. In J. Simpson & W. Rholes (Eds.), *Attachment theory and close relationships* (pp. 46–76). New York: Guilford Press.

Bretherton, I. (1985). Attachment theory: Retrospect and prospect. In I. Bretherton & E. Waters (Eds.), Growing points of attachment theory and research. *Monographs of the Society for Research in Child Development, 50*(1-2, Serial No. 209), 1–38.

Butz, M., & Austin, S. (1993). Management of the adult impulsive client: Identification, timing, and methods of treatment. In W. McCown, J. Johnson, & M. Shure (Eds.), *The impulsive client: Theory, research, and treatment* (pp. 323–344). Washington, DC: American Psychological Association.

Byng-Hall, J. (1999). Family and couple therapy: Toward greater security. In J. Cassidy & P. Shaver (Eds.), *Handbook of attachment: Theory, research, and clinical applications* (pp. 625–645). New York: Guilford.

Carrère, S., Buehlman, K., Gottman, J., Coan, J., & Ruckstuhl, L. (2000). Predicting marital stability and divorce in newlywed couples. *Journal of Family Psychology, 14,* 42–58.

Carstensen, L. (1991). Selectivity theory: Social activity in life-span context. In K. Schaie (Ed.), *Annual review of gerontology and geriatrics,* (Vol. 11, pp. 195–217). New York: Springer.

Carstensen, L., Gottman, G., & Levenson, R. (1995). Emotional behavior in long-term marriage. *Psychology and Aging, 10,* 140–149.

Cassidy, J. (1999). The nature of the child's ties. In J. Cassidy & P. Shaver (Eds.), *Handbook of attachment: Theory, research, and clinical applications* (pp. 3–20). New York: Guilford.

Cobb, R., Davila, J., & Bradbury, T. (2001). Attachment security in marital satisfaction: The role of positive perceptions and social support. *Personality and Social Psychology Bulletin, 27,* 1131–1143.

Cohn, D., Silver, D., Cowan, C., Cowan, P., & Pearson, J. (1992). Working models of childhood attachment and couple relationships. *Journal of Family Issues, 13,* 432–449.

Collins, N. (1996). Working models of attachment: Implications for explanation, emotion, and behavior. *Journal of Personality and Social Psychology, 71,* 810–832.

Collins, N., & Read, S. (1990). Adult attachment, working models, and relationship quality in dating couples. *Journal of Personality and Social Psychology, 58,* 644–663.

Creasey, G. (2002). Associations between working models of attachment and conflict management behavior in romantic couples. *Journal of Counseling Psychology, 49.* 365–375.

Creasey, G. (2005). *Adult Attachment Q-sort (Version 2).* Unpublished manuscript, Illinois State University, Normal, IL.

Creasey, G. (2006). *Romantic Partner Attachment Q-sort (Version 1).* Unpublished manuscript, Illinois State University, Normal, IL.

Creasey, G., Kershaw, K., & Boston, A. (1999). Conflict management with friends and romantic partners: The role of attachment and negative mood regulation expectancies. *Journal of Youth and Adolescence, 28,* 523–543.

Creasey, G., & Ladd, A. (2004). Negative mood regulation expectancies and conflict behaviors in late adolescent college student romantic relationships: The moderating role of generalized attachment representations. *Journal of Research on Adolescence, 14,* 235–255.

Creasey, G., & Ladd, A. (2005). Generalized and specific attachment representations: Unique and interactive roles in predicting conflict behaviors in close relationships. *Personality and Social Psychology Bulletin,* 31, 1026–1038.

Creasey, G., Ladd, A., Dansfield, M., Giaudrone, L., & Johnson, K. (2005). *Predicting romantic relationship status: The role of attachment representations and conflict tactics.* Paper presented at the Biennial Meetings of the Society for Research in Child Development. Atlanta, GA.

Crowell, J., Fraley, C., & Shaver, P. (1999). Measurement of individual differences in adolescent and adult attachment. In J. Cassidy & P. Shaver (Eds.), *Handbook of attachment: Theory, research, and clinical applications* (pp. 434–465). New York: Guilford.

Crowell, J., Treboux, D., Gao, Y., Fryffe, C., Pan, H., & Waters, E. (2002b). Assessing secure base behavior in adulthood: Development of a measure, links to adult attachment representations, and relations to couples' communication and reports of relationships. *Developmental Psychology, 38,* 679–696.

Crowell, J., Treboux, D., & Waters, E. (2002a). Stability of attachment representations: The transition to marriage. *Developmental Psychology, 38,* 467–479.

Cummings, E. M., & Davies, P. (1994). *Children and marital conflict: The impact of family dispute and resolution.* New York: Guilford.

Curran, M., Hazen, N., Jacobvitz, D., & Feldman, A. (2005). Representations of early family relationships predict marital maintenance during the transition to parenthood. *Journal of Family Psychology, 19,* 189–197.

Das Eiden, R., Teti, D., & Corns, K. (1995). Maternal working models of attachment, marital adjustment, and the parent-child relationship. *Child Development, 66,* 1504–1518.

Davila, J., & Bradbury, T. (2001). Attachment insecurity and the distinction between unhappy spouses who do and do not divorce. *Journal of Family Psychology, 15,* 371–393.

Davila, J., Bradbury, T., & Finchman, F. (1998). Negative affectivity as a mediator of the association between adult attachment and marital satisfaction. *Personal Relationships, 5,* 467–484.

Davila, J., Karney, B., & Bradbury, T. (1999). Attachment change processes in the early years of marriage. *Journal of Personality and Social Psychology, 76,* 783–802.

Dickstein, S., Seifer, R., Albus, K., & Magee, K. (2004). Attachment patterns across multiple family relationships in adulthood: Associations with maternal depression. *Development and Psychopathology, 16,* 735–751.

Dickstein, S., Seifer, R., St. Andre, M., & Schiller, M. (2001). Marital Attachment Interview: Adult attachment assessment of marriage. *Journal of Social and Personal Relationships, 18,* 651–672.

Doherty, W., & Jacobson, N. (1982). Marriage and the family. In B. B. Wolman (Ed.), *Handbook of developmental psychology* (pp. 667–680). Englewood Cliffs, NJ: Prentice-Hall.

Dozier, M., Stovall, K., & Albus, K. (1999). Attachment and psychopathology in adulthood. In J. Cassidy & P. Shaver (Eds.), *Handbook of attachment: Theory, research, and clinical applications* (pp. 497–519). New York: Guilford.

Dutton, D., Saunders, K., Starzomski, A., & Bartholomew, K. (1994). Intimacy-anger and insecure attachment as precursors of abuse in intimate relationships. *Journal of Applied Social Psychology, 24,* 1367–1386.

Fairchild, A., & Finney, S. (2006). Investigating validity evidence for the Experiences in Close Relationships—Revised Questionnaire. *Educational and Psychological Measurement, 66,* 116–135.

Feeney, J. (1994). Attachment style, communication patterns, and satisfaction across the life cycle of marriage. *Personal Relationships, 1,* 333–348.

Feeney, J. (1998). Adult attachment and relationship-centered anxiety: Response to physical and emotional distancing. In J. Simpson & W. Rholes (Eds.), *Attachment theory and close relationships* (pp. 189–218). New York: Guilford.

Feeney, J. (1999). Adult attachment, emotional control, and marital satisfaction. *Personal Relationships, 6,* 169–185.

Fincham, F. (1998). Child development and marital relations. *Child Development, 69,* 543–574.

Fincham, F., & Bradbury, T. (1987). The impact of attribution in marriage: A longitudinal analysis. *Journal of Personality and Social Psychology, 53,* 510–517.

Fraley, R., & Waller, N. (1998). Adult attachment patterns: A test of the typological model. In J. Simpson & W. Rholes (Eds.), *Attachment theory and close relationships* (pp. 77–114). New York: Guilford.

Fraley, R. C., Waller, N., & Brennan, K. (2000). An item response theory analysis of self-report measures of adult attachment. *Journal of Personality, and Social Psychology, 78,* 350–365.

Fuller, T., & Fincham, F. (1995). Attachment style in married couples: Relation to current marital functioning, stability over time, and method of assessment. *Personal Relationships, 2,* 17–34.

Furman, W., & Simon, V. (2006). Actor and partner of adolescents' romantic working models and styles of interactions with romantic partners. *Child Development, 77,* 588–604.

George, C., Kaplan, N., & Main, M. (1996). *Adult Attachment Interview* (3rd ed.). Unpublished manuscript, Department of Psychology, University of California, Berkeley.

Glenn, N. (1998). The course of marital success and failure in five American 10-year marriage cohorts. *Journal of Marriage and the Family, 54,* 559–569.

Gottman, J. (1993). A theory of marital dissolution and stability. *Journal of Family Psychology, 7,* 57–75.

Gottman, J. (1994). *What predicts divorce? The relationship between marital processes and marital outcome.* Hillsdale, NJ: Erlbaum.

Gottman, J. (1996). *What predicts divorce? The measures.* Mahwah, NJ: Erlbaum.

Gottman, J., & Krokoff, L. (1989). Marital interaction and satisfaction: A longitudinal view. *Journal of Consulting and Clinical Psychology, 57,* 47–52.

Gottman, J., & Levenson, R. (1986). Assessing the role of emotion in marriage. *Behavioral Assessment, 8,* 31–48.

Gottman, J., & Levenson, R. (1992). Marital processes predictive of later dissolution: Behavior, physiology, and health. *Journal of Personality and Social Psychology, 63,* 221–233.

Gottman, J., & Notarius, C. (2002). Marital research in the 20th century and a research agenda for the 21st century. *Family Process, 41,* 159–197.

Griffin, D., & Bartholomew, K. (1994). The metaphysics of measurement: The case of adult attachment. In K. Bartholomew & D. Perlman (Eds.), *Advances in personal relationships* (Vol. 5, pp. 17–52). London: Jessica Kingsley.

Hatch, L., & Bulcroft, K. (2004). Does long-term marriage bring less frequent disagreements? *Journal of Family Issues, 25,* 465–495.

Hazan, C., & Shaver, P. (1987). Romantic love conceptualized as an attachment process. *Journal of Personality and Social Psychology, 52,* 511–524.

Hazan, C., & Shaver, P. (1994). Attachment as an organizational framework for research on close relationships. *Psychological Inquiry, 5,* 1–22.

Heaton, T., Albrecht, S., & Martin, T. (1985). The timing of divorce. *Journal of Marriage and the Family, 47,* 631–639.

Heavey, C., Christensen, A., & Malamuth, N. (1995). The longitudinal impact of demand and withdrawal during marital conflict. *Journal of Consulting and Clinical Psychology, 63,* 797–801.

Hesse, E. (1999). The adult attachment interview. In J. Cassidy & P. Shaver (Eds.), *Handbook of attachment: Theory, research, and clinical applications* (pp. 395–433). New York: Guilford.

Heyman, R. (2001). Observation of couple conflicts: Clinical assessments applications, stubborn truths, and shaky foundations. *Psychological Assessment, 13,* 5–35.

Hollist, C., & Miller, R. (2005). Perceptions of attachment style and marital quality in midlife marriage. *Family Relations, 54,* 46–57.

Holtzworth-Munroe, A., Stuart, G., & Hutchinson, G. (1997). Violent versus nonviolent husbands: Differences in attachment patterns, dependency, and jealousy. *Journal of Family Psychology, 11,* 314–331.

Jacobson, N., Waldron, H., Moore, D. (1980). Toward a behavioral profile of marital distress. *Journal of Consulting and Clinical Psychology. 48,* 696–703.

Johnson, T., & Dye, D. (2005). *Indicators of marriage and fertility in the United States from the American Community Survey: 2000–2003.* Population Division, US Bureau of Census. Washington, DC.

Julien, D., & Markman, H. (1991). Social support and social networks as determinants of individual and marital outcomes. *Journal of Social and Personal Relationships, 8,* 549–568.

Kachadourian, L., Fincham, F., & Davila, J. (2004). The tendency to forgive in dating and married couples: The role of attachment and relationship satisfaction. *Personal Relationships, 11,* 373–393.

Karney, B., & Bradbury, T. (1995). The longitudinal course of marital quality and stability: A review of theory, method, and research. *Psychological Bulletin, 118,* 3–34.

Karney, B., Bradbury, T., Fincham, F., & Sullivan, K. (1994). The role of negative affectivity in the association between attributions and marital satisfaction. *Journal of Personality and Social Psychology*, *66*, 413–424.

Kashy, D. A., & Kenny, D. A. (2000). The analysis of data from dyads and groups. In H. Reis & C. M. Judd (Eds.), *Handbook of research methods in social psychology* (pp. 451–477). New York: Cambridge University Press.

Kelly, E., & Conley, J. (1987). Personality and compatibility: A prospective analysis of marital stability and marital satisfaction. *Journal of Personality and Social Psychology*, *52*, 27–40.

Kenny, D. A., Kashy, D. A., & Cook W. L. (in press). *Dyadic data analysis*. New York: Guilford.

Kirkpatrick, L. (1998). Evolution, pair-bonding, and reproductive strategies: A reconceptualization of adult attachment. In J. Simpson & W. Rholes (Eds.), *Attachment theory and close relationships* (pp. 353–393). New York: Guilford.

Kirkpatrick, L., & Davis, K. (1994). Attachment style, gender, and relationship stability: A longitudinal analysis. *Journal of Personality and Social Psychology*, *66*, 502–512.

Kobak, R. (1993). *The Attachment Q-sort*. Unpublished manuscript, University of Delaware.

Kobak, R., & Hazan, C. (1991). Attachment in marriage: Effects of security and accuracy of working models. *Journal of Personality and Social Psychology*, *60*, 861–869.

Kobak, R., & Sceery, A. (1988). Attachment in late adolescence: Working models, affect regulation, and representations of self and others. *Child Development*, *59*, 135–146.

Kobak, R., Cole, H., Ferenz-Gilles, R., Fleming, W., & Gamble, W. (1993). Attachment and emotional regulation during mother-teen problem solving: A control theory analysis. *Child Development*, *64*, 231–245.

Kreider, R. (2001). *Number, Timing, and Duration of Marriages and Divorces: 2001*. Current Population Reports, P70-97. U.S. Census Bureau, Washington, DC.

Kurdek, L. (1993). Predicting marital dissolution: A 5-Year prospective longitudinal study of newlywed couples. *Journal of Personality and Social Psychology*, *64*, 221–242.

Latty-Mann, H., & Davis, K. (1988). Attachment theory and partner choice: Preference and actuality. *Journal of Social and Personal Relationships*, *13*, 5–23.

Levenson, R., Carstensen, L. & Gottman, J. (1993). Long-term marriage: Age, gender, and satisfaction. *Psychology and Aging*, *8*, 301–313.

Levinger, G. (1976). A social psychological perspective on marital dissolution. *Journal of Social Issues*, *32*, 21–47.

Locke, H., & Wallace, K. (1959). Short marital adjustment prediction tests: Their reliability and validity. *Marriage and Family Living*, *21*, 251–255.

Lussier, Y., Sabourin, S., & Chantal, T. (1997). Coping strategies as mediators of the relationship between attachment and marital adjustment. *Journal of Social and Personal Relationships*, *14*, 777–791.

Main, M., Kaplan, N., & Cassidy, J. (1985). Security in infancy, childhood, and adulthood: A move to the level of representation. In I. Bretherton & E. Waters (Eds.), Growing points of attachment theory and research. *Monographs of the Society for Research in Child Development*, *50*, (1-2, Serial No. 209), 66–106.

Markman, H. (1981). Prediction of marital distress: A 5-year follow-up. *Journal of Consulting and Clinical Psychology*, *49*, 760–762.

Martin, T., & Bumpass, L. (1989). Recent trends in marital disruption. *Demography*, *26*, 37–51.

Mayseless, O., Sharabany, R., & Sagi, A. (1997). Attachment concerns of mothers as manifested in parental, spousal, and friendship relationships. *Personal Relationships*, *4*, 255–269.

Mikulincer, M., Florian, V., Cowan, P., & Cowan, C. (2002). Attachment security in couple relationships: A systemic model and its implications in family dynamics. *Family Process*, *41*, 405–434.

Mikulincer, M., Horesh, N., Levy-Shiff, R., Manovich, R., & Shalev, J. (1998). The contribution of adult attachment style to the adjustment to infertility. *British Journal of Medical Psychology*, *71*, 265–280.

Mills, R., Grasmick, H., Morgan, C., & Wend, D. (1992). The effects of gender, family satisfaction, and economic strain on psychological well-being. *Family Relations*, *41*, 440–445.

Morgan, S., & Rindfuss, R. (1985). Marital disruption: Structural and temporal dimensions. *American Journal of Sociology, 90*, 1055–1077.

National Center for Health Statistics. (2003). *Marriage and divorce.* Centers for Disease Control, Atlanta GA.

National Vital Statistics Reports. (2006). *Births, marriages, divorces, and deaths: Provisional data for August, 2005.* U.S. Department of Health and Human Services, Washington, DC.

Oggins, J., Veroff, J., & Leber, D. (1993). Perceptions of marital interaction among black and white newlyweds. *Journal of Personality and Social Psychology, 65*, 494–511.

Orbach, T., House, J., Mero, R., & Webster, P. (1996). Marital quality over the life course. *Social Psychology Quarterly, 59*, 162–171.

Paley, B., Cox, M., Burchinal, M., & Payne, C. (1999). Attachment and marital functioning: Comparison of spouses with continuous secure, earned-secure, dismissing, and preoccupied attachment stance. *Journal of Family Psychology, 13*, 580–597.

Paley, B., Cox, M., Kanoy, K., Harter, K., Burchinal, M., & Margand, N. (2005). Adult attachment and marital interaction as predictors of whole family interactions during the transition to parenthood. *Journal of Family Psychology, 19*, 420–429.

Pasch, L., & Bradbury, T. (1998). Social support, conflict, and the development of marital dysfunction. *Journal of Consulting and Clinical Psychology, 66*, 219–230.

Pasch, L., Bradbury, T., & Davila, J. (1997). Gender, negative affectivity, and observed social support behavior in marital interaction. *Personal Relationships, 4*, 361–378.

Pottharst, K. (1990). *Explorations in adult attachment.* New York: Peter Lang.

Powers, S., Pietromoaco, P., Gunlicks, M., & Sayer, A. (2006). Dating couples' attachment styles and patterns of cortisol reactivity and recovery in response to a relationship conflict. *Journal of Personality and Social Psychology, 90*, 613–628.

Roisman, G., Collins, W., Sroufe, L. A., & Egeland, B. (2005). Predictors of young adults' representations of and behavior in their current romantic relationship: Prospective tests of the prototype hypothesis. *Attachment and Human Development, 7*, 105–121.

Schumm, W., Paff-Bergen, L., Hatch, R., Obiorah, F., Copeland, J., Meens, L., & Bugaighis, M. (1986). Concurrent and discriminate validity of the Kansas Marital Satisfaction Scale. *Journal of Marriage and the Family, 48*, 381–387.

Senchak, M., & Leonard, K. (1992). Attachment styles and marital adjustment among newlywed couples. *Journal of Social and Personal Relationships, 9*, 51–64.

Shaver, P., & Mikulincer, M. (2002). Attachment-related psychodynamics. *Attachment and Human Development, 4*, 133–161.

Sibley, C., Fischer, R., & Liu, J. (2005). Reliability and validity of the Revised Experiences in Close Relationships (ECR-R) self-report measure of adult romantic attachment. *Personality and Social Psychology Bulletin, 31*, 1524–1536.

Simpson, J., Rholes, W. S., Campbell, L., Tran, S., & Wilson, C. (2003). Adult attachment, the transition to parenthood, and depressive symptoms. *Journal of Personality and Social Psychology, 84*, 1172–1187.

Simpson, J., Rholes, W.S., Orina, M., & Grich, J. (2002). Working models of attachment, support giving, and support seeking in a stressful situation. *Personality and Social Psychology Bulletin, 28*, 598–608.

Simpson, J., Rholes, W. S., & Phillips, D. (1996). Conflict in close relationships: An attachment perspective. *Journal of Personality and Social Psychology, 71*, 899–914.

Slade, A. (1999). Attachment theory and research: Implications for the theory and practice of individual psychotherapy with adults. In J. Cassidy & P. Shaver (Eds.), *Handbook of attachment* (pp. 575–594). New York: Guilford.

Smith, D., Vivian, D., & O'Leary, K. (1990). Longitudinal prediction of marital discord from premarital expressions of affect. *Journal of Consulting and Clinical Psychology, 58*, 790–798.

Spanier, G. (1976). Measuring dyadic adjustment: New scales for assessing the quality of marriage and similar dyads. *Journal of Marriage and the Family, 38*, 15–28.

Sroufe, L. A. (2005). Attachment and development: A prospective, longitudinal study from birth to adulthood. *Attachment and Human Development, 7*, 349–367.

Stein, H., Koonz, A., Fonagy, P., Allen, J., Fultz, J., Brethour, J., Allen, D., & Evans, R. (2002). Adult attachment: What are the underlying dimensions? *Psychology and Psychotherapy: Theory, research, and practice, 75*, 77–91.

Thompson, R. (1999). Early attachment and later development. In J. Cassidy & P. Shaver (Eds.), *Handbook of attachment: Theory, research, and clinical applications* (pp. 265–286). New York: Guilford.

Treboux, D., Crowell, J., & Waters, E. (2004). When "New" Meets "Old": Configurations of adult attachment representations and their implications for marital functioning. *Developmental Psychology, 40*, 295–314.

United State Census Bureau. (2004). *2004 American Community Survey.* Washington, DC.

van IJzeendoorn, M., & Sagi, A. (1999). Cross-cultural patterns of attachment: Universal and contextual dimensions. In J. Cassidy & P. Shaver (Eds.), *Handbook of attachment: Theory, research, and clinical applications* (pp. 713–734). New York: Guilford.

Volling, B., Notaro, P., & Larsen, J. (1998). Adult attachment styles: Relations with emotional well-being, marriage, and parenting. *Family Relations, 47*, 355–367.

Wallerstein, J., & Lewis, J. (2004). The unexpected legacy of divorce: Report of a 25-year study. *Psychoanalytic Inquiry, 21*, 353–370.

Waters, E., Corcoran, D., & Anafarta, M. (2005). Attachment, other relationships, and the theory that all good things go together. *Human Development, 48*, 80–84.

Waters, E., Crowell, J., Elliott, M., Corcoran, D., & Treboux, D. (2002). Bowlby's secure base theory and the social/personality psychology of attachment styles: Work(s) in progress. *Attachment and Human Development, 4*, 230–242.

Watson, D., Klohnen, E., Casillas, A., Simms, E., Haig, J., & Berry, D. (2004). Match makers and deal breakers: Analyses of associative mating in newlywed couples. *Journal of Personality, 72*, 1029–1068.

Weiss, R., & Heyman, R. (1990). Observation of marital interaction. In F. Fincham & T. Bradbury (Eds.), *The psychology of marriage: Basic issues and applications* (pp. 87–119). New York: Guilford.

Werner, E., & Smith, R. (2001). *Journeys from childhood to midlife: Risk, resilience, and recovery.* Ithaca, NY: Cornell University Press.

West, M., & Sheldon, A. (1988). The classification of pathological attachment patterns in adults. *Journal of Personality Disorders, 2*, 153–160.

Whisman, M., & Bruce, M. (1999). Marital dissatisfaction and incidence of major depressive episode in a community sample. *Journal of Abnormal Psychology, 108*, 674–678.

Chapter 11

The Influence of Family Relationships on Adult Psychological Well-Being and Generativity

Nadine F. Marks and Emily A. Greenfield

> The happiest moments of my life have been the few which I have passed at home in the bosom of my family.
>
> —Thomas Jefferson

> Family love is messy, clinging, and of an annoying and repetitive pattern, like bad wallpaper.
>
> —Friedrich Nietzsche

> Happiness is having a large, loving, caring, close-knit family—in another city.
>
> —George Burns

Introduction

From statesmen to philosophers to entertainers, the role of families in shaping the quality of adults' lives has been the topic of discussion in many domains, including social scientific research. Contemporary scholarship suggests that one way or another, our relationships (or lack of relationships) with family members importantly shape our development in adulthood as well as childhood. As the above ideas together suggest, however, the ways in which families affect development can be myriad and complex. The purpose of this chapter is to present theories and empirical findings that not only demonstrate that families contribute to adult development, but that also advance understanding of the various and nuanced ways in which families do so. This chapter focuses specifically on how families influence adult development in terms of individuals' experiences of psychological well-being and their development of generativity (i.e., caring for and taking responsibility for others).

This chapter first provides a brief overview of theoretical work—specifically, the life course perspective, bioecological systems theory, and structural symbolic interactionism's role-identity theory—that orients attention to how family relationships influence adult development, particularly their psychological well-being and generativity. This chapter then presents current conceptualizations and measurement of psychological well-being and generativity as important domains of adult development. Next, this chapter selectively reviews research related to how family relationships in adulthood—including intimate partnerships, relationships with children, relationships with older parents, and relationships with other kin—influence adult psychological well-being, as well as attitudinal and clinically-rated generativity. We also review empirical studies regarding the psychological effects of family caregiving as a behavioral indicator of generativity in each of the four family relationship areas. We conclude by considering the limitations of this review, as well as offering suggestions for new directions in future research.

Theoretical and Conceptual Background

There are a number of theoretical perspectives that can guide scholars in considering family relationships as critical factors that help to shape adult developmental outcomes, including psychological well-being and generativity. In particular, we focus here on the life course perspective, bioecological systems theory, and structural symbolic interactionism's role-identity theory.

The Life Course Perspective

The life course perspective is an interdisciplinary perspective drawing insights from across the fields of psychology, sociology, anthropology, history, and biology to help understand human development across the life span (Elder, Johnson, & Crosnoe, 2003; Featherman, 1983; Settersten, 2003). While the life course perspective offers a rich theoretical foundation for considering many factors that can contribute to continuity and discontinuity within and between people's lives, several concepts from the perspective explicitly orient attention to family-related processes. For example, one of the key principles of the life course perspective is the concept of "linked lives" (Elder et al., 2003). Linked lives implies that people in salient relationships with each other, such as family members, occupy mutually influential interlocking developmental trajectories that extend throughout their lives (Elder et al., 2003). Accordingly, important events in the life of one person are posited to have implications for the developmental outcomes of a related person, and vice-versa. For example, adult children who get divorced with young children might have needs that change the developmental trajectories of aging parents who step in to provide support to younger generations. Likewise, when older adult parents become ill, their illness can affect the trajectories of their midlife children, who might need to accommodate their parents' needs for support into their lives.

The life course perspective's attention to linked lives indicates its orientation to processes of reciprocal causality between family relationships and adult development. Reciprocal causality suggests that although family relationships can influence adult developmental outcomes, adult developmental outcomes such as psychological well-being and generativity also can impact family relationships. While we acknowledge this reciprocity of influence, we restrict our focus in this review chapter to the preponderance of studies that emphasize evidence for the influence of family relationships on adult psychological well-being and generativity.

Another concept that has emerged in the literature related to the life course perspective is the idea of life course "convoys" of social support (Kahn & Antonnuci, 1980; see also Moen, Kelly, & Maginnis, chapter 13, this volume). This concept suggests that individuals have social networks that move along the life course with them—sometimes for longer and sometimes for shorter periods of time. Family members tend to be convoy members of some of the longest duration periods. For example, siblings are likely to be the most longstanding members of most adults' convoys of support.

The life course perspective further suggests the dynamic and contextual ways in which family members can affect individuals' development. For example, the life course perspective posits the importance of considering the sociohistorical context in which developmental processes occur (Elder et al., 2003). Sociohistorical influences include period effects—which are large-scale, sociohistorical events that are likely to affect groups of individuals who are at diverse points in their lives—as well as cohort effects—which differentiate groups of people who experience sociohistorical influences at similar points in their lives (Ryder, 1965). Given that family experiences in most contemporary societies are undergoing rapid and significant social change (Bumpass, 1990; Cherlin, 2004; Popenoe, 1993; Stacey, 1990), progressive cohorts of adults are likely to experience family relationships across adulthood in dynamic and often nontraditional ways, such as by remaining single, entering into nonmarital, cohabiting partnerships, being a stepparent, and caregiving for grandchildren. The life course perspective suggests that these changes in family relationships might pattern the ways through which families influence adult development.

In addition to considering large-scale sociohistorical factors as important contextual factors that influence how families affect individuals' development, the life course perspective also directs attention to the effects of time in terms of the micro-histories of specific relationships (Elder et al., 2003). This consideration leads to a recognition that the developmental effects of family relationships are not only a function of the "real time" challenges and rewards of those relationships, but also of the entire history of a given relationship (Wheaton, 1990). For example, the developmental effects of caregiving for a spouse might be contingent on the prior duration and quality of relationship an individual had with that spouse (Kramer, 1993), and likewise, the impact of a divorce might have a different effect on an adult's well-being depending on the prior duration and quality of that marital relationship (Wheaton, 1990).

The life course perspective also has added to theorizing on contexts of development by orienting attention to the potential developmental salience of family members beyond the nuclear group. This focus on the breadth of family relationships marks a noteworthy departure from longstanding developmental theories that largely limited the influence of social relationships to current nuclear family members. Freud (1940/1964), for example, emphasized the family of origin for understanding child development, and family development theory (Duvall, 1962) traditionally discussed adult development as corresponding to stages applying exclusively to one's family of procreation. The life course perspective includes attention to both these family domains, but also adds more attention to intergenerational relationships across multiple generations and horizontal relationships to all kin and at all ages (Bengtson & Allen, 1993; Rossi & Rossi, 1990).

Bioecological Systems Theory

Bronfenbrenner's bioecological systems theory (Bronfenbrenner, 1989; Bronfenbrenner & Morris, 1998) is another open-systems perspective on development, which is very compatible with the life course perspective (Settersten, 2003). Bioecological systems theory emphasizes the importance of person, process, context, and time factors that collectively contribute to lifespan development (Bronfenbrenner & Morris, 1998). Person factors include individual characteristics of the target person—such as their gender, age, genetic inheritance, and relatively enduring personality characteristics—as well as the individual characteristics of the persons that the target person encounters in developmental settings. Process factors draw scholars' attention to actual interaction processes that are expected to influence development, such as attentiveness in interaction and affectual quality in interaction.

Bronfenbrenner's theoretical articulation of the components of context is one of the major contributions of this theory to developmental scholarship. Bronfenbrenner posits a systems model in which developmental processes occurring in proximal settings are shaped by more distal systems of context (and vice versa). The most primary level of context is that of microsystems, which consist of immediate settings where a target individual interacts with others and their physical environment. An adult's microsystems often include one or more family microsystem settings, including his or her family of origin household(s), the adult family or family of procreation household, and/or other family members' households.

The next systems level posited by Bronfenbrenner is the mesosystem, which consists of interactional relationships across microsystems. For example, the interaction between an adult's parent's household and an adult's own family household can be an important level of context in shaping that individual's development.

The third level is the exosystem, which consists of microsystem settings that do not include the target adult, but that indirectly impact him or her, as well as of larger social contexts within which microsystems are embedded. For example, an adult's exosystem might include their partner's workplace, as well as the neighborhood, social services system, and legal system within which they live.

Finally, the macrosystem refers to the ideology and values of the society of which an individual is part (i.e., the "blueprint" for the culture), which helps determine the structure and processes of the embedded exosystems, mesosystems, and microsystems. For example, in the United States, the values of individualism and democracy potentially affect many levels of developmental influence, from the structure of social institutions to patterns of interactions in interpersonal relationships. Bronfenbrenner has also added that the structuring of life course opportunities and hazards, such as socioeconomic stratification systems, are elements of the macrosystem.

In addition to person, process, and context, Bronfenbrenner's model also includes time—the chronosystem—as a factor that shapes individuals' development. Bronfenbrenner posits multiple systems of time—including within episodes of interaction (microtime), across episodes of an interaction (mesotime), and across personal biography and history (macrotime)—as collectively comprising the chronosystem.

Overall, bioecological systems theory suggests that multiple and embedded levels of context, many of which include structural and interpersonal process family factors, are important for adult development. The chronosystem, in particular, indicates that historical time might change the context in which family relationships are embedded and thereby influence how family relationships affect adult development.

Structural Symbolic Interactionism's Role-Identity Theory

Structural symbolic interactionism's role-identity theory (Stryker, 1980, 2001; Stryker & Statham, 1985) is one additional complementary theoretical perspective that can enhance understanding of how family relationships are important for adult development. Similar to the life course perspective and bioecological systems theory, symbolic interactionism is a contextualistic perspective that recognizes a dynamic interplay between structural and societal constraints along with individual agency and initiative (LaRossa & Reitzes, 1993). Symbolic interactionism places particular emphasis on the influence of a person's subjective appraisal of meanings and concept of self for a person's behaviors and experiences of well-being (LaRossa & Reitzes, 1993).

Stryker and colleagues' role-identity theory, which developed from structural symbolic interactionism and blends the strengths of traditional structural-functionalist role theory and symbolic interactionism (Stryker, 1980, 2001; Stryker & Stratham, 1985), is particularly relevant when considering how families might influence individuals' development. Drawing from the concept of role as behavioral expectations for an individual occupying a given social position, Stryker has posited that individuals take on roles that social organizations at any historical time have established. Families typically consist of multiple roles, including marital partner, cohabiting partner, biological parent, stepparent, and adult child. When a person internalizes a role, a role-identity is formed, and the accumulation of role-identities combine to form the person's self.

The relation between role-identities and individuals' well-being constitutes a classic theme of social philosophy (Thomas & Biddle, 1966). Emile Durkheim, one of the principal founders of modern sociology and anthropology, wrote extensively in the 19th century on roles as a mechanism through which society and social groups promote individuals' mental and physical health (Durkheim, 1897/1951). Likewise, Turner (1978) considered competently performing within roles to be a germinal process through which people validate their self and gain esteem. Thoits (1983) and Burton (1998) further postulated that role-identities from social roles give structure and meaning to life, thereby helping persons to avoid negative mental health and disorganized behavior. Other theoretical work has suggested how negative experiences in social roles—such as through role overload and conflict—can jeopardize individuals' optimal well-being (e.g., Goode, 1960).

In sum, when considering that families are a primary social institution through which adults can derive salient role-identities, structural symbolic interactionism's role-identity theory suggests how family relationships importantly contribute to adult development, particularly in terms of their psychological well-being.

Psychological Well-Being: A Multidimensional Construct

Psychological well-being is an important component of adult development. Research on linkages between family relations and psychological well-being have focused most consistently on psychological well-being in terms of negative affect, which is often operationalized as depressive symptoms (e.g., Radloff, 1977). However, dating back to Bradburn (1969), scholars have increasingly recognized that positive and negative moods and emotions are not two ends of a linear, bipolar continuum; rather, they can be activated simultaneously or independently by a single stimulus. Drawing on this idea of the multidimensionality of affect, Diener, Suh, Lucas, and Smith (1999) have posited the concept of subjective well-being, which includes the dimensions of negative affect, positive affect (often measured as global happiness), and life satisfaction. In addition, scholars have sometimes considered constructs like self-esteem and self-efficacy as aspects of psychological well being that address how an individual evaluates his or her self (Bryant & Veroff, 1982).

Further developing the idea that psychological well-being is a multidimensional construct, Ryff drew from theoretical insights of Maslow (1968), Rogers (1961), Jung (1933), Allport (1961), Buhler (1935), Neugarten (1968), Jahoda (1958), and Erikson (1950) regarding positive psychological functioning and adults' highest potential to develop and validate six new constructs and scales of psychological well-being (Ryff, 1989; Ryff & Keyes, 1995). Specifically, the Ryff Psychological Well-Being Scales assess autonomy (sense of self-determination), environmental mastery (the capacity to manage effectively one's life and surrounding world), purpose in life (the belief that one's life is purposeful and meaningful), positive relations with others (having quality relations with others), personal growth (feelings of continued growth and development as a person), and self-acceptance (positive evaluations of oneself and one's past life). Keyes, Shmotkin, and Ryff (2002) more recently synthesized theoretical and measurement work in this area and provided additional empirical evidence lending support for distinguishing between evaluations of subjective well-being, self-esteem, and self-efficacy from assessments of Ryff's six well-being scales.

The concept of subjective well-being, in conjunction with Ryff's psychological well-being constructs, has formed the basis for making an empirically validated distinction between hedonic and eudaimonic approaches to conceptualizing psychological well-being (Ryan & Deci, 2001). Hedonic approaches consider well-being to be a state in which individuals experience maximum amounts of pleasure and minimal levels of pain (Kahneman, Diener, & Schwartz, 1999), whereas eudaimonic approaches conceptualize well-being as the actualization of human potentials and optimal psychosocial functioning and engagement with life (Waterman, 1993).

In this review, we focus on dimensions of hedonic-based subjective psychological well-being (positive affect, negative affect, and life satisfaction), as well as eudaimonic-based psychological well-being (personal growth, self-acceptance, environmental mastery, positive relations with others, purpose in life, autonomy, self-esteem, and self-efficacy). Because of space constraints, we do not review work focusing on severe mental illnesses and pathology.

Generativity

The concept of "generativity" was first introduced in Erikson's (1950) psychosocial theory of development. Erikson posited an eight-stage lifespan theory in which an individual's healthy development resulted from overcoming a series of psychosocial challenges (i.e., trust versus mistrust, autonomy versus shame and doubt, initiative versus guilt, industry versus inferiority, identity versus role confusion, intimacy versus isolation, generativity versus stagnation, ego-integrity versus despair). Erikson posited "generativity versus stagnation" as the seventh critical period for human development. This seventh critical period was posited to occur during middle adulthood—an unclearly defined age period of the life course, but roughly occurring between the ages of 40 to 60 (Brim, Ryff, & Kessler, 2004).

In Erikson's (1950) initial exposition regarding generativity, the focal aspect was the development of care, concern, and commitment to the next generation. This developmental "task" could, and often does, include the bearing and care for one's own children, but Erikson also suggested that generativity could include care of many types, including care in a broader societal sense. In fact, in his book on Gandhi, Erikson (1969) articulated a generative story about a broader, more inclusive type of care for others and the generations to come that went greatly beyond taking care of one's own children. Erikson characterized stagnation, by contrast, as a focus solely on self and self-indulgence. Stagnation was posited to sometimes include pseudo-intimacy or mutual self-indulgence with a partner, but nonetheless without an expansion of personhood to authentic caring and taking responsibility for others, particularly the next generation (Erikson, 1950).

Erikson's concept of generativity remained relatively unexplored empirically until a new generation of scholars studying adult development brought new interest to it (e.g., Browning, 1975; Kotre, 1984; McAdams, 1985; Peterson and Stewart, 1990). The most major resurgence of interest in generativity has come with the work of McAdams and his colleagues (de St. Aubin, McAdams, & Kim, 2004; McAdams 2001, 2006; McAdams & de St. Aubin, 1992; McAdams, Hart, & Maruna, 1998). McAdams has contributed to the field by developing a more expansive conceptual model for generativity and by developing a scale measure of generative concern, the Loyola Generativity Scale (LGS).

McAdams' theoretical formulation (McAdams & de St. Aubin, 1992; McAdams et al.,

1998; McAdams, 2001) draws from Erikson's writings as well as that of Becker (1973), Browning (1975), Kotre (1984), McAdams (1985), and Peterson and Stewart (1990). McAdams and de St. Aubin (1992) conceptualize generativity as a "configuration of seven psychosocial features constellated around the personal (individual) and cultural (societal) goal of providing for the next generation" (p. 1004). *Cultural demand* and *inner desire* are posited as motivational sources for generativity. These two factors then combine to promote a conscious *concern* for the next generation. If grounded in a supportive *belief* in the goodness of the human species, concern might stimulate generative *commitment*, or an internal striving toward generativity. Generative *action* might be motivated directly by cultural demand or inner desire, but also can be derived from the adult's commitments to generative activities and goals. Generative action—which includes the behaviors of creating, maintaining, and offering to others—might reciprocally influence later generative commitments. Finally, the meaning of the complex relations among all these features is determined by the person's *narration* of generativity.

Contemporary scholars have differed as to whether the development of generativity is particularly important for adults in midlife (versus other periods of the life course). McAdams and de St. Aubin explicitly reject a stage model of development (and generativity), such as that proposed by Erikson (1950). They posit that although generativity is typically more expected in adulthood than childhood, in part due to certain cultural demands associated with adulthood, it is not expected to be exclusively a feature of any particular age period. Stewart and Vandewater (1998), on the other hand, have suggested a model for how different forms of generativity might become more or less salient across adulthood based on their developmental studies. They posit that: (a) generative desires peak in early adulthood and decline in middle and later age, (b) felt capacity for generativity rises from early to middle adulthood and then shows some bit of decline, and (c) a sense of generative accomplishment might rise across adulthood and peak in old age. Middle age might then include relatively high levels of all three forms, but capacity for generativity is likely to be greater during this period than during earlier and later periods of the life course.

In addition to developing a conceptual model of generativity, McAdams and de St. Aubin (1992) also have advanced studies on generativity by developing the LGS. This scale primarily assesses individual differences in generative concern, with items about passing on knowledge and skills, especially to the next generation; concern with making significant contributions to improving one's community; doing things that will be remembered for a long time and have lasting impact; being creative; and caring for and taking responsibility for other people. To avoid bias for persons without children, the scale does not include items about caring for children, except for one item about adopting children.

In many cases, families serve as a primary context in which generativity as "caring for and taking responsibility for others" occurs. Accordingly, this chapter examines how family relationships are associated with clinical ratings of generativity and attitudinal generativity, assessed most typically by the McAdams and de St. Aubin (1992) Loyola Generativity Scale of generative concern. Additionally, we describe how family caregiving as one specific type of family-related behavioral generativity is associated with adult psychological well-being. In considering caregiving across multiple family relationships, we are explicitly expanding the conceptualization of generativity to include caring for others regardless of their age or generational standing relative to the focal individual.

Scholars have not yet often explored family caregiving as a manifestation of generativity (Keyes & Ryff, 1998, McAdams, 2001). Clearly, however, caring for a person who is unable to take total care of themselves due to a mental or physical condition or disability is a form of taking care and responsibility for others. Because of several recent changes in individual and family life, such as increasing longevity and smaller family size (Biegel, Sales, & Schulz, 1991), the prevalence and salience of family caregiving beyond the routine care for children has mushroomed in the years since Erikson developed his theory. A U.S. national sample study in 2003 estimated there were 44.4 million U.S. caregivers aged 18 and older, or 21% of the population at these ages, providing unpaid care to one or more adults who needed help due to some level of functional limitation (Caregiving in the U.S., 2004). The vast majority of caregivers (83%) indicated their primary caregiving was done in the context of a family relationship, and 4 out of 10 caregivers were men. These prevalence rates suggest the importance of family caregiving as an increasingly important manifestation of behavioral generativity to take into account in adult development.

In addition to the increasing prevalence of the caregiving role, another reason for the importance of considering caregiving within discussions on family relations and generativity is the relatively large body of research on how family caregiving influences individual well-being. This literature adds understanding to the complex ways in which generativity—as one dimension of adult development—is associated with individuals' psychological well-being—as another dimension of adult development. While levels of attitudinal and clinically-rated generativity have been generally linked to better psychological well-being (McAdams, de St. Aubin, & Logan, 1993; McAdams, 2001), considerable research indicates that family caregiving is associated with increased psychological distress, lower positive affect, and a decreased sense of self-adequacy (Biegel et al., 1991; Chappell, 1990; Gallagher-Thompson et al., 1998; Horowitz, 1985; Pinquart & Sorensen, 2003; ; Schulz, O'Brien, Bookwala, & Fleissner, 1995; Schulz, Visitainer, & Williamson, 1990), particularly if it includes care for a family member with cognitive impairment (Ory, Hoffman, Yee, Tennstedt, & Schulz, 1999; Schulz et al., 1995). Yet there are also indications that when studies include measures that capture more eudaimonic dimensions of psychological well-being, such as feelings of purpose in life and experiences of positive relations with others, findings suggest that caregiving also can be associated with psychological and developmental gains (Kramer, 1997; Lawton, Rajagopal, Brody, & Kleban, 1992; Marks, 1998; Marks, Lambert, & Choi, 2002). In this chapter, we review studies on the implications of family caregiving across multiple relationships for caregivers' well-being to illustrate how behavioral generativity can intersect with other dimensions of adult development, such as psychological well-being.

Partner Relationships, Psychological Well-Being, and Generativity

Partnership and Psychological Well-Being

The consequences of intimate partnerships for mental health has been the most frequently studied topic related to the effects of family relationships on adults' psychological well-being. Given major transformations in the social institution of marriage during the last 50 years—such as individuals marrying at later ages, increasing rates of marital dissolution, ideological changes regarding the purpose of marriage, changes in gendered partner/marriage role expectations, and a greater number of individuals living in open same-gender partnerships (Bumpass, 1990; Cherlin, 2004; Kurdek, 2004; Seltzer, 2004)—scholars have been particularly active in tracking how the association between marriage and psychological well-being might be staying the same or changing for both women and men. In this section, we first consider the literature on linkages between marital status (i.e., being married versus being never married or previously married) and psychological well-being, and we then review studies that draw attention to subgroup differences among single and partnered adults and studies that have examined the psychological well-being of adults in nonmarital cohabiting relationships (versus being married). We then note suggestions for future research to advance this relatively large and longstanding literature on intimate partnerships and adult psychological well-being.

Married versus Single.   Jessie Bernard fired up scholarly debate in 1972 with the publication of *The Future of Marriage*, in which she proposed that there were actually two marriages taking place within every union—"his" and "hers." "His" marriage included the traditional narrative about how marriage was a sacrifice of much-prized male freedom, but a long-desired arrangement among women. "Her" marriage included the traditional narrative that all women wanted to marry and become mothers, making marriage their most natural and desired adult status. Yet empirical evidence from that era cited by Bernard suggested that when compared with single men, married men benefited greatly from marriage physically, socially, and psychologically, whereas married women were more likely to exhibit higher rates of mental distress and illness than single women. Bernard hypothesized that the traditional housewife role, with its frustrations and devaluation, was part of what was making women psychologically suffer.

Gove and Tudor (Gove, 1972; Gove & Tudor, 1973), as well as Radloff (1975), brought forward additional evidence that marriage provided greater mental health benefits for men than women in terms of rates of psychological dysfunction. Yet work from the later 1970s through the present has been relatively consistent in providing evidence of less psychological distress for both married men and women in contrast to their unmarried peers (Booth & Amato, 1991; Gore & Mangione, 1983; Gove, Hughes, & Style, 1983; Horwitz, White, & Howell-White, 1996; Marks, 1996a; Marks & Lambert, 1998; Menaghan & Lieberman, 1986; Mirowsky & Ross, 1989; Pearlin & Johnson, 1977; Simon 2002; Williams, 2003).

Overall, the debate about the relative benefits of marriage for women in contrast to men is inconclusive. There has been evidence in both directions, as well as for similarity, across studies depending on the sample, age group, design comparison, and measures used. For example, there has been some evidence that partnership dissolutions (versus remaining married) are associated with more depression for women than men (Aseltine & Kessler, 1993; Marks & Lambert, 1998; Simon, 2002; Willitts, Benzevel, & Stansfeld, 2004). On the other hand, considering marital status differences at middle age and older ages (Earle, Smith, Harris, & Longino, 1998; Gove & Shin, 1989; Peters & Liefbroer, 1997; Willitts et al., 2004), there is also evidence that unmarried men have poorer psychological well-being than unmarried women. A number of recent studies and reviews have concluded that, overall, there are more gender similarities than differences in marital status and marital transition effects (Bierman, Fazio, & Milkie, 2006; Mastekaasa, 1994; Simon, 2002; Strohschein, McDonough, Monette, & Shao, 2005; Waite, 1995, 2000; Waite & Gallagher, 2000; Williams, 2003). This conclusion suggests that marital status today, if not in 1972, has relatively equal importance for the well-being of men and women, although scholars have noted that the effects might work through different mechanisms for men and women. For example, Waite (2000) has suggested that marriage might promote women's psychological well-being by providing them better economic security, whereas for men, marriage might promote psychological well-being through the provision of social support and regulation of health behaviors.

In addition to these studies' focus on associations between marital status and psychological distress among men and women, other studies have considered linkages between marital status and global happiness, particularly over historical time. Earlier studies in this area found that married men and women indicated a happiness advantage in comparison to their nonmarried peers (Glenn, 1975; Glenn & Weaver, 1979, 1988; Lee, Seccombe, & Shehan, 1991). U.S. national trend data from the General Social Survey spanning the 1970s and the 1980s, however, revealed a narrowing of the happiness gap between married and never married adults. This trend was noted particularly for men and for younger adults (ages 25–39). There was a significant increase in the proportion of never married men who indicated that they were "very happy" between 1972 and 1982, as well as a significant decrease in the proportion of younger married women during this period who indicated high levels of positive well-being (Glenn & Weaver, 1988). Waite (2000) did additional analyses of marital status over historical time using national General Social Survey data by examining trends in reported happiness (on a 3-point scale) from 1972 to 1996. She found that adjusting for age, education, race, health, and income, never married and previously married men and women all reported somewhat less happiness than their married peers. She found no evidence for a marital status by year of study interaction, and she concluded that, overall, the association between marital status and happiness had not significantly changed over these years.

In addition to these studies that draw on U.S. national data, evidence for the psychological advantages of being married in contrast to being single has been found in studies drawing on data from numerous countries. For example, Stack and Eshleman (1998) found evidence that being married (versus single) was associated with happiness across 17 industrialized nations. The strength of association did not vary from the United States in 14 of the 17 nations studied. Mastekaasa (1994) also examined marital status and various indicators of well-being across 19 countries, including several non-Western ones. He found evidence of differences in psychological well-being favoring the currently married in contrast to the previously married and never married in nearly all countries.

Differences across Singles.   Increasingly, research on marriage and well-being has moved from examining a simple unmarried versus married dichotomy to examining more subgroup differences. One important subgroup difference is with respect to individuals' specific type of single status. Dating back to the 1970s, scholars who evaluated outcomes across marital status groups found that the unmarried were not all equally distressed; formerly married persons were found to report more distress than never married persons (Pearlin & Johnson, 1977).

Additionally, studies have found that among the formerly married, divorced and widowed individuals sometimes differ. For example, using data from a U.S. national sample interviewed in the mid-1970s, Gove and Shin (1989) found that the psychological well-being of divorced males, divorced females, and widowed females was roughly comparable and better than the psychological well-being of widowed men. Each group was considerably lower than respective married peers on all but self-esteem; the widowed and divorced were also more disadvantaged than never married persons on happiness, life satisfaction, psychological distress, feeling trapped, meaninglessness, and home life satisfaction. No major gender differences were found among divorced individuals, but gender differences were found among the widowed, with men doing poorer than women.

Numerous studies from the 1980s through the present have continued to confirm that divorced persons, compared with married individuals, report lower levels of psychological well-being, including lower happiness, more symptoms of psychological distress, and poorer self evaluations (Davies, Avison, & McAlpine, 1997; Demo & Acock, 1996;

Doherty, Su, & Needle, 1989; Kitson, 1992; Lorenz et al., 1997; Marks, 1996a; Mastekaasa, 1994, 1995; Menaghan & Lieberman, 1986; Robins & Regier, 1991; Ross, 1995; Shapiro, 1996; Simon, 1998, 2002; Simon & Marcussen, 1999; Umberson & Williams, 1993; White, 1992). Longitudinal studies have also provided evidence that the transition to divorce (in contrast to remaining married) is associated with greater psychological distress and less happiness, mastery, and self-confidence (Aseltine & Kessler, 1993; Booth & Amato, 1991; Hope, Power, & Rodgers, 1999; Johnson & Wu, 2002; Marks & Lambert, 1998; Simon, 2002; Wade & Pevalin, 2004). The transition to widowhood (in contrast to remaining married) has been similarly linked to increased psychological distress (Carnelley, Wortman, & Kessler, 1999; Simon, 2002; Stroebe & Stroebe, 1987; Turner, Killian, & Cain, 2004; Turvey, Carney, Arndt, Wallace, & Herzog, 1999; Wade & Pevalin, 2004; Wilcox et al., 2003; Wortman, Silver, & Kessler, 1993).

In addition to examining subgroup differences among single adults in terms of their specific type of single status, researchers also have examined subgroup differences among adults occupying the same type of single status. For example, recent research suggests that the psychological disadvantage of being previously married is lessened if the marriage that terminated was conflictual or problematic (Aseltine & Kessler, 1993; Carr et al., 2000; Futterman, Gallagher, Thompson, Lovett, & Gilewski, 1990; O'Connor, Cheng, Dunn, & Golding, 2005; Wheaton, 1990; Williams, 2003). For example, Williams (2003) used three waves of national data from 1986 to 1994 and found that as pre-loss marital quality declined, increases in depression and decreases in life satisfaction diminished for people transitioning to divorce, separation, or widowhood (versus remaining married). She found no evidence of gender differences in these associations.

Differences across the Married.   Even the married are not a homogeneous group—some individuals are first married and some are remarried, and some individuals perceive being in high quality partnerships, whereas others do not. Regarding subgroup differences among partnered adults in terms of diverse marital histories, Weingarten (1985) was one of the first to evaluate differences between first-married, currently divorced, and remarried adults using national survey data from 1976. She found that remarried adults were similar to first married adults on happiness, self-acceptance, self-esteem, personal control, zest, worry, and anxiety. However, other studies since have found that persons continuing in first marriages have better psychological well-being than the remarried (Bierman et al., 2006; Demo & Acock, 1996; Marks, 1995; Shapiro, 1996).

Adopting a life course approach, Barrett (2000) and Peters and Liefbroer (1997) provide further evidence indicating that higher order marriages might be associated with fewer benefits for mental health than first marriages. Barrett's study did not find major differences across currently remarried adults' psychological well-being by the previous type of marital loss (i.e., divorce or widowhood). However, among single adults who were formerly married, multiple divorces (two losses versus one loss) were associated with more depression, and multiple transitions to widowhood (two losses versus one loss) were associated with more anxiety and substance use. Additionally, Peters and Liefbroer (1997), using life history data from older adults in the Netherlands, found that more lifetime dissolutions predicted more loneliness among singles.

There is some evidence to suggest that a history of divorce and separation can have longstanding influences on well-being. Using data from 2,085 participants in the British National Survey of Health and Development (who were born in 1946 and were 43 years old at the time of the study), Richards, Hardy, and Wadsworth (1997) reported that a history of divorce and separation (versus remaining in one's first marriage) was associated with greater anxiety, depression, and risk of alcohol abuse. Adjusting for many childhood and demographic factors, including early vulnerability and current stressors, time since first separation or divorce did not moderate associations between having ever divorced or separated (versus remaining in a first marriage) and mental health outcomes, even though half of the divorced or separated were remarried or reunited with spouses at the time of analysis. These results suggest the possible significant long-term impact of divorce and separation on psychological well-being.

In addition to examining subgroup differences among married adults in terms of variations in their marital histories, scholars also have examined differences in individuals' reports of the quality of their partnerships. Marital quality has been found to be among the strongest correlates of psychological well-being. In a study by Gove and colleagues (1983), marital happiness explained more of the variation in well-being among married persons than income, education, race, age, or family background. When studies have taken marital quality into account, findings suggest that married persons in low quality marriages report lower levels of psychological well-being in comparison to single persons (Gove et al., 1983; Williams, 2003). There is consistent evidence that marital dissatisfaction is associated with higher levels of depressive symptoms (Whisman, 2001). The evidence from longitudinal studies is generally congruent with findings from cross-sectional studies (e.g., Beach, Katz, Kim, & Brody, 2003; Fincham, Beach, Harold, & Osborne, 1997; Kurdek, 1998; Whisman & Bruce, 1999). For example, Beach and colleagues (2003) found that higher levels of marital discord reported by either spouse predicted more depressive symptoms among married couples. Vega, Kolody, and Valle (1988) likewise found that more marital strains were associated with more depressive symptoms among a sample of non-Hispanics from Chicago, as well as among a sample of Mexican-American women in San Diego.

Regarding gender differences in the influence of marital quality on well-being, the results are inconsistent. For example, Acitelli and Antonucci (1994) found that in a sample of older married couples, more social support in marriage was associated with better general well-being and greater marital satisfaction; these associations were stronger among wives than husbands. This evidence is also congruent with an early finding by Gove and colleagues (1983) that suggested that marital quality matters more for women's than men's well-being. Yet Williams (2003) used three waves of U.S. national data from 1986 to 1994 to provide evidence that lower marital harmony and greater marital stress were associated to a similar extent with greater depression and less life satisfaction over time for both men and women.

Given these findings regarding marital quality, the continuing evidence of a well-being advantage among the married in contrast to the single (when marital quality is not taken into account) may be a reflection of the fact that most married people today report high marital quality. This trend has remained relatively stable over recent decades (Waite, 2000), during which time flexible divorce laws have allowed a significant proportion of unhappy marriages to terminate.

Cohabitation.   Research on cohabitation as an alternative partnership status has boomed during the last decade. Although there is some limited evidence that cohabitors might experience somewhat better well-being than noncohabiting singles (Kurdek, 1991), overall, research suggests that cohabitors do not experience the psychological gains that married persons do (Brown, 2000; Kim & McKenry, 2002; Marcussen, 2005; Stack & Eshleman, 1998; Waite, 2000). For example, Brown (2000) reported that cohabiting men and women reported higher levels of depression and lower levels of life satisfaction than married men and women, mainly because they viewed their relationships as less stable. Cohabitors reported rates of relationship instability about 25% higher than marrieds, and higher levels of relationship instability were found to be especially detrimental for cohabitors who had been in long-standing unions. Longitudinal analyses correcting for selection bias also confirmed that lower levels of well-being of cohabitors were not due to selection of types of people who choose to cohabit.

Dush and Amato (2005) used longitudinal U.S. national data and found that married individuals reported higher levels of subjective well-being than cohabitors, even when statistically controlling for relationship happiness. Their longitudinal analysis suggested that shifting into more committed relationships led to improvements in subjective well-being, and they, too, found little support for the idea that people with high well-being select into more committed relationships.

Willitts, Benzevel, and Stansfeld (2004) reported a somewhat more mixed pattern of findings. They used nine waves of British Household Panel Survey data and found that among women, being in a first marriage (though not in a first cohabiting partnership) led to a significantly better age-standardized mental health score (as measured by the General Health Questionnaire) than the mean mental health score for all women. However, among men, being in a first cohabiting partnership (though not in a first marriage) led to a better age-standardized mental health score than the mean mental health score for all men.

Suggestions for Future Research.   Contemporary research on linkages between partner relationships and psychological well-being has largely addressed several major methodological and conceptual limitations of previous studies. For example, historically, many of the empirical findings noting differences in levels of psychological well-being between married versus single adults have been based on studies with cross-sectional designs. Cross-sectional studies do not allow scholars to disentangle processes of causation (i.e., partnership status leading to well-being) from selection (i.e., well-being leading to partnership status).

As might be expected from a systems perspective positing processes of reciprocal causality, whereby individuals' psychological well-being and likelihood to marry and remain married are mutually reinforcing, more recent studies employing longitudinal designs have generated evidence for both directions of causation (see Booth & Amato, 1991; Mastekaasa, 1992; Simon, 2002, for some evidence for selection effects). However, there is considerable evidence now for social causation, particularly in the instance of gaining a marital partner as opposed to remaining single (Simon, 2002; Waite, 2000; Waite & Gallagher, 2000). Longitudinal data analyses that include assessments of individuals' partnership status, partnership quality, and psychological well-being across multiple times points are necessary to further decouple processes of causation from selection and to better understand the dynamic nature of linkages between partnership processes and individuals' psychological well-being over time.

Furthermore, although research studies on associations between partnerships and psychological well-being have increasingly recognized important subgroup differences among both single and married adults, there are likely many other dimensions of subgroup differences that can pattern how the marital domain influences adults' psychological well-being. First, although there is a sizeable and growing number of same-gender partnerships (Kurdek, 2004), there is not much evidence yet about same-gender partnerships and psychological well-being. One exception is Grossman, D'Augelli, and Hershberger (2000) who studied the social support networks of 416 lesbian, gay, and bisexual adults aged 60–91. Those living with domestic partners were less lonely and rated their physical and mental health more positively than those who lived alone.

Second, given that individuals with lower incomes are less likely to be married, more research is needed to evaluate if marriage is as beneficial for the well-being of poorer persons. Evidence suggests that individuals with low income still aspire to marriage, but only if it includes economic security and maturity, which might be challenging to attain in disadvantaged environments (Edin, Kefalas, & Reed, 2004). The decoupling of marriage and parenthood (Ventura & Bachrach, 2000), particularly among the socioeconomically disadvantaged, might be changing its meaning and influence on psychological well-being and development. Nevertheless, an empirical basis for evaluating whether such is the case is currently not available.

Third, understanding of linkages between marriage and well-being in different racial-ethnic and cultural contexts is also necessary. Individuals within particular ethnic groups, such as Latinos, have been found to be more committed to marriage than other racial-ethnic groups in the United States, but this greater commitment might differ depending on the acculturation status of a Latino individual and their family (Oropesa & Landale, 2004).

Fourth, it would be valuable for more research on partnership and well-being to explore potential age differences in the effects of partner relationships and psychological well-being and connect them to adult developmental theory in a more explicit way. For example, the idea that being never married is associated with fewer disadvantages in psychological well-being among younger men (as opposed to younger women) received some additional support by more recent evidence from a U.S. national 1995 study (Marks, Bumpass, & Jun, 2004). Analyses revealed that never married younger men (ages 25–39) reported less dysphoria than never married middle-aged men (ages 40–59). By contrast, middle-aged never married women reported no more dysphoria than their first married counterparts, yet younger never married women reported significantly more dysphoria than middle-aged never married women. These results suggest an interesting gender difference where never married status might be more problematic for younger women than younger men—possibly due to "biological clock" issues (i.e., the desire to have children with a partner at younger ages).

Additionally, some research has suggested that marital transitions to divorce or widowhood are less detrimental for the psychological well-being of midlife men and women than younger men and women (Marks & Lambert, 1998), and that remarriage, cohabitation, and divorced/widowed statuses are less problematic for psychological wellness (as measured by a composite measure of Ryff's psychological well-being scales) among midlife women than younger women (Marks, Bumpass, & Jun, 2004). Greater developmental gains in self-management, resilience, and capacity to deal with nontraditional role-identities acquired by midlife (cf. Brim, 1992) might help to explain these differences.

Finally, results from a limited number of studies suggest that different patterns of associations between partnership status and psychological well-being can emerge when considering diverse dimensions of psychological well-being. For example, despite findings that single adults often report higher levels of distress than their married peers, separated or divorced adults also have been found to report higher levels of autonomy and personal growth (Kitson, 1992; Marks, 1996a), and divorced women interviewed in depth have reported gains in their sense of control and personal confidence (Riessmann, 1990). Future studies including diverse and multiple measures of psychological well-being would contribute to a more complete understanding of the linkages between partnerships and adults' total experiences of psychological well-being.

Partnership and Generativity

Scholarship on the linkage between marriage or partnership and generativity is limited. In an early study of the correlates of generativity, Vaillant and Milofsky (1980) found that among college-educated men at age 47, as well as among same-aged men from working-class inner city backgrounds, enjoyment of first marriage was a correlate of achieving higher levels of clinically-assessed generativity.

Building on Vaillant and Milofsky's (1980) study, Snarey, Son, Kuchne, Hauser, and Vaillant (1987) reexamined longitudinal data from ever-married men in the same working-class sample of men to further examine differences in generativity by subgroups who had also experienced challenges with infertility (or not) in their first marriage. They found that for the group of men who experienced infertility challenges and subsequently divorced, none had achieved clinically-rated generativity by age 47. For men who experienced infertility challenges and remained married "without enjoyment," 18% were rated as having achieved generativity, whereas among men who experienced fertility challenges and enjoyed their marriage, 52% had achieved generativity. Among the men who had not had challenges with infertility, only 14% of divorced men and 18% of the unhappily married, yet 53% of the happily married were rated as having achieved generativity.

Furthermore, Westermeyer (2004) investigated longitudinal data from 96 college graduate men first studied at age 21 and found that having a successful long-term marriage helped predict clinical ratings of generativity by age 53. Additionally, using data from a U.S. national sample in 1995 and controlling for parental status, Marks, Bumpass, and Jun (2004) found evidence that midlife remarried women reported even more generativity (assessed by an adapted version of the LGS) than first married women. This study also revealed trend-level evidence that never married midlife men reported less generativity than first married men.

Overall, the existing literature suggests that marriage, particularly a high quality marriage, is associated with greater generativity in adulthood. This association might be due to the fact that the role-identity expectations for marriage and partnership include expectations of caring for and taking responsibility for one's partner, and that opportunities to enact this role-identity can lead to more evidence of behavioral care and perception of self as a caring person. Yet the empirical base is limited in this area, and more research is needed to establish linkages, consider issues of causal direction, rule out the potential confounding association with the parenting role (which is not adjusted for in most of the studies reviewed), and develop understanding of the possible mechanisms underlying associations.

Spouse/Partner Caregiving and Psychological Well-Being

Cantor (1979) suggested that there is a normative "hierarchy of succession" in the United States for who should provide caregiving for a person with functional limitations; according to this hierarchy an individual's spouse (if available) is "first in line" to assume that role. In the national Caregiving in the U.S. survey conducted in 2003 (Caregiving in the U.S., 2004), 6% of caregivers responded they were currently providing care to a spouse.

The literature on spousal caregivers is relatively consistent in suggesting that spousal caregiving is associated with increased psychological distress (Biegel et al., 1991; George & Gwyther, 1986; Harper & Lund, 1990; Hoyert & Seltzer, 1992; Marks et al., 2002; Seltzer & Li, 1996; 2000; Young & Kahana, 1989). Caregiving for a spouse, when compared with filial caregiving, usually has been found to be more problematic for psychological well-being (Biegel et al., 1991). This is likely due to the high salience of the spousal role and relationship (making negative health-related changes in this role-relationship particularly distressing), the greater likelihood for spousal caregiving to occur in-household and be very time-intensive, and the greater likelihood that spousal caregiving might include even more demanding personal care tasks.

A life course approach to caregiving is now becoming more typical in the literature, with scholars studying different transitions in the caregiving career and recognizing that different periods of caregiving might have different effects on well-being (Pearlin & Aneshensel, 1994). For example, Seltzer and Li (2000) longitudinally studied the transition to spousal caregiving and found that wives experienced increased psychological distress and a trend toward lower mastery, but bereavement after caregiving was accompanied by an increase in personal growth.

Although the majority of family caregivers are women, a sizeable proportion of spousal caregivers are men (Marks, 1996b; Stone et al., 1987). Men who are spousal caregivers might face unique challenges from assuming this role, given that husbands are the oldest subgroup of caregivers, report spending the greatest number of extra hours in providing caregiving, and are more likely to provide care for partners diagnosed with dementia (Fitting, Rabins, Lucas, & Eastham, 1986; Stone et al., 1987). Early studies of spousal caregiving often failed to include men, but contemporary research is increasingly filling this gap (Kramer & Lambert, 1999; Kramer & Thompson, 2002). For example, examining U.S. national data, Kramer and Lambert (1999) found that husbands 60 years and older who transitioned to caregiving for their spouse reported a greater increase in depression and a greater decrease in happiness than their noncaregiving men peers.

Links between Empirical Findings and Theory.   The multiple literatures on linkages between partner relations and adult psychological well-being and generativity reflect principles from the three major theoretical perspectives reviewed in this chapter. For example, the research linking partnership status to adults' psychological well-being and generativity provides support for structural symbolic interaction's role-identity theory, which directs attention to the psychological benefits of occupying social positions and enacting well-defined role-identities. Furthermore, studies that have focused on individuals' marital histories—as opposed to single marital statuses—are congruent with the life course perspective's attention to how cumulative experiences in a role can influence the psychological impact of that role. Additionally, the literature on spousal caregiving suggests support for the "linked lives" tenet of the life course perspective; the health-related needs of a partner and the demand characteristics set up by these needs have an important influence on an individual's well-being. Finally, research on how day-to-day quality of interactions in partnerships (as reflected in partnership quality assessments) are associated with well-being is congruent with bioecological systems theory's attention to marital partners as potentially important process components of the family microsystem, which can influence adult development.

Parenthood, Psychological Well-Being, and Generativity

Parenthood Status and Psychological Well-Being

Although one might anticipate declining rates of parenthood among U.S. adults given recent social changes—e.g., advances in birth control, women's greater participation in the labor force, and a growing number of adults who remain single throughout the childbearing years—parenthood still remains a normative role during the adult life course.

About 90% of midlife and older adults report having biological, adopted, or stepchildren (Marks, Bumpass, & Jun, 2004). What has changed, however, is that with greater fluidity in marital-partnership status in recent decades, more adults are experiencing the developmental challenges and rewards of parenting in new role-relationships, such as by serving as stepparents and parents of children in cohabiting and same-gender unions (Marks, 1996c; Seltzer, 2004).

Results from studies comparing all adults who are not parents to adults who have ever had children have been inconsistent, suggesting either no difference across these groups (Aneshensel, Frerichs, & Clark, 1981) or suggesting that parents overall report greater psychological distress than nonparents (Evenson & Simon, 2005). In exploring the associations between parenthood and psychological well-being, scholarship has evolved to recognize that exploring this linkage is most helpfully undertaken by taking into account subgroup differences among parents and nonparents. These next subsections focus on studies examining how parenthood is associated with adult psychological well-being in the context of voluntary versus involuntary childlessness, children's developmental characteristics, parents' marital status, social structural conditions surrounding parenthood, and parents' role identity and role quality. We then note suggestions for future research to advance this relatively large literature on parenthood and adult psychological well-being.

Voluntary versus Involuntary Childlessness. Given recent advances in birth control and greater cultural social acceptance of voluntarily childfree adults in contemporary society, an important issue that has emerged within the literature on parenting and well-being is the distinction between voluntary and involuntary childlessness (Letherby, 2002). Overall, it appears that adults who are involuntarily childless are at a greater risk for poorer psychological well-being than are parents. In an early study, Beckman and Houser (1982) compared voluntary childlessness, involuntary childlessness, and semivoluntary childlessness (i.e., respondents who gave neither reason for childlessness). Their results indicated no group differences on morale, depression, or social isolation. However, Connidis and McMullin (1993) compared levels of happiness, depression, and life satisfaction among men and women over age 55 in groups of parents with close ties to children, parents with distant ties to children, voluntarily childless men and women, and involuntarily childless men and women. Their results suggested that parents with close ties and the voluntarily childless had the highest levels of well-being with no differences in levels of happiness between these groups. The lowest ratings of happiness and satisfaction with life and highest depression scores were experienced by the involuntarily childless. Jeffries and Konnert (2002) similarly found differences in psychological well-being between voluntarily and involuntarily childless women and mothers. They found that compared to involuntarily childless women, voluntarily childless women reported higher levels of overall well-being and reported themselves as having more autonomy, more environmental mastery, more purpose in life, as well as smaller present/ideal self discrepancy on autonomy and self-acceptance. In this small study, mothers reported scores on well-being that were in between and not significantly different from those of either of the two groups of childless women.

Children's Developmental Characteristics. Given that parent-child relationships typically extend across children's childhoods and much of their adulthoods, several studies have examined whether associations between parenthood and psychological well-being are contingent upon the child's developmental characteristics, including their age and sociodevelopmental progress. For example, when childless parents are compared with parents of minor children, parenthood is often associated with poorer psychological well-being (Evenson & Simon, 2005; McLanahan & Adams, 1987, 1989; Umberson & Gove, 1989). But when childless adults have been compared to parents of older children, especially widowed parents and parents of relatively independent adult children, evidence suggests that parenthood is associated with higher levels of well-being (Aneshensel et al., 1981; Glenn, 1975; Marks et al., 2004; Ross & Mirowsky, 1988; Umberson & Gove, 1989).

Using U.S. national data from 1995, Marks and colleagues (2004) similarly studied whether children's ages patterned differences among associations between parental status and psychological well-being; this study also took into consideration parents' age and gender. Results from this study indicated that among midlife women ages 40 to 59, having a youngest child ages 5 years old or younger was associated with more dysphoria than having no children, but this effect was significantly reduced for women aged 25 to 39. The authors suggested that this difference might be due to the fact that having young children is more developmentally expected between the ages of 25 and 39. Furthermore, among men, having older adult children was associated with less dysphoria than having no children, and men reported more psychological wellness than women whether parenting young, school-aged, or only adult children. These findings suggest the potentially greater benefits of the parenting role for psychological well-being among men in contrast to women.

Other studies have investigated parents' psychological well-being as a function of their children's developmental transitions. For example, Silverberg (1996) studied 129 two-parent families with a firstborn target child between ages 10 and 15 at the first time of interview. Their aim was to examine linkages between changes among adolescents and parents' well-being. Daughters' pubertal maturation was associated with more midlife concerns for mothers, and sons' pubertal maturation was associated with declines in self-esteem for mothers. Adolescents' higher levels of dating behavior and involvement in mixed-sex activities were associated with parents' poorer psychological well-being, such as their greater midlife identity concerns, lower self-esteem, lower life satisfaction, and more frequent psychological symptoms—but only among parents not strongly invested in a paid-work role. Moreover, emotional autonomy of sons reduced levels of life satisfaction among fathers, particularly among blue-collar fathers.

Also examining associations between children's developmental transitions and parents' psychological well-being, Ryff, Lee, Essex, and Schmutte (1994) studied 215 midlife parents to evaluate the extent to which their feelings about how adult children had "turned out" would influence their psychological well-being. Perceived adjustment (though not accomplishment) of children predicted parents' scores on six of seven psychological well-being outcomes (Ryff's six well-being scales and depression). Furthermore, parents who saw their children as being better adjusted than themselves as young adults had lower well-being. Similar to the study by Ryff and colleagues (1994), other studies focusing on the psychological well-being of parents of adult children have found that adult children's problems are associated with parents' poorer well-being (Greenberg & Becker, 1988; Greenfield & Marks, 2006; Pillemer & Suitor, 1991).

Parents' Marital Status and Family Structure.   In addition to considering developmental processes set in motion by parents' children, studies also have considered parents' relationships (or lack of relationships) with intimate partners as another factor that can influence associations between parenthood and psychological well-being. Studies that have examined marital status interactions have usually found single parenting to be more distressing than parenting with a partner (Aneshensel et al., 1981; Evenson & Simon, 2005; McLanahan & Adams, 1989; Menaghan, 1989a, 1989b; Umberson & Gove, 1989). Stepparenting (versus parenting biological and/or adopted children) has also sometimes been associated with greater distress (Ihinger-Tallman, 1988; White & Booth, 1985).

Some studies have considered additional subgroup differences among parents occupying particular marital status groups. For example, Zhang and Hayward (2001), using data from a U.S. nationally representative sample of adults aged 70 and older, found patterns of gender differences in the associations between parental status, marital status, and psychological well-being. Findings suggested overall that childlessness did not increase the prevalence of loneliness and depression among parents at these ages, net of other factors. However, childlessness did increase loneliness and depression for divorced, widowed, and never married older adults. Divorced, widowed, and never married men who were childless had significantly higher rates of loneliness compared with women in comparable circumstances; divorced and widowed men who were childless also had significantly higher rates of depression than divorced and widowed women. Patterns for adults with stepchildren did not differ greatly from those with biological children.

Using U.S. national data from 1987 to 1988, Evenson and Simon (2005) examined whether differences in levels of psychological well-being among childless adults, parents of stepchildren, and parents of biological children were patterned by whether parents were "empty nest" parents (i.e., had no children at home), "full nest" parents (i.e., had children under ages 19 at home), or parents with adult children at home. Results indicated that in comparison to the well-being of nonparents, elevated levels of psychological distress were reported among parents with minor children at home, noncustodial parents, and parents with nonresidential adult stepchildren, but not among parents with adult children at home or parents with minor stepchildren at home. In comparison to the well-being of "full nest" parents, noncustodial parents, parents with adult children at home and parents with nonresidential adult stepchildren reported higher levels of distress. But contrary to expectation, parents with minor stepchildren at home were no different than other "full nest" parents. These results suggest that associations between parenthood and psychological well-being are likely contingent upon a complex array of family structural arrangements under which parenting occurs.

Parental Role Identity and Role Quality.   Much of the work related to parenting and adult psychological well-being has focused on whether or not adults occupy the parent role itself; a much more limited amount of research has addressed role identity and role quality differences in parenting and their associations with adults' psychological well-being. One study that has contributed to understanding linkages between parental role identity and role quality and adults' psychological well-being is that of Simon (1992). Findings from this study indicated that parental identity was more salient for women's self-conceptions than men's self-conceptions, and women, compared to men, reported higher levels of parental strains. This study did not, however, find evidence that parental strains more strongly jeopardized women's psychological well-being than men's. Instead, there was evidence that the relationship between parental strains and distress was stronger among fathers than among mothers.

In another study of parent role quality using data from 180 full-time employed dual-earner couples, and controlling for many demographic and marital quality characteristics, Barnett, Brennan, and Marshall (1994) found that greater satisfaction as a parent was associated with less overall psychological distress to a similar degree among both men and women. The authors discussed their findings as providing evidence that family roles are beginning to have similar psychological significance for men and women (Barnett, 1993; Pleck 1993; Thoits, 1991, 1992).

Other studies have focused on how characteristics of parent-child relationships pattern associations between parenthood and adult psychological well-being. For example, in Silverberg's (1996) study of parents of young adolescent children, mother-daughter conflict was associated with adults' lower self-esteem and life satisfaction and more psychological distress symptoms, and mother-son conflict was also associated with lower levels of life satisfaction. Longitudinally, more reports of challenge/distancing in parent-child relationships over time were associated with more psychological symptoms among mothers of daughters and less life satisfaction among most parents.

Umberson (1992) explored the influence of relationships with adult children on their parents' psychological distress. Overall, more negative aspects of parent-child relationships—such as greater relationship strain with children and parental dissatisfaction—were predictive of psychological distress of parents, particularly among parents with lower levels of education. Other important subgroup differences in the associations emerged. For example, frequency of contact with children was found to be associated with more beneficial psychological functioning among divorced parents in contrast to married parents, but frequency of contact was associated with higher depression among widowed parents in contrast to married parents. Furthermore, social support from adult children was associated with better psychological functioning among parents who had adult children living at home in contrast to parents whose adult children lived elsewhere.

A few additional studies have focused on social exchange given to and received from adult children and its impact on midlife or older adults' psychological well-being. The results have suggested that at least for U.S. midlife and older adults, overall, being able to give to adult children, whether reciprocated or not, is associated with better psychological well-being than being overbenefitted in exchanges with adult children (Davey & Eggebeen, 1998; Marks, 1995; Mutran & Reitzes, 1984; Rook, 1984; Stoller, 1985). However, Davey and Eggebeen's (1998) contingency theory of intergenerational exchange adds an additional empirically validated perspective: In certain transitional periods—such as during a parent's transition to widowhood, decline in health, significant drop in income, transition out of employment, and birth of a grandchild—greater support received from adult children among older parents leads to increases in their psychological well-being.

Suggestions for Future Research.   Similar to studies on partnerships and psychological well-being, the literature on parenthood and psychological well-being has increasingly recognized potentially important subgroup differences among parents and nonparents; however, many other dimensions of subgroup differences have yet to be explored. For example, few studies have addressed the experiences of gay and lesbian parents (Ross, 2005). It also would be valuable to explore the psychological well-being consequences of parenthood resulting from new types of conception. For example, findings from a study of 42 surrogacy families compared with 51 egg-donation families and 80 natural conception families suggested the psychological well-being and adaptation to parenthood was better among the surrogacy and egg-donation parents than that of mothers and fathers of children born by natural conception methods (Golombok, Murray, Jadva, MacCallum, & Lycett, 2004).

The empirical literature on parenthood and psychological well-being can also be advanced by drawing on theoretical advances in scholarship on parent-child relationships. For example, focusing primarily on relationships between parents and adult children, Leuscher and Pillemer (1998) have drawn attention to the issue of intergenerational ambivalence. With respect to parents' experiences, ambivalence can be conceptualized as perceiving contradictory expectations for behavior as a parent of an adult child, as well as having simultaneously negative and positive feelings toward an adult child. This concept can contribute to moving the examination of linkages between parenthood and psychological well-being beyond investigations of parents' feelings and behaviors of solidarity or conflict.

Additionally, within contemporary theorizing on parenthood and adult development, there continues to be speculation that the social role of parenthood has both emotional benefits and emotional costs. Nevertheless, scholars continue to assess the costs much more frequently than the potential rewards. By adding more eudaimonic-based measures of psychological well-being—such as purpose in life, self-acceptance, positive relations with others, and personal growth—future empirical studies will be better able to capture how and when parenthood promotes individuals' optimal psychological well-being.

Finally, guided by a life course perspective and bioecological systems theory, we expect it would be very valuable for more scholarship on parenthood and developmental outcomes to adopt a more macrohistorical and ecological lens on the role of parenting. The social context of parenting is likely to pattern how parenthood affects adults' well-being. For example, because of decreasing levels of societal support for parenting and less societal-wide valuing of the parental role over the last half century (Evenson & Simon, 2005; Hewlett, Rankin, & West, 2002; Hewlett & West, 1998), we might anticipate that parenting will be associated with greater stresses and fewer rewards, thereby leading to poorer well-being among contemporary cohorts of parents.

Generating empirical support for this idea, Bird (1997) explored associations between U.S. parents' number of children under age 18 and their psychological distress. Although having a greater number of children was associated with higher levels of distress, this effect was mediated by social and economic burdens associated with having more children, including more perceived economic hardship, difficulty arranging child care, and lower quality of marriage. The author suggests that if these factors were ameliorated, having children would lead to less psychological distress for women and eliminate differences in psychological distress for men. By contrast, in a country that provides child allowance and state-subsidized childcare—Finland—evidence suggests that children have no negative effect on the psychological well-being of Finnish women and a positive effect on Finnish men (Savolainen et al., 2001).

Parenthood and Generativity

Parenthood constitutes the family role most typically considered within studies on family relationships and generativity. This fact comes of little surprise given the traditional conceptualization of generativity as "caring for and contributing to the next generation." Overall, the literature suggests that being a parent is conducive to engendering generativity, but that the quality of one's parenting role also influences generativity.

One of the earliest studies examining the link between parenthood and generativity was Vaillant and Milofsky's (1980) study. They assessed Eriksonian life stage at age 47 from two different samples of men (varying by socioeconomic status) and found that achieving generativity was correlated with emotional closeness to adolescent children. As noted previously, building on the Vaillant and Milofsky (1980) study, Snarey and colleagues (1987) examined data from the 343 married men in the working-class sample study with an interest in the influence of infertility problems on men's generativity. Overall, ranking of generativity rates by fertility status suggested generativity was highest among the infertile adoptive fathers, followed by the initially infertile fathers who eventually became birth fathers, then fertile birth fathers, and finally infertile men who remained childless.

McAdams and de St. Aubin (1992) explored associations between parenting and generativity in an adult sample ages 19–68. They found that having children, as opposed to not having children, was significantly associated with higher scores on the LGS, and an additional significant interaction suggested this effect was greater among men than women.

Results reported by Marks, Bumpass, and Jun (2004) are also consistent with this suggestion of a gender difference in the association between parenthood and generativity. They used U.S. national data and controlled for marital status and other demographic characteristics, and employed a modified version of the LGS. Findings indicated two gender differences in the influence of parenthood on generativity. Men with adult children reported significantly more generativity than women with adult children, and men with preschool children showed a trend toward more generativity than women with preschool children. Men (but not women) consistently reported more generativity when they had children; the only exception was young men with school-aged children whose predicted scores were lower than for young men without children.

It is possible that the role-identities of women and men remain sufficiently gendered such that women are encouraged to adopt caring and nurturing attitudes and behaviors in all roles (e.g., Gilligan, 1982), thereby leading them to have relatively similar levels of reported generativity whether they are childfree or parents. In contrast, the parenting role-identity for men might be the most important major role-identity to bring a particular emphasis on caring for and taking responsibility for others, and, as such, the parent role-identity might be the role-identity most closely linked to men's development of generativity. Palkovitz and colleagues' (2001) in-depth interviews with fathers provides additional empirical support for the proposition that the transition to fatherhood provides an important "jolt" to men to become more generative by being less self-centered, more giving, and more involved in taking care of the next generation.

A few studies have specifically explored the types of child involvement activities that promote generativity. Snarey (1993) studied different types of child care involvement among fathers to evaluate their relative influence on men's societal generativity. Results indicated that the strongest catalyst for the development of societal generativity among fathers was their involvement in activities that promoted the social and emotional development of their children. Building on this work, McKeering and Pakenham (2000) studied 134 White Australian parents and found that childcare activities promoting children's social-emotional development were related to fathers' societal generativity, whereas activities promoting academic-intellectual development for children were related to mothers' societal generativity. Bailey (1992) studied White middle-class fathers and found that fathers' social interaction in play with their children was weakly associated with self-reports of generativity; however, men's higher levels of providing routine childcare were not associated with scores on generativity. Finally, focusing on college-educated women in their 40s and using a personal characteristic cluster-based measure of generativity, Peterson and Klohnen (1995) found that the correlates of generativity included being a parent, felt adequacy in the motherhood role, health concerns for children or partner, agreement that motherhood promotes own growth, and having fewer problems with children.

Two studies have valuably extended the study of generativity to other racial-ethnic-national groups of parents. Hart, McAdams, Hirsch, and Bauer (2001) studied 253 adults, ages 34 to 65, about evenly split between African American and White parents. They found that among both African American and White parents, assessments of generativity (as measured by the Loyola Generativity Scale) were associated with emphasizing prosocial values and viewing oneself as a role model and source of wisdom for one's children. Nevertheless, African American adults scored higher than Whites on the measure of generative concern and generative acts, as well as on indices of parenting as a role model and source of wisdom. Extending the study of generativity to an Asian cultural context, Kim and Youn (2002) found that among Korean women, reports of better quality within one's parenting role and, interestingly, more childcare stress were associated with higher scores on the LGS.

Although many of the previous studies provide evidence for linkages between parenting/parenthood and generativity, several major methodological limitations indicate the critical need for additional studies to further investigate these linkages. First, more longitudinal work in this area can help to establish a better understanding of causal processes. Cross-sectional studies that assess parental status and generativity at the same time cannot decouple processes through which earlier levels of generativity heighten individuals' likelihood of becoming a parent from processes through which becoming a parent leads to increased levels of generativity. Additionally, more work that seeks to unconfound the effects of the marital role and the parental role on generativity would be helpful in better understanding the extent to which different family relationships influence adults' development of generativity.

Caregiving for a Child with a Disability and Psychological Well-Being

Parents providing care for a child with a disability sometimes have been found to experience the highest levels of stress in comparison to other types of caregivers (Biegel et al., 1991). The evidence on this issue is mixed, however, likely due to variation in ages, duration of care, and illness types included in different caregiving studies involving children with disabilities (Neal, Chapman, Ingersoll-Dayton, & Emlen, 1993). Mash and Johnson (1983) reviewed studies on parents of children with physical and mental disorders and concluded that findings overall revealed that mothers with children who have conditions such as hyperactivity, cerebral palsy, epilepsy, and developmental delay have interactions with young children that are more stressful and that can be experienced as less rewarding than do mothers of children without disability.

Caregiving for a child with special needs is not limited, however, to special care in childhood. Some disabilities are lifelong (e.g., mental retardation, cerebral palsy, and developmental delay) and others only occur in adulthood (e.g., schizophrenia and disabilities due to an accident or onset of a health condition). The psychological effects of being a parent of an adult child with special needs also appear to depend on the child's type of condition. For example, studies have indicated few differences in levels of psychological well-being among predominantly European-American midlife and later life mothers parenting adult children with mental retardation compared to samples of other-caregiver and noncaregiver age peers (Ramey, Krauss, & Simeonsson, 1989; Seltzer & Krauss, 1989; Seltzer, Krauss, Choi et al., 1996). Parents of adult children with a serious mental health problem, however, have been found to demonstrate elevated levels of depression and alcohol symptoms at midlife in comparison to parents who do not report having an adult child with mental health problems (Seltzer & Greenberg, 2001), possibly due to the greater unpredictability of behaviors associated with serious mental illnesses like schizophrenia, in contrast to mental retardation.

Important subgroup differences might exist even among parents of children with similar conditions. In a valuable comparison study, Blacher, Lopez, Shapiro, and Fusco (1997) reported that Latina mothers with a child with mental retardation experienced more depression in contrast to Latina mothers who did not have a child with mental retardation. The authors suggested that the poorer well-being of Latina mothers of children with mental retardation might be due to their poorer access to interpersonal support (particularly spousal support) when they had a child with this particular disability. This report of more depression among Latina mothers of children with mental retardation contrasts with the finding of few negative effects noted previously based on studies of primarily European-American mothers of children with a similar condition (Ramey, Krauss, & Simeonsson, 1989; Seltzer & Krauss, 1989; Seltzer, Krauss, Choi et al., 1996), and highlights the importance of considering diversity in social contexts (as emphasized in the life course perspective, bioecological systems theory, and structural symbolic interactionism) in more comprehensively understanding the effects of family factors on adult developmental outcomes.

Links between Empirical Findings and Theory.   Similar to the research on partner relations and adults' psychological well-being and generativity, studies on the extent to which being a parent influences adult developmental outcomes demonstrate several of the core ideas from the life course perspective, bioecological systems theory, and structural symbolic interactionism's role-identity theory. Overall, consistent with structural symbolic interactionism's role-identity theory, research on parenthood and well-being suggests that having the role-identity of parent—as a position that typically carries with it expectations for taking responsibility and caring for children—can promote meaning in adults' lives and foster their development of generativity. Additionally, congruent with bioecological systems theory's attention to interpersonal relations within the family microsystem, the literature suggests that the interactional demands of parenting and caregiving for a child with certain health conditions can be distressing, but that this distress is moderated by other factors in the family microsystem (such as by the presence of a partner, the characteristics of the child and their health condition, and the quality of relationship with the child). The influence of relationships with adult children on parents' well-being provides additional support for the life course perspective's emphasis on linked lives across time.

Relationships with Parents in Adulthood, Psychological Well-Being, and Generativity

Experiences in the Adult Child Role and Psychological Well-Being

An important part of adult life is now spent in relationships with parents who are still alive across individuals' adulthood. Today, more men and women reach adulthood with both parents alive than in the early 20th century, and men and women from contemporary adult birth cohorts are likely to spend more years with one or more parents aged 65 and older than they are to spend with children under age 18 (Watkins, Mencken, & Bongaarts, 1987). Despite these demographic trends, relatively little family research outside of work on filial caregiving has focused on adults in their adult child role vis-à-vis their aging parents and how this adult child role might be related to adults' well-being. In this section, we review the few studies that have examined linkages between being an adult child and psychological well-being, as well as studies on the psychological effects of losing one's role as an adult child through the experience of parent death.

Adult-Child Parent Relationship Quality and Adult Child's Psychological Well-Being.   Influenced by Freudian theory, Parsonsian family theory from the 1940s and 1950s emphasized the need for adult children to "disconnect" from their parents after adolescence and to focus almost exclusively on their own adult nuclear family formed by marriage (Parsons, 1943). Nevertheless, family research in the United States over the last 40 years has confirmed that ties between adult children and their midlife and aging parents remain considerable (Bengtson, Rosenthal, & Burton, 1990; Cooney & Uhlenberg, 1992; Eggebeen & Hogan, 1990; Rossi & Rossi, 1990; Shanas et al., 1968; Spitze & Logan, 1992), and that early life relationships with parents help shape later life relationships with parents (Rossi & Rossi, 1990). Indeed, as family structures become more vertical (i.e., more typically comprised of persons from three or more generations) and less horizontal (i.e., more typically comprised of fewer persons from the same generation, such as siblings and cousins), continuing relations across generations and interdependency across generations become even more common and important to adults (Bengtson, 2001; Bengtson et al., 1990; Cooney & Uhlenberg, 1992; Eggebeen & Hogan, 1990; Rossi & Rossi, 1990).

Only a few scholars have studied adult-child parent relationship quality and its impact on adult children's well-being. Barnett, Marshall, and Pleck (1992) reported that adult sons with sisters who had better quality relationships with mothers, as well as better quality relationships with fathers, reported less psychological distress. When relationships with both mothers and fathers were included in statistical models, quality of relationship with fathers was less strongly associated with men's psychological distress than relationship quality with mothers. Additionally, associations were stronger for younger sons and fathers, as well as for sons with less education.

Barnett, Kibria, Baruch, and Pleck (1991) also examined associations between the quality of adults' relationships with their parents and psychological well-being by examining levels of subjective well-being and psychological distress among adult daughters. They found that, overall, having a positive relationship with a parent was associated with daughters' reports of higher well-being and lower distress. Associations between the quality of relationship with parents and psychological well-being were particularly robust for younger and single childless women, as well as when considering women's relationship with their mothers. Results did not vary by adults' race/ethnicity or socioeconomic status.

Umberson (1992) explored the influence of functional and affectual aspects of adult child-parent relationships on adult children's psychological distress. Overall, more negative aspects of parent-child relationships, including greater relationship strain with mothers and fathers, were predictive of greater psychological distress among adult children. Furthermore, the receipt of more social support from mothers and greater frequency of contact with mothers was associated with adult children's lower levels of psychological distress.

Amato and Afifi (2006) explored another dimension of adult children's experience of their parent-child relationship—feeling caught between two parents. This outcome was assessed as being involved in parents' conflicts, feeling it difficult to be more close to one parent without being less close to the other, and feeling parents are competing for the adult child's affection. As hypothesized, adult children experiencing higher levels of feeling caught between parents reported lower scores on a composite measure of psychological well-being. Interestingly, feeling caught between two parents was not associated with parental divorce—which had taken place, on average, about 11 years in the past among study participants who experienced this event—but it was associated with parents' high-conflict continuing marriage.

Death of Parents.   Very few scholars have examined parent loss and adult well-being, but the little work that has been done in this area does suggest that parent loss in adulthood is associated with some negative effects on psychological well-being. Most of this literature is clinically-based, utilizing small nonrepresentative samples of persons who are recruited for study only after a parent loss has occurred. The clinical literature that has examined this issue has suggested that grief reactions after a parent's death can lead to depression, thoughts of suicide, and other psychiatric problems (Birtchnell, 1975; Horowitz et al., 1981; McHorney & Mor, 1988; Sanders, 1979–80).

Scharlach (1991) examined initial and residual grief reactions among a convenience sample of 220 adults, ages 36 to 60 who experienced the death of a parent within the last five years. Results from this study indicated that bereaved adult children reported a wide range of initial symptoms related to parent death, including difficulties sleeping and working and getting along with certain people, as well as residual reactions including becoming upset when thinking about the parent, finding it painful to recall the parent's memory, being unable to avoid thinking about the parent, and crying when thinking about the parent. Scharlach did not find differences in initial or residual grief reactions to the loss of mothers in contrast to fathers.

Moss and colleagues (1993) evaluated responses from 102 daughters ages 40 to 65 who had recently experienced the death of a mother. They found substantial evidence of depression, grief, and somatic reactions, but they also noted considerable heterogeneity in responses that was associated with differential characteristics of the daughter, their deceased mother, and the quality of their relationship. In additional research, Moss and colleagues (1997) examined gender differences in response to the death of a last surviving parent and found that, overall, daughters reported being more upset and experiencing more somatic symptoms in response to parent death than sons.

A prospective, population study of psychological and physical health outcomes associated with parent death was undertaken by Umberson and Chen (1994) by using a 1986–1989 U.S. national sample study to examine parent loss over a 3-year survey interval. The researchers found that loss of a mother, in contrast to no such loss, was associated with a greater increase in psychological distress over time for daughters and sons, although additional moderator analyses suggested this effect applied to only particular subgroups. Sons who lost functionally impaired mothers to death experienced more distress than sons who lost unimpaired mothers, while daughters whose unimpaired mothers died experienced greater increases in distress than daughters who lost impaired mothers to death. Sons who recalled mental health problems of fathers in childhood also reported a greater increase in psychological distress upon the death of a father than did other sons or daughters.

Umberson (2003) also followed up this quantitative research with qualitative interviews of persons who had experienced the loss of a parent. These interviews provide even more striking evidence of the major life change that a parental loss can provoke. Most of the people interviewed spoke about the dramatic changes that their parents' death had created and how those who had not experienced parent death yet did not understand what they were going through. Respondents remarked on how little place had been made for filial bereavement in contemporary American society. Themes from the qualitative analyses of these interviews also revealed how the general societal underestimation of the impact of filial bereavement can also lead to marital misunderstanding and marital problems, which has been confirmed by quantitative analyses on this topic (e.g., Umberson, 1995).

Marks, Bumpass, and Jun (2004) explored linkages between adult child status and parental well-being using data from a 1995 U.S. national survey of midlife adults. Results suggested women with a sole-surviving unhealthy mother reported more dysphoria than women peers who had two healthy parents. Furthermore, Marks, Jun, and Song (2001) also prospectively examined parental death and adult children's well-being using longitudinal U.S. national data. Results indicated that compared to matched-gender peers who continued to have two parents alive over a 5-year period, men and women who reported the death of their father and/or mother reported more problematic changes in psychological well-being.

The Adult Child Role and Generativity

There is very limited work considering how adult child status might be linked to adult generativity—probably due to the fact that generativity has been most typically conceptualized as involving attitudes and behaviors directed toward subsequent and not prior generations. One exception is a study by Peterson (2002) that looked at this linkage prospectively by using a California Adult Q-sort (CAQ) measure of psychosocial generativity among a sample of educated midlife women to examine social relationship factors 10 years later. This study found that CAQ scores at age 43 predicted greater investment 10 years later in intergenerational roles (e.g., daughter and mother) but not in nongenerational roles (e.g., sister and friend). More generative women reported less subjective burden caring for aging parents and more knowledge about community elder care programs. Marks, Bumpass, and Jun (2004) also explored the associations between having living parent(s) alive and/or having parents in poor health and attitudinal generativity. Findings indicated no significant associations across subgroups by adult child status. Additional quantitative studies, as well as qualitative work, in this area would enhance understanding of the ways in which experiences as an adult child can foster the development of generativity.

Filial Caregiving and Psychological Well-Being

Caregiving for parents is the most common type of family caregiving (Hirst, 2005; Marks, 1996b; Stone, Cafferata, & Sangl, 1987). The 2004 Caregiving in the U.S. Study (2004) found that 28% of caregivers in their national sample mentioned giving care to a mother, 8% to a father, and 7% to a mother-in-law. Caregiving for parents tends to be particularly common among midlife adults. Using U.S. national data collected in 1987 to 1988, Marks (1996b) found that about one in 10 U.S. adults between the ages of 35 and 64 reported providing some level of care for a parent either in-household or out-of-household during the previous 12 months. These estimates suggest that for many older parents, adult children are important members of their life course convoy of social support.

Most studies examining filial caregiving have concluded that filial caregiving (in contrast to no caregiving) is associated with an increased sense of burden and psychological distress (e.g., Brody, 1990; George & Gwyther, 1986; Horowitz, 1985; Hoyert & Seltzer, 1992; Marks et al., 2002; Schulz et al., 1990; Schulz & Williamson, 1991; Stephens & Townsend, 1997; Strawbridge, Wallhagen, Shema, & Kaplan, 1997; Young & Kahana, 1989). However, as scholars increasingly examine caregiving as a dynamic life course role, as well as subgroup differences among adult child caregivers and parent care recipients, a more nuanced understanding of the associations between filial caregiving and psychological well-being has emerged.

First, regarding filial caregiving as a dynamic life course role, a number of recent studies have focused specifically on the transition to filial caregiving using a prospective research design. Seltzer and Li (2000) examined data from a representative sample of adult daughters caring for older adults in Wisconsin and found that entry into filial caregiving was associated with a decline in personal mastery. Similarly, Turner, Killian, and Cain (2004) examined the transition to caregiving for parents using data from 952 women ages 50 to 59 participating in the 1992 and 2000 Health and Retirement Study. They found that the transition to a caregiving role for a parent was associated with increases in depressive symptoms. Lawton and colleagues (2000) also prospectively examined the transition to caregiving among a relatively small sample of daughters and daughters-in-law and found no evidence of negative mental health effects. Marks and colleagues (2002), using U.S. national data, found that transitioning into filial caregiving both in-household and out-of-household was associated with negative effects on a number of dimensions of mental health for both women and men; however, out-of-household caregiving was also associated with higher levels of purpose in life among women. Overall, in-household filial caregiving was more problematic for women's than men's psychological well-being, but out-of-household filial caregiving was more problematic for men's than women's psychological well-being. Finally, Hirst (2005) conducted a prospective investigation of becoming a caregiver, continuing caregiving, and multiple types of exiting caregiving using data from 3,000 would-be caregivers, 2,900 former caregivers, and 11,100 noncaregivers participating in the British Household Panel Survey during the 1990s. Results of this study indicated that the onset of caregiving for a parent or parent-in-law living in another household (in contrast to no caregiving) was associated with higher odds of problematic levels of distress for both men and women. Onset of care and the end of care (in contrast to no caregiving) were found to be the most distressing periods of the caregiving career.

In addition to examining subgroup differences among filial caregivers by gender and the stage of their caregiving career, other subgroup differences in the associations between filial caregiving and psychological well-being have been explored. For example, Li, Seltzer, and Greenberg (1999) found that levels of mastery remained high when the caregiving role was shared with a sibling, and levels of mastery decreased if the daughter had other caregiving responsibilities and the parent care recipient had elevated behavior problems.

A few studies have considered subgroup differences among caregivers in terms of whether they provide care to a parent versus a parent-in-law. Overall, results from these studies have generated inconsistent results. Spitze, Logan, Joseph, and Lee (1994) found that adult children reported more distress when caring for a biological parent than caring for a parent-in-law; however, Ingersoll-Dayton, Starrels, and Dowler (1996) found no role relationship differences in caregiver stress. Peters-Davis, Moss, and Pruchno (1999) found few well-being differences between coresident caregiving daughters and daughters-in-law and their husbands. Furthermore, Marks, Lambert, and Choi (2002) found no negative effects on psychological well-being among caregivers for parents-in-law compared to noncaregiver peers.

Links between Empirical Findings and Theory.   Studies on experiences as an adult child further demonstrate primary insights from the life course perspective, bioecological systems theory, and structural symbolic interactionism's role-identity theory. For example, the literature linking the adult child role to adult well-being provides evidence that this relationship is typically experienced as a life course relationship; in other words, the effects of this relationship are not limited to the time when the target person is a child. Also, research on the psychological effects of parent death is congruent with attention from the life course perspective and structural symbolic interactionism's role-identity theory on how family transitions and changes in family roles can influence individuals' development. Furthermore, consideration of linkages between adult-child parent relationship quality and psychological well-being is fitting with bioecological systems theory's emphasis on interactional processes as influencing individuals' development.

Relationships with Other Kin in Adulthood, Psychological Well-Being, and Generativity

Relationships with Other Kin and Psychological Well-Being

While there are sizeable empirical literatures on linkages between adults' partnership and parenthood relationships and their psychological well-being, as well as a smaller literature on the psychological implications of being an adult child, there is much less research examining linkages between other types of kin relationships and adult psychological well-being. In this section, we review the limited research available on linkages between sibling relationships and psychological well-being, as well as grandparent-grandchild relationships and psychological well-being.

Siblings.   The sibling relationship is for most adults the most longstanding family relationship across the life course. Jackson (1997) reported that having a sibling (in contrast to being a singleton) is associated with better mental health among adults from a variety of ethnic groups, including non-Hispanic Whites, African Americans, and Mexicans (though not Puerto Ricans) (Jackson, 1997).

Studies also have indicated that characteristics of individuals' sibling relationships are associated with adults' psychological well-being. Riggio (2000) developed a new measure of sibling relationships, the Lifespan Sibling Relationship Scale (LSRS), to attempt to address the dearth of studies on sibling relationships in adulthood. Scale factors include frequency of positive behavior toward siblings, affect toward siblings, and beliefs about siblings and sibling relationships. Using this measure, Riggio found that more satisfactory sibling relationships were associated with better psychological well-being (Riggio, 2000). Furthermore, Milevsky (2005) found that more sibling support was associated with adults' lower levels of loneliness and depression, as well as higher levels of self-esteem and life satisfaction. Also, more sibling support was associated with adults' better outcomes by compensating for some of the psychological disadvantages of receiving lower levels of support from parents and peers. Stocker, Lanthier, and Furman (1997) also found that more warmth, less conflict, and less rivalry within sibling relationships in young adulthood were associated with siblings' better mental health.

Siblings of persons with disabilities have unique experiences in sibling relationships, in part, because they participate in a family where special attention is often focused on a particular sibling, and also because parents often make it clear to a healthy sibling that they might be "next in line" to provide care to the affected sibling. Seltzer, Greenberg, Krauss, and colleagues (1997) studied siblings of adults with mental retardation and compared them with siblings of adults with mental illness. They found that siblings of adults with mental retardation had higher scores on a composite measure of Ryff's psychological well-being subscales than siblings of adults with mental illness. Moreover, among siblings of adults with mental retardation, more emotional closeness with their affected sibling was associated with higher levels of psychological well-being, whereas among siblings of adults with mental illness, perceiving a less pervasive impact of the affected sibling on their life was associated with higher levels of psychological well-being.

Grandparents and Grandchildren.   The grandparent role is another common role of midlife and older adults, yet relatively little research has emerged specifically examining how this role is associated with grandparents' psychological well-being outside of more recent research on custodial grandparenting (see caregiving for other kin section below). One of the only studies available in this area is by Reitzes and Mutran (2004), who found that having more positive grandparent role identity meanings were associated with greater self-esteem and less depression among grandparents. In addition to the necessity of additional studies on linkages between grandparenting and psychological well-being, there is also a need for research exploring how being an adult grandchild can influence adult developmental outcomes, including psychological well-being and generativity.

The need for this research is particularly critical given demographic changes in grandparent-grandchild relationships, which render it increasingly likely that being an adult grandchild and having an adult grandchild has developmental consequences. First, with greater longevity and greater family emphasis on intergenerational relations extending across at least three, if not four, generations, a growing number of adults are experiencing multiple levels of intergenerational relationships (Bengtson, 2001). Additionally, as more grandparents assume primary caregiving responsibilities for grandchildren (Fuller-Thomson, Minkler, & Driver, 1997), it also might be expected that the relationships between grandchildren and grandparents are becoming increasingly salient in the 21st century. Also, grandchildren are more commonly becoming caregivers for aging grandparents. The 2003 Caregiving in the U.S. Study found that 9% of adult caregivers in that study mentioned a grandparent as the main person for whom they provided care (Caregiving in the U.S., 2004). These trends suggest the importance of examining the potentially reciprocal developmental influences across this important relationship throughout the life course.

Other Kin and Generativity

Relatively little has been written about how relationships with other kin can promote generativity, with the exception of some suggestive work related to childless women. These studies have found that women without children often report very rich family lives that include major generative connections to siblings, nieces, nephews, and other kin (Allen, 1989; Rubinstein, 1996). For example, Rubinstein (1996) reported on in-depth interviews with 109 childless older women in older age. Many of the participants reported having attempted to create ties with siblings' children or developing family-like ties with younger nonrelatives. Never married childless women were quite generative through family-like relationships, as well as through the creation of a social legacy through careers in supportive professions like teaching, nursing, and being a secretary. Overall, these women indicated a strong urge to pass on a legacy, and those who felt there was no one or no purpose for doing this expressed sadness and sometimes despair.

Another interesting, innovative study related to this issue is that of Milardo (2005), who explored uncle-nephew relationships using in-depth interviews in New Zealand and the northeastern U.S. (Maine). He explicitly used dimensions of generativity—including mentoring, doing the family work of serving as mediators of intergenerational disputes and differences, meaning keeping (of family history), and serving as fellow travelers (in friendship)—to code and understand the narratives of his respondents. Considerable evidence emerged that for study participants, nephew-uncle relationships were nontrivial, often of longstanding duration, and very important to the development of both uncles and nephews.

Caregiving for Other Kin and Psychological Well-Being

Overall, there has been much less scholarship exploring individuals' experiences of caregiving for kin other than spouses, parents, and children (for exceptions, see Gerstel & Gallagher, 1993; Marks, 1998; Mui & Morrow-Howell, 1993). Nevertheless, there has been considerable research during the past decade regarding the dynamics and impact of one increasingly recognized family arrangement—grandparents providing major custodial caregiving for grandchildren. In the 2000 U.S. Census, 2.4 million adults (two-thirds women) identified themselves as "grandparent caregivers" for grandchildren younger than 18 years of age, representing about 8.6% of all U.S. households (Simmons & Dye, 2003). Additionally, more than one in 10 American grandparents reported raising a grandchild for at least six months, with most of these grandparents providing care for three years or more (Fuller-Thomson et al., 1997).

A growing body of literature has documented the deleterious psychological effects of assuming full-time care for grandchildren. Comparisons of adults with and without this responsibility have shown that grandparent caregivers are almost twice as likely as their peers to report clinically relevant levels of depression (Fuller-Thomson & Minkler, 2000), and those most at risk are younger, women, in poor health, and new caregivers (Minkler, Fuller-Thomson, Miller, & Driver, 1997). Smaller homogeneous samples also provide evidence that some grandmothers raising grandchildren experience lower levels of psychological well-being (e.g., Burton, 1992; Giarrusso, Feng, Wang, & Silverstein, 1996; Jendrek, 1993; Kelley, 1993; Minkler & Roe, 1993; Minkler, Roe, & Price, 1992; Shore & Hayslip, 1994; Strawbridge et al., 1997).

As in the studies on the psychological effects of filial caregiving, research on grandparents providing full-time care for children also has recognized the potentially dynamic nature of this role. In a study of transitions into and out of grandparent-grandchild coresidence, with the implicit expectation that this arrangement indicated caregiving by the grandparent, Szinovacz, DeViney, and Atkinson (1999) used U.S. national data across all adult ages and found that grandchildren moving into the household increased depressive symptoms among grandmothers. Grandchildren's transitions into the household also decreased happiness for both grandmothers and grandfathers. Interestingly, grandchildren leaving the household also led to reduced well-being among grandfathers. The finding that custodial care for grandchildren is somewhat less detrimental for the psychological well-being of grandfathers than grandmothers is supported by another study that matched grandfathers and grandmothers on care for grandchildren (Kolomer & McCallion, 2005). This study found lower levels of depression among grandfathers than grandmothers, but no gender differences in mastery. These gender differences might be explained by considering the typically gendered nature of family carework (see Horowitz, 1985, for a discussion). For example, grandmothers might suffer more because they take on even more responsibility for children's custodial care than grandfathers, engage in even more challenging personal care tasks (e.g., change diapers, bathe, and interact with schools about behavioral challenges and medical authorities about health challenges), and provide care with less social support from others (e.g., a spouse or other adult children).

A study by Blustein, Chan, and Guanais (2004) suggests that in addition to gender, other characteristics of grandparents can make them more or less vulnerable to experiencing higher levels of psychological distress. This study drew on U.S. national data from grandparents ages 53 to 63 and tracked the movement of grandchildren into and out of grandparents' homes between 1994 and 2000. Overall, grandparents had a greater probability of elevated depressive symptoms with grandchildren in their home, but single grandparents—particularly single women of color—and those without coresident adult children experienced the greatest probability of elevation in depressive symptoms when a grandchild was in residence.

Pruchno and McKenney (2002) drew on data from 867 grandmothers raising a child without the child's parent present to further explore race/ethnicity as a contextual factor for the associations between custodial grandparenthood and psychological well-being. Results revealed similar patterns of variables predicting positive and negative affect among Black and White grandparents, although findings also indicated that the caregiving role was of greater centrality among Black grandmothers, and the quality of relationship with grandchild's parents was related to caregiving satisfaction for White grandmothers, but not Black grandmothers.

Examining differences within ethnic groups in associations between custodial grandparenthood and psychological well-being, Goodman and Silverstein (2005) found that among Latina custodial grandmothers, higher levels of acculturation were associated with more positive affect, and lower levels of acculturation were associated with lower negative affect. Nevertheless, less acculturation was associated with higher life satisfaction. Differences favoring the more acculturated mothers were explained by the finding that more acculturated grandmothers were likely to have more social resources, be married, and have the grandchild's parent at home; furthermore, fewer of the more acculturated grandmothers were assuming care because of the parent's substance abuse problems. The difference favoring less acculturated mothers in terms of life satisfaction might reflect the fact that less acculturated Latina grandmothers might perceive caregiving for a grandchild as more part of a traditional woman's role, whereas more acculturated Latina grandmothers might view custodial grandparenting to be more in conflict with other desired activities.

Results from Szinovacz and Davey's (2006) study on grandchild care and grandparents' retirement status present an additional contextual factor that can pattern associations between caring for grandchildren and adults' psychological well-being. Using data from the U.S. Health and Retirement Study, they found that retirement moderated the influence of grandchild care obligations on depressive symptoms, although the nature of this interaction differed somewhat for men and women. Among retired men, not having (versus having) grandchild care obligations was associated with heightened well-being, whereas among women, continued employment protected against the potential negative effects of having extensive grandchild care obligations on well-being.

Links between Empirical Findings and Theory.   Overall, the research linking relationships with other kin beyond spouse, parent, and adult children to well-being and generativity is further suggestive of the life course perspective, bioecological systems theory, and structural symbolic interactionism's role-identity theory. Congruent with the life course perspective and bioecological systems theory, findings suggest the importance of considering the developmental implications, as well as the cultural and role contexts, of family relationships beyond the nuclear family. Additionally, structural symbolic interactionism's role-identity theory indicates the promise of deepening understanding of how being a grandchild, grandparent, aunt, and uncle—as roles rooted within family structures—can influence adult psychological well-being and generativity.

Caveats and Conclusions

This chapter has provided an overview of broad theoretical perspectives that encourage attention to how family relationships can impact the adult development in terms of psychological well-being and generativity. It also has selectively reviewed the current literature related to family relationships and psychological well-being, family relationships and generativity, and generative family caregiving and well-being. Despite the strengths of this review—including the breadth of family relationships that it addresses, its inclusion of both psychological well-being and generativity as important developmental outcomes, and its tracking of historical trends within several areas of the literature—important limitations remain.

First, this review includes many studies with the shared limitation of using self-report data on family relationships, psychological well-being, and generativity. Because this methodological feature might bias the veridity of associations reported, additional work that includes other types of data offers potentially important contributions to this area of research. For example, future studies might gather observational data on the quality of interactions among adult family members and test for linkages with individuals' self-reported psychological well-being. Additionally, this review must be considered as culturally and historically delimited; it emphasizes literature from mainly the U.S., Canada, the United Kingdom, and occasionally European countries across the last 20 years. Both a life course perspective and bioecological systems perspective would predict that there are likely differences in developmental outcomes across national and subgroup cultural contexts that we have not been able to access and address here. Additionally, within the literature on family relationships and well-being, there are numerous additional studies that examine important issues of how family roles (including caregiving roles for family members), employment roles and characteristics, and other community roles interact to impact well-being. Given limitations of space and comprehensiveness, we were not able to include attention to the literature that addresses these important contextual interactions.

Nonetheless, the literature reviewed here provides ample evidence supporting the propositions of the life course perspective, bioecological systems theory, and structural interactionism's role-identity theory. These perspectives provide rationale and suggest mechanisms whereby family relationships can influence adult development—for better or for worse, and sometimes at the same time. Yet many gaps remain for future research to fill. First, future empirical studies, guided by contextual principles of the life course perspective and bioecological systems theory, might further consider developmental consequences of the growing diversity in family relationships, such as being a partner and a parent in cohabiting relationships, remarriages, two household relationships, and same-gender relationships. Similarly, research on caregiving might fruitfully address the experiences of caregiving in a greater variety of family roles, such as caring for a grandparent, sibling, or niece/nephew. Second, guided by the life course perspective's proposition that it is important to consider cumulative effects and role trajectories over time, life histories in roles as partner, parent, adult child, sibling, grandparent, uncle, aunt, "fictive" kin, and other family relationships warrant further exploration for their cumulative impact on psychological well-being and generativity. Third, it would be valuable for future research to continue to move beyond assessments of negative and positive affect to explore a larger array of psychological well-being outcomes that represent more explicitly developmental outcomes (e.g., personal growth, meaning in life, positive relations with others, self-acceptance, environmental mastery, autonomy, as well as generativity). Attention to these dimensions would better inform our understanding of ways in which interlocking family members influence trajectories of adult development. Fourth, subgroup differences within and between adults' experiences of particular family roles merit additional scholarly attention. For example, the importance of socioeconomic and cultural context for shaping potential differences in developmental outcomes needs further exploration in almost all areas of the literature covered in this chapter. Fifth, given the changing role expectations for both men and women in family life, continued explicit attention to gender differences remains in order, notwithstanding evidence of gender convergence in the effects of family roles on well-being. Finally, additional attention to age differences in family influence also would help to inform a more developmentally nuanced understanding of how family relationships shape individuals' life course trajectories.

Despite these critical directions for future research, current research on family relations and adult development overall suggest that family relationships (or lack of family relationships) help pattern profiles of adults' psychological well-being and generativity. By drawing on well-developed theories of individual and family life, as well by orienting empirical attention to gaps identified from previous decades of research, scholars can enhance the depth and breadth of understanding important familial contexts for adult development.

References

Acitelli, L. K., & Antonucci, T. C. (1994). Gender differences in the link between marital support and satisfaction in older couples. *Journal of Personality and Social Psychology, 67,* 688–698.

Allen , K. R. (1989). *Single women/family ties: Life histories of older women.* Newbury Park, CA: Sage.

Allport, G. W. (1961). *Pattern and growth in personality.* New York: Holt, Rinehart, & Winston.

Amato, P. R., & Afifi, T. D. (2006). Feeling caught between parents: Adult children's relations with parents and subjective well-being. *Journal of Marriage and Family, 68,* 222–235.

Aneshensel, C. S., Frerichs, R. R., & Clark, V. A. (1981). Family roles and sex differences in depression. *Journal of Health and Social Behavior, 22,* 379–393.

Aseltine, R. H., & Kessler, R. C. (1993). Marital disruption and depression in a community sample. *Journal of Health and Social Behavior, 34,* 237–251.

Bailey, W. T. (1992). Psychological development in men: Generativity and involvement with young children. *Psychological Reports, 71,* 929–230.

Barnett, R. C. (1993). Multiple roles, gender, and psychological distress. In L. Goldberger & S. Breznitz (Eds.), *Handbook of stress: Theoretical and clinical aspects* (2nd ed., pp. 427–445). New York: The Free Press.

Barnett, R. C., Brennan, R. T., & Marshall, N. L. (1994). Gender and the relationships between parent role quality and psychological distress: A study of men and women in dual-career couples. *Journal of Family Issues, 15,* 229–252.

Barnett, R. C., Kibria, N., Baruch, G. K., & Pleck, J. H. (1991). Adult daughter-parent relationships and their associations with daughters' subjective well-being and psychological distress. *Journal of Marriage and the Family, 53,* 29–42.

Barnett, R. C., Marshall, N. L., & Pleck, J. H. (1992). Adult son-parent relationships and their associations with sons' psychological distress. *Journal of Family Issues, 13,* 505–525.

Barrett, A. E. (2000). Marital trajectories and mental health. *Journal of Health and Social Behavior, 41,* 451–464.

Beach, S. R. H., Katz, J., Kim, S., & Brody, G. H. (2003). Prospective effects of marital satisfaction on depressive symptoms in established marriages: A dyadic model. *Journal of Social and Personal Relationships, 20,* 355–371.

Becker, E. (1973). *The denial of death.* New York: Free Press.

Beckman, L. J., & Houser, B. B. (1982). The consequences of childlessness on the social-psychological well-being of older women. *Journal of Gerontology, 37,* 243–250.

Bengtson, V. L. (2001). Beyond the nuclear family: The increasing importance of multigenerational bonds. *Journal of Marriage and Family, 63,* 1–16.

Bengston, V. L., & Allen, K. R. (1993). The life course perspective applied to families over time. In P. G. Boss, W. J. Doherty, R. LaRossa, W. R. Schumm, & S. K. Steinmetz (Eds.), *Sourcebook of families, theories and methods: A contextual approach* (pp. 469–499). New York: Plenum.

Bengston, V. L., Rosenthal, C., & Burton, L. (1990). Families and aging: Diversity and heterogeneity. In R.H. Binstock & L. K. George (Eds.), *Handbook of aging and the social sciences* (3rd ed., pp. 205–226). San Diego, CA: Academic Press.

Bernard, J. (1972). *The future of marriage.* New York: Bantam.

Biegel, D., Sales, E., & Schulz, R. (1991). *Family caregiving in chronic illness: Heart disease, cancer, stroke, Alzheimer's disease, and chronic mental illness.* Newbury Park, CA: Sage.

Bierman, A., Fazio, E. M., & Milkie, M. A. (2006). A multifaceted approach to the mental health advantage of the married: Assessing how explanations vary by outcome measure and unmarried group. *Journal of Family Issues, 27,* 554–582.

Bird, C. E. (1997). Gender differences in the social and economic burdens of parenting and psychological distress. *Journal of Marriage and the Family, 59,* 809–823.

Birtchnell, J. (1975). Psychiatric breakdown following recent parental death. *British Journal of Medical Psychology, 48,* 379–390.

Blacher, J., Lopez, S., Shapiro, J., & Fusco, J. (1997). Contributions to depression in Latina mothers with and without children with retardation: Implications for caregiving. *Family Relations, 46,* 325–334.

Blustein, J., Chan, S., & Guanais, F. C. (2004). Elevated depressive symptoms among caregiving grandparents. *Health Services Research, 39,* 1671–1690.

Booth, A., & Amato, P. (1991). Divorce and psychological stress. *Journal of Health and Social Behavior, 32,* 396–407.

Bradburn, N. M. (1969). *The structure of psychological well-being.* Chicago: Aldine.

Brim, O. G. (1992). *Ambition.* New York: Basic Books.

Brim, O. G., Ryff, C. D., & Kessler, R. C. (2004). The MIDUS National Survey: An overview. In O. G. Brim, C. D. Ryff, & R. C. Kessler (Eds.), *How healthy are we? A national study of well-being at midlife* (pp. 1–34). Chicago: University of Chicago Press.

Brody, E. (1990). *Women in the middle: Their parent-care years.* New York: Springer.

Bronfenbrenner, U. (1989). Ecological systems theory. In R. Vasta (Ed.), *Annals of child development* (Vol. 6, pp. 187–249). Greenwich, CT: JAI Press.

Bronfenbrenner, U., & Morris, P. A. (1998). The ecology of developmental processes. In R. M. Lerner (Ed.), *Handbook of child psychology: Theoretical models of human development* (5th ed., Vol. 1, pp. 993–1028). New York: Wiley.

Brown, S. L. (2000). The effect of union type on psychological well-being: Depression among cohabitors versus marrieds. *Journal of Health and Social Behavior, 41,* 241–255.

Browning, D. (1975). *Generative man.* New York: Dell.

Bryant, F. B., & Veroff, J. (1982). The structure of psychological well-being: Sociohistorical analysis. *Journal of Personality and Social Psychology, 43,* 653–673.

Buhler, C. (1935). The curve of life as studied in biographies. *Journal of Applied Psychology, 19,* 405–409.

Bumpass, L. (1990). What's happening to the family: Interactions between demographic and institutional change. *Demography, 27,* 483–98.

Burton, L. M. (1992). Black grandparents rearing children of drug-addicted parents: Stressors, outcomes, and social service needs. *Gerontologist, 32,* 744–751.

Burton, R. D. (1998). Global integrative meaning as a mediating factor in the relationship between social roles and psychological distress. *Journal of Health and Social Behavior, 39,* 201–215.

Cantor, M. A. (1979). The informal support system of New York's inner city elderly: Is ethnicity a factor? In D. Gelfand & A. Kutzik (Eds.). *Ethnicity and aging: Theory, research, and policy.* New York: Springer.

Caregiving in the U.S. Study. (2004). Bethesda, MD/Washington, DC: National Alliance for Caregiving and AARP.

Carnelley, K. B., Wortman, C. B., & Kessler, R. C. (1999). The impact of widowhood on depression: Findings from a prospective survey. *Psychological Medicine, 29,* 1111–1123.

Carr, D., House, J., Kessler, R. C., Nesse, R.M., Sonnega, J., & Wortman, C. (2000). Marital quality and psychological adjustment to widowhood among older adults: A longitudinal analysis. *Journal of Gerontology: Social Sciences, 55,* S197–S207.

Chappell, N. L. (1990). Aging and social care. In R. H. Binstock & L. K. George (Eds), *Handbook of aging and the social sciences* (3rd ed., pp. 438–454). San Diego, CA: Academic Press.

Cherlin, A. (2004). The deinstitutionalization of American marriage. *Journal of Marriage and Family, 66,* 848–861.

Connidis, I. A., & McMullin, J. A. (1993). To have or have not: Parent status and the subjective well-being of older men and women. *Gerontologist, 33,* 630–636.

Cooney, T., & Uhlenberg, P. (1992). Support from parents over the life course: The adult child's perspective. *Social Forces, 71,* 63–84.

Davey, A. & Eggebeen, D. J. (1998). Patterns of intergenerational exchange and mental health. *Journal of Gerontology: Psychological Sciences, 53,* P86–P95.

Davies, L., Avison, W. R., & McAlpine, D. D. (1997). Significant life experiences and depression among single and married mothers. *Journal of Marriage and the Family, 59,* 294–308.

de St. Aubin, E., McAdams, D. P., & Kim, T. (Eds.). (2004). *The generative society: Caring for future generations.* Washington, DC: American Psychological Association.

Demo, D. H., & Acock, A. C. (1996). Family structure, family process, and adolescent well-being. *Journal of Research on Adolescence, 6,* 457–488.

Diener, E., Suh, E. M., Lucas, R. E., & Smith, H. L. (1999). Subjective well-being: Three decades of progress. *Psychological Bulletin, 125,* 276–302.

Doherty, W. J., Su, S., & Needle, R. (1989). Marital disruption and psychological well-being. *Journal of Family Issues, 10,* 72–85.

Durkheim, E. (1951). *Suicide: A study in sociology* (J. A. Spaulding & G. Simpson, Trans.). Ontario, Toronto: The Free Press. (Original work published 1897)

Dush, C. M. K., & Amato, P. R. (2005). Consequences of relationship status and quality for subjective well-being. *Journal of Social and Personal Relationships, 22,* 607–627.

Duvall, E. M. (1962). *Family development* (2nd ed.). New York: Lippincott.

Earle, J. R., Smith, M. H., Harris, C. T., & Longino, C. F., Jr. (1998). Women, marital status, and symptoms of depression in a midlife national sample. *Journal of Women and Aging, 10,* 41–57.

Edin, K., Kefalas, M. J., & Reed, J. M. (2004). A peek inside the black box: What marriage means for poor unmarried parents. *Journal of Marriage and the Family, 67,* 1007–1014.

Eggebeen, D., & Hogan, D. P. (1990). Giving between generations in American families. *Human Nature, 1,* 211–232.

Elder, G. H., Jr., Johnson M. K., & Crosnoe, R. (2003). The emergence and development of life course theory. In J. T. Mortimer & M. J. Shanahan (Eds.), *Handbook of the life course* (pp. 3–22). New York: Plenum.

Erikson, E. H. (1950). *Childhood and society.* New York: Norton.

Erikson, E. H. (1969). *Gandhi's truth: On the origins of militant nonviolence.* New York: Norton.

Evenson, R. J., & Simon, R. W. (2005). Clarifying the relationships between parenthood and depression. *Journal of Health and Social Behavior, 46,* 341–358.

Featherman, D. L. (1983). The life-span perspective in social science research. In P. B. Baltes & O. G. Brim, Jr. (Eds.), *Life-span development and behavior* (Vol. 5, pp. 1–57). New York: Academic Press.

Fincham, F. D., Beach, S. R. H., Harold, G. T., & Osborne, L. N. (1997). Marital satisfaction and depression: Different causal relationships for men and women? *Psychological Science, 8,* 351–357.

Fitting, M., Rabins, P., Lucas, M. J., & Eastham, J. (1986). Caregivers for dementia patients: A comparison of husbands and wives. *Gerontologist, 26,* 248–252.

Freud, S. (1964). An outline of psychoanalysis. In J. Strachey (Ed.), *The standard edition of the complete psychological works of Sigmund Freud* (Vol. 23). London: Hogarth Press. (Original work published 1940)

Fuller-Thomson, E., & Minkler, M. (2000). African American grandparents raising grandchildren: A national profile of demographic and health characteristics. *Health and Social Work, 25,* 109–118.

Fuller-Thomson, E., Minkler, M., & Driver, D. (1997). A profile of grandparents raising grandchildren in the United States. *Gerontologist, 37,* 406–411.

Futterman, A., Gallagher, D., Thompson, L., Lovett, S., & Gilewski, M. (1990). Retrospective assessment of marital adjustment and depression during the first two years of spousal bereavement. *Psychology and Aging, 5,* 277–283.

Gallagher-Thompson, D., Coon, D. W., Rivera, P., Powers, D. E., & Zeiss, A. M. (1998). Family caregiving: Stress, coping, and intervention. In M. Hersen & V. B. Van Hasselt (Eds.), *Handbook of clinical geropsychology* (pp. 469–493). New York: Plenum.

George, L. W., & Gwyther, L. P. (1986). Caregiver well-being: A multidimensional examination of family caregivers of demented adults. *Gerontologist, 26,* 253–259.

Gerstel, N., & Gallagher, S. K. (1993). Kinkeeping and distress: Gender, recipients of care, and work-family conflict. *Journal of Marriage and the Family, 55,* 598–607.

Giarrusso, R., Feng, D., Wang, Q., & Silverstein, M. (1996). Parenting and co-parenting of grandchildren: Effects on grandparents' well-being and family solidarity. *International Journal of Sociology and Social Policy, 16,* 124–154.

Gilligan, C. (1982). *In a different voice: Psychological theory and women's development.* Cambridge, MA: Harvard University Press.

Glenn, N. D. (1975). Psychological well-being in the postparental stage: Some evidence from national surveys. *Journal of Marriage and the Family, 37,* 105–110.

Glenn, N. D., & Weaver, C. N. (1979). A note on family situation and global happiness. *Social Forces, 57,* 960–967.

Glenn, N. D., & Weaver, C. N. (1988). The changing relationship of marital status to reported happiness. *Journal of Marriage and the Family, 50,* 317–324.

Golombok, S., Murray, C., Jadva, V., MacCallum, F., & Lycett, E. (2004). Families created through surrogacy arrangements: Parent-child relationships in the first year of life. *Developmental Psychology, 40,* 400–411.

Goode, W. (1960). A theory of role strain. *American Sociological Review, 25,* 483–496.

Goodman, C. C., & Silverstein, M. (2005). Latina grandmothers raising grandchildren: Acculturation and psychological well-being. *International Journal of Aging and Human Development, 60,* 305–316.

Gore, S., & Mangione, T. W. (1983). Social roles, sex roles and psychological distress: Additive and interactive models of sex differences. *Journal of Health and Social Behavior, 24,* 300–312.

Gove, W. R. (1972). The relationship between sex roles, mental illness, and marital status. *Social Forces, 51,* 34–44.

Gove, W. R., Hughes, M., & Style, C. B. (1983). Does marriage have positive effects on the psychological well-being of the individual? *Journal of Health and Social Behavior, 24,* 122–131.

Gove, W. R., & Shin, H. (1989). The psychological well-being of divorced and widowed men and women. *Journal of Family Issues, 10,* 122–144.

Gove, W. R., & Tudor, J. F. (1973). *Adult sex roles and mental illness.* Chicago: The University of Chicago Press.

Greenberg, J., & Becker, M. (1988). Aging parents as family resources. *Gerontologist, 28,* 786–791.

Greenfield, E. A., & Marks, N. F. (2006). Linked lives: Adult children's problems and their parents' psychological and relational well-being. *Journal of Marriage and Family, 68,* 442–454.

Grossman, A. H., D'Augelli, A. R., & Hershberger, S. L. (2000). Social support networks of lesbian, gay, and bisexual adults 60 years of age and older. *Journal of Gerontology: Psychological Sciences, 55,* P171–P179.

Harper, S., & Lund, D. A. (1990). Wives, husbands, and daughters caring for institutionalized and noninstitutionalized dementia patients: Toward a model for caregiving burden. *International Journal of Aging and Human Development, 30,* 241–262.

Hart, H. M., McAdams, D. P., Hirsch, B. J., & Bauer, J. J. (2001). Generativity and social involvement among African Americans and White adults. *Journal of Research in Personality, 35,* 208–230.

Hewlett, S., & West, C. (1998). *The war against parents*. New York: Houghton Mifflin.

Hewlett, S., Rankin, N., & West, W. (2002). *Taking parenting public: The case for a new social movement*. New York: Rowman and Littlefield.

Hirst, M. (2005) Carer distress: A prospective, population-based study. *Social Science and Medicine, 61*, 697–708.

Hope, S., Power, C., & Rodgers, B. (1999). Does financial hardship account for the elevated psychological distress in lone mothers? *Social Science and Medicine, 29*, 381–389.

Horowitz, A. (1985). Sons and daughters as caregivers to older parents: Differences in role performance and consequences. *Gerontologist, 25*, 612–617.

Horowitz, A. V., White H. R., & Howell-White, S. (1996). Becoming married and mental health. *Journal of Marriage and Family, 58*, 895–907.

Horowitz, M., Krupknick, J., Kaltreider, N., Wilner, N., Leong, A., & Marmar, R. C. (1981). Initial psychological response to parental death. *Archives of General Psychiatry, 38*, 316–323.

Hoyert, D. L., & Seltzer, M. M. (1992). Factors related to the well-being and life activities of family caregivers. *Family Relations, 41*, 74–81.

Ihinger-Tallman, M. (1988). Research on stepfamilies. *Annual Review of Sociology, 14*, 25–48.

Ingersoll-Dayton, B., Starrels, M., & Dowler, D. (1996). Caregiving for parents and parents-in-law: Is gender important? *Gerontologist, 36*, 483–491.

Jackson, P. B. (1997). Role occupancy and minority mental health. *Journal of Health and Social Behavior, 38*, 237–255.

Jahoda, M. (1958) *Current concepts of positive mental health*. New York: Basic Books.

Jeffries, S., & Konnert, C. (2002). Regret and psychological well-being among voluntarily and involuntarily childless women and mothers. *International Journal of Aging and Human Development, 54*, 89–106.

Jendrek, M. P. (1993). Grandparents who parent their grandchildren: Effects on lifestyle. *Journal of Marriage and the Family, 55*, 609–621.

Johnson, D. R., & Wu, J. (2002). An empirical test of crisis, social selection, and role explanations of the relationship between marital disruption and psychological distress: A pooled time-series analysis of four-wave panel data. *Journal of Marriage and Family, 64*, 211–224.

Jung, C. G. (1933). *Modern man in search of a soul* (W. S. Dell & C. F. Baynes, Trans.). New York: Harcourt, Brace, & World.

Kahn, R. L., & Antonucci, T. C. (1980). Convoys over the life course: Attachment, roles and social support. In P. B. Baltes & O. G. Brim, Jr. (Eds.), *Life-span development and behavior* (Vol. 3, pp. 254–283). Boston: Lexington.

Kahneman, D., Diener, E., & Schwartz, N. (Eds.) (1999). *Well-being: The foundations of hedonic psychology*. New York: Russell Sage.

Kelley, S. J. (1993). Caregiver stress in grandparents raising grandchildren. *Image: Journal of Nursing Scholarship, 25*, 331–337.

Keyes, C. L. M., & Ryff, C. D. (1998). Generativity in adult lives: Social structural contours and quality of life consequences. In D. P. McAdams & E. de St. Aubin (Eds.), *Generativity and adult development: How and why we care for the next generation* (pp. 227–263). Washington, DC: American Psychological Association.

Keyes, C. L. M., Shmotkin, D., & Ryff, C. D. (2002). Optimizing well-being: The empirical encounter of two traditions. *Journal of Personality and Social Psychology, 82*, 1007–1022.

Kim, G., & Youn, G. (2002). The role of education in generativity differences of employed and unemployed women in Korea. *Psychological Reports, 91*, 1205–1211.

Kim, H. K., & McKenry, P. C. (2002). The relationship between marriage and psychological well-being. *Journal of Family Issues, 23*, 885–911.

Kitson, G. C. (1992). *Portrait of divorce: Adjustment to marital breakdown*. New York: Guilford.

Kolomer, S. R., & McCallion, P. (2005). Depression and caregiver mastery in grandfathers caring for their grandchildren. *International Journal of Aging and Human Development, 60*, 283–294.

Kotre, J. (1984). *Outliving the self: Generativity and the interpretation of lives*. Baltimore: Johns Hopkins University Press.

Kramer, B. J. (1993). Marital history and the prior relationship as predictors of positive and negative outcomes among wife caregivers. *Family Relations, 42*, 367–375.

Kramer, B. J. (1997). Gain in the caregiving experience: Where are we? What next? *Gerontologist, 37*, 218–232.

Kramer, B. J., & Lambert, J. D. (1999). Caregiving as a life course transition among older husbands: A prospective study. *Gerontologist, 38*, 658–667.

Kramer, B. J., & Thompson, E. H., Jr. (2002). *Men as caregivers: Theory, research, and service implications*. New York: Springer.

Kurdek, L. A. (1991). The relations between reported well-being and divorce history, availability of a proximate adults, and gender. *Journal of Marriage and the Family, 53*, 71–78.

Kurdek, L. A. (1998). The nature and predictors of the trajectory of change in marital quality over the first four years of marriage for first-married husbands and wives. *Journal of Family Psychology, 12*, 494–510.

Kurdek, L. A. (2004). Are gay and lesbian cohabiting couples really different from heterosexual married couples? *Journal of Marriage and Family, 66*, 880–900.

LaRossa, R., & Reitzes, D. C. (1993). Symbolic interactionism and family studies. In P. G. Boss, W. J. Doherty, R. LaRossa, W. R. Schumm, & S. K. Steinmetz (Eds.), *Sourcebook of family theories and methods: A contextual approach* (pp. 135–163). New York: Plenum.

Lawton, M. P., Moss, M., Hoffman, C., & Perkinson, M. (2000). Two transitions in daughters' caregiving careers. *Gerontologist, 40*, 437–448.

Lawton, M. P., Rajagopal, D., Brody, E., & Kleban, M. (1992). The dynamics of caregiving for a demented elder among black and white families. *Journal of Gerontology: Social Sciences, 47*, S156–S164.

Lee, G., Seccombe, K., & Shehan, C. (1991). Marital status and personal happiness: An analysis of trend data. *Journal of Marriage and the Family, 53*, 839–844.

Letherby, G. (2002). Childless and bereft? Stereotypes and realities in relation to 'voluntary' and 'involuntary' childlessness and womanhood. *Sociological Inquiry, 72*, 7–20.

Li, L. W., Seltzer, M. M., & Greenberg, J. S. (1999). Change in depressive symptoms among daughter caregivers: An 18-month study. *Psychology and Aging, 14*, 208–219.

Lorenz, F. O., Simons, R. L., Conger, R. D., Elder, G. H., Jr., Johnson, C., & Chao, W. (1997). Married and recently divorced mothers' stressful events and distress: Tracing change across time. *Journal of Marriage and Family, 59*, 219–232.

Leuscher, K., & Pillemer, K. (1998). Intergenerational ambivalence: A new approach to the study of parent-child relations in later life. *Journal of Marriage and the Family, 60*, 413–425.

Marcussen, K. (2005). Explaining differences in mental health between married and cohabiting individuals. *Social Psychology Quarterly, 68*, 239–257.

Marks, N. F. (1995). Midlife marital status differences in social support relationships with adult children and psychological well-being. *Journal of Family Issues, 16*, 5–28.

Marks, N. F. (1996a). Flying solo at midlife: Gender, marital status, and psychological well-being. *Journal of Marriage and the Family, 58*, 917–932.

Marks, N. F. (1996b). Caregiving across the lifespan: National prevalence and predictors. *Family Relations, 45*, 27–36.

Marks, N. F. (1996c). Social demographic diversity among American midlife parents. In C. D. Ryff & M. M. Seltzer (Ed.), *When children grow up: Development and diversity in midlife parenting* (pp. 29–75). Chicago: University of Chicago Press.

Marks, N. F. (1998). Does it hurt to care? Caregiving, work-family conflict, and midlife well-being. *Journal of Marriage and the Family, 60*, 951–966.

Marks, N. F., Bumpass, L. L. & Jun, H. (2004). Family roles and well-being during the middle life course. In O. G. Brim, C. D. Ryff, & R. Kessler (Eds.), *How healthy are we? A national study of well-being at midlife* (pp. 514–549). Chicago: University of Chicago Press.

Marks, N. F., Jun, H., & Song, J. (2007). Death of parents and adult psychological and physical health: Prospective evidence from a U.S. national study. *Journal of Family Issues, 28*, 1611–1628.

Marks, N. F., & Lambert, J. D. (1998). Marital status continuity and change among young and midlife adults: Longitudinal effects on psychological well-being. *Journal of Family Issues, 19,* 652–686.

Marks, N. F., Lambert, J. D., & Choi, H. (2002). Transitions to caregiving, gender, and psychological well-being: Prospective evidence from the National Survey of Families and Households. *Journal of Marriage and Family, 64,* 657–667.

Mash, E. J., & Johnson, C. (1983). Parental perception of child behavior problems, parenting self-esteem, and mothers' reported stress in younger and older hyperactive and normal children. *Journal of Consulting and Clinical Psychology, 51,* 86–99.

Maslow, A. H. (1968). *Toward a psychology of being* (2nd ed.). New York: Van Nostrand.

Mastekaasa, A. (1992). Marriage and psychological well-being: Some evidence on selection into marriage. *Journal of Marriage and the Family 54,* 901–911.

Mastekaasa, A. (1994). Marital status, distress, and well-being: An international comparison. *Journal of Comparative Family Studies, 25,* 183–205.

Mastekaasa, A. (1995). Marital dissolution and subjective distress: Panel evidence. *European Sociological Review, 11,* 173–185.

McAdams, D. P. (1985). *Power, intimacy, and the life story: Personological inquiries into identity.* Homewood, IL: Dorsey Press.

McAdams, D. P. (2001). Generativity in midlife. In M. Lachman (Ed.), *Handbook of midlife development* (pp. 395–443). New York: Wiley.

McAdams, D. P., (2006). *The redemptive self.* Oxford, UK: Oxford University Press.

McAdams, D. P., & de St. Aubin, E. (1992). A theory of generativity and its assessment through self-report, behavioral acts, and narrative themes in autobiography. *Journal of Personality and Social Psychology, 62,* 1003–1015.

McAdams, D. P., de St. Aubin, E., & Logan, R. L. (1993). Generativity among young, midlife, and older adults. *Psychology and Aging, 8,* 221–230.

McAdams, D. P., Hart, H. M., & Maruna, S. (1998). The anatomy of generativity. In D. P. McAdams, & E. de St. Aubin (Eds.), *Generativity and adult development: Psychosocial perspectives on caring for and contributing to the next generation* (pp. 7–43). Washington, DC: American Psychological Association.

McHorney, C. A., & Mor, V. (1988). Predictors of bereavement depression and its health services consequences. *Medical Care, 26,* 882–893.

McKeering, H., & Pakenham, K. I. (2000). Gender and generativity issues in parenting: Do fathers benefit more than mothers from involvement in child care activities? *Sex Roles, 43,* 459–480.

McLanahan, S. S., & Adams, J. (1987). Parenthood and psychological well-being. *Annual Review of Sociology, 5,* 237–258.

McLanahan, S. S., & Adams, J. (1989). The effects of children on adults' psychological well-being: 1957–1976. *Social Forces, 68,* 124–146.

Menaghan, E. G., & Lieberman, M. A. (1986). Changes in depression following divorce: A panel study. *Journal of Marriage and the Family, 48,* 319–328.

Menaghan, E. G. (1989a). Role changes and psychological well-being: Variations in effects by gender and role repertoire. *Social Forces, 67,* 693–714.

Menaghan, E. G. (1989b). Psychological well-being among parents and nonparents: The importance of normative expectedness. *Journal of Family Issues, 10,* 547–565.

Milardo, R. M. (2005). Generative uncle and nephew relationships. *Journal of Marriage and Family, 67,* 1226–1236.

Milevsky, A. (2005). Compensatory patterns of sibling support in emerging adulthood: Variations in loneliness, self-esteem, depression, and life satisfaction. *Journal of Social and Personal Relationships, 22,* 743–755.

Minkler, M., Fuller-Thomson, E., Miller, D. & Driver, D. (1997). Depression in grandparents raising grandchildren: Results of a national longitudinal study. *Archives of Family Medicine, 6,* 445–452.

Minkler, M., & Roe, K. M. (1993). *Grandmothers as caregivers.* Newbury Park, CA: Sage.

Minkler, M., Roe, K. M., & Price, M. (1992). The physical and emotional health of grandmothers raising grandchildren in the crack cocaine epidemic. *Gerontologist, 32*, 752–760.

Mirowsky, J., & Ross, C. E., (1989). *The social causes of psychological distress.* New York: Aldine de Gruyter.

Moss, M. S., Moss, S. Z., Rubinstein, R., & Resch, N. (1993). Impact of elderly mother's death on middle age daughters. *International Journal of Aging and Human Development, 37*, 1–22.

Moss, M. S., Resch, N., & Moss, S. Z. (1997). The role of gender in middle-age children's responses to parent death. *Omega, 35*, 43–65.

Mui, A. C., & Morrow-Howell, N. (1993). Sources of emotional strain among the oldest caregivers: Differential experiences of siblings and spouses. *Research on Aging, 15*, 50–69.

Mutran, E., & Reitzes, D. C. (1984). Intergenerational support activities and well-being among the elderly: A convergence of exchange and symbolic interaction perspectives. *American Sociological Review, 49*, 117–130.

Neal, M., Chapman, N., Ingersoll-Dayton, B., & Emlen, A. (1993). *Balancing work and caregiving for children, adults and elders.* Newbury Park, CA: Sage.

Neugarten, B. L. (1968). The awareness of middle age. In B. L. Neugarten (Ed.), *Middle age and aging* (pp. 93–98). Chicago: University of Chicago Press.

O'Connor, T. G., Cheng, H., Dunn, J., & Golding J. (2005). Factors moderating change in depressive symptoms in women following separation: Findings from a community study in England. *Psychological Medicine, 35*, 715–724.

Oropesa, R. S., & Landale, N. S. (2004). The future of marriage and Hispanics. *Journal of Marriage and Family, 66*, 901–920.

Ory, M. G., Hoffman, R. R., III, Yee, J. L., Tennstedt, S., & Schulz, R. (1999). Prevalence and impact of caregiving: A detailed comparison between dementia and nondementia caregivers. *Gerontologist, 39*, 177–185.

Parsons, T. (1943). The kinship system of the contemporary United States. *American Anthropologist, 45*, 22–38.

Palkovitz, R., Copes, M. A., & Woolfok, T. N. (2001). "It's like...you discover a new sense of being": Involved fathering as an evoker of adult development. *Men and Masculinities, 4*, 49–69.

Pearlin, L. I., & Aneshensel, C. S. (1994). Caregiving: The unexpected career. *Social Justice Research, 7*, 373–390.

Pearlin, L. I., & Johnson, J. S. (1977). Marital status, life-strains, and depression. *American Sociological Review, 42*, 704–715.

Peters, A., & Liefbroer, A. C. (1997). Beyond marital status: Partner history and well-being in old age. *Journal of Marriage and the Family, 59*, 687–699.

Peters-Davis, N. D., Moss, M. S., & Pruchno, R. A. (1999). Children-in-law in caregiving families. *Gerontologist, 39*, 66–75.

Peterson, B. E. (2002). Longitudinal analysis of midlife generativity, intergenerational roles, and caregiving. *Psychology and Aging, 17*, 161–168.

Peterson, B. E., & Klohnen, E. C. (1995). Realization of generativity in two samples of women at midlife. *Psychology and Aging, 10*, 20–29.

Peterson, B. E., & Stewart, A. J. (1990). Using personal and fictional documents to assess psychosocial development: A case study of Vera Brittain's generativity. *Psychology and Aging, 5*, 400–411.

Pillemer, K., & Suitor, J. J. (1991). "Will I ever escape my child's problems?" Effects of adult children's problems on elderly parents. *Journal of Marriage and the Family, 53*, 585–594.

Pinquart, M., & Sorensen, S. (2003). Differences between caregivers and noncaregivers in psychological health and physical health: A meta-analysis. *Psychology of Aging, 18*, 250–267.

Pleck, J. H. (1993). Are "family supportive" employer policies relevant to men? In J. C. Hood (Ed.), *Men, work, and family* (pp. 217–237). Newbury Park, CA: Sage.

Popenoe, D. (1993). American family decline, 1960–1990: A review and appraisal. *Journal of Marriage and the Family, 55*, 527–555.

Pruchno, R., & McKenney, D. (2002). Psychological well-being of Black and White grandmothers raising grandchildren: Examination of a two-factor model. *Journal of Gerontology: Psychological Sciences, 57*, P444–P452.

Radloff, L. S. (1975). Sex differences in depression: The effects of occupation and marital status. *Sex Roles: A Journal of Research, 1*, 249–265.

Radloff, L. S. (1977). The CES-D scale: A self-report depression scale for research in the general population. *Applied Psychological Measurement, 1*, 385–401.

Ramey, S. L., Krauss, M. W., & Simeonsson, R. J. (1989). Research on families: Current assessment and future opportunities. *American Journal on Mental Retardation, 94*, ii–vi.

Reitzes, D. C., & Mutran, E. J. (2004). Grandparent identity, intergenerational family identity, and well-being. *Journal of Gerontology: Social Sciences, 59*, S213–S219.

Richards, M., Hardy, R., & Wadsworth, M. (1997). The effects of divorce and separation on mental health in a national UK birth cohort. *Psychological Medicine, 27*, 1121–1128.

Riessmann, C. K. (1990). *Divorce talk: Women and men make sense of personal relationships.* New Brunswick, NJ: Rutgers University Press.

Riggio, H. R. (2000). Measuring attitudes toward adult sibling relationships: The Lifespan Sibling Relationship Scale. *Journal of Social and Personal Relationships, 17*, 707–728.

Robins, L. N., & Regier, D. A. (1991). *Psychiatric disorders in America: The Epidemiologic Catchment Area Study.* Free Press: New York.

Rogers, C. R. (1961). *On becoming a person: A therapist's view of psychotherapy.* Boston: Houghton Mifflin.

Rook, K. S. (1984). The negative side of social interaction: Impact on psychological well-being. *Journal of Personality and Social Psychology, 46*, 1097–1108.

Ross, C. E. (1995). Reconceptualizing marital status as a continuum of social attachment. *Journal of Marriage and the Family, 57*, 129–140.

Ross, C. E., & Mirowsky, J. (1988). Child care and emotional adjustment to wives' employment. *Journal of Health and Social Behavior, 29*, 127–138.

Ross, L. E. (2005). Perinatal mental health in lesbian mothers: A review of potential risk and protective factors. *Women and Health, 41*, 113–128.

Rossi, A. S., & Rossi, P. H. (1990). *Of human bonding: Parent-child relations across the life course.* New York: Aldine de Gruyter.

Rubinstein, R. L. (1996). Childlessness, legacy, and generativity. *Generations, 20*, 58–60.

Ryan, R. M., & Deci, E. L. (2001). On happiness and human potentials: A review of research on hedonic and eudaimonic well-being. *Annual Review of Psychology, 53*, 141–166.

Ryder, N. B. (1965). The cohort as a concept in the study of social change. *American Sociological Review, 30*, 843–861.

Ryff, C. D. (1989). Happiness is everything, or is it? *Journal of Personality and Social Psychology, 6*, 1069–1081.

Ryff, C. D., & Keyes, C. L. M. (1995). The structure of psychological well-being revisited. *Journal of Personality and Social Psychology, 69*, 719–727.

Ryff, C. D., Lee, Y.H., Essex, M. J., & Schmutte, P. S. (1994). My children and me: Midlife evaluations of grown children and self. *Psychology and Aging, 9*, 195–205.

Sanders, C. M. (1979–80). A comparison of adult bereavement in the death of a spouse, child, and parent. *Omega, 10*, 303–322.

Savolainen, J., Lahehna, E., Silventionen, K., & Gauthier, A. H. (2001). Parenthood and psychological well-being in Finland: Does public policy make a difference? *Journal of Comparative Family Studies, 32*, 61–70.

Scharlach, A. E. (1991). Factors associated with filial grief following the death of an elderly parent. *American Journal of Orthopsychiatry, 61*, 307–313.

Schulz, R., O'Brien, A. T., Bookwala, J., & Fleissner, K. (1995). Psychiatric and physical morbidity effects of dementia caregiving: Prevalence, correlates, and causes. *Gerontologist, 35*, 771–791.

Schulz, R., Visitainer, P., & Williamson, G. M. (1990). Psychiatric and physical morbidity effects of caregiving. *Journal of Gerontology: Psychological Sciences, 45*, 181–191.

Schulz, R., & Williamson, G. M. (1991). A two-year longitudinal study of depression in Alzheimer's caregivers. *Psychology and Aging, 6*, 569–579.

Seltzer, J. A. (2004). Cohabitation in the United States and Britain: Demography, kinship, and the future. *Journal of Marriage and Family, 66,* 921–928.

Seltzer, M. M., & Greenberg, J. S. (2001). Life course impacts of parenting a child with a disability. *American Journal on Mental Retardation, 106,* 265–286.

Seltzer, M. M., Greenberg, J. S., Krauss, M. W., Gordon, R., & Judge, K. (1997). Siblings of adults with mental retardation or mental illness: Effects on lifestyle and psychological well-being. *Family Relations, 46,* 395–405.

Seltzer, M. M., & Krauss, M. W. (1989). Aging parents with mentally retarded children: Family risk factors and sources of support. *American Journal on Mental Retardation, 94,* 303–312.

Seltzer, M. M., Krauss, M. W., Choi, S. C., & Hong, J. (1996). Midlife and later-life parenting of adult children with mental retardation. In C. D. Ryff & M. M. Seltzer (Eds.), *The parental experience in midlife* (pp. 459–489). Chicago: University of Chicago Press.

Seltzer, M. M., & Li, L. W. (1996). The transitions of caregiving: Subjective and objective definitions. *Gerontologist, 36,* 614–626.

Seltzer, M. M., & Li, L. W. (2000). The dynamics of caregiving: Transitions during a 3-year prospective study. *Gerontologist, 40,* 165–178.

Settersten, R. A., Jr. (2003). Propositions and controversies in life-course scholarship. In R.A. Settersten (Ed.), *Invitation to the life course: Toward new understandings of later life* (pp. 15–45). Amityville, NY: Baywood..

Shanas, E., Townsend, P., Wedderburn, D., Fris, H., Milhof, P., & Stehouwer, J. (1968). *Old people in three industrial societies.* New York: Atherton.

Shapiro, A. D. (1996). Explaining psychological distress in a sample of remarried and divorced persons: The influence of economic distress. *Journal of Family Issues, 17,* 186–203.

Shore, R. J., & Hayslip, B., Jr. (1994). Custodial parenting: Implications for children's development. In A. E. Gottfried & A. W. Gottfried (Eds.), *Redefining families: Implications for children's development* (pp. 171–218). New York: Plenum.

Silverberg, S. B. (1996). Parents' well-being at their children's transition to adolescence. In C. D. Ryff & M. M. Seltzer (Eds.), *The parental experience in midlife* (pp. 215–254). Chicago: University of Chicago Press.

Simmons, T., & Dye, J. L. (2003). *Grandparents living with grandchildren: 2000.* (Census 2000 Brief Report C2KBR-31). Washington, DC: U.S. Census Bureau.

Simon, R. W. (1992). Parental role strains, salience of parental identity, and gender differences in psychological distress. *Journal of Health and Social Behavior, 33,* 25–35.

Simon, R. W. (1998). Assessing sex differences in vulnerability among employed parents: The importance of marital status. *Journal of Health and Social Behavior, 39,* 38–54.

Simon, R. W. (2002). Revisiting the relationships among gender, marital status, and mental health. *American Journal of Sociology, 107,* 1065–1096.

Simon, R. W., & Marcussen, K. (1999). Marital transitions, marital beliefs, and mental health. *Journal of Health and Social Behavior, 40,* 111–125.

Snarey, J. (1993). *How fathers care for the next generation.* Cambridge, MA: Harvard University Press.

Snarey, J., Son, L., Kuchne, V. S., Hauser, S., & Vaillant, G. (1987). The role of parenting in men's psychosocial development: A longitudinal study of early adulthood infertility and midlife generativity. *Developmental Psychology, 23,* 593–603.

Spitze, G., & Logan, J. (1992). Helping as a component of parent-adult child relations. *Research on Aging, 14,* 291–312.

Spitze, G., Logan, J. R., Joseph, G., & Lee, E. (1994). Middle generation roles and the well-being of men and women. *Journal of Gerontology: Social Sciences, 49,* S107–S116.

Stacey, J. (1990). *Brave new families: Stories of domestic upheaval in late 20th century America.* New York: Basic Books.

Stack, S., & Eshleman, J. R. (1998). Marital status and happiness: A 17-nation study. *Journal of Marriage and the Family, 60,* 527–536.

Stephens, M. A. P., & Townsend, A. L. (1997). Stress of parent care: Positive and negative effects on women's other roles. *Psychology and Aging, 12,* 376–386.

Stewart, A. J., & Vandewater, E. A. (1998). The course of generativity. In D. P. McAdams & E. de St. Aubin (Eds.), *Generativity and adult development: Psychosocial perspectives on caring for and contributing to the next generation* (pp. 75–100). Washington, DC: American Psychological Association Press.

Stocker, C. M., Lanthier, R. P., & Furman, W. (1997). Sibling relationships in early adulthood. *Journal of Family Psychology, 11,* 210–221.

Stoller, E. P. (1985). Exchange patterns in the informal support networks of the elderly: The impact of reciprocity on morale. *Journal of Marriage and the Family, 47,* 335–342.

Stone, R., Cafferata, G. L., & Sangl, J. (1987). Caregivers of the frail elderly: A national profile. *Gerontologist, 27,* 616–626.

Strawbridge, W. J., Wallhagen, M. I., Shema, S. J., & Kaplan, G. A. (1997). New burdens or more of the same: Comparing grandparent, spouse, and adult-child caregivers. *Gerontologist, 37,* 505–510.

Stroebe, W., & Stroebe, M. (1987). *Bereavement and health.* New York: Cambridge University Press.

Strohschein, L., McDonough, P., Monette, G., & Shao, Q. (2005). Marital transitions and mental health: Are there gender differences in the short-term effects of marital status change? *Social Science and Medicine, 61,* 2293–2303.

Stryker, S. (1980). *Symbolic interactionism: A social structural version.* Menlo Park, CA: Benjamin Cummings.

Stryker, S. (2001). Traditional symbolic interactionism, role theory, and structural symbolic interactionism: The road to identity theory. In J. H. Turner (Ed.), *Handbook of sociological theory* (pp. 211–231). New York: Kluwer.

Stryker, S., & Statham, A. (1985). Symbolic interaction and role theory. In G. Lindzey & E. Aronson (Eds.), *The handbook of social psychology: Vol. I. Theory and method* (3rd ed., pp. 311–378). New York: Random House.

Szinovacz, M. E., & Davey, A. (2006). Effects of retirement and grandchild care on depressive symptoms. *International Journal of Aging and Human Development, 62,* 1–20.

Szinovacz, M. E., DeViney, S., & Atkinson, M. P., (1999). Effects of surrogate parenting on grandparents' well-being. *Journal of Gerontology: Social Sciences, 54,* S376–S388.

Thoits, P. A. (1983). Multiple identities and psychological well-being: A reformulation of the social isolation hypothesis. *American Sociological Review, 48,* 174–187.

Thoits, P. A. (1991). On merging identity theory and stress research. *Social Psychology Quarterly, 54,* 101–112.

Thoits, P. A. (1992). Identity structures and psychological well-being: Gender and marital status comparisons. *Social Psychology Quarterly, 55,* 236–256.

Thomas, E. J., & Biddle, B. J. (1966). The nature and history of role theory. In E. J. Thomas & B. J. Biddle (Eds.), *Role theory: Concepts and research.* New York: Wiley.

Turner, R. H. (1978). The role and the person. *The American Journal of Psychiatry, 84, 1–23.*

Turner, M. J., Killian, T S., & Cain, R. (2004). Life course transitions and depressive symptoms among women in midlife. *International Journal of Aging and Human Development, 58,* 241–265.

Turvey, C. L., Carney, C., Arndt, S., Wallace, R. B., & Herzog, R. (1999). Conjugal loss and syndromal depression in a sample of elders aged 70 years or older. *American Journal of Psychiatry, 156,* 1596–1601.

Umberson, D. (1992). Relationships between adult children and their parents: Psychological consequences for both generations. *Journal of Marriage and the Family, 54,* 664–674.

Umberson, D. (1995). Marriage as support or strain? Marital quality following the death of a parent. *Journal of Marriage and the Family, 57, 709–723.*

Umberson, D. (2003). *Death of a parent: Transition to a new adult identity.* Cambridge, UK: Cambridge University Press.

Umberson, D., & Chen, M. D. (1994). Effects of a parent's death on adult children: Relationship salience and reaction to loss. *American Sociological Review, 59,* 152–168.

Umberson, D., & Gove, W. (1989). Parenthood and psychological well-being: Theory, measurement, and stage in the family life course. *Journal of Family Issues, 10,* 440–462.

Umberson, D., & Williams, C. L. (1993). Divorced fathers: Parental role strain and psychological distress. *Journal of Family Issues, 14*, 378–400.

Vaillant, G. E., & Milofsky, E. (1980). Natural history of male psychological health IX: Empirical evidence for Erikson's model of the life cycle. *American Journal of Psychiatry, 137*, 1348–1359.

Vega, W. A., Kolody, B., & Valle, R. (1988). Marital strain, coping, and depression among Mexican-American women. *Journal of Marriage and the Family, 50*, 391–403.

Ventura, S. J., & Bachrach, C. A. (2000). *Nonmarital childbearing in the United States, 1940–1999* (National Vital Statistics Reports, Vol. 48, No. 16). Washington, DC: National Center for Health Statistics.

Wade, T. J., & Pevalin, D. J. (2004). Marital transitions and mental health. *Journal of Health and Social Behavior, 45*, 155–170.

Waite, L. J. (1995). Does marriage matter? *Demography, 32*, 483–507.

Waite, L. J. (2000). Trends in men's and women's well-being in marriage. In L. J. Waite (Ed.), *The ties that bind: Perspectives on marriage and cohabitation* (pp. 368–392). Hawthorne, NY: Aldine de Gruyter.

Waite, L. J., & Gallagher, M. (2000). *The case for marriage*. New York: Doubleday.

Waterman, A. S. (1993). Two conceptions of happiness: Contrasts of personal expressiveness (eudaimonic) and hedonic enjoyment. *Journal of Personality and Social Psychology, 64*, 678–691.

Watkins, S. C., Mencken, J. A., & Bongaarts, J. (1987). Demographic foundations of family change. *American Sociological Review, 50*, 689–698.

Weingarten, H. R. (1985). Marital status and well-being: A national study comparing first-married, currently divorced, and remarried adults. *Journal of Marriage and the Family, 47*, 653–662.

Westermeyer, J. F. (2004). Predictors and characteristics of Erikson's life cycle among men: A 32-year longitudinal study. *International Journal of Aging and Human Development, 58*, 29–48.

Wheaton, B. (1990). Life transitions, role histories, and mental health. *American Sociological Review, 55*, 209–223.

Whisman, M. A. (2001). The association between depression and marital satisfaction. In S. R. H. Beach (Ed.), *Marital and family process in depression: A scientific foundation for clinical practice* (pp. 3–24). Washington, DC: American Psychological Association.

Whisman, M. A., & Bruce, M. L. (1999). Marital dissatisfaction and incidence of major depressive episode in a community sample. *Journal of Abnormal Psychology, 108*, 674–678.

White, J. M. (1992). Marital status and well-being in Canada. *Journal of Family Issues, 13*, 390–409.

White, L. K., & Booth, A. (1985). The quality and stability of remarriages: The role of stepchildren. *American Sociological Review, 50*, 689–698.

Wilcox, S., Evenson, K. R., Aragaki. A., Wassertheil-Smoller, S., Mouton, C. P., & Loevinger, B. L. (2003). The effects of widowhood on physical and mental health, health behaviors, and health outcomes: The Women's Health Initiative. *Health Psychology, 22*, 513–522.

Williams, K. (2003). Has the future of marriage arrived? A contemporary examination of gender, marriage, and psychological well-being. *Journal of Health and Social Behavior, 44*, 470–487.

Willitts, M., Benzevel, M., & Stansfeld, S. (2004). Partnership history and mental health over time. *Journal of Epidemiology and Community Health, 58*, 53–58.

Wortman, C. B., Silver, R. C., & Kessler, R. C. (1993). The meaning of loss and adjustment to bereavement. In M. S. Stroebe, W. Stroebe, & R. O. Hansson (Eds.), *Handbook of bereavement* (pp. 349–366). Cambridge, UK: Cambridge University Press.

Young, R. F., & Kahana, E. (1989) Specifying caregiver outcomes: Gender and relationship aspects of caregiver strain. *Gerontologist, 29*, 660–666.

Zhang, Z., & Hayward, M. D. (2001). Childlessness and the psychological well-being of older persons. *Journal of Gerontology: Social Sciences, 56*, S311–S320.

Chapter 12

The Close Relationships of Sexual Minorities
Partners, Friends, and Family

Lisa M. Diamond and Molly Butterworth

One of the most notable developments in psychological research on adult relationships over the past 20 years has been the explosion of inquiry into the romantic, peer, and family ties of lesbian, gay, and bisexual (collectively denoted *sexual-minority*) individuals. After decades of invisibility, the unique interpersonal challenges facing this population have finally received systematic attention. This has vastly improved not only our basic understanding of the sexual-minority life course, but has contributed to research on adult development more generally, by highlighting how issues of diversity and social context bear on normative life experiences and trajectories.

This also represents an advance with respect to our specific understanding of sexual minorities. The first wave of substantive psychological research on this population in the mid-1980s tended to focus disproportionately on their most salient and distinctive experiences, such as coming out as lesbian-gay-bisexual (to themselves and to other people) and coping with stigma and discrimination. Yet as the years went by, researchers began to turn their attention to other aspects of sexual-minority individuals' daily lives, seeking to understand how a "master status" variable such as sexual identity affected multiple domains of adult life, from general adjustment to career planning and development to the aging process. The present chapter provides an overview of what we currently know about the interpersonal fabric of sexual-minority individuals' adult lives. We focus on four major areas: romantic relationships, friendships, relationships with families-of-origin, and parenting.

Importantly, despite the ongoing expansion of research into these topics, this field as a whole remains relatively underdeveloped compared to similar programs of inquiry into the relationships of heterosexual individuals. This is, perhaps, to be expected, given the late start of research on sexual minorities. Hence, in this chapter we will review what is known, but in many cases we will be limited to scant prior research, and will simply identify some of the most promising avenues for additional investigation. We firmly believe that inquiries into these areas will not only advance our understanding of sexual minorities, but adult relationship processes more generally. Given that the structure of the American family has undergone drastic changes over the past 50 years, involving increases in alternative family forms such as stepfamilies, blended families, single parent households, etc., it is of considerable importance to understand how exactly individuals go about breaking from traditions and crafting new ways of understanding intimacy, support, and interdependence with a variety of different individuals, both kin and otherwise. Examining the choices and experiences of sexual minorities provides a fascinating and pertinent model for how these accommodations are made and maintained.

Background: What is the Population Under Study?

Before launching into a review of the research, some basic foundational issues deserve attention. First, what exactly does it mean to talk about the relationship experiences of "sexual minorities?" Why not simply refer to lesbian, gay, homosexual, or bisexual individuals?

Sexual-minority refers to any individual with same-sex attractions or relationships, since these attractions and relationships automatically render him/her a minority with respect to conventional heterosexual norms. The reason for using this term is that not all individuals with same-sex attractions and/or relationships consider themselves lesbian, gay, or bisexual. In fact, a representative survey of Americans found that the number of individuals with same-sex attractions or relationships who do *not* identify as lesbian-gay-bisexual is more than double the number of individuals who *do* identify (Laumann, Gagnon, Michael, & Michaels, 1994). Notably, this survey also found that individuals with bisexual attractions outnumber individuals who are exclusively attracted to the same sex (Laumann et al., 1994), contradicting widespread beliefs that bisexuality is rare or nonexistent.

Yet the majority of research on sexual minorities focuses on openly-identified gay and lesbian individuals, reflecting the fact that research participants are typically recruited by advertising within the lesbian-gay community, and that bisexual individuals have not only been overlooked, but often systematically deleted from research samples (Rust, 2000). Hence, the unfortunate reality is that practically everything psychologists currently know about the sexual-minority life course is based upon a small and relatively unrepresentative subset of the total sexual-minority population. This is not to say that the findings are invalid, but only to indicate that much more research is needed, among much more diverse subsets of sexual minorities, before the findings can be reliably generalized.

What Makes Sexual Minorities Distinct?

Such sampling issues raise a broader question that merits attention: Exactly *why* are the lives of sexual minorities distinctive to begin with? After all, there has certainly been plenty of psychological research conducted over the past 20 years demonstrating that sexual minorities are similar to heterosexuals on most domains of psychological and social functioning, directly contrary to historical notions of homosexuality as a form of psychopathology (reviewed in Kitzinger, 1987). The one salient difference, of course, is that sexual minorities desire and participate in same-sex intimate relationships. Yet determining exactly how this one fact shapes the experiences and developmental trajectories of diverse sexual-minority individuals across contexts is no easy matter. Most generally, it is presumed to expose individuals to "minority stress," defined as the unique strain experienced as a direct result of occupying a socially marginalized category. Minority stress has been advanced as an explanation for the fact that although same-sex sexuality itself is not a mental disorder, sexual minorities do, in fact, have higher rates of anxiety and mood disorders, and these problems are greater among subsets of sexual minorities who report greater prejudice and stigmatization (Meyer, 2003).

Notably, although attitudes toward same-sex sexuality have grown more tolerant in recent years (reviewed in Loftus, 2001), and although the visibility of lesbian-gay-bisexual individuals in mass media and popular culture has surged (Walters, 2001), considerable stigma and intolerance remain pervasive, especially for sexual-minority individuals who do not live in large urban centers with large and visible lesbian-gay-bisexual populations (Lynch, 1992). One large survey found that among a random sample of American lesbian-gay-bisexual adults, three fourths had experienced some form of prejudice or discrimination as a result of their sexuality, and about one third had actually suffered violence against them or their property (Kaiser Foundation, 2001). Most troubling, approximately one third of gay men and one half of lesbians have reported that a friend or family member refused to accept them because of their sexual orientation.

Recent data also indicate a troubling backlash against the recent trend toward greater acceptance of same-sex sexuality, which was particularly evident after the 2003 Supreme Court ruling overturning laws against consensual same-sex relations (Page, 2003). For example, half of American adults oppose legal recognition for same-sex marriages, and believe that such recognition would actually threaten the traditional American family (Kaiser Foundation, 2001). Reflecting this view, in 1996 Congress passed the Defense of Marriage Act, allowing it to override any state legal recognition of same-sex marriage. Opposition to same-sex marriage has become downright mainstream, endorsed by all major candidates for president in the 2000, 2004, and 2008 elections (although some candidates support non-marriage alternatives, such as civil unions or domestic partnerships). Six months after Massachusetts began issuing marriage licenses to same-sex couples in November 2004, 11 states passed ballot measures denying any formal recognition of same-sex marriages. That trend continued in 2006, when seven more states passed same-sex marriage bans. Currently, 45 states have either a constitutional amendment or a state law restricting marriage to one man and one woman. As for other family rights, only about 50% of American adults think that same-sex couples can do as good a job at parenting as traditional heterosexual couples, and less than 50% think that lesbian-gay-bisexual individuals should be allowed to adopt (Kaiser Foundation, 2001), a right that is denied to same-sex couples in about half of states.

The key factor to remember, when considering the influence of minority status and minority stress on sexual minorities' daily lives and relationships, is that the global climate of marginalization, stigmatization and denigration of same-sex sexuality has a diverse range of "local" effects on individual men and women in different environments, with different backgrounds, of different ages, and so on. Consequently, whereas early research on lesbian-gay-bisexual individuals focused on developing a series of universalized models to explain their unique experiences—such as stages of "coming out" (Cass, 1984; Troiden, 1979) and subsequent family adjustment (DeVine, 1984)—research has now shifted toward describing and explaining the incredible variability *within* the sexual-minority population. This is often articulated as a *differential developmental trajectories* approach (Diamond & Savin-Williams, 2002; Dubé, Savin-Williams, & Diamond, 2001; Savin-Williams, 2001a; Savin-Williams & Cohen, 2004; Savin-Williams & Diamond, 1998), which replaces the conventional emphasis on normative developmental stages with an emphasis on "variability within a single life, across multiple individual lives, and among diverse groups of individuals" (Savin-Williams, 2001a, p. 9).

This approach entails greater attention to the specific processes and mechanisms through which an individual's sexual-minority status influences his/her relationship experiences and adult development. This process-oriented focus on within-group diversity is important for guarding against the exaggeration of differences between heterosexuals and sexual minorities, and the incorrect assumption that sexual minorities belong to a monolithic "gay culture" that opposes conventional American norms. To the contrary, sexual minorities have undergone exactly the same socialization into mainstream cultural values as have heterosexuals, and espouse largely similar norms and beliefs regarding "family traditions, relational patterns, and parenting models" (Laird, 2003, pp. 186–187). Hence, most sexual minorities simultaneously occupy both heterosexual and sexual-minority cultures, communities, and social groups, and toggle between these worlds.

Even in areas of civil rights, there is no monolithic position agreed upon by the "lesbian-gay-bisexual community." Same-sex marriage provides a salient example. Although many lesbian-gay-bisexual individuals dearly want the right to marry legally, others question the political and social value of conventional marriage (Ettelbrick, 1993; Sullivan & Landau, 1997), and would prefer that the government stop regulating individuals' personal and spiritual lives altogether. Hence, global notions of lesbian-gay-bisexual culture or lesbian-gay-bisexual community are specious, and do not provide sufficient explanations for any observed differences between lesbian-gay-bisexual and heterosexual life paths and choices. Rather, researchers seeking to understand and explain distinct features of sexual-minority individuals' life trajectories must specify exactly which sorts of differences they are interested in, which subsets of sexual minorities they characterize, and how they are created and/or sustained as a function of specific social, interpersonal, or intrapsychic mechanisms. With these cautions and caveats in mind, we begin by reviewing the most widely investigated domain of sexual-minority social life: romantic relationships.

Same-Sex Romantic Relationships: Initiation, Maintenance, and Satisfaction

The publicity surrounding recent legislative battles over same-sex marriage has heightened both popular and scientific attention to the incredible importance that such relationships play in the daily lives of sexual minorities. Studies have found that between 40–60% of gay men and 50–80% of lesbians are partnered (Peplau & Spalding, 2000), and their relationships are a significant part of the American interpersonal landscape. The 2000 census found that 1 in 9 of the 5.5 million cohabiting, unmarried couples in the United States were same-sex couples (Simons & O'Connell, 2003), and the majority of lesbian-gay-bisexual individuals want to have the option of formalizing such relationships through same-sex marriage (Kaiser Foundation, 2001).

Although many psychological theories purport to explain general processes of relationship initiation, maintenance, functioning, and dissolution in adult heterosexual couples, there are currently no formalized theories that specifically explain and predict how these processes might differ in same-sex couples. To some extent, this might be because there appears to be little need for such theories: Numerous investigations directly comparing same-sex and heterosexual couples have found that most of the core dynamics (such as interdependence, power, conflict, control, and attachment) are basically the same (Kurdek, 2004; Peplau & Spalding, 2000).

Yet undoubtedly, one unique characteristic of same-sex couples which has provided a starting point for theorizing about their distinctiveness is, as noted earlier, their minority status in mainstream culture, and the attendant social and psychological challenges. Unlike conventional heterosexual couples, same-sex couples are often denigrated or denied legitimacy by families-of-origin and the culture at large (Caron & Ulin, 1997; Gillis, 1998; LaSala, 2000a; Oswald, 2002; Patterson, 2000). They also face persistent everyday stressors such as difficulty making hotel room reservations as a couple (Jones, 1996), receiving poor service and rude treatment during routine shopping when together

(Walters & Curran, 1996), and awkwardness and discomfort when attending family functions together (Caron & Ulin, 1997; Oswald, 2002).

Another implicit framework underlying research on same-sex relationships emphasizes the gender and/or the *gender identity* of relationship participants. In general, contrary to historical stereotypes of gay men as excessively feminine and lesbian women as excessively masculine, studies of interpersonal attitudes, behaviors, and cognitions have generally found that gay/lesbian men and women show largely the same gender-related patterns as do heterosexuals (e.g., Bailey, Gaulin, Agyei, & Gladue, 1994; Hayes, 1995; Kenrick, Keefe, Bryan, & Barr, 1995). Hence, researchers have investigated whether *combining* two men or two women in the same relationship magnifies such patterns (providing, in essence, a "double dose" of male-typical behavior in male-male relationships and of female-typical behavior in female-female relationships), and have largely found this to be the case (as reviewed below). The results of such research are particularly useful in explaining differences between the relationships of sexual-minority women versus sexual-minority men (rather than simply focusing on differences between same-sex and heterosexual couples), and in identifying instances in which an individual's relationship behavior is as strongly influenced by his/her partner's gender as by his/her own gender. Clearly, such research can make an important contribution not only to understanding sexual-minority relationships, but the role of gender in relationship functioning more generally.

Relationship Initiation

The joint effects of social marginalization, on one hand, and intrapsychic patterns of gendered behavior, on the other, are evidenced from the very beginning of sexual-minority relationship development. Consider, for example, the simple process of identifying dating partners. Whereas older cohorts of sexual minorities tended to rely on lesbian/gay bars and clubs to meet potential partners (Berger, 1990), progressive increases in societal openness and tolerance regarding same-sex sexuality have made it possible for sexual-minority adults *and* adolescents to meet potential partners through a diverse range of channels, including work or school, friends, and recreational activities (Bryant & Demian, 1994; Elze, 2002).

The Internet, too, has begun to play a major role. When the Internet first emerged as a potential meeting ground for sexual-minority individuals, it was largely utilized by individuals who lived in rural, isolated areas with smaller sexual-minority populations (Peplau & Beals, 2004). Currently, however, online dating sites are used by a much broader range of sexual minorities, regardless of whether they have access to more conventional meeting locations. This parallels similar changes in the mainstream heterosexual population. For example, a recent representative survey (Pew Internet and American Life Project, 2005) found that of the 10 million Internet users who are looking for a romantic partner, about three fourths have used online dating resources. Nearly one third of American adults report knowing someone who has visited an online dating site, and over one fourth report knowing someone who actually dated someone they met through such sites. Furthermore, surveys have found that lesbian-gay-bisexual individuals are heavier Internet users than are heterosexuals, and are more likely to use the Internet for dating (Park, 2004). Hence, many of the traditional obstacles to relationship initiation among sexual minorities—secrecy and the difficulty of identifying a wide range of attractive, available partners—have begun to fall away in recent years.

With regard to features of sexual-minority relationship initiation that differ from those of heterosexuals, perhaps the most notable distinction is the tendency for sexual minorities to develop romantic relationships out of close same-sex friendships (Nardi, 1999; Rose & Zand, 2000). Yet notably, lesbians and gay men show substantially gender-differentiated patterns in this regard, consistent with traditional gender roles in which women place greater emphasis on emotional connection than do men, whereas men place greater emphasis on sexuality than do women. For example, lesbians have been observed to follow a "friendship script" in developing new relationships, in which emotional compatibility and communication are of primary importance (Rose & Zand, 2000; Rose, Zand, & Cimi, 1993). Yet gay men's relationship scripts are more likely to involve the establishment of sexual intimacy prior to the development of emotional intimacy (Rose et al., 1993), a pattern that has now become evident in online dating activity as well (Helfand, 2002). Lesbian couples have also been observed to follow a somewhat accelerated pathway to emotional exclusivity and commitment compared to heterosexuals and gay men, with some lesbian couples considering themselves to be exclusively and emotionally involved with one another by the fifth date (Cini & Malafi, 1991). Such findings provide direct examples of ways in which combining two women or two men in a relationship tends to magnify conventional gender differences, producing relationship patterns in which same-sex female couples and same-sex male couples occupy two ends of a gender-differentiated spectrum, with conventional heterosexual couples somewhere in the middle.

Relationship Satisfaction and Stability

Contrary to historical stereotypes portraying same-sex relationships as inherently unhealthy, unstable, and dysfunctional (Testa, Kinder, & Ironson, 1987), research resoundingly confirms that same-sex couples are generally as satisfied *and* dissatisfied as other-sex couples, and for the same basic reasons. The happiest same-sex couples, like the happiest heterosexual couples, are those who perceive that their relationships provide more benefits than downsides (Beals, Impett, & Peplau, 2002; Duffy & Rusbult, 1985), and in which partners have similar attitudes (Kurdek & Schmitt, 1987; Kurdek & Schnopp-Wyatt, 1997), similar social and economic backgrounds (Hall & Greene, 2002), similar expectations and perceptions regarding fairness and equity (Eldridge & Gilbert, 1990; Kurdek, 1989, 1995, 1998; Kurdek & Schmitt, 1986; Peplau, Padesky, & Hamilton, 1982; Schreurs & Buunk, 1996), and similar views and priorities regarding things like shared activities, commitment, and sexual exclusivity (Deenen, Gijs, & van Naerssen, 1994; Eldridge & Gilbert, 1990; Peplau & Cochran, 1981).

Other predictors of relationship quality that have been found to function equivalently for same-sex and other-sex couples include partners' personality characteristics, their communication and conflict resolution skills, appraisals of intimacy, autonomy, equality, and mutual trust, and the degree of support the couple perceives for their relationship from their local community (Kurdek, 1998, 2004). Same-sex and other-sex couples also use the same basic strategies to maintain their relationships, such as sharing tasks, communicating about the relationship, and sharing time together (Dainton & Stafford, 1993; Solomon, Rothblum, & Balsam, 2005). They have even been found to fight about the same core issues: finances, affection, sex, criticism, and household tasks (Kurdek, 2004; Solomon et al., 2005). Also, as with heterosexual couples, same-sex couples with higher levels of overall relationship satisfaction report higher levels of sexual satisfaction (Bryant & Demian, 1994; Deenen et al., 1994; Kurdek, 1991; Peplau & Cochran, 1981; Peplau, Cochran, & Mays, 1997).

Same-sex relationships also have similar levels of stability as do heterosexual relationships. One survey found that 14% of lesbian couples and 25% of gay male couples had been together for 10 or more years (Bryant & Demian, 1994). A 12-year longitudinal study found breakup rates of 19% among gay male couples and 24% among lesbian couples; notably, after controlling for demographic factors such as length of cohabitation, these rates were not statistically higher than the breakup rate of 14% among unmarried cohabiting heterosexuals (Kurdek, 2004). This is consistent with other studies which have consistently found that the absence of structural barriers to dissolution, such as legal marriage, joint property, and the presence of children, is largely responsible for the fact that same-sex couples have higher break-up rates than married heterosexual couples (Kurdek, 1992, 1998, 2000), consistent with Rusbult's (1983) investment model of commitment.

Legal Status

Such findings are obviously notable in light of the ongoing debates over formal recognition for same-sex relationships (for reviews see Brewer & Wilcox, 2005; Herek, 2006). As of 2006, same-sex marriages were only available in Massachusetts, Canada, Spain, Belgium, South Africa, and the Netherlands, whereas 45 American states have explicitly *banned* gay marriages, either through state laws or constitutional amendments. Yet a number of American states and other countries allow same-sex couples to enter into legally-recognized civil unions or domestic partnerships, including Vermont, California, Connecticut, New Jersey, New Hampshire, Maine, and England and New Zealand. Similarly, poll data consistently suggest greater public support for "non-marital" forms of legal recognition for same-sex relationships than for same-sex marriage. The most recent national survey (Pew Research Center for the People and the Press, 2006) found that the majority of Americans (55%) oppose same-sex marriage, yet as reviewed by Brewer and Wilcox (2005), the proportion of Americans supporting civil unions or domestic partnerships consistently exceeds the proportion supporting same-sex marriage, sometimes by nearly 20 percentage points. Furthermore, Brewer's (2005) review found that since 2004, the proportion of Americans supporting *some* form of legal recognition for same-sex relationships has reliably exceeded the proportion favoring *no* recognition whatsoever. Thus, despite consistent opposition to same-sex marriage, most Americans view longstanding, committed same-sex partnerships as deserving of some form of legal recognition.

A growing, and fascinating, area of research concerns (1) which types of same-sex couples seek legal recognition, and (2) the effects of such recognition on couple functioning and stability. A number of recent studies have directly addressed this question by comparing same-sex couples in civil unions to same-sex couples without civil unions (recruited from the friendship networks of the civil union group) and also the married heterosexual siblings of the civil union group (Solomon, Rothblum, & Balsam, 2004; Solomon et al., 2005; Todosijevic, Rothblum, & Solomon, 2005). This series of studies found that the comparison group of heterosexual married couples had been together longer than the same-sex couples, had more conventional household practices when it came to the division of labor and child care, and had more frequent contact with their families of origin. Regarding differences between same-sex couples who did or did not have civil unions, lesbians in civil unions were more open about their sexual orientation than lesbians who were not in civil unions. Among gay men, civil union couples were closer to their families of origin, had more mutual friends as a couple, and were less likely to have considered or discussed ending their relationship. Yet in the dimensions related to relationship quality and functioning, civil union and non-civil union couples were fundamentally similar.

One interesting but unanswered question is whether civil unions will promote relationship stability in same-sex couples over the long term, and whether such effects would be even greater for bona fide same-sex *marriage*. After all, there are multiple bureaucratic steps that many same-sex couples take to formalize and/or protect their relationships, such as naming one another as insurance beneficiaries and/or legal heirs, purchasing property together, giving one another power of attorney, designating one another as medical proxies, legally taking the same last name, or merging finances (Badgett, 1998; Beals et al., 2002; Suter & Oswald, 2003). Do these incremental forms of formalization have discernable effects on relationship stability? Research comparing break-up rates across couples with different legal, logistical, bureaucratic, and religious ties to one another would provide a unique opportunity to examine the relative stabilizing effects of structural versus personal/moral dimensions of relationship commitment (Johnson, 1999).

Gender-Related Dynamics in Couple Functioning

As noted earlier, a unique aspect of same-sex romantic relationships is their potential to magnify gender-related dynamics, and this phenomenon has been observed in a number of different domains. For example, Kurdek (1998) found that female-female couples tend to report greater intimacy (manifested in shared time together and the degree to which partners maintained a "couple" identity) than male-male or male-female couples. Similarly, Zacks, Green, and Marrow (1988) found that in comparison to heterosexual couples, female-female couples reported higher levels of cohesion, adaptability, and satisfaction in their relationships, a result that the authors attributed to women's gender role socialization.

Gender dynamics are also evident with respect to issues of power and equality, manifested in decision-making, influence strategies, household labor, and problem solving. Although stereotypes have historically presumed that same-sex couples implicitly designate one partner to take the stereotypically female role and one partner to take the stereotypically male role in such matters, research does not bear out this view. Rather, relationship dynamics in these domains may follow a variety of patterns. With respect to household responsibilities, for example, research indicates that same-sex couples tend to develop arrangements based on each partner's respective interests and desires (Huston & Schwartz, 2002). Accordingly, it is not uncommon for same-sex partners to mix and match "female-typed" and "male-typed" tasks and roles.

Overall, same-sex couples show more equitable distributions of household labor than do heterosexual couples (Carrington, 1999; Kurdek, 1993; Patterson, 1995; Solomon et al., 2004), although male-male and female-female couples appear to operationalize equity in different ways, with male couples dividing up responsibility for specific tasks, and female couples sharing the performance of each task (Kurdek, 1993). Also, same-sex couples appear to place a higher value on equity between partners, and are less likely to take for granted a lopsided distribution of labor, decision making, and influence. For such reasons, same-sex couples provide a fascinating model for contemporary couples seeking creative relationship and household practices that serve the unique needs of their families more effectively than rigid, traditional, gender-based relationship roles (Steil, 2000).

Gender-magnification effects are also evident with regard to sexual exclusivity. Numerous studies have found that male-male couples are more likely than either male-female or female-female couples to report engaging in extra-dyadic sexual activity, often with the explicit knowledge of their partner (see also Bryant & Demian, 1994; Harry, 1984; Harry & DeVall, 1978; McWhirter & Mattison, 1984; Peplau et al., 1997; Solomon et al., 2004). This is commonly attributed to the fact that men's socialization allows them to separate sex from love more easily than do women, making it possible for two men in a committed, enduring bond to mutually understand and agree that extradyadic sexual activity does not threaten their primary tie to one another. In such arrangements, extradyadic sex may have few negative repercussions for relationship satisfaction or stability, and might actually foster some benefits (Deenen et al., 1994; Hickson et al., 1992). Yet even gay male couples with positive attitudes toward—and explicit agreements permitting—extradyadic sex may find that they need to revise such agreements over time to account for unanticipated reactions and situations (LaSala, 2001).

Finally, violence and abuse in same-sex couples is also heavily influenced by gender. Overall, the correlates of relationship violence in same-sex couples parallel those found in heterosexual couples, including conflicts over dependency, jealousy, money, power, and substance abuse (McClennen, Summers, & Vaughan, 2002). Yet some unique patterns have emerged. For example, a recent study of gay male couples (Regan, Bartholomew, Oram, & Landolt, 2002) found that violent acts which typically occupy the upper end of the severity continuum for heterosexual couples (such as punching and hitting) tended to cluster with lower-severity violent behaviors among gay male couples. Alternatively, some behaviors typically considered lower-severity for heterosexual couples (such as twisting arms, pulling hair, and scratching) cluster with higher-severity violence among gay male couples. The authors interpreted these findings to suggest that male-male couples might be quicker to resort to behaviors such as punching and hitting than male-female couples, given that this behavior has more serious consequences when directed toward a weaker and smaller woman (and also potentially because some boys become accustomed to hitting and punching other boys in the context of childhood fights). As for lesbians, one recent study (Miller, Greene, Causby, White, & Lockhart, 2001) found that physical aggression was more common than outright violence in lesbian relationships, and that it was best predicted by relationship fusion, whereas physical violence was best predicted by measures of control. Such findings raise important questions about how male and female socialization, as well as males' and females' different histories of physically aggressive conflicts in childhood, relate to the patterns of violence and abuse observed in male-female, male-male, and female-female couples.

Overall, then, the factors that make same-sex romantic relationships different from other-sex romantic relationships appear to have far more to do with gender than with sexual orientation. Sexual-minority and heterosexual individuals do not go about the processes of forming and maintaining romantic ties all that differently from one another, *but men and women do,* and such differences are echoed and magnified in same-sex couples. Before leaving the topic of romantic relationships, however, it bears reiterating that over the course of their lives, the majority of sexual-minority individuals will have romantic relationships with *other-sex* as well as same-sex partners. For many sexual minorities, these relationships are most likely to take place in adolescence and young adulthood, before they have developed a sexual-minority identity and before they have had opportunities to meet potential same-sex partners. Among sexual-minority individuals with nonexclusive (i.e., bisexual) attractions, alternating between other-sex and same-sex partners may remain a consistent pattern over the life course. One fascinating, unanswered question is how such individuals perceive and experience similarities and differences between their interactions with same-sex versus other-sex romantic partners, particularly regarding gender-related patterns of thought and behavior. This is clearly an area in which greater attention to the distinctive, under-investigated experiences of bisexual men and women may greatly advance our understanding of romantic relationship dynamics more generally.

Friendships

In comparison with research on heterosexual friendships, relatively little empirical research has been conducted on the friendships of sexual minorities (Weinstock, 1998). In recent years, however, this has begun to change, and researchers are increasingly exploring a broad range of friendship dynamics among diverse samples of sexual minorities (Diamond & Lucas, 2004; Galupo, 2007; Galupo, Sailer, & St. John, 2004; Galupo & St. John, 2001; Griffin, 2000; Oswald, 2000; Schneider & Witherspoon, 2000; Stanley, 2002; Tillmann-Healy, 2001; Yoshikawa, Wilson, Chae, & Cheng, 2004). One seemingly straightforward—but important—finding of such research is that most sexual minorities *have* numerous, treasured, high-quality friendships (Weinstock, 1998), contrary to historical stereotypes of sexual minorities as isolated and lonely. For example, in Nardi and Sherrod's (1994) study of nearly 300 gay men and lesbians, respondents reported an average of 7.5 close friends and 16–17 casual friends. While exact numbers with regard to size of friendship network vary across studies, results consistently demonstrate that gay men and lesbians have similar, and sometimes even greater, numbers of friends in comparison to heterosexuals (Weinstock, 1998).

This is true in adolescence as well as in adulthood. For example, Ueno (2005) found that sexual-minority adolescents did not differ from heterosexuals in terms of the number of school-based friends or the degree to which they perceived that their friends cared about them. Diamond and Lucas (2004), however, found that both age and gender made a difference in this regard: Male sexual-minority adolescents under the age of 18 had significantly smaller peer networks than their heterosexual counterparts, but this was not true among male youths over the age of 18, or female youths overall. Another factor that moderated sexual identity effects, however, was a youth's degree of openness. When "closeted" versus "out" sexual minority youth were examined separately, both heterosexual youths and "out" sexual-minority youths were found to have larger peer networks than did closeted youths (Diamond & Lucas, 2004). Importantly, however, smaller networks do not necessarily represent less availability of social support. In the study by Diamond and Lucas (2004), the networks of young sexual-minority men contained greater proportions of extremely close friends than did those of their heterosexual counterparts, potentially boosting sexual-minority men's access to support and intimacy.

A growing area for future research concerns Internet-based friendship networks. As noted above in the context of romantic relationships, both heterosexual and sexual-minority individuals are increasingly using web-based resources to form and maintain social ties that cut across traditional boundaries of geography. Such resources are likely to be particularly useful and important for sexual minorities living in isolated areas with small or nonexistent lesbian-gay-bisexual communities. As sexual minorities and heterosexuals make progressively greater use of such resources, differences between the size and structure of their friendship networks may gradually diminish.

With Whom Do Sexual Minorities Form Friendships?

As with romantic relationships, studies generally show that sexual minorities form friendships based upon the same basic dynamics that have been observed to operate among heterosexuals (Nardi & Sherrod, 1994). Similarity, for example, plays an important role. As with heterosexuals, sexual minorities tend to become friends with individuals who are similar to themselves on a variety of identity dimensions, such as sex, race, ethnicity, socioeconomic status, and age (Nardi, 1999; Weinstock & Bond, 2002). One similarity, however, appears to be particularly important: sexual-minority status. Numerous studies conducted over the past 25 years have revealed that most adult gay men and lesbians report that the majority of their friends, including their best friends, are also lesbian, gay, or bisexual (Galupo, 2007; Nardi, 1992; Nardi & Sherrod, 1994; Stanley, 1996; Weinstock, 1998).

The advantages of close and important friendships among fellow sexual minorities are obvious. Both Weinstock (1998) and Galupo (2007), for example, emphasized that such friendships may be particularly important in providing mutual support and understanding regarding the stress of living in a heterosexist society. Of course, one need not be a sexual minority in order to provide excellent social support to a sexual-minority friend. Rather, the small number of studies that have been conducted on "cross-orientation" friendships have found that they are frequently described as extremely valuable and enjoyable, providing substantial social support and important mutual learning opportunities (Galupo et al., 2004; Galupo & St. John, 2001; O'Boyle & Thomas, 1996; Weinstock & Bond, 2002). Future research is clearly necessary to investigate how sexual-minority versus heterosexual friendships provide different types of support in different contexts. Sampling issues must also be considered when interpreting findings: Because most research on sexual minorities overrepresents openly-identified lesbian-gay-bisexual individuals, especially those participating in lesbian-gay-bisexual community activities, these studies probably overrepresent individuals with large proportions of sexual-minority friends. Future research using random, representative samples is necessary to gain a more complete picture of the diversity of sexual-minority individuals' friendship networks. Along these lines, a pressing issue for future study is the extent to which Internet friendships, formed among individuals that might never actually meet one another, can provide the same psychosocial benefits as do conventional face-to-face friendships.

Friends and Lovers

As noted earlier, one of the distinctive features of sexual-minority romantic relationships is that they often develop out of existing friendships. Hence, a certain degree of fluidity between friendship and romantic/sexual involvement often characterizes sexual-minority friendships. In order to appropriately interpret this phenomenon, however, we must first investigate our own assumptions about the very concepts of "friend" and "lover." Although our culture commonly views these as fundamentally different types of relationships, studies of sexual-minority women, in particular, have found that they often find it difficult to articulate the specific differences between same-sex friendships and same-sex romantic relationships (Diamond, 2002). Vetere (1982), for example, found that although most self-identified lesbians considered sexual involvement to be a distinguishing feature of lover relationships, about a third of respondents did not see this to be the case, and viewed the distinction between friends and lovers to be one of degree rather than kind (Vetere, 1982).

Nardi and Sherrod's (1994) research further confirms the fluidity between lovers and friends, as he found that the majority of both gay men and lesbians reported having had sexual contact with at least some of their friends. Gay men and lesbians were equally likely to report having had sexual contact with their best friends, whereas gay men were significantly more likely to also pursue sexual contact with casual and other close friends (Nardi & Sherrod, 1994). There were also gender differences regarding whether sex preceded friendship or vice versa. Nardi found that for gay men, friendships often developed *out of* initial sexual relationships. Many lesbians, in contrast, report having initiated their first same-sex relationship in the context of an existing friendship (Peplau & Amaro, 1982; Vetere, 1982).

Fluidity between friendship and lover relationships also extends to "post-break-up" ties. Both lesbians and gay men report higher levels of connectedness to former lovers than is typically the case for heterosexuals (Harkless & Fowers, 2005), with some research finding that this phenomenon is particularly common among women (Nardi & Sherrod, 1994; Weinstock, 2004). For example, one third of the lesbians in Nardi and Sherrod's study reported that their best friend was an ex-lover, whereas this was the case for only one sixth of gay men. Other studies, however, have found comparable rates of post-breakup friendship among gay men and lesbians (Harkless & Fowers, 2005), and it is possible that this phenomenon is sensitive to variations in the overall availability of alternative romantic and friendship ties in one's local community.

Finally, it bears noting that because gay men and lesbians typically report receiving less support from their biological families than do heterosexuals (Harkless & Fowers, 2005), some place a heightened value on close friendships, often explicitly describing them as "families of choice" (Nardi, 1999; Weinstock, 1998; Weston, 1991). Such chosen families may prove particularly important for sexual-minority youths: Ueno (2005) has pointed out that in most other minority groups, such as ethnic minorities, the *entire family* shares minority status, and hence youths receive beneficial help and advice from parents and siblings about coping with stigma and discrimination. Yet this is not the case for sexual minorities, who might find their sexual-minority friends to be substantially more supportive. Such patterns highlight the degree to which friendships—at least in contemporary Western culture—have been traditionally considered less important than familial and romantic ties (Rubin, 1985). The practice of using "friends as family" among sexual minorities indicates that this need not always be the case, and raises fascinating questions about the multiple ways in which individuals can craft supportive, nurturant constellations of intimate social bonds to meet their unique needs.

Parenting

There has been much discussion of a baby boom (often called a "gayby" boom) in the lesbian-gay-bisexual community. Although accurate statistics are hard to come by, it is unquestionably the case that same-sex couples are increasingly becoming parents, either through donor insemination, surrogacy, or adoption. A growing number of studies are investigating how sexual-minority individuals handle the formation and maintenance of these new and ground-breaking families. However, the research to date is limited in a number of ways. Sampling presents a particular problem, given that sexual-minority parents are often a particularly hidden subset of the general sexual-minority population. This is because in addition to the general stigmatization that faces all sexual minorities, parents might be particularly secretive in order to avoid potential custody battles or anti-gay victimization of their children.

Also, most studies of same-sex parenting have focused primarily on lesbian families (defined in this context as families headed by two women, although one or more might identify as bisexual rather than lesbian). Although research on gay fathers began decades ago, the number of rigorous studies of gay fathers lags far behind the number of studies of lesbian mothers. Historically, this imbalance reflected the fact that most sexual minorities raising children were lesbians who had initially had their children in the context of heterosexual marriages and had retained custody of these children after marital dissolution. Because far fewer divorced gay men had primary custody of children from previous marriages, they received much less research attention. In recent years, many more same-sex couples are *choosing* to have children; yet research on such families remains largely focused on women. Studies of gay male fathers are still largely limited to divorced men raising children from previous heterosexual marriages (Patterson, 2004).

How Does Same-Sex Parenting Affect Children?

This is, without a doubt, the most commonly-asked question when it comes to the sons and daughters of same-sex couples. Judicial decisions regarding these families have reflected three main concerns about the potential effects of same-sex parenting: that it will influence a child's sexual identity, that it will have a negative impact on the child's personality and psychological adjustment, and that it will lead to difficulties in social relationships (Patterson, 2002).

Research resoundingly demonstrates that these concerns are unfounded. Numerous studies have found that the children of same-sex couples are just as well-adjusted as the children of heterosexuals (reviewed in Golombok et al., 2003), showing *no* elevations in psychological problems, school difficulties, or gender-atypical behavior (Golombok et al., 2003; Wainright, Russell, & Patterson, 2004). As for sexual identity, research suggests that although young adult women raised by lesbian parents might be more likely to experiment with same-sex relationships, overall the children of lesbians and gay men typically become heterosexual adults (Golombok et al., 2003; Patterson, 2004).

Concerns have also been raised about the possibility that children of same-sex parents will face homophobic bullying (Clarke, Kitzinger, & Potter, 2004). On this point, research has yielded mixed findings. Some studies suggest that children with gay or lesbian parents encounter homophobic teasing, and fear being labeled as gay themselves, particularly during adolescence. Other studies, however, find no increased risk of bullying (Clarke et al., 2004) or ostracization from peers (Patterson, 2002).

What about the lack of a "matched set" of genders in the home? Specifically, will the absence of an adult man (in same-sex female households) or an adult woman (in same-sex male households) have a negative impact on children? To answer this question, Golombok and colleagues (2003) conducted a study comparing four types of families: those headed by heterosexual couples, single heterosexual mothers, lesbian couples, and single lesbian moms. The results were conclusive: "The presence of *two parents* irrespective of their gender, rather than the presence of a parent of each sex, is associated with more positive outcomes for children's psychological well-being than is rearing by a single mother. That is, it may be the involvement of a *second* parent rather than the involvement of a *male* parent that makes a difference" (p. 31, emphasis added).

Furthermore, same-sex households do not typically involve the complete absence of one gender from the child's life. The majority of children raised by lesbian couples, for example, have at least one nurturing adult man in their lives, most commonly their biological father, a grandfather, or a friend of the family (van Dam, 2004).

In sum, there appear to be no significant deficits in children raised by sexual-minority parents (van Dam, 2004, although see Stacey & Biblarz, 2001, for an alternative interpretation of these findings). Rather, and quite sensibly, it appears to be the quality of the parent-child relationship which is most predictive of the child's psychosocial adjustment (Wainright et al., 2004).

Routes to Parenthood

Now that we know that "the kids are all right," we can consider sexual-minority parenting from the parents' perspective. Perhaps the most obvious question concerns how sexual-minority individuals become parents to begin with. Patterson (2004) identified four primary pathways: (1) maintaining custody of children who were born in the context of prior heterosexual relationships; (2) donor insemination (among women) or surrogacy (among men); (3) adoption or foster parenting; (4) conceiving and rearing children in partnership with another individual or couple (i.e., a gay couple and a lesbian might choose to parent collectively and use the sperm from one of the men to inseminate the woman). It is still most typical for children with lesbian or gay parents to have been born in the context of a prior heterosexual relationship (pathway #1), but it is increasingly common for lesbians, gay men, and bisexuals to choose to become parents in the context of an already established same-sex relationship (pathways #2–4).

All of these pathways, however, involve unique challenges, given that contemporary society continues to define kinship in terms of blood and marriage (Weston, 1991). Consequently, same-sex parents often face considerable difficulty in obtaining recognition—not only from courts of law, but also in the eyes of friends, relatives, co-workers, and community members—as a "real" family. Further compounding these difficulties is the lack of established norms and visible role models of successful same-sex parenting (although this may begin to change if the "gayby boom" continues to flourish). The simple decision of *how* to go about the process involves a complex array of decisions. For example, what are the laws regarding adoption in their state? Should they pursue international adoption? Would they be willing to adopt an older or ethnic-minority child, which might increase their chances? If they opt for insemination, which partner should bear the child? Decisions in this domain have enormous implications, since only the biological mother will have a guaranteed legal tie to the child. Although some states will allow the other parent to adopt the child, many others will not. Each partner's respective health (and health insurance) may also be an issue.

Then there is the sperm. Same-sex female couples who want to guarantee that the sperm donor has no legal claim on their child are generally advised to purchase frozen sperm from a reputable sperm bank (which also allows them to select a donor for specific characteristics and to screen his health background), but this can be prohibitively expensive. It is substantially cheaper, of course, to obtain sperm from a known donor, such as a friend or relative. Yet this raises an entirely new set of complex issues regarding the potential parenting role and legal rights of the donor. Some female-female couples may actually *want* the father to take an active parenting role for the child, and to make a long-term emotional and perhaps even financial commitment to the child's care. Other couples may simply want the father to maintain a limited but consistent role—akin to an uncle—in order to ensure that the child has a regular, trusted, adult male presence in his/her life. Some couples might seek to involve a male relative of the non-biological mother in order to ensure that both parents have some biological tie to the child. Regardless of the specific type of arrangement, use of a known donor inevitably requires scrupulous negotiation (and perhaps even legal documentation) ahead of time regarding the specific responsibilities and expectations of the donor and the female parents. Gay men choosing to bear a child with a surrogate mother face similar complexities. As with insemination, involving a female friend or relative as the surrogate can be substantially less expensive, and can ensure a continuing maternal presence in the child's life (and, in some cases, a biological link to the non-sperm-donating male parent), but necessarily entails careful planning and sometimes the establishment of binding legal contracts. Even when such contracts are established, they may be challenged in the future if the surrogate mother eventually reconsiders her decision to relinquish parenting rights. Clearly, the parenting decisions of same-sex couples involve a broader range of complex decisions and logistical plans than typically face heterosexual couples.

The specter of biology in such deliberate planning deserves close attention. Many same-sex couples go to considerable efforts to maximize biological relatedness (or the semblance of such relatedness) to one or both parents. For example, lesbian couples using donor insemination often choose donors who share the same ethnic background, or simply "look like" the non-biological mother, making use of "implied racial and cultural bio-genetic links between donor-conceived children and co-mothers, and co-mothers' extended families" (Jones, 2005, p. 221). Another step taken by some lesbian couples in order to strengthen the biological connections within their family is to use the same donor for each of their children, effectively making their offspring full biological siblings to one another. In one study, 7 of the 8 lesbian couples who used an anonymous donor opted to purchase additional sperm from a single donor so that their future children would be biological siblings (Chabot & Ames, 2004).

The legal status of same-sex families is often tenuous. Whereas a child born to a woman in a heterosexual marriage is legally recognized as the child of the husband, even if the child is not biologically related to the father (Naples, 2004), the same is not true for children born to committed same-sex couples. Lesbian and gay individuals who wish to adopt the biological children of their partners (conceived in previous marriages or relationships) often face considerable legal hurdles. Currently, four states (Colorado, Nebraska, Ohio, and Wisconsin) do not allow second-parent or stepparent adoption by same-sex couples, and in 37 other states the legality of second-parent adoptions is either unclear (due to an absence of court rulings on this issue) or restricted to certain jurisdictions (Human Rights Campaign, 2006). Even in states which permit second-parent adoptions within same-sex couples, the law does not allow for a child to have more than two legal parents (Hequembourg, 2004). Therefore, second-parent adoptions are only an option for lesbian co-parents if the biological father is either legally absent or is prepared to give up his legal rights as father (Hequembourg, 2004).

Clearly, same-sex parenting is a phenomenon that is currently in considerable flux with regard to prevalence, medical options, legal status, and cultural perceptions. It will undoubtedly become an increasingly common and important topic of research in the years to come.

Families of Origin

It is often assumed that sexual-minority men and women are uniformly alienated or ostracized from their families of origin, yet this is not the case. Rather, research has demonstrated incredible diversity in sexual-minority individuals' ties to their families of origin. These relationships can provide support *or* shame; acceptance *or* rejection, joy *or* distress, comfort *or* alienation. Perhaps the only generalization that can safely be made is that the family relationships of sexual minorities pose a unique set of challenges for all members. Unfortunately, rigorous empirical research in this area has lagged behind other topics in sexual-minority psychology. For example, although many studies of sexual-minority *youths* have investigated their ties to parents (reviewed in Crosbie Burnett, Foster, Murray, & Bowen, 1996; Savin-Williams, 2001b), this is less so for studies of sexual-minority adults. This leaves us with an incomplete picture of sexual-minority individuals' socioemotional development, given that immediate and extended family members clearly have powerful influences on one another's opinions, feelings, choices, and well-being across the entire life course, as reviewed below.

Initial Disclosure

How many sexual minorities are completely open about their sexuality to family members? How long does it typically take for them to come out? Reliable answers to these questions are practically impossible to obtain, and estimates vary according to how samples are recruited (Green, 2000). For example, sexual minorities recruited from lesbian-gay-bisexual social activities and organizations tend to report relatively higher rates of family disclosure than do individuals recruited from support groups. Overall, however, studies suggest that about 80% of self-identified lesbian-gay-bisexual individuals have disclosed their sexuality to one or more family member (Kaiser Foundation, 2001), with about 60–77% of respondents reporting that they are "out" to their parents (Bryant & Demian, 1994).

Disclosure of one's sexuality to *some* family members, but not others, is fairly common (reviewed in Green, 2000). In general, mothers and sisters are told more often—and earlier—than other family members, largely because they are perceived as more accepting (reviewed in Savin-Williams, 2001b). Other factors that shape the timing and breadth of disclosure to family members include the degree of pre-disclosure intimacy, openness, support, contact, and conflict in these relationships, issues of economic dependence, the family's cultural background and religious values, and overall appraisals of the relative costs of continued secrecy versus the potential disruption brought about by disclosure (Bryant & Demian, 1994; Green, 2000).

Of course, simply revealing one's same-sex sexuality to family members is not the same thing as establishing an open and honest dialogue about it. Surveys indicate that even among lesbian-gay-bisexual individuals who are "out" to their parents, many do not discuss the issue directly (Kaiser Foundation, 2001). In some cases, the parents may know and quietly tolerate the situation (Brown, 1989; D'Augelli, Grossman, & Starks, 2005; Herdt & Beeler, 1998), and yet make their disapproval subtly known, for example by refusing to acknowledge or validate the sexual-minority individual's romantic relationships. Much remains unknown about the long-term process through which families—and particularly parents—gradually progress from initial disapproval of a family member's same-sex sexuality to increasing acceptance and tolerance, and how issues of disclosure and openness are managed over time in the course of ongoing day-to-day interactions. The dynamics introduced by selective disclosure also warrant greater attention: When sexual minorities choose to reveal their sexuality to some family members, but not others, they inadvertently create "ingroups" and "outgroups" within the family who maintain starkly different perceptions and expectations of the sexual-minority family member (Crosbie Burnett et al., 1996). Over time, these differences may hinder family cohesion.

Is Openness Beneficial?

Some families never accept a family member's same-sex sexuality, which raises an important question: *Why disclose at all?* It is easy to assume that openness is preferable to secrecy, and that sexual minorities who choose never to share their identity, their community, and their romantic lives with family members are less well-adjusted and less psychologically connected to family members.

Yet researchers have increasingly called this assumption into question (Green, 2000; Green & Mitchell, 2002; Laird, 2003; LaSala, 2000b). It is certainly true that many sexual-minority individuals derive distinct benefits from being open about their sexuality with family members, including increased intimacy and communication, heightened connectedness and support, and feelings of validation and legitimacy of one's identity and relationships (Herdt & Beeler, 1998; LaSala, 2000b; Weston, 1991).

However, these effects are largely dependent upon the type of family relationships that existed prior to the disclosure. If a sexual-minority individual has a history of conflict and poor communication with family members, and anticipates that they will sharply disapprove of his/her same-sex sexuality, then secrecy might make more sense than disclosure (Green & Mitchell, 2002). In such cases, secrecy might actually prove psychologically adaptive, since it allows the individual to protect and cherish his or her own personal truth and integrity (Laird, 1993, 1998; Ponse, 1978). Hence, instead of uniformly encouraging full disclosure, it may be preferable for friends, activists, clinicians and social workers to encourage sexual-minority individuals to carefully evaluate their goals and expectations regarding disclosure, and to realistically assess whether—given their own particular family dynamics—these expectations are likely to be met (Green, 2000).

Issues of disclosure also take on a different meaning for sexual minorities at later stages of the life course. As Herdt and Beeler (1998) indicated, when young adults disclose their same-sex sexuality to parents and other family members, family reactions often revolve around thoughts of the future, sometimes involving grieving for lost expectations and fantasies, as well as fears about their loved one's risk for harassment and victimization. Yet when the family member making the disclosure is in his or her 50s or 60s, many of these concerns about the future become moot. The sexual-minority family member has already traversed major milestones involving career, intimate relationships, potentially even children. Hence, disclosure to family members raises more issues about the *past* than the future. Family members may have to substantially revise and reconsider their narratives of family history (Beeler & DiProva, 1999): Was everything involving this person a fabrication? Who else in the family might be keeping a secret of such magnitude? How much do family members *really* know one another, in the final analysis? As Herdt and Beeler (1998) pointed out, reckoning with and undoing decades of duplicity may prove to be a more pressing issue in such cases than wrestling with the fact of same-sex sexuality itself.

Unique Issues for Ethnic-Minority Families

Culture and ethnicity play important roles in structuring sexual minorities' family-of-origin relationships. As noted earlier, reliable estimates are difficult to obtain, but extant research suggests that ethnic minorities are often less likely to disclose same-sex sexuality to family members, largely because they expect more negative responses (reviewed in Green, 2000). Same-sex sexuality obviously has drastically different meanings in different cultures (Blackwood, 2000; Murray, 2000; Williams, 1998), and families with highly traditional or religious backgrounds might have more negative conceptions of same-sex sexuality—or less knowledge about it altogether—than more mainstream Western families (Chan, 1992; Collins, 1990; Espin, 1984; Greene, 1998; Hidalgo, 1984; Icard, 1986; Morales, 1992). For example, some languages do not have positive or neutral terms for "lesbian," "gay," or "bisexual" (Espin, 1997).

Importantly, the nature, parameters, and underlying reasons for the stigmatization of same-sex sexuality vary considerably across different cultures, and these differences have correspondingly distinct implications for sexual-minority individuals' experiences, both in terms of initial decisions to disclose and also with respect to long-term adjustment. For example, Latino, African American, Asian-Pacific Islander, and South Asian communities typically place considerable emphasis on family ties, and same-sex sexuality is often construed as a violation and betrayal of familial cohesion and loyalty (Amaro, 1978; Chan, 1992; Espin, 1984; 1987; Hidalgo, 1984; Jayakar, 1994; Smith, 1997; Tremble, Schneider, & Appathurai, 1989; Vasquez, 1979; Wooden, Kawasaki, & Mayeda, 1983).

Many South Asian families continue to arrange their children's marriages (Jayakar, 1994), and the social ties created by these marriages may have important implications for the family's integration into other social networks. Men and women whose same-sex sexuality leads them to withdraw from this tradition may be viewed by their parents as making a selfish choice that impacts negatively upon the family's entire social system. Within African American communities, same-sex sexuality is often associated with long-standing cultural stereotypes of African Americans as hypersexual and morally bankrupt (Clarke, 1983; Collins, 1990; Greene, 1986; Icard, 1986). Thus, sexual minorities often feel pressured to hide their same-sex sexuality in order to present an image of normalcy to larger Anglo society and to contradict these racist stereotypes (Clarke, 1983; De Monteflores, 1986; Gomez & Smith, 1990; Mays & Cochran, 1988).

For all of these reasons, ethnic-minority men and women may express their sexuality in distinctive ways that run counter to common conceptions of "the lesbian-gay-bisexual experience." For example, some ethnic-minority men might pursue exclusively sexual same-sex behavior with strangers to avoid identifying as gay, and maintain their most important romantic ties to women (Carballo-Dieguez, 1989; Carballo-Dieguez & Dolezal, 1994; Vasquez, 1979). Others might identify as lesbian or gay and regularly pursue same-sex behavior, but might resist larger participation in gay culture, choosing to emphasize the cultural component of their identity in order to maintain their strong cultural and family ties (Icard, 1986; Mays & Cochran, 1988; Mays, Cochran, & Rhue, 1993). These factors must be carefully considered by researchers investigating how sexual minorities from different ethnic groups manage their sexual-minority identity in the context of broader family and community ties.

From the Family's Point of View

In considering how sexual minorities maintain functioning relationships with their families of origin, it is important not to lose sight of the fact that adjustment to a family member's disclosure of same-sex sexuality may be experienced quite differently from the family's point of view than from the point of view of the sexual-minority individual. Overall, there has been far more research from the latter perspective than from the former (Crosbie Burnett et al., 1996). Yet we know from a small number of qualitative, clinically-oriented accounts (Beeler & DiProva, 1999; Oswald, 2000; Strommen, 1989; Walsh, 2003) that many of the psychological hurdles faced by sexual minorities—feelings of invisibility, fears of marginalization and social stigmatization, uncertainty and confusion about the future, feelings of loss for the old, ostensibly "normal" self—are shared by their parents, siblings, aunts, uncles, and grandparents. Family members also face many of the same practical decisions: Should they hide this information from colleagues? Can anyone "tell"? Which friends of the family are likely to be supportive, and which are likely to be judgmental and rejecting? Will people think that it is the family's fault, and that they somehow created a dysfunctional childhood environment that "caused" this to happen? It is also not uncommon for some family members—especially siblings—to question their *own* sexuality. Especially given the public visibility of scientific findings about the potential genetic underpinnings of same-sex sexuality, it is perhaps natural for siblings and even parents to wonder if they are carrying the much-touted "gay gene," and what this might mean for them.

Overall, then, one way to summarize these issues is to note that such families face an extended period of vulnerability during which each member must reconsider old perceptions of the family unit, and must revise and reconstruct his or her relationship with the sexual-minority family member (Beeler & DiProva, 1999; Walsh, 2003). This vulnerability, as noted earlier, need not be interpreted as necessarily dramatic or negative. Some families experience these transitions as positive events that bring them together, whereas others wrestle with significant feelings of anger, resentment, betrayal (Crosbie Burnett et al., 1996; Savin-Williams, 2001b; Strommen, 1989). Perhaps the only reliable predictions that can be made are that (1) families with high-quality ties before the disclosure, characterized by mutual intimacy, support, cohesion, and warmth, generally fare better (Patterson, 2000; Savin-Williams, 2001b), and (2) the family's adjustment must be considered in light of contextual factors such as their local community, their values, religious background, economic status, cultural beliefs (Crosbie Burnett et al., 1996; Rostosky et al., 2004; Savin-Williams, 2001b; Strommen, 1989).

Conclusions and Future Directions

In considering directions for future research on sexual-minority individuals and their close interpersonal ties across the life course, it is important to remain mindful *and* critical of the cultural assumptions that typically underlie current and prior research questions, for example, the assumptions that (1) biological ties between individuals are somehow more enduring or authentic than elective ties, (2) sexual and romantic relationships are generally more intimate and important than friendships, (3) monogamous sexual-romantic partnerships are the most healthy, desirable, and worthy of social recognition (for a range of views on these issues, see Butler, 2002; Ettelbrick, 1993, 2001; Green, Bettinger, & Zacks, 1996; Laird, 2003; Sullivan & Landau, 1997; Warner, 1999; Weinstock, 2004). The unique experiences of sexual minorities demonstrate the degree to which all such assumptions should be rigorously questioned when trying to draw inferences about familial and interpersonal functioning over the life course.

Accordingly, some advocates and activists have called for greater awareness and appreciation of a variety of relationship practices among sexual-minority and heterosexual individuals, such as maintaining separate residences from a primary partner (Hess & Catell, 2001), nurturing long-standing ties with ex-lovers (Weinstock, 2004), pursuing multiple and/or nonmonogamous partnerships (Munson & Stelboum, 1999; Rust, 1996; West, 1996), developing romantic, emotionally primary, but non-sexual relationships (Rothblum & Brehony, 1993), or forgoing "primary" ties altogether in favor of larger "chosen families" comprised of multiple close friendships (Nardi, 1999; Weinstock &

Rothblum, 1996). Researchers must devote increasing attention to the prevalence and long-term implications of such alternative practices, not only among sexual minorities but among all individuals. Close attention to such phenomena at a process level can advance researchers' understanding of the psychological and behavioral mechanisms through which adaptive interpersonal ties are crafted, managed, and maintained over the life course.

Researchers must also broaden their sampling strategies in order to gain the fullest possible perspective on these issues. Several populations of sexual minorities have been consistently underrepresented in prior research, and deserve substantive attention. Bisexuals represent one critical group for additional study, particularly given the accumulating body of research demonstrating that nonexclusive same-sex attractions are not just common, but in fact are more common among sexual-minority individuals than exclusive same-sex attractions (Garofalo, Wolf, Wissow, Woods, & Goodman, 1999; Laumann et al., 1994). Despite this fact, the identity category of "bisexual" has been much slower to receive cultural legitimacy than the categories of "gay" and "lesbian," and is frequently misunderstood and denigrated even within lesbian/gay communities (Mohr & Rochlen, 1999; Mulick & Wright, 2002; Ochs, 1996; Rust, 1995). Researchers must strive to identify and recruit bisexual individuals and assess how their nonexclusive attractions and relationships have shaped their interpersonal experiences across the life course. Similarly, we require greater investigation of ethnic-minority sexual minorities, specifically of the complex interacting influences of race, culture, and class on various features of the sexual-minority life course. Greater research on sexual-minority individuals from a broader range of socioeconomic backgrounds and underrepresented geographic areas (specifically, rural locations) is also needed to accurately represent how sexual-minority individuals from diverse backgrounds craft adaptive constellations of close relationships which meet their distinct needs.

In conclusion, it bears emphasizing that perhaps the single most defining characteristic of sexual-minority individuals' close relationships is that they have no single defining characteristic. The types of casual, intimate, platonic, romantic, and familial ties that these individuals pursue with friends, lovers, parents, relatives, and children are as diverse as the individuals themselves. Thus, in investigating the long-term significance of different bonds for long-term functioning, researchers must remain mindful of their own preconceptions, and must remember to treat all of an individual's relationships as potentially developmentally significant, not simply those that fit neatly into familiar cultural categories. This requires greater awareness of the specific features linking and distinguishing between different types of bonds, and the different processes through which they meet respective partners' psychosocial needs. Along the same lines, we must also remember that interpersonal experiences are always embedded within highly specific sociocultural and interpersonal contexts, and these contexts must be carefully analyzed if we wish to accurately discern how and why particular subsets of sexual minorities have distinctive interpersonal experiences with distinctive psychological and social implications. In contrast to early research on sexual minorities, which emphasized commonalities in their experiences due to their shared experience of stigmatization, researchers now face the more difficult task of charting the multiple, interacting factors producing diversity in long-term developmental pathways. Greater understanding of such diversity will clearly advance not only our knowledge base about sexual minorities, but will deepen our knowledge of how *all* individuals craft and benefit from a range of social ties over the life course.

References

Amaro, H. (1978). *Coming out: Hispanic lesbians, their families and communities.* Paper presented at the National Coalition of Hispanic Mental Health and Human Services Organization, Austin, TX.

Badgett, M. V. L. (1998). The economic well-being of lesbian, gay, and bisexual adults' families. In C. Patterson & A. R. D' Augelli (Eds.), *Lesbian, gay, and bisexual identities in families: Psychological perspectives* (pp. 231–248). New York: Oxford University Press.

Bailey, J. M., Gaulin, S., Agyei, Y., & Gladue, B. (1994). Effects of gender and sexual orientation on evolutionarily relevant aspects of human mating psychology. *Journal of Personality and Social Psychology, 66,* 1081–1093.

Beals, K. P., Impett, E. A., & Peplau, L. A. (2002). Lesbians in love: Why some relationships endure and others end. *Journal of Lesbian Studies, 6,* 53–63.

Beeler, J., & DiProva, V. (1999). Family adjustment following disclosure of homosexuality by a member: Themes discerned in narrative accounts. *Journal of Marital & Family Therapy, 25,* 443–459.

Berger, R. M. (1990). Men together: Understanding the gay couple. *Journal of Homosexuality, 19,* 31–49.

Blackwood, E. (2000). Culture and women's sexualities. *Journal of Social Issues, 56,* 223–238.

Brewer, P. R., & Wilcox, C. (2005). The polls-trends: Same-sex marriage and civil unions. *Public Opinion Quarterly, 69,* 599–616.

Brown, L. (1989). Lesbians, gay men, and their families: Common clinical issues. *Journal of Gay and Lesbian Psychotherapy, 1,* 65–77.

Bryant, A. S., & Demian. R. (1994). Relationship characteristics of American gay and lesbian couples: Findings from a national survey. *Journal of Gay and Lesbian Social Services, 1,* 101–117.

Butler, J. P. (2002). Is kinship always already heterosexual? *Differences: A Journal of Feminist Cultural Studies, 13,* 14–44.

Carballo-Dieguez, A. (1989). Hispanic culture, gay male culture, and AIDS: Counseling implications. *Journal of Counseling and Development, 68,* 26–30.

Carballo-Dieguez, A., & Dolezal, C. (1994). Contrasting types of Puerto Rican men who have sex with men (MSM). *Journal of Psychology and Human Sexuality, 6,* 41–67.

Caron, S. L., & Ulin, M. (1997). Closeting and the quality of lesbian relationships. *Families in Society, 78,* 413–419.

Carrington, C. (1999). *No place like home: Relationships and family life among lesbians and gay men.* Chicago: University Of Chicago Press.

Cass, V. (1984). Homosexual identity: A concept in need of a definition. *Journal of Homosexuality, 9,* 105–126.

Chabot, J. M., & Amer, B. D. (2004). It wasn't 'let's get pregnant and go to it': Decision making in lesbian couples planning motherhood via donor insemination. *Family Relations: Interdisciplinary Journal of Applied Family Studies, 53,* 348–356.

Chan, C. S. (1992). Cultural considerations in counseling Asian American lesbians and gay man. In S. H. Dworkin & F. J. Gutierrez (Eds.), *Counseling gay men and lesbians: Journey to the end of the rainbow* (pp. 115–124). Alexandria, VA: American Association for Counseling and Development.

Cini, M. A., & Malafi, T. N. (1991, March). *Paths to intimacy: Lesbian and heterosexual women's scripts of early relationship development.* Paper presented at the annual meeting of the Association for Women in Psychology, Hartford, CT.

Clarke, C. (1983). The failure to transform: Homophobia in the Black community. In B. Smith (Ed.), *Home girls: A Black feminist anthology* (pp. 197–208). New York: Kitchen Table Press.

Clarke, V., Kitzinger, C., & Potter, J. (2004). 'Kids are just cruel anyway': Lesbian and gay parents' talk about homophobic bullying. *British Journal of Social Psychology, 43,* 531–550.

Collins, P. H. (1990). Homophobia and Black lesbians. In P. H. Collins (Ed.), *Black feminist thought: Knowledge, consciousness, and the politics of empowerment* (pp. 192–196). New York: Routledge.

Crosbie Burnett, M., Foster, T. L., Murray, C. I., & Bowen, G. L. (1996). Gays' and lesbians' families-of-origin: A social-cognitive behavioral model of adjustment. *Family Relations, 45,* 397–403.

Dainton, M., & Stafford, L. (1993). Routine maintenance behaviors: A comparison of relation-ship type, partner similarity, and sex differences. *Journal of Social and Personal Relationships, 10,* 255–272.

D'Augelli, A. R., Grossman, A. H., & Starks, M. T. (2005). Parents' awareness of lesbian, gay, and bisexual youths' sexual orientation. *Journal of Marriage & Family, 67,* 474–482.

De Monteflores, C. (1986). Notes on the management of difference. In T. Stein & C. Cohen (Eds.), *Contemporary perspectives on psychotherapy with lesbians and gay men* (pp. 73–101). New York: Plenum.

Deenen, A. A., Gijs, L., & van Naerssen, A. X. (1994). Intimacy and sexuality in gay male couples. *Archives of Sexual Behavior, 23,* 421–431.

DeVine, J. L. (1984). A systemic inspection of affectional preference orientation and the family of origin. *Journal of Social Work and Human Sexuality, 2,* 9–17.

Diamond, L. M. (2002). "Having a girlfriend without knowing it:" The relationships of adolescent lesbian and bisexual women. *Journal of Lesbian Studies, 6,* 5–16.

Diamond, L. M., & Lucas, S. (2004). Sexual-minority and heterosexual youths' peer and family relationships: Experiences, expectations, and implications for well-being. *Journal of Research on Adolescence, 14,* 313–340.

Diamond, L. M., & Savin-Williams, R. C. (2002). Gender and sexual identity. In R. M. Lerner, F. Jacobs, & D. Wertlieb (Eds.), *Handbook of applied developmental science: Promoting positive child, adolescent, and family development through research, policies, and programs* (Vol. 1, pp. 101–121). Thousand Oaks, CA: Sage.

Dubé, E. M., Savin-Williams, R. C., & Diamond, L. M. (2001). Intimacy development, gender, and ethnicity among sexual-minority youths. In A. R. D'Augelli & C. J. Patterson (Eds.), *Lesbian, gay, and bisexual identities and youth: Psychological perspectives* (pp. 129–152). New York: Oxford University Press.

Duffy, S. M., & Rusbult, C. E. (1985). Satisfaction and commitment in homosexual and hetero-sexual relationships. *Journal of Homosexuality, 12,* 1–23.

Eldridge, N. S., & Gilbert, L. A. (1990). Correlates of relationship satisfaction in lesbian couples. *Psychology of Women Quarterly, 14,* 43–62.

Elze, D. E. (2002). Against all odds: The dating experiences of adolescent lesbian and bisexual women. *Journal of Lesbian Studies, 6,* 17–29.

Espin, O. M. (1984). Cultural and historical influences on sexuality in Hispanic/Latina women: Implications for psychotherapy. In C. Vance (Ed.), *Pleasure and danger: Exploring female sexuality* (pp. 149–163). London: Routledge & Kegan Paul.

Espin, O. M. (1987). Issues of identity in the psychology of Latina lesbians. In Boston Lesbian Psy-chologies Collective (Ed.), *Lesbian psychologies: Explorations and challenges* (pp. 35–51). Urbana: University of Illinois Press.

Espin, O. M. (1997). Crossing borders and boundaries: The life narratives of immigrant lesbians. In B. Greene (Ed.), *Ethnic and cultural diversity among lesbians and gay men* (pp. 191–215). Thou-sand Oaks, CA: Sage.

Ettelbrick, P. (1993). Since when is marriage a path to liberation? In S. Sherman (Ed.), *Lesbian and gay marriage: Private commitments, public ceremonies* (pp. 20–26). Philadelphia: Temple University press.

Ettelbrick, P. (2001). Domestic partnership, civil unions, or marriage: One size does not fit all. *Albany Law Review, 64,* 905.

Galupo, M. P. (2007). Friendship patterns of sexual minority individuals in adulthood. *Journal of Social and Personal Relationships, 24,* 139–151.

Galupo, M. P., Sailer, C. A., & St. John, S. C. (2004). Friendships across sexual orientations: Experi-ences of bisexual women in early adulthood. *Journal of Bisexuality, 4,* 37–53.

Galupo, M. P., & St John, S. (2001). Benefits of cross-sexual orientation friendships among adoles-cent females. *Journal of Adolescence, 24,* 83–93.

Garofalo, R., Wolf, R. C., Wissow, L. S., Woods, E. R., & Goodman, E. (1999). Sexual orientation and risk of suicide attempts among a representative sample of youth. *Archives of Pediatrics and Adolescent Medicine, 153,* 487–493.

Gillis, J. R. (1998). Cultural heterosexism and the family. In C. Patterson & A. R. D' Augelli (Eds.), *Lesbian, gay, and bisexual identities in families: Psychological Perspectives* (pp. 249–269). New York: Oxford University Press.

Golombok, S., Perry, B., Burston, A., Murray, C., Mooney-Somers, J., Stevens, M., et al. (2003). Children with lesbian parents: A community study. *Developmental Psychology, 39,* 20–33.

Gomez, J., & Smith, B. (1990). Taking the home out of homophobia: Black lesbian health. In E. C. White (Ed.), *The Black women's health book: Speaking for ourselves* (pp. 198–213). Seattle, WA: Seal.

Green, R.-J. (2000). "Lesbians, gay men, and their parents": A critique of LaSala and the prevailing clinical "wisdom." *Family Process, 39,* 257–266.

Green, R.-J., Bettinger, M., & Zacks, E. (1996). Are lesbian couples fused and gay male couples disengaged?: Questioning gender straightjackets. In J. Laird & R.-J. Green (Eds.), *Lesbians and gays in couples and families: A handbook for therapists.* (pp. 185–230). San Francisco: Jossey-Bass.

Green, R.-J., & Mitchell, V. (2002). Gay and lesbian couples in therapy: Homophobia, relational ambiguity, and social support. In A. S. Gurman (Ed.), *Clinical handbook of couple therapy* (3rd ed., pp. 546–568). New York: Guilford.

Greene, B. (1986). When the therapist is white and the patient is Black: Considerations for psychotherapy in the feminist heterosexual and lesbian communities. *Women and Therapy, 5,* 41–66.

Greene, B. (1998). Family, ethnic identity, and sexual orientation: African-American lesbians and gay men. In C. Patterson & A. R. D'Augelli (Eds.), *Lesbian, gay, and bisexual identities in families: Psychological perspectives* (pp. 40–52). New York: Oxford University press.

Griffin, C. (2000). Absences that matter: Constructions of sexuality in studies of young women's friendships. *Feminism and Psychology, 10,* 227–245.

Hall, R. L., & Greene, B. (2002). Not any one thing: The complex legacy of social class on African American lesbian relationships. *Journal of Lesbian Studies, 6,* 65–74.

Harkless, L. E., & Fowers, B. J. (2005). Similarities and differences in relational boundaries among heterosexuals, gay men, and lesbians. *Psychology of Women Quarterly, 29,* 167–176.

Harry, J. (1984). *Gay couples.* New York: Praeger.

Harry, J., & DeVall, W. B. (1978). *The social organization of gay males.* New York: Praeger.

Hayes, A. F. (1995). Age preferences for same- and opposite-sex partners. *Journal of Social Psychology, 135,* 125–133.

Helfand, G. (2002). *Gay goes online.* Retrieved May 28, 2005, 2005, from http://www.sfgate.com/cgi-bin/article.cgi?file=/gate/archive/2002/05/30/gayinet.DTL.

Hequembourg, A. (2004). Unscripted motherhood: Lesbian mothers negotiating incompletely institutionalized family relationships. *Journal of Social and Personal Relationships, 21,* 739–762.

Herdt, G., & Beeler, J. (1998). Older gay men and lesbians in families. In C. Patterson & A. R. D'Augelli (Eds.), *Lesbian, gay, and bisexual identities in families: Psychological perspectives* (pp. 177–196). New York: Oxford University Press.

Herek, G. M. (2006). Legal recognition of same-sex relationships in the United States: A social science perspective. *American Psychologist, 61,* 607–621.

Hess, J., & Catell, P. (2001). Dual dwelling duos: An alternative for long-term relationships. In B. J. Brothers (Ed.), *Couples, intimacy issues, and addiction* (pp. 25–31). New York: Haworth Press.

Hickson, F. C. I., Davies, P. M., Hunt, A. J., Weatherburn, P., McManus, T. J., & Coxon, A. P. M. (1992). Maintenance of open gay relationships: Strategies for protection against HIV. *AIDS Care, 4,* 409–419.

Hidalgo, H. (1984). The Puerto Rican lesbian in the United States. In T. Darty & S. Potter (Eds.), *Women identified women* (pp. 105–150). Palo Alto, CA: Mayfield.

Human Rights Campaign. (2006). *Adoption laws: State by state.* Retrieved June 21, 2006, from http://www.hrc.org/Template.cfm?Section=Laws_Legal_Resources&Template=/Tagged-Page/TaggedPageDisplay.cfm&TPLID=66&ContentID=19984.

Huston, M., & Schwartz, P. (2002). Gendered dynamics in the romantic relationships of lesbians and gay men. In A. E. Hunter (Ed.), *Readings in the psychology of gender: Exploring our differences and commonalities* (pp. 167–178). Needham Heights, MA: Allyn & Bacon.

Icard, L. (1986). Black gay men and conflicting social identities: Sexual orientation versus racial identity. *Journal of Social Work and Human Sexuality, 4,* 83–93.

Jayakar, K. (1994). Women of the Indian subcontinent. In L. Comas-Diaz & B. Greene (Eds.), *Women of color: Integrating ethnic and gender identities in psychotherapy* (pp. 161–181). New York: Guilford.

Johnson, M. P. (1999). Personal, moral, and structural commitment to relationships: Experiences of choice and constraint. In J. M. Adams & W. H. Jones (Eds.), *Handbook of interpersonal commitment and relationship stability* (pp. 73–87). Dordrecht, Netherlands: Kluwer.

Jones, C. (2005). Looking like a family: Negotiating bio-genetic continuity in British lesbian families using licensed donor insemination. *Sexualities, 8,* 221–237.

Jones, D. A. (1996). Discrimination against same-sex couples in hotel reservation policies. *Journal of Homosexuality, 31,* 153–159.

Kaiser Foundation. (2001, November). *Inside-out: Report on the experiences of lesbians, gays and bisexuals in America and the public's view on issues and policies related to sexual orientation.* Menlo Park, CA: Kaiser Foundation.

Kenrick, D. T., Keefe, R. C., Bryan, A., & Barr, A. (1995). Age preferences and mate choice among homosexuals and heterosexuals: A case for modular psychological mechanisms. *Journal of Personality and Social Psychology, 69,* 1166–1172.

Kitzinger, C. (1987). *The social construction of lesbianism.* London: Sage.

Kurdek, L. A. (1989). Relationship quality for newly married husbands and wives: Marital history, stepchildren, and individual-difference predictors. *Journal of Marriage and the Family, 51,* 1053–1064.

Kurdek, L. A. (1991). Sexuality in homosexual and heterosexual couples. In K. McKinney & S. Sprecher (Eds.), *Sexuality in close relationships* (pp. 177–191). Hillsdale, NJ: Erlbaum.

Kurdek, L. A. (1992). Relationship stability and relationship satisfaction in cohabiting gay and lesbian couples: A prospective longitudinal test of the contextual and interdependence models. *Journal of Social and Personal Relationships, 9,* 125–142.

Kurdek, L. A. (1993). The allocation of household labor in gay, lesbian, and heterosexual married couples. *Journal of Social Issues, 49,* 127–139.

Kurdek, L. A. (1995). Developmental changes in relationship quality in gay and lesbian cohabiting couples. *Developmental Psychology, 31,* 86–94.

Kurdek, L. A. (1998). Relationship outcomes and their predictors: Longitudinal evidence from heterosexual married, gay cohabiting, and lesbian cohabiting couples. *Journal of Marriage and the Family, 60,* 553–568.

Kurdek, L. A. (2000). Attractions and constraints as determinants of relationship commitment: Longitudinal evidence from gay, lesbian, and heterosexual couples. *Personal Relationships, 7,* 245–262.

Kurdek, L. A. (2004). Are gay and lesbian cohabiting couples really different from heterosexual married couples? *Journal of Marriage & Family, 66,* 880–900.

Kurdek, L. A., & Schmitt, J. P. (1986). Relationship quality of partners in heterosexual married, heterosexual cohabiting, and gay and lesbian relationships. *Journal of Personality and Social Psychology, 51,* 711–720.

Kurdek, L. A., & Schmitt, J. P. (1987). Partner homogamy in married, heterosexual cohabiting, gay, and lesbian couples. *Journal of Sex Research, 23,* 212–232.

Kurdek, L. A., & Schnopp-Wyatt, D. (1997). Predicting relationship commitment and relationship stability from both partners' relationship values: Evidence from heterosexual dating couples. *Personality and Social Psychology Bulletin, 23,* 1111–1119.

Laird, J. (1993). Women's secrets—women's silences. In E. Imber-Black (Ed.), *Secrets in families and family therapy* (pp. 331–362). New York: Norton.

Laird, J. (1998). Theorizing culture: Narrative ideas and practice principles. In M. McGoldrick (Ed.), *Revisioning family therapy: Race, class, and gender in clinical practice* (pp. 20–36). New York: Guilford.

Laird, J. (2003). Lesbian and gay families. In F. Walsh (Ed.), *Normal family processes: Growing diversity and complexity* (3rd ed., pp. 176–209). New York: Guilford.

LaSala, M. C. (2000a). Gay male couples: The importance of coming out and being out to parents. *Journal of Homosexuality, 39*, 47–71.

LaSala, M. C. (2000b). Lesbians, gay men, and their parents: Family therapy for the coming-out crisis. *Family Process, 39*, 67–81.

LaSala, M. C. (2001). Monogamous or not: Understanding and counseling gay male couples. *Families in Society, 82*, 605–611.

Laumann, E. O., Gagnon, J. H., Michael, R. T., & Michaels, F. (1994). *The social organization of sexuality: Sexual practices in the United States.* Chicago: University of Chicago Press.

Loftus, J. (2001). America's liberalization in attitudes toward homosexuality. *American Sociological Review, 66*, 762–782.

Lynch, F. R. (1992). Nonghetto gays: An ethnography of suburban homosexuals. In G. Herdt (Ed.), *Gay culture in America: Essays from the field* (pp. 165–201). Boston: Beacon Press.

Mays, V. M., & Cochran, S. D. (1988). The black women's relationships project: A national survey of black lesbians. In M. Shernoff & W. A. Scott (Eds.), *The sourcebook on lesbian/gay health care* (pp. 54–62). Washington, DC: National Lesbian and Gay Health Foundation.

Mays, V. M., Cochran, S. D., & Rhue, S. (1993). The impact of perceived discrimination on the intimate relationships of black lesbians. *Journal of Homosexuality, 25*, 1–14.

McClennen, J. C., Summers, A. B., & Vaughan, C. (2002). Gay men's domestic violence: Dynamics, help-seeking behaviors, and correlates. *Journal of Gay and Lesbian Social Services: Issues in Practice, Policy and Research, 14*, 23–49.

McWhirter, D. S., & Mattison, A. M. (1984). *Male couple: How relationships develop.* Englewood Cliffs, NJ: Prentice Hall.

Meyer, I. H. (2003). Prejudice, social stress, and mental health in lesbian, gay, and bisexual populations: Conceptual issues and research evidence. *Psychological Bulletin, 129*, 674–697.

Miller, D. H., Greene, K., Causby, V., White, B. W., & Lockhart, L. L. (2001). Domestic violence in lesbian relationships. *Women and Therapy, 23*, 107–127.

Mohr, J. J., & Rochlen, A. B. (1999). Measuring attitudes regarding bisexuality in lesbian, gay male, and heterosexual populations. *Journal of Counseling Psychology, 46*, 353–369.

Morales, E. (1992). Latino gays and Latina lesbians. In S. H. Dworkin & F. J. Gutierrez (Eds.), *Counseling gay men and lesbians: Journey to the end of the rainbow* (pp. 125–139). Alexandria, VA: American Association for Counseling and Development.

Mulick, P. S., & Wright, L. W., Jr. (2002). Examining the existence of biphobia in the heterosexual and homosexual populations. *Journal of Bisexuality, 2*, 45–64.

Munson, M., & Stelboum, J. P. (Eds.). (1999). *The lesbian polyamory reader: Open relationships, non-monogamy, and casual sex.* New York: Haworth Press.

Murray, S. O. (2000). *Homosexualities.* Chicago: University of Chicago Press.

Naples, N. A. (2004). Queer parenting in the new millennium. *Gender & Society, 18*, 679–684.

Nardi, P. M. (1992). That's what friends are for: Friends as family in the gay and lesbian community. In K. Plummer (Ed.), *Modern homosexualities: Fragments of lesbian and gay experience* (pp. 108–120). London: Routledge.

Nardi, P. M. (1999). *Gay men's friendships.* Chicago: University of Chicago Press.

Nardi, P. M., & Sherrod, D. (1994). Friendship in the lives of gay men and lesbians. *Journal of Social and Personal Relationships, 11*, 185–199.

O'Boyle, C. G., & Thomas, M. D. (1996). Friendships between lesbian and heterosexual women. In J. S. Weinstock & E. D. Rothblum (Eds.), *Lesbian friendships: For ourselves and each other* (pp. 240–248). New York: New York University Press.

Ochs, R. (1996). Biphobia: It goes more than two ways. In B. A. Firestein (Ed.), *Bisexuality: The psychology and politics of an invisible minority* (pp. 217–239). Thousand Oaks, CA: Sage.

Oswald, R. F. (2000). Family and friendship relationships after young women come out as bisexual or lesbian. *Journal of Homosexuality, 38*, 65–83.

Oswald, R. F. (2002). Inclusion and belonging in the family rituals of gay and lesbian people. *Journal of Family Psychology, 16*, 428–436.

Page, S. (2003, July 28). Poll shows backlash on gay issues. *USA Today.*

Park, E. (2004). *Gay users prefer online for politics.* Retrieved May 28, 2005, 2005, from http://www. imediaconnection.com/content/3431.asp.

Patterson, C. J. (1995). Families of the baby boom: Parents' division of labor and children's adjustment. *Developmental Psychology, 31,* 115–123.

Patterson, C. J. (2000). Family relationships of lesbians and gay men. *Journal of Marriage and the Family, 62,* 1052–1069.

Patterson, C. J. (2002). Lesbian and gay parenthood. In M. H. Bornstein (Ed.), *Handbook of parenting: Vol. 3: Being and becoming a parent* (2nd ed., pp. 317–338). Mahwah, NJ: Erlbaum.

Patterson, C. J. (2004). Gay fathers. In M. E. Lamb (Ed.), *The role of the father in child development* (4th ed.; pp. 397–416). New York: Wiley.

Peplau, L. A., & Amaro, H. (1982). Understanding lesbian relationships. In W. Paul, J. D. Weinrich, J. C. Gonsiorek, & M. E. Hotvedt (Eds.), *Homosexuality: Social, psychological, and biological issues* (pp. 233–248). Beverly Hills: Sage.

Peplau, L. A., & Beals, K. P. (2004). The family lives of lesbians and gay men. In A. L. Vangelisti (Ed.), *Handbook of family communication* (pp. 233–248): Mahwah, NJ: Erlbaum.

Peplau, L. A., & Cochran, S. D. (1981). Value orientations in the intimate relationships of gay men. *Journal of Homosexuality, 6,* 1–19.

Peplau, L. A., Cochran, S. D., & Mays, V. M. (1997). A national survey of the intimate relationships of African American lesbians and gay men: A look at commitment, satisfaction, sexual behavior, and HIV disease. In B. Green (Ed.), *Ethnic and cultural diversity among lesbians and gay men. Psychological perspectives on lesbian and gay issues* (pp. 11–38). Thousand Oaks, CA: Sage.

Peplau, L. A., Padesky, C., & Hamilton, M. (1982). Satisfaction in lesbian relationships. *Journal of Homosexuality, 8,* 23–35.

Peplau, L. A., & Spalding, L.R. (2000). The close relationships of lesbians, gay man, and bisexuals. In C. Hendrick & S. S. Hendrick (Eds.), *Close relationships: A sourcebook* (pp. 111–123). Thousand Oaks, CA: Sage.

Pew Internet and American Life Project. (2005). *Online dating.* Retrieved May 28, 2005, 2005, from http://www.pewinternet.org/pdfs/PIP_Online_Dating.pdf.

Pew Research Center for the People and the Press. (2006, March 22).*Less opposition to gay marriage, adoption and military service.* Retrieved online at http://people-press.org/reports/display. php3?ReportID=273.

Ponse, B. (1978). *Identities in the lesbian world: The social construction of self.* Westport, CT: Greenwood Press.

Regan, K. V., Bartholomew, K., Oram, D., & Landolt, M. A. (2002). Measuring physical violence in male same-sex relationships: An item response theory and analysis of the conflict tactics scales. *Journal of Interpersonal Violence, 17.*

Rose, S., & Zand, D. (2000). Lesbian dating and courtship from young adulthood to midlife. *Journal of Lesbian Studies, 6,* 85–109.

Rose, S., Zand, D., & Cimi, M. A. (1993). Lesbian courtship scripts. In E. D. Rothblum & K. A. Brehony (Eds.), *Boston marriages* (pp. 70–85). Amherst: University of Massachusetts Press.

Rostosky, S. S., Korfhage, B. A., Duhigg, J. M., Stern, A. J., Bennett, L., & Riggle, E. D. B. (2004). Same-sex couple perceptions of family support: A consensual qualitative study. *Family Process, 43,* 43–57.

Rothblum, E. D., & Brehony, K. A. (Eds.). (1993). *Boston marriages.* Amherst: University of Massachusetts Press.

Rubin, L. (1985). *Just friends: The role of friendship in our lives.* New York: Harper & Row.

Rusbult, C. E. (1983). A longitudinal test of the investment model: The development (and deterioration) of satisfaction and commitment in heterosexual involvements. *Journal of Personality and Social Psychology, 45,* 101–117.

Rust, P. C. R. (1995). *Bisexuality and the challenge to lesbian politics: Sex, loyalty, and revolution.* New York: New York University Press.

Rust, P. C. R. (1996). Monogamy and polyamory: Relationship issues for bisexuals. In B. A. Firestein (Ed.), *Bisexuality: The psychology and politics of an invisible minority* (pp. 127–148). Thousand Oaks, CA: Sage.

Rust, P. C. R. (2000). Criticisms of the scholarly literature on sexuality for its neglect of bisexuality. In P. C. R. Rust (Ed.), *Bisexuality in the United States: A reader and guide to the literature* (pp. 5–10). New York: Columbia University Press.

Savin-Williams, R. C. (2001a). Differential developmental trajectories. In R. C. Savin-Williams (Ed.), *Mom, dad. I'm gay. How families negotiate coming out* (pp. 7–21). Washington, DC: American Psychological Association.

Savin-Williams, R. C. (2001b). *Mom, Dad. I'm gay.* Washington, DC: APA Press.

Savin-Williams, R. C., & Cohen, K. M. (2004). Homoerotic development during childhood and adolescence. *Child and Adolescent Psychiatric Clinics of North America, 13,* 529–549.

Savin-Williams, R. C., & Diamond, L. M. (1998). Sexual orientation. In W. K. Silverman & T. H. Ollendick (Eds.), *Developmental issues in the clinical treatment of children and adolescents* (pp. 241–258). Boston: Allyn & Bacon.

Schneider, M. S., & Witherspoon, J. J. (2000). Friendship patterns among lesbian and gay youth: An exploratory study. *Canadian Journal of Human Sexuality, 9,* 239–246.

Schreurs, K. M. G., & Buunk, B. P. (1996). Closeness, autonomy, equity, and relationship satisfaction in lesbian couples. *Psychology of Women Quarterly, 20,* 577–592.

Simons, T., & O'Connell, M. (2003). *Married-couple and unmarried-partner households: 2000.* Retrieved May 23, 2006, from http://www.census.gov/prod/2003pubs/censr-5.pdf.

Smith, A. (1997). Cultural diversity and the coming-out process: Implications for clinical practice. In B. Greene (Ed.), *Ethnic and cultural diversity among lesbians and gay men* (pp. 279–300). Thousand Oaks, CA: Sage.

Solomon, S. E., Rothblum, E. D., & Balsam, K. F. (2004). Pioneers in partnership: Lesbian and gay male couples in civil unions compared with those not in civil unions and married heterosexual siblings. *Journal of Family Psychology, 18,* 275–286.

Solomon, S. E., Rothblum, E. D., & Balsam, K. F. (2005). Money, housework, sex, and conflict: Same-sex couples in civil unions, those not in civil unions, and heterosexual married siblings. *Sex Roles, 52,* 561–575.

Stacey, J., & Biblarz, T. J. (2001). (How) does the sexual orientation of parents matter? *American Sociological Review, 66,* 159–183.

Stanley, J. L. (1996). The lesbian's experience of friendship. In J. S. Weinstock & E. D. Rothblum (Eds.), *Lesbian friendships: For ourselves and each other* (pp. 39–59). New York: New York University Press.

Stanley, J. L. (2002). Young sexual minority women's perceptions of cross-generational friendships with older lesbians. *Journal of Lesbian Studies, 6,* 139–148.

Steil, J. M. (2000). Contemporary marriage: Still an unequal partnership. In C. Hendrick & S. S. Hendrick (Eds.), *Close relationships: A sourcebook* (pp. 125–136). Thousand Oaks, CA: Sage.

Strommen, E. F. (1989). "You're a what?": Family members' reactions to the disclosure of homosexuality. *Journal of Homosexuality, 18,* 37–58.

Sullivan, A., & Landau, J. (Eds.). (1997). *Same-sex marriage: Pro and con.* New York: Vintage.

Suter, E. A., & Oswald, R. F. (2003). Do lesbians change their last names in the context of a committed relationship? *Journal of Lesbian Studies, 7,* 71–83.

Testa, R. J., Kinder, B. N., & Ironson, G. (1987). Heterosexual bias in the perception of loving relationships of gay males and lesbians. *Journal of Sex Research, 23,* 163–172.

Tillmann-Healy, L. M. (2001). *Between gay and straight: Understanding friendship across sexual orientation.* Lanham, MD: AltaMira Press.

Todosijevic, J., Rothblum, E. D., & Solomon, S. E. (2005). Relationship satisfaction, affectivity, and gay-specific stressors in same-sex couples joined in civil unions. *Psychology of Women Quarterly, 29,* 158–166.

Tremble, B., Schneider, M., & Appathurai, C. (1989). Growing up gay or lesbian in a multicultural context. *Journal of Homosexuality, 17,* 253–267.

Troiden, R. R. (1979). Becoming homosexual: A model of gay identity acquisition. *Psychiatry, 42,* 362–373.

Ueno, K. (2005). Sexual orientation and psychological distress in adolescence: Examining interpersonal stressors and social support processes. *Social Psychology Quarterly, 68,* 258–277.

van Dam, M. A. A. (2004). Mothers in two types of lesbian families: Stigma experiences, supports, and burdens. *Journal of Family Nursing, 10,* 450–484.

Vasquez, E. (1979). Homosexuality in the context of the Mexican American culture. In D. Kukel (Ed.), *Sexual issues in social work: Emerging concerns in education and practice* (pp. 131–147). Honolulu: University of Hawaii, School of Social Work.

Vetere, V. A. (1982). The role of friendship in the development and maintenance of lesbian love relationships. *Journal of Homosexuality, 8,* 51–65.

Wainright, J. L., Russell, S. T., & Patterson, C. J. (2004). Psychosocial adjustment, school outcomes, and romantic relationships of adolescents with same-sex parents. *Child Development, 75,* 1886–1898.

Walsh, F. (2003). *Normal family processes: Growing diversity and complexity* (3rd ed.). New York: Guilford.

Walters, A. S., & Curran, M. C. (1996). "Excuse me, sir? May I help you and your boyfriend?": Salespersons' differential treatment of homosexual and straight customers. *Journal of Homosexuality, 31,* 135–152.

Walters, S. D. (2001). *All the rage: The story of gay visibility in America.* Chicago: University of Chicago Press.

Warner, M. (1999). *The trouble with normal: Sex, politics and the ethics of queer life.* New York: The Free Press.

Weinstock, J. S. (1998). Lesbian, gay, bisexual, and transgender friendships in adulthood. In C. J. Patterson & A. R. D'Augelli (Eds.), *Lesbian, gay, and bisexual identities in families: Psychological perspectives* (pp. 122–153). New York: Oxford University Press.

Weinstock, J. S. (2004). Lesbian ex-lover relationships: Under-estimated, under-theorized and under-valued? In J. S. Weinstock & E. D. Rothblum (Eds.), *Lesbian ex-lovers: The really long-term relationships* (pp. 1–8): New York: The Harrington Park Press/The Haworth Press.

Weinstock, J. S., & Bond, L. A. (2002). Building bridges: Examining lesbians' and heterosexual women's close friendships with each other. *Journal of Lesbian Studies, 6,* 149–161.

Weinstock, J. S., & Rothblum, E. D. (Eds.). (1996). *Lesbian friendships: For ourselves and for each other.* New York: New York University Press.

West, C. (1996). *Lesbian polyfidelity.* San Francisco: Bootlegger Publishing.

Weston, K. (1991). *Families we choose: Lesbians, gays, kinship.* New York: Columbia University Press.

Williams, W. L. (1998). Social acceptance of same-sex relationships in families: Models from other cultures. In C. Patterson & A. R. D'Augelli (Eds.), *Lesbian, gay, and bisexual identities in families: Psychological perspectives* (pp. 53–71). New York: Oxford University Press.

Wooden, W. S., Kawasaki, H., & Mayeda, R. (1983). Lifestyles and identity maintenance among gay Japanese-American males. *Alternative Lifestyles, 5,* 236–243.

Yoshikawa, H., Wilson, P. A.-D., Chae, D. H., & Cheng, J.-F. (2004). Do family and friendship networks protect against the influence of discrimination on mental health and HIV risk among Asian and Pacific Islander gay men? *AIDS Education and Prevention, 16,* 84–100.

Zacks, E., Green, R.-J., & Marrow, J. (1988). Comparing lesbian and heterosexual couples on the Circumplex Model: An initial investigation. *Family Process, 27,* 471–484.

Chapter 13

Gender Strategies

Socialization, Allocation, and Strategic Selection Processes Shaping the Gendered Adult Life Course

Phyllis Moen, Erin Kelly, and Rachel Magennis

Adulthood is a fundamentally different experience for women and men, even those with similar backgrounds growing up. Why is this the case? Research and theory pose several alternative explanations, grounded in ideas about nature and nurture. Most common historically has been a *biological explanation* (nature), pointing to the impacts of genetic, hormonal, and physiological differences between women and men. There are, to be sure, male and female traits rooted in biology or nature. But if this were the only reason for gender differences, we wouldn't find variations in the distinctive experiences and expectations of women and men across cultures, social classes, geographical regions, and history.

Alternatively, the nurture or *cultural explanation* proposes that gender is learned: Even young children begin to grasp the rules of what is expected for boys and girls, men and women (Maccoby & Jacklin, 1974). *Structural explanations* also fall in the "nurture" camp, pointing to the differing opportunity structures confronting women and men, that is, the social and economic rules and regulations opening up or closing off certain roles, relationships, and resource options based on one's gender (Kramer, 2005; McCall, 2001; Moen & Roehling, 2005). For example, some religious positions (such as pope, bishop) are explicitly reserved for men, and some jobs are typed by gender (until recently, nurses, librarians, secretaries were almost exclusively women; construction workers, pilots and firefighters almost exclusively men), even though this typing may not be "official."

Due in part to the women's movement and the corresponding increase in feminist scholarship since the 1960s, researchers emphasize the social basis of gender, debunking the previously held belief that gender is determined exclusively by biology (Acker, 1992; Anderson, 2005; Bem, 1994; Collins, Chafetz, Blumberg, Coltrane, & Turner, 1993; Folbre, 2001; Moen, 2001). Now, increasingly, social and behavioral scientists use the term "sex differences" when referring to variations in biological traits, reserving the term "gender differences" to represent the actions and characteristics of being a man or a woman that are learned or mandated, in other words, the result of cultural and structural influences. Most scholars have concluded that gender differences can only be understood by considering the *combination* of biological, social, economic, organizational and cultural forces as they intersect throughout the life course (Downey, Eccles, & Chatman, 2005; Kimmel & Aronson, 2000; Moen & Chermack, 2005; Moen, Elder, & Lüscher, 1995; Moen & Spencer, 2006a).

The answer to the question "nature or nurture," in relation to the distinctive lives of women and men is, "both." What is key is that while some differences between women and men are rooted in biology, disparities in the roles, relationships, and resources available to women and to men are the result of institutionalized beliefs, policies, and practices—the culture and structure of gender as enacted in families, portrayed in the media, taught in schools, reinforced at work, and taken-for-granted in communities (Kramer, 2005; Kimmel & Aronson, 2000). The preponderance of evidence is that gender differences are less about nature (biology) than *second nature* (institutionalized arrangements), that is, the taken-for-granted gender schema, stereotypes and strictures permeating every aspect of contemporary life (Acker, 1992; Bem, 1994; Moen, 2001; Moen & Spencer, 2006b; Ridgeway & Correll, 2004; Risman, 1998).

In this chapter we focus on the socially constructed components of being a man or a woman in contemporary society, noting that gender opens up or closes opportunities differently throughout the adult course. We describe three related social processes that both produce and perpetuate gender differences and gender disparities throughout adulthood. First are *socialization* processes: the ways women and men learn cultural schema (taken-for-granted beliefs). Socialization teaches each new generation, directly and indirectly by example, what is expected for people of each gender at different ages and life stages (see Parson & Bales, 1955; Rose, 1979; Settersten & Owens, 2002). Socialization processes foster gendered identities as well as different preferences, expectations and motivations for women and men. Second are *allocation* processes: the structural arrangements and power differences in groups, organizations and societies that open up some possibilities for men or for women, while closing others (Acker, 1992; Bem, 1994; Moen, 1992, 2001; Moen & Spencer, 2006a; Ridgeway & Correll, 2004; Risman, 1998; West & Zimmerman, 1987; Williams, 2000). Third are *strategic selections*: Women and men choose to enter or exit some roles and relationships and not others at different points in their lives (Moen & Chermack, 2005; Moen & Chesley, 2008; Moen & Wethington, 1992).

Our goal is to demonstrate that women and men live different adulthoods because they develop different preferences (Becker, 1981; Hakim, 1997) as a result of bringing different expectations and values (socialization) to each fork in the life-course road. Moreover, each fork in the life-course is stratified by gender, offering women and men different opportunities and constraints (allocation). Even whether or not adults perceive that there is a "fork in the road" (i.e., a decision point) sometimes depends on their gender. Choosing which road to take (strategic selections) is guided by both socialization and allocation processes that persist across the life course through ongoing social relationships and institutionalized gender regimes (what we term "convoys"). Still, large-scale transformations can render old gender scripts (learned through socialization and allocation processes) out of date, opening up new opportunities to women and/or men. Wars, economic dislocations, technological innovations, and social movements, for example, can transform gender strategies, as can changes in social policies and regulatory practices (Elder, 1974; Moen, 1992). The early 21st century is just such a time of social transformation. Demographic, cultural, economic, and technological changes are rewriting the nature of gendered adult roles and relationships at work, family, education, religion, community and government. Still, the fundamental mismatch between old scripts and old rules and new realities perpetuates gender inequality (e.g., Moen, 2003, 2005; Moen & Chesley, 2008; Moen & Roehling, 2005).

This chapter consists of five sections. The first provides theoretical and conceptual underpinnings bringing gender front and center in the framing of human development—an *ecology of the gendered life course* approach. The next three sections describe processes of socialization, allocation and strategic selection. Throughout we discuss the three dynamic themes: the concepts of *social convoys*, *institutional convoys* and *cycles of control*. The chapter concludes with a discussion of converging divergences in the adult development of women and men.

Ecology of the Gendered Adult Course

Most scholarship on human development does not explicitly incorporate gender, but focuses instead on "generic" (i.e., non-gendered) processes presumed to operate in the same way regardless of gender. Three prevailing theories of (generic) human development are framed in terms of ecology (Bronfenbrenner, 2005), the life span (Baltes & Baltes, 1990), and the life course (Elder, 1974). We draw upon all three in our ecology of the gendered life course approach (Moen & Chesley, 2008; Moen, Elder, & Lüscher, 1995) in order to provide a vocabulary for understanding and studying gendered development in adulthood. Four concepts are central to our ecology of the gendered life course framing. In addition to *process* (described in the preceding section about the processes of socialization, allocation and strategic selection), this perspective emphases the importance of time, context, and *linked lives*. Putting them together and in motion reveals the convoys of relationships (i.e., social convoys) and of rules and regulations (i.e., institutional convoys) that shape the gendered life course. We consider each of these concepts through a gender lens.

Gendered Time, Timing, and Age

Understanding adult development requires attention to the meaning, measurement, and management of *time* over the life course of individuals and across historical periods. Gendered adult development is rooted in child and adolescent development (Moen & Roehling, 2005; Putney & Bengtson, 2002). It also changes with age. And, age itself has multiple meanings: as a biological time clock, as multiple social and institutional clocks and calendars, and as historical (and biographical) chronologies of those born at different time periods (i.e., cohorts). Life course scholars have sensitized researchers to the multiple meanings of age (Elder, 1974, 1992; Hagestad & Neugarten, 1985; Moen, 1995; Riley, 1987; Riley, Foner, & Waring, 1988). We add to this the multiple meanings of gender. This matters because the scripts people follow depend on the combination of their age and gender. Age and gender constitute the backbone of key socialization and allocation regimes in adulthood, creating distinctive sets of challenges and limiting the adaptive strategies (strategic selections) of women and men as they move through adulthood. What is key is that both age and gender are intersecting statuses setting expectations, options and resources throughout the adult years. Moreover, gender and age are not simply markers; rather, they play out as biological, social and historical forces. Note that race and class are also important statuses shaping the gendered adult course (McCall, 2001), but space constraints limits our focus to the age and gender intersection.

Biological Forces across Age and Gender.   First, age is an indicator of biological changes in physical and cognitive functioning that set limits on social behavior. Changes in workers' health over the adult course, for example, can affect their decision making regarding labor force exits, including opting out for a short time, seeking a different job, or earlier timing of retirement.

Biology is an important aspect of gender as well. For example, women's biological clocks (the span of years when they can bear children) have enormous repercussions over both men's and women's decisions about marriage and parenting, although medical advances are stretching out women's childbearing years. By contrast, the fact that men can father children over a wide age span means that some men launch second families with (new) younger wives in later adulthood. Biology, in the form of cognitive as well as physiological characteristics tied to both age and gender, is heightened by social forces (including social policies) that can accentuate or mitigate gender distinctions over the adult course (Caspi & Elder, 1988; Caspi, Lynam, Moffitt, & Silva, 1993).

Social Forces across Age and Gender.   Second, age is an important determinant of people's social roles, independent of their capacities and preferences, and is reflected in what Riley (1987) refers to as the age stratification system. Consider common sense notions about the "right" time for doing things. Culturally-grounded norms and policies shape expectations and beliefs about the "right" age to be in school, to marry, to start a family, or to retire from a career (Neugarten, Moore, & Lowe, 1965; Rook, Catalano, & Dooley, 1989; Settersten & Hagestad, 1996a, 1996b). This reflects the institutionalized aspects of adulthood, in terms of life-course convoys of expectations and rules around the time, timing, and duration of roles at different ages and life stages (Moen & Chesley, 2008; Settersten & Hagestad, 1996a, 1996b).

There is also a gender stratification system, allocating some social positions and opportunities to men and others to women throughout the adult course (Bem, 1994; Folbre, 2001; Moen, 2001, 2003; Moen & Chermack, 2005; Moen & Spencer, 2006a; Risman, 1998; West & Zimmerman, 1987; Williams, 2000). Age and aging serve to widen, rather than narrow gender differences and inequalities (Moen, 2001; Moen & Spencer, 2006b). For example, contemporary young people in high school and college often wear similar styles of clothing, earn similar wages, and take similar classes. It is only as they enter and move through adult roles—especially as employees, spouses, and parents—that women's and men's experiences and resources tend to markedly diverge. Whether these are beginning to converge is an issue we take up in the concluding section.

Historical Forces and Cohorts across Age and Gender.   Third, age at a given point in time is an indicator of birth-cohort membership and, thus, of life experiences shared with others of the same generation (Riley, 1987; Riley, Foner, & Waring, 1988; Ryder, 1965). People in different cohorts have different attitudes about gender (Schuman & Rieger, 1992), as well as different options, depending on whether they are women or men. Consider the different experiences of the parents of the Baby Boom cohort (young adults in the 1940s and 50s) versus the boomers themselves (young adults in the 1970s and 80s) versus young adults today. Note that what is taken-for-granted at one point in history changes (e.g., men being the exclusive family breadwinners in the 1950s). Today, dual-earner households are very much the expected norm.

Gendered Contexts (Ecologies) as Dynamic Convoys Shaping the Adult Course

"Context" is another key concept within an ecology of the life course perspective. Social and institutional contexts or *ecologies* (see also Bronfenbrenner, 2005; Dannefer, 1984, 2000) typically differ by both age and gender. "Ecology" refers to the relationship between organism and environment. We view adult development as dynamic ecological processes of interaction between individuals and their psychosocial environments as both change over time. Individuals are not passively located within particular contexts or ecological niches, however. Rather, they make strategic selections into and out of roles and relationships (and the corresponding ecologies) in an effort to meet both their own needs and goals and others' expectations of them. Still, the array of possible adaptive strategies is always constrained by the social and cultural environments available to women and men of different ages and in different cohorts.

Social Convoys (Linked Lives).   Another key concept in the ecology of the life course tool box is that of *linked lives*, the fact that people go through their adult course within a web of relationships. The life-course concept of linked lives (Elder, 1974, 1985) highlights the ways individuals' choices are always embedded in and shaped by the people in their lives.

Kahn and Antonucci (1980) coined the term "social convoy" to capture this notion of linked lives, of people connected in some way, moving through life at different rates and in different ways. Kahn and Antonucci depict such convoys as supportive of human development (in the same way that escorting ships provided protection to transports during World War II). We broaden the meaning of social convoy to recognize that while relationships with children, siblings, parents, spouses, and close friends may indeed be "supportive," they can be sources of conflict and strain as well. Lives are also linked with those of coworkers, neighbors and other social network members. Moreover, a person's social convoy of relationships can shift in size, supportiveness and strain over the adult course as various relationships emerge, end, change or persist throughout adulthood.

What is key is that the nature of linked lives differs for women and men. Jessie Bernard (1981) pointed out that each marriage is, in reality, two marriages: "his" and "hers." So, too, do we find two prevailing ecologies of adult development: "his" and "hers." Yet, as we discuss in the concluding section, there is also evidence of growing within-gender variation as well.

Most people's social networks consist of women and men of different ages, and of different salience (one's parent versus a neighbor, for example). Adulthood for many Americans involves managing their (often conflicting) relationship goals, expectations, and obligations—as parents, as adult children of aging parents, as siblings, as neighbors and friends, as husbands and wives. For example, young adults are often surprised to find that their parents continue to have certain expectations for them, no matter how old or financially independent they may be. And couples must coordinate two careers and, increasingly, "blended" families (including children from prior marriages). Single parents often have to also coordinate children's schedules with their former spouses and current partners.

Institutional Convoys.   Social convoys are the *people* that accompany individuals through their life course development. But lives are also linked with organizations and institutions. Mothers and fathers must coordinate with their children's schooling and recreational rules and timetables. Caregivers to aging or infirm relatives seek to understand and coordinate with health care, Medicare, long-term care and other bureaucratic institutions. And all of this often occurs in tandem with coordination of employers' rules and timetables, as well as those of federal and state governments and community organizations.

We developed the term "institutional convoys" to capture the cultural and organizational expectations, norms, rules, and regulations that open or close role, relationship and resource options for women and men at different ages and life stages. These expectations, norms, rules, and regulations are often age-graded and gender-differentiated. Indeed, gender itself is something of a social institution (Martin, 2004). Most people are unaware of how much their lives are linked to organizational convoys (such as schools, families, businesses, government, hospitals, military, churches, synagogues, and membership groups) from birth to death. These institutions shape individual behavior in both obvious and more subtle ways. Moreover, even when individuals seem to violate institutionalized expectations, norms, rules or regulations for someone of their gender

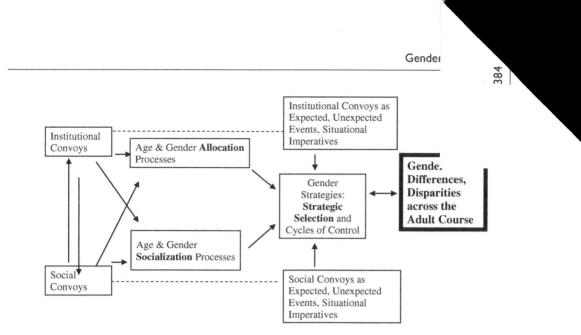

Figure 13.1 Socialization, allocation, and strategic selection processes shaping the gendered adult course.

and age, their accounts (i.e., explanations to themselves and to others) are contrasted with existing institutional "givens" (West & Zimmerman, 1987).

The next sections follow our model of factors leading to both inequality and life quality for contemporary men and women, as depicted in Figure 13.1.

Gendered Socialization

DiRenzo (1977) defines socialization as the process and/or structure of social learning in which uniquely human attributes are developed and/or actualized in the human organism. Liao and Cai (1995) define socialization as a process in which individuals learn and maintain the morals and values of society (see also Kramer, 2005).

Learning Gender

There is an early literature describing how we learn to be men and women, focusing on the role of families in socializing each new generation (Lash, 1979; Mead, 1949, 1970; Parson & Bales, 1955). But people also learn gender and age "scripts" in schools and neighborhoods, as well as from the media, churches, mosques, synagogues, peer groups, coworkers and civic group members.

As a result of both formal and informal learning (socialization), gender and age are, literally, in our heads, as "scripts" guiding our own behavior and expectations of self and others (Fenstermaker & West, 2002). We develop age and gender stereotypes and values by hearing, seeing, and using polarizing language, categories, expectations, and assessments as short-hand heuristics and habits (Moen & Spencer, 2006a; Ridgeway & Smith-Lovin, 1999; West & Zimmerman, 1987). Consider, for example, the ways gender permeates how we think about and refer to people (e.g., "ask that woman over there"), roles (e.g., about nurses, "where is she?" and physicians, "is he in yet?"), and divisions of labor (e.g., "taking out the garbage is a man's job"). Gender and age as ways of categorizing and dividing behavior and beliefs, risks and resources combine to shape adult roles and relationships in ways that seem "natural" (i.e., second nature). Beliefs about men's greater status and competence implicitly shape the expectations of both men and women about their own competence and performance compared to others, independently of their actual underlying abilities (Ridgeway & Correll, 2004).

The Long Arm of Early Socialization

A life-course formulation emphasizes the importance of early experiences. This is especially true in terms of what children learn about gender (Liao & Cai, 1995; Fenstermaker & West, 2002). Liao and Cai (1995) find that contemporary American mothers continue to encourage very different gender-role behaviors in boys and girls.

To understand behavior at any one life stage requires knowledge of prior processes of socialization. Heinz, for instance, describes young people's "biographical action orientation" (Heinz, 1999, 2002a, 2002b) that serves as a guide to behavior as they move into and through adulthood. As an example of the cumulative processes of early decisions, young women are less apt to take calculus in high school, a choice (reflecting earlier gender socialization) that has enormous implications in terms of their subsequent majors in college. For instance, this choice to opt out of high school calculus considerably reduces the odds that women will move into careers in engineering or the natural sciences, given that these careers require training in mathematics, which is widely seen as a valued, but male-typed task (Nosek, Banaji, & Greenwald, 2002).

Such early socialization plays out throughout adulthood. In a recent four-year (2000–2003) Norwegian study of an entering cohort of undergraduate students in varying professions, Daehlen (2005) found preferences for work to be deeply rooted in a person's early socialization, acquired well before the choice of a higher educational program and sustained through such programs. This study offers evidence that gendered preferences are formed well before the transition to adulthood.

But socialization processes are ongoing throughout the life course, shaping adult beliefs, values and expectations (Mortimer & Simmons, 1978). Daehlen (2005) also found that job values do change with education, more or less in the same direction for male and female students (see also Johnson, 2001). Another recent study by Goodwin and O'Connor (2005) reanalyzed data from interviews of young men (who were ages 16–18 in 1962), following up with 94 re-interviews in 2001. They found that the career paths of the respondents they located were extremely gendered. Almost all the men had found jobs through male relatives, they all stressed making money as important, and reported that years ago the Youth Employment Office had steered them into traditionally male jobs.

Socialization into Cohorts

Recall that adults born around the same time period are often grouped together as identifiable cohorts. People of the same cohort share similar experiences and are often socialized in similar ways, experiencing the same technologies, historical circumstances, and social policies and practices. The result is often greater differences across than within cohorts in beliefs and values related to gender and adult pathways. Members of, for example, the aging Baby Boom cohort (born after World War II, from 1946 through 1964), and Generation X (born 1965 through 1975) have somewhat different beliefs about women's and men's roles. Note that family members, neighbors, friends, and coworkers of different ages are also members of different cohorts, socialized differently and viewing their lives—past, present and future—from vastly different vantage points.

What gives each cohort its distinctiveness are the shared events and experiences of people who are roughly the same age when major historical events occur. For Americans moving into adulthood in the early 1960s, a defining moment was the death of John F. Kennedy. For those not yet born, Kennedy's death is the stuff of history books and documentary films. For most Americans who were adults or adolescents at the turn of this century, *the* transformative experience of their lives occurred on September 11, 2001, when planes flew into the World Trade Center and the Pentagon.

There are other ways that *when* people are born—which birth cohort they belong to—has enormous implications for the course of their adult years. Men in certain cohorts have gone to war while their younger or older brothers (in different cohorts) watched these same wars on newsreels or television, safely at home. And the cohort of young women today is the first participating actively in the military in roles previously allocated to men.

Cohort differences are especially evident in societal expectations and gender norms around paid work and unpaid family work. Men in the post-war boom years of the 1950s and 60s were socialized into the American Dream and American values about a *career mystique* of hard work, independence, and occupational success (Moen & Roehling, 2005) even though large segments (minorities, poorly educated, immigrants) could never climb the career mystique ladder.

The career mystique myth crystallized in tandem with the *feminine mystique* (Friedan, 1963)—a belief in the 1950s and early 60s that women were socialized to be exclusively wives and mothers, finding total fulfillment in full-time domesticity. The problem was that many working-class and poor women couldn't afford to be out of the workforce, often moving in and out of marginal jobs, and middle-class women in college were learning different lessons about using their skills and training in the world of work. Friedan's book (1963) tapped a nerve, revealing many homemakers longing for a different kind of engagement and, in doing so, (re) launched the Women's Movement.

The cohort of women coming of age in the 1970s and 80s rejected the feminine mystique, only to learn and embrace the *career* mystique instead. The Women's Movement became an important socializing force encouraging women to want and even demand "men's" jobs, "men's" career aspirations, and "men's" salaries and occupational achievements—as the path to gender equality. But the career mystique—that a lifetime of working hard always pays off in occupational and economic success—was a false myth, never accessible to most workers. *And* it was predicated on having *someone else* (a wife) to take care of all the details of daily living. Accordingly, feminists began to call for men to do their fair share of the unpaid family care work, not recognizing that the structure and culture of paid work made doing so difficult for all workers, regardless of gender.

The feminine mystique is gone, although women are still socialized and allocated to the nation's carework of youth, the disabled, and the older frail and infirm. The career mystique remains dominant in American culture, however; the epitome of independent adulthood, the accepted path of optimal adult development to success, fulfillment, and gender equality for men and women (Becker & Moen, 1999; Moen & Roehling, 2005; Stewart & Healy, 1989). The result is role conflicts, strains, time pressures and overloads for employees in demanding jobs and/or high occupational aspirations who also have family demands and/or high family aspirations.

The result? Contemporary 21st-century cohorts of young workers—men and women—are being socialized to simultaneously both embrace and question the career mystique. Recall that socialization involves learning from observations. Many young people can no longer see the payoffs of following the lock-step career mystique path in light of corporate downsizing, mergers, and outsourcing, as well as the strains they observe in the lives of their parents' generation. Their beliefs about adulthood, gender equality and the path to success are often inconsistent, ambivalent, and vague (Orrange, 2007; Moen & Orrange, 2002).

Old scripts are increasingly out of date with new realities on a variety of levels. Consider how young people are socialized to embrace marriage and parenthood *and* to challenging these as fundamental to adulthood. Rates of marriage decreased from 143 per 1000 in the mid-1940s to 76 per 1000 by 1988. Those who do marry are doing so later. For example, in the U.S. the median age for women rose from 21 to 25 and from 23 to 27 for men from 1970 to 1997 and rose slightly again to 25.3 for women and 27.1 for men from 1997 to 2005 (U.S. Bureau of the Census, 1997, 2006). The age at first childbirth has followed a similar pattern. In 1970 the average age for first childbirth was 22.1 whereas in the year 2000 it is 24.6 (Mathews & Hamilton, 2002). There is also diversity in adult experiences across cultural groups. For example, African American women are much less likely to marry. In 1990, fewer than 75% of them married, and by 2004 less than half (48%) of them married, compared with 90% of white women in 1990 and 66.1% in 2004 (American Community Survey, 2004). Hispanic women have similar patterns; in 2004, 49.5% married versus 64.3% of non-Hispanics (American Community Survey, 2004).

Women who gave birth to the large Baby Boom cohort in the post-World War II economic growth years of the 1950s often had mothers or older sisters with small families, given that fertility had previously dipped in the lean Great Depression years in the 1930s. Since then, fertility rates have declined significantly (from a high of 3.0 children to current rates of 1.5). There is also an increasing number of women who are choosing not to bear children. Others groups are becoming parents for whom parenting might have not been possible in the past (e.g., gay and lesbian parents; see Anderson, 1999).

Socialization involves taking things for granted, as the way things are, and as the way things should be. Azar (2002) observes that what we think of as the typical life course—a sequence of leaving home, marriage, child rearing, launching and survival at age 50 with the first marriage still intact (unless broken by divorce) was not, in fact, the dominant pattern of family timing prior to the early 20th century. Before 1900, only about 40% of women in the U.S. experienced this life pattern (Uhlenberg, 1974, cited in Harevan, 1982). The remainder either never married, never reached marriageable age, died before childbirth, or were widowed while their children were still young.

Socialization is On-Going

Social and institutional convoys are the sources of on-going socialization processes: they transmit to the next generation taken-for-granted norms and expectations about how adulthood should unfold—such as the incidence, timing, durations and trajectories of relationships and roles. In particular, both social and organizational ties foster gendered and age-related expectations about the sequencing, duration and timing of the roles and responsibilities of employment, marriage, and parenthood. Socialization is also subject to changes in the life course of an individual and their social networks (Liao & Cai, 1995). For example, consider the transition to parenthood with the birth of a child. This new member of the parents' social convoy invokes all kinds of responses in adults who suddenly are mothers and fathers—changes in their sleep patterns, their identities, their values and priorities, their working hours and leisure, their relationships with one another and with friends, neighbors, parents, parents-in-law, and other extended kin. Fast forward 30 years, and this social convoy member at age 30 is very different, as is the relationship between parents and the now-adult child. Fast forward yet another 30 years, and this adult child at age 60 may well be helping to care for her aging parents.

Becoming a parent cannot be understood separately from the taken-for-granted norms and scripts that define what it means to be a mother or a father in distinctive ways. Mothers are (still) expected to do most of the child care and fathers (still) expected to do most of the breadwinning, even though both are likely to be in the workforce. Different expectations and beliefs about those who make the transition to parenthood "early," "on time," or else "late" in life according to existing social norms. Institutional convoys give social relationships structure and meaning and they constrain options around motherhood and fatherhood and differ by culture, locational differences by social class, marital status, immigrant status, race and ethnicity.

Adult opportunities still follow informal gender norms and expectations although they are no longer formally regulated by gender. Consider, as a case in point, educational socialization. On the surface, educational policies are gender-neutral. But Goodwin and O'Connor (2005) find that "schools reinforce different cultural values, dominant masculinity types, vocational preferences, and, via the curriculum, link types of knowledge and skills with masculinities and femininities" (p. 453). This accentuates men's traditional expectations and values about male adulthood as years of breadwinning and continuous, full-time hard work (see also Moen & Roehling, 2005; Townsend, 2002). Individuals learn through socialization processes the institutionalized nature of the life course. That, in turn, provides individuals at different life stages with "available lists of reasons, motives, and aspirations" (Meyer, 1986, p. 205), such as expectations regarding parenthood, employment, and retirement (see also Altucher & Williams, 2003; Brines & Joyner, 1999; Carr, 1997; Clausen, 1995; Cooney & Mortimer, 1999; Freund, 1997; Gerson, 1985; Han & Moen, 1999a, 1999b; Moen, Sweet, & Swisher, 2005; Pixley & Moen, 2003; Wethington, Pixley, & Kavey, 2003).

Socialization to Later Adulthood

Socialization to later adulthood is also changing. In their study of pre-Baby Boom workers, Han and Moen (1999a, 1999b) found that the age employees began planning their retirement has gotten progressively earlier for each successive cohort. Respondents who were born in the 1920s typically began to plan at age 54. By contrast, those born between 1935 and 1943 started planning in their mid forties (on average, at age 46). Early planning appears to be related to an earlier expected retirement age, with the most recent cohort in their study (born between 1935 and 1943) expecting to retire from their career jobs in their late 50s.

Given the new uncertainties surrounding both occupational career progression and retirement, we would expect the Baby Boom cohort and those following in their wake to be particularly aware of the need for planfulness. A study of Baby Boomers' saving patterns reveals that almost half (46%) save regularly, with another three in ten (30%) saving occasionally (Gist, Wu, & Ford, 1999). The two most frequent explanations for saving are for precautionary reasons related to life course risks, such as unemployment, illness, security (28.8%) and for retirement (23%).

Moen, Huang, Plassmann, and Dentinger (2006) found that dual-earner spouses' levels of retirement planfulness are positively related, but in different ways, depending on gender, cohort, and family circumstances. Husbands tend to plan more financially, while wives tend to plan more in terms of their lifestyles following retirement. Perceived control (mastery), income adequacy, and work load all positively predict both husbands' and wives' planfulness. Husbands' planfulness tends to shape their wives' planfulness. But in couples without children at home and in the leading edge of the Baby Boom cohort, it is wives' planfulness that influences their husbands' level of planning, not vice versa. Spouses in younger couples (those in the trailing edge Baby Boom cohort) typically make plans independently of one another.

Gendered Allocation of Roles, Resources, and Relationships

Gender Systems of Stratification

Gender socialization—the ways adults as well as children learn how to be male or female (see Figure 13.1)—can explain part of the story, but scholars increasingly focus on processes of gender *allocation*. This is the institutionalized packaging of resources, constraints and options by gender within families, schools, workplaces, religious, civic and other organizational structures and groupings. As Ridgeway and Correll (2004) point out, gender used to be described as an identity or role that is taught in childhood and enacted in family relations. Now the definition is moving toward thinking of gender as an institutionalized system of social practices. These practices divide people into two groups, men and women, and works to maintain the inequality between the two based on these made up differences.

Gender socialization is about *learning* gender, fostering differences in women's and men's beliefs, values, and identities. Gender stratification is about *dividing* by gender, allocating positions, power and material resources based on whether one is male or female. It is the systematic way that roles, resources and rewards are distributed that perpetuates gender inequality. This takes place in large part because organizational rules, routines, and regulations serve to structure the adult course in gendered ways (Mayer & Tuma, 1990).

Why is there inequality—economic, political, social and interpersonal—between women and men? Even more important than socialization processes are the institutional arrangements that stratify women and men by their gender. Kohn and Schooler (1983) define stratification as the hierarchical distribution of power, privilege, and prestige. Groups and organizations of all types allocate roles, resources and relationships—along with power—based on a range of factors. The allocation of power, privilege and prestige in society and in organizations depends on one's social background, race and ethnicity, educational achievement, and occupational level, of course, but also on the combination of age and gender (Anderson, 2005; Kramer, 2005; Kimmel & Aronson, 2000; McCall, 2001).

Gender stratification is fundamentally about disparities in economic power (Anderson 2005; Blumberg 1984) between men and women. Serguino (2007) argues that socialization forces in the form of gender ideology, norms and stereotypes reinforce material inequality between women and men, thereby reinforcing the gender stratification system.

Social Policies as Gender Systems

Twentieth century social policies and practices have created, reinforced, and perpetuated different life courses for men and women. First were efforts to institutionalize life into segments predicated on middle-class men's experience. In fact, the very notion that adulthood consists of distinctive and identifiable paths is a product of primarily mid-20th-century policies and practices developing in Europe and America around the institutions of education, employment, and retirement (see Kohli, 1986a, 1986b; Marshall, Heinz,

Krueger, & Verna, 2001; Meyer, 1986). In the middle of the 20th century, educational, employment, and pension legislation and regulation forged *a lock-step life course*, consisting of first full-time public education as preparation for adult roles, then an adulthood of continuous, full-time employment, followed by full-time leisure during the "golden years" of retirement. This adult path of continuous, full-time, year-round employment, bracketed by schooling at one end and retirement (or death) at the other, became institutionalized as the (only) route to adult fulfillment and success—the structure of the career mystique (Moen & Roehling, 2005). Government policies (e.g., Social Security, unemployment insurance, Medicare, disability regulations, the Fair Labor Standards Act) all took as a given both the lock-step path of (men's) continuous, full-time employment and the breadwinner-homemaker gender divide. These policies, together with the regulations guiding business practices, constitute an age-graded regime giving structure to the life course: the shared understandings and taken-for-granted rules, roles, relationships, resources and risks associated with adulthood at different ages and life stages.

But note that this lock-step arrangement was predicated on *men's*, not women's, lives. Most middle-class women's adulthood in the middle of the 20th century gave primacy to marriage and mothering, with only intermittent ties to the workforce. The primacy of family goals and obligations continues to shape women's lives even though most are entrenched in the workforce (Carr, 1997; Garey, 1999; Gerson, 2001; Han & Moen, 1999a, 1999b, 2002; Ridgeway & Correll, 2004). Thus the social organization of the life course is *gender-graded* as well, typically producing diverging pathways for men and women, even though they may begin life with similar backgrounds and abilities (Moen, 1996a, 1996b, 2001; Moen & Roehling, 2005) fostering work-family conflicts and strains for women and their families. The life course as an institution allocating roles and resources overtime is also replete with informal norms that shape women's and men's cognitive assessments, their "ambitions, stock-taking, and self-image at various times during their lives" (Kruger & Baldus, 1999, p. 356; see also Altucher & Williams, 2003; Becker & Moen, 1999; Blossfeld & Huinik, 1991; Moen & Orange, 2002; Townsend, 2002).

Today, age divides are more visible (often written into policies, such as kindergarten for five-year-olds or retirement for 65-year-olds) than are gender divides. It is easy to "see" the life course as a convoy of institutionalized rules and regulations when we think about the ages one can purchase alcohol, marry, vote, or retire. By contrast, there are few overt regulations about gender. Yet this was not always the case.

Consider the ways jobs were allocated by whether or not one was male or female (or pregnant), or how workers were allocated Social Security credits, both of which disadvantaged women. Until the late 1960s, job want ads in newspapers specified the gender of the employee, with clerical and secretarial positions specifically seeking women (Pedriana, 2004). Teachers in some school districts in the 1960s and 1970s could not continue to teach if pregnant. Before 1978 one could not receive a year's Social Security credit except by remaining in the workforce continuously throughout the year, something problematic for women, given they were likely to move in and out of paid work for caregiving or other reasons (Institute for Women's Policy Research, 2005). Both of these policies were revised in tandem with both the women's movement and the influx of married women into the workforce (Moen & Roehling, 2005).

Work Organizations as Gender Systems

Employment has been a "master" adult role, the path to economic independence, self-esteem, meaning, and security. It is the fundamental public ecology and institutional convoy in which adult life plays out. But jobs remain gendered, even though they are no longer labeled "for men only" or "for women only." Employers commonly steer women (or men) toward some jobs rather than others, contributing to the ongoing gendering of jobs (Fernandez & Sosa, 2005). Ridgeway and Correll (2004) describe how small biasing effects such as these accumulate over careers and lifetimes to result in substantially different employment experiences and rewards for men and women who are otherwise similar in social background.

Characteristics of jobs, career paths, and the working environment are extremely consequential for the developing individual and tend to differ by gender. Considerable theoretical progress and empirical evidence link high demands on the job and low levels of job latitude with heightened feelings of strain (Elsass & Viega, 1997) leading to poor health outcomes such as cardiovascular disease and elevated blood pressure. But men are more apt than women to occupy jobs with both high demands and high control (Bosma, Stansfield, & Marmot, 1998; Cheng, Kawachi, Coakley, Schwartz, & Colditz, 2000; de Jonge, Bosma, Peter, & Siegrist, 2000; Dwyer & Ganster, 1991; Fox, 1993; Schnall, Landsbergis, & Baker, 1994). Moreover, Marshall, Barnett, and Sayer (1997) find evidence suggesting that the demand-control model may be more applicable to employees in manufacturing sector jobs (typically men) than to those in service jobs (typically women). They find that, for employees in the service sector, job control does not moderate job demands, while the intrinsic rewards associated with serving others tend to benefit service employees' health.

Families and Work-Family Linkages as Gender Systems

Contemporary adulthood is replete with ostensibly gender-neutral paths. Even the career mystique of continuous full-time employment, often in the same occupation or organization throughout most of adulthood, is now seen as available to men and women alike. However, family obligations are neither gender-neutral nor integrated into the designs of jobs and career paths. Most women find it patently impossible to pursue the career mystique and simultaneously their own (and others') caregiving role expectations as wives, mothers, and adult daughters (Pavalko & Artis, 1997). The result? Men have typically reaped greater advantages than have women, with their lock-step work histories enhancing future career options and expectations (O'Rand & Henretta, 1996).

When all adults in a household are in the workforce, an increasing number of employees are experiencing work-family conflicts and strains. "Good" jobs (those with benefits, for example) were designed for workers (men) without family responsibilities. The "man in the grey flannel suit" office worker and the unionized blue-collar worker in the 1950s could follow the career mystique of working long hours on a continuous basis throughout their adult years precisely because they had wives working as full-time homemakers. They also had jobs paying a living wage, and could expect both their wages and their job security to increase as they gained seniority by remaining with the same employer throughout a lifetime of employment (Moen & Roehling, 2005).

Supposedly ungendered pathways are, in fact, *not* gender neutral so long as jobs are designed for people without family responsibilities, and gender schema and cultural expectations continue to assign women responsibility for society's unpaid family care as well as for kin-keeping and community-building. Moen and Roehling (2005) conclude that most employing organizations are "work-friendly," not family-friendly. Mennino, Rubin, and Brayfield's (2005) analysis of the 1997 National Study of the Changing Workforce reveals that not only is the workplace environment typically *not* supportive of employees with family responsibilities, but the environment is worse for women. Women report higher levels of both home to job and job to home spillover than men. Purportedly supportive workplace policies are often merely band-aids, doing little to reduce time pressures and strains. Absent are authentically supportive workplace cultures and supervisors.

Family life and occupational careers are both typically examined exclusive of other social roles and of each other. Life course scholars are beginning to look at the ways in which gender, relationships and roles intersect across the life course, at the interdependency between work and family obligations as well as the interdependency between the lives of different family members. Some innovative research (Home, 1998; Wethington, 2000) examines "contagion," that is, the spill over of stress from one family member to another (see, for example, Bolger, DeLongis, Kessler, & Wethington, 1989).

Social Clocks as Gender Systems

Yet another framing of the adult course is to consider the ways individual lives unfold in the face of institutional clocks and the correlative taken-for-granted culture of what constitutes being "on" or "off" time in adult passages (Neugarten, 1968; Hagestad & Neugarten, 1985). People leave old roles and enter new ones—such as that of retiree— at particular points in their life biographies. Han and Moen (1999a, 1999b) term this *biographical pacing*, defined as the age at which individuals undergo key status passages— whether and when one marries, has children, takes a job, goes back to school, changes jobs, retires, goes back to work, remarries, or moves (see also Sweet & Moen, 2006). Viewing adulthood from the vantage point of biographical pacing emphasizes the life-course concept of timing and the social clock aspects of gender systems, with individuals defining the passages in their lives (and the lives of others) as being either on or off time—for example, retiring earlier or later than the conventional norm (Brim & Ryff, 1980; Neugarten & Hagestad, 1976; Settersten & Hagestad, 1996a, 1996b; Hagestad & Neugarten, 1985; Mortimer & Simmons, 1978; Mortimer, Oesterle, & Kruger, 2005; Mortimer, Vuolo, Staff, Wakefield, & Xie, 2006; Wheaton, 1990). Social clocks are often different for women and men, with women having more temporal latitude around job and retirement clocks and men having more temporal latitude around marriage and parenting clocks. Institutionalized clockworks shape not only individual life pathways but the subjective side of adulthood as well, coloring women's and men's expectations, self-concepts, goals, identities, and affinities (Downey et al., 2005; Moen, Sweet, & Swisher, 2005). Thus, the predictability, timing and clustering of role occupancies or transitions change their meaning and their implications for identity and adult development more generally.

An emerging issue in life course research is the effect of variation in the pacing and clockworks of life events. Mortimer, Staff, and Oesterle (2003), for example, find alternative paths of labor force participation on the way to adulthood among high schoolers. Similar proportions (~26%) of both boys and girls follow a high investment employment path of high duration, and high intensity. Similar portions (~23%) of both boys and girls also follow an occasional employment path towards adulthood. But young men are almost twice as likely as young women to not work at all throughout high school (9.9 to 4.6%). Young men are also more apt to have a sporadic work history of low duration but high intensity (28.2 to 14.3%), and are less likely than their female classmates to follow a steady (i.e., high duration, low intensity) employment pathway during the high school years (18.2 to 30.6%). Moreover, Mortimer and colleagues (2003) find that those in sporadic paths—disproportionately men—experience more stress, but also more opportunities for learning, as well as having greater potential for advancement. By contrast, those persons engaged in steady, low intensity occupational paths—disproportionately women—obtain lower earnings and have less stress, but they also have fewer opportunities for human capital development. There has been, to date, little research on biographical pacing as a predictor of behavior or beliefs, and yet it makes intuitive sense that life stage experiences and location—in terms of occupational and family pathways—should shape adult identities as well as plans and expectations for the future.

One manifestation of the unraveling of the social clock aspect of adult development path is the fact that first women and now men as well are increasingly returning to school as adults, often after marriage and childbearing, or even as they approach or enter retirement (Bradburn, Moen, & Dempster-Mc-Clain, 1995; Settersten & Lovegreen, 1998; Suitor, 1987; Sweet & Moen, 2006).

Biographical pacing is patterned by social class, race and ethnicity, and other social markers, as well as by health and ability, age and gender, and chance events. Recall that a life course theoretical lens (e.g., Elder, 1985, 1998a, 1998b; Moen & Wethington, 1992) also points to the importance of prior as well as coterminous events for understanding the gendered nature of adulthood. People's lives thus reflect the interplay between their past experiences, ongoing social and institutional convoys, and large-scale technological, economic, and policy shifts. While considerable advance has been made in capturing the patterned constellations of paths shaping adolescent development (Booth, Crouter, & Shanahan, 1999; Moen, 2003; Mortimer, Staff, & Lee, 2005; Mortimer, Staff, & Oesterle, 2003; Shanahan, 2000), we know little about the dynamic interplay between work, family, gender and human development in middle and later adulthood. This points to the need to capture, through life histories or longitudinal data, the patterned dynamics and social clocks of adult lives and identities as they are constructed and reconstructed over time.

Changes in Gender Systems

Institutional convoys—the taken-for-granted regime of age-graded (and often gender-graded) norms, rules, and regulations allocating options and risks at different ages and life stages—do change as a result of historical events, scientific and technological advances, demographic and economic shifts, policy initiatives and other social transformations.

Most contemporary workers are single, single-parents or dual-earners—without homemakers as back up for family and other obligations. Regardless of status or tenure, both men and women in all kinds of occupations and at all ages confront global economic changes fostering greater job and economic insecurity, along with concerns about health insurance, prospects for advancement, and/or retirement pensions. New information and communication technologies are escalating work demands and speeding up the pace and pressures related to the time and timing of work. The reality is that very few contemporary adults—women or men—have the time, option, or inclination to devote themselves exclusively to their jobs. Moreover, doing so is no guarantee of an adequate income, job security, health care and other protections.

It is only in the last four decades that employers have even attempted to help employees reconcile work and family responsibilities by adding maternity leaves and later gender-neutral family leaves (Kelly & Dobbin, 1999) and creating new child care benefits (Kelly, 2003). Recent research confirms that access to family-supportive policies like leaves and child care benefits has an important effect on women's pattern of labor force attachment, including whether they leave the labor force (Estes & Glass, 1996; Liebowitz &

Klerman, 1995), how quickly they return to full-time work (Hofferth, 1996), and whether they change jobs around the time of a birth (Glass & Riley, 1998). Those employment decisions, in turn, affect mothers' wages and career advancement (see Kelly, 2005a, for a review). Employers have not added these family-supportive policies out of the goodness of their hearts, or even because the evidence of their benefit to the organization was clear and convincing, but instead because public policies and the public's expectations have changed over this period (Kelly, 2005b). In other words, women's decisions about how they will try to "balance" work and family are shaped by company policies and practices that are, in turn, shaped by public policies and by broader cultural shifts about what we expect from good employers.

The notion of orderly career paths embedded in the career mystique dream is no longer a reality even for most middle-class men. In their follow-up study of boys in Great Britain (who were first interviewed at ages 16–18 in 1962–64 and then reinterviewed in 2001), Goodwin and O'Connor (2005) found that as this group proceeded through adulthood they did not follow single careers paths as they had expected, but moved in and out of positions, occupations, and employment based on the fluctuations of the local labor market.

In sum, whether reflective of reality or not, the lock-step institutional life course represents time structures and cultural clocks and calendars that constitute both informal timetables and norms (at what age young people should, for example, become financially independent of their parents) and formal policies (such as at what age people become eligible for Medicare). The multilayered clockworks of the adult course are important because they open up or close opportunities (such as the "right" age to attend college) that can have enormous long-term impacts on life chances and life quality. They also infuse the same transition—such as parenthood—with different meanings and consequences, depending on whether the new parent is a father or mother, and whether that new father or mother is age 15, 25, or 45.

Thus far we have described the life course as an institution that is historically constructed and reconstructed, showing that the rules and regulations around age and gender change for different cohorts of people in light of historical events (such as the women's movement), technological and economic transformations, the move to a service economy (and now a global economy), and social policy development (such as the Family and Medical Leave Act and Social Security). But they change slowly, often lagging behind alterations in the real-world experiences of adults.

Gender Strategies (Strategic Selection)

Both gender learning (socialization) and gender systems (allocation) shape the gendered adult course in the form of preferences and options. In this section we describe processes of *doing gender*, that is, following expected gender scripts in daily life. We propose that doing gender involves processes of strategic selection within the array of options and expectations available in light of prevailing gender beliefs and values.

Doing Gender

Following gender scripts in daily life is what West and Zimmerman (1987) call "doing gender," that is, people engaging in what they believe is behavior expected for their gender. In this way gender distinctions (and therefore gender inequality) are reified, created and recreated through everyday social interactions. As individuals enter public settings that require them to define themselves in relation to others, their default expectation is that others will treat them according to socialized *gender beliefs*. Most people, most of the time, largely and often unwittingly comply with the pressure of gender-based expectations in most of their behavior (Ridgeway & Correll, 2004). This is especially the case since deviating from gender norms leads to social stigma, anxiety, and distress (Serguino, 2007).

We add to this our assessment that adults in fact are doing age *and* gender, following their own expectations, as well as their beliefs about the expectations of others that perpetuate existing age and gender divides. But age/gender socialization and allocation processes are shifting. The early 21st century is a time of opening up of an unprecedented array of both options and risks to women and men at different ages and stages.

An ecology of the life course perspective views doing gender as a series of adaptive strategies as men and women attempt to regain control over the circumstances of their lives (see Figure 13.1). Life course scholars focus on active decision making; people are agents in shaping their own life courses (Clausen, 1991; Elder, 1985; Krüger & Baldus, 1999; Marshall, Heinz, Krüger, & Verma, 2001; Mortimer & Shanahan, 2003; Shanahan, 2000; Shanahan, Hofer, & Miech, 2002). Unfortunately, their choices often reproduce gender differences and disparities that are then accentuated across the life span.

In times of relative stability, when there are few social transformations in the ecologies of adulthood, development seems predictable, and the adaptations women and men make throughout their adult years tend to follow culturally endorsed and taken-for-granted age and gender scripts. In such times of social stability, adult development means following in the footsteps of (same sex) parents, older siblings, aunts, uncles, and cousins. In times of social change, by contrast, the "right" strategies for moving into and through the adult years are suddenly ambiguous, often requiring people to make deliberate, unscripted choices in the face of uncertainty (e.g., strategic selections about whether and when to get additional schooling, marry, have children, switch employers, leave the workforce, retrain for a new career, move aging parents to live geographically closer, change jobs, divorce, move, retire, or even to act a certain way in a particular social setting). Moreover, adults make these strategic choices within an outdated social and cultural environment replete with the last century's gender scripts and gendered structural arrangements.

Cycles of Control and Life-Course "Fit"

Building on theories of stress as a consequence of a disjuncture between resources and needs or demands, life course scholars view individuals and families as making strategic selections (of roles and relationships, but also behavior) as a way of (re)gaining a sense of mastery or control over their lives. Such patterned responses to current (or anticipated) gaps between resources and needs throughout adult life we term *cycles of control* (Elder, 1974; Moen & Chermack, 2005; Moen & Spencer, 2006a; Moen & Yu, 1999, 2000). Individuals or groups seek to remedy any disjuncture between the pressures or needs they experience and their available resources by seeking better life course "fit"—either increasing their available resources, reducing their pressures or needs, or redefining the situation to make it more acceptable (see Figure 13.1). Note that enacted role behavior shapes beliefs and values to be more congruent with that behavior (see Kohn & Schooler, 1983; Lioa & Cai, 1995; Moen & Erickson, 1995).

A sense of personal control or mastery (also called efficacy) is defined as a perception of being in charge of the circumstances of one's life (Bandura, 1982, 1989), and is typically higher among men than women. It has been and remains an important concept in social science research. Bandura (1982) holds that "self efficacy is concerned with judgments about how well one can organize and execute courses of action required to deal with prospective situations containing many ambiguous, unpredictable, and often stressful elements" (p. 23). Bandura and others (Heckhausen & Schulz, 1993, 1995; Rodin, 1987, 1989; Zarit, Pearlin, & Schaie, 2002) theorize personal mastery as a key psychological resource, one that is particularly important in the face of stressful events or chronic strains. It has been linked theoretically and empirically with both direct and buffering effects in reducing the risks of distress and the impacts of stressors on psychological well-being (Koeske & Kirk, 1995; Moen, 1997; Rodin, 1989; Spector & O'Connell, 1994; Spector et al., 2001).

But where does a sense of personal mastery come from? Research shows that this sense of efficacy is related to actual experiences of effectiveness, as well as the toolbox of resources (e.g., education, income, social network) individuals can potentially draw on in response to the crises and chronic pressures in their lives. Thus, conceptually we are theorizing two types of control: 1) the degree of autonomy and choice individuals experience within the work and family ecologies in which adulthood is played out; and 2) the subjective assessment by individuals of their abilities to take charge of their lives. Moreover, both men's and women's sense of efficacy varies with shifts in life course "fit" between demands and resources over the adult course (e.g., de Lange, Taris, Kompier, Houtman, & Bongers, 2003; de lange, Taris, Kompier, Houtman, & Bongers, 2004; Downey & Moen, 1987; Karasek, 1979, 1998; Karasek & Theorell, 1990).

Our ecology of the gendered adult course framing underscores the gender- and age-related distributions and combinations of employment and family needs and pressures as well as personal, social and financial resources. Sociologist Glen Elder (1995) describes control cycles wherein individuals feel more or less vulnerable, or more or less able to cope with the exigencies at hand. This is congruent with Heckhausen and Schulz's (1995) life-span theory of control, Baltes and Baltes' (1990) selective optimization with compensation (SOC) theory of human development, and Carstensen's (1992) social-emotional selectivity theory. Each of these theories emphasizes the importance of ecological contexts. Each depicts adult development as an unfolding process whereby individuals seek to maximize their effectiveness at all ages by selectively choosing some relationships and activities over others. Doing so enables adults to both accentuate their resources and play down the intellectual and physical deficits that accrue with age.

Life course scholars propose that it is the *gap* between needs/pressures and resources that produces cycles of control, or, conversely, cycles of stress for women and men at different times in their lives. In particular, the concept of life course "fit" (Moen, Sweet, & Swisher, 2005; Sweet, Swisher, & Moen, 2005; Swisher, Sweet, & Moen, 2004) consists of adults' perceptions of the nexus or gap between pressures and the resources with which to deal with them, as well as expectations of future gaps. This resources-to-needs ratio varies by age, career development, and family stage, as well as by gender and location within the socio-economic structure. Expected or unexpected events can also reduce perceptions of life course fit. People currently undergoing or anticipating a family or workplace transition (a new child, a chronic or acute illness, a layoff or promotion) are at risk of a shift in either pressures or resources, or both, shifts that can precipitate change in adults' control at home and at work, as well as their perceptions of personal mastery.

Adulthood entails a series of adaptive strategies as men and women seek to gain, sustain, or regain life course fit and with it a sense of personal control in the face of insufficient resources to meet their goals, expectations, and the demands upon them (Moen

& Wethington, 1992). Adults of different ages, at different life stages, and with different pressures and resources, strategically select (or are allocated to) roles and relationships, and with them particular ecologies. Such selections concern, for example, the timing and types of education, occupations, employment arrangements, marriage, parenthood, family size, residence, relationships, and proximity to kin. At historical periods when adult roles are tightly age-graded and gender-graded, adulthood consists of established roles and scripts that reify age and gender distinctions. Scholars (Heinz & Marshall, 2003; Kohli, 1986a, 1986b, 1994; Marshall, Heinz, Kruger, & Verma, 2001; Mayer & Tuma, 1990) refer to this as the standardized, lock-step life course that emerged in Europe and North America through the institutionalization of public education, adolescence, occupational paths, retirement, social welfare regimes, and old age. These institutional arrangements are outdated, however, given the enormity of social changes in longevity, technology, the political economy, and gender roles. The result?—an exacerbation of strains across the adult course for women and men.

Five Propositions about Strategic Selections and Gender

Most social and behavior research looks for differences in outcomes based on what Bronfenbrenner terms different "social addresses": ecologically significant categories such as occupation, family composition, educational level, social class, and (of course) gender. But from a cycles of control perspective, we know that women and men are not randomly distributed across different jobs, different work hours, different family types or circumstances. Neither do they necessarily remain in these situations. We summarize our thinking about strategic selections of women and men through the adult course in five propositions.

Adult Development is an Ongoing "Project."   The adult course has become something of a project, as men and women make strategic choices in efforts to regain a sense of control over their lives and improve their life course fit. The adaptive strategies they "choose" remain gendered, however. Women continue to be allocated (and often feel) responsibility for most domestic chores, child care, and family timetables, even though most now have jobs (Barnett & Rivers, 1996; Gerson, 1985; Hertz, 1986; Hochschild, 1989, 1997). Men are seen as—and continue to feelresponsible for "bringing home the bacon," despite the fact that most households require two incomes to survive and men increasingly want to actively participate in parenting. Gender also continues to shape life chances and life quality, even though few people now believe that women and men are inherently different in ways that would justify strict role divisions and resource disparities.

Viewing adult development as a project clarifies strategic selections and course corrections as on-going. For example, women and men construct particular family ecologies by tending to marry people of similar social positions and values or else someone who is their polar opposite (Kalmijn, 1998; Lucas et al., 2004). A considerable body of research also shows the gendered developmental impacts of family conditions and transitions. In reviewing evidence on the transition to parenthood, Demo and Cox (2000) note that studies following people into parenting find variability in their adjustment to it. Their review suggests that parenting stress is similar for both new mothers and fathers. They also conclude that mothers and fathers both report lower stress when fathers take part in child care at home. From the vantage point of cycles of control, life course fit and strategic selection, one can consider how women and men select themselves into or out of parenthood, and into and out of active parenting, including how men opt to take part in the care of their new infants. This also points to the institutional convoys constraining active parenting options of new fathers: the fact that women but not men are expected to do most of the infant care, and men but not women are expected to remain full-time breadwinners throughout adulthood, regardless of family care needs.

Adaptive strategies themselves may shift over the life course, becoming more or less gendered. For example, Josselson (2002) makes the important point that girls learn early to put aside their own feelings to please others, but may rethink such strategies in middle adulthood. Josselson also notes that as a woman's life progresses, she may see that what seemed like a choice at the time was in fact determined by fear, passivity, impulsivity, unconscious wishes, or external pressures.

Thus, the gendered ecologies of adulthood aren't just "out there;" they are both the consequence of men's and women's strategic selections of some roles and relationships and not others, choices made in constrained, shifting, and progressively more ambiguous cultures and structural arrangements (see Figure 13.1).

Structural Constraints Limiting Options Affect Men's and Women's Health and Life Quality. Various strands of research evidence support our theorization of adulthood as a project: dynamic processes of strategic role and relationship selections that position women and men in different circumstances, with different options, resources, challenges and constraints. For example, occupational health scholarship (e.g., Karasek, 1979, 1998; Karasek & Theorell, 1990) demonstrates that adults' job control (in terms of how one does the work) promotes health and well-being. But such latitude on the job is not distributed evenly across men and women in the workforce. Karasek and Theorell (1990) note that men are more likely than women to have high control over their work circumstances. Moreover, they find a negative relationship between decision latitude on the job and workplace demands for women. This means that women tend to be in jobs with low control but high job demands, precisely the arrangement which exacerbates strain. When men work in jobs with high demands, these jobs also tend to offer them greater control over their work circumstances and demands. Karasek and Theorell find that degree of job control becomes the difference between whether job demands promote growth and learning or psychological strain. Another related study shows that having more job autonomy actually increases negative home to job spillover for men, whereas it decreases it for women (Mennino, Rubin, & Brayfield, 2005). These authors point out that this:

> ... illustrates the discrepancy between having more job autonomy, as the men in this study do, and increasing demands on men to be more involved in domestic responsibilities. These combined pressures can only lead to more spillover between home and the workplace unless institutional support is present. (p. 120)

Consider, as another example, how being in gender-atypical occupations plays out in adult development. Evans and Steptoe (2002) examined well-being among men and women in England who were employed in a traditionally male-dominated occupation (accountancy) and in a traditionally female-dominated occupation (nursing). The highest levels of anxiety were found among women in accounting, and the highest rates of absence due to sickness were found among men in nursing. The researchers concluded that "men and women working in jobs in which they are in a minority, and where the culture is dominated by the opposite sex, may be especially vulnerable to stress-related problems" (p. 490). Our control cycles theory of gendered strategic selections encourages analysis of the kinds of people who enter or remain in male- or female-dominated occupations. At the very least, scholars using cross-sectional data should reflect about such selection processes (for example, who is in certain occupations, or not in the work-force and how did that come about), even if it is impossible to establish them empirically with single point-in-time data.

Pavalko and Smith (1999) find that the amount of time that women spend in employment tends to slow the progression of physical health limitations as they age. Conversely, providing care for an aging parent or another infirm relative is negatively related to both physical and emotional well-being. Ali and Avison (1997) investigated women's transitions into and out of paid work in their longitudinal study of single and two-parent families living in London, Ontario. They found single women who leave their jobs suffer a substantial increase in distress due to loss of income, while married women who leave jobs do not. Moreover, when a transition into employment is coupled with significant increases in caregiving strain for married women, their emotional distress increases. From a control cycles vantage point, we can theorize [ask] why some women spend a great deal of time in the workforce, while others move in and out, and some other leave the workforce early or delay entry. We can also theorize possible distinctions in resources and options between women who are married or single, as well as between those who are or are not involved in caregiving.

Strategic Selections have Long Term Consequences. Women and men make ad hoc choices that may make sense at the time but that sometime have long-term deleterious consequences. Men's focus on paid work and women's focus on unpaid family care work perpetuate gender disparities in income, status, benefits, and other resources. Our cycles of control model theorizes individual strategies of adaptation as embedded in a web of social relations and social structures offering, in fact, only a limited number of options. For example, even though most American workers report a desire to put in less time at work (Clarkberg & Moen, 2001), women and men cannot work fewer hours without real penalties in terms of health care, wages, and job security (Kelly, 2005a; Moen & Roehling, 2005), and women are more apt to incur these penalties.

Because women tend to move in and out of paid work and in and out of various (often unrelated) jobs more than do men (Han & Moen, 1999a, 1999b, 2002; Rosenfeld, 1992; Sorensen & McLanahan, 1987; Williams & Han, 2003) they seldom reap the rewards of following the lock-step career mystique, producing widening economic inequalities by gender with age (Blau, Ferber, & Winkler, 1998; Crompton, 2006; Folbre, 2001; Moen & Roehling, 2005; O'Rand & Henretta, 1996; Padavic & Reskin, 2002; Stier & Lewin-Epstein, 2000; Waldfolgel, 1995, 1998).

In this way, both women's and men's strategic role selections—which often do make sense for them and their families—remain gender strategies, unintentionally reinforcing older patterns of gender inequalities for those who chose them, as well as reinforcing stereotypes that affect the possibilities for all women and men. The repercussions are tangible. Looking only at fulltime, year-long employees in 2004, women earned 76.5 percent as much as men. If part time and part year workers are included in this measure, the ratio would be much lower (Institute for Women's Policy Research, 2005).

Strategic Selections are More Deliberate and Difficult in Times of Social Change. Rational choice theory (Becker, 1981) depicts individuals as making optimal decisions, but "optimal" is difficult to cipher within a kaleidoscope of change. Consider the irrelevance of, for example, etiquette manuals developed in Victorian England as guides for behavior today. In times of social change, parents, teachers, and other models and mentors cannot provide to members of the next generation useful preparation and metrics for assessing "optimal" choices throughout the adult experience. Individuals coming to or moving through 21st-century adulthood are offered as their only resource "outdated guidebooks," presenting obsolete blueprints and irrelevant advice. Contemporary young, middle-aged, and older adults are no longer sure about where they are, much less where they are going.

We theorize that women's and men's strategic selections reflect processes of on-going learning—about the world and about oneself—precisely because existing scripts are no longer relevant. But old strategies die hard. Age- and gender-graded institutional arrangements serve to pull people back into traditional adult paths that remain divided by gender as well as age. As Powell and DiMaggio (1991) point out, existing social arrangements provide a guide to action and produce shared expectations that, in turn, foster psychological security. Attempts to change existing arrangements are often resisted because they threaten individuals' sense of security, increase the cost of information processing, and disrupt routines (see also Moen & Orrange, 2002).

Endorsing Gender Equality is not Enough to Change Gendered Institutions.   Most Americans now endorse gender equality in every sphere, and landmark legislation has reinforced the belief in and the right to equal access and opportunity in education, jobs, and community roles. But some variant of traditional gendered divisions of housework, childcare, and paid work persists even when both spouses work full time outside the home.

We argue that gender inequality is now less a consequence of discrimination and patriarchy than a function of a series of mindful, seemingly pragmatic decisions on the part of employers, employees, and families. For example, cultural beliefs presuming that a mother will prioritize family over paid work bias employers' and managers' expectations about her ability, performance, and appropriateness for authority even more strongly than for a woman who is not a mother (Ridgeway & Correll, 2004). There is growing evidence that women who are mothers of dependent children face special disadvantages in the labor force even compared to other women (Budig & England, 2001). Women are more likely than men to work part time or to avoid overtime in order to manage child-rearing and other caregiving work (Institute for Women's Policy Research, 2005) that remain principally "women's work." Many employers' stereotypical expectations that women are not interested in long-term careers are thereby reinforced. Some managers then assume that all women—or at least all mothers—are less committed to their jobs. Of course, such assessments are inaccurate and arguably constitute sex discrimination (Correll, Benard, & Paik, 2007; Kelly, 2005a; Williams & Segal, 2003). Men in turn, continue to embrace the role of family breadwinner, accentuating their willingness to devote enormous amounts of their energy, focus, and time to their jobs.

Two studies of caring for aging or infirm relatives offer suggestive evidence as to the gendered processes and consequences of strategic selection, as well as the absence of institutional supports. Fredriksen (1996) captures some of these control cycle processes in a study of university employees who also have caregiving responsibilities, defined as "assist[ing] an adult family member or friend who has a health problem or disability." Caregiving demand was defined as the number of children in house, number of hours providing informal adult care, and characteristics of care recipient (i.e., age, resides in home, functional impairment). Women are more likely than men to both be caregivers (strategic selection) and to report higher levels of caregiving strain, work interference and role strain (consequences of strategic selection). Not surprisingly, women tend to have fewer resources and higher levels of caregiving demand. While men tend to help spouses, women tend to help everyone (see also Gerstel, 2000; Sarkisian & Gerstel,

2004). Women employees in this study also were more likely to anticipate job termination as a response to their caregiving responsibilities. The women caregivers also endorsed employer-provided benefits more than did their male colleagues.

Marks (1998), drawing on data from the Wisconsin Longitudinal Study, finds that caring for a disabled child or spouse is associated with poorer health for women, while only spousal care was associated with negative effects for men's well-being. Marks also finds caregiving is conducive to well-being, net of work-family conflict. She concludes:

> [I]f steps were taken to make work-family conflict less problematic for employed caregiving women, women caregivers would evidence considerably less distress than they currently do, and some additional psychological benefits of the caregiver role would emerge more clearly. (p. 962)

Contemporary gender strategies have less to do with gender *values* than with outdated government and business policies that limit options in the time and scheduling of jobs and the inflexibility of career paths (Moen & Coltrane, 2005).

Conclusions: Converging Divergences?

The gendered adult course itself may seem "natural," but it is has been constructed historically through cultural beliefs and norms about the ways women's and men's lives should play out, as well as through institutionalized organizational structures that constrain and open options by gender.

In this chapter we have theorized a dynamic ecology of gendered adult development. Our ecology of the life course perspective locates lives in historical time, emphasizes the unfolding of roles and relationships over time, and recognizes the importance of agency as women and men respond to and shape the gendered environments around them. Although gender differentiation is now more subtle than it was in the past, gender remains a visible source of both difference and inequality, especially related to the most gendered role of all—parenthood—and its impacts on employment experiences.

Contemporary adult development is taking place on a moving platform of multilayered social, economic, and technological transformations rendering existing gender scripts and gender systems obsolete. The mismatch between contemporary exigencies and outdated scripts and structures (geared to a very different, 1950s-style adulthood) means that women and men of all ages and stages make strategic adaptations within a climate of uncertainty, ambiguity, and risk.

The result? An increasing degree of variability both within and across gender and age in the experiences and exigencies of adult life. We call this trend *converging divergences* (Moen & Altobelli, 2007; Moen & Chermack, 2005; Moen & Spencer, 2006a), in that neither men's nor women's lives now follow taken-for-granted timelines. "Convergence" invokes processes of increasing similarity (in, for example, women's and men's labor force participation) over historical time. Most men and men women now participate in both paid work and unpaid family carework. Adult insecurities are also converging across gender lines, in that many women and men—even those in the middle class—have neither job nor income security, regardless of their tenure in a particular job or corporation. "Divergence," on the other hand, suggests a widening of within-gender disparities as a consequence of the deinstitutionalization of traditional gendered expectations around paid work, families, and adulthood. We hold that adult development is both converging (across gender) and diverging (within gender categories).

Basic processes of gendered development unfold in the real-world environments of home and work, as adults seek to integrate and gain a sense of control over the disparate aspects of their lives. People today come to each role transition—marriage, employment, parenthood—with no common set of experiences or expectations. Moreover, people are constrained by their own or significant others' prior choices (buying a home, taking one job over another, marrying, having a child) and by multi-layered social transformations that call for pragmatic, rather than optimal, actions. In decisions large and small, gender continues to operate as a master status (Bem, 1999; Merton, 1968), directly and indirectly shaping identities, relationships, risks, and resources, as well as role trajectories and transitions, but there are also significant variations among women as a group and among men as a group.

Our ecology of the gendered life course theorizing of the adult course suggests a complex process of adult development as individuals strategically respond to policies or practices premised on standardization (as reflected in outdated cultural and organizational allocation and socialization of people by age and by gender) along with emerging processes of individualization. A global economy, new technologies, and values of gender equality, along with other transformations, mean that contemporary adulthood is a complicated project; often challenging institutional timetables and expectations related to education, occupational career paths, marriage, parenthood, and retirement (see also Neugarten, 1968; Rossi, 1980; Stewart & Healy, 1989). Today, the linear path of adulthood as a lock-step movement from schooling to employment to retirement is being upended as people return to school at different ages, get laid off from (supposedly) lifetime career jobs, take up jobs in completely different fields, or are often are "encouraged" (through buy-outs and layoffs) to retire earlier than they expected. Older workers function under age stereotypes about their inability to learn new skills, and worry about their job security (Bybee & Wells, 2002).

Family clockworks are in similar disarray. Young adults sometimes move back home when they can't support themselves. As Mortimer, Staff, and Lee (2005) point out, what it means to be an adult is no longer self-evident to young people in the midst of that transition. Women and men are postponing marriage, never marrying, or leaving marriage. Even, parenthood now occurs on many different time tables. Women are having their first child at 15 and 50, or not having children at all. Men in their 80s are fathering kids, often with second or third (younger) wives. Demographic changes are also reconfiguring the adult years as Baby Boomers move toward and through the traditional retirement years. Increasing longevity means that adult children are now more apt to share more years with their aging parents and daughters especially, but sons as well, are likely to care for infirm relatives.

We end this chapter where we began: to understand the gendered nature of contemporary adult development requires attention to time, ecological context and dynamic processes of socialization, allocation, and strategic selection. We have shown that dynamic convoys of institutions and relationships shape how adults spend time—including the entire adult course—in gendered ways. These convoys shift across the adult course as new roles and relationships are entered, others are exited, and still others shift as a result of maturation, experience, or both (such as the changing parent-child relationship over a 60-year period). Moreover, social and institutional convoys around work and family roles and relationships are themselves in flux, as a result of a changing workforce, a global information economy, egalitarian gender norms, and shifting family life. These large-scale social transformations are creating new risks, uncertainties, and challenges, producing considerable absence of life course "fit" in adulthood for women and men at different ages and life stages.

The mismatch between outdated rules and updated but ambiguous realities is producing a sense of ambivalence about current and future ways of living (see also Bourdieu, 1990; Lüscher & Pillemer, 1998; Orrange, 2007; Sewell, 1992; Suitor & Pillemer, 1994) and of "doing" gender (Bem, 1994; Moen & Spencer, 2006a; Orrange, 2007; Risman, 1998; West & Zimmerman, 1987). We propose the future trends of converging divergences across gender divides in adult development, as women and men pursue similarly diverse paths—in whether and when to marry, have children, divorce, move, go back to school, shift jobs, retire.

There are two ways to change the gender stratification system, from the top down and from the bottom up. Some scholars argue that you have to first change beliefs, norms and stereotypes and then concrete changes will appear (such as equitable income). Other scholars suggest that changing gender systems and structures leads to corresponding changes in gender stereotypes, beliefs and norms (Serguino, 2007). We have made the point in this chapter that contemporary gender inequalities are in large part the result of the fact that jobs remain structured for breadwinners with homemakers, even though neither men nor women are apt to have such back up. When couples have children, therefore, it is women's wages and career progression that suffer (Correll, Benard, & Paik, 2007). But the temporal organization of jobs and career paths—the "typical" work day, workweek, work year, work life institutionalized in public and corporate polices and practices—limits employee control and flexibility in arranging their daily schedules, as well as their control and flexibility over arranging their career paths. Gender equality is difficult if not impossible without the development of greater career and schedule flexibilities in the clockworks of workdays, workweeks, work years, and work lives (Kelly & Moen, 2007). Without such fundamental work redesign, the only way to gender equality seems to be for women and men alike to function as if they have no obligations outside of their jobs.

The absence of relevant blueprints for contemporary adulthood can be disconcerting, to be sure. But it also presents opportunity—for individuals, couples, schools, employers, communities, and governments to reimagine and reinvent alternative scripts of the adult experience. Organizations and nations *can* create a range of options for meaningful, productive and integrative pathways that move beyond the gendered adult course. The challenge is to recognize the need and the value in doing so.

References

Acker, J. (1992). Gendered institutions: From sex role to gendered institutions. *Contemporary Sociology, 21,* 565–569.

Ali, J., & Avison, W. R. (1997). Employment transitions and psychological distress: The contrasting experiences of single and married mothers. *Journal of Health and Social Behavior, 38,* 345–362.

Altucher, K., & Williams, L. B. (2003). Family clocks: Timing parenthood. In P. Moen (Ed.), *It's about time: Career strains, strategies, and successes* (pp. 49–59). Ithaca, NY: Cornell University Press.

American Community Survey. (2004). Washington, DC: U.S. Bureau of the Census.

Anderson, M. (1999). *Thinking about women: Sociological perspectives on sex and gender.* New York: Macmillan.

Anderson, M. L. (2005). Thinking about women: A quarter century's view. *Gender & Society, 19*(4), 437–455.

Azar, S. T. (2002). Adult development and parenthood. A social-cognitive perspective. In J. Demick & C. Andreoletti (Eds.), *Handbook of Adult Development* (pp. 391–415). New York: Plenum.

Baltes, P. B., & Baltes, M. M. (1990). Psychological perspectives on successful aging: The model of selective optimization with compensation. In P. B. Baltes & M. M. Baltes (Eds.), *Successful aging: Perspectives from the behavioral sciences* (pp. 1–34). Cambridge, UK: Cambridge University Press.

Bandura, A. (1982). Self-efficacy mechanism in human agency. *American Psychologist, 37,* 122–147.

Bandura, A. (1989). Regulation of cognitive process through perceived self-efficacy. *Developmental Psychology, 25,* 729–735.

Barnett, R. C., & Rivers, C. (1996). *She works/He works: How two-income families are happier, healthier and better-off.* New York: Harper Collins.

Becker, G. S. (1981). *A treatise on the family.* Cambridge, MA: Harvard University Press.

Becker, P. E., & Moen, P. (1999). Scaling back: Dual-earner couples' work-family strategies. *Journal of Marriage and the Family, 61,* 995–1007.

Bem, S. L. (1994). *The lenses of gender: Transforming the debate on sexual inequality.* New Haven, CT: Yale University Press.

Bem, S. L. (1999). Gender, sexuality, and inequality: When many become one, who is the one and what happens to the other? In P. Moen, D. Dempster-McClain, & H. A. Walker (Eds.), *A nation divided: Diversity, inequality, and community in American society* (pp. 70–86). Ithaca, NY: Cornell University Press.

Bernard, J. S. (1981). The good-provider role. *American Psychologist, 36,* 1–12.

Blau, F. D., Ferber, M. A., & Winkler, A. E. (1998). *The economics of women, men and work.* Upper Saddle River, NJ: Prentice Hall.

Blossfeld, H. P., & Huinik, J. (1991). Human capital investments or norms of role transition? How women's schooling and career affect the process of family formation. *American Journal of Sociology, 97,* 143–168.

Blumberg, R. L. (1984). A general theory of gender stratification. *Sociological Theory, 2,* 23–101.

Bolger, N., DeLongis, A., Kessler, R. C., & Wethington, E. (1989). The contagion of stress across multiple roles. *Journal of Marriage and the Family, 51,* 175–183.

Booth, A., Crouter, A. C., & Shanahan, M. J. (1999). *Transitions to adulthood in a changing economy.* Westport, CT: Praeger.

Bosma, H., Stansfield, S. A., & Marmot, M.G. (1998). Job control, personal characteristics, and heart disease. *Journal of Occupational Health Psychology, 3,* 402–409.

Bourdieu, P. (1990). *The logic of practice.* Stanford, CA: Stanford University Press.

Bradburn, E. M., Moen, P., & Dempster-McClain, D. (1995). Women's return to school following the transition to motherhood. *Social Forces, 73,* 1517–1551.

Brim, O., & Ryff, C. (1980). On the properties of life events. In P. B. Baltes, & O. G. Brim (Eds.), *Life-span development and behavior.* (pp. 367–388). New York: Academic Press.

Brines, J., & Joyner, K. (1999). The ties that bind, principles of cohesion in cohabitation and marriage. *American Sociological Review, 64*(3), 333–355.

Bronfenbrenner, U. (2005). *Making human beings human.* Thousand Oaks, CA: Sage.

Budig, M. J., & England, P. (2001). The wage penalty for motherhood. *American Sociological Review, 66,* 204–225.

Bybee, J. A., & Wells, Y. V. (2002). The development of possible selves during adulthood. In J. Demick & C. Andreoletti (Eds.), *Handbook of adult development* (pp. 257–270). New York: Plenum.

Carr, D. (1997). The fulfillment of career dreams at midlife: Does it matter for women's mental health? *Journal of Health and Social Behavior, 38,* 331–344.

Carstensen, L. L. (1992). Social and emotion patterns in adulthood: Support for socioemotional selectivity theory. *Psychology and Aging, 7,* 331–338.

Caspi, A., & Elder, G. H. Jr. (1988). Emergent family patterns: The intergenerational construction of problem behavior and relationships. In R. Hinde & J. Stevenson-Hinde (Eds.), *Relationships within families* (pp. 218–240). Oxford, UK: Oxford University Press.

Caspi, A., Lynam, D., Moffitt, T. E., & Silva, P. A. (1993). Unraveling girls' delinquency: Biological, dispositional and contextual contributions to adolescent misbehavior. *Developmental Psychology, 29*(1), 19–30.

Cheng, Y., Kawachi, I., Coakley, E. H., Schwartz, J., & Colditz, G. (2000). Association between psychosocial work characteristics and health functioning in American women: Prospective study. *British Medical Journal, 320,* 1432–1436.

Clarkberg, M., & Moen, P. (2001). Understanding the time-squeeze: Married couples preferred and actual work-hour strategies. *American Behavioral Scientist, 44,* 1115–1136.

Clausen, J. S. (1991). Adolescent competence and the shaping of the life course. *American Journal of Sociology, 96*(4), 805–842.

Clausen, J. A. (1995). Gender, contexts, and turning points in adults' lives. In P. Moen, G. H. Elder, Jr., K. Luescher (Eds.), *Examining lives in context: Perspectives on the ecology of human development* (pp. 365–392). Washington, DC: American Psychological Association.

Collins, R., Chafetz, J. S., Blumberg, R. L., Coltrane, S., & Turner, J. H. (1993). Toward an integrated theory of gender stratification. *Sociological Perspectives, 36*(3), 185–216.

Cooney, T. M., & Mortimer, J. T. (1999). Family structure differences in the timing of leaving home: Exploring mediating factors. *Journal of Research on Adolescence, 9*(4), 367–376.

Correll, S. J, Benard, S., & Paik, I. (2007). Getting a job: Is there a motherhood penalty? *American Journal of Sociology, 112,* 1297–1338.

Crompton, R. (2006). *Employment and the family: The reconfiguration of work and family life in contemporary societies.* New York: Cambridge University Press.

Daehlen, M. (2005). Change in job values during education. *Journal of Education and Work, 18*(4), 385–400.

Dannefer, D. (1984). Adult development and social theory: A paradigmatic reappraisal. *American Sociological Review, 49,* 100–116.

Dannefer, D. (2000). Paradox of opportunity: Education, work and age integration in the United States and Germany. *The Gerontologist, 40*(3), 282–286.

de Jonge, J., Bosma, H., Peter, R., & Siegrist, J. (2000). Job strain, effort-reward imbalance and employee well-being: A large-scale cross-sectional study. *Social Science & Medicine, 50,* 1317–1327.

de Lange, A. H., Taris, T. W., Kompier, M. A. J., Houtman, I. L. D., & Bongers, P. M. (2003). The very best of the millennium: Longitudinal research and the demand-control-(support) model. *Journal of Occupational Health Psychology, 8,* 282–306.

de Lange, A. H.,. Taris, T. W., Kompier, M. A. J., Houtman, I. L. D., & Bongers, P. M. (2004). The relationships between work characteristics and mental health: Examining normal, reversed and reciprocal relationships in a 4-wave study. *Work & Stress, 18,* 149–166.

Demo, D. H., & Cox, M. J. (2000). Families with young children: A review of research in the 1990s. *Journal of Marriage & Family, 62*(4), 876–895.

DiRenzo, G. J. (1977). Socialization, personality, and social systems. *Annual Review of Sociology, 3,* 261–295.

Downey, G., Eccles, J. S., & Chatman, C. M. (Eds.) (2005). *Navigating the future: Social identity, coping, and life tasks.* New York: Russell Sage:.

Downey, G., & Moen, P. (1987). Personal efficacy, income, and family transitions: A longitudinal study of women heading households. *Journal of Health and Social Behavior, 28,* 320–333.

Dwyer, D. J., & Ganster, D. C. (1991). The effects of job demands and control on employee attendance and satisfaction. *Journal of Organizational Behavior, 12*(7), 595–608.

Elder, G. H. Jr. (1974). *Children of the great depression.* Chicago: University of Chicago Press.

Elder, G. H. Jr. (1985). *Life course dynamics: Trajectories and transitions: 1968–80.* Ithaca, NY: Cornell University Press.

Elder, G. H. Jr. (1992). Life course. In E. F. Borgatta & M. L. Borgatta (Eds.), *Encyclopedia of sociology* (3rd ed., pp. 1120–1130). New York: MacMillian.

Elder, G. H. Jr. (1995). The life course paradigm: Social change and individual development. In P. Moen, G. H. Elder, & K. Luescher (Eds.), *Examining lives in context: Perspectives on the ecology of human development* (pp. 101–140). Washington DC: American Psychological Association.

Elder, G. H. Jr. (1998a). The life course and human development. In R. Lerner (Ed.) *Handbook of child psychology (Vol.1): Theoretical models of human development* (pp. 939–91). New York: Wiley.

Elder, G. H., Jr. (1998b). The life course as developmental theory. *Child Development, 69*, 1–12.

Elsass, P. M., & Viega, J. F. (1997). Job control and job strain: A test of three models. *Journal of Occupational Health Psychology, 2*, 195–206.

Estes, S. B., & Glass, J. L. (1996). Job changes following childbirth: Are women trading compensation for family-responsive work conditions? *Work and Occupations, 23*(4), 405–436.

Evans, O., & Steptoe, A. (2002). The contribution of gender-role orientation, work factors and home stressors to psychological well-being and sickness absence in male- and female-dominated occupational groups. *Social Science & Medicine, 54*, 481–492.

Fenstermaker, S., & West, C. (2002). *Doing gender, doing difference: Inequality, power, and Institutional Change.* New York: Routledge.

Fermandez, R. M., & Sosa, M. L. (2005). Gendering the job: Networks and recruitment at a call center. *American Journal of Sociology, 111*, 859–904.

Folbre, N. (2001). *The invisible heart: Economics and family values.* New York: The New Press.

Fox, M. F. (1993). Making science: Between nature and society. *Contemporary Sociology, 22*(4), 481–483.

Fredriksen, K. I. (1996). Gender differences in employment and the informal care of adults. *Journal of Women & Aging, 8*(2), 35–53.

Freund, A. M. (1997). Individuating age salience: A psychological perspective on the salience of age in the life course. *Human Development, 40*, 287–292.

Friedan, B. (1963). *The feminine mystique.* New York: Bantam Doubleday Dell.

Garey, A. I. (1999). *Weaving work and motherhood.* Philadelphia: Temple University Press.

Gerson, K. (1985). *Hard choices: How women decide about work, career, and motherhood.* Berkeley: University of California Press.

Gerson, K. (2001). Children of the gender revolution: Some theoretical questions and findings from the field. In V. W. Marshall, W. R. Heinz, H. Krueger, & A. Verma (Eds.), *Restructuring work and the life course* (pp. 446–461). Toronto: University of Toronto Press.

Gerstel, N. (2000). The third shift: Gender and care work outside the home. *Qualitative Sociology, 23*, 467–483.

Gist, J., Wu, K., & Ford, C. (1999). *Do baby boomers save and, if so, what for?* Washington, DC: Public Policy Institute.

Glass, J., & Riley, L. (1998). Family responsive policies and employee retention following childbirth. *Social Forces, 76*(4), 1401–1435.

Goodwin, J., & O'Connor, H. (2005). Engineer, mechanic or carpenter? Boys' transitions to work in the 1960s. *Journal of Education and Work, 18*(4), 451–471.

Hagestad, G. O., & Neugarten, B. L. (1985). Age and the life course. In R. H. Binstock & E. Shanas, Associates (Eds.), *Handbook of aging and the social sciences* (pp. 35–61). New York: Van Nostrand Reinhold.

Hakim, C. (1997). Changing forms of employment: Organizations, skills and gender. *Urban Studies, 34*, 713–714.

Han, S. K., & Moen, P. (1999a). Work and family over time: A life course approach. *Annals of the American Academy of Political and Social Science, 562*, 98–110.

Han, S. K., & Moen, P. (1999b). Clocking out: Temporal patterning of retirement. *American Journal of Sociology, 105*, 191–236.

Han, S. K., & Moen, P. (2002). Coupled careers: Pathways through work and marriage in the United States. In H. Blossfeld & S. Drobnic (Eds.), *Careers of couples in contemporary societies: From male breadwinner to dual earner families* (pp. 201–231). Oxford, UK: Oxford University Press.

Heckhausen, J., & Schulz, R. (1993). Optimization by selection and compensation: Balancing primary and secondary control in life span development. *International Journal of Behavioral Development, 16*, 287–303.

Heckhausen, J., & Schulz, R. (1995). A life span theory of control. *Psychological Review, 102*, 284–304.

Heinz, W. R. (Ed.). (1999). *From education to work: Cross-national perspectives.* New York: Cambridge University Press.

Heinz, W. R. (2002a). Transitional discontinuities and the biographical shaping of early work careers. *Journal of Vocational Behavior, 60*, 220–240.

Heinz, W. R. (2002b). Self-socialization and post-traditional society. *Advances in Life Course Research, 7*, 41–64.

Heinz, W. R., & Marshall. (2003). *Social dynamics of the life course: Transitions, institutions, and inter-relations.* Hawthorne, NY: Aldine de Gruyter

Hertz, R. (1986). *More equal than others: Women and men in dual-career marriages.* Berkeley: University of California PressSummer Reading 2000.

Hochschild, A. (1989). *The second shift.* New York: Avon Books Summer Reading 2000.

Hochschild, A. (1997). *The time bind: When work becomes home and home becomes work.* New York: Metropolitan Books Summer Reading 2000.

Hofferth, S. L. (1996). Effects of public and private policies on working after birth. *Work and Occupations, 23*, 378–404.

Home, A. M. (1998). Predicting role conflict, overload and contagion in adult women university students with families and jobs. *Adult Education Quarterly, 48*, 85–97.

Institute for Women's Policy Research. (2005a, June). *Women and social security: Benefit types and eligibility.* (IWPR Publication No. D463). Washington DC.

Institute for Women's Policy Research. (2005b, August). *The gender wage ratio: Women's and men's earnings.* (IWPR Publication No. C350). Washington DC.

Johnson, M. K. (2001). Changes in job values during the transition to adulthood. *Work and Occupations, 28*, 315–345.

Josselson, R. (2002). Processes of development in midlife women. In J. Demick & C. Andreoletti (Eds.), *Handbook of adult development* (pp. 431– 441). New York: Plenum.

Kahn, R. L., & Antonucci, T. C. (1980). Convoys of over the life course: Attachment, roles, and social support. In P. B. Baltes & O. G. Brim (Eds.), *Life-span development and behavior* (pp. 383– 405). New York: Academic Press.

Kalmijn, M. (1998). Intermarriage and homogamy: Causes, patterns, trends. *Annual Review of Sociology, 24*, 395–421.

Karasek, R. A. (1979). Job demands, job decision latitude, and mental strain: Implications for job redesign. *Administrative Science Quarterly, 24*, 285–307.

Karasek, R. A. (1998). Demand/control model: A social, emotional and psychological approach to stress risk and active behavior development. In J. M. Stellman (Ed.) *Encyclopaedia of occupational health and safety.* (pp. 6–34). Geneva: ILO.

Karasek, R. A., & Theorell, T. (1990). *Healthy work: Stress, productivity, and the reconstruction of working life.* New York: Basic Books.

Kelly, E. (2003). The strange history of employer-sponsored child care: Interested actors, uncertainty, and the transformation of law in organizational fields. *American Journal of Sociology, 109*, 606–649.

Kelly, E. (2005a). Discrimination against caregivers? Gendered family responsibilities, employer practices, and work rewards. In L. B. Nielsen & R. L. Nelson (Eds.), *The handbook of employment discrimination researc.* (pp. 341–362). New York: Kluwer.

Kelly, E. (2005b). Work-family policies: The United States in international perspective. In M. Pitt-Catsouphes, E. Kossek, & S. Sweet. (Eds.), *Work-Family handbook: Multi-disciplinary perspectives and approaches.* (pp. 99–123). Mahwah, NJ: Erlbaum.

Kelly, E., & Dobbin, F., (1999). Civil rights law at work: Sex discrimination and the rise of maternity leave policies. *American Journal of Sociology, 105*(2), 455–492.

Kelly, E., & Moen, P. (2007). Rethinking the clockwork of work: Why schedule control may pay off at work and at home. *Advances in developing human resources. Special issue on work-life integration.* M. L. Morris & S. R. Madsen (Eds.). Newbury Park, CA: Sage.

Kimmel, M. S., & Aronson, A. (2000). *The gendered society reader.* New York: Oxford University Press.

Koeske, G., & Kirk, S. (1995). Direct and buffering effects of internal locus of control among mental health professionals. *Journal of Social Service Research, 20*, 1.

Kohli, M. (1986a). The world we forget: A historical review of the life course. In V .W. Marshall (Ed.), *Later life: The social psychology of aging.* (pp. 271–303). Beverly Hills, CA: Sage.

Kohli, M. (1986b). Social organization and subjective construction of the life course. In A. B. Sorensen, F. E. Weinner, & L. R. Sherrod (Eds.), *Human development and the life course: Multidisciplinary perspectives* (pp. 271–292). Hillsdale, NJ: Erlbaum.

Kohli, M. (1994). Work and retirement: A comparative perspective. In M. White Riley, R. L. Kahn, & A. Foner (Eds.), *Age and structural lag* (Chapter 4). New York Wiley.

Kohn, M. L., & Schooler, C. (Eds.). (1983). *Work and personality: An inquiry into the impact of social stratification.* Norwood, NJ: Ablex.

Kramer, L. (2005). *The sociology of gender: A brief introduction* (2nd ed.). Los Angeles, CA: Roxbury.

Kruger, H., & Baldus, B. (1999). Work, gender and the life course: Social construction and individual experience. *Canadian Journal of Sociology, 24*(3), 355–379.

Lash, C. (1979). *Haven in a heartless world: The family besieged.* New York: Basic Books.

Liao, T. F., & Cai, Y. (1995). Socialization, life situations, and gender-role attitudes regarding the family among white American women. *Sociological Perspectives, 38*(2), 241–260.

Liebowitz, A., & Klerman, J. A. (1995). Explaining changes in married mothers' employment over time. *Demography, 32*, 365–378.

Lucas, T. W., Wendorf, C. A., Imamoglu, E. O., Shen, J., Parkhill, M. R., & Weisfeld, C. C., et al. (2004). Marital satisfaction in four cultures as a function of homogamy, male dominance and female attractiveness. *Sexualities, Evolution & Gender, 6*(2-3), 97–130.

Lüscher, K., & Pillemer, K. (1998). Intergenerational ambivalence: A new approach to the study of parent-child relations in later life. *Journal of Marriage and the Family, 60*, 413–425.

Maccoby, E. E., & Jacklin, C. N. (1974). *The psychology of sex differences.* Stanford, CA: Stanford University Press.

Marks, N. F. (1998). Does it hurt to care? Caregiving, work-family conflict, and midlife well-being. *Journal of Marriage and the Family, 60*, 951–966.

Marshall, N. L., Barnett, R. C., & Sayer, A. (1997). The changing workforce, job stress, and psychological distress. *Journal of Occupational Health Psychology, 2*(2), 99–107.

Marshall, V. W., Heinz, W. R., Krüger, H., & Verma, A. (2001). *Restructuring work and the life course.* Toronto: University of Toronto Press.

Martin, P. Y. (2004). Gender as social institution. *Social Forces, 82*, 1249–1274.

Mathews, T. J., Hamilton, B. B. (2002). Mean age of mother, 1970–2000. *National vital statistics reports, 51*(1). Hyattsville, MD: National Center for Health Statistics.

Mayer, K. U., & Tuma, N. B. (1990). Life course research and event history analysis: An overview. In K. U. Mayer & N. B. Tuma (Eds.), *Event history analysis in life course research* (pp. 3–22). Madison, WI: University of Wisconsin Press.

McCall, L. (2001). *Complex inequality: Gender, class and the race in the new economy.* New York: Routledge.

Mead, M. (1949). *Male and female.* New York: Morrow.

Mead, M. (1970). *Culture and commitment: A study of the generation gap.* New York: Natural History Press/Double Day.

Mennino, S. F., Rubin, B. A., & Brayfield, A. (2005). Home-to-job and job-to-home spillover: The impact of company policies and workplace culture. *Sociological Quarterly, 46*, 107–135.

Merton, R. K. (1968). *Social theory and social structure.* New York: The Free Press.

Meyer, J. W. (1986). The institutionalization of the life course and its effects on the self. In F. E. Weinert, & L. R. Sherrod (Eds.), *Human development and the life course: Multidisciplinary perspectives* (pp. 119–216). Hillsdale, NJ: Erlbaum.

Moen, P. (1992). *Women, work and family: A sociological perspective on changing roles.* Unpublished manuscript.

Moen, P. (1995). A life course approach to postretirement roles and well-being. In L. A. Bond, S. J. Cutler, & A. Grams (Eds.), *Promoting successful and productive aging* (pp. 239–256). Thousand Oaks, CA: Sage.

Moen, P. (1996a). Gender, age and the life course. In R. H. Binstock, & L. K. George (Eds.), *Handbook of aging and the social sciences* (4th ed., pp. 171–187). San Diego, CA: Academic Press.

Moen, P. (1996b). A life course perspective on retirement, gender, and well-being. Journal of *Occupational Health Psychology, 1*(2), 131–144.

Moen, P. (1997). Women's roles and resilience: Trajectories of advantage or turning points? In I. H. Gotlib & B. Wheaton. (Eds.), *Stress and adversity over the life course* (pp. 133–156). New York: Cambridge University Press.

Moen, P. (2001). The gendered life course. In L. George & R. H. Binstock (Eds.), *Handbook of aging and the social sciences* (pp. 179–196). San Diego, CA: Academic Press.

Moen, P. (2003). Midcourse: Navigating retirement and a new life stage. In J. T. Mortimer & M. J. Shanahan (Eds.), *Handbook of the life course* (pp. 267–291). New York: Plenum.

Moen, P. (2005). Beyond the career mystique: "time in," "time out," and "second acts." *Sociological Forum, 20*(2), 187–208.

Moen, P., & Altobelli, J. (2007). Strategic selection as a retirement project: Will Americans develop hybrid arrangements? In J. James & P. Wink (Eds.), *The crown of life: Dynamics of the early postretirement period* (Vol. 26, pp. 61–81). New York: Springer.

Moen, P., & Chermack, K. (2005). Gender disparities in health: Strategic selection, careers, and cycles of control. *Journal of Gerontology, 60B*, 99–126.

Moen, P., & Chesley, N. (2008). Toxic job ecologies, lagging time convoys, and work-family conflict: Can families (re)gain control and life-course "fit"? In D. S. Lero, K. Korabik, & D. L. Whitehead (Eds.), *Handbook of work family integration: Research, theory, and best practices* (pp. 95–118). New York: Elsevier.

Moen, P., & Coltrane, S. (2005). Families, theories and social policy. In V. L. Bengtson, A. C. Acock, K. R. Allen, P. Dilworth-Anderson, & D. M. Klein (Eds.), *Sourcebook of family theory and research* (pp. 543–565). Thousand Oaks, CA: Sage.

Moen, P., Elder, G. H., Jr., & Lüscher, K. (1995). *Examining lives in context: Perspectives on the ecology of human development.* Washington DC: American Psychological Association.

Moen, P., & Erickson, M. A. (1995). Linked lives: A transgenerational approach to resilience. In P. Moen, G. H. Elder Jr., & K. Lüscher (Eds.), *Examining lives in context: Perspectives on the ecology of human development* (pp. 169–210). Washington DC: American Psychological Association.

Moen, P., & Han, S. K. (2001). Reframing careers: Work, family and gender. In V. Marshall, H. Heinz, H. Krueger, & A. Verma (Eds.), *Restructuring work and the life course* (pp. 424–445). Toronto: University of Toronto Press.

Moen, P., Huang, Q., Plassmann, V., & Dentinger, E. (2006). Deciding the future: Do dual-earner couples plan together for retirement? *American Behavioral Scientist, 49*(9), 1–22.

Moen, P., & Orrange, R. (2002). Careers and lives: Socialization, structural lag, and gendered ambivalence. In R. Settersten & T. Owens (Eds.), *Advances in life course research: New frontiers in socialization* (Vol. 7, pp. 231–260). London: Elsevier Science.

Moen, P., & Roehling P. V. (2005). *The career mystique: Cracks in the American dream.* Boulder, CO: Rowman & Littlefield.

Moen, P., & Spencer, D. (2006a). Converging divergences in age, gender, health and well being: Strategic selection in the third age. In R. H. Binstock & L. K. George (Eds.), *Handbook of aging and the social sciences* (6th ed., pp. 127–144). San Diego, CA: Academic Press.

Moen, P., & Spencer, D. (2006b). *Changes in latitudes, changes in attitudes? gendered life-course dynamics and ecologies of control.* Unpublished manuscript. Minneapolis, MN.

Moen, P., Sweet, S., & Swisher, R. (2005). Embedded career clocks: The case of retirement planning. In R. Macmillan (Ed.), *Advances in life course research: The structure of the life course: Individualized? Standardized? Differentiated?* (pp. 237–265). New York: Elsevier.

Moen, P., & Wethington, E. (1992). The concept of family adaptive strategies. *Annual Review of Sociology, 18*, 233–251.

Moen, P., & Yu, Y. (1999). Having it all: Overall work/life success in two-earner families. In T. Parcel & R. Hodson (Eds.), *Work and family: Research in the sociology of work* (Vol. 7, pp. 109–139). Greenwich, CT: JAI Press.

Moen, P., & Yu, Y. (2000). Effective work/life strategies: Working couples, work conditions, gender and life quality. *Social Problems, 47*, 291–326.

Mortimer, J. T., Oesterle, S., & Kruger, H. (2005). Age norms, institutional structures, and the timing of markers of transition to adulthood. *Advances in Life Course Research, 9*, 175–199.

Mortimer, J. T., & Shanahan, M. J. (2003). *Handbook of the life course.* New York: Kluwer.

Mortimer, J. T., & Simmons, R. G. (1978). Adult socialization. *Annual Review Sociology, 4*, 421–454.

Mortimer, J. T., Staff, J., & Oesterle, S. (2003). Adolescent work and the early socioeconomic career. In J. T. Mortimer & M. J. Shanahan (Eds.), *Handbook of the life course* (pp. 437–459). New York: Kluwer.

Mortimer, J. T., Staff, J., & Lee, J. C. (2005). *Agency and structure in educational attainment and the transition to adulthood.* Unpublished manuscript.

Mortimer, J. T., Vuolo, M. C., Staff, J., Wakefield, S., & Xie, W. (2006). *Tracing the timing of "career" acquisition in a contemporary youth cohort.* Unpublished material.

Neugarten, B. (1968). *Middle age and aging: A reader in social psychology.* Chicago: University of Chicago Press.

Neugarten, B. L., & Hagestad, G. O. (1976). Age and the life course. In R. Binstock & E. Shanas (Eds.), *Handbook of aging and the social sciences* (pp. 35–55). New York: Van Nostrand Reinhold.

Neugarten, B. L., Moore, J. W., & Lowe, J. C. (1965). Age norms, age constraints, and adult socialization. *American Journal of Sociology, 70*, 710–717.

Nosek, B. A., Banaji, M. R., & Greenwald, A. G. (2002). Math = male, me = female, therefore math ≠ me. *Journal of Personality and Social Psychology, 83*, 44–59.

O'Rand, A. M., & Henretta, J. (1996). *Age and inequality: Diverse pathways through later life.* Boulder, CO: Westview.

Orrange, R. (2007). Draft of book manuscript (untitled).

Padavic, I., & Reskin, B. (2002). *Women and men at work.* Thousand Oaks, CA: Pine Forge Press.

Parson, T., & Bales, R. F. (1955). *Family, socialization, and interaction process.* Glencoe, IL: Free Press.

Pavalko, E. K., & Artis, J. E. (1997). Women's caregiving and paid work: Causal relationships in late mid-life. *Journal of Gerontology: Social Sciences, 52B*, S1–S10.

Pavalko, E. K., & Smith, B. (1999). The rhythm of work: Health effects of women's work dynamics. *Social Forces, 77*(3), 1141–1162.

Pedriana, N. (2004). Help wanted NOW: Legal opportunities, the women's movement, and the battle over sex-segregated job advertisements. *Social Problems, 51*, 182–201.

Pixley, J. E., & Moen, P. (2003). Prioritizing careers. In P. Moen (Ed.), *It's about time: Couples and careers* (pp. 183–200). Ithaca, NY: Cornell University Press.

Powell, W., & DiMaggio, P. (1991). *The new institutionalism in organizational analysis.* Chicago: University of Chicago Press.

Putney, N. M., & Bengtson, V. L. (2002). Socialization and the family revisited. In R. A. Settersten Jr. & T. J. Owens (Eds.), *Advances in life course research: New frontiers in socialization* (pp. 165–194) Elsevier Science.

Ridgeway, C. L., & Correll, S. J. (2004). Unpacking the gender system: A theoretical perspective on beliefs and social relations. *Gender & Society, 18*(4), 510–531.

Ridgeway, C., & Smith-Lovin, L. (1999). The gender system and interaction. *Annual Review of Sociology, 25*, 191–216.

Riley, M. W. (1987). On the significance of age in sociology. *American Sociological Review, 52*(1), 1–14.

Riley, M. W., Foner, A., & Waring, J. (1988). Sociology of age. In N. J. Smelser (Ed.), *The handbook of sociology* (pp. 243–290). Newbury Park, CA: Sage.

Risman, B. J. (1998). *Gender vertigo: American families in transition.* New Haven, CT: Yale University Press.

Rodin, J. (1987). Personal control through the life course. In R. P. Abeles (Ed.), *Life-span perspectives and social psychology* (pp. 103). London: Erlbaum.

Rodin, J. (1989). Sense of control: Potentials for intervention. *The Annals of the American Academy, 503*, 29–42.

Rook, K. S., Catalano, R., & Dooley, D. (1989). The timing of major life events: Effects of departing from the social clock. *American Journal of Community Psychology, 17*, 233–258.

Rose, P. I. (1979). *Socialization and the life cycle*. New York: St. Martin's Press.

Rosenfeld, R. A. (1992). Job mobility and career processes. *Annual Review of Sociology, 18*, 39–61.

Rossi, A. (1980). Life-span theories and women's lives. *Signs: Journal of women in culture and society, 6*(1), 4–32.

Ryder, N. B. (1965). The cohort as a concept in the study of social change. *American Sociological Review, 30* (6), 843–861.

Sarkisian, N., & Gerstel, N. (2004). Explaining the gender gap in help to parents: The importance of employment. *Journal of Marriage and Family, 66*(2), 431–451.

Schnall, P., Landsbergis, P., & Baker, D. (1994). Job strain and cardiovascular disaease. *Annual Review of Public Health. 15*, 381–411.

Schuman, H., & Rieger, C. (1992). Historical analogies, generational effects, and attitudes toward war. *American Sociological Review, 57*, 315–326.

Serguino, S. (2007). Plus ca change? Evidence on global trends in gender norms and stereotypes. *Feminist Economics, 13*(2), 1–28.

Settersten, R., & Hagestad, G. O. (1996a). What's the latest? II. Cultural age deadlines for educational and work transitions. *The Gerontologist, 5*, 602–613.

Settersten, R., & Hagestad, G. O. (1996b). What's the latest? Cultural age deadlines for family transitions. *The Gerontologist, 36*(2), 178–188.

Settersten, R., & Lovegreen, L. (1998). Educational experiences throughout adult life: New hopes or no hope life-course flexibility? *Research on Aging, 20*, 506–538.

Settersten, R. A., Jr, & Owens, T. J. (2002). *Advances in life course research. New frontiers in socialization* Amsterdam: JAI.

Sewell, W. H. (1992). A theory of structure: Duality, agency and transformations. *American Journal of Sociology, 98*, 1–29.

Shanahan, M. J. (2000). Pathways to adulthood: Variability and mechanisms in life course perspective. *Annual Review of Sociology, 2*, 667–692.

Sorensen, A., & McLanahan, S. (1987). Married women's economic dependency, 1940–1980. *American Journal of Sociology, 83*(3), 659–697.

Spector, P. E., Cooper, C. L., Sanches, J. I., O'Driscoll, M., Sparks, K., & Bernin, P. (2001). Do national levels of individualism and internal locus of control relate to well-being: An ecological level international study. *Journal of Organizational Behavior, 22*, 815–832.

Spector, P. E., & O'Connell, B. J. (1994). The contribution of personality traits, negative affectivity, locus of control and type A to the subsequent reports of job stressors and job strains. *Journal of Occupational and Organizational Psychology, 67*, 1–11.

Stewart, A. J., & Healy, J. M., Jr. (1989). Linking individual development and social change. *American Psychologist, 44*, 195–206.

Stier, H., & Lewin-Epstein, N. (2000). Women's part-time employment and gender inequality in the family. *Journal of Family Issues, 21*(3), 390–410.

Suitor, J. J. (1987). Marital happiness of returning women students and their husbands: Effects of part and full-time enrollment. *Research in Higher Education, 27*(4), 311–331.

Suitor, J., & Pillemer, K. (1994). Family caregiving and marital satisfaction. *Journal of Marriage and the Family, 56*, 681–690.

Sweet, S., & Moen, P. (2006). Advancing a career focus on work and family: Insights from the life course perspective. In M. Pitt-Catsouphes, E. E. Kossek, & S. Sweet (Eds.), *The work and family handbook: Multi-disciplinary perspectives and methods* (pp. 189–208). Mahwah NJ: Erlbaum.

Sweet, S., Swisher, R., & Moen, P. (2005). Selecting and assessing the family-friendly community: Adaptive strategies of middle-class, dual-earner couples. *Family Relations, 54*, 596–606.

Swisher, R., Sweet, S., & Moen, P. (2004). The family-friendly community and its life course fit for dual-earner couples. *Journal of Marriage and the Family, 66*, 281–292.

Townsend, N. W. (2002). *The package deal: Marriage, work, and fatherhood in men's lives*. Philadelphia: Temple University Press.

U.S. Bureau of the Census (1997). *Households, families, and children. A 30 year perspective*. Current population reports, Series P. 23, No 181. Washington, DC: US Government Printing Office.

U.S. Bureau of the Census (2006). *Current population survey* (March, 2006) and *Annual social and economic supplements*, 2005 and earlier. Retrieved September 2007 from http://www.census.gov/hhes/income/histinc/f022.html.

West, C., &. Zimmerman, D. H. (1987). Doing gender. *Gender and Society, 1*(2), 125–151.

Wethington, E. (2000). Contagion of stress. In S. Thye, E. J. Lawler, M. Macy, & H. A. Walker (Eds.), *Advances in groups process* (pp. 229–253). Stamford, CT: JAI Press.

Wethington, E., Pixley, J. E., & Kavey, A. (2003). Turning points in work careers. In P. Moen (Ed.), *It's about time: Couples and careers* (pp. 168–182) Ithaca, NY: Cornell University Press.

Wheaton, B. (1990). Life transitions, role histories, and mental health. *American SociologicalReview, 55*, 209–223.

Williams, J. (2000). *Unbending gender: Why family and work conflict and what to do about it*. New York: Oxford University Press.

Williams, J. C., & Segal, N. (2003). Beyond the maternal wall: Relief for family caregivers who are discriminated against on the job. *Harvard Women's Law Journal, 26*, 77–162.

Williams, S., & Han, S. (2003). Career clocks: Forked roads. In P. Moen (Ed.). *It's about time: Couples and careers* (pp. 80–97) Ithaca, NY: Cornell University Press.

Zarit, S., Pearlin, L., & Schaie, K. (2002). *Societal impacts on personal control in the elderly*. New York: Springer.

Chapter 14

Career Development, Work, and Occupational Success

Erik J. Porfeli and Fred W. Vondracek

Introduction

Career development in the 21st century is likely to be quite different than career development in the 20th century, requiring a reconsideration of major career development theories that were initially formulated to explain career development in a less complex world. The globalization of corporations and of regional and national economies has led to massive restructuring and relocation of significant aspects of the first world economy and explosive growth within the third world economy. At the same time, entirely new industries have emerged that include occupational titles that were unknown only two decades ago. Indeed, "the life cycle of many occupations has been shortened and occupational pathways have become much less stable and predictable. A significant number of today's children will work in occupations that have not yet been invented, and a significant number of today's workers will need to find new jobs because their current occupations will become obsolete" (Vondracek, 2001, p. 256).

Technological advances and the globalization of most industrial economies and labor markets have combined to produce a "pluralization" of the life course and of career pathways. Advances in logistics and distribution, coupled with inexpensive labor on one side of the planet, have had a profound impact on the nature of industry, with a shift from production to "big box" retail consumption, on the other side of the planet. The textile industry in the United States is one example that readily comes to mind. In the face of radical economic restructuring and/or explosive growth, careers are also becoming less predictable, less stable, and more changeable as economies come "online" and become more connected to the global arena. Thus, theories of career development that postulated adult career development as occurring in predictable phases or stages, have either been significantly revised (e.g., Super, 1980) or they have become less relevant. Original formulations of stage models, such as Erikson's (1950) stages of ego development, Super's (1957) stages of career development, or the models proposed by Levinson (Levinson, Darrow, Klein, Levinson, & McKee, 1978) or Schein (1978) may have been applicable to mid-20th-century, White, middle-class males, but today their explanatory power is limited when applied to the enormous variability and unpredictability in the patterns of career development experienced by the women and men who make up the workforce of the future or even the workers of today.

The adequacy of stage models has been questioned on a number of additional grounds by researchers in adult development (e.g., Bromley, 1990b; Thomae & Lehr, 1986), sociology (e.g., Dannefer, 1992), and career development (e.g., Vondracek, 2001). For example, Dannefer (1992) proposed that the normative patterns that are frequently described as stages are more likely a reflection of certain kinds of social and economic patterns that have traditionally channeled the career pathways of individuals. Thomae, Lehr, &

Schmitz-Scherzer (1981), after examining important life events in the biographies of men and women, concluded that the great varieties of pathways that are possible in their lives can be understood only when these lives are placed in context. Bromley (1990a) concluded that stage models tend to require analysis at a very high level of abstraction and generality, leading to a corresponding neglect of the wide differences between individuals and the paths they take in life.

The implications of these changes for workers and for the nature of work itself should not be underestimated. In fact, Super and Knasel (1981) were among the first to recognize that the worker and the aspiring worker must become more open to and prepared for change and must be adaptable to change when it occurs in order to maintain career momentum. More recently, Savickas (1997) has argued persuasively for making career adaptability a central construct in career theory across the entire life span. Clearly, the changed realities of modern careers are beginning to be reflected in life-span career theory, in our understanding of the development and functioning of organizations, and the links between them.

In sum, the 21st century will witness an acceleration of the dramatic changes in the nature of work that are already apparent in most parts of the world. A great deal needs to be learned to: (a) help workers to address their career concerns, (b) enhance the ability of employers to create workplaces that meet their needs and are attractive to workers, and (c) help governments shape policy that enhances the economy and the well-being of all segments of the economy including employers and workers (e.g., Hall, 2004). Fundamental assumptions about what constitutes an occupational career will be challenged. Relative to the last 50 years, instability and change will be the norm, with lifetime careers and life-long employment with a single employer becoming a thing of the past. The "career ladder" concept may be supplanted by more flexible change-related concepts like career acceleration, deceleration, and momentum. Life-long learning, career adaptability, serial careers, and the merging of personal lives with work lives will all be increasingly salient issues for workers of the future. Just as work and careers will be much more varied, variable, and differentiated in the future, so will personal judgments and perceptions of what constitutes occupational success. Clearly, the simple life is a thing of the past for most workers. With good reason, they worry about obsolescence of their occupations or even their industries and hence about the security of their jobs. They also need to be concerned about personal obsolescence, and about being unable to mentally and physically keep up with the ever-changing demands of work as they get older.

Research designed to provide answers to challenging issues bearing on the person and multiple levels of the human ecology must utilize interdisciplinary, comprehensive, and complex models and sophisticated methods for studying simultaneous change and development at multiple levels. The interrelatedness of the personal and work lives of individuals, the interdependence of industries and economies, and the globalization of the labor force demand theories and models that cut across disciplinary boundaries, putting an end to the arbitrary segmentation of fields of research that prevent the integration of essential findings in a timely and meaningful fashion.

A critically important prerequisite to our understanding of career development, work, and occupational success is a sophisticated understanding of how humans change over time, how they function in their multiple contexts, and how they determine whether they are successful or not. Although significant progress has been made, especially in the last two decades, much of the accumulated empirical research has relied on (deliberately) oversimplified theories of human development and human functioning. Often, assumptions about causality have been made on the basis of superficial correlation, and questionable assumptions about the linearity of complex relationships have been perpetuated without adequate evidence (and sometimes in the face of evidence to the contrary). Assuming that general laws govern human behavior regardless of the context within which such behavior is expressed has led to findings that are often not valid for any particular individual and, therefore, not generalizeable.

The basic, underlying assumption of research on career development, work, and occupational success in the decades ahead will be that work represents an activity that is central in human existence across the life span. Consequently, theories of human development must concern themselves with how children learn about work, how adolescents transition from school to work, how workers construct a series of careers, and how adults in their later years disengage from work in a variety of ways that reflect not only their histories as workers, but their histories as whole human beings, who have relationships with others and who have families. It should be clear, therefore, that it makes no sense to separate the study of work from the study of human development or to separate the study of human development from the study of work. A complex conceptualization of "human development in context," which is capable of incorporating career development, work, and occupational success, is represented by developmental contextualism.

Developmental Contextualism

Developmental contextualism is a meta-theory of human development derived from contextualism and organicism (Vondracek, Lerner, & Schulenberg, 1986). The contextualism position argues that individual-level development and interindividual differences in developmental pathways are primarily a product of the environment. In other words, human development proceeds in accordance with human history and social institutions. Given the unpredictable nature of human history and events, the plasticity of intraindividual change and the variability of interindividual differences in intraindividual change is theoretically infinite (Ford & Lerner, 1992), but is apparently bounded in part by the relative stability of human social structures. Organicism, in contrast, assumes that humans are the product of biological predispositions and psychological constructions, and human development proceeds along a predetermined, stage-like trajectory leading toward an end state (e.g., Piaget's (1960) theory of cognitive development). Progress toward the end state can be accelerated or retarded, but the end state and the general pathway leading to it cannot be fundamentally transformed by the context. Developmental contextualism adopts aspects of both, contextualism and organicism, by conceiving of humans as complex multi-level systems which engage in, move between, and are "embedded" within multiple contexts (Vondracek & Fouad, 1994). Vondracek and his colleagues (Vondracek & Kawasaki, 1995; Vondracek & Porfeli, 2002) have concluded that researchers and practitioners who employ theoretical models that account for interacting and linked contexts and that take a systems approach to person-level functioning (e.g., Ford, 1987; von Bertalanffy, 1968) are likely to improve our understanding of the complexity of human development and lay the groundwork for developing techniques that make possible meaningful and durable person- and group-level changes.

The developmental-contextual approach supports the assertion that human development proceeds within a context in a "probabilistic epigenetic" fashion (Vondracek et al., 1986). Development is "probabilistic" because humans at any given point during the life span exhibit bio-psycho-social coherence that limits but does not entirely constrain human action and development in context; hence, we can predict, but not perfectly, how a person will react to any given event. Moreover, human history is subject to difficult-to-predict events that can have a dramatic impact on the human ecology. For example, a "little ice age" occurred from as early as the 10th to as late as the 19th century that had a profound impact on the human ecology and the human life span (Fagan, 2000). The probabilistic feature of human development is made obvious when well-designed, executed, and tested interventions produce unanticipated outcomes across diverse groups of people, contexts and/or time.

Implicit in developmental contextualism is the assumption that both human agency and social forces operate to affect person-level functioning and context-level contingencies and that all research questions involving human development should define the unit of analysis as the person embedded within his or her array of contexts (Vondracek & Porfeli, 2002). Thinking in terms of a system (von Bertalanffy, 1968), stimuli directed at one level of analysis affect to varying degrees all other levels of the system either directly, indirectly or both. The developmental contextual meta-model suggests that researchers should enter a research question by employing person-level functions and social structural features (Shanahan & Porfeli, 2002). This way of thinking is consistent with, for example, advances in the identity theory literature, suggesting that social roles shape identity and identity shapes and guides the selection of social roles (Stryker & Burke, 2000). The developmental contextual-perspective challenges the researcher to at least consider collateral effects and associations and to realize that the effects at one level are not as insulated from other levels or aspects as some models or statistical procedures may suggest.

Drawing from Bronfenbrenner's (1979) ecological model of human development, the application of developmental contextualism to career development asserts that contexts, like members of a family or elements in a system, are linked to one another and hierarchically arranged (Vondracek et al., 1986). Linkages may or may not be readily apparent or intentional and the effect of a linkage may be direct and/or indirect. Rather than consider work, the family, and the neighborhood contexts as distinct, developmental contextualism urges the researcher to view all of these contexts as embedded within and defined by the host community and the person as an occupant of a constellation of differing but interconnected contexts. One important distinguishing feature of the systemic nature of a community is the nature and strength of the linkages between subcontexts and the extent to which these connections benefit their citizens. A popular example of context linkage in the vocational literature that varies across communities and nations is research and discussion on the transition from school to full-time work (Grant Foundation, 1988; Hamilton & Hamilton, 1999; Reitzle, Vondracek, & Silbereisen, 1998; Stern & National Center for Research in Vocational Education, 1995). This literature clearly acknowledges that people navigate career pathways on the basis of person and situation characteristics and the nature and strength of their linkages.

Developmental contextualism has made a major contribution by bringing into focus the inescapable fact that individual development and behavior can be understood only when individuals are recognized to function within a complex tapestry of interconnected contexts and people. Developmental contextualism, being essentially a meta-theory, has little to say about the content and processes of human development. That shortcoming has been addressed, however, by two conceptual advances that are based, in part, on the foundation of developmental contextualism. The first of these, Developmental Systems Theory (Ford & Lerner, 1992), integrates Ford's (1987) Living Systems Framework with developmental contextualism. The second is Baltes' (1997) Theory of Selection, Optimization, and Compensation (SOC). We will briefly discuss some of the major implications of these conceptual advances for understanding career development, work, and occupational success.

Developmental Systems Theory

Developmental Systems Theory (DST) is particularly useful because it integratively defines development as:

> incremental and transformational processes that, through a flow of interactions among current characteristics of the person and his or her current contexts, produces a succession of relatively enduring changes that elaborate or increase the diversity of the person's structural and functional characteristics and the patterns of their environmental interactions while maintaining coherent organization and structural-functional unity of the person as a whole. (Ford & Lerner, 1992, p. 49)

DST thus distinguishes its integrative conceptualization of development from other ways of defining change processes in human development, such as growth, maturation, learning, and socialization. Thus, growth has traditionally been associated with a permanent increase in the total mass of the body; maturation has been defined as the progressive differentiation and elaboration of both biological structures and functional capabilities; learning is a process through which knowledge and skills are acquired, and socialization is a process through which individuals acquire the behaviors, beliefs, and values characteristic of their culture (Ford & Lerner, 1992, p. 52). All of these conceptualizations can be viewed as subcategories of development as defined by DST, thus illustrating the integrative nature of this theory. Finally, DST offers a comprehensive articulation of the implications of adopting a developmental contextual/developmental systems approach for framing the most important questions for research, intervention, and social policy. Applied to career development, these implications may be summarized as follows (adapted from Ford & Lerner, 1992, pp. 50–51).

1. Career pathways are not bound by the past, but they are shaped by it.
2. Career pathways can exhibit incremental and transformational change.
3. Career pathways can make unexpected and abrupt changes that are bounded by the bio-psycho-social unity of the person.
4. Career development is an adaptive process. The process is responsive to changes in a person's productive capabilities and it serves to elaborate those capabilities. A person with more elaborate productive capabilities is better able to respond to changing and diverse work opportunities and constraints. The career adaptability construct has become a focus within career development theory (Savickas, 1997) and is a necessary personal characteristic in the pursuit of Hall's (1996, 2004) protean career.
5. Career development occurs in a multidimensional fashion and prepares people for probable work demands as opposed to planned and determined work demands.
6. Career development creates and constrains potentials along the way. Choosing one alternative during the course of a career may limit the possibility that another career alternative can occur in the future.
7. Career development is open-ended, but is constrained through a process of selective-optimization with compensation (SOC, discussed below).
8. We add that career development is associated with aging and aging leads from bio-psycho-social elaboration to decline as a function of biological maturation and learning.

On the basis of these implications, we propose that adaptive career development involves expanding, refining, and integrating constellations of mental processes (including cognition, emotion, and learning), biological maturation, and observable behaviors in the pursuit of (1) relevant, lucrative, and satisfying career interests, values, and skills, (2) a sufficient and effective understanding of the world of work, and (3) the means to translate the two into progress toward and through a rewarding career (or series of careers) through the identification and attainment of socially, occupationally, and self-defined intermediate vocational goals in family, school, work, and other community contexts.

Selective Optimization with Compensation

Propositional models like Selective Optimization with Compensation (SOC; Baltes, 1997, 2003; Baltes & Baltes, 1990) aid in the translation of meta-theoretical concepts like context and human agency into testable hypotheses. The SOC model assumes that human behavior and choice-making is rooted in an organismic theory of human agency (Ford, 1992; Little, 2002; Ryan, Sheldon, Kasser, & Deci, 1996) or the human tendency to select experiences and goals (i.e., selection in SOC) on the basis of one's strengths and weaknesses and opportunity structure. In the moment of experience, humans aim to optimize (in SOC terms) their strengths while compensating (in SOC terms) for the impact of their weaknesses or, in other words, plan and enact efficient and effective behavioral strategies. As applied to career development, adults presumably select and pursue short- and long-term work goals on the basis of personal strengths and weaknesses and contextual conditions facilitating and constraining opportunities in the employment milieu. Although the SOC model seems fairly simplistic, complexity arises in its application.

The elements of the SOC model can only be faithfully applied when the human context is comprehended because SOC mechanisms spring from the human actor interacting with human contexts. How does the present set of environmental contingencies influence whether and to what extent an aspect of a person's bio-psycho-social repertoire is adaptive or maladaptive in the present moment? An exceptionally adaptive vocational behavior or orientation in the present moment can become catastrophically maladaptive under a unique set of contextual conditions in the next moment. This has been observed with great frequency, for example, as soldiers return from war or business people decompress during the evening commute to quickly learn that their occupational bio-psycho-social repertoire that kept them alive or secured the next big contract may be the same repertoire that now threatens their happiness and survival in the family setting. Ruthlessness, for example, may be an adaptive characteristic yielding success in certain business and war-time contexts, but may lead to turmoil and devastation in the family setting.

Combining the distinction between learning, maturation, and development (Ford & Lerner, 1992) with work by Baltes (1997) leads to the proposition that career development is associated with human adaptation in the face of a curvilinear maturation function (see Figure 14.1) and SOC offers a mechanism to account for how humans respond to the direction and level of this function. Early in life, career development proceeds from the vantage of bio-psycho-social elaboration and selective optimization. Later in life, career development occurs from the vantage of bio-psycho-social maintenance and eventually compensation in the face of decline and a more or less supportive work context. SOC has its limits, and all humans face a critical threshold (see Figure 14.1) where SOC fails to further human development, i.e., the developmental gain-loss ratio becomes negative (Smith, 2003), the "coherent organization and structural-functional unity of the person" (Ford & Lerner, 1992, p. 49) disintegrates, and death follows. For some, abrupt injurious events and, for others, the gradual decline in biological functioning lead to the threshold. The developmental functions could, therefore, represent gradual

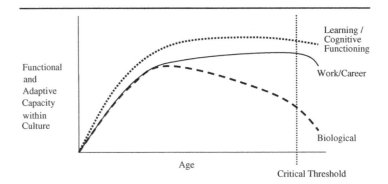

Figure 14.1 The impact of biological and cognitive functioning on career development.

decline across many years or fairly abrupt change caused by an event with the time scale in Figure 14.1 changing in a commensurate fashion.

Although this depiction of career development aids in the understanding of how biology, learning, and career development interact across the life span, it is limited in several important ways. The figure addresses the general change in the gain-loss proportion in functional capacity on a holistic level across the life span, and therefore does not represent the conceptually and empirically supported position that functional gains can yield functional losses and vice versa (Baltes, 2003; Smith, 2003). Figure 14.1 also does not account for potentially abrupt changes in the nature and amount of support afforded to the worker by the work, family, peer, and broader social context. Abrupt adaptive or maladaptive changes in support would lead to sharp changes in the depicted functions because they are all embedded within the human ecology. Sharp changes in these functions could in turn lead to rapid or delayed changes in the supportive nature of the context that may moderate or completely negate detectable changes in one's functional capacity. This possibility then suggests a difficulty in studying the depicted functions in context when the interval between occasions of measurement is a year or longer. Although rapid changes in career adaptive capacity probably occur for a large number of people, relatively resource intensive time series analyses may be necessary to fully apprehend such changes (Molenaar, 2004). Finally, Figure 14.1 does not depict the presumed increasing variability of these career-related functions across the life span (e.g., omnipotentiality) and is therefore limited in the same way that the average number of children in a family (e.g., 1.9 children) does not represent the number of children in any family.

Figure 14.2 is a response to the latter limitation by demonstrating the potential variability of career-related functions across different occupations. The mathematician demonstrates rapid career advancement and innovation through the early 30s and then a slow and steady decline across the remainder of the life span. The philosopher demonstrates a relatively slow incline in work functioning and capacity with a peak relatively late in life. Like the mathematician, the athlete demonstrates rapid career development with a peak relatively early in life, but the athlete demonstrates a much more rapid decline in career functioning and the termination of this career. Like many workers in the 20th century who have lost careers to the massive shifts in the global economy, the professional athlete typically pursues a second career (e.g., coach, sportscaster, or spokesperson) upon the "death" of their career as a professional athlete (see dotted line). As stated earlier in describing Figure 14.1, Figure 14.2 reflects very stereotypical career

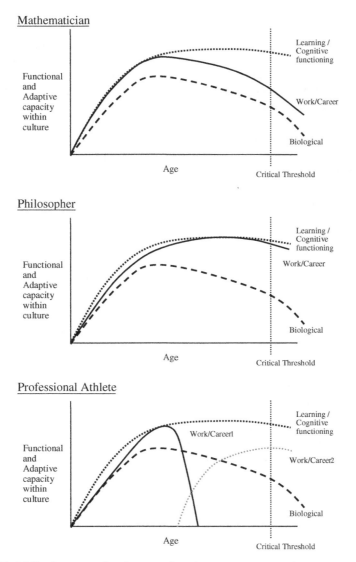

Figure 14.2 Variability in career development functions across occupations.

development functions and exceptions certainly exist in professional sports, mathematics, and philosophy.

Research directly bearing on these theoretically derived functions is mixed. In a review of the literature, Hansson, Dekoekkoek, Neece, and Patterson (1997) found some evidence suggesting that work performance declines across a variety of occupations including technical fields and professional sports, but occupational well-being appears to increase with age. They argue that the changing nature of work across age and cohorts from more to less physically demanding tasks may mask declines in the physiological capacity to work. Other work within the same review suggests that the mechanisms associated with the SOC model appear to be more active and appropriate during the later working years and for those people who engage in work that affords more self control over work tasks and scheduling. Research also suggests that the use of SOC strategies is positively associated with subjective indicators of work success (Wiese, Freund, & Baltes, 2000) and predictive of subjective success at work and job satisfaction across a three year interval (Wiese, Freund, & Baltes, 2002). Finally, some research supports the optimization mechanism by suggesting that the accumulation of work experience across the life span may moderate the impact of a negative maturation function with age, thus mitigating the impact of maturation on work functioning (Warr, 1994). In sum, future research could further examine the link between work functioning and adaptive capacity as a function of age.

SOC theory would predict much more modest declines in work functioning but greater declines in the capacity to make significant career changes because selection and optimization with compensation presumably moderates the impact of biological decline on functioning through a process of increasing specialization rather than generalization of functioning. Future research could look at the capacity of workers to adapt to significant career changes at different points during the life span. The interaction of the theoretical functions suggests that older workers generally have a diminished capacity to make a significant career change necessitating the development of a different skill set (e.g., a 50-year-old office clerk becoming a coal miner or vice versa) because they have presumably selected and optimized certain work skills and capacities at the expense of others while younger workers have not had the time to do so. Older and younger workers may not, however, differ in their capacity to be productive within their respective career fields, with the edge going to older or younger workers depending on the career field (see Figure 14.2).

Issues and Trends Bearing on the Nature of Work and the Structure of Careers

The theoretical and methodological advances we have discussed thus far will be essential tools to help researchers advance our understanding of work and career in the 21st century. Advances in logistics and distribution coupled with inexpensive labor from developing countries has led to a profound shift in developed countries from production to information and service industries and from mom-and-pop retailers to "big box" retail consumption. The applicability of the career construct as reflecting life-span occupational continuity has begun to be revised in the face of rapid and profound economic, social-structural, and cultural changes during the past century (Storey, 2000; Young & Collin, 2000). A much greater fraction of workers and aspiring workers must become more open to and prepared for routine incremental and discontinuous career change, which past generations only rarely experienced, and they must be adaptable to change when it occurs in order to maintain momentum toward at least equally if not more favorable work situations. The pluralization of career and the increasing incidence of serial or boundaryless careers (Arthur & Rousseau, 1996; Littleton, Arthur, & Rousseau, 2000) will have a considerable impact on how we conceptualize, study, and intervene upon work-related phenomena. The employer-employee contract, recurring job loss, lifelong career and job exploration, and retirement are likely to undergo significant changes in the face of significant disintegration and transformation of normative career pathways.

The Employer-Employee Contract

As the labor market becomes more flexible in response to changing market conditions, adults must become more prepared to change jobs and careers. The plasticity of the market hinges in part on a decoupling of the implicit contract whereby the employer pledges a lifelong job and the employee pledges lifelong loyalty. The modern contract will require workers to be more connected to the developmental trajectory of their career field rather than to their employer (Littleton et al., 2000), more adaptable and willing to engage in ongoing learning to keep pace with technological advances and thus ultimately to remain of value to the employer (Hall & Mirvis, 1995). The modern contract may also prompt adults to identify, pursue, and successfully navigate a series of careers akin to the concept of a protean career (Hall, 1996).

In the face of rapid and accelerating technological advances, occupations are becoming obsolete in the space of years rather than decades. Like humans, the modern organization may experience development akin to childhood, adolescence, and adulthood. Moreover, terms associated with maturation like birth, growth, decline, and death may also be aptly applied to organizations because they are increasingly being built with a finite life span in mind or at least implied on the basis of the technology employed to support it. As stated by Hesketh (2000, p. 471), "with the rapid changes facing industry, organizations no longer want to be left feeling responsible for the careers of their employees. Rather, individuals are expected to take personal responsibility for their progress within organizations."

The needs and adaptability of humans and organizations must be considered with respect to notions like timing during the life span to assess when and for how long the needs and resources of both will yield an adaptive synergy and when the organization and/or the worker must acknowledge that the relationship has become imbalanced in some way favoring the organization or the worker, leading to abrogation of the relationship by one or the other. Littleton et al. (2000) aptly depict these issues in their description of the career context of Silicon Valley. Within "the Valley," the formal and informal networks that cut across high tech firms act as a "tacit road map" (p. 106) for situating and projecting one's career within the context of rapidly emerging, developing, and failing firms. Valley employees demonstrate more commitment to their social network and their profession than they do to their present employer, because the network and the profession tend to be less transitory than the employer and/or their fleeting needs. Organizations inside and outside "the Valley" will certainly want to keep abreast of market conditions that may prompt large-scale discontinuities in careers, because at these junctures organizations, particularly those in their growth period(s), have the opportunity to secure expertise that may be hard to come by at other times. Correspondingly, people will want to keep abreast of rapid technological shifts that will prompt a pressing labor demand that may lead to opportunities for rewarding work.

In spite of the predicted decrease in the commitment extended to the worker by the organization, industrial/organizational and vocational psychologists (Riketta, 2005) continue to focus upon constructs like organizational commitment, attitudinal organizational commitment, and the nature of mentoring. These domains essentially focus upon the degree to which workers are psychosocially and behaviorally congruent with the goals and values of their work setting and its leadership. Littleton et al. (2000) argue that the boundaryless career will become much less dictated by the career ladder of the organization and much more governed by workers' personal agency and professional communion across rather than necessarily within organizations. Given the increasingly changeable workforce, what was once thought to be an adaptive quality like, for example, attitudinal organizational commitment, may in fact become generally maladaptive or at least so in certain particularly unpredictable and tenuous sectors of the workforce. The meaning of organizational commitment may change from an enduring partnership to a time-bound but meaningful consultancy like that emerging in Silicon Valley. Moreover, if mentorship is like other human relationships in its dependence on trust and predictability, then the depth of and commitment to emotionally meaningful mentorship (Gibson, 2004; Scandura & Williams, 2004) may become more a function of the mentor and protégé's ties to a shared social network than their commitment to a shared work setting or employer. The relationship may become more focused upon the development of the protégé with respect to not only the immediate needs of the organization but also the career pathways of the protégé and mentor. This relationship may focus upon the enduring needs of the protégé like lifelong learning, marketability, social networks, and career momentum that may, and probably will, translate into the protégé pursuing other jobs in other organizations in the future.

The pluralization of careers and the finite life span of organizations (cast into years rather than decades) may also prompt people to seek and employ role models (e.g., idealized real or imagined figures) rather than mentors to guide their careers, given that this generally involves little or no investment on the part of the role model and the worker can maintain reliance on these role models in the face of changing careers and work contexts (Gibson, 2004). Clearly, the proliferation of the serial career and the disintegration of career boundaries will prompt a serious revision to research and practice bearing on the world of work and career development (Savickas, 2000).

Job Loss and Career Change

Changes in the life span of the modern organization will not only have a bearing on the implicit and explicit employer-employee contract, but it will also have a profound impact on the incidence of job loss and the duration of unemployment during the working years of one's life and the timing and nature of retirement. Research from the late 1990's supports this predicted trend by demonstrating that the incidence of involuntary job loss has increased since 1980 and white collar workers and middle management have experienced the greatest increase in job loss (Hanisch, 1999). This trend may lead to an amendment to the theoretical view of unemployment from being one almost exclusively associated with loss and dysfunction (Jahoda, 1982; McKee-Ryan, Song, Wanberg, & Kinicki, 2005) to one that casts certain forms of job loss, like that associated with industry shrinkage or collapse (as opposed to a person being fired) as normative aspects of a person's working life. This changed perspective may then be most akin to the theoretical view associated with the transition from school to work during the adolescent period. Both involve exploration and career choice and, in the case of re-training for the unemployed, both involve a transition from school to work. Nevertheless, the preponderance of evidence suggests that job loss and unemployment will continue to be a distressing experience (Hanisch, 1999), but the severity of the distress may change in the face of the anticipated change in normative trends. Some research supports this prediction by demonstrating that job loss can have a favorable impact on people when the loss is viewed as an opportunity to make a positive career change (Hanisch, 1999).

With the increasing prevalence of workers pursuing serial careers, career counselors must become prepared for the positive and negative consequences of job and career mobility. A three year-long longitudinal study of 12,140 workers from the Netherlands, which compared a group of workers who changed jobs and employers with a group that did not change jobs, identified a series of antecedent and consequent conditions surrounding a job change (Swaen, Kant, van Amelsvoort, & Beurskens, 2002). Prior to a job change, workers tended to exhibit more strained relationships with supervisors, emotional strain related to work conditions, greater job insecurity, and less job satisfaction relative to those who did not change jobs. On a positive note, those who changed jobs tended to exhibit increased autonomy and task diversity and decreased role ambiguity a year later in their new job relative to those workers who did not change jobs. Those who changed jobs also tended to exhibit improved relations with their new supervisor and coworkers, decreased job insecurity, increased job satisfaction, and a more favorable ratio of income to effort. Interestingly, organizational commitment increased by 33.4% in the group that changed jobs and decreased by 3% for those who did not change jobs. This finding was replicated in more recent research (Kondratuk, Hausdorf, Korabik, & Rosin, 2004). In sum, prior to a job change, workers experience conditions that place them at risk for serious emotional strain on the job, but after the change these workers tend to rebound and actually surpass those who do not change jobs during the same interval.

Relative to job mobility research, much less work has been done to understand the antecedent and consequent conditions surrounding a career/profession change. Theory in this literature is largely based on job mobility theory and suggests that the intent to change careers is largely influenced by external, work-related, and personal factors (Blau & Lunz, 1998). This research suggests, for example, that job satisfaction and the degree of professional commitment predict a worker's intent to change careers (Blau & Lunz, 1998).

A developing body of research suggests that work should be considered on a continuum ranging from full employment to unemployment, with underemployment being the construct situated in between (Dooley, 2003). Handy (1994) conceives of employment in the form of three concentric rings with essential full-time employees representing the smallest inner ring and part-time and subcontracted workers representing the larger outer two concentric rings. The incidence of underemployment is much higher than the incidence of unemployment reported by the U.S. Bureau of Labor Statistics, and data suggests that the incidence of underemployment continued to climb from the 1980s to the early 1990s in spite of a sizeable decrease in the official unemployment rates (Dooley, 2003). This research also suggests that adverse effects of underemployment are more akin to those that spring from unemployment. In the context of serial careers and job loss and the changing nature of the implicit employer-employee contract, this research suggests that underemployment may become the next major threat facing the health of the modern labor force.

Lifelong Job Exploration and Career Redefinition

The notion of a serial career leads to the expectation that adult career development will become more salient in vocational and industrial-organizational psychology in response to ongoing recycling through exploration and choice making (akin to Super's and Erikson's notion of recycling through life stages or crises) across the adult years and the organizational response to the changing nature of those looking for work. The traditional job fair at the local community college or university may be supplemented with increasing efforts by recruiters to track market shifts that may signal the availability of mature, yet transferable talent needing to make career changes. Vondracek (2001) predicted that the rapid creation of new jobs and the proliferation of serial career pathways will prompt a greater demand for the expertise of vocational psychologists. In terms of intervention, it is becoming increasingly clear that vocational psychologists and career counselors must look to constructs like career adaptability (Savickas, 1997; Super, Savickas, &

Super, 1996) and career construction (Savickas, 2005) as constructs that will gain greater meaning as serial careers become more normative. Those individuals who choose, or by necessity pursue, serial careers must not only be ready and able to adapt to meaningful changes in their current work opportunities and constraints, they must also be able to construct a career that can be responsive to anticipated changes in the labor market. At the same time they must strive to remain consistent with salient lifelong career themes and passions that are tied to early developmental periods when the foundations are laid for later career development (Hartung, Porfeli, & Vondracek, 2005).

Retirement

Supported by the tradition of guilds, friendly societies, and fraternal organizations that supported craftsmen who could no longer work, spurred by the Great Depression and bolstered most directly by the social insurance movement first established in Germany in 1889 (Social Security Administration, 2006), the government argued that government-sponsored retirement was preferred to large segments of the population being forced into squalor. As President Roosevelt (1912) stated:

> We must protect the crushable elements at the base of our present industrial structure...it is abnormal for any industry to throw back upon the community the human wreckage due to its wear and tear, and the hazards of sickness, accident, invalidism, involuntary unemployment, and old age should be provided for through insurance. (www.ssa.gov./history/trspeech.html, accessed 7/10/06)

Although P. B. Baltes' (1997) position concerning the incomplete cultural supports available to people in their later years is particularly applicable to the world of work, in certain ways cultural institutions may provide more support than is needed. During the 20th and into the 21st century, the face of retirement has changed from being almost universally defined as the crisp cessation of paid work to a blurred continuum ranging from complete cessation to the beginning of a new career (Hansson et al., 1997; Tempest, Barnatt, & Coupland, 2002). Clearly, this shift in the institution of retirement has been prompted by improved health care that has sustained a much higher quality of life and more adaptive functioning into the later years and has ultimately served to steadily increase life expectancy and population aging. Moreover, the conditions in the labor market have improved to the extent that a large fraction of the human capital of the labor force enters retirement with relatively intact facilities to be productive (Hansson et al., 1997). The image of industrial human wreckage has been replaced with the notion of successful aging and an air of optimism fanned by research suggesting that aging can involve further human development as reflected by the pursuit of personal meaning and the mitigation of cognitive decline through a healthy lifestyle (M. M. Baltes & Carstensen, 2003). Further cause for optimism comes from research suggesting that successive cohorts of older people across the 20th century are exhibiting greater cognitive functioning (Schaie, 2002).

Returning to Figure 14.1, the critical threshold of likely occupational decline has clearly been shifted to later years of the human life span and may no longer coincide with the state instituted retirement age (65 years) that is common in Europe or with the normative expectations of the generation that preceded the Baby Boomers in the United States.

This leads to the reality that within certain human domains and periods of modern societies, cultural supports may overshoot their intended objectives. Many experts believe that the legislated age of retirement is too young given the productive capacity of the labor force at this age. The fraction of the U.S. population over 55 years old is expected to grow to become a projected 34% of the U.S. population by 2010 and only exhibit modest declines toward 28% of the population by 2050 (Wegman & McGee, 2004). Based upon employment exit trends from the 1980s to the present, survival analysis was used to predict at what age certain workers will exit the labor force and work less than 100 hours per year (Wegman & McGee, 2004). The results suggest that blue collar workers are more likely to exit the labor force relative to their white collar age mates even though the latter group is more likely to have the financial assets to support a more comfortable retirement into old age.

In another series of studies, those workers in less prestigious and lucrative occupational sectors were found to exhibit poorer general health, mental health, and physical health and more disabilities than their age mates from more prestigious and lucrative occupations. Adding injury to insult, three of the top four occupational sectors of the U.S. economy with the largest percentage of older workers are predicted to demonstrate decline or weak growth through 2010 (Wegman & McGee, 2004). These results suggest that the modern economy must promote and tap the productive capacity of the older segment of the population. This is particularly true of the blue collar workforce, which contains the largest share of older workers with more rapidly diminishing capacities to pursue their work and it is also true of older workers in declining sectors of the economy because modern societies cannot afford to support their retirement in the face of the relative decline in the number of younger workers who would support them (mainly through taxes they pay).

Reactions to these current and predicted circumstances within the labor market include delaying or staggering the retirement age, with early retirement yielding fewer benefits than later retirement. While large numbers of workers delay retirement, many of those who have already retired seek and successfully pursue occupational careers after they retire from full-time work (Watanabe Muraoka, Kawasaki, & Sato, 1998). Research suggests that older workers are more susceptible to catastrophic injury; and many workers and employers are attempting to alleviate this risk through staggered retirement ages in order to mitigate risk exposure associated with certain occupations (Wegman & McGee, 2004).

For a meaningful fraction of the "retiring" labor force, capabilities developed during the pre-retirement years, such as career adaptability and career exploration skills, may become increasingly important assets during the later working years. These capabilities may be particularly important for those workers who have insufficient retirement income and benefits. Moreover, the impact of unemployment and job loss during the "retirement" years may also take on a meaning traditionally ascribed to the pre-retirement years as "retired" workers develop a growing dependence on gainful employment as a result of the reduction or loss of retirement benefits. The impact of job loss and underemployment for post-retirement workers may be particularly profound given the adverse effects of these circumstances that have been identified in younger workers (e.g., physical and psychological health problems and substance abuse) (Hanisch, 1999). In addition, health problems may be amplified in older workers given that they typically exhibit reduced biological fitness at this point in the life span.

Whether or not a culture is incomplete with respect to institutional structures that support development of its population may partly hinge on abrupt shifts in the size of birth cohorts. During these quick population shifts, a culture may become more or less complete with respect to human development for certain periods during the life span. The population of retirees is expected to increase two to four times its present size in the next 30 years (Tempest et al., 2002). This anticipated quick shift in the size of the retiree population is likely to exacerbate the incomplete nature of modern cultures with respect to health care, living facilities, and financial support. Assuming simple economic principles related to supply, demand, and the availability of capital, the wealth of this cohort is likely to spur development and expansion of the cultural resources needed to meet the demand. As this cohort declines and dies, the cultural resources available to the next (and smaller) cohort of older people will be akin to the infrastructure (e.g., parking, restaurants, and shopping) of a college town during the summer, namely, accessible and abundant. Although this is a rosy picture, the projected high and growing proportion of retirees to working adults is likely to place a greater strain on the overall economy (Tempest et al., 2002) and may lead to clashes between working and retired people with regard to the allocation of cultural resources.

Quick population shifts occur on a smaller but still meaningful scale in communities experiencing rapid increases in certain segments of the life span. For example, many communities in the southeastern U.S. have experienced profound increases in people of childbearing age as they move to seek job opportunities and a more desirable climate. This migration has contributed to a serious teacher and school administrator shortage in states like North Carolina, and local governments in places like the Charlotte community have been unable to build schools fast enough to keep pace with population growth. In such school districts, mobile classrooms are installed before new schools come online because the capacity of the school house has been exceeded before the new schools can be opened. In such places, the culture is incomplete in its capability to support the academic development of children, and legislative efforts are underway to train and attract more qualified teachers. These smaller, but common, population shifts underscore the strain placed on a community to support rapidly growing segments of the life span.

Occupational Success

Throughout this chapter, we have argued for an inclusive, comprehensive, and complex perspective of career development, work, and occupational success. Yet, the very terminology employed suggests a degree of dualism between career, work, and occupation on the one hand and non-work concerns on the other. Although work and non-work distinctions have typically been quite categorical, a progressive blurring of these boundaries has been observed in recent years (Olson-Buchanan & Boswell, 2006). The blurring of the distinction between work and non-work is particularly germane when one addresses occupational success. Some would argue that occupational success is meaningful only when it is achieved as part of a careful balancing act between work and family. Others would maintain that occupational success needs to be defined in relation to one's work values or work aspect preferences (Pryor, 1981). In other words, if a person values money and security above other work outcomes, the measure of that person's occupational success would be money and security. If, on the other hand, a person valued altruism and self-development, then these would be the proper indicators of occupational success.

Hall (2004, p. 3) reported that he asks his students to reflect on the messages about work and careers that they received early in life from their parents and families, and he recounted that one of the messages that he received was that "the success that matters is subjective, how satisfied you feel with your life and work" (p. 3). Is there any reason to abandon this common-sense approach to occupational success at this point in time? Individuals will continue to struggle with finding balance between work and other aspects of life. Their satisfaction and subjective experience of success, however, will not only be determined by the whole of their experience in the work setting, but also in relation to their families, their communities, and the larger environment. If anything has changed in the past 50 years and if anything is to be different in the next 50 years, it will be the multitude of ways in which people can structure their work so that it can be a harmonious part of their lives. Increasingly, people will be able to pursue what Hall (2004) has called a protean career, one in which the person, not the organization, is in charge, where career decisions are guided by the person's core values, and where the criteria for success are subjective. If that model of career development prevails in the future, one of the key issues that must be addressed successfully is the relationship between work and family.

Work-Family Conflict and Work-Family Balance

Much of the research on work and family has been based on the assumption that they necessarily are in conflict with one another. Although this research has been increasingly sophisticated, focusing on both family-to-work and work-to-family conflict, the recognition that family and work influence each other reciprocally has been slow to emerge in industrial/organizational and organizational behavior research (Eby, Casper, Lockwood, Bordeaux, & Brinley, 2005). This is surprising in view of well-known, explicit conceptual formulations that recognize "dynamic interaction" and reciprocal relationships between work and family (Vondracek et al., 1986). Nevertheless, several meta-analyses of research on the relationships between work and family have been conducted in recent years (e.g., Allen, Herst, Bruck, & Sutton, 2000; Eby et al., 2005; Ernst-Kossek & Ozeki, 1998), demonstrating the importance of the topic.

There is reason to believe, however, that future researchers are much more likely to examine work-family balance rather than work-family conflict. The aim of work-family balance is to be engaged in both the worker and family member roles with similar levels of energy, commitment, attentiveness, care, and concern (Greenhaus, Collins, & Shaw, 2003). Research demonstrates that individuals with low involvement in work and family tend to have a lower predicted quality of life than those exhibiting more involvement in both work and family. Interestingly, Greenhaus et al. (2003) found that an involved but imbalanced role structure favoring family over work yielded the highest perceived quality of life. Nevertheless, an involved and balanced approach to work and family is commonly presumed to buffer people from the maladaptive experiences that may occur within one role by virtue of the adaptive nature of the other roles. Moreover, the balanced approach to living permits people to capitalize on the benefits of multiple domains, as they present themselves, when such benefits may not be routinely available in any one role. Although some authors refer to balance in terms of committed time, family functioning clearly hinges more on the nature and amount of interaction than it does on the time spent together (Greenhaus et al., 2003). Finally, it should be noted that time not committed to work or family may be committed to other life fulfilling pursuits like volunteer work in the community or recreational activities that promote individual development, which ultimately serves to improve a person's capacity to make the most of the time committed to work and family.

The Future of Work and Career

Thus far, we have argued for using a more complex, comprehensive, and integrative conceptual model to describe, study, and understand career development, work, and occupational success. We have stressed that the career trajectory and work life of individuals cannot be separated from their overall developmental trajectory and their total life experience, and we have proposed that biological and cognitive development over the life course impact work and career in profound but highly differentiated ways depending on the occupation chosen. We have also stressed that the meaning of work and career has been changing much more rapidly in recent years than in the past, largely due to globalization and technological advances. As a consequence, multiple proposals to advance new conceptualizations and new paradigms for studying work and careers have been published in little more than a decade (Arthur & Rousseau, 1996; Hall & Associates, 1996; Jackson, Arnold, Nicholson, & Watts, 1996; Rifkin, 1995; Young & Collin, 2000).

There is little doubt that the significance and meaning of work, career, and occupational success in the 21st century will be quite different from what it has been in most of the previous century. Individuals will adopt different perspectives on work and family, resulting in different motivations and expectations. Organizations are already in the process of fundamentally changing in the global economy, and theory and research on work, career, and occupational success will experience paradigm shifts that include new methodologies for studying individuals in multiple, rapidly changing contexts (e.g., P. B. Baltes & Smith, 2003; Cairns, Berman, & Kagan, 1998; Molenaar, 2004; Wiese et al., 2000, 2002). While it is clear that the future of work and careers will be very different from the past, making specific predictions is difficult considering the complexity of contributing factors. Nevertheless, some emerging directions for the future of work, career, and occupational success are difficult to ignore and may very well persist for the foreseeable future.

One possible scenario is one in which career development gives way to a series of vocational projects, which "constitute the person's intrinsically oriented and intentional needs to seek outlets through a relationship with the world" (Riverin-Simard, 2000, p. 121). According to Riverin-Simard (2000), these vocational projects play an essential role in the continual redefinition of vocational identity, required by the numerous upheavals and uncertainties of the job market of the 21st century. From a primary and secondary control perspective (Heckhausen & Schulz, 1995), people may aim to influence their social networks to achieve their goals (primary control strategy) and in the face of little or no peer network or an inability to influence it, individuals may develop and manipulate their career pathways in order to achieve their goals (i.e., secondary control strategy). Career may become less characterized by upward mobility through a series of well-defined positions within an organization and more defined by movement through and up the ranks of a peer network that cuts across organizations and may or may not be neatly tied to a clearly hierarchical series of positions. For example, a person may make a lateral or downward move to another organization through connections within the peer network in order to obtain a skill or body of knowledge that may distinguish him/her within the peer network and therefore improve the chances of obtaining more favorable work through the network in the future. A significant aspect of career research may then become a science of peer networks akin to the body of literature on peer networks during the adolescent years. Such theory and research would argue that the career construct is not dead in the face of serial careers (Riverin-Simard, 2000; Young & Valach, 2000), but rather that the conditions that define the career roadmap have changed from being determined by the employer's hierarchical management structure to being defined by one's relative position/standing within professional networks that cut across employers. If true, then what appear to be chaotic career changes (Riverin-Simard, 2000) on a roadmap defined by work organizations and their management hierarchy, may in fact be quite orderly and predictable when the pathway is overlaid on the professional social network. Akin to Kanter's (1989) professional career, the professional social network would not only reveal patterns of socialization, but also possible avenues (linguistically, career = road) for mobility. This research would be informed by empirical studies of adolescent peer networks and cliques and studies of how children navigate within and between these networks.

Although some have criticized the notion of career development as being too centered on the individual (Kanter, 1989), clearly the linguistic source of the word suggesting a roadway connotes that people may choose to turn left or right, but they must remain on a roadway in order to travel. The roadway constrains the possible career routes that one can take. At the risk of abusing the metaphor, entrepreneurs would represent people who have created new roadways. The 21st-century economy may force people to choose alternative markers (like the social network) to define the boundaries of the roadway. The context of these social networks may shift from the pub or club to the virtual world as websites like myspace.com and facebook.com become a part of adults' lives in the way that they have become a central part of adolescents' and young adults' social lives. One's virtual presence may thus become intimately connected with one's occupational opportunities and standing.

Like social networks, the Internet has the potential to blur the boundaries between personal and professional lives. Websites like myspace.com and facebook.com are large, web-based venues for people to develop relationships and reveal the personal side of their lives. As this aspect of the Internet continues to grow, the general public may have the capacity to track the lifestyles of people from childhood to old age. As adolescents today make the transition to the adult world, many of them are finding that their personal lives, as they and others depict them on the Internet, are impacting their chances of securing and maintaining a job. Recent research conducted by Execunet and reported in a variety of online periodicals (e.g., Flesher, 2006) suggests that 75% of recruiters surveyed employ the Internet to learn about the personal lives of prospective employees, and 26% have screened out candidates on the basis of the information they obtained. These sources also suggest that employers are actively searching such web venues to ensure that their employees are not inadvertently disclosing company secrets and/or representing the organization in an unfavorable manner. Reportedly, terminations have been prompted by such material. As a consequence, online periodicals and some universities are warning adolescents and adults to be wary of what they reveal online (Conlin, 2006) and encouraging industry to tap this information to learn more about job seekers and keep tabs on current employees (Baker & Green, 2005). What consequence this new trend will have on the actions of organizations and the vocational and personal behaviors of adults seeking to secure and maintain a job is yet to be seen, but the early signs suggest that profound changes are on the horizon.

Conclusion

The early 21st century is an exciting yet challenging period for the workforce and for those who study it. The rapid and sometimes chaotic changes in the global economy challenge employers and employees to fundamentally revise the implicit employment contract in order to survive and this, in turn, has led to meaningful changes in the content, structure, and course of career development across adulthood and into the retirement years. Researchers have forwarded new theoretical models in an effort to capture the changing ecology of human development and how people define and are defined by their unique array of contexts. These models, as applied to career development, have undergone almost constant revision and expansion in order to explain the apparent transformation in the role of work in people's lives. Current indications and trends suggest that the only constant within the workforce over the next few decades will be change and that we will have to become more adaptive in order to keep up with the pace of change.

Coupling meta-theoretical models like developmental contextualism, meso-theoretical models like developmental systems theory, and propositional models like selective-optimization-with-compensation, yields enough specificity to establish important research questions without becoming so constrained as to risk rapid obsolescence. In this chapter, we have proposed linkages across the three models and demonstrated how they can be employed to predict functional and adaptive career capacity across the life span and how these capacities are influenced by the variability in occupational demands. We further identified what we believe will become more salient issues in career development like the changing nature of retirement and career pathways as defined more by social networks than by organizational structure. Coupling the theoretical model with the salient issues yields a multifaceted agenda for future research.

One of these salient issues may very well be the issue of how social policies and programs may help or hinder individuals as they continually adapt their careers and their work to the brave new world of the 21st century. Any research agenda that aims to answer these questions, if it is based on a developmental-contextual framework, will incorporate individual differences, multiple contexts, and the sociocultural institutions within which individuals function. As Lerner and Simi (2000) note:

> The goal of developmental contextual explanatory research is to understand the ways in which variations in ecologically 'valid' person-context relationships account for the character of actual or potential trajectories of human development, that is, life paths enacted in the 'natural laboratory' of the 'real world.' (Lerner & Simi, 2000, p. 425)

Moreover, from this perspective, policy development and the design, implementation, and evaluation of interventions do not represent secondary or derivative applications after research evidence has been compiled. Instead, developmental contextual research, conducted from a multidisciplinary perspective, considers policies and (intervention) programs as the experimental tools of such research. Applied to career development and work, such research could be instrumental in enhancing our understanding of the role of career and work in the life trajectories of individuals, and in enhancing the career development and work satisfaction of individuals who may experience special challenges because of normative developmental problems associated with aging and risks associated with the larger socioeconomic environment at any given historical moment (Lerner & Simi, 2000, p. 426).

Another salient issue to be included in any agenda for future research on career development and work has to do with the question of what constitutes success in these areas, especially as individuals age and adapt to changing personal capabilities as well as constantly changing work requirements, economic conditions, and life circumstances.

Previously, we introduced the model of selective optimization with compensation (SOC), which was specifically developed to examine and promote successful aging (Baltes & Baltes, 1990). The basic proposition of the model is that selection, optimization, and compensation represent lifelong processes in development that converge around the objectives of maximizing gains and minimizing losses (Baltes, Lindenberger, & Staudinger, 1998). Understanding these processes and helping people to use them effectively could very well represent a major thrust of research in the years to come, primarily because it is becoming evident that the emerging landscape of work and careers demands the development and acquisition of skills in making good decisions (selections), optimizing internal and external resources, and compensating for losses, deficits, declines in capabilities, or changes in the environment throughout the life span into old age.

Selection will be an increasingly important and increasingly frequent task in the environment for career development that is likely to prevail in the decades to come, primarily because of the accelerating pace of change in occupations, industries, and economies. Optimization in career development is likely to be focused on identifying and seeking environments that enhance one's chances for advancement or one's chances of attaining job-related goals or preferences. Optimization could also involve the investment of time and energy in the acquisition of new occupational skills or being able to delay gratification (e.g., in the pursuit of entrepreneurship). In the challenging and rapidly changing occupational environment that is likely to be the norm in the future, optimization in the domains of cognition and intellectual development will be a prerequisite for advancement. Finally, compensation within the SOC model becomes necessary when individuals encounter internal or external limits or losses. Clearly, it is an essential strategy in adult career development and in the maintenance of satisfactory work performance. Adults who used SOC strategies are more likely to maintain a feeling of competency and of successful goal attainment in the occupational domain (Abraham & Hansson, 1995).

At this time, it would be presumptuous to attempt to present a comprehensive agenda for research on career development, work, and occupational success. A constantly recurring theme throughout this chapter has been that the multiple contexts within which individuals will actualize their careers are changing at an ever quicker pace. The conditions of work three or four decades into the future are unknown. At best, we can speculate about what they will be, and thus we can only speculate about the specific questions that will need to be answered by research. More important at this point is to develop and use emerging theoretical formulations that are capable of accommodating the incredible complexity of human development in context and to utilize methodologies that can handle both, complexity and change. It is our hope that we have succeeded in describing some of these and in demonstrating how they can significantly enhance our understanding of career development, work, and occupational success in a future that is exciting and promising, as well as challenging.

References

Abraham, J. D., & Hansson, R. O. (1995). Successful aging at work: An applied study of selection, organization, optimization, and compensation through impression management. *Journals of Gerontology Series B-Psychological Sciences & Social Sciences, 50B*(2), 94–103.

Allen, T. D., Herst, D. E. L., Bruck, C. S., & Sutton, M. (2000). Consequences associated with work-to-family conflict: A review and agenda for future research. *Journal of Occupational Health Psychology, 5*(2), 278–308.

Arthur, M. B., & Rousseau, D. M. (Eds.). (1996). *The boundaryless career: A new employment principle for a new organizational era.* New York: Oxford University Press.

Baker, S., & Green, H. (2005). Blogs will change your business. *BusinessWeek* Online. Accessed July 10, 2006, from http://www.businessweek.com/print/magazine/content/05_18b3931001_mx.htm?chan-tc#monday930anmonday930am

Baltes, M. M., & Carstensen, L. L. (2003). The process of successful aging: Selection, optimization and compensation. In U. M. Staudinger & U. Lindenberger (Eds.), *Understanding human development: Dialogues with lifespan psychology* (pp. 81–104). Dordrecht, Netherlands: Kluwer.

Baltes, P. B. (1997). On the incomplete architecture of human ontogeny: Selection, optimization, and compensation as foundation of developmental theory. *American Psychologist, 52*(4), 366–380.

Baltes, P. B. (2003). On the incomplete architecture of human ontogeny: Selection, optimization and compensation as foundation of developmental theory. In U. M. Staudinger & U. Lindenberger (Eds.), *Understanding human development: Dialogues with lifespan psychology* (pp. 17–44). Dordrecht, Netherlands: Kluwer.

Baltes, P. B., & Baltes, M. M. (1990). Psychological perspectives on successful aging: The model of selective optimization with compensation. In P. B. Baltes & M. M. Baltes (Eds.), *Successful aging: Perspectives from the behavioral sciences* (pp. 1–34). Cambridge, UK: Cambridge University Press.

Baltes, P. B., Lindenberger, U., & Staudinger, U. M. (1998). Life-span theory in developmental psychology. In R. M. Lerner (Ed.), *Theoretical models of human development* (5th ed., Vol. 1, pp. 1029 – 1143). New York: Wiley.

Baltes, P. B., & Smith, J. (2003). New frontiers in the future of aging: From successful aging of the young old to the dilemmas of the fourth age. *Gerontology, 49*(2), 123–135.

Blau, G., & Lunz, M. (1998). Testing the incremental effect of professional commitment on intent to leave one's profession beyond the effects of external, personal, and work-related variables. *Journal of Vocational Behavior, 52*(2), 260–269.

Bromley, D. B. (1990a). Academic contributions to psychological counselling: I. A philosophy of science for the study of individual cases. *Counselling Psychology Quarterly, 3*(3), 299–307.

Bromley, D. B. (1990b). *Behavioural gerontology: Central issues in the psychology of aging.* New York: Wiley.

Bronfenbrenner, U. (1979). *The ecology of human development: Experiments by nature and design.* Cambridge, MA: Harvard University Press.

Cairns, R. B., Bergman, L., R., & Kagan, J. (Eds.). (1998). *Methods and models for studying the individual.* Thousand Oaks, CA: Sage.

Conlin, M. (2006). You are what you post: Bosses are using Google to peer into places job interviews can't take them. Retrieved March 12, 2007, from http://www.businessweek.com.

Dannefer, D. (1992). On the conceptualization of context in developmental discourse: Four meanings of context and their implications. In D. L. Featherman, R. M. Lerner, & M. Perlmutter (Eds.), *Life-span development and behavior* (Vol. 2, pp. 83–109). Hillsdale, NJ: Erlbaum.

Dooley, D. (2003). Unemployment, underemployment, and mental health: Conceptualizing employment status as a continuum. *American Journal of Community Psychology, 32*(1), 9–20.

Eby, L. T., Casper, W. J., Lockwood, A., Bordeaux, C., & Brinley, A. (2005). Work and family research in IO/OB: Content analysis and review of the literature (1980–2002). *Journal of Vocational Behavior, 66*(1), 124–197.

Erikson, E. H. (1950). *Childhood and society.* New York: W.W. Norton.

Ernst-Kossek, E., & Ozeki, C. (1998). Work-family conflict, policies, and the job-life satisfaction relationship: A review and directions for organizational behavior-human resources research. *Journal of Applied Psychology, 83*(2), 139–149.

Fagan, B. (2000). *The little ice age: How climate made history, 1300–1850.* New York: Basic Books.

Flesher, J. (2006). How to clean up your digital dirt before it trashes your job search. Retrieved March 12, 2007, from http://www.CareerJournal.com.

Ford, D. H. (1987). *Humans as self-constructing living systems: A developmental perspective on behavior and personality.* Hillsdale, NJ: Erlbaum.

Ford, D. H., & Lerner, R. M. (1992). *Developmental systems theory: An integrative approach.* Newbury Park, CA: Sage.

Ford, M. E. (1992). *Motivating humans: Goals, emotions, and personal agency beliefs.* Newbury Park, CA: Sage.

Gibson, D. E. (2004). Role models in career development: New directions for theory and research. *Journal of Vocational Behavior, 65*(1), 134–156.

Grant Foundation, W. T. (1988). *The forgotten half—non-college youth in America: An interim report on the school-to-work transition.* Washington, DC: William T. Grant Foundation.

Greenhaus, J. H., Collins, K. M., & Shaw, J. D. (2003). The relation between work-family balance and quality of life. *Journal of Vocational Behavior, 63*(3), 510–531.

Hall, D. T. (2004). The protean career: A quarter-century journey. *Journal of Vocational Behavior, 65*(1), 1–13.

Hall, D. T., & Associates. (1996). *The career is dead—long live the career: A relational approach to careers.* San Francisco: Jossey-Bass.

Hall, D. T., & Mirvis, P. H. (1995). The new career contract: Developing the whole person at midlife and beyond. *Journal of Vocational Behavior, 47*(3), 269–289.

Hamilton, S. F., & Hamilton, M. A. (1999). Creating new pathways to adulthood by adapting German apprenticeship in the United States. In W. R. Heinz (Ed.), *From education to work: Cross national perspectives* (pp. 194–213). New York: Cambridge University Press.

Handy, C. (1994). *The age of paradox.* Boston: Harvard Business School Press.

Hanisch, K. A. (1999). Job loss and unemployment research from 1994 to 1998: A review and recommendations for research and intervention. *Journal of Vocational Behavior, 55*(2), 188–220.

Hansson, R. O., Dekoekkoek, P. D., Neece, W. M., & Patterson, D. W. (1997). Successful aging at work: Annual review, 1992–1996: The older worker and transitions to retirement. *Journal of Vocational Behavior, 51*(2), 202–233.

Hartung, P. J., Porfeli, E. J., & Vondracek, F. W. (2005). Child vocational development: A review and reconsideration. *Journal of Vocational Behavior, 66*(3), 385–419.

Heckhausen, J., & Schulz, R. (1995). A life-span theory of control. *Psychological Review, 102*(2), 284–304.

Hesketh, B. (2000). Prevention and development in the workplace. In S. D. Brown & R. W. Lent (Eds.), *Handbook of counseling psychology* (3rd ed., pp. 471–498). Hoboken, NJ: Wiley.

Jackson, C., Arnold, J., Nicholson, N., & Watts, A. G. (1996). *Managing careers in 2000 and beyond.* Brighton, UK: The Institute of Employment Studies.

Jahoda, M. (1982). *Employment and unemployment.* Cambridge, UK: Cambridge University Press.

Kanter, R. M. (1989). Careers and the wealth of nations: A macro-perspective on the structure and implications of career forms. In M. B. Arthur, D. T. Hall, & B. S. Lawrence (Eds.), *Handbook of career theory* (pp. 506–521). Cambridge, UK: Cambridge University Press.

Kondratuk, T. B., Hausdorf, P. A., Korabik, K., & Rosin, H. M. (2004). Linking career mobility with corporate loyalty: How does job change relate to organizational commitment? *Journal of Vocational Behavior, 65*(2), 332–349.

Lerner, R. M., & Simi, N. L. (2000). A holistic, integrated model of risk and protection in adolescence: A developmental contextual perspective about research, programs, and policies. In L. R. Bergman & R. B. Cairns (Eds.), *Developmental science and the holistic approach* (pp. 421–443). Mahwah, NJ: Erlbaum.

Levinson, D. J., Darrow, C. N., Klein, E. B., Levinson, M. H., & McKee, B. (1978). *The seasons of a man's life.* New York: Knopf.

Little, T. D. (2002). Agency in development. In W. W. Hartup & R. K. Silbereisen (Eds.), *Growing points in developmental science: An introduction* (pp. 223–240). New York: Psychology Press.

Littleton, S. M., Arthur, M. B., & Rousseau, D. M. (2000). The future of boundaryless careers. In A. Collin & R. A. Young (Eds.), *The future of career* (pp. 101–114). New York: Cambridge University Press.

McKee-Ryan, F., Song, Z., Wanberg, C. R., & Kinicki, A. J. (2005). Psychological and physical well-being during unemployment: A meta-analytic study. *Journal of Applied Psychology, 90*(1), 53–76.

Molenaar, P. C. M. (2004). A manifesto on psychology as idiographic science: Bringing the person back into scientific psychology, this time forever. *Measurement: Interdisciplinary Research and Perspectives, 2*(4), 201–218.

Olson-Buchanan, J. B., & Boswell, W. R. (2006). Blurring boundaries: Correlates of integration and segmentation between work and nonwork. *Journal of Vocational Behavior, 68*(3), 432–445.

Piaget, J. (1960). *The psychology of intelligence.* New York: Littlefield, Adams.

Pryor, R. G. (1981). Interests and values as preferences: A validation of the Work Aspect Preference Scale. *Australian Psychologist, 16*(2), 258–272.

Reitzle, M., Vondracek, F. W., & Silbereisen, R. K. (1998). Timing of school-to-work transitions: A developmental-contextual perspective. *International Journal of Behavioral Development, 22*(1), 7–28.

Rifkin, J. (1995). *The end of work: The decline of the global labor force and the dawn of the post-market era.* New York: G.P. Putnam's Sons.

Riketta, M. (2005). Organizational identification: A meta-analysis. *Journal of Vocational Behavior, 66*(2), 358–384.

Riverin-Simard, D. (2000). Career development in a changing context of the second part of working life. In A. Collin & R. A. Young (Eds.), *The future of career* (pp. 115–130). Cambridge, UK: Cambridge University Press.

Roosevelt, T. (1912). Address before the convention of the National Progressive Party, Chicago, IL. Retrieved March 13, 2007, from http://www.socialsecurity.gov.

Ryan, R. M., Sheldon, K. M., Kasser, T., & Deci, E. L. (1996). All goals are not created equal: An organismic perspective on the nature of goals and their regulation. In P. M. Gollwitzer & J. A. Bargh (Eds.), *The psychology of action: Linking cognition and motivation to behavior* (pp. 7–26). New York: Guilford.

Savickas, M. L. (1997). Career adaptability: An integrative construct for life-span, life-space theory. *Career Development Quarterly, 45*(3), 247–259.

Savickas, M. L. (2000). Renovating the psychology of careers for the twenty-first century. In A. Collin & R. A. Young (Eds.), *The future of career* (pp. 53–68). Cambridge, UK: Cambridge University Press.

Savickas, M. L. (2005). The theory and practice of career construction. In R. W. Lent & S. D. Brown (Eds.), *Career development and counseling: Putting theory and research to work* (pp. 42–70). Hoboken, NJ: Wiley.

Scandura, T. A., & Williams, E. A. (2004). Mentoring and transformational leadership: The role of supervisory career mentoring. *Journal of Vocational Behavior, 65*(3), 448–468.

Schaie, K. W. (2002). The impact of longitudinal studies on understanding development from young adulthood to old age. In W. W. Hartup & R. K. Silbereisen (Eds.), *Growing Points in Developmental Science: An introduction* (pp. 307–328). New York: Psychology Press.

Schein, E. (1978). *Career dynamics: Matching individual and organizational needs.* Reading, MA: Addison Wesley.

Shanahan, M. J., & Porfeli, E. J. (2002). Integrating the life course and life-span: Formulating research questions with dual points of entry. *Journal of Vocational Behavior, 61*(3), 398–406.

Smith, J. (2003). The gain-loss dynamic in lifespan development: Implications for change in self and personality during old and very old age. In U. M. Staudinger & U. Lindenberger (Eds.), *Understanding human development: Dialogues with lifespan psychology* (pp. 215–242). Dordrecht, Netherlands: Kluwer.

Social Security Administration (2006). Historical background and development of social security. Retrieved online March13, 2007 from http://www.socialsecurity.gov.

Stern, D., & National Center for Research in Vocational Education, U.S. (1995). *School to work: research on transition programs in the United States.* Washington, DC: Falmer Press for the National Center for Research in Vocational Education.

Storey, J. A. (2000). 'Fractured lines' in the career environment. In A. Collin & R. A. Young (Eds.), *The future of career* (pp. 21–36). Cambridge, UK: Cambridge University Press.

Stryker, S., & Burke, P. J. (2000). The past, present, and future of an identity theory. *Social Psychology Quarterly, 63*(4), 284–297.

Super, D. E. (1957). *The psychology of careers; an introduction to vocational development.* New York: Harper & Row.

Super, D. E. (1980). A life-span, life-space, approach to career development. *Journal of Vocational Behavior, 16,* 282–298.

Super, D. E., & Knasel, E. G. (1981). Career development in adulthood: Some theoretical problems and a possible solution. *British Journal of Guidance & Counselling, 9*(2), 194–201.

Super, D. E., Savickas, M. L., & Super, C. M. (1996). A life-span, life-space approach to career development. In D. Brown, L. Brooks, & Associates (Eds.), *Career choice and development* (3rd ed., pp. 197–261). San Francisco: Jossey-Bass.

Swaen, G. M. H., Kant, I., van Amelsvoort, L. G. P. M., & Beurskens, A. J. H. M. (2002). Job mobility, its determinants, and its effects: Longitudinal data from the Maastricht cohort study. *Journal of Occupational Health Psychology, 7*(2), 121–129.

Tempest, S., Barnatt, C., & Coupland, C. (2002). Grey advantage: New strategies for the old. *Long Range Planning: International Journal of Strategic Management, 35*(5), 475–492.

Thomae, H., & Lehr, U. (1986). Stages, crises, conflicts, and life-span development. In A. B. Sorensen, F. E. Weinert, & L. R. Sherrod (Eds.), *Human Development and the life course: Multidisciplinary perspectives* (pp. 429–444). Hillsdale, NJ: Erlbaum.

Thomae, H., Lehr, U., & Schmitz-Scherzer, R. (1981). Research on aging in behavioral sciences. *Zeitschrift für Gerontologie, 14*(3), 204–223.

von Bertalanffy, L. (1968). *General system theory.* New York: George Braziller.

Vondracek, F. W. (2001). The developmental perspective in vocational psychology. *Journal of Vocational Behavior, 59*(2), 252–261.

Vondracek, F. W., & Fouad, N. A. (1994). Developmental contextualism: An integrative framework for theory and practice. In M. L. Savickas & R. W. Lent (Eds.), *Convergence in career development theories: Implications for science and practice* (pp. 207–214). Palo Alto, CA: CPP Books.

Vondracek, F. W., & Kawasaki, T. (1995). Toward a comprehensive framework for adult career development theory and intervention. In W. B. Walsh & S. H. Osipow (Eds.), *Handbook of vocational psychology: Theory, research, and practice (2nd ed.): Contemporary topics in vocational psychology* (pp. 111–141). Mahwah, NJ: Erlbaum.

Vondracek, F. W., Lerner, R. M., & Schulenberg, J. E. (1986). *Career development: A life-span developmental approach.* Hillsdale, NJ: Erlbaum.

Vondracek, F. W., & Porfeli, E. J. (2002). Counseling psychologists and schools: Toward a sharper conceptual focus. *The Counseling Psychologist, 30*(5), 749–756.

Warr, P. (1994). Age and employment. In H. C. Triandis, M. D. Dunnette, & L. M. Hough (Eds.), *Handbook of industrial and organizational psychology* (2nd ed., Vol. 4, pp. 485–550). Palo Alto, CA: Consulting Psychologists Press.

Watanabe Muraoka, A., Kawasaki, T., & Sato, S. (1998). Vocational behavior of the Japanese in late adulthood: Focusing on those in the retirement process. *Journal of Vocational Behavior, 52*(3), 300–311.

Wegman, D. H., & McGee, J. P. (Eds.). (2004). *Health and safety needs of older workers.* Washington, DC: National Academies Press.

Wiese, B. S., Freund, A. M., & Baltes, P. B. (2000). Selection, optimization, and compensation: An action-related approach to work and partnership. *Journal of Vocational Behavior, 57,* 273–300.

Wiese, B. S., Freund, A. M., & Baltes, P. B. (2002). Subjective career success and emotional well-being: Longitudinal predictive power of selection, optimization and compensation. *Journal of Vocational Behavior, 60*(3), 321–335.

Young, R. A., & Collin, A. (2000). Introduction: Framing the future of career. In A. Collin & R. A. Young (Eds.), *The future of career* (pp. 1–20). Cambridge, UK: Cambridge University Press.

Young, R. A., & Valach, L. (2000). Reconceptualising career theory and research: An action-theoretical perspective. In A. Collin & R. A. Young (Eds.), *The future of career* (pp. 181–196). Cambridge, UK: Cambridge University Press.

Chapter 15

Religious and Spiritual Development in Adulthood

Paul Wink

A surge of interest in religion over the past 20 years has resulted in a number of recent reviews of the relationship between religious involvement and aging. A survey of these publications reveals how little is known, however, about the development of religiousness and spirituality in adulthood. In her review chapter for the *Handbook of Aging and the Social Sciences*, Idler (2006) devotes only two pages to age-related changes in religion and summarizes the existing body of research with the highly general and equivocal statement that "religion remains stable or increases until late life" (p. 283). Spilka, Hood, Hunsberger, and Gorsuch (2003) begin their brief entry on religion and elderly individuals by stating that although "it is widely assumed ... that people in late adulthood are more religious than their younger peers ... the data are often equivocal" (p. 165). A similar conclusion is reached by Levenson, Aldwin, and D'Mello (2005) in their review of findings on religious development from adolescence to middle adulthood.

The paucity of knowledge about religious development in adulthood is not surprising because a methodologically sound inquiry into how religion unfolds over the adult life course would require the continuous study of several different age cohorts over more than half a century. Such a study would need to sample different religious denominations and regions of the United States, assess multiple facets of religious beliefs and practices (e.g., attendance, prayer, use of electronic media), and pay attention to turning points and varied trajectories of change. Clearly, the existing body of research falls short of these requirements. At the same time, a proper evaluation of the available findings is made difficult by the absence of a theoretical framework that should sensitize researchers to reasons why their findings lack consistency, and serve as a guide for designing focused short-term studies aimed at understanding how specific life events or transitions affect religious beliefs, practices, and habits.

According to Idler (2006), the field of religion and aging has been slow in adopting the life course paradigm as the theoretical framework for organizing research because of the perception that the patterns of change in religiousness are not as closely tied to specific life transitions as, for example, work or marriage trajectories. Yet, recently the life course theory has been successfully applied to identifying different trajectories of change, and isolating social forces that influence change in religiosity (see, for example, Dillon & Wink, 2007; Ingersoll-Dayton, Krause, & Morgan, 2002). In this chapter, the existing body of data on religious development in adulthood will be reviewed using life course theory. After introducing the basic principles of this framework, I will discuss: (a) how rates of religious involvement (primarily church attendance) change over the course of early, middle, and late adulthood, (b) how the meaning of religious beliefs and practices evolves from early to late adulthood, (c) the stability of religiousness at an individual, rather than group level, and (d) differences in religious and spiritual seeking development across the life course.

Life Course Theory

Life course theory stresses the importance of understanding the socio-cultural environment for interpreting individual behavior (Elder, 1995). In other words, although humans are active agents, their behavior is inevitably shaped by larger socio-historical forces that provide a context for action. It is not surprising that the development of life course theory coincides with the rapid social changes that have characterized the second half of the 20th century. From a life course perspective, the study of age related changes needs to be multidisciplinary as development is both multidimensional (involving biological, psychological, and sociological processes) and multispheral (involving interrelated changes in various life domains, for example, family, work, and religiousness; Settersten, 2003). Moreover, life long personal development is also multidirectional (involving losses and gains) and is characterized by both continuity and change. Individual lives consist of multiple and interrelated trajectories or patterns of change (e.g., work, marriage, and leisure) that are punctuated by events of abrupt change (e.g., divorce), more gradual transitions (e.g., graduation from college, retirement), and turning points or significant shifts in direction (e.g., religious conversion or apostasy). Events, transitions, and turning points need to be understood in the context of the trajectories in which they are embedded and conversely trajectories can only be understood by paying attention to the role of transitions in promoting stability and change (Elder, 1985; Settersten, 2003). Along with an emphasis on the role of historical context and social structures in interpreting change, life course theory stresses the importance of gender, race, and social class as important context variables for interpreting the trajectories of change.

The power of life course theory for understanding the relationship between religion and age is demonstrated by Ingersoll-Dayton et al. (2002) who applied this framework to retrospective interview data obtained from a group of older adults. Ingersoll-Dayton and her colleagues uncovered the presence of different trajectories of change in religiousness (e.g., an increasing, stable, and curvilinear pattern) whose shapes reflected the dimension of religiousness being considered (e.g., organizational participation, content of religious beliefs, and commitment). For example, whereas religious commitment demonstrated a stable pattern over the life course, organizational participation (church attendance) tended to decrease with age, especially in late adulthood. In addition, the shape of the religious trajectories was influenced by embedded transitions that either promoted (e.g., child rearing) or inhibited (e.g., adverse life events leading to disillusionment) religious involvement. In this chapter, a special consideration will be given to the interrelation between religious dimensions and trajectories and the role of transitions in the process of change. In addition, drawing on Kohli's (1986) tripartite division of the life course, I will discuss separately how religiousness changes in early adulthood, a time of education, training, and entry into the adult world, middle adulthood, a time of social and economic dominance, and late adulthood or the post-retirement period.

Changes in Religious Involvement and Attendance

The most commonly asked question about age related changes in religion is: Do individuals become more religious with age? This question reflects an interest in mean or average level of change in religiousness among the elderly as a group. The answer to this seemingly simple question is complicated by the fact that it requires long-term longitudinal data gathered painstakingly over many decades. Not surprisingly, there exist less than a handful of longitudinal studies that have comparable data on religion for the same group of individuals studied at multiple points in time. In the absence of such data, researchers have either used more focused short-term longitudinal data to explore how religion changes over discrete segments of the life course (e.g., shift from adolescence to early adulthood or from young-old to old-old age) or, alternatively, have resorted to large national cross-sectional data sets that include samples of individuals, albeit not the same, spanning in age the entire life course. While cross-sectional data sets, such as the General Social Survey or the Gallup poll, have the advantage of being representative of the U.S. population as a whole and of being relatively easy to obtain (the data can be collected in a short time), the major drawback of cross-section research is that it inevitably leads to uncertainty whether the findings can be attributed to change in the individual (maturation effect) or whether they are an artifact of cohort and/or period effects. In other words, if today's 60-year-old individuals are more religious than 20-year-olds, this effect could be due to either the fact that persons become more religious with age or, alternatively, that that the older cohort has always been more religious reflecting perhaps a secularization effect. Although longitudinal data are not immune to cohort and period effects, their presence challenges the generalizability of findings but does not undermine the attribution of change to the individual. In discussing how levels of religious involvement change over the life course, I will first consider early and late adulthood, the two segments of the life course that have been researched most extensively, and will then consider middle adulthood, the mostly uncharted segment of the religious landscape.

Early Adulthood.   According to the eminent Berkeley sociologist Robert Bellah and colleagues:

> The self-reliant American is required not only to leave home but to 'leave church' as well... Traditionally, Protestant piety demanded that a young person experiences a unique conversion experience of his or her own, even while specifying more or less clearly the content of that experience. More recently we have come to expect even greater autonomy. (Bellah, Madsen, Sullivan, Swidler, & Tipton, 1985, pp. 62–63)

In view of Bellah and his colleagues' perceptive insight into American culture, it is not surprising that the high school and college years are a period of the life course with highest rate of apostasy (i.e., the abandonment of one's religion) (Beith-Hallahmi & Argyle, 1997; Spilka et al., 2003). The tendency of young men and women to leave the church is only strengthened by the "liberalized social attitudes, greater cosmopolitanism, religious skepticism, and sense of moral and religious relativity" experienced in high school and college (Hoge, Johnson, & Luidens, 1993). Nonetheless, the majority of young Americans resume religious involvement once they marry and become parents; two events that traditionally have been seen as hallmarks of adulthood. As pointed out by Stolzenberg, Blair-Loy, and Waite (1995), "in the U.S. participation in religious organizations is deeply intertwined with values and attitudes that encourage marriage and parenthood" (p. 84).

In a study of Protestant and Catholic boys and girls aged 16 who were reassessed in their late 30s, O'Connor, Hoge, and Alexander (2002) found that the mean age of becoming religiously inactive was in the early 20s, and the mean age of becoming active again was in the late 20s. Over half of the sample indicated that they become religiously inactive with the main reasons being lack of time, lack of interest, and religious doubt. The main reasons for resuming religious involvement were marriage and children, spiritual needs, and influence of spouse. O'Connor et al.'s (2002) findings are supported by a number of other studies indicating that becoming married and a parent decreases the likelihood of apostasy (e.g., Sandomirsky & Wilson, 1990) and increases the chances of "returning to the fold" (e.g., Wilson & Sherkat, 1994). Analyzing data from the National Longitudinal Study of the High School Class of 1972 that traced religious involvement until age 32, Stolzenberg et al. (1995) found that marriage and parenthood increased the likelihood of belonging to a church or synagogue, with the maximum effect of children on church membership occurring when children were on the average 10 years of age. In other words, young married couples with children are more likely to be religiously involved than their peers who are childless and unmarried. According to Wilson and Sherkat (1994), marriage and parenthood have a stronger positive influence on men's religious involvement presumably because men tend to be less religious than women and therefore need an external stimulus to reestablish their church involvement.

Are there factors other than marriage and parenthood that predict religious involvement in early adulthood? In support of social learning theory, Wilson and Sherkat (1994) found that maintaining religious involvement in the transition from adolescence to early adulthood was particularly characteristic of individuals who as children had a close relationship with their parents and those who developed strong religious habits in childhood. In contrast, O'Connor et al. (2002) were surprised by how tenuous was the relation between youth predictors and adult church involvement. They found religious involvement in late 30s was best predicted by current circumstances (e.g., both respondent and partner going to church together) than adolescent religiousness (e.g., strength of belief or frequency of prayer) with the exception of involvement in church youth programs.

In sum, as argued by Wilson and Sherkat (1994), life course transitions play a defining role in understanding the developmental trajectory of religious involvement in early adulthood. But how relevant are findings based on the study of the Baby Boom generation to explaining religious beliefs and practices of the current generations of young adults? In their survey of changes in religious behavior among youth from 1976 to 1996, Smith, Denton, Faris, and Regnerus (2002) found a 10% decline in religious affiliation and an 8% decline in church attendance among Protestants and a corresponding 5% increase in individuals who self-identified as not religious. While significant, the drop in religious participation was relatively small in magnitude meaning that religious involvement among white Protestant American youth continues to exceed that found among their peers in most Western European countries. Nonetheless, Smith et al.'s (2002) findings suggest that the American religious landscape is changing with strongest religious involvement present among African American, Hispanic, and Asian youth and residents of the southern states. Only time will tell whether the United States, like Europe, will become eventually divided into largely secular regions (the Northeast and West) and more traditionally religious areas (the South and parts of the Midwest).

Another feature of early adulthood at the beginning of the 21st century is the tendency among college graduates to delay marriage and parenthood until the late 20s and early 30s. Gone are the days of a lock-step progression from college to a stable career trajectory and family life (see Moen, Kelly, & Magennis, chapter 13, this volume). Instead, the entry into adulthood is marked today by a prolonged interval of several years of exploration. During this period many individuals in their 20s define themselves as being neither an adolescent nor an adult (Arnett, 2004; Settersten, Furstenberg, & Rumbaut, 2005). If, as documented by the older studies, marriage and parenthood play a key role in facilitating religious re-engagement among younger adults, the current trend in delaying commitment to long-term romantic relationships along with the tendency for a growing number of children to be brought up in a single parent family means a need to reconsider the nature of religious trajectories of early adulthood. Clearly, in view of the wide age range in which contemporary Americans marry and become parents, chronological age may have lost its utility as a marker of changes in religious involvement. Whether transition to becoming a marital partner and parent exercise the same effect on "returning to the fold" among current emerging adults remains an open question.

Late Adulthood.   Ever since the times of William James (1902/1961), old age has been associated with heightened religious involvement. The popularity of this belief is based on the view that entering the post-retirement period increases the concern among older adults about mortality (see McFadden, 1999, 2005), and that, at least among Christians, religion assuages not only the existential dread of mortality but also offers the hope of being forever reunited with loved ones (Lemming, 1979–1980). Although persuasive, this view disregards the increasing number of Americans who, upon retirement at the normative age of 65, continue to have relatively healthy and productive 15 to 20 years in front of them (James & Wink, 2007). Being in one's early 80s has lost the aura of survivorship that it had during the time of William James (1902/1961) or even when Erik Erikson (1951) developed his stage theory of development in which he assigned the task of "integrity versus despair" to older adulthood. Not surprisingly, the vast majority of Third Agers (individuals between the ages of 65 and 79) report high levels of life satisfaction, physical health, and vital involvement in everyday activities (e.g., Grafova, McGonagle, & Stafford, 2007; Wink, 2007). Contrary to popular belief, fear of death decreases with age; older adults are significantly less anxious about the prospect of dying than are young adults (Neimeyer & Van Brunt, 1995). The main concern for older adults is not the prospect of death but the fear of dying in a painful and undignified manner (Cicirelli, 1999). The majority of older adults accepts their past and the inevitability of death seamlessly without, as postulated by Erikson (1951) and Butler (1963), the need to review their life and develop a new sense of identity that reconciles the past with the present and leads to the acceptance of their life without undue regret. Using data from the Institute of Human Development (IHD) longitudinal study, Wink and Schiff (2002) found that only approximately a third of older individuals engaged in the process of life review, and these individuals tended to be introspective throughout their adult lives. Further, both Wink and Schiff (2002) and Coleman (1986) found no evidence that older adults who did not review their lives suffered any adverse psychological consequences as a result.

The emerging portrait of the Third Age as a time of high life satisfaction and vital engagement in everyday life does not preclude the possibility that religious involvement increases in the post-retirement period. However, it challenges the idea that such an increase is an inevitable outcome of the existential crises or dilemmas associated with aging. Rather, the view presented here suggests that, if present, the increase in religious involvement among older adults may be equally likely to be due to a greater amount of free time or the need for companionship as the concern over impending mortality or uncertainty about the afterlife.

Given the ubiquity of the assumption that older adults become more religious (e.g., McFadden, 2005), why is there so little empirical data to support this hypothesis? The primary reason is that most short-term longitudinal studies of religiousness and aging appear to have focused on the wrong age period. Instead of tracing changes in religiousness from middle to late adulthood, researchers have focused solely on shifts in religious beliefs and practices among the young-old (age 65–75) and old-old (age 75+) only to find, paradoxically, that religious involvement tended to decrease with age. In an 8-year follow up of Mexican American and Anglos age 60 and over, Markides, Levin, and Ray (1987), for example, found "little evidence that older people increasingly turn to religion as they age and approach death (p. 664)." In fact, it is now well established that attendance at religious services declines with age as a function of increased incidence of illness and disability (e.g., Blazer & Palmore, 1976; Kelley-Moore & Ferraro, 2001; Markides et al., 1987; Mindel & Vaughan, 1978; Idler, Kasl, & Hays, 2001), even though, as reported by Idler et al. (2001), overall church attendance among the elderly remains fairly high—including those with less than six months to live.

A decline in attendance at religious services is not tantamount to a decrease in the importance of religion in the lives of the elderly. It may be the case, after all, that restricted by poor physical health from church attendance, physically incapacitated older Americans turn to other sources such as prayer and electronic media to satisfy their spiritual needs. In support of this hypothesis, Mindel and Vaughan (1978) found that reduction in formal religious participation was compensated by increased involvement in non-organized religion (prayer). However, most other researchers have failed to support the finding that a drop in church attendance is compensated by increase in non-organized or informal religious activities. Rather, the preponderance of evidence suggests that frequency of prayer, ratings of subjective religiosity, and the use of electronic media with religious content remains constant among the elderly whose church attendance declined because of physical disabilities (Benjamins, Musick, Gold, & George, 2003; Kelly-Moore & Ferraro, 2001). This is an important finding in so far as it shows the need of assessing religious involvement in multiple domains. Nonetheless, it fails to support the thesis that signs of impending mortality result in increased religious fervor.

In view of the failure of short-term longitudinal studies to show increased religious involvement as individuals move from their 60s to their 80s, support for the claim that religiousness increases in old age is primarily based on findings from large scale, national, cross-sectional samples spanning the entire adult life course (for an exception, see Wink & Dillon, 2007, discussed below). These studies indicate an overall positive relation between religiousness and age (e.g., Argue, Johnson, & White, 1999; Hout & Greeley, 1987; Ploch & Hastings, 1994; Sasaki & Suzuki, 1987). Although the relationship between age and religion appears to increase linearly for most of adulthood, Argue et al. (1999) report a particularly steep rate of increase in self-reported influence of religion on daily life in early adulthood (ages 18 to 30), and Ploch & Hastings (1994) confirm the tendency of church attendance to decline in the 80s. In addition, several studies indicate slight variation in the pattern of change occurring in middle adulthood, but these findings have largely been ignored in the absence of a theory regarding the meaning of religion in the lives of middle aged individuals. The discussion of these findings will be, therefore, postponed until the next section.

Writing in the early 1990s, Ainlay, Singleton, and Swigert (1992) commented that "30 years of research on the role of religion among older people has produced contradictory findings that have stalled theoretical development" (p. 178). In hindsight, this conclusion seems overly pessimistic. Nonetheless, it reflects the fact that 15 years later we still know relatively little about religion and aging. The preponderance of evidence suggests that although religious involvement increases among the elderly, the magnitude of the change is modest and it does not support the contention that large numbers of older Americans turn to religion in order to deal with issues of mortality. Among the old-old, a decrease in religious participation does not lead to a concomitant decline in other forms of religious involvement, but there is no evidence that such activities increases exponentially as individuals get closer to death. Overall, the findings on religion in old age fit well with the emerging portrait of the Third Age as a time where life satisfaction and engagement in everyday life remain high (Wink & James, 2007) and concomitantly a time when older adults accommodate to life in the post-retirement period by continuing to rely on existing adaptive strategies rather than developing new ones (see Atchley, 1999).

Middle Adulthood.   It is not surprising that less is known about religion in the middle years of life than other segment of the life course. This reflects the fact that until quite recently, middle adulthood has been neglected in general by researchers interested in adult development (see Lachman, 2001) who preferred to focus on early and late adulthood with their better defined points of transitions (e.g., graduating from college, marriage, parenting, retirement, and death and dying). In comparison, the long stretch of middle adulthood lasting from age 30 to the early 60s lacks similar landmarks, perhaps with the exception of the empty nest and menopause for women.

The accumulated body of evidence indicates that middle adulthood is a period of high positive affect for most Americans (Mroczek, 2004; Wink, 2007). The decade of the 40s and 50s is a time of social and personal dominance with middle aged individuals tending to assume positions of responsibility at work and as volunteers (Helson & Wink, 1992; Levinson, 1978; Neugarten, 1968). Although the empty nest was initially depicted as a threat to the well-being of parents, mothers in particular, recent research suggests that children leaving home is a welcome relief for both parents and offspring and, if anything, it enhances rather than detracts from marital satisfaction (Carstensen, Graff, Levinson, & Gottman, 1996). Similarly, although it brings with it unpleasant physical symptoms, menopause does not threaten the sense of self-esteem or "femininity" of most women (Rossi, 2004). Finally, the notorious midlife crisis—far from being omnipresent—is experienced by only approximately 10% of Baby Boomers (Wethington, Kessler, & Pixley, 2004). While the decade of the 50s (dubbed by Karp [1988] as the decade of reminders) is characterized by increased signs of physical limits and aging, the onset of these symptoms is typically gradual and serves to smooth the transition between late middle adulthood and the Third Age (McCullough & Polak, 2007).

Given the dominant societal status of middle aged individuals (Neugarten, 1968), it is not surprising to find them occupying leadership positions in religious congregations and organizations (Argyle, 2000). However, the time pressures associated with maintaining a busy work career, fulfilling volunteer obligations, and the need to take care of elderly parents, coupled with freedom related to the absence of children living at home, and the lack of need to confront issues of impending mortality suggests that midlife is a low point (nadir) for religious involvement (Dillon & Wink, 2007). This hypothesis is supported by a number of older studies indicating a U-curve trajectory of religious involvement over the life course with middle adulthood being characterized by lower participation than either early or late adulthood (see Argyle & Beth-Hallahmi, 1977, for a review). More recently, a midlife (age 50) dip in religious attendance has been reported by Ploch and Hastings (1994) in their national cross-sectional study of religion over the life course. A similar decline in mid 40s to early 50s was found by Miller and Nakamura (1996) and Sasaki and Suzuki (1987) in their analyses of church attendance based on the General Social Survey and Institute of Social Research cross-sectional data sets, respectively. However, lacking a theoretical framework for interpreting these finding, none of the authors discuss the meaning or significance of their results. Whereas the midlife dip in religiousness can be attributed to a shift in social roles at work and in the family, in the case of the current generation of older adults, it also coincides with the turbulent decades of the 1960s and 1970s. According to Hout and Greeley (1987), a temporary drop in church attendance in the 1970s was particularly characteristic of American Catholics (the largest religious denomination in the U.S.) in response to the Church's reaffirmation of papal authority and the ban on contraception (see also Dillon & Wink, 2007).

Although a number of studies suggest a midlife drop in religiousness, these findings are contradicted by research indicating that religious involvement either peaks in middle adulthood or alternatively remains stable after early adulthood. In a 12-year, four wave, panel study of married individuals under the age of 50, Argue et al. (1999), for example, found that religiosity (assessed in terms of self-reported importance of religious beliefs for daily life) increased steadily throughout adulthood, after rapidly accelerating from age 18 to the late 20s. Despite uncovering a slight dip in church attendance around the age of 50, Ploch and Hastings (1994) found an overall tendency for religiousness to steadily increase until age 70 when it begins to gradually decline. A similar pattern of steady age related increases in religiousness was reported by Rossi (2001) in her analysis of cross-sectional data from the MIDUS study.

Findings from Long-Term Longitudinal Studies.   In discussing how mean levels of religiousness change over the adult course, I have omitted thus far the three long-term longitudinal studies that have data on the same individuals assessed over a prolonged period of time. In a 42-year-old follow-up study of male graduates of Amherst college (attending college in the early 1940s), Shand (1990) found considerable stability in rates of religious belief from the early 20s to late adulthood (late 60s). Unfortunately, Shand reports data for only two time points and therefore his study is insensitive to changes in religiousness that may have occurred in the long intervening period.

Both the Terman (McCullough, Enders, Brion, & Jain, 2005) and the Institute of Human Development (IHD; Dillon & Wink, 2007) longitudinal studies consist of California-born, predominantly white, well-educated, Protestant and Catholic men and women who were intensively followed-up throughout the life course. The main differences are that (a) the Terman participants were born somewhat earlier (1910s) than the IHD participants (1920s), (b) whereas the Terman study consists solely of intellectually gifted (IQ within top 1% of the population) individuals who attended public schools in Southern California, the IHD study comprises of a community-based sample of individuals born in San Francisco's East Bay Area, and (c) the Terman data on religious involvement are based on recoding of self-report ratings, whereas the IHD ratings are based on qualitative accounts of religious beliefs and practices obtained from in-depth, semi-structured interviews.

Because the Terman and IHD data were collected from the same individuals at multiple time points, they lend themselves to the use of modern statistical techniques that allow the extraction of multiple trajectories of change. The advantage of growth curve analysis is that it allows the rephrasing of the question: "How does religiousness change over the life course?" to "What are the different patterns of change adhered to by individuals as they progress from adolescence/early adulthood to old age?" As a result, the Terman and IHD data make it possible to test longitudinally Ingersoll-Dayton et al.'s (2002), retrospectively based, life course hypothesis that individuals' religious involvement is contingent on the nature of experienced transitions, life events, and other background factors.

The majority of the Terman and IHD participants remained quite stable in their religious involvement following either a high and slightly increasing, or a low and slightly declining, trajectory of change (McCullough et al., 2005; Dillon & Wink, 2007). In other words, participants in both studies who were religious as young adults tended to maintain (and even increase somewhat) their religious involvement throughout the life course. Conversely, those individuals who were not religious as young adults continued to remain so in middle and late adulthood and, if anything, their commitment declined further with time.

The two stable trajectories were differentiated in both the Terman and the IHD studies by gender, background religiousness, and personality; the high religiousness group included more women, and individuals who as adolescents were religious and whose personality was characterized by warmth and agreeableness. In a separate study of the long-term relation between personality and religiousness, Wink, Ciciolla, Dillon, and Tracy (2007) found that, among the IHD participants, religiousness in late adulthood was predicted by adolescent dependability and conscientiousness and, in the case of women, warmth and agreeableness as well. This effect was independent of any overlap between religiousness and personality. In the Terman study, a similar association between personality and religiousness was obtained in a model predicting religious involvement in early adulthood from adolescent characteristics (McCullough, Tsang, & Brion, 2003).

In addition to the two stable groups, a minority of participants in the Terman and IHD studies followed a parabolic trajectory of change. In the case of the Terman study, an inverse U-curve trajectory reflected the presence of a group of individuals whose initially low level of adult religious involvement increased in their 30s and 40s, followed by a decline from age early 50s onward. Among the IHD participants, a mirror opposite (U-curve) trajectory described individuals whose initial high levels of religious involvement when they were in their early 30s, declined in middle adulthood only to increase in old age (late 60s/mid 70s).

What accounts for these contradictory findings? According to McCullough et al. (2005), a substantial number of the Terman participants who were initially not religious chose to attend church once they became parents—only to revert back to original levels of involvement when the children left home. In support of this hypothesis, members in the parabolic or inverted-U trajectory were distinguished from the low/declining group by a significantly greater number of children. In contrast, the IHD participants who, as a group, were more religious than their Terman counterparts presumably did not feel pressured to become more religious as a result of parenthood. Rather, a portion of the study members chose to reduce their religious involvement in middle adulthood, a time period coinciding with the empty nest, and, the competing demands of life at age 40s and 50s. Despite their different pattern of change, the IHD participants who followed a U-curve trajectory, just like their Terman counterparts, returned in old age to the same levels of religiousness as in early adulthood, which in their case resulted in increased religiousness from age 50s onward. In addition, in the IHD study the midlife decline in religious involvement which coincided with the 1970s was particularly characteristic of Catholics (Dillon & Wink, 2007), thus confirming Hout and Greeley's (1987) finding of a temporary decrease in church involvement among American Catholics following the papal encyclical *Humanae Vitae*.

In sum, both the Terman and the IHD longitudinal studies confirm Shand's (1990) finding that aggregate levels of religious involvement tend to remain substantially unchanged between early to late adulthood, although this does not preclude an intervening ebb and flow in religious participation during the middle years. Further, the two studies highlight the importance of mapping different trajectories of change rather than focusing solely on normative patterns of change that describe the sample as a whole. Finally, the Terman and IHD studies demonstrate the importance of taking a long view of changes in religiousness over the life course. The interpretation of the IHD finding that religiousness increases from late middle to late adulthood, for example, changes considerably once we also know that, despite this increase, the average rate of religious involvement in late adulthood did not differ significantly from that in early adulthood. Taken as a whole, the life long pattern of religious involvement documented by Dillon and Wink (2007) for the IHD participants supports the contention that older aged individuals "return to the fold" by reestablishing levels of religiousness that characterized them as young adults rather than exhibiting heightened religiousness in response to the aging process per se. Similarly erroneous conclusions regarding the drop in religious involvement in the second half of adulthood could be drawn from the Terman study (McCullough et al., 2005) should its findings be interpreted without taking into account the entire adult life course.

Change in Meaning of Religiousness

The fact that rates of religious involvement change or remain stable over the life course has no bearing on whether the actual meaning of religious beliefs and practices alters with age. In other words, even if the level of religious involvement in late adulthood did not differ from that in early adulthood, it is easy to imagine an age-related shift in its meaning from, for example, a more social to a more personal emphasis. Conversely, even a steep increase in church attendance from age early to late 20s, may not result in a change in the personal significance of religious practices.

The hypothesis that the meaning of religious involvement changes (deepens) with age comes from a variety of sources. According to post-Piagetian or post-formal theorists, the development of cognitive abilities and structures continues well into adulthood resulting at midlife in a new appreciation and understanding of the paradoxical and contingent nature of knowledge (e.g., Sinnott, 1994). The post-Piagetian view of adult development has served as a basis for Kohlberg's (1981) stage theory of moral development and James Fowler's (1981) stage theory of faith development. According to Fowler, as people age, their faith becomes less concretistic and more contemplative, and personal yet universalizing in scope. For example, a transition from Stage 3 (synthetic—conventional faith) to Stage 4 (individuative—reflective faith) coincides with a moving away from embracing faith as defined by others and religious institutions and a greater reliance on the self as an arbiter of religious beliefs and practices. At Stage 4, whose emergence typically coincides with the transition from adolescence to early adulthood, "stories, symbols, myths and paradoxes from one's own or other traditions may insist on breaking in upon the neatness of the previous faith" (p. 183). The newly found confidence in self-generated knowledge is, however, undermined in Stage 5 (conjunctive faith) by an emergence, typically in middle adulthood, of a sense of irony reflecting the recognition that all understanding is relative, partial, and distorting of the underlying transcendent reality.

The final stage of universalizing faith (Stage 6) is rarely attained as it involves a total dissipation of self-interests in the service of transforming the "present reality in the direction of a transcendent actuality" (Fowler, 1981, p. 200); a mode of being that can perhaps be discerned in the lives of Mahatma Gandhi, Albert Schweitzer, Mother Theresa, and Martin Luther King. Using cross-sectional data, Fowler found support for his developmental theory with evidence of Stage 4 faith development beginning to emerge only among individuals in their 20s, and Stage 5 narratives coinciding with middle adulthood and increasing in the decade of the 50s.

Another source of support for the idea that the meaning of religiousness deepens with age comes from theories of personality development in adulthood. According to Carl Jung (1953), for example, the primary task of the first part of adulthood is to get to know the workings and intricacies of the external world, including establishing a career and a family. With middle adulthood these priorities change to a greater emphasis on getting to know oneself, a process that includes exploration of archetypes or the propensities and capacities of the mind, including the proclivity to produce an image of God, which, Jung argues, are shared by all humans. A midlife reorientation in personal interests is also embedded in Erikson's (1951) stage theory of psychosocial development. According to Erikson, the early adulthood tasks of identity development and establishing of intimacy give way in the second half of life to a generative concern for others and, subsequently, an emphasis on reconciliation of the past and present in a way that leaves no place for undue regrets. Although based on different intellectual traditions, there are clear parallels among Jung, Erikson, and Fowler—all of whom associate aging with a shift in perspective from the outer to the inner, an emphasis on authenticity, and a deepening of self understanding that ultimately results in an enhanced appreciation of one's limits and a greater sense of compassion for others. These purported age related changes in being-in-the-world are bound to affect religious beliefs and practices by shifting the emphasis from the public to the private role of religion, from reliance on external to internal authority, and by expanding the circle of reference to include a larger segment of humanity.

Empirical support for the view that religious beliefs change with age comes primarily from retrospective studies. Participants in Ingersoll-Dayton et al.'s (2002) study indicated, for example, that older age coincided with a greater tolerance of differing religious beliefs. A new emphasis on caring for others was reflected in a shift in the nature of prayer from request to gratitude and praying less for self and more for others. In a study of faith in late life, Eisenhandler (2003) found that, although most of the participants tended to maintain old habitual (reflexive) means of worship, a number of men and women "stretched their soul" by moving beyond the usual and accepted patterns of faith. These individuals displayed a greater concern for others, an awareness of transpersonal bonds with others, and an emphasis on inner life and reflection (interiority).

Perhaps the strongest empirical support for the view that older age brings with it a new focus and new priorities comes from the work of the Swedish social gerontologist Lars Tornstam, who based his theory of gerotranscendence on data from large scale retrospective and cross-sectional studies of Danish and Swedish adults. In particular, Tornstam (2005) found a positive relation between age and the development of the *Cosmic* dimension of functioning characterized by feelings of being connected with the entire universe and earlier generations, transcendence of time (living simultaneously in the past and present), and strong connection with earlier generations. Age was also associated with an increase in the *Coherence* dimension or the sense of meaning in life. In addition to these cross-sectional findings, retrospective life narratives of older adults indicated less self-preoccupation, a decrease of interest in superfluous social interactions and in material possessions, and a greater need for solitary meditation (positive solitude as opposed to forced disengagement). All of these changes suggest an evolution in late adulthood of religious beliefs and practices from an emphasis on self-interest to a greater stress on the ego-transcendence and the care for the common good. A similar shift has been reported in a number of retrospective studies focusing on highly functioning older adults (e.g., Meddin, 1998; Thomas & Eisenhandler, 1998) and can be also found in fairy tales from around the world that include older age protagonists (Chinen, 1992).

Contravening Tornstam's findings, however, over three-quarters of participants in the Ohio Longitudinal Study of Aging Americans (Atchley, 1999) reported that material things meant more (rather than less) to them; they were likely to take themselves more (not less) seriously, and to see less (not more) connection between themselves and past and future generations.

The presence of similarly worded open questions on religion in the IHD study allowed the testing of aspects of Tornstam's theory using longitudinal data collected in early and late adulthood. Dillon and Wink (2007) coded the study participants' religion narratives to see whether there was an age-related shift in emphasis away from the more social to the more faith-based functions of religiousness. In early adulthood, 55% of the participants referred to religion's social dimensions. In contrast, only 26% commented on religion's personal meaning to them in terms of faith or as a theological resource in trying, in the words of one participant, to apprehend "unanswered questions." This pattern was reversed, however, in late adulthood with only 17% referring to religion's social aspects, and 36% invoking its faith elements. For example, when interviewed in her late 60s, a Presbyterian woman stated, "I enjoy going to church to hear a sermon, but I don't want to be hit for joining committees to do this or that, and have to sit and introduce myself to the people next to me, and all this holding hands." The same woman, in adolescence and early adulthood emphasized the importance of her social involvement in church. Another Presbyterian woman emphasized in late adulthood the importance of faith as a guide to her life and saw it as providing purpose to her life. In early adulthood, this woman expressed "faith in the sense of prayer" but, at the same time, wondered whether church attracted her "as a matter of wanting to belong to a social group" (Dillon & Wink, 2007, pp. 115–116).

In sum, a large gamut of theories and empirical findings suggest that the meaning of religious beliefs and practices evolve with age and that, in particular, older adults place a greater emphasis on the private as opposed to public (social) aspects of religion and use faith to express a concern for others rather than pursue more narrowly circumscribed personal interests. These shifts in the meaning of religion may aid older adults in adapting to the aging process. Nonetheless, it is likely that the age-related changes in meaning of religion, just as changes in church attendance or religious involvement, are likely to follow a variety of different trajectories and as a result apply to some older adults but not others. As documented by Eisenhandler (2003), the majority of older adults are likely to continue using religion throughout their life in a *reflexive* or habitual fashion without evidence of any significant change in its meaning. This should not overshadow, however, the minority of older individuals who approach religious beliefs and practices in a *reflective* way that allows them to use religious resources to grow personally and to seek new answers to life's existential dilemmas. While these individuals may be particularly admired by psychologists who, as a rule, value personal growth and introspection (see Dillon & Wink, 2007), this should not result, however, in labeling as deficient those adults who cope with the vicissitudes of old age by relying on more habitual religious resources. In other words, contrary to Tornstam's (2005) assertion that "the very process of living encompasses a general tendency toward gerotranscendence…which in the West can be accompanied [and impeded] by guilt" (p. 45), it could be argued that many, if not the majority, of older adults cope with the vicissitudes of aging by relying on the same adaptive strategies they used throughout adulthood (see, for example, Coleman, 1986, Wink & Schiff, 2002). Just as it would be erroneous to label this latter group as repressed or lacking in self-realization, so it would be mistaken not to appreciate persons who use the process of aging to develop new modes of psychosocial functioning. Clearly, the welfare of a society depends on the presence of both conservers and innovators at any stage of the life course.

Change at an Individual Rather than Group Level

So far in this chapter I have discussed the connection between age and religious involvement and its meaning at a group level by asking whether older adulthood brings with it a general shift in religious beliefs and practices for most adults or among specific groups of individuals based on anteceding personality and intervening life experiences. However, group level information tells us nothing about individual variation in religious beliefs and practices over the life course. In other words, knowing that older adults as a group become more religious says nothing about whether individual group members retained their rank vis-à-vis each other or not. After all, a sample that is highly stable as a group can show a lot of individual variability as long as increases in religiousness among some of the members are offset by declines in religiousness among other members. Conversely, an increase in religiousness at a group level can be achieved with little individual variability as long as all participants increase at the same rate.

In general, much more is known about group-level change in religiousness over the life course than about its individual (rank order) stability. In contrast to group-level stability, the coefficient of individual stability can be computed only by using data collected on the same individuals over time and this requires longitudinal rather than cross-sectional findings. This is the case because individual stability is calculated using the correlation coefficient which requires data from the same group of persons at two time periods. The need for longitudinal data means that if we want to know whether young adults retain their ranking in religiousness in old age we need to wait for at least 40 years before being able to answer this question.

Recently published findings from the Terman (McCullough et al., 2005) and the IHD (Dillon & Wink, 2007) longitudinal studies indicate a surprisingly high level of individual level stability in religious involvement over the adult life course. In the Terman study the average correlation among measures of religiousness collected at six different time points between the ages of 27 and 77 was .69. In the IHD study the average correlation for religiousness assessed at four time periods spanning age 30s and 70s was .77. In other words, individuals who scored comparatively higher in religiousness in early adulthood tended to also score higher than their peers in late adulthood notwithstanding the ebb and flow of religious involvement for the samples as a whole. In the IHD study, a somewhat lower level of individual (rank order stability) was obtained between religiousness in adolescence and adulthood. The average correlation was .49 with the highest correlation being between religiousness in adolescence and early adulthood (r = .54) and the lowest between adolescence and late adulthood (r = .42). This means that a substantial number of individuals who were highly religious in adolescence became less religious in adulthood and, conversely, some nonreligious adolescents became religious later in life. In short, adolescent religiousness is a robust, but not an overwhelmingly strong, predictor of religiousness in adulthood.

The higher level of individual stability of religious involvement assessed in adulthood compared to that in adolescence confirms findings indicating that radical changes in religious beliefs and practices resulting in apostasy and conversion peak between adolescence and early adulthood (Beith-Hallahmi & Argyle, 1997). There are several explanations for this finding. Adolescent religiousness is more immediately constrained by parents' expectations than is adulthood religiousness. Adolescents who attend church primarily because of parental expectations, boys in particular, are likely to cease doing so once they leave home and gain independence. Some adolescents and young adults may develop an interest in religion for the first time in college, in the military, or through other work and social contacts. For others, these same experiences may serve to dampen their religious involvement. As already indicated, marriage, in particular through spousal influence, is one of the most important predictors of religious affiliation and involvement (Hout & Fisher, 2002; Sherkat, 2003), and, as a result, it may contribute to religious re-engagement or disengagement.

In contrast to adolescence, the high level of rank order stability in adulthood means that relatively few people experience radical religious transformations in adulthood indicative of conversion or apostasy. The finding of high stability in religiousness across adulthood is important because it challenges the view that individuals tend to experience radical changes in religiousness in response to negative (e.g., Ferraro & Kelley-Moore, 2000) or positive (Albrecht & Cornwall, 1989) life experiences. Life events such as, for example, bereavement and poor health tend to affect, at any given point in time, some adults but not others. If these individuals were to respond to these adversities by becoming more or less religious, this should have lowered the correlation among measures of religiousness at different stages of adulthood. This, however, does not appear to be the case.

The Terman and IHD findings do not, of course, preclude the possibility that a small number of individuals respond to adversity by turning to religion or that others decline sharply in their religious involvement. The IHD data, for example, indicate that approximately 3% of the sample did experience a sudden conversion to religion in middle adulthood primarily in response to adversity and a further 3% were characterized by a marked decrease in religious involvement (Dillon & Wink, 2007). The high levels of individual stability across adulthood simply suggest that this was not a normative pattern that applied to the majority of adults.

A final implication of the high correlation between scores on religiousness throughout adulthood means there is a high probability that the social and psychological characteristics associated with religiousness at one point in adulthood can be predicted from religiousness at an earlier time. For example, in the IHD study, the concurrent positive association between religiousness and vital involvement in everyday activities, positive relations with others (Wink & Dillon, 2003), and generativity or altruism (Dillon, Wink, & Fay, 2003) in older adulthood could be predicted from religiousness in early adulthood, a time interval of close to 40 years. This, in turn, means that knowing one's religious involvement at age 30 serves as a good predictor of future patterns of psychosocial functioning.

Life Course Changes in Spiritual Seeking

The review of the literature on religious involvement over the life course has highlighted the importance of considering religion as a multifaceted construct whose various components may follow different trajectories of age-related change. As documented, whereas, for example, prayer and the uses of electronic media with religious content tend to remain unchanged in old age, this does not preclude a decline in church attendance associated with deterioration in physical health. In this section, findings from the IHD longitudinal study are used to consider how life course changes in religious involvement compare to spiritual seeking.

Religiousness and Spiritual Seeking.   In the social science literature, spirituality has been defined in varying ways, with some researchers using it in the context of church-centered piety (e.g., Pargament, 1999) and others using it to refer to the largely non-church based spiritual seeking (e.g., Eastern meditation, New Age practices) that has grown in popularity in America since the 1960s (e.g., Fuller, 2001; Roof, 1999; Wuthnow, 1998). The ambiguity in how contemporary Americans construe their religious/spiritual identity is well captured by Hout and Fischer (2002) who found that over two-thirds of Americans who have a religious affiliation describe themselves as both religious and spiritual. By contrast, among those who had no religious preference, Hout and Fisher (2002) found that 15% thought of themselves as, at most, moderately religious, but 40% describe themselves as spiritual. Clearly, these two groups invoke spirituality to convey different things. Individuals who identify themselves as both religious and spiritual are predominantly church members—"religious dwellers" (Wuthnow 1998)—who use the term spirituality to underscore the sincerity of their beliefs and their personal striving to relate to God within the boundaries of organized or church-focused religion (see Hout & Fischer, 2002; Zinnbauer & Pargament, 2005). Those who identify as spiritual only do so in part to distance themselves from church and organized religion (Hout & Fischer, 2002). In sum, although prior to the 1960s it made little sense to decouple spirituality from religiousness, currently the term "spiritual" is used with equal validity to denote a dimension of traditional religiousness and to signify a growing number of Americans who choose to engage in non-traditional and non-church centered religious beliefs and practices.

Following Wuthnow's (1998) distinction between church-centered religious dwellers and spiritual seekers who actively negotiate among diverse spiritual resources, religiousness and spiritual seeking were operationalized in the IHD study as two separate though overlapping religious orientations (e.g., Dillon & Wink, 2007; Wink & Dillon 2003). Whereas individuals high in religiousness were characterized by a belief in God, an afterlife, prayer, and frequent church attendance, spiritual seekers typically emphasized sacred connectedness with God, a Higher Power, or nature and systematically engage in practices such as mediation, Shamanistic journeying, and centering prayer. The difference between religiousness and spiritual seeking is typified by the response to a question about the afterlife, to which an IHD participant who was high in religiousness stated, "Well, religiously, I go to heaven," compared to the statement offered by a spiritual seeker: "I do believe that I'm part of the universe, and that I get returned somehow—my spirit or my consciousness—to something that is, hopefully, more worthwhile, at a higher level." When asked about religious practices, a woman who was high in religiousness said, "I attend religious services usually every Sunday, but during the year we also have Bible study." In contrast, a woman high on spiritual seeker stated, "If one believes in the universal spirit, 'Our Father in Heaven' doesn't work too well. So I've been introduced to a centering prayer that is an old revival of a Catholic contemplative prayer—not too distant from Transcendental Meditation" (Dillon & Wink, 2007, pp. 219–220).

This distinction between religiousness or religious dwelling and spiritual seeking parallels the analytical distinction made by several scholars; most notably, that between authoritarian and humanist religion (Fromm, 1950), between religious loyalists and highly active seekers (Roof, 1993, 1999), and between religious mystics who embrace religious tradition and spiritual mystics for whom personal authority and experience override the "historical claims of tradition" (Hood, 2003, p. 261). In previous research, the construct validity of the rating of spiritual seeking was evidenced by its closer relation to involvement in non-organized (e.g., meditation and prayer) than organized religious activities (church attendance) (Wink & Dillon, 2003), its significant positive association with personal growth (Dillon & Wink, 2007) and creativity (Wink, 2006), and the personality characteristic of openness to experience (Wink et al., 2007), and its only modest correlation with the IHD measure of religiousness (Wink & Dillon, 2003).

Spiritual Seeking across the Life Course.   In the IHD study, the average scores on spiritual seeking remained stable from early (age 30s) to middle (age 40s) adulthood and then increased significantly in the later stages of adulthood, in particular from age 50s to age late 60s to mid-70s. The late life increase in spiritual seeking was true of men and women, those raised Protestant or Catholic, and of individuals from higher and lower social classes (Wink & Dillon, 2002). Nonetheless, because of a higher rate of spiritual growth, women scored significantly higher on spiritual seeking than men in late-middle (age 50s) and late adulthood (age late 60s, and mid-70s). The overall magnitude of the late life increase in spirituality was of sufficient magnitude to be clinically significant. This means that if we were to meet the IHD participants' socially in middle adulthood and then encounter them 20 years later in late adulthood, their increased spirituality would be clearly evident in casual interaction. In other words, compared to religiousness, the post-midlife increase in spiritual seeking was much more pronounced. In addition, the life course trajectory of spiritual seeking followed a linear path of steady increases from early to late adulthood compared to the curvilinear relation between age and religiousness indicative of a dip in religious involvement in middle adulthood.

What accounts for the increase in spiritual seeking in the second half of adulthood? As discussed in the section on changes in meaning of religiousness, a post-midlife emphasis on a sense of interconnectedness with a Higher Power or nature has been postulated by theorists ranging from Jung to Tornstam. Although this broadening in the meaning of the sacred can be incorporated into traditional religiousness, midlife, as argued by both Fowler and Jung, ushers an additional greater sense of personal autonomy and an appreciation of different religious traditions. It is these latter changes that offer a psychological explanation of the age-related increase in spiritual seeking. As conceptualized in the IHD research, spiritual seeking assumes the willingness to juxtapose and incorporate in one's life different religious traditions and perspectives; a task that entails a sense of personal autonomy, and an appreciation of relativism and contextualism of knowledge.

The post-midlife increase in spiritual seeking among the IHD participants also has a socio-cultural explanation. The study participants entered middle adulthood in the late 1960s, and consequently their negotiation of midlife identity during this time of cultural upheaval may have opened them to the new currents in America's vastly expanding spiritual marketplace (see Roof, 1999). The public accessibility of a new spiritual vocabulary and spiritual resources in the post 1960s era may have generated a new spiritual awareness among the study participants independent of any inner psychological process. In other words, the IHD findings may reflect a period instead of a maturational effect. The cultural explanation for the post-midlife increase in spiritual seeking is supported by the fact that the younger IHD cohort (those born in 1928–29) evidenced a steeper increase in spirituality than the older cohort (those born in 1920–21). Members of the younger cohort had a less firmly set sense of personal identity and they were more likely to have teenagers living at home during the 1960s and 1970s. Both these factors increased, in turn, their chance of being exposed and receptive to the cultural changes of this era (Dillon & Wink, 2007). The significance of cultural context in aiding the post-midlife growth in spiritual seeking does not negate the psychological (maturational) explanation but, rather, reaffirms the life course theory postulate that lives are inevitably lived in a socio-historical context.

Individual Variation in Spiritual Seeking.   Spiritual seeking, unlike religiousness, showed considerable inter-individual variability with the average correlation of .47 among the ratings of spiritual seeking from early to late adulthood. This means that knowing, for example, whether someone ranked high or low in spiritual seeking in early adulthood did not tell much about the person's ranking in late adulthood (r = .30). In fact, the IHD data indicated that spiritual seeking did not stabilize on an individual level until late-middle adulthood, when people were in their fifties (r = .64 between rating of spiritual seeking between late-middle and late adulthood). The relatively low level of rank order stability of spiritual seeking compared to religiousness was due to the fact that relatively few of the IHD participants were rated as high on spiritual seeking in early adulthood.

A direct corollary of the low individual stability was the fact that psychosocial correlates of spiritual seeking in late adulthood, such as its positive relation with creativity, personal growth, interest in gaining new knowledge, and altruism could be predicted by spiritual seeking in late middle adulthood (age 50s), but not earlier (Dillon & Wink, 2007; Dillon et al., 2003; Wink & Dillon, 2003). This once again differentiates spiritual seeking from religiousness; the latter's associations with measures of psychosocial functioning in late adulthood could be predicted from religiousness in early adulthood. The only exception was authoritarianism—obedience to authority, adherence to tradition, and *dis*esteem of minority groups—where its negative relation with spiritual seeking and positive relation with religiousness could both be predicted from early adulthood. This robust and life-long differential effect of religiousness and spiritual seeking on authoritarianism highlights the polarization existing between individuals who are high on religiousness and those who are high on spiritual seeking in the area of submission to authority and attitudes toward minority groups (gay, lesbians, and feminists in particular; Wink, Dillon, & Prettyman, 2007). In all other areas of functioning the effects of religiousness and spiritual seeking on psychosocial functioning were much less polarized.

Finally, the relatively low level individual stability of spiritual seeking raises the question as to who became a spiritual seeker as an older adult. The modal spiritual seeker in late adulthood was a woman who as a young adult was involved in traditional religious practices, who was psychologically minded or incisive, and who subsequently, in her late thirties and forties experienced stressful life events such as divorce, personal or family illness, and untimely death in the family (Wink & Dillon, 2002). The fact that spiritual growth was prompted by personal turmoil indicates a parallel between spiritual seeking and wisdom whose development has been also linked to the experience of stressful life events (see, for example, Wink & Helson, 1997; Kunzmann & Baltes, 2005). In contrast, religiousness was unrelated to personal adversity. In addition, whereas, as discussed in a preceding section, religiousness in late adulthood was predicted by adolescent personality characteristics of conscientiousness and warmth or agreeableness, spiritual seeking was predicted by openness to experience (Wink et al., 2007).

In sum, the different patterns of group and individual change exhibited by spiritual seeking and religiousness confirm the importance of distinguishing not only between various dimensions of religion but also different religious orientations. Just as religiousness is a complex and multifaceted construct, so too is spirituality. Nonetheless, the multiple meanings of the terms should not deter researchers from investigating how spirituality or spiritualities unfold over the life course provided that the investigators offer a clear and precise definition of how the construct is operationalized in their research.

Directions for Future Research

The study of how any psychosocial characteristic changes over time is of necessity a daunting enterprise because it involves the disentangling of maturational, cohort, and period effects. In the case of religion, this task is made more difficult by its multidimensionality and the fact that religion in the Western world is undergoing a dramatic shift not witnessed since the Reformation. Although the forces of secularization are not as strong in the United States as they are in Western Europe, nonetheless, it is hard to imagine that the current generation of young adults will inhabit the same religious landscape in old age as their parents. The best strategy for dealing with this complexity is to ground research on age and religion in specific theories of religiousness and adult development (see McFadden, 1999, 2005) and a methodological paradigm, such as life course theory, that acknowledges the importance of the socio-historical and cultural context for the understanding of human action. Although it is legitimate to ask the question, "How does religiousness change over time," this should not prevent us from answering that it depends on the aspect of religiousness being measured, the cohort being followed, the stage of life cycle being investigated, the particular trajectory of change being adhered to, and the background socio-demographic characteristics of the sample.

Importance of Theory of Religion.   The existing body of research on age and religion indicates the importance of selecting measures of religious beliefs and practices to match the characteristics of life stage under consideration. For example, as demonstrated by numerous studies, it makes little sense to rely on church attendance as an index of religious involvement among the very old; a population where frequency of prayer, strength of belief, and, increasingly, the use of electronic media are likely to provide a much more meaningful measure of religiousness. However, church attendance may be the measure of choice for assessing religious involvement in early adulthood given the prevailing view that many parents "return to the fold" in order to provide their children with religious education. The fact that one or another measure of religiousness may be better suited to research at a particular stage of the life course does not negate, however, the importance of investigating a variety of religious beliefs and practices at any age period.

Whereas the selection of developmentally appropriate measures of religious involvement illustrates the importance of low-level theory, Tornstam's (2005) programmatic research on gerotranscendence demonstrates the power of higher-level theory for understanding the age—religion connection. By conceptualizing religious involvement within an innovative theory of aging, Tornstam is able to not only to shed light on how the meaning of religious beliefs and practices evolves in old age but also highlight the importance of emergent properties of older adulthood that distinguish this segment of the life course from its other stages. In this regard, Tornstam's research not only enhances our understanding of religion in old age but it also helps to promote the view of older adults as valuable members of society with unique skills and insights.

Similarly, findings from the IHD study demonstrate the utility of differentiating religious dwelling from spiritual seeking, a distinction based on Wuthnow's (1998) sociological analyses of the changing American religious landscape in the post 1960s era. Both religiousness and spiritual seeking were found to be associated with different trajectories of change and patterns of individual stability. Yet, each provides older adults with unique resources for positive aging and dealing with the inevitable losses associated with the aging process. Obviously, every research program has its limitations. In the case of Tornstam, these include the lack of longitudinal data and the tendency to generalize findings to older adults as a whole. Whereas the IHD study contrasts spiritual seeking with religiousness, it does not capture the many meanings of spirituality. Nonetheless, these inevitable shortcomings should not overshadow the importance of theory-guided research in furthering the understanding of how religion evolves over the life course.

Importance of Theory of Adult Development.   Perhaps no other stage of the life course illustrates better the importance of theory of adult development for understanding changes in religious involvement than late adulthood. How the evidence of the modest increase in religiousness in the second half of adulthood is interpreted depends squarely on one's theory of aging. Those who subscribe to the view that aging threatens the individual with despair unless he or she gains a new perspective on the past, present, and the future are likely to construe this finding as indicative of the power of religiousness to offer answers to life's existential dilemmas. In contrast, those who construe the post-retirement period as largely an extension of middle adulthood are much more likely to interpret any increase in religiousness in terms of greater availability of free time and/or a desire for more contact with others. For the purpose of the present argument, it does not matter which view of aging is correct, what is important is the inextricable intertwining of fact and theory.

Middle adulthood provides another illustration of the importance of theories of adult development for research on religious involvement. Most studies on age and religion appear to treat the long period of middle adulthood as barren wasteland that is best speedily traversed on the way from youth to old age. As a result, very little is known about religious involvement during this stage of life and the available findings from national cross-sectional studies of the life course are either ignored or treated as random fluctuations. Yet, as a result of the new found interest among social scientists, we know that the middle years of life are an important segment of the life course where individuals shed some of their youthful idealism, begin to confront signs of aging, experience new freedoms resulting from adult children leaving home, confront increased pressure to take care of elderly parents, and, in general, enjoy a dominant status in society reflective of years of experience and expertise at work and in managing volunteer activities. All of these changes are bound to have an impact on religious beliefs and practices that are waiting to be fully explored (see Dillon & Wink, 2007).

Importance of Methodological Framework.   With few exceptions, research on religion and aging tends to ignore the influence of socio-historical context as exemplified by cross-sectional researchers who take great pains to argue away the possibility that their findings are influenced by cohort or period effects. Yet, socio-historical context matters for the ebb and flow of religious involvement over the life course both in terms of more circumscribed and temporary shifts in participation (e.g., decline in church attendance among Catholics in the 1970s) and larger historical trends (e.g., the recent emergence of individuals who define themselves as spiritual but not religious). We should not be afraid, therefore, to interpret findings as contingent and as subject to change depending on age cohort or denominational, regional, ethnic, and racial characteristics of the sample. A reminder of the role played by context in interpreting findings and for designing research is an important contribution of life course theory.

It is not accidental that the emergence of life course theory with its emphasis on multiple trajectories of change and the moderating effect of life's transitions coincided with the advent of new and more powerful statistical techniques that allow researchers to map different patterns of change on a given characteristic. These types of analyses would not have been possible 10 to 15 years ago. Yet, as documented by the findings from the Terman and the IHD study, the use of growth curve analysis has the potential to revolutionize research on age and religiousness by allowing investigators to decompose a single normative curve into its component trajectories. Membership in each trajectory or group can then be predicted from a combination of personality and socio-demographic characteristics.

The drawback of growth curve analysis and path modeling is that it requires longitudinal data (see Holt, chapter 5, this volume). Nonetheless, as shown by Elder and his collaborators, such research does not need to take decades to complete as long as researchers anchor their study on judiciously chosen historical events such as the Great Depression (Elder, 1974) or life transitions such as divorce (Lorenz, Wickrama, Conger, & Elder, 2006). In the case of religiousness, these transitions include, among others, marriage, becoming a parent, children leaving home, and retirement. In other words, the field of religion needs well designed short-term longitudinal studies that will allow the mapping of discrete segments of the life course and, in doing so, to ultimately gain a better perspective on religiousness over the entire life course. These studies need to be obviously grounded in theory of religion and adult development. To gain an understanding of whether, for example, religiousness increases in old age, we need to study the period before and after retirement, or focus on changes associated with moving to a retirement community, bereavement, and physical illness. Participants could be selected based on their degrees of background religious socialization, and their variability by denomination, gender, ethnicity, and personality characteristics. The effectiveness of research on how discrete life transitions, such as marriage and parenthood, affect religious involvement in early adulthood should serve as an example to investigators interested in the shifting role of religiousness at other stages of the life course. While such research can have religion as its primary focus, questions on religious involvement could be also included in studies with other primary aims.

Conclusions

The course of human life is predictable because as the result of an interaction among genetic predispositions, social learning, and life's experiences we develop stable cognitive and personality structures and choose social environments that, in turn, reinforce the stability of our preferred modes of psychosocial functioning. It is not surprising, therefore, that religious beliefs and practices show considerable stability over the life course. Highly religious adolescents and young adults tend to continue being so throughout the life course and, conversely, individuals who enter adulthood with little religious involvement are unlikely to change their practices. Yet, this stability belies the ebb and flow in religious involvement associated with changing social roles, transitions, and movement from one stage of the life course to another. It also does not do justice to the circumscribed group of individuals who experience more radical shifts in religious involvement as a result of a variety positive and negative life experiences. Individual lives are also influenced by the larger socio-cultural and historical context. In this regard, the second half of the 20th century has witnessed a radical change in the prevailing social order and concomitant evolution of religious traditions and habits. Evangelical Christians are the fastest growing religious group in America, but the rates of individuals who identify themselves as spiritual but not religious or simply as not religious are also on the increase. How these changes will influence religious involvement over the life course only time will tell. After all, a true understanding of the human life course can only be achieved in hindsight. Although new trends in religious beliefs and practices do not appear out of the blue, we need a long-term perspective on personal and social history to assess their true meaning and significance.

References

Ainlay, S. C., Singleton, Jr., R., & Swigert, V. L. (1992). Aging and religious participation: Reconsidering the effects of health. *Journal for the Scientific Study of religion, 31,* 175–188.

Albrecht, S. L., & Cornwall, M. (1989). Life events and religious change. *Review of religious research, 31,* 23–38.

Argue, A., Johnson, D. R., & White, L. K. (1999). Age and religiosity: Evidence from a three-wave panel analysis. *Journal for the Scientific Study of Religion, 38,* 423–435.

Argyle, M. (2000). *Psychology of religion: An introduction.* New York: Routledge.

Argyle, M., & Beith-Hallahmi, B. (1977). *The social psychology of religion.* London: Routledge & Kegan Paul.

Arnett, J. J. (2004). *Emerging adulthood.* New York: Oxford University Press.

Atchley, R. (1999). *Continuity and adaptation in aging: Creating positive experiences.* Baltimore, MD: Johns Hopkins University Press.

Beith-Hallahmi, B., & Argyle, M. (1997). *The psychology of religious behavior, belief, and experience.* New York: Routledge.

Bellah, R., Madsen, R., Sullivan, W., Swidler, A., & Tipton, S. (1985). *Habits of the heart: Individualism and commitment in American life.* Berkeley: University of California Press.

Benjamins, M. R., Musick, M. A., Gold, D. T., & George, L. K. (2003). Age-related declines in activity level: The relationship between chronic illness and religious activities. *Journal of Gerontology: Psychological Sciences, 58B,* S377–S385.

Blazer, D., & Palmore, E. (1976). Religion and aging in a longitudinal panel. *The Gerontologist, 16,* 82–85.

Butler, R. (1963). The life review: An interpretation of reminiscence in old age. *Psychiatry: Journal for the study of Interpersonal Processes, 26,* 65–75.

Carstensen, L. L., Graff, J., Levenson, R. W., & Gottman, J. M. (1996). Affect in intimate relationships. In C. Magai & S. H. McFadden (Eds.), *Handbook of emotion, adult development, and aging* (pp. 227–242). San Diego, CA: Academic Press.

Chinen, A. B. (1992). Fairy tales and spiritual development in later life: The story of the shining fish. In T. R. Cole, D. D. Van Tassel, & R. Kastenbaum (Eds.), *Handbook of the humanities and aging* (pp. 197–214). New York: Springer.

Cicirelli, V. G. (1999). Personality and demographic factors in older adults' fear of death. *The Gerontologist, 39,* 569–579.

Coleman, P. (1986). *Aging and reminiscence processes: Social and clinical implications.* Chichester, UK: Wiley.

Dillon, M., & Wink, P. (2007). *In the course of a life time: Tracing religious belief, practice, and change.* Berkeley: University of California Press.

Dillon, M., Wink, P., & Fay, K. (2003). Is spirituality detrimental to generativity? *Journal for the Scientific Study of Religion, 42,* 427–442.

Eisenhandler, S. A. (2003). *Keeping the faith in late life.* New York: Springer.

Elder, G. H., Jr. (1974). *Children of the great depression.* Chicago: The University of Chicago Press.

Elder, G. H., Jr. (1985). Perspectives on the life course. In G. H. Elder, Jr. (Ed.), *Life course dynamics: Trajectories and transitions, 1968–1980* (pp. 23–49). Ithaca, NY: Cornell University Press.

Elder, G. H., Jr. (1995). The life course paradigm: Social change and individual development. In P. Moen, G. H. Elder, Jr., & K. Luscher (Eds.), *Examining lives in context* (pp. 101–139). Washington, DC: American Psychological Association.

Erikson, E. H. (1951). *Childhood and society* (2nd ed.). New York: Norton.

Ferraro, K., & Kelley-Moore, J. (2000). Religious consolation among men and women: Do health problems spur seeking? *Journal for the Scientific Study of Religion, 39,* 220–234.

Fowler, J. W. (1981). *Stages of faith*. San Francisco: Harper.

Fromm, E. (1950). *Psychoanalysis and religion*. New Haven, CT: Yale University Press.

Fuller, R. C. (2001). *Spiritual, but not religious*. New York: Oxford University Press.

Grafova, I., McGonagle, K., & Stafford, F. P. (2007). Functioning and well-being in the third age: 1986–2001. In J. B. James & P. Wink (Eds.), *The crown of life: Dynamics of the early postretirement period* (pp. 19–38). New York: Springer.

Helson, R., & Wink, P. (1992). Personality change in women from early 40s to early 50s. *Psychology and Aging, 7,* 46–55.

Hoge, D. R., Johnson, D. B., & Luidens, D. A. (1993). Determinants of church involvement of young adults who grew up in a Presbyterian church. *Journal for the Scientific Study of Religion, 32,* 242–255.,

Hood, R. W. Jr. (2003). The relationship between religion and spirituality. In A. L. Greil & D. G. Bromley (Eds.), *Defining religion: Investigating the boundaries between the sacred and secular*. New York: JAI.

Hout, M., & Fisher, C. (2002). Why more Americans have no religious preference: Politics and generations. *American Sociological Review, 67,* 165–190.

Hout, M., & Greeley, A. M. (1987). The center doesn't hold: Church attendance in the United States, 1940–1984. *American Sociological Review, 52,* 325–345.

Idler, E. L. (2006). Religion and aging. In R. H. Binstock & L. K. George (Eds.), *Handbook of aging and the social sciences* (6th ed., pp. 277–300). Burlington, MA: Academic Press.

Idler, E. L., Kasl, S. V., & Hays, J. C. (2001). Patterns of religious practices and belief in the last year of life. *Journal of Gerontology: Psychological Sciences, 56B,* S326–S334.

Ingersoll-Dayton, B., Krause, N., & Morgan, D. (2002). Religious trajectories and transitions over the life course. *International Journal of Aging and Human Development, 55,* 55–70.

James, J. B., & Wink, P. (Eds.) (2007). *The crown of life: Dynamics of the early postretirement period*. New York: Springer.

James, W. (1961). *The varieties of religious experience*. New York: Collier Books. (Original work published 1902)

Jung, C. G. (1953). On the psychology of the unconscious. In H. Read, M. Fordham, & G. Adler (Eds.), *Two essays on analytical psychology* (pp. 9–119). Princeton, NJ: Princeton University Press.

Karp, D. (1988). A decade of reminders: Age consciousness between fifty and sixty years old. *Gerontologist, 6,* 727–738.

Kelly-Moore, J. A., & Ferraro, K. F. (2001). Functional limitations and religious service attendance in later life: Barrier and/or benefit mechanism? *Journal of Gerontology: Psychological Sciences, 56B,* S365–S373.

Kohlberg, L. (1981). *Essays on moral development. Vol. 1, The philosophy of moral development*. New York: Harper & Row.

Kohli, M. (1986). Social organization and subjective construction of the life course. In A. B. Sorensen, F. E. Weinert, & L. R. Sherrod (Eds.), *Human development and the life course: Multidisciplinary perspectives* (pp. 271–292). Hillsdale, NJ: Erlbaum.

Kunzmann, U., & Baltes, P. B. (2005). The psychology of wisdom: Theoretical and empirical challenges. In R. Sternberg & J. Jordan (Eds.), *A handbook of wisdom* (pp. 110–135). New York: Cambridge University Press.

Lachman, M. (Ed) (2001). *Handbook of midlife development*. New York: Wiley.

Lemming, M.R. (1979-1980). Religion and death: A test of Homans' thesis. *Omega, 10,* 234–239.

Levenson, M. R., Aldwin, C. M., & D'Mello, M. (2005). Religious development from adolescence to middle adulthood. In R. F. Paloutzian & C. L. Park (Eds.), *Handbook of the psychology of religion and spirituality* (pp. 144–161). New York: Guilford.

Levinson, D. (1978). *The seasons of a man's life*. New York: Ballantine.

Lorenz, F. O., Wickrama, K. A. S., Conger, R. D., & Elder, G. H. Jr. (2006). The short-term and decade-long effects of divorce on women's midlife health. *Journal of Health and Social Behavior, 47,* 111–125.

Markides, K. S., Levin, J. S., & Ray, L .A. (1987). Religion, aging, and life satisfaction: An eight-year, three-wave longitudinal study. *The Gerontologist, 27,* 660–665.

McCullough, M. E., Enders, C. K., Brion, S. L., & Jain, A. R. (2005). The varieties of religious development in adulthood: A longitudinal investigation using growth mixture modeling. *Journal of Personality and Social Psychology 89,* 78–89.

McCullough, M. E., & Polak, E. L. (2007). Change and stability during the third age: Longitudinal investigations of self-rated health and religiousness with the Terman sample. In J. B. James, & P. Wink (Eds.), *The crown of life: Dynamics of the early postretirement period* (pp. 175–192). New York: Springer.

McCullough, M. E., Tsang, J., & Brion, S. (2003). Personality traits in adolescence as predictors of religiousness in early adulthood: Findings from the Terman longitudinal study. *Personality and Social Psychology Bulletin, 29,* 980–991.

McFadden, S. H. (1999). Religion, personality, and aging: A life span perspective. *Journal of Personality, 67,* 1081–1104.

McFadden, S. H. (2005). Points of connection: gerontology and the psychology of religion. In R. F. Paloutzian & C. L. Park (Eds.), *Handbook of the psychology of religion and spirituality* (pp. 162–176). New York: Guilford.

Meddin, J. R. (1998). Dimensions of spiritual meaning and well-being in the lives of ten older Australians. *International Journal of Aging and Human Development, 47,* 163–175.

Miller, A. S., & Nakamura, T. (1996). On the stability of church attendance patterns during a time of demographic change: 1965–1988. *Journal for the Scientific Study of Religion, 35,* 275–284.

Mindel, C., & Vaughan, C. E. (1978). A multi-dimensional approach to religiosity and disengagement. *Journal of Gerontology, 33,* 103–108.

Mroczek, D. K. (2004). Positive and negative affect at midlife. In O. Brim, C. Ryff, & R. Kessler, (Eds.), *How healthy are we? A national study of well-being at midlife* (pp. 205–226). Chicago: The University of Chicago Press.

Neimeyer, R. A., & Van Brunt, D. (1995). Death anxiety. In H. Wass & R. A. Neimeyer (Eds.), *Dying: Facing the facts* (3rd ed., pp. 49–88). Wahington, DC: Hemisphere.

Neugarten, B. L. (1968). The awareness of middle age. In B. L. Neugarten (Ed.), *Middle age and aging* (pp. 93–98). Chicago: The University of Chicago Press.

O'Connor, T. P., Hoge, D. R., & Alexander, E. (2002). The relative influence of youth and adult experiences on personal spirituality and church involvement. *Journal for the Scientific Study of Religion, 41,* 723–732.

Pargament, K. I. (1999). The psychology of religion and spirituality? Yes and no. *The International Journal for the Psychology of Religion, 9,* 3–16.

Ploch, D. R., & Hastings, D. W. (1994). Graphic presentations of church attendance using general social survey data. *Journal for the Scientific Study of Religion, 33, 16–33.*

Roof, W. C. (1993). *A generation of seekers: The spiritual journeys of the baby boom generation.* San Francisco: Harper/SanFrancisco.

Roof, W. C. (1999). *Spiritual marketplace; Baby boomers and the remaking of American religion.* Princeton, NJ: Princeton University Press.

Rossi, A. (2001). Developmental roots of adult social responsibility. In A. Rossi (Ed.), *Caring and doing for others* (pp. 227–320). Chicago: The University of Chicago Press.

Rossi, A. (2004). The menopausal transition and aging processes. In O. Brim, C. Ryff, & R. Kessler, (Eds.), *How healthy are we? A national study of well-being at midlife* (pp. 205–226). Chicago: The University of Chicago Press.

Sandomirsky, S., & Wilson, J. (1990). Processes of disaffiliation: Religious mobility among men and women. *Social Forces, 68,* 1211–1229.

Sasaki, M., & Suzuki, T. (1987). Changes in religious commitment in the United States, Holland, and Japan. *American Journal of Sociology, 92,* 1055–1076.

Settersten, R. A., Jr. (2003). Propositions and controversies in life-course scholarship. In R. A. Settersten, Jr. (Ed.), *Invitation to the life course: Toward new understandings of later life* (pp. 15–45. Amityville, NY: Baywood.

Settersten, R. A., Jr., Furstenberg, F. F., Jr., & Rumbaut, R. G. (Eds.) (2005). *On the frontier of adulthood.* Chicago: The University of Chicago Press.

Shand, J. D. (1990). A forty-year follow-up of the religious beliefs and attitudes of a sample of Amherst College grads. *Research in the Social Scientific Study of Religion, 2,* 117–136.

Sherkat, D. E. (2003). Religious socialization: Sources of influence and influences of agency. In M. Dillon (Ed.), *Handbook of the sociology of religion* (pp. 151–163). New York: Cambridge University Press.

Sinnott, J. D. (1994). Development and yearning: Cognitive aspects of spiritual development. *Journal of Adult Development, 1,* 91–99.

Smith, C., Denton, M. L., Faris, R., & Regnerus, M. (2002). Mapping American adolescent religious participation. *Journal for the Scientific Study of Religion, 41,* 597–612.

Spilka, B., Hood, Jr., R. W., Hunsberger, B., & Gorsuch, R. (2003). *The psychology of religion* (3rd ed.). New York: Guilford.

Stolzenberg, R. M., Blair-Loy, M., & Waite, L. J. (1995). Religious participation in early adulthood: Age and family life cycle effects on church membership. *American Sociological Review, 60,* 84–103.

Thomas, L. E., & Eisenhandler, S. A. (Eds.). (1998). *Religion, belief, and spirituality in late life.* New York: Springer.

Tornstam, L. (2005). *Gerotranscendence: A developmental theory of positive aging.* New York Springer.

Wethington, E., Kessler, R., & Pixley, J. (2004). Turning points in adulthood. In O. Brim, C. Ryff, & R. Kessler, (Eds.), *How healthy are we? A national study of well-being at midlife* (pp. 586–613). Chicago: The University of Chicago Press.

Wilson, J., & Sherkat, D. E. (1994). Returning to the fold. *Journal for the Scientific Study of Religion, 33,* 148–161.

Wink, P. (2006). Who is afraid of death? Religion, spirituality, and death anxiety. *Journal of Religion, Spirituality, and Aging, 18,* 93–110.

Wink, P. (2007). Everyday life in the third age. In J. B. James, & P. Wink (Eds.), *The crown of life: Dynamics of the early postretirement period* (pp. 243–262). New York: Springer.

Wink, P., Ciciolla, L., Dillon, M., & Tracy, A. (2007). Religiousness, spiritual seeking and personality: Findings from a longitudinal study. *Journal of Personality, 75*(5), 1051–1070.

Wink, P., & Dillon, M. (2002). Spiritual development across the adult life course: Finding from a longitudinal study. *Journal of Adult Development, 9,* 79–94.

Wink, P., & Dillon, M. (2003). Religiousness, spirituality, and psychosocial functioning in late adulthood: Findings from a longitudinal study. *Psychology & Aging, 18,* 916–924.

Wink, P., Dillon, M., & Prettyman, A. (2007). The relation between religiousness, spiritual seeking and authoritarianism: Findings from a longitudinal study. *Journal for the Scientific Study of Religion, 46,* 321–335.

Wink, P., & Helson, R. (1997). Practical and transcendent wisdom: Their nature and some longitudinal findings. *Journal of Adult Development, 4,* 1–15.

Wink, P., & James, J. (2007). Is the third age the crown of life? In J. B. James & P. Wink (Eds.), *The crown of life: Dynamics of the early post-retirement period* (305–325). New York: Springer.

Wink, P., & Schiff, B. (2002). To review or not to review: The role of personality and life events in life review and adaptation to older age. In J. Webster & B. Haight (Eds.), *Critical advances in reminiscence: From theory to applications* (pp. 44–60). New York: Springer.

Wuthnow, R. (1998). *After heaven: Spirituality in America since the 1950s.* Berkeley: University of California Press.

Zinnbauer, B. J., & Pargament, K. I. (2005). Religiousness and spirituality. In R. F. Paloutzian, & C. L. Park (Eds.), *Handbook of the psychology of religion and spirituality* (pp. 21–42). New York: Guilford.

Part IV

Research on Adult Learning

Chapter 16

A Brief History of Research and Theory on Adult Learning and Cognition

Dennis Thompson

When one examines the research on cognitive aging and the theory on adult learning, one is essentially looking at two different fields which to a large extent developed independently of one another, but today form much of the knowledge base of adult cognitive development. This chapter will seek to explore the history of these areas of inquiry beginning with the pre-scientific era, then will turn to the period ranging from the early 1920s to the 1950s, and then look in more general terms at the modern era. The focus will be on offering a picture of the road traveled leading to where we are today. Attention will be paid to the people, the research, the theory, and some of the dynamics behind what took place.

Early Contributors to the Study of Adult Learning

The scientific study of aging is often said to have begun with Adolphe Quetelet (1796–1874) but there was much work that had been underway by that time. Frederick Zeman (1979) lists literally hundreds of references devoted to the study of aging published before Quetelet. Most of these early reports were made by physicians who were interested in the study of extreme longevity. However, some of this early work conducted by physicians examined cognitive change in old age as well as physical well-being.

One of the physicians to write on cognitive development was Benjamin Rush (1745–1813). Rush who lived in Philadelphia also happened to be Benjamin Franklin's personal physician and refers to Franklin in his later years in several places in his writing. As a tribute to his contributions, Rush appears today as part of the logo of the American Psychiatric Association. Rush includes a chapter on old age in Volume One of his four volume *Medical Inquires and Observations* (1805). In it he makes observations on the aging process, and makes recommendations on ensuring a long life. The sample consisted of observations of his patients aged 80 and above observed over a five-year period. In many ways Rush's observations seem quite modern. One point that he makes in several places in his observations is that older persons benefit from mental activity as much as do younger people. In a section which he labels "Moderate Exercise of the Understanding," he argues that literary people, who he believed to be among the most mentally active, live longer than others. But he goes on to argue that any occupation which is intellectually stimulating will bring about similar benefits. Later in his discussion he presents the case of Jonathan Swift (1667–1745) as an example of his point. According to Rush, Swift refused to use glasses in his old age—which made it impossible for him to read. Gradually, he also withdrew from most of his social contacts. Rush observed that these events "left his mind without its usual stimulus: hence it collapsed into a state of fatuity" (p. 442).

He made a number of observations on memory. He argued that while memory was the first faculty of the mind to fail, "understanding" remained more stable with age. He cites a conversation that he had with Anthony Benezet (1713–1784) in which Benezet provided an argument that failing memory was an advantage:

> You read a book (said he) with pleasure but once, but when I read a good book, I so soon forget the contents of it, that I have the pleasure of reading it over and over; and every time I read it, it is alike new and delightful to me. (as cited in Rush, 1805, p. 441)

In his history of aging, Birren (1961) cites Adolphe Quetelet as the first to produce and to participate in a quantitative psychology of aging. Quetelet was born in Ghent, Belgium in 1796 and received the first doctorate in science from the University of Ghent in 1819 in mathematics. Following his degree, he became interested in probability and began work on what is today known as the normal curve. In 1835 Quetelet published *A Treatise on Man and the Development of his Faculties. On Man,* as it is sometime known, is a marvelous and extensively referenced book. Quetelet was well read on the demographic data of the time, and frequent citations are provided to support his arguments and observations.

Containing data dating back to the 1690s, Quetelet provides us with some of the earliest statistical data that we have on human beings. Individuals interested in the demographics of the aging process will find much of interest here. He reviewed available mortality data in relation to age, gender, urban and rural location, as well as other demographics. Quetelet, however, wanted to go beyond an analysis of the "physical quantities of man" as he put it. In introducing his chapter on the intellectual qualities of man he wrote that:

> An appreciation of the physical qualities of the average man does not present any real difficulty, whether we can measure them directly or whether they only become appreciated by their efforts. It is not so with the moral and intellectual qualities. Indeed I do not know that any real person had thought of measuring them. (p. 73)

In his section on the development of intellectual faculties, he sought to "determine the period in which memory, imagination, and judgment commence, and the stages through which they successively pass in their progress to maturity, then having established the maximum point, we may extend our inquires to the law of their decline" (pp. 72–73). He added that the methods used would need to be objective, and would need to be generalizable across locality.

In order to accomplish this, he presents an analysis examining the relation of age to the production of French and English drama among a group of 71 playwrights. Quetelet argued that very few of the playwrights were producing work before age 25. But by the late 20s, productivity "manifests itself very decidedly" and "continues rigorous until towards the 50th or 55th year" (p. 75). After that there is decline in productivity, especially for works which were judged by Quetelet to be of the greatest artistic success. What is particularly interesting about Quetelet's work is that at one point in the discussion he included an adjustment for longevity of the playwrights. Quetelet reasoned that since some playwrights in his sample lived longer than others, he conducted a subsequent analysis that divided the number of works produced at a certain age by the number of playwrights still living to produce them. By doing this, he found that productivity lasted longer into the older years than was indicated in his initial analysis. In his arguments, he anticipates far more modern analysis (see, for example, Dennis, 1966 and Lehman, 1953).

Birren (1961), in his analysis, argues that Quetelet and his late 19th century colleague Sir Francis Galton (1822–1911) were among the first to question the fatalistic concept popular in the early 19th century under which it was believed that while it was acceptable to study the physical world in terms of natural laws, human behavior could not be acceptably looked upon as a consequence of identifiable biological and social determinants. Quetelet discusses the difficulty that arose after the publication of his first edition in 1835. In the Edinborough English language translation published seven years later in 1842, Quetelet added a detailed preface responding to criticism of the first edition of his book. Because he had sought to identify biological and social determinants behind human behavior, he saw himself as having been accused of denying free will by some and of being a fatalist by others. He felt that the study of the anatomy of man had become an accepted science and called for a time in which the study of the "moral anatomy" of man would be equally accepted.

Birren (1961) writes that if we are looking for an individual following Quetelet who engaged in the purposeful gathering of psychological measurements of development and aging, that individual is certainly Galton. In 1884 Galton established an "anthropometric laboratory" at the International Health Exhibition in South Kensington, London. From this location over the course of a year, 9,337 individuals were tested. A similar laboratory which operated for several years was established in the Sciences Galleries of the South Kensington museum in 1888. In total, these laboratories provided data on approximately 17,000 individuals, with an approximate age range of 11 to 84 years.

For three pence, participants were measured on a variety of physical and functional measures. Physical measures included head length, head breadth, standing height, height to top of knee, arm span, length of lower arm, length of middle finger, and weight. Functional measures included strength of hand squeeze measured by a denominator, vital capacity, visual acuity, highest tone that could be heard, a variety of reaction time measures, and a number of tactile sensitivity measures. Chief among Galton's arguments was the belief that large brains were related to strong mental powers and these were related to a large head, long arm span, strength, rate of movement, visual acuity, and lung capacity.

Galton's data from the anthropometric laboratory were first published in 1885. Here Galton tells us that his observations were based on 4,726 adult males and 1,637 adult females (age not specified). But while Galton's report may be the first to specifically study large numbers of adults, Galton had relatively little to say regarding age changes or age differences across the adult years. In fact, in only two places in the report are specific age differences discussed. A table of breathing capacity reveals data by age and gender. Peak capacity came at about age 30 for both genders with capacity declining about 16% in males and 19% in females by age 55. While he does not provide specific age related data on the subject, he comments on the relationship between breathing capacity and other physical measures such as hand squeeze. Perhaps this report is best remembered as first demonstrating the relationship between age and hearing, noting a significant age related decline in hearing high frequencies. Oddly, the age related decline was greater for females than males, exactly the opposite of most contemporary analyses. Some years later, Galton in describing these results, cites a Dorsetshire proverb, "that no agricultural labourer who is more than 40 years old, can hear a bat squeak" (as cited in Pearson, 1914).

Johnson and colleagues (1985) have argued that Galton understood the relationship between the stability of a statistic and sample size, and while he solved the problem of large scale data acquisition, the problem of analyzing his huge data set was not adequately solved during his lifetime. It was not until the 1920s that Galton's large data set was analyzed in any meaningful way. Perhaps in the best known of these reports, Ruger and Stoessiger (1927), analyzed Galton's data and presented growth curves regarding each of a number of attributes for over 7,000 male subjects. In their report they presented growth curves for Pull, Grip, Swiftness of Blow, Sense of Perpendicularity, Error of Bisection and Error of Trisection for individuals aged between 22 and 42. Decline in scores across these several measures was small, averaging approximately two and one half percent. Slightly later, Elderton and Moul (1928) performed similar analysis on 1800 female subjects. Ruger (1933) and Ruger and Pearson (1933) presented age corrected intercorrelations among a number of Galton's measures. All of these reports were based on the first of Galton's laboratories. A detailed analysis of the second laboratory in the South Kensington Museum can be found in Johnson, McClearn, Yuen, Nagoshi, Ahern, and Cole (1985).

One of Galton's most significant contributions was the opening up of the psychology of aging to objective study. But Galton had no students to carry on his work, and the opening up of the psychology of aging did not exactly occur overnight. Indeed, both Birren (1961) and Irving Lorge (1940) argued that very little occurred following Galton's work until the 1920s. While this statement is perhaps true as a general summary, it is certainly not the whole story. Edmund Sanford at Clark University presented what is arguably the first statement on the life span by an American psychologist in a lengthy article published in 1902. Moreover, Thorndike (1928) cites over 35 references which addressed adults as subjects published between 1896 and 1920.

Modern Contributions to the Study of Adult Learning

When the transition did come, it came quickly. The 1920s was a period of rapid development in the field, not quite like anything which had occurred before. Within a six-year period, from 1922–1928, the foundation for the field which remained up to the beginning of World War II had been laid. Take, for example, the fact that in 1922, G. Stanley Hall published *Senescence* followed by Eduard Lindeman's *The Meaning of Adult Education* in 1926, Harry Hollingworth's *Mental Growth and Decline* in 1927, Edward Thorndike's *Adult Learning* in 1928, and the organization of the Stanford Later Maturity Studies under Walter Miles, also in 1928. Indeed by the time that Floyd Ruch developed his bibliography for use at the Stanford studies in the early 1930s, the available references had burgeoned to nearly 150 entries.

What might have led to this growth of interest? One explanation might simply be the growth of developmental psychology as a whole during this same period. A statement in Dale Harris' *The Concept of Development*, published in 1957, was that there were only three psychologists in a 1919 survey who identified themselves as developmental. By the early 1930s, however, the field had grown so rapidly that two major handbooks had been published each containing two volumes.

But there are other explanations for the growth of interest in adulthood and aging. Much of the early growth of the field of aging had to do specifically with cognitive aging. It would seem that one possible explanation for the growth of the psychology of aging had to do with the emerging interest in better and more widely distributed adult education.

Role of American Universities

Psychology's interest in adulthood and aging may have had several facets. For one, universities began to see their mission as more than educating the few who could afford to attend college. One way this change was expressed was the development of the university extension program. The concept of the university extension program was originally borrowed from England with the first decade of transfer to the United States occurring in the 1880s. Up to this time, American college teachers had been making their knowledge available to the general public, primarily through the use of individual talks and lectures. The pioneer exponent of university extension in America was Herbert Baxter Adams (1850–1901), an historian at Johns Hopkins. In the middle 1880s Adams began to talk and write about the university extension that he had observed in England. What Adams saw in university extension was an alternative to the fragmentation and discontinuities of subject matter inherent in presentation of single lectures unaccompanied by any other discipline than voluntary attendance.

But the British model of extension was still based on education for an elite few. An Americanized version involving education for large numbers did not take shape until the years just before World War I. The new tone was most effectively formulated by Louis E. Reber (1858–1948), director of the extension service at the University of Wisconsin. By 1907 he was able to argue:

> Right or wrong, you will find here a type of University Extension that does not disdain the simplest forms of service. Literally carrying the university to the homes of the people, it attempts to give them what they need—be it the last word in expert advice; courses of study carrying university credit; or easy lessons in cooking and sewing. University Extension in Wisconsin endeavors to interpret the phraseology of the expert and offers the benefit of research to the household and the workshop, as well as to municipalities and the state. (as cited in Grattan, 1955, p. 193)

A second emerging factor had to do with the changing view of apprenticeship and the emerging concept of vocational education. In colonial times what we now call vocational education was covered by home training and apprenticeships, and these sufficed until the end of the eighteenth century. But as techniques of production changed in the 19th century, the domestic apprenticeship system declined in importance, and as the home ceased to be something of a self-contained economic unit, its teaching function narrowed. Yet the need for vocational training continued. But there was no direct and easy road to the institutionalizing of vocational training.

The net result was to help establish adult education as a legitimate activity of the public school system, with the greatest change coming in the 1920s. As late as 1917, several states continued to have laws actually prohibiting the use of public funds for the education of adults. But with World War I, a new factor emerged with fear of the unassimilated immigrant growing at a feverish pace. Out of a mixture of fear and patriotism, there was generated enough concern to do something helpful for the immigrant working through the process of assimilation. One result was the Smith-Hughes Act, the first federal law in the field of vocational education, and signed by President Wilson in 1917. Among other provisions, it provided resources which were useable in public school adult education programs. The result was a rapid expansion of adult education programs offered through the public schools throughout the 1920's. As evidence, for example, Hendrickson (1943) found that during this period the number of cities reporting housing adult education programs reached a peak in 1928, and the numbers enrolled continued to climb until the early years of the Great Depression.

A third factor was the development of programs offered through the YMCA. The YMCA had initiated education programs in the 1850s by offering libraries and reading rooms. By the 1880s it had shifted its emphasis to classes. For some years the emphasis was on elementary school subjects, but by 1895 the focus began to shift to vocational and technical training for adults. Development after 1900 was particularly rapid. So elaborate and extensive did YMCA education become, that a movement to obtain academic recognition for it led to the development of colleges and universities. Northeastern University in Boston is an example of a university that began out of a YMCA program as is Youngstown State University in Youngstown Ohio.

So here we have a number of factors that came together all at about the same time, which placed an emphasis on the education of adults. As this occurred, psychologists too began to address the needs of adults. Thorndike (1928), on the first page of his book *Adult Learning*, specifically mentions psychology's responsibilities to address, "Adult education in all its multifarious forms. Public evening schools, education departments of the Young Men's Christian Association [and] other philanthropic agencies for the welfare of adults" (p. 1). We will turn again a little later in this chapter to the development of theory on adult learning. For now we will look at how the science of aging within psychology developed.

The Transition to a Science of Cognitive Aging

Perhaps the best known work from the 1920s was G. Stanley Hall's *Senescence*. Published after his retirement from Clark University at the age of 78, it represents the author's awareness in his old age of the need for a science of gerontology. In arriving at this realization, Hall writes about the state of affairs in the early 1920s:

> Wishing to know myself as old, I subjected myself upon my retirement to the examination and tests of some half dozen medical experts for eyes, ears, heart, lungs, digestive tract, kidneys, and even sex but was surprised to find out how hard it was to do so. A strong minority of my impulses preferred the ignorance that is often bliss. There are no mental tests of generally recognized validity above the teens, so we have no criteria for determining psychological age for even the elderly, while psychoanalysts refuse on the express authority of Freud to take on patients over forty. When it was well over, I was glad…I realized anew, however, that there are no gerontologists, as there are experts for women, children, etc., and that barring acute attacks I must henceforth, for the most part, be my own physician. (Hall, 1922, p. 196)

Hall recognized the superficiality of regarding aging as merely a period of decline. He argued that senescence like adolescence had its own "feeling, thought, and will," as well as its own psychology. Hall anticipated Daniel Levinson (1978) in speculating on the existence of a mid-life transition, and using his questionnaires, a technique that he had brought from Germany in his youth, proceeded to explore a number of issues about aging. Oftentimes his conclusions parted from popular opinion. For example, it was commonly assumed that older people, approaching death would become more fearful and hence more religious. Hall believed from his questionnaire data that people do not necessarily show an increase in religious interest, nor do they show any fear of death. He felt that almost the opposite holds: That fear of death appeared to be a young man's concern. Gradually following Hall's lead, psychologists began to turn their attention to research in aging and much of this work was focused on cognitive aging. Let us first turn to Edward Thorndike.

Thorndike (1928), in his book *Adult Learning*, cites dozens of previous studies in the subject area. But much of this literature suffered from one of two limitations. If age groups were compared on some variable, the age range was generally limited, with few participants over the age of 35. Much of the available literature, however, simply examined one group of adults and attempted to make an argument about the capabilities of the group being studied. Some of this literature still reads as a bit of fun. For example, Thorndike cites one of his own studies which measured the improvement of 28 adult graduate students, aged 25 to 30, in multiplying mentally, without help of pencil or paper, a three digit number by a three digit number. The task was to perform 95 multiplication problems such as 657×964, 398×367, and 476×479. In the results, he reported that the graduate students in his study when, given seven hours of practice, could reduce the time in performing the task by forty percent. Many years later Owens (1966) used a time-lag design to conduct an analysis regarding change in cognitive performance in the North American culture spanning the time from approximately 1900 to the 1960s. Owens concluded that one skill that has been emphasized significantly less over time in that culture is mathematical ability.

That same year, 1928, saw the beginning of the first research program in aging. To a very large extent its emphasis was on cognitive aging. This was a project called the Stanford Later Maturity Studies under the direction of psychologist Walter R. Miles (1885–1978). What the Stanford Later Maturity Studies provided was the first program in the psychology of aging, using controlled experimental designs, with subjects representing a wide range of ages. In fact, the age range used in some of the research is remarkable even by today's standards. Take, for example, the fact that Miles designed experiments with an age range of 6 to 95 years, in which all of those subjects were compared on the same set of tasks.

Several factors came to play in the formation of the Stanford studies. As has already been mentioned, G. Stanley Hall had set the stage with the publication of his book *Senescence* in 1922. Miles seems to have been very influenced by Hall's book, taking detailed notes and frequently referring to its content in his public lectures on aging.

By the mid-1920s, research on time, fatigue, and work, using adults as participants, had become popular in industry. During his career Miles was very much interested in this subject area. He was particularly drawn to practical problems involving everyday situations. Apparently a newspaper article published in a New York City paper in 1922 caught his attention. The article was about the transition that was taking place regarding milk delivery in that city. At about that time, milk delivery in New York had passed from horse drawn vehicles to motorized trucks. The point was made in the article that middle-aged workers as young as 40 had difficulty in making the adjustment, older workers had even more difficulty, while the youngest workers learned the new task quickly. This interested Miles, and the subject area became one of the first to be studied in the Stanford studies (Jack Botwinick, personal communication, July 1980).

It should also be pointed out that the coming economic depression had affected California earlier than the rest of the country, increasing employment difficulties in the San Francisco area for older workers. As such, there was interest at Stanford in addressing the needs of these workers. In addition, it was anticipated that Miles' work on aging would supplement the longitudinal work on gifted children that Terman had begun in 1921 (Miles, 1967).

Miles, along with Lewis Terman (1877–1956) who was chair of the psychology department at Stanford, had originally applied for funds from the Social Science Research Council, a major avenue of support at the time. In their application, Miles and Terman outlined a "program of psychological research on the later period of maturity" in which over 50 topics of investigation of perceived importance for the new field were presented. These topics spanned sensory development, psychomotor functions, learning and memory, intelligence, fatigue, emotional and personality development, psychiatric issues, along with a series of proposed sociological and anthropological investigations (Terman & Miles, April 4, 1928). Specifics regarding the extent of funding needed were left very general in this document, but towards the end of their argument, they suggested $20,000 to $25,000 a year for 10 years. Funding was denied.

Such an ambitious request, particularly as an initial proposal, with so little justification as to how funds would be spent, may seem rather strange today, but it is important to point out that, beginning in the early 1920s, the Laura Spellman Rockefeller Memorial had been providing large long-term block grants to universities for the purpose of developing programs on research in child development. Generally, these block grants could be spent as the researchers best saw fit. While during its existence (1918–1929), the Laura Spellman Rockefeller Memorial did not provide funds for research on aging (although it did provide some funds for adult education), it was the major funding source in developmental psychology at the time (see Smuts, 2006, for a detailed discussion of the Memorial's work).

Nevertheless by the summer of 1928, Terman and Miles—while still requesting funds for their general project—outlined three specific studies for investigation during the first year. These included E. K. Strong's investigation on changes of interests with age, an investigation on eye movement during reading using elderly subjects, and a series of small scale investigations of psycho-motor ability (Miles, August 16, 1928). This proposal requesting $2,500 in start-up funds was denied, but on the grounds that the research fell more within the field of natural science than of social science (Letter to Terman, Wesley C. Mitchell, September 21, 1928).

By October of 1928, the Stanford group had changed their strategy, arguing for funding of a series of studies of practical importance to industry and in November of that year the Maturity Studies were supported by a $10,000 grant from the Carnegie Corporation. But the reviewers of Miles' grant proposal raised a number of questions regarding the feasibility of the new adventure (Miles to Woodworth, August 18, 1928). One question to be dealt with concerned the motivation of participants. To some degree, it was felt that the participants in these studies would be far more motivated to perform well in the lab than on the job, and this, therefore, would not provide a very useful indication of the competencies of workers in the work place. A more pressing and far less theoretical problem had to do with the procurement of participants. This proved to be more difficult than expected.

In their first attempt, an assistant was hired to canvass the Palo Alto area offering individuals aged 50 and over the premium wage of $1.00 an hour to participate. This approach failed badly.

The second idea was to make use of students in Palo Alto high schools. The first task was to find out which students had parents and grandparents living in the community. These students were introduced to the study and were asked to persuade their parents and grandparents to take part in the study. This proved more popular than the house to house canvass, but was not successful enough to provide adequate data (see Birren, 1961, for a discussion).

Subsequently, they hit upon a third approach. Miles was to approach various community organizations, meeting with the board of each group. The new strategy was that each community group participating would receive an honorarium for each individual sent for testing. Moreover, the honorarium would be based on the age of the participant, with 2 cents paid for each year of the participant's age. Thus, an organization would receive $1.44 for an individual participant of 72 years. By the time of the first study (March to August 1930), approximately $1,400 was distributed.

An additional problem involved procuring enough male participants. For some time, Miles had been offering a supplement of 25 cents for each male subject. But this was only partially successful, and the problem had grown more serious by the second of the two Stanford studies (April to June 1932). By May of 1932, only 125 of 500 participants tested up to that time were male. So, it became necessary to supply bonuses of up to $25.00 to organizations that could supply males who could be tested and included in the data base.

Also associated with Miles in the Maturity Studies were Lewis Terman (1877–1956), Edward K. Strong (1884–1963), and Calvin Stone (1892–1954), all Stanford faculty. Terman was to continue his studies of the gifted, and these lasted long after the termination of the program. During Terman's lifetime, there were three sets of follow-up investigations of the original 1921 sample. There was one in 1925, a set collected between 1940 and 1945, and a third set collected between 1950 and 1955. At the time of the third testing, participants averaged 44 years of age. It was found that most participants remained close to the 99th percentile on intelligence, and there were increases in performance since the previous testing at all educational and occupational levels, in all grades of ability, and at all ages. The data indicated that not only do the mentally superior hold their own, but actually increase in intellectual status (Terman & Oden, 1959).

Strong was to study interests of adults as they changed with development. By 1931, he had tested 2,340 individuals aged 20–40. His data can still be used to support modern continuity theory in that he found that older adults had no more or no fewer interests than do young adults. But also supportive of some aspects of disengagement theory, he found that activities that involved others, such as playing bridge, decrease in popularity, while activities that one can do alone such as reading increase in popularity (Strong, 1931).

Calvin Stone was to work on the maze learning ability of aged rats. This was viewed as very valuable, as learning ability could be studied without the confounds of "cross sections" as the term was used at the time, as was the case with humans. Generally, Stone found very little age related decline in his rats. However, he did argue that older rats tended to become rigid, making repeated errors he called "perseverative" errors, made even when feedback provided that the incorrect choice was being made (Stone, 1929). This concept of rigidity can be seen in more modern research on learning with aged rats (see, for example, Goodrich, 1972) and with people (Botwinick, 1973).

Miles (1931) studied a wide range of subjects on a series of psychomotor and reaction time tasks. He found that age decline with reaction time was greatest on the simplest tasks, such as raising and lowering a finger from a resting position. But slightly more difficult tasks, such as responding to a stimulus that would signal that a response was to be made showed far less decline. He interpreted his results to mean that because decline appeared to be greatest on the easiest tasks and least on the more cognitively demanding tasks, age change in the central nervous system appeared to be modest. While Miles' conclusions are not supported by modern research, the issue continues to be of considerable interest (see, for example, Salthouse, 1985).

Finally, there needs to be some mention of the milk truck drivers that had Miles' attention in the early 1920s. There were five dissertations that resulted from the Stanford studies. The first of these was Floyd Ruch's dissertation conducted in 1930. Ruch, working under Miles' direction, compared the performance of three age groups with forty participants in each group. These groups included a young group (aged 12–17), a second of middle-aged (aged 35–58) and one of older people (aged 60–82). The first of three tasks, consisted of word pairs such as walk-car or white-pink. A task called Nonsense Words consisted of items such as E × G = Z and a third list, Interference Materials had items such as 3 × 5 = 25. Ruch found all age groups did relatively well on the first task. But the difference between the age groups grew greater with the Nonsense Words and grew even greater with the Interference Materials. Ruch concluded that adults do best with learning tasks in which they can draw from past experience and in which that past experience does not interfere with the new task.

Following the conclusion of the Stanford studies, Miles gave his presidential address before the American Psychological Association based on the results of his work at Stanford. He wrote the chapter presenting the research contributions of psychology in the first edition of Vincent Cowdry's *Problems of Aging* (1939), perhaps the most significant work on aging to be published before World War II. But, during the war, his attention turned to defense research and Miles did not again play a major role in aging research.

The Classic Aging Curve

One of the most researched areas of inquiry in the history of psychology has been on the stability of intelligence test scores across the lifespan. Botwinick (1973) noted that at least 1,500 publications had appeared on the subject up to that time. Most of the work had been cross sectional and a common finding was that IQ peaked in the early 1920s before beginning a progressive decline. This set of findings became known as the classic aging curve, and was believed to have had its foundation dating back to the very earliest literature. David Wechsler (1958), for example, in his classic work, *The Measurement and Appraisal of Adult Intelligence,* argued that experimental evidence for the concept began with Galton.

The research community began to focus on the question with the Army Testing Program during World War I. Briefly summarized, when the United States entered the war on April 6, 1917, the Society of Experimental Psychologists was meeting at Harvard. Robert Yerkes arranged a special session to discuss the contributions that psychologists might make to the war effort. By August 9, Yerkes was given an appointment to organize psychological examinations that would be used to select and grade recruits for the Army. Progress was rapid and by December 24, the Surgeon General ordered that all drafted men would be tested with the newly developed group intelligence tests named the Army Alpha for those who were literate and the Army Beta for those who were illiterate or who were not English speaking. The program was extensive and when the testing program ended on January 31, 1919, a total of 1,726,966 individuals had been tested.

It is frequently argued in more contemporary accounts that intelligence data taken from Army recruits during WWI reaffirmed Galton's data of 40 years earlier. Schaie and Willis (1996) state that data taken during WWI from administering the Army Alpha was interpreted to mean that intellectual functioning peaked in childhood, as early as age 13. In another volume from recent times, Achenbaum (1995) argued that Thorndike's review of the Army Alpha and other early data reaffirmed the "curvilinearity" of intelligence test scores across the adult life span.

The case is, however, that early researchers on the subject, including Thorndike and the authors of the Army Alpha data, were well aware of the limitations of cross-sectional data, and were in fact making no such claims regarding the relationship between age and IQ. In fact, in chapter 12 of his book *Adult Intelligence* Thorndike (1928) dismisses the Army Alpha data by arguing:

> Almost nothing has been known concerning the curve of intelligence in relation to age…In the Army Tests the older man did less well, but there is good reason to suppose that they were a selection of the relatively less intelligent. In the infantry, especially, the old sergeants of the regular army who were made captains and lieutenants would be duller than the young college and business men from the officers' training camps. (p. 155)

That this was not a personal interpretation on Thorndike's part can be seen in the excerpt from Yerkes (1921) original publication of the Army Alpha data:

> The dependence of intelligence upon age of adults is a theoretical problem of great interest upon which, however, the results of the psychological examinationof the Army can throw little light. It is possible to draw up tables of intelligence ratings and age as reported on the examination blank…[but] here is still no way of saying to what extent it reflects a fundamental dependence of intelligence upon age or to what extent it may be caused by the selective process always at work…If among the older men only the more intelligent sought to be officers…or if, on the contrary, among the older man only the poorer professional men could leave their businesses to enter the Army…then we should find a very positive relation of one sort or another between intelligence and age in the Army…. (p. 813)

At the same time, other researchers were beginning to experiment with more sophisticated designs. In an early study, W. B. Pillsbury investigated a sample of 58 subjects divided into four age groups (16–19, 20–24, 25–29, and 30–35 years). Tested longitudinally over a period of 5 to 9 years, all four cohorts showed an increase of at least 8 points on Army Alpha test scores (unpublished data, as reported in Thorndike, 1928, p. 157).

Researchers during this period were finding other reasons to be cautious with their age-related intelligence data. Some of the methodological difficulties that researchers had to overcome at this early date are interesting to relate today. One of the issues frequently discussed concerned the motivation of participants. Jones and Conrad (1933) attempted to address this problem by inviting participants to the town hall of several New England villages where a feature film would be shown. Following the film, the strategy was to administer the Army Alpha. The result was a disaster with most of the town's people opting to go home. Subsequently, the methodology was changed in that an intermission would occur at a strategic location in the evening's presentation. At that point the tests were administered. While this proved much more successful, some still declined. For those individuals, attempts were made to contact them a second time for testing at a later date. Those who declined on the second occasion were contacted on yet a third occasion. Each of these two additional waves of solicitation resulted in a few additional participants. In their analysis, Jones and Conrad reported that intelligence test scores were far more stable across age with the original "hall" tested sample. Greater rates of decline were demonstrated for the second wave of subjects, and greater still for those who participated following the third round of requests. It is one of the first studies in the aging literature to report that the volunteer participant as we know him or her in our research may not be entirely representative of the adult and aging population as a whole.

In another sense, however, the results of Jones and Conrad (1933) directly support those of Yerkes, Thorndike, and others. That is to say, researchers realized early on that even with healthy participants the nature of the individuals being tested, and the designs being used, had even a greater effect on the stability of intelligence scores across age than did the effect of age by itself. By the late 1930s, methodological problems of cross-sectional analysis were understood well enough for Pressey, Janney, and Kuhlen (1939) to make reference to limitations to the methodology in several sections of their book, including the chapter on intelligence (see, for example, pp. 172–173).

If first generation researchers such as Thorndike, Yerkes, and others were aware of the limitations in their data in charting age related change, how did the concept of a classic aging curve get started? Hilgard (1987) suggests that the start may have come with the work of Mark May (1891–1977). May, who is best remembered for his work with Hugh Hartshorne (1885–1967) on an early set of investigations on moral development, had served in the Army during WW I as a lieutenant and had worked with the research staff on the Alpha data. May compared the results of the Army Alpha with scores from the Stanford-Binet, which had been administered during the course of standardization of the Army tests. The result was that the mental age (MA) of the American soldier as computed with the Stanford-Binet was between 13 and 14 years. Some years later, May attempted to clarify the issue by explaining the peculiarities of the mental age concept, and the unintended consequences that had been done. (See Hilgard, 1987, pp. 478–480, for an account.)

These data appear in chapter 11 of the Army report (Yerkes, 1921). While it is not clear whether May actually authored it, this chapter too has been interpreted in different ways. The authors of the chapter begin by arguing that there has been much public interest in the question, "How intelligent is the Army?" (p. 785). In attempting to address this question they defend the "transmutation" of Army Alpha scores into mental age because the concept of mental age was, in their reasoning, more familiar than the scales of the Army Alpha. While they made no statements regarding age differences and IQ scores for the Army recruits, it is here that they conclude that, "…the principal sample of the white draft, when transmuted from alpha and beta examinations into terms of mental age, is about 13 years (13.08)" (p. 735).

But here too the authors are far more cautious than they are often given credit for. This caution can be seen in the following excerpt from the introductory section of chapter 11:

> It is customary to say that the mental age of the average adult is about 16 years…. We can hardly say, however, with assurance that these recruits are three years mental age below the average … The draft … is highly selected at the upper end by reason of the fact that men of higher intelligence become officers without being drafted or constituted the greater part of the group of professional and business experts that were exempted from draft because essential to industrial activity in the war. It is impossible to guess the extent of this selection with respect to intelligence…. Undoubtedly the intelligence of the draft is somewhat lower than that of the country at large. (Yerkes, 1921, p. 785)

It is clear from their report that they were well aware of the influence of education on intelligence test scores. Later in the same chapter, for example, they present data indicating that the median educational attainment of the white draft (on which the 13.08 MA was based), was 7.7 years (Yerkes, 1921, p. 795, Table 347). In the previous chapter, chapter 10, they report a correlation of .75 (p. 780, Table 325) between alpha scores and education. Seen in these terms, the average MA of 13 should not have been surprising, although this specific point was not made.

Apparently because of the public interest in the issue, these data, often taken out of context, almost immediately raised a storm of controversy. They were the subject of the first paper in the famous Lippmann-Terman debate published as a series of six articles and letters in the *New Republic* in the fall of 1922. Earlier that year, Lothrop Stoddard, a Harvard Ph.D. had published *The Revolt Against Civilization.* Stoddard in an emotional display ranted,

> Probably never before has the relatively scarcity of intelligence been so vividly demonstrated. It strikingly reinforces what biologists and sociologists have long been telling us: That the number of really intelligent persons is small, and that the great majority of even the most civilized populations are of mediocre or low intelligence....” (1922, pp. 68–69)

In the October 25, 1922, issue of the *New Republic,* Lippmann tore into Stoddard's contentions calling them incorrect and nonsense. But in presenting his argument, Lippmann missed an important point. Instead of recognizing that the reported MA of 13 years was not surprising given the educational attainment of the average recruit, Lippmann choose to attack the fact that there were now two estimates of the mental age of adult Americans. One, an MA of 16, was based on the typical sample used to develop the Stanford-Binet published in 1916. One problem with this, as Lippmann saw it, was that this group was limited to a few hundred participants living in California. The other estimate, an MA of 13, was based on approximately two million recruits entering the Army during World War I. Who are we to believe, Lippmann asked, a few hundred Californians tested in 1913, or a sample of 1,700,000 men when determining what constitutes an average adult intelligence score. Lippmann's point was that both estimates could not be correct. Quick to defend his standardization process, Terman (1922) replied that there were several tests that had actually been given to Army recruits in World War I, and that they all agreed that the average score earned by draftees was less than the average fourteen year old school child. Interestingly, Terman goes on to say that psychologists “were not entirely agreed” as to how this fact should be interpreted.

But others were, in fact, clear on how the data should be interpreted. Harry Hollingworth, in his 1927 text *Mental Growth and Decline,* explained that the average individual,

> would leave school in the eighth grade, with a working knowledge of the fundamentals' a smattering of local geography, a bit of history, and a few elementary facts of physiology...Upon being given intelligence tests of the standard sort involving literate performance, the score would not significantly exceed that which would be made by average adolescents at their fourteenth year. (p. 276)

Hollingworth went on to describe the kind of performance that would be expected from an eighth grader on the Binet. That is to say that if intelligence tests correlate closely with school success, and if the average American leaves school after the eighth grade, then they would be expected to perform on tests of intelligence, such as the Stanford-Binet, with about the same performance capabilities as a thirteen or fourteen year old, or in other words, the average eighth grader.

It may be the case then that the hysteria that resulted from equating Army Alpha data with Stanford-Binet scores set the stage for some of the misunderstandings that followed. If so, it is unfortunate that Lippmann and Terman could not have been more successful in clarifying some of these issues to the general public. What is clear is that several of the first generation psychologists working with life-span intelligence data were well aware of the problems of interpretation and even some of the causes of these difficulties.

The Psychology of Aging During the Second World War and Afterwards

Before World War II, other research was being conducted internationally. In Vienna, Charlotte Bühler (1893–1974) and her students studied age changes in values and the progression of individuals toward their life goals by utilizing biographical data. Tachibana in Japan was conducting work on mental testing and productivity in industrial settings as early as the 1920s. An English language summary of the work can be found in Tachilana (1959). Also, see Riegel (1958, 1959) for a review of the German literature on aging dating back to the mid-1920s.

Following World War II, events in America began to move quickly. The Gerontology Research Center of the National Institutes of Health began in 1940, but was not active until 1946. At the same time, the Gerontological Society of America, the American Geriatric Society, and the Division of Maturity and Old Age of the American Psychological Association were founded. Sidney Pressey, who 10 years earlier had published the first textbook on life-span psychology, founded the division and served as its first president when it met for the first time in 1947. He saw the work of the new division in the following terms:

> We in this division are concerned with a range of years three times that of childhood and youth. During which there are changes probably in total more complex and more controllable ... this division should continue ... until psychologists do think developmentally about the years after 20 as well as the years before, and until problems of adult life which much need study from that point of view are so dealt with. It has contributions to make, to psychology and to human welfare. (Pressey, 1948, p. 109)

At the University of Cambridge, the Nuffield Unit for Research into Problems of Aging was established in 1946. The research of this unit was oriented toward the experimental analysis of the relationship between age and skill. Welford reported the results of these post-WWII studies in *Aging and Human Skill* in 1958.

A review of the rapid expansion of research on the psychology of aging can be found in Riegel (1977). In his review, Riegel argued that the number of articles and books doubled with an interval of 8.3 years for the whole period from 1873 to 1972. That is, after the first publication in 1873 (that he had in his files) there were two publications by about 1881, four at about 1890, and 4,096 by 1972 (p. 93).

Adult Education and Adult Learning Theory

At about the same time that the Stanford Later Maturity Studies were being organized, the origins of adult learning theory were under development. And for some of the same reasons—one of which was interest in addressing needs and problems faced by individuals in the work force. And another reason was that the adult education movement was funded—as were the Stanford studies, by the Carnegie Foundation. Here is some background.

Up to the mid-1920s, adult education was confined to local organizations such as Chautauqua, a cultural organization founded in the 1870s in western New York, or national organizations that focused on a specific mission such as the National Association of University Extension founded in 1915. But no attempt had been made to organize all the people and organizations interested in adult education into a single national effort.

The initiative to create a national umbrella organization for adult educators was taken up by Frederick Keppel (1875–1943) who had become president of the Carnegie Corporation in 1923. He had been dean of Columbia College from 1910 to 1917 and had also served on the university's Administrative Board of Extension Teaching during the same time period. Keppel was also well acquainted with James Russell (1864–1945), dean of the Teachers College, who had pioneered extension at Columbia and who also had become very sympathetic to developing a larger effort in adult education. In June of 1924, Keppel organized an "Advisory Committee on Adult Education to the Carnegie Corporation" with Russell as chairman. Out of the board's work came the first meeting of the American Association of Adult Education held in Chicago in March, 1926. (See Burrell, 1954, and Grattan, 1955, for a more detailed discussion.) One of the founding members of the board that brought this chain of events about was Eduard Lindeman. He was to become one of the most influential theorists to emerge from this period and had interests in both labor education and adult education.

Eduard Lindeman (1885–1953) was born in Saint Claire, Michigan to Danish parents. His father had escaped a German prison during the Prussian Danish war (1864) immigrating to America where he became a salt mine worker. Both of Lindeman's parents died by the time he was 10. During his developmental years, he supported himself with a variety of odd jobs including agriculture and shipbuilding. Without a high school diploma, Lindeman entered Michigan Agricultural College (now Michigan State University in East Lansing) in 1907 classified as a "subfreshman." Most biographers believe that he had only limited English literacy skills at the time (see, for example, Konopka, 1958). By the time he graduated in 1911, he had become editor of the college newspaper, and married the daughter of the chairman of the Department of Horticulture.

His academic career began with a rough start. From 1919 to 1921, he was director of the Sociology Department of the North Carolina College for Women but, due to unorthodox teaching methods (largely self-directed teaching groups) and his liberal political views, he was forced to leave. Subsequently, he was offered a teaching position at the New York School for Social Work (later the Columbia University School of Social Work). He remained on the faculty from 1924 to 1950.

Throughout his career he had a sympathetic understanding of the working class. For example, in 1911 he became editor of the *Gleanor*, an agricultural journal that stood for the interests of small farmers. Under his editorship, the *Gleanor* advocated principles of mutual cooperation and citizen participation in public affairs.

He was very much interested in the place of education in the labor movement which was robust in the United States and Europe in the mid-1920s. He had attended the Trade Union Congress in London in 1925, but was particularly influenced by the Frankfort Academy of Labor, an organization affiliated with the University of Frankfort-am-Main. In 1927 Lindeman, in collaboration with Martha Anderson, wrote *Education Through Experience*. The work was essentially a description and interpretation of the methods used by the Academy of Labor in Frankfort. Early in their report is a section titled "Adragogy" which they had adopted from the original "Andragogik." For Anderson and Lindeman andragogy became the core of adult education. Other works written by Lindeman on adult education included an entry in the *Encyclopedia of the Social Sciences* (1930), an oft-cited but unpublished manuscript, *What is Adult Education* (1925), and his major work, *The Meaning of Adult Education* (1926).

In these works, Lindeman identified four rather broad assumptions about adults and learning. The first of these spoke to the need for relevance. Lindeman argued that adults are motivated to learn as they experience needs and interests. For Lindeman, these were the units for organizing adult learning activities. Second, as he saw it, adults were interested in applying their learning to real life situations. Other assumptions made by Lindeman spoke to the nature of the adult learner. For one, he saw adults as having a desire to be self-directing. The role of the teacher was to facilitate a process of mutual inquiry rather than to transmit knowledge. Also, Lindeman believed that individual differences increase among people with age, and therefore adult education must make optimal provision for differences in style, time, place, and pace of learning.

Lindeman was a friend of John Dewey and Lindeman's emphasis on life situations and not subject matter may have been due to Dewey's influence. Brookfield (1987) notes that Lindeman anticipates critical theorists such as Freire and Mezirow by suggesting in 1925 that adult education is a process in which the adult learns to become aware of and evaluate his or her experience. For Lindeman, adult education is part of a process in which adults understand and interpret their experiences, and through which one is enabled to comprehend the social forces shaping one's conduct. The idea of analyzing one's experiences to achieve independence from social and political forces is a recurring theme in adult education. Arguing along similar lines in the more modern era, Paulo Friere (1974) adopts the term *conscientisation* to describe the process whereby people come to understand that the way they view the world, and their place in it, has been shaped by social forces in their life space which may or may not be in their own best interests. More recently, Jack Mezirow (1991) argues that a central task of adult education is to assist adults to reflect critically on their internalized values, and assumptions. Brookfield (1986), however, argues that both Freire and Mezirow developed their theories more or less independently of Lindeman. Directly influenced by Lindeman was Malcolm Knowles.

Knowles (1913–1997) grew up in Montana, the son of a veterinarian. He enrolled in the Fletcher School of Law and Diplomacy at Harvard, graduating with a B.A. in 1934. His initial intention was to enter into the diplomatic core, but there was a long wait for positions in the State Department in the mid-1930s. Instead, he began his career with the New Deal era National Youth Administration (NYA) in Massachusetts where the focus of his work was with unemployed young adults. At that time, Eduard Lindeman was director of training for the Works Progress Administration and he also supervised training for the NYA. Lindeman became Knowles' mentor and they formed a life long relationship. Knowles later said that Lindeman's *Meaning of Adult Education* became his chief source of information for a quarter of a century (Knowles, 1989).

After World War II, Knowles sought additional training in adult education earning his Ph.D. in 1960 from the University of Chicago. While at Chicago, Knowles was directly influenced by psychologist Carl Rogers. During that period, Rogers was developing his theory of client centered therapy, and he was in his own thinking becoming increasingly humanistic in orientation. (See Rogers, 1970, for an interview of him regarding how his views changed during the course of his career.) Knowles was particularly struck by

Rogers' three characteristics of an effective counselor. These included unqualified positive regard for the client, an orientation to empathize and to think and feel with, rather than about, the patient, and authenticity to behave as a therapist as a real person rather that out of a pre-determined role.

Knowles wrote his major work, *The Modern Practice of Adult Education: Andragogy vs. Pedagogy*, in 1970. In it he expands on Lindeman's earlier thinking and reintroduces the concept of andragogy which had lain dormant since the 1920s. Ten years later the book came out in a new edition, but with the subtitle changed to "*From Pedagogy to Andragogy.*" His thinking was further expanded in 1984 in the book *Andragogy in Action*. In these works Knowles identified andragogy as including five basic assumptions about the characteristics of adult learners:

1. Adults move from a dependent personality to an increasingly self-directed human being.
2. As adults mature, they accumulate a growing body of experience that serves as an increasingly important resource and foundation on which to base new learning.
3. As adults age, motivation for learning is increasingly focused on life tasks, issues, and challenges.
4. As a person ages, focus changes from postponed application of knowledge to current application.
5. Adult learning is problem centered rather than content centered.

Tennant (2006) sees Knowles' most important contribution is the expansion of the concept of self-directed learning. Knowles (1975) identified self-directed learning as a process:

> In which individuals take the initiative, with or without the help of others, in diagnosing their learning needs, formulating learning goals, identifying human and material resources for learning, choosing and implementing appropriate learning strategies, and evaluating learning outcomes. (p. 18)

Knowles maintained that self-directed learners enter into learning with more purpose and ownership of the learning experience. This is not only very motivating, he maintained, but leads to a more effective learning experience coupled with long term retention.

More recently, both Brookfield (1986) and Mezirow (1991) have reformulated the idea of the self-directed learner to include an additional concept of critical awareness. For them, a self-directed learner is able to accurately identify "authentic" needs which are accomplished through processes of critical reflection and critical thinking. Critical thinking is defined by Brookfield (1986) as the experience of carefully questioning concepts that are accepted as part of common sense or of the natural state of affairs by the majority.

In response to critics (e.g., Brookfield, 1986), Knowles acknowledged in his later writing that andragogy and pedagogy are not necessarily a distinct dichotomy in which one process is appropriate for adults and the other for children. Rather, he saw andragogy as appropriate for some children and pedagogy as a process through which some adults continue to learn effectively. He did continue to argue, however, that adults in the majority of situations benefit from self-directed learning as he described it, and benefit from being facilitated to move in that direction. For a very interesting late career interview in which he discusses his early thinking and the evolution of his views, see Knowles (1994).

A Few Parting Thoughts

The research and theoretical lines presented in this chapter continue to develop at an accelerating rate. Self-directed learning continues to be an important area of interest. Some of the more recent areas of interest include the concepts of self-monitoring, which involves the capability of recognizing accurately when one competently knows new material, and the concept of motivation which involves the capability of carrying to completion the task at hand. Recently, Ackerman (1998) laid the foundation for some of the research on the role of motivation in adult learning, and Thompson and Zabrucky (2005) have discussed some of the recent developments in cognitive self-monitoring research.

The research line begun by Miles (1931) on the question of whether there is general slowing of the central nervous system or whether there are specific localized mechanisms continues to be widely discussed. Research has been conducted to date to indicate that there are specific factors as well as general processes associated with the slowing of behavior with advancing age. Whether this slowing is a primary cause of age differences in cognitive processes is a significant question that continues to be researched. A recent review can be found in Hartley (2006).

The research on intellectual change has known many developments of its own. In recent years researchers have turned their attention to new constructs such as wisdom (see Ardelt & Jacobs, chapter 25, this volume). One of the more active teams has been that of Paul Baltes and his colleagues. They define wisdom as an expert knowledge system with which, if present, permits individuals to exercise insight and judgment. To display wisdom one must have knowledge of one's own strengths and weaknesses as well as management strategies that can be used to maximize gains over losses in a wide variety of decision making endeavors. Baltes and his colleagues also argue that, while wisdom does show an increase with age across adulthood, it can be displayed by individuals across the adult age spectrum (Baltes & Staudinger, 2000).

And then there are areas of research that our ancestors could only have imagined. The neurosciences have added a new chapter in the exploration of cognitive aging. To a certain extent, this has arisen out of a need for more accurate diagnosis and treatment for individuals suspected of suffering from pathologies of aging such as Parkinson's disease and Alzheimer's disease. But the work in this area is increasingly contributing to our understanding of memory processes in normal aging as well.

References

Achenbaum, W. A. (1995). *Crossing frontiers: Gerontology emerges as a science.* New York: Cambridge University Press.

Ackerman, P. (1998). Adult intelligence: Sketch of a theory and applications to learning and education. In MC. Smith & T. Pourchot (Eds.), *Adult learning and development: Perspectives from educational psychology.* Mahwah, NJ: Erbaum.

Baltes, P., & Staudinger, U. (2000). Wisdom: A metahuristic [pragmatic] to orchestrate mind and virtue towards excellence. *American Psychologist, 55,* 122–136.

Birren, J. E. (1961). A brief history of the psychology of aging. *Gerontologist, 1,* 69–77.

Botwinick, J. (1973). *Aging and behavior.* New York: Springer.

Brookfield, S. (1986). *Understanding and facilitating adult learning.* San Francisco: Jossey-Bass.

Brookfield, S. (1987). Eduard Lindeman. In P. Jarvis (Ed.). *Twentieth century thinkers in adult education*. London: Croom Helm.

Burrell, J. (1954). *A history of adult education at Columbia University*. New York: Columbia University Press.

Cowdry, E. (1939). *Problems of aging*. Baltimore: Williams & Williams.

Dennis, W. (1966). Creative productivity between the ages of 20 and 80 years. *Journal of Gerontology, 21*, 1–8.

Elderton, E. M., & Moul, M. (1928). On the growth curves of certain characteristics in women and the interrelationship of these characters. *Annals of Eugenics, 3*, 277–336.

Friere, P. (1974). *Education: The practice of freedom*. London: Writers and Readers.

Galton, F. (1885). On the anthropometric laboratory at the late International Health Exposition. *Journal of the Anthropological Institute, 14*, 205–221, 275–287.

Goodrich, C. L. (1972). Learning by mature, young and aged Wistar albino rats as a function of test complexity. *Journal of Gerontology, 27*, 353–357.

Grattan, H. (1955). *In quest of knowledge*. New York: Association Press.

Hall, G. S. (1922). *Senescence: The last half of life*. New York: Appleton.

Harris, D. (1957). *The concept of development*. Minneapolis: University of Minnesota Press.

Hartley, A. (2006). Changing role of the speed of processing construct in the cognitive psychology of human aging. In J. Birren & K. W. Schaie (Eds.), *Handbook of the psychology of aging* (6th ed.; pp. 183–207). New York: Elsevier.

Hendrickson, A. (1943). *Trends in public school adult education in cities of the United States, 1929–1939*. Ann Arbor,MI: Edwards Brothers.

Hilgard, E. (1987). *Psychology in America: A historical survey*. New York: Harcourt, Brace, Jovanovich.

Hollingworth, H. L. (1927). *Mental growth and decline*. New York: Appleton.

Johnson, R., McClearn, G., Yuen, S., Nagoshi, C., Ahern, F., & Cole, R. (1985). Galton's data a century later. *American Psychologist, 40*, 875–892.

Jones, H., & Conrad, H. (1933). The growth and decline of intelligence: A study of homogeneous group between the ages of ten and sixty. *Genetic Psychology Monographs, 13*, 223–298.

Knowles, M. (1970). *The modern practice of adult education: Andragogy versus pedagogy*. New York: Association Press.

Knowles, M. (1975). *Self directed learning: A guide for learners and teachers*. New York: Association Press.

Knowles, M. (1980). *The modern practice of adult education: From pedagogy to Andragogy*. Chicago: Follett.

Knowles, M. (1984). *Andragogy in action*. San Francisco: Jossey-Bass.

Knowles, M. (1989). *Making of an adult educator: An autobiographical journey*. San Francisco: Jossey-Bass.

Knowles, M. (1994). *Human resource development with Malcolm Knowles* [video recording]. Fayetteville, AK: Media Services Production.

Konopka, G. (1958). *Eduard Lindeman and social work philosophy*. Minneapolis: University of Minnesota Press.

Lehman, H. (1953). *Age and achievement*. Princeton, NJ: Princeton University Press.

Levinson, D. (1978). *The season's of a man's life*. New York: Knopf.

Lindeman, E. (1925). *What is adult education?* Unpublished manuscript Columbia University. Lindeman Archive Butler Library.

Lindeman, E. C. (1926). *The meaning of adult education*. New York: New Republic.

Lindeman, E. (1930). Adult education. In *Encyclopedia of the social sciences*. New York: Macmillan.

Lippmann, W. (1922 October, 25). The mental age of Americans. *New Republic, 34*, 263–264.

Lorge, I. (1940). Publications from 1889 to 1940 by E. Thorndike. *Teachers College Record, 41*, 778–788.

Mezirow, J. (1991). *Transformative dimensions of adult learning*. San Francisco: Jossey-Bass.

Miles, W. (1928, August 16). Stanford later maturity research project, communication to the Social Science Research Council, Hanover Conference, Hanover, New Hampshire. Miles papers, Archives of the History of American Psychology, University of Akron.

Miles, W. (1928, August 18). Letter to Professor Robert S. Woodworth. Miles Papers. Archives of the history of American psychology, University of Akron.

Miles, W. (1931). Correlation of reaction and coordination speed with age in adults. *American Journal of Psychology, 43,* 377–391.

Miles, W. R. (1967). W. R. Miles. In E. G. Boring, & G. Lindsey (Eds). *A history of psychology in autobiography* (Vol. 5, pp. 223–252). New York: Appleton Century Crofts.

Mitchell, W. C. (1928, September, 21). Letter to Lewis M. Terman. Miles papers, Archives of the History of American Psychology, University of Akron.

Owens, W. A. (1966). Age and mental abilities: a second adult follow-up. *Journal of Educational Psychology, 57,* 311–325.

Pearson, K. (1914). *Life, letters and labours of Francis Galton.* Cambridge: Cambridge University Press.

Pressey, S. L. (1948). The new division of maturity and old age. *American Psychologist, 3,* 107–109.

Pressey, S. L., Janney, J. E., & Kuhlen, R. G. (1939). *Life: A psychological survey.* New York: Harper and Brothers.

Quetelet, A. (1842). *A treatise on man and the development of his faculties.* Edinburgh: William and Robert Chambers.

Rogers, C. (1970). *Dr. Carl Rogers, Part 1.* Producer: Richard I. Evans. Distributor: Penn State Media Sales, The Pennsylvania State University, University Park.

Riegel, K. F. (1958). Ergebnisse und Probleme der psychologeschen Alterns forschung. *Vita Humana, 1,* 52–64.

Riegel, K. F. (1959). Ergebnisse und Probleme der psychologeschen Alterns forschung. *Vita Humana, 2,* 213–237.

Riegel, K. (1977). History of psychological gerontology. In J. E. Birren & K. W. Schaie (Eds.), *Handbook of the psychology of aging* (pp. 70–102). New York: Van Nostrand Reinhold.

Ruger, H. A. (1933). On the interrelationship of certain characters in man (males). *Annals of Eugenics, 5,* 59–104.

Ruger, H. A., & Pearson, K. (1933). On the interrelationship of certain characters in man (males). Second paper. *Annals of Eugenics, 5,* 364–412.

Ruger, H. A., & Stoessiger, B. (1927). On the growth curves of certain characteristics in man (Males). *Annals of Eugenics, 2,* 76–110.

Rush, B. (1805). *Medical inquires and observations* (2nd ed.). Philadelphia: J Conrad.

Salthouse, T. (1985). *A theory of cognitive aging.* Amsterdam: North-Holland.

Sanford, E. C. (1902). Mental growth and decay. *The American Journal of Psychology, 12,* 426–449.

Schaie, K. W., & Willis, S. (1996). Psychometric intelligence and aging. In F. Blanchard-Fields & T. Hess (Eds.). *Perspectives on cognitive change in adulthood and aging.* New York: McGraw Hill.

Smuts, A. (2006). *Science in the service of children 1893–1935.* New Haven, CT: Yale University Press.

Stoddard, L. (1922). *The revolt against civilization.* New York: Scribner.

Stone, C. (1929). The age factor in human learning. *Genetic Psychology Monographs, 6,* 125–199.

Strong, E. K. (1931). *Changes of interests with age.* Palo Alto, CA: Stanford University Press.

Tachibana, K. (1959). Trends in gerontology in Japan. *Psychologia, 2,* 150–156.

Tennant, M. (2006). *Psychology and adult learning.* New York: Routledge.

Terman, L. (1922). The great conspiracy, or the impulse imperious of intelligence testers, psychoanalyzed and exposed by Mr. Lippmann. *New Republic, 33,* 116–120.

Terman, L., & Miles, W. (1928, April 4). *A program of psychological research on the later period of maturity.* Miles' papers, Archives of the History of American Psychology, University of Akron.

Terman, L., & Oden, M. (1959). *The gifted child at mid-life.* Stanford, CA: Stanford University Press.

Thompson, D., & Zabrucky, K. (2005). Sensory and cognitive development in adulthood (pp.). In O-S. Tan & Alice S.-H. Seng (Eds.), *Enhancing cognitive functions: Applications across contexts* (pp. 275–298). New York: McGraw-Hill.

Thorndike, E. L. (1928). *Adult learning.* New York: Macmillan.

Wechsler, D. (1958). *The measurement and appraisal of adult intelligence.* Baltimore: Williams & Wilkins.

Welford, A. T. (1958). *Aging and human skill.* Oxford: Oxford University Press.

Yerkes, R. M. (1921). *Psychological examining in the U. S. Army.* Memoirs of the National Academy of Sciences (No. 15). Washington, DC: National Academy of Sciences.

Zeman, F. (1979). Medical history of old age. In G. J. Gruman (Ed.). *Roots of modern gerontology and geriatrics and selected studies by other writers.* New York: Arno Press.

Chapter 17

Expertise and the Adult Learner

A Historical, Psychological, and Methodological Exploration

Patricia A. Alexander, P. Karen Murphy,
and Jonna M. Kulikowich

Throughout history, whether chronicled in primitive cave drawings, the annals of past cultures or societies, contemporary biographies, or web blogs, humans have been captivated by remarkable performance. Likewise, humans have remained fascinated by those capable of exceptional feats and unparalleled visions—whether the bravery of the unnamed hunters seen on the cave walls of Lascaux, France; the military genius of Alexander the Great; or the astonishing physical prowess of Lance Armstrong. Expertise is a term that has been applied to those who attain the pinnacle of human performance in specific domains or areas of pursuit; from art to athletics or from physics to politics. Experts are, in effect, the paragons that people have celebrated throughout the ages and the models to which they aspire.

In this chapter we will consider many questions that have been addressed by researchers in their study of expertise. Some questions pertain to the roots of expertise, be they heritable factors (i.e., genes) or those acquired though life experiences (i.e., schooling or professional opportunities). Other questions pertain to the distinctions between experts and novices both in terms of the traits they possess (e.g., intelligence or prior knowledge) and the procedures they execute (e.g., problem-solving strategies). These distinctions are important. By knowing what experts in contrast to non-experts have and can do, researchers have been able to plot potential developmental trajectories that can help guide movement toward expertise in domains (e.g., Ackerman, 2003a; Alexander, 2003b; Lajoie, 2003).

With our eyes toward the emergence of expertise, we undertake a historical, psychological, and methodological analysis of expertise literature. For the historical segment, exploration will be centered on the question: How has expertise been conceptualized in the distant and near past? One of the issues examined in this discussion relates to who, historically, has garnered the label of expert and what evidence has been applied to confirm the authenticity of such determinations. We will demonstrate that two lines of inquiry have directed our understanding of outstanding performance in fields of study. From the late 1800s to the early 1900s, researchers such as Galton and Terman focused extensively on intelligence and the role of heredity factors in the study of exceptional performance, administering a variety of tasks representing a host of domains. This approach planted the seeds of the large-scale testing movement in vogue today.

While the study of intelligence, testing, and the analysis of test scores continued throughout the mid 1900s, scholars began questioning the underlying mechanisms for how learning occurs. During this period, behavioral accounts of learning (e.g., Skinner) were commonplace. Many theorists posited that internal mental mechanisms for thinking and performing were not relevant in the explanation of learning. Instead, behavior and activity described in relation to external, environmental stimuli could account for human performance. Therefore, expertise as a formal study was not of primary interest to behaviorists for their central premises were not tied to variables like reasoning, memory capacity, or problem solving.

However by the late 1960s, views of learning dramatically changed and the study of expertise soon emerged as a dedicated area of investigation. As a metaphor for knowledge storage and retrieval, the computer, became a powerful force in the rebirth of domain-specific expertise. Initially, as we will show, the focus on performance, specifically problem-solving performance, was more closely linked to early turn-of-the-century views on intelligence. As such, problems were highly contrived (Gick, 1986), ensuring that domain-specific knowledge contributed little to correct solutions. Initially, strategic knowledge that was domain independent was of primary interest to scholars. Gradually, this focus changed as problem-solving tasks became tied to domains (e.g., chess and physics) and fields of practice (e.g., medicine and engineering) from which they were sampled. The interaction between domain knowledge and strategies established this nucleus for the study of expertise (Alexander & Judy, 1988). This nucleus still characterizes the central focus of research activity in contemporary research. However, as we will show, the history of research on intelligence continues to move in concert with this cognitive tradition. Additionally, modern programs of research have introduced other variables that play roles in the development of expertise such as beliefs, motivation, and personality factors.

In fact, contemporary views of expertise are significantly more multidimensional than views adopted throughout the majority of the history on expertise. As a result, these programs of research also offer much more complex accounts for examining differences between experts and non-experts, as well as generating explanations for how individuals may potentially become experts in time. Therefore, in the second section of our chapter, we turn to a more detailed analysis of the psychological research on expertise conducted within the last decade. The findings from select programs of expertise research will be scrutinized, along with the relative strengths and seeming shortcomings of this literature for adults working within academic and non-academic arenas.

Our goal is to offer a comparison that can inform research and practice pertaining to adult development. For this analysis, we review four programs of research that have reflected the history of the study of advanced to elite performance in one or more domains that draws on both the research traditions on intelligence and problem solving. Two of these traditions arguably have more narrow foci in that they examine the multidimensional nature of singular variables. For Sternberg and colleagues, the variable is intelligence. In contrast, for Lajoie and colleagues the variable is domain-specific processes and problem solving. The other two traditions explore the relations among complexes or sets of variables that define expertise and describe its developmental trajectory. For Ackerman and colleagues, the histories of intelligence and domain-specific problem solving are brought together in addition to the roles of personality factors. For Alexander and colleagues, the domain-specific lens focuses on the complex interplay of knowledge, strategies, and motivational factors as learners begin their journey toward expertise. Because the Ackerman and Alexander frameworks have many similarities but unique differences that help provide a more robust account of expertise and its development, we attend specifically to these two programs of research in section two of our chapter.

In the third section, we explore the methodological history in the study of expertise. Indeed, the methodologies employed and developed by researchers have been numerous and varied, spanning the gamut from qualitative to quantitative approaches. Aligning to the history of research on intelligence and its impact on the study of expertise, we review how the factor-analytic tradition was born and how it continues to be a mainstay in contemporary research in all of the social sciences. By comparison, as we revisit the historical path of domain-specific, problem-solving research, we will observe that the methodologies have been more qualitative in nature, resting heavily on think-aloud and verbal protocol analyses, as individuals attempt to describe the processing that coincides with performance. We will close this section by discussing how macro-analytic (i.e., intelligence) and micro-analytic (i.e., problem solving) platforms frame a more comprehensive system of methodological approaches that can chart the movement toward expertise.

Finally, we close our chapter by speculating on future developments in the study of expertise. Again, to match each of our three sections (i.e., historical, psychological, and methodological) we envision: a) what expertise research is likely to look like in the next decade; b) what variables (psychological as well as environmental) assume more central roles in describing expertise development; and, c) what types of methodologies must emerge to capture the essence of expertise as well as the landscape and roadmap that led to its development.

Historical Perspective on Experts and Expertise

Through the ages, humankind has recognized and lauded high levels of achievement. Through their writings and experimentation, various historical personages, among them Plato, Galton, and Terman, helped lay the groundwork for 20th- and 21st-century investigations of expertise. Here, we look briefly at the ideas forwarded by those brilliant scholars for clues to the perspectives and procedures adopted by psychological researchers of the late 20th and early 21st centuries. In this brief retrospective, we seek to understand how genetics and effort are intertwined in views of expertise. Historically, genetics has been tied to the study of intelligence, while effort is a key variable in more recent accounts of expertise as a domain-specific phenomenon where deliberate practice (Ericsson, 1996; Ericsson & Kintsch, 1995; Ericsson, Patel, & Kintsch, 2000) and years of training are hallmarks of exceptional performance (Ericsson & Staszewski, 1989). The interplay of intelligence and effort were evidenced in philosophical thinking that dates back to Plato, as we will demonstrate.

Historical Taproots in the Study of Expertise

In his dialogue, *The Republic*, Plato describes the ideal State where "kings are philosophers" and "philosophers are kings" and where humankind strives for justice through the pursuit of knowledge and the logic of science that contemplates "all truth and all existence." Plato railed against an aristocracy ("aristos" meaning best) or a government ruled by those whose powers were derived solely by virtue of their social status or noble birth. Rather, Plato argued for a government where power fell to those who merited the right to rule by the manifestation of their higher states of knowledge and knowing; that is, a meritocracy. Merit, as conceived in this way, was based not only on individuals' intelligence or inherent mental capability, but also on the effortful striving for the ideal. Plato also held that societies, as organic wholes, functioned best when those who excelled at particular roles were free to take on those roles. In essence, Plato's ideal republic was a place where individuals who displayed emerging expertise were supported and encouraged to assume their place of honor and to hone their particular talents through the continued pursuit of knowledge.

Francis Galton, as with Plato, was absorbed in understanding human excellence and in using whatever knowledge of human excellence he might garner to improve social order. However, where Plato began his quest from a philosophical ideal, Galton's pursuit started from a perplexing observation. Specifically, Galton became intrigued when he realized that many of the students achieving honors at Cambridge University, his alma mater, were the sons or brothers of other high achievers. This led Galton to question whether specific factors passed from farther to son, termed *eminence*, could explain this perplexing pattern of exceptional performance. While Plato's contemplation of human performance remained purely philosophical, Galton's moved into the realm of scientific inquiry—inquiry that became the foundation for modern studies of individual differences.

Specifically, Galton (1874/1970) set about testing the hypothesis that eminence begets excellence by amassing incredible amounts of data on hundreds of men and their offspring. His thousands of measurements included meticulous physical data (e.g., height, weight, or strength), as well as academic data (e.g., honors or professions). In order to deal meaningfully with such massive information, Galton ultimately borrowed a mathematical idea from the Belgian astronomer Adolphe Quételet, himself quite knowledgeable in mathematics. That little idea would serve as a fundamental tool in the study of individual differences, which is still alive and well. Specifically, when data are plotted to show how a population differs with regard to a variable of interest such as height or weight, the resulting graph appears bell-shaped. Formally, this bell-shaped curve is called the normal distribution, and its properties work as well in the descriptions of intelligence and expertise as they did in Galton's presentations of height, weight, strength, and academic honors. Without the ability to quantify human variability, researchers would be thwarted in their attempts to systematically study expertise via statistical means.

One side-effect of Galton's quantification of human differences was his founding of the field of eugenics. For Galton, so much of human accomplishment was derived from inherited factors—in contrast to Plato who gave great weight to human striving. In fact, in his well-known work, *Hereditary Genius* (1869/1979), Galton set out to prove that genius is virtually the consequence of ancestry. The determinations he made in his examination of eminence led him to argue that societies should encourage selective breeding so that the desired traits associated with eminence could be encouraged while less desirable factors or conditions could be bred out of society. Even though many others toyed with ideas of selective breeding, including Plato, it was Galton who grounded his arguments in a wealth of "scientific" data. Although Galton's articulation of eugenics was well-intentioned, the negative ramifications of selective breeding or genetic engineering has become only too apparent to those familiar with the horrors of genocide or the infamous Nazi experiments on genetic engineering (Selden, 1999).

One individual who carried some of the premises of eugenics forward into the 20th century was Louis Terman (with Oden, 1947). Terman, drawn into the eugenic movement during its waning years, wanted to investigate what would become of those who showed exceptional intellectual promise early in life. As such, Terman was invested much more into issues pertaining to schooling like curriculum and testing practices than was Galton (Keating, 1990). In 1921, he launched a longitudinal study of children who scored at an exceptional level on a measure of cognitive ability. This approach differed from that of Galton, who worked backward from demonstrated accomplishments among adults to judgments about expertise.

Among Terman's goals was determining whether the *gifted*, as he called them, would be more or less disposed to psychological or physical disorders in the years to come or whether they would naturally emerge as society's leaders? A belief that genius and madness were two sides of the same coin had been a common conception that Terman, himself a precocious youth, hoped to dispel. As with Plato and Galton before him, Terman hoped that his efforts would have positive social consequences. In effect, Terman not only wanted the knowledge he garnered about the highly gifted to put the genius-as-madness belief to rest, but also to contribute to programs that might nurture these children of promise. The outcome, he trusted, would be an improved society.

In order to find his pool of highly gifted children, Terman and associates tested thousands of children in California. The initial basis for identification was exceptional performance on a translated and adapted version of the intelligence test created by Alfred Binet and Theodore Simon (1905). The resulting test, called the Stanford-Binet, remains a mainstay of intelligence testing in the United States. From this extensive pool, Terman (with Oden, 1947) identified 857 boys and 671 girls between the ages 3 and 19 who scored 135 or above on the Stanford-Binet. Extensive psychological, physiological, and academic achievement data were gathered on these "Termites," as they were affectionately called. These individuals were tracked for more than 80 years; more than four decades after Terman's death (Leslie, 2000).

Even though the design of Terman's longitudinal study has repeatedly been questioned, there is no doubt that this momentous study was a landmark in the exploration of exceptionality and served to define contemporary investigations of expertise. Perhaps the major contribution of Terman's (with Oden, 1947) multifaceted, longitudinal study was the realization that those who are intellectually advanced are also more likely than their non-identified peers to be physically and socially capable as well. It is almost inconceivable that present-day researchers could amass such intricate and lifelong portraits of human performance—portraits that span up to eight decades of participants' lives.

Psychological Studies of Expertise: Three Generations and Three Perspectives

The three forerunners to modern-day studies of expertise just considered had certain attributes in common. For one, Plato, Galton, and Terman believed that there were undeniable differences among human beings and that some individuals, whether as a consequence of their genetic endowments or through their own pursuit of ideals, were superior or advanced. Further, they held that those exceptional individuals should be nurtured and lauded by society. Finally, Plato, Galton, and Terman engaged in the philosophical or scientific study of exceptionality, in part, to advance society. Although contemporary researchers share some of the same characteristics as their historic forerunners, they have typically engaged in their studies for more pragmatic reasons.

Specifically, there was a resurgence of interest in eminent or gifted performance beginning in the late 1960s that has carried forward into contemporary research (Gick, 1986; Keating, 1990). In fact, it is helpful to consider this extant literature in terms of generations of psychological inquiry (Holyoak, 1991)—generations that were initially spawned by the notion of Alan Turing and others that machines (i.e., computers) could be made to think. The introduction of the computer had a tremendous impact on the history of the study of expertise. With the computer, scholars recognized that information could be stored and retrieved in a specific location. For cognitive psychologists studying human learning, that location was the brain. The theory of information-processing (IPT) emerged as a result of mapping human knowledge acquisition and use to that of computer storage and retrieval. Information-processing researchers and theorists are therefore cognitivists dedicated to understanding how the mind perceives, internalizes, interprets, stores, structures, and uses information (Anderson, 1983; Patel & Groen, 1986; Simon, 1989). Indeed, much is owed to IPT scholars like Chi (1978, 1997), Ericsson (with Polson, 1988), Glaser (Chi, Feltovich, & Glaser, 1981), and their contemporaries whose programs of research left their indelible mark on expertise research in the 20th century and paved the way for others invested in this line of inquiry.

Not only did the idea of the computer present a rich metaphor to describe human learning, but also the availability of computers as industrial tools allowed for social advances where seemingly innumerable bytes of information could be stored, organized, and accessed for human consumption as challenging problems arose in society (e.g., breaking codes in wartime, detecting submarines, and flying planes). However, to unlock the potential of computers to accomplish multi-step tasks, it was necessary to enhance the programming that directed their actions. Here, the human mind with its potential to be planful and to execute strategies to reach goals served as a means by which computer programmers could learn more about configuring their codes. As a result, researchers set out to discern the characteristics of expert performance (i.e., what do experts do or how do they reason/think?) and to validate them over a variety of problem-solving tasks so that those characteristics could be programmed into non-human systems or "smart" machines that approximated effective human thinking and actions (Alexander, 2003b; Ericsson & Smith, 1991).

Another goal of these researchers was to ascertain the cognitive attributes that would distinguish experts from novices so that those attributes could be trained in non-expert human populations (Chi, Glaser, & Farr, 1988)—a goal that is reflective of the individual difference theory and research of Francis Galton. In this chapter, we look across three generations of contemporary expertise research, comparing them with regard to their purposes, nature of tasks, target populations, and primary findings (see Table 17.1). We focus our discussion in the next section on the first two generations of this work, leaving more detailed treatment of the third and current generation of expertise research for later.

Table 17.1 A Cross-Generational Examination of Contemporary Expertise Theory and Research

	GENERATIONS		
PARAMETERS	*First*	*Second*	*Third*
Purpose	Study experts at generic problem solving	Investigate domain experts engaged in problem solving	Examine the developing and multidimensional nature of expertise
Theoretical Frames	Artificial intelligence and individual differences	Information-processing and individual differences	Information-processing and social constructivism
Structure	Expert/novice dichotomy	Expert/novice dichotomy	Novice to expert development
Tasks	Knowledge-lean, generic problems	Knowledge-rich domain-specific problems	Well-defined and ill-defined tasks
Participants	Identified adult experts and assumed adult novices	Identified experts and assumed novices; primarily adults	Range of novice, competent, and expert performers of varying ages

First Generation: Expertise as Generic Problem Solving

As noted, computers were a particularly powerful influence in the onset of psychological studies of expertise. A bidirectional relation emerged between research on computers and human learning. Computers served as a metaphor to describe memory and how knowledge is structured in memory. In turn, humans' abilities to solve problems provided programmers with the means to make computers "intelligent" machines that could complete cognitive tasks. This influence is evident in various ways within the first generation. Researchers of this generation such as Newell, Simon, and Chase (e.g., Chase & Simon, 1973; Newell & Simon, 1972) hypothesized that the in-depth study of the cognitive processes and mental structures of expert problem solvers would be a key to the effective programming of more intelligent machines. These cognitive-science researchers who were at the vanguard of artificial intelligence (AI) conceptualized expertise as the efficient and effective solution of generic problems; that is, problems for which all critical information was thought to be part of the given problem space. The first generation researchers also relied on computer simulations and computer modeling to test their assumptions about expert problem solving.

The isolation of the specific strategies or solution techniques employed by expert problem solvers required these first generation researchers to create or to select experimental tasks that would maximize cognitive processing data while controlling for the influence of background or content knowledge. Gick (1986), in her review of problem-solving strategies, refers to these as artificial puzzles or problems. Because of the lack of domain specificity, other scholars such as Holyoak (1991) refer to these tasks as knowledge-lean (Holyoak, 1991). The classic cannibal/missionary conundrum is representative of such knowledge-lean problems:

> There are three missionaries and three cannibals on a river bank. The missionaries and cannibals need to cross over to the other side of the river. For this purpose, they have a small rowboat that holds just two people. There is one problem, however. If the number of cannibals on either river bank exceeds the number of missionaries, the cannibals will eat the missionaries. How can all six get across to the other side of the river in a way that guarantees that they all arrive alive and uneaten? (Sternberg, 1986, p. 57)

In addition to these generic problem sets, it was essential for first generation researchers to ensure that the processes and structures they uncovered were indeed unique to experts, for the code used to program computers had to result in not only accurate task completion but also highly efficient performance. Therefore, they contrasted data from presumed or known experts to those considered to be novices. These expert-novice comparisons became a hallmark of this generation and lead to significant characterizations of expert problem solvers (versus novices) as those who:

- Perceive the underlying structure of problems and are not distracted by more surface-level features;
- Have a richer repertoire of heuristic strategies;
- Engage in problem analysis and planning;
- Employ a means-end problem solving strategy in which they combine aspects of forward and backward reasoning during solution, instead of moving forward in a step-by-step process (e.g., Bransford, Brown, & Cocking, 1999; Chi, 1978).

Despite these remarkable advancements in understanding, there remained critical shortcomings to the first generation approach to expertise. Most notable was the inability to acknowledge the structures of knowledge held in memory by experts and how this knowledge base interacted with strategies during problem solving. Thus, it became apparent that generic problem-solving expertise had limited relevance to exceptional problem-solving performance in specific domains (Gick, 1986). What followed, therefore, was a subsequent generation of researchers who wanted to understand the mental processing with the structures of knowledge of those who demonstrated expertise in specific problem-solving domains (Holyoak, 1991).

Second Generation: Expertise as Knowledge-Rich Problem Solving

As with its predecessor, the second generation of expertise researchers continued to focus on problem solving as the mechanism for operationalizing expertise and retained the expert-novice dichotomization indicative of the prior generation. However, the second-generation researchers were no longer interested in general search strategies or generic knowledge-lean problems. Rather, these researchers—many of whom had been part of the initial generation—targeted tasks drawn from particular fields or problem-solving contexts (e.g., chess, typing, waiting tables, or physics) for which knowledge of the domain was perceived as essential (Anderson, 1983; Chi, 1978; Chi et al., 1981).

In effect, their problems of choice were not self-contained, generic problems, but were problems expected to trigger the infusion of domain-specific knowledge and strategies, as well as general problem-solving heuristics. Careful task selection thus allowed second-generation researchers to document that knowledge and strategies were significant determiners of expert performance in selected domains (Ericsson & Smith, 1991). One such problem used in the domain of political science was:

> Assume you are the head of the Soviet Ministry of Agriculture and assume that crop productivity has been low over the past several years. You now have the responsibility of increasing crop production. How would you go about doing this? (Voss, Tyler, & Yengo, 1983, p. 212)

The pioneering research of de Groot (1978/1946) and Chase and Simon (1973; Simon & Chase, 1973) in the domain of chess serves as an illustrative case of early second-generation research. These researchers wanted to uncover the nature and characteristics of expert chess players. Chess was an ideal domain for this research because it is a game with limited but well defined rules yet with incredible variability in the way experts and novices execute those rules. What also made chess appealing as a domain of study was the fact that the strategic moves of players are transparent as pieces move on the gameboard. Therefore, researchers could readily record those moves. Through the use of think-aloud techniques or stimulated recalls, researchers could then prompt the players to verbalize the reasoning behind particular moves, adding to the problem-solving data. Finally, the procedural nature of chess and similar domains allowed researchers like de Groot to create simulations or laboratory versions of these problem-solving tasks. The benefit of these simulations was that the thinking and moves of experts and novices could be investigated in more controlled conditions, without the extraneous influences that might exist in everyday settings (Ericsson & Smith, 1991).

As with their predecessors, these second-generation researchers were able to document clear and significant differences between experts in particular domains and those new to those domains. These differences, it was hoped, could signal the changes that should be prompted in novices in order to transform them into domain experts. For example, these programs of inquiry gave strong evidence that experts possess the following desirable traits:

- Have devoted much time and effort to the target domain and its relevant tasks;
- Possess an extensive body of domain knowledge that is coherently and efficiently organized;
- Rely on their rich prior experiences to analyze the problem at hand deeply and effectively;
- Select and execute domain-specific, as well as general, strategies that are well-matched to the target problem (e.g., Bransford et al., 1999; Byrnes, 2001; Chi et al., 1988; Ericsson & Smith, 1991).

Through this list, one can again see the intertwining of intelligence and effort. Time is essential to expertise as individuals must have multiple and repeated opportunities to interact with bodies of information. This is a domain-specific principle that relates directly to the fact that one hallmark of expertise is principled understanding (Alexander, Murphy, & Woods, 1996) or the ability of experts to organize information around the few central concepts of their domain. However, experts must also have keen perceptual skills that allow them to sift and sort through information and separate problems into classes. These types of pattern finding and detection skills are commonly measured by intelligence tests (e.g., Wechsler 1981).

Despite the many contributions of the second generation, there remained serious limitations to this body of research, particularly in terms of translating its findings to the development of expertise in and out of school. In effect, it was one thing to document how true experts differed from real novices when confronted with prototypic domain problems, but it was quite another to use that knowledge to stimulate the development of expertise. There have certainly been efforts to translate such consistent and significant findings about experts into instructional metaphors, models, and programs intent on facilitating expertise development (Bereiter & Scardamalia, 1993; Brown, Collins, & Duguid, 1989). Still, these efforts have not been particularly easy or readily apparent (Sternberg, 2003).

We must acknowledge that some of the translational difficulties faced by second generation researchers may be attributable to the social/political and academic climates that surround educational or professional development efforts (Alexander et al., 1996; Berliner & Biddle, 1995). Nonetheless, it was the limitations of the first and second generation research on expertise that gave rise to the current and third generation. As a way to introduce the third generation, we will consider several of those limitations and the manner in which current programs of expertise theory and research have sought to counter them.

Third Generation: Expertise as a Multidimensional, Developmental Process

Many within the third generation of expertise research share a commitment to the development of expertise. It is not simply the sharp contrasts between those at the extremes of expertise that matter; it is also all the places in-between. Further, it is the array of forces and experiences that seem necessary to move one along the trajectory from novice to expert that warrants attention. This developmental versus dichotomous orientation toward expertise is thus a hallmark of the third generation.

Another distinguishing feature of this generation of theory and research is the acknowledgment or embracing of non-cognitive or motivational/affective factors as part of expertise development. It has been argued that prior generations of research held to a "coldly cognitive" view of expertise (Pintrich, Marx, & Boyle, 1993). That is to say, these earlier generations did not expressly consider the personality, social, or motivational factors that seem inherent in the attainment of expertise. These motivational/affective dimensions do not supplant or eradicate the significance of cognitive forces, such as knowledge and strategic processing, but have been treated as complementary and integrated elements of expertise development. Growing competence or established expertise in complex domains also entails persistence, interests, curiosities, and other such forces (Ainley, 1998; Reio & Wiswell, 2000).

For example, in the prior generations of expertise research, the conation (will) or intentionality of the learner did not enter strongly into discussions (Sinatra & Pintrich, 2002; Snow, Corno, & Jackson, 1996). Any willful or goal-directed aspects of the transformation of novices to experts were not systematically incorporated into research designs or empirical measures of past generations (Ackerman, Kyllonen, & Roberts, 1999). Third generation researchers do not work under the assumption that individuals not already acknowledged as experts have a voiced or unvoiced goal of becoming experts in any domain, or any intention of committing the requisite time and energy to achieving expertise, even in those cases where the requisite cognitive abilities exist (Bransford et al., 1996; Meece, Blumenfeld, & Hoyle, 1988).

Over the years, there have been attempts to relate expert/novice research to education or professional development (e.g., Bransford et al., 1999), but little of the foundational research in those years considered schools or education as the primary context for research. As we discussed, the experimental tasks from the first and second generations were carefully crafted or contrived to be knowledge-lean or knowledge-rich (Allard & Starkes, 1991; Ericsson & Polson, 1988; Gentner, 1983, 1988; Patel & Groen, 1986). Those actions were perhaps critical to establishing the parameters for expertise research (e.g., Anzai & Yokoyama, 1984). But, those of the third generation have chosen to look explicitly at schools or academic domains as legitimate venues for study or to investigate expertise in everyday, dynamic settings or with complex, less well-structured tasks. As a result, the subject-matter areas represented in expertise research span the continuum from domains that rely heavily on algorithms (e.g., mathematics or physics) to those that rely heavily on heuristics and case-based reasoning (e.g., history, medicine, or psychology).

Even for domains that tend to be algorithmic, such as mathematics, expertise researchers have looked at both well-defined (i.e., correct solutions) and ill-defined (i.e., plausible solutions) tasks to gain insights as to how those who are more knowledgeable regulate deductive and inductive reasoning strategies (Kulikowich & DeFranco, 2003). Finally, even though domain-specific expertise assumes proficiency in one domain, no domain acts in isolation of other subject-matter areas or fields of study. Therefore, cognitive psychologists have paid significantly more attention to interdomain transfer during problem solving (e.g., Bassok & Holyoak, 1989) and crossdisciplinary thinking (e.g., Spiro & Jehng, 1990).

In the section that follows, we take a harder and more detailed look at this third generation of expertise researchers and consider the strengths, limitations, and contributions of this ongoing work for understanding expertise and its development.

Contemporary Programs of Research on Expertise

Research from the early 1900s on intelligence and the 1960s on problem solving (Chi, 1978; Chi et al., 1981; Ericsson & Smith, 1991) laid the foundation for current theories and models of expertise (e.g., Alexander, 1997). Indeed, ongoing programs of research are girded by a number of presuppositions gleaned from previous research. For example, the research programs reviewed herein assume that experts possess both a breadth and depth of knowledge that is highly integrated or principled (Alexander, 1997; Alexander & Murphy, 1998). When solving problems, experts effectively induce or deduce the underlying structure of the set of problems, and are adept at selecting and applying appropriate problem-solving procedures accordingly. Finally, experts proficiently draw on domain knowledge and strategies with limited cognitive effort (Alexander, 2003a). In essence, current models assume that experts are astute cognitively and metacognitively (i.e., the ability to monitor their thinking and reasoning). Of course, implicit within those presuppositions is the understanding that few individuals will achieve expertise in even one domain.

However, as might be expected, current research programs contribute uniquely to understandings about the emergence of expertise within individuals and the instructional and environmental/contextual conditions under which such emergence is more or less likely to occur. Consequently, there remains no grand theory of expertise. The purpose of this section will be to provide an overview of four empirically supported, contemporary programs of research on expertise and to compare and contrast their articulated theories/models along a number of parameters (e.g., theoretical frame/source or intended populations). Following that comparison, we will offer a more comprehensive overview of one theory and one model emerging from these programs of research. Specifically, we detail the Intelligence-as-Process, Personality, Interests, and Knowledge Theory (PPIK; Ackerman, 1996) and the Model of Domain Learning (MDL; Alexander, 1997). It is important to note that we have selected to review models that lend themselves most easily to adult education and expertise.

We have chosen to discuss the PPIK and the MDL because they are highly complementary, and together offer a more comprehensive picture of expertise in adults. Ackerman's (1996, 2000, 2003b) theory draws on the literature bases of intelligence research, personality theory, and domain-specific knowledge acquisition. He posits a developmental trajectory that has many similarities to the historical outline we described earlier. Intelligence factors contribute to personality and interest factors that in turn direct how individuals excel in one or more domains. Alexander also espouses a developmental trajectory. Unlike Ackerman, her model does not explore the roles of intelligence and personality factors on expertise. Instead, she pays attention to interactions among domain knowledge, strategy use, and interest within one subject-matter area (e.g., human biology or physics), even though her model is espoused to generalize variable relations and temporal patterns across domains. As such, the tenets of the MDL can be applied in diverse domains, under varied conditions, and with individuals of varying ages. As we will explain, these details make the MDL a highly versatile model that could be particularly useful for adults in workplace settings.

A Comparison of Contemporary Programs of Research on Expertise

Within the extant research literature, there are several researchers focused on developing and testing models or theories of expertise. Here, we will discuss the research programs of four contemporary scholars (i.e., Ackerman, Alexander, Lajoie, and Sternberg). These four programs were selected because they extend prior expertise research in critical historical, theoretical, methodological, and instructional ways and inform understandings regarding adult development, learning, and expertise. Specifically, three criteria were employed in the selection of these research programs. First, the perspectives offered by these researchers have been subjected to multiple empirical investigations in varied domains, albeit differentially so. Second, to varying degrees, each of these approaches has implications for adult learners. Finally, the perspectives forwarded in these theories and models have direct implications for learning and instruction within complex domains like those that might be found in the workplace.

Specifically, we will compare the various programs of research on nine parameters (see Table 17.2). In selecting the various parameters, our goal was to provide mooring points upon which we could compare the various strengths of the theories and models of expertise proposed within a given research program. As might be expected, we begin

Table 17.2 Comparison Between Current Programs of Expertise Research

Parameters	CURRENT PROGRAMS OF RESEARCH			
	Ackerman	*Alexander*	*Lajoie*	*Sternberg*
Focus (Learning/ Instruction)	Learning	Learning	Learning/ Instruction	Instruction
Theoretical Frame/Sources				
Primary	Information processing	Information processing, Vygotsky	Information processing, Vygotsky	Information processing
Secondary	Cattell, Snow	Piaget, Dewey	Cattell, Chi, Glaser	Gardner
Context (Academic/ Nonacademic)	Academic/ Nonacademic	Academic	Academic/ NonAcademic	Academic
Intended Population (School Age/Adults)	Adults	School Age/Adults	School Age/ Adults	School Age
Dimensions				
Cognitive	Fluid Intel., Crystal Intel., Domain Knowledge, Ability	Subject-Matter, Domain, Topic Knowledge, Strategic Processing	Knowledge, Skill	Analytic, Creative, Practical Abilities, Knowledge
Affective	Interest	Individual, Situational Interest	Confidence	—
Personality	Extroversion, Social Potency, Control[1]	—	—	—
Trajectory (Y/N)	N	Y	N	N
Problem-Based	N	N	Y	N
Domain Specific (Y/N)	Y	Y	N[2]	N

Note 1: Much of Ackerman's work has focused on trait complexes, rather than individual variables. See Ackerman and Heggestad (1997) for a meta-analysis of trait complexes.

Note 2: Lajoie's work has been more focused on problem-solving within particular domains as opposed to the acquisition of principled domain-specific knowledge.

with an overview of the *focus* and supporting *theoretical frame*. In discussing the focus, we also compare the various models in terms of the *context* (i.e., academic or nonacademic) and whether the *intended population* for the theory or model is school age or adults. We also felt that it was important to compare the *individual difference dimensions* incorporated. Certainly one of the shortcomings of previous research on expertise was the lack of a developmental trajectory for the fostering of expertise. As such, we also compared the theories and models on whether the authors present a *developmental trajectory*. Prior generations have considered a domain-general versus domain-specific orientation to problem-solving (Keating, 1990). Thus, we contrast the various theories and models on whether they have a domain-general, domain-specific, or blend of approaches.

Ackerman

Ackerman has spearheaded a program of research on the role of intellectual investment and trait complexes in the development of expertise (Ackerman, 2000; Ackerman & Rolfhus, 1999; Rolfhus & Ackerman, 1999). Ackerman's work, similar to the other theories or models discussed herein, draws on various cognitive learning theories as a theoretical frame. Among the cognitive researchers most influential in his work were Snow and Cattell. As will be discussed, his research has been instrumental in presenting an understanding that expertise is far more complex than a composite of novel and traditional indicators of intelligence. Specifically, the clustering of various cognitive and affective variables (i.e., trait complexes) identified in his research have been repeatedly shown to correlate differentially with specific academic domains (Ackerman & Heggestad, 1997).

Arguably, the most important implications of this line of research for individuals working with adults in various settings were that (a) middle-aged adults often outperform their young adults in domain knowledge, and (b) trait complexes are linked to domain expertise. As the name would suggest, the strength of Ackerman's (1996) theory, Intelligence-as-Process, Personality, Interests, and Knowledge (PPIK), is that it incorporates a number of cognitive (e.g., fluid and crystallized intelligence or domain knowledge), affective (e.g., interest), and personality (e.g., social potency or control) factors in explorations of expertise in adults. A concomitant area for continued research, however, pertains to the role of these particular factors in the development of expertise.

Alexander

Alexander's MDL was derived from extensive research in knowledge acquisition, motivation, and strategic processing (e.g., Pintrich et al., 1993; Pressley, Goodchild, Fleet, Zajchowski, & Evans, 1989). Thus, she draws her theoretical frame from both information processing and more affective classes of learning theory (e.g., social constructivism). In effect, Alexander's work sketches the nature of and changes in the relations among selected cognitive and affective variables as individuals develop expertise in a domain. Unlike prior expertise research, Alexander has considered the interplay among knowledge, interest, and strategic processing at three stages (i.e., acclimation, competence, and proficiency) in the journey toward expertise.

Alexander and colleagues (e.g., Alexander & Jetton, 2000; Alexander, Jetton, & Kulikowich, 1995; Alexander, Sperl, Buehl, Fives, & Chiu, 2004) have found support for the predictions of the MDL in a multitude of domains (e.g., astrophysics, human biology, or special education) and with varying ages (i.e., elementary through adult). The strength of this program of research is that it is one of the first attempts to model the developmental trajectory of expertise. In fact, this is the only model reviewed that forwards a trajectory for expertise. In addition, the domain-specific nature of the model lends versatility to its application in diverse settings like those commonly found in the workplace. More longitudinal research is needed validating the relations among these factors in individuals over time within varied domains.

Lajoie

The programs of research by Lajoie and Sternberg focus on instructional systems and approaches requisite for enhancing the development of expertise. These two programs of research, however, are quite different. Lajoie's research is heavily rooted in the early expertise research by Chi and colleagues (e.g., Chi et al., 1988). One of the primary contentions gleaned from this line of research was that one could study the actions, skills, abilities, and knowledge of experts as a mechanism for creating instructional interventions for novices. Such a premise clearly underlies the creative instructional environments designed by Lajoie and colleagues. In essence, Lajoie has created a series of computer-based learning environments in which she attempts to foster expertise through knowledge scaffolding, deliberate practice, and creative, dynamic assessments.

A major contribution of this work to the expertise literature is the incorporation of dynamic assessments (Lajoie & Lesgold, 1992). Lajoie has been quite successful at creating learning environments in which cognitive tutors (i.e., computers) continually monitor problem-solving as the process is taking place. Given the dynamic nature of this process, the computer can offer direct in-the-moment feedback allowing the novices to make subtle corrections as needed. It is important to note that Lajoie and her colleagues hold to the understanding that there is no ideal solution path, but that the use of cognitive task analysis can aid in revealing similarities in terms of the planning, strategies, actions, and interpretations that experts make and the ways in which they differ from novices (Lajoie, 2003).

Moreover, Lajoie and her colleagues have been successful at fostering expertise in problem-solving within a number of domains including biology (Lajoie, Lavigne, Guerrera, & Munsie, 2001), surgical intensive care (Lajoie, Azevedo, & Fleiszer, 1998), statistics (Lajoie, Lavigne, Munsie, & Wilkie, 1998), and personal finance (Ahmad & Lajoie, 2001). It is important to note that this is the only program of research that we reviewed that continues to take a problem-based approach to learning where transfer of problem-solving expertise within a domain is of primary interest. For this reason, Lajoie's work is characterized in Table 17.2 as being domain general as compared to other lines of research (e.g., Alexander) in which the primary interest is the acquisition of principled, domain-specific knowledge. For example, if adults in the workforce participate in a computer-based learning experience, like those being created by Lajoie, would they be able to transfer the skills and abilities they acquired during the problem-solving environment to other situations? This is certainly a vital question for both teachers and individuals in the work force.

Sternberg

Like Lajoie and colleagues, Sternberg has forwarded an instructional approach aimed at what he has termed *successful intelligence* (Sternberg, 2003). In effect, Sternberg's premise is that current pedagogical approaches in schools are aimed almost exclusively at fostering technical knowledge in given domains. The problem with such an approach is that it does not foster the kind of *real world* thinking requisite to function as an expert in the world beyond school (Sternberg, 2003). Successful intelligence describes a kind of intelligence in which an expert possesses requisite technical knowledge that he or she can apply in flexible ways. This is similar to and supported by Hatano's (1982; Hatano & Oura, 2003) differentiation between adaptive and routine experts. What varies from the work of Hatano are the conditions requisite for the fostering of adaptive expertise. While Hatano and colleagues (e.g., Hatano & Inagaki, 1992) have pointed to the motivational context of adaptive expertise, Sternberg has focused on fostering expertise by tapping novices cognitive aptitudes. He argues that schools have primarily focused on analytic thinking which is most closely aligned to traditional intelligence measures and as a consequence, have fostered technical rather than adaptive expertise.

Within Sternberg's (2003) *Theory of Successful Intelligence*, instruction in schools would be refocused to develop students' analytical (e.g., analyze, critique, or evaluate), creative (e.g., invent, discover, or predict), and practical (e.g., apply, use, or implement) thinking abilities. Additionally, Sternberg suggests that such thinking skills should be developed by solving real world problems, perhaps similar to those created by Lajoie. Sternberg and colleagues (e.g., Sternberg & Clinkenbeard, 1995; Sternberg, Grigorenko, Ferrari, & Clinkenbeard, 1999) have found support for the theory in a number of empirical, intervention studies in varied domains and settings. Among those studies was an aptitude treatment-interaction intervention. That is to say, when students received instruction paralleling their strength (e.g., creative thinking), then they performed better than when instruction was mismatched to their strengths. This finding is reminiscent of Gardner's (1999) notion of teaching to students' unique intelligences. Another major finding was that students taught in accordance with his model outperformed students taught through traditional instruction (Grigorenko, Jarvin, & Sternberg, 2002). The difficulty, of course, is that these results have not been replicated. Such replication opens a vast area for future research. Moreover, it is not clear what implications this instructional program will have for adults in the workforce.

In the sections that follow, we offer a more detailed discussion of one theory and one model emerging from these four lines of research. It is important to note that the use of the terms theory versus model in no way implies greater predictive abilities or stronger empirical support. Rather, in the case of Ackerman and Alexander, the variability in the use of terms is likely more attributable to differences in field of training (i.e., cognitive psychology versus educational psychology). The comprehensive picture of expertise offered across Ackerman's (1996) Intelligence-as-Process, Personality, Interests, and Knowledge (PPIK) and Alexander's (1997) Model of Domain Learning for adult learners is quite impressive in both breadth and depth.

Intelligence-as-Process, Personality, Interests, and Knowledge

Much of Ackerman's research has had intellectual investment as its central focus. Rooted in Cattell's (1971/1987) investment theory, Ackerman has proposed that domain expertise results from the investment of intellectual resources over time. Unlike Cattell, however, Ackerman's (1996) theory PPIK moves beyond the sole reliance on intelligence and includes other variables to account for how individuals move toward expertise. Specifically, the theory includes: a) two different kinds of intelligence (i.e., fluid intelligence [Gf] and crystallized intelligence [Gc]); b) a set of cognitive, affective, and conative trait complexes; and, c) domain knowledge in multiple subject-matter areas (Ackerman, 2003b). Ackerman has defined Gf and Gc traditionally, based on Cattell's work

(1971/1987), in that he views Gf as the psychological capabilities involving in short-term memory (e.g., pattern recognition, induction, or abstract reasoning) that are fairly stable for a substantive portion of the lifespan. By comparison, Ackerman (2003a), again like Cattell, defines Gc as the psychological capabilities based in formal and informal experiences. As such Gf is highly influenced by heredity and peaks in early adulthood, whereas Gc is highly influenced by learning in various settings (e.g., family, schools, or jobs). In contrast to the development of Gf, Gc is heavily influenced by the investment of Gf, and has the potential to mature into middle-age.

Ackerman's trait complexes are conceptually similar to Snow's (1989) aptitude complexes. In a meta-analysis, Ackerman and Heggestad (1997) determined that a moderate number of traits relating to abilities, personality, and interests appear to cluster in the prediction of domain knowledge. The traits identified by these researchers include Science/Math, Intellectual/Cultural, Clerical/Conventional, and Social. As Ackerman (2003b) suggested: "The inference from the overlapping complexes is that individual differences in trait complexes may have useful properties in determining the direction and level of cognitive investment in the acquisition of expertise" (p. 16). Trait complexes such as Clerical/Conventional or Social seem to have a broader range of influence on expertise across domains, whereas the Science/Math complex more heavily influences expertise within a limited set of domains.

Perhaps the most pertinent finding relative to adult learning is that middle-aged adults generally outperform young adults on domain knowledge assessments even in the context of lower Gf scores or slightly higher Gc scores (e.g., Ackerman, 2000; Ackerman & Rolfhus, 1999; Rolfhus & Ackerman, 1999). These results have been replicated in 20 different domains of expertise (Ackerman, 2003a). Traditional investigations of these populations have compared performance primarily using measures of Gf. Given that Gf peaks in early adulthood, this younger group had the advantage:

> These investigations succeeded in showing that a broader representation of adult intellect as including assessment of the breadth and depth of domain knowledge beyond traditional measures of Gc yielded an overall assessment of middle-aged adults as more capable than younger adults. (Ackerman, 2003b, p. 19)

This finding lends support to the fact that expertise development takes time. Older adults, more so than younger adults, may have opportunities to immerse themselves in one academic area with one set of vocational responsibilities. In contrast, younger adults may still have to negotiate shifting interests and investments among domains as they are likely still acquiring the skills necessary for their eventual professions. As a result, they are exposed to numerous subject-matter areas.

Also of importance in various studies by Ackerman are the consistent findings linking trait complexes with particular domains of expertise. For example, knowledge in the Physical Sciences and Technology domains and Gf have been found to be highly correlated with the Science/Math trait complex. Knowledge across Humanities, Civics, and Business/Law domains was highly positively correlated to Intellectual/Cultural trait complex scores. Finally, scores on the social trait complex have been negatively correlated with knowledge across the domains. Such findings could have tremendous implications for career counseling and guidance, as well as workforce placement, since social trait complexes, which include the personality factors, are hypothesized as mediating forces between intelligence and knowledge.

The Model of Domain Learning

The MDL depicts the journey toward expertise in a domain in terms of select cognitive and affective components (i.e., subject-matter knowledge, learner interest, and general strategic processing). These components are positioned within a framework that addresses both stages and phases of domain learning. Long-term characterizations that arise from the interplay of knowledge, interest, and strategies are referred to as *stages*. Similar to other stage-like theories of development and learning, the stages predicted in the MDL are essentially non-regressive and non-recursive (Karmiloff-Smith, 1986; Shuell, 1990). With the exception of a life-changing event or a dramatic change in the domain itself, the tenets of the MDL posit that it is improbable that an individual will easily regress to a lower stage once a particular stage has been reached. One differentiating feature of the MDL is that the stages are not strictly aligned with chronological age. Rather, the stages in the MDL are much more aligned with the experiences, schooling, and work that tends to be age-associated. The stages of the MDL are acclimation, competence, and proficiency/expertise.

The model also addresses the interplay of knowledge, interest, and strategies at a more immediate and situation-specific level. *Phases* refer to the more recurrent, iterative aspects of domain learning and development (Karmiloff-Smith, 1986, 1986; Shuell, 1990) and are derived from the state of knowledge, interest, and strategies at any given moment or with any given task. As would be expected, the situational factors are always in flux. Consequently, there is a constant interplay, perhaps even tension, between the forces that shape, form, or transform one's state within a field of learning. The phases of learning are meant to capture the fluidity within the learning process. It is the recurring patterns emerging from the phases that give rise to the profiles indicative of a particular stage of domain learning.

Components

Transformations in the components of subject-matter knowledge, interest, and strategic processing serve to define domain learning in the MDL. *Subject-matter knowledge* refers to the knowledge an individual possesses relative to a specific field of study (e.g., biology, algebra, or agronomy; Alexander, Schallert, & Hare, 1991). Two forms of subject-matter knowledge are distinguished in the MDL: domain and topic knowledge. *Domain knowledge* represents the breadth or generality of knowledge including all the declarative, procedural, and conditional knowledge relative to a designated field (e.g., genetics or psychology). By comparison, *topic knowledge* characterizes depth of understanding about a topic (e.g., photosynthesis or the battle of the Alamo; Alexander et al., 1991).

As will be discussed in more detail, the MDL depicts domain knowledge and topic knowledge as working in concert. That is, the more topic knowledge learners have, the more domain knowledge they are projected to have. However, these two forms of subject-matter knowledge have also been shown to operate independently in certain learner groups. For example, Alexander, Kulikowich, and Schulze (1994) found that learners with more fragmented knowledge bases could provide information about domain-related topics (e.g., black holes) but were unable to associate those concepts with their associated domains (e.g., astrophysics). In contrast, they identified certain learners with moderate levels of knowledge in a certain domain (e.g., human immunology/human biology), but who were unfamiliar with selected topics drawn from that domain (e.g., bacteriophages). Thus, the correspondence between domain knowledge and topic knowledge, while understandably high, is not perfect and undergoes hypothesized changes over the course of one's domain learning.

The MDL also speaks to the role of affective or motivational variables in the movement toward expertise. *Interest* connotes the processes by which the underlying needs or desires of learners are energized (Ames & Ames, 1989; Dewey, 1913; Murphy & Alexander, 2000). Within the MDL, two forms of interest have been plotted (i.e., individual interest and situational interest). *Individual interest* refers to more long-term investment or deep-seated involvement in a pursuit (Hidi, 1990; Schiefele, 1991). In recent research, Alexander and colleagues have identified two forms of individual interest evident in expertise: general and professional (VanSledright & Alexander, 2002). *General interest* gives energy to pursuits in which an individual might engage in their everyday experience (e.g., watching historical documentaries). *Professional interest*, by comparison, is a more specialized, goal-oriented interest aligned with vocational or career activities (e.g., attending a psychology conference; Alexander, 2003b).

By comparison, *situational interest* represents more temporary arousal or attention and often tied to conditions within the immediate context (Schiefele, 1991). Hidi (1990) has suggested that this type of interest is necessarily fleeting because it is tied to the environment. Despite links to context, there appear to be some universals that appear to generally pique situational interest (e.g., sex or violence; Schank, 1979).

The third primary component in the MDL is strategic processing. Within the MDL, *strategic processing* denotes a form of procedural knowledge purposefully invoked to overcome perceived deficits in understanding or to circumvent potential barriers to learning. Strategic knowledge entails both surface-level strategies (e.g., rereading) and deep-processing strategies (e.g., elaboration). Specifically, surface-level strategies are defined as processes individuals use to make sense of a text. By comparison, deep-processing strategies involve delving into a given text to make meaning. So defined, the general strategy component of the MDL encompasses tools critical in the acquisition, transformation, and transfer of information (Pintrich et al., 1993).

Stages of the Model

As with several other developmental models or learning theories (e.g., Shuell, 1990; Spiro & Jehng, 1990), the MDL entails three stages. Woven through these three stages are the critical forces of subject-matter knowledge, interest, and strategic processing that serve as catalysts for structuring and restructuring within and across each stage. Thus, it is the configuration of these components that bridges the stages and gives them identifiable characteristics.

Acclimation. The initial stage of development toward expertise is referred to as acclimation. This stage is representative of that point when individuals are confronted with a domain for which they possess little if any relevant knowledge. As novices to the domain, individuals must acclimate or orient themselves to the domain by establishing a base of relevant knowledge and skills. During this stage of acclimation, individuals will begin to acquire knowledge but it will be fragmented and unprincipled (Gelman & Greeno, 1989). Due to this fragmentation, acclimated learners may demonstrate difficulties in differentiating relevant form irrelevant knowledge (Alexander, Jetton, Kulikowich, & Woehler, 1994), and experience difficulty associating information within a domain.

While students are acclimating to a domain, interest necessarily has a situation-dependency to it. That is, individuals within the acclimation stage are more apt to be influenced by transitory and short-lived conditions within the immediate context. In other words, they will be guided more by their situational interests than by any individual interest in the domain. Even if students will eventually possess an individual interest in the domain that interest needs time to take root and grow as the individual's knowledge grows. In addition, few deep-level procedures are specified since most of the tasks are novel and challenging (Alexander et al., 1996). Rather, acclimated learners must rely on their surface-level strategic knowledge if they are to build a relevant knowledge base. Overall, individuals in the acclimation stage demonstrate limited and fragmented knowledge of the subject, rely heavily on surface-level strategies, and report relatively higher levels of situational interest than individual interest.

Competence.   A number of changes take place during the phases of acclimation on the road to competence. For example, individuals evidence more principled, coherent subject-matter knowledge. Moreover, they are facile at applying this information in novel ways, and can more easily differentiate between relevant and irrelevant information.

A substantive increase in individual interest is predicted for competent learners. In essence, the rise in domain knowledge is correlated with a growth in individual interest (i.e., a personal investment in the field) and a decreased reliance on situational interest (e.g., Alexander, Kulikowich, & Schulze, 1994; Renninger, Hidi, & Krapp, 1992). In terms of strategic processing, more competent learners are focusing on expanding and elaborating the knowledge base, and necessarily require a period of optimal interplay between surface-level and deep-level. Specifically, there is a reduction in the need for surface-level processing due to prior knowledge acquired by the individual within a given domain. Concomitantly, competent learners have enough domain knowledge to employ deep-level strategies in effective and efficient ways. Moreover, the additional effort required for deep-level processing aligns with the substantive increases in individual interest and the decreasing reliance on situational interest during competence. Thus, the indicators of competence within a domain include a distinct increase in the breadth and depth of subject-matter knowledge, a deeper personal investment in the domain combined with decreased reliance on situationally interesting conditions, and finally a willingness to exert the effort necessary to employ deep-level processing strategies.

Proficiency.   The highest stage in the MDL is proficiency or expertise. Unlike the first stage change in which any one variable could move an individual forward, the change from competence to proficiency requires a synergy among subject-matter knowledge, interest, and strategic processing (Alexander, 2003a). Perhaps understandably, one of the only components, besides surface-level strategies, that do not exhibit a rise to at least a moderate level of intensity during the proficiency stage is situational interest. Rather, situational interest appears to exert a low-to-moderate influence on learning outcomes. The basis for this prediction is the determination that those judged as proficient or as an expert in a field can operate at a level of abstraction that makes them less bound to the conditions within the immediate environment. Thus, while experts may find particular facets of a situation intriguing, their attention or performance is not distracted from relevant goals or important content (Alexander, Jetton, et al., 1994).

Perhaps the most captivating component within the proficiency stage is that of subject-matter knowledge. The proficient or domain expert must go beyond the gradual acquisition of knowledge, and play a role in redefining the very base of knowledge that signifies a domain. In effect, these individuals are creating principled domain understandings. During the process of knowledge creation, subject-matter knowledge and individual interest become inextricably intertwined. Moreover, as the expert continues to generate new knowledge, they will also experience novel problems—problems for which they must also create strategies to solve. Thus, at this stage there is not necessarily an increase in strategy use, but the employment of deep-level strategies in novel ways.

Those individuals fortunate enough to achieve proficiency in a domain are distinguishable from competent learners in several ways. First, the subject-matter knowledge of an expert becomes increasingly dense and cohesive and proficient learners actually generate knowledge. In addition, individual interest and knowledge combine as a unified force. Finally, they may experience a slight rise in deeper strategic processing due to the knowledge generation and solving of novel domain problems, and a concomitant decrease in surface-level strategies.

In the next sections, we survey the vast variety of methodologies used by researchers to study expertise. As we will see, strategies have differed depending on: a) the theoretical framework of the investigators; b) the participants studied; c) the primary variables of interest; and, d) the contexts in which learning takes place (see Table 17.3). Focusing on the theoretical frameworks of Ackerman and Alexander, we compare and contrast the types of methodologies used to address their research questions. Our chapter closes with an overall look at unanswered questions about expertise. Through these questions, we

Table 17.3 Comparison among Methodologies Used by Psychological Sub-Disciplines in the Study of Adult Expertise

Parameters	Intelligence	Cognitive Science	Educational Research
Units of Analysis	Individuals	Individual Experts and Novices; Expert and Novice Teams	Individuals; Classrooms; Schools; Organizations
Sample Size	Large	Small	Small to Large
Variables	Single-/Multiple-Factor Intelligence; Second-/Third-Order Intelligence	Knowledge acquisition, Strategy Use, Problem Solving	Cognitive (e.g., achievement, aptitude); Intelligence (e.g., Crystallized, Fluid); Affective (e.g., Interest, Motivation), Personality (e.g., Introversion/Extroversion; Self-Concept); Beliefs
Tasks	Multiple-choice items, Short-answer items, Analogy problems, Block rotations, Puzzle completions	Think-alouds, Interviews, Group Discussions; Sorting Tasks, Graphical Constructions, Computerized Problem-based Learning Environments	Traditional to Performance Assessments; Rating Scales, Self-Report Inventories; Classroom Discussions/Internet Chatrooms; Hypermedia/Multimedia Tasks, Computerized Problem-based Learning Environments (e.g., Dynamic Assessments)
Methodological Approaches	Factor Analysis, Structural Equation Modeling	Proximity Analysis, General Linear Model (e.g., ANOVA)	Qualitative Methods; Proximity Analysis; General Linear Model (e.g., ANOVA); Latent Variable Modeling Procedures (e.g., IRT, SEM); Cognitive Psychometric Approaches (e.g., Error Analysis, Rule-space Analysis).

offer an agenda of research that may be adopted to not only understand expertise better but also to assist more individuals in reaching the pinnacles of success in their chosen domains of practice.

Methodological Threads in the Study of Expertise

In this section, we examine two methodological threads that have been influential in the study of expertise. First, the testing tradition that emerged from Galton's work on intelligence continues to thrive in research and practice. Starting with Binet's first test of general mental abilities, which Terman used in his study of youths identified with exceptional talent, to Sternberg's program of research, which incorporates principles of cognitive psychology into the study of various types of intelligence, assessment has been a key force in portraying the individual differences of students (Keating, 1990). Related to this point is that there has been no mathematical distribution more important than the normal distribution to depict how individuals' performance based on item and test scores stands relative to one another.

This strand of methodology is suited ideally to study multivariate relations based on performance, product, or self-report scores. Performance, product, or self-report scores such as those derived from intelligence and knowledge measures, interest scales, and self-concept inventories are often treated as outcome measures predicted by latent traits (Barrett, 2005; McGrath, 2005). Latent traits are unobservable psychology constructs like intelligence, creativity, motivation, and interest that predict response patterns on tests and measures (McDonald, 1999). Latent variable modeling (e.g., Item Response Theory [IRT]; Reise, Widaman, & Pugh, 1993; or Structural Equation Modeling [SEM]; Reise, Widaman, & Pugh, 1993), therefore, has been a primary means by which researchers test their hypotheses. These techniques are commonplace in the work of Sternberg, Ackerman, and Alexander.

However, these methods of task development and data analysis have not allowed researchers to study the processing that differentiates experts and novices or that leads to proficiency in any domain. Here, qualitative, descriptive tools such as think aloud and verbal protocol analyses have served as better means to explore individual differences than scores on tests or self-report inventories. The second thread of methodology we review finds its roots in cognitive science and can be seen in the work of Lajoie. Specifically, cognitive scientists were and continue to be interested in how individuals move through problem spaces (e.g., Bransford & Stein, 1993), and what the interaction between knowledge and strategies looks like as they attempt to complete domain-specific tasks. Lajoie has built an entire body of research around the use of dynamic assessments which are essentially computer platforms that capture individuals' movements through complex problem spaces. We now examine each of these threads in turn.

Methods in the Study of Intelligence

The methodologies used to study intelligence have looked quite different from those employed in the study of domain-specific expertise. Yet, both bodies of work contribute to an understanding of what characterizes adult proficiency. The primary difference in these approaches is that expert-novice researchers focused their attention on individuals whose performance characterized extremes of the normal distribution (i.e., the very low and the very high). By comparison, researchers who study intelligence often do so with an eye toward testing where resultant scores represent the complete continuum of performance. Standardized tests of intelligence must yield reliable and valid sets of scores.

Since the fundamental principles of reliability and validity rest on mathematical foundations of the normal distribution (e.g., Campbell & Fiske, 1959; Cattell, 1952; Spearman, 1904; Cronbach & Meehl, 1955), researchers who study intelligence must construct a broad array of verbal and performance tasks that can depict differences with adult populations (e.g., Wechsler, 1981). Because the need to sample a large variety of tasks becomes essential in terms of matching intelligence scores to tasks that incrementally vary in difficulty (Lord & Novick, 1968), intelligence theorists cannot readily afford administering a set of problem-space tasks like cognitive scientists. Simply, conducting think alouds, interviews, sorting tasks, or graph constructions, which we will discuss subsequently, is not a realistic undertaking. It would take too much time, and the scores are not as psychometrically trustworthy as what can be obtained using traditional measures like multiple-choice or short-answer items that can efficiently cover a broad array of topics drawn from multiple domains. Therefore, those who measure intelligence tend to keep their tasks simple. If they do include tasks in their battery, these exercises (e.g., block rotations or puzzle completion) can be assembled and administered quickly to cover the spectrum of abilities that define general views of intelligence (e.g, generalized intelligence, Spearman, 1904; crystallized and fluid intelligence, Cattell, 1941; verbal and performance intelligence, Wechsler, 1981).

The difficulty intelligence theorists soon encountered when faced with the administration a large set of items or tasks is how to reduce the responses to establish that a single set or small group of scores are reliable and valid. Fortunately, developments in theories of intelligence were concurrent with study of mathematical tools that could reduce correlated patterns of item scores. It was common, therefore, to find intelligence theorists such as Cattell (1952) or Thurstone (1938) to be as much an experts in mathematics/statistics as they were in psychology. Factor analysis became the means by which researchers established the underlying constructs that predicted responses to items/tasks (Carroll, 1993). To this day, it remains the primary mathematical tool among researchers in the social sciences to establish construct validity. Further, with ongoing developments in computer programming, factor-analytic methods have progressed to include measurement models with structural equations where dependent latent constructs can be regressed on a set of independent factors or variables. These types of tools have been useful to test theoretical models. As mentioned, these tools are nested in a family of latent variable modeling techniques that include Item Response Theory (IRT; Baker, 1992; Lord, 1980; Lord & Novick, 1968), Multilevel or Hierarchical Linear Modeling (HLM; Bryk & Raudenbush, 1992; Hox, 1995; Singer, 1998), and Structural Equation Modeling (SEM; Bollen, 1989, Browne, & Cudeck, 1993).

Cognitive Science and Task Analyses

When reviewing the types of methodologies utilized by researchers to study expertise from the perspective of cognitive science, one pattern emerges above all others: the methodologies differ significantly from those used by intelligence theorists. Specifically, the cognitive science tradition is one that does not rest on large-scale testing to the degree found in studies on intelligence. For cognitive scientists, many of whom were invested in pioneering work in artificial intelligence (Anderson, 1987; Chase & Simon, 1973; Clancey, 1985; Kolodner, 1983; Shanteau & Stewart, 1992), the primary goal was to compare problem-solving processes of experts and novices in an effort to inform the programming of computer systems that could be accessed for deep stores of knowledge and corresponding decision-making strategies useful for solving problems in a particular domain (e.g., avionics, economics, or medicine).

Cognitive science offered the first formal study of expertise by examining how people interacted with carefully constructed or selected problem spaces (Hoffman, Shadbolt, Burton, & Klein, 1995; Olson & Biolsi, 1991). Initially, these spaces were very artificial or knowledge-lean as in the missionary/cannibal problem. Methodologically, the steps required for solution were rather sequential as these problem spaces introduced much structure when presented to the problem solver.

In time, however, cognitive scientists came to appreciate that not all problems within a given domain are well-structured (e.g., algorithmic steps or correct solutions) and for some domains like economics and marketing (e.g., Cross, 1988), medicine (Arocha & Patel, 1995; Patel, Groen, & Arocha, 1990), and literacy (Scardamalia & Bereiter, 1991), the problem spaces are more ill-defined and ill-structured. As a result, experts employ heuristic strategies (i.e., guidelines). These strategies often result in more nonlinear movements through the space than linear sequences that result in correct or best solutions (Spiro, Vispoel, Schmitz, Samarapungavan, & Boerger, 1987). An entire subdiscipline of cognitive science is dedicated to the study of problem spaces. This realm of research is referred to as cognitive task analysis (e.g., Essens, Post, & Rasker, 2002; Schraagen, Chipman, & Shalin, 2000), and it classifies the various types of problem sets encountered by experts representing various domains.

For some problem spaces, individuals must troubleshoot (e.g., electronics and engineering). That is, the problem requires individuals to fix one or more operations that are not working properly such as in the case of a mechanic who replaces the transmission of an engine so that the vehicle accelerates and decelerates correctly on the road. Troubleshooting tasks, as a result, require individuals to use significant amounts of conditional knowledge (Alexander, 1997). Conditional knowledge is knowledge of when and why a particular concept or procedure would be facilitative. Experts have significantly more conditional knowledge than novices. Experts are not only able to detect why something is not working correctly, but they also possess the suitable strategies to fix the problem efficiently and effectively.

Troubleshooting tasks are not the only types of problem spaces studied by cognitive scientists. Other problem spaces are characterized as novel (e.g., locating submarines, Gray & Kirschenbaum, 2000; navigating the sea, Hutchins, 1996). In these instances, cognitive scientists have no preset notions as to how problem solvers will move toward solution. Hutchins (1996) refers to this type of problem-solving experience as *cognition in the wild*.

A final set of problem-solving spaces require experts to construct or create their problem environments as in the case of inventing or modeling (e.g., human factors engineering, Essens et al., 2000). This form of problem-solving activity allows for creativity, as in the case of architects who sketch blueprints for buildings and landscapes. And, more recently, these types of creative enterprises have been linked with developments in technology. For instance, investigators can study problem spaces that are dynamic and open, permitting one individual or a team of members to move in and out of activity as in the case of a business firm like Ford or General Motors working on new designs for cars and trucks (Gorman, Tweney, Gooding, & Kincannon, 2005). Here, experts who differ in terms of their areas of expertise (e.g., engineering, graphic design, marketing) work together to accomplish complex tasks.

Think-Alouds and Interviews

Independent of the types of problem spaces analyzed by cognitive scientists, two primary methodologies have been used to explore aspects of expertise and what makes experts' knowledge and performance profiles distinguishable from those of non-experts. Specifically, think-aloud protocol analyses and interviews have been the means by which researchers came to understand how memory capacity, strategy use, recovery from error, and storage of knowledge around principles are hallmarks of domain proficiency (Hoffman et al., 1995; Olson & Biolsi, 1991). So rich was the collection of studies on think-aloud methodology that Ericsson and Simon (1993) wrote a classic book entitled, *Protocol Analysis: Verbal Reports as Data* to offer guidelines for eliciting more reliable and valid data about knowledge and problem-solving strategies.

Although the think-aloud methods showcased knowledge and strategy use during the course of problem solving, interviews both for individuals and groups offered reflections on past performance or speculations on future performance (e.g., de Jong & Ferguson-Hessler, 1986). There are many types of interview procedures that can be used depending on the purposes of the researchers. Unstructured interviews are open-ended. Interviewers ask participants a general question such as; *tell me everything you know about the solar system* (Wood & Ford, 1993). The benefit of unstructured interviews is that participants can draw on a wide array of personal and professional experiences, including references to what interests them most, setbacks they have had in their careers, and sources of inspiration to pursue excellence. A limitation of unstructured interviews is that responses can be long or meander around a host of topics without any sense of cohesion. Alternatively, participants may have difficulty elaborating upon the knowledge and ideas they share. This is a common problem among experts as they try to draw from their rich and tightly networked structures of knowledge (Pressley & Afflerbach, 1995). Likewise, this is a common problem among novices who struggle in their attempts to describe fragmented parcels of knowledge that may be interspersed with misconceptions.

A variation on the open-ended interview is the structured interview. Here the researcher introduces more scaffolding into the questions asked of respondents. Questions can be domain-general, domain-specific, or topic-specific, but they are generally based on an inventory of concepts and procedures that are central to the domain of interest and the problems solved within it. Shadbolt and Burton (1990) extended the methods of structured interviews by establishing what are called *probe sets*. Probe sets are constructed around taxonomies. Interviewers begin with questions asked to get a respondent's overall sense of the domain and its scope (e.g., Can you tell me about the latest research projects completed by you and your colleagues?).

Based on the responses provided, the interviewer sets parameters around the next set of questions by focusing on concepts mentioned in the interview (e.g., Can you describe electromagnetism? Can you tell me the difference between the strong and weak nuclear forces?). After querying for concepts, the interviewer then probes for the types of procedures or mechanistic processes that are key to the domain's activity (e.g., How does a supercollider work? What does a Feynman diagram show you?). These procedures can relate to steps used to solve problems in the domain such as use of the scientific method or mathematical proof construction. These procedures can be associated with explanations for how models or tools of the domain work or operate (e.g., Doppler effect or standard model).

Finally, the questions may pertain to the ways the field represents information or how the expert represents information in an effort to communicate concepts, principles, and procedures to others (e.g., diagrams, graphs, or equations). Rounding out the probe set are questions geared toward an understanding of unusual experiences or insights that have reshaped or restructured one's thinking about the field and representing problems within it (e.g., aha! experiences, anomalies in data, or novel discoveries).

Contrived Tasks

Sometimes researchers weave contrived tasks within protocol analysis or interview studies. Introduction of contrived tasks serves as another means to frame participants' responses so they do not roam all over the place. Usually, these contrived tasks are built around principles and procedures of the domain. For example, researchers interested in proficiency in physics may ask respondents to sort a set of word problems into piles dependent on important structural relations among fundamental principles of the domain (e.g., force-mass-acceleration or distance-rate-time). Similarly, investigators attempting to observe the interplay between knowledge and strategies in a domain that is characterized by high levels of motor performance (e.g., athletics or music) may ask participants to compare and contrast characteristics of those who are considered eminent in their fields (e.g., basketball: Larry Bird, Michael Jordan; classical music: Bach, Mozart) in an effort to reflect on the patterns of individual differences that contribute to hallmarks of excellence in their fields.

Ludwig (1995, 1998) and Martindale (1990) have conducted studies to describe how the interaction between knowledge/ingenuity and personality factors contributes to level of productivity in the domain and its quality. Participants rate the degree to which characteristics about an elite performer fall on a low-to-high continuum. Attributes selected to compare individuals might encompass sets related to: a) work patterns; b) styles of human interaction; c) medical histories (e.g., mental illness); d) impact on the field; and, e) onset and longevity of expertise.

What contrived tasks provide researchers that protocols and interviews may not is a way of coding characteristics efficiently so that they may be subjected to statistical analysis (Hoffman et al., 1995; Olson & Biolsi, 1991). Researchers can examine how many piles are sorted or profiles of ratings on various performance and personality factors using proximity analysis techniques. Proximity analyses are basically correlational analyses. Objects or people are examined for how similar or different they are from one another. For example, grapefruits and oranges would likely be related for high similarity of proximity for they are two types of citrus fruits. Grapefruits and lettuce, however, would likely be rated as highly dissimilar with low proximity as one is a citrus fruit and the other is a leafy vegetable.

When there is a large group of objects to be rated as pairs that are similar or dissimilar, the frequency of proximities can make detection of patterns of relation very difficult for investigators. As a result, these researchers subject a matrix of proximities to data reduction techniques that can mathematically determine the basic underlying patterns of similarity. Cluster analysis and multidimensional scaling are two common forms of data reduction techniques for proximity matrices (Olson & Biolsi, 1991). These data-analytic tools also permit investigators an opportunity to reduce the data into patterns that can be observed visually. So for the grapefruit, orange, and lettuce example, the results might show two general groupings of fruits and vegetables. A flexible feature of these quantitative tools is that data can be analyzed just for one individual or a large group of individuals, or for comparison between groups, such as experts and non-experts.

As early as 1974, Shavelson used proximity analysis methods to explore the memory structures of students in science. Following an information-processing model of memory structure (e.g., Badderly, 1992; Norman, 1969), Shavelson assigned participants to treatment and control conditions where each group was assigned two tasks: word associations and graph constructions. Proximity analyses were then used to explore the structural relations among objects and how they changed over time from those who received instruction in science and those who did not. Based on the data, Shavelson made conclusions about which participants were able to move incoming information through their working memory to long-term store where it could be structured in principled form. Not only did those receiving instruction acquire more concepts and procedures in time (based on the word-associations task), but they also made tighter connections among concepts and procedures (based on the graph constructions) than control counterparts. These types of data summaries, therefore, helped researchers in cognitive science support several of the conclusions noted in our introduction. Specifically, from the first generation of expertise studies, these researchers learned that: *Experts perceive the underlying structure of problems whereas novices are distracted by more surface-level features of problems*; and from the second generation: *Experts possess an extensive body of domain knowledge that is coherently and efficiently organized.*

Standard Statistical Procedures

Cognitive scientists have relied on simpler ways to study expertise differences. Comparing means on knowledge-acquisition outcome measures such as free recalls, reading tasks, and word problems using classical analysis of variance (ANOVA) techniques or multiple regression (e.g., Murphy & Alexander, 2002; Renkl, 1997) have been commonplace. These techniques afford researchers an opportunity to conduct meta-analyses (Glass, 1978; Hunter & Schmidt, 1990) to determine whether manipulations in the task environment (e.g., animation, multiple representations, or seductive details) alter differences between expert and non-experts performances.

Meta-analyses are reviews of the literature that gauge the magnitude of a statistical effect over a series of investigations. For example, the use of the worked example in algebra-based word problems has a long and extensive history (e.g., Mousavi, Low, & Sweller, 1995; Sweller & Cooper, 1985); thus there are many quantitative investigations to form a data pool for a meta-analysis (Renkl & Atkinson, 2003). What these analyses attempt to reveal is what amount and type of instructional intervention promote knowledge acquisition for non-experts. Renkl and Atkinson's summary demonstrated that the worked example facilitates problem solving for novices. Yet, for experts, the inclusion of problem solutions can be detrimental as knowledge structures become more tightly organized around principles. As a result, problem solving looks automatic. In short, the worked examples are excess parcels of information that draw knowledgeable individuals away from their solution path.

Educational Researchers: Weaving Together the Methodological Threads

Unlike researchers who study intelligence or cognitive scientists who address questions about problem spaces, educational researchers must weave together both theoretical and methodological traditions in an effort to help school-aged learners or adults in the workplace. Central to their programs of research, investigators in education must address primary questions related to instruction and assessment. As such, their frameworks for understanding adult expertise must include variables that are more common among cognitive scientists (e.g., conceptual change, knowledge acquisition, or strategy use), as well as those of intelligence theorists (e.g., general vocabulary knowledge, spatial reasoning, or speed-of-processing). In addition, educational researchers must include variables that tie more closely to lines of inquiry in motivation and personality, for students come to schools with a plethora of individual differences. As a result, these researchers connect their variables in a system in an effort to explain what contributes to, as well as derails, progress toward expertise. Only within these tests, can these researchers gain insights into instructional methods that can help those who struggle, as well as feed the roots of expertise. Additionally, educational researchers must be mindful of the assessments they use as those assessments serve not only as a means to measure achievement but also as a form of feedback for instruction that can correct errors, eliminate misconceptions (Alexander et al., 1998; Kulikowich & Alexander, 1994, 2003; Lajoie & Lesgold, 1992), or troubleshoot ineffective problem-solving routines (e.g., Lesgold, Lajoie, Bunzo, & Eggan, 1992).

Ackerman and Factor Analysis

To test the tenets of PPIK, Ackerman and colleagues use factor-analytic and correlational methods. Several instruments are used to assess aptitude, trait complexes, and knowledge structures, respectively. In the case of knowledge structures, for example, Ackerman (2003a) built 20 multiple-choice measures to cover the broad spectrum of science and social science subject-matter areas that depicted primary areas in which expertise is likely to become manifest. Scores on these 20 knowledge measures were subjected to factor analysis. Five primary factors emerged representing the knowledge structures (i.e., physical sciences/technology, civics, humanities, current events, and business) represented in his theoretical framework. Factor analyses have also been used to reduce trait measures so that complexes can be formed (Ackerman, Bowen, Beier, & Kanfer, 2001).

Once the factor analyses are used to reduce sets of scores into aptitude complexes, trait complexes, and knowledge structures, Ackerman and colleagues conduct correlation analyses to detect profiles of individual differences across the variable sets. This is how Ackerman is able to determine that individuals with a lot of fluid intelligence are likely to show dispositions toward study of science and mathematical topics that are likely, in turn, to lead to knowledge acquisition and vocational pursuits in the physical sciences and technology. By comparison, correlational patterns reveal that individuals who have significant amount of crystallized intelligence tend also to have strong proclivities to social and cultural affairs and, as a result, demonstrate achievement in civics, the humanities, and business arenas. These individuals are also likely to know much about current events.

Sternberg and Aptitude-Treatment Interactions

Sternberg's methodology is very similar to that of Ackerman. Relying extensively on factor analytic procedures, Sternberg and colleagues attempt to establish the reliability and validity of the various types of intelligence they study. To date, however, Sternberg has been able to study directly aptitude-treatment-interactions (Snow, 1989) using analysis of variance techniques to a greater extent than Ackerman. The ability to test instructional variables in relation to aptitude profiles is largely due to the fact that Sternberg's modeling framework does not include as many variable sets as in the PPIK framework of

Ackerman. Nonetheless, both scholars are interested in how instructional platforms can best be matched to aptitude and personality factors.

For example, Sternberg, Torff, and Grigorenko (1998a, 1998b) studied elementary- and middle-grade students as they learned about topics in science and social studies. They used experimental procedures and assigned students randomly to one of three conditions based on their intelligence theory framework. In condition one, students received regular classroom instruction. In condition two, instruction focused on critical and analytic thinking. In condition three, the intervention focused not only on analytic thinking but also creative and practical thinking. As such, this arm of the intervention represented the successful intelligence condition. Outcome measures included both multiple-choice knowledge measures as well as performance-based assessment tasks. As expected, results of ANOVA procedures supported the researchers' expectations. Students assigned to instruction where successful intelligence was prioritized as key to academic success outperformed peers on knowledge and aptitude outcomes. Similar results from ANOVA procedures have been found for high-school students who may be experiencing academic challenges similar to those one would expect for young adults beginning to choose one or more domains (e.g., biology, engineering, or history) in which they may eventually demonstrate expertise (Grigorenko et al., 2002).

Lajoie and Case Studies

Lajoie's methodologies rest on case studies of adults working through computerized problem spaces given a variety of tasks representing a variety of domains. As a result, Lajoie and her colleagues more so than Ackerman, Sternberg, and Alexander follow the classical cognitive science tradition in terms of their investigations on expertise. Still, like her contemporary colleagues, Lajoie recognizes the importance of both instruction and assessment in moving non-experts along so that they can begin to perform like experts. Her dynamic assessments are computerized problem spaces that evaluate the progress of individuals as they attempt completion of tasks. The assessment systems are also designed to provide feedback so that problem solvers can begin to detect solution paths that effectively and efficiently lead to solutions.

In using case study analyses, Lajoie's work is perhaps the most qualitative of the group of researchers who have espoused contemporary models of expertise. However, her procedures for analysis follow many of the design strategies evidenced in experimental research (Lajoie & Lesgold, 1992). For example, Lajoie and Lesgold built a computer-coaching tool called Sherlock I to teach troubleshooting skills in avionics. Each participant worked through the Sherlock system in a series of stages. First, the participants completed pretests to measure knowledge, strategies, and plans associated with avionics. Then, the participant progressed through a set of three tutorial exercises that incrementally increased in difficulty. The difficulty was determined through comparisons of expert and novice performance. So, when participants finally completed the last task, their performance began to exemplify the knowledge, strategies, and plans used by experts.

To achieve its desired ends, the dynamic assessment system constructed by Lajoie and colleagues is programmed as a smart tool (Bransford et al., 1996). Specifically, as participants interacted with each tutorial, there was a constant stream of feedback to correct misconceptions and provide suggestions for more efficient plans that resulted in problem solutions. After completion of the third tutorial, participants completed a posttest. Experts in avionics were enlisted to evaluate pretest to posttest performance.

As anticipated, there was a noticeable difference between final and initial scores on outcome measures. Initially, participants' strategies and plans were random and incomplete with minimal evidence on monitoring for more efficient solutions. At posttest, strategies were executed efficiently with evidence that both conditional and principled knowledge not only increased but was also used effectively to reach problem-solving goals (Lajoie & Lesgold, 1992).

Alexander and Cluster Analysis

Alexander and her colleagues have studied the developmental trajectory of expertise using tools like those employed by Ackerman, Sternberg, and Lajoie. In addition, cluster analysis and SEM models are prevalent in their work. As mentioned previously, cluster analysis is a data reduction tool. Like factor analysis, it can be used to study how scores on items and tasks fall into particular groupings, but it can also be used to demonstrate how profiles of individuals' response patterns across a set of variables reduce into prototypic cases. In this fashion, Alexander and her colleagues (Alexander et al. 1995; Alexander & Murphy, 1998) have used cluster analysis to characterize groups that emerge based on students' knowledge, strategies, and interest scores. As related examples, Lawless and Kulikowich (1996, 1998) ran cluster analyses to establish profiles among hypertext users. Their hypertext systems traced the paths of readers using time-stamped data collection methods that can be subjected to log-file analysis. Essentially, log files are just performance protocols that can be captured by a computer system (Young, Kulikowich, & Barab, 1997).

What distinguishes the work of Alexander and her colleagues from that of Ackerman and Sternberg is there is a greater emphasis on the types of knowledge students possess in one domain. This is similar to the work of Lajoie, but it is also different in important ways. Whereas Lajoie's work focuses on problem-solving outcomes, Alexander and her colleagues have invested considerable time look at reading-based outcomes. Simply, Alexander's MDL starts with knowledge and it ends with knowledge by means of acquisition of subject-matter information from texts. These types of text-based outcomes have ranged from simple recalls or retellings (Alexander, Kulikowich, & Schulze, 1994) to more complex comprehension exercises, as in the case of understanding arguments presented in persuasive texts (Murphy & Alexander, 2004). Because knowledge begins and ends at important starting and ending points to determine where individuals are located in stages, SEM models have also served as extremely useful tools to establish that students are moving along a trajectory and that variables specified in the MDL, such as strategy use and individual interest contribute to this movement (Alexander, Murphy, Woods, Duhon, & Parker, 1997).

Additionally, and as evidenced in the work of Lajoie, task and test construction for variables of the MDL has drawn extensively from developments in cognitive psychometric theory (e.g., Katz, Martinez, Sheehan, & Tatsuoka, 1998; Mislevy, 1993; Tatsuoka, 1983, 1985). Specifically, both Alexander and Lajoie have attended greatly to the types of errors students make and the misconceptions they hold. For example, Alexander and colleagues (Alexander, Murphy, & Kulikowich, 1998, Kulikowich & Alexander, 1994) built vocabulary multiple-choice items and analogy problems so that errors could be graded in terms of degree of accuracy. The results from this program of research were very informative. These findings showed that the majority of students' error patterns were nonrandom, meaning that a specific gap in knowledge or processing could be isolated. As a result, instruction could be geared toward filling the knowledge gap, providing remediation for misconceptions, or explicitly teaching strategies that could facilitate knowledge acquisition by means of reading and problem solving (Kulikowich, in press).

Finally, in many instances (e.g., Garner, Alexander, Gillingham, Kulikowich, & Brown, 1991; Judy, Alexander, Kulikowich, & Willson, 1998), Alexander and her colleagues have depended greatly on experimental procedures to test tenets tied to hypotheses about when and why knowledge acquisition or strategy use occurs or does not occur. For example, Alexander and her colleagues were among the first to demonstrate that analogical reasoning could be taught to very young children (e.g., White, Alexander, & Daugherty, 1998) in an effort to help them bridge domain knowledge and strategy use. Analogical reasoning remains a mainstay in Alexander's study of adults' developing expertise (e.g., Alexander & Murphy, 1998; Alexander et al., 1998).

While experimental procedures using ANOVA designs have helped to show that use of analogies can lead to knowledge acquisition, intervention studies using ANOVA procedures have also demonstrated that adults can be non-strategic. For instance, insertions of seductive details or highly salient but irrelevant sources of information often pertaining to death, power, or sex in texts can distract readers' attention away from information that should be comprehended as important (Alexander, Kulikowich, & Schulze, 1994). Specifically, mean recalls of students assigned to text conditions with seductive details compared to students assigned to conditions without seductive details showed that the first group recalled significantly less domain-relevant information than the second group which was very good at jotting down the very interesting, but unimportant bit of information (e.g., Stephen Hawking's wager with Kip Thorne for an issue of Penthouse magazine). Collectively, the cluster analysis, SEM, error analysis, and experimental design approaches have contributed to establishing the MDL as a viable framework for the study of developing expertise.

Final Prognostications: The Future of Expertise in Research and Practice

Throughout this chapter, we have explored the distant past of expertise theory and research and three more contemporary generations, each with its own perspective, goals, and methodologies. Our purpose was to understand the nature of expertise and to examine the forces that contribute to expertise development. While it is relatively easy to look back over the centuries and decades in an effort to describe the state of expertise research, it is far more risky to ask what will become. What will the next generation of expertise research bring? What particular trends will capture the foci and contributions of expertise research in the next 10 years? What research methodologies will surface as most useful or informative in that next iteration?

If we are to project forward based on current trends in expertise theory and research, we believe we can at least glimpse some of that future. Thus, we offer five prognostications related to expertise theory and to the influence of expertise research on everyday practice.

The Road to Expertise Will Become as Important as the Final Destination

As we have witnessed, there has been an increased attention to the trajectory or the path that individuals may follow as they progress toward competence or expertise. This emphasis was a distinguishing characteristic of the third and current generation of expertise theory and research. Nonetheless, the trajectories or paths that have been plotted to date remain largely sketchy and speculative, and the expert/non-expert contrasts still dominate the literature. In the future, the paths that mark expertise development will become more richly specified and the expert/non-expert distinctions will give way to a more developmental orientation—an orientation that stresses the process of *becoming* more competent or more expert.

Longitudinal Investigations Will Be Undertaken

Before the developmental orientation toward expertise becomes a reality, several related transformations must occur within subsequent generations. Among the most critical changes in the empirical landscape is that theory and research can no longer be based solely on cross-sectional investigations—regardless of how well conceived or how theoretically grounded. What are needed are longitudinal studies of expertise. We appreciate that extended longitudinal studies, like that conducted by Terman, are unlikely for a multitude of reasons (e.g., funding requirements and human subject guidelines). However, we still see studies that extend over several years as a hallmark of the next generation of expertise research, especially transitional periods (e.g., transition from school to the workplace). As expertise researchers track the specific cognitive and motivational changes that occur in individuals over time, it will be possible to more fully and completely profile individuals at different points in their journey toward expertise. These longitudinal studies will also contribute to more accurate mapping of the developmental paths individuals traverse.

Multidimensionality of Models and Theories Will Be Expanded

Despite the advancements in multidimensionality witnessed between the second and third generations of expertise research, the scope still remains somewhat limited with regard to the variables examined. Yet, several research trends gaining momentum in the literature may well find their way into future studies of expertise development. Among those trends are the growing interest in emotions and their role in human learning and development (e.g., Bell & Calkins, 2000; Bråten & Olauseen, 2005; Van Yperen & Janssen, 2002). Such emotional dimensions, foreshadowed by the trait complexes of Ackerman (2003b) could enrich current efforts to explore the "hot" side of cognition at work within expertise development.

It is also conceivable that the burgeoning studies in neurology, neuroscience, neuropsychology, and related fields will contribute new insights into the cognitive and noncognitive attributes of those at various points in their growth trajectories (e.g., Donald, 2001; Keating, 2004). Are there structural differences in the brains of those who achieve higher levels of expertise than those who do not, for example? What neurological correlates should be considered in the examination of expertise development? Neurological fields may also shed light on the real-time processing of those engaged in domain-specific tasks of varying complexity; thus shaping what we know about expertise development (Berninger & Corine, 1998; Berninger & Richards, 2002). For instance, what can neuroimaging studies reveal about the way that those new to a domain and those considered highly competent or proficient in that domain mentally engage with a given problem or task?

Further, it might be argued that the role of situation or context as a dimension of expertise development has had little place in past or contemporary models or theories. One of the most salient aspects of situation or context that would seem relevant to discussions of expertise development is culture. Are the expertise models and theories articulated to this point presumably generalizable across diverse cultures? Or, will it become essential for expertise researchers to nest the study of expertise within particular sociocultural contexts? There certainly appears to be sufficient sociocultural research that would cast some doubt over arguments for universality of expertise models and theories (Keating, 2004; Walker, Hill, Kaplan, & McMillan, 2002). At a minimum, those invested in furthering existing knowledge about expertise will want to consider the dimension of culture or cultural context in future programs of research.

Interventions Studies Will Become More Commonplace

Overwhelmingly, the patterns and findings reported in the literature on expertise, regardless of which generation, have been built on correlational or descriptive studies. What have been long missing within this literature are intervention investigations that actually seek to create the conditions that should propel individuals forward toward expertise in a given domain. The work of Alexander and colleagues, for example, would seem to lend itself to interventions framed in the tenets of the MDL. For instance, we would expect that interventions formulated around the knowledge principles of a given academic domain in which strategies are explicitly taught within the context of meaningful domain-specific problems and in which individual interest was intentionally nourished should fuel expertise development. We, therefore, predict that the next generation of expertise research will abandon its over-reliance on correlational and descriptive investigations and become known for interventional studies.

The Workplace Will Become a Relevant Context for Expertise Research

Across the contemporary generations of expertise research, we saw significant change in the context deemed suitable for investigation. Within the first and second generation the parameters for study were particular problem-solving contexts that either constrained or augmented the influence of the respondents' background knowledge. In the third generation that context widened to embrace academic domains like history or science. Ackerman's studies also considered the trait complexes associated with expertise in particular professions. It seems logical, therefore, that future investigations will pay greater attention to the workplace as yet another viable context for expertise development.

Expertise development continues across the lifespan—it does not end with the completion of formal schooling, whether one's schooling concludes with high school, college, or even graduate school. It is likely within the realm of work that the knowledge, strategies, and interests acquired through the educational process are extended and elaborated through meaningful application. Thus, our prognostication is that the next generation will represent an era of lifespan expertise development where the workplace is conceived as a relevant and nature venue for systematic investigation.

New Methodologies Will Be Applied or Will Be Devised To Permit More Sensitive Testing of Emergent Expertise

None of the predictions we have made to this point will come to fruition without concomitant developments in the methodologies associated with expertise research. Among the changes that we envision for the next generation will be the incorporation of innovative statistical procedures that will allow for both micro-analytic and macro-analytic studies.

As the questions about the nature and development of expertise become increasingly more complex and the context and tasks become more ill-structured and "messy," it will be critical to adopt and adapt the statistical tools that are plied. For example, one facet of the MDL that has been understudied is the phases—the dynamic interplay of knowledge, strategies, and interests that occurs with each task engagement. Devising the tasks that permit these phases to be evidenced and tracked over time will be a challenge for expertise methodologists, along with the identification of viable statistical procedures to analyze and interpret the resulting data. However, these are just the kind of challenges that will further energize studies of expertise development.

What we have offered are just five predictions about future theory and research that we anticipate within the next ten years. There are clearly other possibilities that could be forwarded for consideration. Yet, whether these particular outcomes are realized or not, we remain confident that the fascination with expertise and experts, evident throughout human history, will continue unabated. The more that we come to understand the nature of expertise and the more skilled we become at mapping its course across the lifespan, the better guides we become for those undertaking the journey toward expertise in schools and in the workplace.

References

Ackerman, P. L. (1996). A theory of adult intellectual development: Process, personality, interests, and knowledge. *Intelligence, 22*, 229–259.

Ackerman, P. L. (2000). Domain-specific knowledge as the "dark matter" of adult intelligence: Gf/Gc, personality and interest correlates. *Journal of Gerontology: Psychological Sciences, 55*(2), 69–84.

Ackerman, P. L. (2003a). Aptitude complexes and trait complexes. *Educational Psychologist, 38*, 85–93.

Ackerman, P. L. (2003b). Cognitive ability and non-ability trait determinants of expertise. *Educational Researcher, 32*, 15–20.

Ackerman, P. L., Bowen, K. R., Beier, M. B., & Kanfer, R. (2001). Determinants of individual differences and gender differences in knowledge. *Journal of Educational Psychology, 93*, 797–825.

Ackerman, P. L., & Heggestad, E. D. (1997). Intelligence, personality, and interests: Evidence for overlapping traits. *Psychological Bulletin, 121*, 219–245.

Ackerman, P. L., Kyllonen, P. C., & Roberts, R. D. (1999). *Learning and individual differences: Process, trait, and content determinants.* Washington, DC: American Psychological Association.

Ackerman, P. L., & Rolfhus, E. L. (1999). The locus of adult intelligence: Knowledge, abilities, and non-ability traits. *Psychology and Aging, 14*, 314–330.

Ahmad, A., & Lajoie, S. P. (2001). The integrated learning model. In J. D. Moore, C. Redfield, & L. W. Johnson (Eds.), *Artificial intelligence in education* (pp. 354–364). Amsterdam: IOS Press.

Ainley, M. D. (1998). Interest in learning in the disposition of curiosity in secondary students: Investigating process and context. In L. Hoffman, A. Krapp, K. Renninger, & J. Baumert (Eds.), *Interest and learning: Proceedings of the Seeon Conference on interest and gender* (pp. 257–266). Kiel, Germany: IPN.

Alexander, P. A. (1997). Mapping the multidimensional nature of domain learning: The interplay of cognitive, motivational, and strategic forces. In M. L. Maehr, & P. R. Pintrich (Eds.), *Advances in motivation and achievement* (Vol. 10, pp. 213–250). Greenwich, CT: JAI Press.

Alexander, P. A. (2003a). Profiling the developing reader: The interplay of knowledge, interest, and strategic processing. In C. M. Fairbanks, J. Worthy, B. Maloch, J. V. Hoffman, & D. L. Schallert (Eds.), *The fifty-first yearbook of the National Reading Conference.* Oak Creek, WI: National Reading Conference.

Alexander, P. A. (2003b). The development of expertise: The journey from acclimation to proficiency. *Educational Researcher, 32*, 10–14.

Alexander, P. A., & Jetton, T .L. (2000). Learning from text: A multidimensional and developmental perspective. In M. L. Kamil, P. B. Mosenthal, P. D. Pearson, & R. Barr (Eds.), *Handbook of reading research: Vol. III* (pp. 285–310). Mahwah, NJ: Erlbaum.

Alexander, P. A., Jetton, T. L., & Kulikowich, J. M. (1995). Interrelationship of knowledge, interest, and recall: Assessing a model of domain learning. *Journal of Educational Psychology, 87,* 559–575.

Alexander, P. A., Jetton, T. L., Kulikowich, J. M., & Woehler, C. (1994). Contrasting instructional and structural importance: The seductive effect of teacher questions. *Journal of Reading Behavior, 26,* 19–45.

Alexander, P. A., & Judy, J. E. (1988). The interaction of domain-specific and strategic knowledge in academic performance. *Review of Educational Research, 58,* 375–404.

Alexander, P. A., Kulikowich, J. M., & Schulze, S. K. (1994). How subject-matter knowledge affects recall and interest. *American Educational Research Journal, 31,* 313–337.

Alexander, P. A., & Murphy, P. K. (1998). Profiling the differences in students' knowledge, interest, and strategic processing. *Journal of Educational Psychology, 90,* 435–447.

Alexander, P. A., Murphy, P. K., & Kulikowich, J. M. (1998). What responses to domain-specific analogy problems reveal about emerging competence: A new perspective on an old acquaintance. *Journal of Educational Psychology, 90*(3), 397–406.

Alexander, P. A., Murphy, P. K., & Woods, B. S. (1996). Of squalls and fathoms: Navigating the seas of educational innovation. *Educational Researcher, 25*(3), 31–36, 39.

Alexander, P. A., Murphy, P. K., Woods, B. S., Duhon, K. E., & Parker, D. (1997). College instruction and concomitant changes in students' knowledge, interest, and strategy use: A study of domain learning. *Contemporary Educational Psychology, 22,* 125–146.

Alexander, P. A., Schallert, D. L., & Hare, V. C. (1991). Coming to terms: How researchers in learning and literacy talk about knowledge. *Review of Educational Research, 61*(3), 315–343.

Alexander, P. A., Sperl, C. T., Buehl, M. M., Fives, H., & Chiu, S. (2004). Modeling domain learning: Profiles from the field of special education. *Journal of Educational Psychology, 96,* 545–557.

Allard, F., & Starkes, J. L. (1991). Motor-skill experts in sports, dance, and other domains. In K. A. Ericsson, & J. Smith (Eds.), *Toward a general theory of expertise: Prospects and limits* (pp. 126–152). New York: Cambridge University Press.

Ames, C., & Ames, R. (Eds.) (1989). *Research on motivation in education: The classroom milieu* (Vol. 3). San Diego, CA: Academic Press.

Anderson, J. R. (1983). *The architecture of cognition.* Cambridge, MA: Harvard University Press.

Anderson, J. R. (1987). Skill acquisition: Compilation of weak method problem solutions. *Psychological Review, 94,* 192–210.

Anzai, Y., & Yokoyama, T. (1984). Internal models in physics problem solving. *Cognition and Instruction, 1,* 397–450.

Arocha, J. F., & Patel, V. L. (1995). Novice diagnostic reasoning in medicine: Accounting for evidence. *The Journal of the Learning Sciences, 4,* 355–384.

Badderly, A. D. (1992). Working memory. *Science, 255,* 556–559.

Baker, F. B. (1992). *Item response theory: Parameter estimation techniques.* New York: Marcel Dekker.

Barrett, P. (2005). What if there were no psychometrics?: Constructs, complexity, and measurement. *Journal of Personality Assessment, 82,* 134–140.

Bassok, M., & Holyoak, K. J. (1989). Interdomain transfer between isomorphic topics in algebra and physics. *Journal of Experimental Psychology: Learning, Memory, and Cognition, 15,* 153–166.

Bell, K. L., & Calkins, S. D. (2000). Relationships as inputs and outputs of emotion regulation. *Psychological Inquiry, 11,* 160–163.

Bereiter, C., & Scardamalia, M. (1993). *Surpassing ourselves: An inquiry into the nature and implications of expertise.* Chicago: Open Court.

Berliner, D. C., & Biddle, B. J. (1995). *The manufactured crisis: Myths, fraud, and the attack on American's public schools.* Reading, MA: Addison-Wesley.

Berninger, V. W., & Corine, D. (1998). Making cognitive neuroscience educationally relevant: Creating bi-directional collaborations between educational psychology and cognitive neuroscience. *Educational Psychology Review, 10,* 343–354.

Berninger, V. W., & Richards, T. L. (2002). *Brain literacy for educators and psychologists*. San Diego, CA: Academic Press.

Binet, A., & Simon, T. (1905). Méthodes nouvelles pou le diagnostic du niveau intellectual des anormaux [New methods for diagnosing the intellectual level of abnormals]. *Année Psychologique, 11*, 191–336.

Bollen, K. A. (1989). *Structural equations with latent variables*. New York: Wiley.

Bransford, J. D., Brown, A. L., & Cocking, R. R. (1999). *How people learn: Brain, mind, experience, and school*. Washington, DC: National Academy Press.

Bransford, J. D., & Stein, B. S. (1993). *The IDEAL problem solver* (2nd ed.). New York: W. H. Freeman.

Bransford, J. D., Zech, L., Schwartz, D., Barron, B., Vye, N., & The Cognition and Technology Group at Vanderbilt [CTGV] (1996). Fostering mathematical thinking in middle school students: Lessons from research. In R. J. Sternberg & T. Ben-Zeev (Eds.). *The nature of mathematical thinking* (pp. 203–250). Mahwah, NJ: Erlbaum.

Bråten, I., & Olauseen, B. S. (2005). Profiling individual differences in student motivation: A longitudinal cluster-analytic study in different academic contexts. *Contemporary Educational Psychology, 30*, 359–396.

Brown, J. S., Collins, A., & Duguid, P. (1989). Situated cognition and the culture of learning. *Educational Researcher, 18*(1), 32–42.

Browne, M. W., & Cudeck, R. (1993). Alternative ways of assessing model fit. In K. A. Bollen & J. S. Long (Eds.) *Testing structural equation models*. Newbury, Park, CA: Sage.

Bryk, A. S., & Raudenbush, S. W. (1992). *Hierarchical linear models: Applications and data analysis methods*. Newbury Park, CA: Sage.

Byrnes, J. P. (2001). *Cognitive development and learning* (2nd ed.). Boston: Allyn and Bacon.

Campbell, D. T., & Fiske, D. W. (1959). Convergent and discriminant validation by the multitrait-multimethod matrix. *Psychological Bulletin, 56*, 81–105.

Carroll, J. B. (1993). *Human cognitive abilities: A survey of factor-analytic studies*. Cambridge, UK: Cambridge University Press.

Cattell, R. B. (1941). Some theoretical issues in adult intelligence testing. *Psychological Bulletin, 38*, 592.

Cattell, R. B. (1952). *Factor analysis*. New York: Harper.

Cattell, R. B. (1971/1987). *Abilities: Their structure, growth, and action*. [Revised and reprinted as *Intelligence: Its structure, growth, and action*]. Amsterdam: North-Holland.

Chase, W. G., & Simon, H. A. (1973). Perception in chess. *Cognitive Psychology, 4*, 55–81.

Chi, M. T. H. (1978). Knowledge structures and memory development. In R. Siegler (Ed.), *Children's thinking: What develops?* (pp. 73–96). Hillsdale, NJ: Erlbaum.

Chi, M. T. H. (1997). Quantifying qualitative analyses of verbal data: A practical guide. *The Journal of the Learning Sciences, 6*, 271–315.

Chi, M. T. H., Feltovich, P. J., & Glaser, R. (1981). Categorization and representation of physics problems by experts and novices. *Cognitive Science, 5*, 121–152.

Chi, M. T. H., Glaser, R., & Farr, M. J. (Eds.). (1988). *The nature of expertise*. Hillsdale, NJ: Erlbaum.

Clancey, W. J. (1985). Heuristic classification. *Artificial Intelligence, 27*, 215–251.

Cronbach, L. J., & Meehl, P. E. (1955). Construct validity in psychological tests. *Psychological Bulletin, 52*, 281–302.

Cross, T. B. (1988). *Knowledge engineering: The use of artificial intelligence in business*. New York: Bradley Books.

de Groot, A. D. (1978). *Thought and choice in chess*. The Hague: Mouton. (Original work published 1946)

de Jong, T., & Ferguson-Hessler, M. G. M. (1986). Cognitive structures of good and poor novice problem solvers in physics. *Journal of Educational Psychology, 78*, 279–288.

Dewey, J. (1913). *Interest and effort in education*. Boston: Riverdale.

Donald, M. (2001). *A mind so rare: The evolution of human consciousness*. New York: Norton.

Ericsson, K. A. (Ed.). (1996). *The road to excellence: The acquisition of expert performance in the arts and sciences, sports, and games.* Mahwah, NJ: Erlbaum.

Ericsson, K. A., & Kintsch, W. (1995). Long-term working memory. *Psychological Review, 102,* 211–245.

Ericsson, K. A., Patel, V. L., & Kintsch, W. (2000). How experts' adaptations to representative task demands account for the expertise effect in memory recall: Comment on Vicente and Wang (1998). *Psychological Review, 107,* 578–592.

Ericsson, K. A., & Polson, P. G. (1988). A cognitive analysis of exceptional memory for restaurant orders. In M. T. H. Chi, R. Glaser, & M. J. Farr (Eds.), *The nature of expertise* (pp. 23–70). Hillsdale, NJ: Erlbaum.

Ericsson, K. A., & Simon, H. A. (1993). *Protocol analysis: Verbal reports as data.* Cambridge, MA: MIT Press.

Ericsson, K. A., & Smith, J. (1991). *Toward a general theory of expertise: Prospects and limits.* New York: Cambridge University Press.

Ericsson, K. A., & Staszewski, J. J. (1989). Skilled memory and expertise: Mechanisms of exceptional performance. In D. Klahr & K. Kotovsky (Eds.), *Complex information processing: The impact of Herbert A. Simon* (pp. 253–267). Hillsdale, NJ: Erlbaum.

Essens, P. J., Post, W. M., & Rasker, P. C. (2000). Modeling a command center. In J. M. Schraagen, S. F. Chipman, & V. L. Shalin (Eds.), *Cognitive task analysis* (pp. 385–400). Mahwah, NJ: Erlbaum.

Galton, F. (1970). *English men of science.* London: Frank Cass. (Original work published 1874)

Galton, F. (1979). *Hereditary genius: An inquiry into its laws and consequences.* London: Julian Friedman. (Original work published 1869)

Gardner, H. (1999). *Intelligence reframed.* New York: Basic Books.

Garner, R., Alexander, P. A., Gillingham, M. G., Kulikowich, J. M., & Brown, R. (1991). Interest and learning from text. *American Educational Research Journal, 28,* 643–659.

Gelman, R., & Greeno, J. G. (1989). On the nature of competence: Principles for understanding in a domain. In L. B. Resnick (Ed.), *Knowing, learning, and instruction: Essays in honor of Robert Glaser* (pp. 125–186). Hillsdale, NJ: Erlbaum.

Gentner, D. R. (1983). Structure-mapping: A theoretical framework for analogy. *Cognitive Science, 7,* 155–170.

Gentner, D. R. (1988). Expertise in typewriting. In M. T. H. Chi, R. Glaser, & M. J. Farr (Eds.), *The nature of expertise* (pp. 1–21). Hillsdale, NJ: Erlbaum.

Gick, M. L. (1986). Problem-solving strategies. *Educational Psychologist, 21,* 99–120.

Glass, G. V. (1978). Integrating findings: The meta-analysis of research. *Review of Research in Education, 5,* 351–379.

Gorman, M. E., Tweney, R. D., Gooding, D. C., & Kincannon, A. P. (Eds.), (2005). *Scientific and technological thinking.* Mahwah, NJ: Erlbaum.

Gray, W. D., & Kirschenbaum, S. S. (2000). Analyzing a novel expertise: An unmarked road. In J. M. Schraagen, S. F. Chipman, & V. L. Shalin (Eds.). *Cognitive task analysis* (pp. 275–290). Mahwah, NJ: Erlbaum.

Grigorenko, E. L., Jarvin, L., & Sternberg, R. J. (2002). School-based tests of the triarchic theory of intelligence: Three settings, three samples, three syllabi. *Contemporary Educational Psychology, 27,* 167–208.

Hatano, G. (1982). Cognitive consequences of practice in culture specific procedural skills. *Quarterly Newsletter of the Laboratory of Comparative Human Cognition, 4,* 15–17.

Hatano, G., & Inagaki, K. (1992). Desituating cognition through the construction of conceptual knowledge. In P. Light & G. Butterworth (Eds.), *Context and cognition* (pp. 115–133). Hemel Hempstead, UK: Harvester.

Hatano, G., & Oura, Y. (2003). Commentary: Reconceptualizing school learning using insight from expertise research. *Educational Researcher, 32,* 26–29.

Hidi, S. (1990). Interest and its contribution as a mental resource for learning. *Review of Educational Research, 60,* 549–571.

Hoffman, R. R., Shadbolt, N. R., Burton, A. M., & Klein, G. (1995). Eliciting knowledge from experts: A methodological analysis. *Organizational Behavior and Human Decision Processes, 62,* 129–158.

Holyoak, K. J. (1991). Symbolic connectionism: Toward third-generation theories of expertise. In K. A. Ericsson, & J. Smith (Eds.), *Toward a general theory of expertise: Prospects and limits* (pp. 301–335). New York: Cambridge University Press.

Hox, J. J. (1995). *Applied multilevel analysis.* Amsterdam: TT-Publikaties.

Hunter, J. E., & Schmidt, F. L. (1990). *Methods of meta-analysis: Correcting error and bias in research findings.* Newbury Park, CA: SAGE.

Hutchins, E. (1996). *Cognition in the wild.* Cambridge, MA: MIT Press.

Judy, J. E., Alexander, P. A., Kulikowich, J. M., & Willson, V. L. (1998). Effects of two instructional approaches and peer tutoring on gifted and nongifted sixth graders' analogy performance. *Reading Research Quarterly, 23,* 236–256.

Karmiloff-Smith, A. (1986). From meta-processes to conscious access: Evidence from children's metalinguistic and repair data. *Cognition, 23,* 95–147.

Katz, I. R., Martinez, M. E., Sheehan, K. M., & Tatsuoka, K. K. (1998). Extending the rule space methodology to a semantically-rich domain: Diagnostic assessment in architecture. *Journal of Educational and Behavioral Statistics, 24,* 254–278.

Keating, D. P. (1990). Charting pathways to the development of expertise. *Educational Psychologist, 25,* 243–267.

Keating, D. P. (2004). Cognitive and brain development. In R. M. Lerner & L. Steinberg (Eds.), *Handbook of adolescent psychology: Second edition* (pp. 45–84). New York Wiley.

Kolodner, J. L. (1983). Towards an understanding of the role of experience in the evolution from novice to expert. *International Journal of Man-Machine Studies, 19,* 497–518.

Kulikowich, J. M. (in press). Experimental and quasi-experimental approaches to research on new literacies. In D. J. Leu Jr., J. Coiro, M. Knobel, & C. Lankshear (Eds.), *Handbook of research on new literacies.* Mahwah, NJ: Erlbaum.

Kulikowich, J. M., & Alexander, P. A. (1994). Evaluating students' errors on cognitive tasks: Applications of polytomous item response theory and log-linear modeling. In C. R. Reynolds (Ed.), *Cognitive assessment: A multidisciplinary perspective* (pp. 137–154). New York: Plenum Press.

Kulikowich, J. M., & Alexander, P. A. (2003). Cognitive assessment. In L. Nadel (Ed.), The *encyclopedia of cognitive science* (Vol. 1, pp. 526–532). London: Nature Publishing Group.

Kulikowich, J. M., & DeFranco, T. C. (2003). Philosophy's role in characterizing the nature of educational psychology and mathematics. *Educational Psychologist, 38*(3), 147–156.

Lajoie, S. P. (2003). Transitions and trajectories for studies of expertise. *Educational Researcher, 32,* 21–25.

Lajoie, S. P., Azevedo, R., & Fleiszer, D. (1998). Cognitive tools for assessment and learning in a high information flow environment. *Journal of Educational Computing Research, 18*(3), 205–235.

Lajoie, S. P., Lavigne, N. C., Guerrera, C., & Munsie, S. (2001). Constructing knowledge in the context of BioWorld. *Instructional Science, 29*(2), 155–186.

Lajoie, S. P., Lavigne, N. C., Munsie, S. D., & Wilkie, T. V. (1998). Monitoring student progress in statistics. In S. P. Lajoie (Ed.), *Reflections on statistics* (pp. 199–231). Mahwah, NJ: Erlbaum.

Lajoie, S. P., & Lesgold, A. (1992). Dynamic assessment of proficiency for solving procedural knowledge tasks. *Educational Psychologist, 27*(3), 365–384.

Lawless, K. A., & Kulikowich, J. M. (1996). Understanding hypertext navigation through cluster analysis. *Journal of Educational Computing Research, 14*(4), 385–399.

Lawless, K. A. & Kulikowich, J. M. (1998). Domain knowledge, interest, and hypertext navigation: A study of individual differences. *Journal of Educational Multimedia and Hypermedia, 7*(1), 51–70.

Lesgold, A., Lajoie, S., Bunzo, M., & Eggan, G. (1992). SHERLOCK: A coached practice environment for an electronics troubleshooting job. In J. H. Larkin & R. W. Chabay (Eds.), *Computer-assisted instruction and intelligent tutoring systems* (pp. 201–238). Hillsdale, NJ: Erlbaum.

Leslie, M. (2000, July-August). The vexing legacy of Lewis Terman. Palo Alto, CA: *Stanford Alumni Magazine.* Reteived January 30, 2006, from http://www.stanfordalumni.org/news/magazine/2000/julaug/articles/terman.html

Lord, F. M. (1980). *Applications of item response theory to practical testing problems.* Hillsdale, NJ: Erlbaum.

Lord, F. M., & Novick, M. R. (1968). *Statistical theories of mental test scores.* Reading, MA: Addison-Wesley.

Ludwig, A. M. (1995). *The price of greatness: Resolving the creativity and madness controversy.* New York: Guilford.

Ludwig, A. M. (1998). Method and madness in the arts and sciences. *Creativity Research Journal, 11,* 93–101.

Martindale, C. (1990). *The clockwork muse: The predictability of artistic change.* New York: Basic Books.

McDonald, R. P. (1999). *Test theory: A unified treatment.* Mahwah, NJ: Erlbaum.

McGrath, R. E. (2005). Conceptual complexity and construct validity. *Journal of Personality Assessment, 85,* 112–124.

Meece, J. L., Blumenfeld, P. C., & Hoyle, R. (1988). Students' goal orientations and cognitive engagement in classroom activities. *Journal of Educational Psychology, 80,* 514–523.

Mislevy, R. J. (1993). A framework for studying differences between multiple-choice and free-response items. In R. E. Bennett & W. C. Ward (Eds.), *Construction versus choice in cognitive measurement* (pp. 75–106). Hillsdale, NJ: Erlbaum.

Mousavi, S. Y., Low, R., & Sweller, J. (1995). Reducing cognitive load by mixing auditory and visual presentation modes. *Journal of Educational Psychology, 87,* 319–334.

Murphy, P. K., & Alexander, P. A. (2000). A motivated exploration of motivation terminology. *Contemporary Educational Psychology, 25,* 3–53.

Murphy, P. K., & Alexander, P. A. (2002). What counts?: The predictive power of subject-matter knowledge, strategic processing, and interest in domain-specific performance. *Journal of Experimental Education, 70,* 197–214.

Murphy, P. K., & Alexander, P. A. (2004). Persuasion as a dynamic, multidimensional process: An investigation of individual and intraindividual differences. *American Educational Research Journal, 41,* 337–364.

Newell, A., & Simon, H. A. (1972). *Human problem solving.* Englewood Cliffs, NJ: Prentice-Hall.

Norman, D. A. (1969). *Memory and attention: An introduction to human information processing.* New York: Wiley.

Olson, J. R., & Biolsi, K. J. (1991). Techniques for representing expert knowledge. In K. A. Ericsson & J. Smith (Eds.), *Toward a general theory of expertise: Prospects and limits* (pp. 240–285). Cambridge: Cambridge University Press.

Patel, V. L., & Groen, G. J. (1986). Knowledge-based solution strategies in medical reasoning. *Cognitive Science, 10,* 91–116.

Patel, V. L., Groen, G. J., & Arocha, J. F. (1990). Medical expertise as a function of task difficulty. *Memory & Cognition, 18,* 394–406.

Pintrich, P. R., Marx, R. W., & Boyle, R. A. (1993). Beyond cold conceptual change: The role of motivational beliefs and classroom contextual factors in the process of conceptual change. *Review of Educational Research, 63,* 167–199.

Pressley, M., & Afflerbach, P. (1995). *Verbal protocols of reading: The nature of constructively responsive reading.* Hillsdale, NJ: Erlbaum.

Pressley, M., Goodchild, F., Fleet, J., Zajchowski, R., & Evans, E. D. (1989). The challenges of classroom strategy instruction. *Elementary School Journal, 89,* 301–342.

Reio, T. G., Jr., & Wiswell, A. (2000). Field investigation of the relationship between adult curiosity, workplace learning and job performance. *Human Resource Development Quarterly, 11*(1), 1–36.

Reise, S. P., Widaman, K. F., & Pugh, R. H. (1993). Confirmatory factor analysis and item response theory: Two approaches for exploring measurement equivalence. *Psychological Bulletin, 114,* 552–566.

Renkl, A. (1997). Learning from worked-out examples. A study on individual differences. *Cognitive Science, 21,* 1–29.

Renkl, A., & Atkinson, R. K. (2003). Structuring the transition from example study to problem solving in cognitive skill acquisition: A cognitive load perspective. *Educational Psychologist, 38,* 15–22.

Renninger, K. A., Hidi, S., & Krapp, A. (1992). *The role of interest in learning and development.* Hillsdale, NJ: Erlbaum.

Rolfhus, E. L., & Ackerman, P. L. (1999). Assessing individual differences in knowledge: Knowledge structures and traits. *Journal of Educational Psychology, 91,* 511–526.

Scardamalia, M., & Bereiter, C. (1991). Literate expertise. In K. A. Ericsson & J. Smith (Eds.), *Toward a general theory of expertise: Prospects and limits* (pp. 172–194). Cambridge, UK: Cambridge University Press.

Schank, R. C. (1979). Interestingness: Controlling influences. *Artificial Intelligence, 12,* 273–297.

Schiefele, U. (1991). Interest, learning, and motivation. *Educational Psychologist, 26,* 299–323.

Schraagen, J. M., Chipman, S. F., & Shalin, V. L. (Eds.). (2000). *Cognitive task analysis.* Mahwah, NJ: Erlbaum.

Selden, S. (1999). *Inheriting shame: The story of eugenics and racism in America.* New York: Teachers College Press.

Shadbolt, N. R., & Burton, A. M. (1990). Knowledge elicitation: In E. N. Wilson & J. R. Corlett (Eds.), *Evaluation of human work: Practical ergonomics methodology* (pp. 321–345). London: Taylor and Francis.

Shanteau, J., & Stewart, T. R. (1992). Why study expert decision making? Some historical perspectives and comments. *Organizational Behavior and Human Decision Processes, 53,* 95–106.

Shavelson, R. J. (1974). Methods for examining representations of a subject-matter structure in a student's memory. *Journal of Research in Science Teaching, 11,* 231–249.

Shuell, T. J. (1990). Phases of meaningful learning. *Review of Educational Research, 60,* 531–547.

Simon, H. A. (1989). *Models of thought* (Vol. 2). New Haven, CT: Yale University Press.

Simon, H. A., & Chase, W. G. (1973). Skill in chess. *American Scientist, 61,* 394–403.

Sinatra, G., & Pintrich, P. R. (2002) *Intentional conceptual change.* Mahwah, NJ: Erlbaum.

Singer, J. D. (1998). Using SAS PROC MIXED to fit multilevel models, hierarchical models, and individual growth models. *Journal of Educational and Behavioral Statistics, 24,* 323–355.

Snow, R. E. (1989). Aptitude-treatment interaction as a framework for research on individual differences in learning. In P. L. Ackerman, R. J. Sternberg, & R. Glaser (Eds.), *Learning and individual differences. Advances in theory and research* (pp. 13–59). New York: W. H. Freeman.

Snow, R. E., Corno, L., & Jackson, D. (1996). Individual differences in affective and conative functions. In D. C. Berliner & R. C. Calfee (Eds.), *Handbook of educational psychology* (pp. 242–310). New York: Macmillan.

Spearman, C. E. (1904). "General intelligence" objectively determined and measured. *American Journal of Psychology, 15,* 72–101.

Spiro, R. J., & Jehng, J. C. (1990). Cognitive flexibility and hypertext: Theory and technology for the nonlinear and multidimensional traversal of complex subject matter. In D. Nix & R. J. Spiro (Eds.), *Cognition, education, and multimedia* (pp. 163–205). Hillsdale, NJ: Erlbaum.

Spiro, R. J., Vispoel, W. P., Schmitz, J. G., Samarapungavan, A., & Boerger, A. E., (1987). Knowledge acquisition for application: Cognitive flexibility and transfer in complex domains. In B. K. Britton & S. M. Glynn (Eds.), *Executive control processes in reading* (pp. 177–199). Hillsdale, NJ: Erlbaum.

Sternberg, R. J. (1986). *Intelligence applied: Understanding and increasing your intellectual skills.* San Diego, CA: Harcourt Brace Jovanovich.

Sternberg, R. J. (2003). What is an "expert student?" *Educational Researcher, 32,* 5–9.

Sternberg, R. J., & Clinkenbeard, P. R. (1995). The triarchic model applied to identifying, teaching, and assessing gifted children. *Roeper Review, 17*(4), 255–260.

Sternberg, R. J., Grigorenko, E. L., Ferrari, M., & Clinkenbeard, P. (1999). A triarchic analysis of an aptitude-treatment interaction. *European Journal of Psychological Assessment, 15*(1), 1–11.

Sternberg, R. J., Torff, B., & Grigorenko, E. L. (1998a). Teaching for successful intelligence raises school achievement. *Phi Delta Kappan, 79,* 667–669.

Sternberg, R. J., Torff, B., & Grigorenko, E. L. (1998b). Teaching triarchically improves school achievement. *Journal of Educational Psychology, 90,* 374–384.

Sweller, J., & Cooper, G. A. (1985). The use of worked examples as a substitute for problem solving in learning algebra. *Cognition and Instruction, 2,* 58–59.

Tatsuoka, K. K. (1983). Rule space: An approach for dealing with misconceptions based on item response theory. *Journal of Educational Measurement, 20,* 345–354.

Tatsuoka, K. K. (1985). A probabilistic model for diagnosing misconceptions in the pattern classification approach. *Journal of Educational Statistics, 12,* 55–73.

Terman, L. M., & Oden, M. H. (1947). *Genetic studies of genius: Vol. 4. The gifted child grows up.* Stanford, CA: Stanford University Press.

Thurstone, L. L. (1938). Primary mental abilities. *Psychometric Monographs,* No. 1.

Van Yperen, N., & Janssen, O. (2002). Fatigued and dissatisfied or fatigued but satisfied? Goal orientations and responses to high job demands. *Academy of Management Journal, 45,* 1161–1171.

VanSledright, B., & Alexander, P. A. (2002). *Historical knowledge, thinking, and beliefs: Evaluation component of the Corps of Historical Discovery Project* (#S215X010242). United States Department of Education.

Voss, J. F., Tyler, S. W., & Yengo, L. A. (1983). Individual differences in the solving of social science problems. In R. F. Dillon & R. R. Schmeck (Eds.), *Individual differences in cognition* (pp. 205–232). New York: Academic Press.

Walker, R., Hill, K., Kaplan, H., & McMillan, G. (2002). Age-dependency in hunting ability among the Ache of Eastern Paraguay. *Journal of Human Evolution, 42,* 639–657.

Wechsler, D. (1981). *Wechsler Adult Intelligence Scale-Revised.* San Antonio, TX: The Psychological Corporation.

White, C. S., Alexander, P. A., & Daugherty, M. (1998). The relationship between young children's analogical reasoning and mathematical learning. *Mathematical Cognition, 4*(2), 103–123.

Wood, L. E., & Ford, J. M. (1993). Structuring interviews with experts during knowledge elicitation. In K. M. Ford & J. M. Bradshaw (Eds.), *Knowledge acquisition as modeling* (pp. 71–90, Pt. 1). New York: Wiley.

Young, M. F., Kulikowich, J. M., & Barab, S. A. (1997). The unit of analysis for situated assessment. *Instructional Science, 25,* 133–150.

Chapter 18

An Integrative Model of Everyday Problem Solving Across the Adult Life Span

Cynthia A. Berg, Michelle Skinner, and Kelly Ko

In daily life, adults experience a variety of different types of everyday problems. The following examples encompass the wide range of everyday problems mentioned by our research participants who were asked to describe a recent everyday problem they experienced: dealing with a malfunctioning computer at work, deciding on the best medical insurance program for changing family needs, scheduling multiple time demands dealing with work, family, and leisure activities, making a treatment decision for a recent diagnosis of prostate cancer, and dealing with late family members who chronically derail leisure plans. These types of problems have been studied under a variety of labels including everyday competence (Baltes, Mayr, Borchelt, Maas, & Wilms, 1993; Willis 1991), everyday problem solving (Berg, Strough, Calderone, Sansone, & Weir, 1998; Blanchard-Fields, Jahnke, & Camp, 1995; Denney, 1989; Diehl, Willis, & Schaie,1995; Marsiske & Willis, 1995; Sinnott, 1989), everyday cognition (Allaire & Marsiske, 2002; Poon, Rubin, & Wilson, 1989; Rogoff & Lave, 1984), everyday reasoning and decision making (Johnson, 1990; Klaczynski, 2000), and practical intelligence (Sternberg & Wagner, 1986). We use the term "everyday problem solving," because it is the term most commonly applied in the cognitive aging literature. We use the term despite the great diversity in the content, structure, and processes involved in these everyday problems.

The history of everyday problem solving may help to explain how such a diverse set of problems has been grouped together as representative of the concept of "everyday problems." The study of everyday problem solving arose from dissatisfaction with traditional measures of intelligence to assess the intellectual ability of adults. As traditional intelligence tests were designed to predict how successful individuals would be in the academic environment, researchers questioned the utility of such tests for measuring the intelligence of adults who were no longer in the academic environment (Berg & Sternberg, 1995; Demming & Pressey, 1957; Labouvie-Vief, 1982). Thus began the search for a set of tasks that would reflect somewhat uniquely on an individual's ability to solve problems in the "real world." Early attempts to measure everyday problem solving focused on the instrumental tasks of daily living such as finding numbers in a telephone book or how to double a recipe (Demming & Pressey, 1957). The field quickly expanded (Berg, Meegan, & Deviney, 1998; Blanchard-Fields et al., 1995; Cornelius & Caspi, 1987; Denny, 1989) to explore problems where instrumental demands occurred in the context of a rich social context (e.g., dealing with a landlord who refuses to make expensive repairs to your residence; a person who spends time taking care of a relative, but is busy with a family of her own). Although the field has developed a large number of tools to measure everyday problem solving (Marsiske & Margrett, 2006), there has been much less success in assessing whether these new measures of everyday problem solving do a better job of predicting real-world indicators of everyday functioning than traditional intelligence tests (c.f., Allaire & Marsiske, 2002).

The field has traditionally defined everyday problem solving in contrast to "traditional" measures of intelligence (Meacham & Emont, 1989; Sternberg & Wagner & Sternberg, 1986). First, everyday problems are often described as *ill-structured* (as opposed to well-structured) in that there is not a single correct solution and there are many ways to get to each solution. Second, everyday problems occur in a rich interpersonal context where other people can facilitate or impede problem solution (Dixon, 1999; Meacham & Emont, 1989; Meegan & Berg, 2002; Strough & Margrett, 2002). Third, related to the fact that many everyday problems occur within a complex web of interpersonal relationships, these problems frequently require an individual to regulate both emotion and cognition (Blanchard-Fields et al., 1995; Labouvie-Vief, 2003). Fourth, problem solution may occur over an extended time frame of days, weeks, and months, whereas traditional intelligence tests are administered within a very limited time frame. Finally, the content of everyday problems is such that adults frequently experience such problems on an "everyday" basis more so than items found on typical intelligence tests.

Scholars in the field are beginning to make distinctions between different types of everyday problems on the basis of whether the problems are well-defined (i.e., is there a single correct answer and solution strategy or many; see Allaire & Marsiske, 2005; Berg, 2008; Marsiske & Margrett, 2006) or ill-defined (i.e., there are many possible solution strategies and correct answers). We have argued that well-defined and ill-defined problems derive from distinct theoretical traditions in the field (Berg, 2008). Those who examine well-defined problems view everyday problem solving as a manifestation of underlying intellectual abilities (Willis & Schaie, 1986), a view we have termed the "competency perspective" (see also Berg & Klaczynski, 1996). Researchers who focus on the ill-defined nature of everyday problems have frequently examined everyday problem solving as the cognitive, social, motivational, and cultural factors that influence adaptation to specific contexts (Berg & Klaczynski, 2002; Blanchard-Fields & Chen, 1996), reflective of the contextual approach. Although it is true that distinctions are needed in the field to help provide some order to the diverse set of problems currently examined under the umbrella of everyday problem solving, we argue in this chapter that an integrative model is needed that explores the cognitive, emotional, interpersonal, physiological, and personality factors that are involved in solving both well and ill-defined problems.

In this chapter, we first provide a brief review of the current work in the field of everyday problem solving, which is organized around the well-defined versus ill-defined distinctions of everyday problems. We then provide a model of everyday problem solving that encompasses both of these types of problems, and that captures the cognitive, emotional, and physiological processes involved in solving everyday problems. We argue that this model of everyday problem solving will likely lead to an expansion of the outcomes of everyday problem solving beyond those that are simply cognitive to include other markers of successful aging (e.g., social relationships, health, and overall psychological well-being). In this way, everyday problem solving may get closer to its original goal of understanding the multiplicity of factors that lead to successful adaptation to everyday life across the adult life span.

Review of Everyday Problem Solving

Two traditions have guided much of the field of everyday problem solving. The first has focused on designing measures of everyday problem solving that are well-defined, that is they have one correct answer (Allaire & Marsiske, 2002; Willis & Schaie, 1986). The second tradition has examined everyday problem solving on ill-defined problems (where a single correct answer does not exist) that are often embedded in a complex web of inter-personal relationships and involve regulating one's emotions. These two traditions have come to very different conclusions regarding the relationship between everyday problem solving and more traditional measures of intelligence. We will now briefly review the major findings coming from these two traditions.

The Well-Defined Tradition

The well-defined tradition is guided by a perspective that defines everyday problem solving as a manifestation of underlying intellectual abilities (Willis & Schaie, 1986). Thus, the focus within this perspective has been to design everyday problems that are analogues of traditional intelligence tests (e.g., knowledge, reasoning) and compare performance on these two types of problems. For instance, Allaire and Marsiske (1999) devised everyday analogues of inductive reasoning, knowledge, declarative memory, and working memory and compared these measures to traditional measures of these constructs. These everyday analogues involved processing information from nutritional labels and medication labels. Two questions have guided much of the work within this tradition: What is the relationship between traditional intelligence tests and everyday problem solving? Are age-related differences in everyday problem solving similar to those found on traditional measures of intelligence?

The general finding from this tradition is that performance on everyday problem-solving measures is quite similar to performance on traditional intelligence measures (Allaire & Marsiske, 1999; Marsiske & Willis, 1995; Willis & Schaie, 1986; see Thornton & Dumke, 2005, for a review). For instance, in Allaire and Marsiske (1999) correlations between each cognitive analogue were high (ranging from r = .26 to .74), suggesting that everyday problem solving is quite related to traditional measures of intelligence (see also Willis & Schaie, 1986). Furthermore, age-related differences in everyday problem solving were quite similar to those found for measures of fluid intelligence, providing additional evidence of the similarity in abilities underlying everyday problem solving and traditional intelligence.

In sum, the view coming from the literature focusing on everyday problem solving of well-defined problems is that everyday problem solving is determined by one's underlying cognitive abilities. Supportive evidence for this claim comes from the results indicating substantial relationships between measures of everyday problem solving and intelligence items and the similarity in age differences on both traditional intelligence tests and everyday problem-solving measures.

The Ill-Defined Tradition

The ill-defined tradition largely comes from a contextual perspective on everyday problem solving that views everyday problem solving as the abilities that are necessary in order that adults may provide a closer fit between themselves and their environment (Berg & Calderone, 1992; Blanchard-Fields & Chen, 1996). Researchers within this tradition often use adults' own descriptions of the problems that they have recently experienced in daily life as the starting point for measuring everyday problem solving (Berg et al., 1998; Blanchard-Fields et al., 1995) or hypothetical problems based in adults' everyday experience (Berg, Meegan, & Klaczynski, 1999; Blanchard-Fields, Chen, & Norris, 1997; Blanchard-Fields, Chen, Schocke, & Hertzog, 1998; Cornelius & Caspi, 1987). The problems that adults mention typically involve enduring interpersonal relationships

(Blanchard-Fields et al., 1995; Strough, Berg, & Sansone, 1996) that are a substantial part of the problem or are used to assist in the solution of the problem (Berg et al., 1998). Because of the overlap between the types of problems that adults mention experiencing and daily hassles from the stress and coping literature, researchers have often assessed problem-solving strategies utilizing the distinctions found in the coping literature (e.g., problem-focused versus emotion- focused coping strategies of Folkman, Lazarus, Pimley, & Novacek, 1987; Lazarus & Folkman, 1984. The set of skills needed to successfully solve such problems transcend typical cognitive skills and involve regulating emotions (Blanchard-Fields et al., 1995), regulating one's physiological arousal (Uchino, Berg, Smith, Pearce, & Skinner, 2006), drawing on one's interpersonal skills (Berg et al., 1998; Chang, D'Zurilla, & Lawrence, 2004; Meegan & Berg, 2002), and one's ability to cope with daily hassles (Blanchard-Fields et al., 1997; Cornelius & Caspi, 1987; Folkman et al.,1987).

A thorny problem from this perspective is how to determine "optimal" everyday problem-solving performance (see Berg & Klaczynski, 1996, for a more complete treatment of this problem). Some studies rely on the fit between the strategies that are adopted and some standard of optimal performance derived from relevant subgroups of individuals (e.g., experts; Cornelius & Caspi, 1987). Others rely on the participants' own subjective appraisal of strategy effectiveness (Berg et al., 1998) or the extent of contextual fit between strategies and goals (Berg et al., 1998). Optimal problem solving is typically defined more locally and consistent with contextualist principles that focus on the fit between the individual's performance and what is required by the specific context. This does present challenges for the assessment of everyday problem solving such that optimal problem solving in one context may not transcend to another context (Berg & Klaczynski, 2002). However, broad principles of effective functioning (e.g., efficient cognitive strategies, fit between goals and strategies) may transcend specific contexts to index effective problem solving.

Research emanating from this perspective reveals a substantially different picture of the relation between everyday problem solving performance and traditional intelligence tests, than that seen from the well-defined tradition. Everyday problem solving in the contextual perspective is seen as only modestly related to measures of traditional intelligence (r = .27 to .29 in Cornelius & Caspi, 1987; see also Blanchard-Fields et al., 1997). In addition, age-related differences in everyday problem-solving performance are not the same as age-related differences in fluid intelligence. Older adults often perform better than their younger counterparts (Cornelius & Caspi, 1987), especially when the problems deal with high emotional content (Blanchard-Fields et al., 1997; Watson & Blanchard-Fields, 1998) and involve the ability to utilize the interpersonal context by working collaboratively with close-relationship partners (Gould, Kurzman, & Dixon, 1994).

In sum, the contextual perspective examines everyday problem solving largely from an ill-defined perspective, where problems are embedded in a context of interpersonal relationships, emotions, and cognitions. The view from this perspective is that everyday problem solving is substantially different from traditional intelligence and that age-related differences in everyday problem solving diverge from the differences found for traditional fluid measures of intelligence.

Integration of the Well- and Ill-Defined Perspectives

Current positions in the field seem to be moving toward recognition that everyday problem solving consists of both well and ill-defined problems that activate different cognitive and emotional processes in problem solving. Several recent investigations that include both well- and ill-defined measures find that there is little overlap between these measures (Allaire & Marsiske, 2002) and that age differences are found only for performance on well-defined measures (Marsiske & Willis, 1995). This work seems to suggest that everyday problem solving, as it has been studied is multidimensional and that even the component skills that are required to complete a single task are distinct. For instance, Allaire and Marsiske (1999) found that for the same ill-defined task (Denny's (1989) task involving generating as many solutions as possible to hypothetical problems), two measures of performance (outside ratings of the quality of the solution and number of strategies generated) were not significantly correlated (r = .17). These findings suggest that in the realm of everyday problems, the ability to generate multiple solutions does not necessarily map onto perceptions of efficacious solution. This may be particularly important for ill-defined problems where one "tried and true" solution may be adequate for the problem. Further, different problems may require both well and ill defined components where an individual may utilize skills flexibly with relative emphasis on maximizing solution quality.

We have argued (Berg, 2008) that the field may benefit by seeing the well- and ill-defined components of many everyday problems. The balance between well- and ill-defined facets of everyday problems is quite apparent when examining the types of everyday decisions that individuals must make within a specific domain. For instance, within the health domain of managing a condition such as type 2 diabetes, there are well-defined problems like how much medication to take and how to balance carbohydrates with insulin intake. There are also more ill-defined problems such as how to keep on a regular exercise program, how to lose weight, and survive the holidays. In fact, it is possible that what is a well-defined problem for one person (e.g., how much insulin to take) is an ill-defined problem for another person (i.e., the person interprets the task as how to manage the diabetes in ways that avoid insulin). Current models in the decision making field that integrate the analytic and heuristic nature of cognitive processing (Epstein, Lipson, Holstein, & Huh, 1992; Kahneman, Slovic, & Tversky, 1982; Klaczynski, 2000; Stanovich, 1999) may be particularly helpful in seeing that individuals may oscillate between appraising problems as well- and ill-defined even for problems within the same domain (Klaczysnki & Robinson, 2000). We discuss this idea in depth below.

In the present chapter, we argue for an integrative model of everyday problem solving that encompasses both the well- and ill-defined facets of everyday problem solving. This integrative model encompasses the contextual and individual factors involved in problem appraisal as well as the cognitive, emotional, and physiological processes that are involved as adults solve everyday problems. We argue that all everyday problems have the potential to draw on these diverse skill sets for adults. Distinctions between well- and ill-defined problems may lie in the differential activation of one or more of these skill sets. For instance, making a complicated decision regarding whether to take hormone replacement therapy may draw differentially on the cognitive system, whereas making a decision regarding what to do with a struggling adult child may draw on one's ability to regulate one's emotion and physiological arousal together with one's partner or spouse. However, even for the same everyday problem different appraisal processes may make it so that what appears to be a well-defined problem for one person is an ill-defined problem for another individual. We now present this integrative model, drawing from the existing literature.

An Integrative Model of Everyday Problem Solving

This integrative model encompasses many of the defining features of everyday problem solving including the fact that problem solving occurs over an extended temporal frame, draws on a number of different capacities (e.g., cognitive, emotional, social, personality, physiological), and includes problems that are well- and ill-defined. The temporal frame (depicted in Figure 18.1) acknowledges that everyday problems are frequently ones that are anticipated yet infrequently are steps taken to avoid the problem (Berg, Strough, Calderone, Meegan, & Sansone 1997). The problem occurs, strategies are enacted, and often an evaluation process occurs as to how effective one was in dealing with the problem. In some cases, the problem is only mitigated but not ultimately "solved" for the time and may occur in the future. This is not to say that problem solvers do not learn from their experience with solving everyday problems. Experience with similar problems may activate a more automatic appraisal process that facilitates the cognitive, emotional, and physiological responses to the problem.

A key feature of the model is that how an individual solves an everyday problem will depend on how an individual appraises the problem-solving situation. Such appraisals can include the overall "definition" of the problem (Berg, Meegan, & Klaczynski, 1999; Sinnott, 1989), goals for the solution of the problem (Berg et al., 1998), and whether the problem is appraised together with another individual (Berg et al., 1998; Wiebe et al., 2005). We have argued (Sansone & Berg, 1993) that the appraisal of the problem draws from a variety of contextual (e.g., domain) and individual difference (e.g., personality) factors that are activated in a particular situation. Experience with an everyday problem may activate a stored schema for appraisal that serves as a starting part for the solution to the problem (Crick & Dodge, 1994).

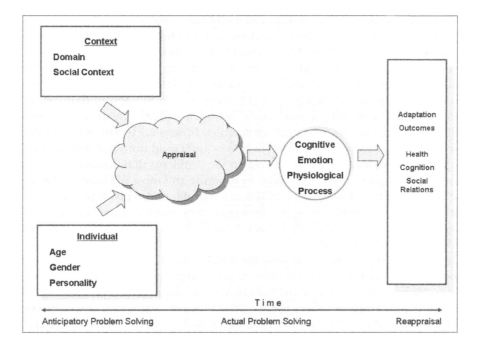

Figure 18.1 Problem solving process.

This differential activation of individual and contextual factors may be responsible for some of the stark distinctions found between well-defined and ill-defined problems. Take the examples of well-defined problems from the work of Willis and Schaie (1986), Marsiske and Willis (1995), and Allaire and Marsiske (2002). These problems are often timed and generally are presented in a multiple-choice format similar to that of traditional intelligence test items. The instructions are to pick the best answer and scoring is conducted based on whether the answer is correct or incorrect. It is likely that this context activates for the individual competence features of the self (Berg et al., 1998) and thereby the cognitive system is activated to solve the problem. Other skills and abilities may not be drawn upon as the context does not evoke interpersonal features (in fact, the interpersonal features are somewhat odd in that the experimenter likely knows the answers to the questions, but is unable to share that knowledge).

In contrast, the ill-defined problems used by investigators like Berg et al. (1998), Blanchard-Fields (Blanchard-Fields et al., 1995, 1997, 1998), Cornelius and Caspi (1987), and Denney and colleagues (see Denney, 1989, for a review) often include a task to be completed that is infused with interpersonal issues and emotional content (e.g., resolving a conflict with a friend). The answers that an individual must make involve inherently subjective assessments such as "how likely is it that you would do the strategy," "generate as many strategies as are possible," or "describe what you did to solve this problem and rate how well you felt you solved the problem." Such a context of everyday problem solving does not suggest to the participant that a "single" correct answer is desirable (particularly in the case where participants are encouraged to generate as many solutions as possible) or required. Rather the context suggests that many strategies are possible and numerous options may be equally desirable. In addition, the content of such problems contain other individuals who may impede or facilitate problem solving, thereby evoking from the individual interpersonal and emotional facets of the self from which the person draws to address the problem in addition to cognitive factors.

Appraisal processes are so crucial that the very same problem may be experienced by one person as a "well-defined" problem, whereas for another individual it is not. Several such examples exist in the literature. For instance, Sinnott (1989) devised a set of logical combination problems (originally devised by Piaget) that were infused with everyday content, as a way to make the problems easier for older adults. She found that young adults clearly identified these problems as a "math" problem and quickly undertook strategies that would get at the correct answer. Older adults, however, identified the problems as ones that they frequently experience in their lives and could not acknowledge that there was a single correct answer. In our own work on the problems that individuals experience on a daily basis, couples have been asked to describe the most difficult problem of the week. In Table 18.1, two descriptions of the same problem are given by a wife and husband; although the problems are quite different in emotional, interpersonal, and task components. This example, and others, point out how crucial appraisal processes are to the solution of everyday problems.

Different appraisal processes may produce a different problem solving process during adulthood. That is, appraisal of the problem as well-defined and contained may involve more of a cognitive system of encoding the elements of the problem, combining information, and selecting a response (Sternberg, 1984) or analytical versus heuristic cognitive processing (Klaczynski & Robinson, 2000). Appraisal of the problem as interpersonal and shared with another person may activate a process of shared decision making, using interpersonal skills to not only solve the task at hand, but to maintain the interpersonal relationship (Meegan & Berg, 2002). Such appraisal processes may vary over time for

Table 18.1 Multiple Perspectives of the Same Everyday Problem

Wife's Description:
I quit my job and got my son in job core up in Oregon because he has been in trouble in Salt Lake. Well job core called and said "oh Michael can't make it" so they shipped him back home and so we said "well you have to get a job and these are things you have to do" because he doesn't like to do those things because he likes mom to take care of him. This makes us so mad. So, we gave him a car and told him there were certain things he would have to get done. He would still come home at 4:30 in the morning, sleep all day, none of the job hunting. So we changed the locks as of Saturday, on the door and told him he had to find a place to live.

Husband's Description:
Having to change the locks on the house. Well I had to go get two bolts and put it on the deadbolt and had to take the knob set over to home depot and have them rekey it to match the dead bolt.

the same problem. Take the case of a couple describing a problem with their adult son. The wife appears to initially appraise the problem as one of assisting her son in successfully securing job skills to be independent. Currently, however, her goals revolve around removing herself from the problem situation and minimizing her distress.

These examples highlight the importance of problem *definition* in activating the process of everyday problem solving. Thus, our integrative framework will detail some of the factors that are involved in the initial appraisal process as it drives solution of both well-defined and ill-defined everyday problems. We briefly focus on how contextual (e.g., domain of problem, social context) and individual factors (e.g., age, gender, personality) affect how problems are appraised. We then provide a more detailed discussion of some of the cognitive, emotional, and physiological processes that are involved as individuals approach problems and enact strategies to deal with the problems.

Contextual Factors

The context of the problem has been an important factor relevant to how problems are solved, particularly within the ill-defined approach to everyday problem solving (Berg & Calderone, 1994; Blanchard-Fields & Chen, 1996). Although there are numerous contextual factors that could be involved, we will focus on the two that have received empirical attention in the everyday problem-solving literature: domain of the problem and the social context of the problem.

Domain of the Problem.   Much of the literature on the ill-defined approach to everyday problem solving has occurred within a contextual perspective to everyday problem solving (Berg & Klaczynski, 2002; Blanchard-Fields & Chen, 1996). Within a contextual perspective, everyday problem solving is examined in terms of the cognitive, social, motivational, and cultural factors that influence adaptation to specific contexts (Berg & Calderone, 1994; Sternberg, 1986). Much of this research has instantiated "context" as domains of problem solving. Multiple domains have been examined (e.g., consumer, health, friends, family), with more recent work contrasting instrumental (involving competence concerns) from interpersonal ones (involving social/interpersonal concerns) (see Berg et al., 1998; Blanchard-Fields et al., 1997).

Context is important for understanding everyday problem solving, as the normative context of everyday problem solving likely varies across adult development (Berg & Calderone, 1994). For example, Sansone and Berg (1993) found that the domains of individuals' actual everyday problems varied across adult development. For college-aged students, multiple contexts were mentioned (e.g., family, friends, work, leisure, school, health), whereas for older adults, the family context and problems dealing with health were most frequently mentioned. For middle-aged adults, everyday problems frequently occurred from the juxtaposition of multiple domains (e.g., conflicts between family and work; work and leisure). These different domains likely reflect that different developmental life tasks (Heckhausen, 1997; Hooker, 1999) and problems (Folkman et al., 1987) actually occur for adults across the life span.

The fact that everyday problems occur within different domains at different points during adult development may be important in understanding aspects of appraisal. Berg et al. (1998) found that interpersonal domains (e.g., family, friends) were largely associated with interpersonal goals, whereas instrumental domains (school, work) were associated with a combination of interpersonal and competence goals. The domain in which a problem occurs also affects the type of problem solving strategy that a person uses. Interpersonal domains draw from interpersonal strategies for their solution (e.g., utilization of others), whereas instrumental domains draw from more problem-focused strategies for their solution (Berg et al., 1998; Blanchard-Fields et al., 1997). There is some evidence that older adults' problem-solving strategies may be most sensitive to the effects of context (Blanchard-Fields et al., 1997), although other studies show no age differences in how strategies relate to context (Berg et al., 1998; Folkman et al., 1987). Problems across domains may be appraised as differentially controllable and familiar and may evoke more perceived ability to resolve the problem (Artistico, Cervone, & Pezzuti, 2003; Blanchard-Fields et al., 1997).

These results suggest that domains may be associated with different cognitive, emotional, and physiological processes. For instance, the school domain may be associated with more well-defined problems appraised in terms of competence and processed with an analytical strategy. However, family domains may activate high emotion and make salient roles and responsibilities that evoke a need to modulate emotion and physiological arousal. Future work will benefit from an understanding of the different appraisal and problem-solving strategies that are evoked as problems occur in different contexts.

Social Context of the Problem.   Everyday problems vary in the extent to which they occur in a social context (Berg, Meegan & Deviney, 1998; Blanchard-Fields et al., 1997). Some everyday problems are oriented toward the solution of a problem that involves only the individual (Berg et al., 1998). However, from the problems that adults report experiencing in their everyday lives, it is clear that other individuals are frequently the source of the problem, involved in the goals that individuals set, and are substantially involved in the solution of the problem (Berg et al., 1998; Meegan & Berg, 2002).

In our work, an important factor in understanding whether others are substantially involved in the solution of everyday problems involves an appraisal of "whose problem is it?" When individuals appraise an everyday problem as "shared" with another close relationship partner, that partner is more likely to be involved in a collaborative manner (Berg et al., in press; Wiebe et al., 2005). Many of the everyday problems examined in the literature (e.g., finances, medical decision making and prescription compliance, interfacing as a consumer with others) are likely ones that individuals share with a spouse, another family member, or a close friend. Older couples report that they prefer to work collaboratively with their spouse (Strough, Patrick, Swenson, Chen, & Barnes, 2003), believe that working with their spouse will be superior to working with other partners (e.g., friends, unacquainted individuals) more so than do than young adults (Dixon, Gagnon, & Crow, 1998), and they collaborate more frequently when they are satisfied in their relationship. As individuals age and lose close relationship partners (most particularly the spouse), other potential collaborators may be important to consider, such as friends and adult children (Cicirelli, 2006).

When an everyday problem is appraised as shared it may initiate a process of collaborative problem solving (Dixon, 1996; Meegan & Berg, 2002; Strough & Margrett, 2002). The collaborative problem-solving literature has focused on (1) how collaboration may optimize problem-solving performance through the utilization of transactive memory or cognitive systems (Johansson, Andersson, & Ronnberg, 2000; Wegner, Erber, & Raymond., 1991) or (2) compensate for cognitive decline experienced in one or both members of the couple (Dixon, 1996). Dixon and Gould (1992) found that older couples performed as well as younger couples on a text memory task, where typically substantial age differences are seen in individual performance. When examining the strategies for remembering text, Gould et al. (1994) indicated that older adults may use collaboration to compensate for cognitive declines through their greater use of strategy discussion at a time in recall when individual-based story recall is waning. Older adults not only benefit from direct forms of collaboration (i.e., when two or more individuals physically work together), but also from mentally evoking the involvement or suggestions of another. Staudinger and Baltes (1996) found that performance on a wisdom problem-solving task benefited as much from an "internal dialogue" with another individual as from actually working side by side with another person.

Very recent research is acknowledging that the interpersonal process of collaboration may vary in ways that either facilitate or impede collaborative performance. Couples vary in the way in which they interact (e.g., affiliation and dominance), which could affect how well the couple works together. Berg, Johnson, Meegan, and Strough (2003) found that couples who were interdependent and warm performed better on an errand running task and a vacation decision task that those who were more separate and less warm. Berg et al. (2007) found that when the person taking control over the task was the more cognitively capable member, performance was enhanced on an errand running task.

In summary, the appraisal of an everyday problem and the types of strategies employed may vary depending on the domain in which the problem is found as well as aspects of the social context (e.g., Whose problem is it? Who is a potential collaborator?). Numerous other contextual factors could be addressed in this literature, such as the cultural context of everyday problem solving, most notably cultural differences in the level of independence and interdependence among individuals (Markus & Kitayama, 2003).

Individual Characteristics

Numerous individual difference characteristics can be examined as important in understanding how individuals appraise everyday problems (e.g., age, gender, personality, self-concept). We will focus on three factors that have been examined in this literature: age, gender, and personality.

Age.   A growing literature exists on how age differences may be involved in how individuals appraise everyday problems. As indicated above from Sinnott's (1989) findings, age may be involved in whether older adults view an everyday problem as one that is well- versus ill-defined. Similar results have been discovered by Laipple (1991) who found that older adults were more likely to interpret logical problems involving plants as experienced problems involving their own plants rather than purely logical hypotheticals. Similarly, Berg et al. (1999) found that adults of all ages will impute their own experience into hypothetical everyday problems they are given to solve, which may alter aspects of the everyday problem-solving process. These results seem to suggest that older adults may be more likely to interpret what researchers view as "well-defined problems" as "ill-defined problems" in that there is not a single correct solution but rather a wide array of solutions based on experiential knowledge.

Older adults may also be guided by different goals in everyday problem-solving situations, in part because their problems are activated within different domains. They may gravitate toward complex interactions between interpersonal and competence goals in everyday problem-solving situations rather than to simply focus on either interpersonal or competence goals (Berg et al., 1998). Further, their interpersonal goals may be less focused on resolving interpersonal problems, but rather on creating interpersonal harmony and positive emotional regard in dealing with everyday interpersonal problems (Carstensen, Isaacowitz, & Charles, 1999; Rook, Sorkin, & Zettel, 2004; Sorkin & Rook, 2006). These different goals may arise from shifts in larger motivational structures (Brandtsadter & Greve, 1994; Heckhausen & Schulz, 1995) that allow for reappraisal of problems and shifting of goals or an acknowledgement that time is more limited (Carstensen et al., 1999).

Gender.   Very little research has focused on gender differences explicitly when examining how individuals may appraise everyday problems. The research that has examined gender has focused on how males and females may be sensitive to the interpersonal goals and strategies present in everyday problems. Strough, Berg, and Sansone (1996) found that females from adolescence throughout late adulthood were more attuned to the interpersonal issues present in everyday problems than were males. In describing everyday problems that they experienced, females were more likely to mention interpersonal relationships and that their goals were more focused on other people than males. However, when the context of the problem was controlled, gender differences in goals were eliminated.

These gender differences in other-focused and interpersonal goals in problem appraisal may relate to the gender differences reported by Watson and Blanchard-Fields (1998) in preferences for strategies for dealing with everyday problems. They found that gender differences were most apparent in interpersonal conflict situations. Women were less confrontational in these situations and sought more social support, whereas men responded with more problem-focused action. Further, gender differences may exist in how individuals collaborate in problem-solving situations in terms of preferences for collaboration and the affiliative process of collaboration (Berg et al., 2007; Margrett & Marsiske, 2002).

Personality.   As personality involves a consistent pattern of interacting with one's environment based on one's thoughts, feelings, and actions (Roepke, McAdams, Lindamer, Patterson, & Jeste, 2001), it may be a factor in how individuals appraise and deal with everyday problems. Consistent with the research on personality and coping, factors such as neuroticism, optimism, and hostility may predispose individuals to identify situations as "problems" and activate different processes of cognitive, emotional, and physiological approaches to everyday problems. Although the role of personality in understanding everyday problem solving has not been addressed, we draw on the work in stress and coping (given the commonality between the hassles examined within the stress and coping literature and problems within the everyday problem literature) to make links between personality and facets of the everyday problem-solving process.

Neuroticism. The role of neuroticism in understanding facets of stress and coping has been well researched in the stress and coping literature. Neuroticism has been described as a heightened sensitivity for negative stimuli that may influence behavior, cognitions, and negative mood (Tellegen, 1985). Individuals with high levels of neuroticism are more inclined to report everyday stressors and deal with them in a less effective manner (Holahan & Moos, 1987; Maitlin, Wethington, & Kessler, 1990). Highly neurotic individuals may create problems for themselves in that they report higher emotional reactivity to situations that contain negative mood and perceive potentially stressful situations in a more negative manner (Larsen, & Ketelaar, 1989).

The relationship between neuroticism and the experience of everyday stressors has recently been explored through daily diary studies. Individuals high in neuroticism were more likely to report stressful events and experience higher levels of distress on a daily basis (Bolger & Schilling, 1991) than individuals low in neuroticism. In addition, when faced with stressful events, individuals high in neuroticism employ less effective coping strategies which may result in higher levels of negative affect and increased everyday problems (Bolger, 1990; Lazarus & Folkman, 1984). Although it remains unclear whether individuals high in neuroticism are actually exposed to more daily stressors or merely more likely to report them, it is apparent that highly neurotic individuals experience higher levels of distress on a regular basis. Thus, it might be expected that highly neurotic individuals might expend energy managing emotion and physiological reactivity when solving everyday problems rather than seeking social support or relying solely on problem-focused solutions, and they may exhibit less cognitive control (Robinson & Tamir, 2005).

Optimism. Optimistic individuals are described as those who have a generalized mentality that they will experience good things in their future (Carver & Scheier, 2001). In contrast to neurotic individuals, optimists may perceive everyday problems in a positive manner. Optimism may not only facilitate the orientation toward accomplishing positive goal states, but also processing negative information relevant to accomplishing the goal (Aspinwall, 2001). Thus, optimism may affect appraisal processes such that optimists report fewer daily stressors and more adaptive coping strategies when stressors do arise (Carver & Scheier, 2001). The positive affect that accompanies optimism may also be associated with cognitive flexibility that encourages the generation of multiple solutions to everyday problems (Fredrickson & Joiner, 2002) and effective decision making (Isen, 2000). In addition, Tugade and Fredrickson (2002) find that positive emotional states may affect interpretative processes after a problem has occurred such that the problems are interpreted in a more positive light. Thus, optimism may be especially beneficial to the solution of everyday problems by affecting appraisal processes, generation of solutions, and re-appraisal after strategies have been implemented.

Previous research has also demonstrated that optimism predicts a host of other health-related outcomes such as longevity, medical outcomes following coronary artery bypass surgery, decreased chance of reoccurring cardiac events following angioplasty, and childbirth (Carver & Gaines, 1987; Carver & Scheier., 2001; Scheier et al., 1999). These findings suggest that optimists may not experience the heightened physiological arousal that neurotic individuals do when faced with stressful events. Further there is some suggestion that predisposition to higher positive emotionality may provide a useful resource in speeding cardiovascular recovery and allaying perceptions of threat when faced with a stressor (Tugade & Fredrickson, 2004).

Hostility.   Hostility can be defined as a set of cognitive, affective, and behavioral characteristics (Smith, 1992) that influence the way in which the individual perceives others, responds to others in social situations, and experiences emotions such as anger. Hostility becomes a particularly relevant personality characteristic for everyday problem solving as so many of the problems that adults experience involve others in rather substantial ways (Berg et al., 1998; Hartley, 1989). Adults describe that others are central to everyday problems (Berg et al., 1998), that their goals often involve goals for other people, and that their problem-solving strategies involve others to address the problem situation. Hostility has been described as a lens through which individuals hold hostile expectations regarding how others will act (Allred & Smith, 1991). Hostile individuals may help to create social environments that are more antagonistic, due in part to their low competence to operate in social situations (Smith, 1992; Smith, Uchino, Berg, Florsheim, Pearce, Hawkins, et al., 2007). Hostile individuals may interpret everyday social problems as ones where the social context is hostile and also not be able to enlist the aid of other individuals when needed to solve their everyday problems. A particularly important way that adults may use their social context is through collaboration with close relationship partners. Hostile individuals, by virtue of their hostile attribution bias, may not be able to configure these collaborative relationships and/or maintain them over time. Further, the negative emotional and physiological reactivity in such everyday interpersonal situations may draw individuals toward expending effort to reduce physiological and emotional reactivity responses.

In summary, these contextual and individual factors transact so that not all contextual factors are activated in the same way for all individuals. The combination of contextual and individual factors affect the appraisal of the problem and are thought to influence the balance of subsequent cognitive, emotional, and physiological processes that are involved as individuals solve everyday problems. We will now review relevant literature that addresses the cognitive, emotional, and physiological processes that may underlie everyday problem-solving performance.

Cognitive Process of Everyday Problem Solving

Although the field of everyday problem solving arose as a way to examine cognitive processes in everyday life, there has been surprisingly little in the aging field that really examines the cognitive processes involved in dealing with an everyday problem either from the ill-defined or well-defined approach. Rather, the focus in the literature thus far has largely been on examining how traditional cognitive tests (e.g., intelligence tests) relate to overall performance on the everyday problem-solving tests (e.g., Allaire & Marsiske, 2002) and whether age differences exist in everyday problem-solving performance (Thornton & Dumke, 2005). Thus, we know relatively little about the role of specific cognitive processes and everyday problem-solving performance.

Much of what we do know about age differences in cognitive processes involved in everyday problem-solving tasks comes from work on everyday decision making and reasoning, which represents in some ways a mid-point along what could be viewed as a continuum between well-defined and ill-defined everyday problem solving. Everyday decision making has examined a range of problems including decisions regarding purchasing cars (Johnson, 1990), over the counter medications (Johnson & Drungle, 2000), financial decisions (Chen & Sun, 2003; Hershey & Wilson, 1997), complex decisions regarding health, nutrition, and finance (Finucane, Mertz, Slovic, & Schmidt, 2005) to medical decisions as to treatments concerning breast cancer (Meyer, Russo, & Talbot, 1995) as well as hormone replacement therapy (Zwahr, Park, & Shiffren, 1999). These problems are not really well-defined in that they contain more than one solution, but perhaps not as ill-defined as are examined in the contextual literature as there are a limited number of decisions that can be made.

Findings from the decision making literature reveal that older adults frequently use less information to make a decision (e.g., Finucane et al., 2005; Johnson, 1990; Johnson & Drungle, 2000; Meyer et al., 1995) and that older adults sometimes attend to different kinds of information (Johnson & Drungle, 2000). Results are much less consistent, however, in whether the quality of the overall decision of older adults is disadvantaged relative to other groups, because of these differences in process. For instance, Meyer et al. (1995) found that although older adults searched for less information prior to making a decision, there were no age differences in the final treatment selected for breast cancer. Johnson and Drungle (2000) found that although older adults were slower to review information about over the counter medications, they displayed more organization in their search patterns. The ability of older adults to make a similar quality decision, despite differences in process may relate to their greater knowledge about treatment decisions (Meyer, Talbot, & Ranalli, 2007, but not always their greater experience with these decisions (Johnson & Drungle, 2000; Meyer et al., 1995). Experience may be important in understanding strategy flexibility (Patrick & Strough, 2004) and information considered (Berg et al., 1999). Age differences in processing have been described as a "mature" style by Sinnott (1989), and includes more of a top-down approach to gathering data and making decisions, as opposed to the bottom-up approach of younger adults (see also Meyer et al., 1995).

The decision-making literature has often linked the type of "mature" processing style of older adults to their greater use of a heuristic that may compensate for declining cognitive function (Chen & Sun, 2003; Johnson, 1990). Klaczynski and his colleagues, however, have explored how individuals of all ages rely on heuristic processing when problems are consistent with one's beliefs (Klaczynski, 2000, 2001; Klaczynski & Robinson, 2000), and that middle-aged and older adults may be more likely to engage in heuristic processing than young adults. Klaczynski's research demonstrates that individuals shift between two different processing systems (one analytical, the other heuristic) across problems that are either consistent with or inconsistent with one's belief systems. For instance, Klaczynski and Robinson (2000) explored how adults reasoned about problems that were either consistent with or inconsistent with their beliefs regarding religion and social class differences. The fact that middle-aged and older adults demonstrated more bias in their reasoning in terms of their beliefs, suggests that adults may rely on their own personal experiences to a greater extent in dealing with everyday problems than young adults.

Two-process theories of cognition have been used successfully in the child development and social psychological literature to address this variability in cognitive functioning in reasoning (Klaczynski, 2005; Stanovich & West, 1999) and decision making (Stanovich, 1999), and may fruitfully be applied to understanding adult age differences in everyday problem solving. In two-process theories (see Figure 18.2), decision making is determined by the interaction of two ongoing cognitive systems. Specific features of the context (e.g., familiarity of the task, accuracy demands) as well as of the individual (e.g., beliefs relevant to the problem) interact to push processing toward one system or the other on a specific problem.

Several properties of the two systems can be distinguished. Heuristic processing is highly contextualized processing that operates on representations where problem

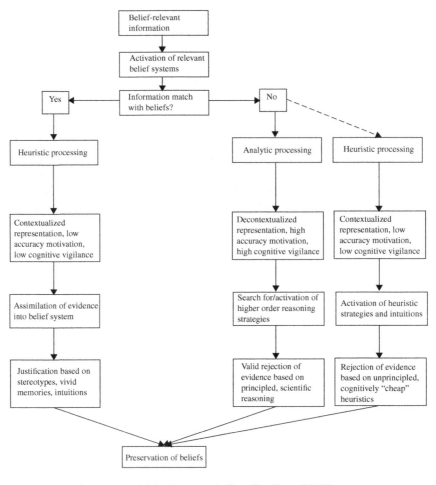

A two-process model of motivated reasoning biases. From Klaczynski (2000).
Adapted with permission of Elsevier Science.

Figure 18.2 A two-process model of motivated reasoning biases.

content is familiar and rich with existing beliefs and schemas (Stanovich & West, 1997). Analytic processing is de-contextualized and is more likely activated when the task is in some sense stripped of its familiarity and the activation of beliefs and schemas. Brainerd and Gordon (1994) relate these two systems to different types of encoding, where analytic processing is associated with verbatim traces and heuristic processing is associated with gist traces. Klaczynski's (2005) research has shown that the heuristic system predominates in daily life and may do so because it is more efficient (i.e., produces the same outcome but in a shorter time with less cognitive effort; see also Scribner, 1986).

We would like to suggest that these two cognitive systems may be useful in understanding the different results found in the well-defined and ill-defined approaches to everyday problem solving. In well-defined problem situations, the task characteristics described above (instructions to circle a single correct answer that makes salient accuracy demands) may activate the analytical processing system. However, ill-defined problems with their rich contextualized features including emotion, interpersonal, and task demands may activate the heuristic processing system. Older adults by virtue of their greater use of gist encoding (Adams, Labouvie-Vief, Hobart, & Dorosz, 1990; James, Burke, Austin, & Hulme, 1998), may gravitate more toward the heuristic processing system even in well-defined tasks.

There is still much to uncover concerning the cognitive processes involved as individuals solve everyday problems. The information that individuals selectively encode and process and how that information is used to select a decision or a problem-solving strategy are important to understand. The two-process model of cognition may be a beneficial framework to begin to explore these processes that may assist in the integration of well- and ill-defined approaches to everyday problem solving. The activation of the heuristic processing system may be especially affected by the emotions made salient by the rich context associated with its activation. We now explore how the processing of emotions in everyday problem-solving situations may be useful in understanding cognitive processing.

Everyday Problem Solving and Emotion

We have argued up to this point that appraisal processes, as defined by contextual and individual factors, pull for enactment of cognitive strategies consistent with problem definition. Similarly, when discussing the contribution of emotion and emotion regulation in everyday problem solving, the distinction between well-defined and ill-defined problems becomes important (Allaire & Marsiske, 2002) in how adults approach problem situations. Researchers using the well-defined approach to problem solving do not typically acknowledge the role of emotion in solving problems. In contrast, the majority of research within the ill-defined tradition, acknowledges the importance of emotion in understanding how individuals approach, solve, and appraise everyday problems (Blanchard-Fields, 1996; Blanchard-Fields et al., 1997). In fact, this research indicates that older adults may solve everyday problems better by virtue of their greater ability to regulate the emotions present in the problem (Blanchard-Fields, 1986; Watson & Blanchard-Fields, 1998). Emotional and cognitive systems appear to have differing developmental trajectories with both developmental changes being important for understanding the solution of everyday problems in adulthood (Diehl, Coyle, & Labouvie-Vief, 1996; Labouvie-Vief & Medler, 2002). In this section we will discuss adult age differences in emotional experience and how these developmental differences shape the importance and structure of emotion in solving everyday problems in terms of the ill-defined and well-defined traditions.

The suggestion that emotional modulation may be a primary strategy for containing everyday problems is reflected in the general literature regarding the emotional expression, experience, and control of emotions in later adulthood. Several studies indicate that older adults process and use emotions to interact with the environment in a more adaptive way than younger adults (Carstensen, Gottman, & Levenson, 1995; Carstensen, Pasupathi, Mayr, & Nesselroade, 2000; Lawton, Kleban, Rajagopal, & Dean, 1992). For example, older adults are less likely than young adults to experience long periods of negative emotion and may strive to regulate these negative emotions (Lawton et al., 1992) such that they often report less distress when these emotions occur (Carstensen et al., 2000). Similarly, Aldwin, Sutton, Chiara, and Spiro (1996) found that older individuals often appraised problems as trivial perhaps indicating that appraisals become less emotionally charged in late life. These findings indicate that as individuals age they may be more likely to appraise everyday problems as less emotionally salient but also may be more effective at regulating negative affect generated by everyday problem situations through the use of cognitive control and reappraisal (Carstensen et al., 1991; Carstensen et al., 2000).

Much of the work within the ill-defined approach to everyday problems has examined emotion modulation strategies borrowed from the stress and coping literature (i.e., emotion-focused coping; see Lazarus & Folkman, 1984). Older adults may utilize more emotion-focused strategies or strategies aimed at controlling the internal environment for managing everyday problems (Blanchard-Fields & Irion, 1988; Folkman, Lazarus, Pimley, & Novacek, 1987; Lazarus & Folkman, 1984; Levine & Bluck, 1997) than do young adults. For example, Folkman et al. (1987) found that older adults were more likely to use strategies for coping that included distancing and positive reappraisal whereas younger adults relied more on instrumental coping strategies for managing stressful experiences. These attempts to regulate emotions may be a function of increased affect reactivity to stressful experiences. Mroczek (2001, 2004) found that older adults show a stronger association between stress and negative affect than younger individuals. However, other research has suggested that older adults do not exclusively use more emotion-focused strategies but rather use strategies that are complimentary to individuals' problem definitions (Berg et al., 1998). For example, if a particular problem was defined as interpersonal, the use of managing or controlling others was employed. These findings suggest that older adults may be more likely to use emotional reappraisal as a way of compensating for negative emotions that arise during problem solving contexts or matching different goals in these situations.

The ability to regulate emotions may be of particular importance for solving interpersonal problems (Blanchard-Fields, 1997; Fredrickson & Carstensen, 1990; Sansone & Berg 1993). Carstensen and colleagues (1991; Carstensen et al., 2000) link older adults' greater ability to regulate emotions with the idea that their goals for social interaction are oriented more toward emotional regulation (i.e., increasing positive mood and minimizing negative mood) than younger adults (Carstensen, 1991; Carstensen, Isaacowitz, & Charles, 1999; Carstensen et al., 2000; Lang, Staudinger, & Carstensen, 1998). Blanchard-Fields et al. (1995) found that in contexts high in emotional salience (e.g., interpersonal domains) older adults used more passive-dependent and avoidant strategies and more emotion regulation strategies than did middle-aged or younger adults.. Further, these differences were confined to problems high in emotional salience; there were no age differences in low or medium emotionally salient problems (Blanchard-Fields et al., 1997). However, this is not to say that older individuals exclusively focused on emotional regulation. When solving interpersonal conflict situations, older adults preferred emotion-focused strategies in combination with problem-focused coping and increased cognitive analysis, whereas younger age groups preferred passive dependent strategies. This might suggest that older adults manage their emotional states in the context of emotionally charged problems by using more suppression of emotion and acceptance of the problem situation, perhaps due to their different goals (Sorkin & Rook, 2006), compared to younger adults who often prefer to understand emotions and use outward expression of emotion (Blanchard-Fields et al., 1995; Blanchard-Fields et al., 1997). Thus, older adults may demonstrate a more diverse and perhaps flexible repertoire of strategies that include both emotion and problem-focused coping regarding everyday problems.

Affective Complexity. Labouvie-Vief and colleagues (Labouvie-Vief et al., 1989a, 1989b) examined a different facet of emotional experience, that is, the role of affective complexity and differentiation in everyday problem situations. This is consistent with her work that views cognitive functioning as becoming increasingly intertwined with affective understanding during middle and late adulthood. Affect complexity involves the ability to analyze emotional reactions at high levels of conceptual complexity and experience the ambiguity of mixed emotions. Diehl, Coyle, and Labouvie-Vief (1996) suggest that the ability to think dynamically about emotion is associated with more adaptive emotional responses linked with mature and flexible coping (e.g., impulse control, acceptance, cognitive restructuring). Labouvie-Vief et al. (1989a) have found that ego level and cognitive ability have been associated with older adults' ability to use mature and flexible coping strategies. Further, they found that middle-aged and older adults were more cognitively and affectively integrated than younger adults, indicating high affect complexity and high maintenance of positive affect (Labouvie-Vief & Medler, 2002). However, there is a potential decline in affect complexity and differentiation in late adulthood (i.e., focus on the positive, minimize the negative), that may prevent rich explorations of affect and problem solution. Thus, cognitive complexity and affective integration may contribute to the use of greater emotion regulatory strategies leading to more effective problem approach.

Emotion Regulation.   Thus far we have discussed the importance of emotion regulation in the context of older adults managing everyday problems that are ill-defined and that are frequently interpersonal. This literature indicates that emotion regulation is an important goal in daily life and a mechanism by which a person copes with problems, especially when the context is fraught with emotional content. Additionally, results indicate that affect and cognition are increasing intertwined in middle age and later adulthood (Labouvie-Vief, 2003). We are now starting to see research emerge as to how emotion may function within the well-defined problem solving literature that may help us identify the overarching contribution of emotion to well-defined problem solving.

In the literature on more traditional or well-defined problem solving tasks, emotion is examined as it may interfere with the ability to manage problems effectively (e.g., heightened arousal from anxiety) and impede the cognitive functioning necessary to generate and implement effective solutions (Lazarus & Folkman, 1984). For example, Phillips, Smith, and Gilhooly (2002) found that induced positive and negative mood influenced older adults', but not younger adults' ability to effectively solve a typical planning problem where the goal was to efficiently achieve the correct solution by using the minimum number of moves to do so. The authors concluded that emotion regulation strategies took priority above cognitive efficiency for older adults. Further, older adults recovered more quickly from the negative mood states than younger adults (Phillips, Smith, & Gilhooly, 2002). These findings might suggest that older adults would be initially impaired in well-defined everyday problem-solving tasks but would be quicker to adjust to emotionally salient problems over time. This is important as many everyday problems are ones that have a long temporal extension.

Although emotion may be a liability when attempting to find a correct solution to a problem, other research has shown that emotion can produce both gains and losses in cognitive control and memory. Dreisbach and Goschke (2004) found in a cognitive set-switching paradigm that affect induction was associated with increased cognitive flexibility and reduced perseveration, but that this occurred at the cost of increased distractibility. This work did not examine the effect that adult age may have on these effects. Older adults seem especially to benefit when the content of the material is positive, termed the positivity effect. For example, Mather and Knight (2005) found that older adults used more elaborative processing when viewing positive images as they remembered more positive images compared to negative images (see also Carstensen & Turk-Charles, 1994; Mikels, Larkin, Reuter-Lorenz, & Carstensen, 2005).

Taken together, the findings on how affect impacts cognitive performance and memory efficiency and flexibility suggests that, to the extent that emotional goals are incompatible with cognitive outcomes (e.g., efficiently solving a puzzle), emotion may relate to lower ability to achieve effective solutions. However, if the emotional goals are consistent with the task (e.g., memory for emotional imagery or content), performance is improved. If emotion regulation strategies take priority, one must be able to shift from cognitive control to mood management. If this control is taxed, the individual may not be able to focus on emotional goals. This fit between goals and strategies harkens back to the literature within the ill-defined tradition where emotion regulation is a goal for older adults and leads to greater emotion-focused coping.

In general, the ill-defined and well-defined traditions of everyday problem solving are rich with the notion that emotion plays an important role in how individuals solve everyday problems. There also appears to be a large overlap between how emotion may be acting in these very disparate contexts. We see that in both traditions emotion is integral to how individuals appraise problem-solving situations, set goals, process the information, enact strategies, and the effectiveness of those strategies. However, these two literatures have as of yet come together to form a comprehensive understanding of where emotional processes come into action with consideration of problem context, individual difference variables, physiological arousal, and social resources.

Physiological Processes

The field of everyday problem solving has focused on cognitive resources and, to some extent, emotion regulation as individuals manage daily problems. The physiological processes involved as adults solve such problems have, however, not been systematically examined. Currently, ongoing research in several laboratories aims to address whether older adults are more physiologically aroused as a result of experiencing everyday problems compared to other aged adults and whether this arousal may impair effective solutions.

The idea that daily stressful events are associated with higher blood pressure reactivity is supported in the work of Kamarck et al. (2005). The extant literature is much less clear on whether there are reliable age differences in reactivity to daily stress. Drawing from the work examining individuals in marital conflict situations, older adults show lower physiological responses (Levenson, Carstensen, & Gottmann, 1994) than middle-aged adults. However, physiological responses to acute stressors (e.g., a prepared speech task) show elevated cardiovascular reactivity in older adults as compared to younger adults (Jennings, Kamarck, Manuck, Everson, Kaplan, & Salonen, 1997; Uchino, Holt-Lunstad, Bloor, & Campo, 2005).

In our research, we have examined the physiological reactivity of middle-aged and older adult couples as they experienced everyday stressors in their daily lives (Uchino et al., 2006). Individuals' ambulatory blood pressure and heart rate were monitored for one day as they completed diaries about mood and experiences of an everyday stressor. Although older adults reported less negative affect to daily stress than younger adults, they experienced greater increases in blood pressure. These results point to the possibility that self-reported affect and physiological responses may be uncoupled in daily life (Cacioppo & Berntson, 1992). Although we do not have data on coping processes, it is possible that coping strategies may be responsible for the uncoupling of affect and physiological reactivity. For example, given the literature, it may be the case the older adults used greater emotion-focused strategies to manage everyday problems, thereby regulating affect but not having benefits for physiological responding.

In other recent work, Tugade and Fredrickson (2004) found that when faced with anticipation of a laboratory stressor, individuals characterized by high resiliency (e.g., flexible management of stressful encounters, modification to meet environmental demands) had faster cardiovascular recovery post stressor. They also found that those characterized by high resiliency were more likely to find positive meaning in everyday problems, in vivo (Tugade & Fredrickson, 2004). Such results are consistent with work on stress exposure and immune system dysregulation, which further details how coping responses that are matched with the appraisal of the stressor may either prolong or reduce physiological arousal. Hawley et al. (2005) found that if a stressor is perceived to be controllable to some extent active coping may temporarily increase heart rate, blood flow and physiological reactivity, and this may be the best way to mobilize resources for problem solution. However, if the stressor is uncontrollable, active coping may unnecessarily activate physiological response without promise of resolution. Here we see the importance of the temporal nature of the everyday problem in understanding physiological dysregulation and chronic stress exposure.

Taken together, these results might suggest that acute well-defined everyday problems may not perpetuate dysregulation of cardiovascular or immune system function. However, when exposure increases or becomes ill-defined and chronic this may lead to health declines. Further, this work reveals that older adults may be at a greater risk for dysregulation in immune system function. Our initial work in this area and the work of others provide fertile ground for additional investigations that are of interest in the field to examine additional elements of physiological response (e.g., galvanic skin response, cortisol) as it relates to coping with daily problems and laboratory stressors.

The physiological processes underlying everyday problem-solving performance may be helpful in understanding how coping with everyday stressors may hold long-term health implications. For example, maladaptive or avoidance coping strategies such as increased substance abuse, wishful thinking, and hostile reaction have been associated with ineffective or negative health outcomes such as increased risk of cancer and cardiovascular disease (Bolger, 1990). Effective coping strategies (e.g., planful problem solving, seeking social support) have been associated with more positive health benefits. The accumulated effects of physiological arousal and the continued utilization of ineffective coping strategies may lead to long term health concerns. Understanding how physiological arousal is experienced and addressed on a daily basis may help address how everyday problems influence physical health.

Our research has also focused on physiological responses as individuals are in collaboration with other individuals. As we have discussed above, a substantial number of the problems that individuals experience on a daily basis involve other individuals and an important way that others are involved is in direct collaboration. The effect of other people as one is engaged in a task on physiological outcomes has been widely explored in the social support literature where social support has been related to several health outcomes such as immune system function, recovery from surgery, and blood pressure reactivity (Scheier, Matthews, Owens, Schulz, Bridges, Magovern, & Carver, 1999; Uchino, Cacioppo, & Kiecolt-Glaser, 1992). Having a marital partner or family member present as one is doing a task is associated with decreased cardiovascular reactivity during social interactions (Holt-Lundstad et al., 2003). The closer the relationship with one's collaborators, the greater is the decrease in physiological arousal experienced (Holt-Lundstad et al. 2003).

In our research, we have examined cardiovascular reactivity as married couples engage in a typical marital conflict task (where couples are asked to engage in a discussion about a typical area of conflict in their marriage) as well as a collaborative problem-solving task frequently used in the everyday problem solving literature (i.e., an errand running task). As couples engage in the tasks, blood pressure and heart rate are taken. Our results indicate that for all groups (except older husbands), cardiovascular reactivity is much lower in the collaborative problem-solving task than in the marital conflict task. However, the physiological reactivity of older husbands in the collaboration task is as high as it is for the conflict task (Smith et al., 2006). The older husbands' reactivity seems to be due, in part, to having to engage in a collaborative manner on a task in which they perceive (and actually are) more cognitively capable in performing than are their wives (Berg et al., 2004).

These results are suggestive of an important, but only recently examined, component of everyday problem solving, that of physiological arousal. As everyday problems are ones that are frequently experienced as stressors with accompanying negative emotions, physiological arousal may help explain when individuals are able to coordinate negative affect and cognition and when the system is sufficiently taxed that regulatory processes become more difficult to implement. Research is needed that incorporates not only the sorts of ill-defined problems that we have examined in our own research, but examines physiological arousal as it occurs when individuals solve well-defined problems.

Summary and Conclusions

We have presented in this chapter an initial model of everyday problem solving that attempts to integrate the well-defined and ill-defined approaches to everyday problem solving. This model extends beyond the traditional focus on cognitive function and everyday problem solving to understand how everyday problem solving exists within different contexts and how individuals come to these contexts with different resources and abilities. In addition, the model explored the cognitive, emotional, and physiological processes that may be involved as individuals deal with everyday problems. As illustrated throughout our review, these processes are not separable, but interact in complex ways that are beginning to be understood.

This model includes numerous factors that have traditionally been outside the realm of everyday problem-solving research (e.g., personality, physiology). However, we posit that such a broad model may assist us in getting closer to the original goal of everyday problem-solving research, which is to understand how everyday problem solving is associated with successful adaptation to everyday life. Very few studies have explored whether performance on everyday problem-solving tasks is important for understanding successful everyday functioning (Allaire & Marsiske, 2002; Diehl, Willis, & Schaie, 1995). These studies have examined adaptation to everyday life through functional ability as assessed by instrumental activities of daily living (Allaire & Marsiske, 2002), observational counterparts of hypothetical problem solving tasks (Diehl et al., 1995), or clinically meaningful outcomes such as mortality and impaired cognitive status (Allaire & Willis, 2006). These attempts are important ones at establishing the validity of everyday problem-solving measures, especially for adults of advanced age. Future work must expand on these attempts to understand a broader range of adaptational outcomes that may extend to young, middle-aged and young-old adults.

As the field explores adaptation outcomes more relevant to adults in young, middle adulthood, and young-old adulthood, the notion of "successful aging" may be useful as a broad starting point for examining possible outcomes. Successful aging has been conceptualized in two primary ways: by identifying domains of successful functioning (Rowe

& Kahn, 1997) and processes whereby individuals achieve a good person-environment fit (e.g., Baltes & Baltes, 1990; Lawton, 1983). According to Rowe and Kahn (1997), successful aging involves achieving success in cognitive functioning, physical health, and social relations. The ways in which everyday problems are solved may play a role in each of these outcomes, as is implied throughout our review, although the literature has focused heavily on the relation between everyday problem solving and success in cognitive functioning.

The link between everyday problem-solving performance and health outcomes has been noted throughout our review. Particularly within the health domain, individuals who appropriately make good decisions regarding chronic health conditions (e.g., breast cancer, hormone replacement therapy, over the counter medications) may directly benefit from making better decisions (Johnson & Drungle, 2000; Meyer et al., 1995; Zwahr et al., 1999). On an everyday basis, individuals who are at risk for how they appraise and deal with everyday problems (e.g., high in neuroticism, low in optimism, high in hostility) are at increased risk for a host of physical health problems including cardiovascular disease (Smith & Ruiz, 2004), suppressed immune function (McGuire, Kiecolt-Glaser, & Glaser, 2002), and negative health behaviors (Carney, Freedland, Rich, & Jaffe, 1995). An important area for future research will be to examine if these personality risk factors are associated with poor health outcomes as a function of poorer everyday problem solving performance and emotional dysregulation.

Similarly, the role of everyday problem solving in understanding successful social relationships will be an important area for future research. As noted throughout our review, a large part of what makes up a good everyday problem solver is one who can effectively deal with other individuals (see also Hartley, 1989). D'Zurilla and colleagues (Chang et al., 2004) have established that solving social problems is associated with less distress for college students. Additional work linking the ways in which adults solve everyday problems and their goals and strategies in interpersonal situations will be important as negative social exchanges detract from life satisfaction (Sorkin & Rook, 2006).

A second approach to successful aging has emphasized how individuals manage their goals, motivations, and approach to problems in a way that maximizes life satisfaction (see Freund & Riediger, 2003, for a review) and mood. With aging, individuals may shift their goals from assimilating to stressors to accommodating and shifting goals (Brandtstadter & Greve, 1994), change the balance of primary and secondary control attempts (Heckhausen & Schulz, 1995), and increasingly use strategies such as selective optimization with compensation (Baltes & Baltes, 1990). The role of these broader developmental processes in everyday problem solving would be a very fruitful direction for future research and may help to explain some of the age-related differences seen in the strategies individual use to deal with everyday problems and the emotions that they experience.

Consistent with the focus in this volume on adult learning, our integrative model has implications for the study of adult learning. In late life, older adults are faced with many new everyday problems (e.g., health concerns, changes in health insurance, problems oriented around relocation, loss of spouse), which pose challenges for their routine ways of approaching problems. As adults learn to deal with these new types of problems, the broad integrative approach described here may be fruitfully applied to the study of adult learning. Understanding not only the cognitive processes that an individual uses to approach a problem, but the emotional and physiological processes that are activated in a learning environment may shed light on the design of effective learning environments for adults.

In summary, we hope that the broad approach outlined here to work on everyday problem solving across the adult life span will serve to integrate the work on ill-defined and well-defined everyday problems in a way that fosters cross-fertilizations rather than increasing separateness in these literatures. Such an integration is important as the daily problems that adults experience likely involve both well- and ill-defined problems. The field of everyday problem solving has amassed an impressive array of tasks and strategies that adults use as they deal with their everyday world. The task for the future will be to understand how performance on these tasks relates to the complex ways that adults can achieve success in their everyday lives.

Note

Cynthia Berg was supported by grant R01 DK063044-01A2 from the National Institute of Diabetes and Digestive and Kidney Diseases. Some of the research reported in this article was supported by a grant from the National Institutes of Aging R01 AG 18903 awarded to Timothy Smith (PI) and Cynthia Berg (co-PI).

References

Adams, C., Labouvie-Vief, G., Hobart, C. J., & Dorosz, M. (1990). Adult age group differences in story recall style. *Journal of Gerontology, 45*, 17–27.

Aldwin, C. M., Sutton, K. J., Chiara, G., & Spiro, A. (1996). Age differences in stress, coping, and appraisal: Findings from the normative aging study. *Journal of Gerontology: Psychological Sciences, 51B*, 179–188.

Allaire, J. C., & Marsiske, M. (1999). Everyday cognition: Age and intellectual ability correlates. *Psychology and Aging, 14*(4), 627–644.

Allaire, J. C., & Marsiske, M. (2002). Well- and ill-defined measures of everyday cognition: Relationship to older adults' intellectual ability and functional status. *Psychology & Aging, 17*(1), 101–115.

Allaire, J. C., & Willis, S. L. (2006). Competence in everyday activities as a predictor of cognitive risk and mortality. *Aging, neuropsychology, and cognition, 13*, 207–224.

Allread, K .D., & Smith, T.W. (1991). Social cognition in cynical hostility. *Cognitive Therapy and Research, 15*, 399–412.

Artistico, D., Cervone, D., & Pezzuti, L. (2003). Perceived self-efficacy and everyday problem solving among young and older adults. *Psychology & Aging, 18*(1), 68–79.

Aspinwall, L. G. (2001). Dealing with adversity: Self-regulation, coping, adaptation, and health. In A. Tesser & N. Schwarz (Eds.), *The Blackwell handbook of social psychology, Vol. 1. Intrapersonal processes*. Malden, MA: Blackwell.

Baltes, M. M., Mayr, U., Borchelt, M., Maas, I., & Wilms, H.-U. (1993). Everyday competence in old and very old age. An interdisciplinary perspective. *Ageing and Society, 13*, 657–680.

Baltes, P. B. & Baltes, M. M. (1990). Psychological perspectives on successful aging: The model of selective optimization with compensation. In P. B. Baltes & M. M. Baltes (Eds.), *Successful aging: Perspectives from the behavioral sciences* (pp. 1–34). New York: Cambridge University Press.

Berg, C. A. (2008). Everyday problem solving in context. In S. Hofer & D. Alwin (Eds.), *Handbook of cognitive aging: Interdisciplinary perspectives* (pp. 207–208). Newbury Park, CA: Sage.

Berg, C. A., & Calderone, K. S. (1994). The role of problem interpretations in understanding the development of everyday problem solving. In R. J. Sternberg & R. K. Wagner (Eds.), *Mind in context: Interactionist perspectives on human intelligence* (pp. 105–132). New York: Cambridge University Press.

Berg, C. A., Johnson, M. M. S., Meegan, S. P., & Strough, J. (2003). Collaborative problem-solving interaction in young and old married couples. *Discourse Processes, 35*, 33–58.

Berg, C. A., & Klaczynksi, P. (1996). Practical intelligence and problem solving: Searching for perspectives. In F. Blanchard-Fields & T. M. Hess (Eds.), *Perspectives on cognition in adulthood and aging*, (pp. 323-357). New York: McGraw-Hill.

Berg, C. A ., & Klaczynski, P. (2002) Contextual variability in the expression and meaning of intelligence. In R. J. Sternberg & E .L. Grigorenko (Eds.), *The general factor of intelligence: How general is it?* (pp. 381–412). Mahwah, NJ: Erlbaum.

Berg, C. A., Meegan, S. P., & Deviney, F. P. (1998). A social contextual model of coping with everyday problems across the life span. *International Journal of Behavioral Development, 22*(2), 239–261.

Berg, C. A., Meegan, S. P., & Klaczynski, P. (1999). Age and experiential differences in strategy generation and information requests for solving everyday problems. *International Journal of Behavioral Development,23*, 615–639.

Berg, C., Smith, T., Ko, K., Beveridge, R., Allen, N., Florsheim, P., et al. (2007). Task control and cognitive abilities of self and spouse in collaboration in middle-aged and older couples. *Psychology and Aging, 22*, 420–427.

Berg, C. A., & Sternberg, R. J. (1985). A triarchic theory of intellectual development during adulthood. *Developmental Review, 5*, 334–370.

Berg, C. A., Strough, J., Calderone, K. S., Meegan, S. P., & Sansone, C. (1997). The social context of planning and preventing everyday problems from occurring. In S. L. Friedman, & E. K. Scholnick (Eds.), *Why, how, and when do we plan? The developmental psychology of planning* (pp. 209–236). Hillsdale, NJ: Erlbaum.

Berg, C. A., Strough, J., Calderone, K. S., Sansone, C., & Weir, C. (1998). The role of problem definitions in understanding age and contexteffects on strategies for solving everyday problems. *Psychology and Aging, 5*, 334–370.

Berg, C. A., Wiebe, D. J., Butner, J., Bloor, L., Bradstreet, C., Upchurch, R., Hayes, J., Stephenson, R., Nail, L., & Patton, G. (in press). Collaborative coping and daily mood in couples dealing with prostate cancer. *Psychology and Aging.*

Blanchard-Fields, F. (1986). Reasoning on social dilemmas varying in emotional saliency: An adult developmental perspective. *Psychology and Aging, 1*, 325–333.

Blanchard-Fields, F., & Chen, Y. (1996). Adaptive cognition and aging. *American Behavioral Scientist, 39*(3), 231–248.

Blanchard-Fields, F., Chen, Y., & Norris, L. (1997). Everyday problem solving across the life span: Influence of domain specificity and cognitive appraisal. *Psychology and Aging, 12*, 684–693.

Blanchard-Fields, F., Chen, Y., Schocke, M., & Hertzog, C. (1998). Evidence for content-specificity of causal attributions across the adult life span. *Aging, Neuropsychology, and Cognition, 5*, 241–263.

Blanchard-Fields, F., & Irion, J. (1988b). The relation between locus of control and coping in two contexts: Age as a moderator variable. *Psychology and Aging, 3*, 197–203.

Blanchard-Fields, F., Jahnke, H. C., & Camp, C. (1995). Age differences in problem-solving style: The role of emotional salience. *Psychology and Aging, 10*, 173–180.

Bolger, N. (1990). Coping as a personality process: A prospective study. *Journal of Personality and Social Psychology, 59*, 525–537.

Bolger, N., & Schilling, E. A. (1991). Personality and the problems of everyday life: The role of neuroticism in exposure and reactivity to daily stressors. *Journal of Personality, 59*, 355–386.

Brainerd, C. J., & Gordon, L. L. (1994). Development of verbatim and gist memory for numbers. *Developmental Psychology, 20*, 163–177.

Brandtstadter, J., & Greve, W. (1994). The aging self: Stabilizing and protective processes. *Developmental Review, 14*, 52–80.

Cacioppo, J. T., & Bernston, G. G. (1992). Social psychological contributions to the decade of the brain. Doctrine of multilevel analysis. *American Psychologist, 47*, 1019–1028.

Carstensen, L. L., Gottman, J. M., & Levenson, R. W. (1995). Emotional behavior in long-term marriage. *Psychology and Aging, 10*, 140–149.

Carstensen, L. L., Isaacowitz, D. M., & Charles, C. T. (1999). Taking time seriously: A theory of socioemotional selectivity. *American Psychologist, 54*, 165–181.

Carstensen, L. L., Pasupathi, M., Mayr, U., & Nesselroade, J. R. (2000). Emotional experience in everyday life across the adult life span. *Journal of Personality and Social Psychology, 79*, 644–655.

Carstensen, L. L., & Turk-Charles, S. (1994). The salience of emotion across the adult life course. *Psychology and Aging, 9*, 259–264.

Carney, R. M., Freedland, K. E., Rich, M. W., & Jaffee, A. S. (1995). Depression as a risk factor for cardiac events in established coronary heart disease: A review of possible mechanisms. *Annals of Behavioral Medicine, 17*, 142–149.

Carver, C. S., & Gaines, J. G. (1987). Optimism, pessimism, and post-partum depression. *Cognitive Therapy and Research, 11*, 449–462.

Carver, C. S., & Scheier, M. F. (2001). Optimism, pessimism, and self-regulation. In E. C. Chang (Ed.), *Optimism and pessimism: Implications for theory, research, and practice* (pp. 31–52). Washington, DC: American Psychological Association.

Chang, E. C., D'Zurilla, T. J., & Lawrence, S. (Eds.). (2004). *Social problem solving: Theory, research, and training.* Washington, DC: American Psychological Association.

Chen, Y., & Sun, Y. (2003). Age differences in financial decision-making: Using simple heuristics. *Educational Gerontology, 29*, 627–635.

Cicirelli, V. (2006). Caregiving decision making by older mothers and adult children: Process and expected outcome. *Psychology and Aging. 21*, 209–221.

Cornelius, S. W., & Caspi, A. (1987). Everyday problem solving in adulthood and old age. *Psychology and Aging, 2*, 144–153.

Crick, N. R., & Dodge, K. A. (1994). A review and reformulation of social information processing mechanisms in children's social adjustment. *Psychological Bulletin, 115*, 74–101.

Demming, J. A., & Pressey, S. L. (1957). Tests "indigenous" to adult and older years. *Journal of Counseling Psychology, 4*, 144–148.

Denney, N. W. (1989). Everyday problem solving: Methodological issues, research findings, and a model. In L. W. Poon, D. C. Rubin, & B. A. Wilson (Eds.), *Everyday cognition in adulthood and late life* (pp. 330–351). New York: Cambridge University Press.

Diehl, M., Coyle, N., & Labouvie-Vief, G. (1996). Age and sex differences in strategies of coping and defense across the life span. *Psychology and Aging, 11*(1), 127–139.

Diehl, M., Willis, S. L., & Schaie, K. W. (1995). Everyday problem solving in older adults: Observational assessment and cognitive correlates. *Psychology and Aging, 10*(3), 478–491.

Dixon, R. A., Gagnon, L. M., & Crow, C. B. (1998). Collaborative memory accuracy and distortion: Performance and beliefs. In M. J. Intons-Peterson & D. L. Best (Eds.), *Memory distortions and their prevention* (pp. 63–88). Mahwah, NJ: Erlbaum.

Dixon, R. A., & Gould, O. N. (1996). Adults telling and retelling stories collaboratively. In P. B. Baltes & U. M. Staudinger (Eds.), *Interactive minds: Life-span perspectives on the social foundation of cognition* (pp. 221–241). New York: Cambridge University Press.

Dixon, R. (1999). Exploring cognition in interactive settings: The aging of N+1 minds. In T. M. Hess & F. Blanchard-Fields (Eds.), *Social cognition and aging* (pp. 297–290). San Diego, CA: Academic.

Dreisbach, G., & Goschke, T. (2004). How positive affect modulates cognitive control: Reduced preservation at the cost of increased distractibility. *Journal of Experimental Psychology, 30*(2), 343–353.

Epstein, S., Lipson, A., Holstein, C., & Huh, E. (1992). Irrational reactions to negative outcomes: Evidence for two conceptual systems. *Journal of Personality and Social Psychology, 62*, 328–339.

Finucane, M. L., Mertz, C. K., Slovic, P., & Schmidt, E. S. (2005). Task complexity and older adults' decision-making competence. *Psychology and Aging, 20*(1), 71–84.

Folkman, S., Lazarus, R. S., Pimley, S., & Novacek, J. (1987). Age differences in stress and coping processes. *Psychology and Aging, 2*, 171–184.

Fredrickson, B. L., & Carstensen, L. L. (1990). Choosing social partners: How old age and anticipated endings make people more selective. *Psychology and Aging, 5*, 335–347.

Fredrickson, B. L., & Joiner, T. (2002). Positive emotions trigger upward spirals toward emotional well-being. *Psychological Science, 13*(2), 172–175.

Freund, A. M., & Riediger, M. (2003). Successful aging. In R. M. Lerner, M. A. Easterbrooks, & J. Mistry (Eds.), *Handbook of psychology: Vol. 6: Developmental psychology* (pp. 601–628). New York: Wiley.

Gould, O. N., Kurzman, D., & Dixon, R. A. (1994). Communication during prose recall conversations by young and old dyads. *Discourse Processes, 17*, 149–165.

Hartley, A. A. (1989). The cognitive ecology of problem solving. In L. W. Poon, D. C. Rubin, & B. A. Wilson (Eds.), *Everyday cognition in adulthood and late life.* New York: Cambridge University Press.

Hawley, L. C., Berntson, G. G., Engleland, C. G., Marucha, P. T., Masi, C. M., & Cacioppo, J. T. (2005). Stress, aging, and resilience: Can accrued war and tear be slowed? *Canadian Psychology, 46*(3), 115–125.

Heckhausen, J. (1997). Developmental regulation across adulthood: Primary and secondary control of age-related challenges. *Developmental Psychology, 33,* 176–187.

Heckhausen, J., & Schulz, R. (1995). A life-span theory of control. *Psychological Review, 102,* 284–304.

Hershey, D. A., & Wilson, J. A. (1997). Age differences in performance on a complex financial decision making task. *Experimental Aging Research, 23,* 257–273.

Holahan, C. J., & Moos, R. H. (1987). Personal and contextual determinants of coping strategies. *Journal of Personality and Social Psychology, 52*(5), 946–955.

Holt-Lunstad, J., Uchino, B. N., Smith, T. W., Cerny, C. B., & Nealey-Moore, J. B. (2003). Social relationships and ambulatory blood pressure: Structural and qualitative predictors of cardiovascular function during everyday social interactions. *Health Psychology, 22,* 388–397.

Hooker, K. (1999). Possible selves in adulthood: Incorporating telonomic relevance into studies of the self. In T. M. Hess & F. Blanchard-Fields (Eds.), *Social cognition and aging* (pp. 97–116). New York: Academic Press.

Isen, A. M. (2000). Positive affect and decision making. In M. Lewis & J. M. Haviland-Jones (Eds.), *Handbook of emotions* (pp. 417–435). New York: Guilford.

James, L. E., Burke, D. M., Austin, A., & Hulme, E. (1998). Production and perception of "verbosity" in younger and older adults. *Psychology and Aging, 13*(3), 355–376.

Jennings, J. R., Kamarck, T., Manuck, S., Everson, S., Kaplan, G., Salonen, J. (1997). Aging or disease? Cardiovascular reactivity in Finnish men over the middle years. *Psychology and Aging, 12,* 225–238.

Johansson, O., Andersson, J., & Ronnberg, J. (2000). Do elderly couples have a better prospective memory than other elderly people when they collaborate? *Applied Cognitive Psychology, 14,* 121–133.

Johnson, M. M. S. (1990). Age differences in decision making: A process methodology for examining strategic information processing. *Journal of Gerontology, 45,* 75–78.

Johnson, M. M. S., & Drungle, S. C. (2000). Purchasing over-the-counter medications: The influence of age and familiarity. *Experimental Aging Research, 26,* 245–261.

Kamarck, T. W., Schwartz, J. E., Shiffman, S., Muldoon, M. F., Sutton-Tyrrell, K., & Janicki, D. L. (2005). Psychosocial stress and cardiovascular risk: What is the role of daily experience? *Journal of Personality, 73*(6), 1–26.

Kahneman, D., Slovic, P., & Tversky, A. (1982). *Judgment under uncertainty: Heuristics and biases.* New Yorj: Cambridge University Press.

Klaczynski, P. A. (2000). Motivated scientific reasoning biases, epistemological beliefs, and theory polarization: A two-process approach to adolescent cognition. *Child Development, 71,* 1347–1366.

Klaczynski, P. A. (2001). Framing effects on adolescent task representations, analytic and heuristic processing, and decision making: Implications for the normative-descriptive gap. *Journal of Applied Developmental Psychology, 22* 289–309.

Klaczynski, P. A. (2005). Metacognition and cognitive variability: A dual-process model of decision making and its development. In J. E. Jacobs & P. A. Klaczynski (Eds.), *The development of judgment and decision making in children and adolescents* (pp. 39–76). Mahwah, NJ: Erlbaum.

Klaczynski, P. A., & Robinson, B. (2000). Personal theories, intellectual ability, and epistemological beliefs: Adult age differences in everyday reasoning biases. *Psychology and Aging, 15,* 400–416.

Labouvie-Vief, G. (1982). Dynamic development and mature autonomy: A theoretical prologue. *Human Development, 25,* 161–191.

Labouvie-Vief, G. (2003). Dynamic integration: Affect, cognition, and the self in adulthood. *Current Directions in Psychological Science, 201–206.*

Labouvie-Vief, G., DeVoe, M., & Bulka, D. (1989a). Speaking about feelings: Conceptions of emotion across the life span. *Psychology and Aging, 4,* 425–437.

Labouvie-Vief, G., Hakim-Larson, J., DeVoe, M., & Schoeberlein, S. (1989b). Emotions and self-regulation: A life span view. *Human Development, 32,* 279–299.

Labouvie-Veif, G., & Medler, M. (2002). Affect optimization and affect complexity: Modes and styles of regulation in adulthood. *Psychology and Aging, 17*(4), 571–588.

Laipple, J. S. (1991). *Problem solving in young and old adulthood: The role of task interpretation.* Unpublished doctoral dissertation, West Virginia University, Morgantown.

Lang, F. R., Staudinger, U. M., & Carstensen, L. L. (1998). Perspectives on socioemotional selectivity in late life: How personality and social context do (and do not) make a difference. *Journal of Gerontology: Psychological Sciences, 53B*(1), 21–30.

Larsen, R. J., & Ketelaar, T. (1989). Extroversion, neuroticism and susceptibility to positive and negative mood induction procedures. *Personality and Individual Differences, 10,* 1221–1228.

Lawton, M. P. (1983). The varieties of wellbeing. *Experimental Aging Research, 9*(2), 65–72.

Lawton, M. P., Kleban, M. H., Rajagopal, D., & Dean, J. (1992). The dimensions of affective experience in three age groups. *Psychology and Aging, 7,* 171–184.

Lazarus, R. S., & Folkman, S. (1984). *Stress, appraisal, and coping.* New York: Springer.

Levenson, R. W., Carstensen, L. L., & Gottman, J. M. (1994). The influence of age and gender on affect, physiology, and their interrelations: A study of long-term marriages. *Journal of Personality and Social Psychology, 67,* 56–68.

Levine, L. J., & Bluck, S. (1997). Experienced and remembered emotional intensity in older adults. *Psychology and Aging, 12*(3), 514–523.

Maitlin, J. A., Wethington, E. M., & Kesser, R. C. (1990). Situational determinants of coping and coping effectiveness. *Journal of Health and Social Behaviour, 31,* 103–122.

Margrett, J. A., & Marsiske, M. (2002). Gender differences in older adults' everyday cognitive collaboration. *International Journal of Behavioral Development, 26,* 45–59.

Markus, H. R., & Kitayama, S. (2003). Culture, self, and the reality of the social. *Psychological Inquiry, 14,* 277–283.

Marsiske, M., & Margrett, J. (2006). Everyday problem solving and decision making. In J. E. Birren & K. W. Schaie (Eds.), *Handbook of the psychology of aging* (6th ed, pp. 315–342). Burlington, MA: Academic Press.

Marsiske, M., & Willis, S. L. (1995). Dimensionality of everyday problem solving in older adults. *Psychology and Aging, 10,* 269–283.

Mather, M., & Knight, M. (2005). Goal directed memory: The role of cognitive control in older adults memory. *Psychology and Aging, 20*(4), 554–570.

McGuire, L., Kiecolt-Glaser, J. K., & Glaser, R. (2002). Depressive symptoms and immune function in community dwelling older adults. *Journal of Abnormal Psychology, 111,* 192–197.

Meacham, J. A., & Emont, N. C. (1989). The interpersonal basis of everyday problem solving. In J. D. Sinnott (Ed.), *Everyday problem solving: Theory and applications* (pp. 7–23). New York: Praeger.

Meegan, S. P., & Berg, C. A. (2002). Contexts, functions, forms, and processes of collaborative everyday problem solving in older adulthood. *International Journal of Behavioral Development, 26,* 6–15.

Meyer, B. J. F., Russo, C., & Talbot, A. (1995). Discourse comprehension and problem solving: Decisions about the treatment of breast cancer by women across the life-span. *Psychology and Aging, 10,* 84–103.

Meyer, B. J. F., Talbot, A. P., & Ranalli, C. (2007). Why older adults make more immediate treatment decisions about cancer than younger adults. *Psychology and Aging, 22*(3), 505–524.

Mikels, J. A., Larkin, G. R., Reuter-Lorenz, P. A., & Carstensen, L. L. (2005). Divergent trajectories in the aging mind: Changes in working memory for affective versus visual information with age. *Psychology and Aging, 20*(4), 542–553.

Mroczek, D. K. (2001). Age and emotion in adulthood. *Current Directions in Psychological Science, 10,* 87–90.

Mroczek, D. K., & Almeida, D. M. (2004). The effect of daily stress, personality, and age on daily negative affect. *Journal of Personality, 72*(2), 355–378.

Patrick, J. H., & Strough, J. (2004). Everyday problem solving: Experience, strategies, and behavioral intentions. *Journal of Adult Development, 11*(1), 9–18.

Phillips, L. H., Smith, L., & Gilhooly, K. J. (2002). The effects of adult aging and induced positive and negative mood on planning. *Emotion, 2*(3), 263–272.

Poon, L. W., Rubin, D. C., & Wilson, B. A. (1989). *Everyday cognition in adulthood and late life.* Cambridge, UK: Cambridge University Press.

Robinson, M. D., & Tamir, M. (2005). Neuroticism as mental noise: A relation between neuroticism and reaction time standard deviations. *Journal of Personality and Social Psychology, 89*(1), 107–114.

Roepke, S., McAdams, L., Lindamer, L., Patterson, T., & Jeste, D. (2001). Personality profiles among normal aged individuals as measured by the NEO-PI-R. *Aging and Mental Health, 5*(2), 159–164.

Rogoff, B., & Lave, J. (Eds.). (1984). *Everyday cognition: Its development in social context.* Cambridge, MA: Harvard University Press.

Rook, K. S., Sorkin, D. H., & Zettel, L. A. (2004). Stress in social relationships: Coping and adaptation across the life span. In F. Lang & K. Fingerman (Eds.), *Growing together: Personal relationships across the lifespan* (pp. 21). New York: Cambridge University Press.

Rowe, J. W., & Kahn, R. L. (1997). Human aging: Usual and successful. *Science, 237,* 143–149.

Sansone, C., & Berg, C. A. (1993). Adapting to the environment across the life span: Different process or different inputs? *International Journal of Behavioral Development, 16,* 215–241.

Scheier, M. F., Matthews, K. A., Owens, J. F., Schulz, R., Bridges, M. W., Magovern, G. J., et al. (1999). Optimism and rehospitalization after coronary artery bypass graft surgery. *Archives of Internal Medicine, 159,* 829–835.

Scribner, S. (1986). Thinking in action: Some characterisitcs of paractical thought. In R. J. Sternberg & R. Wagner (Eds.), *Practical intelligence: Origins of competence in the everyday world* (pp. 143–162). New York: Cambridge University Press.

Sinnott, J. D. (1989). (Ed.), *Everyday problem solving: Theory and applications.* New York: Praeger.

Smith, T. W. (1992). Hostility and health: Current status of a psychosomatic hypothesis. *Health Psychology, 11,* 139–150.

Smith, T. W., Berg, C. A., Uchino, B. N., Florsheim, P., Pearce, G., Hawkins, M., et al. (2006). *Conflict and collaboration in middle-aged and older married couples: Sex, age, and interaction context as moderators of cardiovascular response.* Unpublished manuscript.

Smith, T. W., & Ruiz, J. M. (2004). Personality theory and research in the study of health and behavior. In T. Boll (Series Ed.), R. Frank, J. Wallander, & A. Baum (Vol. Eds.), *Handbook of clinical health psychology: Vol. 1. Models and perspectives in health psychology* (pp. 143–199). Washington, DC: American Psychological Association.

Smith, T. W., Uchino, B. N., Berg, C. A., Florsheim, P., Pearce, G., Hawkins, M., & Hopkins, P. N. (2007). Hostile personality traits and coronary artery calcification in middle-aged and older married couples: Different effects for self-reports versus spouse ratings. *Psychosomatic Medicine, 69,* 441–448.

Smith, T. W., & Zautra, A. J. (2002). The role of personality in exposure and reactivity to interpersonal stress in relation to arthritis disease activity and negative affect in women. *Health Psychology, 21*(1), 81–88.

Sorkin, D. H., & Rook, K. S. (2006). Responding to negative social exchanges in later life: coping strategies, goals, and effectiveness. *Psychology and Aging, 21,* 715–725.

Stanovich, K. E. (1999). *Who is rational? Studies of individual differences in reasoning.* Mahwah, NJ: Erlbaum.

Stanovich, K. E., & West, R. F. (1997). Reasoning independently of prior belief and individual differences in actively open-minded thinking. *Journal of Educational Psychology, 89,* 342–357.

Stanovich, K. E., & West, R. F. (1999). Discrepancies between normative and descriptive models of decision making and the understanding/acceptance principle. *Cognitive Psychology, 38,* 349–385.

Staudinger, U. M., & Baltes, P. B. (1996). Interactive minds: A facilitative setting for wisdom-related performance. *Journal of Personality and Social Psychology, 71, 746–762.*

Sternberg, R. J. (1984). A contextual view of the nature of intelligence. *International Journal of Psychology, 19,* 307–334.

Sternberg, R. J., & Wagner, R .K. (Eds.). (1986). *Practical intelligence.* New York: Cambridge University Press.

Strough, J., Berg, C. A., & Sansone, C. (1996). Goals for solving everyday problems across the life span: Age and gender differences in the salience of interpersonal concerns. *Developmental Psychology, 32,* 1106–1115.

Strough, J., & Margrett, J. (2002). Overview of the special section on collaborative cognition in later adulthood. *International Journal of Behavioral Development, 26,* 2–5.

Strough, J., Patrick, J. H., Swenson, L. M., Cheng, S., & Barnes, K. A. (2003). Collaborative everyday problem solving: Interpersonal relationships and problem dimensions. *International Journal of Aging and Human Development, 56,* 43–66.

Tellegen, A. (1985). Structures of mood and personality and their relevance to assessing anxiety, with an emphasis on self-report. In A. H. Tuma & J. D. Maer (Eds.), *Anxiety and the anxiety disorders* (pp. 681–706). Hillsdale, NJ: Erbaum.

Thornton, W. J. L., & Dumke, H. A. (2005). Age differences in everyday problem-solving and decision-making effectiveness: A meta-analytic review. *Psychology and Aging, 20,* 85–99.

Tugade, M. M., & Fredrickson, B. L. (2004). Resilient individuals use positive emotions to bounce back from negative emotional experiences. *Journal of Personality and Social Psychology, 86*(2), 320–333.

Uchino, B., Berg, C. A., Smith, T. W., Pearce, G., & Skinner, M. (2006). Age-related differences in ambulatory blood pressure during daily stress: Evidence for greater blood pressure reactions in older individuals. *Psychology and Aging, 21,* 231–239.

Uchino, B., Cacioppo, J., & Kiecolt-Glaser, J. (1996). The relationship between social support and physiological processes: A review with emphasis on underlying mechanisms and implications for health. *Psychological Bulletin, 119,* 488–531.

Uchino, B. N., Holt-Lunstad, J., Bloor, L. E., & Campo, R. A. (2005). Aging and cardiovascular reactivity to stress: Longitudinal evidence for changes in stress reactivity. *Psychology and Aging, 20*(1), 143–143.

Watson, T. L., & Blanchard-Fields, F. (1998). Thinking with your head and your heart: Age differences in everyday problem-solving strategy preferences. *Aging, neuropsychology, and cognition, 5,* 225–240.

Wegner, D. M., Erber, R., & Raymond, P. (1991). Transactive memory in close relationships. *Journal of Personality and Social Psychology, 61,* 923–929.

Wiebe, D. J., Berg, C. A., Korbel, C., Palmer, D. A., Beveridge, R. M., Upchurch, R., Lindsay, R., Swinyard, M. T., & Donaldson, D. L. (2005). Children's appraisals of maternal involvement in coping with diabetes: Enhancing our understanding of adherence, metabolic control, and quality of life across adolescence. *Journal of Pediatric Psychology, 30,* 167–178.

Willis, S. L. (1991). Cognition and everyday competence. In K. W. Schaie (Eds.), *Annual Review of Gerontology and Geriatrics* (Vol. 11, pp. 80–109). New York: Springer.

Willis, S. L., & Schaie, K. W. (1986). Practical intelligence in later adulthood. In R. J. Sternberg & R. K. Wagner (Eds.), *Practical intelligence: Nature and origins of competence in the everyday world* (pp. 236–268). New York: Cambridge University Press.

Zwahr, M. D., Park, D. C., & Shifren, K. (1999). Judgments about estrogen replacement therapy: The role of age, cognitive abilities, and beliefs. *Psychology and Aging, 14,* 179–191.

Chapter 19

Changes in Goal-Striving Across the Life Span

Do People Learn to Select More Self-Concordant Goals as They Age?

Kennon M. Sheldon

This handbook as a whole addresses adult development and learning across the life span. Most of the authors on this topic will focus on *cognitive*-developmental issues, such as literacy, problem solving, expertise, and wisdom. However in this chapter, I propose to consider an important *personality*-developmental issue: namely, the question of how people learn to select the best goals for themselves—that is, the ones that will be most adaptive, personally expressive, and promoting of health and happiness. Obviously, we all focus our energies in innumerable different directions over the course of our lives. Surely, some of these choices are "wrong" for us, that is, they lead us towards dependency, frustration, and a failure to thrive. In contrast, other types of choices are likely more right for us, more "self-concordant," leading us towards continued positive change and growth (Sheldon & Elliot, 1999; Sheldon & Houser-Marko, 2001). If this is true, then the decision process by which people continuingly select particular goals and intentions from among the numerous available options may be a crucial meta-cognitive skill—one with important implications for thriving and adaptation.

The primary question of this chapter is: Do people get better, over time, at this vital skill? Consistent with the emerging positive psychology perspective (Seligman & Csikszentmihalyi, 2000), my proposed answer is "yes." Several recent studies are described, to support the personality-developmental proposal that self-concordance typically increases over the life span. In the latter part of the chapter, I consider several other contemporary motivationally-based theories of positive aging, including the selective optimization with compensation model (Baltes, 2003), the primary and secondary control model (Heckhausen & Schulz, 1999), and the socio-emotional selectivity model (Carstensen, 1992; Charles & Carstensen, 1999). I show that these theories both converge with, and somewhat diverge from, the self-determination theory perspective (Deci & Ryan, 1985, 2000) that grounds the current inquiry.

Relevant Meta-Perspectives on Human Nature

Again, the chapter thesis is that there is a normative trend towards more self-appropriate goal selection in older compared to younger adults—in terms of the well known folk expression, we "get better as we get older." Of course, in many ways, people do decline as they get older—becoming less physically strong and agile, and losing cognitive acuity and flexibility (Wilson et al., 2002). Still, this does not mean that the process of personality development and maturation ceases. In fact, there are several prominent theories and theoretical paradigms that are consistent with the claim that positive personality development is normative and continues across the life span.

Perhaps most prominent is Erik Erikson's (1963) epigenetic perspective upon lifelong personality development. According to the Eriksonian stage model, there is an inherent drive within human nature to resolve life tasks, adapt to changing role demands, and consolidate one's identity. According to this psychosocial perspective, society continually expects more from its aging adults (at least, up to a point of decline near the end of life), as exacted by the changing role requirements they face—becoming first novices, then mentors, then leaders; first parents, then grand-parents, then great grand-parents; first learners, then disseminators, then integrators of family, organizational, and cultural wisdom. Of course, some people fail to address or resolve life-tasks and identity conflicts, thereby becoming "stuck" at a particular stage of development. Still, for most, the process of wrestling with the new tasks that each phase of life tends to bring greater maturity and integration over time. In a similar vein, Werner's orthogenetic principle (Werner, 1957) states that people develop both greater differentiation and integration over time, and Loevinger's (1997) psychosocial model assumes that people reach higher levels of ego-development as they age. Indeed, such assumptions are true of most "evolving systems" approaches to human nature, which view developmental elaboration as a near-inevitable outcome of the process of adapting to change.

Organismic and humanistic perspectives also make generally positive assumptions about human nature. Piaget's (1971) organismic perspective on development emphasized the active agency of the learner, which leads to cognitive development via the process of equilibration. According to Piaget, learning does not stop at the end of childhood; because a given person's model of the world can never be complete, cognitive development should continue throughout the life span, assuming conditions are reasonably supportive of the process. Humanistic perspectives converge upon this conclusion, with their emphasis on how people can become self-actualized (Maslow, 1971) and fully-functioning individuals (Rogers, 1961) over time. For example, Rogers said that people develop to a greater extent as they learn to contact and follow their "organismic valuing process," an innate (though subtle) internal compass that points in health-relevant directions (Rogers, 1964; Sheldon, Arndt, & Houser-Marko, 2003). However, Rogers also agreed with the Piagetian view that development may cease if conditions are not supportive (i.e., if important others show only contingent positive regard for the person, or if the social surround is too controlling or punitive). Because of such difficulties, not everybody develops. Still, however, the organismic perspective holds that development occurs more often than not—that is, on average, there is more progression than regression within aging individuals, at least until near the end of life.

Self-Determination Theory

The organismic/humanistic perspective is perhaps best represented within contemporary research psychology by Deci and Ryan's self-determination theory (SDT). This theory, under development for more than thirty years (Deci, 1972, 1975; Deci & Ryan, 1985; Deci & Ryan, 2000), addresses the nature of "optimal motivation" (i.e., self-determined motivation). To be self-determined is to "endorse one's actions at the highest level of reflection. When self-determined, people experience a sense of freedom to do what is interesting, personally important and vitalizing" (Deci & Ryan, 2006). Over time, SDT has provided an elaborated account of the social-contextual and personality processes that promote self-determination in life, as well as demonstrating the many positive consequences of such motivation, via experimental, longitudinal, and applied research. I outline the theory below.

Historically, the earliest SDT research focused on intrinsic motivation, demonstrating the surprising "undermining effect" in which people sometimes lose their desire to do formerly enjoyable behaviors after being rewarded to do those behaviors. In other words, "extrinsic" motivation can usurp intrinsic motivation (Deci, 1972, 1975), to the person's detriment. Research in the late 1970s and early 1980s showed that people's "cognitive evaluations" of rewards is crucial; rewards are only undermining when they are perceived to be coercive or controlling, that is, when authorities use them in a way that threatens peoples' sense of autonomy. Thus, whereas Csikszentmihalyi's (1997) "flow" theory focused on inadequate competence (i.e., low match between skills and task-demands) as an underminer of flow and intrinsic motivation, Deci and Ryan's (1985) analysis suggested that inadequate autonomy (i.e., feelings of being coerced or controlled) can also undermine such positive motivational states.

Commencing in the late 1980s, SDT expanded further to acknowledge that some kinds of extrinsic motivation may be internalized into the self, and may thus feel self-determined even if they are not enjoyable. This covers many important but unpleasant duties and obligations, such as tax-paying and diaper-changing. As will be seen below, it also provides an important means for conceptualizing the nature of maturity and personality integration.

SDT specifies five basic types of motivation, which vary in their location upon a continuum of internalization (Deci & Ryan, 2000; Ryan & Connell, 1989). Figure 191 presents this continuum, and is worthy of some discussion. At the leftmost end of the figure is amotivation, in which the person's behavior is non-regulated and non-intentional. Amotivation typically results when people experience continued failure and have few positive expectancies. To the right of amotivation are four forms of intentional motivation, the first three of which are considered extrinsic (i.e., contingency-focused). External extrinsic motivation exists when people act only because of the rewards they will thereby accrue or punishments they will thereby avoid. In such cases the activity typically has no self-relevance or meaning to the person. Introjected extrinsic motivation exists when people act to avoid internally-imposed recriminations and guilt. In such cases the activity has been partially internalized, so that the behavior might occur even in the absence of external contingencies. Identified extrinsic motivation exists when people act to express an important self-identification or value. According to SDT, such activities have been internalized into the self and thus are self-determined, despite being extrinsic. Finally, at the rightmost end of the figure, is intrinsic motivation, distinct from the three extrinsic motivations. Intrinsic motivation exists when people act for reasons of inherent interest and enjoyment, rather than to achieve some separable contingency. Intrinsic motivations are considered to be automatically internalized, that is, a direct expression of the evolving self (Csikszentmihalyi, 1997). Of course, more than one of these motivations can exist at the same time; behavior is multiply determined. However, many behaviors are characterized by a predominance of one type over the other types.

Considerable research has supported the proposal that the different motivations can be aligned on a continuum, and has also shown that peoples' performance and affective tone are higher when the motivations in the right half of the Figure 19.1 continuum predominate over the motivations in the left half of the figure. These patterns have been shown to apply to a wide variety of positive outcome variables (i.e., persistence, creativity, and mood) within a wide variety of domains (i.e., medicine, sport, education) and within a wide variety of cultures (i.e., Japan, Korea, Bulgaria, and Russia, as well as in western cultures; see Deci & Ryan (2000), for a recent summary of this research).

Notably, SDT also assumes that there is an "organismic integration process" (Deci & Ryan, 1991) by which motivations are naturally internalized and integrated over time—that is, there is a tendency for goals to migrate to the right in Figure 19.1, such that the

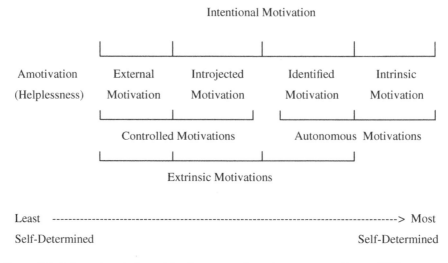

Figure 19.1 Schematic relation of the five types of motivation, according to SDT.

motives underlying then become more internalized. Consider a 4-year-old child who is being asked to share a toy with her friend. For most children of this age, there is not much internalization of the value of sharing, so when the child shares it is only because her mother makes her (external motivation). Hopefully a positive socialization process occurs, so that by the age of 8 the child shares spontaneously, even if mother is not there to make her do it. Still, she might only do it to avoid feeling like a bad girl (introjected motivation). But, hopefully, by the age of 14, the child has internalized this important value so that she does it willingly, without resistance or resentment (identified or even integrated motivation). Eventually, sharing might even become an intrinsic motivation, as the girl learns to take pleasure in giving to others and seeing their pleasure. Again, SDT assumes that such internalization processes take place automatically, assuming that conditions are supportive of them. However, there have been surprisingly few tests of this idea within a life-span context (but see Chandler & Connell, 1987, who showed that older children have more internalized motivation for cleaning up their rooms, i.e., "because I want to know where my stuff is," compared to younger children, i.e., "because my mother makes me").

Self-Determination Theory Applied to Personal Goals

Recently, Sheldon and colleagues have applied the motivation continuum concept in a new way by studying peoples' *self-generated personal goals* (Emmons, 1999; Little, 1993). Past SDT research has focused primarily on variations in domain-specific motivation, i.e., variations in people's reasons for going to school, church, work, or to the gym. Such work has often pinpointed problematic social-contextual features of such domains, i.e., the controllingness (versus autonomy-supportiveness) of important others within the domain. However, Sheldon (2002) has argued that adopting a personal goal focus moves researchers beyond particular life-domains, providing a new means of considering personality as a whole. Furthermore, applying SDT to personal goals affords new means of considering the nature of personality integration and maturity (Sheldon & Kasser, 1995).

In order to illustrate the importance of the shift to a personal goals approach, it is necessary to briefly discuss such approaches. Idiographic personal goal assessments, as developed by Klinger, Little, Emmons and others in the late 1970s and 1980s, usually begin with a blank piece of paper. Participants are asked to think about what they are typically trying to do in life, or what they will be trying to do in the near future, and write down the goals that come to mind. Goal assessment thus shares some characteristics with projective testing (Emmons & McAdams, 1991), which similarly supplies no explicit guidance for responding. In fact, goal assessment is a lot like life itself, in which we must continually make choices about what to do and what not to do, "filling in the blanks," as it were, as best we can. A further positive feature of goal constructs is that, because of their idiographic nature, self-generated goals are likely to have special meaning and significance for participants, providing a direct window into the unique features of their personalities.

Importantly, this does not mean that people cannot be compared using personal goal methodologies. A particularly attractive feature of idiographic personal goal assessment is that once elicited, personal goals can serve as stems for a wide variety of nomothetic comparisons. For example, participants can be asked to rate many aspects of their listed goals, such as their importance, their commitment to them, their expectancy concerning them, and their perceived difficulty. Aggregated across the listed goals, such ratings can provide reliable quantitative measures of various characteristics of a person's motivational and behavioral systems.

Sheldon and colleagues have used this potential by asking participants to rate why they are pursuing each of their listed personal goals, in terms of the reasons specified by the SDT continuum. This research has revealed that people often feel quite controlled and non-self-determined in their goal pursuits, despite the fact that the assessment gives them complete freedom to write down whatever they want; in other words, "Not all personal goals are personal" (Sheldon & Elliot, 1998, 1999). These results also illustrate that the state of feeling controlled can be a global personality characteristic, as well as a characteristic specific to particular domains or areas of life (Deci & Ryan, 1991, 2000).

Sheldon has also argued that, in the case of idiographic personal goal statements, rated self-determination has a somewhat different meaning than that usually ascribed to it; here, these ratings index the extent to which one's listed self-generated personal initiatives express one's underlying values, interests, and identifications, more so than expressing social pressures or partially digested introjects. Sheldon thus called the construct "self-concordance." Self-concordance is defined conceptually as the degree to which one's self-chosen initiatives match and represent one's developing interests and core values. Thus, self-concordance is thought to represent a state of congruence between one's self-generated goals and deeper, growth-relevant aspect of one's personality.

Initial research with this construct showed that pursuing self-concordant goals is concurrently associated with a wide variety of positive characteristics, including greater positive mood, life-satisfaction, openness, empathy, autonomy-orientation, creativity, and role-integration (Sheldon, 1995; Sheldon & Kasser, 1995). Later research evaluated the longitudinal effects of self-concordance upon short-term goal pursuit, showing that self-concordance predicts greater goal-effort and attainment over time (Sheldon & Elliot, 1998) and that it also moderates the effects of goal-attainment upon changes in psychological well-being (Sheldon & Elliot, 1999; Sheldon & Kasser, 1998). In other words, people tend to do better in their self-concordant goals, and independently of this fact, they tend to benefit more when self-concordant goals are achieved.

Selecting self-concordant goals can doubtless be a very complex and daunting task.

First, in order to pick the "right" goals for oneself, one must often be able to resist social pressures, from both peers and well-meaning authorities, which might prompt one to pursue personally inappropriate goals. Example pressures include one's parents' insistence that one attend law school, despite one's talents and interests in a different field; one's boyfriend's urgings for sex, despite one's values and commitments to the contrary; and, especially relevant to aging, one's daughter's admonitions to move to a nursing home, despite one's belief that it is not yet time. In addition, one must sometimes be able to ignore cultural messages, advertising, and conditioning that might orient one in problematic directions, i.e., towards excessive materialism, popularity, and appearance concerns (Kasser, 2002). Not only must one be able to resist problematic goals, one must also be able to figure out which goals are actually "right" for one's self. Thus, Sheldon (2002) has argued that selecting self-concordant goals requires the self-perceptual ability to correctly intuit one's own deeper needs, strengths, dispositions, and talents, so that one's conscious goals can reflect and represent these deeper aspects of personality. It involves not being "a stranger to oneself" (Wilson, 2000).

A Broader Perspective on Personality

What are these deeper aspects? At this point, it is worth pausing to consider a broader view of personality, in order to better explicate the claim that self-concordant goals reflect a state in which one's goals better represent one's deeper personality. Sheldon (2004) introduced a multi-level model of personality which considered four basic aspects of personality: universal foundations (at level 1), traits and dispositions (at level 2), goals and intentions (at level 3), and self and self-narratives (at level 4; see Figure 19.2). This proposal was built upon the earlier proposals of McAdams (1995, 1996, 1998), who suggested that traits, goals, and selves form three distinct "tiers" of personality, none of which are reducible to the others. Sheldon argued for the additional inclusion of a universal foundations level of analysis, because this allows consideration of evolved (or species-typical) human nature—i.e., the psychological needs and personality processes that all humans share beneath their manifest differences.

Sheldon (2004) reviewed evidence showing that goal self-concordance may be a particularly important determinant of an "optimal human being," because the goals and intentions level of personality provides a vital proactive means for people to take self-beneficial action. Goals (at the third level of personality) provide the targets for behavior,

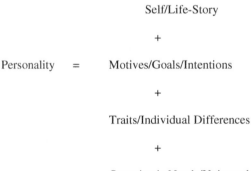

Figure 19.2 Four levels of organization within personality and personality theory.

and ideally, these targets will be ones that allow people to meet their innate psychological needs (at the first level of personality), express their inherited and acquired traits and dispositions (at the second level of personality), and positively develop their identity and life-story (at the fourth level of personality). In contrast, a person who invests energy in pursuing goals that do not correctly represent these other aspects of their personality may waste considerable time and effort. Of course, pursuing non-concordant goals may itself lead people in eventually concordant directions, or teach people important new life-lessons; thus, I do not mean to say that people should *only* pursue goals they personally value and find interest in. However, the existing data suggest that, on average, they will be better off when they do so.

Empirical Support for the Lifelong Development Proposal

The previous discussion sets the stage for a return to the chapter thesis that people improve in their ability to select self-concordant goals as they grow older, and more generally, continue to develop their personalities as they age. Although this life-span idea is implied by SDT's assumptions concerning peoples' inherent tendency to internalize their own motivations over time, the proposition has received very few tests to date. In the section below, I will review the recent published personal goal data that supports this contention.

Sheldon and Kasser (2001) employed two different theoretical perspectives upon personality development and maturity to test the hypothesis of positive motivational change over time. Community participants of widely varying ages were asked to list ten characteristic "personal strivings" (Emmons, 1989, 1999) and to rate why they were pursuing them, in terms of the motivations specified by SDT. This allowed us to test a first hypothesis, that chronological age is correlated with greater self-concordance (computed, as in the past, by summing the intrinsic and identified ratings and subtracting the external and introjected ratings; data were not collected on "amotivation").

In addition, Eriksonian psychosocial theory, already discussed, was employed (Erikson, 1963). Participants' goals were later content-coded in terms of the different life-tasks specified by Erikson's theory. Again, Erikson said that there are different tasks that we face in our lives, depending on our place in the life span, each of which builds on the successful resolution of the task before. In late adolescence we face the "identity" life-task: we have to develop a solid sense of ourselves as a person, persisting over time. Next is the "intimacy" task; we must learn how to relate that identity to other identities, i.e., to connect authentically with other adults. As we approach middle-age, we become more concerned with the next generation and with the thriving of cultural institutions (the "generativity" task). Finally, in the last part of the life span we encounter the task of bringing it all together, to make final meaning of our mortality and the pattern of our lives (the "ego-integrity" task). Based on Erikson's assumption that the latter two themes reflect greater maturity and successful development, we hypothesized that chronological age should be positively associated with the number of generativity and ego-integrity strivings listed by participants, and negatively associated with the number of identity and intimacy strivings.

We also hypothesized that chronological age would be associated with subjective well-being (SWB; Diener, 1994), replicating a number of emerging findings suggesting that age is modestly associated with at least some measures of well-being—in particular, increasing life-satisfaction and decreasing negative affect (Argyle, 1999). Finding evidence for the age-to-SWB hypothesis in the current data would provide another type of support for the "getting older, getting better" idea. Another hypothesis was that our goal-based measures of personality development (i.e., rated self-concordance and coded generativity/integrity goals) would be associated with SWB. The association of self-determination and well-being is a well documented finding in prior SDT research and also in prior research employing the goal self-concordance measure (Sheldon, 2002). Also, Erikson's theory implies that pursuit of later-stage life-tasks is associated with SWB, as those oriented towards generativity and ego-integrity have succeeded in establishing their identities and in connecting with other identities, and are now concerned with meaning-making and cultural contribution. Assuming that the latter two hypotheses received support, we also intended to examine whether greater self-concordance or more advanced life-task pursuit mediates the association between chronological age and SWB. Are older people happier *because* they are more mature?

Participants were 108 adults from Columbia, Missouri, ranging from age 18 to 82, who were called at random and offered two free movie tickets if they participated. Consenters completed a questionnaire in which they first rated their general SWB, then listed their typical personal strivings, then rated those strivings. Supporting our first hypothesis, age was positively and significantly correlated with the aggregate striving self-concordance measure. Turning to the Eriksonian categories, three out of four predictions were supported: older people listed fewer identity strivings, and more generativity strivings and ego integrity strivings, on average. The fact that the correlation between age and intimacy striving was non-significant suggests that striving for intimacy is salient across the life span—it may be that everyone, not just young adults, needs intimacy (Baumeister & Leary, 1995; Deci & Ryan, 2000).

Turning to our third hypothesis, we also found that chronological age was associated with aggregate SWB, providing further support for the idea that increasing age may bring psychological benefits. Fourth, as predicted, self-concordance, generativity strivings, and ego-integrity strivings were positively associated with SWB, whereas identity strivings were negatively associated with SWB. Again, however, intimacy striving was an exception to our hypotheses—although Erikson's theory suggests that intimacy striving is representative of less maturity and thus should be negatively associated with well-being, intimacy striving was instead positively associated with well-being in these data. Although Erikson's stage theory has difficulty explaining this finding, because it presumes that intimacy-concerns are something one grows out of, SDT can explain it because it proposes that humans have a basic need for relatedness that persists across the life span (Deci & Ryan, 2000).

To test the mediational possibility, we created an aggregate goal maturity measure by adding the self-concordance measure, the generativity measure, and the ego-integrity measure, and subtracting the identity measure (the four measures that were associated with SWB as hypothesized). A regression analysis showed that the association of age with SWB fell from .24 to .09 when aggregate maturity was included in the model. Thus, supporting our fifth hypothesis, our measures of maturity could account for most of the fact that older people were also happier people.

Sheldon, Houser-Marko, and Kasser (2006) replicated this basic pattern of results using a somewhat different approach. Instead of employing a cross sectional sample of different ages, they instead obtained a matched sample of college students and their parents. These two groups are similar on many factors, including family income, genetics, hometown, history, and interests. Thus, one can conduct a powerful test by directly comparing a child to his or her parent, to see how they differ. The parents ranged from 38 to 70 in age.

We evaluated the same hypotheses as in the earlier study. However, we tested them in three different ways. First, we examined the current scores for the parents compared to the current scores for their children. Do parents seem happier and more self-concordant now, compared to their child now? Second, we asked parents to think back to what they were like when they were their child's age, and compared parent's scores then to parent's scores now. Do parents report feeling happier and more self-concordant now, compared to when they were their child's age? Although such data may be subject to retrospective biases, we reasoned that if the patterns converged with the other methods, such concerns would be somewhat mitigated. Third, we compared younger parents to older parents, using correlational analyses. This third approach, which focuses on age variations within the parent sample alone, is similar to that used in the first study discussed above (Sheldon & Kasser, 2001).

Participants completed a questionnaire in class and gave us permission to mail a similar questionnaire to their parents. Within the questionnaire, all participants first completed measures of current SWB, then listed their current personal strivings, and rated why they are pursuing those strivings. Parents then rated their SWB when they were their child's age, then listed and rated the strivings they remember pursuing at their child's age.

The data showed that both mothers and fathers reported greater well-being than their child. Mothers were more self-concordant in their goals than their children. Fathers were in the predicted direction on self-concordance, but the difference was not significant. Still, this way of testing our hypotheses yielded fairly good support. A similar pattern of findings resulted in the comparison of parents now to parents then, the one exception being that fathers did not report having higher SWB now, compared to when they were their child's age. However, again, the mean was in the predicted direction, and thus our hypotheses were mostly supported. Finally, we turned to the parent sample alone and correlated parental age with contemporary parental SWB and parental self-concordance. Again, we found good support: maternal age correlated significantly with maternal SWB and maternal self-concordance, and paternal age correlated significantly with paternal well-being and paternal self-concordance. Thus, the older participants in the parent sample were both happier at present than were younger participants, and more self-concordant in their current goals. Finally, we examined the mediational question using the parental datasets. For mothers, we could account for more than half the relation between age and well-being using the self-concordance measure, and for fathers, we could account for about half.

Sheldon, Kasser, Houser-Marko, Jones, and Turban (2005) again tested the "getting older, getting better" hypothesis, using a somewhat different approach. Rather than focusing on personal goals, in this study they focused on social duties. Thus, the question became, "why do people perform the social duties of paying taxes, tipping service people, and voting?" instead of "why do people pursue their goals?" Again, according to Erikson's psychosocial theory, people naturally take on more social-role responsibility as they age. Logically, this should include the doing of important but sometimes unpleasant social duties.

We tested the same hypotheses as before: that chronological age would correlate with a feeling of self-determination in performing unpleasant social duties, that age would be associated with SWB, that self-determination would be associated with SWB, and that self-determination might mediate the age to SWB effect. Ranging from ages 20 to 82, 160 community adults were recruited in doctor's offices or retirement homes, in exchange for being entered into a lottery for a free dinner for two. Participants first rated their SWB then rated why they perform the social duties of voting, paying taxes, and tipping service people (when they perform these duties), again in terms of external, introjected, identified, and intrinsic motivation. We computed an aggregate SWB score for each participant and also computed self-determination scores for each participant, not only for each duty separately, but also aggregated across the three duties.

In this study, chronological age was associated with felt self-concordance aggregated across the three duties. Age was also separately correlated with the motivation for each duty; older people reported voting, paying taxes, and tipping for more self-determined reasons than younger people. Self-determined motivation was associated with SWB, consistent with the earlier studies and supporting our second hypothesis. However, in these data there was no association of chronological age with well-being, perhaps because many of the oldest participants were sampled in retirement homes, which can be depressing places. Because of this, we could not again test the hypothesis that self-determination mediates the link between age and well-being. But from our perspective, the most important thing was to again show that people feel more self-determined as they become older—in this sense, at least, people seem to consistently "get better" as they age.

A fourth study, also reported in Sheldon et al. (2005), addressed an important potential criticism of the earlier studies—namely, that they all employed samples from the United States. Would the results generalize to persons in other nations or cultures? This question is of particular significance because cross-cultural psychologists have recently challenged self-determination theory's claims that self-determination is a basic human need that is universally associated with SWB (Markus, Kitayama, & Heiman, 1996). We reasoned that finding an association between self-determined duty-enactment and SWB in a non-Western culture would lend further cross-cultural support for SDT's universalist claims (see Deci & Ryan, 2000; Sheldon et al., 2004, and Sheldon, 2004, for recent summaries of the evidence supporting the SDT position). Also, we reasoned that finding an association between chronological age and self-determination in such a culture would further support the organismic perspective's optimistic assumptions concerning positive personality development in humans.

This study was conducted in Singapore, considered a collectivist culture. The three assessed duties were modified to fit that context: "helping distant relatives," "obeying authorities (such as teachers, parents, and bosses)," and "staying informed about political issues." Two hundred and thirteen participants ranging in age from 18 to 101 completed the English-language survey. First, they rated their SWB and then they rated their reasons for performing the social duties, using the same measures as before. An aggregate self-determination measure was again computed by averaging across the three duties.

Once again, chronological age was significantly correlated with aggregate self-determination, supporting Deci and Ryan's (2000) claim that the personality developmental processes posited by SDT should occur within every cultural setting. In addition, self-determination was significantly correlated with SWB, supporting Deci and Ryan's (2000) claim that self-determination is a universal psychological need. Once again, chronological age was not associated with SWB, and thus the mediational hypothesis could not be tested. Still, our two most important hypotheses were again supported in this study.

Other Relevant Gerontological Goal Research

In the first part of the chapter, an optimistic perspective was sketched upon the question of whether positive personality development is normative across the life span. Based on SDT and organismic, psychosocial, and evolving systems perspectives, I argued that humans have an innate tendency to internalize their own motivations, becoming more integrated, autonomous, and self-determined over time. This SDT hypothesis has been little tested in life-span research, instead being evaluated primarily in short-term and domain-specific contexts. Several recent goal studies employing the self-concordance construct were discussed that evaluated the hypothesis in a long-term, more global context. Although these studies were only cross-sectional, they offered consistent support for the idea that in this way, at least, people continue to "get better" (i.e., develop) as they grow older. Although older people may experience many new problems and difficulties, at least they no longer waste their energy pursuing goals that they do not believe in. This seems to be quite important for maintaining, and even improving, their well-being.

How do these conclusions concur with other recent theories and findings in the life-span developmental literature? Interestingly, in the last two decades life-span researchers have given increasing attention to motivation, action, and goal-striving (Brandtstadter & Rothermund, 2002; Heckhausen, 2003), echoing the more general trend towards such constructs in the literature that was described earlier in this chapter. These theorists assume that understanding changes in motivation and intentionality over the life span may be the key to understanding the aging process. As will be shown below, action theorists focus primarily on goal performance, and related constructs such as efficacy, efficiency, felt control, and felt competence, based on an argument that successful goal pursuit may be the most important criterion of successful aging (Baltes & Carstensen, 2003).

A number of motivationally-relevant developmental perspectives have originated from the Max Planck group in Germany. This research proceeds under the general rubric of "selective optimization with compensation" (SOC; Baltes & Baltes, 1990; Freund, Li, & Baltes, 1999). According to this view, adjustment in later life involves adapting successfully to loss, in particular the loss of social and cognitive resources. As peoples' action skills and resources narrow, they must learn to *select* goals that better reflect the new realities, then to *optimize* their pursuit of those goals within increasing constraints, by *compensating* for their deficiencies as necessary. For example, an aging athlete must learn to select scaled-down age-appropriate goals, realizing that she can no longer compete at the top level. She must learn to optimize her training so that endurance is maximized and injuries do not occur. Also, she must learn to compensate for increasing deficits such as a slowed reaction time or reduced dexterity. Successful aging means achieving gains that at least partially (if not wholly) counterbalance these losses.

Several variants of this general perspective has been proposed and researched. For example, Brandtstadter (1999) pointed to the surprising finding that peoples' sense of control remains largely unchanged over the life span. He proposed that there are three basic types of processes which interact to determine peoples' sense of control, which might together explain why older people do not feel less control: Assimilation, accommodation, and immunization. Assimilative processes involve modifying how one pursues a goal, in the face of problems and difficulties; accommodative processes involve changing one's goals, when assimilation becomes too difficult; and immunizing processes involve utilizing biases and defenses, in order to avoid recognizing one's (objectively) reduced control. Via the latter two processes in particular, aging people can mount successful rear guard maneuvers (as it were), avoiding feelings of helplessness despite their diminishing capacities.

Relatedly, Heckhausen and Schulz (1999) emphasized two types of control: primary and secondary. Primary control is about pursuing success directly, whereas secondary control is about minimizing the costs of failure. In this model, aging people come to rely to a greater extent upon secondary control as they experience losses in primary control. The SOC perspective and the primary/secondary control perspectives may also be integrated; for example, in a conceptual 2 × 2, Heckhausen and Schulz (1999) delineated both selective and compensatory modes of both primary and secondary control. Once again, however, the general presumption is that as time passes, older persons are shifted inevitably towards more compromised modes of functioning—in this case, towards secondary compensation (i.e., compensating for losses in one's ability to control losses; Heckhausen & Schulz, 1999).

This again points out the most characteristic feature of the European developmental-systems approaches, namely, their focus on competence, control, performance, efficiency, and the like. Although this is indeed a very important set of issues to address, there are other important issues as well, such as those addressed by SDT—namely, peoples' ability to feel a sense of self-determination, identification, and self-expression despite social and intra-personal pressures that might distract them from what is most satisfying or best representative of their personalities. As discussed in the first part of this chapter regarding the intrinsic motivation undermining effect, SDT has long made a distinction between autonomy and competence needs, emphasizing that, although correlated, they can also diverge from each other. For example, one may feel quite competent while also feeling non-autonomous (i.e., a high-performing medical student who desperately wants to be doing something else), or quite autonomous while feeling very incompetent (i.e., a dedicated athlete struggling to master a brand new sport). In the SDT view, the happiest and best-adjusted people are those who feel both competent *and* autonomous at the same time (Sheldon, Ryan, & Reis, 1996).

Based on this reasoning, I propose that the SDT perspective may provide a new way of conceptualizing compensation—although older people may have less energy and resources to devote to their strivings, they may compensate by narrowing their strivings so that unimportant strivings are discarded. Indeed, since felt self-concordance predicts goal effort and achievement (Sheldon & Elliot, 1998, 1999), the observed correlation of age with self-concordance may help to account for the fact that aging people do not experience losses in competence and control (Brandtstadter, 1999). In addition, the SDT perspective may provide a new way of conceptualizing selection; older people may pick not just "easier" goals that they can better attain, but also, goals that better represent who they are and what matters to them. Via more self-attuned goal-selection, older people may gain access to internal resources that younger people do not have.

Another way in which the SDT and action-theory perspectives may diverge is in their consideration of the normative change issue. Again, SDT's organismic approach implies an age-graded trend towards greater motivational internalization over time, a trend which apparently results in more self-concordant motivation in older people compared to younger people. In contrast, the action theory perspective does not presume any normative trends, except perhaps the inescapable trend towards declining cognitive resources that must be counter-acted. Instead, action theories assume that the ratio of gains to losses varies across people, such that some people manage to compensate better than others. Still, given action theory's emphasis on compensation, it appears that if there is a normative trend from this perspective, it is more likely in the negative direction.

It is probably correct that performance is bound to suffer as a person ages, even with the best compensation; again, however, this is not the only important issue. Because it focuses on felt psychological freedom rather than objective performance, SDT provides a plausible way in which people may be said to continue to develop over the life span, even as their basic capacities diminish. Again, although aging people may not be as effective and efficient as they used to be, this may not be so important if they have managed to focus their energies on what is really important to them.

A final way in which the SDT and SOC approaches differ is that SOC theories do not really address personality and psychosocial factors. Attention is primarily focused upon action itself, and the compensatory changes in action-selection and action-enactment that occur over the life span. In contrast, SDT addresses both personality factors (namely, self-concordance and trait autonomy) and social-contextual factors (namely, authority autonomy-support) that impact outcomes. Also, action theories do not typically make assumptions regarding what types of contextual and social factors are most beneficial, beyond saying that factors that support competent performance are desirable. In contrast, SDT emphasizes that factors supporting autonomy and self-determination are also conducive to adaptation and development.

Carstensen's socio-emotional selectivity (SES; Carstensen, 1992; Charles & Carstensen, 1999) theory provides another account of the motivational changes that occur with aging, an account that addresses both personality and psychosocial issues. Carstensen and colleagues hoped to explain the objective fact that older people have diminished social networks and reduced amounts of social contact. Although some perspectives have assumed that this trend is maladaptive and problematic, SES asserts that it is intentionally guided and adaptive. Older people attend, to a greater degree, to their emotional responses and meanings, perhaps because they realize that "time is getting too short" to waste on the superficial. As a result, they discard casual or unsatisfying relationships, instead focusing their energy upon a more select group of intimates and confidantes, who can contribute to the further development of their long-going self-narratives and life-stories. In this way, older people better meet their own changing needs, maintaining or even expanding the quality of their social lives, despite a reduced quantity of social life.

SES theory appears to be consistent with the SDT and self-concordance approach that was described in this chapter. First, SES theory finds that older people attend to a greater extent to their own emotional responses and meanings, and attend to a lesser extent to the social norms and niceties that might lead to superficial relationships. This is conceptually similar our findings that age correlates with self-concordance, since self-concordance refers to the state of pursuing goals that reflect one's interests and identifications rather than goals felt to originate in social pressures and introjects. In terms of the multi-level model of personality presented in Figure 19.2, SES theory implies that as people age, their social goals (at level 3 of personality) become more self-concordant and thus better represent their psychological needs (at level 1 of personality), their dispositional and emotional traits (at level 2 of personality), and their evolving life-story (at level 4 of personality). In particular, their social goals may better reflect their emotional traits and dispositions.

A second point of convergence between SDT and SES concerns the normative change issue. Like SDT, SES theory assumes that people can do more than simply partially compensate for their ever-increasing deficiencies; they might actually become happier (i.e., gains can exceed losses), as a result of attending to internal meanings more so than potentially alienating social forces. In other words, SES theory also provides a way of predicting the normative positive changes in psychological well-being that are often observed in aging samples, whereas simple action theories do not.

Considering SDT, SOC, and SES Theories Together

Each of these three theoretical perspectives provides means of predicting positive (or at least less negative) aging. How, if at all, might they be combined? To offer some preliminary speculations on this issue, let us consider several potential causal models. In one class of models, let us propose that chronological age (representing both the aging process and cumulative experience) positively predicts SOC, SES, and self-concordance. In other words, as people age, they engage to a greater extent in selective optimization with compensation, and become more socio-emotionally selective, and learn to select more self-concordant goals; these may be parallel positive outcomes that have no causal relations or priorities with respect to each other. In another class of models, let us propose that age predicts self-concordance, which then predicts SES and SOC. As in some of the earlier life-span data summarized above, in which attained self-concordance mediated the relation of chronological age to well-being (Sheldon & Kasser, 2001; Sheldon, Houser-Marko, & Kasser, 2006), and consistent with findings that self-concordance is associated with greater quantity and quality of effort (Sheldon & Elliot, 1998, 1999), aging people may first select more self-concordant goals, which in turn leads to greater adjustment (i.e., more SOC and SES). In a third class of models, let us propose that self-concordance is the outcome of SOC and SES, and that SOC and SES mediate the effects of age upon self-concordance. In this view, by learning to favor close social relationships and to better select, optimize, and compensate in their goals, older people are enabled to choose goals that better represent their true values and interests. Finally, in yet a fourth class of models, positive motivational changes might moderate the age effects. For example, age might only predict SES or SOC if the older person is also a more self-concordant person; in this case, in which the older person's goals better represent his/her interests and values, then he/she may evidence more developmentally-appropriate SOC and SES.

Unfortunately, the data do not yet exist to choose between these models, and in any case, the theories (and their associated constructs) may be too abstract and global, or too difficult to measure, to be confidently located in models such as these. Nevertheless, the effort may be worth it, to begin to provide a process understanding of the interplay of positive coping styles, psychosocial personality development, and psychological well-being in the aging process.

Conclusion and Future Research Directions

To summarize, in this chapter I have reviewed recent evidence that personality continues to develop throughout the life span—more often than not. Although peoples' capacities and competencies are almost bound to decline as they age, these trends may be counteracted by a tendency to select more self-concordant goals (i.e., to feel more ownership of their personal initiatives). This conclusion is consistent with organismic and humanistic perspectives on human nature, and is also consistent with traditional psychosocial theories such as Erikson's stage theory and Loevinger's theory of ego-development. Furthermore, it is consistent with SES theory (Carstensen, 1992), which assumes that aging people pay greater attention to internal information and emotions as they construct their social lives. Although it is not inconsistent with SOC theory, the current view addresses issues that SOC theory has not considered, perhaps providing new means of conceptualizing positive selection, optimization, and compensation in the later life span.

Still, much further research needs to be conducted. For example, longitudinal studies of motivational changes through the life span are needed, to extend Sheldon and colleague's recent cross-sectional findings. Do felt inner freedom and appropriate goal-selection really improve over the decades, or might the observed effects instead reflect mere cohort or period effects? In addition, we need to better rule out the possibility of retrospective biases, in both cross-sectional and longitudinal studies. In claiming greater self-concordance, how can we be sure that older persons are not exaggerating?

Brandtstadter's conception of "immunization processes," in which aging people use defensive and biased processing to deny what is happening to them (Brandtstadter, 1999), suggests that this could be the case. Also, recent studies of the bias to think that one is better now than one was in the past (Wilson & Ross, 2001) further suggest that the greater well-being and self-concordance reported by older people may be illusory. Research using peer-reports of the constructs, or implicit measures of the constructs, is needed to rule out such possibilities. Finally, research is needed to try to connect and combine the SDT, SES, and SOC constructs, as in the speculations above, to provide the most comprehensive models of positive aging.

References

Argyle, M. (1999). Causes and correlates of happiness. In D. Kahneman, E. Diener, & N. Schwarz (Eds.), *Well-being: The foundations of hedonic psychology* (pp. 353–373). New York: Russell Sage.

Baltes, M. M., & Carstensen, L. L. (2003). The process of successful aging: Selection, optimization, and compensation. In U. M. Staudinger & U. Lindenberger (Eds.), *Understanding human development: Dialogues with lifespan psychology* (pp. 81–104). Boston: Kluwer.

Baltes, P. B. (2003). On the incomplete architecture of human ontogeny: Selection, optimization, and compensation as foundation of developmental theory. In U. M Staudinger & U. Lindenberger (Eds.), *Understanding human development: Dialogues with lifespan psychology* (pp. 17–44). Boston: Kluwer.

Baltes, P. B., & Baltes, M. M. (1990). Psychological perspectives on successful aging The model of selective optimization with compensation. In P. B. Baltes & M. M. Baltes (Eds.), *Successful aging: Perspectives from the behavioral sciences* (pp. 1–34). Cambridge, UK: Cambridge University Press.

Baumeister, R. F., & Leary, M. R. (1995). The need to belong: Desire for interpersonal attachments as a fundamental human motivation. *Psychological Bulletin, 117*, 497–529.

Brandtstadter, J. (1999). Sources of resilience in the aging self: Toward integrating perspectives. In T. M. Hess & F. Blanchard-Fields (Eds.), *Social cognition and aging* (pp. 125–144). New York: Academic Press.

Brandtstadter, J., & Rothermund, K. (2002). The life-course dynamics of goal pursuit and goal adjustment: A two-process framework. *Developmental Review, 22*(1), 117–150.

Carstensen, L. (1992). Social and emotional patterns in adulthood: Support for socioemotional selectivity theory. *Psychology and Aging, 7*, 331–338.

Chandler, C. L., & Connell, J. P. (1987). Children's intrinsic, extrinsic and internalized motivation: A developmental study of children's reasons for liked and disliked behaviours. *British Journal of Developmental Psychology, 5*, 357–365.

Charles, S. T., & Carstensen, L. L. (1999). The role of time in the setting of social goals across the lifespan. In T. M. Hess & F. Blanchard-Fields (Eds.), *Social cognition and aging* (pp. 319–345). New York: Academic Press.

Csikszentmihalyi, M. (1997). *Finding flow: The psychology of engagement with everyday life.* New York: Basic Books.

Deci, E. L. (1972). Intrinsic motivation, extrinsic reinforcement, and inequity. *Journal of Personality & Social Psychology, 22*, 113–120.

Deci, E. L. (1975). *Intrinsic motivation.* New York: Plenum.

Deci, E. L., & Ryan, R. M. (1985). *Intrinsic motivation and self-determination in human behavior.* New York: Plenum.

Deci, E. L., & Ryan, R. M. (1991). A motivational approach to self: Integration in personality. In R. Dienstbier (Ed.), *Nebraska symposium on motivation: Vol. 38. Perspectives on motivation* (pp. 237–288). Lincoln: University of Nebraska Press.

Deci, E. L., & Ryan, R. M. (2000). The "what" and "why" of goal pursuits: Human needs and the self-determination of behavior. *Psychological Inquiry, 11*, 227–268.

Deci, E. L., & Ryan, R. M. (2006). *Self-determination theory.* Retrieved online at http://www.psych.rochester.edu/SDT/.

Diener, E. (1994). Assessing subjective well-being: Progress and opportunities. *Social Indicators Research, 31*, 103–157.

Emmons, R. A. (1989). The personal strivings approach to personality. In L. A. Pervin (Ed.), *Goal concepts in personality and social psychology* (pp. 87–126). Hillsdale, NJ: Erlbaum.

Emmons, R. A. (1999). *The psychology of ultimate concerns*. New York: Guilford.

Emmons, R. A. & McAdams, D. (1991). Personal strivings and motive dispositions: Exploring the links. *Personality & Social Psychology Bulletin, 17*, 648–654.

Erikson, E. (1963). *Childhood and society*. New York: Norton.

Freund, A. M., Li, K. Z., & Baltes, P. B. (1999). Successful development and aging: The role of selection, optimization, and compensation. In J. Brandtstadter & R.M . Lerner (Eds.), *Action and self-development: Theory and research through the lifespan* (pp. 401–434). Thousand Oaks, CA: Sage.

Heckhausen, J. (2003). The future of lifespan developmental psychology: Perspectives from control theory. In U. M. Staudinger & U. Lindenberger (Eds.), *Understanding human development: Dialogues with lifespan psychology* (pp. 383–400). Boston: Kluwer.

Heckhausen, J., & Schulz, R. (1999). Selectivity in life-span development: Biological and societal canalizations and individuals' developmental goals. In J. Brandtstadter & R. M. Lerner (Eds.), *Action and self-development: Theory and research through the lifespan* (pp. 67–104). Thousand Oaks, Ca: Sage.

Kasser, T. (2002). *The high price of materialism*. Cambridge, MA: MIT Press.

Little, B. R. (1993). Personal projects and the distributed self: Aspects of a conative psychology. In J. Suls (Ed.), *The self in social perspective: Psychological perspectives on the self* (Vol. 4, pp. 157–185). Hillsdale, NJ: Erlbaum.

Loevinger, J. (1997). Stages of personality development. In R. Hogan, J. Johnson, & S. Briggs (Eds.), *Handbook of personality psychology* (pp. 199–208). San Diego, CA: Academic Press.

Markus, H., Kitayama, S., & Heiman, R. (1996). Culture and basic psychological principles. In E. T. Higgins & A. W. Kruglanski (Eds.), *Social psychology: Handbook of basic principles* (pp. 857–913). New York: Guilford.

Maslow, A. (1971). *The farther reaches of human nature*. New York: Viking Press.

McAdams, D. P. (1995). What do we know when we know a person? *Journal of Personality, 63*, 365–396.

McAdams, D. P. (1996). Personality, modernity, and the storied self: A contemporary framework for studying persons. *Psychological Inquiry, 7*, 295–321.

McAdams, D. P. (1998). Ego, trait, identity. In P. M. Westenberg & A. Blasi (Eds), *Personality development: Theoretical, empirical, and clinical investigations of Loevinger's conception of ego development* (pp. 27–38). Mahwah, NJ: Erlbaum.

Piaget, J. (1971). *Biology and knowledge: An essay on the relations between organic regulations and cognitive processes*. Chicago: University of Chicago Press.

Rogers, C. (1961). *On becoming a person: A therapist's view of psychotherapy*. Boston: Houghton Mifflin.

Rogers, C. R. (1964). Toward a modern approach to values: The valuing process in the mature person. *Journal of Abnormal & Social Psychology, 68*, 160–167.

Ryan, R. M. & Connell, J.P. (1989). Perceived locus of causality and internalization: Examining reasons for acting in two domains. *Journal of Personality and Social Psychology, 57*, 749–761.

Seligman, M. E. P., & Csikszentmihalyi, M. (2000). Positive psychology: An introduction. *American Psychologist, 55*, 5–14.

Sheldon, K. M. (1995). Creativity and self-determination in personality. *Creativity Research Journal, 8*, 61–72.

Sheldon, K. M. (2002). The self-concordance model of healthy goal-striving: When personal goals correctly represent the person. In E. L. Deci & R. M. Ryan (Eds.), *Handbook of self-determination research* (pp. 65–86). Rochester, NY: University of Rochester Press.

Sheldon, K. M. (2004). *Optimal human being: An integrated multi-level perspective*. Mahwah, NJ: Erlbaum.

Sheldon, K. M., Arndt, J., & Houser-Marko, L. (2003). In search of the organismic valuing process: The human tendency to move towards beneficial goal choices. *Journal of Personality, 71*, 835–869.

Sheldon, K. M., & Elliot, A. J. (1998). Not all personal goals are personal: Comparing autonomous and controlled reasons as predictors of effort and attainment. *Personality and Social Psychology Bulletin, 24*, 546–557.

Sheldon, K. M., & Elliot, A. J. (1999). Goal striving, need-satisfaction, and longitudinal well-being: The self-concordance model. *Journal of Personality and Social Psychology, 76*, 482–497.

Sheldon, K. M., Elliot, A. J., Ryan, R. M., Chirkov, V., Kim, Y., Wu, C., Demir, M., & Sun, Z. (2004). Self-concordance and subjective well-being in four cultures. *Journal of Cross-Cultural Psychology, 35*, 209–233.

Sheldon, K. M., & Houser-Marko, L. (2001). Self-concordance, goal- attainment, and the pursuit of happiness: Can there be an upward spiral? *Journal of Personality and Social Psychology, 80*, 152–165.

Sheldon, K. M., Houser-Marko, L., & Kasser, T. (2006). Does autonomy increase with age? Comparing the motivation and well-being of college students and their parents. *Journal of Research in Personality, 40*, 168–178.

Sheldon, K. M., & Kasser, T. (1995). Coherence and congruence: Two aspects of personality integration. *Journal of Personality and Social Psychology, 68*, 531–543.

Sheldon, K. M., & Kasser, T. (1998). Pursuing personal goals: Skills enable progress, but not all progress is beneficial. *Personality and Social Psychology Bulletin, 24*, 1319–1331.

Sheldon, K. M. & Kasser, T. (2001). Getting older, getting better? Personal strivings and personality development across the life-course. *Developmental Psychology, 37*, 491–501.

Sheldon, K. M., Kasser, T., Houser-Marko, L., Jones, T., & Turban, D. (2005). Doing one's duty: Chronological age, felt autonomy, and subjective well-being. *European Journal of Personality, 19*, 97–115.

Sheldon, K. M., Ryan, R. M., & Reis, H. R. (1996). What makes for a good day? Competence and autonomy in the day and in the person. *Personality and Social Psychology Bulletin, 22*, 1270–1279.

Werner, H. (1957). The concept of development from a comparative and organismic point of view. In D. Harris (Ed.), *The concept of development* (pp. 125–147). Minneapolis: University of Minnesota Press.

Wilson, A. E., & Ross, M. (2001). From chump to champ: People's appraisals of their earlier and present selves. *Journal of Personality & Social Psychology, 80*, 572–584.

Wilson, R. S., Beckett, L. A., Barnes, L. L., Schneider, J. A., Bach, J., Evans, D. A., & Bennett, D. A. (2002). Individual differences in rates of change in cognitive abilities of older persons. *Psychology & Aging, 17*, 179–193.

Wilson, T. D. (2000). *Strangers to ourselves: Discovering the adaptive unconscious.* Cambridge, MA: Harvard University Press.

Chapter 20

Informal and Incidental Learning in the Workplace

Victoria J. Marsick, Karen E. Watkins,
Mary Wilson Callahan, and Marie Volpe

Periodically, scholars have grappled with the idea of informal and incidental learning, concepts that are typically defined in contrast with formal, structured education and that center around learning from and through experience. Over the past 16 years, Marsick and Watkins (1990, 1999) have evolved a theory of informal and incidental learning that has been used in a number of dissertations and published studies. Growing out of thinking about learning from experience and self-directed learning, their model focused on the learning phases of an individual and added stages of reflective learning that usually occur incidentally but that, with coaching, can deepen this learning.

Over that same period of time, informal learning has moved from an interesting phenomenon at the edges of human resource development and training to mainstream practice (Cross, 2007). Companies in the United States such as IBM have blended formal and informal learning in its On Demand Learning system (IBM Learning Solutions, 2005). Dale and Bell (1999), in a research review, identified many benefits of informal learning at work, for example: flexibility, employability, adaptability of learning to context, rapid transfer to practice, and resolution of work-related problems through regular review of work practices and performance. Dale and Bell also identified drawbacks, namely, a narrow, contextual focus; learning bad habits or wrong lessons; accreditation challenges; and the fact that such learning is so well integrated with work that it may not be recognized. In Europe, as Malcolm, Hodkinson, and Colley (2003) note, "Current EU policies in lifelong learning are raising the profile of informal and non-formal learning. The recognition and enhancement of such learning is seen as vital in improving social inclusion, and increasing economic productivity" (p. 313). Elsewhere in Europe, in support of this observation, the Government of Norway launched the Realkompetanse Project to "give adults the right to document their non-formal and informal learning without having to undergo traditional forms of testing." VOX, the Norwegian Institute of Adult Education (2002), led by Turid Kjolseth, describes realkompetanse as "all formal, non-formal and informal learning acquired by adults" (p. 5).

Recently, Marsick and Watkins have focused on the context (comprised of both the external and internal organizational environments) as a significant component of their model. What is it about this context that so significantly influences informal and incidental learning? As we discuss in this chapter, whole person models of learning (Heron, 1992; Heron & Reason, 1997, 2001; Yorks & Kasl, 2006), theories of artistic learning (Lawrence, 2005), and theories of situated learning (Wenger, 1998) offer partial explanations. Our own evolving work (Cseh, Watkins, & Marsick, 1999; Marsick & Volpe, 1999; Callahan, 1999, Watkins & Cervero, 2000) offers additional perspectives.

Newer research and theory development about workplace learning—including informal and incidental learning—is also moving from a focus on the individual to a deeper understanding of collaborative learning (Raelin, 2000). Learning and action at work is essentially social learning (Brown & Duguid, 2000). Learning is constrained by the rules that govern action in an organization, by the resources available to a learner, and by the receptivity of others within the organization that affect whether or not the learner may try or apply what he or she has learned. Learning is usually undertaken by individuals for group or organizational purposes, may be guided by supervisors, and may be a shared quest with co-workers; it is affected by the mirror of co-workers' responses. Whether undertaken collaboratively or not, the collective nature of the workplace nudges, imprints, or controls what is learned.

This chapter focuses on learning *in the workplace*, although workplace settings are broadly defined to include businesses, not-for-profits, the public sector, educational institutions, and religious venues. We focus on the workplace in part for practical reasons. The range of purposes and settings for informal and incidental learning research is so varied that review and comparison is difficult without some common focus, particularly since many studies of informal and incidental learning are qualitative in nature and use varied theoretical frameworks to guide interpretation of findings. Moreover, we focus on the workplace because a good deal of adult learning takes place at or for work. Even though critics decry the extent to which economic forces have colonized the life-world, to borrow a term from Jurgen Habermas (1987), adults in the "developed world" spend many hours of their lives at work. And while adults rely on education and training to prepare them for work and, increasingly, to update their knowledge and skills, there is simultaneously an emphasis within organizations on learning on the job that is driven by, and integrated with, work routines.

In this chapter, we discuss the historical antecedents of informal and incidental learning, including early work by Marsick and Watkins (1990). We review key themes and trends in recent research to set the stage for rethinking this model of learning. We then recount our own experience in using this model in our own collaborative work together, and how our own use of the model helped us to understand four critical limitations with the way we had constructed our model. We turn to alternative bodies of theory and research that help rethink our theory. We conclude with a critical appraisal of outstanding issues that grow out of our review of research.

Definitions and Model for Understanding Informal and Incidental Learning

Putting definitional and operational boundaries around informal and incidental learning is a challenge. Marsick & Watkins (1990) defined informal and incidental learning as "learning outside of formally structured, institutionally sponsored, classroom-based activities" (pp. 6–7) and asserted that such learning "often takes place under non-routine circumstances, that is, when the procedures and responses that people normally use fail" leading to greater attention to, and awareness, of "tacit, hidden, taken-for-granted assumptions" that may help learners rethink situations in which they find themselves and re-frame their understanding of the kind of learning they might need to undertake. They further distinguished incidental from informal learning by defining it "as a byproduct of some other activity, such as task accomplishment, interpersonal interactions, sensing the organizational culture, or trial-and-error experimentation" (pp. 6–7). They contrasted the sometimes intentional and more possibly planned nature of informal learning with the accidental and often semi-conscious nature of incidental learning.

Informal and incidental learning outcomes depend, in part, on the degree of conscious awareness with which one attends to learning and the environment that brings learning opportunities. Formal learning opportunities heighten awareness, but such learning is divorced from real life action. Informal learning benefits from being linked to meaningful job activities, but it requires greater attention to making the most of the learning opportunity, something that might involve planning and almost certainly involves some conscious attention, reflection, and direction. Incidental learning, while occurring by chance, can be highly beneficial when one moves the accidental learning opportunity closer into the informal learning realm through conscious attention, reflection, and direction.

Marsick and Watkins' (1990) framing of informal and incidental learning is based on theory of learning from and through experience—distinguished from the more designed experiential learning activity described by Kolb (1984). Learning from experience and experiential learning theories rest on Dewey's (1938) pragmatic cycle of problem solving through reflective thought. Reflective thought begins with a disjuncture between what is expected and what occurs, which can lead to re-thinking the nature of the problem and the directions in which one might look for solutions. Solving a problem involves one or more cycles of trial and error in which learning takes place as one seeks to achieve a desired outcome. Observation of what occurs leads to course corrections and eventually to conclusions and planning for how one will address similar situations going forward. Dewey essentially adapted the scientific method to solving problems of everyday life. This same cycle is at the heart of action research, developed by Kurt Lewin (1947) and others based on systematic cycles of problem definition, data gathering, reflection on evidence, learning, and planning based on what was learned. Lewin added an emphasis on collective problem solving of socially shared concerns. Lewin thus moved the more individually oriented learning cycle in interaction with one's environment, as advocated by Dewey, to a group and organizational learning level.

Of the various theorists who built off Lewin's work, Chris Argyris and Donald Schön (1974, 1978) developed action science, a systematic theory for learning from experience in groups and organizations. They developed the idea of a theory of action, comprised of espoused theories, which represent an individual or organizational ideal, and theories-in-use, which represent how such theories are carried out. Argyris and Schön sought ways to close the gap between the ideal and the actual. They adopted Dewey's idea of a disjuncture between what was expected and what occurred (an error) as a trigger for learning how to correct a course of action or tactics (single loop learning) to achieve one's goals. When changes in tactics do not achieve desired ends, they suggest switching to double loop learning in which one examines values, assumptions, and beliefs that influence how a situation or problem is framed. Reframing the situation or problem often leads to more effective desired solutions, which typically one then has to learn how to implement.

Marsick and Watkins (1990) adopted Argyris and Schön's basic framework for their theory of informal and incidental learning. Depending on the degree of awareness, intention, and direction, one might be engaging in either informal or incidental learning. But in both kinds of learning, one's attention might be focused on either single or double loop learning. Marsick and Watkins further adopted Simon's (1965) distinction between routine and non-routine work. They noted the shift, fueled by globalization and high technology, towards rapidly changing environments and a knowledge era that lent itself more often to what the Army Defense College was calling VUCA environments that were volatile, uncertain, complex, and ambiguous. They suggested that increasingly, employees throughout most organizations were likely to find themselves addressing non-routine problems and challenges that call for customized responses that require greater levels of judgment and learning.

They drew on Polanyi's (1967) discussion of tacit knowledge, from which Schön (1983) also drew in developing his theory of reflective practice. Now more widely known through the work of Nonaka and Takeuchi (1995) on knowledge creation, Polanyi pointed out that discoveries in chemistry and other scientific disciplines were not at all rational, value-free, and objective. Instead, Inkster (1987) depicts the thrust of Polanyi's work as shedding light on the "ubiquitous personal coefficient in all knowledge" (p. 114). Polanyi described scientific work as "full of every variety of subjective emotion, including curiosity, exhilaration, frustration, anxiety, and an intense persuasive passion or need to convince others of the correctness of the interpretation of the phenomena he observed." In making interpretations of complex situations, Polanyi noted how our past experience and understanding influences interpretations of present circumstances and how much of that framing of the situation remains outside of our critical awareness and purview.

Roots in Other Definitions

Others have also written about informal and incidental learning. Malcolm Knowles (Overstreet, in Knowles, 1950) differentiated between formal adult education, carried out through systematic instruction—"given in the regular way of teacher, textbook, recitations, examination, and credit"—and informal learning at "times—and these more frequent—when what he most needs is not and could not be found in any formal course of instruction" (p. v). Marsick and Watkins' (1990) contribution was to create a framework and model that could be further researched and tested and that focused more explicitly on the workplace as a context and shaper of such learning. Knowles (1950) dealt more with educational method and did not take into consideration to the same degree the "social contract among individuals who work together to achieve higher-order organizational goals ... (requiring that) individuals learn and work in social units where interactions are not typically subject to design and control by trainers" (p. 35).

Malcolm, Hodkinson, and Colley (2003), in summarizing research commissioned by the Learning and Skills Development Agency of England, used a four-fold heuristic device to discuss differences among formal, informal, and nonformal learning: learning processes, location and setting, purposes, and the nature of what is being learned. They also note that defining informal learning is both problematic and political. Straka (2004), in tracing the genealogy of informal learning, describes it as "a metaphor with a severe problem, namely the lack of systematically and empirically grounded valid evidence on why, where, when, how and what is learned under 'informal conditions'" (p. 2). In an extended discussion of definitions, Gorard, Fevre, and Rees (1999) draw on Eraut, Alderton, Cole, and Senke (1998), whose definition of non-formal learning emphasized a lack of constraints by "prescribed frameworks," to characterize informal learning broadly "such that it includes learning taking place as a process outside formal participation." They thus exclude informal learning that might occur during structured training and education, though our definition of incidental learning includes learning in these circumstances. They go on to describe informal learning, as do we, as characterized by some intentionality despite the lack of formal structure, that is, "non-taught learning ... (that) includes non-certified episodes, and those leading to tacit knowledge ... both at work and at leisure" (pp. 437–438).

Conceptualization of learning as socialization, derived from Vygotsky's cultural-historical psychology, offers a view of informal and incidental learning that differs from Dewey's pragmatic philosophy in which the individual learner acts on his/her world. Vygotsky instead suggested that learning is a natural maturation process shaped by history and culture. External social interaction, over time, becomes internalized and is culturally mediated through the use of language, tools, and artifacts. Learning and development occur through social interaction and culture change (Wertsch & Tulviste, 1996). Learning begins with internalization via socialization, but it can move into a period of innovation through externalization when disruptions call for intentional questioning, critical reflection, and problem solving (Engestrom, 1999). Situated learning (Lave & Wenger, 1991), with antecedents in Vygotsky's work, describes learning that occurs informally and unintentionally through social interaction within a natural workplace context.

Incidental learning might be best understood through socialization theory. Incidental learning has retained a focus on its accidental, unplanned nature over several decades. Postman and Senders (1946) drew on McGeoch (1942) in defining incidental learning as unintentional, accidental, and unstructured. Stokes and Pankowski (1988) emphasized the way learning "occurs by chance while one is engaged in another activity" (p. 89). Jarvis (1987) described incidental learning, using his typology of reflection, as nonreflective and reactive, but he concluded that such learning "should not be minimized since this is a major part of the process whereby people learn and acquire their culture and by which it is maintained through taken-for-granted behavior" (p. 32).

The 1960s saw scholars examining the incidental learning of the "hidden curriculum" in classrooms. These discussions continue. For example, Bloomberg (2006), in studying video-based distance learning communities in Jewish higher education programs, found that: "Much of the 'changed thinking,' or cognitive development as a consequence of participation in this learning community might in fact be attributed to this program's 'hidden' or implicit curriculum ... which offers unintended and often unexpected outcomes or benefits" (p. 248). Reischman (1986) distinguished learning "en passant" from intentional adult learning with a focus on the unintentional learning that might arise from otherwise planned tasks or events. He characterized learning "en passant" as: "integrated, holistic, not compulsory, individualized, uses a wide variety of support, builds on previous learning, can be a basis for further learning, and ... can be especially identified by looking back, i.e., by reflection" (Marsick & Watkins, 1990, p. 34).

Studies and discussions of informal and incidental learning frequently intermingle these two terms, and some authors (for example, Candy & Crebert, 1991) use the terms "informal," "incidental," and "non-formal" in ways other than do Marsick and Watkins (1990). Ellinger (1997) is among those few who pointed out the difference between informal and incidental learning. As did Marsick and Watkins, she hinged the distinction on the issue of learner intent and the planned activity that grows from that intent, while informal learning more clearly grows out of defined learner intentions than incidental learning. However, in a major study of informal learning at work, Bruce, Aring, and Brand (1998) seemed to ignore the concept of incidental learning, but included within informal learning the

> acquisition and application of skills and knowledge; movement along the continuum from inexperience to confidence; and maturity and expertise in regard to specific tasks, skills, and knowledge...[in a learning process that] is neither determined nor designed by the organization. (p. 15)

As we also have done, the authors highlighted the critical role of contextual factors in informal workplace learning, and they listed intrapersonal and interpersonal skills as well as cultural assimilation among the participants' learnings. Another example of how types of learning intermingle is a study of training by Verespej (1998) who also speaks to much incidental learning, including (1) aspects of intrapsychic and interpersonal skills, (2) cultural information, shared values, and goals, (3) ability to devise and communicate ideas, and (4) how to reflect on different approaches to problems. Moreover, the learning situations described align with many settings that nurture incidental learning, such as team participation, meetings, mentoring, peer-to-peer interchanges, and customer interaction. Ultimately, Verespej's conclusion that "if learning is to take place, there must be a culture of openness and trust that is more than empty words" (p. 42) applies to many work settings and underscores the institutional context as an influence on informal and incidental learning in the workplace.

Delimiters and Enhancers

Marsick and Watkins (1990) also identified conditions that might delimit or enhance such learning. Delimiters include framing and capacity. Enhancers include creativity, proactivity, and critical reflectivity.

Argyris and Schön's theory and the work of Polanyi led to the first key delimiter of informal and incidental learning: the way in which we frame our understanding of a situation and the degree to which we are open to re-framing that view. Incidental learning, in particular, is prone to this limitation because little attention is given to such learning in the midst of pursuit of a different task or purpose. The organization's culture and pressures, including time and resource constraints, can reinforce a reluctance to take time out to reframe. Yet problem framing is crucial for informal and incidental learning. Widening one's vision to include aspects of the context in which problems rest opens up multiple definitions of a situation and frees one to examine other learning-related concerns. Problem framing also influences the lens through which one defines a situation. Inkster (1987), for example, noted that Polyani reanalyzed many studies conducted by behaviorists and came to very different understandings of the situation: "Where the behaviorists had seen conditioning, Polyani saw intelligent learning, even in life forms as primitive as worms" (p. 117). The way people frame a situation can thus be a powerful shaper of perception and understanding. Informal and incidental learning benefits when tacit framing is made explicit and thus examinable in light of alternative perceptions.

A second delimiter of informal and incidental learning derived from the work of Elliot Jacques (1988) on work capacity. Jacques describes intellectual capability as the ability to engage in goal-directed behavior in problem solving and everyday work. His extensive research studies focus, in part, on how individuals vary in work capacity, measured in terms of the longest period of time that a person can conceive of a project (in operational terms) and act toward accomplishing the goals of that project without needing feedback. Although controversial, Jacques' work suggests that individuals vary widely in ability to conceive the scope of work and of a learning task.

Developmental theory can be used to support Jacques' claim that all adults may not be ready to conceive the scope of work and learning tasks on their own. Kegan (1982, 1994) argues that as adults mature, they are able to take what has held them subject—that is, what is essentially part of how they perceive their reality—as an object. As adults hold as object what had been subject, their consciousness expands and they are able to deal with increasing levels of complexity. To independently manage one's learning agenda, a person should be "self-authoring," that is, not dependent on others even though one might choose to consult or collaborate with others. Kegan (1994) argues that many adults today are not self-authoring. Instead, they look to follow rules set by others or to follow what respected role models suggest they do. This puts them "in over their heads" when challenged to take on tasks that require independent, critical thinking.

Informal and incidental learning may be shaped by these fundamental mind sets. Jacques does not hold that expanding capacity to move beyond these mindsets is likely. But Kegan and others (e.g., Torbert, 1991) argue that under the right conditions, people can transform the way in which they understand the world, which in turn will influence the lenses they use to learn, and thereby might expand capacity to engage fruitfully in informal and incidental learning that goes beyond current mental models. Those who would facilitate people's capacity for informal and incidental learning at work would want to challenge and support learners to the point where they would "own" their learning goals and intentionally find ways to take advantage of informal learning opportunities that help them meet these goals.

Creativity, the first enhancer of informal and incidental learning, enables people to imagine alternatives and think beyond their current circumstances or points of view. Schön (1983) described a process in new product development in which people were able to imagine new ways of understanding a need or its satisfaction through "seeing as" or "the perception of similarity before one can say 'similar with respect to what'" (p. 182). The example he used was idea generation to improve a paintbrush, a process that was helped when someone compared a paintbrush to a pump, thus opening up a new way of thinking about the nature of product improvements. Creativity helps learners break out of preconceived understandings and mental models that limit their ability to re-frame a situation or problem. Creativity involves playing with ideas in ways that open new possibilities. As discussed later in this chapter, this enhancer was a precursor to current thinking about the role of aesthetics in learning.

Proactivity, the second enhancer of informal and incidental learning, suggests a readiness to take initiative, an alertness to the environment and to opportunities it might afford learning. Its opposite, reactivity, connotes passivity, disempowerment, and in some cases, a somewhat fatalistic stance toward events in which circumstances are allowed to dictate one's response. Proactivity is related, in part, to the concept of autonomy and to empowerment. Autonomy, which is at the heart of self-direction in learning or work, is characterized by independence within the constraints in which one finds oneself. Empowerment, which depends partly on oneself and partly on the social or organizational environment, involves the experience of power to take action.

For critical reflectivity, the final enhancer of informal and incidental learning, Marsick and Watkins (1990) drew on Mezirow's (1985) work on transformative learning, also based on the work of John Dewey (1938), as: "the bringing of one's assumptions, premises, criteria, and schemata into consciousness and vigorously critiquing them" (p. 25). Informal and incidental learning, as we defined it, involves awareness of and reflection on actions and their underlying values and assumptions when desired outcomes do not materialize. Critical reflectivity is the ability to delve deeply into reasons why such desired results do not materialize.

Since Marsick and Watkins first developed their ideas, much has been written from the point of view of adult developmental theory about whether or not the ability to be critically reflective is tied to one's state of consciousness. In other words, building upon Kegan's (1994) subject-object theory, one has to be able to get outside of one's current mental models in order to take them as an object of critique, but the ability to do that is dependent on one's mental capability to see oneself from a broader perspective, and in organizational life, to understand how one's role is part of a larger system. Developmental theorists such as Kegan (1994) and Torbert (1991) suggest that not everyone holds these capabilities, although they would also point out that conditions can be created that enable people to stretch beyond their current mental models and move toward broader, more inclusive mental models that do support critical reflectivity. Everyone, from this viewpoint, is not equally able to think critically, and therefore, may not be as adept when engaging in informal and incidental learning.

Model of Informal and Incidental Learning

Marsick and Watkins (1990) developed a model of informal and incidental learning based on the above definitions and grounding (see Figure 20.1). In this model, people use reflection to become aware of the problematic aspects of the experience, to probe these features, and to learn new ways to understand and address the challenges they encounter. Problem solving steps are located at vertical and horizontal axes, and are labeled (clockwise) as Top, Right, Bottom, and Left. Learning steps are located in between problem solving steps, and are labeled (beginning clockwise just before Top) as Top Left, Top Right, Bottom Right, and Bottom Left.

Problem solving begins when people encounter a new experience (Top). They frame the new experience based on what they learned from past experience (Top Left). They assess similarities or differences and use interpretation to make sense of the new situation. Often, people make these judgments quickly, without much conscious reflection. Reflection slows down the diagnosis, but it also helps a person to become aware of the complexity of the situation and the assumptions used to judge the new challenge.

After diagnosing a new experience, people learn more about the context of the problem (Top Right). They find out what other people are thinking and doing. They try to

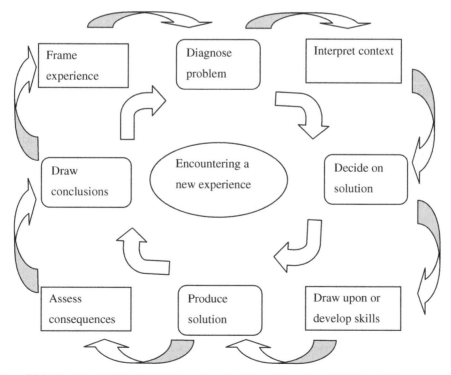

Figure 20.1 Marsick and Watkins' informal and incidental learning original model.

understand the political situation. They may gather information from other people or social groups that are affected by the problem. They might test their thinking with others or conduct mini-experiments before they choose a course of action. Reflection can play a key role in this phase by opening up lines of thinking that would otherwise have remained unexplored. Interpretation of the context leads to choices around alternative actions that are guided by recollections of past solutions and by one's own search for other potential models for action.

Once a decision has been made about a course of action (Right), a person develops or gathers resources to implement the decision (Bottom Right). Reflection might be anticipatory, and lead to the development of new capabilities in order to implement the solution. Often, reflection occurs while the action is being implemented over time. When people reflect-in-action (Schön, 1987), they typically do so when they are taken by some surprise in the course of action. Because they are learning as they implement, people may make quick judgments based on partial information. They may also seek further information during action.

Once an action is taken (Bottom), people assess consequences and decide whether or not outcomes match their goals (Bottom Left). Reflection after the fact allows for a full learning review. It is relatively easy to assess *intended* consequences when goals are reasonably explicit and data are available to make sound judgments. It is harder to recognize *unintended* consequences, although reflection can lead one to ask questions of a wide range of people and explore sources of information that might otherwise be ignored. A learning review leads to conclusions about results (Left) and lessons learned that can be of help in planning future actions. Reflection at this point brings a person full circle to the new understandings (Top Left) that are drawn in a new iteration of the cycle.

Reflection is central to every phase of learning from experience although everyone does not always consciously use reflection to its fullest potential. Reflection sensitizes people to surprises and mismatches that signal the inadequacy of their prior stock of knowledge. Through reflection-in-action (Schön, 1987), people adjust their course of action and learn while they are carrying out the solution. Reflection after the fact helps to draw out lessons learned that are useful for the next problem solving cycle.

Based on subsequent research using the model, Cseh, Watkins, and Marsick (1999) reconceptualized the model to emphasize the pervasive influence of context on all aspects of the model of informal and incidental learning. Cseh (1998) found 143 dissertations between 1980 and 1998 that discussed aspects of informal learning, including over twenty built on the informal and incidental learning model that Marsick and Watkins, separately and together, developed and modified over time. Several studies emphasized the role of context in informal and incidental learning research.

Cseh (1998) examined learning experiences that enabled owner-managers of small private companies in Romania to lead successfully in the transition to a free market economy. She was interested in what triggered their learning, what strategies they used, and what lessons they learned. In-depth, face-to-face interviews using a critical incident technique were conducted with 18 managers, between 28 and 62 years of age, representing both genders and the nationalities (Hungarian and Romanian) specific to the two regions selected. Cseh found that the foremost task faced by her participants was to make sense of the rapidly shifting environment and that, in this, interpretation of context dominated, as "context permeates every phase of the learning process—from how the learner will understand the situation, to what is learned, what solutions are available, and how the existing resources will be used" (Cseh, Watkins, & Marsick, 1999, p. 352).

Review of Research

We conducted a systematic review of research to update our knowledge of what others had found in their research on informal and incidental learning. In 1999, Mary Callahan reviewed research as part of her dissertation study. She selected 39 studies from *Dissertation Abstracts International* using the following criteria:

- Indexed as informal learning, incidental learning, or both
- Concerned with adults in organizational settings (workplace or otherwise)
- Included clear information regarding methodology, sample, and results

Several of these dissertations were read completely, others partially, and some were further discussed in other scholars' work on informal and incidental learning. In 2006, Marie Volpe searched JStor, and ProQuest for published research from 1999 to 2005 using the following key words: Informal and Incidental Learning. Additionally, she searched the Social Science Citation Index for studies that drew on the informal and incidental learning model described in this chapter. Volpe's attention was more directly focused on the workplace. Her search yielded 33 studies. Volpe conducted a search to update this database in early 2007, yielding an additional nine studies. Additionally, the authors drew from six dissertations on this topic that were not included in Callahan's (1999) review, plus articles and books retrieved through a Google search of informal learning, and selected studies relevant to new bodies of theory on which this chapter draws. A number of the articles that Volpe located were conceptual rather than empirical. Examples included Boud and Middleton's (2003) examination of how informal learning can only be partially explained by adopting a Communities of Practice framework (Wenger, 1998), contextuality in such learning (Hager, 2004), and a model of e-learning that incorporates informal learning (Svensson, Ellstrom, & Aberg, 2004).

Methodologically, qualitative studies dominate research on this topic, making it difficult to draw conclusions about the scope and dynamics of such learning across settings. Informal or incidental learning was frequently self-reported and only occasionally observed by the researcher. Qualitative, real-time descriptions by the learners' associates of changes in the learners were absent. A concern with self-reporting emerged during Rossing's study (1991), when he sought to conceptualize the phenomena of informal and incidental learning based on accounts of recalled experience. Interviewing members of rural community enhancement groups, he explored their beliefs about the contexts and actions contributing to effective group performance. His findings clustered into learning attributions, products, modes, strategies, and experience patterns. Rossing found that "participants were most likely to report...a 'learning' experience when strong expectations were contradicted somehow, and the individual subsequently revised his or her beliefs... [Also, participants]...were more likely to view beliefs based on positive outcomes as learning than beliefs based on reversal of negative outcomes." (p. 57). Rossing concluded that his study failed to advance understanding about the *quality* of what was learned, i.e., its accuracy and usefulness.

Taken as a whole, this body of research typically focuses on learning strategies. Perhaps because of the difficulty of grasping what is often a tacit and unstructured process, accounts of the dynamics underlying the use of learning strategies are explained using critical incidents or retrospective recall and retro-fitted into one or more theories of learning from experience. Overall, this research generally supports assertions that the large majority of learning is informal and incidental, yet there was also a recognition of the synergy between formal and informal/incidental modes. Regarding the methods that adults used in learning informally and incidentally, the studies show that:

- Trial-and-error (also referred to as learning from mistakes or from experience) was by far the most often cited.
- Other frequently-cited methods included reading pertinent materials, observing the examples (models) of peers, supervisors, and "veterans," and finally, group involvement.
- The ability to critically reflect on one's own experience and mental models, either pre-existing or developed during the period of study, definitely enhanced learning.
- All types of learning occurred, but chiefly the learning of attitudes (like self-confidence and faith development), and both "hard" and "soft" skills.
- Acquisition of knowledge (information) was generally accomplished through self-directed learning projects.

Marsick and Volpe (1999), in an edited volume including six of the studies that Callahan reviewed, identified patterns of learning methods that echoed those in the Callahan review. They described informal learning as integrated with work and daily routines; triggered by an internal or external jolt; and an inductive process of reflection and action that is often linked to the learning of others.

Earlier research suggested that informal learning is increasingly pervasive and central to learning in organizations. Cross (2007) explicates sources that conclude that informal learning accounts for as much as 80% of workplace learning, even though about 80% of organizations' learning budgets are typically invested in formal training rather than informal learning. Bruce, Aring, and Brand (1998) suggested that as much as 70% of all workplace learning is informal, confirming prior findings on managerial learning at Honeywell (Zemke, 1985). Verespej (1998) concluded that "62% of what employees need to know to do their jobs is acquired through informal learning in the workplace" (p. 42). Mumford (1993) identified informal learning as the heart of managerial problem solving, echoing the findings of earlier studies by Burgoyne and Hodgson (1983) and Davies and Easterby-Smith (1984). Today, these percentages have even become standard rules of thumb for managerial development. GE developed a 70-20-10 leadership development practices rule that also shows up in other companies: that is, that such development should involve 70% on-the-job learning, 20% learning through relationships outside of one's area of focus, and 10% structured learning/training (Corporate Leadership Council, 2004).

Dominant in the research are ways that informal and incidental learning have been affected by external forces in the last few years that have impacted most work organizations, such as downsizing, outsourcing, mergers and acquisitions, cross-cultural and diversity challenges, virtual teaming, networking, and other effects of globalization and increased reliance on advancing computer telecommunications technology. Some studies of informal and incidental learning focus on concerns situated in particular companies or locations, such as the advent of terrorism in the United States and the responses to it at home and abroad (Stahl, 2005).

Downsizing and outsourcing have become predictable responses by organizations to maintain competitiveness and profitability. At the same time, these responses have created more fluid, dynamic, and unpredictable workplace environments. Svennson, Ellstrom, and Aberg (2004) describe organizational problems having to do with the integration of individual and organizational learning and specifically with the lack of time for reflection and learning during conditions of change, restructuring, and downsizing.

The topics of the continuously changing workplace environment and implications for learning, for both organizational leaders and employees at all levels (Alcalde, 2005; Conlon, 2004; Enos, Kehrhahn, & Bell, 2003; Svennson et al., 2004), are well documented. In discussing the influence environment has on learning, Hager (2004) characterizes informal learning as "the daily actions of making contextual judgments" (p. 49). This focus on environment underscores the importance of context as employees try to make sense of contextual changes—what are the new expectations, and how can they meet the demands placed on them in a dynamic and fast paced work environment?

Research suggests that when employees view the environment as highly political, they tend to learn just enough to satisfy what they perceive they need to learn in order to satisfy the demands of their supervisors (Volpe 1992). As Volpe found, employees feel the need to protect themselves from ongoing threats of downsizing and outsourcing. The perceived lack of job security inhibits free exchange of ideas and information, restricting collaboration and cooperation in work groups and teams and causing the breakdown of informal networks as vehicles for learning (Marsick & Watkins, 1997; Skiba, 1999; Volpe, 1992; Walker, 2001).

Ipe (2003) points to the importance of trust as foundational to sharing knowledge and communicating, particularly when this involves informal relationships. Informal learning through such relationships is dependent on the culture of the work environment. As several theorists underscore, such learning is strongly influenced by the workplace environment, the context in which people work (Agashe & Bratton, 1999; Boud & Middleton, 2003; Gorard et al., 1999; Walker, 2001). Relationships, upon which trust is built, are precarious at best in the wake of globalization. Trust is considered critical in knowledge management and communities of practice because of its central role in the building and sharing of social capital (Lesser & Prusak, 2000, drawing on Nahapiet & Ghoshal, 1998). The building of social capital, and its underpinnings of trust, is likely to be critical in informal and incidental learning as well.

Informal learning is often serendipitous and is described as taking place anywhere there are other employees chatting over coffee, at staff and group meetings, and working in teams (Candy & Crebert, 1991). It may involve reaching out to the person in the next cubicle and cultivating relationships by networking, coaching, and mentoring. But such learning has also been influenced greatly by technology. Weintraub (1998), for example, investigated the informal learning strategies, processes, and outcomes of a sales division in a large, technology-savvy corporation. Weintraub found that "while the study focused on how technology plays a role in on-the-job learning, in many instances the problem to be solved was learning the technology itself, and that drove the need to learn" (p. 91). Earlier studies also identified learning strategies for using technology (Cahoon, 1995; Woldesenbet, 1998). Knowledge management was nascent at the time of Weintraub's study, which focused on desktop technologies, and the organization he studied focused extensively on building databases that professionals could use to meet work and customer needs, but an "emphasis on sharing and learning from real experience" was lacking (p. 146).

Informal learning can be supported by widespread access to Internet resources such as search engines, websites, and blogs, as well as other forms of electronic information, but questions can be raised as to whether the organization's culture, rewards, structure and practices support learning as well as "getting the job done." In some ways, technology has brought with it a new openness to informal learning because of the amount and types of information available and the different ways that younger employees have been both socialized and "schooled." Strocchia (2003), whose study was conducted later than Weintraub's and in smaller companies that were also technology-savvy, found that Internet searches were critical to the innovation and learning in three small entrepreneurial firms in Venezuela. But equally as important were informal, interpersonal interactions that helped "innovators to create new ideas, to challenge the current way of solving problems, and to learn competencies" (p. 244). Surprisingly, to Strocchia, who assumed that informal learning would be used more than formal learning, "in the technological field, formal education has a fundamental role in keeping up with technological change" (p. 243). As Weintraub found, the culture and climate were critical to learning and to innovation, but in this case, the three organizations in Strocchia's study fostered "communication, freedom, emotional expression, and autonomy to think and act" (p. 234).

Finally, research involving the assessment of informal learning and its impact on work outcomes is sparse. Fuller et al. (2003) analyzed four regularly conducted national surveys and two one-off surveys in England that purport to assess learning as well as training. Surveys still focus primarily on training and education; an exception is the 2001 National Adult Learning Survey that collected information about both taught and self-directed learning. The authors concluded that "survey evidence on learning is uneven," in part because observation is needed to understand "other forms of learning activity—such as watching, working and learning from others" (p. 33). Fuller et al. also conducted interviews with key informants and prepared case studies of four organizations (hairdressing salon, accountancy practice, primary care trust, and car dealership) to identify links between informal learning in the workplace, product market strategies, and business performance that they might subsequently test in a survey. As will be discussed later in this chapter, indicators used to measure informal and incidental learning at work are in their infancy but promising research focuses on conditions that affect workplace learning (Skule, 2004) and/or learning culture (Watkins & Marsick, 2003).

In fairness, challenges in measuring learning of any kind, formal or informal, are great. It is difficult to isolate the effects of learning as an intervention from other influences on work outcomes, and therefore, to link learning causally to impact. As Raelin (2000) points out in discussing evaluation of work-based action learning interventions, one *can* "establish an intervening effect between the program and financial results" and then look at links between the intervention and the intervening effect, and between the intervening effect and other results, financial or otherwise." Raelin illustrates this approach with a study done at Sears by Boudreau and Ramstad (1997) that looked at relationships between leadership development and employee attitude change, which in turn could be linked to customer satisfaction. Raelin also suggests that one could look at links between reflective practices in programs, known to influence group development, and then examine links between products of action learning groups that are effective and financial indicators. Because of challenges in evaluating outcomes attributed to learning, some workplace scholars are turning to theory-driven evaluation (Chen & Rossi, 1994) that charts and measures anticipated outcomes along a causal chain; and to assessing strategic value contribution to the business rather than trying to prove return-on-investment (O'Driscoll, Sugrue, & Vona, 2005).

Critique and Re-Conceptualization of the Model

Both a review of research and reflection upon our own experience of informal and incidental learning led to the realization that the model requires a fundamental reconceptualization—due in part to limitations of earlier thinking, but also due to trends in theory and practice that necessarily influence the conceptualization of the informal and incidental learning process. Identified problems with the original model can be summarized as follows:

- The model "looks" linear, with beginning and ending points, even though that was not the intent.
- The model "feels" cognitive.
- The model focuses on individual learning within the context of workplaces.
- The model engages context but does not explain the role of context in learning.

Before turning to each of these criticisms and to theory and research that help elucidate how the model needs to be re-conceptualized, Watkins and Marsick turn to reflections on their own experience of informal and incidental learning that illustrates these four basic problems (see Box 20.1).

Although Watkins and Marsick did not distill the lessons of experience into the four key critiques of the original model explored in this chapter, looking back at the story of how they used the informal and incidental learning process, we can tease out elements of each of these reasons for revising our understanding of the informal and incidental learning process in the workplace in the grounded experience of our collaborative writing.

First, even though it was not intended that the model be presented or used in a linear manner—a problem seen in other models such as Kolb's (1984) experiential learning cycle—the positioning of the model using Dewey's problem solving cycle tends to make the process look and feel linear. Learning often began with a disjuncture, such as the need to drastically reduce the number of pages of the manuscript or to speak in one voice to a specific audience. But the actual process of learning about the context of the work—the target audience, the objectives of the effort, prior experience, and new realities—comprise both inspirational insights and painstaking research, some of which seem relatively sub-conscious until ideas are driven to the surface through hours of conversation, often to meet particular deadlines or for the purpose of discussing ideas with other audiences. Learning is more iterative than linear.

Second, learning can be stimulated by frequent experiences of the arts (or nature or physical activity or rest) and by the space allowed for breaking the frame of thinking so one can return to work with the ability to step outside of prior frameworks that constrained deeper understanding of the phenomena being addressed. The best work may occur in the most surprising settings.

Third, intense collaborative work itself led to the understanding that the model focused far too much on the individual. What may appear to be individual accomplishments are often the result of interactions with many others, ranging from the most closely involved to those at several degrees of separation. The model does not adequately theorize the socially constructed learning and knowledge that frequently characterizes informal and incidental learning at work. The model still takes the individual as the unit of analysis, rather than the social units that collectively learn as all participants grapple with mutual interests and problems.

Fourth, the 1999 update of the model focused on the pervasiveness of context, but it did not draw out implications for what context entails. As individuals learning to collaborate, Marsick and Watkins had constructed an environment that supported and fed their collective learning, complete with structures for furthering the work (conference

Box 20.1 *Re-Thinking the Model Based on Our Experience*

Karen E. Watkins & Victoria J. Marsick

We realized that we had only to look at our own learning to identify problems with the informal and incidental learning model. We began to reflect on how we learned to write collaboratively. How did we come to think together, to work out differences in points of view, and to agree on key points that we wished to develop in our work? As we looked back, we could see an evolution in our capacity to write and work collaboratively that was often triggered by jolts in our environment.

We began work together in writing our 1990 book on informal and incidental learning. Our process, at first, was to carve out two halves of the book—one on informal learning with three case examples all written by Victoria as lead author; and the other half about incidental learning with three case examples, all written by Karen as lead author. A disjuncture in our own experience challenged us to re-think the way the book had been written. The challenge came in the form of a publishing take-over when we were suddenly faced with the realization that our manuscript was about a third longer than the new guidelines allowed.

Since increasing the page length of the book was not possible, we began the process of cutting the manuscript. Each of us soon realized she could not cut her own work enough to meet the requirement. We began cutting the other's favorite prose—ruthlessly. We both believe that this was the best thing that ever happened to that book. It was extremely difficult to do within such a short time frame—but it taught us more about how to write together than anything that we had done to that point.

When we decided to write a second book, *Sculpting the Learning Organization: The Art and Science of Systemic Change* (Watkins & Marsick, 1993), we realized that the book would have to read as one voice. This time we discussed our ideas and presented together on the topic. As we spoke of our emerging ideas at conferences, classes, and workshops, our conversations and dialogue with others, both informal and formal, influenced our vision. We interviewed people who said that they were creating a learning organization, and we read everything in sight. We compared what we heard, in all our conversations, with what we read or heard, debated, and had written with one another.

We again divided the outline into sections—with each taking the lead on a given chapter. We read books on sculpting and watched a video in which Henry Moore talked about his art. We decided to go to the Elisabet Ney Museum – a museum about the work of this gifted sculptress and about the art of sculpting. On some level that we could not well articulate, we were clear that sculpting was a significant metaphor that could capture what we wanted to convey about the art and science of systemic change. Throughout our collaboration, art and music breaks were a constant theme. These breaks allowed space for creative juices to flow and inevitably, because of our focus on sculpting, enabled us to do what Schön (1983) had described as "seeing as" (p. 182).

As we look back at learning to write collaboratively, we see that we were learning informally about learning organizations and about sculpting, even as we were learning incidentally about becoming one voice. We followed the problem solving process outlined in our earlier model, but missing from that model were very important elements of the process—how ideas were continually changing through the interpersonal processes of talking and listening to one other, to those with whom we worked, and to those whom we "heard" in print. Similarly, the critical role played by art in helping us to see in a different way is missing in the earlier model. While that fits with our original ideas about creativity as an enhancer, we had conceived of creativity more in terms of personal qualities than in terms of what is now considered aesthetics as a way of knowing. Through the metaphor of sculpting, we were able to convey an idea that was still preverbal for us.

presentations, time set aside for thinking and writing together), a culture of learning that honored each other's work and learning style preferences and family/work commitments, and rewards and incentives to support joint work. Moreover, as scholars steeped in organizational change and learning theory, they had taken for granted that culture, structures, practices, and incentives/rewards were essential to informal and incidental learning, whether of individuals, groups, or the entire organization. But the model fell short of spelling out the kinds of things that eventually found their way into the substance of their later writing on the learning organization (Watkins & Marsick, 1993, 1999). The model also did not include how to diagnose and address the learning culture that is needed to support group and organizational learning.

Reviewing Theory and Research to Reconstruct the Model

These four challenges led to further exploring theory and research to help reconstruct the 1990/1999 model of informal and incidental learning. A search for new insights followed the revised understanding of the learning they sought to understand. Marsick and Watkins were joined by co-authors Callahan and Volpe in this exploration. The process has been messy, non-linear, driven both by systematic search and by accidental surprise, shaped by social interaction with colleagues and clients, and punctuated by forays into the non-rational and intuitive domains captured through aesthetics and artistic ways of knowing.

Non-Linear Work and Learning Approaches.   Implicit learning, like incidental learning, occurs without the learner's awareness. An early example of this was Hamel (1998) who observed that college-to-work transitions via temporary employment were naturally evolving processes, as "apprentices" both learned workplace culture and acquired job skills. The current stream of inquiry into implicit learning in workplaces of all kinds is frequently associated with studies of expertise, tacit knowing, innovation, and organizational learning (Argyris & Schön, 1996; Gleespen, 1997; Kuchinke, 1996; Nonaka & Takeuchi, 1995; Raelin, 1997, 2000). Through tacit learning, people construct the mental, emotional, and interpersonal frameworks for processing all of their experience into knowledge. Unlearning and new learning can occur when frameworks are adjusted or reconstructed to accommodate new experience that does not fit old models. At one extreme, implicit learning and tacit learning can equate to the very basic, even primitive, inputs that might by-pass conscious thought altogether. At the other extreme, such learning includes the abstractions that allow human beings unconsciously to negotiate complex rule-governed signals from the environment (Reber, 1989), which bombard us frequently, often simultaneously, and even contradictorily. Some researchers concentrate on the formation or recognition of attitudes in their discussions of implicit learning, as do Argyris and Schön (1996) in describing the mechanisms of action science. However, as Seger (1994) pointed out, implicit learning also includes the acquisition of skills and habits, again as these result from non-conscious experience or observation.

Seger's (1994) overview of this segment of cognitive psychology was an attempt to sketch the contours of a unified theory of implicit learning. She reported her own research, principally concerning how implicit learning operates within the human nervous system. She acknowledged the elusive nature of the phenomenon—that it is "not fully accessible to consciousness…more complex than a single simple association …does not involve processes of conscious hypothesis testing" (p. 164) and that many issues are controversial, such as the exact organic mechanism whereby implicit becomes explicit knowledge (p.

188). Nevertheless, she was able to certify that incidental learning truly exists, because it survives amnesia. Seger's conclusion that the preponderance of findings—her own and others'—-reveals that, "in the face of strongly held explicit beliefs, knowledge gained through implicit learning is disregarded" (p. 189), is arguable. Reber (1996), for example, is a leader among theorists who hold that implicit learning is more robust and more durable than explicitly mastered skills and beliefs.

Cleermans (1995) echoed the call for more research about the role of implicit learning in training, assessment, and knowledge elicitation, which is central to the design of expert systems. He also provided a clear statement about the relationship between implicit and incidental learning. Implicit knowledge (1) tends not to be expressible through free recall, (2) is associated with incidental learning conditions, (3) gives rise to a phenomenal sense of intuition, and (4) remains robust in the face of time, psychological disorder, and secondary tasks.

Use of Emotion and Intuition along with Cognition.   Goleman (1995) catalyzed awareness of the role that emotions and emotional intelligence plays in work lives. Neuroscientists have likewise broken ground through brain research in debunking the myth that emotions have no place in rational decision making (Damasio, 1995; LeDoux, 1996). Some intimations of the non-cognitive aspects of informal and incidental learning were documented in dissertation findings reviewed in our earlier work. Woldesenbet (1998) found that experts were both motivated and rewarded by recognition and gratitude from their associates. Laverdure-McDougall (1998) found that Native American participants were inspired by a sense of empowerment through informal learning. Finally, Shih (1997) explored the influence of internal non-cognitive drivers, such as mission, values, and personality in triggering a learning search.

Yorks and Kasl (2002) have developed a theory of whole-person learning that bears on what can be learned from implicit/tacit learning theory. They build on the work of Heron (1992) and Heron and Reason (1997, 2001), who use this thinking as the basis for the practice of learning through collaborative inquiry. Yorks and Kasl make the distinction between experience as a noun, i.e., the object of cognitive analysis via learning, and experience as a verb, i.e., the act of learning within experience.

For Heron, the affective is the psychological basis for experiential knowledge. He makes a useful distinction between "feeling" and "emotions," two words often used interchangeably. Heron (1992) refers to feeling as the capacity for participating in wider unities of a whole field of experience. This is distinct from emotion, which is defined as the intense, localized affect that arises from the fulfillment or frustration of individualized needs. Feeling is the phenomenological grounding for the meaning that people eventually make of their experience by conceptualization through reflection and the resultant discrimination. Experiential knowledge is thus considered a pre-linguistic form of knowing gained "through participation in, and resonance with, one or more beings in the unified field of being" (p. 162). For Heron, experiential learning is pre-conceptual, "acquiring knowledge of being and beings through empathic resonance [sic. and] felt participation" (p. 224). Feelings and the experiential knowledge that they hold are brought into awareness through the use of forms of expression that engage the learner's imaginal and intuitive capacities, which connect to new conceptual possibilities. Crossan, Lane, and White (1999) include this pre-conceptual level of communication in their description of learning processes central to learning that individuals do, but that can be shared and communicated with groups and the organization. Their four learning processes—intuiting, interpreting, integrating, and institutionalizing—begin with experience, images, and metaphors as prelude to interpretation via conversation and integration through shared understanding. At the organizational level, this tacit know-ing can be made more explicit and captured in rules, procedures, and systems.

Whole-person learning theory integrates feelings and emotions into the cognitive design of the informal/incidental learning framework. Rather than simply taking emo-tion as an "object" of analysis, this theory makes it possible to look at feeling/emotion as essential components of learning. Tacit/implicit learning can be understood and made evident through what Heron and Reason (2001) describe as presentational knowing: dramatic, participatory, aesthetic, and experience-based formats that convey intuition and tacit knowledge in ways that are precluded by overly-analytic forms of learning.

Aesthetic expression is a way of knowing (Allen, 1995, in Lawrence, 2005) that fits well with informal and incidental learning. Lawrence (2005) asserts that:

> making space for creative expression in the adult education classroom and other learning communities helps learners uncover hidden knowledge that cannot easily be expressed in words. It opens up opportunities for adult learners to explore phe-nomena holistically, naturally, and creatively, thus deepening our understanding of self and the world. (p. 3)

Quoting Allen, Lawrence argues that our earliest ways of knowing are preverbal. What we cannot say in words we can see in our mind as images, colors, or sounds. Dirkx (2001) says that we become aware of our emotional states through images. He calls this "soul work."

Like Schön (1983), Lawrence reminds us that experiencing the art of others helps us see anew. Educators can tie their life experience to aesthetic experience in a way that cre-ates affective connections that cannot be expressed in other ways (Olson, 2005). Olson goes back to Dewey's views on art and experience:

> Works of art that are not remote from common life, that are widely enjoyed in a community, are signs of a collective life. The remaking of the material experience in the act of expression is not an isolated event confined to the artist and to a person here and there who happens to enjoy the work. In the degree in which art exercises its office, it is also a remaking of the experience of the community in the direction of greater order and community. (Dewey, 1934, p. 81, quoted in Olson, 2005, pp. 62–63)

Some of the earliest work on incidental learning occurred in communication theory where scholars explored the unintended consequences of viewing television and film (Stokes & Pankowski, 1988). What makes aesthetic theory interesting at this time is that much art (especially more abstract or impressionistic forms) intends to provoke multiple subjective interpretations. As workplace educators create learning cultures, much of their work is symbolic, creating messages through visions, slogans, posters, quiet spaces and gathering places, and nonverbal means. These aesthetic means of communication provide a core sense of the organization's direction, and simultaneously, allow each per-son to differently interpret how to reach this goal. Weick (2001) argues that a significant role of leaders is to shape the salience of information. Artful, pithy messages signal what is important without constraining action.

Learning in Collaboration with Others.   Informal/incidental learning at work is increasingly understood as socially situated and socially constructed. Research by Oxford (1998), using informal observation as well as interviews and learning measurement instruments, found several instances where team perspectives resulted in new collective knowledge. Gleespen (1997) reported the importance of organizational climate to the formation, effectiveness, and content of relationships and networks that support learning. Cahoon (1995) reported the role of mutual problem solving and coaching by peer experts based on negotiated explicit and implicit rules in mastering computer skills. Larson (1991) used interviews, critical incidents, and observations to uncover the role of relationships, storytelling, and task performance with partners among a group of paramedics. These informal learning studies clearly identify the importance of other people and groups in learning.

Wenger (1998) provides a useful theoretical framework for understanding such learning in his discussion of communities of practice. His social learning theory speaks to the way in which people make meaning of their lives and construct their identity by participation in social practice in natural communities tied by common interests:

> The concept of practice connotes doing, but not just doing in and of itself. It is doing in an historical and social context that gives structure and meaning to what we do. In this sense, practice is always social practice.
>
> Such a concept of practice includes both the explicit and the tacit. It includes what is said and what is left unsaid; what is represented and what is assumed. It includes the language, tools, documents, images, symbols, well-defined roles, specified criteria, codified procedures, regulations, and contracts that various practices make explicit for a variety of purposes. But it also includes all the implicit relations, tacit conventions, subtle cues, untold rules of thumb, recognizable intuitions, specific perceptions, well-tuned sensitivities, embodied understandings, underlying assumptions, and shared world views. Most of these may never be articulated, yet they are unmistakable signs of membership in communities of practice and are crucial to the success of their enterprises. (p. 47)

Wenger explains many of the dynamics of communities of practice using three core concepts: engagement (to create and maintain the community), imagination (which is central to learning), and alignment (which involves social interaction). Wenger argues that "Engagement, imagination, and alignment are all important ingredients of learning—they anchor it in practice yet make it broad, creative, and effective in the wider world" (pp. 217–218). He adds that reflective practice emerges from the joining of engagement and imagination. Among other things, "Imagination enables us to adopt other perspectives across boundaries and time, to visit 'otherness' and let it speak its own language" (p. 218). When alignment combines with imagination, continues Wenger, people can "align our activities" and "understand why" because it is clear that what we do contributes to a larger vision that is meaningful to the community. "Imagination thus helps us direct our alignment in terms of its broader effects, adapt it under shifting circumstances, and fine tune it intelligently" (p. 218).

These three factors—imagination, engagement, and alignment—enhance our understanding of social reflective learning. They add the following to our model: 1) an understanding of how valuing difference enriches social learning; 2) a deepened appreciation of the social context for learning; and 3) respect for the challenges involved in aligning viewpoints as meaning is negotiated within the social context.

Interaction with Context for Sense- and Meaning-Making.   Early and later studies emphasize the role of context in influencing sense- and meaning-making in informal learning. Context comprises both the particular situation in which individuals find themselves, but it can be extended out to include the broader organizational context, with its culture, structures, processes, and practices. Menard (1993) found that 74% of learning incidents were triggered by crises, both personal and combat, among female Vietnam veteran Army nurses. Lo (1996) found that an environment rich in opportunities for on-the-job training, observing others, and document resources supported learning in a Taiwanese not-for-profit organization. Maben-Crouch (1997) emphasized the role of context-based non-routine problems to stimulate reflection and new learning. Foy (1998) reported that organizational support was the most important facilitating factor in continuing professional education by certified management accountants. Weintraub (1998) concluded that the context—the organization's culture and specific stimuli, internal or external, for learning—is key to framing strategies, processes, and outcomes of learning. A culture not conductive to reflection led to an inability to capitalize on the way salespeople used technology to solve job-related problems. Moran (2003) studied 26 team members at a unionized manufacturing plant in the Northeast, many of whom were not English speakers and some of whom were not highly literate. The organization's hierarchical culture made it difficult to change to a team-based plant. Informal learning was relied upon by interviewees despite that fact that "team members had concerns about the competence of other team members, thought that the supervisor restricted information, and believed that informal learning strategies were discouraged by the organization" (p. i). Likewise, Chartrand (2004) found, in a qualitative study of financial advisors who learned to become collaborative team members, that informal learning occurred despite cultural norms in the financial services industry that reward individual accomplishment.

Callahan (1999) identified the critical role of context in a study of 82 critical incidents provided by 16 participants coming from divergent professional cultures who worked together to create innovative new businesses in a publicly-funded small business incubator in Georgia. She showed that incidental learning helped to bridge professional cultures (entrepreneurs, investors, and the incubator's professional staff). In addition to functional learning to achieve mastery in work performance, she identified bridging learning, comprised of both the exertion and the result of conscious and unconscious efforts to enhance empathetic understanding of another's meaning, to bridge professional cultures and jargon to share meaning. For example, Callahan found that members of all three professional groups at the business incubator referred to "karma in the walls and halls"—identifying a real, if intangible, asset of the environment, experienced as a distinctive electricity in the atmosphere, associated with the inhabitants, facilities, and activities of the center. Participants generally agreed that the "karma" exerted an influence, particularly by encouraging them to work even harder and more creatively. One entrepreneur remembered feeling buoyed by the successes of other members and noting that observing other start-up companies at the business incubator gave him a "virtual blueprint" that provided some guidelines until he was able to create his own business plan. Another environmental factor was the influence exerted on incubator inhabitants and activities by elements beyond the economic development center, such as individuals, institutions, and political, economic, social, or demographic forces.

In a study to determine whether two different organizational settings of CPA practice produced substantially different or equivalent learning opportunities of a practicing CPA, Watkins and Cervero (2000) examined three sources of data including a work audit, interviews, and surveys from the principal parties. They concluded that the learning opportunities available in each firm were substantially equivalent, and focused on the organization as a context for enhancing informal and incidental learning—the support, structures, and incentives in place to promote an individual's informal and incidental learning. As part of the study, they developed an instrument to assess an organization as a supportive context for informal and incidental learning.

Another way of thinking about context is the broader concept of learning network theory (Poell, Chivers, Van der Krogt, & Wildermeersch, 2000; Poell, Van der Krogt, & Wildermeersch, 1999). Learning varies, according to this theory, by the learning interests and preference for key actors (employees, managers, HRD, etc.), mediated by "the negotiation of power among the actors" (Poell et al., 2000, p. 44). The authors propose four ideal types of networks: vertical, horizontal, external, and liberal. Informal and incidental learning takes place, along with formal learning, within three basic strategy configurations across these networks: extended training, directed reflection, or reflective innovation. The authors see this framework as descriptive rather than normative, and helpful in identifying ways to best support learning by key players, including self-directed learners. Recently, Poell, Yorks, and Marsick (2006) have cross-analyzed data from studies of action learning in the United States and of learning projects in the Netherlands with a view to critiquing the theoretical frameworks guiding the respective studies. One outcome is a combined framework that links the power of understanding informal learning projects with the leverage of better understanding organizational contextual support for learning.

Quantitative research has been almost non-existent in the study of informal and incidental learning. Indeed, Skule (2004) argued that indicators used to measure and assess informal learning at work, at both the national and the organizational level, are underdeveloped. Consequently, current frameworks to measure and benchmark learning are heavily biased towards more readily measured formal education and training. Skule's study, designed to correct this deficit, was based on interviews followed by a survey of 1,300 private sector Norwegians and 200 public sector Norwegians. Jobs were classified as learning intensive or learning deprived based on three variables in the survey: a subjective judgment of learning intensiveness, length of learning needed to master the job, and durability of acquired skills. Factor analysis and theory-based reasoning was then used to identify six key learning conditions: high degree of exposure to change, high degree of exposure to demands, managerial responsibilities, extensive professional contacts, superior feedback, management support for learning, and rewarding of proficiency. Using at best small samples or mixed methods, other studies have sought to measure various aspects of informal learning including creativity (McCracken, 1998) and participation in informal and incidental learning activities by an accountant (Watkins & Cervero, 2000). A recent web-based study examined individual and joint blogging as a form of reflection (Hammond, 2006).

Studies of self-directed learning have been more quantitative—including participation in self-directed learning (see Candy, 1991), and many studies using a validated Self-Directed Learning Readiness Scale developed by Guglielmino (1978). (For a bibliography of research validating this scale, see http://www.guglielmino734.com/newpage3. htm.) Econometric models estimating informal learning at work have also been developed (Carnevale, Meltzer, & Gainer, 1990). Even in this sub-area of informal learning, research has been more often descriptive focusing on the learning process used by adults engaged in learning projects or the nature of the learning (reflective or transformative) during self-directed learning. Research in this area verifies that a significant portion of working adults learn on their own, often for work-related purposes, and this learning is aided by skills in learning how to learn and reflection and access to knowledgeable people and resources.

One of the reasons that there have been few quantitative studies of informal and incidental learning is that by their less predictable nature, they are hard to measure. While one can readily identify ways that people learn informally and to a lesser extent ways that people learn incidentally, the learning process itself is less clear. What is learned is so ubiquitous and sometimes even pre-verbal as to be extremely difficult to measure. Where researchers might be able to do additional research is in the affective experiences of individuals engaged in informal and incidental learning. Related to this is recent brain research that looks at individuals in a state of flow (Csikszentmihalyi, 1991)—a state which the author describes as "the way people describe their state of mind when consciousness is harmoniously ordered, and they want to pursue whatever they are doing for its own sake" (p. 6). Given the self-directed nature of informal and incidental learning, one might hypothesize that it is similar to engaging in any other creative task, hence brain activity may also be similar. Finally, research into the organizational support for informal and incidental learning is greatly needed. Work by Watkins and Marsick (2003) using a validated measure of a learning culture, the Dimensions of a Learning Organization, has contributed to a growing body of work in this area.

Conclusions

Revised Model of Informal and Incidental Learning in the Workplace

A review of experience, theory, and research led us to conclude that a two-dimensional model of informal and incidental learning is not sufficient. Such learning in the workplace is *not* primarily focused on and managed by the individual. Nor is it linear, rational, cognitive, or a-contextual. The basic problem solving and learning cycle depicted in the earlier model through which most people move is still relevant, but it is often a loose framework within which many learners interact in the pursuit of a mix of individual and organizationally-determined goals. Individuals seem to be more self-motivated, self-reliant, and self-directed in setting and reaching goals, and in finding opportunities for learning that aids performance and their own personal agendas. But the context of organizations—culture, structure, processes, practices—plays a key role in enabling or inhibiting the motivation, time, resources, expectations, and rewards for learning.

Perhaps a better analogy for thinking about informal and incidental learning is an amoeba-like process, multi-dimensional in nature, consisting of iterative cycling back and forth among phases of the process—with frequent forays into conversation, work with other people, and exploitation of a wide array of resources, often Internet-based or technology-driven, that provide new stimuli for further inquiry. Typically, the learning process includes an element of collective learning as work groups struggle together to solve a problem or sail forward to creatively address a new challenge. Collective work is increasingly the norm in organizations that acknowledge the value of virtual teams, dispersed across locations, and networks or communities that support learning. Learning is often intertwined with action and sometimes semi-conscious at best. Reflection can take place before, during, or after action. While reflection aids such learning, it can also sometimes embed error into the learning process when it is private or more subjective than evidence-based (Marsick & Watkins, 1990). Finally, the learning is often so intrinsic to action that it remains unarticulated and preverbal, yet evident in the actions taken by individuals and groups.

Such a dynamic process is hard to capture in a model. It looks more like a group of players on a soccer field. All players have individual roles but they also work together in different ways toward their goals. Expert players have internalized tacit knowledge and know the rules. But imagine how different this would look were it more like a group of toddlers on the soccer field—moving as a collective in a sometimes random, sometimes purposeful manner—hitting the ball more often through luck than skill. Their movements are aided through coaching and knowledge about the rules of soccer, but for most of them, these rules of engagement remain abstract and hard to implement in the moment. Similarly, workers engaged in learning as a part of work are often aware of the elements and steps of self-directed learning, but the exigencies of their context are more salient. Our role as workplace educators is to develop ways to build into that context structures and facilitating resources that are sufficiently rich to enable learners to find what they need more readily. Learning has to be the karma in the walls and halls.

Critique and Implications

In organizations, the need to understand informal and incidental learning has grown along with interest in flexible, high performing organizations whose leaders are challenged to take more responsibility for their own and their team's learning, as well as learning by the organization as a whole. Employees are increasingly expected to be self-directed in their learning in order to keep up with rapid changes in knowledge and the knowledge economy. Depending on the company, and on an individual's status/level, learning may need to occur outside of work hours and be paid for by employees. Much lifelong learning in organizations increasingly takes place on the job, sometimes in structured ways, sometimes via growing reliance on coaching and on action learning (Raelin, 1997, 2000), and often supported with technology. An increase in the variety, unfamiliarity, and scope of information sources complicate work. Formerly routine operations have become more non-routine, calling for judgment that may require further learning. Learning demands are magnified by speed and performance pressures. Practical questions arise as to whether and how informal and incidental learning can or should be managed or facilitated; how informal and incidental learning at work intersect with the idea of lifelong learning especially in today's knowledge economies (Faure, 1972); and whether or not trends toward credentialing have led to a decline of informal learning (Gorard et al., 1999).

The fast-paced environment has made learning through day-long or multi-day seminars a luxury, along with other learning experiences that support reflection and/or practice of skills during the work day. Many in the workforce have never attended any of the formal training programs that used to be so prevalent. Smaller companies and non-profit organizations have never been able to provide extensive formal learning opportunities. Some organizations retain training curricula or company universities, but the trend is toward blended and e-learning solutions and learning on the job, often targeted toward specific task performance. Many organizations do not believe there is sufficient return on investment for extended learning opportunities. It appears that efficiency and short-term payback are guiding principles in decisions about training. However, these criteria may not provide employees with all of the learning they need for maximum development (Bloom, 2006; Gill-Webber, 2005). The lack of extensive formal learning programs has increased exponentially the reliance on informal and incidental learning, even when structured training might better prepare employees for their work challenges. Information and knowledge are widely dispersed, but channels for gaining and sharing may be inadequate, as may be the support for learning provided by the organization's culture.

Gorard et al. (1999) observe that "much valuable and non-trivial learning already goes on, and has always gone on, outside formal programmes of instruction" (p. 437).

However, they also point out that informal learning continues to be undervalued in favor of credentials even though this age is characterized as a knowledge era and as a "learning society." In many ways, informal learning is a powerful yet taken-for-granted resource that appears to be deployed only by default. In this regard, Boud and Middleton (2003) point out that "[i]nformal learning is often not acknowledged as learning with organizations. It is typically regarded as being 'part of the job' or a mechanism for 'doing the job properly' and is thus rendered invisible as learning" (p. 194). We have found few direct recommendations in the literature reviewed around a) how organizations can be influenced to view and appreciate the power of informal and incidental learning as a vital mechanism in achieving organizational objectives, and b) how informal and incidental learning can thus become institutionalized without becoming formalized.

The role of workplace educators, in the face of these challenges, may be to pay as much attention to organizational supports and barriers to learning as they do to learning processes and strategies. Some organizations seek frameworks—e.g., communities of practice, social networks, virtual teams, knowledge or learning networks—and strategies that support informal and incidental learning; while other organizations have not aligned structures, processes, and culture in ways that consistently support learning through work even though task demands seem to require this. IBM, for example, which pioneered earlier work on Instructional Systems Design for improved training and development, has recently moved to an On Demand Learning framework that retains some structured education (Work Apart Learning) but relies even more heavily on informal learning catalyzed by work needs (Work Enabled Learning) and incidental learning in the moment to support performance (Work Embedded Learning). Mechanisms have been introduced that aid in such learning, such as After Action Reviews and Quality tools that provide mechanisms for driving out error and for continuous learning.

The implications for organizations are to find ways to create safer, yet stimulating, environments that prize collaboration over competitiveness; focus on helping employees develop transportable skills, including learning skills; and enhance employees' competencies so they become more in charge of their careers and less reliant on the organization. It is that very reliance that can pit employee against employee in the scramble for scarce resources in the modern organization. Perhaps the organization, particularly its leaders, on some conscious or unconscious level, either encourages this tension among employees, ignores it, or neglects it.

Further Research

As we conclude our review, we draw attention to several areas of needed research. Callahan (1999) notes that research on informal and incidental learning has been largely qualitative case studies focused on the types and nature of informal and incidental learning. There are few large-scale studies that draw on what is known to examine the depth and scope of such learning within or across companies and industries. Future research might include intervention research aimed at learning what works to enhance this type of learning.

Deci and Ryan (2000) have broken ground in understanding intrinsic and extrinsic motivation for self-directed learning. Motivation studies of this kind would benefit informal and incidental learning. Such learning depends primarily on individual capability and interest in proactively using opportunities at work to build knowledge and skills. External rewards may not be motivating, and may even be de-motivating. Deci and Ryan point out that "the only necessary 'reward' for these (intrinsically motivated) behaviors is the spontaneous experience of interest and enjoyment that accompanies the activity itself. Curiosity, exploration, and wonder are all aspects of intrinsically motivated learning" (p. 77). Reio, Petrosko, Wiswell, & Thongsjkmag (2006) and Reio and Callahan (2004) have studied curiosity in adult learning, based in part on dissertation research by Reio. Studies in this vein as well can deepen our understanding of the conditions for supporting informal learning even though it is not highly designed.

We do not yet understand how to support informal and incidental learning without making it artificial or destroying it with too many rules and regulations, although a comparative case study of 11 best-practice organizations by the American Quality & Productivity Center (2001) around how organizations build and sustain communities of practice provides helpful guidelines that can be extrapolated to informal and incidental learning. Watkins and Cervero's (2000) work also leads us to explore what conditions, resources, and policies in the workplace support or squelch informal and incidental learning. Given the importance of context, research might more specifically address the role of organizational leaders in designing and updating learning contexts, including physical and symbolic settings, hiring and reward practices, providing learning models, multi-faceted communications, and work assignments. Although challenging to study, what more can we discover about how power and politics influence informal and incidental learning? A step in this direction is post-modern studies of U.S. organizations such as that conducted by Boje (1994, 1995) or the application of Foucault's power concepts to understanding power dynamics that affect learning in Korean companies that embrace Western-imported learning practices even though their hierarchical culture may conflict with decentralized approaches to self-directed and peer learning (Kim, 2003).

Kim's study moves into different cultural definitions and understandings of learning. Yet, little is known about cultural differences in informal and incidental learning. For example, what is the impact of individualistic versus collectivistic traditions or culturally divergent senses of time on informal and incidental learning? Even though the effects of globalization and multi-culturalism have been discussed for years, disciplined research to understand these realities in terms of the entire informal and incidental learning cycle, and particularly, of learning contexts is needed.

Research is needed to increase our knowledge of the impact of new distributed working arrangements (including telecommuting, outsourcing, and use of contingency workers) on informal and incidental learning in workplaces. Finally, further research is needed on measures of informal learning and assessment of its impact on work outcomes. Better measures would improve surveys that are now more attuned to training than informal learning. New assessment tools are needed to help individuals and organizations understand, document, and manage informal and incidental learning. A promising avenue for assessment research is the measurement of learning conditions and learning culture.

References

Agashe, Z., & Bratton, J. (1999). *Exploring the adult learning—leadership interface.* Paper presented at the First International Conference on Researching Work and Learning, University of Leeds, School of Continuing Education, England.

Alcalde, D. (2005). The role of informal learning on engineering students' teaming process. (Doctoral dissertation, The University of Nebraska – Lincoln). *Dissertation Abstracts International, 66/05,* 1659.

Allen, P. B. (1995). *Art is a way of knowing.* Boston: Shambhala Press.

American Productivity & Quality Center (APQC). (2001). *Building and sustaining communities of practice.* Houston, TX: APQC.

Argyris, C., & Schön, D. (1974). *Theory in practice: Increasing professional effectiveness,* San Francisco; Jossey-Bass.

Argyris, C., & Schön, D. (1978). *Organizational learning: A theory of action perspective.* San Francisco: Jossey-Bass.

Argyris, C., & Schön, D. A. (1996). *Organizational learning II: Theory, method, and practice.* Addison-Wesley Series on Organizational Development Practice. Reading, MA: Addison-Wesley.

Bloom, N. (2006). *The development of a trainers' resource for non-professional trainers.* Unpublished doctoral dissertation, Teachers College, Columbia University, New York.

Bloomberg, L. D. (2006). *Adult education and distance learning: A case study of a learning community in Jewish higher education.* Unpublished doctoral dissertation, Teachers College, Columbia University, New York.

Boje, D. M. (1994). Organizational storytelling: The struggles of pre-modern, modern & postmodern organizational learning discourses. *Management Learning, 25*(3), 433–461.

Boje, D. M. (1995). Stories of the storytelling organization: A postmodern analysis of Disney as Tamara-land. *Academy of Management Journal, 38*(4), 997–1035.

Boud, D., & Middleton, H. (2003). Learning from others at work: Communities of practice and informal learning. *Journal of Workplace Learning, 15*(5), 194–202.

Boudreau, J. W., & Ramstad, P. M. (1997). Measuring intellectual capital: Learning from financial history. *Human Resource Management,* 36:3, 343–356.

Brown, J. S., & Duguid, P. (2000). *The social life of information.* Boston: Harvard Business School Press.

Bruce, L., Aring, M. K., & Brand, B. (1998). Informal learning: The new frontier of employee & organizational development. *Economic Development Review, 15*(4), 12–18.

Burgoyne, J. G., & Hodgson, V. E. (1983). Natural learning and managerial action: A phenomenological study in the field setting. *Journal of Management Studies, 20*(3), 387–399.

Cahoon, B. B. (1995). Computer skill learning in the workplace: A comparative case study. *Dissertation Abstracts International,* 56/05A, 1622. (UMI No. AAI9531174)

Callahan, M. H. W. (1999). Case study of an advanced technology business incubator as a learning environment. (Doctoral dissertation. Athens: University of Georgia). *Dissertation Abstracts International, 61/06,* 2142.

Candy, P. (1991). *Self-direction for lifelong learning: A comprehensive guide to theory and practice.* San Francisco: Jossey-Bass

Candy, P. C., & Crebert, R. G. (1991). Ivory tower to concrete jungle: The difficult transition from the academy to the workplace as learning environments. *The Journal of Higher Education, Research & Development, 10,* 3–17.

Carnevale, A. P., Meltzer, A. S., & Gainer, L. J. (1990). *Workplace basics: The essential skills employers want.* San Francisco: Jossey-Bass.

Chartrand, C. (2004). Learning to "transition" from individual contributor to team member. (Doctoral dissertation, Teachers College, Columbia University, New York). *Dissertation Abstracts International, 65/09,* 3247.

Chen, H. T., & Rossi, P. H. (1994). *Theory-driven evaluations,* Newbury Park, CA: Sage

Cleermans, A. (1995). No matter where you go, there you are. *American Journal of Psychology, 108*(4), 589–599.

Conlon.T. (2004). A review of informal learning literature, theory and implications for practice in developing global professional competence. *Journal of European Industrial Training, 28*(2–4), 283–295.

Corporate Leadership Council. (2004, June). *Global leadership development programs.* Catalogue No. CLC1-1KEAZN. Retrieved June 4, 2008, from http://www.corporateleaderhsipcouncil.com.

Cross, J. (2007). *Informal learing: Rediscovering the natural pathways that inspire innovation and performance.* San Francisco: Pfeiffer, John Wiley.

Crossan, M. M., Lane, H. W., & White, R. E. (1999). An organizational learning framework: From institution to institution. *The Academy of Management Review, 24*(3), 522–537.

Cseh, M. (1998). Managerial learning in the transition to a free market economy in Romanian private companies. (Doctoral dissertation. Athens: University of Georgia). *Dissertation Abstracts International, 59/06,* 1865.

Cseh, M., Watkins, K. E., & Marsick, V. J. (1999). Re-conceptualizing Marsick and Watkins' model of informal and incidental learning in the workplace. In K. P. Kuchinke (Ed.), *1999 Proceedings of the Academy of HRD* (pp. 349–355). Baton Rouge, LA: Academy of Human Resource Development.

Csikszentmihaly, M. (1991). *Flow: The psychology of optimal experience.* New York: Harper Collins.

Dale, M., & Bell, J. (1999). *Informal learning in the workplace.* DfEE Research Report No. 134, London: Department for Education and Employment. Retrieved January 3, 2007, from http://www.dfes.gov.uk/research/data/uploadfiles/RB134.doc.

Damasio, A. R. (1995). *Descartes' error: Emotion, reason, and the human brain.* New York: Avon Books.

Davies, J., & Easterby-Smith, M. (1984). Learning and developing from work experiences, *Journal of Management Studies, 21*(2), 167–183.

Deci, E., & Ryan, R. (2000). What is the self in self-directed learning? Findings from recent motivation research. In G. A. Straka (Ed.), *Conceptions of self-directed learning: Theoretical and conceptual considerations* (pp. 75–92). Munster, Germany: Waxmann

Dewey, J. (1934). *Art as experience.* New York: Wideview/Pedigree Books.

Dewey, J. (1938). *Experience and education.* New York: Collier Books.

Dirkx, J. (2001). The power of feelings, emotion, imagination, and the construction of meaning in adult education. In S. Merriam (Ed.), *The new update on adult learning theory. New Directions for Adult and Continuing Education, No. 89* (pp. 63–72). San Francisco: Jossey-Bass.

Ellinger, A. D. (1997). Managers as facilitators of learning and development: A qualitative study in learning organizations. (Doctoral dissertation. Athens: University of Georgia). *Dissertation Abstracts International, 58/08,* 2957.

Engestrom, Y. (1999). Activity theory and individual and social transformation. In Y. Engeström, R. Miettinen, & R.-L. Punamäki-Gitai (Eds.), *Perspectives on activity theory* (pp. 19–38). London: Cambridge University Press.

Enos, M., Kehrhahn, M., Bell, A. (2003). Informal learning and the transfer of learning: How managers develop proficiency. *Human Resource Development Quarterly, 14*(4), 369–387.

Eraut, M., Alderton, J., Cole, G., & Senker, P. (1998). *Development of knowledge and skills in employment.* Final Report of ESCRC Project. Brighton, UK: University of Sussex.

Faure, E. (1972) *Learning to be.* Paris: UNESCO.

Foy, N. F. (1998). Continuing professional education needs of NYNEX certified management accountants and implications for The Institute of Management Accountants' mandates. (Doctoral dissertation. Teachers College, Columbia University, New York). *Dissertation Abstracts International, 51/10A,* 3301.

Fuller, A., Ashton, D., Felstead, A., Unwin, L. Walters, S., & Quinn, M. (2003). *The impact of informal learning at work on business productivity.* Final report to the Department for Trade and Industry. University of Leicester: The Centre for Labour Market Studies. Retrieved February 14, 2007, from http://www.dti.gov.uk/files/file11719.pdf and http://www.dti.gov.uk/files/file11027.pdf.

Gill-Webber, P. (2005). *Change ahead: Working in a post 9/11 world.* Charleston, SC: BookSurge.

Gleespen, A. V. (1997). The development of coworker relationships that support or inhibit continuous learning. *Dissertation Abstracts International,* 58/07A, 2492. (UMI No. AAI9801964)

Goleman, D. (1995). *Emotional intelligence: Why it can matter more than IQ.* New York: Bantam Books.

Gorard, S., Fevre. R., & Rees, G. (1999). The apparent decline of informal learning. *Oxford Review of Education, 25*(4), 437–454.

Guglielmino, L. M. (1978). Development of the self-directed learning readiness scale. (Doctoral dissertation. Athens: University of Georgia). *Dissertation Abstracts International,* 38, 6467A.

Habermas, J. (1987). *The theory of communicative action* (Vol. II). Boston: Beacon Press.

Hager, P. (2004). The importance of contextuality for learning. *Journal of Workplace Learning, 16,* 22–32.

Hamel, J. C. (1998). The college-to-work transition through temporary employment services: A case study in an informal technology company. *Dissertation Abstracts International,* 59/07A, 2300. (UMI No. AAI9831656)

Hammond, M. (2006). Blogging within formal and informal learning contexts: Where are the opportunities and constraints? Retrieved January 6, 2007, from http://www.networkedlearning-conference.org.uk/abstracts/pdfs.

Heron, J. (1992). *Feeling and personhood: Psychology in another key.* London: Sage.

Heron, J., & Reason, P. (1997). A participatory inquiry paradigm. *Qualitative Inquiry, 3,* 274–294.

Heron, J., & Reason, P. (2001). The practice of cooperative inquiry: Research 'with' rather than 'on' people. In P. Reason & H. Bradbury, (Eds.), *Handbook of action research: Participative inquiry and practice* (pp. 179–188). Thousand Oaks, CA: Sage.

IBM Learning Solutions (2005). *On demand learning: Blended learning for today's evolving workforce.* Retrieved January 2, 2007, from http://www.clomedia.com/content/templates/wp_clo_white-paper.asp?articleid=1128&zoneid=26.

Inkster, R. P. (1987). How do you know? Michael Polanyi and adult education. *Proceedings of the twenty-eighth annual Adult Education Research Conference,* Laramie, WY.

Ipe, M. (2003). Sharing knowledge in organizations: A conceptual framework. *Human Resource Development Review, 2*(4), 337–359.

Jacques, E. (1988). Development of intellectual capability. In F. Link (Ed.), *Essays on the intellect.* Alexandria, VA: Association for Supervision and Curriculum Development.

Jarvis, P. (1987). *Adult learning in the social context.* London: Croom-Helms.

Kegan, R. (1982). *The evolving self: Problem and process in human development.* Cambridge: Harvard University Press.

Kegan, R. (1994). *In over our heads: The mental demands of modern life.* Cambridge: Harvard University Press.

Kim, Y.-S. (2003). Power and learning in organizations: The influence of power on learning in Korean organizations. (Doctoral dissertation. Teachers College, Columbia University, New York). *Dissertation Abstracts International, 64/12,* 4314.

Knowles, M. (1950). *Informal adult education.* New York: Association Press.

Kolb, D. A. (1984). *Experiential learning.* Englewood Cliffs, NJ: Prentice-Hall.

Kuchinke, K. P. (1996, March). *Experts and expertise: The status of the research literature on superior performance.* Paper presented at the meeting of the Academy of Human Resource Development, Minneapolis, MN.

Larson, B. K. (1991). Informal workplace learning and partner relationships among paramedics in the prehospital setting. (Doctoral dissertation. Teachers College, Columba University, New York). *Dissertation Abstracts International, 52/02B,* 0732.

Lave, J., & Wenger, E. (1991). *Situated learning: Legitimate peripheral participation.* Cambridge: Cambridge University Press.

Laverdure-McDougall, E. A. (1998). A critical study of informal and incidental learning resulting from civil action within an American Indian community (informal learning). *Dissertation Abstracts International, 54/09A,* 3319. (UMI No. AAI9907413)

Lawrence, R. (2005). Knowledge construction as contested terrain: Adult learning through artistic expression. In R. Lawrence (Ed.), *Artistic ways of knowing: Expanded opportunities for teaching and learning.* New *Directions for Adult and Continuing Education, no. 107* (pp. 3–12). San Francisco: Jossey-Bass.

LeDoux, J. (1996). *The emotional brain: The mysterious underpinnings of emotional life.* New York: Simon & Schuster.

Lesser, E., & Prusak, L. (2000). Communities of practice, social capital and organizational knowledge. In E. L. Lesser, M. A. Fontaine, & J. A. Slusher (Eds.), *Knowledge and communities* (pp. 123–131). Boston: Butterworth Heinemann.

Lewin, K. (1947). Frontiers in group dynamics. *Human Relations, 1,* 5–41.

Lo, P. (1996). Understanding learning in organizations: A case study in Taiwan (China). *Dissertation Abstracts International, 57/04A,* 1440. (UMI No. AAI9622509)

Maben-Crouch, C.L. (1997). In search of learning within work: A collective case study. *Dissertation Abstracts International, 58/05A*, 1540. (UMI No. AAI9734625)

Malcolm, J., Hodkinson, P., & Colley, H. (2003). The interrelationships between informal and formal learning, *Journal of Workplace Learning, 15*,(7/8), 313–318.

Marsick, V. J., & Volpe, M. (Eds.). (1999), *Informal learning on the job.* San Francisco: Berrett-Koehler Communications.

Marsick, V. J., & Watkins, K. (1990). *Informal and incidental learning in the workplace.* London: Routledge.

Marsick, V., Watkins, K. (1999), Lessons from informal and incidental learning. In J. Burgoyne, J., & M. Reynolds (Eds), *Management learning: Integrating perspectives in theory and practice* (pp. 295–311). Thousand Oaks, CA: Sage.

McCracken, J. L. (1998). *Examining the impact of formal and informal learning on the creativity of women inventors.* Proceedings of the Adult Education Reseach Conference. Retrieved February 6, 2007, from http://www.edst.educ.ubc.ca/aerc/1998/98mccracken.htm.

McGeoch, J. A. (1942). *The psychology of human learning.* New York: Longmans Green.

Menard, S. A. W. (1993). Critical learning incidents of female army nurse Vietnam veterans and their perceptions of organizational culture in a combat area. *Dissertation Abstracts International, 55/01A*, 4651. (UMI No. AAI9413556)

Mezirow, J. D. (1985). A critical theory of adult learning and education. In S. Brookfield (Ed.), *Self-directed learning: From theory to practice,* New Directions for Adult and Continuing Education, No. 25. San Francisco: Jossey-Bass.

Moran, L. (2003). A case study of informal learning among production team workers. Doctoral dissertation. (Teachers College, Columbia University, New York). *Dissertation Abstracts International, 64/02*, 370.

Mumford, A. (1993). *How managers can develop managers.* Aldershot, UK: Gower.

Nahapiet, J., & Ghoshal, S. (1998). Social capital, intellectual capital and the organizational advantage. *Academy of Management Review, 23*(2), 242–266.

Nonaka, I., & Takeuchi, H. (1995). *The knowledge-creating company: How Japanese companies create the dynamics of innovation.* New York: Oxford University Press.

O'Driscoll, T. O., Sugrue, B., & Vona, M. K. (2005). The C-level and the value of learning. *T + D, 59*(10), 70–78.

Olson, K. (2005). Music for community education and emancipatory learning. In R. Lawrence (Ed.). *Artistic ways of knowing: Expanded opportunities for teaching and learning. New Directions for Adult and Continuing Education, no. 107* (pp. 55–64). San Francisco: Jossey-Bass.

Oxford, E. F. J. (1998). A study of collective learning in the workplace. Doctoral dissertation. (Teachers College, Columbia University). *Dissertation Abstracts International, 59/07A*, 2303.

Poell, R. F., Van der Krogt, F. J., & Wildermeersch, D. (1999). Strategies in organizing work-related learning projects. *Human Resource Development Quarterly, 10*(1), 43–61.

Poell, R. F., Chivers, G. E., Van der Krogt, F. J., & Wildermeersch, D. A. (2000). Learning-network theory: organizing the dynamic relationships between learning and work. *Management Learning, 31*(1), 25–49.

Poell, R. F., Yorks, L., & Marsick, V. J. (2006). *Understanding, researching, and practicing action learning: Findings from a cross-cultural analysis of data from two projects.* Manuscript submitted for publication.

Polanyi, M. (1967). *The tacit dimension.* New York: Doubleday & Company.

Postman, L., & Senders, V. (1946). Incidental learning and generality of set. *Journal of Experimental Psychology, 36*, 153–165.

Raelin, J. A. (1997). A model of work-based learning. *Organization Science, 8*(6), 563–578.

Raelin, J. A. (2000). *Work-based learning: The new frontier of management development.* Englewood Cliffs, NJ: Prentice-Hall.

Reber, A. S. (1996). *Implicit learning and tacit knowledge: An essay on the cognitive unconscious.* New York: Oxford.

Reber, A. S. (1989). Implicit learning and tacit knowledge. *Journal of Experimental Psychology: General, 118,* 219–235

Reio, T. G., & Callahan, J. (2004). Affect, curiosity, and socialization-related learning: A path analysis of antecedents to job performance, *Journal of Business and Psychology, 19,* 3–21

Reio, T. G., Petrosko, J. M., Wiswell, A. K., & Thongsjkmag, J. (2006). The measurement and conceptualization of curiosity, *Journal of Genetic Psychology, 167* (2), 117–135.

Reischman, J. (1986, October). *Learning "en passant": The forgotten dimension.* Paper presented at the annual conference of the American Association of Adult and Continuing Education, Miami, FL.

Rossing, B. E. (1991). Patterns of informal and incidental learning: Insights from community action. *International Journal of Lifelong Education, 10*(1), 45–60.

Schön, D. A. (1983). *The reflective practitioner.* New York: Basic Books.

Schön, D. A. (1987). *Educating the reflective practitioner: Toward a new design for teaching and learning in the professions.* San Francisco: Jossey-Bass.

Seger, C. A. (1994). Implicit learning. *Psychological Bulletin, 115*(2), 163–196.

Shih, J. F. (1997). How religious professionals learn: An exploration on learning by Buddhist professionals in Taiwan. *Dissertation Abstracts International, 58/06A* (2029) (UMI No. AAI9723284)

Simon, H. A. (1965). Administrative decision making, *Public Administration Review, 25*(1), 31–37.

Skiba, M. (1999). A naturalistic inquiry of the relationship between organizational change and informal learning in the workplace. (Doctoral dissertation.: Teachers College, Columbia University, New York). *Dissertation Abstracts International, 60/07,* 2587.

Skule, S. (2004). Learning conditions at work: A framework to understand and assess informal learning in the workplace. *International Journal of Training & Development, 8*(1), 8–20.

Stahl, T. A. (2005). Executive learning post 9/11: A case study at one major global financial institution. (Doctoral dissertation. Teachers College, Columbia University, New York). *Dissertation Abstracts International, 66/05,* 1597.

Stokes, I., & Pankowski, M. (1988). Incidental learning of aging adults via television. *Adult Education Quarterly, 38*(2), 88–100.

Straka, G. A. (2004). *Informal learning: genealogy, concepts, antagonisms and questions.* ITB-Forschungsberichte 15. Retrieved January 3, 2007, from http://www.itb.uni-bremen.de/downloads/Publikationen/Forschungsberichte/fb_15_04.pdf.

Strocchia, M. (2003). Innovation and learning in three small entrepreneurial firms in Venezuela. (Doctoral dissertation. Teachers College, Columbia University, New York). *Dissertation Abstracts International, 64/02,* 429.

Svensson,L., Ellstrom, P., & Aberg, C. (2004). Integrating formal and informal learning at work. *Journal of Workplace Learning, 16*(7/8), 479–491.

Torbert, W. (1991). *The power of balance: Transforming self, society, and scientific inquiry.* San Francisco: Sage.

Verespej, M. A. (1998). Formal training: 'Secondary' education? *Industry Week, 247*(1), 42–44.

Volpe, M. (1992). The relationship between organizational change and informal learning in the workplace. (Doctoral dissertation. Teachers College, Columbia University, New York). *Dissertation Abstracts International, 53/05,* 1369.

Vox: Norwegian Institute of Adult Education (2002). *Validation of nonformal and informal learning in Norway: The Realkompetanse Project 1999–2002.* Norway: VOX, on the instructions of the Ministry of Education.

Walker, A. R. (2001). A study of informal learning in the context of managerial decision-making. (Doctoral dissertation. Teachers College, Columbia University, New York). *Dissertation Abstracts International, 62/05,* 1685.

Watkins, K., & Cervero, R. (2000). Organizations as contexts for learning: A case study in certified public accountancy. *Journal of Workplace Learning, 12*(5), 187–194.

Watkins, K., & Marsick, V. J. (1993) *Sculpting the learning organization.* San Francisco: Jossey-Bass.

Watkins, K., & Marsick, V. (2003). Summing up: Demonstrating the value of an organization's learning culture. *Advances in Developing Human Resources, 5*(2), 129–131.

Weick, K. (2001). *Making sense of the organization.* Malden, MA: Blackwell.

Weintraub, R. S. (1998). Informal learning in the workplace through desktop technology: A case study in a sales division of a large corporation. (Doctoral dissertation. Teachers College, Columbia University, New York). *Dissertation Abstracts International, 59/07,* 2305.

Wenger, E. (1998). *Communities of practice: Learning, meaning, and identity.* Cambridge: Cambridge University Press.

Wertsch, J. V., & Tulviste, P. (1996). L. S. Vygotsky and contemporary developmental psychology. In H. Daniels (Ed.), *An introduction to Vygotsky* (pp. 53–74). London: Routledge.

Woldesenbet, D. (1998). Local experts: Facilitators of learning about computer technology in public organizations. *Dissertation Abstracts International,* 59/09A, 3966. (UMI No. AAI99910713).

Yorks, L., & Kasl, E. (2006). Toward a theory and practice for whole-person learning: Reconceptualizing experience and the role of affect. *Adult Education Quarterly, 52,* 176–192.

Zemke, R. (1985, August). The Honeywell studies: How managers learn to manage. *Training, 22*(8), 46–51.

Chapter 21

Literacy in Adulthood

M Cecil Smith

Literacy is among the most important facets of adult life in modern societies. The abilities to read and write, perform basic mathematical tasks, and use technologies such as computers are considered to be essential skills of an educated individual who is able to function competently in the everyday world. Literate persons appear to have a number of economic and social advantages compared to illiterates. Adults who are literate are more likely to be employed and employed first. They have ready access to various kinds of text information that serve to inform, direct, enlighten, provoke, inspire, entertain, and keep them healthy. Literate adults can also use their literacy skills to provide assistance to others, including their children as they are learning to read and write. In contrast, adults who struggle with literacy tasks generally find that opportunities for well-paying jobs and advancement within the workplace are limited. Illiterate adults and those whose literacy skills are marginal may be unable to assist their children with homework. They are less able to navigate the health care system with its complex array of insurance documents and related forms. Further, low literate adults are less likely to participate in the activities that are characteristic of citizenship, such as voting or writing letters to local, state, or congressional representatives to advocate on behalf of themselves and others (Kirsch, Jungeblut, Jenkins, & Kolstad, 1993). Performing one's job, raising a family, being a "smart" consumer, fulfilling citizenship roles such as voting, engaging in leisure—all of these roles require some degree of literacy to fully accomplish.

Certain evidence suggests, however, that there is an extensive adult literacy problem in the United States that impedes adults' success in the workplace, impairs opportunities to fully engage in community life, and prevents healthy development. The results of the 1992 *National Adult Literacy Survey* (NALS), which assessed the abilities of adults ages 16 and older to perform various prose, document, and quantitative literacy tasks, revealed that nearly half of the population scored at the two lowest levels of literacy proficiency (Kirsch et al., 1993), suggesting an inability on the part of many adults to accomplish everyday literacy tasks. More recently, the 2003 *National Assessment of Adult Literacy* (NAAL) found that 14 percent of the adult population, ages 16 and older, scored at the "below basic" proficiency level, representing approximately 30 million adults. Another 63 million adults were found to have only a basic level of literacy proficiency. Thus, there has been little improvement in the distribution of adults' literacy skills over the past decade, with low literacy concentrated among minority, immigrant, elderly, and low-education adults. These two national literacy assessments will be discussed in more detail later in this chapter.

Other findings suggest that the apparent U.S. adult literacy "problem" may be overstated. For example, when adults who participated in the NALS were asked to evaluate their own literacy skills, most did not believe that they had a problem with literacy (Kirsch et al., 1993). Data from the 1995 International Adult Literacy Survey (IALS) revealed that 95 percent of American adults thought their literacy skills were satisfactory for meeting their job demands. These self-evaluations might mean that the adults who were assessed at lower literacy levels were not particularly bothered by their apparent lack of literacy. Or, perhaps low-literate adults rarely put themselves in situations where their literacy skills are challenged and, so they do not perceive any difficulty. But, when low-literate adults lose their jobs or have to change jobs, they may not be able to read well enough to find employment—which is clearly a problem for them.

The discrepancy regarding the suitability of adults' literacy skills for meeting the economic, family, and workplace demands of living may also be due to a lack of consensus about how literacy is best defined (Pont & Werquin, 2001; Venezky, Wagner, & Ciliberti, 1990). Discussions of literacy proficiencies require a nuanced view because of the existing differences of opinion regarding the extent of the adult literacy problem. While educational policymakers point to the large numbers of U.S. adults who perform at the lowest levels in assessments such as the NALS, some researchers claim that there is no evidence of a decline in the skill levels—including literacy skills—of workers in the American labor force (Handel, 2005). It is generally agreed, however, that there is an uneven distribution of literacy in the adult population, in a manner that is similar to the uneven distribution of wealth in the United States.

Rather than specifically addressing the problems of low literacy among adults, however, this chapter is concerned with the nature of adults' literacy skills and practices and, in particular, the ways in which literacy may contribute to adult development and learning. There is abundant evidence to show that the lack of literacy is an impediment in life for individuals in modern, rapidly-advancing cultures where knowledge, as acquired through exposure to the written word, is indispensable social capital. Yet, the other side of the coin—what being literate means in terms of promoting and supporting adults' development—is not often directly addressed in the literature. Therefore, in this chapter, I provide some insights on this matter by drawing upon the research that has examined adults' literacy skills, as well as the work that has demonstrated how adults benefit by learning and using literacy. Further, I examine the nature of literacy practices—which extend beyond reading to include writing and mathematical abilities and, to some extent, the everyday uses of technology—and how these practices may impact adults' lives and development.

Plan of Chapter

I begin with a definition of literacy, acknowledging that there are different perspectives on what it means to be a literate person. These different views of literacy play out in the methodological lenses that are fitted to the study of literacy behaviors and skills across the life span, and how the data are interpreted through these lenses. Arguments about the extent to which adults are "literate enough" to function effectively in society largely turn on the particular theoretical perspective that is upheld. These perspectives determine the methodological approaches taken to study literacy skills and practices, the resulting data, and the manner in which the results are interpreted. I next turn to an examination of the relationship between educational attainment and literacy, acknowledging the reciprocal benefits of one for the other. In subsequent sections, I synthesize the research that has investigated adults' literacy practices in regards to reading, writing, basic math skills or numeracy, and the uses of technology. The chapter concludes with a few comments regarding the role that literacy plays in adult development.

Literacy Defined

Definitions of literacy have shifted over time, from so-called signature literacy (Kaestle, 1991), that is, having the rudimentary ability to sign one's name on a document (taken as indicative of the ability to read and/or write), to the amount of education the individual has attained (thereby correlating progress in school with increased reading and writing abilities). More recently, emphasis has shifted to considering what people can do with literacy and the role that literacy plays in assuring one's ability to participate in the workforce—thereby ensuring personal economic well-being—and to engage in civic activities. Thus, literacy of late has been characterized by the functional purposes it serves. For example, the National Literacy Act of 1991 defined adult literacy as

> an individual's ability to read, write, and speak in English, and compute and solve problems at levels of proficiency necessary to function on the job and in society, to achieve one's goals, and develop one's knowledge and potential. (Public Law 102-73, Sec. 3, n.p.)

The current functional conceptions of literacy view reading and writing as enabling individuals to accomplish things in life, to be productive, and to provide for oneself and one's family. This view also implies that literacy contributes to individual growth and development, and to a sense of well-being and personal satisfaction.

Theoretical Perspectives. This functional perspective on literacy is not universally embraced, however, and there are dissenting views and competing definitions of literacy (Venezky et al., 1990). Two theoretical perspectives on literacy (i.e., reading) development are apparent in the literature and therefore deserve attention. These perspectives embrace somewhat different methodological traditions, and they define what it means to be literate in different ways. One perspective focuses on reading as primarily a cognitive skill. This psycholinguistic view—rooted in cognitive psychology, information processing, and studies of language acquisition—holds that reading ability consists of a number of cognitive processes and sub-processes, including letter and word recognition, phonemic awareness (i.e., understanding that spoken words are made up of a series of sounds), and sound-to-letter correspondence. As these component skills are developed, through exposure to print in the environment, explicit instruction and practice, and as the child's oral language skills and sight word vocabulary grows, they contribute to the development of comprehension—the desired goal when reading written text. A long tradition of empirical research in cognitive psychology has been devoted to understanding comprehension processes, generally focusing on how individuals understand, interpret, and remember segments of texts that are presented under varying task conditions (e.g., high vs. low prior knowledge; easy vs. difficult text versions) (Bransford & Johnson, 1972; Kintsch, 1977, 1988). The psycholinguistic view argues that reading is a portable skill that can be applied in any situation involving written text. This skills-based approach to understanding literacy is most closely aligned with the functional literacy perspective.

A second theoretical perspective argues that reading is but one of a number of literacies in which individuals may participate. This view suggests that reading and its associated literacies (e.g., writing, speaking, numeracy) are not simply cognitive skills, but are ways of interacting with others and ways of representing oneself, as well as ways of interacting with, understanding and using the written word (Barton & Hamilton, 2000; Chouliaraki & Fairclough, 1999). Literacy learning is said to be socially constructed and situated in specific contexts such as the home and school, workplace, and the community. Reading ability, therefore, can be fully understood only within the particular social roles and contexts in which the reader participates (e.g., an engineer reading a memo at work; a parent assisting their child with homework; a commuter examining a train schedule).

Individuals' *perspectives* on their own literacy skills and practices are equally important to understanding literacy proficiency as are assessments of their literacy skills (Fingeret & Drennon, 1997; Knobel, 1999; Lewis, 2001). This phenomenological view is sometimes referred to as the social practices perspective of literacy (Barton, 1994; Baynham, 1995; Sheridan, Street, & Bloome, 2000) and is associated with the so-called New Literacy Studies exemplified by the work of Barton and Hamilton (1998) and Street (1984). Pure cognitive abilities, as these relate to reading skills, are less critical in the social practices perspective because there are numerous ways that individuals might acquire meaning from texts and engage in literate acts. Generally, literacy research that is rooted in this perspective is largely qualitative, and ethnographic methods are employed which entail extensive observations of literacy practices (e.g., Barton, Hamilton, & Ivanic, 2000). Critical discourse analysis, which treats language (including written text) as a social practice and which considers the various ways in which people use language and texts, is another method (e.g., Rogers, 2004).

Literacy skills cannot be separated from the social contexts in which literacy takes place or from its social purposes, according to the social practices perspective. Thus, reading as a literacy practice is *situated* in the interactions between people, between individual readers and the texts they use or produce, and their personal literacy goals, as well as the meanings that individuals attach to their reading and writing behaviors. It is possible to engage in a literacy practice such as reading without actually having the ability to read as, for example, when a person relies upon a friend, coworker, or family member to read and interpret a letter, form, or legal document (Reder & Green, 1983). Here, both parties are "literate" in that they inhabit a common social and intellectual space where a given text must be negotiated, interpreted, and shared.

Clearly, the social practices perspective considers reading in a much different manner than does the psycholinguistic perspective—which seeks to examine, measure, and track the development of isolated reading skills, and to determine individual differences in the component processes of reading (Daneman, 1991). From a social practices perspective, attempts at curriculum standardization or assessments of students' reading skills are meaningless and unproductive because these activities do not acknowledge the socially constructed nature of literacy.

Given these different theoretical perspectives, it is important to consider the role of formal education in literacy development, as schools are places where explicit literacy instruction occurs, where literacy demands are greatest for children and youth, where a particular view of literacy is widely embraced (i.e., the cognitive skills perspective), and where students' literacy skills are repeatedly evaluated to determine the need for further (or different) instruction.

Education and Literacy

Traditionally, schools have been the principal setting where the individual's literacy skills are acquired—both through explicit training (i.e., reading instruction) and direct exposure (i.e., to literate role models, to the literacy tasks that make up or which are imbedded in academic work). Certainly, education and literacy are closely entwined and students' progress in school is assumed to denote that they are developing their literacy skills and becoming literate persons. Thus, schooling's contribution to the acquisition of literacy has been termed a *literacy development effect* by Reder (1998). Students who fail to learn to read, or whose progress in reading development is not on par with their peers, are at great risk for academic failure because so much of schooling is dependent upon the individual's ability to comprehend—and subsequently, to produce—written text. Good readers move ahead in school, increasing their vocabulary knowledge through exposure to texts, acquiring world knowledge, and further developing their literacy skills. Poor readers, on the other hand, are stymied in their knowledge development as they struggle to comprehend texts. Over time, poor readers—in particular, those from economically disadvantaged backgrounds—fall further and further behind their more able classmates (Allington, 1980).

Stanovich (1986) referred to the gap between able and less able readers as "Matthew effects," (i.e., the rich [good readers] get "richer," as they improve their reading skills, and the poor [struggling readers] get poorer, falling further behind in school). Specifically, Stanovich identified the mechanisms through which this gap occurs. Students' inability to master the print components of early reading results in failure to acquire adequate vocabulary from print, poor reading comprehension, and the inability to use reading to learn new information. Thus, Stanovich argued, it is essential that schools and teachers focus on helping students acquire print-related skills (e.g., phonemic awareness) through explicit instruction in these skills.

Literacy practices in school are those that are officially sanctioned—i.e., teacher-produced reading and writing assignments, and commercially-produced textbooks. Students are, of course, encouraged to read outside of school (i.e., homework, library books). But, the kinds of literacy practices in which they might engage outside of school (e.g., reading comic books, playing video games, writing poems or plays for their own amusement, creating web pages), and beyond the constraints of the official curriculum, are frequently not recognized or valued by their teachers or parents. Students soon learn that the only literacy that "counts" is that which is assessed at school.

Literacy ability can also be seen to contribute to the educational attainment of individual learners. That is, those students whose literacy skills are sufficiently well-developed (i.e., as determined by standardized tests) to ensure their success in school are more likely to continue their education compared to those students whose skills are deficient. Reder (1998) has referred to this relationship as a *literacy selection effect*. Students who are successful with literacy in school earn good grades, thereby reinforcing their academic efforts and increasing the likelihood that they will continue their schooling. The problem is not, of course, that those students who learn to read do well in school and increase the achievement gap between themselves and those who do not learn to read well. Rather, the problem is that literacy is poorly *distributed*: Schools have not been successfully in closing the reading achievement gap between White and minority, affluent and poor, and learning disabled and normal ability students.

Despite their obvious entanglement, schooling and literacy are not synonymous. Much literacy learning can place before (but often does not, c.f., Hart & Risley, 1995) the child begins formal schooling. Infants, toddlers, and preschoolers acquire language early in life and they participate in a variety of pre-literacy activities (Teale & Sulzby, 1986), and many children are immersed in rich print environments within their homes. Parents and other caregivers read to children to give comfort and establish predictable routines of storybook reading, for example. In doing so, caregivers point to pictures and colorful drawings, and they demonstrate the different features of books to children. Young children observe their parents, siblings, and others reading and writing, and discussing these activities. Through these observations, many young children recognize the apparent importance of books, magazines, and newspapers long before they are able to read these texts themselves (Bus, van IJzendoorn, & Pelligrini, 1995). In addition, many preschoolers watch *Sesame Street* and countless other television programs and videos, listen to music, shuffle magnet letters on the refrigerator door, and play rhyming games with siblings. All of these activities are, in one form or another, socially determined literacy practices having significant meanings for children as well as their caregivers (Heath, 1984). Such literacy practices precede children's abilities to decode, understand, and create written language.

Of course, not all children are raised in homes where they are exposed to positive literacy role models, and they lack exposure to powerful language experiences and opportunities with play with and use written materials (Hart & Risley, 1995). Other children may get rich exposure to oral language at home, but these language interactions do not prepare them for the extensive demands of the print-based curriculum when they enter school (Heath, 1984). A number of investigators have documented the effects of lack of early language and literacy-related experiences on young students' success in school (Baker, Serpell, & Sonnenschein, 1995; Hart & Risley, 1995).

While early literacy experiences are thought to be necessary for success in school, they are not sufficient for literacy learning. Formal instruction in reading, writing, and mathematics are also deemed to be essential. Yet, clearly not all students respond well to literacy instruction and some children will fail to learn to read and write. Often, such circumstances are due to insufficient or improper instruction, undiagnosed learning disabilities or other intellectual impairments, low motivation, or the lack of timely interventions. Too often, these students are simply passed along from one grade to the next, despite their inability to read well. Thus, having earned a high school diploma is no guarantee that the graduate is able to read and write well—or at all.

Nonetheless, it is also true that some people can develop expert literacy skills despite a lack of educational preparation. It is also possible for adults to carry on with their lives, to work and to raise their families without being "functionally" literate in the traditional sense of being able to read, write, or perform basic arithmetic (Fink, 1998). Yet, even those adults whose literacy abilities—as measured through standardized assessments—place them at the very bottom of the skills distribution, often possess a sufficient level of literacy knowledge to "get by" in their everyday lives. Such individuals frequently resort to a variety of compensatory behaviors (e.g., asking others for assistance with reading and writing tasks) and strategies (e.g., guessing, attentive listening, memorizing) that allow them to function in a print-saturated environment (Kozol, 1985; Merrifield, Bingman, Hemphill, & deMarrais, 1997; Reder, 1994; Smith & Locke, 1998). One recent example of an illiterate adult who nonetheless achieved the pinnacle of success in his professional life is that of the former National Hockey League coach, Jacques Demers. Demers, a French Canadian whose team won a Stanley Cup championship in 1993, reported in his biography (Leclerc, 2005) that he was able to hide his illiteracy from nearly everyone, including his wife, by asking secretaries and media relations people to write letters for him, claiming that his English skills were not sufficient to understand contracts and other business-related documents (he was non-literate in his native French as well).

There are substantial data suggesting that large numbers of U.S. adults have limited reading skills. Several recent national assessments of adult literacy have shown that up to 90 million adults display some difficulties with a variety of reading tasks (Kirsch et al., 1993), although there is much disagreement about the source of these observed deficiencies (Sticht, 2001). In the next section of this chapter, I describe three national surveys of American adults' literacy abilities.

Assessing the Literacy Skills of U.S. Adults

Over the past three decades, the U.S. government has conducted periodic assessments of the literacy proficiencies of adults. These efforts have been fueled, in part, by concerns among government and business leaders that the literacy skills needed for the U.S. workforce to remain competitive in the global arena are increasing, while the literacy skills of adults are not keeping pace with workplace demands (U.S. Department of Labor, 1991). Thus, these assessments have been firmly grounded in a functional perspective. Also, literacy as it is used in these assessments is considered to be synonymous with reading. That is, only reading skills have been assessed, although some information was gathered (but never fully reported) about respondents' writing practices and other activities in which they used math.

Young Adult Literacy Survey (1985)

Although a number of assessments of adults' literacy skills had been conducted in the 1970s (Sticht & Armstrong, 1994), the Young Adult Literacy Survey (YALS), conducted by the Educational Testing Service on behalf of the U.S. Department of Education's National Center for Education Statistics, began a new era of literacy assessments (Kirsch & Jungeblut, 1985). The ETS approach was based upon a cognitive information-processing framework for literacy skills assessment. This framework enabled the designers to create items that had a range of information processing requirements, from having the test-taker simply locate and match written information in a document to generating a theme or an organizing principle from a lengthy prose passage. The YALS designers determined the specific information-processing requirements of each literacy task that was included in the assessment.

Factor analyses of the items led to the conclusion that three types of literacy tasks could be represented on different scales: prose, document, and quantitative (PDQ) literacy. *Prose literacy* is "the knowledge and skills needed to understand and use information from texts that include editorials, new stories, poems, and fiction" (Kirsch et al., 1993, p. 3). Examples of prose tasks include finding information in a newspaper article, or inferring a theme from a poem. *Document literacy* is "the knowledge and skills required to locate and use information contained in material that include job applications, payroll forms, transportation schedules, maps, tables, and graphs" (p. 3). Examples include locating an intersection on a street map and entering personal information on a job application form. *Quantitative literacy* is "the knowledge and skills required to apply arithmetic operations...using numbers embedded in print materials" (pp. 3–4). Examples include balancing a checkbook and summing catalog purchases on an order form.

This multi-scale approach was thought to better reflect the multifaceted nature of literacy than would a single measure of literacy. The PDQ assessment thus resulted in a profile of literacy skills. The advantage of this approach is that it eliminates the arbitrary use of cut points or a single standard to distinguish "illiterate" from "literate" adults—a longstanding practice in the history of literacy in western societies (Kaestle, 1991). The three skill domains encompassed the predominate types of text materials and literacy tasks that young adults encounter in their everyday lives. There is some evidence, however, that rather than assessing three dimensions of literacy ability, the PDQ approach actually taps into a generalized form of literacy ability. Reder (1998), in an analysis of the 1992 National Adult Literacy Survey results, found high intercorrelations (> .90) among the three scales—suggesting that these literacy proficiencies are the same. Nonetheless, the three scales were used in two subsequent assessments of adults' literacy skills, described below.

The literacy skills of a nationally representative sample (N = 3,474) of American adults ages 21 to 25 were assessed in the YALS. The results showed a majority of young adults were able to successfully perform literacy tasks at the lower proficiency levels for prose, document, and quantitative literacy. At least 95 percent of the 21- to 25-year-old population achieved the 200 level (on a 500-point scale, with the mean equal to 305). Only slightly more than one-third (37%) of young adults achieved an above-average score of 325 for prose proficiency, document proficiency (38%), and quantitative literacy proficiency (38%). Fewer than one in ten young adults achieved PDQ proficiencies equivalent to 375. Whites and those having more education demonstrated higher PDQ literacy proficiencies than other racial/ethnic groups and those with less education.

National Adult Literacy Survey

The 1992 National Adult Literacy Survey (NALS) was the first comprehensive, nationwide assessment of adults' literacy abilities in the United States—and the largest such study of American adults' literacy that has ever been conducted. More than 26,000 adults, ages 16 and older, participated in the NALS, completing both the PDQ measures and an extensive background interview that gathered data on individuals' demographic characteristics, primary language, labor force participation, educational background, civic participation, and literacy practices.

Employing the same methodology as the YALS, a 500-point scale (with a mean of 250 and a standard deviation of 50) was adopted by ETS to report adults' literacy proficiencies. Five levels of literacy ability were described. Level 1 (score range = 0–225) is the lowest level. The results showed that about one-half of the adult population (estimated at 90 million adults) scored at the two lowest proficiency levels on the PDQ scales. Adults who performed literacy tasks at Level 1 were able to locate single pieces of information in brief texts and could accomplish relatively simple arithmetic operations. Many of those scoring at the two lowest levels were adults who reported having significant health problems or mental or physical disabilities (3% to 87% of those in levels 1 and 2, depending upon disability), or they were disproportionately recent immigrants who did not speak or read English.

In many cases, Level 1 and Level 2 adults were able to complete more complex, higher-level literacy tasks, but they were significantly less likely to do so than are those adults who performed at the higher literacy levels. Adults at Level 5 (score range = 376–500), the highest literacy level, could make high level inferences, using their background knowledge, when reading densely-packed and complex texts. They could also perform multiple quantitative operations sequentially, among other literacy abilities. Level 5 readers represented only about 3 to 4 percent of the adult population, however, and were those individuals most likely to have the greatest amount of education, worked in high-status jobs, and were White.

The NALS results did not go unchallenged, as a number of adult literacy experts questioned the validity of the findings. That a large segment of the adult population has low literacy abilities resulted from the design of the NALS assessment, according to Sticht (2001). To briefly explain, item response theory (IRT) was used to estimate adults' literacy abilities from their responses to a small number of tasks that were administered to each test-taker. IRT is a statistical method for scaling individual test items for difficulty in such a way that a given test item has a known probability of being correctly completed by individuals having particular background characteristics and performing at a given level of proficiency. The criterion for assignment to a skill level was an 80 percent probability of getting the average item correct at a given literacy level (Kirsch et al., 1993, p. 71). The difficulty level of each literacy task was then placed along a scale. The resulting performance of groups of test-takers was also plotted along the same scale. Thus, scoring of the PDQ measures was based on the difficulty of each scale item, the probability of correct responding, and both respondent and task characteristics.

As Sticht (1999, 2001) has noted, the probability level could have been set at either a higher or lower value, but .80 is a fairly high criterion for most everyday literacy tasks. If an individual reads a newspaper article, for example, but does not understand something within the text, the reader has several alternatives. The individual might turn to another information source, such as television news, or might consult a dictionary or encyclopedia. Alternatively, the reader could ask another person to explain the meaning of the unknown word or phrase. None of these alternatives are possible on assessments such as the NALS. The result is that adults appear to be less proficient in their literacy abilities than they actually are. In fact, when asked as part of the NALS background interview, the majority of adults rated their literacy abilities as "good" (Kirsch et al., 1993), apparently confident that they can accomplish most of the everyday literacy tasks that they encounter. Recall also that even adults at the lowest literacy levels could complete some higher-level tasks. Sticht (2001) argued that setting the probability level at .50 (the point at which the errors are equal when claiming that adults either can or cannot perform specific literacy tasks) would have decreased the number of low-literate adults as much as fifty percent. Thus, the number of "illiterate" adults remains open to interpretation.

National Assessment of Adult Literacy

This 2003 assessment of adult literacy was a somewhat smaller follow-up to the NALS. A nationally representative sample of more than 19,000 U.S. adults, again from age 16 up, participated. Like the NALS, prose, document, and quantitative literacy skills were measured. A primary purpose of the NAAL was to track trends in adult literacy over the decade since the NALS.

NAAL scores were grouped into four levels: *Below Basic, Basic, Intermediate, and Proficient*—in contrast to the NALS' five levels of literacy proficiency. Below Basic is the lowest level indicating that adults at this level possess only the most simple and concrete literacy skills. Proficient adults, in contrast, can complete complex, challenging literacy tasks. Although only broad descriptive results from the NAAL were available at the time this chapter was written, there was little change between 1992 and 2003 in adults' abilities to read and understand sentences and paragraphs or to understand documents such as job applications. On one hand, this result is somewhat surprising as there was increased attention, following the release of the 1992 NALS results, to the role of adult basic education programs in developing low-literate adults' literacy skills. Both the National Institute for Literacy (NIFL), established by mandate as part of the 1991 National Literacy Act, and the National Center for the Study of Adult Learning and Literacy, a research and dissemination center funded by the U.S. Department of Education, assumed national leadership roles in promoting and studying adult literacy education, served as resources for adult literacy programs, and in NIFL's case, helped to coordinate literacy services and policy.

On the other hand, the lack of improvement in the distribution of adults' literacy skills is not surprising because of changes in the adult population over the decade from 1992 to 2003. For example, there are more non-English-speaking immigrants in the country (Reder & Edmonston, 2000). Also, the adult population has aged. Cognitive research on aging (Schaie, 1994) has demonstrated there are declines in some aspects of intellectual performance with age. The extent to which such declines might impair older adults' literacy skills is uncertain but is likely to be non-trivial.

More generally, at what level is an adults' literacy ability too low to enable them to function effectively at work, in school, or within the larger community? This is, of course, an important policy question because accurate estimates are needed of the number of adults that require compensatory education programs, such as adult basic education (ABE), to improve their reading skills. Adults scoring at the lowest level of these national assessments are thought to have difficulty navigating daily life. However, only about 1 in 4 of these low-literacy adults indicated that they did not read or write English well! Thus, many adults do not concur with the assumption that they have a literacy handicap—and therefore, are not likely to enroll in ABE programs.

How Low Is Too Low?   Arnbak (2004) conducted a study of 194 Danish adults in adult education programs who were studying to earn the equivalent to a high school diploma. The purpose was to determine the minimum literacy level below which poor reading skills would be detrimental to educational success. Data were gathered on the adults' reading comprehension skills, decoding abilities, primary language spoken, teacher and student ratings of students' reading skills, and course examination grades. Arbak found that the adults who scored in the lowest tenth percentile for reading ability obtained examination grades that were below the mean in classes for which there were substantial reading demands. Thus, for these adults, poor reading ability was a substantial barrier to attaining a diploma. While many adults who perform at low levels on standardized literacy assessments may not view themselves as having a literacy handicap, there is a segment of the low-ability population who do see their lack of literacy as a barrier to workplace advancement, economic success, and life satisfaction. It is these individuals who are most likely to seek out adult literacy education programs.

Improving Adults' Literacy Skills

The Secretary's Commission on Achieving Necessary Skills (SCANS; U.S. Department of Labor, 1991) described five competencies that students must acquire in order to be well-prepared to function in the modern workforce. According to the SCANS report, effective workers possess competencies that help them to productively use *resources* (enabling them to allocate time, money, materials, and space), *information* (enabling them to acquire, evaluate and interpret, and communicate data), *systems* (enabling them to understand, design, and improve social, organizational, and technological systems), and *technology* (enabling them to select equipment and tools, and apply technologies to specific tasks). Further, effective workers have *interpersonal skills* (enabling them to work with teams, teach others, serve customers, and work well with people from diverse backgrounds). These competencies necessitate the development of sophisticated reading, writing, and arithmetic skills. Some experts have expressed concerns that students graduating from high school (and those who fail to graduate) lack the necessary literacy skills to function effectively in the workplace (Landrieu, 2006; Smith, 2000).

While the percentage of high school dropouts decreased during the 1990s (U.S. Census Bureau, 2000), school dropout continues to be a problem—particularly in urban areas and among Black and Hispanic youth. In 2001, more than twenty percent (21.1) of Hispanic youth ages 16–19 had dropped out of school, and nearly 12 percent (11.7) of Black youth ages 16–19 had done so. Some of these dropouts and others go on to earn a GED or high school equivalency diploma. Those whose reading skills are not adequate to take the GED test, and many older adults who are poor readers, enroll in adult basic education (ABE) programs to improve their reading and related literacy skills. Nearly three million adults participated in basic skills courses in 2004–2005, according to the U.S. Department of Education (2006). Non-English speaking immigrants to the U.S. enroll in English-as-a-Second Language (ESL) programs. Of these adults, many are well-educated and literate in their native language but not in English. Others are non-literate in their native language as well as in English. Almost two million adults participated in ESL programs in 2004–2005, according to the U.S. Department of Education (2006).

There are many reasons for poor reading skills among adults, including the following problems: low verbal intelligence and cognitive deficits that impair short-term memory and comprehension; physical disabilities such as low visual acuity; poor oral language comprehension; inadequate word decoding skills; not a native speaker of the language; poor educational preparation and/or inadequate reading and language arts instruction; inadequate exposure to and practice at reading real texts; and having reluctant, hostile or otherwise poor attitudes toward reading (Singer & Donlan, 1989). Strucker, Yamamoto, and Kirsch (2007) investigated the relationship of the "component skills" of reading (e.g., phonics, fluency, oral language, vocabulary) to low-literate adults' literacy proficiency, as measured by the prose literacy test used in the International Adult Literacy Survey (IALS), which was closely related to the NALS. Strucker et al. found that adults at the lowest literacy skill level were poor at word decoding and oral vocabulary, and appeared to have severe short-term memory problems. Thus, these adults have unique cognitive skills deficits.

These deficits can be remediated, however, with appropriate educational interventions. Although adult education programs to improve U.S. adults' literacy skills have existed in one form or another since the post-Civil war era (Gordon & Gordon, 2003; Sticht, 1989), it has only been during the past 40 years that the federal government has played a substantial role in providing support for these programs (Sticht, 2002). Despite the infusion of federal dollars into adult literacy education, there have been remarkably few studies of the effectiveness of these programs for helping adults learn to read. Existing studies suggest that adult literacy programs are ineffective.

Do Literacy Skills Programs Work?

Beder (1999) conducted a meta-analysis of 23 outcomes and impacts studies of adult literacy education conducted over approximately three decades (late 1960s to late 1990s). These studies were selected from an initial sample of 115 such studies, having met a number of criteria, including adequate sample size and the inclusion of comparison or control groups. Beder found the evidence was insufficient for determining if ABE participants improve their basic literacy skills. ABE participants self-reported that their literacy skills and self-image improved as a result of participation, however. Two recent empirical studies provide additional evidence that adults participating in literacy education and basic skills courses do not improve their literacy skills.

Friedlander and Martinson (1996) were able to randomly assign adults to either adult basic education (ABE) classes or to no-ABE (control) conditions. This is the only randomized trials study in the adult basic education literature. Both groups consisted of adults who were school dropouts and received benefits from the Aid to Families and Dependent Children program. ABE program participants did not differ from the non-ABE adults on standardized reading measures following several months of reading instruction. More ABE participants went on to earn a high school equivalence diploma, however, than did the non-ABE adults. Thus, participation appeared to have an impact on learners' educational motivation but not their reading skills.

Drawing upon data from the 1992 NALS, Sheehan-Holt and Smith (2003) analyzed the associations of participation in adult basic skills programs with literacy proficiencies and reading practices (e.g., reading books and periodicals). Two groups were compared: adults who had or had not—based upon self-report—ever participated in a basic skills program to improve their reading, writing, and/or math skills. Both groups were similar in terms of age, native language, educational attainment, and other important background variables. The basic skills program participants were found to be not different from non-participants in regards to their reading abilities. There were only a few group differences in regards to reading practices, with those who participated in workplace basic skills programs having more extensive document reading practices than those adults who took part in basic skills programs in other settings (i.e., community programs, military). The combined findings from these two studies call into question the benefit of such basic skills education programs for low-literate adults.

Although it is evident that a significant portion of the adult population demonstrates limited literacy proficiencies, substantial numbers of adults are able to read, write, and perform basic mathematics sufficiently for the life and work roles that they inhabit. The next section of this chapter describes the research that has examined adults' reading, writing, math (numeracy), and technology skills.

Dimensions of Adult Literacy

Reading

The study of reading is prevalent within cognitive and educational psychology (Smith, Locke, Boisse, Gallagher, Krengel, Kuczek et al., 1998). The principle foci of investigations of adults' reading skill have centered on knowledge acquisition (Stanovich, West, & Harrison, 1995; West, Stanovich, & Mitchell, 1993), comprehension (e.g., Carver, 1977; Magliano & Millis, 2003) and memory for information derived from text (e.g., Meyer, 1975; Rice, 1986). Much less common are studies of adults' reading practices, although there is empirical literature on this topic going back to at least the 1930s (e.g., Waples, 1938). Literate adults read in a skillful manner, for many reasons, and to accomplish a variety of purposes. They read to gain knowledge and acquire information, for recreation and leisure, for personal empowerment, to cope with life problems, to increase work effectiveness, to facilitate social and community interactions, and to participate in civic activities (Guthrie & Greaney, 1991). Adults who read extensively, purposefully, and skillfully have been characterized as mature or expert readers.

Development of Reading Skills.   Few studies have tracked the development of adults' reading skills over time to determine growth in reading ability and the individual and social factors that contribute to such growth. Bray, Pascarella, and Pierson (2004), however, analyzed longitudinal data gathered from a nationally-representative sample of 1,054 college students enrolled in 18 higher education institutions across the United States. Reading comprehension skills and attitude toward literacy were assessed at the beginning and end of the study and data were collected annually across the first three years of college. Linear regression models were tested to determine predictors of reading growth in college and changes in attitude toward literacy. Potentially confounding influences on reading growth were controlled as seven sets of predictor variables were regressed to determine their associations with end-of-third-year reading comprehension and literacy attitude. The predictor variables were: pre-college characteristics (e.g., reading comprehension; gender, race); amount of secondary education (e.g., credits completed); amount of reading (e.g., number of books read); quality of classroom experiences (e.g., perceptions of effective teaching); involvement in academic activities (e.g., library experiences; required writing assignments); patterns of coursework (e.g., math, science, social science, technical, arts courses taken); and, activities not associated with coursework (e.g., work responsibilities).

Young adults' reading comprehension ability upon entry into college was significantly associated with their end-of-third-year reading comprehension. Race was also associated with reading ability at the end of the third year of college, as White students were found to have made significantly larger net gains than did students of color. The number of credit hours completed, the number of assigned books read, and students' perceptions of having been exposed to effective instruction (e.g., organized, clear teaching) were also significantly associated with reading comprehension following three years of college. Pre-college reading ability and literacy attitude, and number of assigned books read in college were associated with literacy attitude at the end of three years of college, as was gender (i.e., males made larger gains), and some aspects of involvement in academic activities (i.e., library experiences). The college experience factors that were associated with reading growth were the amount of college education attained (i.e., number of credit hours earned) and two literacy practices—the amount of reading completed in college (i.e., number of book read) and the amount of writing required (for above-average readers only). Being exposed to effective teaching was also a significant factor in reading growth in college.

Thus, the college years can be a critical period for developing adults' lifelong reading skills and habits. However, to the extent that students enter college with good reading skills, the more likely it is that they will benefit from their college experiences in regards to their reading and other literacy practices.

The Mature Adult Reader.   One of the most ambitious investigations of adults' reading skills was undertaken in the late 1940s by Gray and Rogers (1956) who asked, what is the nature of the *skills, interests, and attitudes* that enable adults to effectively meet the reading demands in their lives? They identified 18 criteria for maturity in reading, and developed 16 scales to assess these maturity criteria. Collectively, the scales covered three broad areas, including interest in and purposes for reading, the complexity of the reading materials, and the individual's reading competence.

Gray and Rogers (1956) described several characteristics of mature readers, including enthusiasm, reading for four or more hours daily and in multiple interest areas, having broad and deep interests that include intellectually challenging text materials, reading for multiple purposes, and having inferential and critical reading skills, and the ability to apply ideas acquired from texts. These characteristics include cognitive, affective and motivational dimensions and encompass the kinds of reading practices in which mature readers engage (i.e., reading for extended time periods).

They conducted three studies with adults from diverse educational and occupational backgrounds to assess levels of reading maturity. The first study was a pilot investigation to develop and refine the measures used to assess reading maturity. The study participants were volunteers and all were employees of a local department store. They were observed while reading, interviewed about their reading practices, and given multiple measures of reading maturity. Participants were asked to read and respond to texts of various sorts, including newsmagazine articles. They were then asked questions such as, "What does the article say?," "What is your immediate reaction?," and "Where does this fit in with your own ideas?" The purpose of these questions was to assess participants' comprehension, ability to integrate new information with prior knowledge, and their facility in evaluating text information. High levels of reading maturity were not found among the participants in this study, however. In fact, most adults demonstrated only a few of the characteristics of reading maturity.

Because Gray and Rogers (1956) failed to find exemplary cases of reading maturity within their department store sample, they then turned to a highly select sample of 21 adults who were reputed to be accomplished readers, based upon peer nomination. The methodology was much the same as in the department store study, with some minor modifications necessary due to time constraints. Overall, Gray and Rogers determined that maturity is domain-specific (i.e., pertaining to only one topic or content area), and that persons may be mature in one aspect of reading (e.g., reading competence) but immature in another (e.g., amount of time spent in reading).

Although no follow-up work was ever conducted in this vein, Gray and Rogers' ideas were confirmed in later studies of adult reading (Lundeberg, 1987; Pressley & Afflerbach, 1995), in which adults were observed to demonstrate expert reading skills in textual domains where they had sufficient prior knowledge, but evidenced rather poor comprehension skills when reading texts on topics with which they were unfamiliar. Gray and Rogers (1956) also noted individual differences in reading maturity and claimed that each adult reader is distinctive, having a mix of interests, skills, reading demands, and attitudes toward reading. They asserted that the social context, including educational attainment and interests, plays a significant role in the development of reading maturity—a perspective which gained prominence in educational psychology with the rediscovery of the work of Vygotsky (Rogoff, 1990; Rogoff & Lave, 1984; Scribner & Cole, 1981) and the emergence of socioconstructivist pedagogy (Edwards, 2001). The outcomes of Gray and Rogers' research suggest that reading maturity takes a long time to develop, requires appropriate social supports and educational experiences, and is relatively rare. These conclusions are consistent with modern perspectives on life-span cognitive development (Baltes, 1987) and the growth of domain expertise (Ericsson & Charness, 1994).

Developing Reading Expertise.   More recently, Alexander (2006) has proposed a life-span developmental model of reading that draws upon her Model of Domain Learning (MDL; Alexander, 1997) to account for changes in the "path to competence" as a reader. The model is based on research in expertise, and describes the significant roles of learner knowledge, topic interest, and strategic skills across three stages of reading development: acclimation, competence, and proficiency/expertise. As individuals' develop domain knowledge about reading (as a specific skill) and topic knowledge about a variety of subject matters, these forms of knowledge are, according to Alexander, increasingly interconnected.

Educators have long understood the importance of learners' interest to learning (Dewey, 1895; Schiefele, 1991). According to Alexander's model (1997), individual interest becomes increasingly important as the reader advances towards competence. Individual interest is described as the individual's long-term investment and involvement in the topic or domain. In contrast, situational interest—described as temporary attention to a topic or domain (and which is important to developing early reading skills)—plays a less important role in reading development.

A third essential component of the Alexander model of reading development is strategic processing, that is, readers' uses of surface- and deep-level processing strategies. While behaviors such as re-reading, varying one's reading rate, and skipping over unfamiliar words are examples of surface-level strategies, cross-text comparisons and questioning the veracity of a text source are deep processing strategies, according to Alexander (1997). It is these deep processes strategies which become more apparent among competent and proficient, or expert readers.

Alexander's Model of Domain Learning characterizes reading in three stages of development—acclimation, competence, and proficiency/expertise—in which aspects of readers' knowledge, interest, and strategic processing become increasingly interrelated. Acclimation occurs early in reading development. Young children possess little domain knowledge about reading and only some topic knowledge (e.g., about dogs, video games, or Pokemon). Illiterate adults who are learning to read, in contrast, may have much topical knowledge as a result of life experiences but, like young children, have little domain knowledge about reading. For example, adult learners often believe that reading means sounding out words, or that words cannot be skipped over when reading (Meyer & Keefe, 1985).

The strategic skills of acclimating readers are surface level rather than deep, and it is through exposure to a variety of texts which exert different reading demands that they can develop deep processing strategies. Acclimating readers may also benefit from specific instruction in the uses of deep processing strategies. According to Alexander, acclimating readers need situationally interesting learning environments which promote reading activity and further serve to nurture the growth of individual interest. Regardless of age, these developing readers need to be exposed to texts that capture their attention and help them to develop specific and enduring interests.

Competent readers have more domain and topic knowledge and their knowledge is more interconnected and cohesive, according to Alexander (1997). As their knowledge of reading increases, they are more efficient and effective in their strategy uses. Competent readers are also driven to read by individual interests more so than by situational interests. Competent readers are more likely to read on their own initiative rather than in response to reading assignments.

Finally, proficient/expert readers possess broad and deep knowledge of reading as well as any of a variety of topic areas (e.g., mathematics, the Civil War, the stock market). Individual interest is high among experts—contributing to the expansion and refinement of their expertise—and they are less reliant upon situational interest to drive their reading activities. Further, learning strategy uses are at a high level and generally consist of deep processing strategies.

Alexander further describes six profiles of readers that include highly competent, knowledge-reliant, seriously challenged, and resistant readers. Effortful and nonstrategic processors round out the six profiles. The profiles may be of particular value for educators in that they suggest different instructional approaches that can be adopted to develop, encourage, and support students' reading skills. Highly competent readers are engaged and active readers who possess a rich repertoire of strategies—both surface-level and deep processing—and who have principled knowledge about reading and a strong base of world knowledge. Further, they display both interest in reading and in the topics that they read about. Knowledge-reliant readers draw upon what they know to support their reading performance, although they lack expert knowledge of reading itself. They are challenged by novel and highly-demanding reading tasks. Effortful processors are goal-directed and generally do well at most reading tasks. They are also strategic readers who can employ appropriate strategies to comprehend texts, although reading is not easy for them. Nonstrategic processors are, as the term suggests, those who use few or inappropriate strategies for comprehending text information. Further, they often fail to understand the demands of different reading tasks and are not good at judging their reading skills. Resistant readers possess the knowledge and strategic skills to become proficient readers but they lack the desire to do so. There are many adults who are quite capable of reading well, but they think of reading as "boring," and find ways to avoid it. Such individuals have been referred to as *aliterates* (Thimmesch, 1984). Aliterate individuals often prefer to "learn by doing" rather than by reading.

Finally, seriously challenged readers have one or more language-processing difficulties, lack sufficient prior knowledge, possess few relevant strategies, and—likely due to these problems—may be unmotivated to read. According to Alexander, such readers require the most intensive level of instruction, without which, they will fail to progress beyond the initial acclimation phase. Alexander's approach to understanding how reading skills develop over the life span is a rich, dynamic, and instructive model that has important implications for reading pedagogy and adult literacy instruction.

The Effects of Reading on Adults

Adult readers, regardless of their level of reading skill, may obtain many benefits from reading. Both Krashen (1993) and Stanovich (2000) have made strong claims about the positive effects of reading on intellectual abilities, for example. Krashen (1993) summarized a number of studies that have demonstrated positive associations between reading activities and a variety of cognitive skills, including reading comprehension, vocabulary development, spelling, writing, grammar development, and oral language. Of course, correlational evidence is not sufficient to demonstrate that reading activity does, in fact, improve intellectual functioning.

Keith Stanovich and his colleagues, however, have provided stronger evidence that reading does strongly contribute to making readers "smarter" in the sense of having more knowledge and possessing larger vocabularies. Stanovich et al. conducted a series of investigations with children, adolescents, and adults that have consistently confirmed the contribution of reading to intellectual development (Cunningham & Stanovich, 1991, 1993; Cunningham, Stanovich, & Wilson, 1993; Cipielewski & Stanovich, 1992; Stanovich, 1993; Stanovich & Cunningham, 1992, 1993; Stanovich, Cunningham, & West, 1998; Stanovich, West, & Harrison, 1995; West et al., 1993).

Stanovich et al. employed a clever methodology to determine individuals' exposure to print. They speculated that individuals who are exposed to a large amount of print (i.e., those who read widely) would be more likely to recognize the names of authors, book and magazine titles, and the names of major metropolitan newspapers (e.g., *Chicago Tribune*), and would recognize more vocabulary words, than would individuals who do not read much. They devised a series of simple recognition tests to distinguish between those persons having high and low print exposure. A checklist-with-foils protocol was used in which both real and fictional names were included for the author, newspaper, magazine, and book recognition tasks, and real and made-up words for the vocabulary recognition task. Stanovich et al. proposed that children, teens, and adults who read are much more likely to correctly identify real authors, actual newspapers and magazine names, book titles, and vocabulary words, and less likely to choose fictional names and titles, and non-words, as compared to nonreaders. Of course, nonreaders may indirectly learn about authors and books through TV viewing and films. Thus, similar recognition tests for television programs, character names, and movie titles were also used as controls for general cultural knowledge.

Print exposure, as determined by participants' scores on the author, book, newspaper, and magazine recognition tests, was significantly associated with reading comprehension, word decoding ability, spelling, word fluency, vocabulary, and abstract reasoning abilities across several samples of children, college students, and adults. While these finding do not identify the causative factors in cognitive development, the converging evidence from these studies points to the important role of reading experience (i.e., practice) in intellectual performance, according to Stanovich (2000). Thus, reading and reading practice truly does make one smarter. This work also demonstrates that exposure to print, through reading activity, is significantly related to reading ability. Thus, as adults are motivated to read and engage in reading, they consequently improve their reading abilities—illustrative of a kind of practice effect (see also Smith, 1996).

Guthrie and Greaney (1991) also noted that those persons who are active users of literacy are more knowledgeable than those who do not use literacy. Reading gives access to many information sources and types that can inform and assist people in their daily lives—at home and in the workplace and within the broader community. The acquisition of information through reading occurs over and above that which is gained through television and radio.

Reading can also be an important activity for personal empowerment. For example, Pitts (2004) conducted a content analysis of personal web pages that were created by women who were ill with breast cancer. These women used the vast resources of the Internet to read about medical findings, acquire knowledge about different treatment regimes, and share what they had learned by posting information on their web pages for others. They also read about the experiences of other breast cancer patients. In doing so, the women felt empowered to take control of their treatments, asked informed questions of their physicians, and explored issues regarding the potential disfiguring of their bodies and how mastectomy impacted their feelings about their femininity and sexuality.

Reading ability also pays some important benefits in the workplace in terms of one's occupational effectiveness. Generally, literacy researchers perceive reading at work as distinct from the kinds of reading done for school, or within the home or community. The principle distinctions have to do with the purpose for reading and the kinds of materials that are consumed. Reading demands vary by occupation, and higher status workers, managers and professional tend to do more reading, and read a greater variety of materials, than do lower status workers, hourly employees, and unskilled laborers (Kirsch & Guthrie, 1984). This distinction is what Brandt (2001) called "stratified literacy" (p. 184). Sticht (1975) described two primary types of reading that take place at work: reading to do and reading to learn. These can be distinguished by occupational status. Blue-collar workers tend to read in order to locate information that helps them accomplish specific tasks; professionals, on the other, hand do more reading for the sake of acquiring new knowledge, solve problems, and evaluate people, products, and processes.

Reading may have a positive impact on adults' civic awareness and participation in society. Venezky, Kaplan, and Yu (1998) found in an analysis of the NALS data that those adults who reported reading more text materials (e.g., newspapers, books) were more likely to have voted than those who read fewer materials. Similar results have been observed in media use studies (Stamm & Fortini-Campbell, 1983). Emig (1995), for example, found in a survey of adults in one southern community that 69.7 percent of those who reported reading newspapers "a lot" also reported that they had voted in the last local election. While it is impossible to discern cause and effect based on cross-sectional and self-report survey data, it seems obvious that people who are inclined to vote may read in order to stay informed and sample a variety of points of view. People who read a lot are likely to be informed about the political and social issues that they find important and may, therefore, be influenced to vote in regards to these issues.

Reading may also contribute to individuals' emotional well-being. Reading has been prescribed by mental health experts, for example, as an adjunct to therapy or as the therapeutic intervention itself. Such prescriptive reading is assumed to give help seekers opportunities to learn about and relate to the experiences of others, as reading others' stories may be a catalyst for change, or provide readers with different perspectives, opinions, and options. Thus, bibliotherapy has been used to treat problems ranging from alcoholism and depression to weight loss. Although some experts have questioned the validity of bibliotherapy (Rosen, 1987), the use of reading to address certain emotional and behavioral problems appears to be moderately effective (Marrs, 1995).

Books Influence Lves.   In a somewhat different vein, Emery and Csikszentmihalyi (1981) demonstrated the powerful impact that book reading can have in socializing individuals and helping to set the course of their lives. They interviewed and compared 30 men who were carefully matched in terms of demographic (i.e., age, religion) and social background factors present when they were children (i.e., parents' education, disruptions in family life such as death of a parent). All were from working-class backgrounds, but 15 grew up to become university professors, while the other 15 grew up to remain in working-class, blue-collar occupations (e.g., furnace repair). Emery and Csikszentmihaly found that the 15 men who became professors reported having books in their homes, were encouraged to read, had read extra materials beyond those required by school, and were able to identify one or more books that had a profound impact during their early lives. The men who remained in working-class jobs did not have books in their childhood homes, were not encouraged to read and rarely did so. Few could identify a book that was significant to them.

Emery and Csikszentmihalyi (1981) argued that the significant childhood books were those that provided answers to the critical problems in the individuals' lives (e.g., poverty and deprivation, homelessness, and loss), helped with identity formation processes, put their personal problems into a proper context and led them to better understanding of these issues, and offered them solutions to their problems. Thus, in the case of the 15 men who had experienced upward social mobility and improved economic status, book reading was profoundly significant to their individual development. Book reading enabled and encouraged them to use their minds, as opposed to their bodies, as the principal manner of interacting and coping with their environments.

Adults' Motivation for Reading

All of the available evidence shows that reading is a good habit to develop. Yet, it is well-established that people do not always do things that are good for them. As noted previously in this chapter, some people have the ability to read, but avoid doing so. What is it, then, that compels or motivates people to read? What are the key components of motivation for reading? What are benefits that adults accrue from their reading activities?

Compulsion to Read. People read for many reasons, of course. Some reasons are self-determined, arising from individuals' personal and professional goals. Other reasons may be prescribed or assigned by others, such as for a school- or work-related assignment. Self-determined reading frequently involves leisure reading materials, such as novels or popular magazines (Guthrie & Greaney, 1991). It is common for leisure readers to say that they find the reading experiences so pleasurable and rewarding that they often get "lost in a book" (Nell, 1988). Some readers become so absorbed in reading that the activity is actually physiologically arousing and results in a kind of trance-like state, according to Nell. He referred to such individuals as *ludic* readers. When reading for pleasure, the reader's attention is often sharply focused, and they can become so deeply absorbed that all sense of time is lost. Typically, ludic readers report having little self-consciousness yet they still feel in control of their actions. Czikszentmihalyi (1991) referred to such mental states as *flow*: "the state in which people are so involved in an activity that nothing else seems to matter" (p. 4).

While flow can be achieved during the course of many kinds of physical activities (i.e., running, mountain climbing), reading has been found to be the most common activity in which individuals report flow experiences. Readers who find particular topics highly interesting may experience flow while reading about them (Schiefele, 1991). Czikszentmihalyi views flow as a highly desirable condition which can potentially lead to personal happiness, life satisfaction, and intrinsic motivation (i.e., engaging in an activity for its own sake). Thus, as many avid readers have noted, reading has many positive psychological benefits (Birkerts, 1994). Equally important to the task of teaching reading skills in the early grades (and in ABE programs) is finding ways to increase students' desire to read for pleasure and to achieve other purposes in their lives.

A Motivation Model. Thus, motivation is a significant variable in developing and sustaining reading skills and practices across the life span (Alexander, 2006; Guthrie & Wigfield, 2000). Although Gray and Rogers (1956) did not identify motivation specifically, they recognized that mature readers were self-directed and needed little prompting from others to engage in reading. Mature readers recognize the value of reading as both an intellectual and pleasurable activity. More recently, Guthrie and Wigfield (1999) have developed a motivational-cognitive model of reading, and have defined reading motivation as "the individual's goals and beliefs with regard to reading" (p. 199). They further describe several motivational processes in regards to readers' *task mastery goals* (i.e., the reader's intentions for a given reader-text interaction), *intrinsic motivation* (i.e., reading for its own sake), *self-efficacy* (i.e., the reader's sense that he or she can read effectively), *personal interest* (i.e., valuing the topics contained within texts), and *transactional beliefs* (i.e., the reader's belief that meaning exists in the mind of the reader and must be actively constructed from the text; Schraw & Bruning, 1999). Adults having high transactional beliefs "are convinced that their knowledge, values, and personal idiosyncrasies are relevant" to understanding texts, according to Guthrie & Wigfield (1999, p. 201).

Wigfield and Guthrie (1995, 1997) found motivation to predict amount of reading among school-age children. After controlling for prior reading activity and intrinsic motivation levels, intrinsic motivation for reading (i.e., reading for its own sake) accounted for 15 percent of the variance in amount of reading students reported, and significantly predicted growth in the amount of reading from fourth to fifth grade. Low self-efficacy (Quigley, 1997), fear of failure, and embarrassment about one's skills (and about one's choices of reading materials; see Cuban, 2001) appear to be variables that diminish motivation for reading and thereby impede reading development among low-literate adults (Linnenbrink & Pintrich, 2003; Ziegler, Bain, Bell, McCallum, & Brian, 2006). Literacy educators should therefore strive to minimize the conditions which might lead to students' feelings of embarrassment or having few success experiences.

Summary

Although the development of reading skills has not been traced over the life span, reading researchers recognize that reading behaviors and the cognitive skills that influence reading undergo significant changes. During college—when young adults are confronted with substantial reading demands—lifelong reading skills and habits may be established. Expert readers possess the requisite skills, interests, and attitudes, and the strategic skills that enable them to comprehend, enjoy, and make use of the text materials they read. There is compelling evidence that reading contributes to making adults smarter insofar that those having greater exposure to and experience with a variety of print sources learn more topic knowledge and acquire larger vocabularies. Reading provides other benefits as well, including personal empowerment and emotional well-being, effectiveness in performing one's job, and being informed about and involved in community life.

Writing

According to the National Commission on Writing (2004), "[w]riting consists of the ability to say things correctly, to say them well, and to say them in a way that makes sense (i.e., grammar, rhetoric, and logic)" (p. 19). Walter Ong observed that writing is necessary to help the human mind achieve its full potential (1982). Given its obvious importance in human communication and in contributing to the intellectual lives of adults, it is rather surprising that, as Brandt (2001) has noted, the study of writing as a literacy practice has been "virtually invisible" (p. 13) in both educational and communications studies. Somewhat more prominent are the numerous investigations of students' composition skills and the development of models that depict the cognitive processes involved in crafting written work to meet academic demands (Bereiter & Scardamalia, 1987; Flower & Hayes, 1977, 1984; Kellogg, 1994).

Brandt (2001), in describing the long historical and cultural divide between reading and writing, notes that writing is less valued than is reading, as writing practices tend to be "embedded in mundane work" (p. 167). However, writing is now overtaking reading as a fundamental, basic literacy skill because writing both documents and comprises the work that many people do. As such, writing is often responsible for activating reading, according to Brandt. Despite this recent shift in the reading-writing relationship, writing remains secondary to reading within the school curriculum. For example, nearly all public grade schools employ reading specialists, yet few—if any—have writing specialists who help children learn to write well. In general, it is expected that *all* teachers should become writing teachers, and writing-across-the-curriculum is increasingly being practiced in U.S. elementary, middle, and high schools (Brewster & Klump, 2004). This approach may, however, only diminish rather than elevate writing's status in school.

In interviews with 80 individuals who were born at different times from the late 19th to late 20th centuries, Brandt (2001) found that they reported generally vivid, pleasurable experiences regarding their first efforts at reading. In contrast, memories of first writing attempts were much more ambiguous events. These were recalled as humiliating and anxiety-producing experiences. Given such circumstances, it is little wonder that few individual—aside from those who enact the role as professionals—develop an identity as a writer. This may be due to writing's ambiguity as a literate activity and its role in daily activities such as bill-paying, grocery lists, and work.

The result of this ambiguity about writing's role as a central literacy practice is that we know very little about the impacts of writing on adults' learning and development. Krashen (1993) claims, however, that writing contributes to cognitive development in much the same manner as does reading. Writing allows the writer to concretize their abstract thoughts and ideas, for example. "Writing is how students connect the dots in their knowledge," according to the National Commission on Writing in America's Schools and Colleges (2003, p. 3). In contrast to Brandt, the National Commission on Writing claims that writing has a central role in everyday life, sustaining both popular culture and western economies, through the production of artifacts such as best-selling books, feature films, inspirational works, instructional manuals, and political campaign materials. Whenever writing is discussed, however, it is typically focused around the creative and productive activities of professional writers—novelists, poets, essayists, and journalists—rather than the behaviors of adults who can and do write—letters, shopping lists, notes to their children's teachers, brief memos at work—but do not consider themselves to be "writers."

Barton and Padmore (1991) found that the English adults interviewed in an extensive study of everyday literacy practices established regular times and created a specific place in their homes for writing. Some were daily diarists, while others were regular letter writers—sending correspondence to friends and family members. Barton and Padmore noted that each person had their own set of writing practices, an important finding which cautions against making broad generalizations about adults' literacy practices.

Nonetheless, adults' opportunities for writing in daily life appear to be not as prevalent as for reading. When writing occurs, it is often in response to environmental demands, rather than enacted out of a desire for leisure. Further, little is known about the condition of adults' writing skills. No large-scale studies of adults' writing abilities have been conducted since 1969 (National Assessment of Educational Progress, 1970). That survey, called the *National Assessment of Writing*, compared the writing abilities of 17-year-old students and adults ages 26 to 35. Across several different types of writing tasks, the percentage of adults whose writing was judged "acceptable" ranged from 38 percent to 57 percent.

In 2002, the National Assessment of Education Progress, administered by the National Center for Education Statistics, assessed the writing skills of 19,000 U.S. high school students (i.e., 12th graders). Students were asked to write three types of documents: narrative, informative, and persuasive. Each student was given two 25-minute writing tasks and they were encouraged to edit and revise their written work. More than one-fourth (26%) of 12th grade students were below basic proficiency, but slightly more than one-half (51%) were at the basic proficiency level, indicating partial mastery of writing skills. Only about one-quarter (24%) of students were judged to be proficient or advanced in their writing abilities. Overall, the results for 12th graders were unchanged from the 1998 assessment, indicating that U.S. public schools must increase their efforts to improve students' writing skills (U.S. Department of Education, 2002).

What do Adults Write?　Social commentators fret frequently about the disappearance of letter writing as a cultural activity due to the near-universal access to cell phones and Email (Ivask, 1990; Kauvar, 1995; Risen, 2005). Email letters tend to be briefer and thus more telegraphic in nature, but more immediate (Baron, 1998). The Pew Internet and American Life Project found that, on a typical day, 58 percent of American adults use the Internet for writing and reading email (Rainie & Horrigan, 2005), attesting to the popularity of this form of written communication. There are few studies evaluating the quality of adults' email writing, but email messages tend to be brief, and writers frequently employ abbreviations such as LOL ("laughing out loud") and symbolized emoticons to convey emotion or tone in an electronic message, such as the sideways smiley face, :-).

Another form of writing that continues to grow in popularity is the online diary or weblog—also known as a "blog." These online journals, on popular web service providers, may be either public or private, depending upon the writer's preference. Individuals who update their blogs on a regular—often daily—basis are referred to as bloggers. Blogging has rapidly evolved into an intriguing mix of personal confession and public journalism. While most bloggers write about their personal experiences, often commenting upon ordinary aspects of their lives, a significant minority address political and social issues in their blogs (Pew Internet & American Life Project, 2006). Thus, for the first time in history, the writing of common folk is being mass distributed—and very quickly.

Some estimates suggest that as many as a half-million weblogs are actively maintained by bloggers (Manjo, 2002). Most bloggers are young (under age 30) and a significant portion (40%) are non-White (Pew Internet & American Life Project, 2006). Many professional writers and journalists are writing blogs, either in connection with the newspapers and magazines by whom they are employed, or independently. Because this is a relatively new medium for writing, few studies have investigated the degree to which such writing activity may be beneficial to improving adults' writing skills or other literacy proficiencies. However, the Pew Internet & American Life Project survey of bloggers found that more than half (52%) indicated that they blog to express themselves creatively—suggesting that blogging may indeed bestow benefits to adults' skills.

Writing at Work.　Surveys show that employers place a high value on employees' writing skills, and writing is considered to be a threshold skill for hiring and promotion among salaried employees (National Commission on Writing, 2004). Yet, relatively few contemporary studies exist regarding the demands for writing in the workplace or of employees' writing competence. Aldrich (1979) surveyed 254 business employees in middle management positions who were responsible for writing substantive document materials. These managers reported that they experienced two basic kinds of writing problems. They first lacked knowledge about how to adequately prepare for writing tasks, and, second, they therefore had negative feelings about writing.

Faigley and Miller (1982) surveyed 200 college-educated adults about their work related writing to determine how much time people spent writing and the kinds of workplace writing tasks required. Participants were administrators and managers in professional and technical occupations, or worked in sales and clerical positions, were employed in crafts and trades, or were blue-collar and service-industry workers. On average, nearly one-quarter (23%) of their time at work was devoted to writing, according to the respondents. This figure varied across occupations: blue-collar workers, for example, wrote for only about 4 percent of their total work time.

The written documents produced by the respondents included letters, memos, reports, and notes for presentations. Workers produced a weekly average of seven different types of documents. These documents were often written collaboratively with other persons—about 25 percent of the time. Respondents reported doing little writing outside of their jobs. Letters and journaling were very infrequent, for example. Only 1 percent of respondents wrote in a daily journal. This study was conducted, however, before the advent of email and the widespread introduction of personal computers into the workplace and home. There is some evidence to suggest that the growth of email has led to a rebirth of writing, of sorts, among adults. Brief letters and notes to family, friends, and acquaintances are much more frequent (The Pew Research Center for The People and The Press, 1999) and appear to be increasing (Bakardjieva & Smith, 2001). It is likely that much of this kind of writing is ordinary and unsophisticated and meant simply to convey information, news, or greetings rather than to present an opposing side to an argument, or to persuade or enlighten the recipient. Thus, there is little to suggest that such writing activities have any pronounced cognitive benefits. Yet, certain kinds of writing may indeed produce intellectual and emotional benefits for adults.

Benefits of Writing.   It has frequently been observed that writing about bothersome things can be beneficial to the writer. Pennebaker (1997), for example, has conducted an extensive program of research demonstrating that writing about emotional upheavals can improve adults' physical and mental health. Across a series of investigations, individuals who were asked to write about their deepest thoughts and feelings regarding important personal emotional issues (without concern that their writing skills would be evaluated) demonstrated a number of benefits. These included reductions in the number of visits to a physician (Pennebaker, Barger, & Tiebout, 1989), improved immune system functioning (Pennebaker, Kiecolt-Glaser, & Glaser, 1988), improvements in academic performance (Pennebaker, Colder, & Sharp, 1990), decreased work absenteeism (Francis & Pennebaker, 1992), and relief from physical symptoms (Pennebaker & Beall, 1986). Writing appears to be equally profitable as talking about emotional issues for improving mental and physical well-being. Further, writing about such issues has been found to have equivalent benefits for young and old as well as for men and women (Pennebaker, 1997).

Klein and Boals (2001) have shown that writing has important effects on cognitive processes. For example, when adults write about important matters in life, such activity leads to improved memory performance. Klein found that freshman college students who were assigned to write about their thoughts and feelings in regards to college life improved their working memory ability as compared to students who wrote about trivial topics. In a subsequent study, students who wrote about negative life experiences improved their working memory compared to students who wrote about either positive experiences or trivial events. Lepore and Smyth (2002) suggest that expressive writing reduces both intrusive thoughts and avoidant thinking about stressful experiences, thus reducing working memory demands. Intrusive thoughts and one's attempts to suppress these thoughts impair problem-solving to the extent that proactive coping in response to life stressors becomes much less likely to occur. This leads to increased stress which, in turn, causes more emotional distress for the individual. Expressive writing is thus a relatively simple and inexpensive way of improving one's mental health.

As noted above, writing is also beneficial for alleviating chronic physical symptoms.

Smyth, Stone, Hurewitz, and Kaell (1999) studied patients with asthma or rheumatoid arthritis who were assigned to write about either the most stressful event of their lives (treatment group) or emotionally neutral topics (control group). At a four month follow-up, asthma patients in the treatment group showed improvements in lung function, while control group patients evidenced no change. Rheumatoid arthritis patients in the treatment group showed improvements in overall disease activity, but controls did not change. The observed improvements were beyond those that could be attributed to the standard medical care that all participants received.

In sum, writing is an under-studied, even somewhat ambiguous, dimension of adult literacy—even though it is increasingly important in adult life. Most writing research has focused on the composition skills of students who are writing for academic purposes. No large-scale evaluations of American adults' writing skills have been conducted in more than a generation, and little is known about the impacts of writing on adults' development. The advent of new technologies has perhaps increased adults' propensity to write, but not necessarily to produce extended prose or narratives. While writing is considered essential in the workplace, more research is needed to understand the scope of workplace writing demands and workers' writing proficiencies. Writing appears to have intellectual, physical, and emotional benefits for adults when they write about difficult life situations or emotion-laden topics.

Numeracy

A third dimension of literacy ability that has received somewhat less attention is numeracy, or quantitative literacy proficiency. Numeracy is a broad concept that encompasses the cultural, social, and functional dimensions of mathematics (Withnall 1995). It is defined as the "skills, knowledge, beliefs, patterns of thinking, and related communicative and problem-solving processes individuals need to effectively interpret and handle real-world quantitative situations, problems, and tasks" (Office of Vocational and Adult Education, 1994, n.p.). More specifically, numeracy consists of the math skills that are needed to function effectively in the workplace and in the other contexts of adults' lives (Gal & Schuh, 1995; Schmitt, 2000). Everyday activities such as balancing a checkbook, calculating the amount of interest paid on a five-year loan, measuring quantities for a recipe, or estimating the length of a board are examples of numeracy tasks. As with reading and writing, adults' numeracy skills are not all or nothing, but fall along a range of abilities which vary among individuals across different kinds of mathematical tasks and problems. The proliferation of technology into all aspects of people's lives has made numeracy equally important as reading and writing for work, family and community life, and civic participation (Moses, 2003). Many everyday activities require people to estimate quantities, magnitudes, or the conditions of things (Sanfey & Hastie, 2000).

The 1992 NALS assessed adults' numeracy abilities (operationalized as quantitative literacy proficiency) by measuring their skills in applying arithmetic operations, either alone or sequentially, using numbers embedded in printed materials (Kirsch et al., 1993, pp. 3–4). Examples of the quantitative literacy tasks on the NALS included the following:

- determining which flight an individual should take to arrive in time to attend a meeting
- calculating the cost per ounce of a jar of peanut butter
- adding shipping and handling charges and then computing the total costs of a purchase on a catalog order form.

Overall, only about 4 percent of U.S. adults performed at the highest proficiency level. Similar tasks were used for the 2003 NAAL survey of adult literacy. Adults' quantitative literacy skills were found to have little changed since 1992. The percentage of adults with below basic quantitative literacy skills decreased by four percentage points, while the percentage of those having "intermediate" proficiency increased by only three percentage points in that time span (National Center for Education Statistics, 2006).

Why do some adults' quantitative literacy skills appear to be inadequate? Ineffective math instruction in school appears to be one culprit (Kahne, Bridge, & O'Brien, 2002), in part due to the lack of satisfactory preparation and credentialing of mathematics teachers. In California, for example, fully 1 in 5 high school math teachers is unprepared or is teaching out of field according to the Center for the Future of Teaching & Learning (2005). Decades of math curriculum reform in public schools across the United States has not resulted in the kinds of achievement gains for K-12 students that are desired. Trend data from the National Assessment of Educational Progress show that while mathematics achievement has statistically significantly increased over the past 30 years (1973–2004) for nine- and 13-year-olds, scores have remained flat for 17-year olds, with no meaningful improvement in high schoolers' scores over three decades (Nation's Report Card, 2004).

Many adults lack confidence in their numeracy abilities. Adults often report feeling anxious about having to perform mathematical tasks, in part because math is associated with unpleasant activities such as paying bills. Math anxiety refers to the feelings of tension, apprehension, or fear that interfere with the manipulation of numbers and the ability to solve numeracy problems in everyday life and academic situations (Tobias, 1993). Math anxiety can contribute to forgetting even obvious solutions to math problems and may lead to a loss of self-confidence in one's abilities to perform numeracy tasks successfully. Unfortunately, few studies of math anxiety and its role in impeding adults' quantitative literacy performance have been conducted. Some educators (Mathison, 1979) have suggested that math anxiety support groups and tutors can be helpful for adults who experience anxiety with numeracy tasks.

Technology Literacy

Some scholars have argued that proficiency with technology (e.g., being able to use a computer to "surf" the Internet, making a withdrawal from a cash machine, programming a VCR) is yet another form of literacy. Certainly, literacy tasks and skills are imbedded in the uses of technology. The student seeking information on the Internet must be able to read and interpret the information contained on the web site, for example. A person withdrawing cash from an ATM needs to be able to count to determine if the correct amount was dispensed. Certainly, anyone who has ever tried to program a VCR using the instruction manual must have high tolerance for ambiguity as the written instructions are often vague or full of technical jargon. Because modern life is imbued with all manner of technology, it is essential that adults are able to employ these tools in ways that are beneficial.

Rapid advances in computer and communications technologies over the past decade have contributed to remarkable social and cultural changes, and arcane terminology once used only among computer programmers and software designers has entered the daily lexicon (e.g., "log on," "bandwidth," and "download," to cite but a few). Today, for example, television commercials and print advertisements for consumer products frequently include an Internet address for the company's web site. Clearly, advertisers understand how computers have become an integral part of many people's lives. The Internet has contributed to a world that has grown, in a sense, much smaller, as events happening on the other side of the world can be widely reported by observers and journalists nearly in synchrony with their occurrence. As computer technology has been infused into many different cultural institutions and activities, and blended with other technologies (e.g., television, radio, cell phones, portable music devices), researchers, policymakers, and social commentators have also become aware of a "digital divide" that distinguishes those persons who have ready access to the technology and those individuals who do not (U.S. Department of Commerce, 1999). The latter groups consist primarily of members of the economic underclass who cannot afford personal computers, do not use public libraries where computer access is free, and whose children attend schools that are not connected to the Internet. Working adults who lack sufficient education or training may be employed in jobs that do not require them to use computer technology (although such jobs appear to be quickly vanishing).

Although the digital world is a part of many people's lives today, very little is known about the extent to which adults engage in technology literacy practices on a day-to-day basis. A survey conducted by The Pew Research Center for The People and The Press (1999) found that nearly half (46%) of all Internet users had begun to use the Internet within the year prior to the survey (i.e., 1998). More than one-third of all adults (35%) used email, and 24 percent used email on a daily basis. Thirty percent of Americans were found to go on-line everyday. Among those adults having less than a high school education, however, only 4 percent go on-line everyday. Nearly 1 in 4 (24%) of these adults do not use the Internet.

More recently, the U.S. Census Bureau (2005) reported that 70 million U. S. households (62% of all U.S. households) had one or more computers as of October, 2003. More than half (55%) of all households had access to the Internet. Generally, if people have a computer, they have Internet access, as 88 percent of those with a home computer also have access to the Internet. It appears that the digital divide—to the extent that it exists—is more of a generational than an economic problem. That is, children are more likely to use computers than adults because they have access to computers at school or in public libraries. Sixty-four percent of adults 18 years of age and older use a computer at home, work, or at school. One technology use favoring adults is that they are slightly more likely to use the Internet (60% vs. 56%) than are children.

Two-thirds of adults have a computer at home and 83 percent of these adults use the computer. Eighty-two percent of adults who have Internet access at home utilize this access. Fifty-six percent of adults use a computer at work and 42 percent access the Internet while at work. Nearly 9 of 10 adult students (85%) use a computer at school, and two-thirds of them (66%) access the Internet at school. In regard to specific computing practices, 88 percent of adults use the Internet for email and 78 percent use the Internet to obtain information on products or services. More than half of all adults (55%) have sent an email or used instant messaging (IM). IM is popular among youth and is beginning to surpass email in terms of volume of use, according to a survey conducted by AOL (2004). It is obvious that, despite concerns about online security and identity theft, more American adults are feeling reasonably confident about conducting personal financial business online. Eighteen percent of adults conducted online banking in 2003, and one-third (32%) used the Internet to purchase a product or service, according to the 2005 Census Bureau report.

The adoption and uses of technology is not limited to the United States, of course. A survey of Internet use in Europe found that Europeans adults now spend more time online than they do reading newspapers and magazines (BBC News, 2006). The average western European adult spends four hours per week online. As might be expected, younger adults (ages 15–24) are more likely to utilize the Internet than are older adults. The trend of greater online usage is firmly established and is but one example of the profound ways in which technology is changing adults' literacy practices.

Health Literacy. Maintaining good health for one's self and family members is a wise and beneficial practice in adulthood, and there is much evidence that literacy plays an important role in health maintenance. Low-literate adults, for example, may ignore instructions that are written at an advanced reading level. They may not seek out procedures that screen for health threats (e.g., mammograms; Davis, Arnold, Berkel, Nancy, Jackson, & Glass, 1996) because they are unable to comprehend insurance forms or other print materials. Rudd, Moeykens, and Colton (1999) state that

> [p]atients' literacy directly influences their access to crucial information about their rights and their health care, whether it involves following instructions for care, taking medicine, comprehending disease-related information, or learning about disease prevention and health promotion. (p. 162)

They reviewed two decades of research in the health field that showed that health-related written materials (e.g., medicine labels and warnings; informed consent documents; post-surgical instructions; insurance forms) are complex and challenging for many adults. Such materials frequently contain medical terminology, scientific jargon, multi-syllabic words, and complex sentences that are confusing to even average-ability readers. In a study of text materials (such as signs and brochures) found in hospitals, Anderson and Rudd (2006) observed that the reading level of these materials ranged from eighth grade to advanced graduate level. As Rudd (2002) has noted, however, professional in health care are now recognizing the connection between literacy and health, and are working with educators to produce visually-appealing health-related materials that are written so that they can be more easily read and understood by laypersons.

In sum, numeracy has garnered less attention than writing, although it is arguably as important as reading and writing, as many daily tasks require facility with numbers—including counting, measuring, and estimating things, and calculating amounts. Low quantitative proficiency is attributable, in part, to poor math instruction and low self-efficacy and high anxiety around math-related tasks. The infusion of technology has led to a new kind of literacy ability—technology literacy. Although the majority of U.S. adults use technologies such as personal computers, many perform relatively low-level tasks, such as sending email. Yet another dimension of literacy pertains to adults' abilities to navigate the health care system, and to read and understand health- and medical-related documents. This is a growing area of research.

Conclusion

This chapter has described adults' literacy in regards to the roles that literacy plays in adult life and the different forms that literacy takes and the diverse kinds of literacy practices in which adults may choose to participate. There has been historically little consensus regarding the definition of literacy, in terms of what it means to be a literate person. At least two distinct perspectives on literacy coexist. The psycholinguistic perspective, which emphasizes the development of cognitive skills, has largely predominated within

American psychology and education. The emphasis on mastery of the discrete skills that collectively contribute to literacy proficiency has had immense influence on reading instruction in schools, and has largely shaped the way in which people think about their reading skills and those of their children and others. Recent large-scale assessments of adults' literacy skills are based in this perspective. These assessments, such as the 2003 National Assessment of Adult Literacy, have shown that sizeable numbers of adults are lacking in their literacy abilities. In contrast, most adults report that they do not have deep concerns with their ability to accomplish everyday literacy tasks. Of course, some adults lack adequate literacy to be socially mobile in terms of getting and holding onto a better job, and they lack confidence in their abilities to assist their children with literacy tasks, or to participate fully in their communities. Often, these adults enroll in adult education programs that are designed to teach reading, writing, and basic math skills. Unfortunately, the available evidence suggests that these programs are not very effective in improving adults' skills. Other evidence has shown that adults who enroll in literacy education benefit in terms of enhanced self-esteem.

The social practices perspective, in contrast to the psycholinguistic model, argues that there are multiple literacies, of which school reading is but one. Literacy is largely determined and defined by the social context in which particular literacy abilities may be required, and pure cognitive skill for decoding texts is not a prerequisite to demonstrating literacy proficiency. Literacy may be enacted and demonstrated in multiple ways, in diverse environments, and can be accomplished in a number of ways. Four obvious dimensions of literacy are reading, writing, math (or numeracy), and using technology (which often involves uses the three preceding literacies in various combinations). Reading has been shown to contribute to adults' knowledge acquisition, in terms of world knowledge and vocabulary, and reading activities clearly return positive benefits for adults in school and out. For example, reading books has been shown to have important psychic and intellectual benefits to those who develop lifelong reading habits. Motivation is, of course, a key variable in reading. Reading is frequently a pleasurable activity for adults, which tends to lead to more reading.

Expressive writing, like reading, also appears to have important benefits to emotional health and well-being for adults. Writing has, however, been much less emphasized in school and researchers have not devoted much attention to studying adults' writing skills and practices. Some kinds of writing practices appear to be on the upswing, however, as the Internet has made it possible to easily and quickly express one's ideas in writing and within public forums, such as with the use of weblogs. While writing is required for many kinds of jobs, workers are not always confident in their workplace writing skills.

Despite decades of curricular reforms, the mathematics achievement of U.S. high school students has shown little improvement over the past 30 years. Quantitative literacy skills and the abilities to think about and use numbers (also known as numeracy) are essential in contemporary culture. Yet many adults, perhaps owning to their anxiety about school math, lack confidence in their numeracy skills. The uses of various kinds of technologies for work, play, and managing personal needs, family responsibilities, and social obligations, are deeply embedded in the everyday experiences of most adults. These technology uses represent another type of literacy practice that involves reading, writing, and numeracy.

The available evidence shows that literacy is beneficial to adults in advanced societies and contributes to adults' development in a number of important ways. People who participate in various literacy practices within and across different communities of practice have access to the knowledge and information that is necessary for personal growth and health maintenance, occupational advancement, and the establishment of social networks.

References

Aldrich, P. G. (1979). *Adult writers: Some factors that interfere with effective writing.* ERIC Document No. 209675. Washington, D.C.

Alexander, P. A. (2006). The path to competence: A lifespan developmental perspective on reading. *Journal of Literacy Research, 37*(4), 413–436.

Alexander, P. A. (1997). Mapping the multidimensional nature of domain learning: The interplay of cognitive, motivational, and strategic forces. In M. L. Maehr & P. R. Pintrich (Eds.), *Advances in motivation and achievement* (Vol. 10, pp. 213–250). Greenwich, CT: JAI Press.

Allington, R. (1980). Poor readers don't get to read much in reading groups. *Language Arts, 57*(8), 873–875.

America Online. (2004, August 24). *America Online Inc.'s second annual instant messaging trends survey shows instant messaging has gone mainstream.* Retrieved October 9, 2007, from http://media. aoltimewarner.com/media/newmedia/cb_press_view.cfm?release_num=55254160

Anderson, J. E., & Rudd, R. (2006, November). Navigating healthcare. *Focus on Basics, 8*(C). Retrieved November 8, 2007, from http://www.ncsall.net/?id=1156

Arnbak, E. (2004). When are poor reading skills a threat to educational achievement? *Reading and Writing: An Interdisciplinary Journal, 17,* 459–482.

Bakardjieva, M., & Smith, R. (2001). The Internet in everyday life. *New Media & Society, 3*(1), 67–83.

Baker, L., Serpell, R., & Sonnenschein, S. (1995). Opportunities for literacy learning in the homes of urban preschoolers. In L. M. Morrow (Ed.), *Family literacy: Connections in schools and communities* (pp. 236–252). Newark, DE: International Reading Association.

Baltes, P. B. (1987). Theoretical propositions of life-span developmental psychology: On the dynamics between growth and decline. *Developmental Psychology, 23,* 611–626.

Baron, N. (1998). Letters by phone or speech or other means: The linguistics of email. *Language & Communication, 18,* 133–170.

Barton, D. (1994). *Literacy: An introduction to the ecology of written language.* Oxford, UK: Blackwell.

Barton, D., & Hamilton, M. (1998). *Local literacies: Reading and writing in one community.* London: Routledge.

Barton, D., & Hamilton, M. (2000). Literacy practices. In D. Barton, M. Hamilton, & R. Ivanic (Eds.), *Situated literacies: Reading and writing in context* (pp. 7–15). London: Routledge.

Barton, D., Hamilton, M., & Ivanic, R. (2000). *Situated literacies: Reading and writing in context.* London: Routledge.

Barton, D., & Padmore, S. (1991). Roles, networks, and values in everyday writing. In D. Barton & R. Ivanic (Eds.), *Writing in the community* (pp. 38–57). London: Sage.

Baynham, M. (1995). *Literacy practices: Investigating literacy in social contexts.* London: Longman.

BBC News. (2006, October 10). *Web browsing beats page-turning.* Retrieved October 10, 2006, from http://news.bbc.co.uk/2/hi/business/6034433.stm.

Beder, H. (1999). *The outcomes and impacts of adult literacy education in the United States.* NCSALL Report No. 7. Cambridge, MA: Harvard University: National Center for the Study of Adult Learning and Literacy.

Bereiter, C., & Scardamalia, M. (1987). *The psychology of written composition.* Hillsdale, NJ: Erlbaum.

Birkerts, S. (1994). *The Gutenberg elegies.* Boston: Faber & Faber.

Brandt, D. (2001). *Literacy in American lives.* New York: Cambridge University Press.

Bransford, J. D., & Johnson, M. K. (1972). Contextual prerequisites for understanding: Some investigations of comprehension and recall. *Journal of Verbal Learning & Verbal Behavior, 11,* 717–726.

Bray, B. B., Pascarella, E. T., & Pierson, C. T. (2004). Postsecondary education and some dimensions of literacy development: An exploration of longitudinal evidence. *Reading Research Quarterly, 39*(3), 306–330.

Brewster, C., & Klump, J. (2004, December). *Writing to learn, learning to write: Revisiting writing across the curriculum in northwest secondary schools.* Portland, OR: Northwest Regional Educational Laboratory. Retrieved February 7, 2008, from http://www.nwrel.org/request/2004dec/Writing.pdf

Bus, A. G., van IJzendorn, M. H., & Pelligrini, A. D. (1995). Joint book reading makes for success in learning to read: A meta-analysis of intergenerational transfer of literacy. *Review of Educational Research, 65*, 1–21.

Carver, R. (1977). Toward a theory of reading comprehension and rauding. *Reading Research Quarterly, 13*(1), 10–63, 77–78.

Center for the Future of Teaching & Learning (2005, April). California's approach to math instruction doesn't add up. *CenterView: Insight and analysis on California education policy.* Retrieved October 3, 2007, from http://www.cftl.org/centerviews/april05.html

Chouliaraki, L., & Fairclough, N. (1999). *Discourse in late modernity.* Edinburgh: Edinburgh University Press.

Cipielewski, J., & Stanovich, K.E. (1992). Predicting growth in reading ability from children's exposure to print. *Journal of Experimental Psychology, 51A*, 531–560.

Csikszentmihalyi, M. (1991). *Flow: The psychology of optimal experience.* New York: Harper & Row.

Cuban, S. (2001, August). Reading for pleasure. *Focus on Basics, 5A.* Retrieved September 15, 2006, from http://www.ncsall.net/?id=276.

Cunningham, A. E., & Stanovich, K. E. (1991). Tracking the unique effects of print exposure in children: Associations with vocabulary, general knowledge, and spelling. *Journal of Educational Psychology, 83*, 264–274.

Cunningham, A. E., Stanovich, K. E., & Wilson, M. R. (1993). Cognitive variation in adult college students differing in reading ability. In T. Carr & B. A. Levy (Eds.), *Reading and its development: Component skills approaches* (pp. 129–159). San Diego, CA: Academic Press.

Daneman, M. (1991). Individual differences in reading skills. In R. Barr, M. L. Kamil, P. B. Mosenthal, & P. D. Pearson (Eds.), *Handbook of reading research* (Vol. 2., pp. 512–538). Hillsdale, NJ: Erlbaum.

Davis, T., Arnold, C., Berkel, H., Nancy, I., Jackson, R., & Glass, J. (1996). Knowledge and attitude on screening mammography among low-literate, low-income women. *Cancer, 78*(9), 1912–1920.

Dewey, J. (1895). *Interest in relation to training of the will.* Chicago: University of Chicago Press.

Edwards, A. (2001). Researching pedagogy: A sociocultural agenda. *Pedagogy, Culture & Society, 9*(2), 161–86.

Emery, O. B., & Csikszentmihalyi, M. (1981). The socialization effects of cultural role models in ontogenetic development and upward mobility. *Child Psychiatry and Human Development, 12*(1), 3–18.

Emig, A. G. (1995). Community ties and dependence on media for public affairs. *Journalism & Mass Communication Quarterly, 72*(2), 402–411.

Ericsson, K. A., & Charness, N. (1994). Expert performance: Its structure and acquisition. *American Psychologist, 49*, 725–747.

Faigley, L., & Miller, T. P. (1982). What we learn from writing on the job. *CollegeEnglish, 44*, 557–569.

Fingeret, H., & Drennon, C. (1997). *Literacy for life: Adult learners, new practices.* New York: Teachers College Press.

Fink, R. (1998). Literacy development in successful men and women with dyslexia. *Annals of Dyslexia, 48*, 311–346.

Flower, L. S., & Hayes, J. R. (1984). Images, plans, and prose: The representation of meaning in writing. *Written Communication, 1*, 120–160.

Flower, L. S., & Hayes, J. R. (1977). Problem-solving strategies and the writing process. *College English, 39*, 449–461.

Francis, M. E., & Pennebaker, J. (1992). Putting stress into words: The impact of writing on physiological, absentee, and self-reported emotional well-being measures. *American Journal of Health Promotion, 6*(4), 280–287.

Friedlander, D., & Martinson, K. (1996). Effects of mandatory basic education for adult AFDC recipients. *Educational Evaluation and Policy Analysis, 18*, 327–337.

Gal, I., & Schuh, A. (1995, March). *What counts in adult literacy programs? A National survey of numeracy education.* NCAL Brief No. BP94-08. Philadelphia: National Center on Adult Literacy.

Gordon, E. E., & Gordon, E. H. (2003). *Literacy in America: Historic journey and contemporary solutions.* Westport, CT: Praeger.

Gray, W. S., & Rogers, B. (1956). *Maturity in reading: Its nature and appraisal.* Chicago: University of Chicago Press.

Guthrie, J., & Greaney, V. (1991). Literacy acts. In R. Barr, M. Kamil, P. Mosenthal, & D. Pearson (Eds.), *Handbook of reading research, Vol. 2* (pp. 68–96). New York: Longman.

Guthrie, J. T., & Wigfield, A. (2000). Engagement and motivation in reading. In M. L. Kamil, P. B. Mosenthal, P. D. Pearson, & R. Barr (Eds.), *Handbook of reading research* (Vol. 3, pp. 403–422). Mahwah, NJ: Erlbaum.

Handel, M. J. (2005). *Worker skills and job requirements: Is there a mismatch?* Washington, DC: Economic Policy Institute.

Hart, B., & Risley, T. (1995). *Meaningful differences in the everyday experiences of young American children.* Baltimore: P.H. Brookes.

Heath, S. B. (1984). *Ways with words: Language, life, and work in communities and classrooms.* New York: Cambridge University Press.

Ivask, I. (1990). The letter: A dying art? *World Literature Today, 64*, 213–214.

Kaestle, C. F. (1991). Studying the history of literacy. In C. F. Kaestle, H. Damon-Moore, L. C. Stedman, K. Tinsley, & W. V. Trollinger, Jr. (Eds.), *Literacy in the United States: Readers and reading since 1880* (pp. 3–32). New Haven, CT: Yale University Press.

Kahne, J., Bridge, C. A., & O'Brien, J. (2002). Teacher learning counts: Improving instruction in one urban high school through comprehensive professional development. In V. E. Lee (Ed.), *Reforming Chicago's high schools: Research perspectives on school and system level change.* Chicago: Consortium on Chicago School Research.

Kauvar, E. (1995). *Notes toward editing a contemporary writer's letters. Studies in the Novel, 27.* Retrieved April 27, 2006, from http://www.questia.com/PM.qst?a=o&se=gglsc&d=5001654481

Kellogg, R. T. (1994). *The psychology of writing.* New York: Oxford University Press.

Kintsch, W. (1977). Reading comprehension as a function of text structure. In A. S. Reber & D. L. Scarborough (Eds.), *Toward a psychology of reading.* New York: Wiley.

Kintsch, W. (1988). The role of knowledge in discourse comprehension: A construction-integration model. *Psychological Review, 95*, 163–182.

Kirsch, I. S., & Guthrie, J. T. (1984). Adult reading practices for work and leisure. *Adult Education Quarterly, 34*, 213–232.

Kirsch, I. S., & Jungeblut, A. (1986). *Literacy: Profiles of America's young adults.* Princeton, NJ: Educational Testing Service.

Kirsch, I. S., Jungeblut, A., Jenkins, L., & Kolstad, A. (1993). *Literacy in America: A first look at the results of the National Adult Literacy Survey.* Washington, D.C.: National Center for Education Statistics.

Klein, K., & Boals, A (2001). Expressive writing can increase working memory capacity. *Journal of Experimental Psychology: General, 130*(3), 520–533.

Knobel, M. (1999). *Everyday literacies: Students, discourse, and social practice.* New York: Peter Lang.

Kozol, J. (1985). *Illiterate America.* New York: Penguin.

Krashen, S. (1993). *The power of reading: Insights from the research.* Englewood, CO: Libraries Unlimited.

Landrieu, M. (2006, September 13). Why we need more mathematicians, scientists and engineers to win the global economic battle. *The Hill: The Newspaper For and About the U.S. Congress.* Retrieved September 14, 2006, from http://www.hillnews.com/thehill/export/TheHill/News/Frontpage/091306/special_landrieu.html

Leclerc, M.(2005). *Jacques Demers en toutes lettres* [Jacques Demers from A To Z.]. Canada: Stanke.

Lepore, S., & J. Smyth (2002). *The writing cure: How expressive writing promotes health and emotional well-being.* American Psychological Association: Washington, DC.

Lewis, C. (2001). *Literacy practices as social acts: Power, status, and cultural norms in the classroom.* Mahwah, NJ: Erlbaum.

Linnenbrink, E. A., & Pintrich, P. R. (2003). The role of self-efficacy beliefs in student engagement and learning in the classroom. *Reading and Writing Quarterly, 19*(2), 119–137.

Lundeberg, M. (1987). Metacognitive aspects of reading comprehension: Studying understanding in legal case analysis. *Reading Research Quarterly, 22*(4), 407–432.

Magliano, J. P., & Millis, K. K. (2003). Assessing reading skill with a think-aloud procedure and latent semantic analysis. *Cognition and Instruction, 21*(3), 51–83.

Manjoo, F. (2002, February 18). Blah, blah, blah and blog. *Wired News.* Retrieved April 27, 2006, from http://www.wired.com/news/culture/0,1284,50443,00.html

Marrs, R. W. (1995). A meta-analysis of bibliotherapy studies. *American Journal of Community Psychology, 23*, 843–870.

Mathison, M. A. (1979, April). *Interventions in math anxiety for adults.* Paper presented at the annual meeting of the American Educational Research Association, San Francisco.

Merrifield, J., Bingman, M. B., Hemphill, D., & deMarrais, K. P. B. (1997). *Life at the margins: Literacy, language, and technology in everyday life.* New York: Teachers College Press.

Meyer, B. J. F. (1975). *The organization of prose and its effects on memory. North-Holland studies in theoretical poetics* (Vol. 1). Amsterdam: North-Holland.

Meyer, V., & Keefe, D. (1985). Models of the reading process held by ABE and GED instructors. *Reading Horizons, 25*(2), 133–136.

Moses, R. (2003, September 1). Math as a civil rights issue—Working the demand side. *Harvard Graduate School of Education Newsletter.* Retrieved September 15, 2006, from http://www.gse.harvard.edu/news/features/moses09012003.html

National Assessment of Educational Progress (1970). *The national assessment of writing.* Washington, DC: U.S. Department of Education.

National Center for Education Statistics. (2006). *A first look at the literacy of America's adults in the 21st century.* Washington, DC: Author. Retrieved September 26, 2006, from http://nces.ed.gov/NAAL/PDF/2006470.PDF

National Commission on Writing in America's Schools & Colleges (2003). *The neglected "R": The need for a writing revolution.* New York: The College Board.

National Literacy Act of 1991, Pub. L. No. 102-73, § 3, Stat. 333 (1991). Nation's Report Card (2004). *National Assessment of Educational Progress, selected years, 1973–2004, long-term trend mathematics assessments.* Washington, D.C.: U.S. Department of Education, Institute of Education Sciences, National Center for Education Statistics.

Nell, V. (1988). The psychology of reading for pleasure: Needs and gratifications. Reading *Research Quarterly, 23*, 6–50.

Office of Vocational and Adult Education (1994). *Proceedings: Conference on adult mathematical literacy.* Washington, DC: Author.

Ong, W. (1982). *Orality and literacy: The technologizing of the word.* London: Methuen.

Pennebaker, J. W. (1997). *Opening up: The healing power of expressing emotion.* New York: Guilford.

Pennebaker, J. W., Barger, S. D., & Tiebout, J. (1989). Disclosure of traumas and health among Holocaust survivors. *Psychosomatic Medicine, 51*, 577–589.

Pennebaker, J., & Beale, S. K. (1986). Confronting a traumatic event: Toward an understanding of inhibition and disease. *Journal of Abnormal Psychology, 95*, 274–281.

Pennebaker, J. W., Colder, M., & Sharp, L. K. (1990). Accelerating the coping process. *Journal of Personality and Social Psychology, 58*, 528–537.

Pennebaker, J. W., Kiecolt-Glaser, J., & Glaser, R. (1988). Disclosure of traumas and immune function: Health implications for psychotherapy. *Journal of Consulting and Clinical Psychology, 56*, 239–245.

Pew Research Center for The People and The Press (1999, January 14). *Online newcomers more middle-brow, less work-oriented: The Internet news audience goes ordinary.* Retrieved September 20, 2001, from http://www.people-press.org/content.htm.

Pew Internet & American Life Project. (2006, July 19). *Bloggers: A portrait of the internet's new story-tellers.* Washington, DC: Author. Retrieved July 19, 2006, from http://www.pewinternet.org/PPF/r/186/source/rss/report_display.asp.

Pitts, V. (2004). Illness and internet empowerment: Writing and reading breast cancer in cyberspace. *Heath: An Interdisciplinary Journal for the Social Study of Health, Illness and Medicine, 8*(1), 33–59.

Pont, B., & Werquin, P. (2001, March). How old are new skills? *OECD Observer.* Retrieved July 18, 2006, from http://www.oecdobserver.orog/news/printpage.php/aid/428/how_old_are_new_skills_html

Pressley, M., & Afflerbach, P. (1995). *Verbal protocols of reading: The nature of constructively responsive reading.* Hillsdale, NJ: Erlbaum.

Quigley, B. A. (1997). *Rethinking literacy education: The critical need for practice-based change.* San Francisco: Jossey-Bass.

Rainie, L., & Horrigan, J. (2005, January). *A decade of adoption: How the internet has woven itself into American life.* Washington, DC: Pew Internet & American Life Project.

Reder, S. (1994). Practice engagement theory. In B. M. Ferdman, R.-M. Weber, & A. G. Ramirez (Eds.), *Literacy across languages and cultures* (pp. 33–74). Albany, NY: SUNY-Albany Press.

Reder, S. (1998). Literacy selection and literacy development: Structural equation Model of the reciprocal effects of education and literacy. In M C. Smith (Ed.), *Literacy for the 21st century: Research, policy, practices and the National Adult Literacy Survey* (pp. 139–158). Westport, CT: Praeger.

Reder, S., & Edmonston, B. (2000). *Demographic changes and literacy development in a decade.* NCES Working Paper Series. Washington, DC: National Center for Education Statistics. Retrieved September 15, 2006, from http://www.nces.ed.gov/pubs2000/200009.pdf

Reder, S., & Green, K. R. (1983). Contrasting patterns of literacy in an Alaska fishing village. *International Journal of the Sociology of Language, 42,* 9–39.

Rice, G. E.. (1986). The everyday activities of adults: Implications for prose recall: I. *Educational Gerontology, 12*(2), 173–186.

Risen, C. (2005, July 6). Sincerely yours LOL. *The Morning News.* Retrieved July 19, 2006, from http://www.themorningnews.org/archives/culture/sincerely_yours_lol.php

Rogers, R. (2004). Storied selves: A critical discourse analysis of adult learners' literate lives. *Reading Research Quarterly, 39*(3), 272–305.

Rogoff, B. (1990). *Apprenticeship in thinking: Cognitive development in social context.* New York: Oxford University Press.

Rogoff, B., & Lave, J. (Eds.). (1984). *Everyday cognition: Its development in social context.* Cambridge, MA: Harvard University Press.

Rosen, G. M. (1987). Self-help treatment books and the commercialization of psychotherapy. *American Psychologist, 42*(1), 46–51.

Rudd, R. E. (2002, February). A maturing partnership. *Focus on Basics, 5*(C), 1, 3–8.

Rudd, R. E., Moeykens, B. A., & Colton, T. C. (1999). Health and literacy: A review of medical and public health literature. In J. Comings, B. Garner, & C. Smith (Eds.), *The annual review of adult learning and literacy, Vol. 1* (pp. 158–199). San Francisco: Jossey-Bass.

Sanfey, A. G., & Hastie, R. (2000). Judgment and decision making across the adult life span: A tutorial review of psychological research. In D. C. Park & N. Schwarz (Eds.), *Cognitive aging: A primer* (pp. 253–273). New York: Psychology Press.

Schaie, K. W. (1994). The course of adult intellectual development. *American Psychologist, 49,* 484–493.

Schiefele, U. (1991). Interest, learning, and motivation. *Educational Psychologist, 26*(3–4), 299–323.

Schmitt, M. J. (2000, September). Developing adults' numerate thinking: Getting out from under the workbooks. *Focus on Basics, 4*(B). Retrieved October 18, 2001, from http://gseweb.harvard.edu/~ncsall/fob/2000/schmitt.html.

Schraw, G., & Bruning, R. (1999). How implicit models of reading affect motivation to read and reading engagement. *Scientific Studies of Reading, 3,* 281–302.

Scribner, S., & Cole, M. (1981). *The psychology of literacy*. Cambridge, MA: Harvard University Press.

Sheehan-Holt, J. K., & Smith, M C. (2000). Does basic skills education affect adults' literacy proficiencies and reading practices? *Reading Research Quarterly, 35*(2), 226–243.

Sheridan, D., Street, B. V., & Bloome, D. (2000). *Writing ourselves: Mass-observation and literacy practices*. Cresskill, NY: Hampton Press.

Singer, H., & Donlan, D. (1989). *Reading and learning from text* (2nd ed.). Hillsdale, NJ: Erlbaum.

Smith, MC. (2000). What will be the demands of literacy in the workplace in the next millennium? *Reading Research Quarterly, 35*(3), 378–379.

Smith, MC. (1996). Adults' reading practices and literacy proficiencies. *Reading Research Quarterly, 32*, 196–219.

Smith, MC., & Locke, S. (1999). From GED to college: Perspectives, practices and goals of GED students and GED recipients. *Research & Teaching in Developmental Education, 16*(1), 49–56.

Smith, MC., Locke, S. G., Boisse, S. J., Gallagher, P. A., Krengel, L. E., Kuczek, J. E., McFarland, J. E., Rapoo, B., & Wertheim, C. (1998). Productivity of educational psychologists in educational psychology journals, 1991–1996. *Contemporary Educational Psychology, 23*, 173–181.

Smyth, J. M., Stone, A. A., Hurewitz, M. D., & Kaell, A. (1999). Effects of writing about stressful experiences on symptom reduction in patients with asthma or rheumatoid arthritis: A randomized trial. *Journal of the American Medical Association, 281*, 1304–1309.

Stamm, K. R., & Fortini-Campbell, L. (1983). The relationship of community ties to newspaper use. *Journalism Monographs, 84*, 1–27.

Stanovich, K. E. (1986). Matthew effects in reading: Some consequences of individual differences in the acquisition of literacy. *Reading Research Quarterly, 21*, 360–407.

Stanovich, K. E. (1993). Does reading make you smarter? Literacy and the development of verbal intelligence. In H. Reese (Ed.), *Advances in child development and behavior, Vol. 24* (pp. 133–180). San Diego, CA: Academic Press.

Stanovich, K. E. (2000). *Progress in understanding reading: Scientific foundations and new frontiers*. New York: Guilford.

Stanovich, K. E., & Cunningham, A. E. (1992). Studying the consequences of literacy within a literate society: The cognitive correlates of print exposure. *Memory & Cognition, 20*, 51–68.

Stanovich, K. E., & Cunningham, A. E. (1993). Where does knowledge come from? Specific associations between print exposure and information acquisition. *Journal of Educational Psychology, 85*, 211–229.

Stanovich, K. E., Cunningham, A. E., & West, R. F. (1998). Literacy experiences and the shaping of cognition. In S. Paris & H. Wellman (Eds.), *Global prospects for education: Development, culture, and schooling* (pp. 253–288). Washington, DC: American Psychological Association.

Stanovich, K. E., West, R. F., & Harrison, M. (1995). Knowledge growth and maintenance across the life span: The role of print exposure. *Developmental Psychology, 31*, 811–826.

Sticht, T. G. (2002). *The "scientific" understanding of reading and the "reading potential" of adults assessed by measuring listening and reading abilities*. Retrieved June 1, 2006, from http://www.nald.ca/library/research/sticht/feb02/page1.htm

Sticht, T. G. (1975). *Reading for working*. Alexandria, VA: HumRRO.

Sticht, T. G. (1999, March). *How many low literate adults are there in Canada, the United States, and United Kingdom? Should the IALS estimates be revised?* Retrieved June 1, 2007, from http://www.nald.ca/library/research/sticht/resnote.htm

Sticht, T. G. (2001). The International Adult Literacy Survey: How well does it represent the literacy of adults? *The Canadian Journal for the Study of Adult Education, 15*, 19–36.

Sticht, T. G., & Armstrong, W. B. (1994). *Adult literacy in the United States: A compendium of quantitative data and interpretive comments*. San Diego, CA: San Diego Community College District.

Street, B. (1984). *Literacy in theory and practice*. Cambridge, UK: Cambridge University Press.

Teale, W., & Sulzby, E.. (1986). *Emergent literacy: Writing and reading*. Norwood, NJ: Ablex.

Thimmesch, N. (1984). *Aliteracy: People who can read but won't*. New York: AEI Press.

Tobias, S. (1993). *Overcoming math anxiety*. New York: W. W. Norton.

U.S. Census Bureau. (2005, October). *Computer and internet use in the United States: 2003.* Washington, DC: Author.

U.S. Census Bureau (2000, March). *Educational attainment in the United States (update): Population characteristics.* Washington, DC: Author.

U.S. Department of Commerce (1999, October 14). *Computer use up sharply; one in five Americans uses Internet, Census Bureau says* [Press release]. Washington, D.C.: U.S. Census Bureau. Retrieved October 20, 2000, from http://www.census.gov/.

U.S. Department of Education (2006). *National household education surveys program of 2005: Adult education participation in 2004–05.* Washington, DC: National Center for Education Statistics.

U.S. Department of Education (2002). *The nation's report card: Writing highlights 2002.* NCES 2003-531. Washington, DC: National Center for Education Statistics.

U.S. Department of Labor (1991). *The secretary's commission on achieving necessary skills.* Washington, DC: Author.

Venezky, R. L., Kaplan, D., & Yu, F. (1998, August). *Literacy practices and voting behavior: An analysis of the 1992 National Adult Literacy Survey.* Washington, DC: National Center for Education Statistics.

Venezky, R. L., Wagner, D. A., & Ciliberti, B. S. (1991). *Toward defining literacy.* Newark, DE: International Reading Association.

Waples, D. (1938). *People and print: Social effects of reading in the Depression.* Chicago: University of Chicago Press.

West, R. F., Stanovich, K. E., & Mitchell, H. R. (1993). Reading in the real world and its correlates. *Reading Research Quarterly, 28,* 34–50.

Wigfield, A., & Guthrie, J. T. (1995). *Dimensions of children's motivations for reading: An initial study* (Reading Research Report No. 34). Athens, GA: National Reading Research Center.

Wigfield, A., & Guthrie, J. T. (1997). Relations of children's motivation for reading to the amount and breadth of their reading. *Journal of Educational Psychology, 89,* 420–432.

Withnall, A. (1995). *Older adults' needs and usage of numerical skills in everyday life.* Lancaster, UK: Lancaster University.

Ziegler, M. F ., Bain, S. K., Bell, S. M., McCallum, R. S., & Brian, D. J. G. (2006). Predicting women's persistence in adult literacy classes with dispositional variables. *Reading Psychology, 27*(1), 59–85.

Chapter 22

Service-Learning, Civic and Community Participation

Contributions to Adult Development

Susan R. Jones and Anna Gasiorski

The picture portrayed of "bowling alone" in Robert Putnam's (2000) oft-cited book spurred national dialogue about an isolated and disengaged populace who would rather engage in solitary activity than participate in community activities. The rhetoric of "bowling alone" was tempered by national legislation and programs to promote active participation in volunteering and civic engagement (e.g., Points of Light, Corporation for National Service, Teach for America, Freedom Corps). Indeed, recent data from the Independent Sector (2001) suggested that 44% of all adults in the U.S. volunteer, contributing a total value of $280 billion in volunteer hours (Independent Sector, 2005). The Bureau of Labor Statistics (2006) reported that 65.4 million people volunteered for a community organization at least once in 2004–2005, which represents 28.8% of the population. However, how these statistics, inferring civic participation, translate into adult development and learning, or what outcomes are promoted for individuals and communities from such participation, is less clear.

The research on the relationships between service-learning, community involvement and civic participation among adults is disparate and diffuse, thus making a holistic picture difficult to ascertain. Few would argue against the importance of adults leading lives of civic and community participation and indeed, some would suggest this activity is vital to maintaining and supporting a democratic society (Barber 1984; Boyte & Kari, 2000). Further, civic participation, community involvement, and volunteerism all provide ways in which adults may engage in generative activities that promote contributions to communities as well as personal development and learning. However, great diversity exists in perceptions about government sponsored incentives for public service, motivations to serve, influences on community and civic participation, and outcomes associated with community involvement (Dionne & Meltzer Drogosz, 2003). Nonetheless, growing evidence supports the prevailing rhetoric of civic participation contributing to a public good, documents the developmental and personal outcomes associated with civic and community participation, identifies the influences on civic engagement, and outlines the economic, social and political implications of service in the adult years.

One of the challenges in examining adult development and patterns of service-learning and civic and community participation is the overlapping yet distinctive meanings in these terms and how they are used. As interest in discussions about an engaged populace increases, a myriad of terms are being used interchangeably in both public discourse and the scholarly literature. These terms include: volunteering, community service, service-learning, citizenship, civic engagement, civic participation, civic development, civic learning, and community involvement. Although overlapping along some dimensions and complementary in vision and values, important distinctions exist. Both methodological and philosophical issues emerge when using terms interchangeably which make any definitive statements about adult development and civic participation difficult to assert.

For example, much of the research situated in the service-learning literature base includes "studies of community service, field education, youth service, and community service learning programs" (Furco, 2003, p. 14). Similarly, discussion of community service appears both in the literature on service-learning (e.g., "There is broad based agreement that service-learning is a form of the broader model of experiential education, with community service as the fulcrum," Howard, 2003, p. 2) and volunteering (e.g., performing service of one's own free will, doing charitable work without pay, and contributing to a common good, Safrit & Merrill, 1996). Civic participation is often identified as a central element and outcome of service-learning (e.g., Barber, 1992, Eyler & Giles, 1999; Howard, 1998) and implies active involvement in socially responsible ways in the life of a larger community, which can also be accomplished in other than formalized service-learning programs. Civic participation is frequently tied to discussion of community engagement, citizenship development, and democratic values, goals and behaviors (Boyte & Kari, 2000). A common thread in the literature is an emphasis on the need to cultivate the skills and habits of civic life and that community involvement, often through community service, is a cornerstone of civic engagement and participation. Colby, Ehrlich, Beaumont, and Stephens (2003) offered one description of a civically involved individual:

> In general terms, we believe that a morally and civically responsible individual recognizes himself or herself as a member of a larger social fabric and therefore considers social problems to be at least partly his or her own; such an individual is willing to see the moral and civic dimensions of issues, to make and justify informed moral and civic judgments, and to take action when appropriate. A fully developed individual must have the ability to think clearly and in an appropriately complex and sophisticated way about moral and civic issues; he or she must possess the moral commitment and sense of personal responsibility to act, which may include having moral emotions such as empathy and concern for others; moral and civic values, interests, and habits; and knowledge and experience in relevant domains of life. (pp. 17–18)

Also relevant to any discussion of civic engagement is political participation, which incorporates central components of leading a civically responsible life such as voting, holding public office, and representing the interests of "the people." Political participation is defined by Verba, Schlozman, and Brady (1995) as "activity that has the intent or effect of influencing government action—either directly by affecting the making or implementation of public policy or indirectly by influencing the selection of people who make those policies" (p. 38). The Civic Voluntarism Model, created from their research on political participation, provides a framework for understanding political participation by focusing on "the *motivation* and *capacity* to take part in political life" (p. 3, italics in original).

For the purposes of this chapter, our primary focus is on general patterns of civic participation and adult development. We use the term *civic participation* to integrate key elements of other terms such as civic learning, service-learning, citizenship development, political participation, and social responsibility. While we recognize that points of departure exist in the definition and understanding of these terms, civic participation captures important features of each such as service, community involvement, volunteerism, political participation, and action toward a greater good. It incorporates a focus on the *civic*, which emphasizes concern for community and public good, and *participation*, which suggests action and commitment directed toward that concern. In those instances where the research is specific about one form or another of civic participation, (e.g., volunteerism, service-learning), we will make this focus explicit. Because an entire body of scholarship on political participation exists, it is beyond the scope of this chapter to delve into this area; however, we do want to acknowledge that political participation is perceived by some as an integral component of civic engagement.

In this chapter, we synthesize literature and research to provide a snapshot of societal, definitional, educational, psychological, and developmental influences on civic participation and adult development. We also discuss the significant contexts in which civic participation and involvement take place for adults, such as the workplace, religious affiliations, political activity, grassroots activism focused on specific issues, and community service. We conclude by identifying future issues for research, teaching, and practice.

Societal Context for Civic Participation

Civic participation in the United States has long been heralded as central to democratic ideals and practices. Oft-cited as one of the first observers of this tradition, Alexis de Tocqueville (1835/1966) wrote: "Americans of all ages, all stations in life, and all types of dispositions are forever forming associations" (p. 485). Dionne and Meltzer Drogosz (2003) pointed out, "Our public rhetoric has always laid heavy stress on the obligations of citizenship" (p. 23). Irrespective of political party, national leaders encouraged, supported, and even mandated service and greater attention to civic responsibilities. This resulted in more active involvement in community concerns. Heightened interest in service and civic responsibility and community mobilization around issues of concern has been prompted by national and international tragedies such as September 11th, 2001, the tsunami in Southeast Asia, the Pakistani earthquake, and Hurricane Katrina as well as large scale national scandals such as Enron and the charges against Washington, D.C. lobbyist Jack Abramoff, for bribery and embezzlement. According to Dionne and Meltzer Drogosz (2003) in a provocatively written essay entitled *United We Serve: The Debate over National Service*:

> Underlying the debate over national service is an argument over whether service is necessary or merely "nice." If service is just a nice thing to do, it's easy to understand why critics...express such strong reservations about government-led service programs. But is it possible that service is something more than nice? What if it is...a means to strengthen the ties that bind us as a nation? What if it creates bridges across groups in our society that have little to do with each other on any given day.... What if it fosters civic and political participation in a society that seems not to hold the arts of public life in the highest esteem? In sum, what if service is not simply a good in itself, but a means to many ends? (p. 25)

Any understanding of adult development and civic participation must be understood within the larger societal context which provides multiple and conflicting perspectives on the purpose, role, and effectiveness of service.

Presidential Mandates for Service

Presidential administrations, although often disagreeing over the purpose and goals of civic participation, have consistently encouraged service and suggested the connection between civic engagement and the overall health of the nation. Presidential mandates, and the resulting priority given community participation in the federal government, have created a national context for service. Since President Kennedy introduced the Peace Corps in the 1960s, successive presidents continued to sound the call to service. This call has grown even louder in the last 20 years as national leaders and pundits identified the loosening of the tight-knit fabric in communities. In his inaugural address in 1989, President George H. W. Bush reinforced his "thousand points of light" program and his commitment to the development of community organizations and civic participation.

In 1994, President Clinton continued the trend by signing legislation that created the Corporation for National and Community Service (CNCS, n.d.) which includes national programs dedicated to recruiting more people to participate in community service programs. President Clinton's action to consolidate a number of disparate programs was a continuation of the work begun by President George H.W. Bush. The CNCS currently includes Senior Corps, Americorps, and Learn and Serve America. Senior Corps is made up of three different programs through which more than 500,000 senior citizens volunteer. Americorps provides opportunities for more than 70,000 people of all ages to participate in "intensive" service programs like Teach for America and Volunteers in Service to America (VISTA). Finally, Learn and Serve America provides support to K-12 schools, higher education institutions, and community organizations to encourage and develop service-learning programs (CNCS, n.d.).

Even after another change in administration in 2000, the federal government continued to encourage civic participation. President George W. Bush stated that "faith-based and other community organizations are indispensable in meeting the needs of poor Americans and distressed neighborhoods" (Brooks, 2005, p. 2). In 2002, in his "call to service," President George W. Bush called on Americans to spend the equivalent of two years of their lives (4,000 hours) dedicated to community service (CNCS, n.d.). He created the USA Freedom Corps to recognize and to continue the overwhelming service participation that started in response to the tragic events that took place on September 11, 2001. Bush also started the Students in Service to America (SISTA) program to encourage young adults to participate in service. The emphasis on national programs, as well as growth in other local and regional volunteer opportunities, led to an unprecedented number of 64.5 million Americans engaged in volunteer work in 2004, an increase of 5 million people from the same period two years before (Bureau of Labor Statistics, 2006). This record rate of volunteerism may be interpreted as a response to the collective national push for service.

However effective the push toward community service, political participation, and volunteerism coming from the federal government, recent research noted a "scissor effect" between community service and political participation, particularly among college students (Longo & Meyer, 2006; Sax et al., 2003). This phenomenon refers to the inverse relationship between community service and political participation, such that college students did not perceive the political dimensions of community service.

Demographics and Politics of Service Participation

Examining volunteer demographics provides a clearer picture of who is committing time to civic participation. Among different age groups, those between ages 35 and 44 were most likely to volunteer. Women volunteer at a higher rate than men, and volunteers spend, on average, 52 hours per year involved in volunteer work (Bureau of Labor Statistics, 2006). Of all those who reported serving as volunteers, 34.4% of them volunteer through religious organizations and 27% volunteer through educational and youth services organizations. Forty percent of individuals who reported being involved in community service activities became involved of their own initiative while 42% were responding to an invitation by an organization to become a volunteer (Bureau of Labor Statistics, 2006).

The contexts through which individuals volunteer and individual goals for civic participation vary significantly. One trend in civic participation is that individuals, and particularly students, are more engaged and drawn toward community service to "help others," rather than to participate in social or political activism (Astin, Oseguera, Sax, & Korn, 2002; Coles, 1993; Kahne & Westheimer, 1996). Participation in community service activities has continued to increase even as interest in social and political participation decreased (Longo & Meyer, 2006; Putnam, 2000). As a result, the ways in which individuals are engaging civically is more synonymous with community service and less with political participation, advocacy, and activism. However, a recent study measuring America's Civic Health Index reported a resurgence from the decline in the 1990s of voting and other forms of political participation (Center for Information and Research on Civic Learning and Engagement [CIRCLE] & Saguaro Seminar, 2006). A longitudinal study examining civic engagement across time and generations suggested significant differences between Generation X members, who are lagging behind, and their Baby Boomer predecessors (Jennings & Stoker, 2004).

Although on the surface, these rates of participation appear as a positive response to a societal context pushing the value of civic engagement and volunteerism. However, some perceive volunteerism and service as only a temporary solution to the larger problem of decreasing support for social services. Federal support for social services has been decreasing in the United States at the same time that the number of people living in poverty and the need for social services is increasing (Densmore, 2000). This creates an imbalance and national and local leaders have invoked the rhetoric of civic and community participation as a way to resolve pressing social problems. Individuals who participate in community service programs provide an invaluable service to others that is filling a gap created by shrinking resources allocated to social service. With an estimated 44% of all adults volunteering, an enormous financial contribution is made by such participation (and savings to federal support of social and human services). However, it is also clear that the privilege of volunteering is only available to those with the time and resources to do so, thus potentially widening the gap between those who serve and those who receive. Thus, the politics of service become clear as "citizenship requires that individuals work to create, evaluate, criticize, and change public institutions and programs. And such action is unavoidably political" (Westheimer & Kahne, 1999, p. 34).

The national push for service and civic participation, and the variety of responses to this push, is integrally related to the way in which service is constructed in the literature. A variety of competing discourses surrounding service and civic participation exist, which influence what is known and how these constructs are researched.

Discourses of Civic Participation

Although definitions of community engagement, service-learning, citizenship, and civic participation may be found in the literature, competing discourses about the meaning of these terms exist and ultimately influence research and practice focused on these activities and goals. However, while "everyone now seems to believe that citizenship is important" (Westheimer & Kahne, 2003, p. 1), consensus about what it means to be a "good citizen" cannot be presumed. It does appear that what it means to act in a socially responsible way in today's world is increasingly complex. In their study of 100 adults who were leading lives of commitment to the common good, Parks Daloz, Keen, Keen, and Daloz Parks (1996) described the challenges of civic participation as "being thrust into a larger sphere of responsibility, one calling for a keener recognition of the diversity, complexity, and ambiguity that have become the warp and woof of the common life we all share" (p. 3).

In most cases, what constitutes citizenship is quickly connected to promoting a democratic society. Westheimer and Kahne (2003) further illuminated the competing ideas about citizenship:

> For some, a commitment to democracy is a promise to protect liberal notions of freedom, while for others democracy is primarily about equality or equality of opportunity. For some, civil society is key, while for others, free markets are the great hope for a democratic society. For some, good citizens in a democracy volunteer, while for others they take active parts in political processes by voting, protesting, and working on political campaigns. (p. 2)

Based upon their results from a two-year study of ten programs in the United States, each with an intended goal to promote the democratic purposes of education, Westheimer and Kahne (2004) developed three conceptualizations of citizenship: the personally responsible citizen, the participatory citizen, and the justice-oriented citizen. Each of these conceptualizations reflects differential goals and motivations (e.g., moral, political, intellectual), strategies or ways in which an individual participates in the community (e.g., direct or indirect service, advocacy and investment in changing social structures), and outcomes associated with involvement (e.g., character building, charity or social change) (Kahne & Westheimer, 1996; Westheimer & Kahne, 2004). Applying this model to community participation in a food drive, Westheimer and Kahne noted that the personally responsible citizen would contribute food, the participatory citizen would help organize the food drive, and the justice-oriented citizen would actively work toward elimination of hunger (p. 240).

This template is useful when examining adult development and civic participation because it helps locate individual motivations and goals for civic involvement as well as those of sponsoring organizations, government initiatives, and educational programs. Ironically, Westheimer and Kahne (2004) found that although the conception of the personally responsible citizen receives the most attention (and programs supporting this conceptualization are well funded), it is least robust in reflecting the necessary collective and systemic dimensions of citizenship and civic participation. Programs such as the Points of Light Foundation, Freedom Corps, and high school graduation requirements that include community service are all examples of high profile, well-endorsed service initiatives that emphasize personal obligations to "help others" and care for the "underprivileged" without ever linking these volunteer efforts to larger social issues, the political process, and social change. A recent example of this phenomenon occurred when a group of Latino Boy Scouts hoping to earn their "citizenship in the community" merit badge by participating in a demonstration on immigration legislation were warned that their presence was a violation of the Boy Scout's organization's policy (*Washington Post*, April 16, 2006).

The terms *civic participation* and *community involvement* are often used when describing community service and service-learning initiatives. As Saltmarsh (2005) noted, "Civic engagement pursued through teaching and learning found kinship in the pedagogy of service-learning" (p. 52). Service-learning has been defined as a pedagogy, philosophy, and program (Jacoby & Associates 1996) that incorporates active learning grounded in community based experiences, an emphasis on responding to real community needs and issues that have been determined by the community itself, and intentionally designed reflection that connects learning with service. Responding to the need to address the complexities involved in service-learning work, Butin (2005) conceptualized service-learning as a "culturally saturated, socially consequential, politically contested, and existentially defining experience" (p. x). By this he suggested that service-learning reflects normative cultural processes, carries the potential for impact on individuals and communities, is fundamentally about power relations, and forces all participants to take a stance rather than remain neutral in the face of complex social issues.

Discourse surrounding community service, service-learning, and volunteering is sometimes used interchangeably and other times intentionally chosen to portray a certain philosophy or defining characteristic (e.g., the centrality of reflection in service-learning). Political implications can shape the language that certain individuals and programs use. For example, volunteering is typically considered a more conservative word based on the idea that individuals on the local level can solve their own problems without addressing systemic injustices (Densmore, 2000). By definition, volunteering eliminates the possibility that someone will be reimbursed for their service, whereas some community service activities come with remuneration (e.g., the federally funded work study program America Reads America Counts pays college students for community service work). Community service also carries different connotations, such as an association with forced community service as restitution for a violation of policy or the law.

The service-learning and community service movements, as forms of civic participation requiring community involvement, have been critiqued as primarily the activities of White, privileged, and educated individuals providing *service to* those less privileged and underserved. Nieto (2000) captured this dynamic well:

> The term *charity* always bothered me because it implies a detached beneficence that comes from privilege. Civic obligation is missing in charity work. Similarly, there is no sense of civic responsibility in some conceptions of community service learning. *Community service*: the very phrase conjures up images of doing good deeds in impoverished (primarily Black and Brown) communities by those (mostly White people) who are wealthier and more privileged. (p. ix)

Further, as Stukas and Dunlap (2002) pointed out, the research on community involvement typically focuses on the individuals performing community service, rather than on the communities in which such service takes place. However, individuals and communities both stand to gain from community involvement. Understanding community involvement requires a conception of community as both a place and set of relationships (Saltmarsh, 1998) or as Stukas and Dunlap suggested as "territorial" and "relational" (p. 413). Active involvement in community then may be:

> conceived of as virtually identical to the types of unpaid work activities traditionally engaged in by volunteers, but may also involve civic participation such as working with nonprofit organizations, serving on community boards and committees, or organizing block clubs....expanding the definition of community involvement to encompass acts that go beyond those traditionally performed by volunteers brings

elements of the social structure surrounding such acts of community involvement to the foreground of discussion. (p. 414)

Of note is a social class analysis of the kinds of community involvement and civic participation to which individuals are drawn, which ultimately serves to reinforce the social and economic barriers community service and service-learning programs are intended to penetrate. As Mosle (2003) persuasively argued,

> Most volunteers are concentrated in affluent suburbs far from the blighted urban neighborhoods, where their assistance is needed more…time and money tend to stay in a donor's immediate social—and economic—world. When people talk about giving, they are often talking about contributions to institutions, like the Metropolitan Museum of Art or the New York City Opera that confer prestige on the donor and improve the quality of life primarily for the middle class. (p. 31)

Returning to Putnam's (2000) *Bowling Alone,* the idea of social capital and its importance to a community is relevant to a discussion of competing discourses of civic participation and service. Social capital consists of "the networks, norms, and social trust that facilitate coordination and cooperation for mutual benefit" (Putnam, 1995, p. 67), and is measured by community participation and political engagement (Smith, 2001). Putnam's (2000) argument was that America's social capital was in decline as evidenced by decreasing forms of civic engagement and political participation. Voluminous data was collected and supported his thesis in which he argued persuasively that the American community was in trouble.

Challenges to Putnam's theory have surfaced and take issue with his conclusion that American social capital is declining. For example, Lenkowsky (2000) argued that

> ebbs and flows in organizational membership should be seen as stemming not from any broad disaffection with civic groups or public life per se but from uncertainty about how best to work together during changing times. The very concern sparked by Putnam's lament was itself…a sign of America's still abundant supply of social capital. (p. 58)

However, others suggested that it is hard to argue with the copious data Putnam (2000) collected demonstrating that individuals were less interested in joining clubs, civic and religious organizations or participating in any political activities including voting. This pattern is concerning because the existence of social capital is associated with safer, more economically prosperous, better educated, and healthier communities (Smith, 2001).

Social capital is also deeply entwined with cultural capital which Bourdieu (1977) described as "society's symbolic resources in religion, philosophy, art, and science" (p. 187). Cultural capital includes an individual's academic qualifications, or as Bourdieu stated, "Academic qualifications are to cultural capital what money is to economic capital" (p. 187). The amount of cultural capital available to an individual is determined by race, class, language, and citizenship status and also influences how individuals are either accepted or rebuffed as participants in civic activities (Martinez-Cosio, 2004). Bourdieu's cultural capital theory makes it clear that cultural knowledge is not transparent for all individuals and that universal inclusiveness in civic activities is a myth. As Martinez-Cosio noted, "The civic engagement rules are not known to all participants," (p. 4) and cultural capital accrues fastest to those who already have it. Social and cultural capital then may be seen as determining factors in who is most commonly involved in civic activities and how those activities are defined.

What is important to the case we are making in regard to adult development and civic and community participation is recognition of the competing conceptualizations of citizenship and what a civically engaged adult looks like exist. The prevailing discourse of civic participation privileges service and volunteerism that is accessed more readily by some adults, occupying certain positions in society. Using a cultural capital analysis, it becomes clear that some adults are better equipped as those providing service and others as those receiving—thus bolstering the discourse of charity, being nice, and personally responsible citizenship. Both the societal and national contexts for civic participation, as well as competing discourses of service and citizenship, provide the larger landscape in which adult development and civic participation may be understood and the influences on such participation.

Influences on Civic Participation

Having described the larger societal, national, and discourse landscape in which civic participation is researched, understood, and practiced, we now turn to a discussion of influences on civic participation. A review of the literature on civic engagement, civic participation, volunteerism, and community service in the context of adult participation and development suggested the significance of educational, developmental, psychological, and contextual factors. That is, civic participation is influenced by—and influences—a myriad of factors including one's educational experiences and attainment, identity development across several developmental domains, individual personality characteristics and motivations, and the contexts in which civic participation is encouraged and supported.

Educational Influences

One of the primary pathways to adult development and civic participation is through education. We do not mean to suggest that the only means to civic involvement is through formal education or that all those who are engaged civically are college educated. Indeed, civic participation can be cultivated through venues such as continuing education classes and community based courses and activities. Although the research results are mixed, the preponderance of the existing evidence suggests that educational attainment does influence civic participation. From their meta-analysis of the research on how college affects students, Pascarella and Terenzini (2005) concluded:

> The considerable variety in the forms of community service and the varying nature of the samples make it difficult to develop precise estimates, but our analyses suggest that individuals with a bachelor's degree or higher are, on average, perhaps 30 percentage points more likely than those with no postsecondary education to volunteer for a community service group....With few exceptions...the association between educational level and community service is positive, linear, and consistent. (p. 278)

Our focus here on educational influences is included also because a growing body of evidence does suggest that if individuals cultivate the habit of civic involvement during the college years, the pattern may then continue into their adult, post-college years.

The mission of many institutions of higher education includes language about the development of citizenship and the preparation of future leaders in a democratic society. Recent reform literature in higher education emphasizes both the importance of an "engaged institution" and the need to educate students for socially responsible leadership after graduation (Boyte & Kari, 2000; Campus Compact, 1999; Colby, Ehrlich, Beaumont, & Stephens, 2003; Kellogg Commission on the Future of State and Land-Grant Universities, 1999). Further, documents identifying "hallmarks of a college educated person" (Student Learning Imperative, 1994), learning outcomes for students (Greater Expectations, 2002), and the characteristics of a transformative education (Learning Reconsidered, 2004) include an emphasis on civic responsibility, preparation for participation in the democratic process, and citizenship. As noted in Learning Reconsidered (2004): "Our society expects colleges and universities to graduate students who can get things done in the world and are prepared for effective and engaged citizenship" (p. 3).

Many colleges and universities are responding to these calls for engagement and civic responsibility by becoming more intentional in educating for citizenship (Colby, Ehrlich, Beaumont, & Stephens, 2003; Kezar, Chambers, & Burkhardt, 2005; Musil, 2003). Capturing this momentum, London (2001) wrote:

> A new movement is taking shape in American higher education, one aimed at educating for democracy, nurturing community, and promoting civic participation. Across the country, colleges, universities, and academic associations are striving to make civic engagement an integral part of the way they do their work. (p. 45)

This "movement" is anchored by Ernest Boyer's (1990) conceptualization of a "scholarship of engagement" and his clarion call to universities to become more vigorous in their pursuits to address the most pressing problems of our times. Here he evoked this purpose:

> Increasingly, I am convinced that ultimately, the scholarship of engagement also means creating a special climate in which the academic and civic cultures communicate more continuously and more creatively with each other, helping to enlarge what anthropologist Clifford Geertz describes as the universe of human discourse and enriching the quality of life for all of us. (pp. 19–20)

The movement is also buoyed by economic, civic, and demographic realities that call upon institutions of higher education to be more involved in their local communities, more connected to complex social issues (and their resolution), and responding effectively to diverse student populations (Musil, 2003). However, as noted by Zlotkowski (2000) "…the new developments coming to the forefront may very well make civic responsibility and citizenship skills less foreign to higher education's agenda but they do not by any means guarantee that change—even educationally progressive change—will lead to significant civic results" (p. 318).

This renewed commitment to engaging their civic missions has also resulted in specific curricular and programmatic efforts on the part of colleges and universities to cultivate the development of citizenship. These efforts include service-learning courses, community service programs, and diverse democracies projects to name a few among a burgeoning list. A growing body of research documents the positive outcomes associated with these initiatives, including an increased commitment to helping others, developing efficacy related to making a difference in the world, and developing skills of citizenship (e.g., Astin & Sax, 1998; Eyler & Giles, 1999; Gray, Ondaatje, Fricker, & Geschwind, 2000;

Jones & Hill, 2001; Sax, 2000; Vogelgesang & Astin, 2000). Indeed, Pascarella and Terenzini (2005) summarized:

> Even when previous volunteer community service experience and other self-selection factors are accounted for, however, with few exceptions, the weight of the evidence indicates that participation in community service activities has statistically significant and, in some studies, substantial positive effects on a wide array of civic values and activities. The operational forms these concepts take vary, but the relation between community service and civic and community-oriented or "other-oriented" attitudes and values is clear. (pp. 307–308)

Although research has documented that any form of community service produces positive effects on students' civic attitudes, values, and participation (Pascarella & Terenzini, 2005), the outcomes associated with service-learning are strongest, including plans to continue service and civic participation in the future (Vogelgesang & Astin, 2000). In their study comparing the effects of community service and service-learning, Vogelgesang and Astin (2000) found that students participating in community service and service-learning were more likely than those students who did not participate to indicate they were planning for a service-related career; and those students participating in service-learning were significantly more likely.

Of course for the purposes of a discussion on service-learning and civic participation among adults, the question of whether or not college graduates continue their involvement in the community is of utmost importance. Several studies have examined college students' *intentions* to continue service (e.g., Astin & Sax, 1998; Vogelgesang & Astin, 2000), but very few studies follow students beyond their college years into their adult life to explore the longer term influences of community service. We highlight the three studies located that did just that (Astin, Sax, & Avalos, 1999; Jones & Abes, 2004; Vogelgesang & Astin, 2005).

Using data from the Cooperative Institutional Research Program (CIRP), Astin, Sax, and Avalos (1999) surveyed past participants nine years after the first administration during their first year in college. The independent variable used was a measure of time spent each week in volunteer work. Dependent variables included 18 outcome measures. Results indicated that "the habit of volunteering persists over a relatively long period of time" (p. 196). More specifically, 13 of the 18 outcomes measures demonstrated significant effects from service participation during the college years, including helping others in difficulty, socializing with persons from different racial/ethnic groups, participating in service after college, and attending graduate school.

In a constructivist study of students two-four years after their participation in a service-learning course, Jones and Abes (2004) discovered a shift in the nature of commitments, including career plans and aspirations, among their participants. They noted a growing sense of efficacy which resulted in commitments to socially responsible work. Every participant described a shift in career goals and plans as a result of service-learning experiences. For example, one participant in medical school, mentioned that she had included a quote she had read in service-learning class on her medical school applications ("Service is the rent we pay for living," from Marian Wright Edelman, 1992) and that her goals had changed from becoming a private practice physician to working with the Peace Corps as a doctor or with the organization Doctors Without Borders. She explained:

[The service-learning course] definitely influenced my career choice and where I see myself going in my life, and what's important to me, and what I feel I need to accomplish within a day, a week, a year, whatever, in my life. I think it definitely put my goals in perspective. (Jones & Abes, 2004, p. 157)

Other enduring influences identified in this study were the construction of a more integrated identity as evidenced by complexity in thinking about self and relationships with others and openness to new ideas and experiences. Participants also spoke about how the service-learning courses continued to influence their attitudes, values, decision making, and actions (Jones & Abes, 2004).

Drawing from the Higher Education Research Institute's (HERI) longitudinal study of post college civic engagement among graduates, Vogelgesang and Astin (2005) studied patterns of civic engagement in relation to gender and institutional type. The results of this study show that civic engagement and service participation declines somewhat during the years immediately following college. According to Vogelgesang and Astin, despite the fact that 80.3% of students surveyed had participated in community service during their senior year in high school, only 74.4% were participating in the last year of college and 68.1% six years after completing college (p. 2). Further, and related, declines were also found for values such as "helping others in difficulty," "participating in a community action program," "becoming a community leader," or "influencing social values."

Surveyed six years post-graduation, those alumni who were involved in the community reported that their service was most often "through a school or educational organization (59.7%), their employer (57.7%), a religious or faith-based organization (49.4%), or a sports or recreational organization (44.3%)" (p. 4). With less emphasis on social change, advocacy, or political participation, it is not surprising that these researchers found that motivations were more closely aligned with helping others (82.5%), than working toward a more equitable society (14.5%) or changing laws or policies (6.9%) (Vogelgesang & Astin, 2005). Differences existed between men and women in the nature of civic participation with women more involved in volunteering for educational and civic organizations and men more engaged in the political process. Differences across institutional types also surfaced and revealed intriguing patterns in relation to institutional missions and required service. Alumni from Catholic colleges were least likely to report volunteering post-college (62.7%), while alumni from other religiously affiliated institutions weighed in with the highest (77%), and 63.1% of public institution graduates—a finding that some may find surprising given the public purposes of land grant and public universities (Curris, 2006). An earlier study conducted by Knox, Lindsay, and Kolb (1993) emphasized the importance of the educational credential (e.g., bachelor's degree) to patterns of civic and community participation, rather than the institutional type.

Although not explicitly studied in these studies, the impact of increasing numbers of high schools requiring community service as a graduation prerequisite may influence the decline in participation in community service and civic participation during and after college. Although community service requirements do provide for a short term influx of volunteers and expose individuals to community service, perhaps for the first time, some evidence does exist that suggests that high school community service requirements do not result in the intended outcomes related to civic participation and social responsibility and do contribute to declining participation after the requirement has been met (Jones & Hill, 2003; Marks & Jones, 2004). An emphasis on performing service because it was expected and required did little to help students understand why service was important and remained an external motivator (Jones & Hill, 2003). Similarly, in a study with college students enrolled in a service-learning class, Stukas, Snyder, and Clary (1999) found:

> In the context of a mandatory volunteerism program, behavioral intentions to engage in volunteer work in the future were positively related to past histories of volunteerism—but only for students who did not feel that the program had overly controlled their behavior. These results support the findings of earlier research demonstrating that external constraints to act, in the form of requirements or rewards, may reduce interest in an activity. (p. 61)

One unintended outcome of requiring service is that students learned to provide service only when it was required (Marks & Jones, 2004; Stukas, Snyder, & Clary, 1999). Required service participation then tended to be short-lived, segmental, and unrelated to personal values and enduring commitments (Marks & Jones, 2004).

Although very little research exists, a discussion of educational influences, adult development, and civic participation is not complete without some attention to community colleges. Given a mission that emphasizes close involvement in and collaboration with local communities, community colleges provide a good exemplar of service-learning and adult development. Furthermore, the just over 1100 community colleges in the United States educate 11.6 million students, 46% of all U.S. undergraduates, with an average age of 29 years (American Association of Community Colleges, n.d.). Indeed, many community college students are already very involved in their communities and bring their track records for exemplary civic participation with them to the community college setting (Elsner, 2000). Although most of the literature on community colleges and service-learning highlights best practices and "how-to" information, the research that does exist provides some evidence of the positive outcomes associated with service-learning (e.g., Barnett, 1996; Hodge, Lewis, Kramer, & Hughes, 2001) for a mostly "adult" (post-22 years old) student population. In addition, service-learning courses seem particularly well-suited to adult learning (Schlossberg, Lynch, & Chickering, 1989). However, as Lewis (2002) pointed out, much of the reason that a dearth of research exists on service-learning and adults is because service-learning educators have both situated service-learning only in the context of schools and universities as sponsors and seniors as recipients of service-learning rather than active participants. Nonetheless, with 71% of community colleges offering service-learning courses (American Association of Community Colleges, 2003), this remains an untapped and vitally important area for research on adult development and civic participation.

In considering the question of how adults can be socialized and encouraged to develop and sustain values, motives, and habits that produce a lifetime of community engagement (Clary & Snyder, 2002), educational settings are certainly one potentially potent pathway. With mission statements that reflect the importance of citizenship and civic engagement and educational curricula and programs designed to promote such outcomes, colleges and universities are often the sites of such learning and development.

Intersections of Developmental Influences and Civic Participation

The question of whether or not service-learning and civic participation is an influence on adult development and if so, which developmental outcomes are most likely promoted, is an important one for which there is little empirical evidence. The relationship between adult development and service-learning and civic participation is speculated and presumed, but not well researched and understood. Eyler and Giles (1999) commented that "service-learning provides an ideal environment for connecting these disparate elements of student development [values, knowledge, skills, commitment connected to social responsibility] into effective citizenship development" (p. 157). As noted earlier in this chapter, a growing body of research does suggest that service-learning and community service experiences during the young adulthood and college years promotes developmental outcomes and well designed service-learning increases this likelihood (Eyler & Giles, 1999). In the absence of a number of longitudinal studies, Eyler (2000) synthesized research from the youth development literature and the few studies in higher education and suggested "The mediating factor appears to be the development of civic identity, i.e. the personal efficacy and social responsibility that are the outcomes of both community service and service-learning" (p. 11).

Developmental theories are anchored in the social psychological perspective that individual development "represents the organization of increasing complexity" (Sanford, 1967, p. 47) and that domains for development include cognitive, psychosocial, moral, spiritual, physical, vocational, and in dimensions represented by social identities (McEwen, 2003; Smith, 2005). The developmental theory literature typically treats these domains of development as discrete areas (Jones & McEwen, 2000). As conceptualized by developmental theorists, development is triggered by a developmental readiness in the individual, which interacts with conditions in the environment that disrupt the individual's psychological equilibrium and result in processes of differentiation and integration (Sanford, 1962). Some evidence exists that community service promotes development by situating individuals in contexts that introduce cognitive dissonance and disequilibrium and prompts an individual to increasing complexity in understanding the self and the environment (Baxter Magolda, 2000; Jones & Abes, 2003, 2004). The scope of this chapter does not permit a full explication of all developmental theories (some of which appear elsewhere in this handbook). And in the absence of much empirical research on the relationship between civic participation, service-learning, and adult development, our focus is on those developmental theories for which the connections appear most persuasive (drawing from what we know from research on early adult development) or provocative (what we could know from newer conceptualizations of development).

Psychosocial Theories.   Much of what has been written about adult development is grounded in psychosocial perspectives on development and emphasizes such factors as the sequential and age-related nature of development, the intersection of biology, environment, and psychological influences, the importance of life events and their timing, and the social roles individuals play (Evans, 2003; Josselson, 1996; Levinson, 1978; Levinson & Levinson, 1996; Neugarten, 1979; Schlossberg, Waters, & Goodman, 1995). Most notable, and widely cited, is the pioneering work of Erik Erikson. Erikson's approach covers the lifespan and suggests that development proceeds epigenetically along an age and stage trajectory. Each stage is characterized by a crisis or conflict and an accompanying set of developmental tasks that must be resolved (more or less successfully) before moving on (Erikson, 1980; Evans, 2003). The stage most connected to adult development, and related to discussions about civic participation, is that of *generativity vs. stagnation/self-absorption.* The developmental task of this stage is cultivating concern for the next generation, which Erikson framed in relation to parenting and raising children. However, the psychosocial virtue is that of caring and learning to contribute to individuals, issues, and purposes outside of oneself. Clearly, civic participation and community involvement can be viewed as generative activities.

Because of the sequential nature of psychosocial development, the seeds of generativity are planted earlier in life. In their study of 100 individuals leading lives of commitment to a common good, Parks Daloz et al. (1996) discovered that these individuals learned about community and civic involvement by growing up in homes with a "public parent" and with opportunities for "listening from the stairway in which children sitting at the top of the stairway overheard adult conversations about community affairs that nourished their sense of connection to a larger world" (pp. 29–30). Developmental influences are also evident in several studies that suggested that community involvement as young adults does cultivate an ethic of caring and an ability to begin to see the importance of seeing life outside of oneself. In a study of high school students several years after graduating, Youniss and Yates (1997) found that students maintained an identity that embraced "an empathetic outlook toward the other, reflectivity on the self's agency, and relating one's own agency to helping less fortunate individuals" (p. 129). In Rhoads's (1997) study of college students engaged in community service, he emphasized the learning about self and other that emerged as a result of active engagement in a community context that challenged stereotypes and generalized assumptions about those with whom students came into contact. In the most comprehensive research to date on the outcomes associated with service-learning, Eyler and Giles (1999) identified developmental impact on such characteristics as personal awareness, efficacy, interpersonal skills, leadership development, reduced stereotyping, and appreciation of diversity. In these studies, it appears that the community service context contributed to developmental outcomes related to personal, interpersonal, and moral development.

Cognitive and Moral Development.   In addition to psychosocial theories of adult development, theories of cognitive and moral development are important to civic participation among adults. Cognitive theories focus on *how* individuals think, rather than on *what* they think about, and generally describe a process of moving from more concrete, simple ways of thinking to more abstract and complex meaning making (Perry, 1981). Moral development is related to cognitive development because "one's level of complexity of moral development can be no greater than one's general cognitive development" (McEwen, 1996, p. 63). The focus of moral development is on the process of moral reasoning, or how individuals make decisions of an ethical or moral nature. Because service-learning and civic participation are ripe with opportunities to work on *ill-structured problems* (Eyler & Giles, 1999; Kitchener & King, 1981) and experience moral dilemmas (McEwen, 1996), there is good reason to consider the relationship between these developmental outcomes and civic participation.

Although theories of cognitive and moral development were based upon research with college students, none suggest that all developmental tasks are resolved in early adulthood. In fact, given the complexities of current times, moral and cognitive claims are made on adults regularly (Gilligan, 1982; Kegan, 1994; Kohlberg, 1976; Parks Daloz et al., 1996; Rest, 1986). According to Park Daloz et al., the context for their study of 100 individuals who met criteria for leading lives committed to a common good was "a widening gap between the generosity of which the American people are capable and the increasingly fortressed, self-preoccupied, sloganesque, and single-issue orientation that has come to characterize much of public life" (p. 9). They then suggested that new ways of thinking or "habits of mind" (p. 107) are required to deal with the ambiguity, diversity, and complexity of contemporary times. The habits demonstrated by their participants included those of dialogue, interpersonal perspective-taking, critical, systemic thought, dialectical thought, and holistic thought (p. 108).

The work of Carol Gilligan (1982) is particularly congruent with service-learning and community engagement. Departing from Kohlberg's theory which emphasizes a justice orientation, Gilligan's work focuses on developing an ethic of caring, which is consonant with research on service-learning and community service (e.g., Rhoads, 1997). Moral reasoning, particularly for women, is rooted in experiences of connection and relationship. Connecting Gilligan's conceptualization of moral development with community service, Rhoads (1997) wrote, "In essence, students explore the self while learning about and experiencing the other. Gilligan's research supports the idea that experiences gained through different kinds of relationships are linked to changes in one's conception of responsibility and thus may influence the development of an ethic of care" (p. 54). A limited body of research has explored the development of reasoning in service-learning, particularly as service-learning and community involvement cultivate an ethic of care, concern, and compassion (Eyler & Giles, 1999; Markus, Howard, & King, 1993; Rhoads, 1997).

In a meta-analysis of research on moral and civic development, the intersection of cognitive and moral growth and change is also evident (Colby, Ehrlich, Beaumont, & Stephens, 2003). Colby et al., identified three clusters of *capacities* that are crucial to "fully mature moral and civic functioning" (Colby et al., p. 99):

1. Moral and civic understanding (capacity to interpret and understand complex issues).
2. Motivation to "do the right thing" (individual goals, values, commitments, efficacy, compassion, and sense of self).
3. Skills and competencies (capacity for effective communication, to work with diverse groups of people, political action. (pp. 99–100)

Of note, Colby et al. pointed out that these clusters may exist independently of one another and are only loosely connected developmentally, if at all. As example, they wrote, "There is no reason to assume that people who are highly caring and generous will understand the systemic dimensions of the issues they are dealing with on a person-to-person level" (p. 100). Interestingly, the idea that these developmental capacities are loosely connected relates directly to the differing conceptions of service and citizenship explored earlier in this chapter and by extension, suggests that "moral and civic functioning" depends upon definitions of citizenship that include social and political action, rather than the more charitable emphasis on helping through volunteerism.

Social Identities. Service-learning, community service, and civic participation often are constructed as an "encounter with strangers" (Radest, 1993), working with "the other" (Rhoads, 1997), or confronting "otherness" (Parks Daloz et al., 1996). In fact, Parks Daloz et al., reported that "the single most important pattern we have found in the lives of people committed to the common good is what we have come to call "a constructive, enlarging engagement with the other" (p. 63). What often goes missing in the research on service-learning and civic participation is the interplay of power, culture, and identity (Rhoads, 1997) that gives way to the persistent presence of "the other" in the research and discourse of service. An understanding of theories of social identities and the influence of social identities on the way in which individuals participate in community based work helps fill this gap.

Social identities are "roles [e.g., parent] or membership categories [e.g., Latino/a] that a person claims as representative" (Deaux, 1993, p. 6) and cannot be understood outside of the sociohistorical and sociocultural context in which they developed (McEwen, 2003). In the developmental literature, social identities are typically portrayed as discrete categories and represented in the growing body of theories focused on racial identity (including theories of Black racial identity, White racial identity, and multiracial identity for example), cultural identity, social class, and sexual orientation, to name a few (e.g., Cross, 1995; Fassinger, 1991; Helms, 1995). In general, these theories describe a developmental progression from the absence of awareness of a particular social identity (e.g., race) to a more complex and integrated worldview that includes a positive self-concept with regard to the specific social identity dimension.

Important to any discussion of social identity theories is sociohistorical and cultural context and the recognition that power and privilege operate differentially in some social identities. What this means, for example, is that racial identity cannot be understood without attention to racism and sexual orientation identity development cannot be considered outside a discussion of heterosexism. This is not to dismiss the intersecting and interlocking of social structures such as racism and sexism (Weber, 1998), but to point out the particular salience of certain structures of inequality when exploring social identity.

The conceptual model of multiple dimensions of identity (Jones & McEwen, 2000) is one of a few that brings together social identities in an effort to capture the complexity of identity development and recognize that identity salience is mediated by changing contexts (such as community service and civic engagement experiences). Because service-learning and community based work often places individuals in settings that are unfamiliar or working on social issues with which they are not personally familiar, certain social identities may become more salient as a result. Also significant, and related, is the importance of recognizing that all individuals bring to their community work a variety of social identities with which they may be more or less connected.

The irony cannot be lost on the perspective held by some that the tradition of community service and civic participation in the United States grew out of these very structures of inequality and serves to reinforce the barriers and boundaries created by economic, racial, and social systems that thrive because of differences. As a result, the preponderance of those working in the community is represented by White, middle-class, educated, women, *serving* those from very different backgrounds (O'Grady, 2000). This dynamic creates the impetus for developmental growth as certain social identities become more salient in community settings. King and Baxter Magolda (2005) represented this as "the developmental complexity that allows a learner to understand and accept the general idea of difference from self without feeling threat to self enables a person to offer positive regard to others across many types of difference, such as race, ethnicity, social class, gender, sexual orientation, and religion" (pp. 572–573).

The danger in focusing on social identities in the community service and civic participation context is the risk of focusing only on "the other" and essentializing identities (Jones & Abes, 2004; Jones & Hill, 2001; Rhoads, 1997). For example, in his research on college students working with homeless individuals Rhoads found that social class became particularly salient to students, but their conclusions were represented by the statement "I don't see any difference between me and people who are homeless...They just do not have homes" (pp. 119, 120). Very little research exists that examines the developmental outcomes associated with individuals serving in the communities from which they have come (see Henry, 2005 as a notable example of research exploring the experiences of first generation, low SES students serving communities similar to their own).

Given the contexts in which most community service takes place, the intersection of civic participation and social identities seems unavoidable; however, several studies have found that unexamined privilege associated with certain social identities (e.g., race, social class) buffered individuals from any close scrutiny of their social identities (Jones & Abes, 2003). This then suggests that an individual's social identity development (e.g., racial identity) may both be influenced by civic participation and community involvement as well as influences how one chooses to engage in the community and what one experiences while there. That is, particular social identities may become more salient and developed as a result of civic participation *and* the perceived salience of a social identity may influence the nature of an individual's interests and commitments.

An Integrative Perspective.   Perhaps most instructive to a discussion of adult development and civic participation, recent scholarship is advancing a more holistic perspective on development by suggesting that domains of development are more overlapping and integrated than an isolated view presents, and, as a result, represents the complexity of development more fully. In order to better understand the relationship between civic participation and adult development in general, and whether or not civic participation is influenced by developmental influences or promotes developmental outcomes, requires an integrative framework and perspective. Newer conceptual frameworks, and research anchored in these frameworks, are better capturing the complex and holistic nature of development.

One such framework, which relates directly to dimensions of civic participation, is the developmental model of intercultural maturity (King & Baxter Magolda, 2005), which is based on Kegan's (1994) theory of constructivist developmental lifespan development. Kegan's model highlights the developmental task of "self-authorship" or "an ability to construct knowledge in a contextual world, an ability to construct an internal identity separate from external influences, and an ability to engage in relationships without losing one's internal identity" (Baxter Magolda, 1999, p. 12). King and Baxter Magolda's model emphasizes that intercultural maturity depends upon the integration of the three underlying dimensions of self-authorship: cognitive, interpersonal, and intrapersonal. They "define intercultural maturity as multi-dimensional and consisting of a range of attributes, including understanding (the cognitive dimension), sensitivity to others (the interpersonal dimension), and a sense of oneself that enables one to listen to and learn from others (the interpersonal dimension)" (p. 574) and suggest that the development of intercultural maturity occurs incrementally along a developmental trajectory.

Although intercultural maturity and civic participation are not identical developmental constructs, they are overlapping as the literature on civic participation would suggest that intercultural maturity is necessary for active engagement in community life (Cipolle, 2004). In addition, proponents of service-learning and civic engagement would argue that these community-based activities can be powerful contexts for promoting self-authorship and intercultural maturity. One study makes this very point. In a study of young adults who had been engaged in service-learning during their college years, Jones and Abes (2004) found that service-learning did indeed promote self-authorship reflected in increased awareness of self and other (intrapersonal), shifts in the nature of career plans and aspirations to more socially responsible work (interpersonal), and increased open-mindedness about new people, experiences, and ideas (cognitive). In addition to promoting growth in each of the domains of self-authorship, Jones and Abes also discovered that integration among the domains was fostered because the complicated, challenging, and unfamiliar environments of the community service setting, and ensuing reflection on these experiences, prompted participants to re-construct their identities in relation to others and the social issues they were witnessing.

Although very little research has been conducted that specifically examines the relationship between civic participation and adult development, it appears from a review of the research on college student development, that civic participation may both influence developmental outcomes as well as be influenced by where an individual is located in and across several developmental domains. In the longitudinal study conducted by Jennings and Stoker (2004), several findings related to civic engagement and the life cycle are significant. First, they found that civic participation and volunteerism "first rise and then fall across the adult years" (p. 372) with notable declines from late adolescence to early adult years. Further, although the seeds of voluntary activity may be planted in adolescence in high school, the full impact of this early socialization may not be experienced until middle adulthood. Second, they found that "what inspires civic engagement in early adulthood is not the same as what instigates it in mid-life, nor, perhaps, in the later years" (p. 373). This is clearly an understudied area in need of research, particularly longitudinal in design. Another area explored in a rich body of research that influences civic participation is that of psychological factors such as individual motivation to serve and personality characteristics that seem to predispose some individuals toward volunteering. This domain is explored next.

Psychological Influences

A comprehensive review of community service and participation among adults must consider psychological motivations behind the decision to serve. Although our focus in this chapter thus far has been on civic participation, much of the research on psychological motivations of community involvement is based specifically on volunteering experiences and characteristics of adults who volunteer. Safrit and Merrill (1996) defined a volunteer as "anyone who gives time, talents or energies to an individual or group (other than a family member) in order to advance the common good and without desire for financial profit" (p. 3). Throughout this section on psychological motivations, community service and volunteering will be used interchangeably as reflected in the literature cited.

This section examines basic characteristics of volunteering such as motivations and personality characteristics of volunteers, a functional analysis of volunteering, and situational and organizational characteristics of a community service site. Penner (2002) described volunteering as "long-term, planned, prosocial behaviors that benefit strangers and occur within an organizational setting" (p. 448). Certain factors motivate some individuals to volunteer that do not characterize others, and the exploration of these factors provides a different lens for examining adult community and civic participation.

Determinants of Volunteering.   At a most basic level, deciding to volunteer or participate in community service begins with a goal to better the community (Stukas & Dunlap, 2002). Both an individual and a collective component are involved in making the decision to volunteer, such that an individual is making a personal decision, but also is deciding to participate in an effort to better the larger community. A psychological sense of community, "the sense that one belongs in and is meaningfully a part of a larger collectivity" (Sarason, 1974, p. 1), has been shown to contribute to activism and civic participation.

A socialization process occurs toward community involvement and social activism in that most individuals believe that volunteering is good for the community and is something in which they should participate (Clary & Snyder, 2002). The socialization process occurs on two levels, primary (family and consistent caregivers) and secondary (schools, neighborhood, church, and youth organizations) (Selznick, 1992). If the forces of secondary socialization contradict primary socialization, often only a temporary commitment is produced. Therefore, if a family does not emphasize community participation, but community service is then cultivated at school or church, the commitment may not be a lasting one for individuals (Marks & Jones, 2004). For this reason, a very positive attitude toward community service does not always translate to participation in community service.

Volunteering has been characterized in different ways. Penner (2002) described the four most important attributes of volunteering as longevity, planfulness, nonobligatory helping, and organizational context. According to Penner, volunteering is more than a one-time act and also one for which individuals typically weigh the costs and benefits before it is undertaken. One-time events (e.g., fundraiser or blood drive) do not require the same investment as a long-term commitment to volunteering. Weighing the costs and benefits of contributing cans to a food drive or donating blood is very different than deciding to spend one afternoon a week delivering meals to people living with AIDS/HIV. Penner also proposed that volunteering cannot be required and must take place within an organizational setting. Clary and Snyder (1999) offered similar stipulations for volunteering. The helper seeks out the opportunity to help, arrives at the decision after a period of deliberation, and provides assistance over time. According to Clary and Snyder, the decisions related to beginning to volunteer and then continuing are influenced by whether the particular activity fits with the helper's own needs. Drawing from the results of a study conducted with AIDS volunteers, Penner and Finkelstein (1998) described four structural characteristics of the volunteering process: length of tenure, time spent each week, number of meetings attended, and direct contact with the service recipient (in this case, people with HIV/AIDS). These volunteering process variables can significantly change the experience for the volunteer involved. Penner and Finkelstein (1998) examined how each of these four structural characteristics was related to satisfaction with volunteering. Of these four characteristics, length of tenure at the service site was the most strongly correlated with satisfaction with volunteering. This is consistent with other studies that show that organizational satisfaction is linked with the amount of time spent as a volunteer (Davis, Hall, & Meyer, 2003; Omoto & Snyder, 1995; Penner & Finkelstein, 1998).

Motivations of Volunteers.   Individual motivations and personality characteristics are also related to volunteering. Selznick's (1992) theory of social participation posited that some people are motivated by core motivations (intrinsic reasons, internal values) and others by segmental motivation (extrinsic reasons, motivated by personal interest). Batson, Ahmad, and Tsang (2002) theorized four main motivations to volunteer: egoism (motivation of self-interest), altruism (motivation to help others), collectivism (motivation to increase the welfare of a group), and principlism (motivation to uphold a moral principle). They emphasized that all four motivations are possible and that the interplay among motivations is important to consider.

A long debate exists over whether egoism or altruism is a stronger motivation to volunteer. Egoism works under the assumption that "if someone acts for the welfare of others or for the good of the community, it is only because doing so is an instrumental means to promote one's own welfare or is an unintended consequence of promoting one's own welfare" (Batson, Ahmad, & Tsang, 2002, p. 433). For someone motivated by egoism, the central reason for participating in community service is the personal benefit received from the community involvement. Individuals could serve to receive social or material rewards or to avoid social or material punishments, as well as to eradicate guilt. The problem with egoistic motivations for recruiting volunteers is that they do not typically last. One who is engaging in community service in order to receive some reward will most likely stop after receiving the reward (Marks & Jones, 2004; Stukas, Snyder, & Clary, 1999).

Altruistic motivations involve wanting to improve the welfare of one or more other people. Individuals with altruistic motivations typically exhibit strong feelings of empathy that allow them to feel sympathy, compassion, and tenderness (Batson, Ahmad, & Tsang, 2002). The dilemma with altruistic motivations is that it is difficult to feel empathy for an abstract social problem like homelessness or hunger. The problem is too remote and removed for the individual to feel the empathy that is necessary to serve as a motivation to volunteer. Although these two types of motivation, egoism and altruism, are generally pitted against each other, Clary and Snyder (1999) noted that this dichotomy is false and that individuals can in fact be motivated by both egoism and altruism.

Finally, some individuals do not rely on their own personal motivations, but instead, are required to volunteer as part of a job, punishment, or school requirement. Evidence suggests that individuals who are required to volunteer often lessen their own intrinsic motivation to continue volunteering in the future (Marks & Jones, 2004; Sobus, 1995; Stukas, Snyder, & Clary, 1999). Attribution theory suggests that positive attributions people made toward themselves and received from others are diminished when acts of community service are required (Sobus, 1995). Similarly, these positive feelings or attributions are bolstered when participating in community service is self-determined rather than required. "In fact, a coercive policy should be expected to undermine positive attributions, stifle feelings of self-determination, and ultimately make self-generated acts of community service more scarce" (Sobus, p. 182).

Functional Approach to Volunteering.   Once an individual has made the decision to volunteer, there are different processes that maintain the commitment. The functional approach to volunteering emphasizes the personal and social processes that initiate, direct, and sustain action (Clary & Snyder, 1999). Several studies examining the functional approach to volunteering have identified six functions of volunteering: values (altruistic and humanitarian concern for others), understanding (volunteerism permits new learning and the chance to exercise knowledge, skills, and abilities), social (developing relationships with others), career (obtaining career-related benefits), protective (defense of the ego, reduce guilt over being more fortunate), and enhancement (maintaining or enhancing positive affect) (Clary et al., 1998; Clary & Snyder, 1999). These six functions demonstrate a wide range of personal and social motivations. From this research, Clary et al. developed the Volunteer Functions Inventory (VFI) to determine which of these functions is most important in compelling people to volunteer and to continue the commitment.

The VFI is designed to measure why people perform community service. Using the VFI, Clary and Snyder (1999) established a matching hypothesis that starting to volunteer and continuing to volunteer depend on matching the motivations of an individual with situations that match his or her concerns. Individuals who receive benefits relevant to their functional motivations were not only satisfied with their service, but also intended to continue volunteering in the short and long-term future. Volunteers "who found service opportunities that provided benefits matching their initial motivations more strongly believed that they would make volunteerism a continuing part of their lives than individuals who chose opportunities that did not provide functionally relevant benefits or that provided functionally irrelevant benefits" (Clary & Snyder, 1999, p. 1526). The matching process is essential to finding a good volunteer fit and individuals who are already more predisposed to volunteer have an easier time finding that fit.

Personal Characteristics of Volunteers.   Volunteers possess certain personal characteristics that set them apart from individuals who do not volunteer. Prosocial behavior is behavior that is intended to benefit others and provides a predisposition to volunteer (Carlo & Randall, 2002). Penner (2002) researched the connection between a prosocial personality and the propensity to volunteer. According to Penner and Finkelstein (1998), "A prosocial personality orientation is an enduring tendency to think about the welfare and rights of other people, to feel concern and empathy for them, and to act in a way that benefits them" (p. 526). Prosocial behavior has typically been studied as a one-time act to help a stranger in distress, but recently volunteering has been studied as a longer-term prosocial behavior. Penner (2002) theorized two characteristics of a prosocial personality: other-oriented empathy and helpfulness. Other-oriented empathy describes prosocial thoughts. Individuals who demonstrate high other-oriented empathy are concerned with other people's welfare and feel empathetic and responsible for others. Helpfulness describes prosocial actions and individuals with high helpfulness are less likely to experience personal discomfort when helping others in distress.

Several other personal characteristics are associated with the likelihood of volunteering. Penner (2002) examined several different characteristics and their relationship with volunteering. Individuals who belong to an organized religion are more likely to volunteer. In addition to participation in organized religion, the level of religiosity, or how religious someone is including amount of time spent on religious activities and importance of religious identity to personal identity, is also positively correlated with volunteering. Finally, according to Penner, level of education is also positively correlated with the number of organizations where people volunteer, length of time spent volunteering, and number of times volunteering.

Davis (2005) conducted a study to determine whether personality characteristics matter in deciding to become (and remain) a community volunteer. He used a framework of strong and weak situations to show different personality characteristics. "*Strong situations* are those that contain clear features that tend to evoke predictable responses from most individuals; such situations exert a more powerful guiding force on individual behavior, thus reducing the degree of control that individual characteristics such as personality can have" (p. 67, italics in original). In contrast, "*Weak situations* are those in which clear situational cues and characteristics are absent; as a result, they allow individual characteristics more room to operate" (p. 68, italics in original). Personality has been shown not to have much effect on strong situations (e.g., responding to an emergency), but little data existed on whether it affected weak situations (e.g., deciding to volunteer).

In a series of three different studies, Davis (2005) looked at the relationship between anticipated empathy and distress on a volunteer's decision to volunteer, satisfaction with volunteering, and likelihood to volunteer in the future. He found that although other variables such as desire to acquire skills, meet other people, gain self-knowledge, and develop a role identity as a volunteer affect individual's decisions to begin and continue volunteering, personality variables provide more mixed results. Personality characteristics of empathy and distress do have an impact on the decision to volunteer, they sometimes have an influence on satisfaction with volunteering, and the evidence is inconclusive on whether they effect the development of a long-term commitment to volunteer. One important result from this study was that the individual characteristic of distress was found to have a significant influence on volunteering. Davis suggested, "minimizing this distress may be one of the most effective ways of increasing volunteer satisfaction, which may in turn increase the level of volunteer involvement" (p. 80).

Organizational Characteristics.   Organizational characteristics also play a role in retaining community volunteers. Individuals are affected by their own perceptions of and feelings about the way that they are treated by an organization (Penner, 2002). The organization's reputation and personnel practices also seem to play a role in their ability to recruit and retain volunteers. Numerous studies found that satisfaction with the organization was linked with length of tenure as a volunteer (Davis, Hall, & Meyer, 2003; Omoto & Snyder, 1995; Penner & Finkelstein, 1998).

Outcomes Associated with Civic Participation by Adults

This section explored diverse influences on civic participation including educational, developmental, and psychological factors and processes. Much of the research to date is based upon college students engaged in service-learning and community service or adults who volunteer. Although each lens provides a different perspective on adult development and civic participation, none alone fully illuminates the phenomenon of civic participation among adults and the outcomes associated with such involvement. In the absence of research that explicitly addresses the consequences to adult development as a result of participation in service-learning, volunteerism, and/or civic participation, we use existing research as a springboard for speculation about what some of these outcomes might be.

First, with greater numbers of adults enrolling in higher education, it seems reasonable to speculate that greater numbers will also enjoy the developmental outcomes associated with service-learning opportunities. Although the developmental realities and life situations of older adults may be qualitatively distinct from those traditionally aged students (upon which much of the service-learning research is based), outcomes such as personal development, cognitive complexity, self-efficacy, stereotype reduction, and empathy may be promoted by adult participation as well. Second, adult development as a result of civic participation may also be promoted in the cultivation of a "civic identity" and generativity. As adults enter into a generative life stage, caring about individuals and social issues is expected to gain in importance. By extension, we might speculate that a civic identity is most congruent with generativity and that civic participation may both be influenced by generativity and a civic identity and influence the development of generativity and a civic identity. The realization of a civic identity, and the participation in which it is grounded, may then result in greater psychological well-being, self-efficacy, and life satisfaction. Finally, with huge numbers of Baby Boomers preparing to retire, increased numbers of individuals may be looking for ways to stay involved and active. Organizations dependent upon volunteers may see a graying in their volunteer force as retired adults with discretionary time seek out purposeful and meaningful service opportunities. Thus, both individuals and communities stand to gain by Baby Boomer patterns of engagement.

Contexts for Service

Civic and community service participation among adults occurs in many different contexts. Within this chapter, we have already mentioned community service programs, volunteer opportunities, and service-learning courses, to name a few. Community service opportunities are also increasingly common in the workplace as corporations partner with community organizations to provide community involvement experiences for their employees (Peterson, 2004). Religious organizations have long encouraged community service and provided opportunities for service participation. Finally, grassroots activism provides opportunities for people to become civically involved by working for a cause about which they feel exceedingly strong. These groups are often developed in specific racial, ethnic, or cultural communities and are typically left out of discussions about civic participation. A discussion of these service contexts adds to the conversation about the integration of civic participation and adult development because such inclusion provides for acknowledgement of the settings in which community involvement and adult development occur and describes service contexts that are amenable to adult development and civic participation.

Volunteering in the Workplace

Community involvement and civic participation are increasingly becoming part of workplace norms, expectations, and environments. Many different types of workplace environments are offering opportunities for employees to participate in community service and become involved in the local community. Such programs are perceived to be good for employee morale, productivity, and engagement as well as for the business in promoting a positive image of the company actively involved in building community capacity. Government workers tend to volunteer more often than private sector workers. This could be the result of "self-selection" in that people who are more interested in community involvement probably choose government work over that in the business sector (Wilson, 2005). Employers in the private sector are also adding volunteer opportunities to their portfolio of experiences for their employees.

Corporations have emerged as leaders in the movement towards promoting more socially responsible citizens and businesses. The Center for Corporate Citizenship (CCC) at Boston College developed four core principles for corporations to follow: (1) minimize harm; (2) maximize benefit; (3) be accountable and responsive to key stakeholders; and (4) support strong financial results (CCC, n.d.). Although corporations are still largely focused on the "bottom line," they are also sensitive to the rise in social awareness of their employees and the nation in general. The core principles support providing corporate volunteer programs so that employees and management together will "minimize harm and maximize benefit" for the community. With such programs, business and industry contributes to the development of a "civic identity" for employees. Although companies may favor and support employee volunteerism and community service for the purposes of "good business," such community engagement through volunteer programs can also be integral to an employee's personal development (Peterson, 2004).

Currently about one in five employees surveyed had volunteered through the workplace in the last year (Burnes & Gonyea, 2005). Corporate volunteer programs have experienced rapid growth in the last ten years (Peterson, 2004). High profile companies such as Hewlett-Packard, Motorola, and Dell were listed in the top 10 of *Business Ethics* magazine's top 100 corporate citizens (Raths, 2006). Approximately 79% to 92% of firms in the United States include corporate volunteer programs. These programs vary in terms of their targets with the most common focused on education, health and welfare, and the environment (Peterson, 2004).

A wide range of support also exists in terms of the corporation's commitment to the corporate volunteer program. Some corporations commit large amounts of resources, while others simply promote volunteer opportunities to their employees and use it as a public relations campaign. Regardless of motivation and level of support, individuals are more willing to work for companies that are not only concerned with their financial profits (Peterson, 2004). However, if these programs move to mandatory participation or a workplace culture in which individuals feel pressured to participate some of the same problems with requiring service that have been mentioned in other parts of this chapter will also emerge in the workplace (Clary & Snyder, 2002).

Keeping track of corporate volunteer activity is difficult because it is typically informal and varies in whether or not it is externally or internally organized. Less than one in three companies kept track of the volunteer activity of their companies (Peterson, 2004). It is generally hypothesized that corporate volunteer activity leads to more positive attitudes about jobs, but few studies exist that actually test this theory. Peterson conducted an exploratory study of different individuals who work in companies with or without corporate volunteer programs to determine if corporate volunteer programs were related to job satisfaction, job-related skills, and organizational commitment. Several findings emerged from the study. Employees who participated in corporate volunteer programs are much more likely to think that they can learn job-related skills from these programs than employees who do not. The results about the connection between organizational commitment and volunteer programs were mixed, but Peterson did find that organizational commitment is higher among volunteers in organizations with volunteer programs. Finally, a significant positive relationship existed for women between participation in corporate volunteer programs and job satisfaction, but this relationship did not exist for males.

Demographic characteristics within the workforce are contributing to the importance of corporate volunteer programs and making them more enticing. The American workforce is aging, with nearly one-fifth of the workforce projected to be 55 or older by the year 2015 (Burnes & Gonyea, 2005). The American Association of Retired Persons (AARP, n.d.) reported that more than half of their 35 million members are still in the workforce. Eighty percent of all Baby Boomers indicate that they will work in retirement (Burnes & Gonyea, 2005). Businesses will soon have to address this aging workforce and currently retirees are not a strategic part of the corporate volunteer programs, according to Burnes and Gonyea. Retirees could be used to add to the numbers of corporate members who volunteer and serve as trainers and mentors for other volunteers. Evidence exists that retirees might be most likely to volunteer because they are typically motivated by intrinsic rewards (e.g., ability to develop new skills and interests, making a contribution to the community) (Burnes & Gonyea, 2005). Corporations could increase their impact through volunteer programs by tapping into the so far untouched resource of aging Baby Boomers.

Religious Organizations

Religious organizations have provided a place for community service throughout the history of the United States. Community and service are emphasized in most faith traditions and individuals are often called to service irrespective of their specific religious beliefs. The use of the term *faith traditions* is intended to be inclusive of both larger, organized religions and smaller, spiritual groups. Research has demonstrated that adults involved in religious organizations are more likely to volunteer than those adults who are not (Hart, Southerland, & Atkins, 2003; Verba, Schlozman, & Brady, 1995; Vogelgesang

& Astin, 2005). Vogelgesang and Astin's (2005) study of recent college graduates found that those alumni who attended religious services (72.7%) were much more likely than their peers to volunteer (54.8%). The study also found that even though women are more likely to volunteer than men, they are both equally likely to say that their faith is a major motivation for service participation.

Individuals who volunteer through religious organizations appear to possess different characteristics than other volunteers. Volunteering in coordination with a church encourages a longer-term commitment to service (Wilson, 2005). A study of hospital volunteers suggested that participants were volunteering because of religious teachings and beliefs. Volunteers who indicated that their religion was a motivation for service participation were also rated more dependable by their supervisors. However, this could be explained by the fact that "religious congregations provide more solid infrastructural support for the volunteer role than other voluntary associations and therefore make it possible to contribute help over several years" (Wilson, p. 24).

An individual's level of religiosity is also strongly correlated with volunteer activities. The more involved and committed someone is to his or her religious identity, the more likely he or she is to be involved in volunteering (Penner, 2002). Penner found that individuals who reported strong religious beliefs were more likely to work for a number of community organizations, their tenure as volunteers was longer, and they spent more time working as a volunteer.

Grassroots Organizations

> Democracy has been enlarged in our lifetimes when individuals have been driven not by a desire to serve but by an effort to overcome indignities they themselves have suffered…we become civic by joining with others in common enterprise, common work, common prayer, or common struggle. (Schudson, 2003, p. 18)

Community participation typically involves becoming connected with an already established cause or organization. Another context for community involvement not typically covered in discussions of civic participation is grassroots organizations committed to a certain cause. Grassroots organizations are often the civic participation pathway for marginalized groups that have not been included in large scale service efforts for mainstream causes (or that may not want to participate in what is seen as perpetuating the status quo). Participation in grassroots organizations is an underresearched phenomenon because, by nature, grassroots organizations are new, small, and difficult to track. Further, as Verba, Schlozman, and Brady (1995) suggested "a participatory system that seems adequately representative of the public from one point of view may be quite unrepresentative from other, quite significant, perspectives (pp. 2–3).

One such example of significant grassroots efforts is the civic engagement and activism around the HIV/AIDS epidemic. In the 1980s, when AIDS and HIV was epidemic in the gay community, gay men became seriously stigmatized and marginalized. As a result, they responded to this crisis in large numbers. As noted by Ramirez-Valles & Diaz (2005), "The vast majority of activists and volunteers in the AIDS movement … have been middle-class White gay men" (p. 51). White gay men's participation in the grassroots AIDS movement was largely motivated by empathy for the large numbers of gay men who were dying from the disease and recognition that mainstream social and human services were not responding to members of their community. "Those who suffer the illness, either directly or indirectly through relatives and friends, are likely to get involved as activists or volunteers in the organizations or movements related to the illness" (Ramirez-Valles & Diaz, p. 52). Participation in this movement led to increased self-esteem and a network of social support, which had not been accessible to the same extent for gay men in other community movements (Ramirez-Valles & Diaz, 2005).

A long history and tradition of community participation and grassroots activism is found in the African-American community. Survival necessitated taking care of others in this community and contributed to the cultivation of a cultural value of giving back to the community. Exclusion from social and political structures provided the momentum for leadership in such movements as civil rights and anti-poverty (Mattis et al., 2004). African American social thought, led by leaders like W.E.B. Dubois and Ida B. Wells-Barnett, has long championed efforts to use teaching and service to overcome oppression and to help other people rise out of impoverished circumstances, well before the terms community service and service-learning were fashionable (Stevens, 2003). Musick, Wilson, and Bynum Jr. (2000) found that African Americans do not participate in volunteer experiences in the same percentages that Whites do, however, this does not take into account less organized and more spontaneous involvement like grassroots activism or participation in service through social and cultural organizations such as Black Greek Letter fraternities and sororities. This phenomenon may also be understood as differences in how "service" and "volunteering" are culturally constructed and experienced. Serving one's community may be perceived by African Americans not as something one *does*, but central to who one *is*.

Space here limits a discussion of civic contributions by particular groups. Countless other groups could be profiled for their valuable and underappreciated work. More attention to this avenue for civic participation and research in the area of grassroots activism is needed as this provides a viable outlet for community participation for large numbers of people who have yet to be counted but are making significant collective and individual impact.

Directions for Future Research

In this chapter, we outlined how community service, service-learning, and civic participation play a part in adult development. However, from this review of the literature it is clear that further research, assessment, and evaluation are needed. As noted, research that specifically focuses on civic participation and adult development is diffuse, making a clear picture of the relationship between civic participation and adult development difficult to ascertain. Individual contributions to this body of literature have been made in education, psychology, political science, and sociology fields. Interdisciplinary research could fill the gaps in the existing literature by integrating the various concepts and constructs that seem to make a difference when working to understand adult development and civic engagement. The competing discourses and definitions around civic participation and adult development make this challenging, but interdisciplinary research, drawing from rich theoretical traditions, could begin to address this tension by providing a more common discourse that also acknowledges complexity and wholeness.

In addition to common discourses and definitions, the scope of civic participation needs to be expanded to include groups and activities that have not traditionally been included. Racial, ethnic, and cultural groups who have consistently been held out of civic participation or have participated on the margins in the form of grassroots activism or other small movements should be included in both the literature and outreach of civic participation. Expanding the definition of civic participation to include other previously marginalized groups will necessitate further research to explore how civic participation is defined, understood, and realized by diverse groups of adults and what difference this makes to adult development.

In examining the literature, an absence of longitudinal research on adult participation in civic activities, as well as how civic participation as a youth influences the continuation of civic participation as an adult is obvious. Longitudinal research is needed in order to see how civic participation affects adult development over time and in the transition from adolescence to adulthood. Development can never be fully understood only as a developmental snapshot—a more comprehensive and longitudinal look would greatly add to what we know about this topic.

The educational contexts that have been explored throughout this chapter have primarily included traditional educational settings (e.g., colleges and universities). Further research needs to be conducted in the area of community-based classes, vocational educational programs, community programs, and continuing education classes that incorporate service and the relationship to adult development. Adults are returning to school in greater numbers and pursuing more education than ever before. This new population of adult learners is a rich resource for both researching and encouraging civic participation.

Another population of adults who will make an immense impact on civic participation is the Baby Boomer generation. Different strategic initiatives already exist to try and engage this population in service (e.g., Corporation for National and Community Service) because they represent such a large proportion of the population and a great untapped resource. Further research is called for to determine what motivates Baby Boomers to participate in civic activities and how this participation influences adult development and learning.

When considering future directions, the importance of reflection cannot be undervalued. Nearly all the research and literature on service-learning emphasizes the importance of structured reflection to the learning process. Many of the programs in place that rely on volunteers, many of whom are adults, do not include any structured reflective component. Future research might examine whether intentionally designed reflection improves volunteer satisfaction and leads to a longer-term commitment. The presence of reflection could greatly impact adult development as well as further civic participation among adults.

The influence of community service, service-learning, and civic participation on adult development is an under researched and burgeoning field that would benefit from the attention of future scholars and researchers. It is our hope that this chapter will provide a starting point for future conversations about this topic as well as serve as a trigger for civic participation.

References

American Association of Community Colleges. (2003). *Service-learning in community colleges: 2003 National survey results.* Retrieved April 21, 2006, from, http://www.aacc.nche.edu/Content/NavigationMenu/ResourceCenter/Projects_Partnerships/Current/HorizonsServiceLearningProject/Publications/2003_Survey_RB.pdf.

American Association of Community Colleges. (n.d.). *Community college fact sheet.* Retrieved April 21, 2006, from http://www.aacc.nche.edu/Content/NavigationMenu/AboutCommunityColleges/Fast_Facts1/Fast_Facts.htm.

American Association of Retired Persons. (n.d.). *America's aging workforce.* Retrieved May 1, 2006, from http://www.aarp.org/money/careers/employerresourcecenter/.

American College Personnel Association. (1994). *The student learning imperative: Implications for student affairs.* Washington, DC: Author.

Association of American Colleges and Universities. (2002) *Greater expectations: A new vision for learning as a nation goes to college.* Washington, DC.

Astin, A. W., Oseguera, L., Sax, L. J., & Korn, W. S. (2002). *The American freshman: Thirty-five year trends.* Los Angeles: Higher Education Research Institute, UCLA.

Astin, A. W., & Sax, L. J. (1998). How undergraduates are affected by service participation. *Journal of College Student Development, 39*(3), 251–263.

Astin, A. W., Sax, L. J., & Avalos, J. (1999). Long-term effects of volunteerism during the undergraduate years. *Review of Higher Education, 22,* 187–202.

Barber, B. R. (1984). *Strong democracy: Participatory politics for a new age.* Berkeley: University of California Press.

Barber, B. R. (1992). *An aristocracy of everyone. The politics of education and the future of America.* New York: Oxford University Press.

Barnett, L. (1996). Service learning: Why community colleges? *New Directions for Community Colleges, 24*(1), 7–15.

Batson, C. D., Ahmad, N., & Tsang, J. (2002). Four motives for community involvement. *Journal of Social Issues, 58*(3), 429–445.

Baxter Magolda, M. B. (1999). *Creating contexts for learning and self-authorship: Constructive-developmental pedagogy.* Nashville, TN: The Vanderbilt University Press.

Baxter Magolda, M. B. (2000). Interpersonal maturity: Integrating agency and communion. *Journal of College Student Development, 41,* 141–156.

Bourdieu, P. (1977). *Outline of a theory of practice.* New York: Cambridge University Press.

Boyer, E. L. (1990). *Scholarship reconsidered: Priorities of the professoriate.* Princeton, NJ: Carnegie Foundation for the Advancement of Teaching.

Boyte, H. C., & Kari, N. N. (2000). Renewing the democratic spirit in American colleges and universities: Higher education as public work. In T. Ehrlich (Ed.), *Civic responsibility and higher education* (pp. 37–59). Westport, CT: American Council on Education and Oryx Press.

Brooks, A. C. (2005). Does social capital make you generous? *Social Science Quarterly, 86*(1), 1–15.

Bureau of Labor Statistics. (2006, February). *Volunteering in the United States, 2005.* Retrieved March 27, 2006, from http://www.bls.gov/opub/mlr/2006/02/ressum.pdf.

Burnes, K., & Gonyea, J. G. (2005). *Expanding the boundaries of corporate volunteerism.* Retrieved May 1, 2006, from http://www.bcccc.net/ index.cfm?fuseaction=Page.viewPage&pageId=800&nodeID=1&arented=490.

Bush, G. H. W. (1989). *President George H. W. Bush's inaugural address.*

Butin, D. W. (2005). Preface: Disturbing normalizations of service-learning. In D. W. Butin (Ed.), *Teaching social foundations of education: Contexts, theories, and issues* (pp. vii–xx). Mahwah, NJ: Erlbaum.

Campus Compact. (1999). *Presidents' declaration on the civic responsibility of higher education.* Providence, RI: Author.

Carlo, G., & Randall, B.A. (2002). The development of a measure of prosocial behaviors for late adolescents. *Journal of Youth and Adolescence, 31*(1), 31–44.

Center for Corporate Citizenship. (n.d.). *What is corporate citizenship?* Retrieved May 16, 2006, from http://www.bcccc.net/.

Center for Information and Research on Civic Learning and Engagement & Saguaro Seminar (2006). *America's civic health index: Broken engagement.* Report by the National Conference on Citizenship. Retrieved October 7, 2006, from http://www.ncoc.net/conferences/2006civichealth.pdf.

Chickering, A. W., & Associates (1981). *The modern American college.* San Francisco: Jossey-Bass.

Cipolle, S. (2004). Service-learning as a counter-hegemonic practice: Evidence pro and con. *Multicultural Education, 11,* 12–23.

Clary, E. G., & Snyder, M. (1999). The motivations to volunteer: Theoretical and practical considerations. *Current Directions in Psychological Science, 8*(5), 156–159.

Clary, E. G., & Snyder, M. (2002). Community involvement: Opportunities and challenges in socializing adults to participate in society. *Journal of Social Issues, 58*(3), 581–591.

Clary, E. G., Snyder, M., Ridge, R., Copeland, J., Haugen, J., & Miene, P. (1998). Understanding and assessing the motivations of volunteers: A functional approach. *Journal of Personality and Social Psychology, 74,* 1516–1530.

Colby, A., Ehrlich, T., Beaumont, E., & Stephens, J. (2003). *Educating citizens: Preparing America's undergraduates for lives of moral and civic responsibility* San Francisco: Jossey-Bass.

Coles, R. (1993). *The call of service: A witness to idealism.* Boston: Houghton Mifflin.

Corporation for National and Community Service. (n.d.). *Our history and legislation.* Retrieved January 15, 2006, from http://www.cns.gov/about/role_impact/history.asp.

Cross, W. E., Jr. (1995). The psychology of Nigrescence: Revising the Cross model. In J. G. Ponterotto, J. M. Casas, L. A. Suzuki, & C. M. Alexander (Eds.), *Handbook of multicultural counseling* (pp. 93–122). Thousand Oaks, CA: Sage.

Curris, C. W. (2006, April 7). The public purposes of public colleges. *The Chronicle of Higher Education,* p. B24.

Davis, M. H. (2005). Becoming (and remaining) a community volunteer: Does personality matter? In A. M. Omoto (Ed.), *Processes of community change and social action* (pp. 67–82). Mahwah, NJ: Erlbaum.

Davis, M. H., Hall, J. A., & Meyer, M. (2003). The first year: Influences on the satisfaction, involvement, and persistence of new community volunteers. *Personality and Social Psychology Bulletin, 29,* 248–260.

De Tocqueville, A. (1835/1966). *Democracy in America* (G. Lawrence, Trans.). New York: Harper & Row.

Deaux, K. (1993). Reconstructing social identity. *Personality and Social Psychology Bulletin, 19,* 4–12.

Densmore, K. (2000). Service learning and multicultural education: Suspect or transformative? In C. R. O'Grady (Ed.), *Integrating service learning and multicultural education in colleges and universities* (pp. 45–58). Mahwah, NJ: Erlbaum.

Dionne, E. J., Jr., & Meltzer Drogosz, K. (2003). United we serve? The promise of national service. In E. J. Dionne, Jr., K. M. Drogosz, & R. E. Litan (Eds.), *United we serve: National service and the future of citizenship* (pp. 1–12), Washington, DC: Brookings Institution Press.

Edelman, M. W. (1992). *The measure of our success: A letter to my children and yours.* Boston, Beacon Press.

Elsner, P. A. (2000). A community college perspective. In T. Ehrlich (Ed.) *Civic responsibility and higher education* (pp. 211–226). Washington, DC: The American Council on Education and The Oryx Press.

Erikson, E. H. (1980). *Identity and the life cycle.* New York: Norton (Original work published in 1959)

Evans, N. J. (2003). Psychosocial, cognitive, and typological perspectives on student development. In S. R. Komives & D. B. Woodard, Jr. (Eds.), *Student services: A handbook for the profession* (pp. 179–202). San Francisco: Jossey-Bass.

Eyler, J. (2000). What do we most need to know about the impact of service-learning on student learning? *Michigan Journal of Community Service Learning* (Special Issue), 11–17.

Eyler, J., & Giles, D. E., Jr. (1999). *Where's the learning in service-learning?* San Francisco: Jossey-Bass.

Fassinger, R. E. (1991). The hidden minority: Issues and challenges in working with lesbian women and gay men. *Counseling Psychologist, 19,* 157–176.

Furco, A. (2003). Issues of definition and program diversity in the study of service-learning. In S. H. Billig & A. S. Waterman (Eds.) *Studying service-learning: Innovations in education research methodology* (pp. 13–34). Mahwah, NJ: Erlbaum.

Gilligan, C. (1982). *In a different voice: Psychological theory and women's development.* Cambridge, MA: Harvard University Press.

Gray, M., Ondaatje, E. H., Fricker, R., & Geschwind, S. (2000, March/April). Assessing service learning: Results from a survey of "Learn and Serve America, Higher Education." *Change, 32,* 30–39.

Hart, D., Southerland, N., & Atkins, R. (2003). Community service and adult development. In J. Demick, & Andreoletti, C. (Eds.), *Handbook of adult development* (pp. 585–597). New York: Kluwer Academic/Plenum.

Helms, J. E. (1995). An update of Helms's White and People of Color racial identity models. In J. G. Ponterotto, J. M. Casas, L. A. Suzuki, & C. M. Alexander (Eds.), *Handbook of multicultural counseling* (pp. 181–198). Thousand Oaks, CA: Sage.

Henry, S. E. (2005). "I can never turn my back on that": Liminality and the impact of class on service-learning experience. In D. W. Butin (Ed.), *Teaching social foundations of education: Contexts, theories, and issues* (pp. 45–66). Mahwah, NJ: Erlbaum.

Hodge, G., Lewis, T., Kramer, K., & Hughes, R. (2001). Collaboration for excellence: Engaged scholarship at Collin County Community College. *Community College Journal of Research and Practice, 25,* 675–690.

Howard, J. (2003). Service-learning research: Foundational issues. In S. H. Billig & A. S. Waterman (Eds.) *Studying service-learning: Innovations in education research methodology* (pp. 1–12). Mahwah, NJ: Erlbaum.

Howard, J. P. (1998). *Academic service learning: A counternormative pedagogy.* New Directions for Teaching and Learning, 73, 21–29.

Independent Sector. (2001, November). *Giving and volunteering in the United States.* Retrieved December 15, 2005, from http://www.independentsector.org/programs/ research/gv01main.html.

Independent Sector. (2005). *Value of volunteer time.* Retrieved January 15, 2006, from http://www.independentsector.org/programs/research/volunteer_time.html.index.cfm?fuseaction=Page.viewPage&pageId=567&nodeID=1&parentID=473.

Jacoby, B., & Associates. (1996). *Service-learning in higher education: Concepts and practices.* San Francisco: Jossey-Bass.

Jennings, M. K., & Stoker, L. (2004). Social trust and civic engagement across time and generation. *Acta Politica: International Journal of Political Science, 39,* 342–379.

Jones, S. R., & Abes, E. S. (2003). Developing student understanding of HIV/AIDS through community service-learning: A case study analysis. *Journal of College Student Development, 44,* 470–488.

Jones, S. R., & Abes, E. S. (2004). Enduring influences of service-learning on college students' identity development. *Journal of College Student Development, 45*(2), 149–166.

Jones, S. R., & Hill, K. (2001). Crossing High Street: Understanding diversity through community service-learning. *Journal of College Student Development, 42,* 204–216.

Jones, S. R., & Hill, K. (2003). Understanding patterns of commitment: Student motivation for community service involvement. *The Journal of Higher Education, 74*(5), 516–539.

Jones, S. R., & McEwen, M. K. (2000). A conceptual model of multiple dimensions of identity. *Journal of College Student Development, 41,* 405–414.

Josselson, R. (1996). *Revising herself: The story of women's identity from college to midlife.* New York: Oxford University Press.

Kahne, J., & Westheimer, J. (1999). In the service of what? The politics of service learning. *In J. Claus & C. Ogden (Eds.), Service learning for youth empowerment and social change* (pp. 25–42). New York: Peter Lang.

Kegan, R. (1994). *In over our heads: The mental demands of modern life.* Cambridge, MA: Harvard University Press.

Kellogg Commission on the Future of State and Land-Grant Universities. (1999). *Returning to our roots: A learning society.* Washington, DC: National Association of State Universities and Land-Grant Colleges.

Kezar, A. J., Chambers, T. C., Burkhardt, J. C., & Associates (2005). *Higher education for the public good.* San Francisco: Jossey-Bass.

King, P. M., & Baxter Magolda, M. B. (2005). A developmental model of intercultural maturity. *Journal of College Student Development, 46*, 571–592.

Kitchener, K. S., & King, P. M. (1981). Reflective judgment: Concepts of justification and their relationship to age and education. *Journal of Applied Developmental Psychology, 2*, 89–116.

Knox, W., Lindsay, P., & Kolb, M. (1993). *Does college make a difference? Long-term changes in activities and attitudes.* Westport, CT: Greenwood Press.

Kohlberg, L. (1976). Moral stages and moralization: The cognitive-developmental approach. In T. Lickona (Ed.), *Moral development and behavior: Theory, research, and social issues* (pp. 31–53). New York: Holt, Rinehart and Winston.

Lenkowsky, L. (2000). Still "Bowling Alone"? *Commentary, 110*(3), 57–60.

Levinson, D. J. (1978). *The season's of a man's life.* New York: Ballantine.

Levinson, D. J., & Levinson, J. D. (1996). *The season's of a woman's life.* New York: Ballantine.

Lewis, M. (2002). Service learning and older adults. *Educational Gerontology, 28*, 655–667.

London, S. (2001). *The civic mission of higher education: From outreach to engagement.* Dayton, OH: Kettering Foundation.

Longo, N. V., & Meyer, R. P. (2006). *College students and politics: A literature review.* College Park, MD: The Center for Information and Research on Civic Learning & Engagement. Retrieved October 7, 2006, from http://www.civicyouth.org/PopUps/WorkingPapers/WP46LongoMeyer.pdf.

Marks, H. M., & Jones, S. R. (2004). Community service in the transition: Shifts and continuities in participation from high school to college. *Journal of Higher Education, 75*, 307–339.

Markus, G., Howard, J., & King, D. (1993). Integrating community service and classroom instruction enhances learning: Results from an experiment. *Educational Evaluation and Policy Analysis, 15*, 410–419.

Martinez-Cosio, M. (2004). It's not just who you know: Cultural and social capital and civic participation, 1–18. *2004 Annual Meeting of the American Sociological Association.* San Francisco.

Mattis, J. S., Beckham, W. P., Saunders, B. A., Williams, J. E., McAllister, D., Myers, V., et al. (2004). Who will volunteer? Religiosity, everyday racism, and social participation among African American men. *Journal of Adult Development, 11*(4), 261–272.

McEwen, M. K. (1996). Enhancing student learning and development through service-learning. In B. Jacoby (Ed.), *Service-learning in higher education: Concepts and practices* (pp. 53–91). San Francisco: Jossey-Bass.

McEwen, M. K. (2003). New perspectives on identity development. In S. R. Komives & D. B. Woodard, Jr. (Eds.), *Student Services: A Handbook for the Profession* (pp. 203–233). San Francisco: Jossey-Bass.

Mosle, S. (2003, Winter). The vanity of volunteerism. *Campus Compact Reader, 27–37.*

Musick, M. A., Wilson, J., & Bynum, W. B., Jr., (2000). Race and formal volunteering: The differential effects of class and religion. *Social forces, 78*, 1539–1571.

Musil, C. M. (2003). Educating for citizenship. *Peer Review, 5*(3), 4–8.

Nation in brief. (2006, April 16). *The Washington Post*, p. A02.

National Association of Student Personnel Administrators, & American College Personnel Association. (2004). *Learning reconsidered: A campus-wide focus on the student experience.* Washington, DC: Author.

Neugarten, B. L (1979). Time, age, and the life cycle. *American Journal of Psychiatry, 136*, 887–894.

Nieto, S. (2000). Foreword. In C. R. O'Grady (Ed.), *Integrating service learning and multicultural education in colleges and universities* (pp. ix–xi). Mahwah, NJ: Erlbaum.

O'Grady, C. R. (2000). Integrating service learning and multicultural education: An overview. In C. R. O'Grady (Ed.), *Integrating service learning and multicultural education in colleges and universities* (pp. 1–19). Mahwah, NJ: Erlbaum.

Omoto, A. M., & Snyder, M. (1995). Sustained helping without obligation: Motivation, longevity of service, and perceived attitude change among AIDS volunteers. *Journal of Personality and Social Psychology, 68*, 671–686.

Parks Daloz, L. A., Keen, C. H., Keen, J. P., & Daloz Parks, S. (1996). *Common fire: Leading lives of commitment in a complex world.* Boston: Beacon Press.

Pascarella, E. T., & Terenzini, P. T. (2005). *How college affects students: A third decade of research.* San Francisco: Jossey-Bass.

Penner, L. A. (2002). Dispositional and organizational influences on sustained volunteerism: An interactionist perspective. *Journal of Social Issues, 58*(3), 447–467.

Penner, L. A., & Finkelstein, M. A. (1998). Dispositional and structural determinants of volunteerism. *Journal of Personality and Social Psychology, 74*(2), 525–537.

Perry, W. G., Jr. (1981). Cognitive and ethical growth: The making of meaning. In A. W. Chickering & Associates (Eds.), *The modern American college* (pp. 76–116). San Francisco: Jossey-Bass.

Peterson, D. K. (2004). Benefits of participation in corporate volunteer programs: employees' perceptions. *Personnel Review, 33,* 615–627.

Putnam, R. D. (1995). Bowling alone: America's declining social capital. *Journal of Democracy, 6*(1), 65–78.

Putnam, R. D. (2000). *Bowling alone: The collapse & revival of American community.* New York: Touchstone Books/Simon & Schuster.

Radest, H. (1993). *Community service: Encounter with strangers.* Westport, CT: Praeger.

Ramirez-Valles, J., & Diaz, R. M. (2005). Public health, race, and the AIDS movement: The profile and consequences of Latino gay men's community involvement. In A. M. Omoto (Ed.), *Processes of community change and social action* (pp. 51–66). Mahwah, NJ: Erlbaum.

Raths, D. (2006). 100 best corporate citizens 2006 [Electronic version]. *Business Ethics, 20.*

Rest, J. R. (1986). *Moral development: Advances in research and theory.* New York: Praeger.

Rhoads, R. A. (1997). *Community service and higher learning: Explorations of the caring self.* Albany: State University of New York Press.

Safrit, R. D., & Merrill, M. (1996). In search of a contemporary definition of volunteerism. *Echo, 3,* 1–4.

Saltmarsh, J. (1998). Exploring the meanings of community/university partnerships. *NSEE Quarterly, 23*(4), 21–22.

Saltmarsh, J. (2005, Spring). The civic promise of service learning. *Liberal Education, 91*(2), 50–55.

Sanford, N. (1962). *The American college.* New York: Wiley.

Sanford, N. (1967). *Where colleges fail: A study of the student as a person.* San Francisco: Jossey-Bass.

Sarason, S. B. (1974). *The psychological sense of community: Prospects for a community psychology.* San Francisco: Jossey-Bass.

Sax, L. (2000). Citizenship development and the American college student. In T. Ehrlich (Ed.), *Civic responsibility and higher education* (pp. 3–18). Phoenix, AZ: Oryx Press.

Sax, L., Astin, A., Lindholm, J., Korn, W., Saenz, V., & Mahoney, K. (2003). *The American freshman: National norms for fall 2003.* Los Angeles: Higher Education Research Institute, UCLA Graduate School of Education and Information Studies.

Schlossberg, N. K., Lynch, M. L., & Chickering, A. W. (1989). *Improving higher education environments for adults.* San Francisco: Jossey-Bass.

Schlossberg, N. K., Waters, E. B., & Goodman, J. (1995). *Counseling adults in transition* (2nd ed.), New York: Springer.

Schudson, M. (2003). How people learn to be civic. *Campus Compact Reader: Service-learning and Civic Education, 3*(3), 14–21.

Selznick, P. (1992). *The moral commonwealth: Social theory and the promise of community.* Berkeley: University of California Press.

Smith, M. C. (2005, October). *Does service-learning promote adult development? Theoretical perspectives and directions for research.* Paper presented at Linking Adults with Community: A Symposium on Adult Education and Service Learning, DePaul University, Chicago.

Smith, M. K. (2001). Social capital. *The encyclopedia of informal education.* Retrieved April 11, 2006, from http://www.infed.org/biblio/social_capital.htm.

Sobus, M. S. (1995). Mandating community service: Psychological implications of requiring prosocial behavior. *Law & Psychology Review, 19,* 153–182.

Stevens, C. S. (2003). Unrecognized roots of service-learning in African American social thought and action, 1890–1930. *Michigan Journal of Community Service Learning, 9*(2), 25–34.

Stukas, A. A., & Dunlap, M. R. (2002). Community involvement: Theoretical approaches and educational initiatives. *Journal of Social Issues, 58*(3), 411–427.

Stukas, A. A., Snyder, M., & Clary, E. G. (1999). The effects of "mandatory volunteerism" on intentions to volunteer. *Psychological Science, 10,* 59–64.

Theoretical perspectives and directions for research. Paper presented at Linking Adults with Community: A Symposium on Adult Education and Service-Learning, DePaul University, Chicago, IL.

Verba, S., Schlozman, K. L., & Brady, H. E. (1995). *Voice and equality: Civic voluntarism in American politics.* Cambridge, MA: Harvard University Press.

Vogelgesang, L., & Astin, A. W. (2000). Comparing the effects of community service and service learning. *Michigan Journal of Community Service Learning, 7,* 25–34.

Vogelgesang, L., & Astin, A. W. (2005). *Post-college civic engagement among graduates* (HERI Research Report Number 2). University of California, Los Angeles: Higher Education Research Institute.

Weber, L. (1998). A conceptual framework for understanding race, class, gender, and sexuality. *Psychology of Women Quarterly, 22,* 13–22.

Westheimer, J., & Kahne, J. (2003, Winter). What kind of citizen? Political choices and educational goals. *Campus Compact Reader,* 1–13.

Westheimer, J., & Kahne, J. (2004). What kind of citizen? The politics of educating for democracy. *American Educational Research Journal, 41*(2), 237–269.

Wilson, J. (2005). Some things social surveys don't tell us about volunteering. In A. M. Omoto (Ed.), *Processes of community change and social action* (pp. 11–27). Mahwah, NJ: Erlbaum.

Youniss, J., & Yates, M. (1997). *Community service and social responsibility in youth.* Chicago: University of Chicago Press.

Zlotkowski, E. (2000). Civic engagement and the academic disciplines. In T. Ehrlich (Ed.), *Civic responsibility and higher education* (pp. 309–322). Washington, DC: The American Council on Education and The Oryx Press.

Chapter 23

Attention-Deficit/Hyperactivity Disorder in Adults

Lisa L. Weyandt

It has been estimated that 8% to 10% of American children 3 to 17 years has a learning disability, 3% to 7% has Attention Deficit Hyperactivity Disorder (ADHD), and approximately 4% has both ADHD and a learning disability (American Psychiatric Association, *DSM-IV-TR*, 2000; Blackwell & Tonthat, 2002; Waldman & Perlman, 2004). Vogel and colleagues (1998) reported that the proportion of college students with a specific learning disability varied among universities from .5% to 10%. Recently cross-cultural studies have examined learning disabilities in adults from various countries and results have revealed differences in prevalence, type, manifestation, and treatment of learning disabilities in the adult population (e.g., Chapman, Tunmer, & Allen, 2003; Magajna, Kavkler, & Ortar-Krizaj, 2003; Vogel & Holt, 2003).

According to the definition put forth by the federal government in the Individuals with Disability Act (IDEA 1997, Public Law 105-17), the term "learning disability" means a "disorder in one or more of the basic psychological processes involved in understanding or in using language, spoken or written, that may manifest itself in an imperfect ability to think, listen, write, spell, or to do mathematical calculations." The term does not include learning problems due to hearing, vision, physical, motor, or emotional disorders. In other words, learning disabilities interfere with the cognitive processes necessary for learning and they are neurologically based. On December 3rd, 2004 IDEA was amended and signed into law, and although substantial changes were made with respect to procedures for identifying learning disabilities, the definition of specific learning disability was maintained from IDEA 1997. In contrast to the federal definition of learning disability, the essential feature of ADHD is a persistent pattern of inattention and/or hyperactivity-impulsivity that is developmentally more frequent and more severe than is expected. These symptoms can interfere with an individual's ability to concentrate, attend, and complete assignments, ultimately affecting one's learning. ADHD symptoms have an early childhood onset, are pervasive, and cause impairment at home, school, or place of employment (American Psychiatric Association, *DSM-IV-TR*, 2000). Therefore, by definition, ADHD is not a learning disability, but it is a disorder that often impacts one's learning. Research indicates that individuals with ADHD frequently have a coexisting learning disability (i.e., 25% to 50%, Pennington, Willcutt, & Rhee, 2005) and the most common type is reading disability. Brook and Boaz (2005) recently reported that 94% of a group of adolescents with ADHD attending a high school devoted to special education had been diagnosed with a coexisting learning disability. An abundant amount of information is available concerning learning disabilities and it is well recognized that learning disabilities are chronic conditions that continue throughout childhood and into adulthood (e.g., Osmon, Braun, & Plambeck, 2005; Pennington, Willcutt, & Rhee, 2005; Shaywitz & Shaywitz, 2005; Vogel & Holt, 2003). It is only recent that ADHD has been recognized as a valid disorder in adults although this diagnosis is not without controversy. The purpose of this chapter is to summarize the research literature concerning ADHD in adults and to consider the practical implications of these findings for adults living with ADHD.

Attention-Deficit/Hyperactivity Disorder

Existence and Prevalence

Some regard ADHD is a controversial disorder in childhood and have questioned the validity of ADHD in adulthood. Indeed, the National Institutes of Health (NIH) released a consensus statement concerning the diagnosis and treatment of ADHD and indicated that "despite the progress in assessment, diagnosis and treatment of children and adults with ADHD, the disorder has remained controversial...the controversy raises questions concerning the literal existence of the disorder" (National Institutes of Health 2000, p. 182). The NIH consensus statement following thorough review of the scientific evidence concluded that ADHD is a valid disorder and this perspective is endorsed by the American Academy of Pediatrics, the American Medical Association, the American Psychiatric Association, the American Psychological Association, the National Association of School Psychologists, the U.S. Surgeon General and others. In 2002, a consortium of international scientists addressed the assertion that ADHD is a fraud by reviewing the scientific evidence to the contrary and issued the International Consensus Statement on ADHD (2002). In addition, Faraone et al. (2000) sought to determine whether ADHD is a valid disorder in *adulthood* using the validity criteria of Robins and Guze (1970), and they reviewed clinical, family, psychopharmacologic, neurobiological, and adult ADHD outcome studies. Faraone et al. concluded that adult ADHD is indeed a valid disorder, although the authors emphasized that additional studies are needed to understand the specific nature of ADHD in adulthood.

ADHD is estimated to affect 3% to 10% of children and adolescents and 3% to 4% of adults (Biederman, Mick, & Faraone, 2000; Wender, Wolf, & Wasserstien, 2001). Prevalence rates vary depending on factors such as age of the individuals investigated, gender, raters (e.g., parents, teachers) and diagnostic criteria employed. The disorder occurs worldwide, and prevalence estimates are similar to the USA in many countries while some studies report substantially higher estimates (Faraone, Sergeant, Gillberg, & Biederman, 2003; Weyandt, 2006). For example, in India, Bhatia, Nigam, Bohra, and Malik, (1991) reported that 29.2% of adolescents ages 11 and 12 displayed significant ADHD symptoms. Recently, a study of 600 Ukrainian children reported an overall prevalence rate of 19.8% for ADHD with the highest subtype ratings for ADHD hyperactive-impulsive type (8.5%) followed by the inattentive type (7.2%), and combined type (4.2%) based on parent and teacher ratings (Gadow et al., 2000). Pineda and colleagues (1999) reported 19.8% of boys and 12.3% of girls ages 6 to 11 (among a sample of 540 children) living in Manizales, Columbia met *DSM-IV* (1994) criteria based on parental ratings alone. Prevalence rates in other countries such as Japan, Canada, China, Italy, Thailand, Australia, and New Zealand have been similar to U.S. estimates (Benjasuwantep, Ruangdaraganon, & Visudhiphan, 2002; Faraone et al., 2003; Graetz et al., 2001; Kanbayashi, Nakata, Fujii, Kita, & Wada, 1994; Luk, Leung, & Lee, 1988; Mugnaini et al., in press; Schaughency, McGee, Raja, Feehan, & Silva, 1994; Szatmari, 1992). Brownell and Yogendran (2001) investigated physicians' diagnosis rates for ADHD in the province of Manitoba and found an overall rate of 1.52%.

Once considered a disorder of childhood, research, however, suggests that the ADHD symptoms often persist throughout adolescence and into adulthood. For example,

Weyandt, Rice, and Linterman (1995) found a substantial percentage of college students reported significant levels of ADHD symptoms (7%). This percentage decreased, however, when both childhood symptoms and current symptoms were considered (2.5%), as is required by *DSM-IV-TR* criteria. DuPaul et al. (2001) examined the prevalence of ADHD symptoms in college students from three countries (Italy, New Zealand, and the United States) and found the prevalence rates varied from 0% (Italian females) to 8.1% (New Zealand males). Recently, a NIMH-funded survey tracking the prevalence of attention deficit/hyperactivity symptoms in adults found that approximately 4.4% of adults ages 18–44 experience significant ADHD symptoms (Kessler et al., 2006). Symptom prevalence varies substantially from diagnostic rates, however, and studies that have followed-up adults who had been diagnosed with ADHD during childhood have produced variable results. Specifically, the studies have reported that 5% to 70% or more of children with ADHD continue to have symptoms in adulthood (Barkley, Fischer, Smallish, & Fletcher, 2002; Biederman et al., 1993; Claude & Firestone, 1995; Hechtman & Weiss, 1983; Mannuzza, Klein, & Moulton, 2002). As Barkley et al. (2002), noted, follow-up studies often rely on self-report and this method may underestimate the persistence of ADHD into adulthood. For example, Barkley et al. (2002) followed children who had been diagnosed with ADHD into adulthood and found that only 5% of the sample of 147 still met the criteria for ADHD when relying on self-report. However, when parent reports were also considered, the figures rose to 66% of cases met the criteria for ADHD.

Although the exact percentage of adults with ADHD is unknown, it has been estimated that 1% to 5% of adults have ADHD, and the expression of ADHD symptoms changes over time (Barkley, 1998; Biederman et al., 2000; Faraone et al., 2003; Goldstein, 2002; Hill & Schoener, 1996; Shekim, Asarnow, Hess, Zaucha, & Wheeler, 1990; Barkley, 1998; Spencer, Biederman, Wilens, & Faraone, 1994). Specifically, research suggests that symptoms of hyperactivity and impulsivity decline with age while inattention symptoms appear to persist into adulthood (Mick, Faraone, & Biederman, 2004). For example, according to the *DSM-IV-TR* diagnostic criteria (2000), hyperactivity in adolescents and adults "may be limited to subjective feelings of restlessness" (criterion 2.c). Indeed, Weyandt et al. (2003) recently found that college students with ADHD reported significantly higher levels of internal restlessness than students without the disorder, and other studies have reported that college students with a history of ADHD in childhood report more intrusive thoughts and task-unrelated thoughts than control subjects (e.g., Hines & Shaw, 1993; Shaw & Giambra, 1993). Although speculative, one might hypothesize that high levels of internal restlessness and intrusive thoughts are associated with compromised attention skills and academic performance. Kessler et al. (2005) recently studied factors that predict whether ADHD persists into adulthood and found only two factors that predicted persistence: severity of ADHD in childhood and treatment during childhood. It is also important to note that *DSM* diagnostic criteria are not age-referenced and are limited in number with regard to hyperactivity and impulsivity relative to inattention (i.e., nine for inattention, six for hyperactivity, and three for impulsivity) which has lead researchers such as Spencer, Biederman, Wilens, and Faraone (2002) to suggest that the current criteria for ADHD may minimize, or underestimate, the actual rate of persistence of ADHD into adulthood.

With regard to gender, the American Psychiatric Association (2000) indicates that boys are more likely to be diagnosed with ADHD than girls, with ratios ranging from 2:1 to 9:1 depending on the subtype of ADHD. Other studies have provided male-female ratios of 3:1 in the general population, and 6:1 in children referred to clinics (Gaub & Carlson, 1997; Gershon, 2002). In general, research has supported that girls with ADHD tend to be less hyperactive, have fewer acting out problems, are less likely to have a learning disability, and are more likely than boys to have ADHD predominately inattentive type (Biederman & Spencer, 2002). Boys tend to be more hyperactive, have more aggression and acting out problems, and fewer attention and anxiety problems than girls with ADHD (Levy, Hay, Bennett, & McStephen, 2005; Newcorn et al., 2001). Recently, however, research by Joseph Biederman and colleagues at Massachusetts General Hospital, Boston, found that ADHD combined type was predominant in both boys and girls, and girls had the same relative risk for adverse outcomes as boys with ADHD even in adulthood (e.g., Biederman et al., 2004; Biederman & Faraone, 2004). Biederman et al. (2004) studied 219 adults with ADHD and concluded that higher rates of depression, anxiety, substance use disorders, and antisocial personality disorders were associated with ADHD in *both* genders. Learning disabilities (e.g., reading, math) appear to be equally prevalent in males and females with ADHD, although they are more common among males than females in the general population. Quinn (2005), however, has argued that ADHD is often a "hidden disorder" in females and has advocated for gender-sensitive diagnostic and treatment approaches for females with ADHD. Research has also found different patterns of cortical activity in adolescent males and females based on EEG recordings (Hermens, Kohn, Clarke, Gordon, & Williams, 2005) although the clinical relevance of these findings is unclear. What is clear is that ADHD affects both male and female adults, and they are at greater risk for a variety of difficulties including interpersonal problems and psychiatric comorbidity.

In summary, research indicates that ADHD symptoms appear in children, adolescents, and adults from various countries throughout the world. A variety of factors contribute to the inconsistent prevalence rates among studies. An important distinction is whether rates reflect the prevalence of ADHD symptoms or actual diagnosed cases of ADHD.

Outcome Studies and Comorbidity

A number of prospective follow-up and longitudinal studies have reported that children with ADHD are at risk for a wide range of pathology in adolescence and adulthood. For example, Lily Hechtman and colleagues conducted several follow-up studies in the 1970s and 1980s and reported that adolescents and young adults with ADHD had poorer social skills, lower self-esteem, completed fewer years of education, were involved in more automobile accidents, had more geographical moves, and greater academic and conduct problems compared to control subjects (e.g., Hechtman, Weiss & Perlman, 1980; Hechtman & Weiss, 1983; Weiss et al., 1979). Eakin et al. (2004) recently found that married adults with ADHD reported more family dysfunction and poorer overall marital adjustment than control families. In addition, Hechtman and Weiss (1986) conducted a 15-year prospective follow-up study and found greater alcohol use and antisocial behavior in those with ADHD compared to control subjects. Mannuzza and colleagues (1989) followed 103 adolescent and adult males who had been diagnosed as hyperactive as children and compared the arrest records to a control group. Results revealed that significantly more males with a history of hyperactivity had been arrested, convicted, and incarcerated compared to control subjects. Further analyses indicated, however, that it was not the persistence of ADHD that was associated with arrest history but rather the presence of antisocial/conduct disorder in adolescence and adulthood. In a later study, Mannuzza, Klein, Bessler, Malloy, & LaPadula (1993) followed 91 males with a history of childhood ADHD and found that 18% had antisocial personality disorder and 16% had drug abuse disorders. These figures were significantly higher than those of the control group compared (2% and 4%, respectively). More recently, Mannuzza, Klein, and Moulton (2002) conducted a 12-year follow-up study and found 29% of the children with pervasive ADHD had antisocial personality disorder. In addition, Mannuzza et al. found the ADHD group failed a significantly greater number of academic subjects, and completed less formal schooling than the control group.

Similar to Mannuzza et al. (1989), Barkley, Fischer, Smallish, and Fletcher (2004) found that adults with a history of childhood ADHD committed a variety of antisocial acts such as property theft, disorderly conduct, assault, carrying a concealed weapon, and illegal drug possession compared to control subjects. In addition, adults with ADHD had been arrested more frequently, primarily for drug possession, use, and sale of drugs. Kollins, McClernon, and Fuemmeler (2005) found that self-reported ADHD symptoms were significantly associated with risk of smoking and several studies have found that adults with ADHD are more likely to smoke cigarettes compared to control subjects (e.g., Wilens & Dodson, 2004). Lambert and Hartsough (1998) found 42% of adults with ADHD smoked cigarettes compared to 26% of controls and 35% of the subjects with ADHD smoked daily compared to 16% of age-matched control subjects. Biederman et al. (2006) recently suggested that cigarette smoking might serve as gateway to alcohol and illicit drugs among adolescents with ADHD. Specifically, Biederman et al. found that adolescents with ADHD who smoked were significantly more likely to subsequently use and abuse alcohol and illicit substances compared to adolescents with ADHD who did not smoke cigarettes.

Recently, Fischer, Barkley, Smallish, and Fletcher (2005) followed a large sample (147) of children with ADHD into early adulthood (average age 20 years) and found that they continued to have problems with executive functions, that is, inattention, disinhibition, and slowed reaction time compared to control subjects. In a related study, Barkley, Murphy, DuPaul, and Bush (2002) found that adults with ADHD and executive function deficits had received significantly more traffic citations, speeding citations, license suspensions, and had been involved in more vehicular crashes compared to adults without ADHD. Howell, Huessy, & Hassuk (1985) conducted a 15-year longitudinal study of 369 children who exhibited behaviors associated with ADHD and found that, in adulthood, they were more likely to have dropped out of school, been rejected for military service, to have used marijuana daily, and to be employed as manual laborers.

In addition to antisocial behaviors, research indicates that adults with ADHD are at risk for psychiatric comorbidity. For example, Mannuzza et al. (1993) compared adult psychiatric status of those who had been diagnosed with ADHD in childhood compared to those without the disorder and found that 16% of subjects with ADHD had drug abuse disorders (compared to 4% of control subjects). In addition, 50% had a history of conduct disorder by adolescence and as adults, were seven times more likely to have antisocial personality disorder. Other studies have also reported that adults with ADHD are more likely to use and abuse alcohol and illicit drugs. For example, Lambert and Hartsough (1998) reported that 21% of adults with ADHD were cocaine dependent compared to 10% of age-matched control subjects. Carroll and Rounsaville (1993) found that 35% of nearly 300 individuals seeking treatment for cocaine dependence had ADHD. Preliminary studies also suggest that cocaine dependence may be more difficult to treat in adults with ADHD, as individuals with ADHD are less likely to complete treatment than those without the disorder (Levin et al., 2004). Saules, Pomerleau, and Schubiner (2003) have suggested that severity of ADHD symptoms is associated with a greater likelihood of using and becoming addicted to cocaine among adults with ADHD.

With regard to alcohol and other substances, studies have found that 20%–50% of adults with ADHD have a comorbid substance use disorder (Johann, Bobbe, Putzhamer, & Wodarz, 2003; Schubiner, 2005). Murphy, Barkley, and Bush (2002) compared adults with two different subtypes of ADHD (ADHD combined type, ADHD predominantly inattentive type) and control subjects and found that both groups of adults with ADHD had a greater risk of alcohol use and dependence as well as marijuana use and dependence. Johann et al. (2003) found that adults with ADHD and coexisting alcoholism had an earlier onset of alcohol dependence, a higher frequency of suicide ideation, and a higher daily and monthly use of alcohol compared to control subjects and adults with alcoholism but not ADHD. Studies also indicate that individuals with ADHD and alcoholism (and other substance use disorders) are at greater risk for failing to complete treatment and relapse (Levin, Evans, & Kleber, 1999; White et al., 2004). Schubiner et al. (2000) studied the prevalence of ADHD and conduct disorder among adults in chemical dependency centers and found 24% of the participants met *DSM-IV* criteria for ADHD (28% of men, 19% of women). Thirty-four of the 48 adults with ADHD in this study also had conduct disorder. Given the high rate of co-occurrence of conduct disorder with ADHD, several researchers have argued that conduct disorder, not ADHD, increases the risk of substance disorders in adults with ADHD (e.g., Flory, Milich, Lynam, Leukefeld, & Clayton, 2003; Lynskey & Hall, 2001). Barkley et al. (2004) noted that adults with ADHD have a greater likelihood of using substances (and other antisocial behavior), but those with co-existing conduct disorder appear to engage in a greater variety of more frequent use of substances.

With regard to comorbid psychiatric conditions, the findings have been mixed. For example, Mannuzza et al. (1993) did not find a higher incidence of mood or anxiety disorders among the adults with a history of ADHD. Biederman and colleagues (1993), however, studied 84 adults with childhood-onset ADHD and found significantly higher rates of major depression and anxiety disorders compared to control subjects. McGough et al. (2005) reported that 87% of adults with ADHD had at least one psychiatric disorder and 56% had two or more psychiatric disorders, including anxiety and mood disorders. Kennemer and Goldstein (2005) reported that major depression was the most common psychiatric condition for adults with ADHD who were treated in an inpatient setting. Nierenberg et al. (2005) studied adults with bipolar disorder and found that 14.7% of the males and 5.8% of the females had coexisting ADHD. In addition, Biederman et al. (1993) found a significantly greater percentage of adults with ADHD had been divorced or separated, were of lower socioeconomic status, had antisocial personality disorder, had a lower full-scale IQ, and while in school had experienced higher rates of learning disabilities, placement in special education, and repeated grades.

Some have questioned whether use of stimulant medication for ADHD in childhood increases the likelihood of drug use and abuse in adolescence and adulthood. Several long-term studies have investigated this issue and have found that for most individuals the use of medication on a regular basis is not associated with an increased risk of drug involvement and in many cases is actually associated with a *decreased* risk (Chilcoat & Breslau, 1999; Huss & Lehmkuhl, 2002; Weiss & Hechtman, 1993). Barkley, Fischer, Smallish, and Fletcher (2003) followed children with ADHD for 13 years and during adolescence and young adulthood were interviewed about their length of stimulant medication treatment and their drug use. Results revealed that stimulant-treated children had no greater risk for experimenting with drugs during adolescence or frequency of drug use in adulthood. Biederman (2003) also found that stimulant medication treatment appeared to serve a protective role against substance use disorder in adults as substance use disorder rates were 3 to 4 times higher in adults with untreated ADHD. Recently, Katusic et al. (2005) reported that 21.8% of young adult males treated for ADHD had substance use disorder compared to 36.4% of untreated males with ADHD. Among treated females, however, 15.2% had substance use disorder compared to 10.3% of untreated females with ADHD.

Etiologic Theories

One factor that contributes to the controversy surrounding ADHD in adulthood is that the precise etiology of ADHD is unknown. Findings from genetic, neurochemical, neuroimaging, and neuropsychological studies, however, collectively support a neurobiological basis for the disorder. For example, twin and adoption studies have demonstrated that genetic factors are important in the expression of ADHD, and monozygotic twins are significantly more likely than dizygotic twins to meet the criteria for ADHD (78% and 35%, respectively) (Sherman, Iacono, & McGue, 1997; Willcutt, Pennington, & DeFries, 2000). Familial studies have also found that individuals with ADHD are more likely to have siblings or parents with ADHD relative to families with no history of ADHD (Biederman et al., 1993). Wilens et al. (2005a) recently reported that children of parents with ADHD and substance use disorder were at greater risk for ADHD compared to children of parents with ADHD only or, substance use disorder only or neither diagnosis.

Neuroanatomical, neurochemical, and neuroimaging studies collectively have supported a physiological basis for ADHD although some findings have been inconsistent. Several studies, for example, have reported differences in size and symmetry of anatomical brain structures (e.g., corpus callosum, cerebellum, striatum) when comparing individuals with and without ADHD, while other studies have not replicated these findings (e.g., Castellanos et al., 2002; Giedd et al., 1994; Hynd et al., 1991; Mostofsky, Reiss, Lockhart, & Denckla, 1998). Numerous neurotransmitter, neurometabolite, cerebral blood flow, and glucose metabolism studies have also reported differences between those with and without ADHD although the factors responsible for these differences remain unclear (e.g., Schulz et al., 2005; Teicher et al., 2000; Volkow, Wang, Fowler, & Ding, 2005; Weyandt, 2006; Yeo et al., 2003; Zametkin et al., 1990).

It is critical to note that anatomical and neuroimaging findings are correlational in nature and do not reveal the underlying cause of the morphological or functional differences between those with and without ADHD. Studies that have investigated neuropsychological functioning in adults with ADHD have focused primarily on intelligence and executive function tasks. Although some studies have reported differences in IQ (e.g., Biederman et al., 1993) in adults with and without ADHD, other studies have not found these differences (Katz et al., 1998; Weyandt, Mitzlaff, & Thomas, 2002). Several studies have also reported differences between adults with and without ADHD on executive function tasks (e.g., Bekker et al., 2005; Fischer, Barkley, Fletcher, Smallish, 2005; Weyandt, Rice, Linterman, Mitzlaff, & Emert, 1998) but others have not (e.g., Schoechlin & Engel, 2005). It is plausible that executive function deficits influence IQ test performance and it is equally plausible that intellectual capacity influences performance on executive function tasks. Murphy, Barkley, and Bush (2001) have argued that that ADHD shares a portion (i.e., 10%) of the variance with IQ and executive function performance is negatively correlated with ADHD symptom severity. Furthermore, Murphy et al. argued that executive function performance is positively correlated with IQ and they found that performance differences attenuated on several neuropsychological tasks when IQ was controlled for in subjects with and without ADHD. Given these findings, Murphy et al. suggested that future studies should report and control for IQ group differences.

In general, research indicates that neuropsychological tasks do not reliably discriminate among adults with and without ADHD (Schoechlin & Engel, 2005; Weyandt, 2005a). Indeed, as Weyandt (2005b) noted, impairments in certain types of executive function deficits may be characteristic of individuals with ADHD but executive function deficits are not unique to individuals with ADHD. Several neurobiological theories have been advanced to explain the underlying pathophysiology of ADHD and most converge on abnormalities of frontal-subcortical networks, i.e., structures involving regions such as the basal ganglia pathways leading to and from prefrontal cortices (e.g., Schulz et al., 2005). Although the precise etiology of the structural and functional abnormalities implicated in ADHD is unknown, it is likely due to interactions between genetic, physiological, and environmental factors that ultimately affect brain development and neuronal functioning. For example, evidence suggests that ADHD may be due in part to polymorphisms in dopamine genes that modulate neurotransmission in subcortical and cortical regions (Madras, Miller, & Fischman, 2005). It is also plausible that prenatal factors such as exposure to teratogens and other risk factors result in morphological and functional abnormalities within the frontal-subcortical region (Lou, 1996; Rodriguez & Bohlin, 2005). These morphological and functional abnormalities may contribute to the dysregulation of cognitive and behavioral systems that mediate the core behaviors deficient in ADHD, such as attention, self-regulation, motor behavior, and executive functions. Future genetic and neurophysiological studies are needed to fully understand the complex underpinnings of ADHD.

Treatment

Various types of treatments are available for adults with ADHD including pharmacotherapy and non-pharmacotherapy approaches. Compared to the child literature, relatively few well-designed medication studies have been conducted with adults with ADHD. For example, in 2002, over 200 controlled studies evaluating the effectiveness of stimulants (methylphenidate) in children and adolescents had been conducted in contrast to six controlled studies with adults (Biederman & Spencer, 2002). Of those that have been conducted, results support the effectives of medication in the treatment of ADHD. Several types of medication have been studied in the treatment of adult ADHD including stimulants, non-stimulants, and antidepressants. Commonly used stimulants, non-stimulants, and antidepressants are presented in Table 23.1.

Stimulant Medications

Stimulants are the most commonly used medication to treat ADHD, and, according to Zito et al. (2000), 80% of children treated with stimulants are treated with methylphenidate. Faraone, Spencer, Montano and Biederman (2004b) reported that 84% among a sample of approximately 900 adults with ADHD were treated with stimulants. Although the precise mode of action of stimulants in still uncertain, studies using neuroimaging techniques have revealed that methylphenidate results in an increase of the neurotransmitter dopamine by blocking the mechanism by which dopamine is removed from the point of cellular communication (e.g., Rosa-Neto et al., 2005; Volkow, Fowler, Wang, Ding, & Gatley, 2002; Volkow, Wang, Fowler, & Ding, 2005). Matochik and colleagues (1993) also found that stimulants (methylphenidate) increase glucose metabolism throughout

Table 23.1 Commonly Used Stimulants, Non-stimulants, and Antidepressants

	Generic Name	Trade Name
Stimulant Medications		
	Methylphenidate	Ritalin, Concerta, Metadate, Methylin
	Dextroamphetamine Dexmethylphenidate	DexedrineFocalin
	Amphetamine Salts	Adderall
Non-Stimulant Medications		
	Atomoxetine	Strattera
Antidepressant Medications		
Tricyclics	Imipramine	Tofranil
	Desipramine	Norpramin
	Nortriptyline	Pamelor
SSRIs	Sertraline	Zoloft
	Fluoxetine	Prozac
	Paroxetine	Paxil
	Fluvoxamine	Luvox
Other	Bupropion	Wellbutrin

the brain, not in restricted regions as expected. Rosa-Neto et al. (2005) reported that stimulants (methylphenidate) evoked specific changes in the striatal region of the brain and increased dopaminergic transmission in this area.

Although relatively few studies have been published concerning the use of stimulant medications with adults with ADHD, those that have generally support the effectiveness of stimulants with this population. For example, Wood, Reimherr, Wender, and Johnson (1976) were among the first to study the effects of methylphenidate on 15 adults with ADHD and found that 8 adults showed a "good" response to the medication. In a later study, Wender, Reimherr, Wood, and Ward (1985) found that 57% of adults treated with methylphenidate showed a significant reduction in ADHD symptoms compared to 11% who receive a placebo. Mattes, Boswell, and Oliver (1984) reported a lower response rate (25%) in adults with ADHD who were treated with methylphenidate for a three-week period. More recently, Kooij, Burger, Boonstra, et al. (2004) studied the effectiveness of methylphenidate (versus placebo) in the treatment of 45 adults with ADHD. Results revealed that 38% of those treated with methylphenidate compared to 7% placebo showed a significant favorable response based on outcome measures; however, 82% of adults treated with methylphenidate reported adverse side effects such as loss of appetite, sleeping problems, headaches, dizziness, and abdominal complaints. Bouffard et al. (2003) described methylphenidate as having minimal side effects in adults with ADHD and found significant improvements on adult rating scales, neuropsychological measures, and anxiety and depression scales. Overall, the researchers reported a 63% to73% response rate to methylphenidate, which is higher than the Kooij et al. study (2004). Wilens, Spencer, and Biederman (2002) noted that variability in response rates across studies might be related to diagnostic criteria, doses of medication, co-morbidity rates, and methods of assessing medication effectiveness.

Stimulant medications have also been associated with improved neuropsychological functioning. For example, Riordan et al. (1999) studied the neuropsychological functioning of adults with ADHD before and after approximately one-month treatment with methylphenidate. Results revealed significant improvements in various measures including sustained attention, distractibility, problem solving and memory. Lastly, Dorrego and colleagues (2002) compared the effectiveness of methylphenidate and lithium in treating ADHD in adults and reported that the medications produced similar rates of improvement on measures of aggressiveness, anxiety, depression, irritability, and antisocial behavior. A greater number of side effects were associated with the lithium treatment compared to methylphenidate. Biederman and Spencer (2002) reported that responses to methylphenidate were less robust in adults with ADHD compared to improvements found in children and adolescents. However, in a recent meta-analysis of the efficacy of methylphenidate for treating adult ADHD, Faraone and colleagues (2004a) concluded the degree of efficacy was similar to the child literature.

Cylert and Adderall.   A handful of studies have explored the effectiveness of other stimulants including Cylert (pemoline) and Adderall in the treatment of adult ADHD. For example, Wood, Reimherr, Wender, and Johnson (1976) and Wender, Reimherr, and Wood (1981) found that pemoline was significantly more effective than placebo at reducing ADHD symptoms in adults. Cylert is no longer considered a first line of treatment for ADHD, however, due to concerns about liver toxicity (Horrigan, 2001). Adderall is a mixture of amphetamine salts (75% D-amphetamine, 25% L-amphetamine), and research supports its effectiveness in treating ADHD in children and adolescents (Manos, Short, & Findling, 1999; McGough, Pataki, & Suddath, 2005)—particularly those who show no response or an adverse response to methylphenidate (Pliszka, Browne, Olvera, & Wynne 2000). With regard to the use of Adderall with adults, Spencer, Biederman, Wilens, et al. (2001) found that 70% of adults with ADHD showed a 30% or greater reduction in ADHD symptoms following a 7-week treatment with Adderall. Horrigan and Barnhill (2000) used Adderall to treat 24 adults with ADHD and found that 54% showed significant improvement on ADHD rating scales after a 16-week period. Thirty-eight percent, however, were regarded as poor responders and acute anxiety symptoms occurred in the majority of the adults who had co-existing anxiety disorders. Additional questions have been raised about the safety of Adderall following the sudden death in 12 boys (ages 7–16) who had been taking the medication. As a result of the deaths, the Canadian drug regulatory agency suspended the sale of Adderall in the Canadian market in February of 2005. The United States FDA investigated the cases, did not remove Adderall from the market, and issued a statement that patients (and parents of patients) taking Adderall should discuss any concerns with the prescribing physician.

Illegal Use of Stimulants.   Although thousands of studies attest to the safety and effectiveness of stimulants in treating ADHD in children and adolescents, stimulants do have the potential for abuse with adolescents and adults. For example, Low and Gendaszek (2002) surveyed undergraduate students at a small college in Maine, and found that 35% of the students sampled reported illicit use of stimulants. Common reasons for using stimulants illegally included a) to improve intellectual performance (23%), b) to be more efficient on academic assignments (22%), and c) for recreational purposes, i.e., in combinations with alcohol (19%) (known as "pharming"; Kadison, 2005). Studies have found that male college students tend to report greater illicit use of stimulants than female college students. However, Teter and colleagues (2003) found only 3% of college students from the

University of Michigan reported illicit use of stimulants and males and females did not differ in their use. Hall, Irwin, Bowman, Frankenberger, and Jewett (2005) conducted a study in the Midwest, and found that 17% of male college students and 11% of female college students reported illicit use of stimulant medication. McCabe and colleagues (2005) surveyed more than 10,000 college students from 119 colleges across the United States and found that 6.9% of students reported illicit use of stimulants. Illicit use of stimulants varied tremendously across universities, however, with the highest use among students who attended universities in the Northeast region of the United States. Upadhyaya et al. (2005) surveyed college students regarding current ADHD symptoms and drug use and found 25% of those prescribed medication for ADHD reported using for recreational purposes and 29% reported giving it or selling it to someone else at least once.

Although methylphenidate can be and is sometimes misused by adolescents and young adults, it is thought to be relatively non-addictive (Volkow et al., 2002). Kollins (2003) reported that the pharmacokinetic properties of methylphenidate are substantially different from other types of stimulants that are often abused (e.g., cocaine) therefore lessening its abuse and addiction potential. Interestingly, Levin et al. (2006) found that adults with ADHD who participated in a methadone treatment program did not misuse methylphenidate when treated with this medication to improve their ADHD symptoms. Wilens, Faraone, Biederman, and Gunawardene (2003a) conducted a meta-analysis to determine whether treatment of ADHD with stimulants increased the risk of substance abuse in adolescence and adulthood. Results revealed a *reduction* in risk for those treated with stimulants for ADHD compared to those with the disorder who did not receive stimulants. Similar findings were reported by Barkley et al. (2003) after following children with ADHD for 13 years during adolescence and young adulthood and interviewing them about their length of stimulant medication treatment and their drug use. Results revealed that stimulant-treated children had no greater risk for experimenting with drugs during adolescence or frequency of drug use in adulthood.

Non-Stimulant Medication

The FDA approved the use of Strattera (atomoxetine) for the treatment of ADHD in children, adolescents, *and* adults in 2002. Strattera is a non-stimulant, non-antidepressant medication that prevents the reuptake of norepinephrine (stimulants target dopamine) at the cellular level causing more of this neurotransmitter to be available at the synapse. Since its approval, a fair amount of studies have supported the effectiveness of Strattera for improving ADHD symptoms in children and adolescents, including both males and females (e.g., Biederman & Spencer, 2002; Kaplan et al., 2004; Kelsey et al., 2004; Simpson & Plosker, 2004; Spencer et al., 2002; Weiss et al., 2005). At least one study has reported that Strattera is equally effective as methylphenidate at treating ADHD in children (Kratochvil et al., 2002). With regard to adults, Simpson and Plosker (2004) and Faraone et al. (2005b) found Strattera significantly reduced ADHD symptoms relative to placebo with very few side effects. Recently, however, concerns have been raised about the possibility that Strattera increases suicidal thoughts in children and adolescents, and in September 2005 the FDA ordered that the manufacturer of Strattera, Eli Lilly, carry a prominent "black box" warning on its label. This is the FDA's most serious alert and was based on Eli Lilly's research with 1,357 children who were taking Strattera compared to children who were not taking the medication. Results revealed that 5 of the 1,357 children reported suicidal thoughts while no children in the control group had reported these thoughts. It is unknown whether Strattera is associated with suicide ideation in adults.

Antidepressant Medication

Antidepressants, including tricyclics and Selective Serotonin Reuptake Inhibitors (SSRIs) are used less often than stimulants to treat ADHD, although a few studies have supported their effectiveness with adults with ADHD (e.g., Maidment, 2003; Wilens et al., 1996). Tricyclic antidepressants sometimes used for individuals with ADHD include imipramine (Tofranil), desipramine (Norpramin), and nortriptyline (Pamelor). These medications are usually reserved for adults with ADHD due to their ability to increase blood pressure and rapid heart rate in some children and adolescents (Popper, 2000). Tricyclic antidepressants are slower acting than stimulants and may take four to six weeks to show effects. Tricyclic antidepressant medication may be useful for individuals with ADHD who do not respond to stimulants or for those who may misuse stimulants. For example, Williams and colleagues (2004) found that 23% of 450 adolescents referred for substance abuse treatment reported non-medical use of methylphenidate and Dexedrine and therefore suggested that antidepressants or other non-stimulant medications be used with substance abusing individuals with ADHD. Tricyclic antidepressants and selective serotonin reuptake inhibitors (SSRIs) have also been used with individuals with ADHD who have coexisting affective disorders such as depression. As Waxmonsky (2005) noted, there has been increasing interest in combining medications, such as stimulants and antidepressants to attenuate treatment effects. Horrigan (2001) reported, however, that the use of tricyclic antidepressants is dwindling perhaps out of concern for the potential for cardiac problems, particularly in those with a history of heart arrythmias. SSRIs can be used in conjunction with stimulants to treat coexisting anxiety disorders or depression and include sertraline (Zoloft), fluoxetine (Prozac), paroxetine (Paxil), and fluvoxamine (Luvox). SSRIs have been found to have fewer side effects and therefore are often better tolerated than tricyclics in adults with ADHD. A third type of antidepressant is bupropion (Wellbutrin), believed to affect multiple neurotransmitter systems, and has been found to be effective at treating ADHD in adults (Daviss et al., 2001; Wender & Reimherr, 1990; Wilens et al., 2001; Wilens et al., 2003b; Wilens et al., 2005b).

It is important to note that research indicates that stimulants are superior to antidepressants at improving ADHD symptoms, and far more research is available concerning the use and safety of stimulants than antidepressants in treating ADHD in adults. Furthermore, the FDA has *not* approved the use of antidepressants for the specific treatment of ADHD in children or adults. In addition to stimulants, antidepressants, and non-stimulants, researchers have explored the role of other medications (e.g., cholinergic agents) in the treatment of ADHD in adults but less information is available concerning the safety and efficacy of these medications. For now, stimulant medications represent the "gold standard treatment for ADHD across the lifespan" (Horrigan, 2001, p. 582). Additional studies are needed, however, to better understand the pharmacology of stimulants and the safety and effectiveness of these medications in the treatment of adult ADHD.

Non-Pharmacological Interventions

A large number of non-pharmacological interventions have been studied in the treatment of ADHD including biofeedback, dietary supplements, dietary restrictions, fatty acids, massage, yoga, exercise, caffeine, music therapy, and sensory integration training to name a few (Weyandt, 2006). A review of these studies is beyond the scope of this chapter and it is important to note that nearly all of these studies have been conducted with children and adolescents, and therefore information is limited with respect to adults. Moreover, most of the non-pharmacological interventions studies are fraught with methodological problems thereby limiting their usefulness. In general, research indicates that stimulant medications are far superior to alternative approaches in the treatment of ADHD. Biofeedback (i.e., neurofeedback) has received considerable attention recently and a few studies have reported adults with ADHD showed a decrease in symptoms following treatment with biofeedback (Butnik, 2005). Loo and Barkley (2005), however, conducted an extensive review of the literature concerning biofeedback and ADHD and concluded "there is much work to be done to demonstrate EEG biofeedback provides that alternative and that actually changing EEG is the mechanism of change in ADHD symptoms" (p. 73). A handful of studies have examined whether structured-skill building interventions are beneficial to adults with ADHD (Safren, Sprich, Chulvick, & Otto, 2004). For example, adults with ADHD often have issues with disorganization, anger management, financial management, stress management and social skill deficits, and structured skill building programs seek to train and improve the skill level of adults with ADHD in these and other areas. Some programs have used cognitive behavioral and metacognitive approaches to help improve skill deficits of adults with ADHD and the results have been mixed (e.g., Hesslinger et al., 2002; Safren et al., 2005; Wasserstein & Lynn, 2001). Other non-pharmacological interventions targeted for adults with ADHD include psychotherapy (Murphy & Gordon, 1998; Young, 2002), career and vocational counseling (Crawford & Crawford, 2002), marital therapy (Kilcarr, 2002), and life coaching (Ratey, 2002) to name a few. It is important to recognize that non-pharmacological interventions are skill focused, are not uniquely associated with ADHD, and do not address the underlying core symptoms of ADHD.

Assessment of Adult ADHD

The American Academy of Pediatrics (2000) has recommended a multi-method assessment approach be followed in the assessment of ADHD in children and adolescents. A similar multifaceted approach has been recommended for the assessment of ADHD in adults, using multiple assessment measures and multiple informants (Murphy & Gordon, 1998). The process should involve documenting past and current symptoms consistent with *DSM-IV-TR* criteria, establishing that symptoms cause impairment, thorough developmental, social, educational, psychiatric, and medical histories, and use of multiple measures to collect objective data. Methods useful in collecting information about an adult evaluated for ADHD include interviews, behavior rating scales, self-report measures, record review, standardized-normed referenced tests (e.g., intelligence, achievement), and possibly laboratory measures such as continuous performance tasks. Each measure yields a different type of information that is useful in determining whether an individual has ADHD and/or some other problem(s) and requires collaboration among medical personnel, and possibly parents, spouses, employers, or other significant individuals.

Obtaining information from a variety of sources (e.g., adult and spouse/parent/roommate) is critical, as research indicates that diagnoses based on a single informant are likely to be inaccurate (i.e., invalid) (Mitsis, McKay, Schulz, Newcorn, & Halperin, 2000). Although many advocate this multi-method assessment for adults, McGough and Barkley (2004) noted the *DSM-IV-TR* criteria are problematic as they a) have never been validated in adults and b) do not include developmentally appropriate symptoms for adults. Asherson (2005) has argued many cases of adult ADHD may go unrecognized as clinicians may be unfamiliar with symptoms of ADHD in adults.

Implications of Research Findings

Until relatively recently, ADHD was considered a disorder of childhood however, longitudinal and retrospective studies indicate that the majority of individuals continue to have symptoms throughout adolescence and adulthood. ADHD occurs more often in adult males than females but both sexes have a similar relative risk for adult outcomes. Adults with ADHD are at increased risk for antisocial personality disorder as well as depression, anxiety, and substance use disorders. Studies also indicate that adults with ADHD are more likely to have completed fewer years of education, received special educational services, repeated grades, received traffic citations, speeding citations and license suspensions, and been involved in more vehicular crashes compared to adults without ADHD. In addition, adults with ADHD are more likely to experience executive function deficits, family dysfunction and poorer overall marital adjustment. Secnik, Swensen, and Lage (2005) recently reported that employees with ADHD have a higher percentage of comorbidities (e.g., anxiety, asthma, bipolar disorder, substance abuse), higher medical costs, and more absences and unofficial absences compared to employees without the disorder. ADHD in adults is clearly a valid disorder, one that impairs the daily functioning and quality of life of individuals with the disorder. Treatment can significantly improve the symptoms of ADHD, however, and stimulant medication has received the most empirical support. Non-pharmacological interventions are numerous although little information is available concerning the effectiveness of these interventions in the treatment of ADHD. Compared to knowledge concerning ADHD in children and adolescents, a dearth of scientific information is available concerning ADHD in adults. Methodologically rigorous studies are sorely needed to better understand the nature of ADHD in adulthood and to develop ways to effectively improve the symptoms associated with this disorder.

References

American Academy of Pediatrics. (2000). Clinical practice guideline: Diagnosis and evaluation of the child with attention-deficit/hyperactivity disorder. *Pediatrics, 105*, 1158–1170.

American Psychiatric Association. (2000). *Diagnostic and statistical manual of mental disorders* (4th ed., text revision). Washington DC: Author.

Asherson, P. (2005). Clinical assessment and treatment of attention deficit hyperactivity disorder in adults. *Expert Review of Neurotherapy, 5*, 525–539.

Barkley, R. A. (1998). *Attention-deficit/hyperactivity disorder: A handbook for diagnosis and treatment* (2nd ed.). New York: Guilford.

Barkley, R. A., Fischer, M., Smallish, L., & Fletcher, K. (2002). The persistence of attention-deficit/hyperactivity disorder into young adulthood as a function of reporting source and definition of disorder. *Journal of Abnormal Psychology, 111*, 279–289.

Barkley, R. A., Fischer, M., Smallish, L., & Fletcher, K. (2003). Does the treatment of attention-deficit/hyperactivity disorder with stimulants contribute to drug use/abuse? A 13-year prospective study. *Pediatrics, 111*, 97–109.

Barkley, R. A., Fischer, M., Smallish, L., & Fletcher, K. (2004). Young adult follow-up of hyperactive children: Antisocial activities and drug use. *Journal of Child Psychology and Psychiatry, 45*, 195–211.

Barkley, R. A., Murphy, K. R., DuPaul, G. I., & Bush, T. (2002). Driving in young adults with attention deficit hyperactivity disorder: Knowledge, performance, adverse outcomes, and the role of executive functioning. *Journal of the International Neuropsychological Society, 8*, 655–672.

Bekker, E. M., Overtoom, C. C., Kooij, J. J., Buitelaar, J. K., Verbaten, M. N., & Kenemans, J. L. (2005). Disentangling deficits in adults with attention-deficit/hyperactivity disorder. *Archives of General Psychiatry, 62*, 1129–1136.

Benjasuwantep, B., Ruangdaraganon, N., & Visudhiphan, P. (2002). Prevalence and clinical characteristics of attention deficit hyperactivity disorder among primary school students in Bangkok. *Journal of the Medical Association of Thailand, 85*(Suppl. 4), S1232–S1240.

Bhatia, M. S., Nigam, V. R., Bohra, N., & Malik, S. C. (1991). Attention deficit disorder with hyperactivity among pediatric outpatients. *Journal of Child Psychology and Psychiatry, 32,* 297–306.

Biederman, J. (2003). Pharmacotherapy for attention-deficit/hyperactivity disorder (ADHD) decreases the risk for substance abuse: Findings from a longitudinal follow-up of youths with and without ADHD.

Biederman, J., & Faraone, S. V. (2004). The Massachusetts General Hospital studies of gender influences on attention-deficit/hyperactivity disorder in youth and relatives. *Psychiatric Clinics of North America, 27,* 225–232.

Biederman, J., Faraone, S. V., Monuteaux, M. C., Bober, M., & Cadogen, E. (2004). Gender effects on attention-deficit/hyperactivity disorder in adults, revisited. *Biological Psychiatry, 55,* 692–700.

Biderman, J., Faraone, S. V., Spencer, T., Wilens, T., Norman, D., Lapey, K. A., et al. (1993). Patterns of psychiatric comorbidity, cognition, and psychosocial functioning in adults with attention deficit hyperactivity disorder. *American Journal of Psychiatry, 150,* 1790–1798.

Biederman, J., Mick, E., & Faraone, S. V. (2000). Age dependent decline of ADHD symptoms revisited: Impact of remission definition and symptom subtype. *American Journal of Psychiatry, 157,* 816–818.

Biederman, J., Monuteaux, M. C., Mick, E., Wilens, T. E., Fontanella, J. A., Poetzl, K. M., et al. (2006). Is cigarette smoking a gateway to alcohol and illicit drug use disorders? A study of youths with and without attention deficit hyperactivity disorder. *Biological Psychiatry, 59,* 258–264.

Biederman, J., & Spencer, T. (2002). Methylphenidate in treatment of adults with attention-deficit/hyperactivity disorder. *Journal of Attention Disorders, 6,* S101–S107.

Blackwell, D. L., & Tonthat, L. (2002). Summary health statistics for U. S. children: National Health Interview Survey, 1998. *Vital and Health Statistics, 10,* 1–46.

Bouffard, R., Hechtman, L., Minde, K., & Iaboni-Kassab, F. (2003). The efficacy of 2 different dosages of methylphenidate in treating adults with attention-deficit hyperactivity disorder. *Canadian Journal of Psychiatry, 48,* 546–554.

Brook, U., & Boaz, M. (2005). Attention deficit and hyperactivity disorder (ADHD) and learning disabilities (LD): Adolescents perspective. *Patient Education and Counseling, 58,* 187–191.

Brownell, M. D., & Yogendran, M. S. (2001). Attention-deficit hyperactivity disorder in Manitoba children: Medical diagnosis and psychostimulant treatment rates. *Canadian Journal of Psychiatry, 46,* 264–272.

Butnik, S. M. (2005). Neurofeedback in adolescents and adults with attention deficit hyperactivity disorder. *Journal of Clinical Psychology, 61,* 621–625.

Carroll, K. M., & Rounsaville, B. J. (1993). History and significance of childhood attention deficit disorder in treatment-seeking cocaine abusers. *Comprehensive Psychiatry, 34,* 75–82.

Castellanos, F. X., Lee, P. P., Sharp, W., Jeffries, N. O., Greenstein, D. K., Clasen, L. S., et al. (2002). Developmental trajectories of brain volume abnormalities in children and adolescents with attention-deficit/hyperactivity disorder. *Journal of the American Medical Association, 288,* 1740–1748.

Chapman, J. W., Tunmer, W. E., & Allen, R. (2003). Findings from the International Adult Literacy Survey on the incidence and correlates of learning disabilities in New Zealand: Is something rotten in the state of New Zealand? *Dyslexia, 9,* 78–98.

Chilcoat, H. D., & Breslau, N. (1999). Pathways from ADHD to early drug use. *Journal of the American Academy of Child and Adolescent Psychiatry, 38,* 1347–1362.

Claude, D., & Firestone, P. (1995). The development of ADHD boys: A 12 year follow up. *Canadian Journal of Behavioral Science, 27,* 226–249.

Crawford, R., & Crawford, V. (2002). Career impact: Finding the key to issues facing adults with ADHD. In S. Goldstein & A. T. Ellison (Eds.), *Clinician's Guide to Adult ADHD: Assessment and Intervention,* pp. 187–204. Boston: Academic Press.

Daviss, W. B., Bentivoglio, P., Racusin, R., Brown, K. M., Bostic, J. Q., & Wiley, L. (2001). Bupropion sustained release in adolescents with comorbid attention-deficit/hyperactivity disorder and depression. *Journal of the American Academy of Child and Adolescent Psychiatry, 40,* 307–314.

Dorrego, M. F., Canevaro, L., Kuzis, G., Sabe, L., & Starkstein, S. E. (2002). A randomized, double-blind, crossover study of methylphenidate and lithium in adults with attention-deficit/hyperactivity disorder: Preliminary findings. *Journal of Neuropsychiatry and Clinical Neurosciences, 14,* 289–295.

DuPaul, G. J., Schaughency, E., Weyandt, L. L., Tripp, G., Kiesner, J., Ota, K., et al. (2001). Self-report of attention-deficit/hyperactivity disorder symptoms in university students: Cross-national prevalence. *Journal of Learning Disabilities, 34,* 370–379.

Eakin, L., Minde, K., Hechtman, L., Ochs, E., Krane, E., Bouffard, R., et al. (2004). The martial and family functioning of adults with ADHD and their spouses. *Journal of Attention Disorders, 8,* 1–10.

Faraone, S. V., Biederman, J., Spencer, T., Michelson, D., Adler, L., Reimherr, F., et al. (2005a). Atomoxetine and stroop task performance in adult attention-deficit/hyperactivity disorder. *Journal of Child and Adolescent Psychopharmacology, 15,* 664–670.

Faraone, S. V., Biederman, J., Spencer, T., Michelson, D., Adler, L., Reimherr, F., et al. (2005b). Efficacy of atomoxetine in adult attention-deficit/hyperactivity disorder: A drug-placebo response curve analysis. *Behavioral and Brain Functions, 1,* 16.

Faraone, S. V., Biederman, J., Spencer, T., Wilens, T., Seidman, L. J., Mick, E., et al. (2000). Attention-deficit/hyperactivity disorder in adults: An overview. *Society of Biological Psychiatry, 48,* 9–20.

Faraone, S. V., Sergeant, J., Gillberg, C., & Biederman, J. (2003). The worldwide prevalence of ADHD: Is it an American condition? *World Psychiatry, 2,* 104–113.

Faraone, S. V., Spencer, T., Aleardi, M., Pagano, C., & Biederman, J. (2004a). Meta-analysis of the efficacy of methylphenidate for treating adult attention-deficit/hyperactivity disorder. *Journal of Clinical Psychopharmacology, 24,* 24–29.

Faraone, S. V., Spencer, T. J., Montano, C. B., & Biederman, J. (2004b). Attention-deficit/hyperactivity disorder in adults: A survey of current practice in psychiatry and primary care. *Archives of Internal Medicine, 164,* 1221–1226.

Fischer, M., Barkley, R. A., Fletcher, K., & Smallish, L. (2005). Executive functioning in hyperactive children as young adults: Attention, inhibition, response perseveration, and the impact of comorbidity. *Developmental Neuropsychology, 27,* 107–133.

Flory, K., Milich, R., Lynam, D. R., Leukefeld, C., & Clayton, R. (2003). Relation between childhood disruptive behavior disorders and substance use and dependence symptoms in young adulthood: Individuals with symptoms of attention-deficit/hyperactivity disorder and conduct disorder are uniquely at risk. *Psychology of Addictive Behaviors, 17,* 151–158.

Gadow, K. D., Nolan, E. E., Litcher, L., Carlson, G. A., Panina, N. Golovakha, E., et al. (2000). Comparison of attention-deficit/hyperactivity disorder symptom subtypes in Ukrainian schoolchildren. *Journal of the American Academy of Child and Adolescent Psychiatry, 39,* 1520–1527.

Gaub, M., & Carlson, C. L. (1997). Gender differences in ADHD: A meta-analysis and critical review. *Journal of the American Academy of Child and Adolescent Psychiatry, 36,* 1036–1045.

Gershon, J. (2002). A meta-analytic review of gender differences in ADHD. *Journal of Attention Disorders, 5,* 143–154.

Giedd, J. N., Castellanos, F. X., Casey, B. J., Kozuch, P., King, C. A., Hamburger, S. D., et al. (1994). Quantitative morphology of corpus callosum in attention deficit hyperactivity disorder. *American Journal of Psychiatry, 151,* 665–669.

Goldstein, S. (2002). Continuity of ADHD in adulthood: Hypothesis and theory. In S. Goldstein & A. T. Ellison (Eds.), *Clinician's Guide to Adult ADHD: Assessment and Intervention,* pp. 25–45. Boston: Academic Press.

Graetz, B. W., Sawyer, M. G., Hazell, P. L., Arney, F., & Baghurst, P. (2001). Validity of DSM-IV ADHD subtypes in a nationally representative sample of Australian children and adolescents. *Journal of the American Academy of Child and Adolescent Psychiatry, 40,* 1410–1417.

Hall, K. M., Irwin, M. M., Bowman, K. A., Frankenberger, W., & Jewett, D. C. (2005). Illicit use of prescribed stimulant medication among college students. *Journal of American College Health, 53,* 167–174.

Hechtman, L., & Weiss, G. (1983). Long-term outcome of hyperactive children. *American Journal of Orthopsychiatry, 53,* 532–541.

Hechtman, L., & Weiss, G. (1986). Controlled prospective fifteen year follow-up of hyperactives as adults: Non-medical drug and alcohol use and anti-social behaviour. *Canadian Journal of Psychiatry, 31,* 557–567.

Hechtman, L., Weiss, G., & Perlman, T. (1980). Hyperactives as young adults: Self-esteem and social skills. *Canadian Journal of Psychiatry, 25,* 478–483.

Hermens, D. F., Kohn, M. R., Clarke, S. D., Gordon, E., & Williams, L. M. (2005). Sex differences in adolescent ADHD: Findings from concurrent EEG and EDA. *Clinical Neurophysiologist, 116,* 1455–1463.

Hesslinger, B., Tebartz van Elst, L., Nyberg, E., Dykierek, P., Richter, H., Berner, M., et al. (2002). Psychotherapy of attention deficit hyperactivity disorder in adults—A pilot study using a structure skills training program. *European Archives of Psychiatry and Clinical Neuroscience, 252,* 177–184.

Hill, J., & Schoener, E. (1996). Age-dependent decline of attention deficit hyperactivity disorder. *American Journal of Psychiatry, 153,* 1143–1146.

Hines, A. M., & Shaw, G. A. (1993). Intrusive thoughts, sensation seeking, and drug use in college students. *Bulletin of the Psychonomic Society, 31,* 541–544.

Holdnack, J. A., Noberg, P. J., Arnold, S.E., Gur, R. C., & Gur, R. E. (1995). Speed of processing and verbal learning deficits in adults diagnosed with ADHD. *Neuropsychiatry, Neuropsychology and Behavioral Neurology, 8,* 282–292.

Horrigan, J. P. (2000). Low-dose amphetamine salts and adult attention-deficit/hyperactivity disorder. *Journal of Clinical Psychiatry, 61,* 414–417.

Horrigan, J. P. (2001). Present and future pharmacotherapeutic options for adult attention deficit/hyperactivity disorder. *Expert Opinion on Pharmacotherapy, 2,* 573–586.

Horrigan, J. P., & Barnhill, L. J. (2000). Low-dose amphetamine salts and adult attention-deficit/hyperactivity disorder. *Journal of Clinical Psychiatry, 61,* 414–417.

Howell, D. C., Huessy, H. R., & Hassuk, B. (1985). Fifteen-year follow-up of a behavioral history of attention deficit disorder. *Pediatrics, 76,* 185–190.

Huss, M., & Lehmkuhl, U. (2002). Methylphenidate and substance abuse: A review of pharmacology, animal, and clinical studies. *Journal of Attention Disorders, 6,* S65–S71.

Hynd, G. W., Semrud-Clikeman, M., Lorys, A. R., Novey, E. S., Eliopulos, D., & Lyytinen, H. (1991). Corpus callosum morphology in attention deficit-hyperactivity disorder. *Journal of Learning Disabilities, 24,* 141–146.

Individuals with Disabilities Education Act of 1997, 20 U. S. C. § 1400-1485.

International consensus statement on ADHD. (2002). *Clinical Child and Family Psychology Review, 5,* 89–90.

Johann, M., Bobbe, G., Putzhammer, A., & Wodarz, N. (2003). Comorbidity of alcohol dependence with attention-deficit hyperactivity disorder: Differences in phenotype with increased severity of the substance disorder, but not in genotype (serotonin transporter and 5-hydroxytryptmanine-2c receptor). *Alcoholism: Clinical and Experimental Research, 27,* 1527–1534.

Kadison, R. (2005). Getting an edge—Use of stimulants and antidepressants in college. *New England Journal of Medicine, 353,* 1089–1091.

Kanbayashi, Y., Nakata, Y., Fujii, K., Kita, M., & Wada, K. (1994). ADHD-related behavior among nonreferred children: Parents' ratings of *DSM-III-R* symptoms. *Child Psychiatry and Human Development, 25,* 13–29.

Kaplan, S., Heiligenstein, J., West, S., Busner, J., Harder, D., Dittman, R., et al. (2004). Efficacy and safety of atomoxetine in childhood attention-deficit/hyperactivity disorder with comorbid oppositional defiant disorder. *Journal of Attention Disorders, 8,* 45–52.

Katusic, S. K., Barbaresi, W. J., Colligan, R. C., Weaver, A. L., Leibson, C. L., & Jacobsen, S. J. (2005). Psychostimulant treatment and risk for substance abuse among young adults with a history of attention-deficit/hyperactivity disorder: A population-based, birth cohort study. *Journal of Child and Adolescent Psychopharmacology, 15,* 764–776.

Katz, L. J., Wood, D. S., Goldstein, G., Auchenbach, R. C., & Geckle, M. (1998). The utility of neuropsychological tests in evaluation of attention deficit/hyperactivity disorder (ADHD) versus depression in adults. *Assessment, 5,* 45–51.

Kelsey, D. K., Sumner, C. R., Casat, C. D., Coury, D. L., Quintana, H., Saylor, K. E., et al. (2004). Once-daily atomoxetine treatment for children with attention-deficit/hyperactivity disorder, including an assessment of evening and morning behavior: A double-blind, placebo-controlled trial. *Pediatrics, 114,* 1–8.

Kennemer, K., & Goldstein, S. (2005). Incidence of ADHD in adults with severe mental health problems. *Applied Neuropsychology, 12,* 77–82.

Kessler, R. C., Adler, L. A., Barkley, R., Biederman, J., Conners, C. K., Faraone, S. V., et al. (2005). Patterns and predictors of attention-deficit/hyperactivity disorder persistence into adulthood: Results from the national comorbidity survey replication. *Society of Biological Psychiatry, 57,* 1442–1451.

Kessler, R. C., Adler, L. A., Barkley, R., Biederman, J., Conners, C. K., Demler, O., et al. (2006). *American Journal of Psychiatry, 163,* 716–723.

Kilcarr, P. (2002). Making marriages work for individuals with ADHD. In S. Goldstein & A. T. Ellison (Eds.), *Clinician's Guide to Adult ADHD: Assessment and Intervention* (pp. 220–239). Boston: Academic Press.

Kollins, S. H. (2003). Comparing the abuse potential of methylphenidate versus other stimulants: a review of available evidence and relevance to the ADHD patient. *Journal of Clinical Psychiatry, 64*(Suppl. 11), 14–18.

Kollins, S. H., McClernon, F. J., & Fuemmeler, B. F. (2005). Association between smoking and attention-deficit/hyperactivity disorder symptoms in a population-based sample of young adults. *Archives of General Psychiatry, 62,* 1142–1147.

Kooji, J. J., Buitelaar, J. K., van den Oord, E. J., Furer, J. W., Rijnders, C. A., & Hodiamont, P. P. (2005). Internal and external validity of attention-deficit hyperactivity disorder in a population-based sample of adults. *Psychological Medicine, 35,* 817–827.

Kooij, J. J., Burger, H., Boonstra, A. M., Van der Linden, P. D., Kalma, L. E., & Buitelaar, J. K. (2004). Efficacy and safety of methylphenidate in 45 adults with attention-deficit/hyperactivity disorder. A randomized placebo-controlled double-blind cross-over trial. *Psychological Medicine, 34,* 973–982.

Kratochvil, C. J., Heiligenstein, J. H., Dittmann, R., Spencer, T. J., Biederman, J., Wernicke, J., et al. (2002). Atomoxetine and methylphenidate treatment in children with ADHD: A prospective, randomized, open-label trial. *Journal of the American Academy of Child and Adolescent Psychiatry, 41,* 776–784.

Lambert, N. M., & Hartsough, C. S. (1998). Prospective study of tobacco smoking and substance dependencies among samples of ADHD and non-ADHD participants. *Journal of Learning Disabilities, 31,* 533–544.

Levin, F. R., Evans, S. M., Brooks, D. J., Kalbag, A. S., Garawi, F., & Nunes, E. V. (2006). Treatment of methadone-maintained patients with adults ADHD: Double-blind comparison of methylphenidate, bupropion and placebo. *Drug and Alcohol Dependence, 81,* 137–148.

Levin, F. R., Evans, S. M., & Kleber, H. D. (1999). Practical guidelines for the treatment of substance abusers with adult attention-deficit hyperactivity disorder. *Psychiatric Services, 50,* 1001–1003.

Levin, F. R., Evans, S. M., Vosburg, S. K., Horton, T., Brooks, D., & Ng, J. (2004). Impact of attention-deficit hyperactivity disorder and other psychopathology on treatment retention among cocaine abusers in a therapeutic community. *Addictive Behaviors, 29,* 1875–1882.

Levy, F., Hay D. A., Bennett, K. S., & McStephen, M. (2005). Gender differences in ADHD subtype comorbidity. *Journal of the American Academy of Child and Adolescent Psychiatry, 44,* 368–376.

Loo, S. K., & Barkley, R. A. (2005). Clinical utility of EEG in attention deficit hyperactivity disorder. *Applied Neuropsychology, 12,* 64–76.

Lou, H. C. (1996). Etiology and pathogenesis of attention-deficit hyperactivity disorder (ADHD): Significance of prematurity and perinatal hypoxichaemodymanic encephalopathy. *Acta Pediatrics, 85*, 1266–1271.

Low, K. G., & Gendaszek, A. E. (2002). Illicit use of psychostimulants among college students: A preliminary study. *Psychology, Health, & Medicine, 7*, 283–287.

Luk, S. L., Leung, P. W. L., & Lee, P. L. M. (1988). Conners' Teaching Rating Scale in Chinese children in Hong Kong. *Journal of Child Psychology and Psychiatry, 29*, 165–174.

Lynskey, M. T., & Hall, W. (2001). Attention deficit hyperactivity disorder and substance use disorders: Is there a causal link? *Addiction, 96*, 815–822.

Madras, B. K., Miller, G. M., & Fischman, A. J. (2005). The dopamine transporter and attention-deficit/hyperactivity disorder. *Biological Psychiatry, 57*, 1397–1409.

Magajna, L., Kavkler, M., & Ortar-Krizaj, M. (2003). Adults with self-reported learning disabilities in Slovenia: Findings from the international adult literacy survey on the incidence and correlates of learning disabilities in Slovenia. *Dyslexia, 9*, 229–251.

Maidment, I. D. (2003). The use of antidepressants to treat attention deficit hyperactivity disorder in adults. *Journal of Psychopharmacology, 17*, 332–335.

Mannuzza, S., Klein, R. G., Bessler, A., Malloy, P., & LaPadula, M. (1993). Adult outcome of hyperactive boys: Educational achievement, occupational rank, and psychiatric status. *Archives of General Psychiatry, 50*, 565–576.

Mannuzza, S., Klein, R. G., Konig, P. H., & Giampino, T. L. (1989). Hyperactive boys almost grown up: Criminality and its relationship to psychiatric status. *Archives of General Psychiatry, 46*, 1073–1079.

Mannuzza, S., Klein, R. G., & Moulton, J. L., III. (2002). Young adult outcome of children with "situational" hyperactivity: A prospective, controlled follow-up study. *Journal of Abnormal Child Psychology, 30*, 191–198.

Manos, M. J., Short, E. J., & Findling, R. L. (1999). Differential effectiveness of methylphenidate and Adderall in school-age youths with attention-deficit/hyperactivity disorder. *Journal of the American Academy of Child and Adolescent Psychiatry, 38*, 813–819.

Matochik, J. A., Nordahl, T. E., Gross, M., Semple, W. E., King, A. C., Cohen, R. M., et al. (1993). Effects of acute stimulant mediation on cerebral metabolism in adults with hyperactivity. *Neuropsychopharmacology, 8*, 377–386.

Mattes, J. A., Boswell, L., & Oliver, H. (1984). Methylphenidate effects on symptoms of attention deficit disorder in adults. *Archives of General Psychiatry, 41*, 1059–1066.

McCabe, S. E., Knight, J. R., Teter, C. J., & Wechsler, H. (2005). Non-medial use of prescription stimulants among US college students: Prevalence and correlates from a national survey. *Addiction, 99*, 96–106.

McGough, J. J., & Barkley, R. A. (2004). Diagnostic controversies in adult attention deficit hyperactivity disorder. *American Journal of Psychiatry, 161*, 1948–1956.

McGough, J. J., Pataki, C. S., & Suddath, R. (2005). Dexmethylphenidate extended-release capsules for attention deficit hyperactivity disorder. *Expert Review of Neurotherapeutics, 5*, 437–441.

McGough, J. J., Smalley, S. L., McCracken, J. T., Yang, M., Del'Homme, M., Lynn, D. E., et al. (2005). Psychiatric comorbidity in adult attention deficit hyperactivity disorder: Findings from multiplex families. *American Journal of Psychiatry, 162*, 1621–1627.

Mick, E., Faraone, S. V., & Biederman, J. (2004). Age-dependent expression of attention-deficit/hyperactivity disorder symptoms. *Psychiatric Clinics of North America, 27*, 215–224.

Mitsis, E. M., McKay, K. E., Schulz, K. P., Newcorn, J. H., & Halperin, J. M. (2000). Parent-teacher concordance for *DSM-IV* attention-deficit/hyperactivity disorder in a clinic-referred sample. *Journal of the American Academy of Child and Adolescent Psychiatry, 39*, 308–313.

Mostofsky, S. H., Reiss, A. L., Lockhart, P., & Denckla, M. B. (1998). Evaluation of cerebellar size in attention-deficit hyperactivity disorder. *Journal of Child Neurology, 9*, 434–439.

Mugnaini, D., Masi, G., Brovedani, P., Chelazzi, C., Matas, M., Romagnoli, C., et al. (in press). Teacher reports of ADHD symptoms in Italian children at the end of first grade. *European Psychiatry*.

Murphy, K., Barkley, R. A., & Bush, T. (2001). Executive functioning and olfactory identification in young adults with attention deficit-hyperactivity disorder. *Neuropsychology, 15*, 211–220.

Murphy, K., Barkley, R. A., & Bush, T. (2002). Young adults with attention deficit hyperactivity disorder: Subtype differences in comorbidity, educational, and clinical history. *Journal of Nervous and Mental Disease, 190*, 147–157.

Murphy, K. R., & Gordon, M. (1998). Assessment of adults with ADHD. In R. A. Barkley (Ed.), *Attention-deficit hyperactivity disorder* (pp.345–372). New York: Guilford.

National Institutes of Health (NIH). (2000). Consensus and development conference statement: Diagnosis and treatment of attention-deficit/hyperactivity disorder. *Journal of the American Academy of Child and Adolescent Psychiatry, 39*, 182–193.

Newcorn, J. H., Halperin, J. M., Jensen, P. S., Abikoff, H. B., Arnold, L. E., Cantwell, D. P., et al. (2001). Symptom profiles in children with ADHD: Effects of comorbidity and gender. *Journal of the American Academy of Child and Adolescent Psychiatry, 40*, 137–146.

Nierenberg, A. A., Miyahara, S., Spencer, T., Wisniewski, S. R., Otto, M. W., Simon, N., et al. (2005). Clinical and diagnostic implications of lifetime attention-deficit/hyperactivity disorder comorbidity in adults with bipolar disorder: Data from the first 1000 STEP-BD participants. *Society of Biological Psychiatry, 57*, 1467–1473.

Osmon, D. C., Braun, M. M., & Plambeck, E. A. (2005). Processing abilities associated with phonologic and orthographic skills in adult learning disability. *Journal of Clinical and Experimental Neuropsychology, 27*, 544–554.

Pennington, B. F., Willcutt, E., & Rhee, S. H. (2005). Analyzing comorbidity. *Advances in Child Development and Behavior, 33*, 263–304.

Pineda, D., Ardila, A., Rosselli, M., Arias, B. E., Henao, G. C., Gomez, L. F., et al. (1999). Prevalence of attention-deficit/hyperactivity disorder symptoms in 4- to 17-year-old children in the general population. *Journal of Abnormal Child Psychology, 27*, 455–462.

Pliszka, S. R., Browne, R. G., Olvera, R. L., & Wynne, S. K. (2000). A double-blind, placebo-controlled study of adderall and methylphenidate in the treatment of attention-deficit/hyperactivity disorder. *Journal of the American Academy of Child and Adolescent Psychiatry, 39*, 619–626.

Popper, C. W. (2000). Pharmacologic alternatives to psychostimulants for the treatment of attention-deficit/hyperactivity disorder. *Child and Adolescent Psychiatric Clinics of North America, 9*, 605–646.

Quinn, P. O. (2005). Treating adolescent girls and women with ADHD: Gender-specific issues. *Journal of Clinical Psychology, 61*, 579–587.

Ratey, N. (2002). Life coaching for adult ADHD. In S. Goldstein & A. T. Ellison (Eds.), *Clinician's guide to adult ADHD: Assessment and Intervention* (pp. 261–277). Boston: Academic Press.

Riordan, H. J., Flashman, L. A., Saykin, A. J., Frutiger, S. A., Carroll, K. E., & Huey, L. (1999). Neuropsychological correlates of methylphenidate treatment in adult ADHD with and without depression. *Archives of Clinical Neuropsychology, 14*, 217–233.

Robins, E., & Guze, S. B. (1970). Establishment of diagnostic validity in psychiatric illness: Its application to schizophrenia. *American Journal of Psychiatry, 126*, 983–987.

Rodriguez, A., & Bohlin, G. (2005). Are maternal smoking and stress during pregnancy related to ADHD symptoms in children? *Journal of Child Psychology and Psychiatry, 46*, 246–254.

Rosa-Neto, P., Lou, H. C., Cumming, P., Pryds, O., Karrebaek, H., Lunding, J., et al. (2005). Methylphenidate-evoked changes in striatal dopamine correlate with inattention and impulsivity in adolescents with attention deficit hyperactivity disorder. *Neuroimage, 25*, 868–876.

Safren, S. A., Otto, M. W., Sprich, S., Winett, C. L., Wilens, T. E., & Biederman, J. (2005). Cognitive-behavioral therapy for ADHD in medication-treated adults with continued symptoms. *Behaviour Research and Therapy, 43*, 831–842.

Safren, S. A., Sprich, S., Chulvick, S., & Otto, M. W. (2004). Psychosocial treatments for adults with attention-deficit/hyperactivity disorder. *Psychiatric Clinics of North America, 27*, 349–360.

Saules, K. K., Pomerleau, C. S., & Schubiner, H. (2003). Patterns of inattentive and hyperactive symptomatology in cocaine-addicted and non-cocaine-addicted smokers diagnosed with adult attention deficit hyperactivity disorder. *Journal of Addictive Diseases, 22*, 71–78.

Schaughency, E., McGee, R., Raja, S. N., Feehan, M., & Silva, P. (1994). Self-reported inattention, impulsivity, and hyperactivity in ages 15 and 18 years in the general population. *Journal of the American Academy of Child and Adolescent Psychiatry, 33,* 173–183.

Schoechlin, C., & Engel, R. R. (2005). Neuropsychological performance in adult attention-deficit hyperactivity disorder: Meta-analysis of empirical data. *Archives of Clinical Neuropsychology, 20,* 727–744.

Schubiner, H. (2005). Substance abuse in patients with attention-deficit hyperactivity disorder: Therapeutic implications. *CNS Drugs, 19,* 643–655.

Schubiner, H., Tzelepis, A., Milberger, S., Lockhart, N., Kruger, M., Kelley, B .J., et al. (2000). Prevalence of attention-deficit/hyperactivity disorder and conduct disorder among substance abusers. *Journal of Clinical Psychiatry, 61,* 244–251.

Schulz, K. P., Tang, C. Y., Fan, J., Marks, D. J., Newcorn, J. H., Cheung, A. M., et al. (2005). Differential prefrontal cortex activation during inhibitory control in adolescents with and without childhood attention-deficit/hyperactivity disorder. *Neuropsychology, 19,* 390–402.

Secnic, K., Swensen, A., & Lage, M. J. (2005). Comorbidities and costs of adult patients diagnosed with attention-deficit hyperactivity disorder. *Pharmacoeconomics, 23,* 93–102.

Shaw, G., & Giambra, L. (1993). Task-unrelated thoughts of college students diagnosed as hyperactive in childhood. *Developmental Neuropsychology, 9,* 17–30.

Shaywitz, S. E., & Shaywitz, B. A. (2005). Dyslexia (specific reading disability). *Biological Psychiatry, 57,* 1301–1309.

Shekim, W., Asarnow, R. F., Hess, E., Zaucha, K., & Wheeler, N. (1990). A clinical and demographic profile of a sample of adults with attention deficit disorder—residual type. *Comprehensive Psychiatry, 31,* 41–425.

Sherman, D. K., Iacono, W. G., & McGue, M. K. (1997). Attention-deficit hyperactivity disorder dimensions: A twin study of inattention and impulsivity-hyperactivity. *Journal of the American Academy of Child and Adolescent Psychiatry, 36,* 745–753.

Simpson, D., & Plosker, G.L. (2004). Spotlight on atomoxetine in adults with attention-deficit hyperactivity disorder. *CNS Drugs, 18,* 397–401.

Spencer, T., Biederman, J., Wilens, T., & Faraone, S. V. (1994). Is attention-deficit hyperactivity disorder in adults a valid disorder? *Harvard Review of Psychiatry, 1,* 326–335.

Spencer, T., Biederman, J., Wilens, T., & Faraone, S. V. (2002). Overview and neurobiology of attention-deficit/hyperactivity disorder. *Journal of Clinical Psychiatry, 63,* 3–9.

Spencer, T., Biederman, J., Wilens, T., Faraone, S. V., Prince, J., Gerard, K., et al. (2001). Efficacy of a mixed amphetamine salts compound in adults with attention-deficit/hyperactivity disorder. *Archives of General Psychiatry, 58,* 775–782.

Szatmari, P. (1992). The epidemiology of attention-deficit/hyperactivity disorders. In G. Weiss (Ed.), *Child and adolescent psychiatry clinics of North America: Attention deficit disorder* (pp. 361–372). Philadelphia: Saunders.

Teicher, M. H., Anderson, C. M., Glod, C. A., Maas, L. C., & Renshaw, P. F. (2000). Functional deficits in basal ganglia of children with attention-deficit/hyperactivity disorder shown with functional magnetic resonance imaging relaxometry. *Nature Medicine, 6,* 470–474.

Teter, C. J., McCabe, S. E., Boyd, C. J., & Guthrie, S. K. (2003). Illicit methylphenidate use in an undergraduate student sample: Prevalence and risk factors. *Pharmacotherapy, 23,* 609–617.

Upadhyaya, H. P., Rose, K., Wang, W., O'Rourke, K., Sullivan, B., Deas, D., et al. (2005). Attention-deficit/hyperactivity disorder, mediation treatment, and substance use patterns among adolescents and young adults. *Journal of Child and Adolescent Psychopharmacology, 15,* 799–809.

Vogel, S. A., & Holt, J. K. (2003). A comparative study of adults with and without self-reported learning disabilities in six English-speaking populations: What have we learned? *Dyslexia, 9,* 193–228.

Vogel, S. A., Leonard, F., Scales, W., Hayeslip, P., Hermansen, J., & Donnells, L. (1998). The national learning disabilities postsecondary data bank: An overview. *Journal of Learning Disabilities, 31,* 234–247.

Volkow, N. D., Fowler, J. S., Wang, G., Ding, Y., & Gatley, S. J. (2002). Mechanism of action of methylphenidate: Insights from PET imaging studies. *Journal of Attention Disorders, 6*(Suppl. 1), S31–S43.

Volkow, N. D., Wang, G. D., Fowler, J. S., & Ding, Y. S. (2005). Imaging the effects of methylphenidat on brain dopamine: New model on its therapeutic actions for attention-deficit/hyperactivity disorder. *Society of Biological Psychiatry, 57*, 1410–1415.

Waldman, H. B., & Perlman, S. P. (2004). Children with attention deficit disorder and learning disability: Findings from the first national study. *Journal of Dentistry for Children, 71*, 101–104.

Wasserstein, J., & Lynn, A. (2001). Metacognition remediation in adult ADHD. Treating executive function deficits via executive functions. *Annals of New York Academy of Sciences, 931*, 376–384.

Waxmonsky, J. G. (2005). Nonstimluant therapies for attention-deficit hyperactivity disorder (ADHD) in children and adults. *Essential Psychopharmacology, 6*, 262–276.

Weiss, G., & Hechtman, L. (1993). *Hyperactive children grown up: ADHD in children, adolescents, and adults* (2nd ed.). New York: Guilford.

Weiss, G., Hechtman, L., Perlman, T., Hopkins, J., & Wener, A. (1979). Hyperactives as young adults: A controlled prospective ten-year follow-up of 75 children. *Archives of General Psychiatry, 36*, 675–681.

Weiss, M., Tannock, R., Kratochvil, C., Dunn, D., Velez-Borras, J., Thomason, C., et al. (2005). A randomized, placebo-controlled study of once-daily atomoxetine in the school setting in children with ADHD. *Journal of the American Academy of Child and Adolescent Psychiatry, 44*, 647–655.

Wender, P. H., & Reimherr, F. W. (1990). Bupropion treatment of attention-deficit/hyperactivity disorder in adults. *American Journal of Psychiatry, 147*, 1018–1020.

Wender, P. H., Reimherr, F. W., & Wood, D. (1981). Attention deficit disorder ('minimal brain dysfunction') in adults: A replication study of diagnosis and drug treatment. *Archives of General Psychiatry, 38*, 449–456.

Wender, P. H., Reimherr, F. W., Wood, D., & Ward, M. (1985). A controlled study of methylphenidate in the treatment of attention deficit disorder, residual type, in adults. *American Journal of Psychiatry, 142*, 547–552.

Wender, P. H., Wolf, L. E., & Wasserstien, J. (2001). Adults with ADHD: An overview. *Annals of the New York Academy of Sciences, 931*, 1–16.

Weyandt, L. L. (2005a). Executive function in children, adolescents, and adults with attention deficit hyperactivity disorder: Introduction to the special issue. *Developmental Neuropsychology, 27*, 1–10.

Weyandt, L. L. (2005b). Neuropsychological performance in adults with attention deficit hyperactivity disorder. In D. Gozal & D. L. Molfese (Eds.), *Attention Deficit Hyperactivity Disorder: From Genes to Patients*, pp. 457–486. Totowa, NJ: Humana Press.

Weyandt, L. (2006). *ADHD primer* (2nd ed). Boston, MA: Allyn and Bacon.

Weyandt, L., Iwaszuk, W., Fulton, K., Ollerton, M., Beatty, N., Fouts, H., et al. (2003). The Internal Restlessness Scale: performance of college students with and without ADHD. *Journal of Learning Disabilities, 36*, 382–389.

Weyandt, L. L., Mitzlaff, L., & Thomas, L. (2002). The relationship between intelligence and performance on the test of variables of attention (TOVA). *Journal of Learning Disabilities, 35*, 114–120.

Weyandt, L., Rice, J. A., & Linterman, I. (1995). Reported prevalence of attentional difficulties in a general sample of college students. *Journal of Psychopathology and Behavioral Assessment, 17*, 293–304.

Weyandt, L. L., Rice, J. A., Linterman, I., Mitzlaff, L., & Emert, E. (1998). Neuropsychological performance of a sample of adults with ADHD, developmental reading disorder, and controls. *Developmental Neuropsychology, 14*, 643–656.

White, A. M., Jordan, J. D., Schroeder, K. M., Acheson, S. K., Georgi, B. D., Sauls, G., et al. (2004). Predictors of relapse during treatment and treatment completions among marijuana-dependent adolescents in an intensive outpatient substance abuse program. *Substance Abuse, 25*, 53–59.

Wilens, T. E., Biederman, J., Prince, J., Spencer, T. J., Faraone, S. V., Warburton, R., et al. (1996). Six-week, double-blind, placebo-controlled study of desipramine for adult attention deficit hyperactivity disorder. *American Journal of Psychiatry, 153*, 1147–1153.

Wilens, T. E., & Dodson, W. (2004). A clinical perspective of attention-deficit/hyperactivity disorder into adulthood. *Journal of Clinical Psychiatry, 65*, 1301–1313.

Wilens, T. E., Faraone, S. V., Biederman, J., & Gunawardene, S. (2003a). Does stimulant therapy of attention-deficit/hyperactivity disorder beget later substance abuse? A meta-analytic review of the literature. *Pediatrics, 111*, 179–185.

Wilens, T. E., Hahesy, A. L., Biederman, J., Bredin, E., Tanguay, S., Kwon, A., et al. (2005a). Influence of parental SUD and ADHD in their offspring: Preliminary results from a pilot-controlled family study. *American Journal of Addiction, 14*, 179–187.

Wilens, T. E., Haight, B. R., Horrigan, J. P., Hudziak, J. J., Rosenthal, N. E., Conner, D.F., et al. (2005b). Bupropion XL in adults with attention-deficit/hyperactivity disorder: A randomized, placebo-controlled study. *Society of Biological Psychiatry, 57*, 793–801.

Wilens, T. E., Prince, J. B., Spencer, T., Van Patten, S. L., Doyle, R., Girard, K., et al. (2003b). An open trial of bupropion for the treatment of adults with attention-deficit/hyperactivity disorder and bipolar disorder. *Society of Biological Psychiatry, 54*, 9–16.

Wilens, T. E., Spencer, T. J., & Biederman, J. (2002). A review of the pharmacotherapy of adults with attention-deficit/hyperactivity disorder. *Journal of Attention Disorders, 5*, 189–202.

Wilens, T. E., Spencer, T. J., Biederman, J., Girard, K., Doyle, R., Prince, J., et al. (2001). A controlled clinical trial of bupropion for attention deficit hyperactivity disorder in adults. *American Journal of Psychiatry, 158*, 282–288.

Willcutt, E. G., Pennington, B. F., & DeFries, J. C. (2000). Etiology of inattention and hyperactivity/impulsivity in a community sample of twins with learning difficulties. *Journal of Abnormal Child Psychology, 28*, 149–159.

Williams, R. J., Goodale, L. A., Shay-Fiddler, M. A., Gloster, S. P., & Chang, S. Y. (2004). Methylphenidate and dextroamphetamine abuse in substance-abusing adolescents. *American Journal of Addiction, 13*, 381–389.

Wood, D. R., Reimherr, F. W., Wender, P. H., & Johnson, G. E. (1976). Diagnosis and treatment of minimal brain dysfunction in adults. *Archives of General Psychiatry, 33*, 1453–1460.

Yeo, R. A., Hill, D. E., Campbell, R. A., Vigil, J., Petropoulos, H., Hart, B., et al. (2003). Proton magnetic resonance spectroscopy investigation of the right frontal lobe in children with attention-deficit/hyperactivity disorder. *Journal of the American Academy of Child and Adolescent Psychiatry, 42*, 303–310.

Young, S. (2002). A model of psychotherapy for adults with ADHD. In S. Goldstein & A.T. Ellison (Eds.), *Clinician's Guide to Adult ADHD: Assessment and Intervention*, pp. 148–162. Boston: Academic Press.

Zametkin, A. J., Nordahl, E. T., Gross, M., King, C. A., Semple, W. E., Rumsey, J., et al. (1990). Cerebral glucose metabolism in adults with hyperactivity of childhood onset. *New England Journal of Medicine, 323*, 1361–1366.

Zito, J. M., Safer, D. J., dosReis, S., Gardner, J. F., Boles, M., & Lynch, F. (2000). Trends in the prescribing of psychotropic medications to preschoolers. *Journal of the American Medical Association, 23*, 1025–1030.

Part V

Aging and Gerontological Research

Chapter 24

What Do We Know About the Aging Brain?

Implications for Learning in Late Life

Benjamin T. Mast, Jennifer Zimmerman, and Sarah V. Rowe

The breadth of topics covered in this volume suggests that the intersection of adult development and learning is exceptionally complex and influenced by a wide variety of processes. This chapter focuses on how the brain changes in the context of adult development (with particular attention given to later life) and the ways in which these changes affect learning. To begin, we offer several general observations.

First, empirical investigation of direct links between age-related brain changes and the learning activities of older adults is largely uncharted territory. It has been noted that neuroscience and educational psychology have developed as separate fields with very little interaction (Blakemore & Frith, 2005). Much of the existing work that seeks to draw these fields together has focused largely on the first quarter of the developmental spectrum, with relatively little emphasis on later life. It is in this context that we approach the specific issue of how the changes observed in the aging brain affect learning. To accomplish this, we draw on evidence from the fields of cognitive aging, neurology/neuropathology, neuroscience, geriatric neuropsychology, and life-span developmental psychology. Empirical evidence is described where it is available and considerable attention is given to conceptual links in the absence of direct empirical evidence.

Second, the last decades of life are characterized by considerable heterogeneity; therefore when we consider the aging brain and learning, we must ask whether the discussion is focused on so-called "normal aging" or learning in the context of impaired brain functioning such as in Alzheimer's disease? This review focuses on both normal aging and dementia literatures because we believe that both offer important insights into the link between brain changes and late life learning, and because (as will be discussed) the boundary line between normal aging and certain forms of dementia such as Alzheimer's disease is not always clear.

Third, the learning activities of older adults rely on multiple cognitive skills which emerge from a complex interaction of multiple brain systems. Consider a 75-year-old woman who has decided to learn to use a computer so that she can communicate with her friends and family via email, research her genealogy, and write using basic word processing programs. She has several options to accomplish her goal of learning to use a computer. She could enroll in a formal computer literacy class offered at a local college. In this setting, the class will likely be structured for her (syllabus, lectures, textbook, and exercises designed by the instructor), but she will likely be required to focus her attention on the lectures while taking notes (drawing on working memory, inhibition of irrelevant stimuli, processing speed), as well as study and memorize terms and concepts for exams (sustained attention, inhibition of irrelevant stimuli, semantic and episodic memory). Alternatively, she may choose to learn to use a computer on her own outside of a classroom setting. This self-directed learning process will require her to develop a plan for learning the skills needed, finding and acquiring resources, carrying out the plan and modifying as needed, and evaluating whether the learning was effective (Lamdin & Fugate, 1997). This form of learning is clearly less structured than formal classroom learning and places greater demands on the organizational, planning, and problem solving skills of the older learner. On the other hand, it may be advantageous in that there is less dependence upon processing speed and memory resources. Learning clearly relies upon a wide variety of cognitive skills and brain structures that interact with one another to produce successful learning outcomes, but some forms of learning may rely more heavily on specific cognitive skills than others. Furthermore, some of these skills are more affected by age and disease than others. Therefore, the various types of learning activities (e.g., formal learning vs. self-directed learning) may be differentially affected by age-related changes in cognition.

This chapter focuses on cognitive changes that are most notable among older adults and that appear to be most relevant to these two broad learning activities (formal learning and self-directed learning). The probability that learning will be disrupted by age and the diseases of aging is great because learning relies on a multitude of cognitive abilities and declines in any one component skill could have an impact on learning. On the other hand, to the extent that aging does not affect all cognitive abilities equally, spared cognitive abilities may enhance the opportunity for compensation (Baltes & Baltes, 1990; Marsiske, Lang, Baltes, & Baltes, 1995).

In the sections that follow, we first review common structural brain changes in the later decades of life as well as the most common cognitive changes observed in normal aging. As part of this discussion, we review results from selected cognitive intervention studies, using these results as evidence of learning potential among older adults (Baltes & Baltes, 1990; Willis, 1985). The second section includes a discussion of brain changes and their cognitive correlates in Alzheimer's disease (AD) and preclinical AD syndromes. We also review the results from a series of studies that used cognitive training paradigms from the normal cognitive aging literature to examine learning potential in dementia. Finally, using the Selective Optimization with Compensation model (SOC; Baltes & Baltes, 1990) as a broad framework, we describe how the brain and cognitive changes observed in the normal aging and dementia literature might affect the learning activities of older adults and how older adults might compensate for these changes. SOC provides a framework for understanding how cognitive changes lead elders to shift learning goals, methods, and contexts to maintain learning activities despite significant brain changes. Using this framework, we conclude the chapter by discussing how elders with dementia might achieve successful learning outcomes and thereby enhance functioning.

Normal Cognitive Aging

The last several decades have seen tremendous growth in research addressing the pattern of cognitive change observed in later life, particularly in the absence of dementia or other major neurological syndromes. Rigorous empirical efforts such as the Seattle Longitudinal Study (SLS; Schaie, 1994, 2005) have demonstrated that the long held assumption that aging is necessarily accompanied by declines in most, if not all, cognitive abilities is an oversimplification of the actual pattern of change in cognitive and intellectual abilities over time. Among SLS participants without dementia or other neurological conditions, results indicate that many basic intellectual abilities continue to improve or remain stable over the life span (Figure 24.1) until at least age 60, and that when abilities begin to show decline these are somewhat modest until the 80s (Schaie, 1994, 2005). Verbal memory had a slightly positive trajectory through age 60 after which

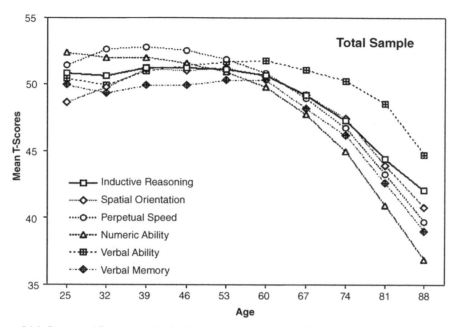

Figure 24.1 Estimated 7-year longitudinal changes in cognitive abilities (measured as latent variables) over the adult lifespan in the Seattle Longitudinal Study. *Source:* Schare (2005), *Developmental influences on adult intelligence: The Seattle Longitudinal Study.* New York: Oxford University Press. Reprinted with permision.

declines began and continued into the 80s. Verbal ability was relatively stable until the 80s. Numeric ability began declining earlier in the life span, but the greatest declines did not occur until the late 60s and 70s. Thus, the general pattern across abilities measured was one of improvement or relative stability in primary mental abilities until later in life (generally 70s and 80s), where declines have been consistently observed across abilities. One notable exception was processing speed, which does show fairly regular declines from middle adulthood until late life. This exception is critical because many of the abilities considered in cognitive aging research rely heavily on processing speed, such that once this variance is controlled the magnitude of age related changes in other abilities is significantly reduced (Salthouse, 1993, 1994; Schaie, 1994). Thus, although studies like the SLS demonstrate later life cognitive declines, some abilities demonstrate relatively greater decline, and some of these changes may be at least partly responsible for deficits observed in other cognitive abilities.

The inhibitory control deficit proposed by Hasher and Zacks "attributes age-related differences in memory and other cognitive functions to a decline in attentional inhibitory control over the contents of working memory" (Zacks, Hasher, & Li, 2000, p. 296). This hypothesis suggests that older adults have difficulty inhibiting stimuli that are not relevant to the task (e.g., thoughts or external stimuli such as noise), and lead to "mental clutter." Two implications of increased mental clutter include (1) less efficient encoding of information into long-term memory, and (2) slower and more error-prone retrieval of information from long-term memory (Zacks, Hasher, & Li, 2000). Thus, the inhibitory deficit model has implications for attention, working memory, and long-term memory encoding and retrieval.

The basic cognitive functions emphasized in the processing speed and inhibitory deficits hypotheses are highly relevant to the efficiency and methods of learning in later life.

As will be discussed later in this chapter, declines in processing speed and the inability to focus attention while inhibiting irrelevant information have both conceptual and empirical links to learning potential among older adults. However, we first turn our attention to the research concerning the underlying brain changes that occur in normal aging and the extent to which these are related to observed cognitive changes in later life.

Brain Changes in Normal Aging

Advances in neuroimaging technologies have allowed investigators to examine the underlying brain changes accompanying the aging process, and consider how they are linked to cognitive changes like those described above. Just as there is "no uniform pattern of age-related changes in adulthood across all intellectual abilities" (Schaie 1994, p. 306), there is similarly no uniform pattern of change across all brain regions. The normally aging brain does experience atrophy (or shrinkage) in general (i.e., whole brain volume) but the changes of aging are better characterized by differential volume loss in terms of gray vs. white matter volumes and within specific brain regions.

Raz (2005) notes that, despite variability across studies, the pattern of change observed in cross-sectional studies generally suggest that gray matter volumes show a negative gradient with increasing age, beginning early in life, and a leveling or plateau in later life. White matter changes, on the other hand, follow an inverted U function with increases in white matter volume into the early 20s, leveling through midlife until the 60s when declines begin and appear to accelerate with advancing age (see Raz, 2005, for review). Some studies reviewed by Raz suggest greater declines in frontal brain regions when compared to other brain regions. This is largely confirmed in his analysis of cross-sectional studies of normal age changes. Cross sectional results were presented as bivariate correlations between chronological age and regional brain volumes. Among cortical regions, prefrontal cortex (PFC) volumes show the strongest negative correlation with chronological age when compared with other brain structures. For example, frontal gray and white matter volumes show stronger correlations with age than do temporal, parietal or occipital cortex volumes. Not surprisingly, PFC changes have received considerable attention in normal aging reviews (West, 1996; Hedden & Gabrieli, 2004). However, although PFC volumes show the strongest cross-sectional correlation with age, it should also be noted that certain limbic structures, particularly the hippocampus, also show significant negative correlations with age in structural imaging studies of normal aging (Raz, 2005). Moreover, within the striatum, caudate and putamen volumes also show substantial negative correlations with age on a similar magnitude as the hippocampus (see Raz, 2005).

The reviews by Raz (2005; Raz & Rodrigue, 2006) also provided comprehensive summaries of median effect sizes based upon longitudinal studies of the normally aging brain (although there are fewer longitudinal studies). Areas of the brain that show relatively greater shrinkage over time include (in order): entorhinal cortex, hippocampus, caudate nucleus, and prefrontal cortex. These are important because these are regions of the brain that may be most critical for optimal learning in later life. Incidentally, these are also regions that are most affected by abnormal aging syndromes such as Alzheimer's disease (entorhinal cortex and hippocampus) and cerebrovascular disease (prefrontal cortex and striatum) in late life, but the changes observed here are generally of lower magnitude than in pathological conditions (Campbell & Coffey, 2001; Jack, Shiung, Gunter, O'Brien, Weigand, Knopman, et al., 2004).

Small white matter lesions (or white matter hyperintensities; WMH) are a key component of the white matter volumetric changes described above. WMH occur in greater frequency and severity in the aging brain, and frequently have vascular etiologies and are linked to cerebrovascular risk factors (Campbell & Coffey, 2001; O'Brien, 2006; O'Brien, Erkinjuntti, Reisberg, Roman, Sawada, Pantoni, et al., 2003; Roman, 2003). In fact, Raz notes that in empirical studies of normal aging, the extent of white matter changes is likely affected by inclusion or exclusion of individuals with cardiovascular disease and related risk factors because they contribute to white matter lesions (Raz, 2005; Raz & Rodrique, 2006). This raises the key issue concerning the nature and definition of normal aging because many cardiovascular risk factors, such as hypertension, increase in prevalence with age. Many authors have noted that WMH are ubiquitous in older brains, but historically their significance was not clear (Campbell & Coffey, 2001; Gunning-Dixon & Raz, 2000). WMH are more common in the brains of individuals with dementia and depression (Campbell et al., 2001), but also occur in individuals without dementia, depression, or clinically significant cognitive impairment (Gunning-Dixon et al., 2000).

Changes in Specific Cognitive Abilities Relevant to Learning

Thus far we have provided a brief overview of the structural brain changes observed in normal aging and selected cognitive changes that are prominent in later life. Yet, the most relevant issue for our purposes concerns how strongly these age-related changes affect learning in later life, which is dependent upon how strongly these brain changes are linked to the observed cognitive changes discussed in the broader aging literature (e.g., processing speed, memory, and inhibition). Ideally, it would be helpful to have direct empirical links between volumetric brain measurements and actual learning performance, or at minimum, longitudinal studies linking changes in brain volumes with performance changes on cognitive tests. However, recent reviews suggest that the evidence linking structural brain changes with cognitive change is not strong or consistent across studies (Raz & Rodrique, 2006). Although there are positive results linking regional brain volumes and cognitive functioning in normal aging, Raz and Rodrigue (2006) argue that because most studies are cross-sectional, and utilize diverse measurement approaches across studies, that "the true magnitude and even direction of association between regional volumes and cognitive functions in normal aging cannot be assessed at this stage" (p. 737).

The evidence is somewhat stronger for the link between WMH and cognition in late life. In a recent review, O'Brien (2006) suggested that although there are a variety of cerebrovascular changes that affect cognition, subcortical white matter changes may be the most common form of cerebrovascular/white matter pathology and is typically linked to changes in attention, processing speed, and executive functions thought to be mediated by the frontostraital circuitry. An earlier meta-analysis by Gunning-Dixon and Raz (2000) revealed a similar conclusion. Their analysis of twenty-three structural neuroimaging studies considered the relationship between WMH and cognitive functioning in elders without dementia or other cognitive impairment. Their findings suggest a significant relationship between WMH and global cognitive functioning, executive functioning, episodic memory (immediate and delayed recall) and processing speed. WMH's were not associated with measures of crystallized or fluid intelligence. Moreover, there was some evidence to suggest that WMH have relatively greater effects on executive functioning and processing speed. Lastly, each of these relationships was significant even after controlling for age (Gunning-Dixon & Raz, 2000).

As we consider the implications for learning in later life, several possibilities emerge from this study. First, measurable brain changes have a greater impact on cognitive changes independent of chronological age, suggesting that when considering learning in later life, individual difference variables such as white matter integrity may be more important than the age of the individual learner. Second, these individual differences in WMH were not significantly linked to general intelligence, but were linked to other cognitive functions including executive functioning, processing speed and recall of episodic memories. Relatively preserved intellectual functioning may enable older adults to continue learning new information, but changes in more vulnerable abilities may alter the setting and methods for continued learning. Individuals with changes in these abilities may learn more slowly, need more externally structured learning opportunities, and may choose to avoid formal learning settings which rely upon delayed recall of learned information (e.g., via exams).

Despite a limited yet developing empirical base bearing on the question at hand, there has been considerable conceptual synthesis of relevant literatures that can be used to make reasonable inferences about the links between normal aging brain changes and learning. In particular, West (1996) has integrated neuroimaging and cognitive aging literatures and concluded, consistent with later reviews by Raz (2005; Raz & Rodrique, 2006), that the prefrontal cortex (PFC) is the brain region that is most susceptible to aging in that it is the earliest and most severely affected in the context of normal aging. His proposed prefrontal cortex function theory of cognitive aging also incorporates more circumscribed cognitive aging literatures that focus on specific functions (e.g., sustained attention, inhibition, working memory) that are highly relevant to learning. Although the model was developed as a broad cognitive aging model, here we emphasize its potential application to learning in late life.

This model proposes the PFC has both primary and secondary cognitive functions. The primary function of the PFC "is to support the temporal organization of behavior through the formation and execution of temporal gestalts or complex behavioral sequences that are both novel to the organism and complex in nature" (West, 1996, p. 280). In other words, PFC is crucial for organizing and carrying out complex behavioral plans (e.g., new learning). The older learner described at the beginning of this chapter could accomplish her goal of learning to use a computer via a formal or self-directed learning (SDL) approach. Although both approaches require organizational and executive skills, the SDL approach may place greater demands upon the primary, organizational function of the PFC because it is less structured. For this learning project to be successful, the older learner would need to develop and carry out a plan of learning, whereas if she had opted for a formal learning experience, this organization may have been provided to a greater degree by an external source (e.g., the instructor).

West (1996) also delineates secondary functions of the PFC that support the primary organizational function: provisional memory, prospective memory, and interference control. Provisional memory is the process that recalls and holds relevant information in working memory while the behavioral plan is formed or, as West explains, "provisional memory serves to maintain task relevant information in an active state while the behavioral structure is constructed" (p. 280). Prospective memory builds upon provisional memory by working to initiate and execute the behavioral plan, or in some cases remembering to construct and execute this plan. Interference control is an inhibitory mechanism of the PFC that is similar to the concept highlighted by Zacks, Hasher, and Li (2000), which seeks to filter out irrelevant stimuli which could be external (competing noise or visual stimuli) or internal (thoughts or memories that are not task relevant).

Thus in our learning example, the older learner must be able to keep relevant information in working memory while developing and executing her learning plan (provisional memory), remembering to act upon the plan at appropriate times (prospective memory), and filtering out irrelevant information that reduces her ability to successfully engage in the learning plan (interference control).

Thus far we have observed (1) some limited empirical connection between structural brain changes and cognitive change in late life, and (2) a conceptual model that seeks to describe links between normal age related brain changes and cognition. In the section below, we examine the cognitive training literature as more direct evidence of the learning potential of older adults, and the extent to which the brain changes described above limit that learning potential. If the conceptual analysis above is correct, then (1) older adults should demonstrate lower learning potential than younger adults because of these brain changes (especially PFC), and (2) those older adults with evidence of age or disease induced cognitive deficits should demonstrate lower learning potential than those who do not.

Cognitive Training Research: Learning Potential and Limits in Normal Aging

In attempting to answer questions related to learning potential later in life, we discuss empirical literature related to cognitive interventions, also referred to as cognitive training studies. Here we take the perspective of Willis (1985) who argues that the short-term changes observed over a cognitive intervention trial have the "most direct and immediate implications for an educational/instructional psychology of the adult learner (p. 819)." In this view, cognitive training studies are well-controlled learning experiments that provide a unique perspective on the potential and limits of learning in later life, and the extent to which learning potential is affected by characteristics of the learner. Below we review selected cognitive training studies to highlight issues related to learning rather than seeking a comprehensive review of the cognitive training literature. Interested readers should consult Kramer & Willis (2002) and Salthouse (2006).

Cognitive intervention studies generally provide positive results concerning learning potential (often referred to as cognitive plasticity) among non-demented elders including those who have demonstrated modest declines in intellectual functioning (i.e., declines not sufficient to warrant a diagnosis of dementia). Elders in the SLS who demonstrated declines in specific abilities (e.g., inductive reasoning) over 14 years were selected to participate in one of two cognitive interventions. After receiving a pre-test assessment, they received cognitive training in the ability on which they had demonstrated decline. As described in Schaie (1994), "Approximately two thirds of our experimental subjects showed significant improvement, and about 40% of those who had declined significantly over the prior 14 years were returned to their pre-decline level" and "training was also somewhat more effective for those individuals who declined prior to the intervention" (p. 311). He goes on to conclude that the results from the SLS "suggest that observed ability declines in many community-dwelling older people are probably due to disuse and are consequently reversible, at least in part, for many persons" (p. 311).

On the other hand, older adults have been shown to improve their performance on cognitive tests after practice alone (i.e., repeated assessment without intervention; Rabbitt, Diggle, Smith, Holland, & McInnes, 2001), and therefore studies that compare specific interventions to control conditions which involve repeated assessment—but no intervention—are needed. In this regard, the most systematic evidence comes from the ACTIVE study, which is a large cognitive intervention study involving 2,832 relatively healthy and cognitively intact adults aged 65 to 94 (Ball et al., 2002). Individuals were excluded if they demonstrated cognitive impairment (Mini-Mental State Exam (MMSE) <23), had experienced functional loss, had a self-reported diagnosis of AD, or had conditions that could lead to functional decline (e.g., stroke). Participants were randomly assigned to a control group (n = 704) or to intervention groups receiving memory training (n = 711), reasoning training (n = 705), or training in speed of processing (n = 712) over a 10 week training period. Immediately after training, roughly 87 percent of speed trained elders, 74 percent of reasoning trained elders, and 26 percent of memory trained elders showed reliable improvement (at least one standard error of measurement over baseline), and these improvements were largely retained over one- and two-year follow-up assessments. Those who received booster speed and reasoning training sessions 11 months after the initial training demonstrated even greater benefit but memory booster sessions did not have a significant effect. Similar results were obtained at five-year follow up. Training gains were maintained in all three abilities and booster sessions enhanced processing speed and reasoning, but not memory (Willis, Tennstadt, Marsiske, Ball, Elias, Koepke et al., 2006).

These results are consistent with the conclusions of prior reviews that although older adults experience cognitive changes in the context of normal aging, they clearly benefit from cognitive intervention programs (Kramer & Willis, 2002; Schaie, 1994). Interestingly, the ACTIVE study also supports the finding from the SLS that the magnitude of training gains roughly approximate the amount of decline experienced by nondemented elders over a 7 to 14 year period (Ball et al., 2002; Schaie, 1994).

In this context then, the question may be less concerned with the extent to which cognitive declines associated with normal aging contribute to learning problems in later life, but rather to what extent new learning might remediate the cognitive changes that many older adults experience. On the other hand, it would seem premature to suggest that the training literature indicates that all age-related cognitive changes can be reversed via training (Salthouse, 2006). Indeed, although findings from the SLS and ACTIVE studies indicate that the magnitude of training gain is similar to the magnitude of age related loss over the preceding periods, there is evidence from memory training studies that suggests younger adults derive greater benefit from training than do older adults (see Kliegl, Smith, & Baltes, 1989; Jones, Nyberg, Sandblom, Stigsdotter, Ingvar, Magnus et al., 2006; Singer, Lindenberger, & Baltes, 2003). This finding has led to the conclusion that although older adults benefit from training, they may demonstrate less cognitive plasticity or learning potential. Recent results from the Berlin Aging Study (BASE) concerning the plasticity of episodic memory among those aged 75 to 101 appear to support both of these points (Singer et al., 2003).

Ninety-six survivors from the ongoing BASE study were taught a mnemonic technique for improving episodic memory. Because this was part of an ongoing longitudinal study of cognitive aging, it was possible to track changes in cognitive abilities (memory, processing speed, verbal fluency, verbal knowledge) that had occurred in the six years prior to memory training. Change in memory performance in the six-year pre-intervention period predicted both pre- and post-intervention performance on tests of memory, but did not predict learning gains associated with the intervention. Interestingly, the best predictor of learning gain was processing speed, including change in processing speed in the six years prior to intervention. Older adults who had demonstrated greater declines in processing speed were less likely to benefit from memory training (i.e., show less new learning). The authors conclude that although memory plasticity was generally preserved in this old-old sample, it was significantly reduced, particularly among those who had demonstrated declines in processing speed in the years preceding the intervention. These findings provide some evidence that the extent to which older adults maintain learning potential depends upon individual differences in their cognitive status, specifically whether they have been demonstrating greater cognitive decline.

Jones and colleagues (2006) build upon this theme in their discussion of the limits of cognitive and neural plasticity among older adults. They also discuss age-related reductions in new learning (plasticity) and seek to explain individual differences in plasticity or new learning using neuroimaging techniques. They review findings from their research group that examined neural correlates of learning gain using mnemonic training (Nyberg, Sandblom, Jones, Neely, Petersson, & Ing, 2003). Reductions in learning potential were observed in that younger adults demonstrated greater learning gain from the training procedure than did older adults. To explain this change using PET imaging, the older adults were divided into two groups: those who benefited from the training and those who did not. These two groups were compared to each other and to the younger participants to determine differences in regional brain activation. When using the mnemonic technique, younger adults demonstrated greater activation in the dorsolateral prefrontal cortex (DLPFC) than the older adults in general, which they interpreted as indicating that older adults had less overall processing resources. Both younger adults and older adults who benefited from training demonstrated increased activity in the left occipital/parietal region, whereas the older adults who did not benefit failed to demonstrate this pattern of activation. Importantly, follow-up questioning of participants regarding the mnemonic strategy indicated that older adults who failed to benefit from training understood the technique but had difficulty implementing it during the task, a result generally consistent with the predictions of the West PFC model of cognitive aging.

Further re-analysis of the Nyberg et al. (2003) data suggested that there were differences between the groups in medial temporal lobe (MTL) activation during use of the mnemonic strategy when compared to pre-training levels of activation. Young adults demonstrated greater bilateral MTL activation, and older adults, who benefited from training, demonstrated increased activity only in the left MTL. Older adults who did not benefit did not show increased MTL activation. Jones and colleagues concluded that there are age-related reductions in cognitive and neural plasticity (the basis for new learning) and that these "may reflect both a general processing (frontal) deficit, and a more task-specific utilization deficit (pariental, MTL)" (p. 870).

These findings suggest that there are limits in terms of new learning in late life, and that these limits may be associated with underlying brain changes. They also provide some support for the notion that PFC dysfunction and its related cognitive deficits may reduce learning potential in late life by limiting both processing resources (such as speed) or by interfering with one's ability to utilize obtained skills (executing behavioral plans). These findings also point to the importance of other brain structures that decline with age in predicting new learning. The finding that MTL activation was associated with training outcomes (learning potential) is particularly intriguing in that it is not only one of the structures most affected by aging (Raz, 2005), but it is also the region that is the earliest affected in Alzheimer's disease, which we turn our attention to in the next section.

Alzheimer's Disease and Dementia Syndromes

Alzheimer's disease (AD) is the most common cause of dementia in late life, and age is the strongest risk factor for AD. As such, any consideration of age-related changes in the brain and their impact on learning must consider AD. Recent estimates suggest that approximately 4.5 million individuals in the United States have AD, and that by 2050 this number will grow to over 13 million with the greatest growth occurring among those over the age of 85 years (Hebert, Scherr, Bienias, Bennett, & Evans, 2003). Although the cause of AD is still unknown, the characteristic neuropathological changes (neuritic plaques and neurofibrillary tangles) have been well-described. These changes initially accumulate in the medial temporal lobe structures in the earliest stages of disease, but eventually spread to other cortical regions including parietal and frontal cortex. Because AD can only be confirmed by neuropathological evidence, the clinical diagnosis of AD must be considered either "possible" or "probable" prior to death (McKhann, Drachman, Folstein, Katzman, Price, & Stadlan, 1984).

Clinically, AD is characterized by progressive declines in cognitive functioning with particularly prominent changes in learning and episodic memory early in the disease process, and additional impairments in executive functioning, language, apraxia, and visual-spatial functioning as the disease progresses (Grober & Kawas, 1997; Stout, Bondi, Jernigan, Archibald, Delis, & Salmon, 1999; Welsh, Butters, Hughes, Mohs, & Heyman, 1991, 1992).

In this context of a progressive dementia, it is not particularly surprising that as more cognitive abilities are compromised by AD, learning will become considerably less efficient. Over the past two decades, considerable neuropsychological research has emphasized the inability to retain information over time as the core deficit of AD throughout the duration of the disease (i.e., episodic memory; Bondi, Salmon, Galasko, Thomas, & Thal, 1999; Welsh et al., 1991). The inability to retain newly learned information poses clear problems to late life learning, such that AD may largely prevent new explicit learning. Moreover, Grober and Kawas (1997) have demonstrated that, in addition to the commonly cited retention failures, individuals with AD also exhibit deficits in new learning, and that this learning deficit may precede the onset of other cognitive problems.

Grober and Kawas (1997) followed 537 non-demented elders from the Baltimore Longitudinal Study of Aging (BLSA) for up to seven years. Twenty participants developed clinically diagnosed AD and were matched with control participants (those who did not develop dementia) based on age and gender. Total learning and retention on the Free and Cued Selective Reminding (FCSR) test were taken both at baseline (when no participants had clinical AD) and at three-year follow-up (when the AD participants were in a mild AD stage). At the baseline assessment, those with preclinical AD demonstrated poorer learning over multiple trials but had similar retention performance over a 30 minute delay when compared with controls (see Figure 24.2). These findings suggest that learning is impaired in AD even before the onset of other cognitive problems including retention which is typically thought to be the earliest symptom of AD (e.g., Bondi et al., 1999). Furthermore, at the three-year follow-up, AD patients continued to show declines in both learning ability and retention of information learned, while controls had stable performance in both learning and retention.

Not surprisingly, these studies have been taken as evidence that AD leads to profound disruption in the learning process. Margaret Baltes and her colleagues (1992, 1995, 1996) took this perspective one step further to suggest that reduced learning potential is the core deficit in dementia, particularly AD. A series of studies by M. Baltes and her colleagues provide some of the most compelling evidence concerning the link between AD and reduced learning potential.

Baltes, Kühl, and Sowarka (1992) studied 81 community dwelling elders in Berlin, Germany, of whom 25 were determined to be at risk for dementia based upon a standardized

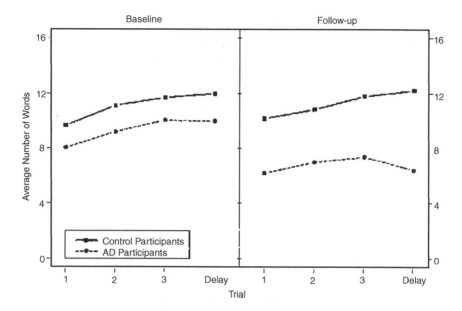

Figure 24.2 Learning and recall over trials baseline and at 3 year follow-up in participants with and without Alzheimer's disease (AD). *Source:* Grober and Kawas (1997). Learning and retention in preclinical and early Alzheimers disease. *Psychology and Aging, 12*, 183–199. Reprinted with permission of the American Psychological Association.

psychiatric interview conducted by a psychiatrist specializing in dementia. Twenty-one of these were determined to have early Alzheimer's type dementia syndromes. All participated in a standardized cognitive training protocol aimed at improving figural relations (fluid intelligence). They hypothesized that elders with early dementia would demonstrate less benefit from the cognitive training (i.e., less pre-post training change) than normal controls. Pre-test figural relations scores did not differentiate controls from those with early dementia and did not predict individual differences in training gain. Individuals with dementia (or at-risk) did not demonstrate statistically significant training gains, whereas controls did. In short, "only the trained subjects identified as healthy significantly improved their scores from pretest to posttest" (Baltes et al., 1992, p. 166). These findings were interpreted as indicating that elders with early AD do not have sufficient learning potential (or reserve capacity) to benefit from cognitive training procedures.

In a follow-up study, M. Baltes, Kühl, Gutzmann, and Sowarka (1995) sought to replicate these findings and extend them to consider (1) whether similar results could be obtained using other fluid intelligence tests (inductive reasoning) and (2) whether the relative difference in training gains would better differentiate between demented and control elders than standard psychometric tests used in AD assessments (Word List and Digit Span memory tests from the Nurenberg Age Inventory). Of 108 participants trained in either figural relations or inductive reasoning, 59 had scores in the mild impairment range or worse on the Structured Interview for the Diagnosis of Alzheimer or Multi-Infarct Dementia (SIDAM). In multiple regression analyses, individual differences in training gains and free recall on the Word List assessment measure were the strongest predictors of dementia status. Figural relations training gains explained the greatest portion of variance in SIDAM scores, followed by free recall of the Word List, and inductive reasoning training gains, respectively. These findings confirm the findings of Baltes and colleagues (1992) that learning potential (cognitive reserve) was a strong, unique predictor of dementia, even after controlling for performance on other measures of memory. Moreover, this effect generalized to different training protocols addressing different fluid abilities (inductive reasoning and figural relations).

M. Baltes and Raykov (1996) followed this study with a longitudinal extension to determine whether the training gains would predict dementia status two years after the initial post-test. Structural equation model results indicated that training gains in figural relations predicted dementia status at the two-year follow-up after controlling for the impact of pre-test dementia status and pre-test figural relations performance. It was determined that the differential training gains (figural relations post-test) was as strong a predictor of two year dementia status (two year SIDAM score) as was pre-test dementia status (i.e., pre-training SIDAM score). They concluded:

> The findings indicate that learning gain, namely posttest scores, predict later mental status even when Time 1 mental status and pretest are controlled for. In fact, we found no difference between the predictive power of posttest scores and initial mental status. (p. 555)

Recently, Fernández-Ballesteros and colleagues (2005) created a clinical assessment battery for dementia that builds upon the work of Baltes and colleagues. The Battery of Learning Potential for Assessing Dementia (BEPAD) involves pretesting on four cognitive domains (visual-spatial, verbal recall, executive functioning, and verbal fluency), followed by standardized training and a post-test in each domain. In one study, the learning potential (training gain) scores were better able to differentiate individuals with AD, Mild Cognitive Impairment (MCI), and controls than did pre-test scores. Overall, 89% of participants were correctly classified using learning potential scores.

These studies indicate that those who are in the early stages of dementia or who are at high risk for dementia show significantly less learning (training gains) even after being taught specific techniques for improving their performance. As a result, Baltes and colleagues suggest that reduced learning potential is a better marker for AD than standard psychometric tests given as part of a one-time static neuropsychological assessment. Baltes and Raykov (1996) suggest the reason for this is that the underlying brain pathology of AD affects cognitive reserve or learning potential.

Neuroimaging and clinico-pathology studies provide evidence concerning why this might occur by identifying the earliest and most notable changes in the brains of individuals who have probable AD. In the sections below, we review selected studies that address links between the AD brain changes and their corresponding cognitive change with the dual goal of (1) identifying the locus of reduced learning efficiency in elders with AD and (2) understanding the extent to which AD related brain changes might affect the learning of older adults who are not yet experiencing clinical AD. As will be seen, the links between underlying AD and reduced learning potential may be highly relevant to understanding learning among a portion of non-demented elders.

For example, one analysis from the Nun Study included both neuropathological and common imaging indicators of AD (Mortimer, Gosche, Riley, Markesbery, & Snowdon, 2004). Using postmortem MRI and autopsy results, the Nun Study investigators found that delayed recall of a word list was associated with temporal lobe volume, and the number of neurofibrillary tangles (NFT) in CA-1 and subiculum. Individuals with a greater number of NFTs and smaller temporal lobe volumes recalled fewer words after a short delay. Hippocampal volume was a better predictor of learning and recall than autopsy indicators of AD pathology. But, perhaps most importantly for our current purposes, hippocampal volume was associated with poorer recall of learned information in *both* demented and non-demented research participants. It has long been hypothesized that AD changes are present in the brain long before cognitive impairment appears or the clinical expression of AD occurs, and as a result, there are many individuals who have AD pathology but have not yet demonstrated cognitive changes sufficient to draw clinical attention (Collie & Maruff, 2000).

The findings of Mortimer and colleagues (2004) suggest that these underlying changes may have cognitive and functional consequences, even when the individual does not meet criteria for a dementia syndrome and provide a compelling rationale for considering the impact of early AD brain changes on learning in individuals who do not have dementia or significant cognitive impairment. The Baltes intervention studies suggest that AD reduces learning potential. Therefore, a key question is whether the underlying brain changes observed by Mortimer et al. also lead to subtle changes in cognition that affect learning potential in non-demented elders? In the next section, we consider this question among those elders who fall in the gray area between the normally aging elders considered in cognitive aging studies and the clinical cases considered in research on neuropsychological aspects of AD.

MCI and Preclinical AD Changes in Cognitively Intact Elders

Cognitive changes that fall short of dementia are common in late life (Panza, D'Intiono, Colacicco, Capurso, Del, Caselli, et al., 2005; Unverzagt, Gao, Baivewu, Ogureuvi, Gureje, Perkins, et al., 2001) and have been linked with AD pathology (Markesbery, Schmitt, Kryscio, Davis, Smith, & Wekstein, 2006). These changes appear to be very important for understanding links between the aging brain and learning in late life. Of particular interest are the earliest detectable brain and cognitive changes in AD, and in some cases, changes that precede the development of AD. Emphasis on Mild Cognitive Impairment (MCI) syndrome as a possible transition between normal aging and AD has grown in recent years with the hope that identifying a clinical state the reliably precedes the development of AD will enhance treatment and prevention outcomes (Petersen, Doody, Kurz, Mohs, Morris, Rabins et al., 2001).

MCI can likely take a number of forms, but the amnestic MCI type has received the most research to date. This syndrome occurs in non-demented individuals and is characterized by an isolated impairment in memory accompanied by subjective memory complaints in the context of otherwise normal cognitive functioning (i.e., no other cognitive decline) and no impairment in activities of daily living (Petersen et al., 2001). Some investigators have concluded that amnestic MCI represents very early AD based upon high conversion rates to clinical AD in comparison to individuals who were cognitively normal at baseline (Morris, Storandt, Miller, McKeel, Price, Rubin, et al., 2001). For example, Morris and colleagues (2001) observed that 100% of participants with MCI (CDR score of 0.5) progressed toward greater dementia severity over the study period (up to 9.5 years). At five years, only 6.8% of cognitively normal elders had developed dementia (CDR = 1). Moreover, of the 25 autopsied MCI cases, 24 demonstrated AD neuropathology.

Recent studies confirm the hypothesis that the amnestic form of MCI is characterized by AD pathology on autopsy and likely represents early AD. Bennett and colleagues (2005) followed 180 Catholic clergy with annual clinical evaluations until death and brain autopsy. Thirty-seven had MCI, 60 had no cognitive impairment, and the remaining 83 had dementia at the last clinical evaluation (the average lag between the last clinical evaluation and autopsy was 6–7 months across groups). More than half of the MCI participants met pathological criteria for probable or definite AD using CERAD criteria. The MCI group fell between the normal control and AD groups in terms of severity of AD pathology and in the frequency of cerebral infarction (Bennett, Schneider, Bienias, Evans, & Wilson, 2005).

Markesbury and colleagues (2006) compared 10 amnestic MCI patients with 10 early AD and 10 controls on the neuropathological features of AD: neuritic plaques and neurofibrillary tangles. Participants had been followed longitudinally through the transition from normal cognition to MCI and early AD, and had an average period of roughly nine months between their last clinical evaluation and death across all three groups. Patients with amnestic MCI demonstrated greater AD pathology than normal controls including greater neuritic plaques in the frontal, temporal and parietal cortices, posterior cingulate gyrus, and amygdala, and greater neurofibrillary tangles (NFT) than controls in the parietal lobe, amygdala, entorhinal cortex, CA1, and subiculum. Amnestic MCI patients were similar to early AD patients in terms of the number of neuritic plaques in the neocortical regions, CA1, and entorhinal cortex, but had fewer neuritic plaques in the amygdala and subiculum. Early AD patients had greater neurofibrillary tangles than MCI patients in the frontal, temporal, amygdala and subiculum, but were similar in terms of tangle counts in other regions such as CA1, entorhinal cortex, the parietal lobe and posterior cingulate gyrus. Moreover, delayed recall of a word list was correlated with several neuropathologic indicators of AD. Greater NFT counts in the entorhinal cortex and CA1 region were associated with poorer recall of the word list after a short delay. These findings suggest that amnestic MCI patients demonstrate early AD pathology and that this pathology may interfere with cognitive functions that are key to optimal learning (i.e., poorer retention).

Longitudinal studies of amnestic MCI suggest that these individuals will progress toward AD at a much higher rate than non-MCI elders (Morris et al., 2001) and, by implication, will experience increasing difficulty with the learning process as memory impairment worsens and other cognitive functions are compromised. As has been suggested by the clinico-pathology correlation studies above, these core deficits appear to be linked predominantly to AD pathology, which is thought to be linked to reduced learning potential in those persons with early AD (Baltes et al., 1996; Baltes, Kuhl, Gutzmann, & Sowarka, 1995; Baltes, Kuhl, & Sowarka, 1992; Raykov, Baltes, Neher, & Sowarka, 2002). Below we consider more direct evidence that patients with MCI demonstrate reductions in learning potential (Darby, Maruff, Collie, & McStephen, 2002; Schrijnemaekers, de Jager, Hogervorst, & Budge, 2006).

Schrijnemaekers et al. (2006) examined the verbal learning and recall performance of elders with AD, to those with MCI, and to normal controls. On repeated testing over a two year test interval, those with AD demonstrated mild decline, and normal controls demonstrated improvement on the Hopkins Verbal Learning Test (HVLT). Elders with MCI were less likely than normal elders to demonstrate improvement on the HVLT, consistent with the hypothesis that MCI (in addition to dementia) is associated with reduced learning potential. In this study, this reduction was partially attributable to lack of strategy use at follow-up testing. The cognitively intact controls appeared to utilize a semantic clustering learning strategy (likely learned on the previous testing) and used this to their advantage in learning and recalling more words over time, whereas elders with MCI were less likely to recall and incorporate this learning strategy at the two-year follow-up, which led to recall of fewer words.

This result is consistent with earlier results from Darby et al. (2002) who found that MCI patients were less likely than matched normal elders to demonstrate practice effects over a three hour test battery on tests of reaction time and working memory. In their protocol, both MCI and normal cognition elders repeated very short, simple cognitive tasks over four occasions within three hours. On initial testing, the MCI patients were not significantly different from normal controls, but these two groups did differ in terms of their changes in performance over the next three testing occasions. The controls clearly demonstrated learning via improved reaction time on a simple reaction time task, and greater speed and accuracy on a simple working memory task (one-back test). MCI patients, on the other hand, demonstrated relatively flat performance over trials suggesting an absence of new learning.

Taken together, the literatures above suggest that amnestic MCI and AD pathology are linked to problems in learning via two core cognitive deficits. The first is reduction in learning capacity, as demonstrated by poorer performance on list learning memory tasks and by failure to benefit from repeated exposure of items to be learned (or a practice effect). Second, failure to employ strategies to optimize learning over trials or repeated exposures may contribute to poorer learning outcomes, which is consistent with predictions made by West's PFC theory. These conclusions are particularly intriguing in light of the training results discussed above in the context of normal aging indicating that learning potential may be reduced in normal aging, and that this reduction may be linked to dysfunction within the MTL and PFC (Nyberg et al., 2003; Singer et al., 2003), which are the same regions which appear to experience greatest volume losses in normally aging longitudinal samples (Raz, 2005; Raz & Rodrigue, 2006; West, 1996).

Recognizing that AD and its pathology may lie on a continuum both in terms of the underlying severity of brain changes and corresponding cognitive changes, in the section below we turn our attention to the question of whether early, preclinical AD pathology interferes with cognitive functioning and learning in those who have not yet demonstrated cognitive impairment. The notion of preclinical AD is based upon the hypothesis that AD changes are present in the brain long before cognitive impairment or the clinical expression of the underlying AD pathology appears. Individuals with preclinical AD are believed to have underlying AD pathology but have not yet demonstrated changes sufficient to draw clinical attention. In the context of the literature concerning the link between AD pathology and reduced learning potential, a key issue is whether the preclinical AD involves subtle changes in cognition that affect learning potential.

Longitudinal clinical studies indicate that individuals at risk for AD demonstrate isolated weakness in multiple areas of cognitive functioning, particularly delayed recall (explicit memory), executive functioning and processing speed. For example, Bäckman and colleagues (2005) performed a meta-analysis on 47 longitudinal studies which examined preclinical AD in clinically non-demented elders. Those who were free of clinical dementia at baseline but went on to receive a diagnosis of AD at follow-up were considered cases of preclinical AD (n = 1207) and were compared with those who did not receive a subsequent diagnosis of dementia at follow-up (normal controls, n = 9097). Those with preclinical AD demonstrated significantly poorer (effect sizes > 1.0) global cognitive functioning, processing speed, executive functioning, and episodic memory (particularly delayed recall). Verbal ability, visual-spatial functioning, and attention were also affected in preclinical AD, but to a lesser extent (Backman, Jones, Berger, Laukka, & Small, 2005).

Clinicopathological studies also appear to support the notion of preclinical AD and appear to be highly relevant to learning in late life. A recent study (Bennett, Schneider,

Arvanitakis, Kelly, Aggarwal, Shah, et al., 2006) examined 134 older adults without cognitive impairment. They observed that, although participants in this study were cognitive normal (i.e., no impairment), those who had pathology consistent with AD demonstrated subtle yet significantly poorer episodic memory than elders without significant AD pathology. An earlier study by Schmitt and colleagues (2000) yielded similar findings in that non-demented elders who had AD pathology on autopsy demonstrated poorer immediate paragraph recall and delayed recall of a word list at their last clinical evaluation when compared to those who did not have AD pathology on autopsy (Schmitt et al., 2000). Both studies suggest that preclinical AD may interfere with memory functions that contribute to optimal learning.

Galvin, Powlishta, Wilkins, McKeel, Xiong, Grant, et al. (2005) studied 41 community dwelling elders without clinical evidence of dementia prior to death (i.e., normal cognitive functioning over repeated longitudinal neuropsychological assessments) and found that 34% had pathological evidence of AD on autopsy. These elders generally did not demonstrate cognitive differences from those without AD pathology, but they did demonstrate a subtle yet detectable difference over repeated assessments. Because the cognitive testing was repeated on an annual basis, most participants received the same tests multiple times (mean number of assessments per participant = 6), and the elders without AD pathology demonstrated the typical practice effect on these tests (i.e., their performance improved over time). However, the elders with AD pathology demonstrated significantly less improvement over time on a test of learning paired associated and demonstrated no improvement on a test of object naming. At one level of explanation, this is yet another cognitive difference between two groups of non-demented elders—those who have autopsy evidence of AD (preclinical AD) and those who do not demonstrate AD. At another level, this finding suggests the possibility that the absence (or reduction) of new learning over time is associated with underlying AD pathology that has not been clinically expressed (preclinical AD; Galvin et al., 2005). This lends further support to Baltes' hypothesis that learning potential is a sensitive marker for dementia and underlying dementia risk (Baltes et al., 1992) and extends this hypothesis to elders who are not yet expressing clinical dementia.

In summary, AD clearly interferes with new learning, and indeed may be primarily a disorder characterized by a deficit in learning. In addition, other clinical states that typically precede AD, such as MCI, also appear to affect learning. Furthermore, a portion of older adults who do not demonstrate cognitive impairment, may nonetheless have underlying AD pathology which is associated with poorer, yet unimpaired performance in episodic memory, executive functioning, and processing speed.[1] There is emerging evidence that these changes interfere with learning over time (Galvin et al., 2005). These findings are consistent with the cognitive intervention studies described above in which both cognitive (processing speed) and neuroimaging indicators (medial temporal and prefrontal cortex activation) were significantly associated with reduced ability to benefit from cognitive training (memory).

Across normal aging and AD syndromes there are brain changes, particularly in the MTL and PFC regions, that contribute to cognitive changes associated with reduced learning potential. This conclusion is consistent with prior reviews (e.g., Hedden et al., 2004) that suggest that PFC changes (including WMH) may be more influential in normal age related cognitive change, and that the medial temporal lobe (MTL) structures are more affected and influential in early AD, although there is considerable overlap between these changes (de Leeuw, Barkhof, & Scheltens, 2004, 2006) and the boundary lines in this context are unclear.

The PFC changes described above may interfere with the efficiency of learning activities by reducing the ability to organize behavior, selectively focus attention, filter irrelevant stimuli, and process information quickly. On the other hand, the underlying AD changes in the MTL also interfere with long-term storage of information that is to be learned, and this deficit is superimposed upon the organizational changes associated with PFC dysfunction. Thus elders with dementia may have both the normal age related reductions in PFC functioning combined with MTL deficits, and therefore may fail to benefit from the learning activities described in cognitive intervention studies.

Thus far, we have highlighted cognitive changes and their links to learning. In the section below, we address social and emotional changes associated with PFC dysfunction that may interfere with learning in late life: depression, apathy, and theory of mind. We include these here because these problems have been linked to PFC dysfunction and because the research literature indicates that learning activities fulfill not only cognitive but also social and emotional needs as individuals grow older (Willis, 1985).

Depression and Apathy

Although depression and apathy are not a part of the normal aging process, they are associated with common brain changes observed among older adults. Significant white matter lesions, particularly within the frontostriatal circuitry are relatively common among older adults (Alexopoulos, 2002; Alexopoulos et al., 1997a; Alexopoulos et al., 1997b; Campbell et al., 2001). The frequent vascular etiology for lesions within the frontal-subcortical circuitry has led to the vascular depression hypothesis which suggests that vascular diseases increase risk for late life depression via small vessel disease in these regions of the brain (Alexopoulos et al., 1997a; Lyness et al., 1998). Empirical studies support the link between depression and vascular lesions within the frontal-subcortical regions (Kales, Maixner, & Mellow, 2005; Krishnan, Hays, & Blazer, 1997; Krishnan, Taylor, McQuoid, Macfall, Payne, Prvenzale, et al., 2004; Steffens, Helms, Krishnan, & Burke, 1999; Steffens, Krishnan, Crump, & Burke, 2002) and between depression and cerebrovascular risk factors (Lyness, King, Conwell, Cox, & Caine, 2000; Mast, MacNeill, & Lichtenberg, 2004; Mast, Neufeld, MacNeill, & Lichtenberg, 2004). Other consequences of frontal lobe disruption, such as executive dysfunction, have been emphasized in geriatric depression as well (Alexopoulos, 2003; Alexopoulos, Kiosses, Klimstra, Kalayam, & Bruce, 2002; Alexopoulos, Raue, & Arean, 2003; Mast, Yochim, MacNeill, & Lichtenberg, 2004). The presentation of vascular depression and depression with executive dysfunction syndromes have emphasized apathy, loss of interest in activities, loss of initiative and social withdrawal (Alexopoulos et al., 2002; Krishnan et al., 2004; Mast, 2004).

The relevance of these depression syndromes to learning in late life is highlighted not only by their association with cognitive inefficiency in key domains such as memory, executive dysfunction and processing speed (Alexopoulos, 2003; Lichtenberg, Ross, Millis, & Manning, 1995; Massman, Delis, Butters, Dupont, & Gillin, 1992; Nebes et al., 2000), but also in their effects on initiative and social activity. The presence of such syndromes would reduce the probability that those affected would engage in new learning project, and if initiated, they would experience greater difficulty due to cognitive dysfunction associated with depression. Thus, depression is one individual difference variable that could affect motivational and emotional aspects of learning in late life. Below, we discuss an emerging construct that could interfere with social aspects of learning.

Theory of Mind

Theory of Mind (ToM) is a relatively new social cognitive construct which describes "the ability to attribute independent mental states to other people to explain and predict their behavior" (Keightley, Winocur, Burianova, Hongwanishkul, & Grady, 2006, p. 559). ToM abilities enable individuals to infer or understand what others are thinking based on nonverbal cues or indirect information (Frith & Frith, 1999) ToM appears to be distinct from other social cognitive constructs, such as personality and emotion processing, and has been used along with other measures of social cognition to predict social functioning (Keightley et al., 2006; Phillips, MacLean, Allen, et al., 2002; Washburn, Sands, Walton, et al., 2003). Thus, ToM appears to be a very important and unique element in social behavior across the life span.

Intact ToM abilities may aid learning across the life span in both formal and self-directed learning settings. Formal learning settings, while characterized by the direct verbal exchange of information, still contain many elements that require the correct interpretation of social nuances: assignments that must be carried out by working with others in groups, the nonliteral interpretation of an instructor's dry wit or tongue in cheek presentation of material, and the appropriate timing of a student comment or question. In self-directed settings, ToM abilities may become even more important, as the expertise and assistance of others (librarians, bookstore clerks, friends, and spouses) become primary resources. In the self-directed learning situation, then, the learner's progress may depend directly on his or her ability to carry out basic social exchanges.

The majority of research on ToM has focused on the relatively late emergence of ToM in childhood (approximately age 3), and its developmental relationship to language, inhibition, and executive function. More recently, researchers have begun exploring ToM in older adults, seeking to understand whether ToM abilities are maintained throughout the life span, increase through the acquisition of wisdom, or decrease through age-related cognitive decline. Studies of age-related differences in ToM in later life have had mixed results with some suggesting age-related improvement in performance on some ToM tasks, other suggesting no changes, and still others demonstrating age-related declines (German & Hehman, 2006; Happe, Winner, & Brownell, 1998; Keightley et al., 2006; Maylor, Moulson, Muncer, & Taylor, 2002; Phillips et al., 2002; Sullivan & Ruffman, 2004). More studies, both cross-sectional and longitudinal, are needed that utilize a breadth of ToM measures in order to fully understand its developmental course at the end of the life span in healthy adults.

It has been suggested that ToM abilities may rely on distinct neuroanatomical circuitry (Baird et al., 2006; Rowe, Bullock, Polkey, & Morris, 2001; Stuss, Gallup, Jr., & Alexander, 2001). Evidence from fMRI studies demonstrate increases in blood flow during ToM tasks in several regions of interest including the medial prefrontal cortex, both temporal poles, anterior superior temporal sulcus, and from the bilateral temporo-parietal junction to the posterial superior temporal sulcus (Gallagher, Happe, Brunswick, Fletcher, Frith, & Frith, 2000; Saxe & Kanwisher, 2003; Saxe, Carey, & Kanwisher, 2004). Some diseases associated with aging that disrupt these brain regions have demonstrated differential effects on ToM abilities. On simple ToM tasks that do not require working memory, patients with Alzheimer's disease (AD) tend to score similarly to healthy controls. However, ToM tasks that rely heavily on working memory do reveal significant differences between elders with AD and healthy controls, although these differences may be attributed to increased demands on working memory and not deficits in ToM in AD patients, as the deficits are seen in both control conditions and ToM conditions (Zaitchik, Koff,

Brownell, Winner, & Albert, 2004, 2006). ToM, like other cognitive domains involved with learning, has been linked to the prefrontal cortex. ToM deficits have also been observed in non-demented Parkinson's patients (Mengelberg & Siegert, 2003; Saltzman, Strauss, Hunter, & Archibald, 2000) and in patients with frontotemporal dementia (FTD; Gregory et al., 2002). Diseases associated with age, then, may produce deficits in ToM abilities in older adults that can be expected to compound increasing problems with learning. These deficits may, in turn, lead to increases in social isolation due to the decreased ability to understand and respond appropriately to others.

ToM has been studied in relation to domains that have demonstrated key influences on learning, such as fluid intelligence, working memory, and executive functioning. Some studies have demonstrated that ToM is significantly associated with fluid intelligence (Maylor et al., 2002; Sullivan & Ruffman, 2004), while others have not (Phillips et al., 2002). Many ToM tasks, particularly second-order false belief tasks, have demonstrated dependence on working memory, a finding which has major implications for late-life learning. Researchers have sought to mitigate the confound of working memory in ToM studies by allowing older adult subjects to refer back to scenarios as often as needed before answering (Maylor et al., 2002) and by employing tasks that require less storage of verbal information (Washburn et al., 2003; Zaitchik, Koff, Brownell, Winner, & Albert, 2004). Similar modifications in formal learning settings may increase their appeal for the older learner. Maylor et al. (2002) have also provided evidence that ToM abilities are independent of executive functioning as associations between ToM and executive functioning disappeared when age was partialled out. Therefore, when considered in conjunction with cognitive constructs associated with successful learning toward the end of the life span, it appears that ToM may uniquely contribute to the older adult's learning process, particularly social aspects of common learning activities. PFC changes may impact learning in late life via both the cognitive abilities delineated by West and others, but also via non-cognitive changes reflecting mood, motivation and social functioning.

Observations about General Learning Trends in Later Life

We have identified a range of neuropsychological changes that likely affect learning in late life and in this final section we consider the more direct ways in which these changes influence the learning activities of older adults. A comprehensive survey of the educational gerontology and lifelong learning literatures is beyond the scope of this chapter. However, several general themes have been observed that we wish to highlight here in the context of considering the impact of neuropsychological changes associated with aging and age-related disease. These general observations described below can be understood in the context of the Selective Optimization with Compensation (SOC) model (Baltes & Baltes, 1990) which will be explained in greater detail below. In short, changes in memory, processing speed and executive functioning may force elders to select a smaller number of learning projects, optimize the use of existing strengths and expertise, and incorporate compensatory techniques and environmental support in order to continue learning effectively. It is our view that the basic principles of the SOC model contribute to the following three observations about learning in later life.

First, participation in formal adult education appears to decline with increasing age. Data from the most recent Adult Education and Lifelong Learning Survey of the 2001 National Household Education Surveys Program indicate that 22% of respondents over the age of 65 participated in formal adult education classes, as compared with 53%–55% of individuals between the ages of 16 and 55 (Kim, Hagedorn, Williamson, & Chapman,

2004). Among older survey respondents, participation in formal learning took the form of work-related classes or personal interest courses, rather than formal university or college degree programs (Kim et al., 2004). Yet, despite this apparent decline, the broader gerontological literature suggests that most older adults continue with some type of learning activities (Tough & Ontario Institute for Studies in Education, 1999). Although learning potential may decline, this is not sufficient to prevent new learning in most cases. Empirical studies of learning activities of older adults and the results of cognitive intervention studies (e.g., Ball, Berch, Helmers, Jobe, Levech, Marissle, et al., 2002; Willis et al., 2006) clearly dispute this claim. As we will discuss below, there is some evidence that even in the case of advancing AD, which involves a clear deficit in learning potential (Baltes et al., 1992, 1995, 1996; Raykov et al., 2002), some new (albeit limited) learning remains possible. The key to successful learning in the context of cognitive decline is to shift methods of learning appropriately to compensate for lost skills and optimize remaining functions (Baltes & Baltes, 1990).

Second, the learning activities of many elders differ from those of younger adults. Several authors have reported a shift away from formal learning settings (e.g., college and university courses) toward informal self-directed learning (SDL; Lamdin et al., 1997; Tough, 1979; Willis, 1985). SDL has been described as "independent learning projects," that are "self-initiated and self-designed" and "constitute a direct response to the learner's own interests, needs, and life style choices" (Lamdin et al., 1997). Tough reports that 90% of adults engage in some form of learning (at least one major learning project per year) and that up to 80% of learning efforts are SDL projects (Lamdin et al., 1997; Tough, 1979, 1999). These projects typically involve several stages, including generating the idea for a learning project, developing a plan for learning, conducting a search for resources, and carrying out the actual learning process (Lamdin et al., 1997). The core of SDL is that the planning, process, and evaluation of learning are taken on by the learner, whereas in most formal learning opportunities the learning objectives, methods, and evaluation are already structured and planned by an instructor.

Both normal age-related and pathological changes in the brain will likely alter the goals, methods and setting of new learning. Thus, although learning potential may be reduced in later life, many older adults compensate by changing the types of learning they engage in, the learning goals targeted and the methods used to achieve their specific learning goals. In a report to a U.S. Department of Education conference on lifelong learning, one scholar noted:

> In summarizing his research on adult learners, Penland (1978, p. 6) noted that adults 'often feel a strong need to establish the pace and control the character of their learning experiences.' Most adults express a preference for independent learning over formalized courses for a number of reasons: pacing, learning style, flexibility and the ability to change, control of structure, lack of classes, immediacy, time limitations, dislike of a classroom setting, expense, and transportation. (Tough, 1979, p. 39, cited by Van Fleet, 1995)

Although not frequently emphasized in the existing literature, it is likely that the cognitive changes discussed thus far (e.g., declining processing speed, memory retention, executive functioning) play a key role in the learning preferences described above. We discuss this hypothesis further in our discussion of Selective Optimization with Compensation below.

Finally, the context of learning in later life is often increasingly social and often serves both social and emotional needs, whereas in earlier developmental periods the goals of learning tend to be more focused on educational attainment and occupational needs. For example, Lamdin and Fugate (1997) report results from the Elderlearning Survey (ES) indicating that 68% of older respondents prefer learning in groups, as compared to 22% who prefer learning on an individual basis. This mirrors a general shift observed in interpersonal aspects of aging as described in Carstensen's socioemotional selectivity theory (SST) in which social relationships functions shift away from informational purposes toward emotion regulatory functions (Carstensen, Isaacowitz, & Charles, 1999). SST observes that when individuals are younger, a broad social network serves achievement oriented goals and functions (e.g., educational and occupational attainment), but as individuals grow older and perceive they have less time left to live, they pare down their social network and focus on those relationships that are emotionally fulfilling and enhance meaning (Carstensen, 2006). Just as relationship functions shift with age, it appears that the needs served by learning in later life may follow a similar shift and may serve more than just informational functions.

In the sections below, we consider in greater detail how the Selective Optimization with Compensation (SOC) framework described by Baltes and Baltes (1990) can provide a conceptual model for understanding how the neuropsychological changes described in this chapter are related to these three observations about late life learning. Specifically, SOC provides a framework for understanding how, despite significant changes in functioning, older adults continue learning, and how new learning might be promoted in the context of dementia.

SOC and Shift in Ways and Means of Learning in Normal Aging

The SOC model was developed by Baltes and Baltes (1990) in their life-span development research related to intellectual and cognitive changes, and it seeks to answer the following question: "Can we envision a prototypical strategy of effective aging that allows for self-efficacy and growth in the context of increasing biological vulnerability and reduced reserve capacity?" (1990, p. 21). This question is remarkably similar to the central question of this chapter: Can we envision a strategy which allows for effective learning in the context of increasing biological vulnerability (both age and disease related change) and reduced learning potential? As noted by Marsiske and colleagues (1995), this model is sufficiently broad and flexible that it can be applied to a wide variety of life-span developmental issues, and here we apply it to the issue of how older adults can continue with successful learning activities in the face of cognitive decline and reduced learning potential.

The three processes (selection, optimization, and compensation) interact with one another to make it possible for elders experiencing reductions in learning potential and greater cognitive vulnerability to continue learning. The first process (selection) refers to a shift toward a reduction in the number of domains a person maintains as he or she grows older and greater specialization that occurs in line with one's priorities (Baltes & Baltes, 1990; Marsiske et al., 1995). According to SOC, as individuals age they may no longer seek to focus their attention on multiple domains of functioning, but may instead seek to shift their focus to selected domains due to limited time or declining cognitive resources. However, it should be noted that "although selection connotes a reduction in the number of high-efficacy domains, it can also involve new or transformed domains and goals of life" (Baltes & Baltes, 1990, p. 22). The shift therefore in relation to learning may involve a focus on a smaller number of projects in valued domains or taking on a new goal or domain (e.g., computer learning for enhanced communication). The prediction of SOC for learning might be that in the face of declining cognitive resources, individuals will reduce the number activities they engage in, and focus in on only those deemed to be most important or valuable.

Optimization suggests that older adults are more likely to select those domains of functioning which make use of and enhance their remaining skills and cognitive strengths and thereby serve to improve quality of life and functioning (Baltes & Baltes, 1990; Marsiske et al., 1995). Thus the older learner may choose to focus attention on specific learning projects which have high value in terms of maintaining interest and efficacy rather than focusing attention more broadly as might have been done at earlier developmental periods. Optimization is a process that necessarily focuses on enhancing function within selected domains, and therefore the older learner may also take advantage of and build upon existing areas of specialization or strength (Marksiske et al., 1995).

Finally, the process of compensation is activated "when specific behavioral capacities are lost or reduced below a standard required for adequate functioning" (Marsiske et al., 1995, p. 22) and, as a result, the "individual and their contexts are challenged to reassess their earlier means-ends, and/or to construct alternative strategies" (p. 44).

An elder learner who places a priority on learning, but is nevertheless faced with declining cognitive resources, may choose a smaller number of focused learning projects (selection), or build upon remaining cognitive strengths (optimization). If cognitive functioning has been compromised such that old methods of learning are no longer adequate, the elder learner may seek to find alternate strategies for continued learning in the focused domains selected (compensation).

Changes in memory, processing speed, and executive functioning may force elders to modify their learning strategies, settings, and goals via the processes of selection, optimization, and compensation. If we return to the computer learning example with which we began this chapter, the elder learner may choose to drop other activities or tasks to focus her resources on the computer learning project (selection) that she views as more important and possibly emotionally fulfilling (optimization) because it allows her to communicate more regularly in key interpersonal relationships. She may also choose to learn via a self-directed learning method rather than a formal class because she prefers to learn at her own pace (compensation for possible declines in processing speed) and has excellent reading ability and can make use of various instructional books (optimization). Instead of taking university computer classes, she may find that other learning opportunities may be more appealing particularly because of the cognitive demands of highly structured courses which move very quickly, rely on dual-task processing (e.g., taking notes while processing the lecture), and draw heavily on delayed recall of information. By selecting and compensating in this fashion, elders may be able to continue learning despite cognitive change, and optimize their current functioning and quality of life.

The observed shift from formal learning to self-directed learning observed in later life appears to represents an example of SOC in response to the cognitive changes that occur secondary to age and disease related changes in the brain. (This is not meant to imply that cognitive change is the sole, or even primary, reason for this shift—which likely reflects a number of changes including financial resources and interests among other factors.) Self-directed learning may allow individuals to optimize intellectual abilities and learning opportunities while compensating for declines in basic cognitive abilities, such as speed or episodic memory, by allowing them to work at their own pace, engage in as much practice as needed, and reducing demands on memory required for many classroom performance indicators. In essence, the SDL approach may reduce demands on cognitive abilities that reliably decline while allowing individuals to select the learning experiences that have the greatest personal value and potential to optimize functioning while building on existing skills or expertise. The positive implication of this framework is that, although cognitive declines are likely to be observed with increasing age, most elders who seek to engage in new learning will have a reasonable probability of being successful because they find ways to compensate for losses, optimize using spared abilities, and select only the most valued domains.

On the other hand, SDL by definition has less external structure which has both positive and negative features for older adults. On the positive side, the SDL approach allows older learners to establish the pace, goals, and methods of learning (Lamdin et al., 1997; Tough, 1979, 1999; Van Fleet, 1995). On the negative side, SDL requires considerable initiative, organization, planning, and problem solving in response to learning activities (i.e., revised plan if the original plan is not successful or needs modification). These prerequisite skills are among those thought to be most affected by aging of the prefrontal cortex (West, 1996). Disruption of both the primary (organization of behavior and cognition) and secondary functions (interference control, provisional/working memory, prospective memory) of the PFC would clearly affect learning in late life quite broadly, but may particularly affect SDL. In addition, to the extent that lesions within the frontal-subcortical circuitry lead to depression, apathy, and lack of initiative (Cummings, 1993; Tekin & Cummings, 2002), a subset of elders will likely have difficulty judging their ability to complete such projects and lack the initiative to develop and carry out a plan for accomplishing the learning. It should be noted however, that it would be expected that these behavioral issues would likely be expected in those with more severe PFC pathology and would be most applicable to only a subset of elders. Yet, as further connections between elderlearning and neurosciences literatures develop further, it will be important to consider these behavioral/motivational factors in addition to the traditional domains of cognitive aging research. For the discussion below, however, we will restrict our focus on the cognitive changes associated with PFC dysfunction.

PFC changes are common in later life (Gunning-Dixon & Raz, 2000; Raz & Rodrique, 2006; Raz, 2005; West, 1996), which conceptually would be expected to be particularly disruptive to SDL. Yet, data indicate many older adults tend to prefer this form of learning (Lamdin et al., 1997; Tough, 1999). Moreover, evidence from cognitive intervention studies suggest that older adults derive similar benefit from self-directed cognitive interventions as they do from interventions that are more structured and led by an instructor (see Thompson & Foth, 2005, for a review). Here again we draw on the SOC framework to understand how older adults might optimize SDL learning in the context of declining PFC functions (organization, interference control, prospective memory). In this context, the SOC processes of selection and optimization will likely function in a very similar fashion as in the computer example given above. Those elders who continue with SDL despite declining PFC resources will likely have narrowed the number of learning projects (or other activities) to focus their cognitive resources more narrowly (selection) on a project which enhances their functioning or quality of life (optimization). Compensation for any apparent weaknesses in cognitive ability will again be important, but in the context of declining PFC, external compensatory techniques to provide structure, guidance and reminders to accomplish specific tasks might become increasingly necessary. The use of external aids or cognitive enhancement strategies (list making, external cues to remember steps to be taken, organizational notebooks) can help to maintain learning in valued domains. Thus the three processes work together to help maintain SDL activities in the context of PFC changes. The conclusion again is that the brain changes observed in normal aging do not prevent new learning for most older adults, but likely will affect the compensatory methods used for optimizing new learning. For some this may take the form of learning in increasingly social settings or with other learners who can help provide structure for SDL. Learning with other individuals may act as an external compensatory strategy in that they can assist in structuring the learning project, provide reminders to carry out the various steps, help obtain needed resources, and provide feedback, assist in problem solving and help utilize strategies for completing the task (see Saczynski, Margrett, & Willis, 2004). In short, learning in social settings may allow for other individuals to serve the functions that were mediated by PFC in the past.

The preference for learning in social settings over individual learning may have a compensatory function as described above, but it is more frequently cited as an example of selection and optimization (Willis, 1985). That is, social learning opportunities serve important social and emotional functions for older learners, such that these individuals select these options over other, less social learning activities (Tough, 1999), and, as a result, the social aspects of these learning activities optimize both quality of life and functioning.

Whether any of the neuropsychological changes observed in late life might affect the success of social learning activities remains an open question. Depression and ToM may be particularly important in this context. If ToM declines with age (the evidence is not clear) and frontal lobe dysfunction occurs, social functioning might become impaired, and older adults may have difficulty getting their social and emotional needs met in this context. As neuropsychological research extends into social contexts the extent to which ToM declines and interferes with social functioning will likely become clearer. Consistent evidence is not yet available to make firm conclusions, but to the extent that cognitive and affect goals and skills become integrated in late life (Labouvie-Vief, 2003; Labouvie-Vief & Diehl, 2000), the ToM construct may prove particularly useful in investigating successful learning activities.

SOC and Learning in AD

Thus far we have focused our discussion of SOC on situations where cognitive decline is not sufficient to warrant a diagnosis of dementia. Yet, despite the lack of clarity as to the boundary line between normal aging and dementia syndromes like AD, a portion of older adults clearly experience brain changes that are sufficient to cause dementia syndromes, and these changes appear to be sufficiently severe to interfere with formal learning (Baltes et al., 1992; Baltes et al., 1995). The combination of significant impairments in episodic memory, the ability to benefit from feedback, and implement plans clearly impact the extent to which elders can learn new information (O'Brien et al., 2003; Royall, 2000; Swanberg, Tractenberg, Mohs, Thal, & Cummings, 2004; Welsh et al., 1991, 1992). Moreover, as discussed above, the cognitive intervention studies conducted by M. Baltes and colleagues clearly demonstrate that both dementia and pre-dementia states interfere with new learning (Baltes et al., 1992, 1995, 1996; Raykov et al., 2002). It is in this context that we turn our discussion to emerging work describing how learning may be possible even in severely impaired individuals. SOC is used as a broad framework to describe how the techniques described below offer ways that those who have AD might be able to compensate for significant cognitive decline while optimizing other cognitive functions (implicit learning and memory) that are relatively spared in AD.

Spaced Retrieval in AD.   As reviewed above, dementia (especially AD) interferes with patients' ability to learn new information in traditional training paradigms, and, as a result, it was thought that little could be done to improve learning outcomes in individuals with dementia. Throughout the past decade, however, this perspective has been challenged by the finding that certain types of memory are relatively spared in persons with AD (Bayles & Kim, 2003; Bondi & Kaszniak, 1991; Mahendra, 2001; Squire & Zola, 1996).

Individuals with dementia experience greater damage to declarative (explicit) memory systems than to non-declarative (implicit) memory systems (Bayles & Kim, 2003). Evidence that learning occurs through preserved implicit memory processes stems from the finding that although people with dementia have the ability to remember target responses successfully, they do not explicitly remember the actual learning process or training sessions (Bayles & Kim, 2003; Camp, Foss, O'Hanlon, & Stevens, 1996; Mahendra, 2001).

Spaced retrieval is one behavioral intervention that capitalizes on spared implicit memory systems and can lead to new learning in individuals with moderate to advanced dementia. Spaced retrieval is essentially a shaping technique that utilizes principles of cognitive rehabilitation (e.g., spacing effect and operant learning) to facilitate learning (Cherry, Simmons, & Camp, 1999). The subject is asked to make a particular response (such as verbally answering a question or physically performing an action) repeatedly over increasing intervals of time (e.g., 15, 30, 60, 90 sec., etc.). If the subject provides an incorrect response, the trainer provides the correct response and then asks the subject to repeat it. The between trial delay then returns to the last time interval that the subject was able to respond correctly. If the subject provides the correct response, the next time delay is increased.

Early spaced retrieval research focused on younger adults but eventually shifted toward individuals with dementia (Camp, Bird, & Cherry, 2000). In Camp's initial studies, he was able to teach one woman and two men diagnosed with Alzheimer's disease to remember face-name associations (Camp & Stevens, 1990). The woman was able to demonstrate a one week retention interval (the ability to remember the to-be-learned information at the beginning of the next training session one week later) after seven weeks of training and the men were able to do so after three weeks of training. Camp also taught six individuals diagnosed with AD to recall the location of common objects (e.g., location of glasses). Three of the participants were able to demonstrate retention of learned material over at least one week during the eight weeks of training and all three demonstrated retention of the target information at a follow-up session (five weeks later). Cherry, Simmons, and Camp (1999) were also able to teach (or re-teach) the names of everyday objects (e.g., carrot, chair) to four older adults with probable AD. In each of these cases, new learning was demonstrated using SR in the context of relatively advanced dementia.

In one report SR was successfully implemented by a patient's caregiver—suggesting that caregivers can incorporate SR techniques to enhance learning in AD (McKitrick & Camp, 1993). The participant was a 77-year-old woman diagnosed with AD, and the training targeted forgotten names of common objects. During 10 weekly one hour visits, the caregiver observed the experimenter train the patient on two initial items (canoe and globe) using the SR method. The caregiver then began training two new objects (toothbrush and mushroom). Lastly, the patient was trained to learn an unfamiliar item (floppy disk). The experimenter began the training of the unfamiliar item and then the caregiver took over training. All items were learned by the participant, including the unfamiliar item. The items were also recalled with greater consistency after the training than before.

Spaced retrieval has also been used with more complex tasks. Because instructions for future actions (i.e., prospective memory) are often forgotten by individuals with AD, investigations of behavioral interventions that could enhance prospective memory abilities in AD patients are needed. McKitrick, Camp, and Black (1992) conducted such an investigation with four participants diagnosed with AD who demonstrated an inability to perform both a verbal and nonverbal prospective memory screening task (McKitrick et al., 1992). The training goal of this study was to learn and demonstrate the ability to accurately choose a pre-selected color coupon to be redeemed for money. At the beginning of each weekly training session, the participants were given the chance to select the correct color coupon (i.e., the color they had been taught to select) out of nine possible colors (shown in a 3 × 3 matrix). If the participant was able to choose the correct color coupon, a new color was chosen to be the target of the next training session. If the participant was unable to select the correct color coupon, SR training for that color coupon continued. Three participants were able to successfully execute the task after one week of SR training and the other participant required five sessions. In addition, all participants were able to successfully adjust their performance when the target coupon color was changed.

Spaced retrieval has also been used to enhance other cognitive interventions and compensatory techniques. Memory wallets and memory books can help individuals with cognitive impairment compensate for their deficits. However individuals with advanced dementia may not be able to utilize these compensatory methods because they forget when to use it, where they left it, or even that it exists (Bourgeois, Camp, Rose, White, Malone, Carr et al., 2003). Bourgeois et al. (2003) investigated the effectiveness of SR and a cueing hierarchy approach to teaching goals (a clinician-identified problem behavior, such as forgetting what activities are available each day) to individuals with dementia through the use of external memory aids (e.g., memory book). Twenty-five participants with dementia worked on individualized goals to decrease identified problem behaviors. Researchers found that the majority of participants were successful in achieving their goals by learning to use the external aids via SR or cueing, but that SR had slightly better outcomes. Camp, Foss, O'Hanlon, and Stevens (1996) also used SR training to teach participants with AD how to successfully use a daily calendar as an external memory aid. Participants were successful in learning to remember to use the calendar and to complete the secondary task (i.e., help with dishes, send a note to a family member) written on the calendar that day.

Brush and Camp (1998) investigated the effectiveness of training speech pathologists to use SR techniques to help patients with dementia use compensatory communication techniques in order to address language problems in dementia. Nine participants who were enrolled in speech language therapy at the Menorah Park Center for the Aging participated in this study. Seven had a diagnosis of dementia and two had a stroke within the year prior to the study. Training took place approximately three times a week during the patient's regularly scheduled speech-language therapy sessions. Using SR, the clients were first taught the name of their speech-language therapists. Once the subject could remember and correctly state the therapists' name in two consecutive sessions, the training for that target stopped. Spaced retrieval was then used to train the subject to remember a piece of meaningful information chosen by the participant, such as date of birth. Again, when the subject successfully remembered the target piece of information at the beginning of two consecutive training sessions, training for that target ended. For each of the training goals, the subject continued to be tested at the beginning of the remaining therapy sessions to determine retention. Finally, SR was used to train a compensatory technique that would facilitate communicative functioning, such as teaching a client to make eye contact when speaking or to properly use a voice amplifier. Training continued until the subject could use the compensatory technique correctly at the beginning of two consecutive therapy sessions. Five out of the seven participants with dementia and both clients with stroke completed the study and progressed toward meeting speech-language therapy goals (Brush & Camp, 1998).

Although there is considerable research to support using the SR method, most of the studies investigating SR do not meet standards typical of clinical trials, in that most "have used small ($n < 10$) sample sizes, have not used control groups, have not randomly assigned patients to conditions, and have not used assessors blind to condition" (Davis, Massman, & Doody, 2001, p. 2). In addition, although SR has been shown to work on teaching specific to-be-learned pieces of information or behaviors, it has not resulted in improvements in overall cognitive functioning or general memory abilities (Camp et al., 1996; Davis et al., 2001).

Davis et al. (2001) conducted a randomized, placebo-controlled study with 37 patients diagnosed with probable AD. The placebo group received five weeks of mock intervention, while the intervention group received five weeks of cognitive intervention consisting of face-name training, SR, and general cognitive stimulation. Intervention patients received individual weekly one-hour clinic visits for five weeks and were instructed to also participate in 30-minute home attention exercises for six days per week. The patients in the intervention group showed significant improvement on recall of personal information and face-name associations but not on standard measures of cognitive performance (e.g., verbal memory, motor speed, verbal fluency), mood or caregiver-rated quality of life).

Camp, Foss, O'Hanlon, and Stevens (1996) investigated the efficacy of SR training on calendar use and also found that, although participants were successfully trained to effectively use daily calendars, this success did not carry over to improvements in general cognitive functioning. In fact, significant cognitive declines were apparent over the course of the study. Therefore, consistent with the broader cognitive training literature (e.g., Ball et al., 2002; Schaie, 1994; Willis et al., 2006), the training effects of SR are highly specific to the trained ability and do not appear to generalize (or transfer) to other functions. On the other hand, the method has demonstrated that individuals with advanced dementia can learn target information and retain this information for a considerable period of time after the initial learning (Cherry et al., 1999).

In this regard SR appears to be a very promising behavioral intervention for persons with dementia. The SR method has been shown to be effective across a number of simple associations (face-name associations, object naming, object location, object selection, and remembering personal information) as well as more complex tasks (using external memory aids such as calendars and memory books, completing prospective memory tasks, and using compensatory speech-language techniques). As noted by Bourgeois et al. (2003), SR has also been shown to work in a number of dementing conditions including Alzheimer's disease, vascular and mixed dementia, post-anoxia dementia, dementia associated with Parkinson's disease, dementia associated with Korsakoff's syndrome, and dementia associated with HIV. Finally, the SR method has been successfully implemented not only by researchers, but by individuals who use spaced retrieval techniques in the real world, such as speech-language pathologists and caregivers.

Perhaps most importantly for our purposes, SR offers some insights into effective procedures to enhance learning in AD and other dementias. Camp and colleagues (2000) have focused much of their efforts on procedural changes to the SR technique that have resulted in a reduced cognitive effort required of the subject and resulted in more social and enjoyable training sessions (Hochhalter, Overmier, Gasper, Bakke, & Holub, 2005). Camp et al. (2000) found that an expanding interval schedule used in early SR research resulted in high error rates, and therefore switched to a more gradual increase in time between recall levels (5, 10, 20, 30, 40, 60, 90, 120 seconds, etc.). Thus, a more gradual recall interval expansion rate is utilized and the length of the between trial delays is based on the subjects, performance on previous trials (Camp et al., 1990, 2000; Hochhalter et al., 2005). In addition, one piece of information is taught at a time versus multiple pieces concurrently (Camp et al., 1990; Hochhalter et al., 2005). Focusing on one target at a time reduces the chance that targets will interfere with one another in the learning process.

The SR techniques used by Camp and colleagues emphasize errorless learning (1990; Hochhalter et al., 2005). According to Mahendra (2001), "errorless learning (EL) is a technique whereby patients are prevented, as far as possible, from making mistakes while they are learning a new skill or acquiring new information" (p. 296). Because common forms of dementia, such as Alzheimer's disease, disrupt episodic and working memory systems, individuals with dementia "cannot use the past as a basis for correcting themselves" (Bourgeois et al., 2003, p. 364). Therefore, "only if they are not allowed to make errors will they learn new information accurately; otherwise, inaccurate learning will take place" (Bourgeois et al., 2003, p. 364). By capitalizing on errorless learning and implicit memory systems, learning occurs "effortlessly" (Camp et al., 1990) with a high frequency of success, resulting in greater self-esteem and mastery (Camp et al., 1990; Brush & Camp, 1998).

The SR technique is also advantageous in that it can be nested within social and leisure activities and, thereby, enhance motivation for training and reduce performance anxiety (Camp et al., 1990, 1996; Mahendra, 2001). The social setting may increase engagement and may fulfill social and emotional needs in later life, which may be a key feature of effective learning in dementia. In the next section, we turn our attention to complementary techniques that have been used to further enhance engagement and thereby enhance learning in AD.

Montessori Techniques in AD

Montessori methods have been utilized to increase the ability of AD patients to engage in and learn appropriately stimulating activities and thereby reduce the frequency of problem behaviors and increase overall quality of life (Orsulic-Jeras, Schneider, & Camp, 2000). We discuss the Montessori method here because it also has the potential to enhance learning in individuals with AD by increasing engagement in selected learning activities, optimizing use of relatively spared cognitive skills, while compensating for declining abilities, particularly processing speed and executive functioning.

The Montessori approach emphasizes "the importance of self-paced learning and developmentally appropriate activities" (Camp & Skrajner, 2004, p. 427) and "modifying learning environments and activities to accommodate adult learners" (Vance, Camp, Kabacoff, & Greenwalt, 2006, p. 11). Many of the Montessori principles and techniques can be utilized to create interventions for promoting learning among individuals with dementia. First, materials are taken from the everyday environment, are designed to give extensive cuing and guidance in terms of how an activity should be completed, and are self-correcting. This allows for immediate feedback to control against error and lets learners know whether or not the task has been completed successfully (Judge, Camp, & Orsulic-Jeras, 2000; Orsulic-Jeras, Schneider, Camp, Nicholson, & Helbig, 2001;

Schneider, Diggs, Orsulic, & Camp, 1999; Vance et al., 2006). Second, larger tasks are often times broken down into smaller steps and are initially taught at the simplest or most concrete level, followed by more complex or more abstract levels if appropriate (Camp & Skrajner, 2004; Judge, Camp, & Orsulic-Jeras, 2000; Orsulic-Jeras et al., 2000; Vance et al., 2006). Third, learning occurs in a sequence that progresses from instructor modeling toward recall and demonstration of the activity by the learner (Orsulic-Jeras et al., 2001). These principles provide the structure and assistance needed to compensate for deteriorating executive functioning in dementia. A more complete list of Montessori principles as they relate to dementia can be found in Orsulic-Jeras et al. (2001).

Like spaced retrieval, Montessori-based activities rely on practice and guided repetition and capitalize on spared implicit memory systems in persons with dementia (Camp & Skrajner, 2004; Orsulic-Jeras, Schneider, & Camp, 2000), thereby improving performance on an activity even if the learner cannot explicitly remember participating in the activity (Orsulic-Jeras, Schneider, Camp, Nicholson, & Helbig, 2001). Modeling is an important aspect of the Montessori method. The person teaching the activity will demonstrate the activity prior to asking the learner to try that same activity (Schneider, Diggs, Orsulic, & Camp, 1999).

The Montessori method stresses the importance of individualizing activities and considering each participant's "past occupations, past interests and present cognitive and physical abilities" when creating activities (Orsulic-Jeras et al., 2001, p. 108). By tailoring activities to an individual's needs, interests, and cognitive ability, the activities become more engaging and can increase the probability of success. This may optimize function in that new learning builds upon spared abilities or expertise to enhance functioning and quality of life (Baltes & Baltes, 1990).

Montessori-based activities can be conducted with both individuals and groups, and can be used with individuals across various stages of dementia (Orsulic-Jeras et al., 2000). Individual Montessori activities may focus on intergenerational programming in which an older adult is paired with a child, or other one-on-one individual activities, in which an older adult is paired with a staff member. Examples of activities that have been used in prior research include "picture and word sorts" and "matching cufflinks and earrings" (Schneider et al., 1999). The interaction with a child gives the individual with dementia the opportunity to serve as a mentor and be successful in an activity (Orsulic-Jeras et al., 2001) and provides for the social and emotional functions of learning in late life as discussed in earlier sections of this chapter.

Small group Montessori activities include Memory Bingo and Question Asking Reading (QAR). These group activities capitalize on a number of Montessori principles to increase engagement including frequent feedback, provision of structure to the activity participation, and considerable practice/repetition (Orsulic-Jeras, Schneider, & Camp, 2000). QAR is "designed to incorporate external cues in order to strengthen participants' focus on the task and improve comprehension and concentration" (Orsulic-Jeras et al., 2000, p. 83). Each participant is given a copy of the story to follow along with, gets a turn to read a paragraph, and is given a color coded statement to read out loud to encourage discussion (Orsulic-Jeras et al., 2001). Although the content of the story may change, the procedure remains the same for each QAR session, allowing for participants to learn the procedure through implicit memory systems and thereby increase the probability of successful engagement and learning.

Several empirical studies have investigated the effect of Montessori activities on learning and engagement in individuals with dementia. For example, Judge, Camp, and Orsulic-Jeras (2000) conducted a study in which nineteen participants with dementia aged 60- to 101-years-old were assigned to either a treatment (9 subjects) or control group (10 subjects) and were matched according to their MMSE scores. Participants in the treatment group participated in both individual and group Montessori-based activities twice a day throughout the study as an alternative to the regularly scheduled activities at the center. Subjects were rated on their level of engagement in the activities over 10-minute segments throughout the day at three different times throughout the study: at baseline, before Montessori-based activities were implemented, and at two follow-up points (four and eight months after baseline). Results indicated that participants in the Montessori condition demonstrated significantly greater constructive engagement when compared to those in the control condition.

Thus far, the Montessori-based activities utilized in these research studies have been implemented by trained investigators. However, to have practical application on a broad scale the activities need to be implemented by others, including caregivers and employees of long-term care nursing facilities. Orsulic-Jeras et al. (2001) investigated whether the activities staff could incorporate Montessori-based activities into their established programming schedules. The activities staff first participated in three half-hour preliminary training sessions (*Understanding Dementia*, *The Montessori Method*, and *Presenting Montessori-Based Activities*) and had access to a training manual developed by Camp and colleagues. The staff was then trained on the Myers Menorah Park/Montessori Assessment System (MMP/MAS), an assessment tool used to examine a subject's "remaining cognitive, motor, sensory, and social skills" (p. 116) to help guide the development of appropriate activities for that individual. The results showed that the activities staff members were able to successfully implement the Montessori-based activities and reported positive changes in both the residents and the staff members themselves after implementing these activities. In a similar study, Schneider, Diggs, Orsulic, and Camp (1999) taught nursing assistants at the Myers Research Institute of the Menorah Park Center for Aging to implement Montessori based activities to residents with dementia. The results of the seven-month study showed that patients were more actively engaged during individual and small group Montessori activities then when participating in their regular activities. Also, the residents showed less negative affect and greater positive affect while participating in Montessori activities compared to their regular environment.

Camp and Skrajner (2004) conducted a study investigating whether dementia patients themselves could learn to serve as group leaders and implement Montessori-based activities for their fellow residents. Four female residents of a senior living facility, diagnosed with either Alzheimer's disease or another form of dementia, were trained to lead Memory Bingo. Training sessions were conducted once or twice a week until the trainee felt comfortable with the game. Data collection began once the leaders indicated that they felt capable of leading the Montessori group activity. Assessments of both the leaders and players (who were residents with more severe dementia) were conducted. The assessments of the leaders revealed a high frequency of at least partial adherence to protocol, which enabled all games to be completed. Players demonstrated greater constructive engagement after the implementation of Montessori program activities.

These findings suggest that Montessori techniques have positive psychosocial effects and that persons with dementia can continue learning successfully when they are engaged in stimulating activities that are matched to their cognitive strengths (optimization) and are accompanied by external compensatory support (e.g., task break down) provided by this approach (Judge et al., 2000; Orsulic-Jeras et al., 2001; Schneider et al., 1999). Taken together, SR and Montessori techniques may enhance learning in dementia by compensating for declines in memory (SR), executive functioning and processing speed (Montessori), and optimizing the use of both implicit learning and memory and environmental structure.

Conclusion

Normal brain aging is accompanied by declines in prefrontal cortex (PFC) volumes, greater white matter lesions, particularly within the PFC. In this context, normally aging elders experience declines in processing speed, executive functioning, and working memory. These brain-behavior changes may lead to modification of the methods and goals of late life learning via the processes of selection, optimization and compensation (SOC), but these changes do not preclude new learning in most older adults. However, more severe forms of cognitive change, such as dementia, do appear to significantly interfere with new learning. Dementia syndromes, such as Alzheimer's disease, lead to more dramatic changes in the brain, particularly within the medial temporal and prefrontal cortex. Nonetheless, even in moderate stages of dementia, some forms of new learning may be possible when the learning techniques can optimize the use of spared cognitive abilities and compensate for affected abilities. The broad SOC framework may serve as a fruitful guide for future research into late life learning, particularly in the context of dementia and other cognitive syndromes. It can also assist both caregivers and educators in appropriate planning for individualized interventions.

Notes

1. The challenge of fully utilizing the concept of preclinical AD lies in the fact that AD pathology cannot be detected prior to death. Until very recently, it was not possible to use neuroimaging methods to image AD characteristic changes in the living brain. Preliminary evidence suggests that a new compound (Pittsburgh compound) can be injected into the body and appears to accumulate in amyloid plaques in the brain imaged with positron emission tomography (PET) methods(Fagan, Mintun, Mach, Lee, Dence, Shah, et al., 2006). This technique has potential for detecting preclinical AD, but will require further replication and development before it is used clinically.

References

Alexopoulos, G. S. (2002). Frontostriatal and limbic dysfunction in late-life depression. *American Journal of Geriatriatric Psychiatry, 10,* 687–695.

Alexopoulos, G. S. (2003). Role of executive function in late-life depression. *Journal of Clinical Psychiatry, 64*(Suppl. 14), 18–23.

Alexopoulos, G. S., Kiosses, D. N., Klimstra, S., Kalayam, B., & Bruce, M. L. (2002). Clinical presentation of the "depression-executive dysfunction syndrome" of late life. *American Journal of Geriatric Psychiatry, 10,* 98–106.

Alexopoulos, G. S., Meyers, B. S., Young, R.C., Campbell, S., Silbersweig, D., & Charlson, M. (1997a). 'Vascular depression' hypothesis. *Archives of General Psychiatry, 54,* 915–922.

Alexopoulos, G. S., Meyers, B. S., Young, R. C., Kakuma, T., Silbersweig, D., & Charlson, M. (1997b). Clinically defined vascular depression. *American Journal of Psychiatry, 154,* 562–565.

Alexopoulos, G. S., Raue, P., & Arean, P. (2003). Problem-solving therapy versus supportive therapy in geriatric major depression with executive dysfunction. *American Journal of Geriatric Psychiatry, 11,* 46–52.

Backman, L., Jones, S., Berger, A. K., Laukka, E. J., & Small, B. J. (2005). Cognitive impairment in preclinical Alzheimer's disease: A meta-analysis. *Neuropsychology, 19,* 520–531.

Baird, A., Dewar, B. K., Critchley, H., Dolan, R., Shallice, T., & Cipolotti, L. (2006). Social and emotional functions in three patients with medial frontal lobe damage including the anterior cingulate cortex. *Cognitive Neuropsychiatry, 11,* 369–388.

Ball, K., Berch, D. B., Helmers, K. F., Jobe, J. B., Levech, M. D., Marsiske, M., et al. (2002). Effects of cognitive training interventions with older adults: a randomized controlled trial. *JAMA, 288,* 2271–2281.

Baltes, M. M., Kühl, K. P., Gutzmann, H., & Sowarka, D. (1995). Potential of cognitive plasticity as a diagnostic instrument: a cross-validation and extension. *Psychology and Aging, 10,* 167–172.

Baltes, M. M., Kühl, K. P., & Sowarka, D. (1992). Testing for limits of cognitive reserve capacity: a promising strategy for early diagnosis of dementia? *Journal of Gerontology, 47,* 165–167.

Baltes, M. M., & Raykov, T. (1996). Prospective validity of cognitive plasticity in the diagnosis of mental status: A structural equation model. *Neuropsychology, 10,* 549–556.

Baltes, P. B., & Baltes, M. M. (1990). Psychological perspectives on successful aging: The model of selective optimization with compensation. In P. B. Baltes & M. M. Baltes (Eds.), *Successful aging: Perspectives from the behavioral sciences* (pp. 1–34). New York: Cambridge University Press.

Bayles, K. A., & Kim, E. S. (2003). Improving the functioning of individuals with Alzheimer's disease: Emergence of behavioral interventions. *Journal of Communicative Disorders, 36,* 327–343.

Bennett, D. A., Schneider, J. A., Arvanitakis, Z., Kelly, J. F., Aggarwal, N. T., Shah, R. C., et al. (2006). Neuropathology of older persons without cognitive impairment from two community-based studies. *Neurology, 66,* 1837–1844.

Bennett, D. A., Schneider, J. A., Bienias, J. L., Evans, D. A., & Wilson, R. S. (2005). Mild cognitive impairment is related to Alzheimer disease pathology and cerebral infarctions. *Neurology, 64,* 834–841.

Blakemore, S. J., & Frith, U. (2005). The learning brain: Lessons for education: A precis. *Developmental Science, 8,* 459–465.

Bondi, M. W., & Kaszniak, A. W. (1991). Implicit and explicit memory in Alzheimers-Disease and Parkinsons-Disease. *Journal of Clinical and Experimental Neuropsychology, 13,* 339–358.

Bondi, M. W., Salmon, D. P., Galasko, D., Thomas, R. G., & Thal, L. J. (1999). Neuropsychological function and Apolipoprotein E genotype in the preclinical detection of Alzheimer's disease. *Psychology and Aging, 14,* 295–303.

Bourgeois, M. S., Camp, C., Rose, M., White, B., Malone, M., Carr, J., et al. (2003). A comparison of training strategies to enhance use of external aids by persons with dementia. *Journal of Communicative Disorders, 36,* 361–378.

Brush, J. A., & Camp, C. (1998). Using spaced retrieval as an intervention during speech-language therapy. *Clinical Gerontologist, 19,* 51–64.

Camp, C. J., Bird, M. J., & Cherry, K. E. (2000). Retrieval strategies as a rehabilitation aid for cognitive loss in pathological aging. In R. D. Hill, L. Backman, & A. Stigsdotter Neely (Eds.), *Cognitive rehabilitation in old age* (pp. 224–248). New York: Oxford University Press.

Camp, C. J., Foss, J. W., O'Hanlon, A. M., & Stevens, A. B. (1996). Memory interventions for persons with dementia. *Applied Cognitive Psychology, 10,* 193–211.

Camp, C. J., & Skrajner, M. J. (2004). Resident-assisted Montessori programming (RAMP): Training persons with dementia to serve as group activity leaders. *Gerontologist, 44,* 426–431.

Camp, C. J., & Stevens, A. B. (1990). Spaced retrieval: A memory intervention for dementia of the Alzheimer's type (DAT). *Clinical Gerontologist, 10,* 58–60.

Campbell, J. J., III, & Coffey, C. E. (2001). Neuropsychiatric significance of subcortical hyperintensity. *Journal of Neuropsychiatry & Clinical Neuroscience, 13,* 261–288.

Carstensen, L. L. (2006). The influence of a sense of time on human development. *Science, 312,* 1913–1915.

Carstensen, L. L., Isaacowitz, D. M., & Charles, S. T. (1999). Taking time seriously. A theory of socioemotional selectivity. *American Psychologist, 54,* 165–181.

Cherry, K. E., Simmons, S. S., & Camp, C. J. (1999). Spaced retrieval enhances memory in older adults with probable Alzheimer's disease. *Journal of Clinical Geropsychology, 5,* 159–175.

Collie, A., & Maruff, P. (2000). The neuropsychology of preclinical Alzheimer's disease and mild cognitive impairment. *Neuroscience & Biobehaioral.Review, 24,* 365–374.

Cummings, J. L. (1993). Frontal-subcortical circuits and human behavior. *Archives of Neurology, 50*, 873–880.

Darby, D., Maruff, P., Collie, A., & McStephen, M. (2002). Mild cognitive impairment can be detected by multiple assessments in a single day. *Neurology, 59*, 1042–1046.

Davis, R. N., Massman, P. J., & Doody, R. S. (2001). Cognitive intervention in Alzheimer disease: A randomized placebo-controlled study. *Alzheimer Disease and Associated Disorders, 15*, 1–9.

de Leeuw, F. E., Barkhof, F., & Scheltens, P. (2004). White matter lesions and hippocampal atrophy in Alzheimer's disease. *Neurology, 62*, 310–312.

de Leeuw, F. E., Korf, E., Barkhof, F., & Scheltens, P. (2006). White matter lesions are associated with progression of medial temporal lobe atrophy in Alzheimer disease. *Stroke, 37*, 2248–2252.

Fagan, A. M., Mintun, M. A., Mach, R. H., Lee, S. Y., Dence, C. S., Shah, A. R., et al. (2006). Inverse relation between in vivo amyloid imaging load and cerebrospinal fluid Abeta42 in humans. *Annals of Neurology, 59*, 512–519.

Fernandez-Ballesteros, R., Zamarron, M. D., & Tarraga, L. (2005). Learning potential: A new method for assessing cognitive impairment. *International Psychogeriatrics, 17*, 119–128.

Frith, C. D., & Frith, U. (1999). Interacting minds—a biological basis. *Science, 286*, 1692–1695.

Gallagher, H. L., Happe, F., Brunswick, N., Fletcher, P. C., Frith, U., & Frith, C. D. (2000). Reading the mind in cartoons and stories: an fMRI study of 'theory of mind' in verbal and nonverbal tasks. *Neuropsychologia, 38*, 11–21.

Galvin, J. E., Powlishta, K. K., Wilkins, K., McKeel, D. W. J., Xiong, C., Grant, E., et al. (2005). Predictors of preclinical Alzheimer Disease and dementia: A clinicopathologic study. *Archives of Neurology, 62*(5), 758–765.

German, T. P., & Hehman, J. A. (2006). Representational and executive selection resources in 'theory of mind': Evidence from compromised belief-desire reasoning in old age. *Cognition, 101*, 129–152.

Gregory, L., Lough, S., Stone, V., Erzinclioglu, S., Martin, L., Baron-Cohen, S., et al. (2002). Theory of Mind in patients with frontal variant frontotemporal dementia and Alzheimer's disease: Theoretical and practical implications. *Brain, 125*, 752–764.

Grober, E., & Kawas, C. (1997). Learning and retention in preclinical and early Alzheimer's disease. *Psychology and Aging, 12*, 183–188.

Gunning-Dixon, F. M., & Raz, N. (2000). The cognitive correlates of white matter abnormalities in normal aging: A quantitative review. *Neuropsychology, 14*, 224–232.

Happe, F. G. E., Winner, E., & Brownell, H. (1998). The getting of wisdom: Theory of mind in old age. *Developmental Psychology, 34*, 358–362.

Hebert, L. E., Scherr, P. A., Bienias, J. L., Bennett, D. A., & Evans, D. A. (2003). Alzheimer disease in the US population: prevalence estimates using the 2000 census. *Archives of Neurology, 60*, 1119–1122.

Hedden, T., & Gabrieli, J. D. E. (2004). Insights into the ageing mind: A view from cognitive neuroscience. *Nature Reviews Neuroscience, 5*, 87–97.

Hochhalter, A. K., Overmier, J. B., Gasper, S. M., Bakke, B. L., & Holub, R. J. (2005). A comparison of spaced retrieval to other schedules of practice for people with dementia. *Experimental Aging Research, 31*, 101–118.

Jack, C. R., Jr., Shiung, M. M., Gunter, J. L., O'Brien, P. C., Weigand, S., Knopman, D. S., et al. (2004). Comparison of different MRI brain atrophy rate measures with clinical disease progression in AD. *Neurology, 62*, 591–600.

Jones, S., Nyberg, L., Sandblom, J., Stigsdotter, N. A., Ingvar, M., Magnus, P. K., et al. (2006). Cognitive and neural plasticity in aging: general and task-specific limitations. *Neuroscience and Biobehavioral Review, 30*, 864–871.

Judge, K. S., Camp, C. J., & Orsulic-Jeras, S. (2000). Use of Montessori-based activities for clients with dementia in adult day care: Effects on engagement. *American Journal of Alzheimer's Disease, 15*, 42–46.

Kales, H. C., Maixner, D. F., & Mellow, A. M. (2005). Cerebrovascular disease and late-life depression. *American Journal of Geriatric Psychiatry, 13*, 88–98.

Keightley, M. L., Winocur, G., Burianova, H., Hongwanishkul, D., & Grady, C. L. (2006). Age effects on social cognition: Faces tell a different story. *Psychology and Aging, 21,* 558–572.

Kim, K., Collins Hagedorn, M., Williamson, J., & Chapman, C. (2004). *Participation in adult education and lifelong learning: 2000–01* (NCES 2004-050).

Kliegl, R., Smith, J., & Baltes, P. B. (1989). Testing-the-limits and the study of adult age-differences in cognitive plasticity of a mnemonic skill. *Developmental Psychology, 25,* 247–256.

Kramer, A. F., & Willis, S. L. (2002). Enhancing the cognitive vitality of older adults. *Current Directions in Psychological Science, 11,* 173–177.

Krishnan, K. R., Hays, J. C., & Blazer, D. G. (1997). MRI-defined vascular depression. *American Journal of Psychiatry, 154,* 497–501.

Krishnan, K. R., Taylor, W. D., McQuoid, D. R., Macfall, J. R., Payne, M. E., Provenzale, J. M., et al. (2004). Clinical characteristics of magnetic resonance imaging-defined subcortical ischemic depression. *Biological Psychiatry, 55,* 390–397.

Labouvie-Vief, G. (2003). Dynamic integration: Affect, cognition, and the self in adulthood. *Current Directions in Psychological Science, 12,* 201–206.

Labouvie-Vief, G., & Diehl, M. (2000). Cognitive complexity and cognitive-affective integration: Related or separate domains of adult development? *Psychology and Aging, 15,* 490–504.

Lamdin, L., & Fugate, M. (1997). *Elderlearning: New frontier in an aging society.* Phoenix, AZ: Oryx Press.

Lichtenberg, P. A., Ross, T., Millis, S. R., & Manning, C. A. (1995). The relationship between depression and cognition in older adults: A cross-validation study. *Journals of Gerontology Series B-Psychological Sciences and Social Sciences, 50,* 25–32.

Lyness, J. M., Caine, E. D., Cox, C., King, D. A., Conwell, Y., & Olivares, T. (1998). Cerebrovascular risk factors and later-life major depression. Testing a small-vessel brain disease model. *American Journal of Geriatriatric Psychiatry, 6,* 5–13.

Lyness, J. M., King, D. A., Conwell, Y., Cox, C., & Caine, E. D. (2000). Cerebrovascular risk factors and 1-year depression outcome in older primary care patients. *American Journal of Psychiatry, 157,* 1499–1501.

Mahendra, N. (2001). Direct interventions for improving the performance of individuals with Alzheimer's disease. *Semininar in Speech & Language, 22,* 291–303.

Markesbery, W. R., Schmitt, F. A., Kryscio, R. J., Davis, D. G., Smith, C. D., & Wekstein, D .R. (2006). Neuropathologic substrate of mild cognitive impairment. *Archives of Neuroogy., 63,* 38–46.

Marsiske, M., Lang, F. B., Baltes, P. B., & Baltes, M. M. (1995). Selective optimization with compensation: Life-span perspectives on successful human development. In Dixon R. A. & Backman, L. (Eds.), *Compensating for psychological deficits and declines: Managing losses and promoting gains.* Hillsdale, NJ: Erlbaum

Massman, P. J., Delis, D. C., Butters, N., Dupont, R. M., & Gillin, J. C. (1992). The subcortical dysfunction hypothesis of memory deficits in depression: neuropsychological validation in a subgroup of patients. *Journal of Clinical Experimental Neuropsychology, 14,* 687–706.

Mast, B. T. (2004). Cerebrovascular disease and late-life depression: A latent-variable analysis of depressive symptoms after stroke. *American Journal of Geriatriatric Psychiatry, 12,* 315–322.

Mast, B. T., MacNeill, S. E., & Lichtenberg, P. A. (2004). Post-stroke and clinically-defined vascular depression in geriatric rehabilitation patients. *American Journal of Geriatric Psychiatry, 12,* 84–92.

Mast, B. T., Neufeld, S., MacNeill, S. E., & Lichtenberg, P. A. (2004). Longitudinal support for the relationship between vascular risk factors and late-life depressive symptoms. *American Journal of Geriatric Psychiatry, 12,* 93–101.

Mast, B. T., Yochim, B., MacNeill, S. E., & Lichtenberg, P. A. (2004). Risk factors for geriatric depression: the importance of executive functioning within the vascular depression hypothesis. *Journals of Gerontology A: Biolical Science & Medical Science., 59,* 1290–1294.

Maylor, E. A., Moulson, J. M., Muncer, A. M., & Taylor, L. A. (2002). Does performance on theory of mind tasks decline in old age. *British Journal of Psychology, 93,* 465–485.

McKhann, G., Drachman, D., Folstein, M., Katzman, R., Price, D., & Stadlan, E. M. (1984). Clinical diagnosis of Alzheimer's disease: Report of the NINCDS-ADRDA Work Group under the auspices of Department of Health and Human Services Task Force on Alzheimer's Disease. *Neurology, 34,* 939–944.

McKitrick, L. A., & Camp, C. J. (1993). Relearning the names of things: The spaced-retrieval intervention implemented by caregiver. *Clinical Gerontologist, 14,* 60–62.

McKitrick, L. A., Camp, C. J., & Black, F. W. (1992). Prospective memory intervention in Alzheimer's disease. *Journal of Gerontology, 47,* 337–343.

Mengelberg, A., & Siegert, R. J. (2003). Is theory-of-mind impaired in Parkinson's disease? *Cognitive Neuropsychiatry, 8,* 191–209.

Morris, J. C., Storandt, M., Miller, J. P., McKeel, D. W., Price, J. L., Rubin, E. H., et al. (2001). Mild cognitive impairment represents early-stage Alzheimer disease. *Archives of Neurology, 58,* 397–405.

Mortimer, J. A., Gosche, K. M., Riley, K. P., Markesbery, W. R., & Snowdon, D. A. (2004). Delayed recall, hippocampal volume and Alzheimer neuropathology: Findings from the Nun Study. *Neurology, 62,* 428–432.

Nebes, R. D., Butters, M. A., Mulsant, B. H., Pollock, B. G., Zmuda, M. D., Houck, P. R., et al. (2000). Decreased working memory and processing speed mediate cognitive impairment in geriatric depression. *Psychological Medicine, 30,* 679–691.

Nyberg, L., Sandblom, J., Jones, S., Neely, A. S., Petersson, K. M., Ingvar, M., et al. (2003). Neural correlates of training-related memory improvement in adulthood and aging. *Proceeding of the National Academy of Science U.S.A, 100,* 13728–13733.

O'Brien, J. T. (2006). Vascular cognitive impairment. *American Journal of Geriatric Psychiatry, 14,* 724–733.

O'Brien, J. T., Erkinjuntti, T., Reisberg, B., Roman, G., Sawada, T., Pantoni, L., et al. (2003). Vascular cognitive impairment. *Lancet Neurology, 2,* 89–98.

Orsulic-Jeras, S., Schneider, N. M., & Camp, C. J. (2000). Special feature: Montessori-based activities for long-term care residents with dementia. *Topics in Geriatric Rehabilitation, 16,* 78–91.

Orsulic-Jeras, S., Schneider, N. M., Camp, C. J., Nicholson, P., & Helbig, M. (2001). Montessori-based dementia activities in long-term care: Training and implementation. *Activities, Adaptation, & Aging, 25,* 107–121.

Panza, F., D'Intiono, A., Colacicco, A. M., Capurso, C., Del, P. A., Caselli, R. J., et al. (2005). Current epidemiology of mild cognitive impairment and other predementia syndromes. *American Journal of Geriatric Psychiatry, 13,* 633–644.Penland, P. R. (1978). *Self planned learning in America.* ERIC Document Reproduction Service No. ED 152 987. Washington, D.C.

Petersen, R. C., Doody, R., Kurz, A., Mohs, R. C., Morris, J. C., Rabins, P. V., et al. (2001). Current concepts in mild cognitive impairment. *Archives of Neurology, 58,* 1985–1992.

Phillips, L. H., MacLean, R. D. J., & Allen, R. (2002). Age and the understanding of emotions: Neuropsychological and sociocognitive perspectives. *Journals of Gerontology: Series B: Psychological Sciences and Social Sciences, 57*B, 526–530.

Premack, D., & Woodruff, G. (1978). Does the chimpanzee have a theory of mind? *Behavioral and Brain Sciences, 1,* 515–526.

Rabbitt, P., Diggle, P., Smith, D., Holland, F., & McInnes, L. (2001). Identifying and separating the effects of practice and of cognitive ageing during a large longitudinal study of elderly community residents. *Neuropsychologia, 39,* 532–543.

Raykov, T., Baltes, M. M., Neher, K. M., & Sowarka, D. (2002). A comparative study of two psychometric approaches to detect risk status for dementia. *Gerontology, 48,*185–193.

Raz, N., & Rodrigue, K. M. (2006). Differential aging of the brain: Patterns, cognitive correlates and modifiers. *Neuroscience and Biobehavioral Reviews, 30,* 730–748.

Raz, N. (2005). The aging brain observed in vivo: Differential changes and their modifiers. In R. Cabeza, L. Nyberg, & D. Park (Eds.), *Cognitive neuroscience of aging: Linking cognitive and cerebral aging* (pp. 19–57). Oxford University Press.

Roman, G. C. (2003). Vascular dementia: Distinguishing characteristics, treatment, and prevention. *Journal of the American Geriatric Society, 51,* S296–S304.

Rowe, A. D., Bullock, P. R., Polkey, C. E., & Morris, R. G. (2001). "Theory of mind" impairments and their relationship to executive functioning following frontal lobe excisions. *Brain, 124,* 600–616.

Royall, D. R. (2000). Executive cognitive impairment: a novel perspective on dementia. *Neuroepidemiology, 19,* 293–299.

Saczynski, J. S., Margrett, J. A., & Willis, S. L. (2004). Older adults' strategic behavior: Effects of individual versus collaborative cognitive training. *Educational Gerontology, 30,* 587–610.

Salthouse, T. A. (1994). The nature of the influence of speed on adult age-differences in cognition. *Developmental Psychology, 30,* 240–259.

Salthouse, T. A. (1993). Speed mediation of adult age-differences in cognition. *Developmental Psychology, 29,* 722–738.

Salthouse, T. A. (2006). Mental exercise and mental aging. *Perspectives on Psychological Science, 1,* 68–87.

Saltzman, J., Strauss, E., Hunter, M., & Archibald, S. (2000). Theory of mind and executive functions in normal human aging and Parkinson's disease. *Journal of the International Neuropsychological Society, 6,* 781–788.

Saxe, R., Carey, S., & Kanwisher, N. (2004). Understanding other minds: Linking developmental psychology and functional neuroimaging. *Annual Review of Psychology 55,* 87–124.

Saxe, R., & Kanwisher, N. (2003). People thinking about thinking people. The role of the temporo-parietal junction in "theory of mind." *Neuroimage., 19,* 1835–1842.

Schaie, K. W. (1994). The course of adult intellectual development. *American Psychologist, 49,* 304–313.

Schaie, K. W. (2005). *Developmental influences on adult intelligence: The Seattle longitudinal study.* New York: Oxford University Press.

Schmitt, F. A., Davis, D. G., Wekstein, D. R., Smith, C. D., Ashford, J. W., & Markesbery, W. R. (2000). "Preclinical" AD revisited: Neuropathology of cognitively normal older adults. *Neurology, 55,* 370–376.

Schneider, N. M., Diggs, S., Orsulic, S., & Camp, C. J. (1999). NAs teaching Montessori activities. *Journal of Nurse Assistants, 6,* 13–15.

Schrijnemaekers, A. M., de Jager, C. A., Hogervorst, E., & Budge, M. M. (2006). Cases with mild cognitive impairment and Alzheimer's disease fail to benefit from repeated exposure to episodic memory tests as compared with controls. *Journal of Clinical & Experimental Neuropsychology, 28,* 438–455.

Singer, T., Lindenberger, U., & Baltes, P. B. (2003). Plasticity of memory for new learning in very old age: A story of major loss? *Psychology and Aging, 18,* 306–317.

Squire, L. R., & Zola, S. M. (1996). Structure and function of declarative and nondeclarative memory systems. *Proceedings of the National Academy of Sciences of the United States of America, 93,* 13515–13522.

Steffens, D. C., Helms, M. J., Krishnan, K. R., & Burke, G. L. (1999). Cerebrovascular disease and depression symptoms in the cardiovascular health study. *Stroke, 30,* 2159–2166.

Steffens, D. C., Krishnan, K. R., Crump, C., & Burke, G. L. (2002). Cerebrovascular disease and evolution of depressive symptoms in the cardiovascular health study. *Stroke, 33,* 1636–1644.

Stout, J. C., Bondi, M. W., Jernigan, T. L., Archibald, S. L., Delis, D. C., & Salmon, D. P. (1999). Regional cerebral volume loss associated with verbal learning and memory in dementia of the Alzheimer type. *Neuropsychology, 13,* 188–197.

Stuss, D. T., Gallup, G. G., Jr., & Alexander, M. P. (2001). The frontal lobes are necessary for "theory of mind." *Brain, 124,* 279–286.

Sullivan, S., & Ruffman, T. (2004). Social understanding: How does it fare with advancing years? *British Journal of Psychology, 95,* 1–18.

Swanberg, M. M., Tractenberg, R. E., Mohs, R., Thal, L. J., & Cummings, J. L. (2004). Executive dysfunction in Alzheimer disease. *Archives of Neurology, 61,* 556–560.

Tekin, S., & Cummings, J. L. (2002). Frontal-subcortical neuronal circuits and clinical neuropsychiatry: An update. *Journal of Psychosomatic Research, 53,* 647–654.

Thompson, G., & Foth, D. (2005). Cognitive-training programs for older adults: What are they and can they enhance mental fitness? *Educational Gerontology, 31*, 603–626.

Tough, A. (1979). *Choosing to learn.* Toronto: Ontario Institute for Studies in Education.

Tough, A., & Ontario Institute for Studies in Education (1999). *Reflections on the study of adult learning. NALL Working Paper.* NALL: New Approaches to Lifelong Learning, Ontario Institute for Studies in Education, University of Toronto.

Unverzagt, F. W., Gao, S., Baiyewu, O., Ogunniyi, A. O., Gureje, O., Perkins, A., et al. (2001). Prevalence of cognitive impairment: Data from the Indianapolis Study of Health and Aging. *Neurology, 57*, 1655–1662.

Van Fleet, C. (1995). *Public libraries, lifelong learning, and older adults: Background and recommendations.* National Institute on Postsecondary Education, Libraries, and Lifelong Learning. U.S. Department of Education. Washington, D.C. Retrieved June 30, 2008, from http://www.ed.gov/pubs/PLLIConf95/vanfleet.html.

Vance, D., Camp, C., Kabacoff, M., & Greenwalt, L. (2006, Winter). Montessori-method: Innovative interventions for adults with Alzheimer's disease. *Montessori LIFE, 10*–12.

Washburn, A. M., Sands, L. P., & Walton, P. J. (2003). Assessment of social cognition in frail older adults and its association with social functioning in the nursing home. *Gerontologist, 43*, 203–212.

Welsh, K., Butters, N., Hughes, J., Mohs, R., & Heyman, A. (1991). Detection of abnormal memory decline in mild cases of Alzheimers-disease using cerad neuropsychological measures. *Archives of Neurology, 48*, 278–281.

Welsh, K. A., Butters, N., Hughes, J. P., Mohs, R. C., & Heyman, A. (1992). Detection and staging of dementia in Alzheimer's disease. Use of the neuropsychological measures developed for the Consortium to Establish a Registry for Alzheimer's Disease. *Archives of Neurology, 49*, 448–452.

West, R. L. (1996). An application of prefrontal cortex function theory to cognitive aging. *Psychological Bulletin, 120*, 272–292.

Willis, S. L., Tennstadt, S. L., Marsiske, M., Ball, K., Elias, J., Koepke, K. M., et al. (2006). Long-term effects of cognitive training on everyday functional outcomes in older adults. *JAMA, 296*, 2805–2814.

Willis, S. L. (1985). Towards an educational psychology of the older adult learner: Intellectual and cognitive bases. In J. E. Birren & K. W. Schaie (Eds.), *Handbook of the psychology of aging (2nd ed.)* (pp. 818–847). New York: Van Nostrand Reinhold.

Zacks, R. T., Hasher, L., & Li, K. Z. H. (2000). Human memory. In F. I. M Craik & T. A. Salthouse (Eds.), *The handbook of aging and cognition* (2nd ed., pp. 293–357). Mahwah, NJ: Erlbaum

Zaitchik, D., Koff, E., Brownell, H., Winner, E., & Albert, M. (2004). Inference of mental states in patients with Alzheimer's disease. *Cognitive Neuropsychiatry, 9*, 301–313.

Zaitchik, D., Koff, E., Brownell, H., Winner, E., & Albert, M. (2006). Inference of beliefs and emotions in patients with Alzheimer's disease. *Neuropsychology, 20*, 11–20.

Chapter 25

Wisdom, Integrity, and Life Satisfaction in Very Old Age

Monika Ardelt and Steve Jacobs

What is wisdom? Although wisdom is an ancient and time-honored concept and there has been a renewed interest in the role of wisdom with respect to human development and aging during the past 25 years, contemporary researchers have been unable to reach consensus on a single, all-encompassing definition of wisdom (Dittmann-Kohli & Baltes, 1990; Kramer, 2000).The multifaceted nature of wisdom tends to evoke different connotations depending on the philosophical and theoretical orientation of a particular researcher (e.g., Achenbaum & Orwoll, 1991; Ardelt, 2003, 2004b; Arlin, 1990; Assmann, 1994; Baltes & Staudinger, 2000; Labouvie-Vief, 1990; Meacham, 1990; Sternberg, 1998; Sternberg & Jordan, 2005). According to Birren and Svensson (2005), the earliest "wisdom literature" was written more than 5000 years ago by the ancient Sumerians and consisted of practical advice for daily living, whereas the wisdom texts of the ancient Egyptians (circa 3000 B.C.) focused on good and proper behavior. The ancient Greeks were known as the "lovers of wisdom" and a thorough analysis of the concept can be found in the Platonic dialogues (Robinson, 1990). Yet, even today it remains difficult to define and conceptualize the elusive concept of wisdom.

Defining Wisdom

Contemporary definitions of wisdom can be categorized according to whether they arise from explicit (expert) theories or implicit (lay) theories of wisdom. These definitions can be further classified according to wisdom traditions of the West or the East and whether they refer to personal or general wisdom (Sternberg & Jordan, 2005). Western explicit theories have defined wisdom as:

1. expert knowledge in the fundamental pragmatics of life (including life planning, life management, and life review) and in the conduct and meaning of life (Baltes & Smith, 1990; Baltes & Staudinger, 2000; Baltes, Staudinger, Maercker, & Smith, 1995; Dittmann-Kohli & Baltes, 1990; Smith & Baltes, 1990; Smith, Staudinger, & Baltes, 1994);
2. as "the application of tacit knowledge as mediated by values toward the achievement of a common good through a balance among multiple (a) intrapersonal, (b) interpersonal, and (c) extrapersonal interests in order to achieve a balance among (a) adaptation to existing environments, (b) shaping of existing environments, and (c) selection of new environments" (Sternberg, 1998, p. 347);
3. as the transformation of intrapersonal, interpersonal, and transpersonal experiences in the domains of personality, cognition, and conation (Achenbaum & Orwoll, 1991);

4. as "seeing through illusion," which requires (a) realizing the illusion of a false belief, (b) not being tempted by the illusion, and (c) having sympathy for others who are still under the spell of the illusion (Mckee & Barber, 1999);

5. as the art of questioning (Arlin, 1990) or the balance between knowing and doubting (Meacham, 1990);

6. as the balance between emotion and detachment, action and inaction, and knowledge and doubt in dealing with life's vicissitudes (Birren & Fisher, 1990); or

7. as self-transcendence (Levenson, Jennings, Aldwin, & Shiraishi, 2005).

As Takahashi (2000) has pointed out, explicit theories of wisdom might differ for the philosophical wisdom traditions of Western and Eastern cultures. The wisdom traditions of the West tend to emphasize the cognitive dimension of wisdom (i.e., knowledge and analytical ability), whereas the Eastern wisdom traditions tend to integrate the cognitive, reflective, and affective elements of wisdom.

Implicit wisdom theories refer to common-sense, folk approaches to wisdom and describe how lay people tend to perceive wisdom. Based on respondents' characterizations of wisdom, the concept has been defined as a combination of cognitive, reflective, and affective personality qualities (Clayton & Birren, 1980), as exceptional understanding, judgment and communication skills, general competencies, interpersonal skills, and social unobtrusiveness (Holliday & Chandler, 1986), as reasoning ability, sagacity, learning from ideas and environment, judgment, expeditious use of information, and perspicacity (Sternberg, 1990a), or as an integration of self-knowledge, understanding of others, judgment, life knowledge, life skills, and willingness to learn (Brown, 2004). Bluck and Glück (2005) identified five subcomponents of wisdom that emerged in five studies on implicit wisdom theories: cognitive ability, insight, reflective attitude, concern for others, and real-world skills. Moreover, Takahashi and Bordia (2000) found that Western undergraduate students tend to highlight the cognitive dimension of wisdom, whereas Eastern undergraduate students tend to combine the cognitive and affective dimensions of wisdom. Takahashi and Overton (2005) argue that implicit wisdom theories correspond to the ideal self in a particular culture and, therefore, often vary between Western and Eastern cultures. They recommend that wisdom definitions should avoid cultural egocentrism and instead consist of the broadest and most inclusive characterizations of wisdom.

Other researchers have tried to determine the characteristics of wisdom by inquiring about situations or events during which adolescents, young adults, and older respondents said, thought, or did something wise (Bluck & Glück, 2004; Glück, Bluck, Baron, & McAdams, 2005; Montgomery, Barber, & McKee, 2002). Bluck and Glück (2004) found that adolescents and adults most often experienced wisdom when they were able to transform an event or situation that was initially perceived as negative into a positive outcome. Furthermore, young and older adults were more likely than adolescents to report that they had learned a life lesson or gained a life philosophy from the wisdom experience. The wisdom experiences that respondents described consisted either of empathy and support for others, self-determination and assertion, or knowledge and flexibility (Glück, Bluck, Baron, & McAdams, 2005). Similarly, Montgomery, Barber, and McKee's (2002) in-depth analysis of semi-structured interviews with six older adults between the age of 60 and 88 produced six characteristics of experienced wisdom: guidance, knowledge, experience, moral principle, perspective of time, and compassion.

Following the suggestion by Takahashi and Overton (2005) to define wisdom in a

Table 25.1 Definition of Wisdom as a Three-Dimensional Personality Characteristic

Dimension	Definition
Cognitive	• An understanding of life and a desire to know the truth, i.e., to comprehend the significance and deeper meaning of phenomena and events, particularly with regard to intrapersonal and interpersonal matters.
	• Includes knowledge and acceptance of the positive and negative aspects of human nature, of the inherent limits of knowledge, and of life's unpredictability and uncertainties.
Reflective	• A perception of phenomena and events from multiple perspectives.
	• Requires self-examination, self-awareness, and self-insight.
Affective	• Sympathetic and compassionate love for others.

Adapted from Ardelt, M. (2004). Wisdom as expert knowledge system: A critical review of a contemporary operationalization of an ancient concept. *Human Development, 47,* 257–285.

broad and culturally inclusive way, we believe that wisdom is best characterized as an integration of cognitive, reflective, and affective personality qualities, given the fact that most definitions and descriptions of wisdom contain cognitive, reflective, and affective (emotional) components that are inherently related to each other (Baltes & Staudinger, 2000; Bassett, 2005, 2006; Manheimer, 1992; Sternberg, 1990b; Sternberg & Jordan, 2005; Taranto, 1989; Vaillant, 2002; Webster, 2003). This definition was originally based on Clayton and Birren's groundbreaking empirical research on implicit wisdom theories (1980), but has evolved to incorporate explicit theories of wisdom from both the Western and Eastern wisdom traditions (see Table 25.1).

The cognitive dimension of wisdom refers to the search for truth (Osbeck & Robinson, 2005). This dimension is characterized by the quest for a clear and comprehensive understanding of the significance and deeper meaning of life, particularly with respect to intrapersonal and interpersonal phenomena and events (Ardelt, 2000b; Blanchard-Fields & Norris, 1995; Chandler & Holliday, 1990; Kekes, 1983; Sternberg, 1990a). To achieve such an understanding of life, one must come to accept both the positive and negative aspects of human nature, the fundamental limits of knowledge, and life's unpredictability and uncertainties. However, one can only develop such a deep and unbiased view of life after one has "seen through illusion" (McKee & Barber, 1999) and transcended one's own subjectivity and projections to perceive reality as it is. Subjectivity and projections tend to cause people to blame circumstances and others for their failures and to credit their own skills and abilities for their successes instead of taking all possible factors into account (Bradley, 1978; Green & Gross, 1979; Riess, Rosenfeld, Melburg, & Tedeschi, 1981; Sherwood, 1981). The transcendence of one's subjectivity and projections is the task of the reflective dimension of wisdom. It requires a perception of phenomena and events from many different perspectives as well as self-examination, self-awareness, and self-insight. A gradual transcendence of one's subjectivity and projections also tends to reduce ego-centeredness, which makes it easier to perceive and accept the reality of the present moment and to obtain a more thorough and sympathetic understanding of oneself and others (Csikszentmihalyi & Rathunde, 1990; Hart, 1987; Kekes, 1995; Levitt, 1999; Taranto, 1989). A diminished sense of ego-centeredness and the acknowledgement and acceptance of one's own negative aspects of the self will make it easier to develop sympathetic and compassionate love for others that are similarly not perfect. A general sentiment of good-will and sympathetic, compassionate love for all beings describes the affective dimension of wisdom (Achenbaum & Orwoll, 1991; Clayton & Birren, 1980; Csikszentmihalyi & Rathunde, 1990; Hart, 1987; Holliday & Chandler, 1986; Kramer, 1990; Levitt, 1999; Orwoll & Achenbaum, 1993; Pascual-Leone, 1990). Thus, wisdom is comprised of three distinct but interrelated dimensions. This parsimonious, yet comprehensive definition of wisdom appears to be compatible with most contemporary as well as ancient explicit and implicit theories of wisdom from both the wisdom traditions of the East and the West (Blanchard-Fields & Norris, 1995; Curnow, 1999; Levitt, 1999; Manheimer, 1992; Sternberg, 1990b, 1998; Sternberg & Jordan, 2005; Takahashi & Bordia, 2000).

Methodological Issues in Wisdom Research

How do we determine what constitutes wisdom and who is wise? Various researchers have implemented diverse techniques in an effort to assess and measure wisdom empirically (Ardelt, 1997, 2003; Baltes & Staudinger, 2000; Helson & Srivastava, 2002; Kitchener & Brenner, 1990; Staudinger, Dörner, & Mickler, 2005; Takahashi & Overton, 2005; Webster, 2003; Wink & Dillon, 2003; Wink & Helson, 1997). This research can be divided into two types of studies: those that (a) assess the implicit theories or the meaning of wisdom as described by lay people and others that (b) use either explicit or implicit theories of wisdom to measure people's wisdom or their wisdom-related performance (Ardelt, 2003).

Assessment of Implicit Wisdom Theories

Clayton and Birren (1980) conducted a study to assess how young, middle-aged, and older adults define wisdom. Each person was given a list of 12 wisdom descriptors generated from an earlier study and asked to pair up the descriptors with the words "wise," "aged," and "myself," rating the similarity of all possible, non-redundant word pairs. A multidimensional scaling analysis of the similarities between the pairs resulted in three wisdom dimensions, which Clayton and Birren (1980) labeled cognitive (knowledgeable, experienced, intelligent, pragmatic, and observant), reflective (introspective and intuitive), and affective (understanding, empathetic, peaceful, and gentle).

Holliday and Chandler (1986) used a similar approach in their study of young, middle-aged, and older adults. They first asked the adults to describe the concept of wisdom, which resulted in 79 distinct wisdom attributes. Those attributes were rated in a second study by a different group of young, middle-aged, and older adults on a scale from 1 (almost never true of wise people) to 7 (almost always true of wise people). A principal component analysis of the descriptors yielded five wisdom factors, which Holliday and Chandler (1986) termed exceptional understanding, judgment and communication skills, general competencies, interpersonal skills, and social unobtrusiveness. Interestingly, four of these factors represent cognitive, reflective, and/or affective attributes.

Along the same lines, Sternberg (1990a) asked laypersons to describe a wise individual and professors of art, business, philosophy, and physics to describe the ideal wise person in their respective field. Sternberg (1990a) gave the obtained descriptors to a second group of laypersons and professors in the same fields and asked them to rate the descriptors on a scale from 1 (behavior extremely uncharacteristic for a wise person in my occupation/in general) to 9 (behavior extremely characteristic). The 40 highest ranked behaviors were arranged by college students under as many category headings as desired. A nonmetric multidimensional scaling analysis of these arrangements resulted in six wisdom dimensions, which Sternberg (1990a) named reasoning ability, sagacity, learning from ideas and environment, judgment, expeditious use of information, and perspicacity. Once again, these dimensions pertain to cognitive, reflective, and/or affective attributes of wisdom.

Measurement of Wisdom or Wisdom-Related Performance

Few researchers have thus far attempted to measure individuals' degrees of wisdom or their wisdom-related performances. However, Baltes and colleagues from the Max Planck Institute for Human Development and Education in Berlin have conducted rather extensive empirical work on the subject. Proceeding from a theoretical definition of wisdom as expert knowledge and judgment in the fundamental pragmatics of life, these researchers attempt to assess wisdom-related knowledge or performance by asking people to respond to hypothetical life problems in the areas of life planning, life management, and life review (Baltes & Staudinger, 2000; Smith & Baltes, 1990). At least two independent judges then rate the respondents' answers according to the presence of five wisdom criteria: rich factual knowledge, rich procedural knowledge, life span contextualism, value relativism, and the recognition and management of uncertainty. Wisdom-related performance was positively associated with openness to experience, psychological mindedness, creativity, and certain cognitive thinking styles (Staudinger, Lopez, & Baltes, 1997; Staudinger, Maciel, Smith, & Baltes, 1998). Furthermore, wisdom nominees and clinical psychologists tended to be rated higher on the five wisdom criteria than did other professionals, although wisdom nominees did not perform significantly better on the wisdom criteria than clinical psychologists (Baltes, Staudinger, Maercker, & Smith, 1995; Smith, Staudinger, & Baltes, 1994; Staudinger, Maciel, Smith, & Baltes, 1998; Staudinger, Smith, & Baltes, 1992). To define, operationalize, and measure wisdom as expert knowledge in the fundamental pragmatics of life might be problematic, however, if this approach is unable to distinguish between wisdom and mere intellectual or theoretical knowledge in the fundamental pragmatics of life (Ardelt, 2004b). We suggest instead that wisdom is inherently embodied by individuals, and it is the wisdom of people that should be measured, not the wisdom of their knowledge (Ardelt, 2004a).

Kitchener and Brenner (1990) use the Reflective Judgment Interview to measure individuals' wisdom-related performances. This research rates people according to their ability to solve complex decision problems that are devoid of a clear solution. Individuals who reach the highest stage of the Reflective Judgment model are deemed wise and are characterized by judgments that "reflect a recognition of the limits of personal knowledge, an acknowledgment of the general uncertainty that characterizes human knowing, and a humility about one's own judgments in the face of such limitations" (Kitchener & Brenner, 1990, p. 226). Ratings on the Reflective Judgment Interview were positively correlated with education and with age among high school and college students and young adults.

Similarly, Brugman's (2000) 15-item epistemic cognition questionnaire (ECQ15) intends to measure wisdom as expertise in uncertainty. The ECQ15 consists of three components that assess acknowledgement of uncertainty, emotional stability despite uncertainty, and the ability to act in the face of uncertainty. Epistemic wisdom was positively associated with the personality trait openness to experience in samples of young and older adults.

In contrast to wisdom-related knowledge, which is considered "a cultural and collective product" (Baltes & Staudinger, 2000, p. 127) and "too large and complex to be stored in one individual's mind" (Staudinger & Baltes, 1996, p. 748), personal or self-related wisdom has been measured as rich self-knowledge, availability of heuristics for growth and self-regulation, interrelating the self, self-relativism, and tolerance of ambiguity (Staudinger, Dörner, & Mickler, 2005). Similar to wisdom-related knowledge, self-related wisdom was positively related to openness to experience and psychological mindedness.

Wink and Helson (1997) selected cognitive, reflective, and mature adjectives from the Adjective Check List (ACL) to measure "practical wisdom" and rated the respondents' examples of their own wisdom development to assess "transcendent wisdom." To receive a high rating on transcendent wisdom, "…the statement needed to be abstract (transcending the personal), insightful (not obvious), and to express key aspects of wisdom, such as a recognition of the complexity and limits of knowledge, an integration of thought and affect, and philosophical/spiritual depth" (Wink & Helson, 1997, p. 6).

In a later study, Helson and Srivastava (2002) measured wisdom as a latent variable with practical wisdom, transcendent wisdom, and scores on a wisdom task from the Berlin wisdom group (Baltes, Staudinger, Maercker, & Smith, 1995) as the effect indicators. The wisdom task consisted of a hypothetical life problem that asked respondents what they would do if a friend telephoned to inform them that he or she has decided to commit suicide. In contrast to the Berlin wisdom studies, responses to the wisdom task were given in writing rather than verbally, and the answers were rated according to the respondents' cognitive differentiation, procedural knowledge, emotional understanding, and acknowledgement of moral complexity. With the exception of procedural knowledge, those ratings differed from the Berlin group's wisdom criteria.

Levenson, Jennings, Aldwin, and Shiraishi (2005) developed the Adult Self-Transcendence Inventory (ASTI) to measure self-transcendent wisdom. The ASTI was unrelated to gender and educational status.

Takahashi and Overton (2002) assess the analytic and synthetic modes of wisdom. The analytic mode is measured by the size of one's knowledge database and abstract reasoning skills, whereas the synthetic mode of wisdom consists of reflective understanding, emotional empathy, and emotional regulation. In a study of 136 middle-aged and older American and Japanese men and women, American respondents tended to score significantly higher on the five wisdom variables than did Japanese respondents (Takahashi & Overton, 2002).

Webster's (2003, 2007) Self-Assessed Wisdom Scale (SAWS) consists of five components (critical life experiences, reflectiveness/reminiscence, emotional regulation, openness to experience, and humor), which were selected to measure the non-cognitive aspects of wisdom. The SAWS was unrelated to education but significantly associated with perceived health and gender in the original 2003 study. Women tended to score higher on the SAWS than men. However, the revised SAWS (Webster, 2007) was not significantly correlated with gender.

Brown and Greene's (2006) self-administered Wisdom Development Scale (WDS) contains five factors, which were derived from Brown's (2004) Model of Wisdom Development in reference to integrated learning outcomes. The factors are self-knowledge, altruism, inspirational engagement, judgment, life knowledge, life skills, and emotional management.

Ardelt (1997, 2000a, 2003) measured wisdom as a three-dimensional latent variable with cognitive, reflective, and affective effect indicators. In a secondary data analysis of a sample of 120 white older adults (age range: 58–82 years) from Berkeley, California, items from Haan's Ego Rating Scale (Haan, 1969) and the California 100-item Q-sort (Block, 1971) were selected at face validity to assess the cognitive, reflective, and affective dimensions of the latent variable wisdom. The respondents were interviewed in 1968/69 as part of a 40-year follow-up project (Maas & Kuypers, 1974). At least two clinically experienced and trained coders read the transcribed semi-structured interviews and rated the respondents. To measure wisdom in large, standardized surveys, Ardelt (2003) developed a self-administered three-dimensional wisdom scale (3D-WS) with the cognitive, reflective, and affective dimensions as effect indicators of the latent variable wisdom. A study of 180 older adults between the age of 52 and 87 supported the validity and reliability of the 3D-WS. Confirmatory factor analyses in the rating and the survey study confirmed that the latent variable wisdom can be assessed through cognitive, reflective, and affective effect indicators. The cognitive wisdom dimension measures the ability and desire to understand a situation or phenomenon thoroughly, the reflective dimension assesses the perception of phenomena and events from different perspectives and the absence of subjectivity and projections, and the affective wisdom dimension measures sympathy and compassion for others, that is, the presence of positive and the absence of indifferent or negative emotions and behavior toward others.

Wink and Dillon (2003) also used items from the California 100-item Q-sort (Block, 1971) to assess a person's degree of wisdom in a longitudinal study of 157 predominantly white adults from Berkeley and Oakland, California. Individuals who were characterized by independent panels of expert raters as straightforward, clear thinking, introspective, insightful, philosophically concerned, and unconventional in thinking were considered high in wisdom. Spirituality in late middle and late adulthood was significantly correlated with wisdom in late adulthood, suggesting that highly spiritual individuals maintain complex thought patterns and insight into the human condition. Furthermore, religiousness but not spirituality in early adulthood was significantly associated with wisdom in late adulthood, whereas religiousness in late middle and late adulthood was unrelated to wisdom in late adulthood.

Development of Wisdom across the Life Course

Erik Erikson (1963, 1982) was probably the first contemporary researcher who outlined the development of wisdom across the life course. In the following section we will introduce Erikson's stage model of human development and point out differences between his theoretical model and empirical findings. The next section focuses on social factors that might influence the acquisition of wisdom throughout the life course, such as the family and the social environment. The subsequent section explores the question of whether wisdom increases with age. Finally, we examine whether crises and hardships in life might be pathways to wisdom.

Erikson's Stage Theory of Human Development and the Development of Wisdom

According to Erikson's (1963, 1982) stage model of human development, the life course can be understood as a series of developmental tasks starting in early infancy with the psychosocial crisis of basic trust versus basic mistrust and ending in old age with the crisis of ego integrity versus despair. If a crisis is resolved successfully, a person will gain a specific strength or virtue that is necessary to solve the next and all subsequent developmental crises. For Erikson (1963, 1982), wisdom is the highest virtue that results when the eighth psychosocial crisis, ego integrity versus despair, is resolved in old age (Glover, 1998).

The first crisis that an infant encounters is the feeling of basic trust versus basic mistrust. When basic trust in the environment outweighs a basic mistrust in the environment, hope emerges. The second crisis during early childhood is characterized by autonomy versus shame and doubt, and its successful resolution results in the strength of will. In the next two stages, during a child's play and school age, a child first struggles with initiative versus guilt and then with industry versus inferiority. The virtues that emerge from those two stages are purpose (play age) and competence (school age). During adolescence, a person is in search for his or her identity and is threatened by identity confusion. The strength gained by the resolution of this crisis is fidelity. The early adulthood years are characterized by a search for intimacy and the avoidance of isolation. The successful resolution of this crisis leads to the discovery of mature love, which should not to be confused with the feeling of "being in love" at the beginning of a new romance. The task during middle and late adulthood is to engage in generativity to help the next generation succeed and move forward rather than being resigned to personal stagnation or self-absorption. Care for others is the basic strength that evolves if this crisis is resolved successfully. The final crisis of ego integrity versus despair occurs in old age and requires the integration of an individual's entire life course into a coherent whole without despairing over missed opportunities or mistakes in the past or the inevitable approach of life's end. Wisdom is the virtue and strength that results from the resolution of this crisis.

If a person fails to successfully resolve a developmental task either due to a reluctance to face a certain crisis (foreclosure) or an inability to resolve a psychosocial crisis (psychological moratorium), the mastery of subsequent life stages might be severely impaired. If this is the case, the psychosocial development of an individual might be halted and fixated at an earlier stage, thereby thwarting the developmental potentials of all later stages (Clayton, 1975). Hence, to gain the basic strengths or virtues of later life stages, the developmental tasks of all previous life stages need to be resolved first. As Markstrom, Li, Blackshire, and Wilfong (2005, p. 86) point out, "... the likelihood of ascendance of later ego strengths is enhanced through positive resolutions of earlier psychosocial crises and ascendance of ego strengths." This can either be done at the appropriate time when the crisis is acute or at a later life stage (Meacham, 1989). For example, a young man who is still confused about his identity (Stage 5) is unlikely to experience mutual, mature love (the resulting strength of Stage 6). Only after he has resolved the crisis from Stage 5 and accepted a certain identity for himself will he be ready to address the next crisis of intimacy versus isolation featuring love as its emerging strength.

From this perspective, wisdom is the result of the successful resolution of a long series of psychosocial crises or developmental tasks. Yet, although wisdom appears in Erikson's theory only as the positive end result of the final crisis, integrity versus despair, its emergence depends on the successful resolution of all previous crises. This indicates that wisdom develops gradually over the life course according to a person's ability to master each developmental task (Clayton & Birren, 1980; Orwoll & Perlmutter, 1990).

Erikson's model of life stages and their accompanying crises can be understood as an ideal type (Weber, 1980) of human development that is rarely if ever achieved in reality. Most people do not actually resolve all of the crises in the appropriate order as they pass through the stages of life, and many might never reach the last virtue, wisdom, if they remain stuck in earlier developmental stages (Clayton, 1975). This might happen due to foreclosure or a prolonged psychological moratorium. Furthermore, some people might deal with a crisis only to the extent that they are able to function "normally," that is, without showing any obvious signs of psychological impairment. Yet, having never solved the crisis thoroughly, their future psychological development might be unstable and sometimes even regress until the crisis reappears and is finally resolved (Clayton, 1975).

In addition, each developmental task is present at each and every stage of the life course, although in various strengths. The crisis of ego integrity versus despair, for example, is felt only weakly during childhood, but it is not totally absent. From this perspective, wisdom is as much the desired end result of human development as it is a virtue with potential development already beginning shortly after birth. Conversely, each developmental task emerges again during all subsequent life stages, but with different qualities. No crisis can be fully solved once and for all, and although the successful resolution of a crisis at an earlier stage facilitates its resolution at a later stage, there is no guarantee that the task will be successfully accomplished. Foreclosure or a psychological moratorium is again possible and sometimes even partial regress might be unavoidable. Hence, all psychosocial crises and their resulting virtues are related to each other, and the emergence of wisdom is not confined to old age alone. Individuals might struggle with any of Erikson's developmental tasks at any stage in the life cycle (Kivnick, 1993). The only safe conclusion one can draw is that a person is less likely to be strongly negatively affected by a psychosocial crisis whose ascendance has not yet been reached than by the predominant and all previous crises. Indeed, in a cross-sectional study which implicitly included different age groups, Nicholson (1980) was unable to detect any universal age-related life crises.

The emergence of wisdom is, therefore, less clearly attributable to the last stage of life than Erikson's theory first suggests. Instead, it appears that the development of wisdom takes place continuously over the whole life course and that a person's degree of wisdom at each life stage depends as much on the extent of its acquisition during earlier life stages as on the successful resolution of the individual's past and current crises. This statement is in accordance with the life course perspective, which posits that a certain stage of life, such as old age, can only be completely understood when one considers all previous life stages of an individual (Elder, 1994; Elder & Liker, 1982; Meacham, 1989).

Personality and Social Factors Influencing the Acquisition of Wisdom throughout the Life Course

Even though Erikson's theory focuses primarily on psychological factors of human development, the influence of personality and environmental factors, particularly during an individual's early years of life, cannot be neglected. Childhood experiences play a crucial part in Erikson's theory of development. Half of the eight psychosocial crises described by Erikson take place in childhood, when an individual's physical and psychological well-being depends largely on interactions with other family members. Therefore, childhood experiences lay the foundation for a person's capacity to deal with later psychosocial crises during adolescence and adulthood.

Past studies demonstrate that the social environment has an impact on a person's psychosocial development (Ewens, 1984; Kohn, 1977; Kohn & Schoenbach, 1983; Meyers, 1989; Schneewind, 1995; Thalberg, 1978; Vaillant, 1977). Although "… early-emerging individual differences in personality shape how individuals experience, interpret, and respond to the developmental tasks they face across the life course" (Caspi, Roberts, & Shiner, 2005, p. 417), research has also shown that even innate personality predispositions can be fashioned by the social environment. Reiss, Neiderhiser, Hetherington, and Plomin (2000) report that parents are likely to reinforce their children's innate personality dispositions. For example, parents tend to be more protective of a shy and withdrawn child than a child that is socially adept and outgoing. This parenting behavior, in turn, prompts changes in the child's brain that cement the personality dispositions of the child even further. Thus, the very structure of an individual's brain is molded in part by the social environment, as environmental stimuli determine which of the brain's neurons will flourish (Eisenberg, 1999; Reiss, Neiderhiser, Hetherington, & Plomin, 2000).

Twin and adoption studies suggest that genes have a greater impact on the cognitive development than on the psychosocial development of the child. For example, a longitudinal study that assessed the intelligence of adopted and biological children from their first to their sixteenth birthday showed that similar to biological children, the IQ of adopted children during their middle childhood and adolescent years resembled more the IQ of their biological parents than the IQ of their adoptive parents (Plomin, Fulker, Corley, & DeFries, 1997). By contrast, twin studies demonstrate that the psychosocial development of the child can be directly affected by parenting behavior. For example, in a study of five-year old monozygotic twin pairs and their mothers, the twin who received more maternal warmth and less emotional negativity was less likely to exhibit antisocial behavior problems than the other twin (Caspi et al., 2004).

A difficult social environment and behavior problems in childhood are often predictors for a negative developmental trajectory across the whole life course. For example, a 25-year longitudinal study by Fergusson, Horwood, and Ridder (2005a, b) linked childhood behavior problems and adverse family circumstances to unfavorable psychosocial development in adulthood ranging from relationship and mental health problems to substance abuse and criminal behavior. Those results lend support to earlier findings by Caspi, Bem, and Elder (1989), which showed that ill-tempered children had a tendency to become ill-tempered adults. Furthermore, ill-tempered boys were more likely than other boys to experience divorce, unemployment, and downward occupational mobility as adults, and ill-tempered girls had a higher chance than other girls to marry men with lower occupational status and get divorced later in life. The negative spiral is likely to repeat itself when adults with a history of psychosocial problems become parents. A longitudinal study by Jaffee, Belsky, Harrington, Caspi, and Moffitt (2006) showed that parents with a history of conduct disorder during early and late adolescence were less likely to engage in positive parenting behavior with their 3-year old toddlers and more likely to have children with difficult-to-manage behavior problems than parents without a history of conduct disorder.

Other aspects of the social setting in which an individual is raised have ramifications on psychosocial development as well. For instance, neighborhood structure has been shown to account for antisocial behavior, whereas the presence of adult supervision and adult interventions tends to reduce delinquency and negative outcomes in children (Eisenberg, 1999; Furstenberg, Cook, Eccles, Elder, & Sameroff, 1999). The quality of communication with parents and interactions with teachers also directly affect adolescents' behavioral and psychological adjustment (Estevez, Musitu, & Herrero, 2005). Besides families, schools might facilitate children and adolescents' psychosocial development (Jax, 2005; Sternberg, 2001). The engagement in structured extracurricular activities is also likely to stimulate psychosocial development among adolescents. A study by Markstrom, Li, Blackshire, and Wilfong (2005) revealed that involvement in student government, issues groups, sports, or volunteer activities was associated with the ego strengths of hope, will, purpose, competence, and wisdom. Additionally, involvement in student government or volunteer activities was correlated with the ego strength of fidelity, and participation in the creative arts, issues groups, sports, and volunteer activities was related to the ego strength of care.

Yet, what exactly is the role of environmental stimuli in the development of wisdom throughout the life course? Even if it is true that a supportive social environment during childhood and adolescence will foster psychosocial development and that unfavorable circumstances can have long-lasting detrimental effects (e.g., Brooks, 1981; Erikson, 1963; Ewens, 1984; Heath, 1991; Horney, 1970; Maslow, 1970; Meyers, 1989; Vaillant, 1977), this does not mean that positive or negative childhood experiences determine the destiny of a person (Allport, 1961; Clausen, 1993; Vaillant, 1993, 2002). Yet, longitudinal research on the long-term effects of a person's childhood and social environment on the cultivation of wisdom are extremely rare. Ardelt (2000a), for example, found that a supportive social environment in early adulthood had a positive effect on women's wisdom over forty years later, whereas the quality of the women's childhood or mature personality characteristics in early adulthood were unrelated to their level of wisdom in old age. By contrast, in a different longitudinal study of women by Helson and Srivastava (2002), certain personality characteristics at the age of 21 (low repression, tolerance of ambiguity, achievement via independence, psychological mindedness, and tolerance) and a sense of meaning in life and benevolence toward others at the age of 43 were positively associated with the women's degree of wisdom at the age of 61. However, the authors did not investigate if the women's social environment in childhood and early adulthood had an impact on their personality in early adulthood or their sense of meaning in life and benevolence in middle adulthood. It is likely, for example, that an affectionate, emotionally supportive, and stable family environment promotes the development of personality characteristics, such as tolerance, open-mindedness, sincerity, equanimity, and independence that facilitate the acquisition of wisdom (Ardelt, 2000a). Hence, positive social conditions early in life might be conducive for the development of wisdom, but they are neither necessary nor sufficient.

Wisdom and Age

Sternberg (2005) notes five generalized views of the relationship between wisdom and age:

1. the "received" view, which suggests that wisdom develops as a spiritual awakening of sorts in old age;
2. the "fluid intelligence" view, which suggests that wisdom follows the same pattern of incline and decline as the ability to think in novel ways, increasing until early adulthood, then leveling off until starting to decline in late middle age;
3. the "crystallized intelligence" view, which suggests that wisdom follows the same path as crystallized intelligence, increasing strongly relatively early in life and continuing to increase at a lower rate until old age when disease might halt its development;
4. a combination of "fluid" and "crystallized" intelligence views, which suggests that the increase in crystallized intelligence might not be enough to offset the decline in fluid intelligence and, hence, prevent a decrease in wisdom with age; and
5. the view with little empirical support suggesting that wisdom declines monotonically throughout the life course beginning early in life.

Most wisdom researchers concur that wisdom does not automatically increase with age, as wisdom is relatively rare even among the older population (Ardelt, 1997; Assmann, 1994; Baltes, 1993; Baltes & Freund, 2003; Baltes & Staudinger, 2000; Dittmann-Kohli & Baltes, 1990; Jordan, 2005; Staudinger, 1999; Sternberg, 1990b; Webster, 2003). Kekes (1983, p. 286) states that "one can be old and foolish, but a wise man is likely to be old, simply because such growth takes time." Hence, wisdom might increase with age, particularly among people who actively pursue its development and successfully master Erikson's eight psychosocial developmental tasks (Ardelt, 2000b; Erikson, 1963, 1982; Erikson, Erikson, & Kivnick, 1986; Kramer, 1990; Moody, 1986; Taranto, 1989).

For example, the task of the reflective dimension of wisdom involves transcending one's subjectivity and projections. However, such transcendence is not easily achieved and can only be accomplished through determination and constancy (Kekes, 1983). A person who is determined to engage in constant self-examination and self-awareness is likely to view problems and events with increased objectivity rather than from an ego-centered point of view and without being overwhelmed by any negative emotions that the situation might have brought forth (Hart, 1987; Kunzmann & Baltes, 2003; Levitt, 1999). If a person feels insulted by someone, for instance, the first reaction is often a negative emotion, such as anger. Yet, if the person becomes immediately aware of the arising anger, the negative emotion will less likely become as strong as if the anger immediately overpowers the person's perception. This, in turn, will enable the person to see the whole situation more clearly, thoroughly, and objectively, which might lead to a better discernment of the other individual's motives and motivations and, most likely, to greater tolerance and forgiveness.

With time, determination, and constancy, taking such a perspective might eventually enable a person to transcend subjectivity and projections and to dissolve negative emotions (Pascual-Leone, 2000). This process of transcendence results in "a weakening of ego-centered characteristics, which leads to greater intuition and empathic understanding of Other, self, world, and nature as equally strong concerns. From this perspective, wisdom is the rarely attained, asymptotic state of normal human growth toward maturity" (Pascual-Leone, 1990, p. 272; emphasis in the original).

However, whether wisdom increases with age and at what point of the life course wisdom develops might also depend on the definition, operationalization, and measurement of wisdom. If wisdom is defined and operationalized as an expert knowledge system in the fundamental pragmatics of life and measured as wisdom-related knowledge, it is not surprising that age-related gains can be found during the period between adolescence and young adulthood when most members of modern societies first learn about their society's stock of accumulated expert knowledge in the fundamental pragmatics of life (Pasupathi, Staudinger, & Baltes, 2001; Richardson & Pasupathi, 2005). In adulthood, increases in this kind of knowledge appear to depend more on the chosen occupation than on age as occupations that require knowledge in the fundamental pragmatics of life, such as clinical psychologists, are at a clear advantage when it comes to solving hypothetical life problems in the area of life planning, life management, and life review (Jordan, 2005; Smith, Staudinger, & Baltes, 1994; Staudinger, 1999; Staudinger, Maciel, Smith, & Baltes, 1998; Staudinger, Smith, & Baltes, 1992).

Yet, if wisdom is defined as a combination of cognitive, reflective, and affective characteristics, its development can be considered a lifelong process (Ardelt, 2000b). Whereas wisdom might grow throughout the life course, the later years of life provide particular opportunities for the emergence of wisdom, as depicted, for example, in Erikson's stage theory of human development (Erikson, 1963, 1982; Erikson, Erikson, & Kivnick, 1986). Moreover, older people are more likely to have the time to engage in wisdom tasks that people at earlier stages of the life course are often too busy to pursue, such as developing a reflective mode of thinking, contemplating the meaning of life, engaging in a quest for self-fulfillment and spiritual advancement, and coming to terms with one's past as a preparation for physical and social decline and ultimately death (Ardelt, 2000b; Erikson, 1963, 1982; Jarvis, 1992; Mason, 1974; Moody, 1986; Shuldiner, 1992; Thornton,

1986). In fact, Takahashi and Overton (2002, 2005) found higher performances by older adults (mean age = 70 years) than by middle-aged adults (mean age = 45 years) on their wisdom measure, consisting of knowledge database and abstract reasoning (analytic wisdom mode) and reflective understanding, emotional empathy, and emotional regulation (synthetic wisdom mode).

Of course, cross-sectional studies are ultimately unable to address whether wisdom tends to increase with age. Although longitudinal studies on the development of wisdom are extremely rare, longitudinal research by Wink and Helson (1997) shows that practical wisdom (measured by self-reported cognitive, reflective, and mature adjectives from the Adjective Check List) tended to increase between the age of 27 and 52 and that clinical psychologists were more likely to gain higher levels of practical wisdom during that time period than were non-psychologists. Helson and Srivastava (2002) also report that a psychological or spiritual career path earlier in life was positively related to women's level of wisdom (measured as a latent variable with practical wisdom, transcendent wisdom, and scores on a wisdom task as the effect indicators) at age 61.

Coping with Crises and Hardships as a Pathway to Wisdom

Although crises and obstacles throughout life tend to be categorized as negative experiences, they ultimately might be of benefit if they stimulate the development of wisdom (Bluck & Glück, 2004; Pascual-Leone, 2000). Past studies indicate that people who experience negative life situations as an opportunity for psychosocial growth and who successfully overcome crises and obstacles in their lives are more likely to develop wisdom (Ardelt, 1998, 2005; Bianchi, 1994; Giesen & Datan, 1980). Elder (1991, p. 14) suggests that crises and obstacles in life might be perceived as a "form of apprenticeship .. in learning to cope with the inevitable losses of old age." Similarly, Pascual-Leone (2000) states that "*ultimate limit situations* that cannot be undone and are nonetheless faced with consciousness and resolve—situations like death, illness, aging, irremediable oppression or loss, extreme poverty, rightful resistance or rebellion, guilt, absolute failure, danger, uncontrollable fear, etc., lead to the natural emergence of a transcendental self, if they do not destroy the person first" (p. 247; emphasis in the original). If crises and hardships can facilitate the emergence of wisdom, older people have a higher chance to be wise than younger ones because the number of life crises a person encounters tends to increases with age (Baltes & Smith, 1990; Kekes, 1983; Kramer, 1990; Taranto, 1989). Yet, it is equally true that some people are easily defeated by crises and might become depressed or desperate rather than wise when confronted with hardships. Hence, growth in wisdom might not depend on what people experience throughout life but on how they deal with life events (Holliday & Chandler, 1986).

During a crisis, routine behaviors and normal problem solving habits tend to be ineffective. To overcome a crisis a person is often forced to approach the problem from a novel angle. This change in perspective promotes reflective thinking and is likely to increase awareness of one's subjectivity and projections. The resolution of crises and obstacles in life often requires the elimination of certain projections, which tends to decrease ego-centeredness and increase maturity and wisdom (Kramer, 1990). For example, the experience of prolonged unemployment or a life-threatening illness might cause a person to question his or her sense of invulnerability (i.e., the projection that bad things only happen to other people who deserve it) which, in turn, might lead to increased compassion and empathy toward the less fortunate members of society. Such a reflection on priorities and values might also trigger a reevaluation of life's meaning, which can prompt major life changes that ultimately might result in a more meaningful and satisfactory life (Bianchi, 1994; Lehr, 1978; Marris, 1986; Park, Cohen, & Murch, 1996; Taylor, Lichtman, & Wood, 1984).

Yet, many people might be unwilling to face the uncertainty and psychological disequilibrium that the process of reevaluating and reordering of life priorities and values entails and instead prefer to utilize their previous coping styles and behavior patterns when dealing with a crisis, even if it is maladaptive and leads to psychological deterioration rather than growth (Bursik, 1991). For example, in a study of families during the Great Depression, explosive and irritable men tended to become even more explosive and irritable if they were directly affected by Depression hardship (Elder, Caspi, & Nguyen, 1986). As past longitudinal research has shown, crises and hardships in life can have opposing effects on people's psychosocial growth. For example, adults who were rated as relatively high on the cognitive, reflective, and affective dimensions of wisdom in old age (in 1968/69) and who experienced economic hardship in early adulthood during the Great Depression tended to become psychologically healthier after the Depression years (Ardelt, 1998). By contrast, the psychological health of men and women who were characterized as relatively low on the cognitive, reflective, and affective dimensions of wisdom in old age and who experienced similar hardships during the Great Depression declined after the Depression years. The psychological health of respondents who were not affected by economic deprivation during the Great Depression remained relatively stable during and after the Great Depression, but respondents who were rated as relatively high in wisdom in old age tended to have better psychological health during those early adulthood years than respondents who were rated as relatively low in old age wisdom. Similarly, in a study of women, marital separation led to either growth or regression in ego development, depending on the women's level of adjustment one year after the separation or divorce (Bursik, 1991).

This research confirms that crises and hardships in a person's life are neither a necessary nor a sufficient condition for the development of wisdom. Rather, the path to wisdom requires a willingness to learn life's lessons and to be transformed in the process (Moody, 1986). Randall and Kenyon (2001, p. 99) note that "wisdom is not a matter of putting a Band-Aid over a problem, or even of coping, in a sense of merely getting by on the basis of a clever coping strategy. It involves the possibility for real growth and transformation." Without a commitment to psychological growth and personal transformation, crises and hardships might result in psychological disintegration rather than wisdom (Allport, 1961; Bianchi, 1994).

Yet, how exactly do wise individuals deal successfully with crises and obstacles in life? A recent exploratory study examined this question through an in-depth qualitative analysis of semi-structured interviews with six respondents between the ages of 59 and 85 who were interviewed about the most pleasant and unpleasant events in their lives (Ardelt, 2005). The respondents were chosen based on their quantitative scores on the 3D-WS (Ardelt, 2003) and the ratings they received from three independent judges on the cognitive, reflective, and affective dimensions of wisdom. Results showed that the three elders who scored and were rated relatively high on wisdom first mentally distanced themselves from the unpleasant event to relax, calm down, and not become overwhelmed by the situation. Second, they engaged in active coping that consisted of a mental reframing of the situation and of taking active mental and/or physical control of the crisis. Third, relatively wise elders were able to apply the lessons that life had taught them when they encountered crises and hardship. They learned from their experiences and, as a consequence, recognized and accepted life's unpredictability and uncertainty.

By contrast, the three older people who scored and were rated relatively low on wisdom did not try to deal with a crisis in an active manner and instead relied on passive coping strategies, such as passive acceptance and/or reliance on God, to deal with unpleasant events. As a consequence, they did not learn from their experiences, did not gain wisdom and insight into the nature of life, and remained extremely vulnerable and defenseless when experiencing severe hardship in life.

It should be noted, however, that success in coping with crises and hardships is not equivalent to wisdom. Rather, successful coping might initiate stress-related growth (Park, Cohen, & Murch, 1996; Park & Fenster, 2004), which can serve as a catalyst for the development of wisdom. The major difference between these three concepts is that successful coping with crises and hardships does not require the development of sympathy and compassion for others that characterizes the affective dimension of wisdom and that stress-related growth is only one possible pathway to wisdom.

The relatively wise elders in the above mentioned qualitative study learned to engage in active mental and physical coping during crises and obstacles in life, which prepared them to face the physical and social challenges of old age, such as declines in physical health and the loss of loved ones (Ardelt, 1998; Bianchi, 1994; Caspi & Elder, 1986; Giesen & Datan, 1980). The successful mastery of crises and hardships earlier in life led to stress-related growth (Park, 1998; Park & Fenster, 2004), which resulted in decreased ego-centeredness (Kramer, 1990) and gains in wisdom manifested by greater insight, understanding, and sympathy and compassion for others (Ardelt, 2005). However, both the qualitative and the earlier quantitative study demonstrated that crises and hardships are a possible pathway to wisdom only for people who successfully deal with negative life events (Ardelt, 1998, 2005; Erikson, 1964, 1980, 1982; Erikson, Erikson, & Kivnick, 1986; Pascual-Leone, 2000).

The Association between Wisdom, Integrity, and Life Satisfaction

We will explore the association between wisdom, integrity, and life satisfaction by first examining the relation between wisdom and integrity and then the relation between wisdom and life satisfaction in old age.

Relation between Wisdom and Integrity

The task that needs to be solved during Erikson's eighth stage of human development in old age is the acceptance of one's life and the acknowledgement of the "inalterability of the past" (Erikson, Erikson, & Kivnick, 1986, p. 56). If people are satisfied with the way they have lived and with what they have accomplished, ego-integrity can be achieved (Wrightsman, 1988). On the other hand, psychological despair is likely to occur if people have major regrets in life, believe that life is generally unfair, and wish that they could live their life over again to change the past. Despair also emerges when people are unable to accept the deterioration of the body and the accompanying personal limitations. Those elders might despair over the loss of their physical mobility and the fading acuteness of their senses, and they might fear that they lose control over their lives and end up helpless and dependent on the mercy of others.

This does not mean that only individuals who have lived a successful life without any hardships, disappointments, and setbacks and who retain their physical health in old age can reach ego-integrity. On the contrary and as mentioned above, the successful resolution of crises and obstacles in life is one of the pathways to wisdom. People who have achieved ego-integrity know that crises, obstacles, and setbacks are aspects of life that cannot be avoided, and they can acknowledge and accept that they, like everyone, are not perfect and that they might have made mistakes in the past (Deci, 1980). However, they do not brood over past misfortunes, mistakes, and missed opportunities, but instead learn from their mistakes and view negative events and their personal imperfections as opportunities for growth (Ardelt, 2005).

Individuals who are able to accept themselves and their whole life course can also better cope with the inevitable losses of old age and the approach of their own deaths. Although they are aware that their life course will soon come to its natural end, they are not bitter or remorseful because they feel that they have successfully completed the cycle and can, therefore, accept death in the same way that they accept life. Nicholson (1980) notes that "paradoxically, it is the person who believes that his or her life has been most worthwhile who seems to have least qualms about the prospect of it coming to an end" (p. 252).

According to Erikson (1963, 1982), the successful resolution of the eighth psychosocial crisis of ego-integrity versus despair in old age results in wisdom. Takahashi and Overton (2002, 2005) point out that Erikson's model highlights the synthetic/transformational and synthetic/integrative features of wisdom. The synthetic/transformational feature of wisdom refers to reflective understanding and "an informed and detached concern with life" (Erikson, 1982, p. 61). The synthetic/integrative feature of wisdom is represented by ego-integrity, which can be described as "a sense of coherence and wholeness" (Erikson, Erikson, & Kivnick, 1986, p. 65). Yet, wisdom and ego integrity are not the same. Wisdom consists of cognitive, reflective, and affective elements and has the potential to increase throughout life (Ardelt, 2000b). Ego integrity, defined as an acceptance of one's whole life course including the positive and the negative aspects of life, can ultimately only be obtained in old age. However, a person who has grown in wisdom throughout life is probably more likely to achieve ego integrity in old age. Wise elders experience ego-integrity, which includes an accepting attitude toward physical and social losses and the closeness of death. Taranto (1989) explains that "with acceptance, detachment, and humor about failing physical and social potential, aged [wise] people may still take charge of their lives and develop a new level of autonomy, because such an attitude makes one impervious to the vicissitudes of life" (p. 16). It is in this way that wise elders become role models for successful aging.

Most researchers in human development would concur with Erikson that a wise person is characterized by an integrated personality, exceptional maturity, and the ability to cope with life's vicissitudes and the nearing of death (Ardelt, 2000a, 2000b; Assmann, 1994; Baltes & Freund, 2003; Bianchi, 1994; Clayton, 1982; Kekes, 1983, 1995; Kramer, 2000; Kunzmann & Baltes, 2003; Sternberg, 1990b, 1998; Vaillant, 1993, 2002). In fact, past studies have found empirical support for this statement. Wink and Helson (1997) demonstrated that ego development, insight, and autonomy at age 43 and psychological mindedness at age 52 was positively related to practical and transcendent wisdom at the age of 52. Generativity at age 43, Erikson's seventh developmental task, was also associated with practical wisdom. This finding was confirmed in a different study by Wink and Dillon (2003) who reported a significant association between generativity (characterized as giving, protective, sympathetic, warm, socially perceptive, and having broad interests) and wisdom in late adulthood (late 60s to late 70s). Similarly, in a study of adults ranging in age from 22 to 78 years, ego integrity and generativity were positively and significantly correlated with Webster's (2003) Self-Assessed Wisdom Scale (SAWS). In a later study of participants between the ages of 17 and 92 years, generativity was again positively associated with the revised SAWS (Webster, 2007). Staudinger, Dörner, and Mickler (2005) found that orientation toward personal growth, purpose in life, ego-development, and benevolent values were positively associated with self-related wisdom. In research by Orwoll and Perlmutter (1990), wise nominees received significantly higher scores on ego-integrity than did creative nominees and were also more likely than creative nominees to support a generative perspective. Finally, among older adults between the age of 52 and 87, the Three-Dimensional Wisdom Scale (3D-WS) was positively correlated with mastery and purpose in life and negatively associated with death avoidance and death anxiety (Ardelt, 2003).

This empirical evidence lends support to the Eriksonian claim that wise elders are able to integrate and make sense of their past and present life and be content with what they have accomplished (Thomas, 1991; Wrightsman, 1988). They do not despair over the finitude of life or missed past opportunities but appear to be integrated into the natural flow of life through the succession of generations (Erikson, 1980, 1982; Erikson, Erikson, & Kivnick, 1986). It is in this way that wisdom can be described as "detached concern with life itself in the face of death itself" (Erikson, 1964, p. 133).

Relation between Wisdom and Life Satisfaction

Most people believe that wisdom is a good predictor of successful aging because it teaches "the art of living" or how to lead a life that is good for oneself, others, and society at large (Baltes & Freund, 2003; Baltes, Glueck, & Kunzmann, 2002; Baltes & Staudinger, 2000; Hart, 1987; Kekes, 1995; Kramer, 2000; Kunzmann & Baltes, 2003, 2005; Kupperman, 2005; Sternberg, 1998). If wise elders can avoid despair and instead achieve ego-integrity through the acceptance of their whole life, they should be satisfied with life even if objective conditions, such as their physical health or marital status, are less than ideal (Ardelt, 2000b; Assmann, 1994; Bianchi, 1994; Clayton, 1982; Kekes, 1995; Kramer, 2000; Sternberg, 1990b; Vaillant, 1993). The contentment that wise individuals feel does not depend on external circumstances, because they have learned how to be aware of and accept both the positive and negative aspects of reality as it is (Assmann, 1994; Blanchard-Fields & Norris, 1995; Gadamer, 1960; Hart, 1987; Maslow, 1970; Strijbos, 1995; Weinsheimer, 1985). Hence, wise elders can handle even the most difficult situations, such as the physical and social losses that accompany old age, with equanimity (Ardelt, 1997, 2000a; Clayton, 1982; Kramer, 2000).

Of course, older adults' objective circumstances do have an impact on life satisfaction in old age. In a review of the literature, for example, Veenhoven (1991, 1994) found that people's happiness depends on their objective living conditions and that individuals who experience negative life situations, such as poverty, illness, and loneliness, tend to be less happy than those who are spared from misfortune. Most people are unlikely to be satisfied with their life unless basic physical and psychological needs are met (Cantril, 1965; Ikels et al., 1995; Maslow, 1970; Oishi, Diener, & Lucas, 1999). However, the fulfillment of these basic needs is not a sufficient condition for life satisfaction (Diener & Biswas-Diener, 2002; Diener & Seligman, 2004). In fact, past studies indicate that people's life satisfaction and subjective well-being are ultimately more affected by their cognitive perception and appraisal of events than by the events themselves (Colerick, 1985; George, 1990; George & Clipp, 1991; Larson, 1978; Lohmann, 1980; Rudinger & Thomae, 1990; Spreitzer & Snyder, 1974).

This might explain why wise elders who have learned to cope successfully with the vicissitudes of life tend to be most satisfied in old age. For example, among older adults between the ages of 58 and 82 in 1968/69, the latent variable wisdom (measured by cognitive, reflective, and affective effect indicators) was a significantly stronger predictor of life satisfaction than objective circumstances, such as older adults' finances, physical health, socioeconomic status, physical environment, and social involvement (Ardelt, 1997, 2000a). In fact, the inclusion of wisdom in the analysis models generally reduced the effects of objective circumstances on life satisfaction. Furthermore and unlike life satisfaction, wisdom was unrelated to objective life conditions with the exception of physical health, which was positively correlated with wisdom. Similarly, wisdom (measured by the 3D-WS as a latent variable) was positively related to general well-being and subjective health and negatively related to depressive symptoms in a contemporary sample of older adults between the age of 52 and 87 (Ardelt, 2003). Interestingly, wisdom was unrelated to income (an objective life condition) but negatively correlated with feelings of economic pressure (the cognitive appraisal of the financial situation). Epistemic wisdom was also positively correlated with subjective well-being among young and older adults (Brugman, 2000). Finally, Takahashi and Overton (2002) report that the analytic and synthetic modes of wisdom were positively associated with life satisfaction in a study of American and Japanese middle-aged (age 36 to 59 with a mean age of 45 years) and older (age greater than 65 with a mean age of 70 years) adults.

It appears that wisdom and integrity are important but not necessary conditions for life satisfaction in old age. People can be satisfied if they live a life that is blessed by good fortune, physical and mental health, and friends (Rowe & Kahn, 1998). Yet, it is during times of crises and misfortune that wisdom is necessary for subjective well-being as it allows people to actively and effectively cope with negative life events (Ardelt, 2005). Moreover, the pursuit and realization of wisdom might be intrinsically rewarding and result in positive emotions, such as joy and serenity, through a transcendence of ego-centeredness (Csikszentmihalyi & Nakamura, 2005).

However, it should be noted that not all studies reveal a positive association between wisdom and life satisfaction. Both practical wisdom and transcendent wisdom, as measured by Wink and Helson (1997), were unrelated to life satisfaction or marital satisfaction at the age of 52. Similarly, wisdom-related knowledge was not significantly correlated with measures of autonomy, environmental mastery, positive relations, purpose in life, and self-acceptance from the Ryff Inventory of Psychological Well-Being (Ryff, 1989) among adults between the age of 19 and 87 with a mean age of 45 years (Staudinger, Lopez, & Baltes, 1997). Self-related wisdom was equally unrelated to life satisfaction and positive or negative emotions (Staudinger, Dörner, & Mickler, 2005).

It might be that a significant correlation between wisdom and life satisfaction only exists in advanced old age when social and physical losses become more prevalent and death is more than an abstract and remote possibility. However and as mentioned above, the results of Brugman's (2000) and Takahashi and Overton's (2002) research included a positive correlation between wisdom and subjective well-being among young and middle-aged adults. Hence, an alternative explanation for the contradictory results might be that the association between wisdom and subjective well-being depends in part on the operationalization and assessment of the variables under investigation. Because the measurement of wisdom and subjective well-being varies widely between studies, results might differ due to the researchers' underlying philosophy of what wisdom and subjective well-being really is and how those concepts can best be operationalized and assessed (Ardelt, 2004a, b).

Future Directions

In what directions is the future of wisdom research heading? Some researchers are examining social contexts that might foster the cultivation of wisdom. One such focus is education. Is it possible that wisdom can be taught in schools (Bassett, 2006; Reznitskaya & Sternberg, 2004; Schwartz & Power, 2000; Sternberg, 2001) or at the college level (Brown, 2004) so that people can reap its benefits throughout the life course and particularly in old age and at the end of life? An education that consists primarily of learning cognitive skills and knowledge, however, is insufficient for the development of wisdom (Jax, 2005; Sternberg, 2001). Wisdom is not equivalent to advanced intellectual understanding and knowledge (Ardelt, 2000b, 2004b; Chandler & Holliday, 1990; Clayton, 1982; Csikszentmihalyi & Rathunde, 1990; Kekes, 1983; Taranto, 1989) but "… transcends the intellect" (Naranjo, 1972, p. 225). In fact, "… wisdom is not simply one aspect of knowledge, but knowledge is only one aspect of wisdom" (Blanchard-Fields & Norris, 1995, p.105). As Jax (2005, p. 37) states, wisdom "… is the use of knowledge in light of spiritual purpose."

Table 25.2 summarizes the major differences between intellectual knowledge and wisdom in the domains of goals, approach, acquisition, effects on the knower, and relation to aging. A thorough discussion of this table can be found in Ardelt (2000b). However, it should be noted that the acquisition of wisdom, in contrast to intellectual knowledge, requires a profound personal transformation (Achenbaum & Orwoll, 1991; Ardelt, 2004b; Assmann, 1994; Kekes, 1983; Kupperman, 2005; Moody, 1986).

The problem is that purely intellectual learning does not stimulate the kind of personal transformation that is fundamental to the realization of wisdom. Thus, Jax (2005) and Sternberg (2001) suggest that the function of schools should not just be to instill knowledge in students but also to impart wise and appropriate uses for such knowledge. Sternberg (2001) lists four reasons why wisdom-related skills should be taught in schools. First, wisdom but not knowledge is related to subjective well-being (Ardelt, 1997, 2000a, 2003). Second, wisdom leads to mindful, deliberate judgments. Third, wisdom provides an avenue for the creation of a more harmonious world. And fourth, wisdom teaches students to become better parents, leaders, and members of their community. Although wisdom cannot be taught directly, Sternberg (2001) believes that schools can at least offer the scaffolding for the development of wisdom by teaching students how to think and not just what to think. Yet, if wisdom were to be included in the curriculum, some essential changes in the delivery of education would be required. For instance, to teach the acquisition of wisdom, teachers should be encouraged to pursue wisdom themselves so that they can serve as good role models for their students (Jax, 2005; Kupperman, 2005). Sternberg and colleagues (Reznitskaya & Sternberg, 2004; Sternberg, 2001) are currently working on a project to examine the effects of a wisdom-related curriculum on middle school students.

Brown (2004) suggests that wisdom can potentially be taught in colleges if they provide an environment that is conducive to the learning-from-life process, which consists of reflection, integration, and application. For growth in wisdom to take place, however, students need to have a well-developed and positive orientation to learning, a variety of experiences, and positive interactions with others. Colleges can play a crucial role in creating an orientation and environment that transform fragmented campuses into seamless learning environments (Brown, 2004).

Other researchers examine the role of spiritual practices in the development of wisdom throughout life. For example, Pascual-Leone (2000) suggests that meditation can serve as a path to wisdom as this practice leads to a reduction in ego-centeredness and

Table 25.2 Differences between Intellectual Knowledge and Wisdom

Domain	Intellectual Knowledge	Wisdom
Goals	• quantitative: accumulation of knowledge and information	• qualitative: deeper understanding of salient phenomena and events
	• discovery of new truths	• rediscovery of the significance of old truths
	• descriptive knowledge	• interpretative knowledge
	• *how* to do certain things	• *should* I do certain things?
	• mastery of the outside world through liberation from outside forces	• mastery of the inner world through liberation from inner forces
	• change of reality	• acceptance of reality
	• striving for certainty, regularity, and predictability to plan for the future	• acceptance of uncertainty, irregularity, unpredictability, and impermanence
	• knowing how to deal with the expected	• knowing how to deal with the unexpected and the unknown
Approach	• scientific	• spiritual
	• theoretical	• applied
	• abstract, detached	• concrete, involved
	• impersonal	• personal: intrapersonal and interpersonal
Acquisition	• intelligence/cognition	• combination of cognition and self-reflection
	• detached experience, i.e., studying books, listen to lectures, conducting experiments, objective observations	• personal life experiences together with self-awareness, determination, and constancy to transcend subjectivity and projections
Effects on the knower	• increased self-centeredness because one believes that one knows	• diminished self-centeredness because one knows that one does not know
	• concerned about individualistic and particularistic issues	• concerned about collective and universal issues
	• pride and a feeling of superiority towards people with less intellectual knowledge	• sympathy and compassion for others
Relation to aging	• reversed u-shaped pattern	• potentially positive
	• might become outdated and obsolete with time	• important at all stages of the life course

Adapted from Ardelt, M. (2000). Intellectual versus wisdom-related knowledge: The case for a different kind of learning in the later years of life. *Educational Gerontology: An International Journal of Research and Practice, 26,* 771–789.

ultimately to self-transcendence. He emphasizes that different paths are appropriate for different people but "any major modality/mode of human processing that can lead to *mindful* ritualization (and so to *attention-getting* but *repetitive* practices that can be partly *automatized* and *habituated*) should, *when coupled to a suitable philosophy*, yield a way to wisdom and transcendental self development" (pp. 252–253; emphasis in the original). In fact, practicing meditation was positively correlated with self-transcendent wisdom (Levenson, Jennings, Aldwin, & Shiraishi, 2005).

What directions should future wisdom research take? Longitudinal studies should assess the development of wisdom and its relation to subjective well-being throughout life to illuminate the effects of the pursuit of wisdom at each stage of the life course. Unfortunately, however, longitudinal studies tend to be rather costly and difficult to conduct (Vaillant, 2002). Yet, longitudinal studies are necessary to answer questions about the consequences of the development of wisdom: Are wise people more successful in life? Are they happier, healthier, and wealthier than those with comparatively little wisdom, or does the development of wisdom have its costs (Staudinger, Dörner, & Mickler, 2005)? Is transcending one's subjectivity and projections to perceive reality more clearly intrinsically rewarding and joyful (Csikszentmihalyi & Nakamura, 2005) or does it lead to the realization of the Buddha's First Noble Truth that life is suffering? However, Buddha did not only proclaim that life is suffering but also taught that the origin of suffering is attachment, that the cessation of suffering is attainable, and how to follow the path that leads to the cessation of all suffering (Nanamoli, 2001). Does this mean that wise people remain subjectively content and at peace during objectively negative life situations?

Future research should also address the role of wisdom in the workplace and public policy. Moral and ethical decisions in particular require wisdom so that people can live a life that is good for themselves, good for others, and good for the larger society (Kupperman, 2005). What could be done to emphasize the importance of wisdom in the workplace and public policy (Etheredge, 2005; Solomon, Marshall, & Gardner, 2005)? According to Etheredge (2005), wisdom in public policy or political wisdom is defined by good judgment and commitment to the well-being of all present and future members of society and also to members of other nations in international politics. Hence, wise policies require a balance sheet of effects (good, nil, evil) across populations and time. Wise policies can be characterized by eight values for human betterment: power, enlightenment (education and personal growth), wealth, physical and mental well-being, skill, affection, rectitude, and respect (Etheredge, 2005). Yet, at this point it is not clear how political wisdom could pragmatically be implemented to achieve a better world. Perhaps political wisdom begins with teaching wisdom in schools and universities to produce wise citizens who have the ability to understand different perspectives and contexts, can communicate well across cultures, honor the environment, are compassionate, understanding, and able to make wise decision, and strive to establish a just world, where no citizen is left behind (Jax, 2005; Sternberg, 2001).

References

Achenbaum, A. W., & Orwoll, L. (1991). Becoming wise: A psycho-gerontological interpretation of the Book of Job. *International Journal of Aging and Human Development, 32,* 21–39.

Allport, G. W. (1961). Pattern and growth in personality. New York: Holt, Rinehart, and Winston.

Ardelt, M. (1997). Wisdom and life satisfaction in old age. *Journal of Gerontology: Psychological Sciences, 52B,* P15–P27.

Ardelt, M. (1998). Social crisis and individual growth: The long-term effects of the Great Depression. *Journal of Aging Studies, 12,* 291–314.

Ardelt, M. (2000a). Antecedents and effects of wisdom in old age: A longitudinal perspective on aging well. *Research on Aging, 22,* 360–394.

Ardelt, M. (2000b). Intellectual versus wisdom-related knowledge: The case for a different kind of learning in the later years of life. *Educational Gerontology: An International Journal of Research and Practice, 26,* 771–789.

Ardelt, M. (2003). Development and empirical assessment of a three-dimensional wisdom scale. *Research on Aging, 25,* 275–324.

Ardelt, M. (2004a). Where can wisdom be found? — A reply to the commentaries by Baltes and Kunzmann, Sternberg, and Achenbaum. *Human Development, 47,* 304–307.

Ardelt, M. (2004b). Wisdom as expert knowledge system: A critical review of a contemporary operationalization of an ancient concept. *Human Development, 47,* 257–285.

Ardelt, M. (2005). How wise people cope with crises and obstacles in life. *ReVision: A Journal of Consciousness and Transformation, 28,* 7–19.

Arlin, P. K. (1990). Wisdom: The art of problem finding. In R. J. Sternberg (Ed.), *Wisdom: Its nature, origins, and development* (pp. 230–243). Cambridge, UK: Cambridge University Press.

Assmann, A. (1994). Wholesome knowledge: Concepts of wisdom in a historical and cross-cultural perspective. In D. L. Featherman, R. M. Lerner, & M. Perlmutter (Eds.), *Life-span development and behavior* (Vol. 12, pp. 187–224). Hillsdale, NJ: Erlbaum.

Baltes, P. B. (1993). The aging mind: Potential and limits. *The Gerontologist, 33,* 580–594.

Baltes, P. B., & Freund, A. M. (2003). The intermarriage of wisdom and selective optimization with compensation: Two meta-heuristics guiding the conduct of life. In C. L. M. Keyes & J. Haidt (Eds.), *Flourishing: Positive psychology and the life well-lived* (pp. 249–273). Washington, DC: American Psychological Association.

Baltes, P. B., Glueck, J., & Kunzmann, U. (2002). Wisdom: Its structure and function in regulating successful life span development. In C. R. Snyder & S. J. Lopez (Eds.), *Handbook of positive psychology* (pp. 327–347). London: Oxford University Press.

Baltes, P. B., & Smith, J. (1990). Towards a psychology of wisdom and its ontogenesis. In R. J. Sternberg (Ed.), *Wisdom: Its nature, origins, and development* (pp. 87–120). Cambridge, UK: Cambridge University Press.

Baltes, P. B., & Staudinger, U. M. (2000). Wisdom: A metaheuristic (pragmatic) to orchestrate mind and virtue toward excellence. *American Psychologist, 55,* 122–136.

Baltes, P. B., Staudinger, U. M., Maercker, A., & Smith, J. (1995). People nominated as wise: A comparative study of wisdom-related knowledge. *Psychology and Aging, 10,* 155–166.

Bassett, C. (2005). Emergent wisdom. Living a life in widening circles. *ReVision: A Journal of Consciousness and Transformation, 27,* 6–11.

Bassett, C. L. (2006). Laughing at gilded butterflies: Integrating wisdom, development, and learning. In C. Hoare (Ed.), *Handbook of adult development and learning* (pp. 281–306). New York: Oxford University Press.

Bianchi, E. C. (1994). *Elder wisdom. Crafting your own elderhood.* New York: Crossroad.

Birren, J. E., & Fisher, L. M. (1990). The elements of wisdom: Overview and integration. In R. J. Sternberg (Ed.), *Wisdom: Its nature, origins, and development* (pp. 317–332). Cambridge, U.K.: Cambridge University Press.

Birren, J. E., & Svensson, C. M. (2005). Wisdom in history. In R. J. Sternberg & J. Jordan (Eds.), *A handbook of wisdom. Psychological perspectives* (pp. 3–31). New York: Cambridge University Press.

Blanchard-Fields, F., & Norris, L. (1995). The development of wisdom. In M. A. Kimble, S. H. McFadden, J. W. Ellor, & J. J. Seeber (Eds.), *Aging, spirituality, and religion: A handbook* (pp. 102–118). Minneapolis, MN: Fortress Press.

Block, J. (1971). *Lives through time.* Berkeley, CA: Bancroft Books.

Bluck, S., & Glück, J. (2004). Making things better and learning a lesson: Experiencing wisdom across the lifespan. *Journal of Personality, 72,* 543–572.

Bluck, S., & Glück, J. (2005). From the inside out: People's implicit theories of wisdom. In R. J. Sternberg & J. Jordan (Eds.), *A handbook of wisdom. Psychological perspectives* (pp. 84–109). New York: Cambridge University Press.

Bradley, G. W. (1978). Self-serving biases in the attribution process: A reexamination of the fact or fiction question. *Journal of Personality and Social Psychology, 36,* 56–71.

Brooks, J. B. (1981). Social maturity in middle age and its developmental antecedents. In D. H. Eichorn, J. A. Clausen, N. Haan, M. P. Honzik, & P. H. Mussen (Eds.), *Present and past in middle life* (pp. 244–265). New York: Academic Press.

Brown, S. C. (2004). Learning across the campus: How college facilitates the development of wisdom. *Journal of College Student Development, 45,* 134–148.

Brown, S. C., & Greene, J. A. (2006). The Wisdom Development Scale: Translating the conceptual to the concrete. *Journal of College Student Development, 47,* 1–19.

Brugman, G. M. (2000). *Wisdom: Source of narrative coherence and eudaimonia.* Delft, The Netherlands: Eburon.

Bursik, K. (1991). Adaptation to divorce and ego development in adult women. *Journal of Personality and Social Psychology, 60,* 300–306.

Cantril, H. (1965). *The pattern of human concerns.* New Brunswick, NJ: Rutgers University Press.

Caspi, A., Bem, D. J., & Elder, G. H., Jr. (1989). Continuities and consequences of interactional styles across the life course. *Journal of Personality, 57,* 375–406.

Caspi, A., & Elder, G. H., Jr. (1986). Life satisfaction in old age: Linking social psychology and history. *Journal of Psychology and Aging, 1,* 18–26.

Caspi, A., Moffitt, T. E., Morgan, J., Rutter, M., Taylor, A., Arseneault, L., Tully, L., Jacobs, C., Kim-Cohen, J., & Polo-Tomas, M. (2004). Maternal expressed emotion predicts children's antisocial behavior problems: Using monozygotic-twin differences to identify environmental effects on behavioral development. *Developmental Psychology, 40,* 149–161.

Caspi, A., Roberts, B. W., & Shiner, R. L. (2005). Personality development: Stability and change. *Annual Review of Psychology, 56,* 453–483.

Chandler, M. J., & Holliday, S. (1990). Wisdom in a postapocalyptic age. In R. J. Sternberg (Ed.), *Wisdom: Its nature, origins, and development* (pp. 121–141). Cambridge, UK: Cambridge University Press.

Clausen, J. A. (1993). *American lives. Looking back at the children of the Great Depression.* New York: The Free Press.

Clayton, V. (1975). Erikson's theory of human development as it applies to the aged: Wisdom as contradictory cognition. *Human Development, 18,* 119–128.

Clayton, V. (1982). Wisdom and intelligence: The nature and function of knowledge in the later years. *International Journal of Aging and Development, 15,* 315–323.

Clayton, V. P., & Birren, J. E. (1980). The development of wisdom across the life-span: A reexamination of an ancient topic. In P. B. Baltes & O. G. Brim Jr. (Eds.), *Life-span development and behavior* (Vol. 3, pp. 103–135). New York: Academic Press.

Colerick, E. J. (1985). Stamina in later life. *Social Science and Medicine, 21,* 997–1006.

Csikszentmihalyi, M., & Nakamura, J. (2005). The role of emotions in the development of wisdom. In R. J. Sternberg & J. Jordan (Eds.), *A handbook of wisdom. Psychological perspectives* (pp. 220–242). New York: Cambridge University Press.

Csikszentmihalyi, M., & Rathunde, K. (1990). The psychology of wisdom: An evolutionary interpretation. In R. J. Sternberg (Ed.), *Wisdom: Its nature, origins, and development* (pp. 25–51). Cambridge, UK: Cambridge University Press.

Curnow, T. (1999). *Wisdom, intuition, and ethics.* Brookfield, VT: Ashgate.

Deci, E. L. (1980). *The psychology of self-determination.* Lexington, MA: Lexington Books.

Diener, E., & Biswas-Diener, R. (2002). Will money increase subjective well-being? *Social Indicators Research, 57,* 119–169.

Diener, E., & Seligman, M. E. P. (2004). Beyond money: Toward an economy of well-being. *Psychological Science in the Public Interest, 5,* 1–31.

Dittmann-Kohli, F., & Baltes, P. B. (1990). Toward a neofunctionalist conception of adult intellectual development: Wisdom as a prototypical case of intellectual growth. In C. N. Alexander & E. J. Langer (Eds.), *Higher stages of human development. Perspectives on adult growth* (pp. 54–78). New York: Oxford University Press.

Eisenberg, L. (1999). Experience, brain, and behavior: The importance of a head start. *Pediatrics, 103,* 1031–1034.

Elder, G. H., Jr. (1991). Making the best of life: Perspectives on lives, times, and aging. *Generations, 15,* 12–17.

Elder, G. H., Jr. (1994). Time, human agency, and social change: Perspectives on the life course. *Social Psychology Quarterly, 57,* 4–15.

Elder, G. H., Jr., Caspi, A., & Nguyen, T. V. (1986). Resourceful and vulnerable children: Family influences in hard times. In R. K. Silbereisen, K. Eyferth, & G. Rudinger (Eds.), *Development as action in context: Problem behavior and normal youth development* (pp. 167–186). Berlin: Springer.

Elder, G. H., Jr., & Liker, J. K. (1982). Hard times in women's life: Historical influences across forty years. *American Journal of Sociology, 88,* 241–269.

Erikson, E. H. (1963). *Childhood and society.* New York: Norton.

Erikson, E. H. (1964). *Insight and responsibility. Lectures on the ethical implications of psychoanalytic insight.* New York: Norton.

Erikson, E. H. (1980). *Identity and the life cycle.* New York: Norton.

Erikson, E. H. (1982). *The life cycle completed. A review.* New York: Norton.

Erikson, E. H., Erikson, J. M., & Kivnick, H. Q. (1986). *Vital involvement in old age: The experience of old age in our time.* New York: Norton.

Estevez, E., Musitu, G., & Herrero, J. (2005). The influence of violent behavior and victimization at school on psychological distress: The role of parents and teachers. *Adolescence, 40,* 183–196.

Etheredge, L. S. (2005). Wisdom in public policy. In R. J. Sternberg & J. Jordan (Eds.), *A handbook of wisdom: Psychological perspectives* (pp. 297–328). New York: Cambridge University Press.

Ewens, W. L. (1984). *Becoming free: The struggle for human development.* Wilmington, DE: Scholarly Resources.

Fergusson, D. M., Horwood, L. J., & Ridder, E. M. (2005a). Show me the child at seven II: Childhood intelligence and later outcomes in adolescence and young adulthood. *Journal of Child Psychology and Psychiatry, 46,* 850–858.

Fergusson, D. M., Horwood, L. J., & Ridder, E. M. (2005b). Show me the child at seven: The consequences of conduct problems in childhood for psychosocial functioning in adulthood. *Journal of Child Psychology and Psychiatry, 46,* 837–849.

Furstenberg, F. F., Jr., Cook, T., Eccles, J. S., Elder, G. H., Jr., & Sameroff, A. (Eds.). (1999). *Managing to make it: Urban families and adolescent success.* Chicago: University of Chicago Press.

Gadamer, H.-G. (1960). *Wahrheit und Methode. Grundzüge einer philosophischen Hermeneutik* [*Truth and method. Outline of a philosophical hermeneutics*]. Tübingen: Mohr.

George, L. K. (1990). Social structure, social processes, and social-psychological states. In R. H. Binstock & L. K. George (Eds.), *Handbook of aging and the social sciences* (3rd ed., pp. 186–204). New York: Academic Press.

George, L. K., & Clipp, E. C. (1991). Subjective components of aging well. *Generations, 15,* 57–60.

Giesen, C. B., & Datan, N. (1980). The competent older woman. In N. Datan & N. Lohmann (Eds.), *Transitions of aging* (pp. 57–72). New York: Academic Press.

Glover, R. J. (1998). Perspectives on aging: Issues affecting the latter part of the life cycle. *Educational Gerontology, 24,* 325–331.

Glück, J., Bluck, S., Baron, J., & McAdams, D. P. (2005). The wisdom of experience: Autobiographical narratives across adulthood. *International Journal of Behavioral Development, 29,* 197–208.

Green, S. K., & Gross, A. E. (1979). Self-serving biases in implicit evaluations. *Personality and Social Psychology Bulletin, 5,* 214–217.

Haan, N. (1969). A tripartite model of ego functioning: Values and clinical research applications. *Journal of Nervous and Mental Diseases, 148,* 14–30.

Hart, W. (1987). *The art of living: Vipassana meditation as taught by S. N. Goenka.* San Francisco: Harper.

Heath, D. H. (1991). *Fulfilling lives: Paths to maturity and success.* San Francisco: Jossey-Bass.

Helson, R., & Srivastava, S. (2002). Creative and wise people: Similarities, differences and how they develop. *Personality and Social Psychology Bulletin, 28,* 1430–1440.

Holliday, S. G., & Chandler, M. J. (1986). *Wisdom: Explorations in adult competence.* Basel, New York: Karger.

Horney, K. (1970). *Neurosis and human growth.* New York: W.W. Norton.

Ikels, C., Dickerson-Putman, J., Draper, P., Fry, C. L., Glascock, A., Harpending, H., & Keith, J. (1995). Comparative perspectives on successful aging. In L. A. Bond, S. J. Cutler, & A. Grams (Eds.), *Promoting successful and productive aging* (pp. 304–323). Thousand Oaks, CA: Sage.

Jaffee, S. R., Belsky, J., Harrington, H. L., Caspi, A., & Moffitt, T. E. (2006). When parents have a history of conduct disorder: How is the caregiving environment affected? *Journal of Abnormal Psychology, 115,* 309–319.

Jarvis, P. (1992). *Paradoxes of learning: On becoming an individual in society.* San Francisco: Jossey-Bass.

Jax, C. (2005). No soul left behind: Paths to wisdom in American schools. *ReVision: A Journal of Consciousness and Transformation, 28,* 34–41.

Jordan, J. (2005). The quest for wisdom in adulthood: A psychological perspective. In R. J. Sternberg & J. Jordan (Eds.), *A handbook of wisdom: Psychological perspectives* (pp. 160–188). New York: Cambridge University Press.

Kekes, J. (1983). Wisdom. *American Philosophical Quarterly, 20,* 277–286.

Kekes, J. (1995). *Moral wisdom and good lives.* Ithaca, NY: Cornell University Press.

Kitchener, K. S., & Brenner, H. G. (1990). Wisdom and reflective judgment: Knowing in the face of uncertainty. In R. J. Sternberg (Ed.), *Wisdom: Its nature, origins, and development* (pp. 212–229). Cambridge, UK: Cambridge University Press.

Kivnick, H. Q. (1993). Everyday mental health: A guide to assessing life strengths. *Generation, 17,* 13–20.

Kohn, M. (1977). *Class and conformity: A study in values.* Homewood, IL: Dorsey.

Kohn, M., & Schoenbach, C. (1983). Class, stratification, and psychological functioning. In M. Kohn & C. Schooler (Eds.), *Work and personality: An inquiry into the impact of social stratification* (pp. 154–189). Norwood, NJ: Ablex.

Kramer, D. A. (1990). Conceptualizing wisdom: The primacy of affect-cognition relations. In R. J. Sternberg (Ed.), *Wisdom: Its nature, origins, and development* (pp. 279–313). Cambridge, UK: Cambridge University Press.

Kramer, D. A. (2000). Wisdom as a classical source of human strength: Conceptualization and empirical inquiry. *Journal of Social and Clinical Psychology, 19,* 83–101.

Kunzmann, U., & Baltes, P. B. (2003). Beyond the traditional scope of intelligence: Wisdom in action. In R. J. Sternberg, J. Lautrey, et al. (Eds.), *Models of intelligence: International perspectives* (pp. 329–343). Washington, DC: American Psychological Association.

Kunzmann, U., & Baltes, P. B. (2005). The psychology of wisdom: Theoretical and empirical challenges. In R. J. Sternberg & J. Jordan (Eds.), *A handbook of wisdom: Psychological perspectives* (pp. 110–135). New York: Cambridge University Press.

Kupperman, J. J. (2005). Morality, ethics, and wisdom. In R. J. Sternberg & J. Jordan (Eds.), *A handbook of wisdom: Psychological perspectives* (pp. 245–271). New York: Cambridge University Press.

Labouvie-Vief, G. (1990). Wisdom as integrated thought: Historical and developmental perspectives. In R. J. Sternberg (Ed.), *Wisdom: Its nature, origins, and development* (pp. 52–83). Cambridge, UK: Cambridge University Press.

Larson, R. (1978). Thirty years of research on subjective well-being of older Americans. *Journal of Gerontology, 33,* 109–125.

Lehr, U. (1978). Kontinuität und Diskontinuität im Lebenslauf [Continuity and discontinuity in the life course]. In L. Rosenmayr (Ed.), *Die menschlichen lebensalter: Kontinuität und krisen [The human life stages: Continuity and crises].* München: R. Piper.

Levenson, M. R., Jennings, P. A., Aldwin, C. M., & Shiraishi, R. W. (2005). Self-transcendence: Conceptualization and measurement. *International Journal of Aging & Human Development, 60,* 127–143.

Levitt, H. M. (1999). The development of wisdom: An analysis of Tibetan Buddhist experience. *Journal of Humanistic Psychology, 39,* 86–105.

Lohmann, N. (1980). Life satisfaction research in aging: Implications for policy development. In N. Datan & N. Lohmann (Eds.), *Transitions of aging* (pp. 27–40). New York: Academic Press.

Maas, H. S., & Kuypers, J. A. (1974). *From thirty to seventy: A forty-year longitudinal study of adult life styles and personality.* San Francisco: Jossey-Bass.

Manheimer, R. J. (1992). Wisdom and method: Philosophical contributions to gerontology. In T. R. Cole, D. D. Van Tassel, & R. Kastenbaum (Eds.), *Handbook of the humanities and aging* (pp. 426–440). New York: Springer.

Markstrom, C. A., Li, X., Blackshire, S. L., & Wilfong, J. J. (2005). Ego strength development of adolescents involved in adult-sponsored structured activities. *Journal of Youth and Adolescence, 34,* 85–95.

Marris, P. (1986). *Loss and change* (revised ed.). London: Routledge and Kegan Paul.

Maslow, A. H. (1970). *Motivation and personality* (2nd ed.). New York: Harper & Row.

Mason, W. D. (1974). Aging and lifelong learning. *Journal of Research and Development in Education, 7,* 68–76.

McKee, P., & Barber, C. (1999). On defining wisdom. *International Journal of Aging and Human Development, 49,* 149–164.

Meacham, J. A. (1989). Autonomy, despair, and generativity in Erikson's theory. In P. S. Fry (Ed.), *Psychological perspectives of helplessness and control in the elderly* (pp. 63–98). Amsterdam: Elsevier Science.

Meacham, J. A. (1990). The loss of wisdom. In R. J. Sternberg (Ed.), *Wisdom: Its nature, origins, and development* (pp. 181–211). Cambridge, UK: Cambridge University Press.

Meyers, D. (1989). *Self, society, and personal choice.* New York: Columbia University Press.

Montgomery, A., Barber, C., & McKee, P. (2002). A phenomenological study of wisdom in later life. *International Journal of Aging and Human Development, 54,* 139–157.

Moody, H. R. (1986). Late life learning in the information society. In D. A. Peterson, J. E. Thornton, & J. E. Birren (Eds.), *Education and aging* (pp. 122–148). Englewood Cliffs, NJ: Prentice-Hall.

Nanamoli, B. (2001). *The life of the Buddha. According to the Pali Canon.* Seattle, WA: BPS Pariyatti Editions.

Naranjo, C. (1972). *The one quest.* New York: Viking.

Nicholson, J. (1980). *Seven ages. The truth about life crises — Does your age really matter?* Glasgow: William Collins Sons & Co.

Oishi, S., Diener, E. F., & Lucas, R. E. (1999). Cross-cultural variations in predictors of life satisfaction: Perspectives from needs and values. *Personality and Social Psychology Bulletin, 25,* 980–990.

Orwoll, L., & Achenbaum, W. A. (1993). Gender and the development of wisdom. *Human Development, 36,* 274–296.

Orwoll, L., & Perlmutter, M. (1990). The study of wise persons: Integrating a personality perspective. In R. J. Sternberg (Ed.), *Wisdom: Its nature, origins, and development* (pp. 160–177). Cambridge, UK: Cambridge University Press.

Osbeck, L. M., & Robinson, D. N. (2005). Philosophical theories of wisdom. In R. J. Sternberg & J. Jordan (Eds.), *A handbook of wisdom: Psychological perspectives* (pp. 61–83). New York: Cambridge University Press.

Park, C. L. (1998). Stress-related growth and thriving through coping: The roles of personality and cognitive processes. *Journal of Social Issues, 54,* 267–277.

Park, C. L., Cohen, L. H., & Murch, R. L. (1996). Assessment and prediction of stress-related growth. *Journal of Personality, 64,* 71–105.

Park, C. L., & Fenster, J. R. (2004). Stress-related growth: Predictors of occurrence and correlates with psychological adjustment. *Journal of Social and Clinical Psychology, 23,* 195–215.

Pascual-Leone, J. (1990). An essay on wisdom: Toward organismic processes that make it possible. In R. J. Sternberg (Ed.), *Wisdom: Its nature, origins, and development* (pp. 244–278). Cambridge, UK: Cambridge University Press.

Pascual-Leone, J. (2000). Mental attention, consciousness, and the progressive emergence of wisdom. *Journal of Adult Development, 7,* 241–254.

Pasupathi, M., Staudinger, U. M., & Baltes, P. B. (2001). Seeds of wisdom: Adolescents' knowledge and judgment about difficult life problems. *Developmental Psychology, 37,* 351–361.

Plomin, R., Fulker, D. W., Corley, R., & DeFries, J. C. (1997). Nature, nurture, and cognitive development from 1 to 16 years: A parent-offspring adoption study. *Psychological Science, 8,* 442–447.

Randall, W. L., & Kenyon, G. M. (2001). *Ordinary wisdom: Biographical aging and the journey of life.* Westport, CT: Praeger.

Reiss, D., Neiderhiser, J. M., Hetherington, E. M., & Plomin, R. (2000). *The relationship code: Deciphering genetic and social influences on adolescent development.* Cambridge, MA: Harvard University Press.

Reznitskaya, A., & Sternberg, R. J. (2004). Teaching students to make wise judgments: The "Teaching for Wisdom" program. In P. A. Linley & S. Joseph (Eds.), *Positive psychology in practice* (pp. 181–196). New York: Wiley.

Richardson, M. J., & Pasupathi, M. (2005). Young and growing wiser: Wisdom during adolescence and young adulthood. In R. J. Sternberg & J. Jordan (Eds.), *A handbook of wisdom: Psychological perspectives* (pp. 139–159). New York: Cambridge University Press.

Riess, M., Rosenfeld, P., Melburg, V., & Tedeschi, J. T. (1981). Self-serving attributions: Biased private perceptions and distorted public descriptions. *Journal of Personality and Social Psychology, 41,* 224–231.

Robinson, D. N. (1990). Wisdom through the ages. In R. J. Sternberg (Ed.), *Wisdom: Its nature, origins, and development* (pp. 13–24). Cambridge, UK: Cambridge University Press.

Rowe, J. W., & Kahn, R. L. (1998). *Successful aging.* New York: Pantheon Books.

Rudinger, G., & Thomae, H. (1990). The Bonn Longitudinal Study of Aging: Coping, life adjustment, and life satisfaction. In P. B. Baltes & M. M. Baltes (Eds.), *Successful aging: Perspectives from the behavioral sciences* (pp. 265–295) Cambridge: Cambridge University Press.

Ryff, C. D. (1989). Happiness is everything, or is it? Explorations on the meaning of psychological well-being. *Journal of Personality and Social Psychology, 57,* 1069–1081.

Schneewind, K. A. (1995). Impact of family processes on control beliefs. In A. Bandura (Ed.), *Self-efficacy in changing societies* (pp. 114–148). New York: Cambridge University Press.

Schwartz, A. J., & Power, F. C. (2000). Maxims to live by: The art and science of teaching wise sayings. In W. S. Brown (Ed.), *Understanding wisdom: Sources, science, and society* (pp. 393–412). Philadelphia: Templeton Foundation Press.

Sherwood, G. G. (1981). Self-serving biases in person perception: A reexamination of projection as a mechanism of defense. *Psychological Bulletin, 90,* 445–459.

Shuldiner, D. (1992). The older student of humanities: The seeker and the source. In T. R. Cole, D. D. Van Tassel, & R. Kastenbaum (Eds.), *Handbook of the humanities and aging* (pp. 441–457). New York: Springer.

Smith, J., & Baltes, P. B. (1990). Wisdom-related knowledge: Age/cohort differences in response to life-planning problems. *Developmental Psychology, 26,* 494–505.

Smith, J., Staudinger, U. M., & Baltes, P. B. (1994). Occupational settings facilitating wisdom-related knowledge: The sample case of clinical psychologists. *Journal of Consulting and Clinical Psychology, 62,* 989–999.

Solomon, J. L., Marshall, P., & Gardner, H. (2005). Crossing boundaries to generative wisdom: An analysis of professional work. In R. J. Sternberg & J. Jordan (Eds.), *A handbook of wisdom. Psychological perspectives* (pp. 272–296). New York: Cambridge University Press.

Spreitzer, E., & Snyder, E. E. (1974). Correlates of life satisfaction among the aged. *Journal of Gerontology, 29,* 454–458.

Staudinger, U. M. (1999). Older and wiser? Integrating results on the relationship between age and wisdom-related performance. *International Journal of Behavioral Development, 23,* 641–664.

Staudinger, U. M., & Baltes, P. B. (1996). Interactive minds: A facilitative setting for wisdom-related performance. *Journal of Personality and Social Psychology, 71,* 746–762.

Staudinger, U. M., Dörner, J., & Mickler, C. (2005). Wisdom and personality. In R. J. Sternberg & J. Jordan (Eds.), *A handbook of wisdom. Psychological perspectives* (pp. 191–219). New York: Cambridge University Press.

Staudinger, U. M., Lopez, D. F., & Baltes, P. B. (1997). The psychometric location of wisdom-related performance: Intelligence, personality, and more? *Personality and Social Psychology Bulletin, 23,* 1200–1214.

Staudinger, U. M., Maciel, A. G., Smith, J., & Baltes, P. B. (1998). What predicts wisdom-related performance? A first look at personality, intelligence, and facilitative experiential contexts. *European Journal of Personality, 12,* 1–17.

Staudinger, U. M., Smith, J., & Baltes, P. B. (1992). Wisdom-related knowledge in a life review task: Age differences and the role of professional specialization. *Psychology and Aging, 7,* 271–281.

Sternberg, R. J. (1990a). Wisdom and its relations to intelligence and creativity. In R. J. Sternberg (Ed.), *Wisdom: Its nature, origins, and development* (pp. 142–159). Cambridge, UK: Cambridge University Press.

Sternberg, R. J. (Ed.). (1990b). *Wisdom: Its nature, origins, and development.* Cambridge, UK: Cambridge University Press.

Sternberg, R. J. (1998). A balance theory of wisdom. *Review of General Psychology, 2,* 347–365.

Sternberg, R. J. (2001). Why schools should teach for wisdom: The balance theory of wisdom in educational settings. *Educational Psychologist, 36,* 227–245.

Sternberg, R. J. (2005). Older but not wiser? The relationship between age and wisdom. *Ageing International, 30,* 5–26.

Sternberg, R.J., & Jordan, J. (Eds.). (2005). *A handbook of wisdom: Psychological perspectives.* New York: Cambridge University Press.

Strijbos, S. (1995). How can systems thinking help us in bridging the gap between science and wisdom. *Systems Practice, 8,* 361–376.

Takahashi, M. (2000). Toward a culturally inclusive understanding of wisdom: Historical roots in the East and West. *International Journal of Aging and Human Development, 51,* 217–230.

Takahashi, M., & Bordia, P. (2000). The concept of wisdom: A cross-cultural comparison. *International Journal of Psychology, 35,* 1–9.

Takahashi, M., & Overton, W. F. (2002). Wisdom: A culturally inclusive developmental perspective. *International Journal of Behavioral Development, 26,* 269–277.

Takahashi, M., & Overton, W. F. (2005). Cultural foundations of wisdom: An integrated developmental approach. In R. J. Sternberg & J. Jordan (Eds.), *A handbook of wisdom. Psychological perspectives* (pp. 32–60). New York: Cambridge University Press.

Taranto, M. A. (1989). Facets of wisdom: A theoretical synthesis. *International Journal of Aging and Human Development, 29,* 1–21.

Taylor, S. E., Lichtman, R. R., & Wood, J. V. (1984). Attributions, beliefs about control, and adjustment to breast cancer. *Journal of Personality and Social Psychology, 46,* 489–502.

Thalberg, I. (1978). Socialization and autonomous behavior. *Tulane Studies in Philosophy, 28,* 21–37.

Thomas, L. E. (1991). Dialogues with three religious renunciates and reflections on wisdom and maturity. *International Journal of Aging and Human Development, 32,* 211–227.

Thornton, J. E. (1986). Life span learning and education. A conceptual progression in the life course. In D. A. Peterson, J. E. Thornton, & J. E. Birren (Eds.), *Education and aging* (pp. 62–92). Englewood Cliffs, NJ: Prentice-Hall.

Vaillant, G. E. (1977). *Adaptation to life.* Boston: Little, Brown.

Vaillant, G. E. (1993). *The wisdom of the ego.* Cambridge, MA: Harvard University Press.

Vaillant, G. E. (2002). *Aging well: Surprising guideposts to a happier life from the landmark Harvard study of adult development.* Boston, MA: Little, Brown.

Veenhoven, R. (1991). Is happiness relative? *Social Indicators Research, 24,* 1–34.

Veenhoven, R. (1994). Is happiness a trait? Tests of the theory that a better society does not make people any happier. *Social Indicators Research, 32,* 101–160.

Weber, M. (1980). *Wirtschaft und Gesellschaft. Grundriss der verstehenden Soziologie [Economy and society. An outline of interpretive sociology]* (5th revised ed.). Tübingen: Mohr.

Webster, J. D. (2003). An exploratory analysis of a self-assessed wisdom scale. *Journal of Adult Development, 10,* 13–22.

Webster, J. D. (2007). Measuring the character strength of wisdom. *International Journal of Aging & Human Development, 65,* 163–183.

Weinsheimer, J. C. (1985). *Gadamer's Hermeneutics: A reading of Truth and Method.* New Haven: Yale University Press.

Wink, P., & Dillon, M. (2003). Religiousness, spirituality, and psychosocial functioning in late adulthood: Findings from a longitudinal study. *Psychology and Aging, 18,* 916–924.

Wink, P., & Helson, R. (1997). Practical and transcendent wisdom: Their nature and some longitudinal findings. *Journal of Adult Development, 4,* 1–15.

Wrightsman, L. S. (1988). *Personality development in adulthood.* Newbury Park, CA: Sage.

Part VI

Policy Perspectives on Aging

Chapter 26

Social Trends and Public Policy in an Aging Society

Judith Treas and Twyla Hill

Changes in American society will shape the context for social programs in coming decades. The changing composition of the U.S. population is altering the needs, capacities, and resources of Americans. Of particular importance is the aging of America and the policy challenges posed by a growing contingent of older adults. Besides demographic changes, economic and political developments are creating a new context for national policies on aging. Public policy is defined as governmental decisions and actions affecting a considerable number of persons (MacRae & Wilde, 1979), but private sector policies made possible by government action (or inaction) also impinge on individuals over the life course. While a comprehensive description of national aging policy is beyond the scope of this chapter, several excellent discussions are available (e.g., Binstock & Quadagno, 2001; Clark, Burkhauser, Moon, Quinn, & Smeeding, 2004; Meyer & Herd, 2001).

In many countries, the ethos of the capitalist welfare state is being questioned. There are cutbacks in the public safety net and government social insurance that once protected citizens from risks to their security and dignity. Welfare provisions are eroding. Market forces have been given free play. Workers navigate the labor market with fewer traditional protections, and private enterprise is touted as offering consumers products to meet the threats to their health and welfare. Individuals and their families are assuming more responsibility for their health, education, and well-being over the life course. This new "ownership society" arrives at a time when industrial restructuring and global outsourcing have many Americans worried about their long-run economic prospects. Because these changes bring income volatility and shift more risk to individuals, the cognitive skills necessary to negotiate the workplace and everyday life are increasing.

In aging policy, there is new interest in the continued productivity of older Americans. This goal is desirable, given concerns that a large, dependent population of older adults will cripple pension and health care systems. It is also consistent with an older population that is expected to be healthier and wealthier. Adult education is an important component of policies to encourage successful aging. Life-long learning as an adaptive strategy for rapid social change squares with a new policy orientation which de-emphasizes old-age dependency in favor of programs that promote the continued productivity, health, and self-sufficiency of older adults.

Thus, various forces—the need to maintain the productivity of an aging population, the desire to maintain competitiveness in a global economy, the cognitive demands of an ownership society where people make complex choices with their own money—all signal a vital role for adult learning and cognitive development. A brief review of recent and prospective welfare, social security, private pension, and health care initiatives suggests how aging policy is responding to pressures from market forces that raise the stakes for Americans confronting critical decisions in their lives.

The Aging of America

At the beginning of the 20th century, the United States had a very young population. Given persistent high fertility, half of Americans in 1900 were younger than age 23 (Hobbs & Stoops, 2002). As the U.S. entered the 21st century, the threshold of middle age, not young adulthood, marked the middle of the age distribution. In 2000, the median age of the population stood at 35 years (Hobbs & Stoops, 2002).

This population aging was the result of long-run fertility declines (interrupted only by the baby boom) coupled with medical advances extending life expectancy. The aging of the baby boom generation born after World War II (1946–1964) will compound this trend toward an older American population. The first baby boomers will turn 65 in the year 2011. By 2030, 72 million Americans will be 65 or older compared to 35 million in 2000 (He, Sengupta, Velkoff, & DeBarros, 2005). Their share of the population will also increase from 12.4% to 19.6%. The aging of the general population will slow after 2030 as baby boomers die off and are replaced by the small baby bust cohorts born in the decades of the 1960s and 1970s. However, the older population itself will undergo aging as the baby boomers move from sixty-somethings to eighty-somethings.

The growth of the older population is a policy concern, because old age is associated with higher rates of chronic illness. Fully 80% of older adults have at least one chronic health problem; 50% have two or more (He et al., 2005). The prevalence of health conditions rises steeply with advancing age. The risk of having a heart or circulatory condition, for example, is 54% higher for persons 75 or older than for those 65 to 74. Policy concerns not only include the costs of treating chronic illness, but also the challenges of dealing with the accompanying disabilities. Over one-quarter of women 65+ say that they cannot walk three blocks, and 71% report a serious limitation in their ability to perform at least one of eight simple physical tasks (He et al., 2005).

Cognitive limitations are also an issue. While most older Americans will escape severe impairment, the prevalence of dementia increases with age. Up to 7% will experience dementia, with the two most common types being Alzheimer's disease and vascular dementia (Watari & Gatz, 2002). Rates of Alzheimer's disease differ by sex, although women's greater longevity may be a factor in their higher rate. Men and African Americans are more likely to have vascular dementia (Watari & Gatz, 2002). Functional limitations, whether physical or cognitive, interfere with older adults' ability to work, to go about their daily lives, and to manage independently.

The illness and disability in an aging population will increase usage of Medicare, Medicaid, and public services as well as the dependence of older Americans on their families. Leaving aside their greater needs, the aging population has important implications for the balance between the retirement-age and the working-age populations. Old age support ratios (persons 65+ to those 20–64) will climb from 21.4 in 2000 to 36.2 in 2040 (He et al, 2005, p. 25). (By contrast, the child support ratio—8.8 in 2000—will hold steady.) Thus, responsibilities will increase for the population of young and middle-aged adults who will face higher taxes to support the nation's retirees and greater demands for the care of frail family members.

Discussions of Medicare or Social Security often imply that demographic data is an adequate tool for informing national policy debates. Certainly, demographic projections yield reasonably good estimates of the future older population. After all, tomorrow's elderly are young people today. Demographic data are often weighted more heavily in debates on societal "caring capacity" than are more uncertain—but arguably more important—factors, including long-run performance of the economy and the efficiency of public programs. Reassuringly, the future has already arrived in some places without extraordinary social or economic dislocation. In Florida, long a retirement destination for Northeasterners, nearly 18% of the population was 65 or older in 2000 (Hobbs & Stoops, 2002).

Optimism about Baby Boomers

A somber demographic picture underpins pessimistic assessments of the long run future of Medicare, Social Security, and other age-related programs. Another, brighter perspective exists on the aging of the baby boom. Coupled with generational profiling that asserts that baby boomers are too adventuresome, stubborn, or self-indulgent to accept the limitations of old age, improvements in the health and welfare of older Americans support a degree of optimism.

Coming cohorts of older Americans will be healthier, wealthier, and better educated. Older people are more financially secure. Poverty in the older population has declined from one in three persons in 1959 to one in ten (He et al., 2005). Since Social Security constitutes at least 90% of income for one-third of retired recipients (He et al., 2005), the prosperity and "self-reliance" of today's older Americans shows the historical success of aging policies. Baby boomers, at least those who finished high school, appear to be on track to be as well-off as their parents in old age (Easterlin, Schaeffer & Macunovich, 1993).

Older adults' lives are not only longer, but also healthier. Disability has been declining among the older population for decades (Crimmins & Saito, 1997; Schoeni, Freedman, & Wallace, 2001). We owe these gains to healthier lifestyles, earlier diagnosis and better medical treatment of disease, increased income and education of the older population, and more widespread usage of enabling devices like walkers and hearing aids. Not only are physical disabilities on the decline, but rates of cognitive impairment have decreased, a development traced, in part, to rising educational attainments (Freedman & Martin, 1999).

This positive vision of the capacities and resources of older adults is a key philosophical component of new aging policies, which seek to encourage or compel continued contributions of older people, rather than assume their dependency. However, it is important to recognize that many older Americans remain vulnerable and disadvantaged. In 2003, 12.5% of older women and 7.3% of older men lived in poverty (He et al., 2005). Poverty characterized 8% of older non-Hispanic whites, but the figures were 23.7% for African Americans and 19.5% for Latino/as. Other risk factors are being unmarried, living alone, and having less than 12 years of schooling. Similarly, poorer health prospects affect some older Americans. Compared to whites, older African-Americans have significantly higher death rates from heart disease, cancer, and strokes (He et al., 2005). Policies stressing old age self-reliance must contend with vulnerable populations that will not be able to work longer or manage successfully on their own.

Interdependent Generations: Needs, Capacities, and Resources

Population aging alters the nature of societal needs and resources as well as their mix. As the baby boom grows older, there will be more retired adults—people with the time, money, and know-how to contribute to their families and communities. However, proportionately fewer workers, taxpayers, and caregivers will be available to support the nation and its retirees. New labor force entrants with the latest training will be in short supply unless immigrants fill the gap. Health care costs face upward pressure from growing numbers of older adults. More people will need personal assistance in managing daily life (e.g., transportation, household chores, money management). Challenges for some Americans will pose opportunities for others who step into new occupations or create products and services to meet new needs.

Responding to an aging population is not as simple as reallocating resources from the young to a growing older population. Short-changing children will only require families to reallocate time and money from older family members to younger ones. Today's children will be tomorrow's workers and taxpayers. Meeting the diverse needs of the generations will depend on young people's preparation for productive employment. Investments in child health and education remain important even as their population share declines. This mutual dependency is recognized by innovative intergenerational programs that bring together children and retirees to support one another in mentoring, tutoring, and care giving activities (Newman, Faux, & Larimer, 1997). Research has demonstrated the importance of early life experiences for a host of cognitive, psychological, health, family, and socioeconomic outcomes in adulthood (Blackwell, Hayward, & Crimmins, 2001; Sigle-Rushton, Hobcraft, & Kiernan, 2005). Whether older adults in the future are healthy and independent or sick and dependent depends, in part, on the nutrition, medical care, nurturing, and education that they receive as children today.

Summary

Population aging presents the challenge of supporting older adults who need health care, economic support, and assistance with daily living. Although some populations will remain very vulnerable in old age, the baby boom is apt to be healthier and wealthier than previous generations of older Americans. This meshes with a new philosophy for old age policies that emphasizes self-reliance and continued productivity. Because older adults rely on younger workers, taxpayers, and caregivers, the interdependence of generations means that the well-being of older adults in the future depends on the investments made in child welfare today. The educational system is one institution challenged to meet the needs of both young and old.

Education and Competencies

Educational attainment has risen over time. In 1960, 41% of Americans, 25 and older, had at least a high school diploma (U.S. Census Bureau, 2006b, Table 214). By 2004, this figure was 85%. Only 8% of Americans had a college degree in 1960, but 28% reported being a college graduate in 2004. People of Asian and Pacific Islander descent were particularly well-educated, with 49% reporting a college degree. Other racial and ethnic minorities lagged. In 2004, only 12% of Latino/as and 17% of African Americans had graduated from college although their educational attainments, too, rose since 1960. All racial and ethnic groups have completed more years of schooling, but African Americans and Latino/as are at a disadvantage.

Recent cohorts are better educated than earlier ones. Although 24% of persons ages 65 to 74 had not finished high school, that figure dropped to 14% of 55- to 64-year-old Americans (U.S. Census Bureau, 2006b, Table 216). Older Americans in the future will have even more education than those today. This trend is consistent with the global expansion of higher education in the 20th century driven by a world view that education is appropriate for everyone and "that education creates generalized human capital that benefits both individuals and society" (Schofer & Meyer, 2005, p. 902). If everyone is educable, higher expectations of general numeracy and literacy are also appropriate. This leads, however, to an even greater divide between those who have education and those who do not, because access to education continues to be stratified.

How Valuable is Schooling?   Limited education limits economic prospects. Among adults, ages 25 to 34, earnings averaged $18,920 for workers without a high school diploma, $26,073 for high school graduates, and $51,040 for college graduates (U.S. Census Bureau, 2006b, Table 217). Although a high school diploma now conveys a relatively modest advantage, the advantages of college have grown (DiPrete & Buchmann, 2006). The favorable economic situation of better educated Americans reflects more than a bias toward formal credentials. More schooling translates into skills (Kaestle, Campbell, Finn, Johnson, & Mikulecky, 2001). Educational attainment is positively associated with literacy. For those who finish high school, a higher level of literacy increases the likelihood of being employed. When they are employed, those with only minimal literacy are laborers, not managers. Education also equips adults to be more informed citizens, more savvy consumers, and better parents.

Many adults beyond traditional school ages seek additional education. In 2001, 648,000 Americans earned their GED credentials by examination (U.S. Census Bureau, 2006b, Table 262). In 2003, there were 6.1 million adults, 25 and older, enrolled in colleges, where they made up one in three students (U.S. Census Bureau, 2006b, Table 270). Millions more pursued some sort of adult education, including continuing education requirements for their occupation, English as a second language courses, basic skills education, apprenticeship programs, and vocational and technical diploma programs (U.S. Census Bureau, 2006b, Table 292).

Adult Learning.   Much adult education is employment-related—designed to help the displaced worker or welfare recipient find and keep a job. With its narrow economic orientation, adult education policy is now labor market policy. This philosophy invites a minimalist approach—providing no more schooling than is needed to get the student a job. Learning-for-learning's-sake is now a luxury good marketed via university extension courses, eco-tourism packages, and public radio fund drives. Fortunately, a good deal of learning in adulthood is informal and incidental (Marsick & Watkins, 2001; Marsick, Watkins, Callahan, & Volpe, chapter 20, this volume).

Enhancing labor market success is a worthy educational goal, but it falls short of the needs of an aging society. Educational policies and informational programs are necessary to maintain the health and functioning of mature Americans (Uhlenberg, 1992). Forestalling disease and disability promises pay-offs in continued productivity, improved quality of life, and reduced need for costly medical services. Education confers benefits in physical health and cognitive functioning. The recognition that individuals can play an important part in managing their own medical conditions has led health care providers to devote more effort to educating patients about diet, exercise, and medication. In the cognitive domain, the prospects for maintaining capacities with suitable interventions are bright. Although older adults experience declines in cognitive functioning in various areas, even modest treatments (e.g., a five-hour training program) yield remarkable improvements in spatial orientation and inductive reasoning (Schaie, 2005). Despite their potential, learning activities that promote healthy adult functioning have yet to become a primary objective of adult education.

Do Americans Know Enough?   Is a high school graduate today as knowledgeable as in earlier generations? Despite concerns with the quality of public schools, standardized tests for young people approaching the end of high school do not suggest much deterioration. From the early 1980s to late 1990s, science and math scores improved somewhat while reading and writing scores were either stable or down slightly (U.S. Census Bureau, 2006b, Table 254).

Trends in the cognitive abilities and knowledge of American adults are less reassuring. Alwin (1991) tracked the verbal ability of representative adults from 1974 to 1990. Despite little change from year to year, there were notable differences between cohorts. Vocabulary scores rose steadily across cohorts from those born at the beginning of the 20th century until the middle, but declined for those born later. Although better educated Americans know more words than less educated Americans, word recognition declined even as educational attainment rose. The culprit was not the schools, because vocabulary gains to an additional year of schooling did not decline (Glenn, 1994). Rather, lower verbal ability reflected changing leisure-time habits. Adults reading the newspaper daily declined from 67% to 53% from 1975 to 1990. Daily hours of television viewing climbed. Controlling for schooling and age, recent cohorts—those with lower vocabulary scores--watched more television and read fewer newspapers. Even if technology turns the tide by creating a generation of on-line bloggers, the digital divide means that poor people without computer access will miss out on any verbal benefits of the Internet.

Another important proficiency is English language ability. Because of high immigration, more Americans (one-in-five adults, ages 25–44, in 2000) speak a language besides English in the home (He et al., 2005, p. 172). A small minority (6%) of Americans, ages 18 to 64, report that they do not speak English very well (U.S. Census Bureau, 2005a). Persons with limited English proficiency are at a clear disadvantage in negotiating an English-speaking culture, including communicating with health care professionals, following product usage instructions, and understanding legal matters.

Even college graduates, however, lack the skills to deal with the complex challenges that they confront in signing up for a credit card, adhering to a medical regimen, or choosing an insurer. In 2003, only 31% of Americans with a bachelor's degree could read long, complex English-language text and then reach complicated conclusions (Dillon, 2005). This proportion declined from 1992 when 40% of college graduates had this high proficiency.

According to cross-national studies of adult skills, Americans are not well-equipped to balance their own checkbooks much less deal with global economic competition. In 2003, the U.S. was one of six nations in the Adult Literacy and Life Skills Survey (National Center for Educational Statistics, 2005). On both numeracy and literacy, the U.S. fell below Norway, Bermuda, Switzerland, and Canada. The poor showing by American adults cannot be attributed to educationally disadvantaged groups dragging down the overall average, because the top 10% of Americans scored lower than their high-performing counterparts in Bermuda, Canada, and Norway. In a brief test of scientific knowledge, Americans ranked seventh out of 20 countries (Science, 1995) with younger people scoring better than older ones (Gendall, Smith, & Russel, 1995).

Summary.   Despite rising educational attainments, many Americans lack basic skills like literacy and numeracy (c.f., Smith, chapter 21, this volume). They do not have the higher order thinking skills to evaluate and manipulate complex information in order to inform their life choices. More than rudimentary computational skills like multiplication and decimals, numeracy demands the competency to deal with everyday situations such as pricing out alternatives and maintaining numerical records. This means confidence in one's ability to know when and how to apply what one knows in various situations (Cohen, 2000).

As we note below, the proliferation of choices in our society has raised the cognitive complexity of the decision making required of individuals—especially to manage the increasing risk associated with policies that limit public and employer responsibility for education, illness, or old age. The MetLife 2004 Study of Employee Benefit Trends argues that better access to financial advice and education is critical, because employers expect employees to help pay for benefits and increasingly offer voluntary rather than set benefits. Only 38% of employees say they fully understand which company benefit options best meet their needs (MetLife, 2005). Only 14% of employers identify helping employees to make better benefits decisions as their most important human resources objective, compared to 53% that choose controlling costs (MetLife, 2005). Clearly, employees want and need more advice and education than employers currently are providing.

Aging Policies: From Dependency to Productivity

Writing about aging policy in the early 1990s, Uhlenberg (1992) observed that there had been few systematic efforts in U.S. public policy to promote the productive contributions of older Americans, despite the increase in the life expectancy, human capital, and functional capacity of the older population. Public policy assumed idleness and dependency were the hallmarks of old age. The main accomplishment of decades of American social policy on aging had been to create a population of retirees cut loose from the labor force. Today, fewer than one-in-five men and about one-in-ten women, 65+, work, even part-time (He et al., 2005). Older Americans enjoy relatively good health, but are dependent on federal programs for much of their support. In the middle of the last century, gerontologists worried about the "roleless role" of old age, because there were so few behavioral expectations for later life. Since then, retirement has become institutionalized as leisure time. In the past, public polices, dating as far back as Civil War pensions (Costa, 1998), encouraged this development.

The absence of policies fostering the productivity of older adults, Uhlenberg (1992) argued, was problematic given concerns about the long-run capacity of society to afford the pensions and health care needed by a growing population of retirees. Decreasing the dependency of the older population, he concluded, called for restructuring the life course—breaking down the assumptions that education was appropriate only for the young, that adulthood required single-minded devotion to work, that old age was the time for leisure. Some modest reforms—raising the age for receipt of full Social Security benefits and outlawing mandatory retirement—moved in this direction. Labor force participation rates, which had declined for older men and held steady for older women since the 1950s, inched up beginning in the 1990s (He et al., 2005, p. 83). Without draconian economic incentives, however, older Americans have little reason to extend their work lives, given the strong retirement norm that has taken hold. Although some retirees still regard themselves as being forced to retire, perhaps due to poor health or inflexible employers, about one-third of retirees (aged 50–67) want more time with family and over one-quarter say that they want to do other things (Haider & Loughran, 2001).

Educational Policy as Aging Policy

To reduce the segmentation of the life course, greater attention must be paid to capacities instead of deficits. Life-long education—ranging from employer-sponsored educational programs to federally funded job training to Elderhostel leisure-learning—is one way to maintain the productivity of adults over the life course. Besides educational programs geared to adults, tax credits, student loans, and flexible employment schedules encourage adults to pursue human capital investments.

Many argue that the large, rapidly growing older population constitutes a great social resource (e.g., Freedman, 2002). One-quarter of the 65+ population volunteered during 2004, primarily for religious organizations (U.S. Census Bureau, 2006b, Table 575). Older adults provide social services of many types, including eldercare and childcare for family members and others. Some public policies actively support intergenerational programs (e.g., foster grandparenting) that involve older persons in children's day care (Larkin, 1998–1999). While opportunities for highly educated volunteers exist (e.g., the Senior Corps of Retired Executives), they are few and far between (Freedman, 2002). Most supervisors and managers have yet to be educated to value the abilities of older volunteers (Freedman, 2002; Larkin, 1998-1999). Arguably, educational opportunities for older adults make them more capable volunteers, even if they do not continue in paid employment.

The 1965 Older Americans Act included the policy goal that older adults have access to educational and training opportunities (Binstock, 1991). The act has consistently been underfunded (Binstock, 1991), and the Administration on Aging has focused on access to and provision of health services, broadly defined (U.S. Administration of Aging, 2005). Adult education has not been a high priority. Funding education (e.g., in health literacy) would be a good idea. Medicare beneficiaries who can read material about health and follow prescription drug instructions are better able to compare plan information and feel more confident about making good choices (Greene, Hibbard, & Tusler, 2005).

The agenda for the 2005 White House Conference on Aging also incorporated educational issues, such as financial literacy throughout the life cycle and continuing higher education for the older learner. There were resolutions on improving health decision making through promotion of health education, health literacy, and cultural competency. Proposals promoted incentives for older adults to continue working and for job training and retraining programs to better serve older workers. Another resolution called for developing a national strategy for promoting new, meaningful volunteer activities and civic engagements for seniors.

Promoting productivity of the older population is consistent with the direction of broader public policies. As Meyer and Herd (2001) observe, social policies on aging have evolved away from a preoccupation with social problems to an emphasis on social solutions that are often informed by cross-national comparisons. Since the 1990s, governments have looked to productive aging as a remedy for labor force skills shortages. A global "active aging" movement has emerged, promoted by the World Health Organization and the Organization for Economic Cooperation and Development (Davey, 2002). Life-long learning, a response to rapid technological change in the 1960s, was identified in the 1990s as one element of a set of policies to permit older adults to work longer, stay healthier, remain active, and maintain independence. These upbeat aspirations for education are not without basis, because education contributes to employability and health (Freedman & Martin 1999). The enthusiasm for life-long learning also meshes with broader policy developments placing the responsibility for successful aging squarely on the shoulders of the individual. Despite continuing interest, however, programs fall short of potential.

Political Engagement of Older Americans

Before examining major public policies on aging, older Americans' place in the political process merits attention. Older adults are among the most engaged political constituencies. They are more likely to vote than younger people. Voter turnout increases with age (Binstock & Quadagno, 2001). Some of this seems to be a cohort effect, perhaps reflecting differences in early socialization towards civic duty or exposure to specific political events (e.g., Watergate) at a critical moment in the development of political consciousness. Other age differences in political participation are due to life cycle effects. As people age, they become more interested in politics and public affairs. Their higher voting rate gives older Americans clout with their political representatives.

Older adults do not necessarily agree on all issues. It is assumed that older people consistently vote to maintain and expand old age benefits out of self interest (Binstock & Quadagno, 2001). Older adults' political beliefs, however, vary along income, race/ethnicity, education, social class, and party lines, just like those of younger voters (Binstock & Quadagno, 2001; Day, 1990). While a higher percentage of older people vote, there are more 25- to 44-year-olds voting than persons 65 and older (He et al., 2005). The aging of the baby boom cohort will increase the number, and presumably the power, of older voters (He et al., 2005). Certainly, their electoral significance argues for educational and informational initiatives to insure that older Americans continue to be active and knowledgeable.

More than 100 national organizations—including mass membership associations like AARP, single issue advocacy groups, and organizations for service providers and professionals—focus on aging policy (Binstock & Quadagno, 2001). Their constituencies and tactics vary, as do their priorities and stands on political issues. Without unifying goals, the power of the "gray lobby" is limited. Any group's power may be hampered by the diversity of its membership. AARP has over 35 million members to satisfy. Major developments in aging policy, such as the enactment and amendment of Medicare and Social Security, have owed more to the initiative of public officials than advocacy organizations (Binstock & Quadagno, 2001). While advocacy groups have benefited from stereotypes of the elderly as needy and deserving, their political legitimacy has been eroding (Binstock & Quadagno, 2001). The political power of older adults, then, owes more to perceptions that they vote as a bloc than to their effective activism.

Market Fundamentalism: The Changing Context of Public Policies

Market fundamentalism has become the dominant policy perspective in the U.S. over the past two decades (Somers & Block, 2005). Market fundamentalism is "the idea that society as a whole should be subordinated to a system of self-regulating markets" (Somers & Block, 2005, p. 261) and individuals should be responsible for themselves. With the decline of organized labor, workers have been stripped of traditional employment protections, made to pay more for employer-provided benefits, and even redefined as independent contractors who bear the cost of doing business. Even private insurers have transferred risk to individuals by excluding more conditions from coverage and pulling out of some markets altogether. We have also seen a breakdown of the government safety net as expressed in living wage protections, federal welfare programs, and social insurance. In the past, the social contract held that citizens had mutual obligations to each other. These obligations were met through diverse public initiatives, including public education, health care for the poor and elderly, child labor laws, and social insurance against the risk of becoming impoverished through bad luck or illness (Reich, 1998–1999).

Currently in the U.S. and around the world, public policy is shaped by a neo-liberal political agenda based on twin pillars (Rubenson, 2005). First is the questioning of the social contract that provided a public safety net to citizens in need. In the United States, this trend is seen in many areas. There are new time limits and work requirements for welfare recipients, an erosion of Pell grants for low-income students, and cut-backs in various public services. Second, there is a shifting relationship between the market and the state. The U.S. government is morphing from a neutral service provider to an enthusiastic sales intermediary for largely unregulated private enterprises. Americans have seen not only proposals for private Social Security accounts with brokerages, but also a new Medicare prescription benefit that is notable for sacrificing cost control in favor of a dizzying array of private drug plan options. This "market-oriented approach to social welfare" (Gilbert, 2002, p. 44) is supposed to encourage personal responsibility, which invariably requires high levels of knowledge and individual competency.

Welfare Reform.   Public income-support programs illustrate the new market fundamentalism. Privatization, as seen in recent proposals for Social Security and Medicare reform, leaves intact broad-based eligibility and benefits, but reduces the redistributive elements that transfer money from the rich to the poor (Herd, 2005b). This philosophical shift is seen in the rebranding of Aid to Families with Dependent Children (AFDC) as Temporary Assistance to Needy Families (TANF). The title of the 1996 welfare reform legislation—Personal Responsibility and Work Opportunities Reconciliation Act—clearly shows this paradigm change.

Through most of the last century, there was support for the social contract protecting all citizens, particularly children. By 1920, 40 states had enacted mother's pensions, promoting the idea that families with children deserved support; this was codified by the 1935 federal act (Skocpol, Abend-Wein, Howard, & Lehmann, 1993; Somers & Block, 2005). By 1996, perceptions had changed. Individuals are now viewed as responsible for themselves and their children. Only short-term assistance is regarded as appropriate (Somers & Block, 2005). The 1996 welfare reform legislation not only mandated time limits for assistance, child support enforcement, and work requirements (Lee, Slack, & Lewis, 2004), but also excluded "undeserving" groups like older adults who had recently immigrated (Treas, 1997). Ironically, the tough stance toward welfare belies how many ordinary Americans need public assistance to make ends meet. According to Rank and Hirschl (2002), two out of every three Americans (aged 20–65) at some point will live in a household that receives means-tested welfare benefits of one sort or another.

Whether the new welfare policy has been a success or failure is much debated. The welfare rolls are smaller now. In 1980, 3,712,000 families received AFDC compared to 1,987,000 in 2003 (U.S. Census Bureau, 2006b, Table 555). However, inequality grew. Although the average income of families in the poorest quintile increased by $2,664 from 1981 to 2002, the average in the richest quintile increased by $45,101. The income ratio of the top to bottom quintiles went from 5.5 to 7.3 (Bernstein, McNichol, & Lyons, 2006). Many people who left government assistance found that work did not keep them above the poverty line. Work often meant the loss of Medicaid and food stamps, leaving people worse off (Mink, 1999). During an economic boom, the mean wages of those leaving welfare ranged between $5.60 and $6.60 per hour in 1998 (Mink, 1999). States now face growing pressure from the federal government to insist on immediate employment instead of schooling that would lead to better jobs.

Although some adults got jobs, TANF has not improved the lives of American children. The poverty rate for children was 17.9 in 1980 and 17.8 in 2004. Work requirements removed parents from the home for longer periods of time, and promised childcare fell short. There are fears that more children are growing up without adequate supervision and shouldering adult household responsibilities. These changes led to concern that welfare reform is hindering the education and development of children at the bottom of the economic ladder. The question is whether they will be able to acquire the literacy, numeracy, and educational credentials to support themselves, manage their affairs, and contribute to the broader economy and society.

Social Security Reform.   Poverty rates for the elderly have declined since 1959; a development largely attributable to the expansion of Social Security benefits (Clark et al., 2004). For two-thirds of Americans aged 65 and older, Social Security makes up at least half their income (He et al., 2005). In January, 2006, fully 33,595,000 people received benefits. The average benefit was $959 monthly or $11,504 annually (Social Security Administration, 2006). With the 2005 poverty line for one person 65+ at $9,060 (U.S. Census Bureau, 2006a), Social Security offers a modestly secure and dignified old age for many, but not all. In 2004, 3.5 million older people (9.8% of those 65+) were still living in poverty. African American, Asian American, and Latino/a seniors are more likely to be poor than non-Hispanic Whites. Singles and women are at greater risk. Single older women of color are most likely to live out their lives in poverty (He et al., 2005).

Alterations in the program are necessary. Demographic projections inform the estimates that Social Security's payments will exceed its income in 2017 and exhaust the trust fund by 2041, when only 74% of promised benefits could be paid (Social Security Administration, 2005). These predictions have led to suggested reforms which have been widely discussed. None have yet to be implemented, perhaps due to political cross-pressures in Congress or to fears of the wrath of elderly voters. Although the proposals would appear to be dead, they deserve a closer look, because they illustrate the complexity and risks involved in reform and because they spell out how market fundamentalism shapes thinking about public policy.

Market fundamentalism favors privatization. Two different measures were recently suggested for Social Security. First, investing trust funds in the stock market, it is argued, would buoy the system with greater returns, as stocks generally outperform government bonds. Second, individual retirement accounts have been advocated. Although Social Security reform floundered, these proposed provisions and their implications merit scrutiny.

President Bush directed the 2001 President's Commission to Strengthen Social Security that proposed reforms had to include voluntary, individually-controlled, personal retirement accounts. The President did not endorse any of the Commission's three proposals, but Model 2 in the Commission report came the closest to what he had endorsed (Copeland, 2005). It was two-tiered. A minimum benefit would be figured under the traditional formula and then combined with money from the individual account (President's Commission, 2001). Individuals would choose whether to have individual accounts. For these individual accounts, workers would choose from a limited number of investment funds. If workers did not participate, their benefits would be computed similar to the current program. As there is currently no minimum Social Security benefit, the

Commission predicted some low-income workers would benefit. To get a minimum benefit equal to the poverty line would require 40 years of earnings, however. Thus, women—having shorter work lives—were disadvantaged by this provision (Herd, 2005a).

The Commission predicted that individual accounts would produce higher benefits (assuming the historical rate of stock market returns) than traditional Social Security. If the new accounts grew more than 2% above inflation, individuals would be better off than if they had stayed in the traditional plan. It is unclear what would happen if growth rates were less than 2% above inflation. Critics call attention to Chile, where the stock market lost 25% of its dollar value, and many saw returns drop from an average 12% to nothing (Gilbert, 2002, p. 106). Managing individual accounts would cost more than under the current Old Age & Survivors' Insurance (OASI) program, which spends just 1% of its budget for administration. Skeptics also are concerned about those individuals who choose their investments poorly or simply have bad luck.

Due to market ups and downs, large differences in individual retirement account outcomes can be predicted based on when someone is born and how much s/he earns. According to estimates by Burtless (1999), private retirement accounts—had they existed—would have replaced as little as 19% of the income for a typical male worker retiring in 1942 as compared to up to 104% for one retiring in 1969. Estimated replacement rates vary widely by birth cohort because of stock market fluctuations. By contrast, the current Social Security program replaces about 40% of income, on average, regardless of birth cohort (Burtless, 1999). Of course, the success of privatized investments will depend on whether the equity market continues with historical levels of return and whether legislators are willing to subject future retirees to benefits that could prove to be lower than currently guaranteed (Copeland, 2005). One thing is certain: including private savings accounts in OASI would shift risk to individuals while the current program spreads risk across cohorts.

Other reforms also have their critics. Proposals to increase the number of years of income used to calculate benefits tend to hurt those with intermittent employment or lower paid jobs, namely, women and people of color. Poorer than whites, older African Americans and Latino/as are less able to continue working given higher rates of disability; raising the benefit eligibility age affects them negatively and disproportionately (Green, 2005; Treas, 2004). Latino/as, in particular, are less likely to have private pensions to fill the gap. Longer work expectations, however, are consistent with the improved health and life expectancy of older adults as well as with the general philosophical commitment to encouraging the continued productivity of older Americans.

Employer Pension Plans.   Private pension plans are an important supplement to Social Security benefits. The earliest American pensions honored military service by Revolutionary War soldiers who were injured protecting American colonists and their property (Clark et al., 2004). Civil War pensions for Union soldiers were so generous and widespread that they are thought to have retarded the development of a social security system in the U.S. Although public sector employee pensions began in the middle of the 19th century, private pensions came later. Only a few companies had retirement plans in 1900.

Private pensions grew slowly until after WWII when they increased rapidly. By 1974, roughly half of the private labor force was covered, but progress stalled, in part because of the increased fiduciary and reporting requirements of the Employee Retirement and Income Security Act (ERISA). Currently, 50% of workers are covered, but this varies widely by occupational class. Fully 60% of white collar workers have pension coverage, compared to 50% of blue collar workers and only 22% of those in service industries (U.S.

Census Bureau, 2006b, Table 543). In 2002, 43% of male workers were covered compared to 41% of female workers, and 43% of whites compared to 40% of African Americans and 26% of Latino/as (U.S. Census Bureau, 2006b, Table 545). If employer pensions are to supplement Social Security for all workers, more employers will have to offer them. Recent developments suggest this is unlikely. The increased requirements placed on companies under The Pension Protection Act of 2006, while making pension plans more secure, may decrease employers' willingness to implement pension plans.

The past 30 years have seen a shift from defined benefit pension plans (guaranteeing a given pension benefit to retirees) to defined contribution plans (where the benefit amount depends on the investment return on contributions) or to hybrid plans. Between 1990 and 2000, the number of defined benefit plans fell from 113,100 to 48,700; the number of defined contribution plans increased from 599,200 to 687,300 (U.S. Census Bureau, 2006b, Table 542). While both types have some advantages for employers and employees, under ERISA legislation, the costs to employers of defined benefit plans are higher than those of defined contribution plans (Clark et al., 2004). As the media reports, businesses are free to move workers from defined-benefit to riskier defined-contribution pension plans—increasing uncertainty for workers planning retirement.

Defined benefit plans generally provide a specified benefit based on years of service and earnings. The company determines the formula, although limited by federal regulations. It may include incentives to retire at a given age or after a specific number of years of employment. The company bears the investment risk, makes the contributions, and covers all qualified employees. Rewarding workers who stay with the company, they require less financial literacy on the part of the employee. With typical defined contribution plans, contributions are voluntary, and the company makes contributions only if the worker also contributes. Workers bear the investment risk. Benefits are paid out as a lump sum. These plans require greater financial literacy. The employee must grasp the long-run benefits of contributing, make good investment decisions from what may be a broad portfolio of investment options, and be able to make the large lump sum payout last until death. Many companies are changing to hybrid plans: all workers are covered and the company makes all contributions, but the benefits are paid out as a lump sum (Clark et al., 2004). Hybrid plans require less financial savvy than defined contribution plans, but more than defined benefit plans.

Medicare Reform. Health insurance is an important component of financial security. Medicare (for older adults) and Medicaid (for the impoverished) were implemented in 1965. Medicare increased the proportion of older people with health insurance from about 50% in 1965 to 97% in 1970 (Clark et al., 2004). The proportion has remained high, providing an important resource for almost all seniors. In 1997, the government established Medicare+Choice, a managed care version of Medicare. With traditional Medicare, the federal government acts as the insurer, bearing the risk of covering the costs of care. Private insurers run Medicare+Choice programs, providing all Medicare benefits for a fixed monthly payment and bearing the risks of the cost of care.

Medicare+Choice was consistent with the general movement in employer-based insurance towards managed care, which is supposed to reduce costs. The Choice plans often provide more benefits than traditional Medicare, but they also tend to enroll healthier-than-average older people, leaving the sicker, more expensive enrollees in traditional Medicare (Clark et al., 2004). Originally, the federal government seemed to overpay the HMOs, but HMOs dropped out when reimbursements were lowered. Because Congress boosted reimbursements in 2002 to encourage HMO participation (Herd, 2005b), it is doubtful these plans actually save money. Given traditional fees for service and private Medigap insurance against costs not covered by Medicare, the expense of the newly required Part D Medicare prescription drug plan creates an incentive to enroll in HMOs (Herd, 2005b).

Rebranding was included in the Medicare Prescription Drug, Improvement, and Modernization Act of 2003, Public Law 108-173. So nobody misses the point, the HMOs are now called Medicare Advantage rather than Medicare+Choice. The act also established "an educational and publicity campaign for Medicare Advantage and Medicare Advantage Prescription Drug plans" (U.S. Department of Health and Human Services, 2004, p. 21). In other words, a campaign was designed to encourage people to switch from traditional fee-for-service Medicare to managed care—illustrating how the government acts as an intermediary for corporate enterprise. This state role is even more apparent in Medicare Part D.

The New Medicare Drug Policy.   Under the Medicare Prescription Drug, Improvement, and Modernization Act of 2003, a variety of plans are offered through private insurance companies, and individuals decide which plan is best for them. They decide whether to continue with traditional fee-for-service Medicare or go to a HMO (if offered). They choose whether to keep their private Medigap insurance, if they have one. People on both Medicaid and Medicare are expected to pick a plan, because Medicare takes over drug coverage from Medicaid. These dual-coverage patients are likely to be the sickest, poorest, and least able to make informed decisions; they are also the heaviest users of prescription drugs. Medicare enrollees were encouraged to use websites and interactive pages to inform their deliberations. They could call toll-free telephone numbers although insufficient staffing led to many complaints. Information was made available in writing and also on the Internet. Pharmaceutical providers must indicate changes to formularies on their websites; there is no requirement for paper copies of notifications (U.S. Department of Health and Human Services, 2004).

Individuals need financial and computer literacy to make good decisions. For example, in Kansas 40 different drug plans are available (HMO options differ by county). All plans offer coverage up to $2250 annually, some between $2250 and $3600, and all above $3600. The types and amounts of coverage vary between $2250 and $3600. Some plans provide generic drugs, others generic and brand name drugs. Premiums, deductibles, and drugs covered also vary. If a person is on multiple medications, it can be very hard to determine which plan is best. There is a 1% per month penalty for not signing up immediately, creating the dilemma of whether it pays to wait to get more information on prescription needs and the performance of various plans. Even if not currently taking medication, older adults were compelled to pick a plan in the face of great uncertainty. Most people can change plans only once a year. Despite discussions of limiting the number of plans in order to decrease complexity and confusion, the cognitive requirements to make the best decision are apparent.

The emphasis on websites for information and enrollment in Medicare Part D surely came from people who are younger and more computer savvy than most Medicare recipients. Only 48% of people, 65 to 74, have a computer in their household, and only 26% of those 75 or older access the Internet from home (Hill & Wright, 2006). While it is possible to access the Internet elsewhere, only 3% of those ages 55 and older use the Internet somewhere besides home (Hill & Wright, 2006). Therefore, most people who have Medicare do not have easy access to its information. Later birth cohorts will be more computer literate, but computer and Internet usage are highly stratified by income and education (Day, Janus, & Davis, 2005). Thus, poor older people will have even greater difficulties getting access to the information that they need.

Health Care.   Disturbingly, 45.8 million Americans did not have any health insurance in 2004 (U.S. Census Bureau, 2005b). The number remained steady from 2003, because declines in employer-sponsored health insurance were offset by increases in the numbers eligible for government-sponsored health insurance programs. Those relying on government programs increased from 76.8 million to 79.1 million between 2003 and 2004.

Under the banner of privatization, the market is being given freer reign at the same time that the welfare state is being downsized. Voicing concern with rising health care costs, employers are eliminating health care benefits or asking workers to pay more, even though corporate profits are increasing (MetLife, 2005). In addition, many companies are redefining employees as contingent workers or independent contractors who must bear the cost and uncertainty of doing business. Fewer workers can expect their health care benefits to continue into retirement. Although 28% of companies offer at least some benefits to retirees (MetLife, 2005), the number continuing health insurance benefits to new retirees has declined since 1993 (Mercer, 2001). The proportion of large firms (200+ employees) with retiree health benefits plummeted from 66% in 1988 to 34% in 2002 (Kaiser, 2002).

President Bush endorsed Consumer Directed Health Plans, including Health Savings/Reimbursement Accounts. Only 15% of employers without such plans are receptive to the idea of offering them. Of workers, only 16% say they would be very interested in enrolling (MetLife, 2006). These accounts also demand financial literacy and a highly developed planning ability on the part of the employee. According to one argument, the more money that individuals spend out of their own pockets for health care, the more likely they are to become frugal health care consumers. Health care, however, is a complex and sophisticated industry. Relatively few consumers have sufficient medical knowledge or information to conduct a good cost-benefit analysis of alternative treatments or providers. Persons suffering from disabling medical conditions often lack the ability and resilience for comparison shopping, especially in emergencies.

Summary.   Although population aging points to the need for Social Security and Medicare reform, the lack of resolution on the issue means that Americans face a moving target in retirement planning. In an ownership society where individuals can no longer count on being protected by the state from life course contingencies, programmatic changes could increase the insecurity of the poorest Americans. New programs with new rules (like Medicare Part D) will place greater demands on individuals to be sophisticated managers of their finances, career, and life course. Many Americans lack the necessary education, knowledge, skills, and cognitive ability to deal with choices having serious financial implications. Thus, successful new programs of public old age support demand considerable resources to educate Americans about the viability of their options. The inadequate planning for the educational and counseling component in the Medicare prescription drug plan raises concerns about any programs that confront Americans with high-stakes, but very complex, choices.

Putting Aging Policy in Context

Bernard and Phillips (2000) summarize the market-oriented trend that threatens the traditional protections that older adults came to expect from the welfare state:

> Terms such as empowerment; advocacy; user involvement and participation; consumerism; care management; purchasers and providers; enablers and facilitators; internal markets; and packages of care, to name but a few, have come into everyday parlance. However, behind this new rhetoric, we can discern the continuing erosion of state responsibility for the care of older people. (p. 39)

These developments are not limited to old age policies. They affect all age groups. Whether school vouchers for children or drug plans for seniors, the thrust of policy developments has been to rely more on the market and less on the state to meet health, education and welfare needs across the life course.

Privatization means a wider number of choices for individuals, but these choices can demand an extraordinary level of cognitive sophistication and motivation to make good decisions. This is no small matter, because the choice of employer, insurer, and physician has not only immediate consequences, but also significant long-run implications for well-being over the life course. Average Americans may not be up to the challenge. Many do not know enough or have the skills to manage the sophisticated decision making being thrust on them. For disadvantaged Americans—those who are poorly educated or non-English speakers or socially isolated or cognitively impaired—the tasks of an ownership society are formidable. Undoubtedly, many will fall by the wayside, victims of bad judgment or even fraud. This is not to say that people who are poorly equipped for complex decision making could not function in the new privatized welfare state, but it would take a high level of outreach, education, support, and counseling. This situation poses real opportunities for those who would empower consumers, engage patients in the management of their own illnesses, implement cognitive interventions for older adults, or provide impartial financial advising. To date, however, the public commitment to life-long learning and empowerment has been inadequate to incorporate those who most need knowledge, skills, and advice in the ownership society.

Cut-backs in state support parallel other developments that undermine the security of individuals and their families. The traditional employment contract promising a living wage and job security has been rewritten, a corporate change rationalized by the need for global competitiveness. More Americans work in nonstandard employment (Kalleberg, Reynolds, & Marsden, 2003). These jobs are usually substandard, characterized by lower pay, part-time or irregular work hours, no guarantees of continuity, scant promotion or training opportunities, and little in the way of employer-paid benefits (Kalleberg, Reskin, & Hudson, 2000). Fewer jobs offer the firm financial foundation to equip workers to manage a lengthy illness, a financial setback, or a bout of unemployment on their own. Although manufacturing employment has been shipped abroad, even the jobs of highly educated workers are being outsourced to other countries. More U.S. companies rely on India for their skilled financial work, for example. This trend raises questions about the limits of retraining and education in addressing the problems of Americans who are out of work or in dead-end jobs.

Family income has become increasingly unequal as high income Americans have pulled ahead (Bernstein, McNichol, Mishel, & Zahradnick, 2000). Family income has also become increasingly volatile (Gosselin, 2004). More workers find periods of employment and prosperity to be punctuated by job loss and income decline. Unemployed workers are less likely to receive unemployment insurance benefits now than they were 30 years ago, even though the percentage of workers eligible has increased (Bernstein et al., 2006). In addition, personal saving fell from 7% of disposable personal income in 1990 to 1.2% in 2004 (U.S. Census Bureau, 2006b, Table 659). The growth of the credit card industry means that Americans at all economic levels bridge short-term financial short-falls by taking on what can become long-term debt. One-quarter of families with credit cards say they hardly ever pay off their monthly balance (U.S. Census Bureau 2006b, Table 767). New legal barriers, however, limit bankruptcy relief, long the last resort to manage burdensome debt. The rise in medical insurance co-payments and the shift from defined benefit to defined contribution pension plans add to the conclusion that individuals are shouldering more of the risk in a precarious world. As the welfare reform and social security debates show, these economic changes have been coupled with political developments that have frayed the government safety net.

Even as volatility and uncertainty mean that families are hard pressed to educate their children, educating adults becomes a more critical enterprise. New developments have placed a premium on knowledge to navigate uncertain waters and on retraining to keep workers afloat in a rapidly shifting economy. As the 2005 White House Conference on Aging pointed out, the need for economic literacy and financial planning over the life course has increased due to economic changes and political developments. Declining newspaper readership (U.S. Census Bureau, 2006b, Table 738) and the rise of new information media that are subject to fewer constraints on truth claims suggest some of the challenges ahead. Although a host of national policies have made life-long learning critical, the success of public policies must be gauged by the learning opportunities that they extend to Americans of all ages.

Conclusion

A growing population of older adults raises the prospect of more people in need of medical care, income support, and assistance with daily living. The baby boom, however, promises to be healthier and wealthier than any prior generation of older Americans. Their vitality, coupled with the projected shortfall in Social Security and Medicare funds, has encouraged a new philosophy toward aging policy. Rather than supporting old age dependency, public programs are slowly changing to encourage the continued productivity of older adults. Older Americans are encouraged to stay healthy, keep working, and remain independent.

Productive aging dovetails with a broader development in public policy—market fundamentalism. This philosophy seeks the solution to societal problems in self-regulating markets while scaling back government programs that traditionally protected workers and their families from poverty, unemployment, natural disasters, illness, disability, and old age. As a consequence of this ideological shift, individuals assume greater responsibility for their own lives. This comes at a time of global economic restructuring that has shaken not merely the perennially disadvantaged groups in society, but also the solid middle class. The growth in non-standard jobs offering no security or promotion prospects, the decline in employer-provided benefits, the increasing volatility of family income, all signal economic challenges to families working to provide for themselves.

Public policy has responded to market fundamentalism with a host of proposals and social programs that cast the individual as consumer, private enterprise as supplier, and government as the business-friendly broker. From the roll-out of a Medicare drug plan featuring a dizzying array of private insurers to calls for individual Social Security accounts invested in the stock market, social insurance has ceased to mean simple, one-size-fits-all programs. The upshot is that public programs entail greater personal risk, and public policy innovations make increasing cognitive demands on Americans who must make choices of enormous consequences to their lives.

While job training has been touted for welfare recipients transitioning to work and manufacturing workers displaced by foreign competition, the limitations and complexities of public and employer-sponsored insurance programs make life-long learning even more necessary. Unfortunately, adult education policy has not been aging policy. It has been employment policy with only fitful attention paid to other pressing concerns. Americans, however, are poorly informed, and many lack the basic literacy and numeracy skills to process the information that they need to evaluate benefit options, follow a medical regimen, or manage their business affairs.

Older Americans pose special challenges and opportunities. For all the optimism about the baby boom's resources, there will invariably be vulnerable populations who require special assistance. Often on the wrong side of the digital divide, many older adults have trouble keeping up with the shift of information from printed to web-based media. Special approaches are needed to educate and inform adults (Smith & Reio, 2006). Beyond enrichment, there is a significant role for life-long learning in fostering productive aging. Adult education promises not only to make older adults more valuable workers and volunteers, but to promote health and maintain cognitive functioning in later life. If aging societies can no longer afford to cultivate old age dependency, the promise of adult learning must become a reality.

References

Alwin, D. F. (1991). Family of origin and cohort differences in verbal ability. *American Sociological Review, 56*, 625–638.

Bernard, M., & Phillips, J. (2000). The challenge of ageing in tomorrow's Britain. *Ageing and Society, 20*, 33–54.

Bernstein, J., McNichol, E., & Lyons, K. (2006). *Pulling apart: A state-by-state analysis of income trends.* The Center on Budget and Policy Priorities. Retrieved March 20, 2006, from http://www.cbpp.org/1-26-06sfp.pdf.

Bernstein, J., McNichol, E. C., Mishel, L., & Zahradnik, R. (2000). *Pulling apart: A state-by-state analysis of income trends.* Washington, DC: Center on Budget and Policy Priorities.

Binstock, R. (1991). From the great society to the aging society: 25 years of the Older Americans Act. *Generations, Summer/Fall*, 11–18.

Binstock, R., & Quadagno, J. (2001). Aging and politics. In R. Binstock & L. George(Eds.), *Handbook of aging and the social sciences* (pp. 333–351). San Diego, CA: Academic Press.

Blackwell, D., Hayward, M. D., & Crimmins, E. M. (2001). Does childhood health affect chronic morbidity in later life? *Social Science and Medicine, 52*, 1269–1284.

Burtless, G. (1999). Putting retirement at risk. *Aging Today.* Retrieved March 4, 2006, from http://www.agingtoday.org/at/index.cfm?page=http://www.asaging.org/at/at-201/toc.html.

Clark, R. L., Burkhauser, R. V., Moon, M., Quinn, J. F., & Smeeding, T. M. (2004). *The economics of an aging society.* Malden, MA: Blackwell.

Cohen, D. (2000). Numeracy, mathematics, and adult learning. In I. Gal (Ed.), *Adult numeracy development: Theory, research, practice* (pp. 33–50). Cresskill, NJ: Hampton Press.

Copeland, C. (2005). Comparing social security reform options. *EBRI Issue Brief* No. 281. Retrieved May 5, 2005, from http://www.ebri.org.

Costa, D. (1998). *The evolution of retirement: An American economic history.* Chicago: University of Chicago Press.

Crimmins, E. M., & Saito, Y. (1997). Trends in disability-free life expectancy in the United States, 1970–1990. *Population and Development Review, 23*,555–572.

Davey, J. A. (2002). Active ageing and education in mid and later life. *Ageing and Society, 22*, 95–113.

Day, C. (1990). *What older Americans think: Interest groups and aging policy.* Princeton, NJ: Princeton University Press.

Day, J. C., Janus, A., & Davis, J. (2005). *Computer and internet use in the United States: 2003.* Washington, DC: U.S. Census Bureau.

Dillon, S. (2005, December 16). Literacy falls for graduates from college, testing finds. *New York Times,* A34.

DiPrete, T. A., & Buchmann, C. (2006). Gender-specific trends in the value of education and the emerging gender gap in college completion. *Demography, 43,* 1–24.

Easterlin, R., Schaeffer, C., & Macunovich, D. (1993).Will the baby boomers be less well off than their parents? Income, wealth, and family circumstances in the United States. *Population and Development Review, 19,* 497–522.

Freedman, M. (2002). Civic windfall? Realizing the promise in an aging America. *Generations, 86–89.*

Freedman, V. A., & Martin, L. G. (1999). The role of education in explaining and forecasting trends in the functional limitations among older Americans. *Demography, 36,* 461–473.

Gendall, P., Smith, T., & Russel, D. (1995). Knowledge of scientific and environmental facts: A comparison of six countries. *Marketing Bulletin, 6,* 65–73.

Gilbert, N. (2002). *Transformation of the welfare state: The silent surrender of public responsibility.* New York: Oxford University Press.

Glenn, N. D. (1994). Television watching, newspaper reading, and cohort differences in verbal ability. *Sociology of Education, 67,* 216–230.

Gosselin, P. G. (2004, December 12). The poor have more things today—including wild income swings. *Los Angeles Times,* A1.

Green, C.A . (2005). Race, ethnicity, and social security retirement age in the U.S. *Feminist Economics, 11(2),* 117–143.

Greene, J., Hibbard, J., & Tusler, M. (2005). *How much do health literacy and patient activation contribute to older adults' ability to manage their health?* Washington, DC AARP Public Policy Institute.

Haider, S., & Loughran, D. (2001). *Elderly labor supply: Work or play?* RAND Working Paper Series, DRU-2582.

He, W., Sengupta, M., Velkoff, V. A., & DeBarros, K. A. (2005). *65+ in the United States: 2005.* Washington, DC: U.S. Census Bureau.

Herd, P. (2005a). Ensuring a minimum: Social security reform and women. *The Gerontologist, 45,* 12–25.

Herd, P. (2005b). Universalism without the targeting: Privatizing the old-age welfare state. *The Gerontologist, 45,* 292–298.

Hill, T. J., & Wright, D. W. (2006). *Older Adults, computers, and the internet.* Paper presented at the annual meeting of the Midwest Sociological Society, Omaha, NE.

Hobbs, F., & Stoops N. (2002). *Demographic trends in the 20th century.* Washington, DC: U.S. Census Bureau.

Kaestle, C. F., Campbell, A., Finn, J. D., Johnson, S. T., & Milulecky, L. J. (2001). *Adult literacy and education in America: Four studies based on the national adult literacy survey.* Washington, DC: National Center for Educational Statistics.

Kaiser Family Foundation and Health Research and Educational Trust. (2002). *Employer health benefits, 2002 annual survey.* Washington, DC: Kaiser Family Foundation. Retrieved March 4, 20006, from http://www.kff.org/insurance/upload/ 2002-Employer-Health-Benefits-Survey-Chartpack.ppt.

Kalleberg, A., Reskin, B., & Hudson, K. (2000). Bad jobs in America: Standard and nonstandard employment relations and job quality in the United States. *American Sociological Review, 65,* 256–278.

Kalleberg, A., Reynolds, J., & Marsden, P. (2003). Externalizing employment: Flexible staffing arrangements in U.S. organizations. *Social Science Research, 32,* 525–552.

Larkin, E. (1998–1999, Winter). The intergenerational response to childcare and after-school care. *Generations,* 33–36.

Lee, B. J., Slack, K. S., & Lewis, D. A. (2004). Are welfare sanctions working as intended? Welfare receipt, work activity, and material hardship among TANF-recipient families. *Social Service Review, 78,* 370–403.

MacRae, D., Jr., & Wilde, J. A. (1979). *Policy analysis for public decisions.* North Scituate, MA: Duxbury Press.

Marsick, V. J., & Watkins, K. E. (2001). Informal and incidental learning. In S. B. Merriam (Ed.), *The new update on adult learning theory: New directions for adult and continuing education, 89* (pp. 25–34). San Francisco: Jossey Bass.

Mercer, W. M. Inc. (2001). *Fifteenth annual Mercer/Foster Higgins national survey of employer-sponsored health plans.* Retrieved March 4, 2006, from http://www.imercer.com/us/imercercommentary/BB-final.pdf.

MetLife. (2005). *The MetLife study of employee benefits trends: Findings from the 2004 national survey of employers and employees.* Metropolitan Life Insurance Company. Retrieved March 4, 2006, from http://www.metlife.com/WPSAssets/14195940071116862808V1FFINAL%20EBTS.pdf.

MetLife. (2006). *The MetLife study of employee benefits trends: Findings from the 2005 national survey of employers and employees.* Metropolitan Life Insurance Company. Retrieved March 4, 2006, from http://www.metlife.com/WPSAssets/12884679701139323230V1FTheMetLifeStudyofEmployeeBenefitsTrends2006.pdf.

Meyer, M. H., & Herd, P. (2001). Aging and aging policy in the U.S. In J. R. Blau (Ed.), *The Blackwell companion to sociology* (pp. 375–388). Malden, MA: Blackwell.

Mink, G. (1999). Introduction. In G. Mink (Ed.), *Whose welfare?* (pp. 1–4). Ithaca, NY: Cornell University Press.

National Center for Education Statistics. (2005). *Highlights from the 2003 international literacy and life skills survey (ALL).* Issue Brief (May), 1–3.

Newman, S., Faux, R., & Larimer, B. (1997). Children's views on aging: Their attitudes and values. *The Gerontologist, 37L,* 412–417.

President's Commission. (2001). *Final report of the president's commission to strengthen social security.* Retrieved March 25, 2006, from http://www.ssa.gov/history/reports/pcsss/Final_report.pdf.

Rank, M. R., & Hirschl, T. A. (2002). Welfare use as a life course event: Toward a new understanding of the U.S. safety net. *Social Work, 47,* 237–248.

Reich, R. B. (1998–1999, Winter). Broken faith: Why we need to renew the social compact. *Generations,* 19–24.

Rubenson, K. (2005). Social class and adult education policy. In T. Nesbit (Ed.), *Class concerns: Adult education and social class: New directions for adult and continuing education* (Vol. 10; pp. 15–25). San Francisco: Jossey Bass.

Schaie, K. W. (2005). *Developmental influences on adult intelligence: The Seattle longitudinal study.* Oxford, UK: Oxford University Press.

Schoeni, R. F., Freedman, V. A., & Wallace, R. (2001). Persistent, consistent, widespread, and robust? Another look at recent trends in old-age disability. *Journals of Gerontology Series B: Psychological and Social Sciences, 56,* S206–S218.

Schofer, E., & Meyer, J. W. (2005). The worldwide expansion of higher education in the twentieth century. *American Sociological Review, 70,* 898–920.

Science. (1995). Environmental knowledge gap. *Science, 268,* 647.

Sigle-Rushton, W., Hobcraft, J., & Kiernan, K. (2005). Parental divorce and subsequent disadvantage: A cross-cohort comparison. *Demography, 42,* 427–446.

Skocpol, T., Abend-Wein, M., Howard, C., & Lehmann, S. G. (1993). Women's associations and the enactment of mothers' pensions in the United States. *American Political Science Review, 87,* 686–701.

Smith, MC., & Reio, T. G., Jr. (2006). Adult development, schooling, and the transition to work. In P. A. Alexander, & P. H. Winne (Eds.), *The handbook of educational psychology* (2nd ed.; pp. 115–138). Mahwah, NJ: Erlbaum.

Social Security Administration. (2005). *Status of the social security and medicare programs: A summary of the 2005 annual reports.* Retrieved March 27, 2006, from http://ssa.gov/OACT/TRSUM/trsummary.html.

Social Security Administration. (2006). *OASDI monthly statistics, January 2006.* Retrieved March 27, 2006, from http://www.ssa.gov/policy/docs/statcomps/oasdi_monthly/2006-01/table02.html.

Somers, M. R., & Block, F. (2005). From poverty to perversity: Ideas, markets, and institutions over 200 years of welfare debate. *American Sociological Review, 70,* 260–287.

Treas, J. (1997). Older immigrants and U.S. welfare reform. *International Journal of Sociology and Social Policy, 17*(9/10), 8–33.

Treas, J. (2004). Population ageing in the United States of America: Retirement, reform and reality. In *Policy responses to population decline and ageing: Population Bulletin of the United Nations, 44/45 2002* (pp. 358–370). New York: Population Division, Department of Economic and Social Affairs, United Nations.

Uhlenberg, P. (1992). Population aging and social policy. *Annual Review of Sociology, 18,* 449–474.

U.S. Administration on Aging. (2005). *2004 Annual report: Aging well, living well.* U.S. Department of Health and Human Services. Washington DC. Retrieved March 11, 2006, from http://www.aoa.dhhs.gov/about/annual_report/2004_ar.pdf.

U.S. Census Bureau. (2005a). *Census 2000 summary file 4 sample data QTP17: Ability to speak English: 2000.* Retrieved from http://factfinder.census.gov/servlet/QTTable?_bm=y&-geo_id=D&-qr_name=DEC_2000_SF4_U_QTP17&-ds_name=D&-_lang=en&-redoLog=false.

U.S. Census Bureau. (2005b, August). *Income, poverty, and health insurance coverage in the United States: 2004.* Washington, DC: U.S. Department of Commerce.

U.S. Census Bureau. (2006a*). Poverty thresholds 2005.* Retrieved March 27, 2006, from http://www.census.gov/hhes/www/poverty/threshld/thresh05.html.

U.S. Census Bureau. (2006b). *Statistical abstract of the United States: 2006.* Washington, DC: U.S. Government Printing Office.

U.S. Department of Health and Human Services. (2004). *CMS legislative summary of H.R. 1: The Medicare prescription drug improvement and modernization act of 2003, Public Law 108-173.* Retrieved March 27, 2006, from http://www.cms.hhs.gov/relevantlaws/downloads/legislativesummary-forMMAof2003.pdf.

Watari, K., & Gatz, M. (2002). Dementia: A cross-cultural perspective on risk factors. *Generations, 26*(1), 32–38.

Postscript

On February 14, 2008, an emotionally disturbed former student walked into a lecture hall on the campus on Northern Illinois University. Armed with a shotgun and handguns, he killed five NIU students and injured 16 others before taking his own life. This handbook is dedicated to these vibrant young adults whose lives were so tragically and swiftly taken.

Gayle Dubowski, 20, was a young woman of deep faith who was studying to become an anthropologist. Proud of her Eastern European heritage, she was also studying Russian at the university.

Catalina Garcia was a 20-year-old sophomore who was majoring in elementary education. Shortly before her death, she was hired to work at NIU's Center for Latino and Latin American Studies.

Julianna Gehant, 32, was a 12-year veteran of the U.S. Army and Army Reserves. A junior at NIU, Julianna was majoring in elementary education.

Ryanne Mace was a 20-year-old sophomore who was majoring in psychology. She wanted to earn a doctorate so that she could become a counselor.

Daniel Parmenter, 20, was a staff member at the NIU campus newspaper, a rugby player, and finance major. He died shielding his girlfriend from the gunman.

Contributors

Elisa Abes
Miami University
Oxford, OH

Patricia A. Alexander
University of Maryland
College Park, MD

Monika Ardelt
University of Florida
Gainesville, FL

Jeffrey Jensen Arnett
Clark University
Worcester, MA

Cynthia A. Berg
University of Utah
Salt Lake City, UT

Fredda Blanchard-Fields
Georgia Institute of Technology
Atlanta, GA

Cory R. Bolkan
Washington State University Vancouver
Vancouver, WA

Molly Butterworth
University of Utah
Salt Lake City, UT

Mary Wilson Callahan
Magellan Center
Longmont, CO

Harris Cooper
Duke University
Durham, NC

Gary Creasey
Illinois State University
Normal, IL

Lisa M. Diamond
University of Utah
Salt Lake City, UT

Anna Gasiorski
University of Maryland
College Park, MD

Emily A. Greenfield
Rutgers University
New Brunswick, NJ

Twyla Hill
Wichita State University
Wichita, KS

Carol Hoare
The George Washington University
Washington, DC

Janet K. Holt
Northern Illinois University
DeKalb, IL

Karen Hooker
Oregon State University
Corvallis, OR

Steve Jacobs
University of Florida
Gainesville, FL

Patricia Jarvis
Illinois State University
Normal, IL

Susan R. Jones
University of Maryland
College Park, MD

Antje Stange Kalinauskas
Georgia Institute of Technology
Atlanta, GA

Erin Kelly
University of Minnesota
Minneapolis, MN

Eva-Marie Kessler
Jacobs University Bremen
Bremen, Germany

Kelly Ko
University of Utah
Salt Lake City, UT

Jonna M. Kulikowich
Pennsylvania State University
State College, PA

Julie A. Leis
Johns Hopkins University
Baltimore, MD

Rachel Magennis
University of Minnesota
Minneapolis, MN

Marcia Baxter Magolda
Miami University
Oxford, OH

Nadine F. Marks
University of Wisconsin
Madison, WI

Victoria J. Marsick
Teachers College
Columbia University
New York, NY

Benjamin T. Mast
University of Louisville
Louisville, KY

Patricia Meierdiercks
Oregon State University
Corvallis, OR

Phyllis Moen
University of Minnesota
Minneapolis, MN

P. Karen Murphy
Penn State University
University Park, PA

Erik J. Porfeli
Northeastern Ohio Universities
Colleges of Medicine & Pharmacy
Rootstown, Ohio

Sarah V. Rowe
University of Louisville
Louisville, KY

Kennon M. Sheldon
University of Missouri
Columbia, MO

Jan D. Sinnott
Towson University
Towson, MD

Michelle Skinner
University of Utah
Salt Lake City, UT

M Cecil Smith
Northern Illinois University
DeKalb, IL

Ursula M. Staudinger
Jacobs University Bremen
Breman, Germany

Jennifer L. Tanner
Rutgers University
New Brunswick, NJ

Dennis Thompson
Georgia State University
Atlanta, GA

Vasti Torres
Indiana University
Bloomington, IN

Judith Treas
University of California

Jeffrey C. Valentine
University of Louisville
Louisville, KY

Marie Volpe
Teachers College
Columbia University
New York, NY

Fred W. Vondracek
Pennsylvania State University
University Park, PA

Karen E. Watkins
University of Georgia
Athens, GA

Lisa L. Weyandt
Central Washington University
Ellensburg, WA

Paul Wink
Wellesley College
Wellesley, MA

Jennifer Zimmerman
University of Louisville
Louisville, KY

Index

CPSIA information can be obtained at www.ICGtesting.com
Printed in the USA
LVOW03s1917281213

367247LV00006B/323/P